THE ANCIENT EGYPTIAN COFFIN TEXTS

Spells 1–1185 & Indexes

R. O. Faulkner

Aris & Phillips

Aris & Phillips is an imprint of Oxbow Books

Published in the United Kingdom by
OXBOW BOOKS
10 Hythe Bridge Street, Oxford OX1 2EW

and in the United States by
OXBOW BOOKS
908 Darby Road, Havertown, PA 19083

Originally published in three volumes:
Volume I published 1973, reprinted 1978, 1994
Volume II published 1977, reprinted 1978, 1994
Volume III published 1978, reprinted 1996
Reprinted as a single volume with corrections 2004, 2007, 2015

ISBN 978-0-85668-754-9

A CIP record for this book is available from the British Library.

Oxbow Books is part of the Casemate group

CONTENTS

The pagination of the original three volumes is retained throughout

ABBREVIATIONS

Abubakr, *Kronen*	A. el M. Abubakr, *Untersuchungen uber die ägyptischen Kronen.*
AEO	A. H. Gardiner, *Ancient Egyptian Onomastica.*
Amarna	N. de G. Davies, *The Rock Tombs of El Amarna.*
Ann. Serv.	*Annales du service des antiquités de l'Égypte.*
Barns, *Ram.*	J. W. B. Barns, *Five Ramesseum Papyri.*
Bersh.	F. Ll. Griffith and P. E. Newberry, *El Bersheh.*
BD	E. A. W. Budge, *The Book of the Dead,* Text (1898 edition).
Bibl. Or.	*Bibliotheca Orientalis.*
BIFAO	*Bulletin de l'institut français d'archéologie orientale.*
BH	P. E. Newberry, *Beni Hasan.*
Book of Hours	R. O. Faulkner, *An Ancient Egyptian Book of Hours.*
Boylan, *Thoth*	P. Boylan, *Thoth the Hermes of Egypt.*
Bremner-Rhind	*The Bremner-Rhind Papyrus*, ed. R. O. Faulkner.
Brit. Mus. Cat. Eg. Coll.	*British Museum Catalogue of Egyptian Antiquities.*
Caminos, *L.-Eg. Misc.*	R. A. Caminos, *Late Egyptian Miscellanies.*
Caminos, *Lit. Frag.*	R. A. Caminos, *Literary Fragments in the Hieratic Script.*
C. T. Transl.	R. O. Faulkner, *The Ancient Egyptian Coffin Texts (= this book)*
Ch. B.	A. H. Gardiner, *Hieratic Papyri in the British Museum. Third Series: Chester Beatty Gift*
COA	J. S. Pendlebury, *The City of Akhenaten.*
Concise Dict.	R. O. Faulkner, *A Concise Dictionary of Middle Egyptian.*
CT	A. de Buck, *The Egyptian Coffin Texts.*
D. el B.	E. Naville, *The Temple of Deir el Bahari.*
D. el Geb.	N. de G. Davies, *The Rock Tombs of Deir el Gebrâwi.*
Dav. *Ptah.*	N. de G. Davies, *The Mastaba of Ptahhetep and Akhethetep.*
Eb.	*Ebers Medical Papyrus.*
Ed. Smith Pap.	*Edwin Smith Surgical Papyrus.*
Edel, *Altäg. Gramm.*	E. Edel, *Altägyptische Grammatik.*
Edel, *Qubbet el Hawa*	E. Edel, *Die Felsgräber der Qubbet el Hawa bei Assuan.*
Edel, *Weltkammer*	E. Edel, *Zu den Inschriften auf den Jahreszeiten-reliefs der "Weltkammer" aus dem Sonnenheiligtum des Niuserre* in *Nachrichten ... Göttingen*, 1961; 1963.
Eg. Gramm.^{3}	A. H. Gardiner, *Egyptian Grammar,* 3rd edition.
Erman, *Religion*	A. Erman, *Die Religion der Ägypter.*
Festival-Hall	E. Naville, *The Festival-Hall of Osorkon II in the Great Temple of Bubastis.*
Fischer, *Dendera*	H. G. Fischer, *Dendera in the Third Millennium B.C.*
GAS	A. H. Gardiner, *The Admonitions of an Egyptian Sage.*

Gauthier, *Dict. géogr.*	H. Gauthier, *Dictionnaire des noms géographiques contenus dans les texts hiéroglyphiques.*
GES	B. Gunn, *Studies in Egyptian Syntax.*
GNS	A. H. Gardiner, *Notes on the Story of Sinuhe.*
Hamm.	J. Couyat et P. Montet, *Les inscriptions hiéroglyphiques et hiératiques du Ouadi Hammâmât.*
Harris, *Minerals*	J. R. Harris, *Lexicographical Studies in Ancient Egyptian Minerals.*
Horus and Seth	*The Contendings of Horus and Seth*, in A. H. Gardiner, *The Chester Beatty Papyri No. I*
Hymnen	A. Erman, *Hymnen an das Diadem der Pharaonen,* in *Abhandlungen der königlichen preussischen Akademie* ..., 1911.
James, *Hekanakhte*	T. G. H. James, *The Hekanakhte Papers.*
JAOR	*Journal of the American Oriental Society.*
JARCE	*Journal of the American Research Center in Egypt.*
JEA	*Journal of Egyptian Archaeology.*
Jéquier, *Frises*	G. Jéquier, *Les frises d'objets des sarcophages du Moyen Empire.*
JNES	*Journal of Near Eastern Studies.*
JEOL	*Jaarbericht van het Voor-aziatisch-egyptisch Genootschaap 'Ex oriente lux'.*
Komm. Pyr.	K. Sethe, *Übersetzung und Kommentar zu den altägyptischen Pyramidentexten.*
L. to D.	A. H. Gardiner and K. Sethe, *Egyptian Letters to the Dead.*
Lacau, *Textes rel.*	P. Lacau, *Texts religieux égyptiennes.*
Lanzone, *Mitologia*	R. v. Lanzone, *Dizionario di Mitologia.*
Leb.	P. Berl. 3024, *Gespräch eines Lebensmüden mit seiner Seele.*
Leps. *Denkm.*	R. Lepsius, *Denkmäler aus Ägypten und Äthiopien.*
Les.	K. Sethe, *Aegyptische Lesestücke zum Gebrauch in akademischen Unterricht.*
Mar. *Mast.*	A. Mariette, *Les mastabas de l'Ancien Empire.*
Meir	A. M. Blackman, *The Rock Tombs of Meir.*
Mill.	The Millingen Papyrus, *Revue d'Égyptologie,* 15 (1963), 29ff.
Möller, *Pal.*	G. Möller, *Hieratische Paläographie.*
M.u.K.	A. Erman, *Zaubersprüche für Mutter und Kind,* in *Abhandlungen der königlichen preussischen Akademie* ..., 1911.
P. Kah.	F. Ll. Griffith, *Hieratic Papyri from Kahun and Gurob.*
Peas.	*The Story of the Eloquent Peasant*, in F. Vogelsang and A. H. Gardiner, *Die Klagen des Bauern.*
Pr.	The Prisse Papyrus, in Z. Žába, *Les Maximes de Ptahhotep.*
PSBA	*Proceedings of the Society for Biblical Archaeology.*
Pt. (LII)	British Museum Papyrus No. 10509 (duplicate of *Pr*).
Pyr.	K. Sethe, *Die altaegyptischen Pyramidentexte.*
Pyr. Suppl.	R.O. Faulkner, *The Ancient Egyptian Pyramid Texts.* Translation and hieroglyphic supplement.
Pyr. Transl.	As above.
RB	A. de Buck, *Egyptian Reading-book.*

Rec. trav.	*Recueil de travaux relatifs à la philologie et à l'archéologie égyptiennes et assyriennes.*
Rev. d'Ég.	*Revue d'Égyptologie.*
Saqq. Mast.	M. A. Murray, *Saqqara Mastabas.*
Säve-Söderbergh, *Hippotamus*	T. Säve-Söderbergh, *On Egyptian Representations of Hippopotamus Hunting as a Religious Motive, Horae Soderblomianae*, III.
SDT	K. Sethe, *Dramatische Texte zu den altägyptische Mysterienspielen.*
Sethe, *Alphabet*	K. Sethe, *Der Urspring des Alphabets*, in *Nachrichten ... Göttingen*, 1916.
Sethe, *Amun*	K. Sethe, *Amun und die acht Urgötter von Hermopolis*, in *Abhandlungen per preussischen Akademie* ... 1929.
Sethe, *Komm. Pyr.*	K. Sethe, *Übersetzung und Kommentar zu den altägyptischen Pyramidentexten.*
Sethe, *Lauf*	K. Sethe, *Altägyptische Vorstellungen von Lauf der Sonne*, in *Sitzungsberichte der preussischen Akademie* ... 1928.
Sh. S.	*The Story of the Shipwrecked Sailor*, in A. M. Blackman, *Middle Egyptian Stories.*
Sin.	*The Story of Sinuhe.*
Sitzb. Bayer. Akad.	*Sitzungberichte der bayerischen Akademie.*
Siut	F. Ll. Griffith, *The Inscriptions of Siut and Der Rifeh.*
Stud. Griff.	*Studies presented to F. Ll. Griffith.*
Th. T. S.	*Theban Tomb Series*, ed. A. H. Gardiner.
Urk. I	K. Sethe, *Urkunden des alten Reichs.*
Urk. IV	K. Sethe, *Urkunden der 18. Dynastie*, continued by W. Helck.
Urk. V	H. Grapow, *Religiöse Urkunden.*
Wb.	A. Erman and H. Grapow, *Wörterbuch der ägyptischen Sprache.*
Wenamun	*The Misfortunes of Wenamün*, in A. H. Gardiner, *Late Egyptian Stories.*
Westc.	*The Westcar Papyrus*, in A. Erman, *Die Märchaen des Papyrus Westcar.*
ZÄS	*Zeitschrift für ägyptische Sprache und Altertumskunde.*

NOTES TO READERS

Square brackets [ ] denote a restored passage.
Square brackets with dots [. . .] denote a lacuna.
Angle brackets ⟨ ⟩ denote words or suffixes omitted in the original.
Round brackets ( ) denote English words supplied to bring out the sense.
Dots . . . not in brackets indicate that a word or words are untranslatable.

'Osiris N', representing the name of the owner of the coffin, whether with or without titles or epithets, has been rendered everywhere simply as 'N'; the constant repetition of 'Osiris' as epithet of the deceased becomes almost meaningless, and can make nonsense, as in e.g. 'O Osiris, this Osiris N is your son'. Similarly the demonstrative in *N pn* 'this N' has not been translated, since again constant repetition renders it meaningless. It might be noted here that *pn* and *pw* not infrequently serve as the definite article. The translations have been made in the 1st person where that appears to be original; it is of frequent occurrence and usually too obvious to justify a note.

THE ANCIENT EGYPTIAN COFFIN TEXTS

Volume I Spells 1–354

To
PHYLLIS AND CYRIL SPAULL

In token of a long friendship
and of many kindnesses received

PREFACE

The Coffin Texts take their title from the fact that they are inscribed in ink on the inside walls of the large rectangular wooden coffins which were much used for the burial of wealthy Egyptians during the Middle Kingdom; texts written on papyrus are very rare, though of course they must once have existed to provide the necessary copies for the scribes working on the coffins. The first attempt to publish these texts as a whole was made by Pierre Lacau, who produced a printed text of eighty-four spells in *Receuil de Travaux relatifs à la Philologie et à l'Archaéologie égyptiennes et assyriennes*, vols. 26–31, reprinting them in *Textes religieux égyptiens*, Paris, 1910. Quotations from these texts were used by J. H. Breasted in his *Development of Religion and Thought in Ancient Egypt*, New York and London, 1912. Lacau was prevented by other preoccupations from carrying this work any further, so Breasted and (Sir) Alan Gardiner, after the end of the war of 1914–18, and with Lacau's full consent and co-operation, took up again the idea of making a complete collection of all known Coffin Texts, and of publishing them in autograph in vertical columns with the signs in their original arrangement and order. This colossal task was undertaken by Professor Adriaan de Buck, at first in collaboration with Gardiner, but later by himself, with the whole-hearted support of the Oriental Institute of the University of Chicago, which also made itself responsible for the publication of the copied texts. The magnificent result of de Buck's labours is the seven volumes of *The Egyptian Coffin Texts*, published at intervals between 1935 and 1961. The versions of the Pyramid Texts which appear in the Coffin Texts are not, generally speaking, included in de Buck's published copies, for reasons which he states on p. xi of his first volume. It was his original intention to publish these later, but sadly he did not live to do so. But his edition of the Coffin Texts is complete, apart from any later discoveries there may have been, and these seven large volumes are the lasting monument to the acumen and industry of a very great scholar.

Had he been spared to do so, de Buck himself would doubtless have carried out the task for which he was uniquely competent, namely the translation of this great corpus of texts into a modern language, but this was not to be, save for one spell published in the *Journal of Egyptian Archaeology*, vol. 35. This rather formidable duty has now been undertaken by one who lacks de Buck's long familiarity with the material, but who can at least plead a life-long active interest in Egyptian religious texts. As justification for the attempt he can quote Gardiner's dictum in *JEA* 32, 56: 'Scholars should not shrink from translating difficult texts. At the best they may be lucky enough to hit on the right rendering. At the worst they will have given the critics a target to tilt at'.

In general the present work follows the model of my translation of the Pyramid Texts, except that there are no italicized headings to the spells, and the same conventions of translation have been followed. The notes on the spells are confined mostly to textual and philological matters, as a work of this nature does not lend itself to lengthy exposition; discussions of this sort in respect of individual spells of especial interest by various authors will be found in the periodical literature of Egyptology. In such cases the reader is referred in the note or notes following the translation to the relevant article; in the interest of economy the discussions to be found there have not been repeated in the present work. Furthermore, owing to the recent phenomenal rise in the costs of book-production, other economies have had to be employed if the price of this work were to be kept at all with reasonable bounds. Thus hieroglyphic signs and groups have been reproduced by zincograph instead of hieroglyphic type, and the indexes, which are intended for inclusion in vol. II, now in course of preparation, will also have to undergo some economy, though in any case the mere mass of the material would have enforced something of the sort.

In preparing this work for publication one of my greatest pleasures has been the great encouragement I have had from friends and colleagues, especially those of my old Department in University College, London; in fact it is not too much to say that without their support this book would not have seen the light. I also acknowledge most gratefully the friendliness and help I have had from Mr. Adrian Phillips of Aris and Phillips Ltd., the publishers of this book. I further express my great thanks to the Sir Alan Gardiner Settlement for Egyptological Purposes for a generous subvention towards the costs of publication.

R. O. Faulkner

The complete work is now in three volumes, with The Index in Vol. III. (1978)

TRANSLATIONS AND NOTES

Spell 1

HERE BEGINS THE BOOK OF VINDICATING A MAN IN THE REALM OF THE DEAD.[1] I, 1
Ho N! You are the Lion, you are the Double Lion, you are Horus, Protector
of his father,[2] you are the fourth of these four gods | who are powerful[3] and 4
strong(?),[4] who bring water[5] and make the Nile[6] | through the power of their 6
fathers.[7] O N, raise yourself on your left side, put yourself on your right side.[8]

1. T1L adds 'and of not going upside down in the realm of the dead'. M.C.105[a] substitutes 'pronouncing recitations'.

2. T9C (originally also M.C. 105[b]) inserts: 'You are Thoth the vindicated'.

3. Written in T9C and both versions of M.C. 105 as if it were the word for 'spirits'. The 1st person of M.C. 105[a], Y1C and S10C may be secondary, in view of the 'Ho N!' of most texts.

4. *'Itpw*, meaning doubtful. This word is omitted in B15C, and four texts omit the passage entirely. *'Itp* occurs again is a similar context in *CT* III, 270*d* = 271*b.d.*

5. Two texts insert here: 'who make inundation'.

6. For *ḥp* 'Nile' B1P has corruptly *ḥkȝw* 'magicians'. The translation follows the text of B3Bo and four others, as it seems most likely to be closest to the archetype. Several texts add ***irr hy hnw*** 'who make jubilation', and T9C adds still further ***irr bʿbʿ*** 'who make the stream'; these two phrases are muddled in M.C. 105[b]. 5*g* (BH5C only) is a somewhat corrupt alternative text to 4*b*–6*a*.

7. Varr, B4C: 'their divinity'; Y1C: 'the children of their fathers'; so also originally S10C. The damaged T1L has an allusion to Osiris.

8. T1L ends with a broken passage (6*d*) the last word of which is *ḥmst* 'sitting'.

Spell 2

Gēb has commanded, and the Double Lion has repeated, that you be given I, 8
your soul which is in the earth and your shade which is in the hidden places.
Ho N! | Raise yourself, that you may be vindicated against your foes.[1] 9

1. Four texts expand this clause into the common formula: 'against your foes, male or female, against those who would harm you, male or female, against those who hate you, male or female, and those who would have judgement against you on this day'; M.C. 105 omits 'against those who hate you'.

Spell 3

I, 10 Ho N! Take your staff, your loincloth and your sandals, and go down to the Tribunal, that you may be vindicated against your foes, male or female, against those who would harm you,[1] and those who would have judgement against you in the Tribunal[2] on this happy day.

1. M.C. 105 adds: 'in the realm of the dead', and stops.
2. B15C: 'all the Tribunal'; B6C 'all the Tribunal of Osiris'.

Spell 4

I, 11 O N, the earth opens its mouth for you, Gēb throws open his jaws on your
12 account.[1] May you eat your bread and receive your plenty, | may you go to the Great Stairway, may you come to the Great City, may you kindle your warmth
14 upon earth,[2] may you become Osiris.[3] | O N, their great ones stand up for you, the scribes who are upon their mats tremble at you in your presence, and you have knit on for yourself the heads of the mottled snakes in Ōn.[4]

1. I.e. the earth opens to let the deceased leave his grave. Th.T. 319 adds: 'You are vindicated against [your] fo[es]', and with B15C and B6C introduces the next clause with the vocative 'Ho Osiris N!' M.C. 105 introduces this spell with the title: Recitation of the spells of vindication'.
2. Presumably the erstwhile warmth of his living body.
3. The variants expand this into: 'May you become this fair young god who is yonder. May you have power over your foes, male or female, those who would harm you, male or female, those who hate you, and those who would have judgement against you on this day'.
4. An obscure sentence; presumably the deceased himself assumes the heads, and thus the qualities and attributes, of these mysterious snakes, which in *Pyr.* § 1211 are spoken of as decapitated; see also *JEA* 29, 36 (33).

Spell 5

I, 15 Ho N![1] Take possession of the sky, inherit the earth![2] Who is he who shall
16 take away this sky from you,[3] you fair young god?[4] | You are vindicated against your foes, male or female, etc.[5]

1. Omitted in all but two texts, which suggests that originally this spell was intended to be a continuation of Spell 4.
2. M.C. 105 reads: '[N] has taken possession of the sky, N has inherited the earth'.
3. All texts except B2Bo and B3Bo use the future construction *in-m ir·f nḥm·f*, which yields a slightly better sense. For 'from you' M.C. 105 has 'from N'.

4. The *m* before *nṯr* (dittograph *m m* in B2Bo) has been regarded here as the *m* of equivalence. In B3Bo, B2Bo and B6C the adjective *nfr* has an unusual ending , as if it were assimilated to the imperfective active participle (*Eg. Gramm.*[3] § 357), and has an unusual determinative. B4Bo has an obvious corruption arising from a copyist failing to understand the abnormal det. of *nfr*. M.C. 105 and S10C substitute for this clause the words: 'even Rēʿ, the eldest of the gods, and Horus, the successor of Osiris' (15*d*).

5. B15C and B6C omit *ḥmt-rꜣ* 'etc.'

Spell 6

How great is the monthly festival of the height of heaven, even the festival of
the New Moon![1] The finger is removed from upon you, | your trembling is 17
taken away, since you have planted the plume[2] at the horizon, at the place
where are those who know you. You suck at your mother Sothis as your nurse
who is in the horizon, | Isis squats (?)[3] by you, she makes you bright,[4] she 18
makes for you fair ways of vindication against your foes, male and female,
etc.,[5] | and those who would have judgement against you in the realm of the 19
dead[6] on this happy day.

1. This spell deals with the rebirth of the deceased at this festival. B15C has carelessly substituted *pt* for *ꜣbd*.

2. Hardly 'tuft', despite Gardiner's rendering of a passage from *ZÄS* 57, 10* (*Eg. Gramm.*[3] p. 290, second example); in *M.u.K.* 1, 2 *śwt* with hair-det. undoubtedly means 'feather', see also Spell 8, n.6. The bearing of this passage on the context is not obvious.

3. *Pꜣg* is unknown to *Wb.* The translation 'squats' rests upon the det. and the possible identity with the later *pgꜣ* 'mode of sitting', *Wb.* I, 562,8.

4. I.e. cleans up the new-born child? Two texts substitute the inferior reading *sḫp·s ṯn* 'she conducts you' (fem.).

5. So B3Bo and B1P. Several texts omit *ḥmt-rꜣ* and read 'who would harm you' or 'who hate you'; M.C. 105 has: 'against your foes, male or female, on this day'.

6. *M ḫrt-nṯr* 'in the realm of the dead' occurs in three versions only out of nine; nevertheless the text seems the better for its inclusion.

Spell 7

The vindication of a man against his foes is brought about in the realm of the
dead.[1] The earth was hacked up when the Rivals[2] fought, their feet scooped
out | the sacred pool in Ōn.[3] Now comes Thoth adorned with his dignity, for 20
Atum[4] has ennobled him with[5] strength, and the Two Great Ladies[6] are
pleased with him.[7] |So the fighting is ended, the tumult is stopped, the fire 21
which went forth is quenched, the anger in the presence of the Tribunal of
the God is calmed,[8] and it sits to give judgement in the presence of Gēb. | 22

Hail to you, magistrates of the gods![9] N is vindicated before you[10] on this day,[11] even as[12] Horus was vindicated against his foes on that day[13] of acces-
23 sion.[14] | May he be joyful before you[15] even as Isis was joyful in that her happy day of playing music,[16] when her son Horus had taken possession of his Two Lands in triumph.

1. So B2Bo; M.C. 105 reads: 'To be uttered: the spells of recitations for vindication in the realm of the dead'. The other texts omit the title.

2. Horus and Seth.

3. An aetiological myth regarding the sacred pool in the temple of Heliopolis. T1N.Y. and T1L have corrupted *šdyt* 'pool' into *šdwty* and *šdty* respectively. Note the abnormal writing of *nṯr* in B2Bo and B3Bo, which recurs elsewhere.

4. Varr. 'Rēʿ-Atum' or 'Lord of All' (*nb tm*). The former variant is so common that henceforward it will not normally be recorded.

5. The *m-ḫrt* of B3Bo, B2Bo and B1P seems inferior to *m* (B4Bo, S10C) or *ḫr* (B6C, B4C, T9C); the same comment applies to *m-ḫr* of T1N.Y. and T1L.

6. Presumably Isis and Nephthys.

7. Thoth, the traditional pacifier, comes equipped to stop the fight and so to relieve the anxieties of the goddesses, who were Isis and Nephthys, the respective spouses of the combatants.

8. Lit. 'censed'; T1L has: 'all the Tribunal'.

9. Var. 'magistrates of heaven, magistrates of earth'.

10. Two texts omit *ḫr·tn* 'before you'.

11. There are minor variants of this sentence which do not affect its sense.

12.  (B3Bo) and  (B2Bo) represent the older form of *my* of the other texts.

13. Var. 'that happy day'.

14. On *ḫʿw* see *JEA* 39,23; Horus takes over his father's kingship.

15. Varr. 'on this day' and 'before you on this day'.

16. For *ḫnt* 'play music' cf. the late *ḫn* of *Wb.* III, 286,2 ff. Presumably we have here the infinitive of a 3 inf. verb. Three texts have failed to understand this word and have substituted *ḫnt* 'rowing'.

Spell 8

I, 24 Hail to you, Tribunal of the God who shall judge me[1] concerning what I have
25 said, I being ignorant, at ease and having no care.[2] | O you who surround me and stand at my back, may I be vindicated in the presence of Gēb, chiefest of
26 the gods.[3] |Yonder god shall judge me[4] according to what I know.[5] I have arisen with my plume[6] on my head and my righteousness on my brow, my
27 foes are in sorrow,[7] | and I have taken possession of all my property in vindication.

1. The 1st person appears to have been original, see B4Bo and B1P in 24*b* and 25*a*. Three texts add 'on this day'.

2. An obscure passage which seems to have puzzled the ancient copyists, judging by the many varr. The text followed in the translation is B2Bo. *Ḫm* and *nḏm* are old perfectives. *N* in *n ḳsnt·f* has been regarded as the old equivalent of the classical Middle Egyptian *nn* in the sense of 'without'. In B4Bo the strange group  after the name of the deceased must surely be intended for the demonstrative *tn* 'this', and it seems that some inexplicable corruption has occurred, since the reading is confirmed by de Buck, p. 24, n. 1.* The other varr. are:– B1P: 'concerning what I have said, being ignorant, young, at ease and having no care'; B6C: 'concerning what he has said, being ignorant; concerning what he has said, being young; [. . .] care'; B4C: 'concerning what he has said and done, being ignorant [. . .] youthfulness, and N is troubled about it'; M.C. 105 and T9C: 'concerning what she (he) has said and done, being ignorant, young and having no care'; S10C: 'concerning what N has done, being ignorant and not knowing [. . .]'; T1L: 'concerning what he has said, being young; concerning what he has done, being ignorant [. . .]'.

3. B4Bo omits 'vindicate N', while T1L perverts the whole sentence into: 'N has stood up vindicated against his foes, male and female, and against those who would have judgement with you (*sic*) on this day'. S10C omits the whole sentence, and after the name of the deceased M.C. 105 inserts: 'against his foes, male and female'.

4. *Ḫr*+ subject + participle is apparently a development of the participial statement, and the particle *ḫr* seems to imply future time. S10C and T1L omit.

5. *Ḫft rḫ·f* is corrupted in B1P into *ḫft·f*, and in B6C into *ḫr·f*, while M.C. 105 has: 'who shall judge the case (*ḫt*) according to what he knows'. The subject of *rḫ* 'know' apparently refers to the deceased, who is to be judged only on his conscious acts, not on unwitting conduct.

6. *Šwt* certainly means 'feather', 'plume' here (see Spell 6, n.2), since the context shows that it is the feather symbolic of 'truth', 'righteousness' which is envisaged. Some copyists seem to have had difficulty with this passage and to have emended it, and the following versions result:– B6C: 'He is vindicated, his plume is on his head, righteousness is on his brow'; M.C. 105 and T9C: 'N has stood up in the presence of Gēb, her (his) plume is on her (his) head and her (his) righteousness is on her (his) brow'; S10C: 'N has come forth vindicated in the presence of Gēb with his plume on his head and his brow'. T1L 'N has arisen, his plume on his [head and his righteousness on his brow]'.

7. *Ḳmw* is unknown to *Wb.*, but cf. *iḳmw*, 'sorrow', *Pyr.* § 1989.

Spell 9

Hail to Thoth and his Tribunal.[1] Hail to you, O Thoth, in whom is[2] the peace
of the gods, and all the Tribunal[3] | who are with you! Command that they 28
shall come forth at the approach of N, that they may hear all that he has to
say[4] that is good on this day, | because[5] to you belongs this plume[6] which 29
arose in God's-land, which Osiris brought to Horus,[7] that he might set it on
his head as a reward,[8] | being vindicated[9] against his foes, male and female. It 30

was he who tore off (?) the testicles of Seth;[10] he neither perished nor died,[11]
31 for you[12] are | that star which the West bore,[13] which neither perished nor was annihilated; this N shall neither perish nor be annihilated; and no evil im-
32 pediment shall be imposed[14] | against N—so says Atum.[15] As for anything evil
33 which they may say or do against N in the presence of Gēb,[16] | they are[17] against them and they will be against them.[18]

1. B2Bo only. This is the title of the spell.

2. So, rather than the normal 'who is in'; Thoth the great pacifier is responsible for the peace of the gods. B2Bo omits these words, while T1L omits nearly all this spell.

3. M.C. 105 and T9C: 'this Tribunal'; S10C: 'the Tribunal of the Gods'.

4. For *ḏdt·f nbt* three texts substitute *mdw N* 'the word of N.' M.C. 105 inserts a superfluous suffix after *mdw*.

5. *Ntt* for ⟨*n*-⟩*ntt*; three texts have the synonymous *ḥr-ntt*. B6C has *n* alone.

6. So B3Bo, B4Bo and B6C; B2Bo omits the pronoun after *ntt*. B1P and B4C are in the 3rd person, while M.C. 105 and T9C (which is corrupt) have the name of the deceased; S10C has simply 'Osiris', having doubtless omitted the name of the deceased in error. The version in the 2nd person is to be preferred, since Thoth is more likely to be the owner of the plume than is the deceased. For the demonstrative *tw* of B3Bo, B2Bo, B4Bo, B6C and B4C, we find *tw pw* in B1P, M.C. 105 and S10C; *pw* is superfluous.

7. Var. 'to his son Horus'; B4Bo omits 'to Horus'.

8. Four texts have: 'as the reward of (his) vindication'.

9. B4Bo and B1P insert the suffix *f* after *ẖrw*.

10. Four texts add an apparently unnecessary and misplaced dative *n·f* at the end of the sentence. M.C. 105, S10C and T9C have *ꜥfꜣ·n·f* instead of *swt ꜥfꜣ*; T1L, which starts here, is corrupt. B4C has a word *isnwy* for 'testicles' which appears as *isn* in *CT* III, 124*i* but is better known in the form *insw* in *CT* IV, 236*b* (M4C), cf. also *Wb.* I, 100, 15. A late form which has lost the *n* is *iswy* in *Wb.* I, 131, 12.

11. Reading *n sk·f n mt·f* with B4Bo and B1P. B3Bo is corrupt; B2Bo (before *mt·f* only), B6C and T1L have *iwty* instead of *n*, apparently anticipating 31*b*. The other texts run:—B6C and T1L: 'who neither perished nor was annihilated (*ḥtm*)'; M.C. 105 and T9C: 'N neither died nor perished nor was annihilated'; S10C 'N neither died nor was annihilated'.

12. Thoth?

13. Var. B1P and B6C: 'the beautiful West'; B4C inserts after *sbꜣ pw pw* (*sic*) the words *iry s*(*m*)*t* 'the warden of the desert'.

14. Var. B1P: *iwty dmyt sḏb nb ḏwy*.

15. M.C. 105, S10C and T9C may have understood *in* 'so says' as *in* 'by', for they refer to gods, spirits and men.

16. B2Bo omits 'or do'; note the omission of the repeated suffix in *irt·sn* in B3Bo, B4Bo, B6C and S10C. B1P inserts 'in the presence of Osiris' after the name of the deceased, and B6C is similar, while four texts omit the 'in the presence of' phrase.

17. An inexplicable *n* has found its way into *iw·sn* in six texts; again in 52*d*.

18. M.C.105, S10C and T9C add 'that is what they say', followed by a further reference to the vindication of the deceased.

Spell 10

Ho N! The portal is opened for you by Seshat,[1] | fair paths are opened up for I, 34
you by Wepwawet,[2] and there is no god who has turned himself about con-
cerning what he has said.[3] This is what he has said:[4] N is vindicated against
his foes, male | or female,[5] and against those who would have judgement 35
against him on this day.[6]

1. The deceased is admitted to the other world. For the sense of *wḏꜥ* here cf. *wḏꜥ rꜣ* 'open the mouth', *Wb.* I, 406,11.
2. B4Bo shortly: 'a road is opened up for you'.
3. I.e. has not gone back on a previous verdict favourable to the deceased. Cf. *JEA* 35,93, n.1.
4. B4Bo omits; S10C had: 'what they have [said]'.
5. B1P and B4C substitute *ḥmt-rꜣ* 'etc.' and B4C ends.
6. M.C. 105, S10C and T9C add 'those who hate him or would injure him' in more or less garbled forms.

Spell 11

Welcome, welcome! The statue (?)[1] is brought to you; so say I (?).[2] Welcome,
welcome! | The great statue (?) is brought to you.[3] Encompass N,[4] do all that I, 36
he shall say,[5] give him praise, you gods.[6] Come, you gods,[6] | that you may see 37
him, he having come forth safely[7] and having been vindicated against his
foes;[8] he has taken possession of the crown,[9] he has mounted (?)[10] the thrones
of Gēb, | he has taken and destroyed the other.[11] 38

1. The word *Tw* as a divine name does not carry conviction, and despite the unanimity of the texts in 35*e* and the near unanimity in 36*a*, it is hard not to believe that this is in fact a misspelling of *twt* 'statue', which is actually found in B1P in 36*a*. Even so the sense remains obscure. In 35*e* B6C omits all but the opening words; B4C appears to read: 'Welcome, welcome today! My statue(?) is made. Welcome, welcome!'
2. 𓇋𓀁 perhaps for *i·i* 'so say I', in three texts only. At the end of 35*e* M.C. 105 and T9C add the name of the deceased.
3. Var. B1P: 'the statue (*twt*) is brought to you, the statue of the great one is brought to you'; T9C has: 'his statue(?) (*tw*) is brought to him.'
4. An imperative addressed to the gods.
5. Five texts omit.
6. Two texts omit 'gods'; one is damaged.
7. T9C has bungled *ḥtp* and added 'on account of his eye', perhaps thinking of the Eye of Horus.
8. Three texts omit and B4Bo is corrupt.
9. Varr. B3Bo, B4Bo: 'her two crowns'; B1P: 'his crown'.

10. The translation is a guess, for no verb *ḫnt* with an appropriate meaning appears to be known; can the literal sense be 'has confronted the thrones'? The ancient copyists seem also to have felt the difficulty, for four texts out of the surviving seven have added the boat-determinative, as if the verb meant 'sail upstream', which in this context yields no sense. M.C. 105 continues with a broken passage referring to the vindication and heritage of the deceased.

11. Probably a reference to Seth. B1P adds *ḥmt-r3* 'etc.' at the end of the spell, and, together with B6C and B4C, has corrupted *ḥḏ·f* into *ḥḏ sw*. B4C also inserts *sw* after *nḥm*.

Spell 12

O N, go forth great and mighty[1] even as Rēʿ went forth great and mighty |
I, 39 on the east side of the sky. The gods who spoke on behalf of Horus and over-
40 threw Seth for him,[2] they shall speak on behalf of N | and overthrow his foes for him.[3]

1. B6C has a dittograph of *pr n·k*, while M.C. 105 omits this imperative and T2C omits the initial invocation of the deceased.

2. The context clearly demands this rendering rather than the imperative of B3Bo and B4Bo. For 'Seth' T9C substitutes: 'his foes who hate him'.

3. T2C adds: 'those who would injure him, who hate [him] and who would have judgement [against him] on this day'; similarly in M.C. 105, S10C and T9C. S10C has *ḥmt-r3* instead of *irwt r·f*, etc. in 40*b*.

Spell 13

Title: To be recited: The spells for causing a spirit's tomb (*is*) to flourish in the necropolis; the spell for opening the tomb (*ḥ3t*) for the double of the blessed N.[1]

41 Ho N! Go forth[2] from your house, from your seat and from any place where
42 you are, as Horus was vindicated when he[3] inherited | the inheritance and had acquired power;[4] go forth vindicated from the presence of this Tribunal of
43 the gods of Pe, Dep and Ōn, | even as Horus went forth vindicated against Seth from the presence of this Tribunal of the Lord of Suffering(?).[5]

1. This title is in T2C only, see de Buck's note p. 40, n.4.

2. The interjection *h3* clearly desiderates an imperative, here with reflexive dative. M.C. 105, which omits the prefatory summons, puts the text into the 3rd person: 'N has gone forth from her house'; so clearly also S10C, though the verb is lost. These two damaged texts differ in other details from the other versions.

3. B4C wrongly has the 2nd person, an example of the not infrequent confusion of pronouns in the Coffin Texts.

4. Lit. 'had powered power'; B4C is again wrongly in the 2nd person, as also T2C, which stops at this point.

5. For *gmwt* 'suffering(?)' cf. *BD* 29,11; P. Bremner-Rhind, 26,13. The 'Lord of Suffering' is presumably Osiris, who suffered at the hands of Seth.

Spell 14

Go forth from the dispute, | go forth from the dispute, for it was Horus[1] who I, 44
went forth from the dispute. Be far from N,[2] O you who should be far from
him;[3] do not approach him, O you who would approach him,[4] | for he will 45
judge the Wilful One[5] in Ōn.

1. Var. S10C *ṯwt Ḥr* 'It was you, Horus . . .'.

2. The 1st person of B2Bo and B1P seems in error, for the spell opens with an imperative addressed to the deceased, and the pronoun of the 2nd person *ṯwt* in 44*b* (S10C) confirms this.

3. The clause introduced by *nt(y)* shows some variations. Instead of the construction *nty* + old perfective employed by the B3Bo group, B15C, etc., use the participle *ḥr*, while B6C wrongly inserts  before *ḥrt*. B4C has two imperatives *ḥr ṯn . . . ḥr ṯn*; note the fem. dependent pronoun reinforcing the imperative. B4C is a woman's coffin.

4. See the last note. B15C is corrupt.

5. *'Imr·f*, lit. 'he wishes' is here a *nomen divi*, apparently an epithet of Seth, since he is judged by Osiris in the person of the deceased.

Spell 15

O you whom the Bull begot, O you whom the Bull begot,[1] pull off the bonds
of the Bull | and appear in order that he may give orders against those foes of I, 46
his, male or female, who would revile N or do anything evil against N.[2]

1. The Bull is presumably Osiris, whom his son Horus is summoned to rescue.

2. From 'appear' onwards B4C and the related texts have a variant version of which S10C has the most complete and intelligible text. It reads: 'Neith appears against that evil word, Neith appears against that evil Power; Neith appears against those who would smite N; Neith appears against those who would drive out (*rdy* for *dr*, cf. *Stud. Griff.* 72) N. Horus has crossed over from Ōn to(?) his father(?), who is pre-eminent in the *ṯnnt*-shrine, because of the conspirators' (*wꜣtw*, cf. *Wb.* I, 245,2). For Neith as protectress of the dead, cf. *Pyr.* §1314; *BD* 112,13; 158,3; *JEA* 4, pl. 11,3.6; Turin 2202.

Spells 16 and 17[1]

I, 47 Be seated,[2] O N, in the presence of Gēb, chiefest of the gods,[3] for you are
48 Horus with his White Crown on his head.[4] | Isis[5] bore him, Nekhbet[6] brought
49 him up, the nurse of Horus nursed him, the powers of Seth | served him over
and above his own powers,[7] his father Osiris gave him these two staffs of his.[8]
50 N has come | and he exults over it[9] in vindication, there are given[10] to him
51 these two great and mighty Enneads, he rages against[11] the gods | with his
power, he controls the life of the gods. In truth there is an invocation-offering
for Rēʿ, and Horus who is at the head of the living protects his father Osiris, |
52 he has stopped[12] the movements of him who slew[13] his father. As for anyone
53 who shall commit any evil robbery against N, N will use an arm upward |and
downward[14] against their great ones in Ōn in the presence of the risen Osiris.
This N has taken possession of his Two Lands in vindication; you are Horus,
Lord of Justice.[15]

1. Despite the separation mark at the end of Spell 16 in B1P, these two spells form a continuous text.

2. Shown to be imperative by the 2nd person of the next clause. M.C. 105 and doubtless S10C have *sḏm·n·f* forms, see n.4 below. B3Bo omits the verb, clearly a copyist's error.

3. Cf. *JEA* 39,10.

4. Var. 'upon him'. B4Bo adds 'righteousness on his brow'; M.C. 105 and S10C: 'N has sat down to judge in the presence of Gēb as Horus with his White Crown upon him'; B15C: 'N has sat down in the presence of Gēb; you are Horus', etc.; B.H. 5C: 'Ho N! I sit down for N to judge in the presence of Gēb, for you are Horus with his Double Crown on [his] head'.

5. Var. 'his mother Isis'. B.H. 5C is corrupt.

6. *Ḫꜣbt* or *ḫꜣbyt*, determined with a vulture, is clearly the original of the vulture-shaped breast-ornament recorded under *ḫꜣbyt* in *Wb.* III, 229.14. Here *Ḫꜣb(y)t* is a goddess, a nurse of the young Horus.

7. Apparently even Seth was unable to avoid adding his strength to that of the young Horus, a most unexpected phenomenon.

8. Var. S10C: 'his two standards' through an obvious misunderstanding. T2C seems to have had a different text.

9. For *ḥkn* B2Bo and M.C. 105 read *ḥk;* the latter omits 'in vindication'.

10. Spell 17 begins here.

11. *Ḏnḏn*, varr. *dndn*, *ḏnd*, is recorded in *Wb.* V, 471,21 ff., 579,6.7, only as an intransitive verb, but the transitive sense is found in *dndn·s tn m dndn·s* 'it shall rage against you with its wrath', Bremner-Rhind, 25,7; the present passage takes the usage back to the Middle Kingdom.

12. Lit. 'caused to be taken away'. B4Bo omits the *s* of the causative *snḥm*.

13. Var. B15C and S10C: 'those who slew'.

14. I.e. will strike a heavy blow.

15. Var. S10C (52*d–g*): 'As for any who may say or do anything evil against you, they will be (again *iw·n·sn* for *iw·sn*, see Spell 9, n.17) destroyed because of (read *r swn·sn n*) this which they have said, and this N will be vindicated against his foes, against those who would injure him and against those who would have judgement against him (*ḫft⟨·f⟩*) on this day.

Spell 18

Ho N! You shall cross the sky and traverse the firmament, those who are in the Winding Waterway shall worship you | and see you when you arise in the I, 54
eastern horizon, those who are in the Netherworld having permitted your beautiful appearing; you shall come forth from the Night-bark and go aboard the Day-bark as Horus Lord of Patricians himself commands you.

Ho N! You shall go up upon the great west side of the sky and go down 55
upon the great east side of the earth[1] among those gods who are in the suite of Osiris, in peace, in peace with Rēʿ who is in the sky.

1. This unexpected reversal of the points of the compass is incomprehensible. We would expect the deceased to go up on the east and down on the west as does the sun. Perhaps we have here a blunder in an early copy which no-one has noticed or at least attempted to correct.

Spell 19

Ho N! You are a god and you shall be a god, you shall have no foes or opponents with Rēʿ who is in the sky or with Osiris the great god who is in Abydos.

Spell 20

Ho N! | Gēb will open for you your blind eyes,[1] he will straighten for you I, 56
your bent knees,[2] there will be given to you your heart (*ib*) which you had from your mother, your heart (*ḥꜣty*) which belongs to your body,[3] your soul which was upon earth, your corpse which was upon the ground.[4] There will be bread for your body, water for your throat, and sweet air for your nostrils. |
The owners of tombs will be kindly to you,[5] the owners of coffins will come to 57
you,[6] they will bring to you your members which were far from you, | when 58
you are re-established in your original shape(?)[7]

1. T9C wrongly: 'his eyes'.
2. An allusion to the crouched posture of the early burials, which suggests that this is a very ancient text; on *mꜣst* 'knee' see my note *JEA* 45,104. *BD* 436,3 has 'legs' for 'knees'.

3. The passive *rdyw* of B3Bo is preferable to the active *rdy·n·i* of B1P and B4C; all texts except B.N.5C and the damaged T9C agree in stating the dead man had his *ib* from his mother, but that his *ḥȝty* was simply part of his physical body; this suggests that in this context at least *ib* represented the inherited characteristics—temperament, intelligence and the like—which had their supposed seat in the physical heart (*ḥȝty*), though it is not to be supposed that the Egyptians made this clear-cut distinction in all cases where *ib* and *ḥȝty* appear side by side. For *mwt* 'mother' B.H. 5C substitutes *ẖt* 'body' in contrast to its synonym *ḏt* at the end of the clause.

4. B6C omits 'your soul'. *BD* 436,5 describes the corpse as 'under' the ground.

5. I.e. those already dead whom the deceased will meet: var. B1P and B6C: 'those who are in their tombs'. B1P, B6C and B4C introduce this sentence with 'Ho N!'; B.H. 5C omits it.

6. All the other versions have *wn* 'open', but 'come' of B3Bo yields the better sense. The prospective *sḏm·f* forms *iwt* and *int* (below) give the clue to the future tense of this spell.

7. , varr. 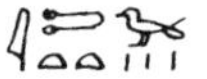 M.C. 105, 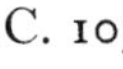 *BD* 436,8, is quite obscure; following Barguet, *Livre des Morts*, 249, I have taken it to be a corruption of 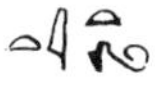 'form', 'shape'. B.H. 5C omits this last clause.

Spell 21

Ho N!, Come,[1] that you may ascend to the sky;[2] the ladder to the side of Rēʿ
I, 59 is put together for you | among the gods, who remove[3] the pestilence of the
60 streams[4] so that you may drink water from them. You shall | walk upon your feet,[5] you shall not walk head downwards.[6] Those who are in the midst of the earth shall go up ⟨to⟩ you,[7] but there will not go up to you ⟨those who would destroy your⟩ gate or wall[8] or who would throw down your fences[9] for
61 you, | or your tomb[10] which your city gods made for you. You are pure, you
62 are pure! As Rēʿ lives, you are pure! Your front is in | purity, your back parts are in cleanness,[11] and your cleanliness[12] is by means of natron and incense,
63 milk of ⟨the mother of⟩ | Apis[13] and beer of the beer-god.[14]

1. *'Iw* is shown to be imperative by the following enclitic, further strengthened in B3Bo by a reflexive dative. B6C has *iw in r·k;* B4C employs the prospective form *iwt·ṯ*. T1L is destroyed, and the other texts omit the *iw*-clause; T9C and T1C leave out all the earlier parts of this spell.

2. M.C. 105, T1L and B.H. 5C, which have omitted the archaic imperative *iw*, begin here with the imperative 'ascend to the sky!'; the ending *-t* in *prt* of M.C. 105 is probably due to the fact that the owner of this coffin was a woman. Other examples of this rare form are *mȝt ptrt . . . sḏmt wnt im* 'See! Behold! . . . Hear! Be yonder!', *CT IV*, 383*a–b* (B3C woman's coffin); *ḥfȝwt ẖrt ḥr ḥr·tn* 'O you female snakes, fall on your faces', V, 42*a:* Cf. *Eg. Gramm.*[3], p. 257, n. 1a.

3. For *ẖsr* 'remove' B1P has *sẖr*, an obvious slip. B.H. 5C has *sẖn* with a peculiar determinative.

4. Minor varr. in M.C. 105 and B.H. 5C; this sentence shows that the Egyptians had some knowledge of the consequences of drinking contaminated water.

5. Before this clause four texts insert: 'Ho N!'.

6. M.C. 105 has corrupted the negation *n* into the interrogative *in*.

7. All texts seem to be corrupt to some extent. The simplest emendation is to read *prr* ⟨*n·*⟩*k ḥryw-ib nw tꜣ*, compare 60*d*.

8. All texts are obviously corrupt; the reading *ʿryt* 'gate' seems to be authentic, but before it we must assume the loss of a participle of a verb for 'destroy' or the like, and after it of a suffix 2nd sing., as also after *inb* 'wall'. This clause would then fall in to line with 60*e* and 61*a*, which refer to damage to the deceased's fences and tomb. The preposition *m* in B3Bo or *r* (T1L, B.H. 5C) before *ʿryt* is hard to account for; in B1P and B6C we have *rw* in this position.

9. Read *wḥn n·k*, participle + dative, not *sḏm·n·f;* the deceased would not throw down his own fences. M.C. 105 has merged the two successive *n*'s; B3Bo, B.H. 5C and T1L omit the suffix after *inbwt*.

10. Reading *ḥꜣḥꜣt*, a reduplicated form of *ḥꜣt* 'tomb'. B6C has corruptly *gꜣgꜣt;* M.C. 105 and T9C have *ḥꜣ·t̠(k) sp 2* 'Get back! Get back!' which is nonsense in this context, and they also omit the suffix after 'gods'. T1L is corrupt; B.H. 5C has *ḥꜣ* and omits the rest of the clause.

11. Var. T9C: 'in incense'.

12. *St-swʿb(t)* appears to be an abstract noun of the type collected in *Concise Dict.* 206 f. The preceding *m* in B3Bo is superfluous.

13. 'Milk of Apis' (so also *BD* 437,1) is a physical impossibility; read presumably 'milk of the mother of Apis'.

14. This deity is the masculine counterpart of *Ṯnmyt* the beer-goddess, on whom see *JEA* 13, 198. The name of the god has been corrupted in T1L and B.H. 5C.

Spell 22

An image of wax[1] which dispels evil. Tefēnet the daughter of Rēʿ feeds you |
with what her father Rēʿ gave to her,[2] the Valley gives you bread from the I, 64
burial of her father Osiris,[3] Rēʿ bites on | something sweet, and he will give it 65
to you.[4] Your trio[5] are in the sky[6] with Rēʿ, they are of[7] twisted[8] barley of
Lower Egypt.[9] Your quartette[10] are on earth with Gēb, they are of Lower
Egyptian barley of *'Ibw*.[11] | Their[12] two millers are yours, are piled up (?)[13] the 66
offerings which they place before you.

Ho N! You shall go forth into the day, you shall have power in | your legs[14] 67
in the morning, you shall have power in your legs in the evening,[15] you shall
have power in your legs at the lamp-lighting, | you shall have power in your 68
legs at all seasons, at any hour in which you desire to go forth,[16] you shall have
power in your legs in every tribunal | in every court;[17] you shall have power 69
in your legs in every place from which your heart desires to go forth at any time.

1. Presumably of Tefēnet, in view of what follows.

2. M.C. 105 omits 'Rēʿ' after 'her father' and ends here. B1P inserts an unnecessary *n* before *it·s* and before the final 'Rēʿ'.

3. B.H. 5C omits this clause.

4. T1L omits the pronoun *st;* T9C has *m dd·f n·k* 'when he gives to you' or 'being what he gives to you'.

5. Of foodstuffs. T1C has 'your bread'; B.H. 5C omits 65*c–d.*

6. For *r pt* of B3Bo we have *m* in T1C and *ḥr* or *r–ḥr* in the other texts. *R* is the best reading, cf. *Pyr.* §§121; 717; 2156.

7. B3Bo, B1P and B6C have *nt,* presumably in concord with *ẖmt(t)* 'trio'; B4C has *n,* T1L has *n-st,* T1C has *n-sw.* T9C omits this clause.

8. *Snḥ,* used elsewhere of 'binding' hair, *Pyr* §1950*f*; a prisoner (*Urk.* I, 305, 18; IV, 617,13) and of a snake 'entwining' a stem (*Hymnen,* 8,3), seems to refer here to stalks of barley twisted together. T1L has *sꜥḥ* here, T1C *sryw,* both corruptions of *snḥ.*

9. For 'barley of Lower Egypt' T1L substitutes 'emmer'.

10. Var. T1C: 'bread' again.

11. *'Ibw* is obscure to me. For 'barley' T1L again substitutes 'emmer'. T1C has 'Your bread is on earth with Gēb, it is of twisted barley of Lower Egypt'; T9C is corrupt.

12. 'Their' presumably refers to Rēꜥ and Gēb. These 'protectresses' are apparently Tefēnet and 'the Valley', since these are the only two female entities hitherto named. T1L and T9C have: 'the protectresses protect them for you'; B.H. 5C refers to 'the two protectresses of Rēꜥ': the text is corrupt, but seems originally to have supported T1L. T1C has shortly: *iw nḏty nḏt.*

13. *Sẖt* is obscure, and the sense here given to it is a guess. T1L, B.H. 5C and T1C have confused this word with *sḫt* 'field', thinking of the 'Field of Offerings', and the latter two are otherwise corrupt.

14. I.e. freedom of movement. For 'legs' B.H. 5C has 'heart'. At this point B6C omits a good deal, running straight on into the middle of 68*a.*

15. T1C only.

16. Following B3Bo.

17. *Rꜣ-ꜥwy* (see also 77*a*) is apparently a variant of *rꜣ-ꜥꜣ* 'entry', on which see *ZÄS* 70,84; the gate was the traditional place for a bench of judges to sit. Compare *ꜥry* of B.H. 5C and *rꜣ-ꜥry* of T1L, reminiscent of *ꜥryt,* also a place of judgement. B4C has *rꜣ-pr* 'temple', B6C takes a leap to the middle of 69*c.* T1L ends here.

Spell 23

I, 70 Ho N! You shall not be examined, you shall not be imprisoned, you shall not
be restrained,[1] you shall not be fettered, you shall not be put under guard,[2]
71 you shall not be put in the place of execution in which rebels are put,[3] | and
sand shall not be put on your face.[4] Be watchful, be weighty,[5] and no-one will
cause you to be opposed.[6] Beware that you do not go forth.[7] Take your staff,[8] |
72 your loincloth, your sandals, and your arrows[9] for the road, that you may cut
off the heads and sever the necks of your foes male and female[10] who draw
73 near when you are dead.[11] | 'Hasten[12] and come' are the words of the god who
brings him on the day of accusation.[13]

1. T9C and B.H. 5C omit the clause with *ḏdḥ*; T1C omits both the *ḏdḥ* and the *ẖnr* clauses.

2. Varr. B6C: 'you shall not be fettered' only; B4C *mnyt* corruptly for *n inṯ;* T1L: 'you shall not be fettered, you shall not be imprisoned': T1C: 'you shall not be put under guard, you shall not be fettered'. T9C and B.H. 5C omit.

3. B.H. 5C transfers this clause to 71*g*.

4. I.e. not buried in a hole in the desert. T9C and T1C transfer this and the two following imperatives to 71*e.f*.

5. This use of 'be weighty' in the sense of 'be careful' survives in modern Egyptian and Sudanese colloquial Arabic, as I have been informed by Dr. Haikal and by Dr. A. J. Arkell.

6. Lit. 'none will place opposition against you'.

7. I.e. unequipped, for in what follows the dead man is adjured to equip himself adequately for the journey. On the texts of B.H. 5C, T1L and T9C see nn. 3.4 above.

8. Varr. B4C, T1L: 'take your scrip and your staff': T9C: 'take your scrip'; B.H. 5C: 'take your [. . .], your scrip and your staff'; T1C omits this clause. *Šṯ, šṯ,* here translated 'scrip' as being an essential part of a traveller's equipment, is shown by the dets. to be a different word from *šṯ* 'a garment', *Wb.* IV, 558,5 ff.

9. Varr. B4C: 'your loincloth and sandals'; T9C 'your loincloth and your arrow'; T1L: 'your bow, your loincloth, your sandals and your arrow'. B.H.5C writes the word for 'arrow' as *iꜣḥ*, metathesis for *iḥꜣ*; for this var. of the stem *ꜥḥꜣ* cf. *Urk.* V, 54,10.

10. For *sinn* 'sever' B6C and B.H. 5C have *ꜥnn;* T9C, T1L and T1C have *in.* For 'your foes male and female' T9C substitutes 'all dead male and female'; similarly T1L, B.H. 5C, T1C.

11. B6C misreads *sꜥr* as *sꜥꜥ;* T9C has: 'who make your death'; T1L omits *mt·k*.

12. From T9C to T1C, all texts are to some extent corrupt.

13. For *ẖbnt* 'accusation' B.H. 5C has *ẖprt:* T1C is also slightly corrupt at the end.

Spell 24

Ho N! The Falcon has screamed for you,[1] the Goose has cackled for you.[2] I, 74
A hand is extended to you by Thoth, the arm of your foe is chopped off for you, the Two Kites, who are Isis and Nephthys, scream for you,[3] striking for you on two gongs[4] in the presence of the gods. Anubis[5] is upon you as[6] your protection, Wepwawet has opened up fair paths for you.[7]

Ho N! The doors of the sky are opened for you by Rēꜥ, the doors are thrown 75
open on your account by Gēb, the doors are opened for you in Abydos, the doors of the firmament[8] are thrown open for you by your mother Nūt, because your power is so great;[9] the portals on earth are thrown open for you by Gēb, because[10] the knowledge of your name is so effective.

1. Note the many varr. of *ḥꜣ* 'scream'.

2. B3Bo corruptly: 'you have cackled as a goose' and ends, as do T1L, B.H. 5C and T1C. A long omission in T9C.

3. B1P is slightly corrupt, inserting *in* unnecessarily before *ḏrty*.

4. The same expression recurs in I, 248*b* (Spell 60). For *skr* 'strike' instruments of sound cf. *Festival Hall*, 11 (drum) and *Ti*, 60 (harp). Here the objects struck are clearly of metal, hence the translation 'gongs'.

5. Var. 'the arms of Anubis'.

6. B4C omits 'are upon you as'.

7. B1P wrongly: 'for him'.

8. B6C omits.

9. So B6C; var. B1P, T9C: 'it is the greatness of your power'.

10. *N* 'because' only in B1P; the construction with *pw* is common to all texts.

Spell 25

I, 76 Ho N! There has been given to you a field-plot in the Valley[1] and the food of the West;[2] it is power, it is speech,[3] it is opening up the West, which is pleasing to the heart of Rēʿ and satisfactory to the hearts of his tribunal who
77 watch over men.[4] 'Give to him', says Rēʿ, 'and lead him'.[5] | May he[6] be gracious to you at the stairway of any tribunal in any court[7] and at any place in which your god[8] is gracious to you.

1. Varr. B6C: 'by the Valley'; B4C to B.N. 5C: 'of the Valley'; T1C is corrupt.

2. Var. B6C: 'of the Westerners'.

3. Var. B.H. 5C: 'it is effectiveness, it is speech, it is power'. A long omission in T9C.

4. An omission in B6C.

5. So B1P and B4C. T1L omits 'and lead him'; T9C and B.H. 5C read: 'Give to him, O Rēʿ, that he may lead him'.

6. Rēʿ.

7. Compare I, 68*c*–69*a* (Spell 22), with n.17 thereon, B.H. 5C alone has a completely intelligible text, because it omits the incomprehensible words *smsty wꜣty* of all the others at the end of 77*a*.

8. So B1P and B6C. The other texts omit the suffix to *nṯr*.

Spell 26

Ho N! I have set your power among the spirits[1] because so great is your
I, 78 strength, | in order that the fear of you may be ever in their bodies;[2] I have set the awe of you in their hearts, and the sun-folk are in joy because of N, for he is vindicated against his foes, male and female.

Ho N! Sail on the lakes of the Netherworld,[3] row on the waters of this great god who is in Ōn, whose soul is in Djedu, whose dignity is in Ninsu, and the awe of whom is in Abydos.

1. B4C precedes this statement with 'I have set the awe of you in their hearts', anticipating *78c*.

2. Two texts insert needlessly: 'Ho Osiris N!'

3. Var. B15C: 'the pleasant lakes'.

Spell 27

O Isdes, give speech to N. ⟨O N⟩, it is your righteousness which makes your I, 79
power, it is your character(?) which makes you noble,[1] and you[2] live on the food of falcons. You are[3] the seed of the Great One who protects his[4] father at the head of the two Conclaves, vindication is yours on this day[5] like him who took possession of the great *ṯnnt*-shrine[6] in order to transfer(?) [. . .].[7] Rēʿ has made you lift up your limbs,[8] so raise yourself up, O N, | for you have not 80
died.[9] O N, to you belongs the fear which went forth from Isis to Horus[10] when [he] was vindicated against his foes who would have had judgement against him on that day.[11]

1. There is confusion of persons here. M.C. 105 and T9C have: 'it is her (his) righteousness which makes your power'; S10C has 'it is your righteousness which makes your power'; a similar confusion arises in the next clause, where the feminine suffixes of the 2nd person sing. in B4C suggest that both these sentences originally referred to the deceased, and that a vocative 'Osiris N' has been omitted by haplography between *79a* and *b*, so that the suffixes of the 2nd person sing. should be understood throughout; only by rendering the passages thus can a clear sense be obtained:—Isdes is called on to permit the dead man to speak because the latter's virtues justify the privilege. In *79c* *inṯt* (B4C) is obscure; *snṯt*, lit. 'foundation', of the other texts has been regarded as a figurative word for 'character' or 'disposition'.

2. Var. 'N lives'.

3. Three out of the four texts insert, somewhat unnecessarily, the invocation 'O N' before this clause.

4. T9C wrongly: 'your'.

5. Here follows in B4C a long omission and a lacuna.

6. Following T9C; what is preserved in M.C. 105 seems to be an inferior text.

7. So M.C. 105 and S10C; not in T9C.

8. So S10C; T9C has 'he has made him lift up his two limbs' etc., with a garbled det. to *ʿty* 'two limbs'; M.C. 105 may have had something similar.

9. Here B4C ends a longish lacuna with '[. . .] for you the number of your limbs', clearly the remnant of a variant of *79m*.

10. I.e. the awe and dread which Isis bestowed on Horus; T9C has: 'from the throne of Horus'.

11. Following S10C. B4C has: 'the fear of (i.e. the respect inspired by) his vindication is the fear of Osiris N [. . .]. M.C. 105 is lost except for the first word 'fear'; T9C has: 'the fear of his vindication' and stops.

Spell 28

Recitation: Hail to the Spirit![1] Hail to you, my lord! Hail to you, O N![2] I have come to you on this day since(?) the night, I have given *Nwt·k-nw* to you,[3] I bring for you your heart into your body even as Horus brought the heart of his mother,[4] even as Isis brought the heart of her son Horus.

1. M.C. 105 only.
2. Var. T9C: 'Hail to this N!'
3. On the obscure expression *Nwt·k-nw* see *Komm. Pyr. IV*, 109 ff. In an attempt to emend it, M.C. 105 has: 'I have granted to you to hunt (*nwt*)'. See also 282*h*.
4. Not in T9C.

Spell 29

I, 81 Be silent, be silent, O men! Hearken, hearken, O men! Hear it, this great word which Horus made[1] for his father Osiris. He lives thereby,[2] he has a soul thereby, he has honour thereby.[3] Ho N! You shall live thereby, be a soul thereby, have honour thereby;[4] you shall have power in your body, you shall ascend to Rēʿ, and shall hear[5] words of vindication in the presence of Rēʿ, in the presence of the great god. You shall not perish, your members shall not be destroyed, your [members] shall not suffer, and you shall not be wiped out for ever and ever. May you live, grow old, have dominion, have permanence in your (*sic*) presence, and live after old age through what Horus himself has done for you, (he) the Lord of Patricians, when you ascend to Rēʿ in the horizon.

1. T9C omits 'which Horus made'.
2. T9C: 'he becomes a spirit thereby'.
3. T9C omits 'thereby'.
4. T9C omits 81*f.g* and continues (81*h* onward) in the 3rd person.
5. T9C omits the rest of this spell with the exception of the last words 'in the horizon', which it attaches to 81*i*.

Title of Spells 30 ff.

I, 83 RECITATION:[1] TO CAUSE THE WEST TO LOVE A MAN AND TO CAUSE THE WEST TO REJOICE OVER A MAN BY MEANS OF EVERYTHING THAT IS DONE FOR HIM IN ALL THE SEASONAL FESTIVALS OF THE NECROPOLIS, IN ALL THE YEARLY FESTIVALS AND AT ALL DAYS AND TIMES.

1. *Ḏd mdw* in S1C only. The rubric is from S1C and S2C; varr. B1L: 'to cause the spirit to raise himself on his left side over to his right side' (in black); T1L[b]: 'Recitation: [. . .] the Great One, and the West shall give her hands to a man' (in red). See de Buck's note on p. 83, n.5.*

Spell 30

A cry issues from the mouths of the great ones, the lords of the people, and a I, 82
shout from the mouths of the sceptred ones,[1] because of the thundering
noise | of the gods who are in the horizon[2] when they see the terror on their 84
faces,[3] who have never seen the like of it[4] when they see | N[5] proceeding 86
peacefully on the beautiful paths of the West[6] in his shape of a god-like spirit,[7]
having acquired all powers[8] | when the great ones who preside over the horizon 88
spoke to him.[9] The young god is born of the beautiful West,[10] having come
here from the land of the living;[11] | he has got rid of his dust,[12] he has filled 90
his body with magic, he has quenched his thirst with it, those who watch for
him tremble at it[13] | like a bird[14]—so say the gods of the horizon concerning 92
N who is in the West.[15] They shall say to him: | Go, row to the Field of Rushes 94
within the Islands of the Sky, navigate therein to Him who is on his *ḳ3dt*-plant[16]—so shall the gods say to N.[17]

1. For *ḏsyt*' 'shout' cf. *Wb.* V, 609,6; *ḏsryt* of B1P and of several other texts is an obvious corruption of a rare word, a derivative of the verb *ḏsw* 'call', ibid. 609,4. S1C and S2C omit 'from the mouths of'. For *nḥbtt* 'the sceptred ones', a fem. collective, all texts of the group beginning with S6C have *ḥbsw* 'the veiled ones'.

2. B3Bo and the following texts omit 'the gods'.

3. Presumably the great ones and the sceptred ones notice the terror on the faces of the noisy gods, but the text is a trifle ambiguous.

4. B1L omits the suffix after *p3*; B3L omits *p3·sn* entirely; S11C has *p33 mytt* for *p3·sn m33 mytt*, and the writings of S12C are eccentric.

5. B3Bo ff. have: 'N who is in the West': S6C stops here.

6. Four texts omit 'beautiful'. For *sḏ3* B3Bo and the texts following substitute : B2Bo omits this clause.

7. S2C omits *n 3ḫ* 'of a spirit', reading 'in his god-like shape'.

8. Var. S11C *ᶜpr·n·sn s3ḫ nb*, clearly corrupt.

9. Some texts omit the dative; B3L and L2Li are corrupt; S11C ends.

10. Varr. 'Welcome ⟨to⟩ the West, you young god, born of the beautiful West'; 'Here comes the young god . . .'. S10C and S12C end here; B3L omits *iy* 'having come' before *myn* 'today'.

11. L2Li has a fragmentary version of its own of 87*a* ff; see 89*c*. For *myn* 'here' see James, *Hekanakhte*, 111–2.

12. I.e. of the tomb. T1L renders this and subsequent clauses in the 2nd person. *R·f* at the end of the clause is the enclitic.

13. Lit. 'tremble at it (*scil.* the magic, cf. I, 149*d*) his watchers for him'; so ten texts. The remainder omit *im·f* at the end; it seems hardly necessary. For *sdꜣ* 'tremble' B3Bo has wrongly *ḥtm*, repeated from the preceding clause; S5C reads *wḫꜣ n·f wrw·f* 'his great ones seek him'.

14. S1C, S2C, S5C and M25C end here.

15. Var. T1L: 'the great ones of the horizon concerning this N'. The other texts omit the reference to the gods of the horizon. B4L, B12C[b] and B13C insert a long formula which crops up again and again in this group of texts, but which can hardly belong to the present spell. Its source seems to be Spell 38, where apparently it is original, see *JEA* 48, 37, n.*c*. Here the wording runs: 'so say they concerning that father of mine, that attendant of mine, that champion of mine, that one to whom I have gone down in the West'. The allusion to the father of the deceased is quite out of place here, and this formula is certainly an interpolation.

16. L2Li has *šmt* for *iṯ* and the rest is lost.

17. Var. 'to you'.

Spell 31

I, 96 The complete one[1] is joyful at what has been done to him and at what they[2]
98 said to him; therefore I[3] will cause N to see[4] the falcons on their nests,[5] | I will cause N to see the birth of the Apis-bull in the byres of the dappled cattle,[6] I
100 will cause N to see | Osiris in Djedu in his dignity of Bull of the West.[7]

1. *T(w)t*, referring to the restoration of the body of the deceased by the magic of the funerary rites.

2. Possibly referring to the embalmers and other officiants at the obsequies.

3. Presumably the lector reading the spell.

4. So B1P; T1L has 'they say to him: Therefore you shall see . . .'. The other texts omit 'they said to him' and vary between 'therefore I will cause this N to see . . .' and 'therefore you shall see . . .'. All the other texts evade the initial sentence of B1P; probably the copyists found it incomprehensible.

5. Some texts interpolate: 'the young god is like you'.

6. Varr, 'the dappled serpents(!)': 'the white cattle'. Here again in a few texts comes the interpolation of n.5.

7. S10C omits the words after 'Djedu'.

Spell 32

Hail to you! He calms your pain,[1] | O Osiris in Djedu.[2] N[3] has come to where I, 102
Your Majesty is, | he will dispel your pain, he will make your foes tremble, he 104
will raise up your ornaments to the rank of(?) summer,[4] You shall cause the
beautiful West to know that he is your beloved son | whom Māʿet bore,[5] and 106
she enfolds him and loves him as your son,[6] as your child[7] of your shape whom
you yourself have made. Hear this with both your ears![8]— | so says Osiris to 107
the Majesty[9] of the West. Come in peace, that you may perform good jour-
neys[10] and that I may enfold you— | so says she, the beautiful West, to N.[11] 108
She has come to meet him[12] in her attire of *sndw*-garment and her necklaces
of carnelian(?).[13] Her offerings are extended on her hand, | her provisions 110
follow after her, and she says to him: Come, be welcome![14] Make yourself
into a god in the suite of the Bull of the West,[15] | your dignity being according 111
to your desire, for you are the son of the Lord of the House.

1. There is a characteristic confusion of pronouns among the various texts of this spell, but the context shows that it is Osiris who is addressed in the sentences down to and including 106*c*, the deceased playing the role of Horus succouring his father. Thereafter Osiris speaks to the West, and the West addresses the deceased. L2Li as usual is damaged and corrupt.

2. Most texts are correctly in the vocative, invoking Osiris, but B1L and B3L wrongly append the name of the deceased, who in fact is speaking;  of B1P could be the interjection, cf. 111*d*. This text interpolates after 'Djedu' the words 'in his dignity of Bull of the West'.

3. B4L, B12C (both texts) and B13C have incorrectly substituted for the name of the deceased the formula noted in Spell 30, n.15.

4. Meaning obscure. S10C, S11C and S12C end here.

5. Var. 'whom she (the West) bore to you. Māʿet is here identified with Isis.

6. B2Bo ff. have a minor variant of this. T1L[a·b] have 'as this son of yours' and T1L[a] ends here.

7. Var. T1L: 'your offspring' (*mswty*). All texts except B1P and L2Li omit *is* after *sḏty*.

8. The fem. suffix in *msḏrwy·s* is due to the fact that this sentence is addressed to the West.

9. B12C (both texts) and B13C have *r* for *n* before *ḥmt*. T1L, S1C and S2C have a variant text: ' "Hear this with both your ears, O beautiful West"—so says Osiris, Bull of the West'.

10. S1C, S2C and M25C end here.

11. T1L omits 'to this Osiris N'. The B4L group again interpolate the formula referred to in Spell 30, n.15.

12. T1L has 'meet you'.

13. All texts are confused to some extent; the best seems to be B1P. The translation assumes the original reading to have been *m škrw·s n sndw m wꜣḥw·s n ḥrswt*. For *sndw* cf. also *Pyr.* §661; *Urk.* I, 296,9; *CT* III, 82*a*; the basic meaning may be 'cloth'. For *wꜣḥw* as 'necklace' rather than 'garland' cf. the cord determinative and the material, which must have consisted of beads, not flowers. For *ḥrswt* (*et varr.*) 'carnelian(?)', T1L has *ṯḥnw* 'fayence'.

14. Var. B12C[a]: 'Come in peace, be welcome'; T1L omits 'be welcome'.

15. Var. T1L: 'in his dignity of Bull of the West'.

Spells 33–35[1]

I, 112 O you gods who are in Chaos,[2] O[3] you Nine Gods | who are in the Mysterious
Places: see him,[4] you gods, this god-like spirit[5] whom Osiris has made into
113 his son,[6] whom Isis has made into her child,[7] | to whom is given the praise due
to the gods.[8] Come, see him who has come forth in peace, having been vindi-
114 cated.[9] Rejoice at meeting him, O you who shall travel to her(?);[10] | the Majesty
115 of the West herself meets N,[11] and she says to him:[12] | Welcome, my son, you
soul with shining horn;[13] travel[14] in peace that I may enfold you. So has
Osiris commanded.

116 |Hail to you, O beautiful West![15] See, N has come to you[16] that he may greet
117 you | daily as your son; your child whom you have borne to Osiris. He has come
that he may greet you in the Island of Fire,[17] he has got rid of the dust[18] which
118 was on him, | he has filled his body with magic, he has quenched his thirst
119 with it, those who watch for him tremble at it like a bird,[19] |he has mastered
the land by means of what he knew[20] like those to whom he has descended,[21]
120 saying to her:[22] Hail to you, O beautiful West in the suite of Osiris— | and
vice versa.[23] I have come here[24] as I desired, I have got rid of the injury of
Osiris,[25] I make his foes to tremble.[26]

121 Travel in peace that I may enfold you—so says the beautiful West to N.[27]
She is joyful indeed at meeting him, and she says to him: Welcome! Your
son who is on earth has sent you, you soul [. . .] I get rid of your complaint,
I hear the speech of my god-like equipped son, I do your business in accordance
with what he has said. Osiris has commanded [. . .] for(?) you.

122 I will cause[28] you to see[29] Osiris in Djedu, and you shall travel[30] with him
to Abydos, for the young god is like you.[31]

123 I will cause you to see the Wine-press God with his knives[32] in his shape of
'Slaughterer', for the young god is like you.

124 I will cause you to see the Fields of Ducks, for the young god is like you.[33]

125 I will cause you to see the magician[44] clad in his dignity of 'He controls
offerings for the blessed ones', for the young god is like you.

126 I will cause you to see[35] Nūt, that she may institute offerings, standing in
charge of things, for the young god is like you.

127 Welcome, | O you whom Osiris has sent;[36] see[37] these gods at the word of
the beautiful West to N.[38]

129 I will cause him to be pure in the Lake of the Jackal[39] among the blessed
ones.[40]

130 I will cause him to be cleansed in the Lakes of the Dwellers in the Nether-
world[41] among the blessed ones.

I will cause the Two mighty in magic to cense[42] him among the blessed ones. 131
I will cause him to enter into[43] the Great Shrine among the blessed ones. 132
I will cause him to enter into the Mysterious Places among the blessed ones. 133
I will cause him to enter into the Place of Ferrying among the blessed ones. 134

1. Spells 33–35 seem originally to have been a unity and have been translated as such here. The deceased is identified with Horus son of Isis and Osiris and is promised all due benefits on arrival in the next world.

2. *Ḥḥw*, despite the writing, probably refers to the primeval chaos out of which the world arose, cf. Sethe, ***Amun***, §§128. 147. 148[c]; to translate it as 'millions' or 'myriads' makes no sense.

3. *'I* is almost certainly the interjection, though here, as in 102*a*, B1P determines it with .

4. I.e. the deceased.

5. The B4L group of texts omit the demonstrative and several texts determine *ꜣḫ* with ; L2Li mispells it; B12[a] has the plural 'spirits'; T1L (both texts) omits the invocation 'to the gods' and reads 'this young god, a god-like spirit'.

6. Varr. B3L: 'whom Osiris has made into his beloved son'; B12C[a]: 'whom Osiris has made' and ends; B13C has confused *sꜣ* and *Gb*; L2Li has for .

7. B3Bo and B4L ff. corruptly: 'his child'. L2Li attaches *sḏty·f* to the preceding clause.

8. T1L (both texts) and L2Li: 'to whom praise is given'; B4L ff. 'the sailor (of the boat of the sun) to whom praise is given'.

9. Seven texts omit this clause.

10. Some corruption has surely occurred here. B1P has *sḏꜣt·s r·s*, but all the other versions have *sḏꜣt r·s* except L2Li (*sḏꜣ r·s*) and T1L which omits it. The almost complete unanimity as to the final *t* suggests that it is archetypal, and the clear plural imperative *ḥꜥw* 'rejoice' shows that these last words must refer to the persons addressed. Since there is no reason to suppose that they were exclusively feminine, it is difficult to account for this final *-t* except on the assumption that *sḏꜣt·s* is a corruption of *sḏꜣ·ty·sn* 'they who shall travel', the 3rd person here being in accord with Egyptian usage. Possibly the omission of *s* in the other texts arose from misunderstanding it as an erroneous feminine suffix. *R·s* at the end refers to the West, named in the next clause.

11. So B1P, with *m ḥsfw*; most of the other texts have: 'the Majesty of the West herself is she who meets N', with *ḥst m*, but B1L and B3L have the meaningless 'the Majesty of the West herself is in this N', omitting *ḥst*, while the B4L group append to *ḥst m* the formula referred to in Spell 30, n.15. B12C, B13C and B16C have misread and have omitted 'the West'.

12. *R·f(s)* 'to him (her)' not in B1P. At this point T1L[a] interpolates in a corrupt version (114*c*): 'He says: "My son who belongs to the Shining of horn", he says to him', influenced by 115*a*, while T1L[b] has simply 'he says to him'. In both instances Spell 30 follows.

13. B3Bo has: 'my daughter Pillar-of-his-mother, shining of horn', while B2Bo has: 'my son, Pillar shining of horn', and B12C ff. have: 'my son, shining of horn'.

14. B1L determines *ḥp* with as if it meant 'die'; similarly B12C and B16C.

15. B4L omits 'beautiful'.

16. Var. B1L: 'has come in peace to you'. The B4L group interpolate the formula of Spell 30, n.15.

17. B3Bo and B2Bo omit *ḥr·ṯ* after *nḏ*. B12C and the following texts have: 'he has come here into the Island of Fire'.

18. *Scil.* of the tomb.

19. For the four last sentences cf. 90*a–d*. Instead of *sdꜣ* 'tremble', which is clearly the correct reading in 118*c* as in 90*d*, four texts have repeated *ḥtm* from the preceding sentence, cf. Spell 30, n.14.

20. Var. 'with what he did not know', which is nonsense. In the text as accepted here it appears that by means of his knowledge of magic the dead man has mastered (or 'acquired') the earth just as once did the elder dead whom he is now joining. The sense here given to *ꜥpr* is a development of the now well-known meaning 'acquire' attached to this verb, in this instance probably implying not physical acquisition of the earth but acquisition of control over it. The commonest meaning of *ꜥpr*, namely 'equip', does not at all suit the present context.

21. Var. S1C, S2C: 'like what he has done for those to whom he has gone down'. B1P omits the datival *n* after *hꜣw·n·f*.

22. Several texts omit the suffix in *ẖft·s*. B12C has corrupted *ḏd* into *dr*.

23. Three texts omit *ṯs pẖr*, which seems meaningless here unless it is intended to suggest mutual greetings. S1C, S2C and probably M25C have: 'you make yourself into a follower of Osiris'; L2Li reads: 'Hail to you, O follower of Osiris in the beautiful West'.

24. So four texts, carrying on the speech of the deceased. The 1st person here is superior to the 3rd person of the majority of texts.

25. S1C, S2C and M25C stop here. B1P var. 'your injury, O Osiris'.

26. Read 'his foes' as B2Bo and B4L ff. L2Li interpolates: 'so says this N'.

27. Var. 'to (this) N who is in the West'. B4L and the allied texts substitute the formula of Spell 30, n.15. All texts except B1P end Spell 33 here.

28. Here begins Spell 34, continuing the speech of the West, to whom presumably the pronoun 'I' refers.

29. B1P, B1L and B3L insert the name of the deceased instead of the suffix 2nd sing. after *mꜣꜣ*, and so throughout this series of promises.

30. B16C substitutes *sꜥḥ* for *sḏꜣ*.

31. L2Li has: 'this N is like you, this young god who comes as children whom you have sent'. The young god referred to is Horus, whose role the deceased is filling; B12C omits this clause here and below.

32. In B4L and the allied texts *nsꜣw* has an odd rectangular determinative. This word for 'knife' is unknown to *Wb.*, but may be a formative in *n* from *sꜣw* 'cut off' nose or ears, *Wb.* III, 419,12. *Ḥr nsꜣw*, lit. 'upon his knives', is probably to be understood as 'having knives upon him', compare *Eg. Gramm.*[3] §§165,9.

33. L2Li has: 'I cause you to see the catch(?) of [. . .], for the young god, who comes as children whom Osiris has sent, is like you'.

34. Var. L2Li: 'the Nile-god'.

35. By inadvertence the verb *mꜣꜣ* has been omitted from B1P.

36. For the text of L2Li see n.33 above.

37. B1P and L2Li show the imperative *mꜣ* as a plural, probably wrongly.

38. Some texts omit the name of the deceased, and all except L2Li have the formula of Spell 30, n.15, with some confusion of pronouns. Here, as elsewhere, it appears to be an interpolation,

and it has therefore been ignored in the translation. The B4L group have added on p. 128 several formulae borrowed from 129*c–f*, see n.39 below.

39. Spell 35 begins here, clearly as a continuation of Spell 34. The B4L group read: 'Osiris has commanded him to be pure', and similarly throughout the spell. For the Lake of the Jackal cf. *Pyr.* §§ 372; 457; 1164; 2170; plural. 1083; 1847.

40. Here begins a series of six promises each starting with: 'I will cause . . .'. To each of these promises is appended a refrain of doubtful translation and meaning which has every appearance of being an interpolation from another source; note the abrupt change of person and the fact that whereas the promises in question are spoken by the West in favour of the deceased, in this refrain the speaker appears to be the dead man's living representative in earth who is responsible for his funerary offerings. The refrain has therefore been omitted from the running translation. The least obscure version is that of B1P-B1L, which runs: 'your quartette which are upon me belong to life and lasting (for *w3ḥ* of the other texts B1P has strangely *ḥs*). I am your company (*wnḏwt*, once determined as if it were the like word for 'cattle') on earth, I am your soul who lives on earth, who makes for you invocation-offerings on earth in your house which is in the Island of Fire'. Here the 3rd person of B1P and B3Bo is clearly wrong, since the speaker on earth is addressing the deceased. The B4L group have a variant version which reads: 'See, his quartette for life and lasting are on his cattle (*wnḏwt*, here in all cases determined with ) through me, they being alive; I am his soul who lives on earth'. L2Li has a damaged version, see 134*e*.

41. Reading *sfḫ·tw·f* with B1L; the B4L group apparently employ the passive *sḏm·f* form. For 'lakes' of B1P the other texts have 'islands', but the former reading is to be preferred, cf. *Pyr.* §§ 1432; 1530.

42. Var. L2Li: 'Osiris has commanded that the Two mighty in magic examine him'.

43. Here and below B1P consistently omits *ʿk·f r ẖnw*.

Spell 36

O Osiris, Bull of the Great Ones,[1] controller of the living, behold N has come I, 135
to you,[2] | so that he may[3] see your beauty,[4] that he may worship you, that he 136
may serve you, get rid of your injury, and set your movements aright | in his 137
shape of a god-like spirit. He has come here from the land of the living,[5] he
has got rid of the dust which was on him,[6] he has filled his body with magic, |
he has quenched his thirst with it, those who watch for him tremble at it like 138
a bird;[7] he has mastered the land through what he knew[8] like those | who went 139
down to him for themselves, he has brought all power in his hand[9] from[10] the
Island of Fire.[11] He knows those two sentences which Ḥa spoke to | Him on 140
whom is the ram's head(?).[12] He has brought[13] (something) in his hand in
order to join your head on to it[14] and in order to make your neck firm with it.[15]
He has brought to you your wig(?)[16] of your dignity of Bull of the West. He
has brought to you the living waters which are in the hands of Iḥy;[17] he has
caused Ḥeḳes and Ḥepḥep to know what he has foretold to you about it(?).[18]

141 Receive him,[19] let him enter in to me—so says Osiris to the beautiful
West.[20] Nurse him, proclaim him,[21] for you have placed him within your
arms since he came equipped[22] from[23] the Island of Fire. Usher him in to me,
142 uncover for him my injured privy parts,[24] | let him see my wounds[25]—so
says Osiris.

In what manner shall he come, this renewed[26] spirit?—so says the beautiful West.[27]

143 He shall enter[28] in his dignity of a god-like spirit, | he shall be ennobled[29]
in the House of Sothis, he shall be suckled[30] in the Mansion of the Great
Bulls, he shall receive the divine state[31] in the Mansion of the White Bull
144 which is in the necropolis | when they[32] hear the words of the gods. It is the
Two mighty of magic who cleanse him and he shall enter when you have got
rid of[33] his complaint[34] by means of his cattle[35] which are upon earth. Let
him not shout,[36] but let him remember what I detest, for my detestation is
145 the shouter; he shall not enter[37] into my Mansion— | so says Osiris.[38]

Here comes the god who guards the earth; travel happily in peace that I may enfold you—so says the beautiful West to N who is in the West.[39]

1. Var. B3L: 'Osiris, Bull of the West and the Great Ones'.

2. The B4L group read: 'behold this father of mine (etc.) have come to you'. Cf. Spell 30, n.15.

3. The parallels indicate that *mꜣn·f* of four texts is but the known var. of the *sḏm·f* form *mꜣ·f*, cf. *Eg. Gramm.*³ § 448.

4. Four texts add: 'which belongs to the great god who is in the West'.

5. L2Li adds: 'with his face true'.

6. Cf. I, 90*a* ff.; 117*c* ff.

7. Cf. Spells 30, n.13.

8. Cf. Spells 33–5, n.20.

9. The B4L group read: 'he brought all power—and nothing (thereof) was left over—in his hand as power from (or 'in') the Island of Fire'.

10. Or 'into'.

11. B1P, B1L and B3L end here.

12. For *iꜣw* see also *CT* II, 405 *h*; no such word is known to *Wb*.

13. Four texts have *n·k* 'to you' instead of *m-ʿ·f* 'in his hand'.

14. Var. L2Li: 'the eyes of Osiris on to it'.

15. Instead of the adverb *im*, L2Li has senselessly *iw nṯr*, and for 'your neck' has 'his neck'.

16. Adopting the reading *fẖt* of B3Bo, supported by L2Li; the translation 'wig' (lit. 'cover') depends on the dets. in B3Bo. In any case, we appear to have here a mark of rank. The other texts have replaced *fẖt* by the colourless *rẖt n·k m* 'what is known to you as' (*rẖt* bungled in B16C).

17. For *ʿwy* 'hands' B3Bo has *ḫfʿ·f* 'his grasp'. L2Li inserts 'Osiris' unnecessarily twice, once *after* the name of the deceased and once after the name of Iḥy.

18. Obscure; what was foretold? *Wnt·f sr* is perhaps the perfective relative form of the auxiliary verb with the main verb *sr* in the old perfective; B3Bo has the fem. form of the 3rd person *sr·t(y)*. L2Li is corrupt.

19. The deceased; Osiris is speaking.

20. L2Li adds: 'concerning this N', omitting the dative before 'West'.

21. B3Bo alone uses the reflexive dative after the imperative.

22. B3Bo inserts *ꜣḫ·t(y)* 'spirit-like' (fem.) between 'came' and 'equipped'.

23. Or 'into'.

24. *Bꜣg* with det. is not known to *Wb.*, but cf. *bꜣgg* with the same sense II, 162*i*. In view of the next clause it probably refers to the severed genitals of Osiris; B3Bo has 'my weariness'; cf. de Buck's note *JEA* 35, 92, n.10. The same text interpolates 'so says Osiris' here instead of in 142*b*, where the other texts have it.

25. For *sḳr* 'wound' see *Concise Dict.* 250.

26. Despite the writing of *mꜣwty* with in three texts out of five, it surely has nothing to do with 'seeing' here, but must be regarded as a derivative of *mꜣwy* 'be new, renewed', analogous to the similarly constructed *mrwty* 'the well-beloved', *Concise Dict.* 111.

27. Two texts add *r N tn* 'concerning N'.

28. Var. B3Bo: 'has entered'.

29. The B4L group wrongly have the 2nd person, as also in the following sentences.

30. For the sense given to *sbnn* cf. *sbnt* 'woman who gives suck', *Peas.* B2, 120; also used of cattle, 'cows in suck', *Pyr.* §716. The det. in B3Bo is due to confusion with *sb(y)n* 'make bad'.

31. B3Bo has *st·s-nṯryt*, an abstract expression compounded with prefixed *st*, cf. *Concise Dict.* 206 f.; so too L2Li; the other texts have simple *nṯrwt* without the prefix and without personal suffix.

32. The bulls? B3Bo and L2Li omit *imy ẖrt-nṯr* to *mdw nṯrw*.

33. For *dr·n·ṯ* of the other texts B3Bo has *dr* alone.

34. For the strange group which B16C substitutes for *iw* 'wrongdoing' cf. de Buck's n.2*.

35. Determined with in all texts except L2Li, which has no det. Possibly we may have here the notions either of an expiatory sacrifice or of the scapegoat; the former seems more probable.

36. B4L ends here.

37. Two texts have *ꜥḳ·f* and two have *ꜥḳ·n·f;* the latter is preferable.

38. L2Li only, but probably rightly, cf. *CT* I, 150*c.d*.

39. So B3Bo; B12C and B16C have 'to that father of mine', etc., see Spell 30, n.15.

Spell 37[1]

O my father N![2] You have been ennobled in the House of Sothis, and have I, 146
been suckled[3] in the Mansion of the Great Bulls, so that you may receive the
divine state[4] in | the Mansion of the White Bull, the Two mighty of magic 147
cleanse[5] you.[6] When you speak and | cry out, it is got rid of for you in order to 148
do things according to all that you have said.[7] See, Your Majesty has come,[8]

you have acquired all power, and nothing has been left behind by you[9] in |
149 the Island of Fire. You have filled your body with magic, you have quenched
150 your thirst with it, those who watch for you tremble at it | like a bird, you[10] have mastered the land with what you know[11] like those to whom you have gone
151 down. Do not shout, for the detestation of Osiris is a shouter,[12] | and he shall never go in to him.[13]

Hail to you, Osiris in Djedu, in your dignity of Bull of the West. See, N[14]
152 is | in your presence. Advance[15] his position, establish[16] his dignity, hear |
153 his word, get rid of his complaint,[17] vindicate him[18] against his foes, may his arm be strong in your tribunal, he having parted from(?) his companions |
154 upon earth.[19] Powerful is Osiris—so shall men say about it.[20] The dog which thwarts its master is beaten.[21] See that foe[22] who is among men and gods and the inhabitants of the necropolis[23] has come[24] to break your house,[25] to ruin
155 your gate and to cause your foes to exult | over you who are in the Island of Fire. O Osiris, see that foe who is among men[26] and who is in the necropolis has come, having joined with Seth.[27] He has disturbed[28] your weariness,[29] he has said that your wounds are hidden,[30] he has said: 'Sore be the pains of
156 your suffering which are on you.' | May your soul be strong[31] against him,[32] see the others[33] who are rebellious at heart, that they may show forth[34] your power and make report of your majesty. May you break and overthrow your foes[35] and set them[36] under your sandals.[37]

157 TO BE SPOKEN[38] OVER A FIGURE OF THE FOE | MADE OF WAX AND INSCRIBED WITH THE NAME OF THAT FOE ON HIS BREAST[39] WITH THE BONE(?)[40] OF A SYNODONTIS FISH: TO BE PUT IN THE GROUND IN THE ABODE OF OSIRIS.[41]

1. Partly an alternative version of Spell 36.
2. Var. 'O you shapes', an invocation which hardly fits the sing. suffix after *sꜥḥ*.
3. See Spell 36, n.30. For *sbnn* B3Bo and B2Bo have *sḥnn*, which is quite obscure.
4. See Spell 36, n.31.
5. For *swꜥb* L2Li has *stfn*.
6. The texts of the B4L group insert: 'there having been brought in what belongs to the interior of the great shrine, the mysterious places, the place of ferrying'. Cf. I, 132 ff.
7. Referring to the dirt of the tomb? The dative before *r irt* occurs only in B3Bo. B16C has the peculiar periphrasis for *iw* already noted by de Buck, p. 144, n.2*.
8. The fem *iy·t(y)* of B3Bo is due to the female sex of the owner. In L2Li,  after *mk* is probably due to a misreading of .
9. Five texts add *m ꜣḫ nb* 'namely all power'.
10. An abrupt change of person in the text; in copying from an original like 138*a*, the scribe has forgotten to alter his pronouns to the 2nd person to fit his present context.

11. See Spells 33–5, n. 20.
12. Four texts omit *pw nhm* in 150*d*.
13. Var. 'into his mansion'. B3Bo omits 150*c*.
14. Var. 'behold this father of mine', etc., see Spell 30, n.15. For the opening sentences of this section L2Li substitutes: 'so says the beautiful West to N', and ends.
15. B3Bo has erroneously determined *sẖnt* with .
16. For *smn* 'establish' B3Bo and B2Bo substitute *smnẖ* 'embellish'.
17. B3Bo and B2Bo only.
18. B3Bo and B2Bo omit the suffix in *ḫrw·f*.
19. Regarding *sby*, apparently unknown to *Wb.*, as a verb of motion in the old perfective, cf. the det.  in B3Bo. The writing of the other texts, with det. , recalls the Late Egyptian *sby* 'laugh', *Wb.* IV, 89,4, which makes no sense here. All texts except B3Bo insert *im·i*, apparently superfluously, before *tp tꜣ*.
20. Reading *kꜣ·t(w) r·s*.
21. Doubtless a true aphorism, but it is not clear what this saying is doing here, unless it is to hint at the fate of him who disobeys Osiris. For *ẖꜣy* 'thwart' cf. *Pyr.* §§ 588; 651.
22. Some texts add *ḥmt-rꜣ* 'etcetera' after 'foe'.
23. So B3Bo and B2Bo. For the sense given to *ꜥwt* here and in 155*b* cf. *ꜥwt špst* 'noble cattle', i.e. human beings, *Westc.* 8,17; the B4L group have garbled this passage.
24. *R·f* after *iy* appears to be the enclitic; so also in 155*b. h*.
25. Here and in what follows the 2nd person is to be preferred; *mk* in 154*d* shows that the deceased is directly addressed.
26. On *ꜥwt* 'men' see n.23 above.
27. For the name of Seth B16C substitutes the incomprehensible periphrasis noted by de Buck, p. 144, n.2*.
28. *Šd mdw* appears to be analogous to *šd ḫrw* 'disturbance', *Concise Dict.* 274.
29. B3Bo and B2Bo insert: 'for Seth'.
30. Or 'enduring'?
31. For this sense of *wꜣš* cf. *Urk.* IV, 430,12; *ZÄS* 57,7*.
32. *R·f* 'against him' only in B3Bo and B2Bo.
33. Read probably *mꜣꜣ⟨·k⟩ kywy*. The B4L group have: 'see your rebellious foes'.
34. B12C and perhaps B20C have misread *dy* as *spd*.
35. The B4L group have: 'may you break and overthrow him, that foe, etc.'
36. Some texts are in the singular.
37. B3Bo adds (156*f*): 'may N set them under her sandals for ever'. The B4L group end with a phrase taken from Spell 42: 'O Osiris, help your double, that it may rest'.
38. This rubric only in B4L, B12C and B20C; in the last it is almost entirely lost.
39. For *šnꜥ* 'breast' cf. *Wb.* IV, 506,14.
40. A hitherto unrecorded word for part of a fish; since it is to be used for writing on wax, a sharp-pointed bone or spine are the only possibilities. Cf. Parker, *Eg. Astronom. Texts*, I, pl. 26, nos. 36 and 10. I owe this reference to Mr. Spaull.
41. Presumably meaning that the figure is to be laid in the dust to be trodden under foot. For this mode of annihilating hostile beings cf. Bremner-Rhind 22,5; 23,5; 28,16; 29.14.

Spell 38[1]

Causing him who is in the realm of the dead to be kindly to a man.

The newly deceased son speaks: O you of the Great East, O you of the
158 Great West, you beings of the Broad Hall,[2] I speak before you. | See that father of mine, that attendant of mine, that guardian of mine, that champion of mine, that one to whom I have descended, him who is in the West, him who is in the realm of the dead.[3] He has announced me to the Tribunal, he has said that your utterance will fetch me, for my days have been brought to
159 an end in this land of the living | in which I was. He has said that I may take over his seat and assume his dignity in that sacred land in which he is.

Have you said that I may be brought to you in order that that father of mine may give place(?) to me, in order that I may inherit his seat and assume his dignity? Do you say that I may bring you his utterance?

160 *The speech of the previously deceased father:* |Although he knows your abode and is aware of all that you have done, yet I have seen the chest of Sia and I know what is in it;[4] I have made sharp knives which will destroy the foe in the Broad Mansion on behalf of her who is in Ḳedem—so says that father of mine who is in the realm of the dead.

The son speaks: Do you say that I should be brought to this sacred land in which you are, your seat which is in the realm of the dead, that I may inherit
161 your dignity? Transfer to me your power | in order that I may take over for myself your office and say: My power is equal to yours.

The father speaks: My son has come into the Island of Fire in order to disturb(?) me, in order to open up the interior of the twilight, to make a doorway into the Netherworld, to take possession of his father's seat, to inherit his dignity, to emulate his power, and to take over his offices, so that his[5] foes who are in the Island of Fire may exult over him, even those who
162 are in the sacred land in which he is, | who wish to throw down his house, to break up his gate, and to despoil his inheritance upon earth and in the Island of Fire—so says my father who is in the West.

The son speaks: God-like power is on you in the West in this sacred land in which you are. You have your soul, your power is with you, for you have desired your soul from me upon earth. Do you say that I am indeed brought to the sacred land in which you are in order to break up your house, to throw
163 down your gate, and to despoil your inheritance | so that your foes may exult over you? See, I am here in this land occupying your seat and pulling together your weakness. See, I . . .[6] your companions, bringing up your orphans, strengthening your gate, perpetuating your name upon earth in the mouths

of the living, and setting up your door and your tomb at your stairway. Be kindly, be god-like, be god-like, in this sacred land in which you are, in your office and in these possessions of yours in this sacred | land in which you are. 164

When I was in this land of the living, I built your altars, I established your invocation-offerings in your funerary domain which is in the Island of Fire. I heard the word of the Wilful One(?)[7] within the Island of the Living in front of the robing room of the Pure Ones. I shall not perish, I shall not pass away, I shall not die because of them, | I shall not die suddenly. O you Kindly Ones 165
whose speech is not known, who are held in veneration, command that I endure upon earth at my desire(?),[8] for I am one who eats his meals in this land of the living.[9]

1. For a full discussion of this and the two subsequent spells see my article in *JEA* 48, 36 ff. They are remarkable in that on the one hand the dead man expects his previously deceased father to sponsor him before the tribunal of the dead and the father agrees to do so, yet on the other hand the son claims the right to eject his father from his rank and dignity in the next world and to arrogate them to himself.

2. The beings here invoked are the judges of the dead.

3. All these epithets apply to the dead man's father. This is the constantly occurring formula noted in Spell 30, n.15; here it seems original and in place.

4. The father is appealing for consideration from the gods in view of his impending displacement by his son; Sia was the deified intelligence, and by knowing the contents of his chest the father himself becomes all-wise.

5. From this point on the end of the speech the pronouns are erroneously in the 2nd person. Confusion of pronouns is not a rare phenomenon in funerary texts, cf. de Buck, *JEA* 35, 88 ff.

6. An expression which I cannot translate.

7. Perhaps to be emended into *mrrt·k*, see *JEA* 48, 39, n.*gg*.

8. Emending *mr·f*, var. *mrf·f*, into *mrt·i*.

9. I.e. the deceased returns to the present world to consume the offerings presented at his tomb.

Spell 39

The mats of Thoth are laid down in the Mansion of the Prince which is in I, 16
Ōn—so say all the gods, Māʿet being at the Great Palace to greet the primeval god who is superior to the primeval gods, who are on their bellies and make greeting, she having turned back and gone into the Island of Fire. My double has been found there with them, living among those who had lived on earth and who are in the Island of Fire. | It has heard from the mouths of those who 167
perform rites that that father of mine who is in the West has raised me up at the bringing about of the ending of my days in this land of the living when I

had not yet brought up my fledgelings, when I had not yet hatched my eggs,
168 before I had attained my lifetime, before I had eaten the bread of my | nurse,
before I had drunk my due measure of milk, before I had furnished my house
of the living in the Island of Fire.

Do you say that I shall be brought to the place of that father of mine, that
attendant of mine, that guardian of mine, that champion of mine, that one to
169 whom I have descended? | Indeed I know your nature, I have seen your
abode. As for him who brought me to birth, he has made me into a body of his
own flesh, the seed which issued from his phallus.

You have said that I shall receive his dignity and take over his seat, so that his foes will exult over him when he is seen coming from the Island of Fire to yonder sacred land in which he is.

You have said that his abode in the Island of Fire is to be overthrown. See,
170 to me belongs his *ḥbnnt*-bread which is on earth | and the *ḫnfw*-loaves which
have been made(?). See, I will act, that I may occupy his seat which is in the
land of the living in the Island of Fire; may it not be destroyed upon earth. I
have heard the word of the Wilful One(?) within the Island of the Living, in
the midst of the robing room of the Pure Ones, because of whom I die not by
171 slow death; I perish not because of them, I do not perish suddenly. | See, my
being is created in this land of the living because of what has been created(?),
there are established for me the offerings to the gods and the invocation-
offerings to the spirits, for I am their survivor, it is indeed I who shall exist
in this land of the living, my will shall create my members. My flesh obeys me,
it lifts me up, for I am the Old One. I come to you, for I have loved you, O
you who are very far away, while that father of mine who is in the West is my
172 guardian who is in the Tribunal of the God, whether | in his office, in his
yearly income, in his dignity, in his affairs, or in wherever he is in the realm of
the dead, in that sacred land in which he is.

The father speaks: While I am in this sacred land of the living, I will be in it as your guardian who is in the Tribunal of Men.

Spell 40

I, 173 *The son speaks:* I am he who is created; he is created and endures in this land
according as he desires. There is no testimony against me, there is no complaint
against me, I have no falsehood, I have no crookedness, I have no wrongdoing,

I have no enemy, I have no accuser, I have sent nothing against him, I have
not implanted an obstacle against him with evil intent, that he should speak
evilly against me in the Tribunal. I am the Old One, and I detest death until
I have become aged, until I pass to the blessed state. My bread is in my hand
and the inheritance which my father had shall not be taken from me(?), for
it is I who am upon his seat, and Rēʿ has commanded that I bring life to an
end| in this land of the living among the blessed ones who attain to food- 174
offerings, until I come to you as I have desired. While I was in this land of the
living I built a shelter(?) in the realm of Rēʿ through fear lest he should see the
wrong which was being done in the Island of Fire. I am the Old One who has
attained his blessed state, I greet(?) that father of mine who is in the Tribunal,
to whom I have descended: See,[1] it is said that I am brought to you in order to
be with you in this sacred land in which you are; a word to you yourself is
indeed spoken in order to bring me to occupy your seat, so that I may receive
your dignity, that I may oust you| from this place of yours in this sacred land 175
in which you are, and in order that the spirits who are with you may speak
against you. The son comes to oust his father from his place and from his
dignity [. . .] having commanded [. . .] until I become aged, [until I come] to
you, for I love the very distant ones. See, you are in this land content as my
guardian who is in [the Tribunal of the God].

The father speaks: See, I am here as [your] speaker who is in the Tribunal of
Men, I establish your landmark, I pull together your weakness [. . .] so that
the spirits who are your equals may say of you [. . .] the realm of the dead
[. . .]. Your statue is made for you upon earth, your associates have given
orders| to(?) the land for you, your gate is strengthened for you by means of 176
what I have done, I am [. . .] the blessed state. You are here in this sacred
land in which you are through my speaker who is in the Tribunal of the [God].

The son speaks: Indeed I am here in this land of the living [through] your [speaker] who is in the Tribunal of Men until I come to you, for I love the very distant ones. Do not [hinder?] or oppose me [. . .] when I had not yet brought up my fledgelings, when I had not yet hatched my eggs, when I had not yet pressed out the marrow(?) of [. . .] in the Island of Fire [. . .] his spirits who speak on my behalf, who are sent on my behalf, I am the Old One, THE EQUAL OF [. . .][2].

1. The actual words spoken by the son to his father.
2. Written in red.

Spell 41

I, 177 Now I [. . .] I occupy [your seat][1] which is upon earth, I bring up your [orphans], I strengthen your gate, I set up your [doors . . .I] build [your altars], I establish [your] invocation-offerings [of bread and beer], oxen and fowl [. . .] your house which is in the Island [of Fire].

1. For the restorations see de Buck's notes. This spell is in the same vein as Spells 38–40.

Spells 42–43[1]

I, 178 O N, help your double that it[2] may be pleased thereat. You are the eldest son of Gēb, his first-born, and the Nine Gods have put for you your foes under you. He[3] has said: He is longer (-lived) than I in this name of his of Osiris. Horus has caused your magic to be greater than his in this name of yours of Great of Magic. Horus has borne you aloft in the *ḥnw*-bark,[4] he has raised you up as Sokar, for he is this son whom my (*sic*) father raised up. Be mighty[5] in the *Ḥn*-water as this Horus; you shall have power through it that you may guard yourself from your foes. Ho N! The White-crown Eye of Horus[6] goes up from your head;[7] Horus has given you his Eye, and the Chemmis-crown Eye of Horus[8] goes up from your head, and you appear as King of Upper and Lower Egypt. O N, may you be mighty and crush your foes.

179 O Thoth,[9] be friendly with the King of Upper and Lower Egypt. May you[10] be mighty and crush your foes, may you have peace; Osiris has given you . . .[11] that you may be pleased with it.[12] Horus has given you his Eye that you may see with it. You are the great god, Lord of Abydos,[13] who governs the blessed for himself,[14] to whom is given honour in the Island of Fire,[15] to whom is given the rulership of the sacred land, Thoth having given to him the thrones of Gēb, while Horus is heir. Horus is concerned with the business of the vindication of his father N;[16] may he be content, content![17]

O Osiris, son of Nūt, Bull of the West, Foremost of the Great Ennead:
180 Ho N! I have granted respect of you as of Horus of the gods, | and the awe of you is in the dwellers[18] in the Netherworld; I have set your sceptre among[19] those who are[20] on earth, I have put the fear of you into the ill-disposed. Ho N! The patricians and the plebs come to you prostrate[21] and the sun-folk crawling, and they see N vindicated.[22] O Osiris who shoots at his foes, for whom is made acclamation in heaven, it is the Unwearying Stars who will see N's power when he goes down into the earth as the god himself[23] who is there.[24]

1. These spells seem originally to have been a unity. They give the impression of having been taken over bodily from the rites of coronation, with some later adaptation for funerary purposes. In any case the deceased is quite unmistakably promoted to royal rank.

2. For 'it' B2Bo has 'you'.

3. Gēb.

4. The bark of Sokar.

5. Optative old perfective 2nd sing.

6. Note the writing for 'Horus' in B2Bo.

7. I.e. towers up on the king's head; both crowns are tall.

8. *'Irt Ḥr ꜣḫt*, the last word determined in B2Bo with .

9. Spell 43 begins here.

10. The fact that the pronoun changes in gender shows that the deceased is regarded as king, whether man or woman.

11. The texts are corrupt here. The object of *rdy·n* has been omitted in both texts; the suffix in *ḥr·s* in the next clause shows that the missing noun was of feminine gender. Further, although the suffix of the 2nd person in the dative after *rdy·n* shows that it is the deceased who is being addressed, the copyists have mechanically appended the name of the dead person to that of Osiris, where in fact the god himself is clearly meant. On this common corruption see *JEA* 35,89, bottom.

12. B3Bo omits *ḥtp·ṯ* before *ḥr·s*.

13. The deceased as king is identified with Osiris, the embodiment of kingship.

14. B2Bo omits.

15. Read *rdy n·f imꜣḫy m 'Iw Nsrsr*; B2Bo has blundered the writing of *imꜣḫy*.

16. The name of the deceased is probably out of place here.

17. *Ḥtp* again is probably hortative old perfective.

18. For the rendering of *imy* as plural see n.20 below.

19. B3Bo omits *m* after *sḫm*.

20. B2Bo shows the plural ending which the sense demands; doubtless we should read *imyw Dwꜣt* above.

21. So B2Bo. On *ḥdb* see *GNS* 91. B3Bo substitutes *m ḥfꜣt* 'crawling', borrowed from the next clause; for *ḥfꜣt* cf. also *Les.* 82,3.

22. B2Bo omits.

23. B3Bo omits *m* after *tꜣ* and inserts  after *nṯr*; except that B2Bo has omitted the suffix in *ḏs·f*, its reading is superior.

24. So B2Bo; B3Bo substitutes 'her foes are fallen'.

Spell 44

The doors of the sky are opened because of your goodness;[1] may you ascend I, 181
and see Ḥatḥōr, may your complaint be removed,[2] may your sin be erased by those who weigh in the balance on the day of reckoning characters, may it be granted that you join those who are in the Bark by those who are in the Suite,[3]

182 they having been made spirit-like[4] with lustration[5] like Rēᶜ: | appear[6] as the
Lone Star. Life is yours, there shall be [water for] you,[7] that it may be well
with your members. Be watchful[8] over your corpse, for you shall not be held
back by the . . . who are in . . .[9] may your soul have a heart, that it may
remember your corpse, that it may make fortunate the egg which creates you.[10]
183 Betake yourself to me,[11] draw near to me, be not far from your tomb,[12]
turn to me,[13] for I am your son, O you who are greatly sleepy and mightily
weary,[14] who buried his father, Lord of the West. May Isis and Nephthys
favour you when you appear[15] in the crown Mighty-of-magic; rub(?),[16] that
you may redden(?) the cords,[17] for your head belongs to the Mistress of Imet.[18] |
184 Your impediment will be removed by Ḥatḥōr, for you are the son of Gēb.
The earth is illumined for you, the sky shines for you, there will come[19] to you
the Old Ones who are in the horizon and the Great Ones will bend down their
arms to you, saying: Ḥeḳes! Ḥepḥep![20] May you sail southward in the Night-
185 bark and northward in the Day-bark; | may you recognize your soul[21] in the
upper sky, while your flesh, your corpse,[22] is in Ōn. May Nephthys favour
you, may she grant your call like her call, may she put the terror of you into
the spirits as when Rēᶜ rises from the Double Gates.[23] Oho *Nt*-crown! Oho
186 *in*-crown![24] Oho Mighty-of-magic! Oho Fiery Serpent!, | even you who
fashioned N, and from whom he has gone forth—and *vice versa*.[25]

Ho N! The Serpent-goddess has borne you, the Great Goddess has fashioned you.

Ho N! Rise up and sit down at your thousand of bread, your thousand of
187 beer, your thousand of oxen and fowl, that you may be glad | and that he who has
injured you may be apprehensive.[26] Stand up, that you may see Māᶜet; behold
she is before you like the daily rising of the sun.

Ho N! You have departed living, you have not departed dead.[27]

188 Ho N! Go down and bathe with Rēᶜ within the lotus tanks(?);[28] | don the
clean garment upon the refuge[29] with him who lives[30] in his shroud. May N
be encircled by Orion, by Sothis and by the Morning Star, may they set you
within the arms of your mother Nūt, may they save you from the rage of the
189 dead who go head-downwards, for you are not among them | and ⟨you⟩ shall
not be among them,[31] you shall not go down to the butchery of the first of the
decade among those who suffer the lamentations of the West. I fight for you
with this staff of mine, for I am your son, O you who are greatly sleepy and
mightily weary, even your heir who is among the gods.

You have appeared as Lord of the West, having ruled the Egyptians who
190 are on earth. | Rise up to life, for you have not died.[32] Raise yourself upon your

left side, put yourself upon your right side, receive these dignities of yours
which your father Gēb has given you. Ḥatḥōr has provided clothing for you;
betake yourself to me, draw near to me,[33] be not far from me ⟨in⟩[34] your
tomb; | turn to me,[35] for I am your son Horus,[36] and I enclose you within the 191
arms of your mother Nūt—may you live for ever![37]

1. Or 'beauty'.

2. B12C has wrongly *nḏr* 'lay hold of' instead of *ḏr* 'remove'.

3. Of Rēꜥ.

4. Apparently old perfective 3rd plur., which would have to refer to the Suite. *Sȝt* of B12C is surely a corruption.

5. Lit. 'pouring' (of water). On ritual lustration see Blackman's articles in *JEA* 5,117 ff. 148 ff.

6. *Ḥꜥ·ty* is old perfective 2nd sing., probably in the hortative sense.

7. Reading *wnn [mw n·]k*; the restoration is probable but not certain. The position of the dative in the preceding clause, and by inference here also, is abnormal, but was possibly intended to stress the thing possessed; cf. *Eg. Gramm.*[3] § 507, 1.

8. *Rs·t(y)*, again hortative old perfective.

9. *Sḏtyw* is obscure; the determinatives, especially in B12C, speak against the translation 'children'. *ꜥftt* is also unintelligible to me.

10. An allusion to the soul re-visiting the body and the consequent re-birth after death?

11. 183*d* suggests that this is Horus addressing Osiris in the person of the deceased.

12. Cf. also 190*h*.

13. B10[c] omits. For *mḏr r* 'turn to' someone cf. *Pyr.* §§ 484; 498.

14. B12C appears to have the best text. The allusion is apparently to the dead man.

15. Var. B13C: 'rejoice'.

16. The sense of *syn* here is very doubtful, but since the homophonous verbs for 'wait' and 'run' normally take the det. 𓂻, *sin* 'rub' seems the only alternative.

17. *Ṯms·k* is also obscure. The only transitive verb recorded by *Wb.* under *ṯms* is a Late Egyptian verb meaning 'bury', but the dets. here do not correspond, so that the word has been taken here as a transitive verb derived from *ṯms* 'red'. But even so the sense of this passage entirely escapes me, unless it be that the deceased is urged to rub life (reddening) into his muscles.

18. Compare *tp·k n rpwt 'Iwnt* 'your head belongs to the Mistress of Denderah', *Pyr.* § 207*e*. For *n* of B10C[b] and B12C, B10C[c] has *m*.

19. The prospective *sḏm·f* form *iwt*.

20. The deceased is presumably identified with these deities, for whom cf. also I, 140*g*. *ȝḳs* of B10C[a,b] and B12C is a var. of *Ḥḳs*, cf. *Wb.* III, 175,13.

21. For *sip·k bȝ·k* 'may you recognize your soul'. B10C[a] has corruptly *sȝ·k [. . .]k* 'your son and your [. . .]'.

22. *'If·k* and *ẖȝt·k* are presumably in apposition; the co-ordination 'your flesh *and* your corpse' makes poor sense.

23. Var. 'in the east of the sky'.

24. For the *in*-crown cf. *Pyr.* §§ 196; 198; it is clear that the copyists had no knowledge of this name of the crown of Lower Egypt. B10C[c] and B13C differ from the other texts in the order

of the crown-names, and the former also inserts an additional invocation: 'Oho Great One!', while this text and B12C include *hy nsrt* 'Oho Fiery Serpent!' which is lacking in the other versions. From 186*b* onwards B13C has a long omission which extends into 188*a*, see n.28 below.

25. So three texts; B10C[c] writes out in full: 'he has gone forth from you, you have gone forth from him'.

26. For *ḥwꜥ ib* see also *Peas.* Bl, 271. B10C[a] ends here.

27. Cf. *Pyr.* § 134, and on the interpretation as a present perfect cf. *Komm. Pyr.* I, 2.

28. With *šw sšnt* compare *sšnt* with det. ⊏⊐ in I, 212*f*, cf. Spell 48, n.5. For 186*b*–188*a*, B13C has only a badly damaged passage 187*h* which reads '[. . .] like the fear of you; [who causes?] the love of him to be like the love ⟨of you⟩; who puts the fear of him ⟨into⟩ the foes [. . .]'. 187*h* is followed by 188*f*, and B13C joins 188*a* at *ibw*.

29. A puzzling and possibly corrupt passage. *Wnḫ·k wꜥbw* of the B10C texts seem straightforward, though B12C omits the noun, probably by inadvertence. B12C then continues with *tp ibw ḥnꜥ ꜥnḫ m tꜣyt·f*, while the B10C texts appear originally to have read *n tp ibw*, etc. 𓈖 is preserved in B10C[b] but not in B10C[c], while *tp* is lost in both texts. In any case, the sense of these words escapes me; we can translate only as 'the clean garment upon (or 'of the top of') the refuge', which seems meaningless; nor does the continuation 'together with him who lives in his shroud' help at all. The dets. of *ibw* in B10C[b] and B12C are curious; the latter especially appears to represent a structure of wooden lattice-work. There may be a reference here to the 'tent of purification' discussed by Grdseloff in *Ann. Serv.* 51, 129; see also Griffiths, *Osiris*, 44–5.

30. B13C wrongly determines *ꜥnḫ* with .

31. B12C only; the suffix after *wnn* is omitted in error.

32. B12C and B13C insert at this point, rather tautologically: 'raise yourself to life, for you have not died'.

33. *Kw* of four texts is doubtless the old writing of the dependent pronoun 2 m. sing., which suggests that this spell, or at least this part of it, is of considerable antiquity; B1Y has the normal spelling *ṯw*. B13C has mistaken *ms kw* for the old perfective 1 sing.

34. A preposition, probably *m*, has been omitted before *is·k* in all texts.

35. B10C[c] omits *mḏr·k r·i*.

36. B10C[b] omits 'Horus'.

37. This royal ascription, which ends the spell, suggests that it was originally written for a king's burial, and the sentences 189*f.g* support this view; cf. also the invocation of the crown of Lower Egypt in 185*g*.

Spell 45

I, 192 Fall and tremble[1] in the eastern horizon;[2] show[3] the paths in the holy places[4] to N, he having appeared ⌈ as Rēꜥ and having been exalted as Atum. Ḥatḥōr has anointed him, she has daily given him life in the West[5] like Rēꜥ.

Ho N! There is no god or goddess who will vent anger on you[6] on the day of reckoning characters[7] in the presence of the Great One, the Lord of the

193 West.[8] May you eat bread from upon the ⌈altars of Rēꜥ together with the Great Ones who are in the Portals.[9] I open your path[10] and fell your foe for you, I

cut off for you his confederates who come against you, against your meals, and against your dignities.[11] I have stretched out my hand to you because of it[12]
on that day in which your double and your soul went to rest. | I open the paths,[13] 194
(even I) the heir of the Two,[14] the son of Osiris.

O N, may you be vindicated through your protection,[15] for the power of Isis is your strength; see, you are more spirit-like and more soul-like than the southern or northern gods.[16] The Great Ones who are in the horizon appear,
the Followers of the Lord of All rejoice, the crews | and servants of the Bark 195
are glad, and those who are in the horizon are happy[17] when they see you in this dignity of yours.[18] Your father Gēb has helped you, he has put your foes who rebelled against you into the embalmer's workshop,[19] Anubis makes
your savour sweet in front of your seat | in the Sacred Booth,[20] he gives you 196
incense at all seasons, and there is no deduction therefrom at the festival of the New Moon. They[21] save you from the *mꜣstyw*,[22] the messengers of the mysterious place of execution.[23] You have appeared at the bow of the Bark[24] and you have authority over the starboard side; no-one has power over your
soul, no-one takes away your heart, no-one causes you to go down | into the 197
Great Void[25] among those who commit blasphemy,[26] when is broken[27] the misconduct(?)[28] of him who does it(?);[29] you shall not be taken to those who are in the place of execution.[30] You are the son of the king, the heir,[31] your soul[32] shall indeed[33] exist, so that your heart may be with you and that Anubis
may remember you[34] | in Djedu. May your soul rejoice in Abydos and your 198
corpse which is in the desert-plateau[35] be glad, may the embalmed one[36] rejoice wherever he is. Would that you were examined and made whole in this your mummy which is in my presence![37] May Anubis be glad with what
is under his hands, | may he who presides over the Sacred Booth be glad when 199
he sees this good god, lord of those who exist, ruler of those who do not exist.[38]

I am your son Horus,[39] I have given you vindication in the Tribunal, Rēʿ has given command to me to give you your head, so that your spine may be
made secure for you and your foes felled for you. I am your son,[40] | your 200
offspring upon earth;[41] all the gods have assembled and all those who are on earth have come[42] to follow you,[43] that they may worship you. I am the *sꜣ-mr·f* priest,[44] the hearer who hears; I am your son and would that you were seen every day!

1. Apparently imperatives addressed to the denizens of the Beyond by the officiating priest.
2. B13C adds: 'of heaven'.
3. The various writings of *sr* here suggest that the scribes were in doubt as to the meaning;

'foretell' makes no sense. The writing appears to be the most correct; it is not allotted a meaning in *Wb.* IV, 190, 20 ff., but here and in *CT* I, 211*a*; 404*c*, *sr wꜣt n* appears to mean 'show the way to', while in 229*d* the verb is used of 'showing' the crowns. The frequently occurring giraffe-sign is common to both verbs *sr*, and may be a phonogram rather than a determinative.

4. B10C^{b} appends the suffix *s* to *ḏsrw*, presumably in reference to *ꜣḫt* 'horizon'.

5. B1Y omits 'the West' and 'daily'.

6. So B10C^{b}; tautologically expanded in the other texts.

7. The spellings of *ḳdw(w)* with doubled *d* in B10C^{c} and B1Y may well be genuine variants, cf. *ḳd* and *ḳdd* 'sleep'. See also 212*a*.

8. A clear allusion to the Last Judgement.

9. Possibly the guardians of the gates of the Netherworld.

10. A long omission in B10C^{c}.

11. B12C and B13C, possibly also B1Y, append the demonstrative *(i)pn* 'these' to *šbw* 'meals' and to *sꜥḥw* 'dignities'. B10C^{b} adds 'against these god's offerings', somewhat tautologically, since 'meals' have already been mentioned.

12. For *ḏꜣ·n·⟨i⟩* of B10C and B1Y, there is substituted in B12C and doubtless originally B13C the clearly faulty reading *r ḏꜣt n·i*. The suffix in *ḥr·s* doubtless refers generally to the giving of food and dignities.

13. B12C and B1Y were apparently intended to read: 'I am Wepwawet', judging by the det. . B13C has: 'your roads', later assimilated to B12C and B1Y by the addition of a small . B10C^{c} resumes here.

14. The 'Two' are probably Osiris and Seth, and the 'heir' is the officiant in his role of Horus son of Isis.

15. So B10C^{b}; B10C^{c} and B12C have: 'O you vindicated N, I have set my arms as your protection'; for 'my arms' B1Y reads 'magic'.

16. So B10C^{b} and B1Y; B10C^{c} and B13C insert *sḫm·ty* 'mighty'; B12C omits *ꜣḫ·ty* 'spirit-like', as does B13C, which adds *spd·ty* 'effective'.

17. B1Y here inserts the sentence 194*g*.

18. Var. B10C^{c} and B1Y: 'when they see you having come in this dignity of yours'.

19. I.e. has killed them. For the sense of *pr-nfr* cf. *Th.T.S.* I, p. 73, with n.2. With the next sentence B16C and B17C appear.

20. An allusion to the embalming of the deceased.

21. Presumably Gēb and Anubis.

22. For these obscure beings cf. *BD* 280,5; expanded into *nṯrw mꜣstyw* 'the *m.*-gods' in *BD* 319,10; *Book of Hours*, 14,16.

23. B12C, B16C and B17C omit 'the messengers of' and make *nmt* 'place of execution' depend directly on *mꜣstyw*.

24. B16C corruptly: 'at the head of the doubles', having misread as .

25. For *šꜣꜥt* 'void' cf. *GES* 101, n.5; B16C and B17C have completely corrupted this clause.

26. Lit. 'who make a reviling of (or 'a quarrel with') God'.

27. The interpretation of *sḏ* as a passive *sḏm·f* is partly confirmed by the var. *sḏ·t(w)* of B17C.

28. *ꜥwꜣ*, lit. 'robbery', here perhaps in a more general sense of ill-behaviour.

29. The masc. pronoun *sw* presumably refers back to *ꜥwꜣ*. Four texts insert *ḥr* between *n* and

ir, but the significance of this insertion is obscure; the interpretation of the whole clause from *sḏ* onward is uncertain.

30. The readings of the last word vary between *ḫb*, *sbḫwt* and *ḫsbw*: *ḫb* seems to be the best reading, cf. the var. of B10C[c]: 'you shall not be taken among those who are in the place of execution, among those who use long knives'.

31. I.e. Gēb, cf. *JEA* 39,10.

32. Var. B12C: 'your son' a scribal slip of the pen.

33. *Wnnt* is the enclitic particle of *Eg. Gramm.*[3] §§ 124,4; 249.

34. B10C[c] wrongly inserts *ib* after *sḫꜣ*.

35. I.e. that part of the desert where tombs were dug, cf. *GNS* 30.

36. So, not 'embalmer'; it is the deceased to whom the text refers.

37. The funerary priest is apostrophizing the mummy of the deceased over whom he is performing the funeral rites.

38. These high-flown epithets refer to the deceased, who has come into the hands of Anubis of the Sacred Booth for embalming.

39. The funerary priest who impersonates Horus is speaking.

40. Three texts omit 'your son'.

41. Var. B10C[b]: I am your offspring who survived you' (*tp·k tꜣ*).

42. Three texts insert *ḫrt* (in error for *grt*?) before *iw* 'have come'.

43. Perhaps an allusion to the funeral cortège.

44. I.e. the principal officiant at the rites; either the dead man's son or his representative. Var. B10C[c]: 'I am your son'.

45. *Ḥw* + dependent pronoun + old perfective 2nd sing.

Spell 46

The Followers of the Lord of the Horizon rejoice, those who are in the Bark I, 201
are glad[1] when they see you[2] coming crowned as[3] Horus, Protector of his
father, the offspring of his father Osiris, to whom I have given vindication
against his foes[4] on this happy day.[5] I am he who illumines the young god for
ever,[6] | I bring to him the breezes of the north-wind,[7] I have set Truth on his 202
brow for him like Atum,[8] I have established him as Lord of the Gods,[9] I have
spoken with him in the presence of Thōth, I have put gladness in his heart
and joy in the heart of Rēʿ(?)[10] when he sees my father speaking to me.[11]

1. All texts are to some extent corrupt; B1Y is the most reliable.

2. For *ṯw* 'you' B12C has *mn pn* 'this so-and-so', while B16C and B17C have the name of the deceased.

3. For *m* B10C[b] and B1Y wrongly have *iw*; B16C and B17C have corrupt versions of *nḏ it·f*.

4. So all texts except B10C[b], saving that B10C[c] has wrongly *n·k* for *n·f* and *ḫftyw·k* for *ḫftyw·f;* the suffix of the 1st person presumably refers to the officiating priest at the funeral. B10C[b] has less well; 'who caused vindication against his foes'. The pronoun 'his' refers to the deceased.

5. B10C^b and B1Y omit 'happy'; B10C^c omits the whole phrase B12C, B16C and B17C add unnecessarily: 'which I did for him on that day'.

6. 'I' again presumably refers to the officiant. B12C, B16C and B17C read: 'the young god, Lord of Eternity'. *Rnpw* 'young god' presumably refers to the deceased in his role of Horus son of Osiris.

7. All texts are to some extent corrupt, and there is confusion of persons. There seem to be two distinct versions of this passage; one, represented by B10C^b and B1Y, probably read originally: *in* ⟨*·i*⟩ *n·f ṯꜣww mḥyt* 'I bring to him the breezes of the north-wind'; the 3rd person of B10C^b seems preferable to the 2nd person of B1Y, which is otherwise correct. *Mḥtyw* of B10C^b is an obvious corruption of *mḥyt* 'north-wind'. The other version seems to have read: *iy·n·i dy*⟨*·i*⟩ *n·f ṯꜣww, smꜣꜥ·n·i n·f mḥyt* 'I have come that I may give to him the breezes, I have set the north-wind aright for him', cf. B12C, B13C, B16C and B17C; for *iy·n·i dy*⟨*·i*⟩ B10C^c substitutes *in* ⟨*·i*⟩ 'I bring'.

8. Following B10C^b. For 'Atum' B10C^c has a faulty writing of *nb tm* 'Lord of All'.

9. Reading *smn·n·i sw m nb nṯrw*; note again the persistent confusion of persons.

10. All texts seem more or less corrupt. The verbs *ꜣw* and *ḥꜥ* do not seem to be known in the sense apparently employed here, but from the confusion of the texts I venture to extract the reading *ꜣw·n·i m ib·f, ḥꜥ·n· i m ib n Rꜥ* 'I have put gladness in his heart and joy in the heart of Rēꜥ'. The verb-forms vary between the *sḏm·n·f* and the *sḏm·in·f*, with omission of the subject-suffix, presumably 1st sing.: the suffix after the first *ib* vacillates between *·k* and *·i*, where *·f* would certainly be correct.

11. Three texts omit the final dative 'to me'.

Spell 47

I, 204 How good it is[1] that my father should receive bread and beer from my hand,[2]
for he has no adversaries among the gods! Ho N! I have given you these
offerings which Ḥatḥōr, Lady of Punt, has given you;[3] she[4] gives you myrrh
205 in the Great Mansion among those who go forth | within the Bark of Flesh(?).[5]
You have appeared as Lord of the West at the head of all the gods, oblations
are given to you as to Rēꜥ. He who presides over the Sacred Booth cleanses
you,[6] and you ascend to the sky on the day of the Sixth-day festival.[7] The
horizon trembles at you[8] as at Rēꜥ, your character is praised within the Court[9]
206 in the presence of the Potentate.[10] | The gods acclaim you when you arrive at
interment,[11] the Westerners[12] speak to you in giving praise,[13] as when they
see[14] this god[15] devising it.[16] Isis rejoices when she sees you,[17] she is happy
when she sees your appearings, for you are beautiful and made anew[18] like
207 Rēꜥ | you have appeared as Horus of the distant ones(?).[19] Arise, raise yourself
to life, for you have not died.

Ho N! You are my[20] father and I am your son. As for any god, any spirit or any dead person[21] who shall oppose themselves against these dignities of

yours, they shall be . . . in the confederacy of | Him who is dangerous.[22] O 208
Thoth, set[23] your hand against them and your knife into them, turn them
back upon the roads which are . . .[24] among the possessors of gifts,[25] may
those who are in the Netherworld destroy them[26] among the doers of evil.
This god who is in the horizon awakes, acclamation[27] is given to him in the
Two Conclaves, the Followers appear | within the Bark,[28] the Westerners pull 209
on their ropes.[29] Spacious is your seat within the Disk, you weigh in the
balance like Thoth, your character is recognized by Him who is in his Disk as
that of a god who is in his presence.[30] You eat bread within the Court,[31] meals
are given to you as to Rēꜥ | by those who are in charge of the establishments of 210
Ōn; you have your heart, and it will not be stolen by those who are on the
paths. Receive oblations in Djedu, may your evil be purged in Ninsu, may
Thoth ennoble you with his[32] beauty, may *Wnwt*[33] make firm your head for
you, may you receive a sceptre in the Bark of Night, | may the roads of the Lord 211
of All be shown to you.[34] Ho N! Raise yourself to life for ever![35]

1. The speaker is the son of the deceased acting as funerary priest. B12C and B13C omit *w(y)* 'how'; B17C omits *nfr* as well, and in fact is thoroughly corrupt all through this spell.

2. Var. 'this bread of mine'; 'beer' in B10C[b] only.

3. B12C reads: 'these offerings which Ḥatḥōr gave to me for you when he (*sic*!) saw his father speaking ⟨to⟩ the Lady of Punt', a senseless elaboration of a perfectly straightforward statement.

4. B16C: 'he'; again confusion of personal pronouns.

5. So four texts out of five; B10C[b] has *wḥꜥw* 'fishermen(?), which seems equally out of place. Perhaps *ḥꜥw* 'rejoicing' may have been the original reading.

6. An allusion to the process of mummification. For *wꜥb* B10C[c] substitutes *sḥ* 'enwrap(?)', which is not known to *Wb*. B1Y may originally have had the same or a similar reading.

7. Miswritten in B13C with eight numeral strokes.

8. Reading *sdꜣ n·k ꜣḫt* with B10C[b.c] *sꜣdd* of the other texts is almost certainly corrupt.

9. Var. B16C: 'the horizon'.

10. Presumably either Atum or Rēꜥ as president of the divine tribunal.

11. B17C is quite corrupt; B16C miswrites *smꜣ*.

12. B10C[c] may have had [hieroglyph] wrongly before *mdw*, but the reading is not certain; B16C has *wḏ-mdw* 'command', which yields no sense.

13. Var. 'in praise'.

14. B17C omits *my* and misspells *mꜣꜣ*.

15. Var. 'the god', without the demonstrative.

16. Presumably the advent of the deceased into the Beyond.

17. B10C[c] has the archaic form *kw* of the dependent pronoun 2 m. sing. B17C and B16C omit the suffix to *mꜣꜣ*.

18. Reading *mꜣty* 'made anew' with four texts; bungled in B10C[b] and 317C.

19. So all texts except B10C[b], which has *Ḥr iꜣ*; B16C has *wr* 'great one' for 'Horus'.

20. B12C, B16C and B17C have 'his/my father', another instance of muddled pronouns.

21. B10C[b] has less well the plural 'spirits' and omits 'any dead person'.

22. All texts are corrupt. *'Iw·sn r* must originally have been followed by a verb in the infinitive; the misreading of the preposition *r* as  or  seems to be due to the general incomprehension of this passage by the copyists. The *w* before *smꜣyt* in B10C[b] is to be eliminated, while in B16C  has been rendered by an obscure sign. The pronoun *ṯw* after *smꜣyt* in both texts of B10C is also to be discarded, the correct reading being *smꜣyt nt Nḥꜣ-ḥr*. On the last expression, a designation of an evil spirit, cf. *Wb.* II, 290,15–18, and on the significance of *nḥꜣ* see *GAS* 48. B16C has corrupted  of *Nḥꜣ-ḥr* into .

23. The imperative *imy* is abbreviated into  or .

24. The meaning of *ꜥftt* (cf. also I, 182*e*) is not known.

25. *'Iwt* is badly corrupted in B17C.

26. Reading *sḥtm st imyw dwꜣt* with B10C[c].

27. Reading *hn* with B12C, etc., as against *ḥꜥw* or *ḥꜥy* of B10C.

28. B12C omits the last word, and B16C has miswritten *šmsw* 'Followers'.

29. I.e. to tow the solar bark.

30. B16C and B17C have corrupted *nṯr nty r-gs·f* into a meaningless jumble.

31. For *wsḫt*, lit. 'broad court', of the other texts, B16C has *ḫtm* 'closed place'.

32. B1Y: 'your beauty'.

33. The ancient hare-goddess of Hermopolis, cf. Sethe, *Amun*, §§ 68 f.

34. Reading *sr* with B12C ff., cf. Spell 45, n.3; B10C[c] has *sꜥr*, while B17C begins 211*a* with a *vox nihili*.

35. Reading *ṯs tw n ꜥnḫ ḏt* with B12C, B16C and B17C. B17C ends with a rubric: 'Words spoken by the *itfꜣ-wr*, the steward N'. *'Itfꜣ-wr*, lit. perhaps 'saw of the Great One', according to *Wb.* I, 144,3 is known only as a name for a shrine of Osiris, so it would appear that 'the steward N' was its priest and took its name as his title.

Spell 48

Hail to you, N! is what Isis, Lady of the Deserts, says. Be pre-eminent in the
I, 212 Sacred Booth,[1] for she speaks your good name within the Bark | on the day of reckoning characters.[2] May you cross the sky as one who is on his throne, and tread on the heart of him who would exclude you.[3] You have your heart, and it will not be seized among those who are in strife.[4] Go down and bathe in the
213 lotus-tank;[5] the Chaos-gods will raise you with their hands,[6] | the Imperishable Stars will fear you, those who are in their seats will come to you, Rēꜥ will worship (*sic*!) you when he rises,[7] and acclamation[8] will be given to you in the Double Gates[9] by those who are in Rostau.[10]

Ho N! Raise yourself up to life,[11] for you have not died. As for him who
214 shall oppose himself | to the meal of Ḥatḥōr or who shall oppose himself to this which I have set down for N on this day, namely a boon which Gēb grants[12] to his son N; take ⟨. . .⟩[13] for purity is from the king,[14] and I am your son and heir.

1. Reading *sḥ-nṯr* with B1oC[c].

2. See Spell 45, n.7.

3. For *šꜣs* 'tread on' cf. *Pyr.* § 444; for *ẖm* 'exclude' cf. *Pyr.* §§ 309; 313.

4. Var. B12C: 'by those who are in robbery'; B17C is corrupt.

5. *Sšnt* is unknown to *Wb*. The translation as 'lotus-tank' rests on an assumed connexion with *sšn* 'lotus'; the det. ▭ shows that an artificial construction is envisaged. In 187*g*, a similar sentence, the expression used is the plural *šw sšnt* 'lotus tanks'. In *CT* IV, 43*a* the 'lotus-tank' is a haunt of birds.

6. The translation in the future tense is indicated by the prospective *sḏm·f* form *iwt·f* in 213*b*.

7. B12C and B17C add: 'in the eastern horizon'.

8. So three texts; the others have *iꜣ* 'praise'.

9. For *sbꜣty* 'the double gates' of the sky cf. also I, 185*f*; 223*b*, which also show the corruption *sbṯy*.

10. Name of the Memphite necropolis, later generalized as a term for the other world.

11. *Ṯs ṯw* in B1oC (both texts) and partly in B1Y; the other texts have *ꜥḥꜥ* 'arise'.

12. *Ḥtp dy Gb*, var. *ḥtp dy nsw Gb*, is in apposition to *nn wꜣḥ·i* 'this which I have set down', and specifies it. At the end of the clause B1oC[c] adds: 'on this day'.

13. Imperative with reflexive dative addressed to the deceased; the object appears to have been omitted. This appears to be the main clause which refers back to *ir ḏꜣ·t(y)·f(y) sw m* . . . and as such it implies that the deceased can ignore any opposition to his enjoyment of the funerary repast.

14. B12C and B17C meaninglessly repeat *iw wꜥb*.

15. B17C adds in red: 'A blessed one is N.'

Spell 49

Fall and tremble in the eastern horizon because of a sound of mourning[1] in 215
the Great Place, Isis moaning greatly and Nephthys weeping because of this
god, Lord of the gods,[2] conspiracy being in seeing him in the Great Place by
him who would harm him:[3] he transformed himself into a louse[4] | and crept[5] 216
under his[6] flank. Be vigilant, you who are in the Pure Place! Beware, you who
are in the Great Place![7] See, the god himself is afraid of the Evil Ones . . .[8].
Light a torch, you Wardens of the Chambers, you gods who are in darkness,[9]
set your protection about your lord, | divide up the hours[10] for the Lord of 217
the White Crown until Horus[11] comes from Ōn, (even he) to whom the great
crowns have been given. The sceptre of Him who is in the place of embalming
appears, the Wardens of the Chambers are glad, the Great Ones[12] have
received their leopard-skins, the staffs stand before the Great Place, for it is
Anubis who comes in peace, | having appeared as Vizier.[13] He says: Guard 218
yourselves, you whose faces are . . .,[14] who see the Pure Place, who come in
the following[15] | of the Evil One;[16] who enter into the choice places(?),[17] who 219
create(?)[18] their breaths(?)[19] ⟨for him⟩, who prepare the daily offerings for

this great god, the Lord of the gods, who awaken the *nʿw*-snakes[20] because of their lords. Go, hold fast within the castle the great . . .[21] within[22] the . . .[23]
220 on account of this god ǀ who is in the Presence, that he may make fear within his castle—so says Anubis.

There is no happiness in the hearts of those who are in the Presence. What is said in their hearts: Injury has been done to him in his castle[24] by him who would harm him. Seize the Evil One[25] who is in darkness, execute sentence[26] upon his confederates, and the heart of Him who presides over the Sacred
221 Booth will be glad ǀ when he sees the rejoicing in the Great Place by Isis, Lady of the Deserts. Thus said Anubis to Osiris: Awake to life, observe your accession, and execute sentence on him who harmed you.[27]

1. For 'a sound of mourning', two texts have 'great mourning'.

2. Var. 'this oldest god, the Lord of the gods'; presumably Osiris is meant. B16C omits the words after 'weeping'; B10C[c] and B17C are corrupt.

3. For *wꜣ* 'conspire' cf. *Concise Dict.* 52. B10C[c] omits the *m* before *mꜣn·f* (infinitive with objective suffix, cf. *Eg. Gramm.*[3] § 299). B17C and B16C have bungled *in ḫt r·f*; the plural *irw* of B12C is also an error, see the next clause.

4. Note the det. in B13C and B17C; so probably also B10C[b].

5. A word unrecorded elsewhere.

6. The pronoun refers to the god against whom the louse has evil intent.

7. Following B10C[b].

8. *'Ir·n ḫprw* lacks a subject and appears to have no connexion with what follows. Apparently somewhere in the line of descent from the archetype a copyist has skipped the rest of the sentence.

9. B10C[c] determines *snkt* with  and inserts *m·ṯn nṯr ḥʿw·f* 'see the god himself'.

10. I.e. set an hourly watch split up among the guardian gods.

11. Var. B12C, B16C and B17C: 'the Great One'.

12. Var. 'the Elders'. B16C is corrupt in 217*d–f*.

13. So B10C[b]. B10C[c] has *tꜣyty ṯꜣ*; B12C has *tꜣyty sꜣb ṯꜣ*, so also corruptly B16C and B17C, recalling the Old Kingdom form of the title of the Chief Executive.

14. *ʿḳn* is a stem of unknown meaning which occurs also as a name of the celestial ferryman, cf. *Wb.* I, 235,1; the whole of this speech of Anubis is obscure. Between 218*b* and *c* B17C inserts a corrupt duplicate of part of the text (de Buck's 218*d*).

15. B10C[c] inserts an unnecessary suffix after *šmswt*.

16. Four singulars as against two plurals. B17C has *bḏ*.

17. *Sṯpw*, otherwise unknown. B17C has become confused between *sṯnw* and *sṯpw*.

18. *Ḳmꜣw*, so B12C ff. B10C has *mꜣꜣw* 'who see' in both texts.

19. Or 'fans', cf. *Concise Dict.* 131.

20. So B12C and corruptly B16C and B17C; B10C has nonsensically 'doors'. B12C omits *sn* after *nbw*.

21. Unintelligible and almost certainly corrupt in all texts.

22. B12C and B16C instead of *m-ḫnw* have an unintelligible expression *m ṯwty*.

23. The meaning of *stt* is not known. B17C has an omission extending to *220b*.

24. Var. B10C: 'to him who sees (*nwꜣ*) the castle'; three texts have 'his castle'. For *wd nkn* cf. *Westc.* 8,15–16; *Urk.* IV, 410,6; the det.  of *wdt* in B10C[b] and B16C suggests that burning was the fate envisaged. The dets.  and 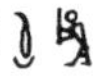 of four texts are due to confusion between *wd nkn* and *wdn n·k* 'is offered to you'.

25. Var. B12C 'the rebel'; B16C and B17C are again corrupt.

26. Cf. IV, 69*g*; 73*a*; *BD* 165,15; 166,2.

27. See de Buck's note 221, n.6*. The sentences on p. 222 have not been translated.

Spell 50

The sky is cleared,[1] the Horizon-dwellers rejoice,[2] when Rēʿ arises from the I, 223
Double Gates.[3] The Followers[4] have given hands to the Chaos-gods,[5] Horus the Protector of his father is glad;[6] the paths to the gates are cleared,[7] Anubis is within[8] his castle in his service of the Sacred Booth,[9] he puts[10] his hands on the Lord of the gods, | who is joyous of appearings on the thrones of Gēb[11] 224
and ⟨to whom⟩ is given praise[12] in Djedu. Horus, pre-eminent in Khem, rejoices at Osiris Onnophris who has come safely to the West with all the gods in his train. See, you are at the bow of the Bark, and a throne in the shrine is given to you; | see, you are king of the sky.[13] Those who are on their thrones 225
shall come[14] to you, for it is you who rule them,[15] to you there belongs one of the two Chaos-gods,[16] to your double belong the riches in Ninsu,[17] your soul is established in Djedu,[18] magic and protection are knit together about you within the Sacred Booth,[19] | your dignity is in the House of the Twin Souls.[20] 226
Again[21] you appear; your evil is purged,[22] and acclamation is given to you in the realm of the dead by those who are in the Field of Offerings;[23] do not go on the roads of the Knife-wielders. The voices of those who would make opposition are raised,[24] but he who is in the Disk greets you,[25] | even he who 227
exercises governance among the gods. Shall I be alone here?[26] Pray is my father here with me?[27] Is there someone who would carry off his brother[28] after the Great Mooring?[29] See, Seth[30] has come in his own shape and has said: I will cause the god's body to fear,[31] I will inflict[32] injury on him, I will slaughter him.[33]

Thus has Atum said:[34] Awake, O Anubis, Lord of Roḳeret, because of this 228
god, son of the Lord of the gods! Isis has put her arms around you as she did for the Lord of All.[35] Awake, you paths! Arise early, you gates! The god appears that he may see the nobles who give praise in the Sacred Booth, who look on the god who drives out the rebel | and who imprisons for himself those who 229
spoke of frightening him. The followers within the ship of the Night-bark are in rejoicing,[36] the Elder Horus is in joy, the crowns are shown[37] in Pe and

Dep when the gods who are in the horizon come; they expel the makers of
230 tumult and the doers of evil to this god.[38] I am son of your son, | seed of your seed. O god who judged between the contestants, whom I have placed upon this great height,[39] says the Lord of the Ennead. He has taught me within the Disk in order that I may pay you honour and that I may fell your foes for you.[40]

231 Ho N! Arise, raise yourself, that I may let myself see you. | I am Thoth, [son of your] son,[41] the god who judged between the contestants; do not hold yourself back from me. I am Thoth, son of your son, seed of your seed, I have taught you within the Disk in order that I may make you spirit-like and that I
232 may fell your foes for you, | they being cast into the slaughter-house of Khemennu.[42]

1. *Ḏsr* used of 'clearing' the sky does not seem to have been recorded, but it is used of 'clearing' roads, *Les.* 71,16; *Hamm.* 114,11; *CT* I, 223*e*; the night, *Pyr.* § 515.

2. B17C has omitted  from *ꜣḫtyw* 'horizon dwellers'.

3. Cf. Spell 48, n.9.

4. Presumably of Rēʿ.

5. So B12C; B16C has a superfluous *·i* after *dy·n* and after *ʿ* 'hand'; B10C^c has *ḥww*: B17C is thoroughly corrupt, and the other texts are damaged.

6. For 'Horus' B16C and B17C, as often, substitute *wr* 'the great one'. B16C retains the epithet of Horus *nḏ it·f* despite the substitution of *wr* for *Ḥr*; B17C is corrupt but clearly descends from the same archetype as B16C.

7. B16C omits *nt ʿrrwt* 'to (lit. 'of') the gates'; B17C is still corrupt.

8. *M-ḫnw* is corrupted in both B16C and B17C.

9. I.e. his embalming operations on Osiris, who is designated in 223*g* as 'Lord of the gods'.

10. B12C has the *sḏm·n·f* form *dy·n·f*; B17C omits the verb.

11. This epithet presumably refers to the 'Lord of the gods'. B16C and B17C are corrupt.

12. The text appears to read 'who gives praise', which is absurd when said of Osiris; *rdy* of B10C^c has the appearance of a perfective passive participle, and if we translate in this sense and supply a dative *n·f* (presumably dropped somewhere in the history of the text) we obtain a perfectly normal epithet of Osiris: 'to whom is given praise in Djedu'.

13. So B10C, presumably addressing Osiris; for 224*f* to 225*a* the B12C group has: 'O Osiris N, see, your son is at the bow of the Bark, and a throne in the shrine is given to him; see, you are king of the nether sky'. It is difficult to decide which is the better reading.

14. *'Iwt*, prospective *sḏm·f* form.

15. So B10C^b; B10C^c puts the clause into the future (construction *ntf sḏm·f*). B16C and B17C have utterly corrupted this clause and the next.

16. Lit. 'a Chaos-god of the two Chaos-gods'.

17. B16C has omitted 'riches', while B17C has omitted the *n* before *kꜣ·k* and has misspelt 'Ninsu'.

18. Since the text is dealing with Osiris, 'Djedu' of the B12C group is more likely to be correct than 'Djedet' of B10C; for the association of Djedu and Ninsu see also I, 210*c.d*.

19. So B10C^{c}; B10C^{b} has: 'magic and protection are knit together [about] you, and protection of you is put within the Sacred Booth': the B12C group reads: 'great magic is knit about you, and your protective cord is put within the Sacred Booth'—N17C omits *ḥkȝw* 'magic'. The reference is to the embalming of Osiris.

20. So B10C; B12C omits 'house' and B16C and B17C are corrupt. On the twin souls in Djedu cf. *CT* IV, 267 ff.

21. B10C omits 'again'.

22. The scribe of the B10C texts has skipped *ḏwt·k* and has taken the determinative  of *wḫȝ* for  of *dy*; B12C ff. misspell *wḫȝ*.

23. Following B17C, which for once is a good text; B13C and B17C are virtually identical, except that B17C omits *m* after *wnw*.

24. For *khȝ* cf. *Concise Dict.* 286–7; for *sḏb* cf. op. cit. 258.

25. On *iʿnw n* cf. *JEA* 16,151. The translation as a verb with *imy-itn* as subject is unavoidable, as if the expression were used vocatively in the sense of 'hail to . . .' or the like, some such word as *in* 'so says' would have to precede *imy-itn*. 'Woe to you', James, *Ḥeḳanahhte*, p. 109, makes no sense here.

26. The next three sentences (*227b.c.d*) are obscure. They appear to be questions asked by Horus son of Isis, with an eye to danger impending from Seth. *227b*, which occurs only in B10C, contains the rare particle *rr(w)*, for which see also I, 168*d*; 227*d* (the B12C group); and *Wb.* II, 438,6.

27. In B10C^{b} only.

28. So B10C^{b} only. The B12C group reads: 'Is there indeed someone who would give his brother to me?'. B10C yields the better sense; 227*f–g* is concerned with danger from the arrival of Seth, who would gladly destroy his brother's body.

29. I.e. death; perhaps more specifically the death of Osiris.

30. B10C refers to the god by his well-known nickname of *wḏʿ* 'the outcast'.  of B17C is an error for the animal of Seth, which in B16C has lost its tail.

31. So B16C; B17C is clearly a corrupt version of this, and what is left of the damaged parallel texts shows no disaccord.

32. All texts except those of B10C have corrupted  of the particle *ḥm* into , unless a collocation of particles *ḥm ȝ* is intended.

33. Lit. 'I will make his slaughtering'; on *šʿt* 'slaughter' cf. *JEA* 37,29.

34. *ʾIn*, var. *i·in* 'so says', 'said', used exceptionally before the quoted speech.

35. B16C and B17C have misread *ḏr* of *Nb-r-ḏr* as *mn*, with resulting nonsense.

36. B17C has distorted *ršrš* into unintelligibility.

37. On *sr* see Spell 45, n.3; 47, n.34.

38. B10C^{c} substitutes the ideogram of a baboon for *ḫnw* 'tumult'; cf. the usual det. of *ḳnd* 'be angry'. B17C is, as usual, distorted.

39. Read doubtless *ḳȝȝ (pn) ḳȝ* in all cases.

40. B16C and B17C are corrupt.

41. So B10C^{c}, partly restored from 231*e*; B10C^{b} omits. The other texts omit this clause, apart from B12C, which has a version of its own, cf. 232*e–g*: '(I am Thoth, son of your son, seed of your seed), the god who judged between the contestants. I have been placed [upon] this great height

by the Lord of . . . in order that [. . .] I have [. . .] you, that your ⌊foes⌋ may be felled for you and that those who confederated against you may be cut off'.

42. For a bungled version by B17C of part of this spell see 232*b–d* with de Buck's note 3*.

Spell 51

I, 233 Groan for the king, for Gēb has no other son;[1] there is no successor,[2] because
injury has been inflicted on him by his brother,[3] and he is[4] in his hand in
continual misery.[5] Awake to life,[6] O N, for you have not died! Lift up your
heart and see the patricians, that praise may be given to you in the Two Con-
234 claves. | Lift yourself up from upon your left side, place yourself upon your right
side, and receive the breezes of the river-side; eat bread with the living and
travel in peace to the beautiful West. The western deserts worship you,
rejoicing at meeting you, and they say to you: Welcome, O N, for you are
235 Lord of the West![7] | I am glad because of you that you are joyful.[8] Rēʿ appears
in the east of the sky and he sees the beauty of your bark;[9] jubilation is in its
bow and stern,[10] and the gods who are in it are in joy when they see this great
god, the son of Gēb, whom his mother Nūt bore.[11]
236 Ho N! | The members of the Two Conclaves in Ōn will kneel to you, the
gods will come[12] to you bowing with their faces to the earth through fear of
you within the arms of Happy Year[13] when you have appeared as Rēʿ, Lord
237 of the Horizon.[14] Horus son of Osiris stands up,[15] | he creates(?)[16] the Sistrum-
player with authority(?).[17] You shall have life, O Lord of the West, you son of
Ḥarakhti, Bull of his mother Nūt. Awake to life, for you have not died! See the
patricians early, for you are dignified as ruler of the horizon; you shall have
238 life from Anubis, for you are dignified in the Sacred Booth. | Betake yourself
to me, mount up to me, be not far from me, for Anubis is glad(?), Khnum is
glad(?) thereby(?).[18]

1. This must originally have been a royal funerary text. The aberrations of B17C henceforward will not normally be noted.

2. With *nn wḥmty* compare *nn wḥmty·fy* 'there will be none else like him', *Äg. Stud.* 1; *JEA* 38,59.

3. After 'his brother' B10C[c] may have added 'who is younger than he', but the reading is doubtful.

4. Var. 'I am', but the 1st person appears to be secondary here. The deceased is addressed in the 2nd person in 233*e*.

5. For this use of *ꜣw* cf. *ḥꜣb ꜣw* 'continual crookedness', *JEA* 28,18(*i*). B16C has changed *ꜣw* into *ꜣwr* under the influence of the following *rs·t*(*y*).

6. Hortative old perfective except in B10C[c], which has the imperative.

7. Var. B10C[b]: 'Welcome, for you are N'; B10C[c]: 'you are N, Lord of the West'.

8. So B10C; the other texts insert *m* before *ib·k*. perhaps to be understood as 'joy is in your heart'. The speaker may be the funerary priest impersonating Horus.

9. The funerary bark which conveys the dead to the necropolis?

10. B17C stops here.

11. So B10C; the B12C group has wrongly 'my mother'.

12. Note the prospective *sḏm·f* form *iwt·f*. Var. B10C: 'the spirits'.

13. Personified as a protecting goddess.

14. B13C here inserts an anticipation of 237*f*–238*a*.

15. B16C has completely bungled this clause.

16. *Ḳmꜣ* 'create' here may perhaps be used figuratively in the sense of 'act the part of'.

17. Var. B10C[c]: 'with jubilation'.

18. *H̱nm*, var. *ẖnm*, is tentatively identified here with *ẖnm* 'be glad', cf. *GNS* 97. Similar collocations occur in 241*c.d*; 244*f*; 246*d.e*. The sense of the final adverb is doubtful but the reading is confirmed by 241*c.d*; 245*g*; 246*d.e*. and in part by 244*f*, with de Buck's note 4*. After the reference to Anubis B16C inserts *m ʿt* 'in the chamber'.

Spell 52

O you gods, come with these kindred of mine,[1] be vigilant as regards this god
who is unconscious,[2] | make for him the contentment(?) of Rēʿ,[3] pronounce I, 239
his name in[4] the Great Hall, that those who are in the Following[5] may be glad. Oho! Oho! say the joyful one and the sorrowful one. Shall I place my arms which are on me over this god, the Lord of the gods, and put groaning and outcries in the Great Hall[6] because of this Destroyer[7] who has come in?
He has acted against[8] this god | in order to frighten the gods in the Pure Place. 240
Begone, you monster![9] See, the Pure Place is guarded.[10]

1. Read *my m m hꜣw·i ipn*, the imperative 'come' + the particle *m* of *Eg. Gramm.*[3] § 250; the second *m* is the preposition, which could be interpreted as either 'with' (cf. *JEA* 25,166; 39,20) or 'as', 'in the capacity of'.

2. Lit. 'who does not know himself', cf. *Sin.* B253; *Sh. S.* 76; here a euphemism for 'dead'.

3. Reading *ir n·f ẖnmw Rʿ* with B10C[b], ignoring the superfluous *n* before *ẖnmw*. Here and in the next clause the imperative of B10C is preferable to the *sḏm·f* forms *ir·n*, *dm·n* of the other texts.

4. For *m* of B10C the other texts have the less suitable *tp*.

5. Of Rēʿ or Osiris? More probably perhaps the former.

6. All this sentence down to *wryt* is omitted in B10C.

7. For *nbd* of B10C the parallel texts substitute *šsr* determined perhaps with a monkey, which in B16C has been misread. This word *šsr* recurs in *Dream-book*, 3,12. It can hardly be identified with *šsr* 'sacrificial bull', *Wb.* IV, 547,8.

8. Lit. 'he has made happenings against'.

9. The emphatic reduplication of the particle *rk* after the imperative *ḥm* is unusual. *Nmyt* is unknown to *Wb.*, but is clearly an offensive epithet; for the det. in B10C[b] cf. the roughly synonymous *hyw* in *Pyr.* § 245.

10. Following B10C[b].

Spell 53

Awake to life; behold, the earth is bright! Nephthys has favoured you, you
I, 241 being renewed[1] daily in the night-time,[2] | being with the Unwearying Stars,
the gods who are in the sky, who are placed as[3] followers of your bark for ever
and ever. Anubis is content(?) thereby(?), Khnum is content(?) thereby(?).[4]
The sky is in light(?),[5] the earth is in rejoicing, and all the gods are joyful[6]
242 when N has appeared in peace in the beautiful West. | Nephthys has favoured
you and you shall not lose your house of joy. Alas, my husband, even my
brother![7] He rules in the realm of the dead and I am not with him.[8] I give
orders to(?) (the women) who are at the Great Hall, who are sick at heart
because of their husbands:[9] Come, let us lament Osiris since he is far from
243 us. | Rise, rise in the morning[10] now that you are a mummy,[11] for you are far
from your house.[12] Nephthys has favoured you, and you shall not lose your
house of life, of life.

1. B10C[c] alone has preserved the correct reading *mꜣ·ty* 'you being renewed'. The other texts apparently misread this as the homophonous *mꜣ·ty* 'you are seen', which makes poor sense in view of the reference to the night-time; this is, nevertheless, a common corruption. The deceased is compared with the sun, which is renewed nightly to rise next day.

2. The B12C group read: 'you being renewed daily and appearing in the night-time', which yields a poorer sense.

3. So B12C and B16C; B10C[c] omits *m*. The remaining texts are defective.

4. See Spell 51, n.18.

5. *Mꜣty* of B10C[b] and B16C is assumed to be the old perfective of a verb from the same stem as *mꜣwt* 'rays of light', *Concise Dict.* 103; *pt m mꜣty* of B12C and *pt mm mꜣty* of B10C[c] may perhaps embody a noun meaning 'light'.

6. B16C is corrupt.

7. B16C is again corrupt. From what follows it appears that Isis is here speaking of her dead husband Osiris, but the connection with the preceding context is not clear.

8. The B12C group preserves the correct reading *nn wi ḥnꜥ·f*, which is garbled in B10C.

9. Apart from B10C[b], which is damaged, all texts seem to have suffered some slight degree of corruption. I would suggest emending *ḥnn·i tpt* (var. *tptt*) *wryt* into *ḥn·i n tpt wryt*, for this clause seems to introduce an exhortation to other widows; in what follows, *irt* of B12C and *ḥrt* of B16C are clearly corruptions of *mrt* of B10C and B13C, which alone yields good sense. In the next sentence, for 'Osiris this N,' we should surely understand 'Osiris' the god.

10. The widowed Isis invokes her dead husband.

11. Var. 'you are in your mummy-shape'.

12. Var. B10C[c]: 'be not far from your house'.

Spell 54

I am content(?)[1] in the booths, I cry out in [the Sacred Booth] because of this god, the Lord of the gods: Rise early in the morning, for the noble one[2] appears, | the heir of the Two Lands. There is given [. . .] all of it, the thrones I, 244
of Gēb in [. . .]. Oho!(?) [. . .] enduring of speech(?).[3] See, you are more soul-like, effective and powerful than all the gods. [Nephthys][4] has favoured you, and Anubis is content(?), Khnum is content(?) [thereby(?)].[5] [. . .] gods, the sun guides us, and loud is our cry:[6] Alas, shall I indeed be alone?[7] I have no brother or son, no [. . .] Osiris. O N, raise yourself to life, for you have not died; receive the god's-offering(?) [. . .] renewed and rejuvenated[8] [. . .] good are(?) the guardians(?). Lift up your heart, see your beauty, having appeared as Horus [. . .] the Two Ladies of Pe and Dep [. . .] western [. . .] meeting N, who has appeared as Lord of the Oar, the Lord of Life within ⟨. . .⟩.[9] The gods of Pe are glad in the Suite [. . . Anubis is content(?),] Khnum is content(?) thereby(?).

1. A badly damaged spell which exists for the most part in only one text, but which is linked to the preceding spells by the *ẖnm* formula with Anubis and Khnum. The speaker is apparently an officiant present in the embalming booth who calls on the dead man to awake.

2. The reference to the 'heir of the Two Lands' in the next clause suggests that here Osiris as heir of Gēb is meant.

3. With *ḏd rꜣ* compare *ḏd m rꜣ* in 246*f*. Its meaning is far from clear.

4. See de Buck's note 2*.

5. See Spell 51, n.18.

6. Here again we seem to be concerned with widows.

7. The clause is introduced by the interrogative *in* and the particle *rr*. For the restoration *wꜥ·k[wy]* see de Buck's note 5*.

8. *Rnpty* 'rejuvenated' indicates that *mꜣ·ty* should be understood not as 'seen' but as 'renewed', cf. Spell 53, n.1.

9. A word or words omitted after *m-ẖnw*.

Spell 55

Woe is in heaven, groaning is in the Netherworld, because [. . .] I [. . .] in I, 245
the Night-bark, I am [raised up(?)][1] in the Day-bark [. . .] within the arms of Anubis in the Pure Place, I have put the rebel into bonds of the warder(?) [. . . Anubis is content(?), Khnum is content(?)] thereby(?).

1. Cf. de Buck, 245, n.1*.

Spell 56

This inert one has raised himself up, and I rejoice [when I?] see [. . .] as one worshipped in peace in the beautiful West because(?) I have cleared my vision.[1] Come to me [. . .] with you so that you shall be Lord of the West.
246 O N, stand up to life, for [you have] not [died]; see [. . .] | cross [the sky with Rēʿ, travel over the sky(?)] with the god who came into being of himself. Anubis is content(?), Khnum is content(?) thereby(?).

1. Lit. 'I have opened the face'.

Spell 57

[. . .] See you . . .[1] health and endurance of speech(?).[2] O my lord, I lament you with groaning,[3] for there is not(?) [. . .] after you [. . .] as(?) one who crosses the sky. Oho! You are Horus, Lord of All;[4] see, you . . . health [. . .] see, you . . . health.

1. The meaning of *ḏꜣm*, which occurs again in 246*m.o*, always followed by *snb*, is not known.
2. See Spell 54, n.3.
3. Another widow's lament.
4. Corrupted into a meaningless 'Lord of the Sledge'.

Spell 58

I, 247 O my lord, [stand up] to life; behold, the earth is bright [. . .] behold [. . .].

Spell 59

[. . .] the Great Hall [. . .] within the darkness [. . .].

Spell 60

I, 248 The god appears within his shrine, he hears the striking for him on two gongs,[1] protection is made for him among the gods, among the Children of Horus Protector of his Father. Gēb is there as your (*sic*) protection, for he is your father to whom you were born.[2] The arms of Nūt who bore you are about you
249 so that your beauty may be upraised, | (even) your living soul which is in Djedet. The ill-disposed are warded off for you, Seth[3] is afraid when he sees you,[4] he discards his strife-making on earth, for the fear of him has fallen on his own body. O you who are fair of face, who are among the gods, (even) Ptaḥ-Sokar in the bow of your bark, their (*sic*) arms bear the seal of the god. |

Bastet the daughter of Atum, the first-born daughter of the Lord of All, she 250
is your protection until day dawns, until you go down to the realm of the dead.
The Eye of Horus glances at you, it comes with you to the realm of the dead.
May you live in their hearts, (even of) those who are in the following of your
brother Seth. What was said to Him who is in his shrine:[5] | Rēʿ himself is the 251
Lord of All, he causes the gods to come in his following when the bark travels,
it being dragged straight on.[6] When the god[7] goes down to the realm of the
dead he is happy, for Horus is king, having acted for him as 'loving-son'. The
rebel is quiet when he sees you, the *sm*-priest, (who is also) lector | and em- 252
balmer, is one of you, overthrowing enemies.

The nurse of the Souls of Ōn has come bearing provisions to the Lord of
All; Anubis who presides over the Sacred Booth offers a meal to the lector at
dawn; the day shines and the god is far from the Great Hall.[8] | Your Great 253
Hall is in the temples, being what Rēʿ made for your protection, that you
might be in it at dawn. The horizon is shut away,[9] the pillars[10] are broken(?),[11]
(even) that which was[12] the protection of Osiris; its pillars are . . .,[13] | its 254
beams[14] are the arms of Nūt when she watches over Osiris, its curtain is the
cloak[15] of Ptaḥ which Tayt herself wove.[16] May the day[17] rise in the east of
the sky, may it shine there over your breast; night belongs to you and day is
yours,[18] O Osiris. | O Horus, Lord of Life, fare downstream and upstream 255
from 'Andjety, make inspection of those who are in Djedu,[19] come and go in
Rostau, clear the vision of those who are in the Netherworld. Fare upstream
from it[20] to Abydos, the primeval place of the Lord of All.

1. See Spell 24, n.5. There are minor varr. in B10C[d] and B4C.
2. So B4C; minor varr. in B10C[b.c], and B10C[d] omits.
3. Var. *wdʿ* 'the Outcast', so too in 250*f*. The name is omitted in B10C[a].
4. Var. 'him'.
5. Or: 'what he who is in his shrine said'.
6. *Mty* has been taken to be an adverbial use of *myt* 'straightforward'.
7. Presumably Osiris, cf. 251*f*.
8. The meaning of this sentence is not clear.
9. For the det. of *sbḫ·t(w)* 'is shut away' in B10C[b.d] and B1Y, cf. *Urk*. IV, 1071,8; the other texts have confused this passive in *·t(w)* with the noun *sbḫt* 'portal', giving it the det ⊏⊐.
10. Var. B10C[d]: 'the pillars of the house', though the supports of the horizon are apparently what is meant.
11. Or 'reckoned up'; it is not clear which sense of *ḥsb* was intended.
12. Everything from 253*d* to 254*c* is obscure, but it seems that the horizon is equated in some way with the booth in which Osiris was embalmed.
13. B10C[a] omits 253*f–h*; these sections are all defective in the other texts, but they equate the pillars with the 'Children of Impotence'; there must surely be some ancient corruption here.

14. The suffix in *sꜣwt·s* refers back to *ꜣḫt* 'horizon' in 253*d*.

15. Following B4C; *srḫtt* of the other texts appears to be corrupt.

16. The last words of 254*c*, namely *sḫtt Tꜣyt ḏs·s* 'which Tayt herself wove', have been corrupted in B10C^{a} into *sḫtyt* with woman-determinative.

17. Miswritten in B1Y.

18. Reading *ntk hrw* with B10C^{c}.

19. I.e. Busiris. B10C^{b,c} have *Ḏdt* 'Mendes', which in this context is certainly in error.

21. From Rostau.

Spell 61

I, 256 Every god at the mouth of his lake goes on the water of your bark,[1] which
Orion lifts up; your hinder parts are in the . . .,[2] Nūt puts her hands on you,
you sit on the mat of Osiris, and Rēʿ makes your seats pre-eminent. You are
257 cleansed in the Lake of Cold Water, Anubis burns | incense for you, you open
the windows[3] upon the Ennead, you see the mysteries which are in them, you
shine in the plumes of Sopd, you have assumed the crowns of Horus,[4] the
White Crown is made firm for you upon the dais, just as was done by Rēʿ for
258 Horus at his coronation. | Men serve you as Horus, leader of the Two Lands,
the falcon-shrines are opened for you and the fledgelings of the gods speak to
you, there is said to you: 'Welcome into the fanes!' by the Great Ones of
Ōn; you are clad in the pure garment of Ptaḥ, in the robe of Ḥatḥōr. Spacious
259 is your seat in the Bark; | you sit in the Ship of God and you harpoon the
hippopotamus[5] in the Winding Waterway, every god being your harpooner.
The old women of Cusae who are in the train of Ḥatḥōr glorify you, there is
brought to you a chest of natron by the priest on monthly duty. Rēʿ is his[6]
260 name, | Horus is his shape, crowns are set on with his titulary, Shu and Tefēnet,
the gods who made the Primeval Ones, glorify you.[7] The soul of the Great
One rejoices at meeting you when(?) you stroke(?)[8] Horus of Shedet. You sit
261 on the mat(?)[9] of turquoise at the bow of the Bark of Rēʿ. | Fair is your rising
like the rising of Rēʿ, you shine like Ḥatḥōr.[10] Osiris desires to see you in
your risings of the pillared hall, when the blocks of silver are dragged[11] for
262 you | on to the bases of turquoise; Ḥatḥōr, Lady of Byblos, makes the steering-
oar of your bark. The stars kindle a light for you, the twin children of Nūt
glorify you, Gēb and Nūt glorify you, even the gods who encompass(?)[12] the
263 plebs. May | you eat the *sn*-bread which came forth from Khem,[13] the pure
bread which came forth from Ōn; may you drink the bowl of milk which came
forth from upon the altar on the day of the Sixth-day festival; may there be

said to you: 'Welcome!' in the Broad Hall by the Great Ones of the temple;
may there be uncovered for you the supports of the sky, may you see the
mysteries which are in it, | may you extend your legs over the supports of the 264
sky.[14]

A sweet breeze to your nose! Orion says to the Great Bear: 'Take from your lake what I take from my lake, that we may prepare a place for N'. Stand upon a *ḏꜣ*-cloth, a six-weave cloth upon your shoulder, grant the crane's way to the sky.[15]

1. Meaning perhaps that every god follows the bark over the celestial waters. The preposition *ḥr* appears to have been omitted before *mw*.

2. The meaning of *bꜣw* is doubtful; *Wb.* IV, 418,9 suggests 'hillock', clearly on the basis of the dets., but in that case we would expect the preposition to be *ḥr* 'on' rather than *m* 'in'. The late Professor Černý, in a letter to me, suggested the meaning 'heap', quoting Coptic ϐⲟⲟⲩ from P. Bodmer XX, Joshua 7,26 and 8,29, i.e. 'your hinder-parts are a heap', but that makes the sense no clearer, and it seems not unlikely that we are here in the presence of some deep-seated corruption.

3. On *ws* 'window' cf. *Ch. B.* Text, p. 71, n.3.

4. Var. 'the great crowns'.

5. Cf. Säve-Söderberg, *Hippopotamus*, p. 33.

6. The pronoun must surely refer to the deceased rather than to the priest. There appears to be an abrupt change of person; the deceased, who has been spoken *to*, is now spoken *of*, in a kind of parenthesis.

7. We return to the 2nd person.

8. For this sense of *sẖr* cf. *Urk.* IV, 294,8. Is the deceased to be regarded as stroking the plumage of the sacred falcon of Shedet?

9. *Psẖ* or *psẖ* is recorded in *Wb.* I, 553,5 as 'etw. auf dem man vorn im Sonnenschiff sitzt'. It may perhaps refer to the mat-like appendage often depicted as hanging from the bows of mythological barks, on the top of which a divine or semi-divine figure is often seated, cf. Erman, *Religion*, p. 17, fig. 5; 18, fig. 6; Sethe, *Lauf*, p. 20; there may also be an etymological connexion with *pšst* 'carpet of matting, *Concise Dict.* 95.

10. At this point B4C inserts: 'Osiris desires to see you (fem., woman's coffin); the Lady of Byblos makes the steering-oars of your bark'; this latter sentence anticipates 262*b*.

11. Var. B10C^{a}: 'chosen'; *sṯꜣ ṯw* of B10C^{c} is surely a miswriting of *sṯꜣ·tw*. For late references to blocks of silver and bases of turquoise cf. the passages from the Ritual of Embalmment and from Brugsch, *Dict. géogr.* p. 413 quoted by Blackman in *JEA* 5, 122.

12. Or possibly: 'the gods whom the plebs question', though the plural strokes after *šnw* in B10C$^{a.b}$ point to a participle rather than to a relative form. In either case doubt exists as to the exact meaning to be given to *šnw*. Note the reference to the *šn-sẖyt* waterway in 268*c*.

13. Letopolis.

14. These two last clauses only in B4C and B1Y, though largely destroyed in the latter.

15. I.e. to the deceased, that he may fly up to heaven.

Spell 62

I, 265 Hail to you, my father Osiris;[1] see, I have come. I am Horus who, with Ptaḥ,
split open your mouth, I make you spirit-like in company with Thoth, I put
your heart into your body for you, that you may remember what you have
266 forgotten. I cause you to eat bread at your desire | in addition to what was done
for you upon earth, I give to you your feet that you may walk and that your
sandals may hurry. I cause you to make a sending in company with the south-
wind, and to run with the north-wind. You cross to look[2] on the face of him
who hastens you[3] in the twinkling of an eye,[4] and I cause you to take shape
267 with the *ḏwyt*-bird. | I cause you to cross the Waterway of the Sky-windows, to
cross the lake[5] and to traverse the sea ⟨with⟩[6] the sole of the foot as if you were
performing on the land; you rule the streams with the heron, and there is
none who opposes you at the District of the Waters.[7] I cause you to act as
268 pilot with a sounding-pole of 40 cubits, of planted wood | of cedar of Byblos,
standing in the Bark of Rēʿ. You have crossed the *Šn-rḥyt* water,[8] you are
vindicated on the Day of Judgement in the tribunal of the Lord of Suffering(?).[9]
There is removed for you him who hacked up the earth, is driven off for you
the rebel who came in the night, the thief of the dawn, who made darkness
in coming, the Great Despoiler(?)[10] of the dependants of the House of Isis.
269 May you traverse the deserts with Rēʿ, | may he cause[11] you to see the places
of those who follow desire, may you find the valleys full of water for your
washings in[12] your cool water, may you pluck papyrus-plants, rushes, lotuses
and lotus-buds. There shall come[13] to you waterfowl in thousands, lying[14] on
your path; you cast your throwstick at them,[15] and it means that a thousand
270 are fallen at the sound of its wind,[16] namely *r*-geese,[17] | green-fronts, *ṯrp*-geese,
and the males of *st*-geese. There shall be brought[18] to you the young of gazelles,
short-horns and the bulls of white cattle; there shall be brought to you males(?)
of ibex and fattened rams of Barbary sheep. A ladder to the sky shall be put
together for you and Nūt will extend her hands towards you, you shall navigate
271 on the Winding Waterway and sail in the eight-boat. | These two crews of the
Imperishable Stars and the Unwearying Stars shall navigate you, they shall
pilot and tow you over the District of the Waters with ropes of iron.

1. So B10C[c] and originally B10C[a]; the other texts add the name of the deceased.

2. Or: 'your crossing is to look . . .', according as we take *nmt* to be verb or noun.

3. *Ḫꜣḫ* as a transitive verb perhaps only here, but the dependent pronoun *ṯw* demands this interpretation.

4. Reading *r ṯrm n irt;* for *ṯrm*, lit. 'wink', cf. *Concise Dict.* 306.

5. B10C^{c} only; all the other texts are damaged, but B10C^{d} may have had something different. For the previously mentioned 'Waterway of the Sky-windows' see *CT* IV, 367*m*.

6. The preposition ***m*** is omitted after *wȝḏ-wr*.

7. B10C^{b} here repeats part of 267*a–b*.

8. Cf. *nṯrw šnw rḫyt* in 262*f*.

9. For *gmwt* cf. Spell 13, n.5.

10. *Thb wr*, again 272*a*. The translation is conjectural.

11. B10C^{c} omits *dy·f*.

12. Lit. 'of'.

13. Prospective *sḏm·f*, setting the tense of what follows.

14. The *n* after *wȝḥ* in B10$^{a.c}$ is inexplicable except as a writing of the obscure suffix *ny*, cf. *Eg. Gramm.*^{3} § 34, Obs. 3.

15. Varr. 'have cast', 'shall be cast for you'. At the end of the sentence *r·s* is for *r·sn*, cf. *JEA* 16, 64 (5).

16. I.e. as the throwstick whines through the air.

17. Var. '*sr*-geese', B10C^{d}. The det in B10C^{b} is not very goose-like.

18. Var. 'I shall cause to be brought'.

Spell 63

Here comes the Great Despoiler(?);[1] guard yourself,[2] guard yourself, go 272
down to . . .,[3] wave[4] the hands. Be put together, be put together, O you who
should be put together(?)[5] Your limbs are released, your bonds are loosed like
Seth who is in *Ḥnt*.[6] Isis has summoned you, Nephthys has called to you, | the 273
spirits are given to you,[7] they come to you bowing. Go to open[8] the mansion
of yon soul. If you find them[9] playing,[10] you shall sit down between them.
If you find the gods seated, you shall sit with them. Receive this sceptre of
yours | which is at the feet of Rēʿ and your rod which is at the feet of the 274
Morning Star; you shall ascend to the sky among the stars which do not perish,
you shall strike with the sceptre and govern with the rod.

1. See Spell 62, n.10.

2. The first *sȝ ṯ* was probably intended for *sȝ ṯw*. *S(ȝ)ṯ* 'make libation' of the other texts is clearly corrupt.

3. Read *hȝ r wrwty* as T2C; the last word is obscure.

4. For *ḏȝm* 'wave' the hands cf. *Pyr.* §§ 743; 1366.

5. 𓈖 after *iʿb* (T1C only) has been borrowed from *wʿb* 'pure', The passage is obscure.

6. Var. *sfḫḫ·k* in T2C; sim. Sq3C. On *Ḥnt*, varr. *Ḥnbt* (T2C), *Ḥnḫnt*, *Pyr.* § 734, cf. Gauthier, *Dict. géogr.* IV, 31.

7. *Rdyw* of Sq3C shows that the passive is intended here. '*Irw* in T9C and Sq3C is probably a corruption of the enclitic *irf* in T2C and T1C.

8. We have here abnormal writings of *sn* 'open', *Concise Dict.* 229; T9C determines *sn* as if it were *snš* 'flow forth'.

9. Isis and Nephthys.

10. *Ḥꜥb* is normally used of playing a board-game, but the dets. in T1C and T9C look more like a 'pat-a-cake' game with the hands.

Spell 64

I, 275 Giving water to a spirit.[1] This your cold water, O my father! This your cold
water, O Osiris! Come[2] to your son, come to Horus; see, I bring it[3] to you that
your heart may be made glad by means of it; I bring to you the Eye of Horus,
that your heart may be made glad by means of it. Whatever you tread under
276 your sandals, | I will be your guide[4] for you, and I will give you water at the
wꜣg-festival and the festival of Thoth.

1. In B10C only. The damaged first word stands for the infinitive *rdyt*; cf. 276*c* (Sq3C).

2. Old imperative *iw* with reinforcing dative.

3. For *inn·i* of T2C and T9C the variants have *in·i*; so also 275*h*. The use of the fem. dependent pronoun *s*(*y*) here and in 275*g* is an anticipation of the fem. *irt* 'eye' of Horus in 275*h*, with which the 'cold water' of 275*b.c* is identified.

4. Reading *ꜥw*, see de Buck's note p. 276, n.2*.

Spell 65

Placing water and bread in a real [. . .][1] I fetch[2] you, my father, I fetch you,
I, 277 my father; go[3] to the Mounds | of Pe, traverse the Mounds of Nekhen. O my
father, Horus is your scribe, Seth is your . . .,[4] and both your hands are on
your possessions. Ascend to the sky and do not give to them, but move about.[5]
278 Horus goes about seeking[6] his father Osiris. | Ho N![7] Your porters go, your
couriers who are on earth run,[8] they tell Rēꜥ, whose hand[9] is raised in the East,
that you have ascended as a god, you have gone as a god, you have descended
as a god, being bandaged[10] in this your name of Sopd; Anubis, Wepwawet
279 and the Eyeless One are those who make you | very glad. You have put him[11]
with your[12] calves,[13] and it is he who watches them for you upon earth. Your
fore-leg offering is in the Thinite nome, your hind-leg offering is in Zety-land.
Your soul is behind you, your strength(?)[14] is before you, having been placed
on your head, and I am your heir, I am your survivor.[15]

1. The title of the spell is at the beginning only in B10C (damaged); a variant: 'Giving water and bread to a real spirit' appears in red ink at the end of the spell in Sq3C.

2. Reading with T1C1;  of the other texts is surely due to a misunderstanding.

3. Hortative old perfective.

4. Unknown word, which, to judge by the variant spellings, is surely corrupt. Here follows a long omission in T1C.

5. Lit. 'go these your goings'.

6. *Sẖn;* corrupt in T2C and T9C.

7. T1C only.

8. 278*d* shows that the 2nd person of T2C, T1C and B10C is to be preferred. Compare *Pyr.* §§ 253*c*; 1861*a*.

9. Var. T2C: 'brow'.

10. *Str* of T2C may be identical with *srt* of *Wb.* IV, 344, 5–7, recorded there only from late times. *Sṯr* of T1C may well be merely a var. This rare verb has been emended in T9C and B10C into *sty* 'shoot', 'throw', 'pour', etc., while Sq3C has tried to combine *sty* and *str*. Since the deceased is here equated with Sopd, who is often represented as a mummified falcon, it seems best to take *str* as meaning 'bandage a mummy'.

11. The pronouns are puzzling. Since the deceased presumably is still being addressed in the 2nd person, *sw* may perhaps refer to the survivor who has inherited the calves, i.e. the dead man's son who is reciting this spell. But in 279*h* he speaks in the 1st person.

12. Note the possessive construction *nw·k n*, an unrecorded anticipation of the familiar *nꜣy·k n*.

13. Sq3C adds: 'who are in the garden'.

14. For *wꜣš* 'be strong' cf. *Urk.* IV, 430,12; *ZÄS* 57,7*.

15. Sq3C ends with the rubric: 'Giving water and bread to a real spirit', see n.1.

Spell 66

Presenting glorifications.[1] O N, be great, be mighty![2] Go to the Great Stairway, I, 280
travel to the Great City, for the earth-gods cannot detain you.[3] O walls of
Shu, release(?) what he has enclosed(?).[4] Horus the Ascender(?) has equipped
you,[5] the earth has been removed for you[6] in the sight of *'Iẖt-wtt* who has
come forth from Ōn—so says Isis.| She shall suckle you,[7] Nephthys shall give 281
you her pendent breast, the Two Ladies of Dep shall give you their locks, your
two mothers who are in Nekheb shall come to you,[9] they shall take their breasts
to your mouth,[10] they shall lift you up[11] and carry you[12]. Recite four times.

1. B10C only. In Sq3C this title, in the form of 'Presenting a spirit', appears in red at the end of Spell 68.

2. Hortative old perfectives. Note the reinforcing particle *rr* in T2C.

3. Var. 'you whom the earth-gods cannot detain'.

4. Virtually incomprehensible. The pronoun *ṯn* obviously refers to the 'walls', but *it* is entirely obscure and to all appearance corrupt; *mḏr·f* may possibly be identified with *mḏry* 'enclose', 'wall in', *Urk.* IV, 1087,10. The translation of the passage is conjectural, but reference seems to be made to giving the dead man freedom of movement.

5. *Šṯ* is given the meaning 'schmucken' in *Wb.* IV, 558, 3–4, but here the sense seems to be

'equip' rather than 'adorn'; the word is corrupted in T1C; see also *CT* V, 26*b*. *ȝḳty*, var. *ȝḳw*, may be a derivative of *iȝḳ* 'ascend', *Pyr.* §§ 139; 452; 941; cf. *ȝḳt* 'ascent' § 1431.

6. An allusion to the resurrection from the tomb. B10C has corrupted *nš n·k* into *nšn n·k*.

7. For the translation as a future cf. the prospective form *iwt* in 281*d*.

9. T2C has miswritten *nḫb*.

10. Cf. *Pyr.* §§ 381; 1119; 1427.

11. T9C and Sq3C precede this clause with 'recite four times' (B10C with 'four times' only). In T2C and T1C this phrase appears at the end of the spells.

12. The meaning of *sḏn* is fixed by the det. in T9C of a man carrying a child; its rarity is shown by the variety of spellings, hinting that it was unfamiliar to the copyists. It is not in *Wb.*

Spell 67

I, 282 Awake, awake, O N! Awake, Osiris; awake, Anubis, at his death! Your kite(s) are Isis and Nephthys;[1] this your cold water,[2] O my father,[3] is what came out of Elephantine;[4] your white loaves are Anubis; your *ḫnfw*-loaves are Osiris; your *ḫbnnt*-bread is *Nwt·k-nw*.[5]

283 O N, awake for this your warm bread which I have prepared for you, your thousand of bread, your thousand of beer, your thousand of oxen, your thousand of poultry, your thousand of figs, your thousand of earth-almonds,[6] your thousand of grapes, your thousand of alabaster, your thousand of linen, your joints of meat on your slaughter-block, your bread which is in the Broad Hall.

284 O N, I have filled your storehouses, I have brought in(?)[7] your jar-stands, I have given to you[8] your bread which does not grow mouldy and your beer[9] which does not grow sour.

O N, beware of the Great Lake; as for death, you shall escape[11] it, you shall avoid[12] the road to it, they shall not[13] carry you off to the house of yon Soul, they
285 shall not make | opposition to you in their name of 'Opponents'.

O N, join the great ones, for arms go down for you,[14] the dancers of Horus Protector of his father dance[15] for you.

O Elder, the fragrance of the Great One is on you; what delights the nostril
is the fragrance of *'Iḫt-wtt*.[16]
O N, I have threshed barley for you, | I have reaped emmer for you,[17] I 286
have celebrated your yearly festivals yonder,[18] I have celebrated your monthly
festivals yonder, I have celebrated your half-monthly festivals yonder.[19]
O N,[20] these are your movements, you being spirit-like and mighty as the
Foremost of the Westerners,[21] as the successor of Min.
O N, | you have not died the death;[22] you have spent the day wakeful, O 287
great one who once spent the day here[23] asleep. You beget[24] in your name of
'Heron',[25] and I cause[26] you to beget in your name of 'Heron'. Raise yourself
in your name of 'Raiser', stand up in your name of 'Stander', receive your
head | and be glad. You are purified with these four pleasant[27] *nmst*-jars 288
wherewith the two Horuses were purified; they weave(?) their . . .[28] against
the gods, so weave(?) your . . . against the living, weave(?) your . . . against
the dead. Adjudge(?) your needs as Horus who is in his house;[29] | may your 289
bonds wind round[30] Seth of *Ḫnt*.[31] Your shape is like to a jackal upon his
shoulders,[32] the spines of Thoth,[33] his gazelles(?)[34] which overleap[35] the
housetop.

1. This and the following clauses 282*c*–*h* have been translated here as sentences with nominal predicate in direct juxtaposition (Gardiner, *Eg. Gramm.*^{3} § 125, end), since to render them as ejaculations, e.g. 'your kite, O Isis and Nephthys', yields poor sense.

2. Construed as a masc. plur. as in 275*b*.

3. The son, acting as Horus, is addressing his deceased father in his role of Osiris. T1C omits this invocation; the other three texts substitute 'O N'.

4. The region of the First Cataract, mythologically the site of the caverns from which the Nile rose, is the traditional source of the water used in ritual.

5. *Nwt·k-nw* is corrupt in all texts except T9C and B10C where it is given the det. of the huntsman; see Spell 28, n.3.

6. See Edel, *Qubbet el Hawa*, II Abt., I Bd., 2. Teil, p. 22.

7. Assuming a transitive sense 'bring in' for *ḥsf* 'draw near'.

8. T1C only.

9. Construed as plural.

11. For this sense of *nh* cf. *Pyr.* § 1453.

12. For the meaning here given to *ꜣb* cf. *Wb.* I, 6,8.

13. Here and in 284*j* T2C has corrupted the negative verb *imy* into *imy* 'who is in', which makes no sense.

14. In the gesture of obeisance.

15. For *rw* 'dance' cf. *Pyr.* § 743; *Urk.* IV, 259,16.

16. Reading *ỉȝmy šrt* 'what delights the nostril'; cf. 294*c*.

17. For these two sentences cf. also *Pyr.* § 657*a*, which, like Sq3C here, is in the passive *sḏm·f*; T2C (with loss of an *n* after *ḥw*), T9C and B10C are in the *sdm·n·f* form. In the first sentence three texts have 'barley' as against 'emmer' of T1C; in the second, all texts have 'emmer'.

18. Some corruption has certainly crept into T2C and possibly also into T1C and Sq3C; in parallel with the preceding sentences we would expect a *sḏm·n·f* form here. I suspect that T9C approximates closely to the archetype, reading *ir·n·i rnpwt·k*, the dative *n·k* of 286*a* being rendered superfluous by the possessive suffix in *rnpwt·k*. The final adverb *im* is lacking in T1C.

19. Despite the odds of four to one, I have rejected the passive form *ir*(*w*)*ty* in 286*c.d* as against  of T1C, which presumably represents the *sḏm·n·f* form, thus carrying on the sequence of 286*a–d*. Again T1C omits the adverb *im* except in 286*d*.

20. T1C omits.

21. Sq3C adds: 'as Osiris'.

22. Sq3C adds: 'I will not let you die the death.'

23. T2C appends  to the adverb *ꜥȝ* as if it were the homophonous word for 'great one'; the passage points the contrast between the former supineness of the dead and his present alertness after resurrection.

24. Cf. *bnn* det.  CT I, 45*b*; *BD* 68,6.

25. So T1C and Sq3C; T2C has *bn* and T9C and B10C have *bȝ*.

26. Following Sq3C. Despite the consensus of the other texts in inserting the negation before *rdy*, its presence makes nonsense of the passage, since *bnn* is a desirable activity, and as such there is no reason for preventing it; the negative here may be a false echo of the genuine negation in 287*a*.

27. For *ꜥȝbt* 'pleasant' T9C and Sq3C have substituted an unknown word *nyt*.

28. I cannot translate *sẖt ḏr*, but the context suggests a precaution or defence against hostile gods or humans, living or dead. The expression occurs again in 293*c*.

29. In T9C followed inexplicably by the figure of a pig.

30. No two texts agree here. T2C has *sẖn mḏwt·k Stẖ* 'your bonds wind round (lit 'embrace') Seth'; T1C: 'your fetters uproot Seth'; Sq3C appears to read: 'woven with your bonds is Seth'; for *sšn* 'weave' cf. Caminos, *Lit. Frag.* p. 13. *Sšm* of T9C is unintelligible, and B10C is too badly damaged to help. For *mḏwt* 'bonds' cf. *Pyr.* § 2202; the det. ▭ here is taken over from *mḏt* 'byre'. For *intt* <*inṯt* 'fetter' cf. *Concise Dict.* 24.

31. On the locality *Ḥnt* or *Ḥnbt* see Spell 63, n.6.

32. Perhaps referring to the funerary priest, though there is no antecedent to *·f*. The reference to the 'jackal on his shoulders' calls to mind the jackal-collar worn by Sekerkhabau in *Saqq. Mast.* I, pl.1. For *sn* of T2C, T9C and Sq3C have the causative *ssn*, while T1C apparently reads *snḏ* 'fear', which yields no sense.

33. For *myȝsw* 'spines' cf. *Pyr.* § 1560, var. *mȝzw* § 1999; the word seems to refer to the shafts of feathers.

34. *Myst*, *mrst* and *sšyt* are all unknown to *Wb.* B10C and possibly T9C determine *myst* with the gazelle-sign.

35. Cf. *Concise Dict.* 231; but the end of this spell is incomprehensible to me.

Spell 68

O N, stand at the doors which keep out the plebs![1] There comes out to you | I, 290
the warden of the two Mansions of Khentymentef,[2] who is a lone star without a companion.

O N, stand at the Two Conclaves! Your mother Seshat clothes you, the Great Mooring-post[3] speaks to you, a stairway is set up[4] for you from the sea, the Slaughterers fall | on their faces at you and the Imperishable Stars bow 291
to you.

O N, stand against them, your sceptre on your shoulder,[5] strike your hand against them, and they will fall for you into the Great Lake, while your bread has flooded in, your beer has flooded in, even the efflux which came out of Osiris.

O N, raise yourself and stand up![6]

1. This injunction already in *Pyr.* § 655.
2. For this deity cf. *Pyr. Transl.* Indexes, p. 324; T1C has corrupted *mnt·f* into *mnyt* 'daily offerings'.
3. An epithet of Isis, cf. ibid. p. 321.
4. For *skr rdw* 'set up a stairway' cf. *Pyr.* § 1090; *CT* V, 399*f.*
5. For 'shoulder' Sq3C and B10C have 'arm(s)'.
6. Sq3C adds the rubric 'presenting a spirit', cf. Spell 63, n.1.

Spell 69

The Great One falls upon his side, he who is in Nedit quakes. O N, lift up I, 292
your head, says Rēʿ. Detest sleep, hate inertness, be far[1] from them[2] as Horus, that you may live; be readier than they as Sopd, | that you may live; 293
be more of a soul than they as the Two Souls, that you may live. Devour[3] their hearts,[4] drink their blood, because you are[5] the judge beside him[6] in Ōn. Live on[7] his brethren, weave(?) your . . .[8] against them for the dead, set your name against them for the living,[9] | because you are[10] Gēb who is at the 294
head of the body of the Nine Gods.[11] O you Elder, the savour of the Great One is on you; the nostrils of the gods are delighted,[12] they snuff up the savour of *'Iḫt-wtt*, and N is one of them.

Ho N! Stand up for this left eye of the Mansion of the Mace, for the gods are protected by it. | You will not be wiped out or obliterated, you will have no 295
efflux, you will have no putrescence, for it will be missing from you through the full power of Osiris.[13] Stand up at the head of the Two Conclaves like

Horus at the head of the Two Conclaves; stand up at the head of the spirits like Wepwawet at the head of the gods.

I, 296 O N! | I am your son, I am Horus, I have come that I may perform these glorifications for you. You are protected(?) . . . my name is saved through you(?); do not say it, O Shu, when you speak.[14]

1. Paronomasia between *ḥr* 'be far' and *Ḥr* 'Horus'; so also *spd* and Sopdu; *bꜣ* and *bꜣwy* below.

2. 'Them', 'they' in what follows can refer only to 'sleep' and 'inertness' as personified aspects of death.

3. *Bꜣs*, unknown to *Wb.*, is doubtless the verb from which the name of the feline goddess Bastet is derived. The rendering 'devour' fits both this association and the present context.

4. Sq6C inserts: 'that you may live'; so also in 293*e*.

5. 293*e–j* omitted from T2C.

6. Presumably Rēʿ, in view of the mention of Ōn, though there is no antecedent for this suffix, which T1C omits.

7. There appears to have been a textual omission after 293*g*, because the suffix of *snw·f* lacks an antecedent, which will have referred to a being hostile to the deceased.

8. On *sḫt ḏr* see Spell 67, n.28.

9. *Dy*, varr. *d(w)*, *rdy*, is to be understood as imperative with reflexive dative, in accord with the context, though in two cases the *n* has been doubled.

10. T2C resumes here.

11. T1C inserts *ʿꜣt* after *psḏt*.

12. Reading *iꜣmy šrt*, cf. T9C and Sq3C. Compare 285*f.g*.

13. For *iꜣṯ*>*iꜣt* 'be missing', cf. *Urk.*V, 173,13, where, however, the following preposition is *r* instead of *m*. For *mḥ m* 'the full power of' cf. *Peas.* R 35, where the expression is used of a 'full measure' of goods.

14. 296*c.d* are unintelligible to me. Sq3C adds the rubric 'Giving bread to a spirit'.

Spell 70

O N, take this your bread which is issued for your sustenance,[1] which Horus who is pre-eminent in Upper Egypt has given to you; be full, for men bring
I, 297 to you.[2] | I prevent you from drowning, and my heart is not weary until he[3] gives to you. GIVING BREAD AND BEER TO A SPIRIT.[4]

1. Lit. 'which goes forth on account of your loaves'; for the last word T2C substitutes the incomprehensible *nḫnmw·k*.

2. Translation uncertain; S9C and B10C seem to have misunderstood *in n·k* as *in·kw*, which makes no sense.

3. The officiant.

4. Sq3C only.

Spell 71

Giving bread to a spirit.[1] Take the Eye of Horus, with which you have refreshed(?) yourself.[2]

1. In B10C only.
2. Identical with *Pyr.* § 64*b*. At end, read *ḥr·s* with *Pyr.* and T2C.

Spell 72

O N, your water is yours, your flood is yours, being abundant. Raise yourself, I, 298
receive these four pleasant brim-full[1] *nmst*-jars.

Wipe off, wipe off for me,[2] libate, libate for me, be silent, be silent for me,
listen, listen for me, that I may hear it, that great word which Horus made
for his father Osiris[3] | that he might become a spirit thereby and that he might 299
become great thereby[4] in the presence of the Ennead.[5]

O my father Osiris,[6] raise yourself;[7] O Anubis, raise yourself (and) your
kites Isis and Nephthys.[8] | May you be satisfied by means of the hand of 300
Rēʿ; may you cross over to the Field of Offerings among your brethren who
are in the midst of them, yonder people of whom it has been said: 'You have
⟨not⟩ died the death',[9] and I will not let you die the death,[10] (even) you who
are heavily sleepy and greatly weary.[11] Barley is cultivated for you, emmer is
reaped for you, wherewith I have made your yearly sustenance;[12] I have
celebrated your half-monthly festivals and I have celebrated your monthly
festivals;[13] | your thousand of figs, your thousand of bread, your thousand of 301
alabaster,[14] your thousand of *ṯrp*-geese, your thousand of *r*-geese upon the
offering table of the Foremost of the Westerners. The gods come to you
bowing, the Morning Star rejoices at you, he brings to you | what is in the 302
Abyss; you strike with the sceptre and rule with the staff. You cross the lake,[15]
you traverse the Waterway of the Two Sheep.[16] Do not say:[17] It is I who say
this.[18] It is Gēb and Osiris who say this to you.

1. For *ʿbḥ* 'fill to the brim' cf. *Pyr.* §§ 1140; 1902. The officiant speaks.
2. Read *sk n·i sp 2* with Sq3C; the deceased is speaking now. T2C omits this clause.
3. T9C omits 298*h–j*.
4. T9C inverts the order of the verbs.
5. T1C inserts: 'that he might be strong thereby, that he might be ready thereby, that he might become Foremost of the Westerners thereby, that he might sit thereby'. This last clause occurs in all texts except T2C.
6. The officiant speaks.
7. So Sq3C; the other texts ring the changes on this theme.

8. Here T2C and B10C add *ḫnfw·k nṯr·k* ‘your bakemeats and your natron’, after which T2C branches off on a text of its own which reads: ‘This is your cold water, my father, which issued from Elephantine, these are your white loaves, O Anubis, your bakemeats, O Osiris, your *ḥbnnt*-loaves of *Nwt·k-nw*. O N, O N, wake up for this your warm bread which I have made for you, your thousand of bread, your thousand of beer, your thousand of figs, your thousand of earth-almonds, your thousand of alabaster, your thousand of clothing, your ribs of meat upon your slaughter-block in the Broad Hall’. At this point T2C joins the main stream of the spell.

9. 300*e* shows clearly that the negation has been omitted from 300*d*.

10. Sq3C and B10C insert an unnecessary *n mt*.

11. Following Sq3C; both T1C and B10C have bungled *bꜣg*.

12. Reading *irw·n·i rnpwt·k im*.

13. Following T1C, which inserts a superfluous *n* after the second *ir·n*.

14. Following T1C.

15. Determined with  in four texts out of five.

16. *Sywy*, var. *srw(y)*, means ‘two sheep’, but the word is determined with ibex-heads.

17. Sq3C wrongly inserts *nw* ‘this’ in anticipation of the next clause.

18. The officiant is disclaiming personal responsibility for the preceding address to the deceased, which in the sequel he attributes to Gēb and Osiris. T9C and Sq3C wrongly put this disclaimer into the negative, making nonsense of it.

Spell 73

I, 303 The *ḏd*-pillar[1] of the Day-bark is released for its[2] lord, the *ḏd*-pillar of the Day-bark is released for its protector.[3] Isis comes and Nephthys comes, one of them from the west and one of them from the east, one of them as a kite and one of them as a screecher,[4] they prevent you from rotting in this your
304 name| of Anubis; they prevent your putrefaction from dripping to the ground in this your name of Jackal of Upper Egypt; they prevent the smell of your corpse from being foul[5] in this your name of Horus of Khati; they prevent Horus of the East from putrefying, they prevent Horus of
305 the Netherworld from putrefying;| they prevent Horus Lord of Patricians from putrefying; they prevent Horus Lord of the Two Lands from putrefying.

Your speech is heard by Gēb, the impediment is removed for you by Atum, you are vindicated by the Ennead;[6] indeed they will not permit Seth to be free of bearing you aloft for ever,[7] O Osiris.

1. B10C begins with *sꜣḫ* ‘making spirit-like’ followed by a lacuna, apparently part of a title for the spell, which is a version of *Pyr.* Utt. 532.

2. I.e. of the bark.

3. Lit. ‘the one behind it’, i.e. backing it up.

4. On the *ḥꜣt*-bird see *Pyr. Transl.* Utt. 532, n.1.

5. T1C wrongly *dḏw* for *ḏw*.

6. Var. B10C: ‘the Enneads’.

7. Sq3C reads *wṯs wdn snd·k Wsir ḏt*, apparently meaning 'bearing aloft the weight of the fear of you, O Osiris, for ever'.

8. Only T2C inserts the name of the deceased here.

Spell 74

Turn about, turn about,[1] O sleeper, turn about in this place which you do I, 306
not know, but I know it. See now, I have found you (lying) on your side,
O Great Inert One. My sister, says Isis to Nephthys, this is our brother.[2] Come,
that we may raise his head. Come, that we may reassemble his bones. Come,
that we may rearrange his members. | Come, that we may make a dam in his 307
side.[3] Let not this one be limp in our hands;[4] there drips the efflux which has
issued from this spirit.[5] The pools are filled for you, the names of the streams
are made for you.[6]

O Osiris, live, O Osiris! The Great Inert One stands up from upon his
side. I am Isis, I am Nephthys; Horus has addressed you,[7] | Thoth has pro- 308
tected you, and your two sons are Lords of the *wrrt*-crown; what you have
done shall be what you shall do.[8] Gēb has seen and the Nine Gods have heard
that your power shall be against the sky and the dread of you among the gods.
Your son Horus has taken possession of the *wrrt*-crown, which has been taken
from that one who would harm you.[9]

Live, Osiris! The Great Inert One stands up from upon his side. I am
Isis, I am Nephthys;[10] raise yourself, O my brother,[11] so that your heart may
live | and that Seth may not exult[12] over you, even he who is subject to[13] this 309
hindrance[14] of you when you are placed[15] on his back for him[16] and he has
run beneath your feet,[17] when he supported you on his[18] shoulders, like what
your father Gēb did for you.

Live, Osiris! The Great Inert One stands up from upon his side. I am Isis, I am Nephthys; . . .[19] I am Isis; rouse up at the voice(?).[20] I am Nephthys; wake up! Awake, put yourself upon this your side, O Great Inert One;[21] traverse water, cross the flood, protect your property from those gods who have fallen on their faces because of you . . . this.[22] Stand up,[23] O Osiris!

Live, Osiris! The Great Inert One stands up from upon his side. I am Isis,
I am Nephthys; | Horus comes lamenting you,[24] O Osiris. You are set for 310
him[25] upon his shoulders[26] and you[27] are firm there through your power.
O Horus of the Netherworld,[28] you have swum to Pe,[29] and the gods who were
given to you by Atum have swum after you,[30] the men who among them have
followed you(?),[31] the women who are among them have turned back[32] faint

through you[33] and through your seed, O Osiris; ⟨so says(?)⟩[34] Sothis who is in Pe.

Live, Osiris! The Great Inert One stands up from upon his side. I am Isis,
311 I am Nephthys; | Horus comes lamenting you, Osiris.[35] You are placed upon his[36] back and he runs under your feet,[37] which ⟨your⟩ father Gēb did for you.[38]

Live, Osiris! The Great Inert One stands up from upon his side. I am Isis, I am Nephthys; you are happy now that you have arisen today as[39] Horus of the Netherworld; now that you have arisen today and have ascended into the Celestial waters. The water of purification is yours by means of these four
312 pleasant *nmst*-jars with which the Ennead have purified you.[40] | I have spoken for you what Gēb said; the obstacle is **removed**; your mother Nūt hears . . . what is upon you.[41] Horus has purified you,[42] Thoth has made you a spirit, your two sons are the two Lords of the *wrrt*-crown, and the evil hatred(?)[43] against you is removed. Stand up on your intact feet,[44] that you may open up
313 the way to the gods, that you may belong to them as[45] Wepwawet. | There is created for you your power over your foes,[46] and I have abandoned weeping.

Live, Osiris! The Great Inert One stands up from upon his side. I am Isis, I am Nephthys.

First title in T2C: Giving bread and giving beer to a spirit in the realm of the dead, having power over water in the realm of the dead; the spells for going out into the day for N.

Second title in T2C: Recitation of many spells and vindication in the realm of the dead for the double of N.

1. T2C begins: 'O limp one, you are limp', and then repeats 305*c* ff. in 306*g–i*. *'Inn* of the other texts has been assumed to be identical with *inn* 'turn round, about, back' of *Pyr.* §§ 214; 218; 1491; 2060. The deceased, identified with Osiris, is summoned to wake from his sleep in the tomb.
2. So Sq3C and perhaps B10C; the other texts omit the suffix.
3. Perhaps an allusion to the costal incision made in the process of embalming, which is now to be stopped up. *Ḏr* is taken to be a writing of *ḏrww* 'side', 'flank', cf. *AEO* II, 254.
4. Sq3C and B10C have borrowed the det. 𓂻 from *nnyw* 'move, turn about', *Pyr.* §§ 310*c*; 314*c*; 1596*a.b*, which, however, would make poor sense here.
5. Sq3C ends in a lacuna and a broken rubric.
6. A reference to Osiris as god of water.
7. For *mdw* with transitive meaning 'address' cf. *Pyr.* § 758; note the rare narrative construction *wn(n) sḏm·n·f* here and in 308*a–d*. T1C omits 307*h*–309*g*.
8. A sentence with the perfective relative clause *wn ir·n·k* as subject and with the *r* of futurity and the imperfective relative form *irr·k* as predicate.

9. An obscure interpolation (308*g*) by T9C and B10C is omitted from the translation as being to all appearance no part of the basic text.

10. T2C omits 308*j*–310*j*.

11. Var. B10C *ity* 'O King'.

12. *Nḥ* 'pray' is clearly an error for *nḥn* 'exult'.

13. Lit. 'under'.

14. Fot *ṯwꜣ* see *Pyr.* § 2086.

15. Read *wn·k dy·ty;* cf. also 310*c*; 311*b*.

16. B10C wrongly: 'your back'.

17. Both texts seem to be slightly muddled; read *bṯ·n·f ẖr rdwy·k.* Seth has to go about carrying Osiris. See further 311*b* (T1C).

18. Both texts are corrupt; read *is⟨t⟩ twꜣ·n·f ṯw ḥr rmnwy·f.*

19. I do not understand *tp ir.*

20. The sense of *sḫsf ḫrw* is doubtful, but it appears to be an exhortation addressed to Osiris; perhaps 'rouse up at(?) the voice' or the like.

21. T1C omits the suffix *·k* after *gs*, while the two parallel texts omit *wrḏ wr.*

22. I can make nothing of *dr ḥm nw.*

23. T9C and possibly B10C insert *im* unnecessarily after *ꜥḥꜥ·k.*

24. *Ḥr iy·k* of T1C and B10C is a corruption of *ḥr iw·k* 'lamenting'. There is a similar error in 311*a*.

25. Cf. n.15 above.

26. I.e. the shoulders of Seth.

27. The suffix *·k* of T1C is clearly the true reading as against *·f* of the parallel texts.

28. Here employed as an epithet of Osiris, see 311*g*.

29. For this sense of *mḥ r* cf. *BD* 105,5.

30. Apparently a reference to some hitherto unrecorded myth.

31. All three texts seem to be corrupted. Possibly they should be emended to read *ṯꜣw imyw·sn šms·n·sn ṯw* 'the men who are among them have followed you'.

32. Cf. *Wb.* IV, 219,3.

33. See de Buck's note 4*.

34. A word or words have been omitted before the name of Sothis, which as the text stands appears *in vacuo;* perhaps the most probable emendation is to supply *in* 'so says' before the name of the goddess.

35. See n.24 above. T2C has only 311*a*–*c* of this spell, which it has appended to Spell 73. T9C and B10C onit 311*a*–*g*.

36. I.e. Seth's.

37. T1C inserts *sṯwꜣ·n ṯw rmnwy⟨·f⟩* 'his shoulders bear you aloft'.

38. Read *it⟨·k⟩* in both texts.

39. *M* after *myn* only in T9C, which for *Ḥr dwꜣt* has *dwꜣty* 'him of the Netherworld'.

40. So T9C. The parallels have *wꜥb·ty n psḏt im·sn* 'you being pure for the Ennead by means of them'.

41. The meaning of 312*a*–*c* is quite obscure; I have translated the Egyptian words, but they convey no sense. It looks as if there must have been a gross error of copying in an ancestral MS which the present texts have perpetuated. This view is borne out by the pronoun *ṯw* in *sḏm*

mwt·k ṯw ḥrt-tp; apart from the wrong word-order, this pronoun cannot be the object of *sḏm*, since that verb takes as direct object the words or sound that are heard and the dative of the person who is listened to; something has clearly been omitted after *mwt·k*, while *ḥrt-tp·k* seems entirely unconnected with what has gone before.

42. Accepting the *sḏm·n·f* form of T9C and B10C; the ending *-ṯ* in *wꜥbt* of T1C is an error.

43. Some emendation seems unavoidable here, as *sfꜣ ḫwḏw* makes no sense; *sfꜣḫ ḏw* also does not convince, for no word *sfꜣḫ* is recorded. Just possibly the original reading may have been *sfꜣ ḏw* 'evil hatred.' and *sfꜣ* may have been corrupted into *sfꜣḫ* under the influence of *sfḫ* preceding.

44. T1C omits the suffix in *rdwy·k*.

45. T9C omits *m* before *Wp-wꜣwt*.

46. T1C omits the suffix in *ḫftyw·k*.

Spell 75

I, 314 SPELL FOR THE SOUL OF SHU AND FOR BECOMING SHU.[1] I am the soul of Shu
316 the self-created god,[2] | I have come into being from the flesh of the self-created
318 god. I am the soul of Shu, the god invisible of shape,[3] | I have come into being
320 from the flesh of the self-created god,[4] I am merged in the god,[5] | I have
become he. I am he who calmed the sky for himself, I am he who reduced the
Two Lands to order for himself,[6] I am stronger and more raging[7] than all the
Enneads.

322 I am he who foretells | him[8] when he ascends from the horizon, I am he who
puts the fear of him into whoever would search out his name. I am he who is
324 among the Chaos-gods[9] and who hears the words of the Chaos-gods: | I am
he who despatches the word[10] of the Self-created to the multitudes, I am he
326 who captains the Bark[11] and its crew, I am stronger | and more raging than all
the Enneads.[12]

I have repeated the words of the ancestral gods and those who came into
328 being after me; they enquire about[13] | my creation from the Abyss, they see me
330 strong and raging in the Bark which the Self-created navigates, | and I have
stood[14] among them, I display splendour in accordance with my nature, I
332 speak and the Enneads are silent | when the gods are censed(?).[15] I tell you
that I come into being in my own shape;[16] do not enquire about my creation
334 from the Abyss. | Nu saw me when I came into being, and I know his name,
I know the place where I came into being, but he did not see me come into
336 being with his own sight, | for I came into being from the flesh of the self-
338 created god. He created me by his wish, | he made me by his power, he exhaled
340 me from his nostril,[17] and I am he whose shape was exhaled,[18] whom | this
august god created,[19] who strews the sky with his beauty, whose name the
342 gods do not know,[20] | whom the sun-folk serve. I have grown at his feet, I

have come into being in his arms, I have ascended by means of his members, | 344
he created me[21] in his heart, he made me[22] with his power when I was not yet
born. There was made for me | herbage in the fields of Asia, I am he who made 346
the loaves of the gods, I am he who is in the midst of his circle,[23] lord of green
fields | in the Netherworld. 348

O Rēʿ-Atum-Nu, I am he who provides provisions, who makes fresh the
sustenance of Osiris,[24] | because I have come into being from the flesh of this 350
august self-created god who strews the sky with his beauty and who assembles
the shapes of the gods, the Lord of Justice who locks up the robber, | who 354
assembles shapes. I am he whose shape was exhaled, he did not fashion me
with his grasp, he did not conceive me with his grasp. | He exhaled me from 356
his nostril, he made me in the midst of his beauty; those who are in | their 358
doorways(?) rejoice[25] when they see[26] his light. I am he[27] | whose shape was 360
exhaled in front of his fields,[28] who gives judgement in the secret matters
which are in the Mansion of the Six.[29]

I have created my soul which is behind me,[30] its flame will not be upon my 362
corpse, my soul will not be restrained | by the guardians of the members of 364
Osiris. I beget, my soul begets, my soul impregnates | the people who are in the 366
Island of Fire, I myself impregnate the goddesses,[31] | there is seen my crown 368
which belongs to him who is in his cavern, and it is he who is in his cavern who
raises aloft | my crown for me,[32] it is he who is in his shape who ennobles me 370
and who raises aloft my dignity. I take | the dignities of those who are in their 372
caverns, I do not obey magic, for I have already come into being.[33]

I have gone forth in front of the self-created god who came into being alone, 374
being older than the gods.[34] | I am he who pierced the height of heaven, I am 376
he who for himself used his power,[35] I am he who for himself united his
myriads of souls who were placed among his associates. | I have extinguished 378
the fire, I have calmed the soul of[36] her who burns,[37] I have quietened her who
is in the midst of her rage.[38] | I am he whom the flame of fire burns, but its fiery 380
blast is not against me;[39] (I am he) | who makes the soul of her who burns to 382
travel,[40] and who makes the pain of the flame of her who is in the midst of her
rage, (even she) the fiery one who severed the tresses of the gods. | Your hearts 384
have spoken to me, you gods, without anything issuing from your mouths,
because there has come into being through me the doing of everything,[41] 385
because of what issued from the mouth of the August One,[42] | the Self-created,
who never goes back on what he has said, because I am he who does everything
in accordance with what was commanded to him.

I have shown respect to[43] the lions,[44] | those who are about the shrine are 386

387 afraid of me, those who encircle the tomb stand up because of me,[45] | I go in
and out of the shrine of the Self-created,[46] I have taken my *Nt*-crown on to my
388 head, and the Red Crown rejoices when it sees the *Nt*-crown.[47] | My *Nt*-
crown is on my head, and the Red Crown is on the head of the Self-Created;
389 the *Nt*-crown rejoices when it sees the Red Crown: | so say the gods who hear
its voice. The god is brotherly to the god who came into being from his flesh;[48]
390 when they saw him,[49] | the *nʿw*-serpents cried out to me in acclaim;[50] they
391 prepare a fair path for me | when they see me issuing from the shrine.

I judge the entourage who are about the shrine, I release him whom I should
392 release, | I nourish him whom I should nourish, I remove the hindrance of
him whose ḥindrance should be removed,[51] I loose my own hindrance; blood
393 is my detestation, | and I will be with the Lord of Life.[52] I am he who assembles
the myriads for him, I am he who knits together the Entourage for him, I am
394 he who makes those who are about the shrine firm | in accordance with what
he has commanded to me.[53] He has created me with my soul behind me,[54] in
395 order to let him know | what I know, for I pervade all the skies and travel
about all the lands. I have done what he commanded me, there is no flame for
396 my soul | on account of its foulness,[55] and my soul will not be restrained by the
397 guardian of the limbs of Osiris.[56] You possess your soul and your power |—so
says the Self-created to me. My soul shall not be gripped by the Falcons, my
398 soul shall not be seized by the Pigs, | my soul shall not be grasped by the Earth-
399 gods, my soul shall not be seized by magic.[57] My soul shall pass[58] | quietly by
400 them until it enters into the shrine. It has taken possession of what is mine[59] |
because I came into being in front of it; it grants me power over my foes, and
401 I have expelled them from their tombs, | I have overthrown them in their
mansions, I have expelled those who are yonder from their seats, I have
402 caused their dignities to pass away,[60] | I have destroyed their magic, I have
cut off their powers.[61] I have allotted them to be purchased serfs, in accordance
403 with what the Self-created commanded | to be done to my foes, whether dead
404 or alive, in heaven or on earth, who shall encroach upon | my pastures or my
405 fields, who will not exalt me and who will not show[62] me the way | to the Bark
of Praise. I am one invisible of shape,[63] I am merged in the Sunshine-god.[64]

1. In translating this spell, which exists in twenty-one copies, I have so far as possible adhered to S1C, which on the whole seems to furnish the best text, though there are exceptions duly noted below. On the role of Shu here and in the spells which follow see *Jaarbericht Ex Oriente Lux*, No. 18 (1964), 266 ff. Cf. the study of this spell by Zandee in *ZÄS* 97, 155 ff.; 98, 149 ff.; 99, 48 ff., which I did not see until after this work was in proof.

2. B6C adds 'N is Thoth, N is Shu [. . .]. 316*a* is omitted in S1C.

3. For *sfg irw* cf. *Pyr.* § 1061; *CT* II, 58*a*; 62*d*; 63*f*. For the suggested translation 'invisible of shape' cf. *Wb.* IV, 118, 6–7; *štȝ sfg* 'mysterious and invisible' *Pyr.* § 665. In 316–7*c*–318*a* several texts repeat 316–7*a*–*b* in a shortened form.

4. For *ḫpr·n·i* the majority of texts have *ṯs·n·i*, but the following *m*, which would be unnecessary after the transitive verb *ṯs*, shows that *ḫpr* is the correct reading, as does the sense of the text, which is not dealing with the restoration of the god's flesh but with the deceased's emergence thence.

5. Lit. 'I am one who is in the side of the god'; for *imy ḏr(w)* cf. *Wb.* V, 586,11.

6. Reading *ink sydd n·f tȝwy* with S14C, B3C, B1Bo, M4C, M5C, G1T and BH2C; S1C wrongly has *isdd*; T3C, M3C and M6C have *sdd*; B1C, B2C and B1P have *idd;* M20C and M28C have *sdr;* A1C has *sḳdd*. The more common sense of *sydd*, namely 'make impotent', *JEA* 4,35,n.2.; Bremner-Rhind, 23,21, hardly suits the present context, and we must fall back on the alternative meaning 'zur Ruhe und Ordnung bringen', *Wb.* IV, 41,8.

7. Reading *wsr·ky ḏnd·ky r*.

8. Presumably the sun-god. Since Shu is god of the air, the 'foretelling' of the sunrise may refer to the atmospheric hues which announce the coming dawn.

9. The eight primeval gods, cf. Sethe, *Amun*, §§ 120 ff.

10. The  after *mdw* in S1C is a slip, read .

11. Of the sun-god.

12. Repetition of 320*c*.

13. Var. G1T and A1C: 'they raise up'; the writing in M.Ann. is clearly a corruption of *nḏ·sn*. *'Is* before *nḏ·sn* in B6C is obscure.

14. Varr. I have sat'; I have stood and sat'; I have sat and stood'. Several texts have corrupted *m-m·sn* 'among them' into 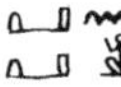 or .

15. More probably so than 'assaulted', despite the det.; for *id* 'assault' cf. *CT* III, 365*b*.

16. Var. 'I come into being of myself'.

17. Apparently attributing the existence of the air (the soul of Shu or Shu himself) to the breath exhaled from the nose of the primeval god. This passage occurs in seven texts only, but it may well have existed in the archetype.

18. Common to nearly all texts.

19. So all texts except S1C and S2C, which both have *pḏ·n·i* 'I extended', which as the text stands makes no sense. I suspect that there has been extensive corruption or omission, and that there was originally a reference to the diffusion of the air from its source as described above; I would suggest that the archetype may have read something like: 'I diffused abroad from his nostril, even I whom this august god created', but actual emendation is not warranted on the present evidence. T3C and BH2C have: 'this august self-created god created me', while M4C has meaninglessly *ʿȝb·n* for *ḳmȝ·n*.

20. Between *rḫ* and *rn·f* a number of texts incomprehensibly insert *sḳdd sw*.

21. Var. BH2C *ir·n·f wi* 'he made me'; N4C corruptly *ʿȝb·n·f wi*.

22. Var. BH2C *ḳmȝ·n·f wi*; M18C obscurely *dns·i*.

23. Var. G1T and A1C; *mḥn·f* 'his coil'.

24. All texts except S1C insert: 'those who are in their caverns fear him', followed by a repetition of 348*c*–*d*.

25. The *n* after *ḥꜥ* in SiC is probably superfluous, though it recurs in M23C; it may be due to the influence of the *sḏm·n·f* forms in the preceding clause. S1C, S2C and M23C are the only texts which show the simplex *ḥꜥ*, which nevertheless I believe to be correct; the majority of texts show the causative *sḥꜥꜥ*, while B2L, B1P and M-Ann. have bungled the word. In the translation I have followed S1C in making *snšw* (or *snw*) in 358*b* follow directly on *ḥꜥ imyw* in 356*b*; the considerable expansion of the other texts appears to be an interpolation, for part of it is virtually a repetition of 340*b* and 352*b*; S5C in particular has a version of its own. *Snšw* or *snw* of 358*b* may be a derivative either of *snš* 'open' ears, *Wb.* IV, 174,4, or of *sn* 'open' doors, cf. the varr. quoted in *Concise Dict.* 229; there may possibly be a connection with *sš* 'threshold', op. cit. 246, where the reading *sn* is not entirely impossible, cf. *GNS* 72. 161.

26. Here the plural suffix of most of the parallel texts is preferable to the 1st sing. of S1C.

27. Varr. 'I am the god'; 'I am the great god'; only G1T and A1C follow S1C.

28. Varr. 'his green fields'; 'his green fields in the Netherworld'. B1Bo is corrupt.

29. *'Imt ḥwt 6* is strangely determined everywhere with , as if an allusion to a judicial robe were intended. Several texts add: 'of Rēꜥ'.

30. In the B3C group there is a considerable interpolation (362*b.e–g*).

31. Most of the parallels insert here: 'my crown (*nms*) is raised aloft for me'; var. G1T, A1C: 'they see my dignity'; M6C, M23C and Sq5C refer to the 'seeing' of the *nms*, anticipating 368*b*, where nearly all texts except S1C and S2C have: 'I have allotted the *nms* to him who is in his cavern'; M3C is obviously corrupt. I adhere, however, to S1C and S2C in the translation.

32. S2C here inserts a repetition of sentences from 359*c* onward, cf. 370*d* ff.

33. All texts except S1C, S2C and T3C here insert: 'my clothing is the breath of life which issued after me from the mouth of Atum'.

34. For 374*d* S2C substitutes 375*e*: 'he brings flame'.

35. Here the parallel texts have clearly the better version; S1C has corrupted *ꜣḫw·f* into *ꜣḫ·ky*, thus depriving *innw* of an object.

36. *Bꜣ* 'soul' only in S1C.

37. For *wpst* cf. *Wb.* I, 305,9.

38. All texts except S1C and S2C add: 'the fiery one who judges and gathers together the gods'.

39. Var. 'the heat of the blast of its mouth is not against me'.

40. *Ssd* in S1C is meaningless and is presumably a corruption of *sḳdd* in the other texts. After this they vary between *Wpst* and *bꜣ Wpst*, with the latter in the majority.

41. *'Irt my r-ḏr*, varr. *irt my-ḳd*, *irt my r·i*.

42. Varr. 'the gods'; 'this august god'.

43. So S1C, S2C and T3C; var. 'I have departed and shown respect to'.

44. Var. 'the souls' (B1Bo). M5C has: 'I have departed ⟨to⟩ the lions, I have shown respect to the jackals'.

45. For *ꜥḥꜥ* 'stand up' of S1C, S2C and M23C, the other texts have the undoubtedly inferior reading *wḏꜥ* 'judge', probably anticipating 391*b*. Seven texts add: 'they prepare a way for me', while to this T3C adds: *mꜣꜣw·s n·i*, perhaps for *mꜣꜣ·sn wi*.

46. Most texts have 'in the presence (*r-gs*) of the Self-created'; S2C omits the mention of 'the shrine' and inserts after this clause a repetition of 385*b*.

47. Reading *ḥꜥꜥ dšrt mꜣꜣ·s nt*; S1C has a mysterious *-t* in *ḥꜥꜥ* and omits the object of *mꜣꜣ·s*. Four texts read *iw dšrt mꜣn·s nt*, omitting any allusion to rejoicing; B1P has erroneously written *mꜣ·sn* for *mꜣn·s*.

48. So S1C; but the suffixes after *snsn* and after the second *nṯr* are absent from all other texts and seem superfluous.

49. Six texts, surely wrongly, insert a negation before *mꜣn·sn*.

50. T3C inserts: 'the entourage about the shrine is in the *sꜣ-tꜣ* festival'.

51. Emending *sḏb·i* at the end of the clause into *sḏb·f*, as the context clearly demands. The parallel texts are either incomplete or corrupt.

52. Compare *CT* I, 255*a*; IV, 72*g*. S2C expands this clause into: 'I will be with the Lord of lords, I will live on what he lives on, he creates [for me] his soul, he repeats for me his majesty, for I pervade the skies and travel about the Two Lands' (393*f–i*) and follows this with another digression which in part repeats 392*d*–393*b*.

53. S2C goes off (398*d–e*) into a damaged digression.

54. Var. 'he has created for me authoritative utterance, my soul being behind me'.

55. I.e. the soul has no foulness which needs cleansing by fire. For this translation of *ẖꜣt* cf. *Wb.* III, 360,6.

56. 'Osiris' omitted in S1C; cf. 364*a*. Some texts have 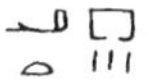 'rooms' for 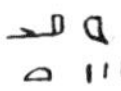 'limbs'.

57. Four texts read: 'the magic of the entourage of Rēꜥ'.

58. The same four texts insert *tmy* before *swꜣ*, but the reason is obscure.

59. S2C ends with a damaged rubric.

60. Var. 'I have destroyed those who are yonder on their thrones'.

61. Var. 'their powers and their dignities'.

62. See Spell 45, n.3.

63. See n.4 above.

64. Cf. n.5 above. This last sentence is not in S1C or T3C. M6C has a damaged text of its own.

Spell 76

ASCENDING TO THE SKY, GOING ABOARD THE BARK OF RĒꜥ, AND BECOMING A II, 1
LIVING GOD.[1] O you eight Chaos-gods who are in charge of the chambers[2] of
the sky, whom Shu made from the efflux of his members,[3] who put together the
ladder of Shu,[4] come and meet your father in me, give me your arms, put
together the ladder for me, for I am he who created you and made you, even
as I was created| by your father Atum. I am weary of the Supports-of-Shu 2
since I lifted up my daughter Nūt from upon myself,[5] so that I might give
her to my father Atum in his realm,[6] and I have set Gēb under my feet.[7] This
god[8] knits up the Two Lands for my father Atum, he gathers together for
himself| the celestial kine; I have set myself among them, but the Nine Gods 3
cannot see me.[9] I indeed am Shu whom Atum created, whereby Rēꜥ came into
being; I was not built up in the womb, I was not knit together in the egg, I
was not conceived,[10] but Atum spat me out| in the spittle of his mouth together 4

with my sister Tefēnet.[11] She went up after me, and I was covered with the
breath of the throat.[12] The phoenix of Rēʿ was that whereby Atum came into
5 being in chaos, in the Abyss, in darkness and in gloom.[13] | I am Shu, father of
the gods,[14] and Atum once sent his Sole Eye seeking me and my sister Tefēnet.[15]
I made light of the darkness for it,[16] and it found me[17] as an immortal.[18] It was
6 I who again begot the Chaos-gods | in chaos, in the Abyss, in darkness and in
gloom. I indeed am Shu who begot the gods.[19]

7 O you eight Chaos-gods whom I[20] created from the efflux of my flesh,
whose names Atum made when the Abyss was created, on that day when
8 Atum spoke in it with Nu | in chaos, in darkness and in gloom: Come to meet
me in joy, give me your hands, put the ladder together for me just as you did
10 for my father Atum, for I am weary of the Supports-of-Shu, | the bank of dusk.[21]

O Lord of Flame guarding the doors[22] of the sky,[23] open the doors of the sky,[24] put the ladder together for me, make a way for me, for I am weary[25] in chaos, in the Abyss, in darkness and in gloom.[26]

11 O you who brighten chaos and lighten the skies,[27] put the ladder together
for me, make a way for me, for I am weary in the Abyss, in chaos, in darkness
and in gloom.

O you *nʿw*-snakes, the seed[28] of Shu, put the ladder together for me, make
12 a way for me, | for I am weary in the Abyss, in chaos, in darkness and in gloom.

O Blood of Shu, Bull of Uraei, put the ladder together for me, make a way for me, for I am weary in the Abyss in chaos, in darkness and in gloom.

13 O Inhaler of the breath which is in the mouth of Shu,[29] | put the ladder
together for me, make a way for me, for I am weary in the Abyss, in chaos,
in darkness and in gloom.

O Bull of Millions who wards off ‘Apep, put the ladder together for me, make a way for me, for I am weary in the Abyss, in chaos, in darkness and in gloom.

14 Shu once became weary of it in the presence of his brethren;[30] put the
ladder together for me, make a way for me, for I am weary in the Abyss, in
chaos, in darkness, and in gloom.

Make a way for Shu[31] that he may go up stout-hearted to the sky;[32] put the
15 ladder together for me, make a way for me, | for I am weary in the Abyss, in
chaos, in darkness and in gloom.

17 Raise up the weary Shu by means of those who are in charge of the dusk.[33]
Make way for Shu[34] that he may go up stout-hearted to the sky; put the ladder
of the weary Shu together for me, make a way for me in the darkness, in
chaos, in the Abyss and in gloom.[35]

1. G1T only. Otherwise the translation in general follows B1C, but with exceptions noted below. See now Zandee, *ZÄS* 100,60.

2. Following B1C; *ʿwt* 'members' of the parallels is meaningless in this context. It may be due to an anticipation of *ʿwt* 'members' in 1*b*.

3. Var. B1Bo and G1T: 'his flesh'.

4. 'Shu' of B1Bo is the better reading, cf. 8 ff. There is a clear tendency to confuse Shu and Atum in this spell. Cf. nn. 31 and 34 below.

5. G1T reads: 'since I lifted up my father and my mother who are upon me'.

6. Cf. *Wb.* V, 586,9.

7. In 2*b*–*e* the deceased identifies himself with Shu the air-god who separated sky and earth, as also in 3*d* and in the following spells.

8. 'This god' appears to refer to Gēb.

9. Because this god is the invisible air. Varr. B1Bo: 'men and gods see him'; G1T 'the Nine gods see me', with *psḏt nṯrw* instead of the usual *psḏt* alone; both varr. are in the affirmative.

10. G1T shows that *ms(w)* is a passive *sḏm·f* construed with a 'complementary infinitive'; B1Bo inserts a superfluous *m*.

11. *Nwt* in B1C is an obvious slip of the pen; read *Tfnt* with the other texts.

12. Var. B1Bo and G1T: 'the breath of life of the throat'. This passage appears to be an attempt to account for the invisibility of the air-god Shu. His covering of air veils him from sight.

13. A description of the inchoate universe before the creation which occurs often below and also in Spells 79 and 80.

14. B1C has corruptly: 'Shu and Tefēnet of the gods', making nonsense.

15. Cf. Junker, *Der Auszug der Hathor-Tefnut aus Nubien*; Sethe, *Zur äg. Sage von Sonnenauge, das in der Fremde war*.

16. Read *ink ir šsp n·s n kkw*; the fem. suffix refers to *wʿt* 'the Sole Eye'.

17. B1C has inserted a superfluous *n* before *wi*.

18. Lit. 'man of eternity'.

19. In G1T this clause is inserted between 5*c* and *d* in the form: 'it was I, Shu, who begot the gods'; here it is repeated in the form 'it was I who begot Atum', in flat contradiction of 3*h*–4*a* where it is stated that Atum produced Shu. In 6*c* ff. there are corruptions, omissions and in G1T virtual duplication, 6*c*–7*b* (in G1T alone) being repeated in a variant version in 7*d* ff. In *Jaarbericht Ex Oriente Lux*, No. 18 (1964), 269–70, I make an attempt to extract an intelligible text from the existing confusion, on the assumption that the invocation 'O you eight Chaos-gods' of 7*c* should in fact begin the next sentence, following directly on 6*b*, and I have made my translation on this basis.

20. 'N' in B1Bo (7*d*) representing the true 1st person as in 1 ff. 'Atum' of G1T is surely secondary and incorrect.

21. 'The bank of dusk' may perhaps be an allusion to low cloud formations at sunrise or sunset which might be thought to resemble great banks propping up the sky.

22. For *tḫ* 'plummet' of B1C, B2L and B1P, B1Bo has 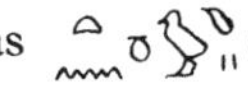 (so also in 1*c*), while G1T has 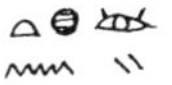 in 10*b* and 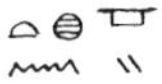 in 10*c*. Since none of the other varr. make sense in this context, it would seem that the true reading is the third one quoted in both 10*b* and *c*, and that we have here an ancient and unrecorded word for 'leaf' of a double door which the Egyptians themselves had forgotten.

23. *Nwt* 'sky' of B1C, B2L and B1P is preferable to *nw* of the other texts; the primeval Abyss can hardly have had doors. The *ḥḥ*-sign at the end of this clause in these three texts frequently recurs and may be a direction to the reader, though its meaning escapes me.

24. This passage is not in B1C and the allied texts, but since it fits the context and therefore may possibly have occurred in the archetype, it has been included in the translation.

25. Following B2L and G1T.

26. B2L here employs *st sk* as a direction to the reader, as also in 11*a*; 12*a.f*; 13*b.f*; 14*c*; 15*a*, where it alternates with the *ḥḥ*-sign noted in n.24; B1P also employs this expression, while B1C has more shortly *sk*.

27. Var. G1T: 'lighten the Two Lands'.

28. Read *mtwt*.

29. B1Bo and G1T add: 'you exhale the breath which is in the mouth of Shu'.

30. Var. B1C: 'his sisters'; B1P omits *ḫnt snw*, leaving only the suffix. B1Bo reads: 'Shu was weary of it . . . raise Shu whom the sunshine wearies'; G1T has 'Shu was ⟨weary⟩ of it in the presence of his brethren; raise Shu because of the sunshine'.

31. The texts have 'Atum', but see n. 4 above.

32. Var. *pr m mnhw*. 15*b*–17*c* are mere repetitions and have not been translated.

33. So B1C and B1P; for *wrḏ* B2L has *m*. Since the general tenor of the text attaches the adjective 'weary' to Shu himself, perhaps we would eliminate *·k* in *wṯs·k* and translate as 'raise up the weary Shu, O you who are in charge of the sunshine', or else insert *m* before *ḥryw* as does B2L and read *wṯs·k Šw wrḏ m ḥryw iḫḫw* 'Raise up the weary Shu by means of those who are in charge of the sunshine'. Of these alternatives I prefer the latter.

34. For 'Atum' read 'Shu', see n.31 above.

35. Following B1C. *Mw3t·k tn* of 17*j* has been corrupted out of *m tnmw*, compare B2L with B1P in 15*d.g; 16a.d.h; 17c.f*.

Spell 77

II, 18 I am this soul of Shu which is in the flame[1] of the fiery blast which Atum kindled with his own hand.[2] He created orgasm[3] and fluid(?)[4] fell from his mouth. He spat me out as Shu together with Tefēnet, who came forth after me[5] as[6] the Great Ennead, the daughter of Atum, who shines on the gods.[7] I was set in it[8] as son and daughter of Nūt,[9] she with the braided hair who bore the gods.[10] Such am I.[11]

1. The reading *tp(y)* of G1T and A1C seems preferable to *tpy*(?)-ʿ of B1Bo. On the other hand, *nby* of B1Bo is known as a word for 'flame', cf. *Concise Dict.* 130, but *nys* (G1T, A1C) with this meaning has not hitherto been recorded. The 1st person of these two texts has been preferred to the 3rd of B1Bo; similarly in Spell 78. See now Zandee, *ZÄS* 100,71.

2. For these varr. of *ḏrt* 'hand' cf. *Wb.* V, 580.

3. In A1C *nḏmmt* has been misread as *nḥmmt*.

4. This translation of *stp* rests on the context and the det. in B1Bo; the word may be the ancestor of the later word *stf* 'liquid(?)', *COA* III, Vol. 1, p. 175. After *stp* B1Bo adds *n r3·f* 'of his mouth'.

5. So G1T and A1C; this reading seems preferable to that of B1Bo, with its forced pun on *tfn*. The latter reads: 'He spat out N as Shu, he expectorated (*tfn·n·f*) him as Tefēnet, the sister of N behind him'.

6. The preposition *m* in B1Bo only; in G1T and A1C *psḏt* seems to be in apposition to *Tfnt*.

7. This clause is dragged in for the sake of the pun on *psḏt* 'Ennead'.

8. The Great Ennead. On B1Bo see n.10 below.

9. Here we have the deceased, who in 18*a* ff. claims to be Shu himself, now assuming the role of Shu's grandchildren, presumably Osiris and Isis.

10. So G1T and A1C. For 18*g* B1Bo has the obviously corrupt reading: 'you place for this N his soul in it as Gēb and Nūt on that day of her who copulated(?) for me and who bore the gods'.

11. B1Bo omits.

Spell 78

I am the soul of Shu, for whom Nūt was placed above and Gēb under his II, 19
feet,[1] and I am between them.[2] O you eight Chaos-gods whom Shu conceived,
whom Shu fashioned, whom Shu created, whom Shu knit together, whom
Shu begot from the efflux which was in his flesh as jackals of the seed of Shu;[3]
| whom Nu begot, whom Atum made, whom Nūt[4] raised up under Atum, who 20
guard the path of Nūt[5] which is under[6] Atum, whose length is that of the sky,
whose breadth is that of the earth.[7] Come, | be joyful[8] in your[9] dignities, be 21
tall[10] with your crowns when meeting Shu in me. Give me your hands, put
together the ladder of Shu.

I am the soul of Shu[11] who ascended on the wings[12] of Shu the father of
the gods. O you bowmen(?)[13] of Shu, regard me, | for I am eternity,[14] the 22
father of the Chaos-gods;[15] my sister is Tefēnet, the daughter of Atum,[16]
who bore the Ennead. O you gods, bow your heads, extend[17] the arms of Shu
until I go up[18] upon the ladder,[19] regard my father Atum in these his proces-
sions with the *wrrt*-crown for ever. I am he who fashioned the Chaos-gods,
whom Atum repeated, and this my sister is eternity.

1. The writing *rdy* of B1C, B2L and B1P is that of the perfective passive participle, so that *tpt* must be either an adverb 'above' or else an error for *tp·f* 'above whom (was placed)' as in B1Bo, G1T and A1C.

2. I.e. the deceased is Shu (air) between earth and sky.

3. B1Bo has corrupted *mtwt* 'seed' into *tꜣw* 'lands'.

4. Var. B1C: 'Nu'. 20*b* is clearly superfluous.

5. So the B1Bo group; the B1C texts have *nw*, surely wrongly, for the path of Atum is the sky, not the Abyss.

6. G1T and A1C have *n* 'of' in place of *ẖr*; B1Bo omits the last two words.

7. So the B1C group; at the end of 20*e*, for 'earth' B1Bo substitutes *nwt* 'sky', and absurdly

puts the whole clause into the plural comparative: 'who are longer than . . . who are wider than . . .', as if the adjectives referred to the guardians.

8. Hortative old perfective, carrying on the imperative in 20*f*.

9. The suffix is omitted in G1T and A1C.

10. *Kꜣ·tywny* has been corrupted in G1T and A1C into *ḳmꜣ·n·i*; these two texts omit the suffix after *ꜣtfw*, both reading: 'I have created crowns', which makes no sense here. *Ḳꜣ* 'be tall' refers to the towering height of the *ꜣtf*-crown. The beings addressed must be the eight Chaos-gods invoked in 19*c*, who are now being adjured to appear in full dress, crowns and all, to meet the deceased in his role of Shu.

11. The original reading was doubtless simply *bꜣ·f* as in B2L, B1P and B1Bo, but in order to remove any ambiguity the other texts have added the name of Shu.

12. The hair-det. of *dnḥ* 'wing' here is given also to *šwt* 'feather' in e.g. *CT* I, 17*b*; 26*b*; *M.u.K.* 1,2.

13. For this word see also the varr. in 22*d* of B1Bo and A1C, cf. n.17 below.

14. So, rather than 'to me belongs eternity', for B1C cannot be translated otherwise than 'N is eternity'. B1Bo has emended this assertion into 'he is Lord of eternity'.

15. So the B1Bo group. The B1C group has *it n tfn ḥḥw* 'father of expectorating (i.e. begetting) the Chaos-gods'.

16. Following B1C–B1P, emending the meaningless  'Ennead' into  'daughter'; B1Bo has *psḏt ꜥꜣt*, carrying the original corruption a stage further. Confirmation of the proposed emendation comes from G1T and A1C, which read: 'she is my eldest sister, the daughter of Atum, who bore the Enneads'.

17. For the plural imperative *pḏw* of B1C, B2L and B1P, we find the meaningless *pḏtyw* 'bowmen' in B1Bo and A1C.

18. Whether the construction be *r* + *sḏmt·f* 'until . . .' or *r* + infinitive with subjective suffix, the gemination of B2L is erroneous.

19. B2L and B1P add: 'of Shu'.

Spell 79

II, 23 O you eight Chaos-gods who went forth from Shu, whose names the flesh of
24 Atum created | in accordance with the word of Nu in chaos, in the Abyss, in darkness and in gloom: you know me,[1] for it was I who created you, begot you and knit you together; we will make you[2] according to the pattern of the word
25 of Nu and Atum,[3] for it was Rēꜥ by means of whom Atum was on high | within his realm (?),[4] and I did not see my father Gēb under my feet, for Shu was in his realm; Shu was within the Abyss when the Earth-gods[5] had not yet been knit together,[6] when the celestial kine of Atum had not yet come into being so that he might come to rest upon them. I am the great one of Shu who climbed upon the
26 ladder of Shu,[7] | I reckon the number of the Chaos-gods in dusk and in sunshine, I am bent on(?)[8] turning to[9] the counting of the pillars which (takes place) in[10] the *ḥṯṯt*-room(?)[11] of the chapel of Atum. I set the *nꜥw*-snake upon

the Supports-of-Shu.[12] | I go down to the ship, I bind together the chapel of 27
Rēʿ with the right-doing which he desires.

1. Var. 'you know (that) . . .'.
2. The text of B1Bo is slightly variant in 24*c–e*.
3. Var. B1Bo: 'Nu and Rēʿ'.
4. Read *m-ḫnw* ⟨*m*⟩ *ḏr·f*? B1Bo reads: 'within Nūt, Shu being in his realm(?)'.
5. I.e. Aker and Gēb.
6. Following B1Bo for 25*c–d;* after 'his feet' the B1C group have only *Šw m ḏr·f*.
7. B1C omits *Šw* after *mꜣḳt*.
8. For this sense of *wdy* cf. *Peas.* B1,206. The words of this sentence can be translated, but its meaning is quite obscure.
9. For *wḏb-ḥr* cf. *Wb.* I, 408,3.
10. The fem. *imt* must refer to *ḥsbt*, not to the masc. *ʿꜣw*.
11. *Ḥṯṯt* means literally 'armpit', cf. Caminos, *Lit Frag.* p. 15, n.1, but here it seems to refer to a chamber in the chapel of Atum.
12. B1C omits 'of Shu'. Following this, B1Bo inserts: 'in the place in which Rēʿ-Atum installed the *ʿnwt* (corruption of *nʿwt* 'female *n.*-snake(?)) when Sia went out facing this N within the sun-disk . . . Kati'.

Spell 80

O you eight Chaos-gods, being veritable Chaos-gods,[1] who encircle the sky
with your arms, | who gather together sky and earth[2] for Gēb, Shu fashioned I, 28
you in chaos, in the Abyss, in darkness and in gloom, and he allots you to Gēb
and Nūt, while Shu is everlasting and Tefēnet is eternity. I am the soul of
Shu[3] | at the head of the celestial kine, who ascends to heaven at his desire, 29
who descends to earth at his wish. Come joyfully at meeting the god in me,[4]
for I am Shu whom Atum fashioned, and this garment of mine is the air of
life.[5] A cry for me went forth(?)[6] from the mouth of Atum, the air opened up | 30
upon my ways. It is I who make the sky light after darkness, my pleasant
colour is (due to) the air which goes forth after me from the mouth of Atum,[7]
and the storm-cloud of the sky is my efflux; hail-storms[8] and half-darkness[9]
are my sweat(?)[10] | The length of this sky belongs to my strides, the width of 31
this earth belongs to my settlements(?). I am he whom Atum created, and I
am bound for my place of eternity. I am Everlasting, who fashioned the Chaos-
gods, reproduced(?) by the spittle of Atum[11] which issued from his mouth
when he used his hand; | his saliva(?)[12] will be made to fall to the earth. 32

Thus said Atum: Tefēnet is my living daughter, and she shall be with her brother Shu; 'Living One' is his name, 'Righteousness' is her name. I live with my two children, I live with my two fledgelings, for I am in the midst

of them, both of them follow after my body,[13] and I lie down and live with
33 my daughter Mā‘et; one within[14] me and one behind me,| I stand up because of them both, their arms being about me. It is my son who will live, whom I begot in my name.[15] He knows how to nourish him who is in the egg in the womb for me,[16] namely the human beings who came forth from my eye which I sent out while I was alone with Nu in lassitude,[17] and I could find no place on which to stand or sit, when Ōn had not yet been
34 founded that I might dwell in it,[18]| when my throne(?)[19] had not yet been put together that I might sit on it; before I had made Nūt that she might be above me,[20] before the first generation[21] had been born, before the Primeval Ennead had come into being that they might dwell with me.

Thus said Atum to Nu: I am on the flood-waters, being very weary, and
35 the patricians are inert;[22] It is Gēb who lives and lifts up my heart,| he nourishes my heart, he has gathered together these very weary members of mine.

Nu said to Atum: Kiss your daughter Mā‘et, put her at your nose, that your heart may live, for she[23] will not be far from you; Mā‘et is your daughter and your son is Shu whose name lives. Eat of your daughter Mā‘et; it is your son Shu who will raise you up.

I indeed am one who lives,[24] son of Atum; he has fashioned me with his
36 nose,| I have gone forth from his nostrils; I put myself on his neck and he kisses me with my sister Mā‘et. He rises daily when he issues from his egg which the god who went up shining(?) fashioned. There is said to him 'Hail!' by those who begot him, who are in the horizon; I make his father to live, the crew of whose bark are the Unwearying Ones,[25] the life of living flesh.[26]

37 I am[27] the living one who knits on heads, who makes necks firm, and who nourishes throats. I knit Atum together, I make firm the head of Isis on her neck, I knit together the spine of Khopri for him, I am the far-travelling sunshine which daily brings the sky to Atum for the nose of Rē‘. I will come[28] and go, I will open the way for Rē‘ that he may voyage to the western horizon.
38 I am . . .[29] at his nose, my arms are under him, I save him from ‘Apep| when he travels to the western horizon. I make to flourish the neck which is in the Night-bark and in the Day-bark,[30] my breath has gone forth today from the west and the east into the body of Nūt. Him whom I fashion daily, he sets me at his nose, does my father Atum; I knit on his head, I make firm his neck[31] and I make firm the head of Isis on her neck,[32] I reassemble the limbs of Osiris, I gather his bones together, I make his seed to flourish, I make his
39 flesh hale,| I give him food-offerings, and the Bull of the West makes him endure.

I am a living one, possessor of years, and I live for ever and ever. Atum
achieved eldership through his power when he fashioned Shu and Tefēnet in
Ōn; when he was alone in his existence, without me; when he separated Gēb
from Nūt, before the first generation had been born, before the primeval
Enneads had come into being, and they shall be with me.[33] He conceived me
in his nose | and I came out of his nostrils. He has set[34] me on his neck and will 40
not let me be far from him; I, my name and my son are alive, (even he) the
Primeval God,[35] I live on the . . .[36] of my father Atum, I am the living one
who is on his neck and my throat is made to flourish,[37] (even I) whom Atum
made[38] into the Grain-god when he caused me to go down into this land, to the
Island of Fire, when I became Osiris the son of Gēb. I am the living one | who 41
made for himself[39] the length of the sky and the breadth of Gēb, that there
might come into existence the food-offerings which were led into me(?)[40] for
the god. My father Atum kisses me when he goes forth from the eastern
horizon, and his heart is at peace at seeing me; he proceeds in peace to the
western horizon, and he finds me in his path; I knit on his head and make
his uraeus to live; I make the head of Isis firm on her neck, I gather the bones
of Osiris together and I make his flesh to flourish daily, | I make his limbs hale 42
daily. There live falcons, ducks, jackals in movement, pigs in the desert,
hippopotami in the marshes, people, corn and shoals of fish, fish in the waters
which are in the Nile,[41] | in accordance with the command of Atum that I 43
should govern them and nourish them with this mouth of mine. My life is
what is in their nostrils, I guide their breath into their throats, I knit on their
heads with this authority of mine which is on my lips, which my father Atum
who came forth from the eastern horizon gave to me, and I nourish the *ḥḏḏw*-fish and the snakes which are on the back of Gēb; I indeed will live beneath
Nūt.

1. Lit. 'being Chaos-god of Chaos-god'. G1T and A1C put the last word in the dual.
2. Lit. 'Aker', earth-god. The B1Bo group omit *pt* 'sky'.
3. G1T and A1C omit 'of Shu'.
4. 29*a–c* in the B1Bo group only.
5. A1C omits 'of life'.
6. The translation of *pr·n ḥꜣ·i* (so the B1C group) is difficult, but the reference to the mouth of Atum suggests that *ḥꜣ* may be connected with the verb *ḥꜣ* 'wail', 'screech', *Concise Dict.* 160, and I have translated with all reserve as 'A cry for me (lit. 'my cry') went forth'. The B1Bo group has: 'he (I) went out behind him(my)self', which is manifest nonsense.
7. Lit. 'the air . . . is my pleasant colour', reading the word following *pw* as *ꜥꜣb* 'pleasant' (op. cit. 38), qualifying *inm* 'colour' (op. cit. 23); I suggest that this sentence attributes the pleasant blue of the sky to the presence of the air, conceived of as appearing blue when viewed in

depth. If so, this would be an unwitting anticipation of a scientific fact, that the blue of the sky is due to the presence of air, which scatters the blue rays of the solar spectrum. The whole passage from *29f–30f* seems to attribute all atmospheric phenomena to Shu.

8. Reading *šnyt* with G1T and A1C rather than the less precise *nšn* 'storm' of the other texts. For *šnyt* cf. *Pyr.* § 336, where the dets. in both texts clearly indicate hailstones; § 1150; *Urk.* IV, 535, 1: *BD* 481,4.

9. '*Iẖẖw* normally means 'twilight', 'dusk', but here it seems to represent the half-darkness of a heavy storm.

10. Lit. 'dew', but here the word refers to a product of the human body.

11. Lit. 'whom the spittle of Atum . . . repeated'. The subsequent reference to the 'hand' alludes to the creation by masturbation, 'spittle' being a euphemism.

12. Unknown word.

13. Reading *wꜥty·sny r-sꜣ ẖt·i*, cf. B2L.

14. The det. of *ẖn(w)* in three texts out of five is surely an error. The two goddesses concerned appear to be Tefēnet and Māꜥet.

15. So B2L; B1C identifies the son of Atum with Gēb, whereas mythologically he should be Shu.

16. Reading *r*⟨*·i*⟩; the following *m* is of equivalence.

17. I.e. resting in the Abyss before the creation. For 'Nu' B2L has wrongly 'Nūt' and B1P *pt*. B1C omits *nnwt* 'lassitude'.

18. B2L and B7C add: 'when my papyrus-stem had not yet been put together that I might sit on it.' B1P has simply *grgw* and omits the rest. Note the masc. suffix used in reference to the town-name '*Iwnw*; usually in Egyptian such names are fem. The use of the imperfective *wnn* here could be to stress the adverbial adjunct *im·f*.

19. *Ḥꜣ·i* lacks a det., and we can only guess at the meaning, but it is something on which Atum can sit. There is a late word *ḥꜣyt* 'chapel' (*Wb.* III, 16,3–5), but a god would sit in (*m*) a chapel, not on it.

20. So B1C and B2L; B1P is corrupt; B2L and B1P add: 'that she might create Gēb'.

21. Cf. *GAS* 82.

22. Still unborn?

23. B1C wrongly 'they'.

24. The deceased speaks. '*Ink* appears to have been omitted from B2L.

25. An obscure passage. after *it·f* can only be the relative adjective *nty* with resumptive suffix in *wyꜣ·f*, but the use of *nty* before a sentence with nominal predicate in direct juxtaposition to the subject (lit. 'who the Unwearying Ones are the crew of his bark') is unexpected, nor is it clear how this bears on the context.

26. It is not clear whether *ꜥnḫ* refers to 'his father' or the 'Unwearying Ones'.

27. It is the deceased, identified with Shu, who now speaks.

28. '*Iwt* is prospective *sḏm·f*.

29. After *ink* (B2L) or N (B1C) comes , which can only be the remains of a word of which part has vanished; the dep. pron. *wi* and *wy* 'coffin' are equally out of the question.

30. Apparently the speaker (= Shu) provides air for the occupants of the bark to breathe.

31. The plural strokes are an echo of *37a*.

32. So B2L; B1C and B1P both omit *smn·i*.

33. The dual suffix *sny* refers to the Enneads. B1C ends 39*h* with *m fnd·f*, anticipating the next clause.

34. *Dwd* as it stands is a *vox nihili;* it appears to be a combination of the two related words *dw* and *wdy*, on which see *JEA* 45,102. 'he has set me on his neck' means 'he carries me on his shoulder with my arm round his neck.' Cf. *JEA* 50, 26–7.

35. *Pȝwtyw* is to be read as a singular adjective, since 'primeval god' is much more likely than 'god of the primeval ones'.

36. *Bsnw* appears to be a name for something edible, not to be confused with *bsn* 'gypsum'.

37. Read *swȝḏ ḥtt⟨·i⟩*, cf. B1C; the other texts have merged 𓎛 and 𓎜.

38. *'Ir·n* appears to be a relative form, the implied antecedent being the speaker.

39. Less probably 'for whom were made', since in this case we might expect the full writing of the passive participle *iry* before the dative.

40. The significance of *sšmt im·i* is uncertain; is the deceased viewed in the role of a collector of offerings?

41. Following B1C; the varr. all show some measure of confusion. The *m* inserted in the middle of l.170 of the diagram in n.2 may have had the significance of something like 'and also'. From here on the deceased is clearly identified with Shu as representing the vital element of the air.

Spell 81

I am Shu, son of Atum;[1] he fashioned me in his nose and I issued from his II, 44
nostrils; he put me on his neck and kissed me every day. He shines and rises when he issues from his egg which the god fashioned as offspring(?).[2] There is said to him: Hail, O you who begot men as one who is in the horizon;[3] I give air to his nose, his bark is alive, his flesh is alive, and I nourish his limbs. TO BE RECITED OVER EIGHT CHAOS-GODS INSCRIBED WITH YELLOW PIGMENT AND NUBIAN OCHRE(?) ON THE HAND OF THE MAN;[4] TO BE RINSED(?)[5] OFF EVERY DAY VERY EARLY.

1. So B1C, with the substitution of *ink* from B2L for the name of the deceased. The version of B2L and B1P: 'I am (N. is) Atum' is out of accord with what follows.

2. On the sense given here to *prt* cf. *Les.* 73,10; *Urk.* IV, 249, 2; 362,4; 1276, 14.

3. Reading *imy* with B2L; the fem. *imt* of the other texts lacks an antecedent, and is probably due to a misunderstanding of *wṯt*, where the *t* is radical.

4. Presumably the images are to be painted yellow and ochre(?); it seems unlikely that the hands of the deceased are to be ochred.

5. Lit. 'licked', cf. *Wb.* II, 334,14, but it does not seem at all probable that actual licking was intended.

Spell 82

My eye is opened[1] for me; my father is in evil case,[2] the eyes of both my souls II, 45
and both my uraei are dead,[3] but I have not given my eyes to my souls or to

my uraei. My eyes[4] are for the grasp of Shu and for the grip of darkness, the distant one who has not[5] my eyes has not slept. My eyes are the doubles of the eyes of Horus; if his eye is firm my eye will be firm whether in sickness or in storm.

1. Surely so, despite the absence of the det.  has been taken to be the enclitic particle.

2. Reading *b(y)n n it·i* rather than *b(y)n it·i* 'my father is evil', which makes no sense.

3. For the association of eyes and uraei cf. *rdy n·k irty·k m iʿrty·k* 'there are given to you your eyes, namely your two uraei', *Pyr.* § 1287.

4. *Ṯwt* with det. here and in 45*e. f* is not recorded, but no translation other than 'eye' seems possible. This spell is most obscure, and its real meaning escapes me, cf. also 82*e.f.*

5. *'Iwty wnt·f* is the relative counterpart of *n wnt·f.*

Spell 83

II, 46 TO BE RECITED[1] OVER THE FOREPART OF A LION MADE FROM CARNELIAN(?) OR FROM THE BONE OF A VULTURE, TO BE GIVEN TO A MAN FOR HIS NECK WHEN HE GOES DOWN TO THE NECROPOLIS ⟨AS⟩[2] PROTECTION FROM THE SOUL OF SHU,
47 THAT A MAN MAY HAVE POWER OVER THE WINDS OF HEAVEN,[3] | HAVING BECOME THIS WORTHY SPIRIT AND KING OF ALL THE WINDS OF HEAVEN. AS FOR ANY MAN WHO KNOWS THIS SPELL, HE WILL NEVER DIE THE DEATH AGAIN,[4] HIS FOES WILL NOT HAVE POWER OVER HIM,[5] NO MAGIC WILL RESTRAIN HIM ON EARTH FOR EVER. IT MEANS A GOING FORTH BY A MAN AT HIS DESIRE FROM THE NECROPOLIS, |
48 IT MEANS BECOMING A WORTHY SPIRIT WITH OSIRIS.

1. The whole of this spell, which is written entirely in red except in M23C, seems to be a rubric to Spell 82.

2. Read ⟨*m*⟩ *mkt* with the two *m*'s merged by haplography.

3. S1C and M23C insert here a much damaged clause which refers to the deceased also having power over water in the necropolis.

4. B1C wrongly repeats before the second *mt*. After this clause S1C add M23C add: 'nothing evil will happen [to him]'.

5. At this point S1C and M23C diverge completely from the main text, but this version is too fragmentary to be translated.

Spell 84

II, 49 BECOMING NEḤEBKAU[1] IN THE REALM OF THE DEAD. I have used(?)[2] myrrh, I have burnt incense, I have hacked up the earth, I have presented offerings before Isis and Nephthys, that they may place holy things upon the arms of
50 Seshat, who is pregnant with me[3] | and holds back[4] from me. She is angry with me and she stabs(?)[5] at me. I have made the front(?) which is between her thighs[6] as Him whose head is raised;[7] I have issued from between the

thighs of Isis[8] as Horus, I have measured out(?) my flesh in the sky as a great
and young wild bull. My libation-jars are of fine gold, my *nmst*(?)-jars[9] are of
electrum(?).[10] I have purified myself in the face of the Two Conclaves, I have
surpassed the spirits,' I have surpassed the sages, and I have said that they 51
shall make for me a standing-place by reason of it(?).[11]

1. On this serpent-deity see *JEA* 21, 41.

2. The verb *ḫꜣ* (the [hieroglyph] is a det.) apparently only here; cf. *Wb.* III, 361,12. *BD* 375, 9–10 has *šd·tw n·i ᶜntyw* 'myrrh has been taken for me'.

3. Following S1C, but ignoring the intrusive *nt* after *tp ᶜwy*, which is lacking in the other texts. G2T likewise refers to Seshat; M22C has 'Selket', while T1L and Sq6C substitute *ḥkꜣw* 'magic'. M22C couples *synt* 'who runs' with *iwr* 'who is pregnant'.

4. Reading *int* with S1C (50*a*) and G2T (49*e*). Sq6C and T1L have *synt m* 'who runs from'. In 50*a* M22C has determined *syn* with the clay-det. (from *syn* 'clay') and the birth-det. For *int* in this sense cf. *CT* I, 231*d*.

5. Following S1C + G2T. For *sšd* 'stab(?)' cf. *Wb.* IV, 310,2, perhaps in allusion to the flash of a knife-blade. For *ḏnd* 'be angry' T1L and Sq6C have a hitherto unknown verb *nḏḏ* (possibly a metathēsis of *ḏnḏ* < *ḏnd*) and invert the order of the two clauses.

6. An allusion to the outward appearance of pregnancy?

7. A mythological serpent.

8. Here Seshat is identified with Isis.

9. *Nmnwt* is otherwise unknown, and looks suspiciously like a corruption of *nmswt*, well-known as a kind of ritual jar.

10. From the context and the det. it would seem that *sšmtt* refers to an alloy of gold; it can hardly be a corruption of *šsmtt*, the word for malachite, which would be an improbable material for jars or vases. Only in G2T; M22C has a broken and distorted version of 50*g*.

11. The significance of *r·s* at the end of the clause is not certain. At the end of the spell G2T inserts the title which the other texts put at the beginning.

Spell 85

N is this *nᶜw*-serpent,[1] Bull of the sky; N is this great one of Atum[2] who swallowed the seven uraei;[3] exalted and fair is N[4] as Neḥebkau. N has come to you, you gods, (even) Neḥebkau who takes away powers. BECOMING NEḤEB-KAU.[5]

1. Var. Sq6C: 'O Osiris N, you are the *nᶜw*-serpent'.

2. Following T1L.

3. So T1L; Sq6C has only four strokes after *iᶜrt* instead of seven.

4. Reading T1L as *ḳꜣ twt N pn*; Sq6C has *ḳꜣ Wsyr N pn wtt Wsyr N pn*, where *wtt* is almost certainly a miswriting of *twt*. Both *ḳꜣ* and *twt* are adjectival predicates. In the similar Spell 86 (52*h*), *ḳꜣwt* is probably a corruption of *ḳꜣ twt*.

5. Rubric in Sq6C only.

Spell 86

II, 52 Becoming Neḥebkau.[1] I am the *nʿw*-serpent, the Bull of the Tribunal, who
swallowed these seven uraei,[2] who is exalted and fair[3] as Neḥebkau, the great
II, 53 Ennead of Atum, who bestows the powers of the gods.[4] | I[5] have come to you,
you gods, I bestow your powers (*kꜣw*) and take away your powers (*ꜣḫw*).

1. Following Sq1C and M14C, which, probably rightly, begin at 52*g*; both texts are in the 1st person. A long insertion at the beginning of Sq6C, which is in the 3rd person, reads (52*b*–*g*): 'O N, you are this *nʿw*-serpent who lifts up the great ones, whom the uraei fashioned. N has come to you, N bestows your powers (*kꜣw*), N has taken away your powers (*wsrw*) as the *nʿw*-serpents (sic), the Bulls of the Enneads.'

2. So Sq6C; cf. also *Pyr.* § 511; *CT* II, 54*a* (M6C). The other texts have the normal plural.

3. The fem. ending in *kꜣwt* (Sq6C) is probably due to a false concord with *iʿrt*, arising from a misunderstanding of an archetypal reading *kꜣ twt*, cf. Spell 85, n.4. The corruption is taken a stage further in Spell 87, where we have two fem. participles *kꜣyt* and *ddt* in M6C which can only be taken as referring to *iʿrt*.

4. So Sq6C; varr. Sq1C: 'I am the Bull of the Tribunal, [the great Ennead(?)] of Atum, who bestows powers'; M14C: 'I am the *nʿw*-serpent, [the Bull of(?)] these [two great Enneads(?)], who bestows powers'.

5. So Sq1C, cf. 52*g*. For 53*a*–*c* M14C has: '. . . [I am] he who assumes [your(?)] powers' (*or* 'the powers [of the gods]'). Here follows in Sq6C the rubric which the other two texts place at the head of the spell.

Spell 87

I am the *nʿw*-serpent, the Bull of the Enneads, who obeys no magic, and to
enter into [. . .] is my detestation. I am the *nʿw*-serpent, the Bull of the
54 Enneads, | who swallows these seven[1] uraei which are exalted[2] as Neḥebkau,[3]
which give power to those who are in their caverns. I will never obey any evil magic and nothing harmful will happen to me. I have gone up and have set my foes under my sandals, that I may have power over them, in accordance with what Rēʿ commanded for me.[4]

1. So M6C.
2. See Spell 86, n.3. M4C has: 'I will be exalted as Neḥ[ebkau].'
3. M4C ends here.
4. M6C is in the 3rd person, but the 1st is certainly original.

Spell 88

I am the *nʿw*-serpent, Bull of the Enneads, who obeys no magic, who is not scorched because of fire, who is not wet because of water. I will never obey magic, I will never be scorched because of fire, I will never be wet because of water, I will be like Rēʿ every day, one who will be fashioned every day by the sun-folk, who saw yesterday [. . .].

Spell 89

SPELL FOR SENDING A MAN AND HIS SOUL AND [. . .] A MAN AGAINST HIS FOE.[1] II, 55
I have come to you, O *ʾIbw-wrt*, gate-keeper of the battle-ground of the gods,
who will ward off the evil ones. | I am he of the sharp knife who went out into 56
the day, and I have power over my foes. I have come,[2] a way has been given
to me, I have control of my foot, | and I will go up against yon foe. I have 57
come here from the Tribunal, my word with him[3] was heard, | and a way has 58
been given to me against him by Him whose shape is invisible.[4] He[5] has taken
away the breath from my nose before my days had come,[6] | he has brought me 59
to this place, while my food is on earth.

1. For the full form of this rubric see Pap. Berl. B4C reads 'Having power over a foe' and S1C (55*d*) has: 'Taking the shape of [. . .]', and at the end of the spell (59*c*) S1C and G1T have: 'Sending a man and his soul'.
2. The B1Bo group only. S1C omits 56*c*–57*a*.
3. Meaning probably 'my contention against him', i.e. against the foe.
4. Cf. Spell 75, n.4.
5. Apparently the invisible one, though the reference is by no means clear.
6. For a similar complaint cf. *CT* I, 167–8.

Spell 90

Not going upside down and going out into the day.[1] I have come[2] to you, II, 60
O *ʾIbw*;[3] protect me.[4] How pleased is my mother's double with me![5] My
father sees me standing on my feet, my staff of fine gold in my hand;[6] | I cut 61
off[7] the flesh of him who lives between the thighs of Sothis.[8] 'Be young, be
young in peace!'[9] say the gods to me; Ḥatḥōr shines.[10]

1. So B2Bo, in black. T1L has in red: '[. . .] that a man may have power over [his] foe[s]'; T1Be in red: 'Spell for going forth [. . .] in the realm of the dead in order to bring according to what he used to do on earth'. The other three texts lack the title.
2. 60*b* in B2Bo only. The translation follows the 1st person of this text.
3. '*Ibw* is clearly an abbreviation of '*Ibw-wrt* of 55*b*; 63*d*.
4. In 60*c* all texts are in the 3rd person. but in 61*a.b* B2Bo, B4Bo and T1Be revert to the 1st person.
5. Reading *ḥtp w(y)*. T1L and T1Be omit the *w* after *ḥtp* and appear to read 'that his mother's spirit may be pleased'; T1Be omits the final *im·f*.
6. B1Bo ends here.

7. T1Be has the *sḏm·n·f* form *šʿ·n* and omits the suffix, as do B2Bo and B4Bo; the other two texts are in the 3rd person.

8. T1Be omits the name of the goddess.

9. Var. T1Be: 'In peace, in peace! Be young!' say [the gods].'

10. The relevance of this last sentence to what has gone before is not clear. B4Bo ends with a defective version of the rubric of B2Bo: '⟨Not⟩ going upside down ⟨by⟩ N', with omission of the negation.

Spell 91

II, 62 I have entered[1] in company with Magic by means of my power[2] | in order to overcome[3] for myself that foe of mine, so that I may go forth into the day. He[4] has been granted to me and he will not be rescued from me, even as He whose shape is invisible has commanded. It is he whose faces[5] are many who sends me for(?) him, and it is he[6] who will approach him.

Going out into the day.[7] I have gone forth from a myriad, I have appeared as the Centipede-god,[8] I have entered into[9] the gates of the horizon; that
63 foe[10] of mine | who was given to me has gone forth, but he will not be rescued from me, for I am vindicated against him.

1. Following the 1st person of B2Bo.

2. Or 'knife,' cf. *Wb.* IV, 24,13.

3. Cf. Caminos, *Lit. Frag.* p. 11.

4. The foe.

5. The writing of the plural *ḥrww* 'faces' indicates that the true original reading of the singular is *ḥrw* rather than *ḥr*.

6. 62*f* should probably be emended to the 1st person, in common with the rest of B1Bo and B2Bo. The use of the old independent pronoun *swt*, the writing of *i(w)·f* in 62*c* and the use of the passive form *sḏmm·f* in 62*c* and 63*b* all point to an early origin for this spell.

7. This sub-title only in B2Bo.

8. B1Bo ends here.

9. Var. 'I have gone up upon'.

10. Shown to be singular by T1L and the suffix in *nḥmm·f* (63*b*). despite the plural strokes in B2Bo.

Spell 92

I [have come] to you, O *'Iby-wrt*, warden of the battle-ground of the gods, I have come in peace to the Island [of Fire(?) . . .], I have hurried myself, my shape is invisible in the presence of yon god who brings [. . .] to my nostril before my days have come [. . .] the ways which are on earth to him. Behold [. . .] has given [. . .] this god. Behold [. . .] I [give (?)] it to you. Go, that you may inspect your fledgelings when comes [. . .].

Spell 93

Spell for going out into the day.[1] O you Sole One who shines[2] as the moon, II, 64
I go forth among the masses to the gates | of the Bark with those who are in the 65
sunshine.[3] The Netherworld has been opened, | for I have gone out in this 66
day;[4] those foes of mine are brought to me, they having been put an end to
in the Great Tribunal.

1. B1C briefly: 'Going out into the day'.
2. B1Bo has *psḏ·f*; B2Bo^{a} has *wbn*; B2Bo^{b} has *wbn psd*, as also S10C$^{b.c}$; S10C^{a} has a bungled conflation of these two words. B1C omits everything down to 65*c*. B2Bo^{b} and S10C$^{a.b}$ for *m iꜥḥ* have the obscure *m ḥnt*; while S10C^{c} has *m* but omits the next word. For a variant text see 259*d–e*.
3. From here on following B1Bo, but using the 1st person of most texts. Varr. of 65*d* read: 'those who are in the sunshine are loosed' and 'in the rejoicing of those who are in the sunshine'; one of these is clearly a corrupt version of the other.
4. B4C ff. add here: 'in my true shape of a living spirit'; in 66*e–h* B1C has a version of its own.

Spell 94

Causing the soul to escape from the corpse: another book for going out II, 67
into the day.[1] I am this great soul of Osiris whom the gods commanded to
copulate with him, | he living on high by day,[2] I have remade Osiris from the 68
efflux which was in his flesh, from the seed which issued from his phallus at
the going out into the day that he might copulate with it.
| I am the son of Osiris, his heir within his rank, I am the soul within his 69
blood, I am he who uncovers this great crown of Lower Egypt | which belongs 70
to Osiris, the uncovering of which the gods fear, because I am this great soul
of Osiris whom the gods commanded to copulate with him, | he living on high 71
by day, I have remade Osiris from the efflux of his flesh, from the seed which
issued from his phallus | at the going out into the day that he might copulate 72
with it. I am he who opened the places of slaughter[3] and the foreparts are
ready.[4]

1. So B1C^{a}; B1L has briefly, in red: 'Going out into the day', while the other texts have no title. *Sḥr r* has been taken to be the causative of *ḥr r* 'be far from'; the alternative possibility 'fly up to' is ruled out because the corpse is buried deep in the earth.
2. For *ḥr ḳꜣ* 'on high' two texts substitute *ḥr iꜣ* 'striding out'; for this rare verb cf. *Pyr.* § 567. Possibly 'living on high' refers to Osiris lying on a lofty bier.
3. So three texts; two have *sbḫwt* 'portals'.
4. Referring to the butchery of animals for food.

Spell 95

II, 73 O Keeper of the Gates.[1] | who inflames[2] wombs and injures[3] faces in the presence
74 of Him who goes forth from his burning, I will go out into the day[4] | with[5] my
soul in my day-time shape to my seat which is in its thicket,[6] and which is in
the midst of . . . on my vertex.[7]

1. For *sn* 'gate' cf. 144*d*; *BD* 163,5.

2. *Stȝȝ*, lit. 'heat' (vb.), is shown from the context to have a connotation of something harmful, but the gemination is unexpected; the passive *sḏmm·f* seems ruled out by the fact that the following verb *snkn*, var. *stkn*, does not show this doubling of the final consonant, and the context suggests that the two clauses in 73*a* are epithets of the gate-keeper. For *idwt* 'wombs' S2C has *tpw* 'heads'.

3. *Stkn* 'make to approach' in B2L yields but poor sense, and *snkn* 'injure' of the other texts is to be preferred.

4. The writing *pry·i* suggests the prospective *sḏm·f* form **peryaf*; B3L has *pr·i*, while M3C and S2C[a] show the *sḏm·n·f* form. S2C adds: 'in this my name of [. . .].'

5. Or 'as'.

6. It is clear from the variants that the copyists did not understand the clause 74*b*. There appear, however, to be two basic versions, one of which apparently reads: 'my seat which devours its flame (or 'power')', while the other runs 'my seat which is in its papyrus-thicket'. Of the two versions, the second is at least intelligible; the 'papyrus-thicket' may be an allusion to the Delta hiding-place of Isis and the infant Horus. Cf. also II, 75*b*; 81*a*.

7. Unintelligible. The meaning of *ḥknw*, var. *ḥnkt*, in this context escapes me, but there may possibly be a connection with the epithet *ḥknw* found associated with the names of Horus and other gods, cf. *Wb.* III, 179, 20–180,3. See also *CT* II, 75*b*; 81*a*.

Spell 96

II, 75 Gēb has opened[1] the door for me, that I may go out from it[2] | to the portal of
. . .[3] north of the Bank of Ḥu. I place the Field of Ḥu in front of ⟨my⟩ seat
77 on the day of ascending ⟨to⟩ the sky[4] | because I am this great soul of Osiris,
with whom the gods commanded him to copulate,[5] he living[6] on high by day. I
78 have remade Osiris from the efflux | which was in his flesh, from the seed
which issued from his phallus at the going out into the day, that he might
79 copulate with it. 'Go forth and copulate with your soul'[7] | say all the gods.[8]
'Go forth into the day' say you yourselves, you gods, ⟨to⟩ Osiris.[9] Osiris has
80 made me into his living soul | according to the word of the gods;[10] I will go out
into the day and will copulate with him; I will go forth as his soul[11] in my
81 (own) shape[12] and I will copulate with him[13] | at my seat which is in the
thicket which is in the midst of . . . on my vertex.[14] Osiris has washed my
82 mouth with the milk of the red cow which came forth | from the sunshine,
83 which bears Rēʿ daily. I have crossed the sky, I have traversed | the sunshine,

I have crossed the west of the sky, I have traversed the east of the sky, it is
Rēꜥ who made my soul for me, and it is I who made a soul for Rēꜥ.[15]

I have come to you, O *Ꜣb(w)-wrt*, door-keeper of the battle-ground of the 84
gods, who wards off[16] the evil ones, to whom the wardens of the fields open
up. | I am he whose knife is sharp,[17] who went out into the day and who has 85
power over his foes; a way has been given to me, I have power | in my legs, I 86
come out into the day against my foe, I have power over him, even as He
whose shape is invisible commanded.[18] I have come here | from the Tribunal, 87
my affair has been judged with it,[19] and I am vindicated.[20] A way has been
given to me by Him whose shape is invisible; | he has taken the breath from 88
my nose[21] before my days had come and he has brought me | to this place, my 89
food being on earth[22] and my magic in my ritual incantations,[23] so that he
might bring to me my foe,[24] | and I have power over him, even as He whose 90
shape is invisible commanded. It is He whose faces are many who sends me to
him;[25] it is he who will judge,[26] for it is he who hears it.[27]

1. For this sense of *wḏꜥ* cf. *CT* I, 33*d*. B1L has the more usual *wn*.

2. S2C inserts repetitions of the obscure passage II, 74*b–c*.

3. *R-ḏꜣwt* is probably a corruption; no such place-name is known, and it recalls the prepositional expression of *Eg. Gramm.*[3] § 180. M3C omits the reference to the portal and reads: 'in order to cross (*r ḏꜣt*) to the north of the Bank of Ḥu'; this has the appearance of an ancient emendation of an obscure passage.

4. This clause is quite obscure and probably corrupt; I translate the words without understanding the meaning of the passage. For 'Field of Ḥu' B1L has 'Field of Rēꜥ-Ḥu'; M3C and M28C have 'Field of 20(!)'; for *ꜥr* 'mount up' M3C has *iꜥb* and M28C has *ḥḏ*.

5. Cf. Spell 94.

6. For *ꜥnḫ* (old perfective) *ḥr kꜣ* (so also 68*a*; 71*a*) B3L has *ꜥnḫ·f im·f ḥr iꜣ*; S2C has *ꜥnḫ ḥr iꜣ*.

7. So B3L and apparently M28C; B1C has *bꜣ* [. . .] *ir·k*; B1L *bꜣ ꜥnḫ*; S2C apparently [*bꜣ*]*·k ꜥnḫ Wsyr*; the lacuna before *bꜣ·k* in M3C is only one square.

8. The M3C group append [*n*?] *Wsyr* to *nṯrw nb*.

9. In B3L for *prt* read *pr* (imperative) as M3C and S2C; all the texts except B3L are quite corrupt, and even this omits the preposition *n* before 'Osiris'.

10. B3L adds 'Osiris' at the end of this clause.

11. The preposition *m* before *bꜣ* only in M3C, and the suffix *·f* after *bꜣ* only in M3C and M28C; the suffix of the 1st person in *bꜣ·i* (B3L, B1C, B1L) makes poor sense. Alternatively one could disregard the suffix in *pr(y)·i* and read *pr(y) bꜣ·i* 'my soul will go forth'; emendation one way or the other is unavoidable.

12. After *irw* B1C and B1L interpolate *m ḥrw*.

13. In B1C and M3C only.

14. Cf. Spell 95, nn. 6,7.

15. Conflated from B3L and B1L, reading *in Rꜥ ir n·i bꜣ·i ink ir bꜣ n Rꜥ*. All texts are corrupt, but M3C less than the others; here for *n* at the beginning read *in*; so also M28C and M30C.

16. B3L *sꜣꜣ nbḏw*; the other texts *sꜣwt(y) nbḏw*.

17. *'Ink mds*; before this M3C has *ink nhs* 'I am one who is wakeful'.

18. In B3L only.

19. The suffix in *ḥnꜥ·f* refers to the masculine membership of the tribunal; the grammatical fem. gender of *ḏꜣḏꜣt* is ignored.

20. *R·f* after *mꜣꜥ ḫrw·i* is apparently the enclitic.

21. 88*a*, in B3L only, is a corrupt anticipation of 88*b*.

22. *Wn* is probably a participle as nominal predicate: 'my food is what is on earth'. The det. of *wn* in B1C is an error.

23. Here M3C and M28C insert 'my praises are in it on earth'.

24. B3L has a dittograph of *ḫfty* 'foe'. M3C and M28C add *im·f* at the end of the clause. The suffix in *im·f* in 90*a*, which refers back to *ḫfty* here, shows that the latter must be singular, despite the plural strokes in N3L and M28C.

25. Following B1L. M28C: *hꜣb mn pn* 'who sends this X'; M3C and M37C: *hꜣb r mn pn*; 'who sends for this X.'

26. For *ir* after *swt* read *ir·f* (enclitic). At the end the M3C group add: 'his soul is with him behind him'.

27. I.e. the case for judgement; 'hears him' would be *sḏm·n·f*, for this verb takes the direct object of the thing and the dative of the person heard.

Spell 97

II, 91 GOING OUT INTO THE DAY.[1] The doors[2] are opened, the contracts(?) are sealed on my behalf(?),[3] for I am Thoth, the trusty one.[4] O Eye of Horus, take me
92 with you,[5] | that I may cause the seeing of your insignia on the vertex of Rēꜥ.[6] O Atum, come, give to me the Eye of Horus,[7] that I may take it[8] and bring it in.

1. B4C only, in red.

2. Most texts vacillate between *wnwt* 'doors' and *wnwt* 'cords', but the former is to be preferred. B4C and S10C are corrupt.

3. Reading *ḥr-tp·i* with M3C and M28C; four texts have *tp·i* (var. *tp N*) 'upon me', while two substitute *rꜥ nb* 'every day'.

4. B1Bo and S10C add: 'who is in it', referring back to *ḫtmt* as if the word meant 'sealed chamber' or the like.

5. Var. S10C: 'O Eye of Horus, come, take me (B1Bo 'this N')', without *ḥnꜥ·ṯ* 'with you'.

6. So B3L; B1L; M28C; B24C and probably T1L. M3C omits *dy·i* and reads: *ptr·i bꜣ·i šwt·i m wpt Rꜥ* 'that I may see my soul and my shadow on the vertex of Rēꜥ'; B4C adds at the end 'father of the gods' as epithet of Rēꜥ; so also apparently T1L; S10C (similarly B1Bo): *smn·i* 'that I may establish' instead of *dy·i ptr*; S10C also strangely writes the fem. suffix in *skrt·ṯ* as .

7. Corrupt in all texts. I suggest an emendation which at least makes sense: *'I 'Itm, m r·k, imy n·i irt Ḥr.*

8. So B3L and B1L; the masc. pronoun *sw* is probably an error for the fem. *sy*, referring to the Eye, which is what is needed here. M28C and M37C have *šd·s wi* 'that it may take me' and end there.

Spell 98

Mine is the sounding pole(?) which went forth from the Abyss. | Yesterday I II, 93
divided the firmament,[1] my soul goes to me ⟨to⟩ the sky, the sky, having
come ⟨from⟩ the earth, the earth.[2] He who is in darkness(?)[3] is he who veils
my back, because I am tomorrow and the Lord of yesterday.[4] Do I forget[5] the
outer chamber of Thoth, does he forget the wish of the dead[6] until my soul
and my shade pass by it?[7]

A MAN SHALL SAY THIS SPELL OVER A LOUSE[8] FROM HIS HEAD; HE SHALL PLACE II, 94
IT ON HIS KNEE, SPITTING(?)[9] UNTIL A FLY COMES TO SNATCH IT.

1. Following the B1C group; S1C and G2T have 'I divided the firmament, (even I) the Lord of yesterday'; the context shows that *psš* refers to the division of sky and earth.
2. As they stand, 93*b.c* are unintelligible, owing to the lack of prepositions, which may be a sign of great age for this text. The most probable emendation is to read *šm n·i bꜣ·i* ⟨*r*⟩ *pt, iy·n·f* ⟨*m*⟩ *tꜣ* in S1C and G2T. The B1C group read *šm·k(y) pt, iw·f tꜣ*; *šm·k* must be understood as the 1st person of the old perfective, since the suffix of the 2nd person yields no sense; the 3rd person in the second clause must refer to the *bꜣ*, although there has been no previous mention of it. Again the prepositions have been omitted before *pt* and *tꜣ*.
3. 93*d* is corrupt in all texts. *Šꜣwt* of G2T and *skt* of the B1C group are both unknown to *Wb.* and the absence of  from *šꜣwt* is suspicious. *Wḥꜣwt* of S1C is likewise unknown, for it cannot be connected in this context with *wḥꜣt* 'cauldron'. If, however,  of S1C be emended into  and the det. ○ into ⊙, we arrive at a word *wšꜣwt* which could be a fem. counterpart of *wšꜣw* 'darkness', *Concise Dict.* 70.
4. S1C and G2T end here. The B1C group continue with sentences which recur in Spells 99 and 101 (S1C, G2T and S2C).
5. Cf. *Wb.* IV, 139,13.
6. After *mt mtt* 'male and female dead' B2P inserts *ḥmt-rꜣ* 'etcetera'.
7. Presumably the 'outer chamber of Thoth'. But what does all this mean?
8. Not in *Wb.*; the translation rests on the determinative.
9. For *pꜥg* see also *Siut*, 11,9. The word may possibly be a miswriting of *psg* in both cases.

Spell 99

Go, my soul, that yonder man may see you; stand opposite him[1] in my shape
and form. 'Just is the living spirit' say these hundreds of Atum[2] who take
possession of you. | Go for the efflux of my flesh and for the sweat of my head. II, 95
You shall ascend from the Netherworld ⟨into⟩ the sunshine, in which they
shine, from which they ascend and into which they descend.[3] It is this god of
smoked(?) grain[4] who lives after his death and who takes you to see yonder
man wherever he is, in my shape, in my form, in my wisdom, the offerings(?)
of a living spirit. Do I forget the outer chamber of Thoth? Does he forget

96 the wish of[1] this man until I pass by it?[5] He does not speak, but the falcons fly up, the antelopes travel,[6] Neith crawls(!) in front of him,[7] he being alive wherever he is.

1. For *ꜥḥꜥ·f* it is probable that *ꜥḥꜥ* (imperative) should be read; G2T and S2C have: 'stand and sit', with defective writings of *ḥms*. Who 'the man' is remains obscure.

2. The stars? Cf. 95*c* and n.3 below.

3. *'Im·f* must refer to *ꜣḫw* 'sunshine', because *Dꜣt* 'Netherworld' is feminine. If our interpretation of this passage be correct, it follows that the 'hundreds of Atum', i.e. as we suppose, the stars, were looked on as detached pieces of sunshine, the ascending referring to the rising of the stars from the last of the sunshine in the evening and the descending to their descent into the light of dawn. It is unfortunate that the ambiguity of the prepositional expression *im·f* prevents us from being certain of this interpretation.

4. *Npr hty*; apparently so, but its real meaning escapes me, as also *Wb.* III, 182,12. The position of *ḥty* after *pw* indicates that it is an adjective qualifying *npr*.

5. Cf. 93*f*. *Sm* in S1C at the beginning of 95*g* is an obvious error for *smhy*, correctly written at the end.

6. Reading the group as *šꜣs ssꜣw*; it would be possible to read *šꜣs šꜣw* 'the swine travel', but not only is this inherently unlikely, but also the det. as written by de Buck is much more like a hornless antelope than a pig. In any case, although individual clauses can be translated, the meaning of the spell as a whole escapes me.

7. So S1C; G2T and S2C insert a damaged and unintelligible passage after *ḫft*. For *ḥfꜣ* 'crawl' cf. *ḥfꜣt* 'crawling posture', *Concise Dict.* 168; the relationship of this word to *ḥfꜣw* 'snake' is obvious.

Spell 100

O messenger who is in the temple, O runner who is in the temple, take my
II, 97 soul to yonder man[1] that he may see it with his eyes, it being alive wherever he is . . . .[1] See, he has taken possession of it, and you shall find[2] the Eye of Horus. Arise . . .[3] this arm of yours is cut off, this hand of yours is . . .,[4] the wardens of sky and earth care for you. You shall stand up and sit down opposite him,[5] and he will see you with his real eyes.

To be recited over an image of the Foremost of the Westerners and to be inscribed upon his hand.[6]

1. An untranslatable insertion after *nt(y)·f im*.
2. So G2T; S1C and S2C appear to be in the 1st person.
3. *ꜥḥꜥt* is hortative old perfective; I cannot translate *mynf*.
4. *Ḏꜥꜥmw* occurs in *Pyr.* §§ 439; 670; 671; 693; but its meaning is not known.
5. Presumably 'yonder man' of 96*i*.
6. In black in G2T.

Spell 101

SENDING A MAN AND HIS SOUL.[1] Go, go, yonder soul of mine, that yonder man II, 98
may see you in your living face wherever you are.[2] He stands up and sits down
when you are in front of him. Shu opens his arms to you; she who does . . .[3] 100
has sent you. | It is this grain-god[4] who lives[5] after death and who removes you from the portal of the sunshine, and you go forth from it by means of the efflux of my flesh and the sweat[6] of my head in the presence of the lifting up(?)
which the Lord of All made,[7] | his sun-folk with him, in order that yonder 102
man may see you,[8] in my real shape of a divine dignitary,[9] wherever he is; | he 104
stands and sits while you are before him[10] until this soul and shade of mine pass by him. Nothing comes forth from his mouth,[11] his lips do not create, |
his mind does not conceive(?).[12] 105

TO BE RECITED OVER [. . .] OF THE HEAD LAID ON THE GROUND IN THE SUNSHINE FROM A WINDOW.[13]

1. Only in B2L.
2. The B1C group: 'Go, go, O soul and shade of mine, to yonder god; permit me to see you wherever you are'. S1C in 98*c*: 'your face of the living'.
3. I cannot translate *smns*, var. *smnys*.
4. B1C and B2L: 'this grain-god and these hundreds of Osiris'.
5. The following *r·f* is apparently the enclitic particle.
6. *Ḳysw*, lit. 'vomit' (n.) must in this context refer to physical exudation, i.e. 'sweat'; cf. 95*a* and 108*g*, which have *fdt* in this context.
7. The translation of *ṯny* as 'lifting up' is not certain, but there may be an allusion here to the primeval god lifting the world from the primal chaos. The suffix in *irw·f* (S1C and G2T) seems superfluous; the writings of *irw* in G2T and B2P suggest an alternative translation: 'in the presence of the lifting up of the shape of the Lord of All'. *Nb tm* 'Lord of All' is corrupted in S1C into the meaningless *nb Rꜥ-'Itm*. For 'yonder man' B1C, etc., have 'yonder god' as in 98*b*.
8. S1C and G2T insert here: 'in my shape, in my form, in my wisdom', cf. 95*f*.
9. S1C, G2T and S2C here insert a garbled version of 93*f*.
10. The same three texts omit 103*c*–104*a*.
11. So S1C and G2T, with impersonal use of *n sḏm·n·f*; the other texts have: 'he does not speak', and then come to an end.
12. *Ṯm* is a hapax, but the contexts suggest that the meaning may be 'think', 'conceive', or the like.
13. G2T (in black) ends here; S1C and S2C continue with illegible traces. For *ws* 'window' cf. *Concise Dict*. 68.

Spell 102

O *Sk-wr*, hunter(?) of Ōn,[1] who lives after his death; ascend, O great one who

issues from the efflux which comes into being from the human body. He will
I, 106 bring[2] me my life that I may see him and send him; | he will go so that yonder
god may see him wherever he is. If there be delayed, go wrong or be held up
your bringing him to me, the Eye of Horus will be against you accordingly.[3]
O my soul, your bread and your food are for riches of the god's bark, which
is splendid, new and long-enduring.[4] You shall put the offering of the first of
the decade in front of the Great One like Thoth and fear the rage of the Great
One (fem.) who is upon Atum;[5] she receives your front in the *pꜣḫt*-bark, your
107 rear in the god's bark. | The great ones quake in their seats at you just as they
quake at the Disturber; Isis gives you this knife[6] of hers which she gave to
Horus[7] after the mourning of the gods. 'You are Authoritative Utterance who
is on our mouths'[8] say the gods. What you did for your own selves, you gods,
do you the like for this living soul. Be strong in the sky,[9] be mighty in the
sky, be mighty on earth, (and also) the uraeus which is on your head; to you
belongs all.
108 Go, go, yonder soul of mine,[10] that yonder god may see you wherever he is
in my form, my shape and my wisdom; may he stand and sit while you are
opposite him. It is the hundreds of the grain-god who rescue you in the portal
of the sunshine; they go up, go down and return by means of it. It is the grain-
god who takes possession of you, and you go by means of the efflux of my flesh
109 and the sweat of my head. | Have control over your foot like a living soul, for
you are the unique one of these companions(?)[11] of Osiris. Festival will never
be made for those who rebel against you,[12] because I am master of the rebels.

1. The translation 'hunter' is no more than a guess on account of the stem *nw*. cf. *Wb.* II, 217,1.

2. Prospective *sḏm·f* form *int·f*.

3. Reading *irt Ḥr r·k my*. *My·f ḳd*(?) of B1C is corrupt and *ḥꜣt·f* of B2L and B2P is an interpolation.

4. Read probably *iw t·k ḥfꜣt·k r wḫdw dpt-nṯr ꜣḫ·t(y) mꜣ·t(y) wꜣḥ·t(y)*. B2P has attempted, not wholly successfully, to convert the side-by-side arrangement of B1C into a single-line text.

5. His uraeus; note the snake-det. of *ḏndt* in B2P.

6. According to *Wb.* IV, 24,13 known only from Graeco-Roman times in the form *sꜣḫt*; here the word is masculine.

7. For this writing of the name of Horus see also 106*c*.

8. Hardly 'who is over names', despite the absence of the stroke-determinative.

9. The deceased's living soul is addressed.

10. Compare Spell 101.

11. Reading and sense alike uncertain. Perhaps *sktyw* is to be preferred to *wꜣḥtyw*, in view of a possible relation to *skw* 'troops', 'companies', *Concise Dict.* 251.

12. *N* + passive *sḏm·f* is used here as a universal negative, like its active counterpart *n sḏm·n·f*. The plural strokes to *irw* in B1C are an aberration.

Spell 103

I am Atum the creator who has no weakness; what is stopped up[1] releases[2] my soul that I may send it to the god of the Netherworld. | Atum takes this soul II, 110
of mine to Gēb, for he knows the governor of the earth. My soul opens the earth for himself, he has opened what was stopped up, he has power over the gods, Atum opens his arms to him, Merty(?)[3] exalts him, he[4] strikes him[5] with his sceptre and governs him with his rod. His vertex is the tongue of Osiris, it is he who divides the south from the north.[6]

Go, go, my soul, that yonder man may see you; stand opposite him wherever he is; go up into his sight in the form of a spirit.

To be recited over an image of clay(?) . . . built(?), [the name of] the man is to be placed upon it in the ground, the ground(?).

1. Cf. *Wb.* IV, 528,1. Here the word may refer to the closed tomb.
2. Lit. 'opens'.
3. A male deity, see the pronouns in 110*f*.
4. The soul.
5. Merty.
6. Participle of *wp* as adjectival predicate with pronominal subject.

Spell 104

You possess your soul, O Horus, when protecting your father. If it be that II, 111
you have the Beloved,[1] you will possess your soul, O Horus, when protecting your father. Take my soul and my shade that yonder man may see them;[2] stand opposite him wherever he is. Be a spirit, so that the wakeful ones may be awake and that the sleepers may sleep; stand up, you of the pillars! Down on your faces,[3] O you who are in darkness! I am he who watches over the sceptres of the town in which I am(?),[4] I am he who sought Osiris, who took this soul and this shade of mine that yonder man might see them standing[5] in front of him wherever he is.

1. The subject of *ir wnn* can only be *mry*; note the unusual position of the pronominal dative here after a noun subject in the presence of *wnn*. The 'Beloved' may be Osiris.

2. The use of the masc. sing pronoun *sw* to refer back to both *bꜣ* and *šwt* may be due to both words being regarded as a single entity representing the dead man who is speaking.

3. G2T unnecessarily inserts  after *ḥr ḥr·ṯn*.

4. Read *imy·i*, which presumably is an error for *imy·f*.

5. *ꜥḥꜥ* is omitted from S1C.

Spell 105

I, 112 Going out into the day and assuming human shape.[1] O Bull, I lift up your
bonds; O Bull, I give you your loosened fetters; O Bull, I am not grasped
by Shu, I am not seized by the earth-gods, I am not driven off by Rēʿ,[2] the
sunshine has no power over me, and the fear of me falls on those who are at
113 the ferry-boat[3] when they see me[4] appearing exalted and having become| this
noble one who is at the land of the Island of Fire. I have opened the dawn of
the day, I have split open (*wḏʿ*) the doors of the tombs, I have greeted Rēʿ who
is in his sun, I have repelled for you him who injured Osiris in his night, the
Great White One is my strength, the great god is in my earthly dignities[5] in
the presence of Rēʿ who is in his shrine,[6] Lord of Terror, greatly majestic,
114 Lord of All, who brings everything.[7] Osiris has said of me:| 'Give him his
bones that he may use his limbs and gather together his body for himself';
and my bones have been given to me, I have used my body and gathered my
limbs together like the eating of my body.[8] My body has been given to me like
the Great Lady, it being fair in his (*sic*) presence, my eyes have been opened
for me by the Eyeless One, my [ears(?)] have been opened for me by *Mḫnt-wr*,
I have heard acclamation from the mouths of the Entourage. My mouth is
115 that of a falcon,| my throat is fresh, the lashings[9] which were on my mouth
have been removed, the coils[10] which were on my entrails have been opened;
I eat with my mouth, I defecate with my hinder parts, and the foulness has
gone out of my mouth. Raise yourself, O Nurse[11] of the land, (even) Gēb,[12]
father of the Five. O you god who ascend and descend, they[13] speak against
me; do not repeat the word, but remember what shall come(?).[14]

1. So G2T, in black; S1C and S2C are in red, but extensively damaged.
2. Var. S2C: 'by the sun-disk (*itn*)'; G2T absurdly *in hrw* 'by the day'.
3. For *ḏꜣw* 'ferry-boat' see also *CT* III, 112*f*.
4. For *n* before the object-pronoun *wi* after the suffix ·*sn* see also 116*k*.
5. S1C shows a dittograph of *m sʿḥw·i tpyw tꜣ*. The obscurity of this clause suggests an omission after *nṯr ʿꜣ*.
6. G2T inserts: 'my third is Osiris who is in his night'.
7. For *my-ḳd* as object of *in* 'bring' see also 116*b. c. w*.
8. I.e. the eating by the body, cf. 117*e*.
9. For *ḥtrw* 'lashings' cf. *Pyr.* § 2080; *CT* III, 196*e*; the reference is to the bandages binding up the mouth of the mummy, which are now taken away so that the deceased may live again.
10. Again a reference to the bandages wound about the body. With *ʿnnw* 'coils' compare *ʿnn* 'coil up', of centipede, *Pyr.* § 425.
11. Read *ꜣṯw* with G2T. S1C probably rightly, inserts *tꜣ* 'land' after *(ꜣ)ṯw*; cf. S2C.
12. An eccentric writing of *Gb*; compare 117*m*.

13. Presumably accusers of the dead.

14. A nominal verb-form, fem. gender; a participle seems more likely than the infinitive.

Spell 106

O boar(?), raise yourself; I cause the boar(?) to be loosed and the boar(?) is II, 116
loosed.[1] 'Have you brought everything?' says Osiris to me. I have brought everything, and I say to Osiris: 'I am the forceful one[2] who is in the sun, I am the mighty one who is in the sunlight'. Those who are in the sun have not driven me off, those who are in the sunlight are powerless against me, fear falls upon the arms of those who cross the sky daily in his[3] train when they see me[4] gone up, crowned, exalted, spiritualized, equipped, ennobled and divine in this dignity of mine in which I was upon earth among the living. There are opened [to] me the paths(?) of the sun, there are opened to me the paths from the doors of the tombs, that I may go to and fro and greet Rēʿ who is in his disk, [and that I may . . .] myself on my feet, for I have removed the injury from the skin of Osiris,[5] so that I may go to and fro, that I may protect my body, that I may be wise in my speech, that I may have power over my foe, that I may have fair fame with Rēʿ who is in his shrine, that I may make plans as Osiris.

'Lord of Terror, greatly majestic, to whom everything is brought, for
whom all is taken,| to whom his bones are brought, for whom his limbs are 117
reassembled': so says Osiris of me as of this great serpent, the figure beside him. My bones are brought to me, my limbs are reassembled for me, what was taken from me is brought to me, [what was taken][6] from me is reassembled for me,[7] so that my body may eat. Give me my meat, for my eyes are opened for me by the Eyeless One, the great star, joined to Khem,[8] and I see with them. My ears are opened for me by this Falcon to whom men do not speak, and I hear with them. I have heard the acclamation in the mouths of the Entourage, and the pillar-amulet is at my throat, the breath is not plucked from my nose, it is not cut off, the wind is lacking(?), its door is . . .,[9] which Gēb, father of the Five, raised and lifted up. My staff is in my hand, and I have power over the Excluder of the Great Ones.

1. '*Ibkꜣ* here and in 118*d* is an unrecorded word determined with the pig-sign; It may possibly mean 'boar' or 'wild pig'; for the normal word *rr* for 'pig' cf. 118*c*. The word recurs in *BD* 147,3.5. The curiously arranged opening passage of this spell appears to read: *ibkꜣ ṯn n·k rdy⟨·i⟩ sfẖ ibkꜣ sfẖ (ibkꜣ)*.

2. Read *ink mds*; the *d* of *mds* has been omitted, but the det. of the knife indicates the reading.

3. The sun-god's.

4. See Spell 105, n. 4.

5. Read *ḫn Wsyr*, honorific transposition.

6. Restore *iṯt* in the lacuna.

7. Probably to be read as *dmḏ·t(w)*, passive.

8. For the sake of better English I have transferred the 'by' clause forward before the 'see' clause; so also in 117*h*.

9. *Ngꜣgꜣw*, an old perfective apparently describing a state or condition, may possibly be a reduplicated form of *ngꜣ* 'lack', 'be destitute', *JEA* 49, 32. *Gnhꜣꜣ* is a hapax, and looks corrupt, but may refer to the effect of the raising of the door by Gēb referred to in the next clause.

Spell 107

II, 118 RECITATION FOR GOING OUT INTO THE DAY. The crocodile and the pig have
slept, the pig has passed by. Do they perish? Then I perish. The boar(?) has
slipped.[1] Does he slip? Then I have slipped. O Nu in company with the
Chaos-gods—and *vice versa*—make for me a way that I may go forth and see
119 men,[2] and that the plebs may worship me.! LIKEWISE:[3] I am he who glitters
with fayence in front of the Sunshine-god,[4] who causes me to go forth in this
secret hour. I am he who judges between this one and that one every day, and
praise is given, acclamation is inaugurated, the two locks[5] are ⟨parted⟩,
while I open the [Upper] Netherworld[6] [. . .]; I go forth with a multitude who
have the figs which were in the produce[7] of the sunshine, while I open[8] the
Lower Netherworld. I am the Sun of this day,[9] I am Horus within his Eye;[10]
120 how much better it is with me today than yesterday!! How happy is Ḥu [. . .]
having the scalp of the sun-disk. Anubis and Thoth guard me, Sha guards me
in company with the Lord of Upper Egypt, the gates of Degneg[11] are opened
to me, the gates of the horizon are opened to me, to me belong the Vulture and
the Lion which issued from my [body],[12] my flood-water is that of the celestial
cattle,[13] my movements are the movements of Anubis. O Dau[14] who knits up
fields and lays hold on fields,[15] I am not opposed by hands.[16]

1. For *snbꜣ* see also *Pyr.* §§ 1021. 1536; G2T curiously determines the word with .

2. Here and in the next clause S1C uses the imperative: 'see me, O men; worship me, O plebs!', but the text of G2T seems preferable from 118*f* on to 118*i*.

3. G2T omits.

4. S1C omits 119*c–h*.

5. cf. Sp. 533. n. 11.

6. 'Upper' (*ḥrt*) is restored on the evidence of 'the Lower (*ẖrt*) Netherworld' in 119*i*.

7. Oddly determined with 

8. S1C resumes here.

9. G2T adds: 'and *vice versa*'.

10. Corrupt in G2T.

11. So G2T and probably originally S2C; S1C has: 'the gates of the Netherworld of Degneg'. Who this being may be is obscure.

12. S1C could have read either *ʿwt* or *ḥʿw*; the last word in G2T is corrupt.

13. *Mḥt·i m mḥt-wrt*; *mḥt* 'flood-water' could refer either literally to rain or metaphorically to the milk yielded by the celestial cattle.

14. A being otherwise unknown.

15. S1C inserts *m* between verb and object in both cases; G2T has wrongly inserted a negation before *nḏr*, where S1C has *m*.

16. Apparently so, but the last word may be corrupt.

Spell 108

Opening the Netherworld and going in and out from it.[1] The Sole One II, 1: shines, and I[2] go forth among his multitudes; I walk side by side with(?) them, namely those who are in the sunshine;[3] I have opened[4] the Netherworld.

1. Only in T1L; the remains of a similar passage in black in P. Gard. III.

2. T1L is in the 3rd person, but that the 1st person is original is indicated by M22C; S10C and P. Gard. III. B1Bo omits *pr·i;* S10C omits the subject of *psḏ*.

3. T1L has *gbꜣ·i sn imyw iꜣḫw* with a transitive verb of motion hitherto unrecorded. It may be a derivative of *gbꜣ* 'side', *Concise Dict.* 288, with the meaning 'walk side by side with' or the like. The other texts have *dgꜣ*, also in an unrecorded transitive sense, but *gbꜣ* seems to suit the context better.

4. So P. Gard. III and B1Bo, in accord with the title of this spell; *wnnw* of T1L does not fit the context and should be emended into *wn·n·i*. S10C has *wn·n·i sbꜣw* 'I have opened the gates'; S2C is both defective and corrupt.

Spell 109

Opening the West. Praise is given and acclamation is inaugurated in giving II, Ḥatḥōr . . .[1]

1. Quite obscure; a variant of 119*e*.

Spell 110

I [. . .] this day—and *vice versa*. I am Horus within his Eye because it is II, much better with me today than yesterday [. . .]. There have been opened for me the three [. . .] of the horizon. How good is the report of me yonder with Ḥatḥōr![1] I lead the noble ones with Atum, I control the Jackal and the Lord of Upper Egypt.

[. . .] HORIZON IN THE FOLLOWING OF ḤATḤŌR.

1. Var M22C: 'my mistress Ḥatḥōr'.

Spell 111

II, 125 COPY OF A SPELL FOR BURIAL IN THE WEST. O Anubis who inters me at this mighty mound[1] among those who are foremost among the Silent Ones, You know that I am not[2] among the Mound-dwellers; I am among the first ones of the . . .,[3] I am the god of reckoning in the Garden of the Silent One,[4] I
126 am the owner of fields in the Great Mound | through burial[5] in the beautiful West.

TO BE SPOKEN OVER SAND OF THE TEMPLE OF ANUBIS, IT BEING PLACED ABOUT HIM.[6] THIS MEANS BURIAL IN THE WEST.

1. Following S1C. G1T reads 'who inters in *ʿnḏr-rn·s* and who inters me at . . .'; S2C is similar and B4C stops short at *ʾInpw smꜣ tꜣ*, see n.5* in de Buck.
2. *ʾIwt* 'that not', negative of *ntt* 'that' after *rḫ*.
3. *Smmtyw*, meaning unknown.
4. Var. G2T: 'of silence'.
5. So S1C; G2T and S2C have: 'through fear of burial', which does not seem to make sense; see also 126*c*.
6. Presumably the deceased.

Spell 112

SPELL FOR NOT LETTING A MAN'S HEART SIT DOWN AGAINST[1] HIM. O knees of
II, 127 Orion[2] | which are on the shoulders of him who flew up and destroyed a full half of Punt,[3] the breaker of bones who wailed when he saw Seth, who was bright behind the Great One and who made disturbance when he saw: This heart of mine sits down against me and it weeps for itself.[4] Withdraw(?) your
128 hands which beg for you. | I have given to you, and you have been allotted to Him who is joyful(?)[5] in the mansion of Him who is broad of face. I present to you sand from the Gate of Khemennu,[6] and this heart of mine has not forsaken me. I am he who is in front of Tjenēnet ⟨. . .⟩ and he cares for(?) this heart of mine in the Field of Offerings which is in the Field of Rushes.[7]
129 O you who are greatly detested, you possessor of powers,[8] your sting is in your tail,[9] but my heart gives the *gyw*-plant to Atum, and if he does not give it, I will not give it. I am the Sole One who is alone, I am this one who belongs to him who made his heart in the Island of Fire.

1. Perhaps meaning 'to give witness against him'; another possibility is that the expression may refer to mental depression (cf. 127*e*). That *r·f* is not the enclitic here is confirmed by *r·i* of 127*e*. G2T places the title, in black, at the end of the spell in 129*h*; B4C omits it. The spell which follows is virtually unintelligible.

2. The reference to 'two shoulders' in 127*a* suggests that *sp* 2 in 126*e* may have been intended to express the duality of *mꜣst Sꜣḥ*.

3. Translation doubtful, but *ipꜣ* cannot be the participle of the 'past time' verb *pꜣw*, since in that case it would have been followed by the infinitive *ḥḏt*. For *gs t(w)t* 'full half of' cf. Urk. I, 105,1; *ZÄS* 57,7*.

4. Reading *rm·f sw ḏs·f*, lit. 'it itself beweeps itself', with G2T. S1C omits the dependent pronoun *sw* and M23C omits the suffix in *rm·f*.

5. So apparently 128*b*. For *ꜣw ib* of G2T and M13C, S1C has *ib* only.

6. For *R-Ḫmnnw* cf. Gauthier, *Dict. geogr.* III, 126.

7. The text is quite corrupt. *Ṯnnt* is a feminine word, and the fact that *nw·f* has a masc. suffix with no antecedent is a clear indication of an omission after *Ṯnnt*. After *sḫt ḥtpw* S1C wrongly inserts *iw*.

8. G2T appears to read 'possessor of necks'.

9. Lit. 'your striking-power is in your hinder parts'; possibly a scorpion is envisaged.

Spell 113

PREVENTING A MAN'S HEART FROM CONTENDING AGAINST HIM[1] IN THE REALM OF II, 130
THE DEAD. 'O Eye-breaker!' says Osiris. He has seen Seth,[2] who has been turned back behind the Wretched One; he waged war against the Double Lion when his heart sat down, and he wept on his own account.[3] His staff is in his hand; complete(?)[4] Osiris, I beg of you. There is given to me ⟨. . .⟩[5] and there are allotted to you the . . .[6] in the Broad Hall. Would that the sand had taken[7] | this heart of mine, that it might ask for help(?) from Atum and 131
that it might control the gardens of Seth,[8] for the maker of hearts has not given to him.

1. For *ḥsf r* 'contend against' cf. *Peas.* B1, 296.
2. Var. 'the Outcast'.
3. Cf. Utt. 112, n.4.
4. Restore his dismembered corpse?
5. An omission; *rdy* lacks an object.
6. *Nꜣtyw ibw*, meaning unknown.
7. Var. B6Bo: 'N is not forsaken [. . .].'
8. B1C originally had 'Atum' in error, see de Buck, p. 131, n.1*.

Spell 114

NOT ENTERING INTO THE GOD'S PLACE OF EXECUTION. I am Shu, (fully) equipped, |

II, 132 I have not been taken to the god's place of execution, for I am covered with the *ḳny*.[1] I have not been made to enter into the god's place of execution, for I am covered with the *ḳny*.[2] I have not been made to enter the god's place of execution, for I have seen Shu and Tefēnet behind me, behind me. I am not encir-
II, 133 cled, encircled, I am not enclosed, enclosed,[3] | I am Neper of the knife,[4] my hinder parts are on my back, my buttocks are on my arms,[5] I am a great one, baboon-shaped, I have not entered into the god's place of execution, the knife has no power over me.

1. On the ceremonial garment *ḳny* cf. *SDT* 211.

2. S2C and M3C omit 132*d–f*; 132*e* consists in G2T of the single word *ink* 'I', and in M4C of *nk·i* 'I copulate', which is probably a corruption of *ink*, possibly due to mis-heard dictation. *'Ink* itself appears to be an error, for it lacks a predicate.

3. Intact only in M3C. For *šny·i* S1C had a different word starting with *f*.

4. So S1C; G2T and S2C are untranslatable, and the sentence is probably corrupt in S1C as well.

5. So 133*b–c*, but the lack of sense in the last sentence is testimony to further corruption.

Spell 115

II, 134 DIGGING A POND, PLANTING ZIZYPHUS-TREES, BUILDING A [TOMB] IN THE NECROPOLIS.[1] Come,[2] O you who know the gods with skulls,[3] who propitiate those who have existed in the past with your blood(?)[4] Come, make for me that guide-line(?)[5], fare upstream for me to this great mansion.[6] I am guardian for them,[7] I make coolness for them upon the threshing-floor [. . .]. Come,[8] O
135 Sharp-knived One in front of the Jackal who is at peace, | make peace(?) for them, for the radiant ones help him[9] in the great storm. Come, place for me this *hp*-cord,[10] make for me that guide-line, set aright this plumb-line, that I may set up the guide-line for these gods . . . within it,[11] in the secret holy places, the Imperishable Ones who are among(?) them. I say to them and(?) to
136 their great fathers: 'This is the day when they went forth from their nest | within the arms of Ḥeneg the Great.'

1. The rubric is defective in all texts, but the only word which is entirely lost is the object of *ḳd* 'build', which the space available suggests was *is* 'tomb', cf. 136*b*. The spell which follows clearly refers to the planning of a building, but is otherwise most obscure.

2. Note the reduplication of the enclitic after the imperative *my* 'come' so also 134*h*; I, 240*b*.

3. *Syꜣtt* appears to be the fem. participle of a transitive verb with *nṯrw* as object, and despite the double *-t* of the ending is probably to be referred to *syꜣ* 'recognize', 'know', *Concise Dict.* 212; *syꜣt* 'mutilate' does not fit the context. At the end of the sentence the reading *ḏnnwt* 'skulls' of S1C is presumably to be preferred to the obscure *ḏnwt* of the varr.

4. Lit. 'redness'; the other words from the stem *ṯms* make even less sense. The fem. suffix of

the 3rd person refers to the being addressed; since we are dealing with a vocative, English usage demands the 2nd person.

5. Despite the plural strokes,  after *ir*, after *ḫnt* in 134*e*, after *dr* in 135*c* and after *ir* in 135*d*, must be the preposition, since in every case it has the suffix 1st sing. The rest of 134*d* is quite corrupt, but should probably be emended into *mꜣꜥ pf*, cf. 135*d*; the 'guide-line' is apparently to be used in laying out the tomb-plan.

6. Read *ḫnt n·i r ḥwt tw wrt*.

7. 134*g*–135*a* only in G2T. Who are 'they'?

8. Again a duplicated enclitic after *my*.

9. The Jackal? Hardly the deceased, who in S1C and S2C is female. G2T and S2C read: 'he who is among the radiant ones'; for the sense of *ꜣsb* cf. *Pyr.* § 324.

10. The reading *d hp* of G2T is surely correct, even though *hp* with det.  is not recorded; the context shows that we are dealing here with the setting of cords for planning a building. *Dr hp* (det. ) of S1C is without meaning here.

11. Surely corrupt. No recorded sense of *ib* seems to fit. The suffix in *m-ḫnw·f* appears to refer to the tomb.

Spell 116

BUILDING A TOMB FOR A MAN IN THE NECROPOLIS. O you who are in his[1] breast, who are over the confederacy of the great ones,[2] | come, place this *hp*-cord for II, 137
me,[3] set up the staves for me, make its[4] guide-line for me, bring me food-offerings, propitiate the Great One[5] in his *wrrt*-crown for me, for to me belongs this altar. Everyone who guards the altar(?) of every god helps himself(?).[6]

1. Whose?

2. So G1T and A1C; for 'great ones' S1C and S2C[a] substitute , meaning unknown.

3. See Spell 115, n.10.

4. The suffix *·f* presumably refers to the tomb to be built.

5. Dual in G2T and S2C[a]; plural in G1T and A1C, omitting *m wrrt·f*.

6. All texts except S1C add *mꜣꜥw* 'aright'.

Spell 117

O you who are over his one-ness,[1] who is in charge of the *hp*-cord, who resembles II, 138
his brother,[2] who is in the middle of his . . .,[3] who bears the plumb-line, who opens out the guide-line(?):[4] Come to place the *hp*-cord for me,[5] make the guide-line for me,[6] set aright[7] this plumb-line on the *wsrt*-posts,[8] control for
me the paths of His-face-is-behind-him, | who loves truth and hates falsehood, 139
who is over the broodings(?)[9] of his heart (and of(?)) Māꜥet,[10] because of whom the gods are guided to ⟨me(?)⟩.[11]

1. Quite obscure; the suffix in *wꜥ·f* apparently refers to the person addressed. G1T and A1C omit 138*a* presumably as incomprehensible, while S2C[b] may have had a slightly different text.

2. The *n* before *sn·f* in S1C is correct, cf. *Urk.* IV, 1509,5, but it is lacking in G2T.

3. *Sht*, meaning unknown.

4. *Mꜣꜥt* here is probably corrupt for *mꜣꜥ* 'guide-line' as in 137*c* (S1C, G1T). G1T and A1C omit the object of *pgꜣw*.

5. So S2C[a]; S1C has *dr* in error as before. G2T omits *my* 'come'; G1T and A1C omit 138*c–d*.

6. S1C omits.

7. Reading *smꜣꜥ* with S1C. G2T and S2C[a] have repeated *mꜣꜥ* 'guide-line'; G1T and A1C have: 'just as this plumb-line is on the *wsrt*-posts'.

8. Posts with a jackal-head to which the lines for laying out the plan of a building were secured.

9. The translation of this passage is doubtful, but the connection of *wꜣw*, despite the det. in most texts, with *wꜣ* 'brood' (*Concise Dict.* 52) is suggested by the following *ib* 'heart'. For *wꜣw* A1C has *wꜣwt* 'roads'.

10. The nexus of *Mꜣꜥt* with what precedes is uncertain. Either the name of the goddess is to be co-ordinated with *Ḥr·f-ḥꜣ·f* in 138*f*, or else that there has been an omission at this point.

11. Taking *sšm(w)* in S1C and G2T as the passive *sḏm·f* followed by the dative *n⟨·i⟩*; on this view the *-t* forms of G1T and A1C will be the passive in *-tw*.

Spell 118

I[1] have come[2] as the Double Lion so that I may go up into the Night-bark
II, 140 and | that I may go down into the Day-bark, that I may judge[3] in the crew of Rēꜥ in these evenings.

See, you have come, spirit-like and equipped. By what path did you go?[4]

By the great path which the Sole One inherited,[5] which men do not know, |
141 and upon which the gods never go, but upon which the Foremost Ones went that they might act as guides on the paths to the Great God.[6]

See, you have come, spirit-like and equipped. By what path did you go?

142 By the great path which the Sole One[7] inherited, | on which Seth could not go down after the fight.

See, you have come, spirit-like and equipped. By what path did you go?

By that path upon which the Opponent went to[8] west and east, to the secret place of the sky.

1. The deceased.

2. Read *ink iy* with S1C + G2T + S3C[a]; G1T and A1C have turned this into a question and read *in iy·n·k im* 'have you come thence?'.

3. S1C adds *m ⟨m⟩ꜥnḏt*.

4. The deceased is questioned, but by whom is not clear.

5. So S1C and G2T, though S1C has *iwꜥ* for *iwꜥt*; G1T and A1C begin the reply with *šm·i* 'I went'.

6. Reading *šmt·n ḫntyw ḥr·s sšm·sn wȝwt n nṯr ʿȝ*. G1T and A1C refer to the *ḫntyw* of Anubis. The rendering of *sšm* here is due to the fact that in English we cannot use 'guide' of roads in the sense here intended.

7. For *wʿ* 'sole one' G1T and A1C have *tm* 'complete (or 'perished') one' and omit *wrt* after *wȝt*.

8. *'In* in 142*e* is a difficulty. The most likely view is to take it as the full form of the preposition *n*, though *ir* rather than *in* is what would be expected here.

Spell 119

Twice he has placed[1] (someone) behind me, so that he[2] cannot reach me. He II, 143
has placed Horus son of Isis behind me, so that he cannot reach me. He has placed Seth behind me, so that he cannot reach me. Twice he has placed (someone) behind me, so that he cannot reach me. He has placed[3] Gēb behind me, even he who went forth from his Eye, so that he cannot reach me on the great path which the Sole One inherited, the way to which is unknown to men and upon which the gods never go.

RECITATION FOR BUILDING A MANSION FOR A MAN IN THE NECROPOLIS, FOR II, 144
DIGGING PONDS AND FOR PLANTING TREES.

1. The lack of antecedent to the suffix *·f* suggests that what we have here is but the latter part of a spell of which the beginning is lost. As a result, the present translation is somewhat uncertain, but it would seem that the deceased is protected from assault from the rear on the part of some unnamed being, by interposing deities between himself and the danger; *pḥ* 'reach' probably has here its not uncommon sense of 'attack'. On any view of this spell, it is hard to see what connection it has with its ostensible purpose, as stated in the rubric 144*a–b*.
2. The would-be attacker.
3. G2T omits *dy·n·f*.

Spell 120

I am the great one who went forth from Gēb,[1] and the Great Ennead opens the doors;[2] I have prepared a way for the Great One, for Gēb.[3]

1. Var. 'from the vertex of Gēb'.
2. Var. P. Gard. III: 'the Ennead of Spirits it is who open the doors of the houses'; so apparently also S2C and P. Gard. II. For *sn* 'door' cf. Spell 95, n.1.
3. P. Gard. II is somewhat corrupt.

Spell 121

I am the son of Atum, the companion of Māʿet; I have come that I may climb II, 145
up, I go forth from upon the vertex of the Ennead.[1]

1. Following P. Gard. II and III, which at least provide a text which is intelligible; note the det. of *ḥfd* 'climb'. S1C and C2T have: 'that I may pluck up the upper temples and that I may judge the Ennead'.

Spell 122

II, 146 I have come to you, you great and mighty gods[1] in the two . . .;[2] my fourth is Shu.[3]

1. P. Gard. III reads: 'I have come, I have made three of you, you gods who follow after them, (namely) the great ones'.
2. *Ḥtrwy*, meaning unknown.
3. So S1C; G2T: 'who stand in the two *ḥtrt;* my four (*sic*) is Shu'; P. Gard. II: 'who stand ⟨in⟩ the two *ḥtrt;* I have come ⟨as(?)⟩ three (*sic*) of Shu'.

Spell 123

I have climbed that I may be high in his place,[1] I have come as the fourth of these four gods who went forth from the vertex of Gēb.

1. To whom does 'his' refer?

Spell 124

II, 147 I have descended in order to see Him who is astray, even your fifth, you neighbouring (*sꜣḥw*) stars in Orion (*Sꜣḥ*).

Spell 125

I have come as your fourth, you Imperishables, who keep the records of Khopri and who reveal the secrets of the thrones.

Spell 126

II, 148 I am he who released Māʿet from the head of the Seven of Māʿet.[1]

1. Var. P. Gard. II: 'I am he who loosed the pain of Osiris and Māʿet; his head is the seventh of Māʿet.' A clear case of corruption.

Spell 127

I am ignorant of the crookedness which the Lord of Khemennu detests, I am their eighth.[1]

1. Following P. Gard. II and III throughout; S1C and G2T are incomprehensible. Note the paronomasia *Ḫmnnw* 'Eight-town' and *ḫmnnw* 'eighth'.

Spell 128

I shine as Rēʿ daily, I set up truth and expel falsehood, I open the doors II, 149
which are in the Abyss.[1]

1. Following S1C and G2T.

Spell 129

TO KNOW THE PATHS TO THE SKY.[1] I have opened the paths in the sky, the sun II, 150
has shone when going downstream to the north from the south, a chamber is their[2] entrance and it is roofed;[3] the north is near the gates of its . . ., the south of the sky is open to the earth, and men drive off . . .[4] from the west and the east. May you go down upon the western path because it is large and pleasant; the eastern is difficult because it is small.

1. So G2T; S1C is damaged.
2. The paths.
3. Cf. *kꜣp* 'cover', 'roof over,' *JEA* 22, 38.
4. *Kt;* hardly the fem. word for 'other'.

Spell 130[1]

The name of the small eastern road[2] is 'Cool is the *Nt*-crown'; the bonds are burnt up(?), he[3] makes the Nt-crown . . . . The name of the large western path is 'Bright is the crown of Lower Egypt'; he lives on *inb*-plants.

1. Apparently a continuation of Spell 129.
2. Lost in S1C except for traces in red.
3. Who? Perhaps the deceased.

Spell 131

THE SEALING OF A DECREE CONCERNING THE FAMILY; THE GIVING A MAN'S II, 151
FAMILY [TO HIM] IN THE REALM OF THE DEAD.

Horus Great and Mighty, Lord of the Field of Rushes.[1]

Gēb, chiefest of the gods, has decreed that there be given to me my family, my children, my brethren, my father, my mother and all my servants and my dependants, they being saved from the acts of Seth and from the numbering by Isis the Great beside Osiris, Lord of the West. Gēb, chiefest of the gods,
has spoken of causing[1] that there be released to me immediately my family, 152

my children, my brethren, my father, my mother, all my servants and all my dependants, they being saved from any god or goddess, from any spirits male or female,[2] or from any dead man or woman.

1. The Horus-name of the divine ruler who grants the decree, i.e. Gēb. The regular heading of royal decrees, cf. Goedicke, *König. Dokumente*, passim. On the group of spells 131–146, see the article by Heerma van Voss, 'Hereniging in het hiernamaals volgens Egyptisch geloof' in *Pro Regno Pro Sanctuario*, Nijkerk, 1950 (*Festschrift* van der Leeuw).

2. G2T only.

Spell 132

I am Atum who created the great ones, I am he who created Shu and fashioned
153 Tefēnet, I am he who divided up his boons(?) in the time of Nu, | I am this
one who belongs to the regions(?)[1] of the dwarfs, I have taken my place that
I may rest[2] thus from searching and going to and fro and from circling round
and round. I have reached my seats, I have overpassed my seats, my staves(?),[3]
my throwsticks(?),[4] and my . . .;[5] I am strong, my staff is beside me, my
speech is that of a Chaos-god, my guide is . . .,[6] I give food to the gods and
154 (the results of) butchery to the Lords of Ōn. I will be with their rope, | because
I am this friend(?)[7] of Rēʿ, weary[8] with wounds; there is given to me strength
through wisdom(?).[9] I have sat with my back to Gēb, for I am he who will
judge in company with Him whose name is hidden on the day when the
princes pass by.[10] This is a reminder that I have found the ropes which were
severed ⟨in⟩ the ferry-boat of the flood; I have knotted them and moored it.
I have gone forth, and there have been given to me my family,[11] my children,
155 my brethren, my father, my mother and all my dependants; the | prisoners[12]
156 have been released to me, and I use my arms.[13] | The horn has been pulled
out[14] for me, and there has been brought to me him who is to be placed under
me together with(?)[15] my father who is in Seḥseḥ.

O you whose head is blind, who are among the Six, be exalted in proportion as I am exalted, and *vice-versa*.[16] You shall come[17] to me, for Pe is mine, Dep is mine, and mine is the . . .[18] which is pre-eminent in Ḥet-wer-iḥut. My mother is Nūt who made the fibres(?)[19] in the hearts of Neith, who has come so that I may see you.[20] I have appeared in lapis-lazuli, Lord of Horns in Ōn, I am the god of 'Adja.

157 Welcome![21] I fashion for you | those who are in their primeval state,[22]
whose names are hidden for me. To me belongs writing, and it is I who will
fashion it—so says Neith.

I have made bread for the great ones, green-stuff[23] for the middle-sized ones and cakes for the little ones who are the least important(?),[24] whose faces are veiled for me.

1. *Šdḥw*, not in *Wb.*
2. *R·i* after *ḥtp·i* is probably the enclitic particle.
3. *Nwwt*, not in *Wb.*
4. *'Imyꜥwt*, not in *Wb.* Possibly a var. of *ꜥmꜣꜥt* 'throwstick', *Concise Dict.* 42.
5. *Ḫnw*, meaning unknown; the object represented by the det. is unidentifiable.
6. I cannot translate *my sw*. There seems no connection with *myw sw* 'he is cat-like', *CT* IV, 288*a*.
7. For the sense given here to *ꜥḳ* cf. *ꜥḳw* 'friends', *Mill.* 1,5; *Pr.* 11, 3.4. it is true that the det.  is absent in all texts, but to translate it as 'food' or 'revenue' as written in S1C and S2C makes no sense; the det.  in G2T may be due to assimilation with  in hieratic.
8. *Gḥ* 'weary' is probably a participle in apposition to *ꜥḳ*.
9. The apparent literal sense of *šsꜣty*, namely 'two female antelopes,' is an absurdity here, and the word has been regarded as a miswriting of a derivative of *šsꜣ* 'be wise'.
10. With 154*c.d* compare *Pyr.* §§ 398*c*–399*b*; the only essential variant is the latter part of 154*d*, namely *hrw swꜣ srw*, which is represented in *Pyr.* § 399*b* by *hrw pw n rḥs smsw* 'on this day of slaughtering the first-born'; *CT* II, 163*b* has *grḥ pw n rḥs wrw* 'on that night of slaughtering the Great Ones'.
11. The list of the family is repeated in tabular form in 155*c–d*, the better text being that of G2T; it runs: 'All my family who are in Pe and Dep, my father in Djedu, my mother in Ōn, my children in Kherꜥaḥa and Sepa, my brethren in Abydos and the realm of the dead, and all my dependants in the Thinite nome, 'Adja, Ḥet-iḥut and Rostau'.
12. Lit. 'bound persons'.
13. I.e. resume normal activities.
14. For this sense of *stꜣ* cf. *Pyr.* §§ 443. 572.
15. Cf. *n sp* 'together', 'at once', *Eg. Gramm.*[3] 205,3; the det.  of *sp* must surely be an error, since to translate 'because of the fault of' yields no sense.
16. Note the abnormal writing of *ṯs pẖr* in S1C.
17. *'Iwt·k*, prospective *sḏm·f*.
18. *Sṯn*, meaning unknown.
19. *ꜣẖꜣẖw*, not in *Wb.* with this det.
20. Surely to be read as *mꜣ·i ṯw*.
21. Corrupt for *iy·tywny*? The plur. suffix in *n·ṯn* demands a plural here, always supposing that our interpretation is correct.
22. *'Imyw pꜣwt·sn;* S1C omits *pꜣwt*.
23. For the sense here given to *wꜣḥ* cf. *Wb.* I, 259,10.
24. For *imyw ḏrw* cf. *Wb.* IV, 586,11.

Spell 133

O you who are in your two mansions, . . ., whom the Great Lady made,[1] to

158 me belongs the Great Lady, to me belongs the eye of the Great Lady,[2] | I have spat on the scalp of *Sw*[3] in order to heal it, there has been given to me everything. I have sat down a vindicated one, I have stood up a vindicated one, and there has been given to me all my family about which I spoke. I am Rēʿ, father of the sun.

1. G2T only, with retrograde order of signs. I cannot translate the second line.
2. Var. S2C: 'the Eye of Horus'.
3. Cf. Spell 139, n.2.

Spell 134

Spell for sealing a decree for a man concerning his family.[1] I have come to you, you lords of appearings, that you may give an order to[2] the Great
II, 159 One who is in the Tribunal, | that there may be sealed a decree concerning this family of mine. I have come here[3] from the Island of Fire, and a share has been found for me in the mouths of those great ones who take. Thoth has said to me; 'The decree which is given to you is sealed'. So said he. How good is this decree, this good document of the lady of appearings, who grants my family and which governs my lands under the authority of my mansion!

1. P. Gard. II only.
2. The preposition *n* omitted in G2T.
3. Cf. James, *Ḥeḳanakhte*, p. 111.

Spell 135

II, 160 O you who are upraised, who are over the execution-block, I am not a papyrus-amulet[1] which passes by, I am the papyrus-amulet which went forth from mankind. Clay is given to me and the decree is sealed.

Recitation for sealing a decree concerning the family and for giving a man's family to him in the realm of the dead.

1. Or 'green-stone', but its significance escapes me.

Spell 136

Assembling a family in the realm of the dead. I am Atum[1] who created
II, 161 the great ones, | I am he who fashioned Shu,[2] I am[3] these Two, male and female.[4] I am he who receives his offerings, I have received my plot of land in the place where I am content;[5] to me belong these field-plots of the dwarfs, also[6] the circumference[7] of . . .[8] I have reached *Nwt·k-nw*,[9] I have trodden

on and overpassed the two throw-sticks(?)[10] . . .[11] My staff is in my hand, |
I give my good things to the possessors of doubles. My speech[12] is that of a 162
Chaos-god, my conduct is doubly good, I am mightier than the mighty ones,
and the mighty ones sail upstream to me[13] on that night of faring upstream to
the great antelopes(?).[14] I carry out the butchery for those who are in Ōn; I
have power over them, they do not have power over me; they conceal my
name and they hide my privy member. I sit with my back to Gēb, | I judge him 163
(*sic*) with Him whose name is hidden on that night of slaughtering the great
ones.[15] This is a reminder that I have found the rope which was severed and
I have knotted it.[16] I have found the ferry-boat which was lost ⟨in⟩ its flood-
waters[17] and I have brought it to land. I have gone forth in it and have ferried
across, I have taken and released the prisoners.[18] | I have directed my feet 164
aright, I have extended my arms, I have ruled the sky,[19] I have taken posses-
sion of the earth, and the Two Enneads are pleased at it. There are given to
me my human connections of whom I spoke, there are given to me my family,
my children and my brethren (with) their relatives and my companions
wherever they may be, and I tread down those who are in . . .;[20] | I have gone 165
forth from the sky and I will be in the waters,[21] alive for ever and ever.

1. So Sq3Sq; B2L has *tk*, B2P *tr*, both incomprehensible, while in Sq4C the name is lost. The reading 'Atum' is confirmed by *ink ms Šw* 161*a*. This spell has much in common with Spell 132, but seems to have undergone corruption.
2. Reading *ms Šw* with Sq3Sq; Sq4C.
3. So, rather than 'to me belong' which in this text would be *nnk*, cf. 161*c*.
4. Reading *pn tn* 'this (masc.) and this (fem.)'. B2L and B2P are clearly corrupt.
5. So Sq3Sq. B2L, B2P have 'the place of my content'.
6. *My nn sp 2*.
7. *Dbn sp 2*.
8. *Ḥnm sp 2*; the meaning of the first word is unknown.
9. See Spell 67, n. 5.
10. See Spell 132, n. 4.
11. The collocation *ḫnw n ʿ* seems to refer to 'clapping the hands', but its connection with the context evades me. For *ḫn* 'clap' cf. *Concise Dict.* 192.
12. Or 'mouth'.
13. Var. Sq4C: 'this N fares upstream to the mighty ones'.
14. Read *šsȝwt wrt*? Cf. 154*b*.
15. Cf. Spell 132, n. 10, but the second clause has been misunderstood; the present text has *wḏʿ sw* for the correct *wḏʿ·f* of 154*d*. Sq3Sq and Sq4C add 'on that day of slaughtering the great ones'.
16. Read *gm·n·i ʿḳȝ wḏʿ ink ṯs sw*.
17. Read *gm·n·i mḫnt iwt ⟨m⟩ mḥw·s*; *iwt* is omitted from Sq3Sq.

18. Cf. Spell 132, n. 12.
19. For *ikr* read *ḥkꜣ* with Sq3Sq.
20. I cannot translate the rest of this clause.
21. Varr. Sq3Sq: 'in the sky'. Sq4C: 'in the earth'.

Spell 137

O Rēʿ-Atum, to me belong herds, I live on what my family[1] desire. If any-
thing be withheld[2] in respect of the sealing for me of these good decrees . . .[3]
II, 166 in order to give to me this family of mine wherever it may be, | the staff(?)[4] shall
be taken away[5] from Rēʿ, and choice cattle and poultry shall not go into the
shambles of the god. To me belongs everything, (even) this son and brother
of mine; I am born and I am stronger than he. The door-bolt(?)[6] closes
the . . .[7] upon its . . .[8] What is my fate?:[9] so say they to me. I am created[10]
and made firm and there is given to me this family of mine. What Rēʿ has
167 made for me is his protection for one who is in his shroud.[11] | The gods speak
of this[12] great Eye of Horus, and I am created and made firm, and I am pleased
about it; there is given to me this family of mine wherever it may be. If there
be withheld anything in respect of giving to me this family of mine wherever
it may be, (even) him who is in Pe and him who is in Dep, this staff(?) shall be
taken away[13] from Rēʿ, and choice cattle and poultry shall not go into the
shambles of the god who is in Ōn and Kherʿaḥa; the staff(?) shall be taken away
from Rēʿ and choice cattle and poultry shall not go into the shambles of the
168 god | who is in Khem and Abydos—[14] in 'Abat and Ḥet-wer;—in the Panopo-
169 lite and Thinite nomes;—in Thinis;—|in the Abyss;—in sky and earth;—in
170 the Waters of the West;—in the East and South;—in the North; |—in Pe and
Dep. (If?) the staff(?) belongs to Rēʿ, there shall be choice cattle and poultry
for the shambles of the god which is Ōn and Kherʿaḥa;—[15] in Khem and
171 Abydos;—in 'Abat and Het-wer; |—in the Panopolite and Thinite nomes;—
in Thinis:—in the Abyss;—in sky and earth;—in the Waters of the West;—in
172 East and South;—| in the North; (if?) the staff(?) belongs to Rēʿ, there will be
choice cattle and poultry for the shambles of the god.[16]

I am he with blue-black hair, Lord of Ōn, and there is given to me the bread of the Great Ones and the loaves of the Little Ones, the primeval beings who are in the horizon; mine are the Great Ones and mine is the Eye of the Great One—so say those Primeval Ones who cover their faces at me. Mine is the writing.

1. stands for *ꜣbt* 'family', cf. 166*i*; 167*d*.

2. This is a different word from 'proceed', *Urk.* I, 216,7; 218, 3.7.

3. I cannot translate the rest of this clause.

4. *Ḥw ib ṯsm* (cf. also 167*f* onward), lit. perhaps 'the authority of the heart of the dog', is clearly an attribute of which Rēᶜ is to be deprived, but its meaning is entirely obscure. In 189*b* we have in its place *ḥb-ib*, apparently a staff of rank, see Spell 146, n.3, and that may be the meaning here, on the assumption that *ḥw-ib* is a corruption of *ḥb-ib*, though *ṯsm* remains unaccountable.

5. *Nḥm·kꜣ·t(w)*.

6. *Ḳꜣt* may be a shortened form of *ḳꜣꜣt*, itself a var. of *ḳꜣrt* 'door-bolt', *Concise Dict.* 276.

7. *Ḥrwdt*, meaning unknown.

8. *'Int*, meaning unknown.

9. Surely corrupt. The use of *iššt* as subject of *iw* is not recorded by Gardiner or Edel, and even if the validity of such a construction be admitted, the necessary *m* of predication is absent. The normal construction would be *iššt pw kꜣ·i.* cf. *Eg. Gramm.*[3] § 500. The apparent meaning of the passage as it stands is 'What is my fate?' The Egyptian here uses the pronoun of the 1st person where English would use the 2nd, 'What is *your* fate?'; the gods are asking the question of the deceased narrator. At the end of 166*g* read *in·sn r·i*; B2P is the least muddled, but (*sy*?) at the end is superfluous.

10. *'Ir·i* omitted in B2L. *'Ir(y)* and *smn* appear to be passive *sḏm·f*; there is suppression of the suffix 1st sing. after *smn.*

11. I.e. the protection usually accorded to the worthy dead. For *wnḫt* 'mummy-cloth' cf. *Adm*, 2,6, which has the fuller form *wnḫyt.*

12. *'Itn* can hardly be other than the fem. demonstrative, cf. *Pyr.* § 591*c*, where also it is used of the Eye of Horus; it is unusual that here it should precede the noun it qualifies, but cf. *pf gs* 'that side' and *tfꜣ pḫrt* 'that remedy', cf. *Eg. Gramm.*[3] § 111. Another example of *itn*, there following its noun, is *Pyr.* § 1755*b*. Here Sq4C has corrupted *itn* 'this' into *it in* 'so says she, namely . . .'.

13. See nn. 4. 5 above.

14. The same sentences are repeated over and over again, the only difference being the abode of the god who is invoked.

15. Again repetition of the phrases except for the different place-names.

16. No locality named.

Spell 138

I am he who fashioned Seṣhat, I have been made into her additional . . .[1]

1. Lit. 'her *ꜣḫꜣ* in addition'; the meaning of *ꜣḫꜣ* is not known.

Spell 139

O you attendants(?)[1] of Neith, I have made festival at the (due) seasons, I have II, 173
spat on[2] him whose name is *Nn-isśw* in order to heal him, for he has given everything to me.[3]

1. *'Ibyt*, at any rate in this spelling, is unknown to *Wb*. It might possibly be a writing of *ibꜣwt* 'dancers', *Wb*. I, 62,15, but the context does not warrant so definite a translation; the word is therefore rendered by the non-committal 'attendants'.

2. This is a therapeutic act, cf. 158*a*; *JEA* 16, 171, n. 4. The fact that the untranslatable name of the being spat on begins with the negation *nn* suggests that he lacked something which was set right by the spitting.

3. Here following Sq4C, but retaining the original 1st person of B2L. *Rmn·f* (apparently a miswriting of *rdy·n·f*) of the latter text lacks an object.

Spell 140

The streams overflow into the ditches(?),[1] and Gēb is covered(?)[2] for me with what went forth from him.

1. This spell refers to the irrigation of the land. *ꜣẖꜣẖ* of B2L may be a reduplication of *iꜣẖ* 'overflow', 'be inundated', cf. Sq3Sq and the *Pyr.* passages quoted below; Sq3Sq reads: 'the streams are full, the ditches(?) overflow'. With this compare *mḥ mrw iꜣẖw itrw* 'the canals are full, the streams overflow', *Pyr.* § 848; *ḥtp šꜣw iꜣẖy mynwt* 'the fields are content, the ditches(?) overflow', § 857. Of the three kinds of waterway named in these passages, their respective importance can be gauged by the order in which they occur; *mrw* 'canals' takes precedence over *itrw* 'streams', which I suggest may be the main channels linking the major canals (*mrw*) with the actual system of irrigation, and the least of the three, the *mynwt*, may be the ditches round the fields which receive the water from the 'streams', and which in turn pass it into the network of runnels which supply the seed-beds. The term *mynt* 'a kind of land', *P. Wilbour*, Index, p. 96, presumably refers or originally referred to land watered by such ditches.

2. The verb *sꜣg* is not recorded, but from the context appears to refer to the covering of the earth (Gēb) with vegetation; B2L would then mean 'Gēb is covered for me with what went forth from him', i.e. as a result of irrigation the earth is covered on the deceased's behalf with the plants which have grown up from it. This version yields a better sense than Sq3Sq, which runs: 'Gēb has covered that from which he went forth'. *Sꜣg* may possibly be connected with the Late-Egyptian *sg* 'woollen covering' or the like, *Wb*. IV, 320,4.

Spell 141

II, 174 O Rēʿ, O Atum, O Gēb, see,[1] N is bound for the sky, for the earth, for the waters, N is seeking his family in the sky, in the earth and in the waters, for N is incomplete.[2]

1. Read certainly as  . For the vocatives which precede, cf. 180*b*.
2. A pun on *tm*.

Spell 142

If anything delay the sealing of this decree of . . .[1] to place N at an assembly

of N's family and dependants for him wherever they may be, there shall be
taken away this staff(?)[2] from Rēʿ, and choice cattle shall not go into the
shambles of the god. But if this decree of . . . be sealed, giving N's family
and dependants to him wherever they may be, the staff(?) shall belong to
Rēʿ and choice cattle shall go into the shambles of the god . . .[3] | The depen- II, 175
dants and family of N are given to him at his burial which Rēʿ made in his
power of those who are (*sic*) in his shroud.[4] He judges them(?)[5]—so says she,
the great Eye of Horus, the Great Ennead. I am created and made firm, and
I am pleased at it.[6] N's family is given to him, N's dependants assemble for
him. . . .[7]

Assembling for him the dependants of N who are in the realm of the dead.

1. *Šswt* is a corruption also found in 165*d* (Sq4C).
2. See Spell 137, n.4.
3. 174*n*–175*b* is untranslatable as it stands; it appears to be a corrupt version of 166*c*–167*b*.
4. 175*c*–*d* appears to be corrupted from 167*c*–*d*. The greater part of 175*d* is repeated meaninglessly in 175*i*.
5. *S* for *sn*? A corrupt version of 163*a*.
6. Cf. 167*b*.
7. See n. 4 above.

Spell 143

N is Rēʿ who went forth in the *hnhnw*-bark, N's power(?) is that of the Double
Lion, N has taken his place, the god who is in the West, with the Eldest God(?).
He opens the mouth of the earth for N, he opens the doors of Gēb for N, | he 176
assembles N's dependants for him, and also his family. N has taken . . .,[1]
Osiris has made what is in [. . .], lying at the food-offerings in the *hnhnw*-bark.
N despatches the *hnhnw*-bark of Khopri, N eats of ⟨that of which the gods
eat, N⟩ lives on ⟨that on which the gods⟩ live, ⟨N breathes⟩ of the air of
⟨which the gods breathe⟩.[2] N has made a writing for the masses, N has taken
possession of those who are on the shores of the Great One, N has heard[3]
those who are in the shrines, N has assembled dependants, so that N's family
may come to him. The masses have served N, N has made a writing ⟨for⟩[3]
these spirits who are hidden in the places of the West, so that they may give a
spirit to N for him, that they may create N's dignity, that they may awaken
N when he sleeps.

N utters a behest to him who hears words and he caused N to enter when Gaḥty speaks, he causes N to open the caverns of those who are in[4] the Abyss.

N frees the movements of the sunshine, N governs those who are in the evening light[5] of the crew[6] of Rēꜥ, who . . .[7] N's sceptre thereby. They send N to the
II, 177 Night-bark, N has gone aboard the Day-bark, | N controls these winds, being mightier than the earth-god and living after death like Rēꜥ every day. If you do not assemble N's dependants for him with this family of his in the West, you shall descend to . . .,[8] you shall go up ⟨in⟩[9] fire, to those who are in the Abyss, and it is the mourners who will quench it.

ASSEMBLING N'S FAMILY FOR HIM IN THE REALM OF THE DEAD AND GIVING HIS FAMILY TO HIM IN THE REALM OF THE DEAD.

1. , quite obscure.

2. *Wnm N pn m ꜥnḫ m ꜥnḫt m ṯꜣw im* is nonsense as it stands, owing to omissions from the text. On the basis of, e.g. *Pyr.* § 129, and using what words are preserved in the present copy, the text has been emended to read: *wnm N pn m ⟨wnmt nṯrw im⟩, ꜥnḫ ⟨N pn⟩ m ꜥnḫt ⟨nṯrw im, sn N pn⟩ m ṯꜣw ⟨snw nṯrw⟩ im.*

3. The preposition *n* omitted after *pn.*

4. Dittograph of *n imyw* on passing from line to line.

5. Read ⟨*m*⟩ *mšrw.*

6. The following fem. genitive shows that we should read *ist*, not *isty.*

7. *Tmyt*, meaning obscure.

8. The words after *hꜣ·k* in 177*e* are unintelligible, and the plural suffix in *ir tm·ṯn dnḏ* has become singular here; so also in *pr·k* in 177*f.*

9. The preposition *m* omitted before *sḏt.*

Spell 144

SPELL FOR ASSEMBLING THE FAMILY. I am he who has come thence, whom the Great Ones created; I am he who made [. . .] he enters, his gifts are in front of his offerings, and I am content,[1] [my?] heart [. . .] this field-plot is brought
II, 178 to me. Creep(?)[2] in peace into the place in which I rest [. . .]. | I am at the head of those whose seats are pre-eminent [. . .] I have come thence, I have found the broken cord [. . .], I have moored the ferry-boat at the town [. . .] my back to my sister the Ennead, I have placed my father [. . .] all of them, those who are in the Thinite(?) nome, those who are in the Elephantine(?) nome, those who are in Djedu and Kherꜥaḥa, those who are in Ōn, those who are in [. . .].

1. Reading *iw⟨·i⟩ ḥtp·k⟨y⟩*; the 2nd person makes no sense here.

2. Reading *ḥnmnm*, but the dct. is strange.

Spell 145

Almost entirely lost, see de Buck's note p. 178, n. 7*.

Spell 146

ASSEMBLING A MAN'S FAMILY FOR HIM IN THE REALM OF THE DEAD.[1] O Rēʿ! O II, 180
Atum! O Gēb! O Nūt! See, N goes down (*sic*) into the sky, | he goes down into 181
the earth, he goes down into the waters seeking his family, seeking his father
and mother, seeking his children and brethren, | seeking his loved ones, seeking 182
his friends, seeking his associates and his servants who worked for N on earth |
and seeking his concubines whom he has known, because N is you (*sic*) whom 183
the Great One created.[2] There are assembled for N his children and his
concubines | whom N's heart has accepted, and there are assembled for N his 184
servants who worked for N on earth. If there delay, be prevented or impeded |
the giving of his father to N and the releasing of his mother to him and the 185
assembling[3] for N of his family, | his father and mother, his men and women; if 186
there be delayed, prevented or impeded the assembling for N of his children |
and the assembling for N of his brethren, his loved ones, his friends, his 187
associates, | ⟨and his servants⟩ who worked for N on earth, the staff(?)[4] shall 189
be taken away from Rēʿ, | there shall be taken away the choice joints from 190
upon the altars of the gods, *pꜣḳ*-cakes shall not be kneaded,[5] white loaves
shall not be mixed, legs of beef shall not be conveyed[6] to the shambles of the
god, | you (plur.) shall not tie the cords, you shall not make ready the ferry- 191
boats; but if N's father be given to him, if N's mother be released for him, | if 192
there be assembled for N his family, his fathers, his mothers, his men and his
women, his children, | his loved ones, his friends and associates, his children 193
and his concubines whom N's heart has accepted, and his servants who worked
for N on earth; | if there be assembled for N his family who are in heaven and 195
earth, who are in the necropolis, who are in the Abyss, who are in the place of
mourning(?),[7] who are in the Nile and the flood, | who are in the Mansion of 196
the Greatest of Bulls, who are in Djedu, who are in Djedet, who are in Ōn
and Khem,[8] who are in Pe of the Great One,[9] who are in Kherʿaḥa and who
are in Abydos: then *pꜣḳ*-cakes shall be kneaded, white loaves shall be mixed,
legs of beef shall be conveyed to the shambles of the god, the cords shall be
tied, | the ferry-boats shall be made ready, this bark of Rēʿ shall be navigated 198
by this crew of Rēʿ who know no weariness.[10] His[11] name is not known | and 199
his name shall not be known, the sistrum-player of Hathōr is N's protector for
life. Now as for this staff, it is the son of N's sister, the woman who is in charge

200 of the Great Field.| Now N's sister, the woman who is in charge of the Great Field, has said: See, you have come joyful and happy-hearted—so said she to
201 N. Answer![12]| Has there been granted to you a decree for this family of yours? N has gone down rejoicing and happy-hearted, for his family has been
202 given to him.| The great ones of N's family have gone down joyfully and their
203 hearts are happy at meeting N. They have stuck their picks (?)[13], their panniers[14], their hoes and their bowls into the earth. N has taken them from the levy[15] of Isis, from the census of Nūt, from the great levy of the Double Lion.

As for any soul or any god who shall cause N's family to be taken away from
205 him,| N shall cause his head to be broken on the . . .[16] of Khnum.[17]

ASSEMBLING THE FAMILY, FATHER, MOTHER, FRIENDS, ASSOCIATES, CHILDREN, WOMEN, CONCUBINES, SERVANTS, WORKERS AND EVERYTHING BELONGING TO A MAN FOR HIM IN THE REALM OF THE DEAD. A SPELL A MILLION TIMES RIGHT.[18]

1. In black in B1L and B4L^{b}; omitted in B2P, B4L^{a} and B3L; B1C more briefly: 'Assembling the family'. There is another longer rubric to the same effect at the end of the spell, see 205*b* ff.

2. In 183*b*, *N pn* and *twt is* are contradictory, one being 3rd person and the other 2nd. B2L has seen the mistake and has omitted *twt is*, while B3L has emended the text into ⟨*r*⟩ *ntt N pn twt Rꜥ* 'because N is the likeness of Rēꜥ'. The passage may well have stood originally in the 2nd person, and later may have been altered to the 3rd without removing the pronoun, but since the text has otherwise been cast into the 3rd person, it has been retained in the translation.

3. Following B2L and thus avoiding vain repetitions.

4. In *Pyr.* § 542 *ḥb-ib* appears to mean 'stairway', but here the det. is a staff of state. In 166*a;* 167*f.j;* 168*b* ff. and 174*h* the corresponding expression is the incomprehensible *ḥw-ib-ṯsm.*

5. For this use of *sḳr* cf. *Wb.* IV, 306, 13.

6. In this context almost certainly so to be understood, despite the universal use of the det. [sign] instead of [sign].

7. Cf. *iꜣkby* 'a part of the Netherworld', *Wb.* I, 34,16; clearly in this context the name of a locality is required.

8. B3L only.

9. Not 'Great Pe'; as a town-name 'Pe' would require a fem. adjective.

10. B1C only: 'who know no destruction or weariness'.

11. Perhaps referring to the deceased. There seems to be an abrupt transition of subject here, and is not impossible that a portion of text following on *iḫmw-wrḏ* has dropped out.

12. *Ḥw r·f,* lit. 'proclaim!'; here the deceased is told to answer the question which follows, but in fact he does not. Perhaps there has been another omission.

13. & 14. The Illustr. London News of 17 Nov. 1928 shows from the Tomb of Tutankhamun two sets of models of a shabti's equipment; from this we can identify in *CT* VI, 1*k-l išrt* 'mattock', ḥnn 'hoe', nbꜣw 'yoke' and ḥnkw 'panniers'. Letter from Mr Spaull dated 27 Feb. 1978.

15. *ʾIrw*; B3C substitutes *kyw*, perhaps meaning 'roll-call', cf. the verb *ky* 'cry'.

16. *Mꜥḏ*, meaning unknown. 'Anvil' is perhaps a possibility.

17. Varr. 'Nephthys', 'Rēꜥ', and in B1C and B2P names of uncertain meaning.

18. B2P adds: 'the being of the Great Lady endures for me'.

Spell 147

BECOMING A FALCON. O *'Itn-ib* who are in the horizon and your places![1] O II, 206
'Itn-ib who are in the Two Fields of Offerings! | Have judgement with Him 207
whose name[2] is hidden on account of(?)[3] those who are pre-eminent in the
Mansion of Osiris; make a way for me, for I am he who swallowed his eye in
front of the clouds[4] of the sky, I have come | and I have opened the Great One,[5] 208
I have released my downpour, I have opened the gates of the Blue One,[6] and
praise is heard | in the mouths of the door-bolts of the gods which go up from 209
the western horizon of the sky.[7]

1. Var. S1P: 'who is in the horizon and who is in his front places(?)'. *'Itn-ib* apparently means 'the contentious one', cf. *ḫt itnt-ib* 'a contentious company', 358*b*.
2. Var. 'mouth', error due to omission of *n*.
3. *Ḥr* is a preposition governing *ḫntyw*; the following det. refers to *'Imn-rn*.
4. Lit. 'covers'; the det. of *k3p* represents the conical clay stopper of a jar. The reference is to the onset of rainfall; this part of the text appears originally to have been a rain-spell spoken by a rain-bringer, and it is not obvious why it was adopted for its present purpose.
5. I.e. the sky.
6. Again the sky; for the stem *ṯfrr* cf. *Wb.* V, 300, 1–4.
7. 'The door-bolts of the gods' may be a term for rain-bearing clouds rising on the horizon.

Spell 148[1]

TAKING SHAPE AS A FALCON. The lightning flash strikes, the gods are afraid, |
Isis wakes pregnant with the seed of her brother Osiris. She is uplifted, (even II, 210
she) the widow, and her heart is glad with the seed of her brother Osiris. | She 211
says: 'O you gods, I am Isis, the sister of Osiris, who wept for the father of the
gods, (even) Osiris who judged the slaughterings of the Two Lands. His seed
is within | my womb, I have moulded the shape of the god within the egg as my 212
son who is at the head of the Ennead. What he shall rule is this land, the heritage
of his (grand-) father Gēb, | what he shall say is concerning his father, what he 213
shall kill is Seth the enemy of his father Osiris. Come, you gods, protect him
within my womb, | for he is known in your hearts. He is your lord, this god who 214
is in his egg, blue-haired of form, lord of the gods, and great and beautiful
| are the vanes[2] of the two blue plumes'. 215

'Oh!' says Atum, 'guard your heart, O woman!'

'How do you know?[3] He is the god, | lord and heir of the Ennead, who made 216
you within the egg. I am Isis, one more spirit-like and august than the gods;
the god is within | this womb of mine and he is the seed of Osiris'. 217

Then says Atum: 'You are pregnant and you are hidden,[4] O girl! You will give birth, being pregnant for the gods, seeing that(?) he is the seed of Osiris. May that villain who slew his father not come, lest he break the egg in its early
218 stages,| for the Great-of-Magic[5] will guard against him'.

Thus says Isis: 'Hear this, you gods, which Atum, Lord of the Mansion of the Sacred Images, has said. He has decreed for me protection for my son within my womb, he has knit together an entourage about him within this
219 womb of mine,| for he[6] knows that he[7] is the heir of Osiris, and a guard over the Falcon who is in this womb of mine has been set by Atum, Lord of the gods. Go up on earth, that I may give you praise.[8] The retainers of your father
220 Osiris will serve you, I will make your name,| for you have reached the horizon, having passed by the battlements of the Mansion of Him whose name is hidden. Strength has gone up within my flesh, power has reached into my flesh, power has reached its strength. . .'[9]

221 '. . .[10] the Sunshine-god is conveyed,| and he has prepared his own place, being seated at the head of the gods in the entourage of the Releaser(?)'.[11]

'O Falcon,[12] my son Horus, dwell in this land of your father Osiris in this your name of Falcon who is on the battlements of the Mansion of Him whose
222 name is hidden. I ask that you shall be always| in the suite of Rēʿ of the horizon in the prow of the primeval bark for ever and ever'.

Isis goes down to the Releaser(?) who brings Horus, for Isis has asked that he may be the Releaser(?) as the leader of eternity.

223 '| See Horus, you gods![13] I am Horus, the Falcon| who is on the battlements of the Mansion of Him whose name is hidden. My flight aloft has reached the horizon, I have overpassed the gods of the sky, I have made my position more prominent than that of the Primaeval Ones. The Contender[14] has not attained
224 my first flight,| my place is far from Seth, the enemy of my father Osiris. I have used the roads of eternity to the dawn, I go up in my flight, and there is no god who can do what I have done. I am aggressive against the enemy of
225 my father Osiris, he having been set under my sandals| in this my name of . . .[15] I am Horus, born of Isis, whose protection was made within the egg; the fiery blast of your mouths does not attack me, and what you may say against me does not reach me, I am Horus, more distant of place than men or
226 gods;| I am Horus son of Isis'.

1. See my article 'The Pregnancy of Isis' in *JEA* 54, 40 ff. My view of this spell has been criticized by Griffiths in *JEA* 56, 194 f., and by Gilula in 57, 14 ff., but I adhere to my original version; see my 'Rejoinder', to appear in *JEA* 59.

2. The feathery part of a plume as distinct from the stem.

3. Isis speaks.
4. An allusion to the pregnant Isis hiding in the marshes of Chemmis.
5. Masculine.
6. Atum.
7. Horus.
8. Said to the unborn Horus.
9. A considerable textual omission.
10. On *ks·f*, the word preceding *sḳdd*, see now Gilula, *JEA* 57,18 (31).
11. Unidentifiable speaker, probably either Isis or Atum.
12. Isis speaks, addressing her son who has now been born.
13. Horus proclaims his power.
14. Seth.
15. *ꜣdmw*, meaning unknown.

Spell 149

BECOMING A HUMAN FALCON,[1] MAKING A MAN A SPIRIT IN THE REALM OF THE II, 227
DEAD, |GIVING A MAN POWER OVER HIS FOES, AND SAYING ⟨TO⟩ A MAN:[2] BE
SHOD WITH A PAIR OF WHITE SANDALS ⟨AND BE CLAD IN⟩[3] A KILT AND SASH(?)
OF RED LINEN. |To me belongs a human body,[4] the *špt*-fish comes from the 228
Island of Fire, men open to me in the Tribunal[5] because of what has been
done to me crookedly by my foes. I have demanded a shape as a human falcon
that I may walk as a man| and go forth thence,[6] no god having hindered me.[7] 230
I am a human falcon who walks as a man and who is not opposed, for I am on
the path of Horus| so that I may shoot at my human foes.[8] I went up into the 232
tribunal of the Foremost of the Westerners, and in the night| I was adjudged 234
with him in the presence of his members of the realm of the dead. His guardian
who is in the Tribunal has stood up[9] with his hands before him and he has
seen| my vindication. It is granted that I have power over that foe of mine, 235
so that I may conquer him in the presence of the people who came to contend|
with me by means of the magic spells which were on their lips. I have appeared 236
as a great falcon, I have grasped him with my talons, my lips are on him as a
gleaming knife, my talons[10] are on him like the arrows of Sakhmet, my horns
are on him as the Great Wild Bull,| my wings are on him as a *ḥꜣw*-bird, my tail 238
is on him as a living soul, I fly up| and alight upon his spine, I cut his throat[11] 240
in the presence of his family, I take out his heart unknown to them,[12] for I
am| a human falcon, to whom has been given existence as a falcon in the 241
Mansion of the Foremost of the Westerners on account of a true phrase.[13]

I have said it because of what was done to me crookedly by that foe of 242
mine, for I speak from my heart, the strength of my soul protects me,[14] (even)

that which turns me away from[15] his family. | I cut it off from its . . .[16] while
244 I speak from my heart to those who are in the Tribunal | in the Mansion of the Foremost of the Westerners.

See,[17] I have come and I have brought my foe, I have crushed his family, |
245 I have thrown down his house, I have crushed his survivor,[18] I have crushed
246 his cultivator who is in his field.[19] The spirits[20] are glad, |Osiris is joyful, when he sees me mount aloft as a falcon, though I walked on my feet when I was mortal. I am the human falcon who speaks in the cavern of Osiris, and I
248 speak[21] in the presence of Osiris, | just as I spoke in the Island of Fire. How spirit-like is he, this god[22]—so says the Foremost of the Westerners. I have come here,[23] I have cried out because of yon foe,[24] and it is decreed in the
250 Tribunal[25] | and repeated in the presence of Mā'et, who has given me power over my foe.

251 Those who are and those who are not cry out,[26] | (even) those who would fight against you, those who would ask for him from you,[27] those who would take him from you,[28] although I (*sic*) am[29] a human falcon—so says the Foremost of the Westerners to me. You are a [human] falcon.

252 The Eye of Horus is my guide, | my magic powers are my strength, (even) those which come after me from the Island of Fire into the Mansion of the Foremost of the Westerners.[30] I crush those who are, I cause those who are not to pass away. There are none who come and oppose me, there are none who raise a hand against me in any evil matter. I am a human falcon, I go down to the Island [of Fire].[31] I eat with my mouth, I defaecate with my hinder
253 parts, | I walk on my feet to the Island of Fire; this is my cavern [. . .] in the Island of Fire. I eat bread, I take the pouring-out of water,[32] I am taken to the cavern[33] of the Foremost of the Westerners, I sit on the banks of the flood, I am among the happy ones, and my name will not be wiped out in this land for ever.

1. Some texts omit *rmṯ*. S2P is the text generally followed in the translation.

2. *Ḏd s* is slightly corrupt, even though it is common to all texts; read *ḏd* (infinitive) ⟨*n*⟩ *s*. The error probably arose from the similarity of *n* and *s* in hieratic, causing them to be merged into one.

3. Either there has been an omission of a verb or else *ṯb* 'be shod' has been clumsily used in respect of garments as well as sandals.

4. '*Ink ḥ'w rmṯ*; some texts interpolate *nw n* before *ḥ'w*, which is construed as a plural. One would have expected *nnk* rather than *ink*, but there can be no doubt as to the sense.

5. Var. 'I have opened the earth in the sight of the Tribunal', referring to the dead man's emergence from interment.

6. Varr. 'and go forth from the horizon'; 'because I am one who goes forth from the horizon'. Cf. Heerma van Voss, *Phoenix*, 17 (1971), 99.

7. Read *n ḫnr wi nṯr* as S1P; so also B2Bo in 232*a*.

8. So S2P–S2C^{a}; the other texts show variants and there is disorder in the sequence of sentences.

9. It is not certain whether *r·f* is to be regarded as preposition + noun 'for him' or the enclitic particle. I have taken the second choice.

10. Var. 'my fingers'.

11. For *ḏȝd* see also *Pyr.* § 402.

12. Lit. 'they do not know'.

13.  has been taken to be a writing of *ṯs* 'phrase', in view of 241*c*, though 'a well-made magic knot' is also a possibility.

14. Reading *ḫw wi nḫtw bȝ·i* with S2C^{d}; *ȝḫw* of three texts makes no sense and two have *sȝ·i* instead of *bȝ·i*; B9C shortly *nḫt bȝ·i* 'my soul is strong'.

15. Var. B9C: 'I have risen up against'; the suffix in *ȝbt·f* following refers to the enemy of the deceased, cf. 244*c–d*.

16. *Ḥdḳ* is used elsewhere of cutting off the nose, *Wb.* III, 206,1; its var. *sdḳ* in S2C^{d} is not known to *Wb.*, nor are *ḥȝʿb* in B9C or *ʿggt* at the end of the sentence. After this clause S1C^{a} inserts a rubric: '[Vin]dicating a man against his foes', as if what follows were a new spell.

17. Reading *m·ṯn wi* with B9C; all the other texts insert a superfluous *n*. In 244*e*, S2C^{d} inserts the same rubric as S1C^{a}, see n. 16.

18. Var. 'his children who are on earth' or 'his surviving children'.

19. S2C^{d} and S1C^{a} only.

20. Varr. 'Rēʿ'; 'the gods'.

21. S2C^{d} and S1C^{a}: . The first sign may read *i* rather than *mdw*. Cf. Heerma van Voss, *Phoenix*, 17 (1971), 99.

22. S2P ends.

23. Or 'today'.

24. S2C^{d} and S1C^{a} add: 'I have come because of my foe; he has been placed for me completely under me'.

25. S2C^{d} and S1C^{a} add: 'the great (tribunal) in the cavern of Osiris'.

26. Var. S1P 'lament him'.

27. Not in S1P. S1Chass. and S1C^{b} end here. 'Him' is presumably the enemy of the deceased; no-one else seems available.

28. S1P ends here.

29. Repeated from 246*d*–247*a*; the second person is needed here, for it is the deceased who is a human falcon, not the Foremost of the Westerners.

30. Var. 'of Osiris who comes with me'.

31. So S2C^{e}; S2C^{d} and S1C^{a} have only *hȝȝ·i* 'I go down'.

32. Following S2C^{d} and S1C^{a}; from here on the other two texts are far too badly damaged to yield a coherent sense.

33. Var. 'mansion'.

Spell 150

II, 254 The lightning-flash strikes, the gods are afraid,[1] those who are in their shrines are frightened, the gods fall into great trembling, the falcons within the eggs are on his (*sic*) belly in the nest of him who is acute of vision.[2] I indeed am Horus within[3] the egg, ⟨one acute of⟩[4] vision, who is on his belly in the nest. There has been brought to me this ⟨one who is acute of(?)⟩[5] vision, all the heavens are united, bulls are given to me, the north-wind conducts me ⟨to⟩ her who is over the falcons(?) of Shu[6] when I go out from my [house(?)]. I have displayed my power, I mount up[7] to the horizon, I am supported on Gēb, I travel on the sunshine, I have power over them[8] but they have no power over me, I have expelled them from their mansions, I have disturbed them in their caverns, I have doomed[9] them, (even) those who are senseless,[10] the . . .[11] who eat the soul. May their souls which are on earth be devoured and destroyed while I am in the bark of Rēʿ for ever. I hear what my mother Isis says to me, for I am the child of Rēʿ(?), the companion[12] of Rēʿ, I am the marvellous one who is in the gate of eternity, my allotted term is everlastingness, and I come to you[13] at will.

1. See *JEA* 54, 41, 2.
2. The parent falcon?
3. ; read *m-ḫnw*.
4. Between *swḥt* and *ḥr* supply *spd*, cf. 254*d*.
5. *Ḥr pw* is meaningless as it stands; possibly *spd* has been omitted again.
6. Read probably *sb w⟨i⟩ mḥt ⟨n⟩ ḥrt bykw Šw.* with omission of the prep. *n*. *Bykw* with fire-det. is a *vox nihili*; for  read almost certainly .
7. Restoring as *iꜣ[k]·i*.
8. The following sentences show clearly that the plural suffix in *im·sn* must refer to beings of whom a previous mention has been omitted.
9. Cf. *syp* 'destine' to a fate, *Concise Dict.* 212.
10. *Ntyꜣw* is a miswriting of *ntyw*.
11. *Ḥꜣtyw*, meaning unknown.
12. Read *smꜣ(y)*, *nisba*-form of *smꜣ* 'side', *Concise Dict.* 227.
13. To whom? Apparently there has been another omission, for the pronoun is plural.

Spell 151

II, 255 Going out from the tomb in th[e] necropolis.[1] The cavern of those who are in
256 the Abyss is opened,[2] the movements of those who are in | the sunshine are extensive,[3] the tomb of the Sole One[4] is opened. When he went out, I went
257 out ⟨from⟩ the tomb,[5] | I went forth from the Great Lake, I descended into
258 the lustral basins(?).[6] My foot is on the . . .,[7] my hand is raised aloft,[8] | I have

laid hold of his lashing which belongs to *Ḥnty-mnyt·f*,[9] I row in my seat which is in the Bark of God,[10] I go down into my seat | which is in the Bark of God,[11] 259 I have taken control without neglect of my seat which is in the Bark of the Controller,[12] my seat which is in the Bark of God did not leave me stranded.[13]

1. So S14C; varr. B3Bo 'Opening the tomb and the going out of the woman at will'; B1C in red: 'Opening the tomb in the night'.

2. So the majority of texts; var. S14C: 'the cavern of the lords of Ōn is opened'. B2Bo has *nwt* 'sky' for *nw* 'abyss'; L1Li omits the last word.

3. B1Bo omits 'those who are in' and adds a repetition of 255*c*.

4. Varr. 'the tomb of the Lion(?)', 'the tomb of Shu'. B2Bo has *wn* only.

5. Following S14C, which, however, omits *m* after *pr·n·i*, as also after *hȝ·n·i* in 257*b*. L1Li has 'when he went out, I opened the tomb'; three texts have only *ps·f* and two omit the clause entirely.

6. . B1C has , which according to *Wb.* III, 363, 10 is the designation of a particular opening into the earth. The dets. of the other texts, however, suggest a lustral bowl or basin; having once issued from the tomb, the deceased would hardly return into the earth.

7. , var. 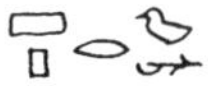 in L2Li, meaning unknown. B3Bo has 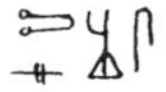 only.

8. 257*d* occurs only in Sq6C and Sq3Sq, B1Bo and B1C, as a substitute for 257*c*. It reads *šsp·n·i sṯs*, var. *sṯwt* or an indecipherable word.

9. Following S14C; of eight texts no two are exactly alike.

10. S14C and L1Li only.

11. Varr. 'which is in the Bark'; 'which is in the Bark of Rēʿ'.

12. Following S14C. For *ḫrp* 'control' four texts have *ḫsr* 'drive away'. B1Bo and B1C are incomplete.

13. So S14C. B1C adds 259*d–e*, which properly belongs to Spell 93.

Spell 152

Going forth into the day and living after death.[1] O you Sole One who rises II, 260 in the moon, O you Sole One who shines in the moon, I will go up[2] to the sky among a multitude of others when those who are in the sunshine are released,[3] while I have gone forth into this day that I may carry off that foe of mine.

1. So B2Bo, in black. Varr. 'going forth into the day', 'going forth into the day, living after death in the beautiful West', both in red.

2. *Pry·i*, probably prospective *sḏm·f*.

3. *Wḥʿʿ* is passive *sḏmm·f*. Apparently the dead ascend to the sky at sunset, having previously gone forth from the tomb into the day to deal with enemies, cf. the next clause *sk wi pr·ky* . . . with old perfective. Cf. also 264*c*.

Spell 153

[. . .].[1] I am Atum who went forth as the Great One of the *hnhnw*-bark, | the II, 261

spirit in the Double Lion, I proclaim[2] your words, O you who were afore-
263 time. Those who are in | their coils[3] come to me, they make to me offerings
of bread and beer of the *hnhnw*-bark, the *hnhnw*-bark raises me up to the two
264 barks of Khopri,[4] | it opens for me the mouth of the earth, it throws open for
me the doors which are in the sunshine, and commands are given to the crew
265 of Rēʿ in the evening | that I may live after death just as Rēʿ lives every day.
It is yesterday's birth of Rēʿ which fashions me, the gods rejoice at me when I
live just as they rejoiced over Ptaḥ when he went forth from the Mansion of
the Prince which is in Ōn.

1. Rubric lost, and also an opening sentence, see de Buck's notes 1* and 4*.
2. Despite the determinatives, the sense of *ḥw* here must surely be 'proclaim' what is said, cf. *Pyr.* §§ 153; 253, and the det. in B1P.
3. Serpent spirits.
4. Omitted in T1L. On what follows in this text see de Buck's note 6*.

Spell 154[1]

II, 266 KNOWING THE LORDS OF ŌN, KNOWING THE SOULS OF ŌN, KNOWING WHAT THOTH
KNOWS OF PROTECTIVE SPELLS, KNOWING EVERY TEMPLE, HAVING POWER IN THE REALM
OF THE DEAD, ENTERING INTO THE SOULS OF ŌN.

268 | I have become greatest of the great, I have come into being among the
beings who clear the vision of his[2] sole Eye, I have opened and built up the
272 injured Eye, for I am one of them. | I KNOW THE ENNEAD OF ŌN, INTO WHICH
THE GREATEST OF THE SEERS WAS NOT INITIATED, THE HUSHING OF THE MOUTH IN
274 THE SNWT-FESTIVAL, THE HOSTILE ACTS[3] BY THE DESTROYER | AGAINST THE
HEIR OF ŌN, I KNOW WHY A BRAIDED LOCK IS MADE FOR A MAN.

276 It so happened that Rēʿ disputed with the *ʾImy-wḥm·f* serpent concerning
the division of Ōn,[4] and his mouth was injured, and that is how the reduction
278 in the monthly festival came about. Then said | *ʾImy-wḥm·f:* 'I will take my
harpoon and I will inherit this city', and that is how the Harpoon came into
280 being. Then said Rēʿ: 'I will erect | my flagstaffs[5] against him, I will oust
him, and that is how the *snwt*-festival came about.

It so happened that Rēʿ met[6] Him who wears bright-red cloth before he
282 could direct his hand against him, | and he set a trap for him, namely a woman
with braided hair, and that is how the man with braided hair in Ōn came into
284 being. A shorn man had power in | the two temples—and that is how the
shorn man came into being—until the Heir came into being, (even) the Great
286 One who sees his father, and that is how the shorn man became | Greatest of

the Seers as a son who acts for his father.

I KNOW THE SOULS OF ŌN;[7] THEY ARE RĒʿ, SHU AND TEFĒNET.| LIVING LONG 288
UPON EARTH, HAVING POWER IN THE REALM OF THE DEAD, ENTERING INTO THE LORDS OF ŌN, ASCENDING TO THE SKY AND OPENING THE NETHERWORLD.

1. Cf. *ZÄS* 57,1 ff. The present translation is based on S2P.
2. The sun-god's.
3. Lit. 'the extending of the arm'.
4. *Ḥr psšt 'Iwnw* is not in S2P, but it is required in order to explain the dispute.
5. Hardly 'brethren' as Sethe. Rēʿ had no brothers, nor is *sʿḥʿ* 'erect' the right verb in such a case. Six texts determine *snw(t)* with , and such poles, bearing streamers and mounted against a temple pylon, seem to have had a purpose of protection against the powers of evil. Further, Sethe's translation of *snwt* (det. ) as 'brotherhood-festival' seems no more than a guess. A more likely explanation is that it was a festival for the dedication or re-dedication of the protecting flagstaffs.
6. Emend into *Rʿ pw* , cf. *ZÄS* 57,22.
7. A final subtitle. S2P has inadvertently omitted *bꜣw* 'souls'.

Spell 155[1]

KNOWING THE SOULS OF THE NEW MOON, ENTERING INTO THE HOUSE OF II, 290
OSIRIS OF DJEDU.

Who is he who enters,| whence comes he who comes forth[2] because of this 292
soul, on whom the earth is high? Such a thing is unknown.

Open to me, for I am a saviour,[3] I am one who keeps secrets, and I belong 294
to the House of Osiris. I am the god in charge of the document-case in the room which contains the ritual robes.[4]| I know what was missing from the 296
Eye of *Tb* on the day of accounting for its parts when the dawn was stronger than the darkness. The fifth part of one Eye and a full half are (available)| for 298
the allotting of its parts between the complete Eye and the injured Eye.

Open to me, you Souls of the New Moon, for I am he who completes it more fully than| the embalmer who resides in the temple knows.[5] I know what 300
is lacking from the corpse in the hand of Anubis on that night of covering| his 302
testicles(?), and on that day of bandaging what is in his mouth. It is something which was not out of Osiris,[6] the front of which was joined to its back| in 304
woodwork of planking.[7]

Open to me, for I am one who knows his spell, I have been inducted into embalming materials(?), and I will never imitate(?)[8] the disaffected ones.

|Open to me, you who are in the New Moon, for I have seen the executioner 306
who came forth from the slaughter-house of the Great One.[9]

308 I know | the Souls of the New Moon: they are Osiris, Anubis and Isdes.[10]

1. Cf. *ZÄS* 57,27 ff. Again S2P is followed.

2. Cf. Edel, *Altäg. Gramm.* §§ 1010. 1012; Gardiner, *Eg. Gramm.*[3] §§ 498. 503,4.

3. I regard *tr* here as the enclitic particle, *pace* Sethe in *ZÄS* 57,29. *Smy* is translated by me as 'saviour' (Sethe, *Ehrfurchterheischenden*); I take *smy* to be a participial formation from *sm* 'help', 'succour', *Concise Dict.* 225. Throughout my translation of the Pyramid Texts I reject Sethe's connection of the stem *sm* with the notion of *Ehrfurcht*.

4. *Dbḥw* with clothes-det., lit. 'clothing of offering'.

5. The stroke after *r* of *rḫt* is to be discarded.

6. See Sethe's note *ZÄS* 57,33 (24).

7. A reference to a wooden coffin which seems remote from the context. Possibly a sentence or sentences may have been omitted after 'Osiris'.

8. Lit. 'repeat'.

9. Fem.

10. I.e. Thoth, compare 324*b*, and cf. Boylan, *Thoth*, 201 ff.; Scharff, *Lebensmüde* (Sitzt. Bayer. Akad., 1937), 19, n. 36.

Spell 156[1]

II.308 I know the Souls of Khemennu.[2] Going in to the dwellers in Khemennu, being among the followers of Osiris of Djedu, having power over water,
312 not walking head downwards, | not dying another time.

314 Knowing the souls of Khemennu. The plume is stuck into | the shoulder of Osiris, the Red Crown shines in the bowl, the Eye is eaten and he who sought
316 it is fetched. I know it, | for I have been initiated into it by the *sm*-priest, and I have never spoken nor made repetition to the gods. I have come on an errand
318 for Rēʿ | in order to cause the plume to grow[3] into the shoulder of Osiris, to make complete[4] the Red Crown in the bowl and to pacify the Eye for him who
320 numbered it. I have entered as a Power | because of what I know, I have not spoken to men, I have not repeated what was said.

322 Hail to you, Souls of Khemennu! Know[5] that Rēʿ desires | the plume which grows and the Red Crown which is complete[6] at this temple, and rejoice[5] at the allotting of what is to be allotted.

324 I know the Souls of Khemennu. | What is small in the full month[7] and great in the half-month,[8] that is Thoth.[9]

1. Cf. *ZÄS* 57, 35 ff.

2. B2Bo only; otherwise I follow S2P.

3. Emend into *r srdt šwt*, cf. *ZÄS* 57,42.

4. Sethe has 'blacken', but what could be meant by 'blackening' the Red Crown? *Skm* 'make complete' yields better sense.

5. Plural imperative, as Sethe, surely rightly; to translate *rḫw* and *ršy* below as participles yields poorer sense.

6. Sethe 'which is black'; cf. n. 4 above.

7. The new moon; in several texts the adjectival participles are determined with .

8. The full moon. Sethe's allocations of the half-month and the full month to the 15th and the 2nd days of the month is correct in terms of the 360-day calendar.

9. Var. B9C wrongly: 'that is Sothis', the moon-god is Thoth. B2Bo ff. have inserted here a passage (324*c–d*) proper to spell 157 (328*a*).

Spell 157[1]

BEING ASSIGNED TO PROVISIONS IN THE REALM OF THE DEAD, BEING FAVOURED II, 326
AND LOVED ON EARTH, BEING IN THE TRAIN OF HORUS AND HIS FOLLOWERS,| A 328
MYSTERY WHICH MEN KNOW IN THE HOUSE.[2] KNOWING THE SOULS OF PE.

O you Souls of the Night, Marsh-dwellers, Mendesians, you of the Fish-
nome, |you of the Mansion of *Ỉ3pw*, Sunshade-bearers of the Adoration,[3] 330
who prepare beer of Nubia, do you know[4] why Pe was given| to Horus? You 332
do not know it, but I know it. It was Rēʿ who gave it to him in compensation 334
for the mutilation in his Eye;| I know it.

It so happened that Rēʿ said to Horus: 'Let me see your Eye since this has
happened to it'. He looked at it| and said: 'Look at that (black) stroke[5] with 336
your hand covering up the sound Eye which is there'. Horus looked at that
stroke and said:| 'Behold, I am seeing it as altogether white'. And that is 338
how the oryx came into being. And Rēʿ said: 'Look again at yonder black pig'.|
And Horus looked at this black pig, and Horus cried out because of the con- 340
dition of his injured Eye, saying: 'Behold, my Eye is like that first wound
which Seth inflicted on my Eye', and Horus became unconscious[6] in his[7]
presence. And Rēʿ said:| 'Put him on his bed until he is well'. It so happened 342
that Seth had transformed himself[8] into a pig[9] and had projected a wound into
his Eye. And Rēʿ said; 'The pig is detestable to Horus'. 'Would that[10] he were
well', SAID THE GODS.| THAT IS HOW THE DETESTATION OF THE PIG CAME ABOUT 344
FOR HORUS'S (SAKE) BY THE GODS WHO ARE IN THE SUITE.[11]

Now when he was a child, his sacrificial animal was a pig before his Eye
had suffered—Imsety, Ḥapy, Duamūtef, Ḳebḥsenuf,| whose father is the 346
elder Horus and whose mother is Isis[12]—and he said to Rēʿ: 'Give me two in
Pe and two in Nekhen| from this second company.[13] May I be in my own 347
right(?) an allotter of eternity,[14] an opener of everlasting, a queller of strife in

348 this my name of| 'Horus who is on his pillar'.

I KNOW THE SOULS OF PE, THEY ARE HORUS, IMSETY AND HAPY.

1. Cf. *ZÄS* 58,1 ff. S2P is followed.
2. Var. S1C: 'in the House [. . .] in Pe'.
3. Groups of female spirits are addressed.
4. Read *in iw·ṯn rḫ·tywny*; [hieroglyph] of S2C is an error.
5. *Dgꜣ my r*| *pf*; cf. Sethe.
6. For this sense of *ꜥm ib* cf. *SDT* 166. S2P omits *ib*.
7. Rēꜥ's.
8. *'Ir·n·f ḫprw r·f*; the meaning is hardly in doubt, but *r·f* is a puzzle, for we would expect *ḫprw·f*. Perhaps the *r* in *r·f* is a dittograph of the *r* in *ḫprw*.
9. The majority of the parallel texts add the adjective 'black'.
10. Equating *ḥy* with *ḥꜣ*, *ḥwy ꜣ*.
11. Emending here according to S3P. [hieroglyphs] *et varr.* at the end of 344*a*, may be possibly an additional note or editorial comment of some kind, but it seems probable that the copyists themselves did not understand it.
12. This mention of Imsety, etc., is either out of place or else very clumsily dragged in, and Sethe would refer it to 'the gods who are in the suite' of 344*a*.
13. S2P and S1C have *ḥkꜣt* 'chieftainess' here, but *snwt* of the other texts seems more likely to be correct.
14. Read perhaps *wn(n)·⟨i⟩ m-ꜥ·i m syp* 'may I be in my own right(?) an allotter'.

Spell 158[1]

II, 349 KNOWING THE SOULS OF NEKHEN. I know the mystery of Nekhen; it is the hands of Horus of his mother's making which were thrown into the water,
350 she saying:| 'You shall be the two severed portions of Horus after you have
351 been found'.[2] And Rēꜥ said: 'This son of Isis is injured| by reason of what his mother herself has done to him; would that we might fetch Sobk from the
352 back of the waters, that he may fish them out| and so that his mother Isis may cause them to grow (again) in their proper place'. And Sobk from the
353 back of the waters said: 'I have fished and I have sought;| they slipped[3] from my hand upon the banks of the waters, but I fished them up in the end with a fish-trap'. THAT IS HOW THE FISH-TRAP CAME INTO BEING.
354 KNOWING THE MYSTERY OF NEKHEN.| Thus said Rēꜥ: 'Has Sobk any fish[4] as well as finding Horus's hands for him?' THAT IS HOW TR-RMW-TOWN CAME
355 INTO BEING.| Then said Rēꜥ: 'Hidden are the mysteries concerning this fish-
356 trap which brought to us Horus's hands; the sight is cleared because of it| in the monthly festival and the half-monthly festival in this *Tr-rmw*'. And Rēꜥ said: 'Nekhen is set in his embrace and the sight is cleared on account of his

hands in this Nekhen which I have given[5] to him, | and what is in them is shut 357
up in the half-monthly festival.'[6]

Then said Horus: 'Indeed I have placed[7] Duamūtef and Kebḥsenuf with
me so | that I may watch over them, for they are a contentious company; further 358
they are to be[8] there while Nekhen is mine, according to the word of Rēʿ:
"Place them in | the prison(?)[9] of Nekhen, for ⟨they⟩[10] have done what used 359
to be done by Her who is in the Broad Hall"; "They are with me", you shall
say, and they will end up with you until Seth knows | that they are with you 360
and complains.'[11] O you who are in Nekhen, power is given to me, and I know
the mystery of Nekhen; | it is the hands of Horus and what is in them, for I 361
have been introduced to the Souls of Nekhen. Open to me, that I may join
with Horus.

I | KNOW THE SOULS OF NEKHEN; THEY ARE HORUS, DUAMŪTEF AND ḲEBḤ- 362
SENUF. NOT TO BE SAID WHEN EATING PIG.

1. Cf. *ZÄS* 58, 57 ff. S2P is followed.
2. Var. *bꜣ·tywny* 'destroyed'.
3. Read *btktk* (Old perfective) with B4L^b; the *n* following *btktk* in all other texts probably arises from a confusion with *tkn* 'approach'.
4. In S2P and B4L^b *rmw* 'fish' is erroneously determined with ⊗, borrowed from the place-name *Tr-rmw* below. All texts except S2P have 'To what purpose has Sobk fish?', ending the sentence with the interrogative *r-m*, apparently as a pun on *rmw* 'fish', but S2P gives the better sense.
5. Note that the town-name *Nẖn* is treated as a masculine word.
6. Var. 'at the monthly festival and the half-monthly festival'.
7. Sethe translates as an imperative, 'gib mir', but the use of the enclitic *ḥm* speaks against this view.
8. *Wnn* may be imperfective *sḏm·f* used impersonally, the subject being sufficiently indicated by the enclitic *r·sn*; the alternative is an abnormal use of the imperative in respect of the 3rd person.
9. Cf. *ZÄS* 58, 75.
10. Suffix 3rd plur. omitted.
11. The speech of Horus ends here.

Spell 159[1]

GOING IN AND OUT FROM THE EASTERN GATES OF THE SKY AMONG THE FOLLOW- II, 363
ERS OF RĒʿ. KNOWING THE SOULS OF THE EASTERNERS.

I know that middle gate from which Rēʿ issues in the east; its south is in 364
the Lake of Waterfowl, its north is in the Waters of Geese, in the place in |
which Rēʿ navigates by rowing or by wind. I am he who has charge of the 366

rigging in the God's Bark, I am he who rows and does not tire in the Bark
367 of Rēʿ;| I know those two sycamores which are of turquoise[2] between which
368 Rēʿ goes forth, which go strewing shade| at every eastern gate from which
369 Rēʿ shines forth. I know that Field of Rushes which belongs to Rēʿ,| the wall of whose enceinte is of iron; the height of its barley is four cubits, its ear
370 is one cubit,| its stalk is three cubits; its emmer is seven cubits, its ear is two
371 cubits, its stalk is five cubits.| It is the horizon-dwellers who reap it, 9 cubits
372 long in the presence of the Souls of the Easterners,| who are Harakhti, the . . .[3] calf and the Morning Star.

1. Cf. *ZÄS* 59,1 ff. S2P is followed.
2. Lacuna in S2P restored from the parallel texts.
3. *Ḫwrr*, meaning obscure; cf. *Pyr.* § 161 ff., where it occurs in an entirely different context. In S2P without det., suggesting an adjective qualifying *bḥs* 'calf', but in the other texts determined with  or .

Spell 160[1]

II, 373 LIVING LONG UPON EARTH, NOT EATING FILTH IN THE REALM OF THE DEAD, NOT
374 DYING BECAUSE OF A SNAKE,| BEING HALE UPON EARTH, GOING IN AND OUT OF THE EASTERN GATES OF THE SKY, KNOWING THE SOULS OF THE WESTERNERS.

376 I know that mountain of Bakhu| upon which the sky rests; it is of crystal(?),[2] 300 rods long and 120 rods wide. Sobk, Lord of Bakhu, is in the east of this mountain, his temple is[3] of carnelian, his serpent is on the summit of that
378 mountain,| 30 cubits long, and 3 cubits of its forepart[4] are of flint. I know the name of this serpent which is upon the mountain, its name is *Whn·f*. Now at
380 eventide he will turn his eye against Rēʿ,| and a stoppage will occur in the crew[5] and a great astonishment(?)[6] in the voyage, and Seth will bend him with his hand.[7]

Spell which he[8] utters as magic: 'I rise up against[9] you and the voyage[10]
382 is directed aright. O you whom I have seen from afar,| close[11] your eye, for I have bound you.[12] I am the Male, so cover your head; I am hostile.[13] I am one great in magic which I have sent forth[14] against you.'

'What is it, this power?'[15]

384 'O you who go on your belly, your strength belongs to your mountain.| See, I go off with your strength in my hand, for I am he who displays strength. I have come that I may take care of the earth-gods; O Rēʿ, may He who is in
386 the evening and Those who travel round the sky be gracious to me.| You[16] are in fetters, which is what was decreed against you in the Presence, and Rēʿ will go to rest in life'.

I know the Souls of the Westerners; they are Rēꜥ,[17] Sobk Lord [of II, 387
Bakhu] and Seth the Lord of Life.[18]

Having power through invocation-offerings which the heir on 388
earth makes for his father.[19]

1. Cf. *ZÄS* 59,73 ff. S2P again is followed.
2. Read *ṯḥn*? Cf. Harris, *Minerals*, 92.
3. The use of the imperfective *wnn* here, and in the two sentences which follow, in all texts but one probably implies duration.
4. For *ḥnt* used of the forepart of a snake cf. *ꜥrḳ sw r ḥnt* 'he was reared up in front', *Sh. S.* 66, from the sailor's description of the magic serpent.
5. Of the solar bark.
6. Cf. *Wb.* IV, 320,9.
7. Seth appears here to be acting in his role as defender of the solar bark. The reading *m ḏrt·f* of B2P ff. seems superior to *m ḏr·f* of S2P–B9C. Elsewhere *kꜥḥ m ḏrt* is used of a gesture of respect, cf. *Urk.* IV, 121,12.
8. Presumably the deceased, who apparently acts as Seth the defender.
9. *M-ḏr* as a compound preposition, common to all texts.
10. Of the solar bark.
11. Emending *ꜥn* of S2P and S2C into *ꜥḥn* of the other texts; for this word see also *CT* V, 369*g*; *BD* 113,16; var. *ꜥḥn* 135,15. B3C^{a} has a version of its own which appears to read: 'Do not close your eye for yourself'.
12. So S2P and S2C. All the other texts have *ṯꜣm n·i* 'be veiled (i.e. blindfolded) for me'.
13. Reading *ḏꜣḏꜣ·ky* as S2P and S2C; for the meaning cf. *Wb.* V, 533,1–4. The other texts have corrupted this into *wḏꜣ·k wḏꜣ·i* 'if you are hale, then will I be hale', which is nonsense in this context.
14. Reading *iw wdy·n·i*; *iw rdy·n·i* of several texts is less forcible.
15. Var. 'this power, what is it?' The serpent asks this question.
16. The serpent.
17. Var. B4Bo: 'Atum'.
18. So S2P. The other texts have 'Sobk, Lord of Bakhu, and Ḥatḥōr, Lady of the Evening', omitting the reference to Seth. B2Bo adds: 'Entering into the gate of the west of the sky'.
19. B2Bo adds: 'to be in the suite of Rēꜥ'.

Spell 161

N. knows the Field of Rushes, it is the city of Rēꜥ [. . .] its ear (of corn) is of two cubits, its[1] stalk is of seven cubits, its leaf(?) is of four cubits, men reap it in the presence of Rēꜥ himself. N knows that middle gate of the Field of Rushes from which Rēꜥ comes forth in the east of the sky; its southern part is in the Lake of Waterfowl, its northern [part] is in the Waters of Geese at the place where Rēꜥ navigates. It is N who rows and does not tire in the Bark of Rēꜥ, N knows those two sycamores which are of turquoise, between which

Rēʿ comes forth, which go strewing shade at the gate at the east of the sky, at the place where Rēʿ rises. N knows the Field of Rushes.

1. The suffix in *mꜣt·f* must refer to the ear (*šms*), not to the fem. noun that fell in the lacuna, where perhaps *bdt* should be restored.

Spell 162

HAVING POWER OVER THE FOUR WINDS OF HEAVEN.[1] These winds have been
II, 389 given to me by these maidens. Such is the north-wind | which circulates about
the Isles, which opens its arms to the limits of the earth and which rests when
391 it has brought the things which I daily desire.[2] | The north-wind is the breath
of life, and what it has granted to me is that I may live by means of it.[3]

392 These winds have been given to me| by these maidens. Such is the east-
wind which opens the celestial windows; the east-wind is opened and a fair
path is made for Rēʿ that he may go forth on it. Rēʿ grasps my hand and sets
394 me in this field of his in the midst of rushes,| and I flourish in it[4] like[5] the
condition of Apis and Seth.[6] The east-wind is the breath of life, and what it
395 has granted to me| is that I may live by means of it.

These winds have been given to me by these maidens. Such is the west-
396 wind, the brother of *Ḥꜣ*,| the offspring of *Iꜣꜣw*, which lives in one body, the
397 second in this land[7] of(?) the north, south,[8] west and east winds,| and what it
has granted to me is that I may live by means of it.

These winds have been given to me by these maidens, Such is the south-
398 wind,| a native[9] of the Southland, which brings water, growth and life; the
south-wind is the breath of life, and what it has granted to me is that I may
live by means of it.

399 Hail to you, you four winds of the sky, the bulls of the sky! I tell you[10] your
names, the names which I give to you.[11] I know that you were brought to
400 birth| and that you came into being before men were born or the gods existed,
401 before birds were trapped or cattle lassoed,| before there were bound up the
jaws of *Mꜣṯrt*,[12] daughter of the Morning Star,[13] before there was created the
402 need for any quarryman(?) of sky or earth. I have requested them (*sic*)| from
the Lord of Powers, and it is he who has given them to me. Come, proceed
403 with me, that I may cause you to see the bark,| that you may go aboard it and
navigate in it without me(?).[14] I have built my own bark, and I cross in it to
404 the lotus-tank,[15] and I will hew out| therein a bark of 1000 cubits over all,[16]
I will navigate in it to the Stairway of Baking just as Rēʿ navigated to the
405 Stairway of Baking,| and I will have bread[17] outside *Tnt*.[18]

1. Varr. M22C: 'having power over the winds in the realm of the dead'; G1T: 'Likewise

having power over the winds'; B2Bo: 'having power over the four winds of the sky by a man in the realm of the dead'. On this spell see Blackman in *ZÄS* 48, 117 ff.; Drioton, 'La chanson des quatre vents', *Revue du Caire*, No. 44 (July 1942), 209 ff.

2. Note the use of the direct object after a relative form here and in *dy*⟨*·i*⟩ *n·k sn* 'which I have brought to you', 399*b*; cf. Eg. *Gramm.*[3] § 385.

3. A variant text of 390*b*–391*b* occurs in B3Bo (390*d*–*e*; 391*d*–*e*); see de Buck's note 7* on p. 390.

4. So B1Bo. Varr. *wnm·i ꜣf·i im·s*, *wnm·i ꜣfꜣf·i im·s* 'I eat and gorge(?) on it', cf. *CT* IV, 23*l*; *wnm·i im·s* 'I eat of it'.

5. *My* 'like' only in T3C and G1T. The other texts have *is* after *ꜥ*.

6. For the name of Seth most texts substitute *wḏꜥ* 'the Outcast'.

7. After *ḫt wꜥt*, for *snnw* of B1Bo, B4C and Y1C have *snty*, as if the word qualified *ḫt;* B2Bo and B4Bo have *sny*, and the other texts read: 'before the two parts(?) had come into being in this land'.

8. B1Bo has a dittograph of *rsw* 'south-wind'; having started off with that word and having reverted to the order 'north, south' of S2C–B4Bo; Y1C has 'south, north, east, west', and the remaining texts name only the 'west-wind' as the breath of life.

9. Lit. 'a *nḥsy* of the south'.

10. Sing., as of the winds were being invoked collectively as one being.

11. See n.2 above.

12. Cf. Edel in *ZÄS* 96,11. Misread as the plant *mꜣtt* in B6C and BH2C.

13. Varr. 'the great god', 'the god'.

14.  for *nn wi*, lit. 'when I am not'.

15. For this word cf. Spell 48, n.5.

16. Lit. 'to its two heads', i.e. between the upstanding portions of bow and stern.

17. Var. B1Bo: 'bread and beer'.

18. Location unknown.

Spell 163

Crossing the Winding Waterway. These winds have been given to N by these maidens, namely this north-wind, and it is the sweet ⟨breath⟩ of life;[1] it has given N his life[2] by means of itself.

These winds [have been given] to N by these maidens. The west-wind [is(?)] the offspring of Him who is in the ram's head(?),[3] who came forth from between the thighs of the West, who makes a butchery of the herds (reserved) for offering. The gods are content with the good and sweet breath of life of N which he (*sic*) has taken[4] for N that N may live by reason of it.

1. Read *m mḥt pw* ⟨*ṯꜣw*⟩ *pw nḏm n ꜥnḫ*, with suppression of the second .
2. Lit. 'it has given to N the life of N'.
3. *'Iꜣw* 'ram's head(?)', also in *CT* I, 140*a*.
4. Read *šd·tw·f*; the form *šdt·f* is fem. with a masc. antecedent.

Spell 164

III, 1 '[My] portion is a meal at the temples;[1] I am the possessor of seven portions, three in the sky and four on earth in the House of Rēʿ[2] and Thoth'.

'Where is it granted to you to eat?'

'I eat in the booth containing the branches of the *imꜣ*-trees of Ḥatḥōr who in front of the *ἰṯnws*-tree'[3]

'Come to me, that the gate may be opened for you.'

'O Great Elder, companion and brother,[4] prepare a way for me.'

2 'Look, where do you go in and out?[5]'

'I go in to *Wns*, I go out from Horus.'

'Come, that you may call to the Inner Gods, the wardens of the middle sky;[6] they[7] will prepare a way for you.'

O Great One, O Seer, O Father of the Primeval Ones of the middle sky,[8]

3 a way is prepared for me. O Great *Ḫns*-lake, I will not fall into you; the Lakes of the Destroyer, I will not fall into them. I have come that I may turn my serpent[9] about, that I may raise up the uraeus, and that I may cure the great god of what he has sorely suffered.

What is it that the great god has sorely[10] suffered from?

4 It is his head, his arm[11] and his leg. I have come that I may spit[12] on the head and arm,[13] cool the scalp and ease the leg of the ailing[14] great god.

Welcome, O equipped spirit; come and go down there, and it will be well.

1. G1T omits *iw išt* and opens with the suffix 1st sing.; with *ʿbt* compare *ʿb* 'meal', Caminos, *Lit. Frag*. pl. 1, 2, 9; 2, 2, 9. This spell consists of a conversation between an unnamed being and the deceased.

2. Var. Horus.

3. '*Iṯnw*, meaning unknown. Cf. Sp. 1029, n. 8.

4. So S2C; var. G1T: 'elder companion'.

5. Following S2C; G1T has the old perfective, to be translated as 'look, where have you gone in and out?'. M22C omits the interrogative *ṯn*.

6. Varr. S2C: 'that you may call to those who are among the primeval gods of the middle sky'; G1T: 'that you may call ⟨to⟩ the wardens of the middle sky'. For *ṯnw* 'warden' cf. *Ann. Serv.* 42,108.

7. For *ir·f* read *ir·sn*, referring back to *ẖnw* 'inner gods'. of S2C is clearly a mis-writing of 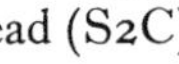.

8. Read (S2C): *i it pꜣwtyw nw pt ḥrt-ib*, cf. 2*e*; G1T omits 2*g*–*h*.

9. So rather than 'my body', in view of the allusion to the uraeus in the next sentence.

10. So G1T.

11. G1T is the clearest of the three texts. of M22C and S2C is to be read *kʿḥ* 'arm', cf. 4*a*, where is a det. of *kʿḥ*.

12. For spittle as medicine cf. *JEA* 16,171.

13. *Ḳꜥḥ* 'arm' is intact only in G1T; see n.11.
14. G1T only.

Spell 165

SPELL FOR EATING BREAD FROM UPON THE OFFERING-TABLES OF RĒꜥ, GIVING OBLATIONS IN ŌN.[1] III, 5

O you who are content with what you[2] have done—four times—and who 6
send Māꜥet to Rēꜥ daily, the liver of Rēꜥ is flourishing[3] daily because of Māꜥet,
and he partakes of the meal of the Great Goddess. I am hale from every ill[4] |
which has gone forth from the mouth of any god, any spirit or any dead person 8
in this year and in this happy day of the *ṯnnt*-sanctuary, and a happy day will not be lacking in the *ṯnnt*-sanctuary, my powers will be bestowed in this happy day in the *ṯnnt*-sanctuary.

O you who are at your altar—four times—| controller of the oblations in 10
Ōn upon the altars of Rēꜥ daily,[5] I am the Sole One;[6] I have gone forth from
the horizon with my oblations in front of me—twice—| and I will continue to 12
go forth with my oblations in front of me—twice—which I have set[7] before
myself that I may eat what is before me.[8] | I am this one who issued from the 13
egg of the great god.[9]

1. Varr. S1C: 'giving oblations at the gates of the necropolis in Ōn'; B3Bo: '[. . .] at the temple of every god'.
2. In the 3rd person in the original, in accord with Egyptian usage, but the pronoun can refer only to the person addressed.
3. *ꜣḫ*, otherwise unrecorded, is clearly the simplex which is reduplicated in *ꜣḫꜣḫ* 'grow green', 'flourish', *Wb.* I, 18,16 ff.
4. S2C, S1C *et varr.* In three texts *sḏb* is qualified by *ḏwy* 'evil'.
5. So four texts; the others add 'for those who love Rēꜥ every day'.
6. Var. 'I am one of them'.
7. Read *rdyw·n·i* 'which I have placed' with S2C, B4Bo and B17C; the reading *rdy·n wi* of the other texts is ruled out by the absence of subject.
8. For *m-ḥꜣt* read *imyt-ḥꜣt*.
9. Var. B5C: 'I am this one, I am the egg of the god'. For *swḥt* 'egg' the B3C group substitute meaninglessly *ḥrst* 'carnelian'.

Spell 166

O Hearer, O Unstopper (of ears),[1] | hear me, unstop me(?)[2]—and *vice versa*— III, 14
for I am the Bull of Kenzet who is in charge of the meals[3] in Ōn; four loaves
are on earth with Horus and three in the sky[4] with Min. | Give me these 16
oblations, and I will depart.

1. Both fem. participles. For *smt* 'hear' cf. *Pyr.* § 1189; *Hatnub*, 26,6; B3Bo, M2C and *CT* III, 74*e* make the reading certain. *Sšn* appears to be a metathetic var. of *snš* 'unstop' ears. *Pyr.* §§ 712; 1673; 1727; 2084, and is in fact written *snš* in M2C.

2. Of thirteen parallel texts, no two are identical, and there has been much corruption. Although seven versions are introduced by *in*, a question is out of place here, for what one would expect is a request from the dead to the two beings invoked. I suggest that the archetype may have read *smt wi, sšn wi* 'hear me, unstop me', and this translation has been adopted, with all reservations.

3. B3Bo has 'seven meals' with the numeral in red.

4. So M2C, with Rēꜥ for Min; B5C and the B3C group have 'on earth'. S2C–B3Bo omit this reference to the place of the offerings.

Spell 167

III, 17 Sit down, sit down for food,| for Rēꜥ sits down for food when the Enneads
have given water. Stand up, O Abundance, upon the altars[1] of abundance.|
18 I have come to you, O butler of Rēꜥ, I have come to you, for Rēꜥ's
countenance is gracious to you, the countenance of the Enneads is bright
19 for you. |You have given me bread and beer when I was hungry and
thirsty, for I am the Eyeless One who is upon the throne of the firmament.
My power belongs to my double, I feed on what is from out of the
20 horizon,[2]| I eat of the *šrt*-plants which are in the field,[3] I partake of a meal in
22 the riparian land of the god.| O Mourner(?),[4] dress your hair[5] for me; O
Forgetter(?),[6] your face is turned to the wall! It is *Ḥmꜣtt*[7] who causes me to
23 speak[8]| that I may(?) . . .[9] those two gods who go down to their food-offerings
at the festival of the seventh day;[10] as snakes they go down to the earth,[11] and
25 I will go down on their coils;| as falcons they ascend[12] to the sky, and I will
ascend[13] on their wings. The festival of the sixth day is for my breakfast,[14]|
26 the festival of the seventh day is for my supper, for I am Rēꜥ-Atum, I have
27 placed food on the altars of Rē|-Atum |in the two-*ḥtrt*-lakes on the eastern
side of the sky, for I am Rēꜥ-Atum, Lord of All—twice.

1. For *wḏḥw* 'altars' three texts substitute *wḏbw* 'river-banks'. Cf. *Pyr.* Utt. 494.

2. Four texts only. For *wšb m* 'feed on' cf. *Pyr.* §§ 736; 803; 1722.

3. B3C group only. The plant *šrt* is probably the source of *šrt*-grain, *Urk.* IV, 747,5. 9. B2Bo and B4Bo add: 'your (var. 'N's') bread is to be *snt*-loaves', but the abrupt change of person shows clearly that this clause is an interpolation.

4. Cf. *ḥꜣyty* 'the two mourning women', *Wb.* III, 7,7. It seems clear that the word puzzled the copyists, for S2C (damaged), S1C, B5C and B4Bo all read *ḥꜣ(w)t*; M22C has 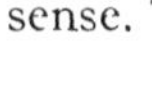; B3C has 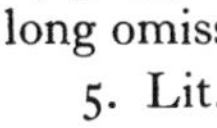 and B17C ff. have *wḏwt*; neither of these variants seems to yield good sense. There is a long omission in B2Bo.

5. Lit. 'your scalp'.

6. Cf. *smhy* 'forget', *CT* II, 93*f*.

7. Varr. *ḥm3t*, *ḥ3t*, *ḥ3ty*, meaning unknown. Other obscure words from the same stem are ? *CT* IV, 83*a*, var. 85*d*, cf. *JEA* 35,96, n.5; and probably also *Pyr.* § 373, which Sethe, *Komm. Pyr.* II, 99 identified with the curl on the Red Crown; see also Abubakr, *Kronen*, 53.

8. So the four texts of the S2C group; the others omit.

9. *D3m*; not recorded in *Wb.* and meaning unknown.

10. *Ḏnyt* is twice determined with and three times with , the latter borrowed from *dnyt* 'dam'. For 22*c*–23*b*, B3C ff. have *in ḥ3t r ḏnyt*; B2Bo and B4Bo (23*c*) have *iw ḥnḳt·k r ḏnyt*.

11. S2C and S1C omit *r t3*, but the contrast with *r pt* in 24*c* shows that *r t3* is original. M22C has only *m ḥf3w*. The use of the imperfective *sḏm·f* here and in 24*c* is apparently to emphasize the adverbial adjuncts *m ḥf3w*, *m bykw*, cf. *JEA* 33, 99 ff., the stress lying on the forms assumed rather than on their actions. Note that in 24*b* the prospective *sḏm·f* is used, indicating the speaker's intention.

12. B3C ff. have *r pr(t)·sn* 'until they ascend', but the parallelism with 24*a* shows that *prr·sn* is the correct reading.

13. S2C and S1C alone have *prr·sn*; M22C–B1C have *pr·sn*; B1Be has the prospective form *pry·i*, and comparison with 24*b* shows that the last is correct.

14. Var B17C ff 'in the festival of the sixth day', B2L adding a superfluous , as apparently also B1Be.

Spell 168

Joining the river-banks.[1] The hair of Isis is knotted to the hair of Nephthys[2]— III, 28
and *vice versa*—putrefaction is left boatless,[3] the streams are dried up,| Gēb 29
has swallowed up the waters, the hands of Shesmu are joined over the lungs of the Two Ladies.[4]

1. Title of spell in M5C only (28*d*). This short spell appears to be a description of Egypt under drought. The following spells 169–171 with similar titles are entirely different in content.

2. In three texts *n šn* is omitted after *3st*.

3. I.e. cannot be removed. This suggests that boats were used for removing and dumping the fouler forms of garbage, but the water is now too low for the purpose.

4. *Et varr.*, an obscure sentence. B2Bo adds a superfluous and irrelevant rubric: 'the gates of the necropolis'.

Spell 169

SPELL FOR JOINING THE RIVER-BANKS. I have brought together the two river III, 30
banks, the west to the east—and *vice versa*. My feet are these four seers,[1] my
sandals are Ḥatḥōr, I will[2] cross the sky,| I will traverse the earth,[3] I will join 32
the river-banks,[4] these are small[5]—twice—having gone forth[6] from the lips
of the *inb3*-plant. Let me not see the father of him whose face is putrid[7] | when 34

he remembers to weep.[8] May I come and go as Shu, for I am Shu, my face is that of the Great Flood,[9] I am born as Horus of Shesmet, and the river-banks
36 are united. Open to me,| for I am the Great Flood.

1. Var. P. Berl. '6', and *ipw* is omitted.

2. Prospective; cf. *ḏꜣy N* of B4Bo.

3. So B5C. Most other texts have 'the Two Lands', but the singular *tꜣ* 'earth' is the usual counterpart of *pt* 'sky'. B4C substitutes *wꜣḏ-wr* 'sea'.

4. B4C adds 'In the realm of the dead' and stops.

5. Var. B5C *snw* 'the two'. *Nw* 'these' presumably refers to the *iḫmty*, while *šrr* is apparently old perfective; for geminated forms of this tense cf. *Eg. Gramm.*[3] § 310 (p. 236. bottom). The meaning of this clause is not obvious, and the whole spell is obscure.

6. B5C has  as against  of all the other texts. The sense of *spty inbꜣ* is obscure.

7. Read *im mꜣꜣ·i it ḥwꜣ ḥr*; for the position of the suffix *·i* cf. Edel, *Altäg. Gramm.* 1104 ff. The suffix in *it·f* in B5C, if correct, must refer in advance to *ḥwꜣ ḥr*, 'his father of . . .', as it has no antecedent.

8. Read ⟨*r*⟩ *rmt*?

9. Reading *ḥr·i m mḥt wrt* with S2C and P. Berl, cf. 36*a*. The alternative reading *ḥḏ wrt* 'harmer of the Great One' yields poor sense.

Spell 170

III, 37 Joining the river-banks in the realm of the dead.[1] O *Ꜣꜣw*,| I am he of the Mansion,[2] the two serpents on the eye of Atum are parted for me, the bulls[3]
39 are led| to their caverns for me. He who united the Two Lands goes forth; cross over, O *Iꜥnw*, to the Abyss when the doubles cross to the earth. I give ⟨to⟩ the swimmers, the river-banks are joined for me, and god is friendly with god, face to face[4] and nose to nose.[5]

1. Title of the spell in B2Be[a]; in B1Bo[b] it is in red at the end of the text, see 40*f*.

2. For *Ꜣꜣw* (with varr.) see also *CT* II, 396*a*. *Ḥwty in* 37*a* has been read as a *nisba*-form. Again many varr.

3. In two texts 'bulls' has a snake-det., implying that the word refers here to powerful serpents, cf. the 'bull-snake' of *Pyr.* § 2254.

4. M5C only.

5. From 38*b* onwards B1Bo[b] and B2Be[b] take a line of their own (39*e* ff.) which reads: 'Shu does not go forth (T3C is in the affirmative and ends), the Two Lands are united from(?) this(?) west ⟨to⟩ this(?) east—and *vice versa*—the god kisses his brother. *Ḏbw* is given, the two banks are joined together, the god is crossing the deserts, N has joined together the two banks on earth, nose is on nose, the two banks are *Ḥw*', followed by the title of the spell. B1Bo[a] and B2Be[a] have yet another version (40*g* ff.): 'I(?) go up to the Abyss, to the House of Shu, the Two Lands are united from the west to the east—and *vice versa*—the god is brotherly to his brother. N has given *ḏbw*, he has united the banks, the god is crossing the deserts, he makes ready(?) the waters of rowing over the Two Lands in the face of(?) the river banks'.

Spell 171

JOINING THE RIVER-BANKS.| Here comes a female spirit—so says a female III, 42
spirit. Here comes a female great one—so says a female great one.[1] | It is 43
Mā‘ety[2] who brings them to me; O western bank, kiss the eastern bank |—and 44
vice versa—bring me to land,[3] for I possess truth.[4] | O god and goddess of the 45
spindle(?)[5]—so says Atum—you shall not lay hold on me for ever.[6]

1. B2Bo and B4Bo insert a repetition of *iy ꜣḫt* before *iy wrt* and for *in* 'so says' have alone.
2. Masc., therefore a *nisba*-form and not a dual 'The Two Truths'.
3. For this sense of *smꜣ-tꜣ m* cf. *Urk.* I, 122,8.
4. Omitted in B1Bo and B2Bo, which likewise omit all 45*a* and substitute 'N is (= I am) there'.
5. *Pnn* with this det. appears not to be recorded and the translation 'spindle(?)' is a guess. In M2NY the det. closely resembles *ḥsf* = a spindle, cf. Gardiner, Sign List U 34. A similar det. is found with *nbꜣ* 'ewer'(?), 133*b*.
6. Note the use of the rare negation *w* in B2Bo–M2NY. P. Berl. omits it, presumably not recognizing it, while B1L–B9C are all more or less corrupt; S10C has transformed *in ꞽItm* into *imy Nt*. In *ḥr·i* the suffix must surely refer to the deceased, not to Atum as would appear at first sight. M5C and M2NY end with curious animal-signs (baboon and ichneumon(?)) which apparently stand for Atum.

Spell 172

The Two Lands are joined for my crossing, the river-bank(s) are joined, the III, 46
god kisses his brother, the Bull gives command ⟨to⟩[1] the river bank(s) with
authority(?). RECITATION: THE RIVER BANKS.

1. Var. *nfꜣ r* 'snorts at'.

Spell 173

NOT TO EAT FAECES AND NOT TO DRINK URINE IN THE REALM OF THE DEAD. What I III, 47
doubly detest, I will not eat. Faeces is my detestation, and I will not eat it.
Filth[1] shall not enter into this mouth of mine, and I will not eat it with my
mouth, I will not touch it with my finger,[2] I will not tread on it with my toes,[3]
because I will not eat faeces for you,[4] | I will not drink urine for you, I will not 48
go upside down for you, I will not accept this mat of Shesmētet for you;[5]
because I will not eat for you this filth which issued from the hinder parts of
Osiris.

'Eat!' say they to me.

'I will not eat for you.'

'Why?' say they to me.

49 'Because I am shod| with the sandals of Sokar.'
'Eat!' say they to me.
'I will not eat for you.'
'Why?' say they to me.
'Because that staff which separated sky and earth is in my hand.'
'Eat!' say they to me.
'I will not eat for you.'
'Why?' say they to me.
'Because I have brought in(?)[6] that stick(?)[7] which is in the acacia'.

50 'Eat this excrement which issued from the hinder parts of Osiris; what (else) can you live on?' say these gods to me. 'What have you come to eat?'[8]

'I eat of bread of white emmer, I drink of beer of red emmer'.

51 'Bread of white emmer will perish,| beer[9] of red emmer will perish. What (else) can you live on?'

'Because seven portions are in this land, there come to me four[10] portions above with Rēʿ and three portions below with Gēb'.

'He who has granted to you to eat; where is he?'

'In the booths under the *imꜣ*-trees of *ꞽIṯnws* in the presence of *Sḥr* who
52 makes (men) subordinate(?),[11]| because I have entered into the rising flame,[12] I have gone forth from Sehēl[13] exercising authority over the two she-asses[14] of Shu, and there have been given to me my father, my mother, my brethren, my home and all my family; because I have a protector as far as Elephantine and at every place where I wish to be that I may dwell there.'[15]

53 I am the Bull, the Old One of Kenzet, in charge of the five (*sic*) portions in this temple; five portions are above with Rēʿ, five portions are below with Osiris. The sacred doors are opened to me, the doors of Kenzet[16] are thrown open for me, my messenger appears, Thoth is on high, the spirits are awake,
54 those who are in Kenzet roar in front of the Great Egret(?)| who opens up ways, who went up from the top of the *sꜣrt*-plant. I wash myself, I cleanse my mouth, my teeth are sharpened, faeces protects me (*sic!*), urine respects me like those detestable ones who cross the sky dead, dead.

55 O you two who cross the sky, fetch me with you,| that I may eat of what you eat of, that I may drink what you drink of. I course over the sky, I travel to and fro in heaven, my booth is in the Field of Rushes, my plenty is in the Field of Offerings, I support the sky with my horns, I toe the earth with my
56 sandals.| I am the Double Lion, older than Atum, I take my throne which is in the deserts and which is in Chemmis. I have taken possession of Powers and their courts(?) on the ways of the Bark of Khopri,[17] I[18] have led those who

are in their booths, I have taken possession of those who are in their caverns, I have made the circlings of the *hnhnw*-bark, which I have guided[19] on the ways of Khopri,ǀ I have stood in the bark of Khopri. I control[20] the crews of Atum 57
in the evening on the day when the god recites his words in power, I cause his word to enter into him whose throat is narrow. I open(?)[21] my mouth, I eat life, I live by air, I live again hereafter. Filth is my detestation and I will not eat it; my detestation is efflux, ǀI will not drink discharge.[22] I will survive the 58
Earth-god. It is I who will protect the son of him who is in control,[23] the son of the great god. Efflux is my detestation, and I will not eat it; I have eaten of Him who is in charge of dates, who is in his shrine, on whom Rēʿ's retainers live.

'Be off!' say they[24] to me. 'Who pray are you?' 59

'I am Horus ⟨on⟩ his tall perch(?)'.[25]

1. *Ḥtp-kȝ* 'what pleases the double' is an euphemistic expression for 'excrement', describing it by the exact contrary to what it really is. Cf. also 48*d*; 80*d*. A parallel expression is the well-known *nb ʿnḫ* 'lord of life' for 'sarcophagus'.

2. So B3C; *tp* 'head' of B1S and B2L is obviously absurd, but suggests that the original reading may have been *tp ḏbʿ·i* 'the tip of my finger'.

3. Following the negation of B3C, though the verb is lost; this gives a sense much superior to *ḥr* 'because' of the other two texts; surely no-one would willingly tread in ordure. See also 80*g*.

4. Plural, referring to the unnamed denizens of the Beyond, who are called 'these gods' in 50*c*, and who want the deceased to consume this foul diet.

5. What the 'mat of Shesmētet' may be is not apparent.

6. For *ḫsf* 'bring in(?)' cf. *CT* I, 284*b*.

7. *Twȝw* only here; the translation 'stick(?)' rests solely on the context.

8. Following B1C. B2L and B3C omit this sentence and insert meaninglessly 'in this land to which you have come'.

9. B1C wrongly 'bread'.

10. B2L wrongly 'seven'.

11. The meaning of *ssiṯn* is uncertain, but cf. *siṯn* 'subordinate(?)' (vb.), *Les.* 81,20.

12. Reading *ʿk·n·i m wṯst* with B3C. *Ṯist* in the other two texts looks like a *vox nihili*, and the preposition after *ʿḳ·n·i* is lacking.

13. The alternative meaning 'Asia' is less likely; cf. the allusion to Elephantine in 52*e*.

14. B1C omits the references to asses, certainly in error. Compare *iʿȝt-ḥmt* 'she-ass', *Pyr.* § 523.

15. The cross-questioning stops here.

16. So B1C; B2L corruptly *sn n·k ʿȝwy·k n imnt*. In B3C the latter part of the sentence is lost.

17. Here is a long omission in B1C and B2L.

18. B3C uses the 3rd person, but the 1st person of the other texts is undoubtedly the original form.

19. B3C has miscopied the *n* of *sšm(w)·n* as *f*.

20. B1C and B2L resume here.

21. Cf. *Wb.* III, 67,8.

22. Read *bwt·i pw ḥs, n wmn·i sw; bwt·i pw rḏw, n swr·i sfẖ*; for the last word see also 141*g*.

23. For *snẖn* 'control' cf. *Concise Dict.* 233. B2L has a superfluous *sw*.

24. Emending *ḏd·n·i* to *ḏd·sn*; the speakers are presumably the gods of 50*c*. *Ḥr·t(y)* is hortative old perfective; B3C has the plural *ḥr·tywny* and reads 'be far from N' as if the gods were being told to depart.

25. Reading conjecturally *Ḥr ⟨ḥr⟩ ḳꜣꜣ·f*; the meaning of the last word is uncertain. Since the stem *ḳꜣ* means 'high', the det. may possibly represent a high perch for the falcon of Horus.

Spell 174

III, 60 I have gone up on Shu, I have climbed on the sunshine,[1] | my meals are in Ōn, three[2] portions in the Field of Rushes. My detestation is faeces, and I will not eat it, I will not smell it; urine, I will not drink it.[3] I eat with my mouth, I defaecate with my anus; I will not go to you . . .[4]

1. 59*f*, in B3C only, has every appearance of an obscure interpolation and has been ignored in the translation.

2. Var. B3C: 'five'.

3. B1C erroneously has the masc. object-pronoun *sw*.

4. The meaning of *bḏn*, var. *bnḏ*, is not known.

Spell 175

III, 61 SPELL FOR ASCENDING TO THE SKY, TO THE PLACE WHERE RĒꜥ IS. I am Horus who presides over the Lake of the Sky, Thoth who presides over the God's Booth, and the White Bull whom the milk-goddess suckled. I am the Great One whom the frog-goddess created, who[1] gathered together these bones of Osiris. If you[2] go up to the sky as vultures, I will go up on the tip of your wings; if you go up to the sky as snakes, I will go up on your coils; if you go up to the sky as uraei, I will go up on the tops of your heads, I have taken possession of my double for my body, and it will take me to the pools[3] of the Field of Offer-
62 ings of Rēꜥ. | I will eat, for my meal is there; the sixth-day festival is for my meal, the seventh-day festival is for my supper,[4] and acclamation is made for me in the train of Rēꜥ.

1. Fem., i.e. Ḥeḳet.

2. The above-mentioned deities.

3. Cf. *ꜥꜣꜥw*, *Pyr.* § 1200.

4. Cf. *Pyr.* § 716.

Spell 176

'The god comes in peace', say they who are in the full moon; they have given to me appearings in glory with Rēʿ. ASCENDING TO THE SKY, TO THE PLACE WHERE RĒʿ IS.

Spell 177

GIVING GIFTS TO A MAN IN ŌN. Hail to you, Ḥu, Baʿḥ, Neper, Sek! Hail to III, 63
you, you gods who make oblations to Rēʿ, [who are] with Ḥu, who are among the celestial kine. I eat of what Rēʿ bites, I sit on the thrones of the sunshine; to me belongs Ōnet,| [I have come from Ōnet . . .] behind me. Tefēnet is on 64
my arms, Wepwawet is on my loin-cloth, (even) he who is in his West;[1] they cause me to be nourished in[2] the Field of Offerings which belongs to Rēʿ. I eat and have gathered ⟨myself⟩ together like Him who presides over his Ennead,[3] who lives[4] among the celestial kine.

1. Both B4C and L1Li seem corrupt and M57C is damaged. Perhaps we should emend into *Wp-wꜣwt ḥr swḥ·i imy wnmw·f.*

2. Emending  of M57C into .

3. For *psḏt·f* 'his Ennead' M57C has *ḫt ẖrt-nṯr* 'the affairs of the necropolis'.

4. L1Li makes this participle feminine, as if it referred to *psḏt.*

Spell 178

GIVING GIFTS IN ŌN. Gifts are given in the Field of Offerings; when you give III, 65
everlasting, give me everlasting, and I will be content for ever.

Spell 179

Bringing bread in Ōn,| giving gifts in Ōn, not eating faeces in Ōn, appearing III, 66
as a god, worshipping the spirit of the Great Goddess.[1] | O Great Provider who 68
presides over houses,[2] to whom goes up the great-bread which is in the Broad Hall in Ōn| and invocation-offerings in Ōn, who gives great-bread[3] to Ptaḥ 69
in Ōn, give me bread and beer,[4] let me eat of the shin of beef[5] together with the *sꜣšrt*-bread.| O my double,[6] bring me some,[7] that I may eat some and be hale 71
thereby;[8] may offerings flourish for me.

1. So S10C; 'Great One' is fem. Varr. 'Giving bread in Ōn' B4C; D1C 'Giving clothes in Ōn', M57C; 'Causing a man's tomb to flourish in the realm of the dead' B2L, see also B3Bo.

2. The imperative *imy* or the optative *dy·k* of five versions of 70*a* as well as inherent probability indicate that the vocative *Ḏfꜣ-wr* is to be preferred to the statement *ink Ḏfꜣ-wr* of the variants. On the var. of B2L see de Buck's note, 68, n.3*.

3. Var. *t* 'bread' instead of *t-wr* 'great bread'.

4. Var. 'bread' only. B2L and B3Bo have the imperfective participle 'who gives'; T1C has 'give to me' only.

5. L1Li is quite clear, if *imy* 'cause', 'allow' be restored before *wnm*. M 57C, which is defective, refers again to *t* 'bread'; all the other texts have *iꜥw pw* with variants; this apparently means 'my breakfast is (shin of beef, etc.)', but the proposed restoration of L1Li fits better with what has gone before. For *ḫnd* in the sense of 'shin of beef' cf. *AEO* I, 17 f.

6. Var. 'O Ferryman of the Field of Rushes'.

7. The reading with *im* is probably secondary, but the sense in either case is clear. S10C has 'bring me this for a leg, water and a *mytf-wr* bird', and follows this up with 'may I be sent(?) like the bark of the god'.

Spell 180

III, 73 Hail to you who preside over abundance and who watch over provisions from out of the Field.[1] Give bread to N that N may eat of grain, that N may become Khopri like Him whose hair is parted,[2] that N may live again[3] among the celestial kine; that N may eat with his mouth like Him whose hair is parted;[4] and N may be loosed in his hinder parts like Selḳet. May breath be in N's nose and seed in his phallus like Him who is invisible of shape. NOT FALLING INTO THE LAKE OF ŠNWNW.[5]

1. Var. 'The Field of Standing'.

2. Var. T1L: 'like the name-repeater at the head of the celestial kine'. T2C omits the comparison. *Wpš* is shown by the dets. to be a faulty writing of *wp šnwy* in 73*g*.

3. Lit. 'repeat', in B2L only.

4. Not in B2L.

5. B2L only.

Spell 181

O Hearer! O Unstopper!—and *vice versa*—hear me, unstop me,[1] save me
III, 75 when I am heard,| for I am the Bull of Kenzet, a possessor of bread in [Ōn];
four portions are in the sky and three portions are on earth. These things have been made for me as gifts in Ōn which have been given to me, for I am the Bull with curly hair, having five portions in the House of Horus and two portions in the House of Seth; three portions are in the sky and three portions are on earth.[2] It is the Night-bark and the Day-bark which are daily taken for me to the House of the God. Faeces is my detestation, and I will not eat it, nor will I drink urine; I will not walk upside down, for it is Isis who rows me every day.

1. The negation is so opposite to the obvious sense of the spell as to be completely inexplicable except as a scribal aberration, and it has therefore been ignored in the translation; compare Spell 166 with n. 2.

2. The scribe has got his arithmetic muddled; here we have six portions only instead of the seven twice referred to above. Probably we should read 'four portions are in the sky'.

Spell 182

I am Isis; I have gone forth from my house and my boat is at the mooring- III, 76
rope;[1] Horus ferries me over, Horus[2] brings me to land[3] just as he brought the boatless Eye of Horus to land; if the Eye of Horus be not boatless, then will I not be boatless.[4] O you who fare downstream or upstream while I am boatless, bring me this,[5] bring me to land, for I have come with this chest of the gods, I have opened this chest of the gods. I have come down from Pe, I have
ferried over from Dep, I have landed[6] from my boat in Ōn,[1] I have tied the 77
mooring-rope in Djedu. Bring me this that I may go up; if this is what you have brought me today, the steering-oar of the god's bark will not be broken, its[7] tiller(?) will not be snapped, the stern-post will not be broken,[8] the warp will not be severed by reason of the crew of Rēʿ. O you who travel in the sky, I will row him with you, I will travel as Isis, for I am he who will ⟨bring⟩ this to him.

[My] boat shall be brought to me,[9] the mooring-post shall be driven in for me, sandals shall be laid down for me, because I am the heir of my father who brings me to this courtyard alone, alone. O you gods, bring me this.

1. S10C[a] omits *r ʿḳꜣ*.
2. Var. 'Seth'.
3. Read *smꜣ·f tꜣ im·i* with S10[b].
4. S10C[b] omits the negation.
5. The regular formula for demanding a ferry-boat, cf. *Urk.* V, 171 ff.
6. Read *smꜣ⟨-tꜣ⟩*.
7. Masc.; should be fem. to agree with *dpt*. On *ḫr-ʿ* and *imy-tp* see Spell 398, nn. 48.47.
8. S10C[a] ends here.
9. Read *dp*[*wt·f*], cf. de Buck, n. 3*. The pronouns of this passage refer to the deceased, and so should be emended from the 3rd person into the 1st, see 77*o.p.q*. On the confusions of pronouns in the Coffin Texts cf. *JEA* 35, 88 f. There is also some confusion in 77 *j–l*, where Isis speaks of the deceased in the 3rd person, and the pronouns of the 2nd person vary between sing. in 77*d* and plur. in 77*j*.

Spell 183

Giving bread in Ōn. Recitation: I am *Ḥwrr*, owner of six (*sic*) meals in the III, 78

Great Mansion; three portions are in the sky with Rēʿ-Atum, and two (*sic*) portions are on earth with Gēb. My[1] gifts are on the record of the Double-Master, scribe of the Field of Offerings; my wealth of food[2] and what appertains to bread are on the record of the Name-Repeater who presides over the celestial kine, because I am mistress[3] in the Great Mansion, one in charge of governance in the Field of Offerings among those counsels which were made on the Second Occasion.

1. Objective suffix, referring to the gifts received by the speaker.
2. *'ḥʿw*.
3. *Sic!* A man's coffin (Ḥarḥotpe).

Spell 184

III, 79 NOT TO EAT FAECES IN THE REALM OF THE DEAD, NOT TO WALK UPSIDE DOWN, TO HAVE POWER OVER WATER AND AIR, TO GO FORTH INTO THE DAY.[1] I am this lotus-haunting heron(?)[2] who acts the *gš*-bird,[3] who overawes[4] myriads.[5]
80 That which I doubly detest, I will not eat;| what I detest is faeces, and I will not eat it; I will not consume filth.[6] I will not go up for it with my hands, I will not tread on it with my sandals, touch it with my fingers.[7]
81 'What will you live on? What will you eat of?' say the gods to me.
'I will live on bread in the Field of Offerings, I will have abundance in the
82 Field of Rushes, my basket of the *nnt*-plant is in my hand,| my cloth-bag is of *twn*-plants.[8] I will never bow down to kiss my father Gēb,[9] I will never drink water from the plume which is on the water. There is given to me power over the pleasure(?) of copulation,[10] joy in pleasure(?) when desire comes,|
83 and contentment at the pleasure(?) of eating bread,[11] because I am this heron(?) which is on the plateau of the horizon of the sky, I fly up on to the eastern side of the sky, I alight on the western side of the sky,[12] I cross the sky like Rēʿ,|
84 I come to land like Thoth,[13] I am unique among them.'

1. This rubric in T1L only. B1L has a title in black (79*a*): 'To repel him who is under the tomb(?)'; this det. of *ḥ3t* 'tomb' seems unrecorded.
2. *Nwr pw sšnty*; for the bird *nwr* with a heron-like det. cf. *Pyr.* § 2179; *CT* III, 393*d*. T1L and B4C add the adjective 'great'. *Sšnty* could mean 'belonging to the lotus'.
3. Doubtless identical with the migratory birds *g3š* mentioned in *Wenamun*, 2,65. *Gš* with det. (T1L) is a *vox nihili*.
4. Cf. *Urk.* IV, 2081,19.
5. Var. 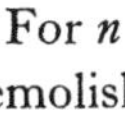 in B1L.
6. For *n ḫmy im·f* cf. also 84*h*; 85*f*; *BD* 123,8; 214,12; 244,1; apparently a figurative use of *ḫm* 'demolish', *JEA* 22, 178. In English we can speak of a hungry person 'demolishing' a meal. Var. T1L, B4C: 'I will not partake of it'.

7. Only in B3Bo and originally in B4C.

8. For *snd*-cloth cf. *Urk.* I, 296,9; *CT* I, 109*a*; *Pyr.* § 661, where the word seems to mean 'sail'. The additional det. ○ suggests that the 'cloth' may be in the form of a round bag, cf. *iw ḳꜣr TMN m ṯwn* 'the King's bag is of the *ṯwn*-plant, *Pyr.* § 557. T1L appears to read: 'my cords (*rwdw*) are of the *ṯwn*-plant'; B4C seems to have confused *rwd* and *sk*.

9. Var. 'I will never bow down to my father Gēb'.

10. Var. *ꜣḫ m nk* 'power over copulation'.

11. T1L and B4C only.

12. B1L and B3Bo reverse the order to 'western' and 'eastern', but B9C accords with the movements of the sun. T1L seems to share the confusion of B1L and B3Bo.

13. Note *mr* for *my* in B3Bo. T1L and B4C omit *tꜣ* after *smꜣ* and for 'Thoth' substitute 'Sothis'.

Spell 185

What I doubly detest, I will not eat. Faeces is my detestation, and I will not eat; I will not consume filth, because I am Anubis, Bull of his Side (*sic*).

Spell 186

What I doubly detest, I will not eat. Faeces is my detestation, and I will not III, 85
eat; I will not consume filth, I will not go to you[1] upside down, I will not drink
urine for you, because I am this Great One who fought the hostile ones(?),[2]
for whom are made nine portions from the store of Osiris; four portions are
in the sky with Rēʿ, three portions are on earth with Gēb, and two portions 86
are in the temple—so says *ꜣẖbẖb* son of *ʾIsḥnn*; so says Nu. 'Enter', said *Ḳꜣḳꜣ*,
for I am he who has power over portions, because[3] I will not eat faeces.

'What will you live on? What will you swallow?' say the gods.

'I will live on that pleasant tree which is in the god's shrine.'

'Where[4] is it granted to you to eat?' 87

'I will eat under[5] this sycamore which is south of Nefrusi, under the branches of the *ỉṯnws*-tree'

1. The gods of the Beyond.

2. So B1L and B3Bo, B9C appears to be corrupt. With *snṯt* here interpreted as a collective 'the hostile ones' compare *znṯ* 'hostile', *Pyr.* § 1837; *snṯw* 'enemies', *CT* IV, 115*f*; VII, 401*a*; *BD* 281,13. The det. suggests that the 'hostile ones' were deemed to have come from the desert, and the plural strokes in two instances out of three point to the word being a collective.

3. *ʾIn* must be the full form of the preposition *n* in its meaning of 'because'; no other interpretation makes sense.

4. B9C adds a superfluous suffix to *ṯn*.

5. B9C omits *ẖr*.

Spell 187

What I doubly detest, I will not eat. Faeces is my detestation, and I will not
III, 88 eat;[l] I will not consume filth, for to me belongs this white bright crown of
Anubis. Its bread is of the zizyphus-tree, its beer is of white emmer, there is
made for it a portion therefrom of red emmer. There have gone forth the
supports(?) of the White Crown, the power-givers of uraei; two fields are in
89 the midst of . . .;[1] I have a throne which the Silent One seized for me[l] in
order to protect his bread, because I will not eat faeces for you.[2]

'What will you live on?' say the gods.

'I will live on those three portions which were made for Osiris; one is for Horus, another for Seth,[3] and another for me, and I am their third.'

'What does Osiris live on?' say the gods.'

90 'He lives on this green plant[l] which is on the river-banks of *Ggws*'.

I have come today into the presence of Ptaḥ, and he has made me with this
baton of their warriors,[4] he has made me a seat on the block(?)[5] which is over
the entrance[6] of the horizon of the sky. I found Khons on the way when he was
going down ⟨to⟩ Punt, and he has caused thousands to stand up for me and
hundreds to sit down for me as my brother and my sister, as the living, male
91 and female,[l] as men, as my family, as my fellow-citizens, male and female,
who are raised up(?). He has come to his realm(?) his entrance is at his hand,
his . . .[7] behind him when he lives.[8]

'May you drink', say the horizon-dwellers to me. 'May you live on what we live on, may you eat of what we eat of, may you drink of what we drink of'.

1. Totally obscure.
2. Read *in tr r·f n wnm·i n·k ḥs*, cf. 86*e*.
3. Var. B1L: 'Osiris'.
4. In B9C *sšm* has det. [hieroglyph] instead of [hieroglyph]. *ꜥḥꜣw* 'warriors' in three texts, lost in B15C, but what can this mean? B1L omits the suffix *·sn* after *ꜥḥꜣw* and ends.
5. *Ḏbꜣt* seems here to mean a block of earth or stone on which one can sit, cf. *ḏbꜣt* 'basis' of shrine, *Wb.* V, 561,13.
6. Regarding *pgꜣ* as sing. with B15C; B3Bo has completely muddled the word.
7. *Nyt, nywt, syt,* meaning unknown.
8. So B9C; the varr. have *ꜥnḫ·sn*. For this obscure plural suffix cf. 90*c*.

Spell 188

III, 92 What I doubly detest, I will not eat. Faeces is my detestation and I will not eat; I will not consume filth. I will not go up for it with my hands, I will not tread on it with my sandals, touch it with my fingers.

'What will you live on[1] in the place into which you have come?' say the horizon-dwellers to me.

'I will live on those seven portions which have gone forth from upon the 93
great altars of the Souls of Ōn. Their[2] four portions are in the sky with Rēʿ, their three portions are on the earth with Gēb.'

'Where has it been granted to you to eat?' say the horizon-dwellers to me.

'I will eat under this myrrh-tree, having the breezes of Nefrusi.'

'Welcome,[3] O swimmer of sheep! We will swim on your tail.[4] We[5] will live 94
on the cakes of your store-chest,[6] we will drink of the contents of your jars'.[7]

'How shall I act? You will live on the cakes of my store-chest, you will drink of the contents of my jars'.

'Act when we dig your ponds, when we plant your trees and build your mansions'.

'There is bread for him who does my work, I will give bread to him who does my work'.[8]

I will knot the ropes for Rēʿ in the sky, I will bring him to land in the beauti- 95
ful West. I will knot my ropes in the sky like Rēʿ, I will land in the beautiful West. Bring me this![9]

'Who are you?' say the . . . to me.[10]

1. B9C and B1L omit the interrogative.

2. *S* in all texts in concord with *ẖt* of 92*m*, which is sing. in Egyptian.

3. Reading *iy wy ḥm* in all texts; *nḥm* of B9C is an obvious slip.

4. *Nb* 'swim' is used here in two different ways. In the first instance it is used transitively of 'swimming' a flock of sheep (*sḥt*, cf. *Wb.* III, 464,2) over an imaginary canal, and secondly it has its more usual intransitive sense. *Ḫr sd·k* is a modern-sounding idiom for 'following after you'.

5. The suffix in *ḥꜣdt·k* shows that this passage continues the speech addressed by the horizon-dwellers to the deceased, but only B1L has the correct reading *ʿnḫ·n*.

6. After *fḳꜣw* 'cakes' B9C adds *ḥnḳt* 'beer'. The translation of *ḥꜣdt* as 'store-chest' rests on the det. and the context, but the word certainly refers to a container of some sort, cf. *ḥꜣd* 'fish-trap', *Concise Dict.* 164, which seems to have consisted of a large basket. *Wb.* III, 36,9, does not allot any meaning to this word.

7. A free translation of *šʿw syft·k*. *Šʿw*, clearly a drink, looks like a masc. var. of *šʿyt* in *Wb.* IV, 421,1; *syft* is not recorded, but from the context appears to refer to jars for storing drink. The same collocation recurs in 94*e*.

8. In 95*a* B1L repeats 94*j*.

9. The regular summons for the celestial ferry-boat.

10. For *in·s* read *in·sn*; who the *ʿꜣw* are is not clear. The text ends here, so that the reply to this question is not forthcoming.

Spell 189[1]

III, 96 What I detest, I will not eat. Faeces is my detestation, and I will not eat; I will not consume filth; I will not tread on them with my feet, I will not touch it with my fingers. I have ploughed, I have reaped, I have made a cake of
97 dough in the Island of Fire, I break my fast on white emmer, I sup on red (?) emmer, my endowment is seven portions which are issued from the great altars of the Souls of Ōn; its four portions are in the sky with Rēʿ, its three portions are on earth with Gēb.

I have tied up the bark to the land, my endowments are with those who are in Ōn. Its papyrus-stems are cut, its lacings(?) are twisted, its hull is frapped.[2] A way to the sky is made for me, and I am king of those who are yonder.

1. For a full account of this spell see my article 'Boat-building in the Coffin Texts' in *Rev. d'Ég.* 24,60.
2. A reference to the building of a reed canoe.

Spell 190

III, 98 What I doubly detest, I will not eat.[1] Faeces is my detestation, and I will not eat; I will not consume filth. I will not go up to it with my fingers, I will not tread on it with my toes.[2] If they[3] say to me: 'What will you live on?' (I will reply) 'I will live on the white emmer which is in the eastern corner of the sky'. I have gone up as a swallow,[4] I have cackled as a goose, I have alighted on this great plateau; as for anyone who alights on it, he will never die, and he whose hands are hidden[5] will be seen as a god. My springs(?) of water[6] go forth for me, the stream is spat out for me, and there are opened to me the gates of the horizon, the good place of the sky wherein I would dwell.

1. B1L only.
2. For *n ḫnd·i ḥr·f* of B1L, B9C has *n bb·i im·f* 'I will not wade in it'.
3. The denizens of the Beyond.
4. So rather than 'great one', despite the writing; in the next sentence the deceased is likened to another bird, the goose; cf. also 130*f.g*. For *wr* 'swallow' cf. *Pyr.* §§ 1130. 1216.
5. I.e. swathed in bandages as a mummy.
6. The translation of *tꜣḥ·i* ⟨*n*⟩ *nt* as 'my springs(?) of water' rests on the next sentence; and on 145*f*; *tꜣḥ*, from the same stem as *tꜣḥt* 'dregs', seems to refer to a small flow of water as contrasted with *itrw* 'streams' in 98*o*. For *nt* 'water' cf. Sethe. *Alphabet*, 153; B1L makes it clear that this word is meant.

Spell 191

III, 99 SPELL FOR NOT EATING FAECES IN THE WEST. O child of faeces, do not bring your faeces to me.

'What will you live on?'[1]

'I am the Bull of *Ḥnnt* which is in[2] the limits of the sky, I am the owner of five great portions with Osiris;[3] | three portions are in the sky and two on 100
earth.[4] 〈. . .〉 has ordained[5] that this name of mine should live for ever; he has vomited me from his mouth and blown me out of his nose. These two great and mighty gods who eat food on the banks of the sky have ordained that when they ascend to the sky as falcons, I am on their wings; | when they des- 101
cend to the earth as snakes, my feet are on their coils. There have been given to me the sixth-day festival for my breakfast and the seventh-day festival for my supper,[6] and I have heard the praises in the mouth of the shorn priest in Ōn.'[7]

1. In red in S1C and S2C.
2. So S1C and the damaged S2C. B9C makes 'the Bull of *Ḥnnt*' the speaker, whereas the repeated *ink* of 99*f* confirms the reading of S1C and S2C in 99*e* and shows that the latter is part of the answer of the deceased. B4C has simply 'Bull of *Sḥnt* who is in . . .', omitting both *ink* of S1C and S2C and *ḥrw·fy* of B9C and B1L, the latter being quite corrupt.
3. B9C and B1L: 'these five great portions'; B4C substitutes (99*g–i*): 'What I doubly detest, this N (*sic*) will not eat; her detestation [. . .]' and ends.
4. Var. B1L: 'three' and 'three'.
5. The subject of *syp·n* has been omitted, cf. 100*e*.
6. S1C has combined the sixth and seventh days into a single group.
7. S1C and S2C only.

Spell 192

NOT TO EAT FAECES AND NOT TO DRINK URINE. What I doubly detest, I will not III, 102
eat. Faeces is my detestation, I will not eat; I will not consume filth,[1] | I will not 104
go up to it with my fingers,[2] I will not tread on it with my toes,[3] filth shall not enter into my belly.

'On what will you live?' say they to me. 106

'On these seven portions. | Four portions are in the sky with Orion and three on earth in the Day-bark,[4] which go forth from upon the altars of the Souls of Ōn, because I am this Sole One to whom Anubis has bowed, whose members Anubis has strengthened'.

'Where will you eat?'[5] 108

'Upon the rushes, upon the rushes which are in front of *Ḥknws*, and I make jubilation for my double'.[6]

NOT EATING FAECES IN THE REALM OF THE DEAD.[6]

1. S1C[a] inserts here an anticipation of 104*c*. 103*d.f* is the correct text.
2. Var. S1C[a]: 'my hands'; B2Bo has omitted *·f* of the dative.

3. Varr. 'sandals', 'feet'.

4. S1C[a] inserts before this clause: 'Four are in the House of Horus, three are in the House of Thoth'.

5. In red in S1C[a].

6. Var. B1Bo: *bꜣ* 'soul'.

7. B1Bo only.

Spell 193[1]

III, 110 O filth,[2] | I will not eat you with my mouth, I will not go up for you with my
111 hands,[3] | I will not tread on you[4] with my feet. | My garden is in the Field of Offerings, my . . .[5] are in the Field of Rushes.[6] Be far from me, O bearer of faeces!

1. B2Bo begins with a rubric 'Spell for not drinking urine', but the spell says nothing about drinking.

2. *Ḥtp-wr* is a variant of *ḥtp-kꜣ*.

3. Var. B1Bo: 'with his fingers, with his hands'.

4. For *ḥr·k* S1C has obscurely *hr·s*.

5. *Ḥꜣwt* is quite obscure.

6. B1Bo and B2Be omit 'in the Field of'.

Spell 194[1]

III, 112 Recitation for not eating faeces. Even if Rēʿ is very hungry and Ḥatḥōr very thirsty, I will not eat the earthy dust(?)[2] with which threshing-floors are covered. O you door-keeper of the mud(?) of the Two Lands, bring me my ferry-boat, take me under your care in this rowing-boat of yours, for I am pure among the pure ones in the presence of the Lords of Eternity,[3] one who chews myrrh and lives by righteousness. I am strong, and I attain to the blessed state.

1. See Spell 189, n.1.

2. *Wṯst Gb* lit. 'the rising thing of the earth'. The context suggests dust flying up into the air.

3. Both texts are corrupt. Read perhaps *wʿb ⟨wi⟩ m-m wʿbw r-gs nbw nḥḥ ḏt*.

Spell 195[1]

III, 113 What N doubly detests, he will not eat. Faeces is N's detestation, N will not eat; N will not partake of filth. N will not eat it with his mouth, this N will not touch it with my fingers.

'On what will this N live?' say the gods of the New Moon Festival.

This N will live on these seven (portions) which are issued from the altars

of the Souls of Ōn; four portions are in the sky with Rēʿ and three portions are on earth with Gēb. O N, cut the papyrus-stems, twist the lacings(?) and frap the hull! N has come, N has cut the papyrus-stems, N has twisted the lacings(?), N has frapped the hull, N is the king of those who are yonder.| N 114
has come today to Ptaḥ, he has made a baton which beats their great ones. N sits on a throne in front of the horizon, N found Khons standing in his path when he came down from Punt, and he has caused N to have stood with thousands and to have sat with hundreds of brethren and fellow-citizens. 'The Follower has come', say they of the New Moon Festival; 'he lives on what we live on, he eats of what we eat of, he drinks of what we drink of'.

1. See Spell 189, n.1.

Spell 196

My heart has . . .,[1] my double has power, I am installed with Rēʿ, and Rēʿ III, 115
instals me with these great gods who descend to their meal in the festival of the seventh day. They have gone down[2] to the earth as snakes, and I have gone down on their coils; they have ascended to the sky as falcons, and I have gone up on their wings. They have installed[3] me on the banks of the horizon, and I have eaten with them the sixth-day festival for my (main) meal and the seventh-day festival for my supper. I hear acclamation in the mouths of the shorn priests—twice.

1. *Bḥ*, meaning unknown, not in *Wb*.
2. Emend into *hꜣ·n·sn*, cf. 115*f* and *pr·n* of 115*g.h*.
3. Read *wdn⟨·n⟩·sn*, cf. *wnm·n·i* of 115*j*.

Spell 197

NOT TO EAT FAECES IN THE REALM OF THE DEAD. I am the companion of those III, 116
two gods who ascend to the sky as falcons and I ascend on their wings; who descend to the earth as snakes,| and I descend on their coils. I will not eat 117
faeces for you, I will not walk upside down for you,[1] I will not depart bowed down for you, I will depart upstanding. My phallus is on me, it being attached;[2] | my anus is on me, it being attached. I eat with my mouth, I 118
defaecate with my anus.

'What will you live on?' say those who are yonder to me.

'I have stopped up the two apertures(?)[3] in Djedu, I have opened up the two fields in *'Irw*,[4] | because I belong to those messengers[5] of If-he-wishes- 119
he-does'.

1. S6C only. To whom the plural 'you' refers is not clear; it may be to 'those who are yonder' mentioned below.

2. The meaning given to *dmy* is based on *GNS* 41. That it is a verb in the old perfective, despite the det., is shown by 118*a*, where we have the fem. *dmy·t*(*y*). Cf. also 121*a.b*.

3. Lit. perhaps 'nostrils'. The det. in two texts is borrowed from *šrt* 'a plant', 21*a*.

4. Var. S6C: 'the quarry'.

5. Qualified by the fem. demonstrative *tw*, by confusion with *wpwt* 'message', as likewise the fem. genitive in 119*b*.

Spell 198

III, 120 I am the third of these gods who ascend to the sky as falcons,| and I ascend on their wings; who descend to the earth as snakes, and I descend on their coils. I will not eat filth for you, I will not depart bowed down for you, I will

121 depart upstanding.| My phallus is on me, it being attached; my anus is on me, it being attached. I eat with my mouth, I defaecate with my anus.

'What will you live on?' say those who are yonder.

122 'Three portions are in the sky with Rēʿ, four portions are on earth with Gēb. It is the Night-bark and the Day-bark which bring them to me daily in the two ships of Rēʿ.

Spell 199

III, 123 What I doubly detest, I will not eat. Faeces is my detestation, and I will not eat; I will not consume filth, I will not approach it[1] with my fingers, I will not tread on it with my toes.

124 'What will you live on?'| say those who are yonder.

'On a *sꜣšrt*-cake of red emmer, on a loaf(?) of twisted(?) barley'.[2]

'Where is it granted to you to eat?' say those who are yonder.

'Under the branches of the sycamores; I desire it, together with the minstrels of Ḥatḥōr, for I am this bull on whom are[3] his testicles,[4] who went forth from Ōn.

1. Note the use of the adverb *n*(*y*) 'thereto' after *n ʿr·i*' instead of *n* + suffix.

2. *Kpyt*, translated as 'loaf' by virtue of the det. and the context, is not recorded. The significance of *snḥ* 'twisted' or 'tied' in relation to barley is not clear.

3. Surely rather than 'who is on', which in this context does not make sense.

4. For *isn* cf. *CT* I, 30*b* (B4C), where the dual is written out.

Spell 200

III, 125 Not to go upside down. O Faeces, 'I-will-not-befoul-her'[1] is your name.

You have befouled Horus who is in his . . .,[2] you have befouled the vessels(?)[3] of the living; if you make presentation to me, you present his night to Rēʿ.[4]

1. *Ḥs* appears to be a denominative verb from *ḥs* 'faeces'. The fem. object-pronoun is due to the coffin being that of a woman.
2. *Ngꜣ*, meaning not known; possibly a garment.
3. Cf. *ḫtw* 'ducts(?)' of eye, *Pyr.* § 451.
4. I.e. consign the sun to outer darkness; despite the absence of a det. for Rēʿ, the suffix in *wḫ·f* implies that the god is meant, and not merely a word for 'day'.

Spell 201

I am the Bull[1] of Darkness, owner of two portions in earth with Gēb and three
in the sky with Rēʿ.[2] | I will be in the arms of the Field,[3] and She who is in the III, 126
pestilence is flourishing.[4] What I doubly detest, I will not eat. Faeces is my detestation and I will not eat; the *ssnnw* of my father are urine[5] and I will not
drink them.[6] I go upstanding, for to be upside down is my detestation. | The 127
Followers of Rēʿ are those who serve me, for I am a child of *Wnpy* the son of Thoth. Impurities are my detestation, and I will never eat them, faeces being (cast away) behind the pleasant things which are in the shrine of the gods.[7]

1. B1Bo omits 'bull'.
2. Var. 'owner of five portions in the temple; its three portions are in the sky with Rēʿ, its two portions are on earth with Gēb'.
3. So S1C; in the other two texts *m-ʿ* follows *wnn*.
4. Var. 'he flourishes in the Winding Waterway; he rests (so BH3Ox) [in(?)] the Field, the Lord of Pestilence'; for *iꜣdw* 'pestilence' see also *CT* VII, 412*c*. The real meaning of 126*a–c* escapes me.
5. Var. '⟨My(?)⟩ *ssnnw* are urine'. The meaning of *ssnnw* is quite obscure; if it were not for the man-det. in S1C, one might have suspected it of being a synonym of *bwt* 'detestation'.
6. Reading *n swr·n* ⟨*·i*⟩ *sn* with S1C. The varr. omit the object of *swr*.
7. Var. 'excretion (for burning) is behind the pleasant things'; for the meaning of *sfẖt* cf. *sfẖw* used of what the body rejects in 58*a*; 141*g*. *Ḥꜣw* 'behind' is to be understood as 'cast away behind'.

Spell 202

What I detest, I will not eat. Faeces is my detestation and I will not eat; filth III, 128
shall not enter into my belly, I will not go up to it with my hands, I will not tread on it with my sandals. I am protected from you who are bowed down,[1] I will not walk upside down. He who serves me is the servant of Horus, for I am one of you.

'What will you live on?' say the lords of Pe.

129 I will live on what they live on, I will eat of what they eat; I will live on what they live on, I will live on that pleasant[2] tree which is in his (*sic*) shrine, on which the Followers of Rēˁ live, for I indeed dwell in his shrine, being pure; I will enter into him and save(?) him.[3]

1. Reading ***mk·i m-ˁ·k*** ***⟨k⟩st*** with S1C; B1Bo has *iw nḥm·n sw Pty* [. . .] *r ks* 'P. has saved him in order to(?) bow down'.
2. *Bnr* omitted in S1C.
3. So B1C; B1Bo has obscurely *ˁk·f šdy n·f*. The exact sense of *šdy* is doubtful.

Spell 203

SPELL FOR POWER IN THE WEST,[1] NOT TO EAT FAECES[2] AND NOT TO WALK UPSIDE
III, 130 DOWN.[3] | O you who reject[4] faeces in Ōn, be far from me, for I am the Bull whose throne is equipped. I have flown up as a swallow,[5] I have cackled as a goose, I have alighted under the sycamore which nurses(?) its . . .,[6] which is in the
131 midst of the flood.[7] As for him who alights on it,[8] | he will not suffer neglect; and as for him who is under it, he will be as the great god.

132 What I doubly detest, I will not eat. Faeces is my detestation, and I will not eat; filth shall not enter into my body. I will not go up to it with my
133 hands, I will not tread on it with my sandals, | I will not flow into bowls,[9] I will not pour(?) for you into ewers,[10] I will not act for you upside down,[11] I will not take (water) for you on the banks of the pools.[12]

134 THUS SAYS THAT ONE WHO CANNOT COUNT: 'WHAT WILL YOU LIVE ON IN THIS LAND TO WHICH YOU HAVE COME THAT YOU MAY BECOME A SPIRIT?'

'I will live on bread of black emmer and on beer of white emmer on the Field of Offerings, for this distinction of mine is more than that of any god;
136 there will be affluence in Kher-ˁaḥa and affluence in Ōn'.[13] | What I detest, I will not eat. Faeces is my detestation, and I will not eat; filth shall not enter into my body. I will not go up to it with my hands, I will not tread on it with my sandals.'[14]

THUS SAYS THAT ONE WHO CANNOT COUNT: 'WHAT WILL YOU LIVE ON IN THIS LAND TO WHICH YOU HAVE COME THAT YOU MAY BE A SPIRIT?'

137 'I will live on seven portions of bread;[15] | four loaves are in the House of Horus and three in the House of Thoth'.

'Who will bring it to you?'

'It is the nurse[16] of the House of Horus and the stewardess(?)[17] of the Souls of Ōn who will bring it to me'.

THUS SAYS THAT ONE WHO CANNOT COUNT: 'WILL YOU LIVE ON SOMEONE ELSE'S GOODS EVERY DAY?'

'There will be ploughed for me two fields in *Ỉꜣw*'.

'WHO WILL PLOUGH THEM FOR YOU?'

'It is the greatest of those who are among the gods of the sky and the gods of earth(?) ⟨who will plough them for me(?)'⟩.[18]

'WITH WHAT WILL ONE THRESH[19] FOR YOU?'

'One will thresh for me as Apis who presides over *Nsꜣw*; one will tread in 138
(seed)[20] for me as Seth, Lord of the Northern sky'.

'WHERE WILL YOU EAT IT?'

'Under the branches of the *ḥs-nfrt* tree[21] which supports *Ḥknws*.[1] As 139
regards the shrouded one(?)[22] of the worship of the Two Lands, a path has been made for me, and here I am, I have brought the supports(?)[23] of the Green Crowns, the [. . .] of the uraei. I have travelled around the sky over its four corners, and I sit in the place where I desire to be'.

1. Var. 'in the knowledge of the god'. The translation in general follows S1C.

2. Repeated in S1C; T3Be: 'by the blessed N'.

3. Only in S1C; T3Be: 'he says'.

4. *Ḥs*, var. *ḥss*, is apparently to be understood in the sense of *ḥsy* 'turn back', here in the sense of 'rejecting' filth to get rid of it; to interpret the word as 'praise' leads to nonsense. In S1C it is written like *ḥs* 'befoul' of 125*b–d*. Since in 130*d* this being is to be avoided by the deceased, there is a suggestion that the 'rejecter of faeces' was thought of as a sanitary worker who collected filth and dumped it; cf. 'be far from me, O bearer of faeces' in 111*e*.

5. See Spell 190, n.4.

6. *Ḥknw*.

7. Varr. T1Be: 'I have caused myself to alight on the twigs of the *ḥs-nfrt* tree (cf 138*d*) which is in the middle of the island of the flood-land': T3Be: 'I have caused myself to alight on the beautiful sycamore which is in the middle of the mound of the two sycamores of the flood-land'.

8. Var. 'he who ascends and alights'.

9. *Sšw* in S1C is dual, but plural in T1Be, with the plural suffix *·ṯn*. T3Be absurdly: 'you shall not drag me into bags'(!). For *šsr* 'bag' cf. *Urk*. IV, 1143,12; if *sšr̦* here is really the same word, it speaks against Gardiner's reading of the Dyn. XVIII word as *šsr*, *BIFAO* 30,179.

10. The verb *pn* (*pnn*) is guessed from the context to mean 'pour'; it could be connected with *pnn* 'strew', *Wb*. I, 510,2. *Nbꜣ* in S1C, with det. , could mean 'ewer', compare *nbꜣ* with det. 'ointment-horn(?)', Brit. Mus. 6655; the same peculiar det. is found with *pnn* 'spindle(?)',

45*a* above. The det. of *nbꜣ* in T3Be is probably due to confusion with *nbꜣ* 'carrying-pole' of litter, *Westc.* 7,12. T1Be omits 133*b*. 133*a.b* may perhaps refer to the disposal of urine, but to whom the plur. *ṯn* in 133*b* ff. refers is not clear.

11. S1C only.

12. For *šdwt* 'pools' the varr. have *šdw* with det. , which makes nonsense of the preceding *spty* 'banks'. After this clause the varr. interpolate: 'because I know you and know your names'.

13. 134*h* in S1C only. 134*i*–135*i* do not occur in S1C and may well be a long interpolation. The text of T3Be is corrupt and yields no intelligible sense, while T2Be is badly damaged, so that these passages have been passed over in the translation.

14. T3Be and T2Be omit 136*e*–*h*.

15. Emending *ẖt 7 w nt ẖt* into *ẖt 7 nt t*, cf. 137*a*. T3Be reads 'I will live on bread'; so apparently T2Be.

16. *H̱nmt* may well be a reduction of *ẖnmtt* 'nurse', *Concise Dict.* 193, though *Wb.* III, 293, 11–13 treats it as a separate but synonymous word.

17. *Ḥṯꜣwtt* is an early spelling of *ḥtꜣty* in *BD* 495,9. The meaning guessed here depends both on the context and the parallelism with *ẖnmt* 'nurse'.

18. Obscure as it stands and probably corrupt. I suggest emending into *in wrw imyw nṯrw pt nṯrw tꜣ* ⟨*skꜣ·sn n·i st*⟩. The presence of *in* at the head of the sentence implies a lost verbal predicate parallel to 137*d*. 137*e*–*i* are omitted in T2Be.

19. Reading the first word as *ḥw·tw*, impersonal *sḏm·f* form.

20. Reading this strangely spelt word as *pys·tw* with donkey-det.; for this verb cf. *JEA* 3, 100, n.1. A normal spelling—without det.—in 139*a* (T2Be).

21. Cf. 130*h* (T1Be). *BD*495, 10 has *ḏbꜣty-nfrt*.

22. Read *ṯꜣyty*; can the allusion be to Osiris? 138*e*–139*b* only in T2Be, which is both damaged and disordered, and appears to be a bungled interpolation.

23. For *smnw* 'supports' cf. *Concise Dict.* 228; the det. here suggests that an abstract sense 'means of support' may be intended.

Spell 204

RECITATION FOR NOT EATING FAECES OR WALKING UPSIDE DOWN IN THE REALM
III, 140 OF THE DEAD.[1] | O Provider of life, bring me this, for I am . . .,[2] I am[3] Apis who is in the sky, long of horns,[4] fair of names,[5] far-sighted,[6] far-striding: I am at
142 nurse,[7] | efflux[8] is my detestation and I will not eat; discharge,[9] and I will not drink.[10] I will not go up with my fingers,[11] I will not tread on it[12] with my sandals, I will walk on my feet, I will not be upside down.[13]

1. The variant texts have only 'not walking upside down', but S10C adds: 'sending a soul into the realm of the dead'.

2. *Hꜣt*, varr. *ꜣht*, *htt*, *ht*, meaning obscure.

3. S1C and B2L omit *ink*.

4. S10C reads: 'who is among the bulls, who is in the sky, mighty of horns, [. . .] of horns'.

5. Var. B1Bo, S10C: 'who makes you fair'.

6. *Pḏ irty*, synonym of *pḏ-ḥr* 'far-sighted', 'prescient'; for the latter cf. Caminos, *L.-Eg. Misc.* 424.

7. Lit. 'I am on my nurse (*mnʿt*)'. S1C repeats this sentence with the synonymous *ꜣṯt* for *mnʿt*.

8. Var. S1C 'efflux of the earth'.

9. For *sfḫ* 'discharge' (med.) see Spell 201, n.7.

10. After this sentence M5C interpolates unnecessarily *wsšt* 'urine'.

11. Var. S1C: 'hands'.

12. For *ḥr·s* read *ḥr·f* as e.g. 136*h*; *ḥs* and *ḥtp-kꜣ* are masc.

13. B3C adds a rubric: 'not to walk upside down in the realm of the dead'. B2L adds an extension of its opening rubric: 'in the realm of the dead in very deed'.

Spell 205

NOT TO WALK UPSIDE DOWN. A voice is raised in the northern sky, wailing is in III, 143
the marshland, because of the voice of the summoning of the blessed one. I
am raised up to the place where Māʿet is, | I have flown up to them as a swallow,[1] 144
like Thoth; I cackle to them as a goose, like[2] the Wine-press God; I fly up as
a vulture[3] | on this great plateau that I may stand on it.[4] I appear as a god, for 145
he who looks at them will never die. The water-springs(?) of the marshes of
the Mansions of the Red Crown[5] are the flame of the Eye of Horus.

Faeces is my detestation, and I will not eat for you; urine is my detestation, 146
and I will not drink for you;[6] walking upside down is my detestation, and I
will on no account perform the recitation for you.

'What will you live on | at this place to which you have come? There will not 147
look at you those seven[7] spirits who lift Rēʿ up, who show Rēʿ, who live on
faeces, | who quench their thirst with urine, who walk upside down'.[8] 148

'I am one equipped against them, | I will sever connection with them on that 149
day of going to the Tribunal of Rēʿ. I will live on what they live on, | I will eat 150
of what they eat of, I will sit in the place where they sit,[9] I will live on cucumbers,
figs, *wnšw* and grapes,[10] | I will travel around[11] to the limit of the horizon, to 151
the place where my double desires to dwell'.

'What have you come for, what have you come for?'

'Seven portions are in the House of Horus,[12] three portions are in the sky
and two are on earth; | it is the Night-bark and the Day-bark which will bring 152
to me all portions from upon the altars of the Souls of Ōn'.[13]

1. Cf. Spell 190, n.4.

2. Var. 'of'; S2C and B2Bo have the direct genitive. B9C omits 'I cackle to them'.

3. The translation of *gbgꜣ* as 'vulture' rests on the detailed det. in B1Bo, which appears identical with Gardiner, Sign-list, G1.

4. B2Be adds: 'that I may sit on it'.

5. Var. 'of Mut' in B2Bo.

6. S1C omits *n·t̲n*; it is not clear who is being addressed.

7. Var. S1C: 'four'.

8. B1Bo inserts: 'This N shall say: He will not give ⟨for(?)⟩ those seven spirits who lift up Rēʿ', etc.; B2Be has a var. of this, reading *ny·f r*.

9. *·Sn* here presumably refers to the tribunal of Rēʿ, hardly to the seven spirits aforesaid. The varr. are oddly in the 2nd person, 'what you (plur.) live on', etc.

10. Varr. B1Bo: 'grapes, *išd* and *wnš*'; B2Be: 'grapes, cucumbers and *wnš*.'

11. S2C, B1Bo and B2Be insert *nn* 'here'.

12. So B1Bo and B2Be.

13. B1Bo and B2Be append the rubric: 'Recitation for not eating filth in the realm of the dead'; note the writing of *wnm* in B1Bo, see also 128*b* above.

Spell 206

III, 153 NOT TO WALK UPSIDE DOWN. An obstacle[1] is built in Djedu, I have ploughed two fields of rushes, two *dōm*-palms are their guardians. I have taken away the
154 tongue of the Silent One, | I grind my food with it. I will not eat faeces, I will not drink urine, I will not walk upside down, but I will dwell in the place where I desire to be; that is Djedu.

1. Apparently a noun derived from *šr* 'stop up', 'block'.

Spell 207

III, 155 RECEIVING GIFTS IN ŌN.[1] O you two who gave birth in the night, come that you may bear me.[2] O you two who conceived Rēʿ, you shall bear me who am in
157 the egg; when you have borne me,[3] | you shall nurse me. My heart is glad at the head of the Netherworld, and the hearts of the gods are glad when they see
159 me young.[4] The sixth-day festival is for my breakfast | and the seventh-day festival for my supper; dappled cows are slaughtered for me for my *wꜣg* festival.[5] I have desired that there be given to me what ought to be given to me,[6] because I am the Bull of Ōn.

NOT TO EAT FAECES NOR DRINK [URINE] IN THE REALM OF THE DEAD[7]

1. G1T substitutes: 'Recitation for being the scribe of Khons'.

2. Reading *my ms·t̲n wi* in S2C ff; B2Bo[a] ff. apparently take *ms* as a second imperative: 'come and bear me'. S1C omits *my*.

3. Read *sk ꜣ ms·n·t̲n wi* as S2C.

4. M22C–P. Gard II omit *rnp·ky*; B2L–P. Gard. II add: 'O young one, your heart is in me'.

5. Cf. *Pyr.* § 716. S1C has miswritten *snt* 'sixth-day festival' as if it were the word for 'shrine'. A majority of texts have the apparently superfluous adverb *im* at the end.

6. It seems impossible to extract a coherent sense from the varying texts as they stand; possibly the archetypal reading was *mr·n·i rdy·tw n·i ddt n·i.*

7. S1C only.

Spell 208

TO BE THE SCRIBE OF ḤATḤŌR AND TO BECOME THE BULL OF ŌN. I am the Bull of III, 161
Offerings, owner of five portions in Ōn. Three portions are in the sky with Horus and two on earth with the Great One; it is the Night-bark and the Day-bark which bring to me daily.

Faeces is my detestation, and I will not eat; urine is my detestation, and 162
there is none with me;[1] it is the Morning Star which serves me daily.[2]

1. B1Bo[c] substitutes: 'he will not drink'.
2. B1Bo[c] adds a rubric: 'Writing down the offerings of Rēꜥ-Atum'.

Spell 209

Get back, you whose body is hot and who lust after(?) your *smꜥt*-plant, III, 163
beware of the *ḳꜣdt*-plant.[2]

1. *Skn* with det.  is not recorded; with det.  as in G1T and A1C it means 'be greedy', 'lust after', with *ḥr*, as in S1C alone, cf. *Concise Dict.* 251, but none of the other texts show *ḥr*, so the meaning remains in doubt.
2. Var. *iꜣḳt* 'leeks'. For *ḳꜣdt* cf. *Wb.* V, 14, 10–12.

Spell 210

NOT TO WORK IN THE REALM OF THE DEAD. I have gone up from Pe, I have III, 164
spent the night in Darkness-town.| O *Ỉḳ*,[1] do this with me.[2] 166

1. On the god *Ỉḳ*, *Ỉḳr* see Fischer, *Dendera*, 13, with n.59.
2. B2L adds a rubric: 'in the realm of the dead'; B1Bo[a–b]: 'becoming the Bull of Ōn'.

Spell 211

I am the bull of the dappled cows, the owner of five portions in the temple;| III, 167
three portions are in the sky with Rēꜥ, two portions are on earth with Gēb.|
Faeces and urine are my detestation; I live on the sweet things which are 168
issued from the shrine of Rēꜥ. It is the Night-bark and the Day-bark which bring to me daily; I walk on my feet, I am not upside-down in the presence of(?) Rēꜥ.[1]

1. *'Imy Rʿ*, common to both texts, is a peculiar phrase to use here, where a preposition is needed; perhaps we should emend into *tp-m Rʿ*, cf. 172*i*. B2Bo and B1Bo[b] substitute: 'He does not walk upside down in the presence of(?) Rēʿ'. B1Bo[b] adds a rubric: 'To be a scribe of Ḥatḥōr'.

Spell 212

III, 169 I am the Bull of the Ennead[1] who goes forth from the horizon, the owner of
five portions in Ōn; three are in the sky and two on earth. It is the . . .-bark[2]
which serves me and brings to me daily, and a path is made for me. I am
N-ḥs·nnf, I am heir(?) of Rēʿ-Atum.[3] It is granted to me that men listen to me
170 in my presence, (even I?) who swallowed the Ass.[4] | Men set down for me[5]
while I am on my way in order to institute[6] my magic at the altars and in order
that men may set down a meal[7] for me. He[8] crosses to the Field of Offerings
and I act on behalf of his desire. Going out of the shrine of Rēʿ.

1. Cf. B1Bo; the writing of S2C and B2Bo is a fanciful variant.
2. *Msw-nb*-bark in B2Bo, partly supported by S2C, but the reference is quite obscure; B1Bo is apparently quite corrupt.
3. The reading of B2Bo seems the most probable; it is the only one that can make sense as it stands, though the translation of *pʿt* as 'heir' is much open to question.
4. Apparently so, but the significance is most obscure.
5. Restore *wd n·i* in S2C, cf. B1Bo.
6. Reading *sgrg* with S2C; *sgr* 'make quiet' of the other texts makes poor sense.
7. *St* here is the prefix of *Concise Dict.* 206–7; for *st-ḫt* 'meal' cf. *Pyr.* § 1182.
8. Rēʿ?

Spell 213

III, 171 Not to eat faeces. What I doubly detest, I will not eat. Faeces is my detestation,
and I will not eat; urine is my detestation, and I will not drink. I will not go
up with my fingers, I will not[1] tread on it with my sandals. Gēb has commanded
to my father Osiris[2] that I shall not eat faeces nor drink urine behind(?) this
172 quartette of my father Osiris. | I eat of red emmer, and seven loaves are in the
sky in Ōn with Rēʿ,[3] seven portions are [on earth][4] with Gēb, seven portions
are with Osiris. It is the Night-bark and the Day-bark which will convey for
me to Ōn.[5] I will have acclamation and my double will have acclamation when
I am in Ōn, and I will live before[6] Rēʿ today.

1. T1C has miscopied the negation as *ḥr*.
2. Read *wḏ·n Gb ⟨n⟩ it·i Wsyr*; T1C has omitted the preposition *n* after *Gb*. B4Bo is quite corrupt.
3. Var. 'four portions are in the sky with Rēʿ, N is for three portions in Ōn'.

4. In T1C there is room to restore : B4Bo omits *r tꜣ*.
5. Following B4Bo; T1C is corrupt.
6. Read simply *tp m*; the second *m* is a dittograph.

Spell 214

Not to walk upside down and to repel Khnum who brings faeces in order to III, 173
make what is in the two districts. Recitation: O *Sḳdy* who speaks in fault(?),
you have come and you have brought me faeces and urine. I will not eat for
you (pl.), I will not drink for you, I will not travel upside down for you. I will
not chew faeces for you; I will not drink urine for you, because I have become
the Bull of the Conclaves; because I am at the head of the Westerners. O
Guardian of five great portions on Ōn, five portions are in the sky with Horus
and on earth with Min. Who will bring them to me? It is the Nurse who
will bring to me, it is the Day-bark which will set down for me. O Guardians
of the Enneads and the Uraei, | wait for me, for I will be with you at the south- 174
ern part of the northern sky. I dress and I undress, I sit on my mat, I govern
the two fields of *Mꜣṯw*. Offerings are for my children and for my servants;
there are brought to me and placed for me under me my family, my father and
my mother by thousands, and tens of thousands are allotted to me.[1]

O *Ḥr·f-ḥꜣ·f*, ferryman of the Winding Waterway, bring me this, ferry me across and set me on yonder side with these bags which are in my hand, because I am become a god.

1. 174*h* is but a dittograph of part of 174*f*.

Spell 215

SPELL FOR NOT EATING FAECES OR DRINKING URINE IN THE REALM OF THE DEAD. III, 175
O Great One,[1] owner of nine portions at the head of the Great Ennead, three
portions are in Djedu,[2] three in Ōn, and three in the Mansion of the Ibis in
the Field of Rushes. | The food of Rēʿ is my food, the hunger of Rēʿ is my 178
hunger, I live on what he lives on. Ptaḥ[3] washes him, he gives bread to those
who are with *Hdw*.[4] | Bread is given to me in the presence of Ptaḥ;[5] my mouth 180
is opened, and the four Ptaḥ-gods open my mouth in the tribunal in which
Horus opened the mouth of Osiris. He[6] says, he says: He is his son, | he is his 182
heir; He is Horus and I am he.[7] Ptaḥ is under his *moringa*-tree, he who is in
front of the great one presides over the *ṯnnt*-shrine, and they give me life just
as Isis gave water to Horus, | Bull of Offerings. 184

I am content, (even I) the guardian of offerings in the temple;[8] three por-

tions are in the sky with Rēʿ and two on earth with Gēb. I am Atum; if I sit
186 down to eat bread, then will Rēʿ[9] sit down to eat bread, | and water will be
given to the Two Enneads.[10] Stand up, O Plenty, you butler of Rēʿ, at my
offering-table,[11] for I have come to you, O Plenty, that you may give me bread
188 when I am hungry and beer when I am [thirsty];[12] your mouth gives me | my
lips that I may . . .[13] them.
Hail to you, O face of Rēʿ![14] May you propitiate the Two Enneads for me.[15] |
189 may you give to me, you gods, of bread and beer,[16] and my hands will be on it.

1. Fem. in S2C; masc. in the other texts. Varr. B3C: 'This N is "Smoked-grain" (*npr ḥty*), lord of great offerings', similarly B1Bo; P. Gard. II (both versions): 'I am the Great One, son of "Smoked-grain" ', etc. S1C does not begin until 178*a*.

2. Var. B2L: 'Abydos'.

3. Var. P. Gard. II[b]: *Hndf.* An eccentric writing of *Ptḥ* in B3C.

4. *Hdw* is everywhere determined with , and so must be a god rather than a place-name. Varr. P. Gard. II[b]: *Hndw*, in dual; B1Bo: *imyw hny* 'who is among the acclaimed ones'. P. Gard. II[b] also has a long and unintelligible variant of its own in 179*c–e*; 180*c*.

5. S1C and S2C omit 'of Ptaḥ'.

6. Ptaḥ?

7. M22C and P. Gard. II[a] only.

8. S2C omits 'in the temple'; varr. M22C, P. Gard. II: 'I am the guardian', etc., omitting *ḥtp·i*; S1C is corrupt.

9. Var. B1Bo: 'the Ennead'.

10. Var. S1C: 'I have given bread to him'.

11. B1Bo omits 'butler of Rēʿ, at my offering-table' and also 186*c*–187*a*.

12. *Ḥnkt iw·i [ib·ky]* only in M22C.

13. *Mṯn*, meaning obscure; hardly to be connected with *mṯn* 'assign', *Pyr.* § 2040.

14. Var. S1C: *nd·i ḥr n Rʿ* 'I greet Rēʿ'.

15. So S1C; S2C is similar. The other texts read: 'the face of the Enneads is propitiated for you'.

16. For *dyt·ṯn* of four texts read *dy·ṯn* as S1C, etc. B3C omits *m t ḥnḳt*.

Spell 216

III, 190 Not to eat faeces. I am a soul[1] in charge of the Two Lands, (even) Wepwawet
in Asyut. Protect me,[2] O faeces; respect me,[3] O urine, just as Thoth was
191 protected[4] from those two great and mighty gods | who traverse the sky. Take
me, that I may traverse the sky with you;[5] I will eat of what they eat of, I will
drink of[6] what they drink of. I will eat a *r*-goose, I will slaughter a *trp*-goose; |
192 my booth is in the Field of Rushes, I have plenty in the Field of Offerings, I
have abundance of what you have abundance of, O gods; I traverse the sky
193 like Rēʿ, | I travel about the sky like Thoth, I have worship like Rēʿ and accla-
mation like Thoth, (even I), Osiris, secret of abodes, whose abodes will endure

as (those of) the gods. NOT TO EAT FAECES OR DRINK URINE IN THE REALM OF THE DEAD.[7]

1. Read *bꜣ*, cf. B1Y.
2. Read *mk wi hs* with S1C. For the translation of *mk* as 'protect' cf. 54*e*.
3. Read *twr wi wsšt* with S1C. Cf. 54*f*.
4. Following B2Bo.
5. 'You' refers to the two gods.
6. For *my* read *m* with S1C and B1Y.
7. See 191 *g–h* and de Buck's note 190, n.1*.

Spell 217

GIVING GIFTS IN ŌN,[1] the gateway of the desert, the secret gate. I am the III, 194
protector of Hare-town, son of the Souls of Ōn; I walk on my feet, and I will
not walk upside down. Faeces is my detestation, and I will not eat; I cleanse[2]
off urine like Rēʿ when asleep and like Atum when dead, because I am the
Bull of Kenzet in Ōn | and ⟨my⟩ fleshy body[3] is in Ōn. Five portions are in 195
Ōn; two are in the sky with Rēʿ and three are on earth with Gēb.[4]

1. The rubric is misplaced in B2L.
2. The writing of *twr* 'cleanse off' in B2L has been bungled.
3. *ʿt⟨·i⟩ nt if*, lit. 'my member of flesh'. Before this B2Bo inserts: 'five portions are in Ōn', which the other texts place in 195*c*.
4. B2L ends with the rubric: 'Not to walk upside down and not to eat faeces'.

Spell 218

GIVING BREAD IN ŌN.[1] I am the curly-haired bull who guides the sky,[2] | Lord III, 196
of celestial appearings(?),[3] the great illuminator who came forth from the
heat(?),[4] leader of every god. My bones are firm and my lengthy lashings
are loosed,[5] and the movement of the sunshine has been given to me.[6] Faeces
is my detestation, and I will not eat it, nor will I drink urine; I walk on my
feet, | and I will not walk upside down. I am the owner of five portions in Ōn;[7] 197
three portions are in the sky with Rēʿ and two are on earth with Gēb.[8] It is the Night-bark and the Day-bark which will bring to me[9] in the house of the god in Ōn. I am stretched out straight,[10] I make ready the ferry-boat,[11] | I ferry across in the west[12] of the sky. I live on what they live on, I eat of what they eat of,[13] I have eaten bread in every pleasant room of the Great Goddess in Ōn.[14]

1. Var. 'good is the giving of bread in Ōn'.
2. Varr. 'the horned bull'; 'the curly-haired one'.

3. Read probably *nb ḫʿw ⟨nw⟩ pt* with *BD* 125,2–3.

4. For *bḫḫw* cf. *Pyr.* §§ 502.503.702.

5. *Wnf* 'be loosed' (S10C) may be the root-meaning of *wnf* 'be joyful', with dets. , *Concise Dict.* 61. Here the reference is probably to the loosening of the mummy-wrappings. *Wnnf* of L1Li and *wnnḏ* of B2L are obvious errors. *ȝw*, despite the dets., makes sense only if interpreted as an adjective qualifying *ḥtrw*; B2L and S10C are both corrupt here.

6.  of B2L is a blunder of obvious origin.

7. Read *ink nb ḫt 5 m Iwnw*.

8. The reading of the archetype was probably *iw ḫt 3 r pt ḫr Rʿ, iw ḫt 2 ḫr Gb*; for the second god B5C has Osiris, B2L Rēʿ and Min, S10C Horus, though Gēb of L1Li is almost certainly the original deity.

9. Var. S10C: 'who will take me from the god's storehouse every day'.

10. Var. L1Li: 'N has stretched out his intestine(!)', but cf. *BD* 125,10.

11. S10C adds 'my ropes are strong'.

12. 'West' of B5C is to be preferred to 'east' of the other three texts.

13. After this L1Li and S10C repeat 198*b*.

14. Var. S10C: 'there is bread of mine with the god'; L1Li has *nṯr* 'god' for *wrt*.

Spell 219

III, 199 A MAN RAISES HIMSELF UPON HIS [LEFT] SIDE.[1] I am raised up from upon my left side, I am placed upon my right side, I eat bread, I drink beer, there is given to me my desire[2] in every place where men give to me. I knot the rope,
200 I frap the ferry-boat, I cross the lakes of the horizon,| I go down to them[3] with eggs, I come forth from them with uraei, I have taken possession of their souls, I have torn out[4] their braided tresses, and fair is the likeness(?)[5] of the god. There have been given to me bread and beer in every place where men give to me. RAISING UP ON THE LEFT SIDE, PLACING ON THE RIGHT SIDE.[6]

1. B2L only.

2. B2L has mistaken the compound noun *šsp-n-ib* for a *sḏm·n·f* construction and has prefixed *iw* and has repeated the group in a dittograph.

3. Who are 'they'? Not the lakes, for 'they' have souls.

4. For *sḫs* 'tear out' cf. *Pyr.* §§ 97. 522; Dav. *Ptah.* II, 13. The det. is borrowed from *sḫs* 'run'.

5. Reading *nfr twt n nṯr*.

6. Not in B2L, which has its rubric at the beginning of the spell.

Spell 220

III, 201 What I doubly detest, I will not eat. Faeces is my detestation, and I will not eat; urine is my detestation, and I will not drink; O filth, I will not consume you. Do not take my hands; I will not tread on it (*sic*) with my sandals, I will not walk upside down for you, for I am the great Power who came forth from

the jar. O you great one and you mighty one who opened this great sky, I
know you and I know your names; this great one is in the company of the
Sunshine-god. If I stand up, you shall stand up; if I sit down, you shall sit
down. | I will walk on that road on which you walk and I will land at the sky, 202
because ⟨. . .⟩[1] the place where I wish to dwell, I will join with the Two Sisterly
Companions. O . . .,[2] I will not eat faeces for you, I will not drink urine for you,
I will not travel upside down for you among those who are . . . faces.[3]

WHY[4] WILL YOU NOT EAT FILTH OR DRINK URINE BECAUSE OF(?) THE EMPTINESS(?) OF HORUS AND SETH?[5]

Because I am made for portions from upon the great altar of Osiris on the
west side of the sky, | *šns*-bread, a jug of beer, *prsn*-bread, and a piece of a limb 203
of the flesh of him who is upon the *ryw*-plant. I travel upon that upper road
of the sky and that lower road of the earth north of the *ỉṯnws*-tree, I eat on the Field
of Offerings, on the Lake of Turquoise, and it is *Ḏꜥꜥ-wtt* who feeds me.

1. Clearly there has been an omission after *n ntt*.
2. 202*e* is quite obscure, except that beings are addressed.
3. *Swnw-ḥr*, meaning obscure.
4. B3L has the negation *n* in mistake for *ḥr*.
5. For the falcon of *Ḥr* B1L has the face-sign *ḥr*, and both texts write the name of Seth as 'the Outcast'.

Spell 221

A MAN DOES WHAT HE WISHES IN THE REALM OF THE DEAD. I am a lion who eats III, 204
what is pure in the field, for whom is done what he wishes; I will be there, for
I have seen with my (own) eyes.[1]

I am a lion who eats what is pure in the Garden of the Standard.[2] | I have gone 205
up, and I will be there, for I have seen with my (own) eyes.

I have gone up from Pe, I have spent the night in Darkness-town, and *Ỉḳ*
has acted with me.[3] I walk when Rēꜥ sees me, | for I am ever among his attend- 206
ants, I shine with those who are in the Abyss, it is Dawn who gives me his
hand, he prevents me from being among the executioners of Osiris | whom 207
Nwt⟨·k⟩-nw has doomed(?), (even he) the gate-keeper of the hidden desert.

1. Following B1Bo^a, but in the 1st person. Cf. also 205*c*.
2. Var. B1Bo^a: 'among the owners of standards'.
3. Cf. Spell 210.

Spell 222

Recitation: the [august god] who is in his egg has commanded[1] that N breathe the air in the realm of the dead, [and that there be given to him the sweet air][2] which is in N's nostrils. O N, seek out that great place which is in [*Wnw*]; O N, [guard][3] this egg of the Great Cackler. [If] N [be strong], it will be strong;[4] if N live, it will live;[5] if N breathe the air, it will breathe the air.

1. Read *iw wḏ·n* [*nṯr šps*] *imy s*⟨*w*⟩*ḥt·f*.
2. Cf. *BD* 127,9.
3. Cf. *BD* 127,9–10.
4. Read [*rwd*] *N rwd·s*, cf. *BD* 127, 11–12.
5. Read *ᶜnḫ*, not *my*, see de Buck, 207, n. 10*.

Spell 223

III, 208 Spell for breathing air in the realm of the dead.[1] O Atum, give me this sweet air which is in your nostrils, for I am this egg which is in the Great Cackler,|
209 I am the guardian of this great prop which separates the earth from the sky.
210 If I live, it will live; if I grow old, it will grow old; if I breathe the air,| it will breathe the air. I am he who splits iron,[2] I have gone round about the egg,[3] (even I) the Lord of Tomorrow.[4]

1. Var. 'Recitation: Becoming air, breathing air in the realm of the dead.' The text which follows has much in common with *BD* Ch. 54 and 56.
2. *Wḏᶜ byꜣ*; var. B3Bo and T1C: *wḏᶜ iᶜb* 'who splits what is joined'. Of the two readings, the first is to be preferred, for we seem to have here an allusion to the splitting of the iron of the sky (cf. *byꜣ n pt*, ⲃⲉⲛⲓⲡⲉ) at the deceased's ascension; there may also be a secondary reference to the splitting of the eggshell in hatching, in which case the reading of B3Bo and T1C, though probably an ancient emendation, will not be altogether inappropriate.
3. The masc. suffix in *swḥt·f* (B2Bo, B1Bo, and Sq12C) has no antecedent and is superfluous; it does not appear in B3Bo and T1C.
4. *Nb bkꜣ* must refer to the deceased, so that *iw* of B3Bo and T1L is to be ignored.

Spell 224

III, 211 Spell for not walking upside down in the realm of the dead.[1] Thus says N: I ⟨will not⟩[2] walk upside down for you; I walk on my feet and I will not walk upside down for you. I walk like Horus,[3] my strides are like those of Atum, my tomb is like that of a spirit, I walk like one who is among the spirits,[4] who open up the mounds of the gods.

1. *Rḫ nṯr* in T3Be is an obvious corruption of *ẖrt-nṯr* in T1Be;  after *sḫd* is a det.

2. A negative has certainly been omitted before *šm·i* in T1Be; the other texts are damaged.

3. Read *šm*[*·i*] *n Ḥr*, with  written for , in T1Be; so also *'Itm* in 211*g* and *ꜣḫ* 'spirit in 211*h*. Here *ꜣḫt* of T3Be is an inferior reading.

4. Read *šm·i wi my imyw ꜣḫw*; for the reflexive *wi* after *šm·i* cf. T2Be and T2L. T3Be reads: 'I walk to those who are in the horizon'; T1Be has: 'like him who is in his power', but *ꜣḫw* 'spirits' is doubtless to be read in both cases.

Spell 225

SPELL FOR THE VINDICATION OF A MAN AGAINST HIS FOE IN THE REALM OF THE III, 21
DEAD.[1] | Ho N! The sky is opened for you, the earth is opened for you, the 214
door-bolts of Gēb are opened for you, the shutters[2] of the sky-windows are
thrown open for you. | Does one guard you and release you? Does one bind 216
his hand to you and thrust his hand into you on earth?[3] The mouth of the
Pelican is opened for you, the mouth of the Pelican is thrown open for you,[4]
the Pelican has caused you to go out into the day[5] | to the place where you 220
wish to be.[6]

Ho N! May you have power in your heart (*ib*), may you have power in your 222
heart (*ḥꜣty*), may you have power in your arms, may you have power in your
legs,[7] | may you have power over the invocation-offerings which are yours,[8] 224
may you have power over water, may you have power over air, may you have
power over the river-waters,[9] | may you have power over the river-banks, may 228
you have power over the streams, may you have power over your enemies, may
you have power over those who would harm you in the realm of the dead, | may 232
you have power over those who would command you to be harmed in the
realm of the dead. Surely it will be[10] according to what I say. May you live
on the bread of Gēb, and that detestation of yours, you will not eat it. | May you 236
live on bread of red emmer, may you swallow beer of red[11] emmer at the pure
place;[12] may you sit under the branches of the myrrh-tree near Ḥatḥōr | who is 240
pre-eminent in *'Itnws* when(?) she travels to Ōn bearing the script of the divine
words, the book of Thoth.[13]

Ho N! . . .[14] may you have power over tamarisk and sand, may you have 242–5
power over every field of yours, | may you have power over those who would 246
harm you in the realm of the dead, may you have power over those who would
command you to be harmed on earth or in the realm of the dead.[15]

Raise yourself upon your left side, | put yourself upon your right side,[16] sit 248
down and stand up, throw off your dust, may your tongue be wise about it(?).[17]

1. *Smꜣʿ* of S2C[b] and Pap. Berl. is to be preferred to *mꜣʿ* of B2Bo; B1Y; Y1C; M2NY. T1L reads: 'Having power over water, going out by day and night by a spirit to every place where his

heart desires to be'; B4C: 'Spell for opening a way [. . .]'; B1L: 'Causing a man to receive invocation-offerings for himself in the morning and evening'; B2L: 'Spell for a man to have power over his foes on earth and in the realm of the dead, (and for) the destruction of all evil magic'; B1C: 'Spell for a man to have power over his foes and in his heart (*ib* and *ḥꜣty*), his arms and his legs'. The titles of B2L and B1C are nearest to the actual tenor of the spell, but the S2C group titles are in the majority.

2. Lit. 'roof', but a roof does not cover windows, nor can it be opened. The translation 'shutters' receives support from B10C (215*g*), where *rwty* 'double-doors' of the sky-windows is substituted for *tp-ḥwt*; 'double doors' is an apt figure for double shutters. The translation 'sky-window' for *ptr* seems certain, cf. *Pyr.* §§ 468. 852. 1058. 1203. 1680.

3. 216*a*–*b* have been taken to be questions with interrogative *in* and impersonal *sḏm·f*. These clauses have been preceded in B4C by a damaged interpolation. T1Be–T2L are corrupt or damaged.

4. A figurative way of referring to the doors of the tomb? B1L, B2L and B1C have the var. 'your mouth is opened by the Pelican, your mouth is thrown open by the Pelican'; B10C reads: 'The Pelican opens your mouth, the Pelican throws open your mouth', with an incomprehensible group of signs for *sn* in 219*c*; T3Be has: 'you open the mouth of the Pelican' (219*b*), while 219*c* is quite corrupt. In 219*e* B10C inserts its version of 216*a* and ends.

5. In 219*d*, five texts omit *rdy·n* before *pr·k*, while B1L has simply ; T3Be again is corrupt. T1L adds: 'and night'.

6. So, with minor varr. Some texts have *nb* 'every' after *bw*; some omit *bw* and others *ib*. B1L and B1C: 'from which you desire to go forth by night': B2L adds: '(or) by day'.

7. In several texts shortened to: 'may you have power in your heart (*ib* and *ḥꜣty*); may you have power in your arms and legs'.

8. Note *n·k imyt*, the fem. of the possessive construction *n·k imy*, here agreeing in gender with *pr(t-r)-ḫrw*, see also 259*g*; cf. Edel, *Altäg. Gramm.* § 384. This inflexion seems to be obsolescent in Middle Egyptian. In T1L this clause is misplaced in 228*c*.

9. *Nt*, varr. *nwt*, *mwyt*, distinct from *mw* in 226*a*, which refers to 'water' in general; *nt* seems to be used here of river- or irrigation-waters. T9C appears to read: 'may you have power over the action of the waters'. Several texts have: 'the river-waters and the river-banks'.

10. Assuming a subjectless use of *iw*, cf. Gardiner, *Eg. Gramm.*[3] § 121. The 1st person survives in S2C[a] and P. Berl. and possibly in Y1C, and refers to the person uttering the good wishes.

11. Var. 'white'.

12. *R bw wꜥb*; var. *bw nb* (B4C); omitted in T1Be and T1L.

13. Var. 'Thoth, Lord of Khemennu'. M2NY has misread 'book' as .

14. 242*a*–246*b* are but a repetition of 220*b*–230*a*, and have been omitted from the translation, except for an addition peculiar to T1L (245 *g*–*i*).

15. So T1L (247*g*–*h*). M.C.105 is slightly variant.

16. These two clauses have become somewhat muddled, and should surely read: 'Raise yourself on your left side, put yourself on your right side', cf. Pyr. §§ 1003. 1047. 1747; *CT* II, 256*e*–*f*. The group of spells S2C[b]–M2NY have only *imy ṯw* 'place yourself'.

17. *Ns·k r·s m sꜣw*, with varr. Most texts determine *sꜣw* with the knife, apparently in reference to the acuteness of wisdom; T1L and M.C.105 stress this point by adding *spd* 'acute' to *sꜣw*. B2L adds a rubric which is but a repetition of what has gone before.

Spell 226

SPELL FOR LETTING A MAN HAVE QUIET(?) BY NIGHT [. . .] THAT [DOOR(?)] III, 251
AND EVERYTHING WHICH IS CUSTOMARILY GIVEN TO [HIM(?)] IN THE [GREAT(?)]
MSW-FESTIVAL AND IN THE W3G-FESTIVAL.

Ho N! Sky and earth are opened for you, the great gates are opened for you,
| the gates of the plebs are thrown open for you,[1] Gēb has opened his jaws on 252
your account, (even he) the chiefest of the gods.

Ho N! | The Ram conducts you to his altars, Sopd being at his . . .[2] 254

Ho N! They remove the dimness of your sight and the wrinkles which are
on your limbs; | they open your blind[3] eyes, they extend your contracted 256
fingers.[4]

Ho N! Lift yourself up upon your left side, place yourself upon your right side.

Ho N! Eat your portion, consisting of this pure bread which is issued, 257
namely the collected loaves of this great god whose name is unknown.

Ho N! Drink of this pure water[5] which is issued upon this plateau of the
citizens, | for that Ram who is in his blood has given to you what is in his 258
redness.

Ho N! Ptaḥ South-of-his-Wall and Sokar have granted to you an appearing in the *Ḥnw*-bark of Gēb, chiefest of the gods.

Ho N! May you go out by day and by night; may you eat bread and drink 259
beer; may you receive the invocation-offerings which are yours. Come, O
invocation-offerings!—four times.[6]

1. M35C inserts: 'that you may go out by night and by day' here and in 253*b*.
2. *Trw*, hardly 'willows' despite the damaged det. in S1C, in view of [hieroglyph] of three other texts.
3. *Š3b*, a dialectical(?) form of *šp* 'be blind'; the meaning is not in doubt.
4. B1L adds: 'they open your mouth for you'.
5. Var. T1L: 'drink your portion, consisting of this pure water'.
6. So B1L and B15C.

Spell 227

BECOMING THE COUNTERPART OF OSIRIS. I indeed am Osiris, I indeed am the III, 260
Lord of All,[1] I am the Radiant One, the brother of the Radiant Lady; I am
Osiris, the brother of Isis. My son Horus and his mother Isis have protected
me from that foe[2] who would harm me;[3] | they have put cords[4] on his arms and 261
fetters on his thighs[5] because of what he has done to me.[6]

I indeed am Osiris, | greatest of the company of the Elders of the Five, heir 262 of my father Gēb.[7] I am Osiris, lord of doubles, alive of front, strong of hinder parts,[8] stiff of phallus, who is in the boundary of the plebs.[9]

263 I am Horus on the day of his accession, I am Orion who treads[10] his Two Lands, who navigates in front of[11] the stars of the sky[12] on the belly of my mother Nūt; she conceives me at her desire and she bears me at her will. I am the Centipede on the Day of the Centipede,[13] I am the White Bull who presides over the field.[14]

264 I indeed am Osiris for whom his father and his mother made a contract(?) on the day of the great slaughter; Gēb is my father and Nūt is my mother, I am Horus the Elder on the day of accession, I am Anubis on the Day of the Centipede,[15] I indeed am the Lord of All, I indeed am Osiris your lord who made you and who takes away him who rebels against you.[16]

1. Following P. Gard. II except where otherwise indicated in the notes. On this spell see Kees, *Göttinger Totenbuchstudien*, 6 ff.

2. Read *m-ʿ ḫft(y) pf* with B2L.

3. Sq3C has: 'his son Horus protects me (*sic*) [from the harm which was done (restoring as *m irw iryt*)] to him by Seth when he issued from the womb of his mother, and there were given to him his flood-waters when [he] was prostrate(?)', 260*g*–261*b*.

4. For *ʿwt* of P. Gard. II and Sq3C read *ʿḳ3w* with B2L, which adds a superfluous suffix; Sq3C has *rdy·n·f* for *dy·n·sn* of P. Gard. II. L1Li, as often, is corrupt.

5. Corresponding to *ḳm3w* of P. Gard. II and Sq3C, B2L has *ndwt*, which may well be a miswriting of *nṯwt* 'bonds' *CT* II, 112*c*, itself a shortened form of *nṯṯwt*, *Pyr.* § 349. B2L has miswritten *iwʿ* 'thigh' as *ʿʿw*.

6. Read *irt·n ⟨·f⟩ r·i*, cf. L1Li and Sq3C. 261*e* consists of a broken and unintelligible passage from M13C, see de Buck's note 4*.

7. 262*a*–*d* are missing from P. Gard. II. For 'my father' the Egyptian has the usual 'his father'.

8. So B2L; L1Li. P. Gard. II and Sq3C have: 'alive of front, dead of hinder parts', which surely is corrupt, and P. Gard. II adds the even more absurd: 'who is under the feet'. At this point Sq3C adds: 'No-one has come to meet this N among the gods because so great is [. . .] of Ptaḥ' (262*g*–*h*).

9. Sq3C omits *nḫt ḥnn* (deceased is a woman) and corrupts *imy ḏrw* into *sḏr*.

10. *S3ḥ*, lit. 'toes' (vb.); see also 55*h*.

11. So B2L and L1Li.

12. In 263*a*–*c* Sq3C reads: 'O N, you are Orion who has made peace for you (pl.) because of what he has done, who has given to you [this(?)] altar in front of the stars of the sky'.

13. Var. B2L: 'I am Anubis in the Day of the Centipede'; cf. 265*a*.

14. Var. Sq3C: 'the Field of Rushes'. After this it inserts 264*a*: 'his need is made up on the Day of Propitiation; his son and [his mother(?)] are gracious to him (*n·f* duplicated) on that day [of slaughter(?)]'. This replaces 264*b*–*d* of the other texts.

15. P. Gard. II omits 264*g*–265*b*. B2L and L1Li end here.

16. Sq3C has a damaged variant of this passage and ends the spell with the rubric: 'Becoming Osiris'.

Spell 228

SPELL FOR ENTERING IN FRONT AND GOING OUT BEHIND IN THE MIDST OF THOSE III, 266
WHO EAT THE BREAD OF OSIRIS IT IS BENEFICIAL ⟨FOR⟩ WHOEVER DOES IT. | AS 267
FOR ANY [MAN] WHO KNOWS THIS SPELL,[1] HE WILL COMPLETE 110 YEARS IN [LIFE], 10 YEARS THEREOF IN THE REALM(?)[2] OF HIS IMPOTENCE,[3] ETC., BEING WHAT A MAN, IGNORANT OR LEARNED, SHOULD DO. IF HE PROCEEDS TO THE REALM OF THE DEAD, HE WILL EAT BREAD IN THE PRESENCE OF OSIRIS.[4]

O Great One who comes in, say to him who collects(?)[5] writings, the door- 268
keeper of Osiris, that I have come great, powerful, strong,[6] | mighty, divine.
I have come here that I may protect[7] my body, | that I may nourish my uraei, 274
that I may sit on the bearing-stool(?) of Osiris and get rid of the sore suffering of the god. I am strong, having appeared as Osiris;[8] I was born with him when
he was very young.[9] | I uncover for you the knees of Osiris,[10] I remove for you 278
this locked chest[11] which contains the side of Osiris, which opens the mouth of the gods, and I sit beside him as Thoth, I write the news: a thousand of
bread and beer[12] | on the altars of my father Osiris; my dappled cattle consist- 282
ing of long-horned bulls and red cows, *r*-geese and *ṯrp*-geese with which I
make offering to Horus and with which I make presentation to Thoth;[13] | my 285
place of slaughter[14] there belongs to Him who is over the blood-offering.[15] I rule Djedu, I travel about on its river-banks, I open up its green fields, I
make its lotus-plants[16] to flourish, | I release[17] the *wnb*-flower, I cultivate 287
emmer,[18] for the offerings to the gods, and they are made content because of
me;[19] I snuff[20] the great east-wind for its tresses,[21] I grip[22] the north-wind | 289
by its braided lock, I grasp[23] the south-wind by its coiffure(?),[24] I seize the
west-wind by its nape(?).[25] I travel around the sky on its four sides, | I give 291
breath to the blessed ones in the presence of their father Osiris, I go in at the front and go out at the back among those who eat bread.[26]

1. The rest of this rubric only in B2L^{c}. In B3L, B2Bo and B2L^{b} it comes at the end of the spell in 292*d*–293*e*. On this spell see Kees, op. cit. 19 ff.

2. For *m ḏr*. cf. Spell 76, n.6.

3. *Sḏb*, lit. 'impediment'.

4. For all this long rubric L1Li substitutes 'Spell for eating [bread]'.

5. *ʾIʿb*, lit. 'unites'.

6. Following the B2Bo group, which here is the most consistent. *ʾItp* of three texts (270*d*) occurs also in *CT* I, 4*a*. B5C has *ʿpr·ky* 'equipped' (271*f*).

7. Var. *šd* 'save'. In 273*f* BH3Ox ends up with '[. . .] equipped with his magic'.

8. B6C–B3L omit *wsr·kw* 'I am strong'. Before this B5C (277*d*) repeats the 'bearing-stool' clause.

9. Four texts have absurdly ***rnp·kw sp 2*** 'when I was very young'. The two B2L texts have further corrupted this into ***rnpy ink***.

10. The lost *n·ṯn* of B2Bo survives in nine texts. B2L^{a} has: 'I uncover the knees of Isis', without dative; the clause is abbreviated in B3Ox, lost in B7C and L1Li and missing in B5C.

11. *Mḫtmt*, var. *ḫtmt*, with box-det. in B1P. On *mḫtmt* cf. *JEA* 41,13.

12. Much expanded in B3Ox.

13. Var. B3C: 'Osiris'.

14. With *mnḥy* 'place of slaughter' compare *imnḥy* 'slayer', *Wb.* I, 87,17; *mnḥ* 'slay' II, 84,2.

15. For this being cf. *Pyr.* § 401, where also he is associated with butchery. Cf. *ṯr* 'blood', *Pyr.* §§ 451. 1263; used also of a red substance, Harris, *Minerals*, 154.

16. Var. B5C: 'its herbage'.

17. Apparently in the sense of making free to grow.

18. Var. B3L: 'Barley and emmer'. Some of the other texts write *bty* 'emmer' twice over.

19. This clause only in B2Bo.

20. *Sn·i* omitted in B2Bo, but present in 11 texts out of 14. BH3Ox apparently 'he grasps the east-wind by its braided lock'; L1Li is mostly destroyed.

21. For *ḏꜣꜣ* cf. *Wb.* V, 520,7.

22. Again B2Bo omits the verb. The other texts vary between *nḏr* and *ḫfꜥ*.

23. The verb varies mostly between *ḫfꜥ* and *ꜣm*. Other varr. are *nfꜥ* B1P; *sꜣm* B2L^{c}; *ḥmꜥ* B15C; *nḏr* B3Ox. B2Bo again omits it.

24. Apparently a mode of coiffure; cf. also *BD* 446,7.

25. 'Nape' is the only part of the head, apart from the hair, which affords a firm grip; L1Li has *mkḥꜣ* 'back of the head'. B1L and B3L, which passed over 289*b*, now substitute 290*b*: 'I grasp the south-wind by its plaited hair'. For the last word B1L has *gꜣbt*, with  instead of  as above in 289*b*, but B3L has *gmḥty*, suggesting a pair of plaits of hair with a resemblance to tapers for lighting. *Gmḥt* also in 289*b* in B1P only.

26. Varr. 'bread of Osiris', 'daily bread', 'bread of N'. For the rubrics of 292*c*–293*e* see n.1 above.

Spell 229

III, 294 Hail to you, you who are on the head of the Great One, you mistress of brow[1]
and neck, ⟨at⟩ whom Rēꜥ is joyful when he sees her on the road which is in the
Sacred Land, offspring of Osiris in the Pure Place who mourns the Bull of
the West, who folds her arms[2] on account of the Inert One within the secret
295 place of the Great Hall; | who knits up the soul, who builds up the shade and
who gives breath to the Inert One in this her name of 'Her who is in attendance
on her lord'. May you place for me my head upon my neck when you gather
together[3] life for the throat. May you make me into a spirit,[4] may you enfold
my members, may you knit on my face and build up my soul, may you save me
296 from the fishers of Osiris | who cut off heads and sever necks and who take
souls and spirits to the slaughter-house of those who eat fresh (meat). My

head will not be cut off, my neck will not be severed, my name will not be
unknown among the spirits, I will not be caught in a net,[5] the food which is
at my mouth will not be taken away, my heart (*ib* and *ḥꜣty*) will not be cut out,
my soul will spend the night watching over my corpse, my face will not be sad,
my heart will not be forgetful, I will not be ignorant of my path to the realm
of the dead, for I am a spirit whose mouth is hale, and magic is what equips me
according to my desire.[6] | I have come free from[7] corruption, I have poured 297
away my foulness, my garment is what I have found, I am one who is missing(?)
from within the secret places of the Great Hall, I am Māʿet, wrongdoing is my
detestation.

Hail to you, Lady of Goodness who raised up the head of Osiris and who
wailed over him in the Pure Place in this your name of 'Headrest(?)[8] which
is under the head': Place my head on my neck for me, gather up life for my
throat, for I am in the following of Osiris among the blessed ones, the possess-
ors of offerings, | for I have come equipped with my magic, I will not die, 298
breath will not be taken away from my nose and I am a possessor of offerings.

1. So T3C. For *ḥꜣt* 'brow' the other texts have [hieroglyph]; read *nḥdt* 'tooth'?
2. Cf. *Pyr.* § 743, where, however, the word refers to arms 'linked' in the dance.
3. Read *sꜣkt·t* with G1T.
4. Read *sꜣḫ·ṯ w⟨i⟩*, cf. 295*e*.
5. The meaning of *Šw* at the end of 296*f* is not clear; it is in G1T only.
6. A sentence with nominal predicate with *ḥkꜣw* as subject and a participle of *ʿpr* as predicate. English requires the 1st person here, as this refers to the deceased, who is the spirit.
7. Lit. 'veiled of'; for this sense of *ḥꜣp* cf. *CT* II, 93*d*; III, 311*c*.
8. *Ḏnyt* with det. [hieroglyph]. As a wooden object which is under the head, 'head-rest' seems the most likely meaning.

Spell 230

A boon which the King gives ⟨to⟩ Osiris, an invocation-offering of a thousand of bread and beer, an altar of alabaster, oxen and fowl:[1] so say Isis and Nepthys to N, the virtuous and vindicated. May your head be raised, may your heart live,[2] may you possess your flesh, . . .[3] on your body, may you ever be in the Following,[4] may you live.

1. Var. 'a thousand of oxen and fowl on an altar'.
2. Var. 'may you live'.
3. *Wnty*, meaning unknown.
4. Of Osiris.

Spell 231

III, 299 Ho N! may your head be purified by Ḥapi, may your eyes be made bright by *Dwꜣ-wr*, may your moth be split open by Thoth with this wondrous book of his wherewith he split open the mouth of the gods.[1] He speaks and splits open[2] the mouth of N that he may speak.

1. T3C ends here. G1T and A1C have 'Osiris' instead of 'gods'.
2. So G1T; A1C has the passive *sḏm·f* 'is split open'.

Spell 232

III, 300 A SPELL FOR THE HEAD-REST.[1] May your head be raised, may your brow be made to live, may you speak for your own body, may you be a god, may you always be a god.[2]

1. G1T only. See de Buck's notes 1* and 3*.
2. G1T adds: 'so says the great god of the two Enneads 〈to〉 N'.

Spell 233

O N, take the Eye of Horus which trod down the enemies of Osiris, that it may tread down your enemies for you; take[1] it, N.

1. Regarding *im* as a miswriting of *m* 'take'; to read it as the preposition yields poor sense.

Spell 234

III, 301 To prepare an offering in the four basins of Khopri and Ḥeḳet, the small, the medium and the large; to present[1] the mooring-post, the bow-warp and the stern-warp;[2] to turn over gifts(?)[3] four times for N, virtuous and vindicated.

1. In G1T *ḥnk* is followed by a superfluous *n*.
2. Loaves representing these objects; the triangular sign is a det. of bread.
3.  is taken to be a det. of *ꜣwtyw*.

Spell 235

You have your legs; lift up your body, gather your members together, that
III, 302 you may tread out the paces to the tribunal,[1] to the place where the gods are, that they may give you the fluid which issued from you. May you never be inert, having it. May you travel and never tire, may you traverse sky and earth and never tire, O N, virtuous and vindicated.[1]

1. The last sentence only in G1T and A1C.

Spell 236

Hail to you, Lady of Goodness, ⟨at⟩ seeing whom those are in the Netherworld rejoice, | who removes[1] the limpness of the Inert One, because of whom III, 303
Osiris has trodden,[2] who made for him the stride[3] of those who walk[4] in his moment of interment, in this your name of 'Dam[5] which is under the feet'. May you give me my legs that I may walk on them, may there be joined together for me what is in the movement of my legs, for I am one who strides far to the limit[6] of my desire, I shall not be turned back at the gates of the Netherworld.[7] | I ascend to the sky with Orion, I receive food-offerings with 304
the Great Ones, my abode is at the high portals of the Entourage of Rēᶜ who give supplies of food; I am one who collects for himself his efflux in front of Rostau.

O you terrible ones, you messengers of Osiris who close the mouths of the spirits because of what is in them,[8] | you are powerless to close my mouth, you 305
cannot take away the movement of my legs, for I am one who will go in and out,[9] the mover of the Pure Place, who kindles a flame for Anubis on the day of treating him who is in his putridity.[10] Be far from me, you executioners[11] of Osiris; you have no power over these feet of mine, | for I possess the funerary 306
meal in Ōn; I know what I should know.[12]

1. Lit. 'dams off'.
2. I.e. has got on his feet again.
3. Reading *nmtt* with A1C.
4. So T3C; A1C determines *šmw* with 𓈗 in 305*b.c.*
5. So T3C; the varr. omit *ḏnyt*, which is required for the pun on 303*a*.
6. T3C *r-ḏr* as against *ḏr* alone in the other texts.
7. So T3L; omitted in the other texts owing to the similar writings of *sbȝw* and *dȝt*.
8. Var. 'what is in their mouths'.
9. Read *ᶜḳ⟨·f⟩ pr·f*.
10. A reference to Anubis as the embalmer.
11. *ᶜḏtyw*, a derivative of *ᶜḏt* 'slaughter', *Concise Dict.* 51.
12. So T3C; G1T has: 'I know what Sia knows, into which the Greatest of the Seers is initiated; a way is made for me and I am Lord of Air'. A1C has *rḫt·n·i* as T3C and then appends 'Sia' to it; it continues as G1T.

Spell 237

Spell for the wall of the Great East. | Hail to you, Mourner[1] of Osiris III, 307
who bewails the limp Great One; who makes a spirit of the Bull of the West; ⟨at⟩ seeing whom the Westerners rejoice; Lady of All in the secret place; | to 308

whom Osiris turns his back[2] in these his moments of inertness; who is in front of the Lord of Abydos; whose place on the paths of the Netherworld is hidden; who bewails her lord at the interment in this her name of 'She who
309 bewails her lord'. | Watch over me, for I am Osiris; spiritualize me, O you who should raise up my members; gather together for me what issued from my flesh; open for me the paths which belong to the Netherworld. I am one spirit-like of speech, healthy of magic, lord of food-offerings in accepting
310 gifts. | I am one who is in front of the funerary workshop, I have come to do ⟨my⟩ duty, to enter into the secret portals into which Anubis is initiated; the
311 secrets of the Pure Place belong to me[3] because of what is in it. | I belong to the House of Osiris,[4] I watch over it; I veil his limpness, I ease his severe suffering for him; I know what Sia knows, and a path is opened for me, for I am the Lord of Air.

312 Hail to you, Mourner of Osiris, | Companion[5] of the Bull of Nedit who makes the mummy-wrappings[6] to breathe, who veils the limpness, to whom Osiris has turned his back, helper of the embalmer Anubis when treating the body of the Inert One. Spiritualize me, O you who split open my mouth for
313 me[7] and | who guide my soul on the paths of the Netherworld; grant to me food-offerings among the Great Ones on the altars of those who possess names, for I am Osiris, I am bound for Abydos, I receive gifts upon the great altar on
314 the day of giving food-supplies and offerings to many persons.[8] | I have reached the high portals of the Entourage of Rēʿ who reckon up the pillared bark,[9] I enter into the great shrine with the Great Ones among the great
315 Followers of Osiris, I have come | that I may veil the limpness of the Inert One, I have covered up what I found missing; open a path for me, for I am Lord of Sepa, I possess the funerary Meal in Ōn.[10]

1. For *ḥꜣṯ* of G1T read *ḥꜣt* with the other texts.

2. I.e. ignores in death, does not know her.

3. Somewhat corrupt in all texts. I suggest the emendation *iw n·i sštꜣ n wʿbt*, the 'Pure Place' being the embalmer's booth.

4. Var. 'House of Osiris, Lord of Djedu'.

5. Var. T1Be: *mnʿtt* 'nurse'; 318*l* indicates that *rmnwtt* is the better reading.

6. Var. T1Be: *if* 'flesh'.

7. Var. A1C: *wp·t n·i r·i* 'split open my mouth for me', optative *sḏm·f*.

8. Lit. 'names'.

9. The latter part of this sentence is quite corrupt in T1Be.

10. Var. 'I possess your funerary meal at Abydos'.

Spell 238

O you who split open my mouth for me and who gathered together for me III, 316
what issued from my flesh, grant to me offerings from[1] the hands of the Great
Ones upon the altars of those who possess names. I enter the Great Shrine
by means of the hands of the Great Ones, I see the god at his oblations, I am
a spirit, and the Sacred Eye is behind [. . .] I am content. I am one who knows
his utterance, I have come from [. . .] because of what I know, there is no
sort of suffering which is on me.

Hail to you,[2] Great One behind your lord; who raises him up [after being]
limp, who gathered my body together, who pulled my flesh together, who
spiritualized me, who split open my mouth for me; I [receive][3] gifts upon the
great altar on the day of giving food-supplies[4] to many persons,[5] for |I am 317
Osiris, I [am bound for] Abydos,[6] I [. . .] the shrine, for I am the Lord of Air.[7]

Hail to you, you who are in attendance on your lord, Mourner of Osiris,
the Great One, the Wailer,[8] Mistress of the *Pr-nw*(?) [. . .] the souls of the
Westerners; grant me the path of those who are on earth at the place of
power(?) which [I(?)] have desired: 'Come[9] in peace' shall be said to me. I
am content, for the causing that my power be great is what *Snpw* does.[10] O
[my] champion[11] in life, lord of knowledge(?), [. . . give] me power like
Anubis, behind whom stood(?)[12] the Two Sisters; cause that the Souls of Ōn
speak to me and that those who accompany Horus be gracious to me. There
is no laying hold of me, no god will utter a curse against me, for I have entered 318
the realm of the dead, this abode[13] of those whose mouths are pure, hatred(?)[14]
is behind me on the day in which I am content in the horizon.| The Nile-
god has given me his hand, I caress(?) Wepwawet, I pass eternity like Neḥeb-
kau [. . .] which goes forth from my mouth, every god being content with his
body; I am satisfied by means of my power. Rēʿ, lord of the sky who is in his
shrine, makes me flourish,[15] and I am a great god. All the lower portions of
the god's-offerings have come to me, (even) the due of Her who is behind her
lord, the Companion of the Bull of Nedit who makes his body to breathe, who
veils the limpness, who spiritualizes the Bull of the West, to whom Osiris has
turned his back,[16] helper of Anubis. [I] receive my body, I know my name, for
I am your offspring. There is no weariness in your body [. . .]. I am he who
ascends at the head of those who are yonder, a spirit(?) [. . .] oblations within
the shrine| [. . .] on the first day of contenting the god with his offerings. 319
Give me [. . .]. I have received my body and I am rejuvenated with life daily,
for I am he who buried his father.[17]

Hail to you [. . .] dead. The god awakes and his members are at rest for him. I have gathered together my power in the hands of the Great Ones; I spend eternity alive, I have come from [. . .] because of what I know, I am a *sꜣ-mr·f* who examines [hearts . . .] I have gathered together my body. Raise me up [. . .] live for ever, because I am one powerful of speech who came forth from Gēb, who knows his speech in the great bark. [I have(?)] come in the protection of her who has reassembled for me [my] members [. . .] like this which that potent god has done[18] after his [. . .][19] this land. What I have done is this which this god has done [. . .] shape [. . .] who goes to rest in life.

1. Here *m-m* serves as single *m*; again 316*e*; 319*h*.
2. Feminine.
3. Restore as *šsp·i*, cf. 313*d*.
4. Read *snmw* with 313*d*.
5. Lit. 'names'.
6. Restore as *iw·i r ꜣbḏw*, cf. 313*c*.
7. For *ink ink ṯꜣw* read *ink nb ṯꜣw*, cf. 311*g*.
8. Read [*ḥ*]*ꜣt*.
9. Read  ?
10. Regarding *dyt* as infinitive, subject of a sentence with nominal predicate, in this case the neuter participle *irt*.
11. Feminine. Lit. 'who is behind me', i.e. backing me up.
12. Guessing that *ḥꜣʿ* may be a corruption of *ʿḥʿ*.
13. Lit. 'mound', 'tell'. Emend into *iꜣt tn n ntyw wʿb rw*.
14. *Sft* perhaps a variant of *sfꜣt* 'hatred' *Concise Dict*. 224.
15. Probably a miswriting of *swꜣḏ*; *swḏ* 'hand over' makes no sense.
16. See Spell 237, n.2.
17. The deceased equates himself with Horus son of Isis.
18. Read *nw irt·n nṯr mnḫ* with intrusive *n* after , see 319*s*.
19. An illegible word, probably a verb with *tꜣ pn* as object.

Spell 239

[II, 320 Hail to you,[1] Mistress of the Old Ones, Lady of (many) faces in the Secret Place, who gives orders to the Bull of Djedu, who guides the Lord of the West, ⟨at⟩ whom Osiris rejoiced when he saw her; Mistress of the hidden mysteries, who announces festivals in the bow(?) of the bark when men navi-
321 gate[2] in the morning, | to whom the Inert One has turned his face in this her name of Mistress of faces. Give me my face, for I am Osiris, I have come into the Island of Fire, I have filled my belly with magic, I have quenched my thirst with it. Clear my vision in the paths of the Netherworld, make hale for

me what is in my mouth, for I haul on(?)[3] the bow-warp of the Bark of Righteousness,[4] | I give supports to those who are in the Great West. I have come that 322
I may restore[5] ⟨my⟩ body, ease ⟨my⟩ wounds and cover up ⟨my⟩ portal because of what is in it. What belongs to ⟨me⟩ is what Anubis who opened to me restored;[6] I am the Lord of faces and I give food-offerings to the Lord of *pꜣt*-cakes, I satisfy those who are over the altars, and I come to land at the region of the horizon in company with those who are in the Bark.[7]

1. G1T and A1C write horizontally and retrograde, G1T in red.
2. Impersonal *sḏm·f*; the varr. have *sḳdwt* for *sḳd·tw*.
3. A hitherto unrecorded verb, but cf. *wnt* 'rope', *Wb.* I, 314,18.19.
4. Var. *wny⟨·i⟩ ḥꜣtt mꜣꜥ⟨·i⟩ sḳdwt* 'I haul on(?) the bow-warp, I direct the navigation.'
5. Read *srwḫ* with G1T and A1C.
6. G1T reverts to the normal direction of writing.
7. Note the eccentric writing of *im(y)w* in T3C.

Spell 240

O you four Horuses,[1] the offspring of Osiris, who announce offerings to those III, 323
who are in the evening, you have no power to take this face of mine to him who is in his shambles who severs the necks of spirits for himself, for I am the companion of Anubis within the secret places of the Great Hall. I have come[2]
that I may wash the towns and overrun the well-brims(?);[3] | my soul is with 324
⟨me⟩, I have power in my body, and I live on white emmer. I have come that I may control offerings, for I am a possessor of gifts.

1. Entirely in red in G1T.
2. So A1C.
3. I do not understand the meaning of these two sentences. *Sḫs* of T3C is probably to be preferred to the obscure *sḫn* of the varr.

Spell 241

Hail to you,[1] Lady of offerings, ⟨at⟩ whom[2] Osiris rejoices when he sees her, whose[3] great wall is an owner of possessions; who brings air, who gives
offerings, | who presides over the throne in the secret places of the Nether- III, 325
world; who clears the vision of the Bull of Djedu, who split open his mouth and split open his eyes when the Inert One asked; who gathered together his arms and legs, who laid Osiris down in [. . .,] who gave abundance to the Lord of the Flood on the desert plateau; who gave offerings. Open a path for the Inert One to the abode of embalming, the pillared bark; may you open

to me, for I am Osiris; I have come to Rostau in order to know the secret of the Netherworld into which Anubis is initiated. My mouth is split open, my
326 eyes are split open, I am made a spirit,[4] | my members are gathered together,[5] I am in possession of offerings in Ōn. Open to me that I may control offerings, for I am he who is in charge of secret matters, I know what Sia did, I am unique as one who does justice, I have come equipped with magic, I have quenched my thirst with it, I live on white emmer, filling the Winding Waterway.

1. Entirely in red in G1T.
2. So A1C.
3. Osiris's(?). One would have expected a fem. suffix.
4. Reading *sꜣḫ·tw·i*.
5. A1C has a superfluous *ṯ* after *sꜣḳ·t(w)*.

Spell 242

III, 327 Spell for opening a door to the soul. Recite: I am Thoth who brings justice, who healed the Sacred Eye in the House of the Double Lion. Open to me that I may see my corpse, for I am a living soul, I have come here into the
328 Island of Fire, | and there has been given to me vindication concerning what I used to do in the presence of Osiris, Bull of the West, who grants power and vindication to me.[1]

1. The text has the personal name instead of the pronoun.

Spell 243

III, 329 Spell for opening up the West and for acquiring . . .[1] of the West in
330 the realm of the dead.[2] | I am the Pelican[3] who saw your (*sic*) birth,[4] I have
331 come that I may inspect my nest; | I ask for a brain (*sic*); do not(?) bite into my breast.[5] I am the Baboon, I am stronger than you.[6]

1. *ʿftt*, meaning unknown. See also 376*a*.
2. So S2P–S3P; T1L and B4C omit the second clause. BH4C has the rubric: 'Spell for going down to the Field of Rushes'; B1Bo postpones the rubric to Spell 264 (393*k*), where it reads: 'Opening up the West in the realm of the dead'. L1Li and S10C omit the rubric.
3. For *ḥnt* 'pelican' L1Li has *mntw*.
4. BH4C omits the suffix after *mst*.
5. Incomprehensible; I translate the words without grasping their sense. For *psḥ* BH4C has *spr*. For *ḳꜣbt* 'breast' (S1C–S3P) cf. *AEO* II, 214*; the other texts have *ḳꜣb* 'intestines' S10C has a version of its own: 'I shall bite into your intestines, I shall take away your brain'. Nowhere is it indicated who is being addressed thus.
6. Plural in S1C–S3P; singular in the other texts.

Spell 244

Horus has placed ⟨. . .⟩,[1] he has not reached the path of the unique of heri- III, 332
tage(?)[2] on which Thoth went; men are afraid of the gods who go on it. It cannot reach me ⟨. . .⟩,[3] the light of those who are among the earth-gods at the domain(?) of Horus the Elder. Those who are in charge of the sky see, those who are in charge of the earth hear that I have inherited its[4] paths, | I 333
have been placed in the ferry-boats[5] like Horus the Elder. Give to me,[6] you nurses of the gods, place your hands on me; may you raise me up,[7] may they (*sic*) set me[8] on their thighs with their breasts on my mouth, may they lift me up[9] and set me in the pure places among the brothers of the pure gods.

1. A textual omission.
2. Reading *wꜣt wꜥt(y) iwꜥt*, an obscure jingle. S1C wrongly inserts *wi* 'me' before *wꜣt*, perhaps anticipating 332*d*. The whole passage appears corrupt.
3. S2C omits *wi*. There must have been an omission in a text ancestral to these, since the passage concerning 'the light' seems quite irrelevant to the context.
4. Of the sky, in view of the fem. suffix.
5. Reading ⟨*m*⟩ *mḫnwt* with S2C.
6. Reading *imy m n·i*; S2C omits the dative.
7. A superfluous *n* before *wi* 'me'. Omitted in S2C.
8. So S1C; S2C has *fꜣ·sn wi* 'may they raise me up . . .'.
9. See n.8 above.

Spell 245

Hail to you, you who arise and come into being in this your name of Khopri. III, 334
This is what I say[1] to you: Would that I had my son that I might appear[2] with my sceptre, and that he might cleanse me and bring me worship in the Pure Land.

See,[3] I have come and I bring you worship and purification in the Pure Land, because I am this seed which conceived ⟨me⟩ for you[4] by means of your mouth, | which bore ⟨me⟩ for you by means of your grasp in orgasm. 335
I am the star which went forth from the plumes of(?) Rēʿ, I am these water-pots[5] by means of which water came into being, by means of which Rēʿ [. . .],[6] by means of which I have come into being, by means of which I have grown.

I will not be taken away to the night-offerings,[7] the god's slaughterers shall not have power over me, Elephantine shall come to an end, and the booth of the god who came forth from the fire at Ro-ḥōnĕ shall not be found. | I have 336
appeared as Sokar, and those who walk in Ro-tjenenet have made acclama-

tion,[8] I have arisen ⟨on⟩ my throne by means of myself; there is no father of mine who has given to me, there is no mother of mine who has given to me. It was the heir of the great one of Kenzet who gave it to me.[9]

1. Or: 'is said'.
2. *H̱ʿy·i* is prospective *sḏm·f*. So also *swʿb·f* and *int·f* following.
3. Khopri speaks.
4. Read perhaps *n ntt ink is nw n mtwt iwrt n·k ⟨wi⟩ m r·k*, cf. 335*a*. Note that both here and in 335*a* S1C has not observed that *iwrt* and *mst* should both be fem. to agree with *mtwt*.
5. The boat-sign after *šḏwt* is meaningless; it may be a reminiscence of *šdw* 'raft'.
6. S2C only.
7. Here probably the deceased speaks again.
8. Expanded but defective in S2C.
9. A construction with *in* + noun + *pw* serving as subject in anticipatory emphasis to the participial statement *swt rdy n·i s(y)*. The first *pw* is a demonstrative adjective qualifying *iwʿ*, and is best translated as the definite article.

Spell 246

III, 337 SPELL FOR ENTERING INTO THE FIRE AND FOR COMING FORTH FROM THE FIRE BEHIND THE SKY. I am this one invisible of form in the midst of the sunshine, I enter into the fire, I come forth from the fire, the sunshine has not pierced me,[1] those who find the Great One have not burnt[2] me, mine is the knife which
338 cuts down him who is in the hand of Thoth.[1] I will not travel around and I have not travelled around, for your[3] arm is that of Horus, your arm is that of the Great One, while the Sacred Eye, the Lady of provisions, is powerful.

I enter into and come forth from the fire, the sunshine has not pierced me, those who find the Great One have not burnt me, mine is the knife which cuts down him who is in the hand of Thoth. I travel round her who is opposite to me, is opposite to me, for your arm is that of Horus the Great One, and the Sacred Eye has power.

1. Read *n dm wi i3ḫw*, cf. S3C and 338*d*. The det.  is misplaced in S1C.
2. Cf. *nswt* 'flame', *Concise Dict.* 139.
3. Whose?

Spell 247

III, 339 GOING FORTH FROM THE FIRE BEHIND THE GREAT GOD. I have entered into the protection of the gods,[1] I have come forth from this . . .[2] on the heart of Thoth, I am the mighty one, lord of speech, who judges the crowd in the

Mansion of the Sistrum-player,[3] I know those names of yours[4] which belong to the Eye of Horus, one mighty against those who work ill against them,[5] (even) those who are in the chest[6] of Rēꜥ, | who bring to him the child of his 340
utterance who loves him.

1. The plural of Sq3C is shown to be correct by the plur. suffix *·ṯn* in 339*f*.
2. *Ꞽkw*, meaning unknown. It can hardly be connected with *ikw* 'stone-quarry' or *ik* 'attack'.
3. So S1C, with *iḥ*(*w*) determined with the side-lock; S2C has *iꜥḥ* determined with the cord.
4. Of the gods mentioned in 339*b*.
5. Read *wsr r irw r·sn* as Sq3C, except that its plur. *wsrw* is in error.
6. Read *ꜥfḏt* with S2C; for the word, cf. *Concise Dict.* 42.

Spell 248

O Fire, weapon[1] of Her who follows after the Eye, who has eaten for herself her father the primeval god,[2] who adjudged Shu for Him who ascended,[3] who destroyed the living, | may you eat and live; *Snw*[4] eats and lives for me, III, 341
I have eaten my father and am alive, my strength is the strength of the Lion; be god-like and eat what is green.[5] Mine is the knife, and my utterance is not opposed. | I have entered in to you,[6] I have gone out ⟨from you⟩,[7] I know you 342
and I know your names, I conduct you behind Rēꜥ—and *vice versa*; his place is my place, his protection is my protection, I have appeared in the Eye of Horus, I[8] eat the gods, I kill him whom I made to live,[9] I bind him whom I loosed, I implant obstacles and remove obstacles, for I am Rēꜥ, I am Authority.

1. Cf. the late word *ḥmyt* 'Art Waffe', *Wb.* III, 82,3.
2. A play on the words *pꜣwty* 'primeval god' and *pꜣty* 'two loaves'.
3. A play on *šw*.
4. The deified *snw*-loaf?
5. Apparently so, but who is addressed?
6. To whom?
7. *Ꞽm·ṯn* omitted.
8. Read *wnm·i*.
9. Read *sꜥnḫ·i*, cf. *wḥꜥ·i* in the next clause.

Spell 249

[. . .] God. I am Thoth who approaches the Great Ladies, I have come that I III, 343
may seek out the Eye of Horus, I have brought and examined it, and I have found it complete, fully numbered and intact. Its flame is to the sky, its breath is above and below, it is high in front of Him of the bird-trap. | You[1] shall 344
rejoice over me,[2] you shall be happy through me, for it is my arm[3] which brings

and guides you, it is my arm which severs[4] you. I lift it up, this arm of mine; if you sever it, it will sever you.[5] I am Thoth, my arm is before me, I[6] guide the heralds(?)[7] of the gods.

1. The Eye.
2. Read *im·i* with S2C^a here and S2C^b in 344*b*.
3. For  of S1C, S2C^b has  'warrant'. In 344*e–g* the reverse is the case, but 'arm' gives the better sense everywhere.
4. *Wḏꜥ* determined with the knife.
5. Read *wḏꜥ·tn sw gr wḏꜥ·f ṯn* as certainly S2C^{a-b}; S1C is corrupt. Despite de Buck's notes 344, nn.1*.2*, the reading *gr* is to be preferred to *ḫr*, which would make no sense here.
6. Read *sšm·i* in both texts.
7. Cf. *ḥw* 'proclaim'; possibly a miswriting of *ḥwtyw* cf. *Pyr.* § 769.

Spell 250

III, 345 SPELL FOR GOING ON THE PATH OF THE GOD. Gēb has come and he has cared for[1] me, the doors of . . .[2] are opened for me, the doors of the firmament are
346 thrown open for me, | he has given to me the sacred images of the Old Ones who preceded me, he guides me on the path of . . .;[3] I am he who is complete,[4] and the Double Lion becomes faint.

1. For *ꜥwꜣ* 'care for' cf. *Urk.* IV, 21,11; 1912,7. Only the woman's coffin B3Bo provides an object (3rd fem. sing.), but the continuations show that this spell was originally in the 1st person.
2. *Sfꜣtyw*, varr. *sfꜣṯw*, *sfꜣṯ*, meaning unknown; the context suggests a part of the sky.
3. *Gmꜣt*, meaning unknown.
4. *Skm* 'complete' has det. , borrowed from the homophone 'be grey-haired'.

Spell 251

III, 347 SPELL FOR THE NURSE OF OSIRIS.[1] I am the centipede-faced,[2] I have gone down[3] that I may protect my father from Him of the snakes, the Bull of the West; he has no power over me.[4] If I protect him,[5] he will protect me, and *vice*
348 *versa.* | My protective amulet(?) is in his hand.[6] I am under[7] the nose of Osiris, I know the names of those two nurses who make this bread for him and who bring air, the mysterious ones who preside over the Mansion of Him of the Two Names; who perceive(?) the eyes of the Mistress of Life and
349 drive away the shape of the Mistress of Death;[8] | who rescue Osiris from inertness and who rescue me from inertness. I know your names, and I shall not die, Seth shall not have power over me.[9] If the bones of Osiris are knit together every day, then my bones will be knit together every day; his bread
350 is my bread, | and I will not go in the head-cloth of the dead. A fly has flown,

a *fnṯ*-snake has crept and Osiris has reached my place; my double is exalted
and it has repeated my name. I do not die while it remains; I am Osiris, I
have counted the two gods with my . . .,[10] (and also) | those two female com- 351
panions, the two Ladies of Pe. This is life which I give to Osiris, for I am the
beloved of my father, the Lord of serpents.

1. Var. T1L: 'Driving away [. . .]' in red.
2. Varr. 'I am the centipede of Horus'; 'this N is the centipede in his mansion'.
3. In S1C^a a long omission follows.
4. T1L adds: 'this N has no power over him'.
5. S1C^a resumes. 'Him' is presumably the aforementioned father.
6. Var. S1C^b: 'his amulet(?) is in my hand and my amulet(?) is in his hand'; the damaged S2C apparently had a similar version.
7. Note the construction of independent pronoun with adverbial predicate.
8. See de Buck's 348, n.3*.
9. S2C has 348*g–h* out of place; for the other two texts see n.8 above.
10. *ʿḏꜣt*, meaning unknown.

Spell 252

To become Rēʿ-Atum.[1] O Hand-in-hand, | make a way for me, for I am the III, 352
Great One who sought out the Great Lady; I have come that I may seek out
this beard of Rēʿ-Atum which is what was taken on that day of rebellion.[2]

1. Var. T3C: 'To be the scribe of Rēʿ-Atum'. S3C has the god's name alone.
2. T3C adds: 'I shall be the scribe of Rēʿ-Atum.'

Spell 253

To become[1] the scribe of Atum.[2] Orion has gathered together his fields III, 353
which are in the house.[3] | Great is Orion in judgement, great is *Rḫt-ḥw* when 354
he is dead; | it is his[4] son who will act ⟨against⟩[5] *Rḫt-ḥw*, because he is for 355
death[6] and it is his son who will make death.[7] | O Shesmu in your nest,[8] I will 356
act on behalf on my [lord] who shall come,[9] I will act on behalf of my lord
when he departs,[10] I will depart at the monthly festival, I will return at the
yearly festival, I will be young . . . .[11]

1. Var. 'to be'.
2. Varr. 'Rēʿ-Atum'; *nb tm* 'Lord of All'; and a meaningless *nb-Rʿ-Ịtm*.
3. So T1L. M22C–B4Bo omit *sẖwt* and S1C–S3C omit *sꜣḳ* also.
4. Orion's son. Several texts omit the suffix in *sꜣ·f* both here and in 355*c*, and S1C^b omits *sꜣ* as well, writing only the det. ; note the use of the enclitic *ꜣ* after *in* in all texts, see de Buck's note 1*.

5. The preposition *r* omitted by haplography.

6. Read *n ntt·f r mt*, cf. S1C–S3C; the other texts have omitted *n* before *ntt*, another case of haplography.

7. Read *in sꜣ·f iry·f mt* with T1L, cf. de Buck, 355, n.4*. Sq6C omits *mt* and substitutes *sb m mt* (356*a*), the translation of which is obscure, for if *sb* were the object of *iry·f* one would expect the infinitive *sbt*. M22C has a text similar to T1L, but in 356*a* adds *sb m sb* [. . .]. The other versions of 355*c* are either incomplete or corrupt, and they end at this point.

8. The invocation of *Šsmw* is unexpected. The 3rd person in *šs·f* is in accord with Egyptian practice, but English requires the 2nd person, if indeed this is an invocation. If it is not, we will have to admit a textual omission between 356*b* and *c*.

9. Reading *iry·i ḥr* [*nb*]*·i*; for the restoration see de Buck, 356, n.11*.

10. Read [*r*]*wy·f* at the end of 356*d*; there seems no need to restore the second *r* as suggested by de Buck, n.12,* for what is needed here is a *sḏm·f* form, without preceding preposition.

11. Untranslatable remains. At the end of the spell Sq6C inserts the rubric which the other texts placed at the beginning of the spell.

Spell 254

III, 357 To be a scribe of Rēʿ. I am *Ḳrḳrw* the scribe of Osiris, I have counted the
number of those who are on the paths, their business is done for me, and
358 Osiris and Rēʿ-Atum[1] are content | ⟨. . .⟩ his head is given to him ⟨. . .⟩
my place.[2] I will never give my place to these . . .[3] who come with oppression
359 by evildoers. My mouth is Anubis, my arm is Thoth, | I am X son of Y, and I
will not be destroyed or obliterated by them[4] for ever.

1. Varr. 'Osiris and Rēʿ'; 'Rēʿ-Atum'.

2. 358*a* appears to have no connection with what precedes, and it would seem that there was a considerable omission before *rdy n·f tp·f*, with another omission between *tp·f* and *st·i*, the latter being quite out of context.

3. *ꜣhrw*, meaning unknown.

4. *ʾIm*, lit. 'thereby', presumably in reference to the *ꜣhrw*.

Spell 255

III, 360 Promoting a man's double[1] in the realm of the dead. | Water[2] is upon me, I
appear as Rēʿ; water is on my hands, I appear as Horus, I am exalted as Him
of Nubet.[3] I have sucked at Isis, Nephthys has nursed me in the Jackal Lake,
361 I am loosed in the Lakes of Peace, | I will wipe my face with these (cloths(?))
which are on the shoulders of Rēʿ,[4] I will receive sandal-straps thence, I will
appear as Horus who ascends in gold from upon the lips of the horizon.
362 Praise is given to me by the lords of the East,[5] | acclamation is made to me by
the lords of the West, homage is done before me by the sun-folk, I go aboard

the ship, I cross to yonder side, I enter the Great Mansion, | they establish me[6] 363
at the head of the Two Conclaves, they assign me at the head of the Two
Conclaves, the Entourage is knit together about me by the Imperishable Stars, | 364
the gates are laid hold of for me by the Unwearying Stars, my double does
not linger, for I belong to the House of Horus.

1. S1C inserts *n·f* after *s* 'man'.
2. S1C inserts the suffix *·i* after *mw*.
3. *Bnwt* is in all probability a metathesis of *Nbt(y)*, an epithet of Seth.
4. Read probably *nw n rmnwty Rʿ*, lit. 'these belonging-to-the-shoulders of Rēʿ'. For the future tense 'will wipe', etc., cf. the prospective *sḏm·f* form *ḥʿy·i* in 361*c*.
5. Var. S1C^{a}: 'West' in error, cf. 362*a*.
6. A superfluous *n* before *wi* in 363*a.b*.

Spell 256

[SPELL FOR] BECOMING THE KING OF THE SKY. I have assaulted(?) and conquered III, 365
the horizon by my own hand,[1] the Netherworld by the hand of Rēʿ, and the
wrrt-crown by the hand of the Ennead; the kingship on the thrones of Horus
is given to me, | he shoots down[2] the slaughterers[3] for me, he makes offerings 366
and oblations for me. I have conquered the horizon and have knit together
the throats of the living.

1. Omitted in S1C^{a}. S1C^{b} has 'by my utterance'.
2. Reading *šsr* with S1C^{c} ff.; for the sense cf. *Wb.* III, 547,5 and *šsr* 'arrow'.
3. Reading *ḫꜣtyw*.

Spell 257

TO BECOME ONE HONOURED WITH THE KING. O you two of the willow(?),[1] you III, 367
belong to me,[2] for I am made divine,[3] | I drive off the slaughterers;[4] prepare a 368
path for me that I may pass on it,[5] | for I am one honoured of Khons,[6] I issue 369
from his mouth in the presence of Rēʿ, I stand up in the midst of the sky, | and 370
those who are above the sky,[7] their hearts are glad.

1. *Ṯrty*; note tree-det. in B2L——B3C; the dual is confirmed by the suffix *ṯn* in 367*c* (S1C^{a}), and by *sp sn* after the word in four texts. *Krkrty* in S1C^{a} is to be read *krty*, the reduplication being in this case a way of expressing the dual; for *k* instead of *ṯ*, compare the old dependent pronoun *kw* with *ṯw* and old *kbw* 'sole', 'sandal' with *ṯbw*.
2. The pronoun *ṯn* only in S1C^{a}; the other texts repeat *ṯrty*. The former is the reading to be preferred.

3. Cf. *Pyr.* §§ 1098. 1378.

4. *H̱ꜣtyw*, written like *ḫꜣꜣ*, in S1C[a]; the other texts substitute *nwnw* 'those with dishevelled hair'.

5. All texts except S1C[a] prefix to this sentence the invocation 'O you gods'.

6. So S1C[a]; S2C[a]–S3C have: 'of the king of the sky'; B2L and B1C: 'with my sister'. Cf. Posener, *ZÄS* 93,116.

7. Before this sentence B2L and B1C insert a repetition of their version of 369*a*.

8. B2L and B1C add: *im·i* 'through me'.

Spell 258

III, 371 NOT PERISHING FOR EVER. O Great Living One, the equipped(?) one who is on his staff,[1] throw out the bow-warps of yonder Great One for(?) the Hidden One(?),[2] yonder Great One who is in the horizon. The Ennead conduct to 372 him the frog-goddesses who bore Rēʿ, | they serve for you your great doubles in the midst of the horizon; rise up wearing[3] the great White Crown, O you whom Nūt bore.[4] A great festival is celebrated for you with offerings of bread 373 and beer with the Souls of Pe, Nekhen and Ōn. | Hear this: The Elder Horus has clothed you with life; to you belongs the speech of those in whom is[5] authority, and the skins are turned over (*sic*).

1. Cf. Sethe, *Komm. Pyr.* IV, 55 f., where he points out that *ḥry-ib* is corrupted out of an original *ḥry-tp*. The sense presumably is that he leans on his staff.

2. The significance of  is by no means clear; in S1C[b] it is inserted after *ḥꜣtt* in 371*c*.

3. Lit. 'upon'; the sense is 'upon whom is', compare *ḥr sḏꜣt* 'having a seal on it'.

4. Read *msw·n Nwt* 'whom Nūt bore'; S1C[a] has the man-det.

5. *Ḥr(y)w* here, lit. 'who are over', is probably to be interpreted as in n.3 above.

Spell 259

III, 374 BEING INTRODUCED TO THEM[1] IN THE HORIZON. O you snakes of the horizon who enter here and who go out of here, ⟨who are in⟩ the . . .,[2] who place hands in 375 the hidden mansion at the chapel of the western horizon: | I travel, my power overpasses the sky, the dread of me is on earth, the terror of me is in the . . .[3] He comes into being[4] as the Eyeless One, he introduces me to your great ones. 376 | I open . . .[5] on the hands of that god who gives orders in accordance with what he knows; I am this one who uncovers[6] Nūt, I support for him[7] him who adjudges the Enneads, I cross on foot with Rēʿ over the Milky Way(?)[8] with 377 Khopri, | I know those who are in sarcophagi, and it is he who is at their head.[9]

1. Presumably the snakes mentioned below.

2. *Ỉmyw* omitted before *ḏnnwt* in S1C[a]. S3C reads: 'who enter into and come out from him who is in the *ḏnnwt*'. For *ḏnnwt* cf. *ḏnnt*, *Wb.* V, 576,12, but why the det.  ? The context implies a place or building which can be entered or left.

3. *Pꜣḳ*, meaning unknown.

4. The dets. refer to *ḫpr·f* as a whole;  , as often in *CT*, stands for .

5. For *ʿftt* see also 329*b*; meaning unknown.

6. *N* + infinitive, lit. 'of uncovering'.

7. Presumably the god of 376*a*.

8. For *msḳt* cf. *Pyr.* §§ 279. 334. 949.

9. For *ḫnty* S1C has *ʿnḫ*, which makes no sense. The doubtful *n* under *pw* at the end of this text is surely no more than a division-line between spells.

Spell 260

O Great Living One who are on[1] your *smʿt*-staff | and your *mʿnḫt*-staff, throw out the bow-warps of the Netherworld, so that those who are in[2] the horizon may live for this spirit, the Ennead being enwrapped(?)[3] and pure because of(?)[4] the great White Crown. I appear upon the great throne | so that I may be potent thereby as Thoth whom the god of the sky fashioned when Rēʿ was born for me, the dwellers in Ōn serve me, (even) the great mighty ones who dwell in the horizon. I order a festival, for mine is the *snwt*-shrine, | oblations and offerings are made for me in Ōn. The Souls of Nekhen[5] hear this; the Great One has clothed me with life in the midst of the Field of Rushes, | I am this double bull who is on the vertex of Rēʿ, who makes brightness[6] in the East according to the books of the Spirits in the West, whose faces turn round on account of their colours(?) [. . .].[7]

III, 378 · 379 · 380 · 381

1. Read *ḥry-tp*, cf. Spell 258, n.1. *Ḥtm ḥr-ib* of three texts out of four is obscure, for the preposition is strange after that verb; we would expect *m* if the sense is 'who are provided with'.

2. S3C omits  of *imyw*.

3. With sheets of linen? Cf. *ḥnkyt* 'bed'.

4. For *ḥr* S1C[b] has *ḥr(y)t-ib* 'who are in the midst of', which does not make sense; similarly S3C.

5. Var. S1C[b] 'of Pe'.

6. Var. S1C[b]: 'who goes forth bright'.

7. S1C[b] only. The mention of 'colours' may perhaps allude to the hues of dawn and sunset; cf. *RB* 113, 12–13.

Spell 261

To BECOME A MAGICIAN. O you nobles[1] who are in the presence of the Lord of All, behold, I have come to you;[2] respect me in proportion to what you know. I am he whom the Sole Lord made[3] | before there came into being the two meals on earth, when he sent his Sole Eye when he was alone,[4] being what

III, 382 · 383

came forth from his mouth; when his myriads of spirits[5] were the protection
384 of his companions;[6] | when he spoke with Khopri, with him,[7] that he might be
more powerful than he;[8] when he took authoritative utterance upon his mouth.
385 I am indeed the son of Her who bore Atum,[9] | I am the protection of what the
Sole Lord commanded,[10] I am he who caused the Ennead to live,[11] I am 'If-
he-wishes-he-does',[12] the father of the gods. The standard is high, the god[13] is
387 endowed in accordance with the command of Her who bore Atum, | the august
god who speaks and eats with his mouth.[14] I have kept silence,[15] I have bowed
388 down, I have come shod ⟨into the presence of⟩ the Bulls of the sky,[16] | I have
seated myself ⟨in the presence of⟩ the Bulls of the sky,[17] in this my dignity
of 'Greatest of the owners of doubles', the heir of Atum.
389 I have come that I may take possession of my throne | and that I may receive
my dignity, for to me belonged all before you had come into being,[18] you gods;
go down and come upon the hinder parts,[19] for I am a magician.[20]

1. B1Bo has: 'O you who are in the presence of the nobles of Atum'.

2. Var. B1Bo: 'behold, N is with you'. Note the superfluous *n* before *wi* in the other three texts.

3. Varr. S1C:[b] 'I am the young one whom the Sole Lord made'; B1Bo apparently: 'because of this name of the Sole Lord'.

4. So four texts; B1Bo has *n wn·f* instead of *m wn·f*.

5. *M wn ḥḥ·f n kꜣ*; B1Bo omits *m*.

6. B1Bo adds: 'who shone in his eye'.

7. B1Bo has *n* for the first *ḥnꜥ* and omits the second.

8. Var. B1Bo apparently *wsr (r)n N pn m wsr·f* 'that N's name might be powerful through his power'.

9. Var. B1Bo: 'as for N, he is the son of Her who bore Atum', and then inserts in contradiction: 'who was born without a mother'.

10. B1Bo omits *sꜣ* 'protection' and misreads  as ; it also inserts thereafter the obscure *N pn ḥwy kꜣw·f* 'N is he who smote his spirits'.

11. Again an obscure and unintelligible addition by B1Bo (385*e*–386*a*).

12. Compare the fuller form of this expression in *Pyr.* § 412.

13. Plural in B1Bo, which reads: 'the gods are endowed in accordance with what the eldest god commanded'.

14. B1Bo omits the reference to eating.

15. Var. B1Bo apparently: *snḏ·n N pn ⟨n⟩ id·n·f* 'N was afraid of him whom he assaulted(?)', but the relation of this to the context is obscure.

16. Emending into *iy·n·i ṯb⟨·ky m-bꜣḥ⟩ kꜣw nw pt*; *kꜣw*, despite the det., surely stands for 'bulls'; so also in 388*a*. B1Bo has: 'he has come so that he may defy (*ksm*) the Bulls of the sky'.

17. B1Bo has corrupted *ḥms·n* into a meaningless group.

18. For *ḫprt* B1Bo has less correctly *ḫpr·n*.

19. *'Iyw* is probably to be understood as the rare old imperative 'come!'; the sense of the whole expression is apparently 'squat down'.

20. Var. B1Bo: 'N is a noble magician'.

Spell 262

To be equipped as [. . .]. I am one,[1] the second of the Ennead; men ferry III, 390
'Ibnwt[2] over, she grinds for me . . .[3] because what is given to me is bread. This of mine is not an estate(?)[4] [. . .][5] who breaks . . .[6] every day. | I have 391
gone up and come down, men have sung for me, acclamation has been made for me. I am the lord who guards(?)[7] the earth; few and small are the banks of . . .,[8] the tomb is intact(?).[9]

1. Read *wꜥ·i*, *sḏm·f* form.
2. An obscure being.
3. *Mꜣtn* with fire-det., meaning unknown. There may have been some corruption here.
4. Reading doubtful; *ḏꜣtt* seems a possibility.
5. A broken passage in S2C^a, omitted in S1C.
6. *Sḏꜣ*, quite obscure.
7. Probably so, despite the det., borrowed from *sꜣy* 'linger'.
8. *Ḥt ꜥbꜣ*; perhaps to be read as *t ꜥbꜣ*, cf. IV, 45j, but even so, quite obscure.
9. Read perhaps *(w)ḏꜣt*, but IV, 45*j* has *ḏꜣt* with boat-det; if anything, the latter is even more obscure.

Spell 263

O Great One (*wr*) who destroys what is detestable, O Great One (*ꜥꜣ*) who wakes III, 392
Nbyt, hide her, my father, from those who are in the Abyss. I am the Pelican[1] who saw your birth, who saw your birth when you were born.[2] I[3] have come here seeking my fledglings.

1. Cf. 393*b*.
2. For 392*a–b*, B2L has: 'O Great One, Great God, who saw ( omitted) your birth'.
3. For the continuing 1st person cf. B2L, which reads: 'I have come seeking all the nests of the god', with the rubric 'Opening up the West' inserted out of place after *iy·n·i m*, see de Buck, 392, n.8*.

Spell 264

O Great One, loud of voice, N is the Pelican who sees your[1] head. He has come III, 393
here that he may seek his fledgelings, and the heron(?) is content, for N is his father. This one who comes is the Great One, N is safe in the sight of the Old One . . .[2] as Seth, upon his wings as Thoth; his plumes are the tails of . . .,[3] he has gone up that he may drive off[4] what Gēb[5] detests. Opening up the West in the realm of the dead.

1. See de Buck, 393, n.1*.
2. Obviously corrupt; something has been lost before and after *n·f*.
3. *Bꜣtyw*.
4. Cf. *dndn* 'subdue', *Concise Dict.* 323, here with a nuance of motion.
5. Written abnormally.

Spell 265

III, 394 NOT [PERISHING FOR EVER].[1] O great living one, O you who are provided in the midst of the sky, throw out the bow-warps of the Great One who is in the city; they will cause the doubles of the great ones in the midst of the horizon to circulate [. . .] Horus wearing[2] the White Crown, I have come that I may pass to[3] the sky, for the fear of me is in the sky and the terror of me is in the hearts of the Fenkhu; I have come that I may be vindicated and that my double may attend on my body. It is Thoth who flew[4] yesterday and who secured[5] the ropes with your doubles; it is this Eye of [Osiris(?)][6] which secured the ropes with the double of Rēʿ in the midst of his field. I am the gall of the Destructive One, the Lord of snakes; I am weary in proportion as Rēʿ is weary. [. . .] at the going of Shu, the messenger of Bastet, I will never be
395 given over to the killer, | the hostile serpents have not eaten me.

O you who lasso and quench,[7] act as a god, Anubis [. . .] . . . the toes of your doubles[8] for the Bull who is in your midst. [I] eat [bread and drink(?)] pure water,[9] I am . . .[10]; you shall come[11] for me, summons being made to you. [See], I am[12] in your midst [. . .] both your wings. I am this one who comes of himself, I am not eaten because of [. . .] who eats on his face, whose belly is empty, who lives on the shorn ones of *Skks*.

1. See 371*a*; this spell is related to Spell 258.
2. Lit. 'in the midst of'.
3. Read *swꜣ·i r*.
4. 'Thoth' is misplaced; the text should have read *in Ḏḥwty wʿr sf*. For this verb cf. 'fly', of javelin, *BD* 219,10.
5. Emend into *smnt* as 394*k*.
6. See de Buck, 394, n.3*. *Wsyr* might be possible.
7. Surely corrupt; probably there have been omissions of text.
8. *Sic*; probably again corrupt.
9. Read perhaps *wnm⟨·i t swr·i⟩ wʿb*, but the space seems barely enough.
10. *Trḥty*. quite obscure.
11. Prospective *sḏm·f* form *iwt·f*.
12. Restore as *m* [·*k*] *wi*.

Spell 266

I am Atum in his name of Rēʿ [. . .]; I am Min(?)[1] in his name of Min(?), I III, 39
am [. . .] and the great monster is on his belly.

1. The ideogram looks more like a door-bolt *s* than the Min-sign, but the det. of the god with two plumes favours Min.

Spell 267

NOT DYING AGAIN. O you great living one who are detained on[1] your staff, | III, 397
throw out the bow-warps of the Netherworld, the living ones[2] who are in the horizon of this spirit; he has conducted to you the fathers[3] of his Enneads.
Appear in this great cool room;[4] | Nūt has borne you according to the birth 398
of Rēʿ, the powers issue from Ōn, the greatest of the snakes who are before the
horizon are enduring, and I live as Thoth,[5] | Pe is given to me, Dep is mine, 399
and an offering is made for me in Ōn. O Souls of Pe and Dep,[6] truly hear this;
I have ennobled you[7] as the Elder Horus[8] in life, | and you are the Double 400
Bull, the Great One who is on the vertex of Rēʿ, and the chief powers issue from the East.

1. Read *ḥry-tp*; see Spell 258, n.1.
2. Perhaps snakes acting as ropes.
3. Apparently so in S1C, where the *n* before *itwy* seems superfluous. B2Bo has 'his women of his Enneads', so too B7Bo; B5C and S10C are quite corrupt.
4. So S1C: each text has a different word here. Further, all texts lack the indirect genitive after *tw*, which indicates that *wrt* is adjectival.
5. Varr. S1C: 'his soul'; S10C: 'Horus'.
6. So B5C; the other texts have 'Pe and Nekhen'.
7. The deceased, for the pronoun of the 2nd person is singular here and in 400*a*. Clearly there has been a textual omission after 399*d*.
8. S1C omits 'Horus'; S10C has *šmsw Ḥr* 'Followers of Horus' and omits *m* before *ʿnḫ*.

Spell 268

BECOMING SOBK, LORD OF THE WINDING WATERWAY. N is the *fnṯ*-snake which IV, 1
issued from the shank and ate the Chaos-god, whom Seth exhaled for him from within the secrets of Gēb.[1] N is a shape who eats (even) when he copu-
lates,[2] who lives on . . .,[3] | who makes for himself . . .[4] to the full extent of 2
his[5] desire. The . . .[6] have descended from the sky for him. His are the bulls,[7] Anubis has made horns for him, because N is a great crocodile, and fair is the flood of the lord of the fens,[8] the greatly majestic, the companion of this

3 Great One who traverses swamps and river-banks. | N has come from[9] the green fens, he has turned the reeds of the fens and the crocodiles[10] of the fens, N traverses swamps and river-banks; N has come[11] that he may eat his brother[12] with his fish-scales;[13] the god comes, having eaten his brother and
4 lived on his scales.[14] | N finds his true brother(?),[15] namely the brother of this Great One, namely this Dep-ite judge who is in the Broad Hall of Abydos. N is a crocodile-spirit,[16] crocodile-faced, dangerous in the reeds of the fens; N has traversed the crossings of the river-banks, for N is a crocodile, lord of the
5 creeks.[17] | Djedu has been given to N to nourish him, with Khabet for his nurse;[18] Edjō the Great has acted for him[19] so as to ferry him over to the Fields of Offerings.

Acclamation to N and to his double![20] N is Sobk, lord of creeks.[21]

1. Var. *Ḫꜣ* in T1L.

2. Var. T1L: 'his *ḥdw*-fish'; on *wnm nk·f* in B1Bo and B2Be see Spell 285, n.4.

3. *'Iꜥnw*, var. B2Be *iꜥrw*, is incomprehensible as a *Lebensmittel*.

4. *Smwt*, meaning unknown, but the dets. suggest something unpleasant. IV, *2a–3c* are absent in T1L and Sq6C.

5. The suffix *·f* here and in what follows appears to refer to the deceased.

6. *'Ityw*, meaning unknown; var. B2Be: *ikw* 'quarrymen'.

7. Var. B2Be: 'he fetters the bulls', obviously a corruption.

8. Not 'fields', since they are places where crocodiles lurk, see also 3*b*.

9. B1Bo omits *m*.

10. For *sbk* as a common noun 'crocodile' cf. 4*g* where it occurs as an equivalent of *msḥ*.

11. Var. T1L and Sq6C: 'this N will be a great one'.

12. B1Bo has the *sḏm·n·f* form *wnm·n·f*; the *sḏm·f* form of B2Be is to be preferred. B2Be omits the suffix after *sn*. The 'brother' apparently is the fish which shares the water with the crocodile and which the latter eats.

13. Var. T1L: 'N lives on his scales', without any indication as to whose scales; Sq6C ends in lacuna.

14. Var. T1L: 'the god comes, having lived on his brother', and adds 'so shall you (plur.) say concerning this N'.

15. As it stands, 4*a* is not only unintelligible, but grammatically impossible, so that there must have been some corruption. One might perhaps emend as *iw N pn gm·f sn·f mꜣꜥ*, but even so the sense remains obscure.

16. 4*d–g* only in T1L and Sq6C.

17. Lit. 'Niles'.

18. T1L reads *iw rdy·n N pn Ḏdw wdnw N pn Ḫꜣbt*, etc.

19. Emending *ir·n·t* of B1Bo into *ir·n*. B2Be omits the words before *Wꜣḏt*; T1L and Sq6C have a version of their own.

20. B2Be differs unessentially; T1L: 'Praise is given to N and acclamation to N's double'. Sq6C was originally very similar.

21. In both B1Bo and B2Be *ḥspw* 'gardens' is an error for *ḫpw* 'creeks', For this last clause T1L and Sq6C substitute 'N lives on something from you (plur.)'. B1Bo and Sq6C insert the rubric at the end of the spell.

Spell 269

BECOMING BARLEY OF LOWER EGYPT. N is this bush of life which went forth IV, 6
from Osiris to grow on the ribs of Osiris and to nourish the plebs, which
makes the gods divine and spiritualizes the spirits, which provisions the 7
owners of doubles and the owners of property, which makes cakes for the spirits, which causes the living to grow, and which makes firm the bodies of the living. N lives on smoked grain, N is the smoked grain of the living, N lives and grows fat on the ribs of Gēb, the desire[1] of N is in sky and earth, in the waters and in the fields.[2] Beneficial is Isis to Horus her god,[3] she is friendly thereby to Horus her god. N lives as Osiris.[4]

1. For *iw mrwt N pn*, Sq6C has corruptly *iw tn Wsyr N pn*, which makes no sense.
2. In Sq6C only.
3. For *ꜣḫ n ꜣst* 'it goes well with Isis' of T1L, read *ꜣḫ ꜣst* 'beneficial is Isis' with Sq6C; the significance of *im·f* in the continuation is not certain.
4. So T1L; Sq6C has: 'it is N who lives and goes forth as Osiris', and ends with the rubric which T1L has at the beginning of the spell.

Spell 270

BECOMING SOPD. N has gone forth upon the water which surrounds him, IV, 8
N's plume is on his head, N's eyes are the powerful ones(?),[1] woe(?) is in the garden(?)[2] . . .[3] N is lord of the deserts,[4] N is Sopd, eldest of the gods.

1. *Kꜣꜣ* as an adjective meaning perhaps 'potent', in reference to the Eye of Horus, occurs in *Pyr.* § 2087. In T1L the det. looks like an insect! *Ḳ* of T1L is an error.
2. Apparently so in T1L; the varr. have 'woe(?) is in the west of *Gmt*'. Neither version is comprehensible to me.
3. 8*g* completely defeats me. *Msprw*, written in T1L as *m⸢ꜥ⸣prw*, may be connected with *Wb.* II, 144,5.6.
4. Var. Sq6C: 'O N, you are lord of the deserts'. Both Sq6C and Sq3C omit the next clause and end with the rubric, which in Sq3C reads: 'Becoming Isis'.

Spell 271

BECOMING AN ꜥWꜥ-BIRD.[1] I have[2] flown up as an ibis, I have alighted as a IV, 9
ḳꜣd-bird, I am he who saw[3] the Unclothed One, the son of Ḥatḥōr.[4]

1. Var. *iwꜥ[w]*-bird in Sq6C (9*f*). In 9*b* (B2L and B2P only) is a corruption of 15*f*.
2. For the 1st person cf. B2L and B2P.
3. Var. Sq6C: 'O N, it is you who saw . . .'.
4. I.e. Iḥy 'the Sistrum Player', who is depicted naked. In Sq6C is the var. 'him whose head is uncovered', while B2L and B2P omit *f* of *kf*, apparently under the delusion that *k* was the suffix.

Spell 272

IV, 10 BECOMING A HERON(?)[1] I[2] am a heron(?) on the limitless desert plateau, and there is brought to me what appertains to the land of Atum.[3]

1. Determined with  in *Pyr.* § 2179.
2. The 1st person in four texts out of seven.
3. 'Of Atum' omitted in the B2L group.

Spell 273

IV, 11 BECOMING A FALCON. I am a falcon[1] on that night of enriching[2] the years. He[3] has set the dread of me in those who are over destruction,[4] and respect
12 for me in the lords of butchery; | I will not be taken to the slaughter-house of the god, the destroyers will not use their whip-lashes[5] on me, for I am the guide to the horizon of the sky.[6]

1. B2L and B2P only; lost in B1Y. The other texts treat this spell as a continuation of Spell 272.
2. Var. B3L: *sgrh* 'making peaceful'.
3. Who?
4. Sq6C: 'who are over the old ones'.
5. *Ḥꜥwt*, here translated as 'whip-lashes', appears to be identical with *ḥꜥt* 'wick', Gardiner, Sign-list V28. A plaited wick would resemble a diminutive lash of plaited leather. B2L and B2P have *ḏḥrwt*, cf. *ḏḥrw* 'leather lacings', *Concise Dict.* 324, supporting the above translation of *ḥꜥwt*. Sq1C has absurdly *wdḥw·s m rꜣ⟨·i⟩* 'her altars in my mouth'.
6. Only in T1L and B3L; Sq6C has the rubric here, with *nwr* 'heron' for *byk* 'falcon'.

Spell 274

IV, 13 BECOMING A DIVINE FALCON IN THE REALM OF THE DEAD. Hail to you, Horus of the East, whom my herald does not know;[1] I will descend[2] and rush on(?)[3] to
14 your stairway.[4] I am uplifted[5] as a divine falcon | ⟨. . .⟩ upon(?) its ribs(?),[6] I will move up and down at starboard and larboard,[7] I will strike with my sceptre and control with my staff.[8] They of the starboard watch are under my control,
15 they of the larboard watch are under my command,[9] I will follow the god, I will make

the descent to the Bank of Rushes,[10] I will go around the northern sky. Make your rope fast.[11] It means that Khnum will make fast.[12]

1. *ʾIḫm* has been regarded as a relative form, since it is *ḥwt*(*y*) who is most likely to be ignorant.

2. *Hꜣy·i*, var. *hꜣy N pn*, looks like a prospective *sḏm·f*; *r·i* (*ir·f*) is the enclitic. Sq6C has the infinitive *hꜣyt* followed by the agential genitive *nt Wsir N pn*.

3. For the sense given to *gwꜣ*, cf. *Pyr.* § 709; Sethe, *Komm. Pyr.* III, 303.

4. B2L and B2P omit the suffix after *rwd*, which in Sq6C is determined with  .

5. B2L and B1Y stress the subject of *ṯny·i* with *ink*; B2P has the 3rd person *N pn* followed by *ṯny·i* with the suffix of the 1st person.

6. Cf. *wgyw* 'ribs(?)' of ship, *Concise Dict.* 71. Since the suffix in *wgw·f* has no antecedent, it is clear that there has been a textual omission before *r-sꜣ* which will have mentioned a masculine word for boat (*im*, *wyꜣ*?); the nautical context of what follows makes this clear. *R-sꜣ* of 14*a* may mean 'on the back of', = 'standing on' ribs, or it may mean 'behind', 'abaft' some construction. Our ignorance of the precise meaning of *wgw* prevents a decision between these alternatives.

7. The significance of the adjective *ꜥꜣ* after *tꜣ-wr* in T1L and after both *imy-wrt* and *tꜣ-wr* in B2L and B2P is not obvious, and it is omitted in Sq6C. From what follows it is clear that the reference here is to the rowing-gangs on either side of the vessel.

8. The deceased keeps order among the rowers with sceptre and staff. B2P is garbled.

9. The plural suffixes in 14*d* of all texts except Sq6C are superfluous. *ʾImyw-wrt ḫr st·i tꜣw-wr ḫr wḏ-mdw·i* of Sq6C (certainly originally in the 1st person) probably represents the archetypal reading.

10. So T1L, Sq6C; var. B2L: 'the descent of the Sunshine-god'; B2P: 'to the bank of the Sunshine-god'.

11. On *hy nwḥ* 'make a rope fast' see *JEA* 57,202. T1L shows only the det. of *nwḥ*, which in Sq6C has been corrupted into *nwtt*.

12. Sq6C is corrupt.

Spell 275

N is one who expels and opposes, who lives by air; N has overturned Osiris IV, 16
from his throne on the day of the Festival of Sokar. Air belongs to N, N has swallowed the Ennead and fed on the Cobra, N is the cedar-tree in front of Osiris, who gives what N needs, and judgement in the matter is what they (*sic*) have done.[1] N has split open the mountains, N lives by air; this means that he shares out what they have given to him.[2] Assuming all forms in the realm of the dead.

1. So rather than 'what was done for them', cf. 16*f.j.*

2. B1Bo omits 16*b–i* and B2Be omits the rubric.

Spell 276

N is this forepart of a lion(?)[1] which lives and shines on the day[2] when he IV, 17 knows of the turning back in the hearts of the gods.[3] She who is high on his vertex is the Lady of the Horizon,[1] a spirit better equipped than any god. N protects[4] men, the gods show respect to him, this Great One (fem.) has appeared in his shape.[5] The Lady of Offerings is in him,[6] he has taken her bow-warp(?)[7] and the great oar within the shrine. N has come that he may set the fear of himself in the gods,[8] he protects the Eye of Horus in the tribunals of every god. TAKING SHAPE AS ḤATḤŌR in the realm of the dead.[9]

1. A star or planet?
2. 𓇳𓀭 is apparently meant for *rꜥ* 'day'; BH1Ox has *hrw*.
3. Meaning a change of mind?
4. Reading with B1Bo rather than with B2Be, which has: 'N is protected by men'. BH1Ox has the senseless *snḏ in N ṯn*.
5. BH1Ox: *iw ḥ3t·t ḥ3t m irw·s*, clearly corrupt.
6. BH1Ox again slightly corrupt.
7. Reading *ḥ3t* as *ḥ3tt* 'bow-warp', with some doubt. *Ḥ3t·s* 'her bow' seems poor sense.
8. So B1Bo; BH1Ox has reduced this to *iy·n dy snḏ ḏs*.
9. The last words only in B1Bo, which writes the rubric in black.

Spell 277

IV, 18 BECOMING THOTH.[1] I have sat down with the Eye of Horus at the head of the
Three[2] who give orders among the gods in the affairs of Thoth. My protection
is Thoth's protection among you. I am a spirit, lord of spirits, and it was a
spirit who made me. . . .[3] I am he who celebrates the monthly festival, and
19 who bears witness to[4] the half-monthly festival; | the circuit[5] of the Eye of
Horus[6] is at my hand[7] in the suite of Thoth. As for any god, any goddess,
any spirit, or any dead, male or female, who shall open(?)[8] his mouth against
me this day, he shall fall to the execution-blocks, (to) the magic which is in my
body, the sore flames which are on my mouth. Those who see me are afraid
20 of me, | for I am high, having gone up aloft,[9] (being) one who has no weakness.
I have expelled him who is hated[10] with my hands; I never judged[11] with
partiality between the Rivals, and I never heard in the Palace anything that
was said[12] when all the Tribunal spoke. The Rivals were satisfied with what
21 I said in judgement. | I never repeated[13] a judgement as one who went forth
because of those who did evil to him(?) when they spoke.[14] I have made for
him the House of Eight in the House of Thirty.[15] I am the Bull of Justice;
men respect my voice and dread my fierceness(?).[16] I am the confidant of the
Palace in the presence of the Bull of Justice. May your souls be quiet, be quiet
22 for me, for I am |Thoth; behold, I have come joyfully, executing judgement on

the destroyer at the desire[17] of Isis the great and making the Rivals content.

1. In black here, in red at the end of B1Bo and in black in B2Be.

2. Cf. the epithet of the sun-god *bꜣ n ḫmt* 'Soul of the Three', *Wb.* III, 283,12. BH2C has corruptly 'three days'; the suffix 2nd plur. in 18*d* can refer only to beings, not to days.

3. I can make nothing of 18*f*, which appears to be quite corrupt. All three texts differ.

4. B1Bo, B2Be *smtr*, BH2C *mtr*, probably incorrectly.

5. *Dbnt*, so B1Bo and BH2C; B2Be has *dbnwt* 'locks' of hair, for which see *M. u. K.* 9,6.

6. B1Bo omits 'of Horus'.

7. *R ʿ·i* (BH2C); B2Be: *r ʿ n N pn*. B1Bo has *ḥr* [hieroglyphs] *n* 'upon the warrant of'.

8. B2Be has *nswt(y)·f(y)*, i.e. *sḏmty·fy* form; *·f* has been omitted in B1Bo. In *Wb.* II, 325,13 the verb is not allotted a meaning, but the context and the possible derivation from *ns* 'tongue' both indicate that the meaning may be to 'open' the mouth in speech. BH2C has preserved only *t* and the det. [hieroglyph] (error for [hieroglyph] by confusion with *ns* 'flame') and the suffix.

9. BH2C is defective, and also omits *m* before *tp*.

10. Following B1Bo in reading *ḫbḏy* 'who is hated' in preference to the collective *ḫryt* 'enemies' of the other texts; the former is more forceful.

11. Both B1Bo and B2Be have *wpt* where one would expect the *sḏm·f* form *wp*. Cf. n.13.

12. I.e. 'I did not eavesdrop'.

13. B1Bo wrongly *wḥmt* for *wḥm*.

14. BH2C possibly *m prt*. The sense of the passage is by no means clear, but it may mean that he never changed a verdict because of adverse comment. All texts appear to be corrupt in part; the archetypal reading may possibly have been *ḥr iryw isft r·f mdw·sn*.

15. Text obscure and translation doubtful.

16. Cf. *nhd* 'grimmig o. ä.', *Wb.* II, 288,2; a word nearly synonymous with *snḏ* is needed. *Kbyt* (B1Bo) or *kbwt* is not recorded, but is guessed from the context to mean 'fierceness' or the like.

17. Read *sḥtm* ⟨*m*⟩ *ib* in all texts. In BH1Bo and B2Be *m* is omitted by haplography; in BH2C *n·f* is superfluous.

Spell 278

I have flown up as a swallow,[1] I have cackled as a goose, it has been granted IV, 23
to me to alight on the plateau of the Great Foreland,[2] and I have stood on it;
I have moored[3] at it and I have sat down on it. I shall appear[4] as a god, I shall
eat and gorge(?)[5] in the Field of Offerings,[6] | I will make descents into the 24
reeds(?),[7] the Doors of Righteousness will be opened for me, the doors of the
firmament will be thrown open for me, for I am saved from my foes.[8] O men
and gods, I am bound for seven meals in the sky(?).[9] Six meals are on earth, so
that I may go up;[10] | I will set up a ladder among the gods, for I am one of 25
them.[11] BECOMING A GOOSE.[12]

1. Not 'great One', despite the writings; this sentence and the next liken the deceased to a bird. For *wr* 'swallow' cf. *Pyr.* §§ 1130. 1216; 1770.

2. Read *ḫnty* (masc.); the qualifying adjective *ꜥꜣ* is masc. in all texts.

3. I.e. 'died', but the fact of death is not to be admitted.

4. The writing *ḫꜥy* of Sq6C suggests the prospective *sḏm·f*. Here this text has slipped back for a moment into the 1st person, to which Sq1Sq has adhered from the first.

5. Cf. *wnm ꜣf* also in *CT* II, 394*a*, see Spell 162, n.4.

6. So T1L; Sq6C has 'by means of magic', while Sq1Sq reads: 'I will eat a meal in the Field of Offerings'.

7. Var. Sq6C: 'the banks of reeds(?)'; compare *BD* 376,16.

8. Var. Sq6C: 'from men and gods', anticipating 24*e*.

9. All texts appear to be corrupt; perhaps to be emended as *iw·i r ḫt 7 r pt* 'I am bound for seven meals in the sky'; Sq1Sq has 'six'.

10. So Sq6C. T1L has: 'N's six meals are so that N may go up to [. . .]'; Sq1Sq: 'my meals are in sky and earth' and omits 24*h*.

11. Sq6Sq writes *wꜥ* 'one' with a single stroke.

12. Sq6C only.

Spell 279

[. . .] you have your soul, you being a soul;[1] go forth![2] you come [. . .], you
IV, 26 will descend, | you will bathe in the basin of the Abyss; you will come to land in the West;[3] you grow as a growing-bird, you glitter[4] as a glitter-bird;[5] you come to land at the Field of Rushes, you eat the cucumbers[6] of the two mysterious mansions[7] [. . .]; you have divided the field-plots of the two Fields of Offerings; you have flown up[8] [. . .]; you have occupied[9] [. . .]. The king
27 sees it,[10] | you who go up on account of it have not moored,[11] you have appeared as the great god. [You] have seen it, you have appeared because of it as the great god,[12] you have eaten the cucumbers [. . .] your eye [. . .]. O N, you are a glitter-bird which lies down and does what it will; [your] wings are those of a sacred image. [BECOMING . . .].

1. Old perfective 2nd sing., referring to the deceased.

2. The absence of the ending of the 2nd person in *pr* precludes this from being an old perfective like *bꜣt*; it appears rather to be imperative with reinforcing dative. Like Spell 806, this text was originally in the 2nd person, see also 27*f*.

3. T1L has *r imntyw*, 'at the Westerners', but this is surely a miswriting of *r imnt*. Sq6C has *r ḫnt nfrt* 'at the beautiful stopping-place'.

4. Cf. *CT* VII, 11*j*.

5. Both texts have a bird as det., which seems to exclude the interpretation as 'starry sky'; cf. also 27*f*.

6. Reading *šspwt*.

7. The reading *štꜣ* in T1L is not quite certain; Sq6C is much damaged here.

8. Sq6C only.

9. For this sense of *sḥn* cf. *Pyr.* § 310; *BD* 127,9.

10. Read *mꜣꜣ nsw*, a case of honorific transposition, cf. *27b*.
11. In the sense of dying; cf. Spell 278, n.3.
12. *M nṯr ꜥꜣ* omitted in T1L.

Spell 280

O N, you are the Elder Horus who took sail(?)[1] at nightfall(?) while you were IV, 28
at rest ⟨in⟩ the tomb of the *Nt*-crowns of the great ones and the lesser ones.[2]

O N, you are he who mourns in the Mansion of Osiris; your eye is Rēꜥ, your arms are Atum,[3] your legs are the centipede-god, your head is Iwnmūtef.

This is a reminder that honour was taken in the House of the Two Thorns for Her who is kneeling(?);[4] you have issued thence with your plume on your head. You possess your mother, and your mother has given (gifts) to you.

ꜥO N, you are the Elder ⟨Horus⟩,[5] you have judged between the Rivals, 29
namely the two who would destroy the sky; you have adzed[5a] Orion with the two adzes of Seth, you have given judgement in this sky for Rēꜥ, light and dark are at your will.[6]

O N, you are the Elder Horus, one who has become the Elder Horus. BECOMING THE ELDER HORUS.

1. For *ṯꜣwt* see also *Urk.* V, 156,15. This spell appears to have been originally in the 2nd person, see also *29a*.
2. Apparently so, but the meaning of *28c–d* escapes me.
3. Var. 'Min'.
4. Lit. 'her who is on the calf of her leg'.
5. Not in Sq3C. The original reading may have been 'the Elder Horus', cf. *28a*; *29f*.
5a. cf. *Pyr.* 2080; JEA 24. pl. 2, 4. Orion is thought of here of as a wooden figure.
6. Lit. 'what N says'. *Ḏdt* of Sq3C is to be preferred to *ḏd* of Sq6C.

Spell 281

Hail to you, you who perceive the wand[1] of the august god! Come and hear it, IV, 30
this word, and empower it, this magic of N; N appears as Horus,[2] great in the ram's-head,[3] the hawk[4] of the gods. N has taken possession of your powers, N has taken away your magic. All the spirits[5] who know their spells are those who shall make their own magic. N has taken possession of everything within the Broad Hall in the eastern horizon of the sky; the Elder Gods rejoice and the two great Enneads are happy when they see the manifestations of this
Neith the Great, Lady of Sais,[6] ꜥ for she has taken for herself the warrant of the 31
Great Ones in her train. Go in peace, in peace; do what you have heard, (namely) what I have said to you,[7] and do not again do harm to N. O N, you are Horus himself, Lord of magic.[8] BECOMING MAGIC.[9]

1. *Syꜣ(w) sḫm* is to be understood as a plural, cf. 30*b*, despite the singular suffix in *inḏ ḥr·k*, which apparently is becoming a more or less fixed expression.

2. Var. Sq6C: 'She (woman's coffin) is made to appear as a falcon'.

3. Conceived as a mask covering the head; cf. *bbwt* 'long wig', *Concise Dict.* 82.

4. For *gnḥsw* as var. of *gmḥsw* cf. *Pyr.* § 1048.

5. *ꜣḫw* is to be interpreted as 'spirits', despite the det. in both texts. The suffix *·ṯn* in Sq6C is probably to be ignored as a carry-over from the preceding sentences. The whole phrase *ꜣḫw nbw rḫw r·sn* is the subject of a sentence of which *irt(y)·sn ḥkꜣ·sn ḏs·sn* is the nominal predicate.

6. The sentences 30*k*–31*d* appear to be an interpolation from another source, for they are not in accord with the general context of this spell.

7. *'Ir n·ṯn sḏmt·n·ṯn ḏdt·i n·ṯn* which pronouns 2nd plur.; 31*d* shows that they refer to beings who are adjured not to harm the deceased. In Sq3C presumably the lector is speaking on behalf of the deceased; this interpretation seems preferable to that of Sq6C: 'what N has said to you'.

8. Var. Sq6C: 'O N, you are Magic himself'.

9. So rather than 'a magician', because both texts have det. , not .

Spell 282

Not to lie down in the shambles. N has swallowed *Wpšt*,[1] N has chewed *Wpšt*.
It is said of N[2] that his savour goes up, and that the dread of him is banished
IV, 32 from the sky | and the fear ⟨of him⟩[3] goes down from[4] the horizon. All the
gods fall dead and the spirits are on their faces when they see[5] N at his going up
upon[6] . . .,[7] and he is exalted within the shrine. N has taken possession of all
the powers of the One, and praise is given to N by those who are with him
when they see N dominating[8] their lord; Tayt has made for him a seat which
belongs to N. BECOMING TAYT.

1. Lit. perhaps 'what is strewn', i.e. grain, here deified.

2. So Sq6C; Sq3C apparently has the imperative: 'Speak, O N', which makes poorer sense.

3. Omitted after *snḏ*, cf. Sq3C, which employs the name.

4. Or 'into'.

5. Apparently a geminated *sḏmt·f* form.

6. Construed as a fem. nisba qualifying the fem. infinitive *prt*.

7. *wt*, meaning unknown. The translation follows Sq6C.

8. After *mꜣꜣ·sn* the *nw* of Sq6C is inexplicable and seems superfluous; this *nw* has no counterpart in Sq3C and has been ignored in the translation. *Ḫꜥ ḥr*, var. *sḫꜥ ḥr*, lit. 'manifested upon' or 'appearing over', in this context implies dominion.

Spell 283

IV, 33 O N,[1] you are a swallow, you are a swallow. O N, you are the father of the *ḥḏḏyt*-bird, the daughter of Rēꜥ. O you gods whose savour is sweet, there is a flame[2] for N when he goes up from the horizon. BECOMING A SWALLOW.

1. Sq6C has a rubric at the end of the spell: 'Becoming a swallow (*mnt*)', with an eccentric spelling of *mnt*; the lost rubric at the beginning of T1L has the merest trace of *w* of *ḫprw*(?), see de Buck's note 33, n.2; Sq1C starts with *tm mt m wḥm* 'not dying again', in red; L1Li has *ḏd mdw N ḏd·f* 'Words spoken by N. He says'. Of the texts which follow, L1Li and Sq1C are in the 1st person, the much battered T1L is in the 3rd person, while Sq6C is in the 2nd person. This last appears to be the best version of the four and has been followed in the translation.

2. *Ns* 'flame' has a superfluous *s* in Sq6C. L1Li reads: 'a flame has gone up from the horizon', as also *BD* 186,6; T1L has 'the flame of N has gone up, N [has gone up from(?)] the horizon'. The text of Sq1C may have read *pr* where de Buck has doubtfully read *prt*; it also obscurely substitutes *sšm* for *ns* and at the end appends 'the blessed, vindicated N'.

Spell 284

O N,[1] you are Horus, who belongs to the Great Lady of the Desert(?), the IV, 34
Lady of Flame, the great one[2] who is between the horns of the Sunshine-god,[3] who bites with her mouth, who looses with her tail(?),[4] who lives also on those who perish in[5] the blast of the flame of her mouth, who rescues Rēʿ from Apep.[6] BECOMING FIRE IN THE REALM OF THE DEAD IN EVERY PLACE OF THE WEST.

1. T1L, again much damaged, starts with the rubric 'becoming [. . .'], which Sq6C, practically intact, places at the end of this spell.

2. *Wrt* in Sq6C; T1L obscurely writes *intt*.

3. So T1L; Sq6C appears to read 'who is between the horns of the disk of the sunshine'. This passage suggests that the goddess in question may be the uraeus, see the next note.

4. The det. of *sd* is damaged in Sq6C, and the sense given to it is doubtful, but this may be a reference to the tail of the uraeus serpent; T1L has preserved only the initial *s*. The previous reference to 'biting' supports the view that the goddess here is the uraeus.

5. Read probably *ʿnḫt ḏdṯ* ⟨*m*⟩ *tmyw m-ḫr-*[*ib*]. *Ḏdṯ* has been taken to be the particle discussed by Edel, *Altäg. Gramm.* §§ 111; 180. This passage is mostly lost in T1L.

6. This sentence only in T1L.

Spell 285

BECOMING SOBK, LORD OF THE WINDING WATERWAY.[1] I am[2] the throwstick IV, 35
of the fen, I traverse the lakes,[3] I am alert when I traverse the shores, I am a shape who eats (even) when he copulates, I eat the Great One,[4] I live on his scales, I live on what he knows and on that through which he has power. There have been given to me[5] the northern swamp-lands for my water-side settlements[6] and my roamings.[7] I live on the great ones who are in the water, the great ones who are in the streams fear me, the *ḫdw*-fish which are in the water protect me, the great ones who are in the streams respect me,[8] I am he
who emerges,[9] the Lord of water;[10] I am Sobk, Lord of the Winding 36
Waterway. BECOMING SOBK, LORD OF THE WINDING WATERWAY.

1. So B2L, but with *Sḥ* for *Sbk*, cf. the rubric of Sq6C in 36*b*, and the identification of the deceased with Sobk in 36*a*. At the end of the rubric in B2L read *mr nḫꜣ* 'the Winding Waterway', cf. 36*a*. Sq6C is in the 2nd person, changing to the 3rd, while B2L is in the 1st; the latter is followed here.

2. *Sic*, not 'belongs to me'; this a metaphor for the crocodile as a predator.

3. 'Lakes' of Sq6C seems preferable to 'islands' of B2L; the two words are apt to be confused.

4. Sq6C: 'O N, you are a shape; N eats the Great One'. B2L (35*f*) suggests that the deceased, in his avatar of a crocodile, is so voracious that he never stops eating whatever he is doing; his prey 'the Great One' is clearly envisaged as a fish, cf. 35*h*. 35*i* gives the reason for devouring this particular prey. Compare 1*f* above.

5. Read *rdy·n·t(w)* ⟨*n·i*⟩ in B2L; Sq6C has *rdy(w) n·f* with the passive *sḏm·f*.

6. Determined with  in B2L. Possibly a reference to the dry banks where the crocodile lies basking in the sun.

7. *ꜥẖt* of Sq6C is to be preferred to *ꜥḫnt* of B2L. The stem *ꜥẖ* means 'fly away', cf. *Concise Dict*. 48, but since a crocodile cannot fly, the word seems to be used metaphorically here for its movements in the swamp-lands.

8. *Ḫdw imyw* of B2L is not in Sq6C, and *ḫdw* in the former text may be a dittograph from the preceding sentence. The det.  after *sw* in Sq6C suggests that the noun *wrw* 'great ones' has been omitted before it, and that the original reading of this passage was *twr sw wrw imyw itrw*, compare 35*b*.

9. *'Iṯṯ* 'fly up', *Concise Dict*. 34, is used here metaphorically of the crocodile's emergence at the surface of the water.

10. Note the writings of *nt* 'water' in these two texts.

Spell 286

IV, 36 BECOMING [A FALCON].[1] The Two Enneads of Horus are afraid of me and tremble at me,[2] (even they) the Primeval Ones who witnessed the separation

37 of the sky from the earth, | when he who in the past brought my father into being was created.[3] Regard me,[4] one who was conceived and born as Horus the heir; I was created for you,[5] (even I) the Lord of the Enneads.[6]

O you plebs, look on me, the son of Isis;[7] I was conceived in Pe and born in Chemmis;[8] I was nursed in my Field of Fire[9] on that day when I was received(?) on the birth-stool,[10] I was taken to my father Atum,[11] and he gave me the ornaments[12] of his father Gēb;[13] I entered into the horizon.[14]

38 TO BECOME A FALCON.[15]

1. For the restoration *m byk* cf. 38*e*.

2. Read *snḏ n·i sdꜣ n·i psḏty nty Ḥr*; for the 1st person cf. Sq1C, which ends abruptly in a lacuna.

3. Reading *m ir·t(w) pꜣ ḫpr it·i* with Sq6C; B1C omits *m ir·t(w)* and has only *pꜣ ḫprt·f*, the meaning of which is not clear, though *tf* could possibly stand for *it·i* 'my father'.

4. Again following Sq6C, where it seems necessary to regard *mꜣ* as an imperative addressed to the Enneads; B1C has *mꜣ·sn* 'they regard'.

5. The pronoun ·*ṯn* presumably refers to the Enneads.

6. Following B1C; in Sq6C some other epithet must have intervened after *N pn*, since there is a lacuna here which is not represented in B1C.

7. In Sq6C the first part of the sentence is lost in lacuna, and this text inserts *ntf* between the name of the deceased and *sꜣ Wsyr* (*sic*).

8. Reading *iwr·i m P ms·i m ꜣḫ-byt*, cf. Sq6C; B1C omits the suffix of *iwr* but inserts it after *ms*.

9. So B1C; Sq6C has *sndm·f N pn m . . . ·f*(?) 'N dwelt in his [. . .]'. The length of the lacuna suggests that *sẖt ḥt·f* is to be restored here, cf. B1C.

10. So Sq6C; B1C has, less probably: 'O you silent ones, N is recognized upon the birth-stool'; *ipp* is apparently the passive *sḏm·f*.

11. The *n* after *iṯt* (*iṯ* in B1C) appears to be superfluous; the absence of an object, as well as the general trend of the text, precludes interpretation as a *sḏm·n·f* form. The deceased, as the young Horus, is describing what happened at his birth and not what he himself did. For *Ꞽtm* B1C has *Rꜥ*.

12. For *ꜥprw* cf. *Urk.* IV, 633,6; 634,12; 669,2.

13. B1C omits the words after *ꜥprw*.

14. So Sq6C; B1C apparently: 'I flew up ⟨to⟩ the horizon', with omission of the preposition. At this point Sq6C inserts (37*n*) a garbled repetition of 37*e–h* which appears to read: 'Look on N, say they(?) (*ḥrt·sn* for *ḥr·sn*?) ⟨concerning⟩ N, who was born in Chemmis, for you (*sic!*) are the son of Osiris.' In its place B1C (38*a–d*) has: 'they dry(?) N, the son of [Osiris(?) . . .] who fashioned (masc.) him. TO HAVE POWER IN THE SKY AND ON EARTH'. *Ḥm·sn*, despite det. , may refer to the drying of the new-born infant.

15. So both texts, but see de Buck's note 2*.

Spell 287

BECOMING A GOOSE. I have flown up as a swallow, I have cackled as a goose, I have [alighted][1] on that great plateau north of the horizon of the sky. Regard me;[2] I am not dead,[3] my glance rests on his regular appearings[4] as great god. I drive out pains, ˡI make the uraei to endure, I drive out the secret trouble of IV, 39
the great god. The great lake, I do not see it; O you five hyaenas(?),[5] I have not fallen among you. I have indeed come, and great is what I have seen;[6] I have come that I may see the fields which the fair firmament has beautified, and that I may dwell in it, (even I), N.

1. For this collocation and for the restoration *ḥn* 'alight' cf. III, 130*f–h*; *BD* 179, 10–11; 493, 12–13.

2. For the translation in the 1st person see what precedes; the deceased was a woman.

3. Read *n mt·n·i*.

4. Read *ḥn ḥr·i r ḫꜥꜥ·f* (imperfective *sḏm·f* construed as a noun); the suffix ·*f* presumably refers to Rēꜥ.

5. Regarding *ḥṯ* as the masc. of *ḥṯt* 'hyaena'; cf., however, *Wb.* III, 203, 15.

6. At the end of this clause read *mꜣt·n·i*; the copyist has got his pronouns completely confused, since in any case Sq1C is a woman's coffin.

Spell 288

IV, 40 Becoming air.[1] I am the Tosser(?),[2] son of the fiery one of Shu, | long-extended of brilliance,[3] when Shu is at the head of the sun-folk.[4] I am a flame (moving) before the wind to the end of the sky and the end of the earth,[5] I travel the air and traverse the earth,[6] I sit[7] on the eastern side of the celestial vault, the sky is brought to me at dawn,[8] I separate the sky from the earth,[9] for I am the son of [the Lord(?)] of the Field of Rushes.[10]

1. Only in Sq1C.
2. This spell is a badly garbled version of *Pyr.* Utt. 261, which at this point reads: 'The King is a heart-tosser(?), the favourite son of Shu'. The point of the *Pyr.* Utterance is that the King is a flash of lightning which makes the heart leap with fright. For *wyṯ* 'tosser(?)' (the true reading) Sq1C has *wṯ* and Sq6C has *wy*.) Sq1C is closer to the original than the other texts in that it brings in the name of Shu, but even so it is quite corrupt. P. Gard. II has read *ꜣsb* as *sꜣb*.
3. So Sq1C, with *ꜣbs* for *ꜣsb*; Sq6C is further corrupted. Cf. *Pyr.* § 324*b*: *ꜣwy ꜣwt ꜣzb iꜣḫw* 'long-extended, fierce of brilliance'.
4. So Sq1C; Sq6C has: 'the hands of Shu grasp the sun-folk in the person of(?) N.' The damaged P. Gard. II, so far as preserved, agrees with *Pyr.* § 324*d*: *ḏr šw·t(y) ꜥ ḥnbw m W* 'when the hand of the lightning is voided of the King'.
5. P. Gard. III agrees with *Pyr.* § 324*c* except that in the original version this passage follows 40*a*. Sq1C has *iw* for *ink*; Sq6C is quite corrupt.
6. For once there is no corruption, except that Sq1C has *sḏm·n·f* instead of *sḏm·f*, but Sq6C omits this sentence, and all texts omit *Pyr.* §§ 325*b*–326*a*. Note the spelling *šꜣꜣs* in Sq1C.
7. *Pyr.* § 326*b* has 'stand' for *CT* 'sit'.
8. *Pyr.* § 326*c* reads: *in n·f iꜥt n ḥrt* 'there is brought to him a way of ascent to the sky.'
9. So Sq1C; Sq6C: 'O N, you are storm'; P. Gard. III: 'I am he who divides (*wp*) the storm'; *Pyr.* § 326*d*: *W py irw wpt nšn* 'It is the King who performs the errand of the storm'. This spell would in fact be incomprehensible without the original Pyramid Text to help it out.
10. Sq1C only.

Spell 289

IV, 41 Becoming an apparitor of Ōn.[1] I have gone forth from Su, I have spent the night in Uu,[2] my skin was turned inside out at the time of nightfall in the West, and I am an apparitor of Ōn.

1. B1Bo and B2L only, in black and in red respectively. In B2L read *'Iwnw* as B1Bo; is merely a complement of the town-det. B1C puts the rubric at the end of the spell, and B9C omits it.

2. The locations of these places are not known; for *Sw* cf. Gauthier, *Dict. Geogr.* V, 61, and for *Ww* see op. cit. I, 188.

Spell 290

Becoming a weaned child.[1] I have indeed become a weaned child, of whom my IV, 42
mother spoke,[2] and of whom record has been made, and mine is the mode of being of every god. THE MAN SHALL BE TRANSFORMED INTO ANY GOD THE MAN MAY WISH TO BE TRANSFORMED INTO.[3]

1. In black in all three texts.

2. In B1Bo these two sentences are in inverted order. We clearly have here an allusion to the registration of births.

3. Not in B1Bo. B1L uses slightly differing wording to the same effect. At the end of the latter  is probably to be read as 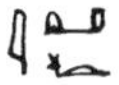 *im·f*.

Spell 291

BECOMING A CHILD.[1] I have indeed become a child, whom my father begot and of whom my mother spoke.[2] Such am I.

1. A variant of Spell 290.

2. Sq1C has completely muddled the suffixes in 42*i*, with the 3rd masc. after 'father' and the 3rd fem. after 'mother', though 42*g* and 42*j* are in the 1st person.

Spell 292

BECOMING A HERON(?)[1] OF THE LOTUS-TANK.[2] I am a heron(?) of the lotus- IV, 43
tank,[3] secluded and hidden.[4] My side-lock is he whose form is distinguished in the midst of his garden, my wings are the throwers of his knives in the midst of his land(?).[5] My neck is he who is fair to see,[6] my fingers are the terrible ones,[7] my eyes are the guides of Rēʿ. I rule the marsh-lands, I stand up and travel to the West,[8] I eat (*sic*) of the flood which is with the Inundation-god
in the Island of the Double Lion,[9] | I eat with Him whose face is wiped in the 44
midst of the Sacred Lake,[10] I have passed by the front of his northern eternal field which belongs to Rēʿ,[11] there is opened to me the sacred place at the Lake of Jackals.[12] O you who are over eternity, who are in your windings, prepare a path for me.[13] It is I who drive away the hornet,[14] I will spear fish at the Field of *Ḥr-wr*.[15] O you who are in(?)[16] Djedu, is there . . .?[17] It is I who eat the . . . which is in Djedu.

1. Cf. Spell 272.

2. For *sšnt* 'lotus-tank' cf. I, 187*g*; 212*f*; the det. implies that it was a haunt of birds.

3. B2L: *ink nwr pw sšnty*; Sq1C: *ink nwr sšnt.*

4. So Sq1C, which seems the better reading; B2L has expanded this into 'what appertains to Atum has been taken for my coming into existence with intent to(?) seclusion and hiding'.

5. Equating *s3ḥw* with *s3ḥ* 'grant of land', *Concise Dict.* 210. Sq1C omits.

6. So B2L; Sq1C has *iw i* [. . .] *nfr m3w*; the last word, for which see op. cit. 100, seems a better reading than *m33wt* of B2L.

7. So B2L, taking *nrytyw* to be a derivative of *nr* 'be terrible', 'fear', 'dread'. Sq1C has 'my two fingers are the Double Lion' and omits the next two sentences except for ⊙ in 43*i* and  in 43*j*.

8. Following Sq1C, which seems superior to B2L here. *M šsp m3m3·f* of B2L is quite obscure; it is omitted in Sq1C and in the present translation.

9. So B2L; Sq1C has simply *3gb byḥ* (*sic*) *m Rwty* without any introductory verb.

10. So B2L; Sq1C obscurely: *Ḥr m ḳ3b ḏsr.*

11. So B2L; Sq1C: *w3wt·i m sḫwt mḥywt in Rʿ* 'my paths are in the fields which are filled by Rēʿ'.

12. So Sq1C; B2L: 'he opens to me with her who is sacred of shape at the Lake of the Jackal'.

13. So B2L; Sq1C omits *nḥḥ*, writes *imy* with a sacred bark sign and omits the suffix after *dbn*.

14. Hardly 'bee' (B2L), which surely would not be driven away; an unpleasant insect is indicated. Sq1C is corrupt.

15. Var. Sq1C 'at the marshes of eternity' and ends.

16. Regarding  as a miswriting of .

17. Reading *in* ⟨*n*⟩*ḏ3t*; for the noun see again below. Its meaning is not known, but it is something which can be eaten.

Spell 293

Opening up the West and becoming a swallow.[1] This spirit of mine is lost, having been put on the river-bank; I have come that I may see you, for you are Ty[2] today. Come, cross over and bring me my beer and your two red cows which enrich you(?);[3] reduced and small is the bank of loaves of the offering-stone of the intact(?) tomb,[4] and the two phoenixes are restrained(?).[5] I have ascended on Shu, I have descended on Horus; I am favoured and I possess favour, and a . . .[6] is made for me. | I have ascended among the stars,[7] I have bathed in the celestial waters(?);[8] put water on me, for I possess favour and acclamation.

1. Read *mnt*; cf. 33*g*; B2L has corrupted it into *ʿrt*. See also 46*f*.

2. An obscure being.

3. 45*i* is quite obscure and the translation doubtful; from here on, though the words can be translated, the real meaning of the text escapes me. For *s3ḫty* of B1C, B1L has *3ḫt*.

4. Compare *CT* III, 391*e*, equally obscure. *D3t* makes no sense, but may be a miswriting of *wḏ3t* 'intact'.

5. 45*k* is quite obscure.
6. *Hmys*, meaning unknown. In 45*o–p* B2L repeats 45*l–n* with variations.
7. *Wnwt*; cf *CT* IV, 347*a*; *Bd* 99,11.
8. *Ssw*, unrecorded; not to be confused with *zzw* 'dust-devil' *Pyr.* §§ 308; 312.

Spell 294

The shape of a swallow[1] is given to me by the Flaming One,[2] Mistress of the
Isles, who ascends in the flame which is on[3] the battlements of the sky. My
head and my back are of lapis lazuli, my belly is of fine gold, my neck is of gold
of Iuu;[4] my . . .[5] and my toes(?)[6] are Iunmūtef, Lord of Bakhu. | I have eaten 47
the *sšt*-fruit,[7] I have borne witness to the provisions(?)[8] in the temple of
Ḥatḥōr, I have travelled around the sky with the Cat,[9] and this land is beneath
me by means of my sandals.

1. Read *mnt*, cf. Spell 293, n.1.
2. The uraeus-serpent, cf. *Hymnen*, 4,4.
3. *Ḥryt* (fem.) is due to confusion with the fem. *nbyt* in 46*f*; read *ḥry*.
4. Unidentified, cf. Gauthier, *Dict. géogr.* I, 51. 215.
5. *Sṯrwt*, meaning unknown, but clearly part of the body.
6. Lit. 'hoofs'.
7. For the fruit *sšt* cf. *Pyr.* 96. 108.
8. Cf. G.–R. , *Wb.* III, 373,4.
9. The sun-god, cf. *CT* IV, 286*c*.

Spell 295

BECOMING A SCRIBE OF THE ALTARS OF ḤATḤŌR. I sit, (even I) the son of Atum,
my writings are in the two Fields of Offerings of Ḥatḥōr, I BECOME THE
SCRIBE OF THE ALTARS OF ḤATḤŌR, reassembly[1] is carried out for me by means
of papyriform amulets, (even for me) | *'Ihmsw*, son of Nefertum, scribe of the IV, 48
altars of the Field[2] of Offerings of Ḥatḥōr. This gate which Ḥatḥōr has
created is opened, the third of the gates of Rēʿ is thrown open; how happy
and well provided am I[3] thereby ! I will be[4] there in the Following.

1. Presumably of the corpse.
2. Not dual as above.
3. Following B2L; *ḥw ꜣ wi* perhaps literally 'how "would that" am I', meaning 'I have got all I want'. For *nfr w(y) ꜣ* B1C has *wḏ·kw ꜣ*; the sense may be 'I am commanded to have all I want'.
4. Reading *wnn·i* with B1C.

Spell 296

O you who are in the city, N has brought Him who guards his coils. Give your hand to N, for N has spent the day in the Island[1] of Fire, N has gone on
IV, 49 an errand and N has returned with the report. | Open to N; then will N tell what he has seen. Horus is commander of the sacred bark,[2] and his father's throne has been given to him. What is in Khem has been allotted [to] N; it means that obeisance has been made at the left hand of Osiris. N has gone to make inspection and N has returned to speak; let N pass, that N may make report on ⟨his⟩ errand. N is one who goes in esteemed and who goes out distinguished at the portal of the Lord of All. N is pure on that great tomb-plateau; N has got rid of his evil, N has discarded his wrongdoing, N has cast down to the earth the evils which were on his flesh. O you keepers of the gate, make a path for N, who is one like you. May N go forth into the day, may N walk on his feet, may N have power over the movements of the sunshine, for N knows the secret ways and the portals of the Field of Rushes; may N be there. See, N has come, N has felled his foes to the ground, and N's corpse is interred.

1. Emend  into , *tꜣ nsrsr* is not otherwise known.
2. Read *iw Ḥr m ḥrp n wyꜣ* as *BD* 186, 10–11;  is det. in both cases.

Spell 297

IV, 50 BECOMING THE FOUR WINDS OF THE SKY AND KNOWING THE NAME OF THE GOD IN CHARGE OF THE SKY-LADDER.[1] The double barrier against the plebs has been opened by *Ḥnw*, Seshat has allotted my abode[2]—four times—the Inert One is in his chapel.[3] If[4] the weather[5] comes as the south-wind, I will dwell in the north-wind, and *vice versa*; if the weather comes as the west-wind, I will dwell in the east-wind, and *vice versa*. I protect ⟨my?⟩ skin,[6] I sit in the sunshine and a drying wind(?)[7]. O *Ḥmtyw*, give me your hand![8]

1. So B1C; B2L has a variant rubric at the end of the spell.
2. The compound *r-pr* here has not its usual sense of 'chapel' or the like. Compare *CT* V, 2*b*.
3. B1C is corrupt; emend perhaps as *ḥms wrḏ-ib r r-pr·f*; compare *CT* V, 2*c*. The translation follows B2L. *R-pr* here has its normal meaning.
4. For the translation as a conditional clause cf. V, 3*a*. *c*; 4*b*; 5*a*. *c*.
5. Lit. 'sky'; see also loc. cit. and compare *Westcar*, 11, 14.
6. V, 7*a*; *BD* 129, 8–9 have in this context *itḥ·i inm n šrt·i* 'I drag the skin of my nose', perhaps meaning 'I blow my nose'; *nḏ* in the present text seems to be the word for 'protect'.
7. 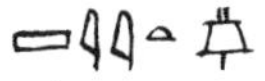 is not known to *Wb*. It is clearly a term for 'wind' or the like, and I have tentatively connected it with the stem *šw* 'dry'.

8. B2L ends with the rubric: 'Knowing the name of the god who guards the sky-ladder. As for him who knows this spell, he shall be at the portal in the sky when he has gone to his double.'

Spell 298

I have come into being in the limit of the land, even more than the gods. IV, 51
I am one who has travelled around, and I have come that I may demand the diadem as Osiris.[1] COMING INTO BEING BY A MAN: A GOD SAYS WHAT HE DESIRES, AND COMING INTO BEING IS BROUGHT ABOUT BY IT.[2]

1. So B1L; *nṯr mn* of B3L appears to mean 'the god so-and-so.'
2. Var. B1L: 'Coming into being as a god, possessor of what he desires'. In B3L the *nb*-sign after *nṯr* appears to be cancelled.

Spell 299

May you conceive me, O Pool; may you fashion me, O Earthly Expanse, for everything is mine, and I am the Lord of the First of the Year, (even) NEPRI.

Spell 300

I have grown on incense, I have climbed up on the sunbeams; O Ḥatḥōr, give IV, 52
me your hand. ASCENDING TO THE SKY.

Spell 301

I have passed by ⟨the House of⟩ the Songstress,[1] and it was an *ibꜣyt*-bird
which brought you to me. Hail to you who flew up to the sky, | you milk-white IV, 53
bird[2] which guards the White Crown. I shall be with you—and *vice versa*; O great god, make a path for me that I may pass on it.[3] TAKING SHAPE AS ANY GOD THAT A MAN MAY WISH,[4] TAKING SHAPE BY MEANS OF IT.

1. For *šmꜥtt* of B3L and B1L read *pr-šmꜥtt* with 65*d*. *Pr-nsw* of L1Li is an obvious misreading of *pr-šmꜥtt*.
2. Connecting *ḥsꜣ* here with the stem *ḥsꜣ* 'milk', 'milky' and regarding the second 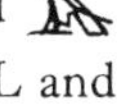 in B3L and B1L as a bird-det. The translation follows B3L, which reads *ḥsꜣ sꜣw ḥḏt*; B1L and P. Gard. II have *ḥsꜣ ḥḏt* only, *sꜣw* 'which guards' being suppressed by haplography. L1Li (52*h*–53*a*) reads: 'who whitens the White Crown and guards the White Crown' and varies 53*b*–*c*.
3. L1Li adds *ḏt r nḥḥ* 'for ever and ever'. P. Gard. II has garbled the passage.
4. Var. B1L: *mrr·f* and omits the rest.

Spell 302

BECOMING A FALCON.[1] I am the great falcon which came into existence in
IV, 54 the egg, | I fly up and alight as a falcon of one cubit measured along[2] its back, my wings[3] are of green-stone of Upper Egypt. I have gone up from the coffer into the Night-bark, I have brought my heart from the horizon, I have alighted in the Day-bark, worship is given to me. The Followers serve me, the gods who are in[4] their primeval state have come to me bowing down. They present all the crowns to me as a fair falcon of gold upon his pointed stone,[5] and Rēᶜ comes in daily to hear his[6] words. I sit with those gods who are the lords of
55 the sky, | the good things of the Field of Offerings[7] are laid down for me, and I eat of them and drink of them to my content and satisfaction;[8] 'Smoked Grain'[9] has risen up before me.

1. So B3L; B1P has 'another spell for ⟨becoming⟩ a falcon in the realm of the dead', with omission of *ḫpr*.

2. Lit. 'resting on'. *BD* 164,11 omits *ḥtp* and reads *mḥ 4 m psḏ·f* 'four cubits along its back'.

3. Read *ḏḥnwy*, cf. 58*m*; *BD* 164,11.

4. B1P omits *imyw*.

5. *Bnwt* is taken here to be a pointed stone on which the falcon rests; cf. *bnbn* 'sacred stone'; *bnbnt* 'pyramidion'.

6. Presumably the falcon's.

7. Read *sḫty-htp* as a *nisba*-form, 'the (good things) of the F. of O.'

8. *R dd ib·i r spr r ib·i*, lit. 'to what my heart gives and to what reaches my heart'; it is necessary to paraphrase to make the expression intelligible in English.

9. For *ḥtyt* read *ḥty* with det. ; for the expression cf. II, 95*e*; III, 176*a*; and in the later version of this spell, *BD* 165,5.

Spell 303

O Falcon,[1] come to Djedu and go all over my mansion—so says Osiris—that you may see it, this new state(?)[2] which I have attained. My paternal brother
IV, 56 has taken action;[3] he has struck me, | and none can speak to me,[4] none of my members can come to me.

O my father Osiris,[5] here am I; I have come to you, for I have smitten Seth for you, I have slain his confederacy, I have smitten them who smote you, I have cut down them who cut you down. I am one who overcomes with strength, the heir of everything; I myself have guarded my body,[6] I have felled my foes, and I have created it, this new state(?) in which I am.

57 Here am I[7]; I have come, having seen my father; | allotment has been made to me, and I have gone out from him, I have guarded him from those who

would rob him, and my name has come into being because my power of protection has gone forth.

1. The deceased in the role of Horus Protector of his father is addressed by Osiris.

2. *Mȝw*, determined with in B3L and in B1P, the latter det. being due to its being a homophone of *mȝwt* 'flute', etc., while *mȝw* with det. appears to be unrecorded; in 56*l* B3L has the det. , which suggests that we have here a derivative of *mȝwy* 'new' with the meaning of 'new condition' or the like.

3. What follows makes it clear that *ir·n* is to be taken in a hostile sense; the brother is Seth, acting against Osiris.

4. *Mdw·n* used without expressed subject.

5. The deceased as Horus replies to Osiris.

6. B1P determines *ḏt* 'body' with , but the sense is not in doubt.

7. The writing of *m·ṯn* in B3L is clearly an error. The remainder of the spell appears to be an address by the deceased to an unnamed third party in which he recounts what he has done for Osiris.

Spell 304

It goes well with me, for my soul has been assigned[1] to me, in my company; my heart is in my body, my corpse is in the earth, and I will not weep for it. My soul is with me and will not go far from me; | magic power is in my body, 58
and it will not be stolen. I have my power, I have my modes of being, so that I may eat my meals with my double who is in this earth of mine,[2] and I go to rest, having been seen to be young.[3]

TO BE SPOKEN OVER A PILLAR OF GREENSTONE OF UPPER EGYPT; TO BE PLACED ON THE NECK OF THE DECEASED.[4]

1. *Ỉp* of B1P is to be preferred to *itp* of B3L as yielding better sense.

2. I.e. my tomb.

3. Two old perfectives, lit. 'I being seen, I being young'.

4. Lit. 'to be given to a spirit on its neck'; *ȝḫ* is used here not of the immaterial 'spirit' but of the spiritualized body of the deceased, cf. *BD* 404,3; 405,1. 5. 9. 15.

Spell 305

The god grows, the god rises up from his nest, he flies and soars to the underside of the sky as that great falcon, sharp of talon,[1] long of plume, of seven cubits along his back, his wings being of greenstone of Upper Egypt. | I[2] have IV
gone up from the coffer[3] into the Night-bark, I have alighted on the Day-bark, I[4] am pure, one who inspires fear(?);[5] I have shaken out my plumage on the bank of the Winding Waterway, I have flown around the Followers[6] on it,

I have assembled the sun-folk, and all the great gods come to me bowed[7] down; all those who appear in glory come to me that they may see me manifested as that great falcon, sharp of talon, long of plume, of seven cubits along my back, my wings being of greenstone of Upper Egypt, and Rēʿ appears daily in order to hear my words. I fly and soar between those two great mountains on which Rēʿ appears; I eat bread with Him whose name is bruited abroad, while the grain-god stands before me, I have tied the two Fields of Offerings tightly together, and to me belongs the All[8] which Atum has given to me.

1. Note the det. of *dꜣt*; the var. with det.  in 59*j* is doubtless influenced by *ꜣt* 'striking power'.

2. For the 1st person cf. also *BD* 164,12. In the later version the whole text is in the 1st person.

3. Determined with  in loc. cit.

4. Here the editor has changed the text to the 3rd person, but 59*g*. *h* show that in fact the falcon is still speaking, as in the *BD* version.

5. *Snšnš* is not recorded, but cf. *snšn* '(das Herz der Feinde) in Furcht verletzen o. a.' *Wb.* IV, 174,6.

6. As a protective act? The 'Followers' may perhaps represent the attendants of the deceased (originally perhaps the dead king) who have bid him farewell as he crosses the celestial waterway.

7.  is a slightly aberrant abbreviation of *ks*, cf. *BD*, 164,15, though with a variant text.

8. *R-ḏr* construed as a noun.

Spell 306

IV, 60 A boon which the king grants,[1] which Rēʿ-Atum grants, which the Nine Gods grant and which Ḥarakhti[2] grants, that he (*sic*) may grant bread and beer, roast meat(?)[3] [. . .] for N from upon the altar of Rēʿ daily. May N eat with the Followers(?) [. . .] which the Nine Gods grant.

Hail to you, Atum, you who made the sky and created what exists, who came forth from [the earth, who created] seed, [Lord of all things], who fashioned the gods.[4]

Hail to you, Lords of pure offerings, whose thrones are secret.[5]

Hail to you, Lords of eternity, whose names are hidden, whose shrines are secret, and the place where you are is unknown.

Hail to you, you gods of . . .,[6] you gods who encircle [the sky(?)],[7] you gods who are in the West, you Nine Gods who are within the Lower Sky.[8] Here am I, I[9] have come to you pure, divine, spiritualized, strong, besouled, mighty; I have brought to you natron and incense, and I have given to you[10] what is in your hearts towards me. I have come that I may expel the evil which is in my heart and that I may remove the wrong that is in it. I have brought

to you what is good, | [I have upraised] Truth to you, for I know you, I know 61
your names, I know your shapes which were unknown and the modes of being which are in you.

I have come to you, [having appeared in glory] as that god who eats men and lives on gods; I am mighty before you as that god who is uplifted [on his standard], to whom come joyfully the gods who are in the Presence, and the goddesses[11] rejoice when they see me. I have come to you, having appeared in glory as [your son];[12] I sit on my seat[13] which is in the horizon, I receive offerings from upon your altars, I drink beer(?)[14] in the evening. Those who are joyful will come to me bowing; praise is given to me by those who are in the horizon in this my rank of the Lord of All, I am exalted as that august god, Lord of the Great Mansion, and the gods rejoice when they see me in my fair movements on the body of the Lower Sky, (even I) whom Nūt fashions daily.

1. This *ḥtp-dy-nswt* formula appears to be an addition to the original spell; it does not occur in the corresponding *BD* Spell 79.

2. It is difficult to see what could have stood in the small lacuna before , and it may in fact not have existed in the original text. De Buck had to make a copy of a copy because the original was not available.  is to be understood as a god-determinative, as regularly in L1Li, cf. e.g. 'Rēʿ-Atum' above.

3. Restore *ꜣš[rt]*.

4. For the restoration cf. *BD* 174,5 f.

5. Read *ḫꜣp swt*.

6. *Nyt*, meaning unknown; *BD* 174, 10 *f.* has *nṯrw imyw tntꜣyt* 'you gods who are in the Radiance(?)'.

7. *BD* 174,12 has *šnw ḳbḥw* 'who encircle the firmament', but the size of the lacuna favours the restoration *pt* rather than *ḳbḥw*.

8. Reading *imt ḫn Nnt* with *BD* 174,14.  may be a misreading of ; *BD* has . This has been taken to be a writing of *ḫnw* 'interior' in a nisba form of the compound preposition *m-ḫnw*.

9. *BD* is in the 1st person, which is what one would expect here after the invoking of the gods; the spell has therefore been translated accordingly, though the ancient editor has effectively transposed the text into the 3rd person.

10. There is a dittograph of *n·ṯn*.

11. Read *nṯrwt-ḥmwt* with *BD* 175,11. On *ḥmwt* as a fem. suffix see my note *JEA* 58,300; the translation as 'goddesses and women' is ruled out because the preceding passage refers to 'gods' only and not to 'gods and men'.

12. Read *sꜣty·tn* as *BD* 175,12; the dead man is said to be a son common to all deities.

13. *Sty* is written as a dual, probably under the influence of the preceding *sꜣty*, now lost in this text, but it is to be interpreted as a singular; the deceased cannot sit on two seats at once.

14. *Sṯꜣ*, written *sṯy* in BD 175,14; the word is probably related to *sṯt* 'beer-jar', *Concise Dict.* 255.

Spell 307[1]

IV, 62 Thus says N: I am a guinea-fowl,[2] I am Rēʿ who issued from the Abyss in this my name of Khopri,[3] and my soul is a god.

I am he who created Authority; wrongdoing is what I detest, and I will not see it, for I am one who does right, and I live by means of it daily.[4]

I am [Authority] who will never [perish in this my name] of 'Soul'.[5] I am prayed to [as] a bull,[6] I am invoked in the Ennead in this my [name] of the guinea-fowl god.[7] I come into being of myself in company with the Abyss in this my name of Khopri; I come into being in it daily, for I am the Lord of light.[8] [Death is my detestation],[9] and I will not enter into the place of execution of them of the Netherworld.[10]

63 I am he who gives power to Osiris, and | I satisfy the hearts of those who are in his service;[11] [I am] he who puts the fear [of himself among those who are in] their [boundaries(?)],[12] for I am raised aloft on my standard above yonder places of the Abyss; the doers of wrong cannot harm me.

I am [the eldest of the primeval ones, the soul of][13] them of the Temple of Eternity.

I am he who created darkness, who set his throne in the limits of the sky. The great soul has come upon [. . .] the limits of the sky.[14] I desire to reach their limits, and I walk afoot, I control [. . .],[15] I cross the firmament[16] of those who make . . .[17] darkness [. . .]. My soul is a (real) soul, my body is the uraei of the Eternal One, possessor of years, and it means that I shall live for ever.

I am one who is raised aloft, Lord of Tatjebu, young in my city, boyish [in the field],[18] and my name will not perish.

I am the Soul who created the Abyss, who made my seat in the realm of the dead; my nest will not be seen nor my egg[19] broken, for I am the Lord of
64 those who are high, and I have made my nest in the limits of the sky. | I will go down to the land of Gēb, I will expel evil, I will see my father, Lord of the evening, I will kiss the body of Him who is in Ōn, I will govern those who are in the hall on the Western Mound of the Ibis.

1. Cf. *BD* 184,2 ff.; 397,12 ff. The former represents L1Li and the latter BH4C.

2. So also *BD* 397,12; for the identification of the bird see *Eg. Gramm.* Sign-list, G21. *BD* 184,2 has *bꜣ* 'soul', written with the ram and not the *bꜣ*-bird.

3. This last clause only in BH4C.

4. *Rꜥ nb* only in BH4C, which also reads: 'I am Osiris who does right'.

5. Restoring the lacuna as *ink Ḥw iwty sk·f m rn·i pw n bꜣ* with *BD* 184, 6–7. BH4C and *BD* 397,15 omit this sentence.

6. Read *nḥḥ·i m kꜣ* with *BD* 397,15–16; *BD* 184,10 omits this sentence.

7. Determined with .

8. At this point BH4C comes to an end.

9. Restoring as *bwt·i pw mny* with *BD* 184,11.

10. At end read *dꜣtyw*; *BD* 184,12 has *dꜣt*.

11. For *ẖrt* [*·f*] *BD* 184,13 has *ẖt mrt*.

12. Restoring as [*ink*] *dd snḏ* [*·i*] *n imyw pẖrw·sn*; cf. *BD* 184, 13–15, which, however, in its full form is too long for the lacuna.

13. Cf. *BD* 185,1; after *pꜣwtyw* there seems space only for *bꜣ*, not for *bꜣ pw bꜣw* of *BD*, which for *ḥwtyw-nṯr nḥḥ* has *nṯrw nḥḥ*, followed by a couple of sentences which are not in *CT*.

14. Not in *BD*; *-rw* of *ḏrw* is preserved.

15. *BD* 185,5–6 has *ḫrp·i m iꜣrt·i*, but L1Li was different.

16. Reading *byꜣ* with *BD* 185,6.

17. *Mḥnd*, meaning unknown. *BD* 185, 6–8 is equally obscure.

18. Cf. *BD* 185,10, but omitting *rn pw*.

19. A new text, Ḳ1T, comes in here.

Spell 308

I appear as [Rēꜥ], Lord of the East, in those processions of the East, [I have come] to the sky, I have sought out my place which is in the East [. . .].[1]

[1] For the restorations see *BD* 398, 3–6. The final lacuna is too short to be filled from *BD*.

Spell 309

SITTING BETWEEN[1] THE TWO GODS, SHOWING[2] THE WAY IN DARKNESS. I sit IV, 65
between the two great gods, I pass by the House of the Songstress, and it is this *ibꜣt*-bird[3] which brings me.

1. *BD* 215,16 has *r-imytw*.

2. For this sense of *sšm* cf. *Urk*. I, 127,9; IV, 247,6; V,75,2. The final *-t* is superfluous, but is probably due to the preceding *ḥmst*, where the ending is correct.

3. For the *ibꜣt*-bird see also *CT* IV, 52*f*; *BD* 164,1. *BD* 216,2 has distorted this word into *bbꜣyt* 'wasp(?)'.

Spell 310

(I am) a spirit in the sky, a spirit in the sky. Greeting to you, you gods who are in the sky, you spirits of the horizon. I am the son of Shezmētet, I am

Khons who sends out the rage which burns(?)[1] hearts; I have entered into the finger and toe of Osiris and the body of Osiris, into the strong arm, into
IV, 66 the knee and into the head. I have grown as do plants, I am covered as does a tortoise[2], I have grown great in death (?),[3] I have come into being, I am one unique, the essence of the gods.[4] I am the seventh of those seven uraei which were taken from it,[5] the Great One who has power in his body, that god who cannot die, on that day of the flame(?),[6] when seed was taken away from that spirit when he had judgement in front of his father with Ōn, when he judged between Horus and Seth, Thoth being between them on that day in which he appeared as that august god who is in charge of judgements. O Henchmen of the gods, be very far removed from me,[7] for I am Khons ⟨who sends out⟩[8] the anger of the Lord of lords, I am he who burns(?) hearts,[9] I am the slayer among you; to me belong the two braided locks which are upon the shorn ones, and to me belongs the Mansion of the Cord in which are the heads of the bulls when they act as bulls(?).[10]

1. For *bḫḫw* as noun 'heat' cf. *Pyr.* §§ 502. 503. 702; *CT* III, 196*b*; *BD* 125,3; here it appears to be a participle.

2. The verb *šṯ* appears to be derived from *šṯ* 'tortoise', meaning 'cover oneself up like a tortoise' or the like.

3. *ʿrwt* is probably the same word as *ʿrt* 'death', *Pyr.* § 505.

4. *BD* 181,7: *ink dḳrw n nṯr nb* 'I am the essence of every god'; *dḳrw*, lit. 'what is pressed out' is a participle of *dḳr* 'press'.

5. From what? There seems to be some corruption here, and *BD* 181, 8 ff. is quite different.

6. Regarding the det.  as a corruption of : *nsr* is not recorded with the former det.

7. Read *ḥr·tywny· ir·i wrt*;  is an error.

8. Supply *sb* before *ḏnd*, cf. 65*j*.

9. *Nb* is intrusive, cf. 65*j*.

10. Utterly obscure.

Spell 311

IV, 67 I have grown up[1] as do plants, I am covered as does a tortoise,[2] I have come into being as Khopri, because I am the fourth of those four uraei who dwell in the eastern side of the sky. I know them and I know their names; it is my strength which created my power, and it is my power which created my strength. I am strong enough to cut off heads, and sharp is the flame which is on my mouth against the knives which are in the hands of the gods. Sakhmet is she who wielded the Cerastes-Mountain knife on the night of the great battle and on the morning of dividing what was complete(?) like the stems(?)[3] of their *ḥsꜣw*-plants. I will not fashion(?) ⟨. . .⟩[4] and I will hear the words of the Red One, the mother of the garden (*sic!*). My bread is with men, my god's-offerings are with the children. The fear of me has caused the gods to . . .[5] the Old One, and it means that I will appear as Khons who lives on hearts.[6] BECOMING KHONS IN THE REALM OF THE DEAD.

1. *Rdy·n* is an error for *rd·n* 'has grown', cf. 66*a*. Like Spell 310, this spell was originally in the 1st person, cf. *ḥtpw-nṯr n·i* in 67*p*.
2. Cf. Spell 310, n.2.
3. Taking *iȝwt* 'old age', which makes no sense here, to be a corruption of *iȝȝt* 'rod', hence 'stem' of plant. This passage is most obscure.
4. An object for *ms* is lacking.
5. A verb has certainly been omitted after *rdy·n·f*.
6. The final *N pn* seems superfluous.

Spell 312

SPELL FOR BEING TRANSFORMED INTO A DIVINE FALCON.[1] IV, 68

Osiris speaks: O Horus, come to Djedu, clear my ways for me, and go all
over my mansion, that you may see my form | and extol my shape.[2] May you 69
inspire fear of me, may you create awe of me, that the gods of the Netherworld
may fear me, that the gates may beware of me. Do not let him who has done me
harm approach me, | so that he sees me in the House of Darkness, and uncovers 70
my weariness which is hidden from him.

The gods: 'Do thus' say the gods, who hear the voices of those who go in the suite of Osiris.

Horus: Be silent, you gods; | let a god speak with a god, let him hear the 71
true message which I shall say to him. Speak to me, Osiris, and grant that
what has come forth from your mouth concerning me be revoked.[3] See your
own form, form your own shape, | and cause him to go forth and to have power 72
over his legs that he may stride and copulate among men, and you shall be
there as the Lord of All. The gods of the Netherworld fear you, the gates
beware of you. You move along with those who move along, while I remain
on your mound like the Lord of Life.[4] I ally myself with the divine Isis, | I 73
rejoice on account of him who has done you harm. May he not come so that
he sees your weariness which is hidden from him. I shall go and come to the
confines of the sky, that I may ask the word from Gēb, that I may demand
authority from the Lord of All. Then the gods shall fear you, even they who
shall see that I send to you one of those who dwell in the sunshine. | I have

made his form as my form, his gait as my gait, that he may go and come to
Djedu, being invested with my shape, that he may tell you my affairs. He shall
inspire fear of you, he shall create awe of you in the gods of the Netherworld,
and the gates shall beware of you.
The messenger: Indeed I am one who dwells in the sunshine, I am a spirit
75 who came into being and was created out of the body of the god, | I am one of
those gods or spirits who dwell in the sunshine, whom Atum created from
his flesh, who came into being from the root of his eye, whom Atum created
and whom he made spirits, whose faces he created in order that they might be
with him, while he was alone in the Abyss, who announced him when he came
forth from the horizon, who inspired fear of him in the gods and spirits, the
76 Powers and Shapes. | I am one of those serpents which the Sole Lord made,
before Isis came into being that she might give birth to Horus. I have been
made strong, I have been made young and vigorous, I am distinguished above
the (other) beings who dwell in the sunshine, the spirits who came into
being along with me. I have made my appearance as a divine falcon, and Horus
77 has invested me with his shape | in order that I might take his affairs to Osiris,
to the Netherworld.
The Double Lion raises an objection: The Double Lion who is in his cavern,
warden of the House of the Royal Wig-cover, said to me: How can you reach
the confines of the sky? Indeed, you are equipped with the form of Horus, but
you do not possess the Wig-cover. Do you speak on the confines of the sky?
78 *The Messenger:* | I am indeed he who takes the affairs of Horus to Osiris, to
the Netherworld. Horus has repeated to me what his father Osiris said to him
in the coffin(?)[5] on the day of burial.
The Double Lion: Repeat to me what Horus has said as the word of his
father Osiris in the . . .[5] on the day of burial, then I will give you the Wig-
cover—so said the Double Lion to me—that you may come and go on the
79 paths of the sky. | Then those who dwell in the horizon shall see you and the
gods of the Netherworld shall fear you.
The messenger: You may jubilate concerning him, he has been initiated into
the words of these gods, the Lords of All, who are at the side of the Sole Lord—
so said he who is high on his dais, who dwells in holiness, concerning me.
The Double Lion is satisfied: Take out the Wig-cover for him—so said the
Double Lion concerning me.
80 *The messenger, now possessed of his passport, the Royal Wig-cover, continues
his journey:* O Heret, clear my way for me. I am high in the form of Horus, and
the Double Lion has taken out the Wig-cover for me, he has given me my

wings, he has established my heart on his great standard. I do not fall on
account of Shu, I am he who pacifies himself with his own beauty, the Lord
of the two mighty royal serpents. | I am he who knows the paths of Nūt, the 81
winds are my protection, and the raging bull shall not drive me back. I go to
the place where dwells he who sleeps, being helpless; who is in the Field of
Eternity; who was conducted to the painful western darkness, (even) Osiris.
I come today from the House of the Double Lion, I have come forth from it to
the House of Isis, to the secret mysteries, I have been conducted to her hidden
secrets, for she caused me to see the birth of the great god. Horus has invested
me with his shape in order that I might say what is there, | in order that I 82
might say . . .[6] which shall drive back the fearful attack. I am the falcon who
dwells in the sunshine, who has power through its light and its flashing.[7] I
go and come to the confines of the sky,[8] there is no-one who thwarts me [. . .]
Horus to the confines of the sky. Horus is upon his seats and his thrones, and
I am he who is in his form. My arms are those of a divine falcon, I am one who
has acquired (the position of) his lord, and Horus has invested me with his
shape. I come forth to Djedu that I may see Osiris, I land at the Mansion of
the Great Dead One;[9] I inspire fear of him and create awe of him among the
gods. I belong to the great shrine, | (even I) the holy one of . . .,[10] in front of 83
whom one walks to and fro, and Nūt shall walk to and fro[11] when she sees me.
The hostile gods have seen that she incites the Eyeless One against those who
shall stretch forth their arms against me. The Powerful One stands up against
the earth-gods, the holy roads are opened for me when they see my form and
hear what I shall say. Down on your faces, you gods of the Netherworld,
whose faces are . . .,[12] whose necks are outstretched, and who hide the face
of the Great Demolisher! Clear the road of . . .[13] towards the majestic shape.

The messenger quotes the command of Horus: Horus has commanded: Lift up
your faces and look at him; he has made his appearance as a divine falcon,
the Double Lion has taken out the Wig-cover for him, | he has come with the 84
word of Horus to Osiris. The Grey-haired Ones have . . .,[14] he has united
himself with the Powers. Get out of the way, you wardens of your gates, for
him in front of me, clear the way for him. Let him pass by, O you who dwell in
your caverns, wardens of the House of Osiris.

The messenger resumes his own speech: I say: How mighty is Horus! I cause them to know that the terror of him is great, and that his horn is sharp against Seth; that Horus has taken authority and that he has acquired the might of Atum. I have followed Horus, the Lord of All.

The gods give the messenger permission to pass: Pass by in peace—so say the gods of the Netherworld to me. The wardens of their caverns, the wardens of the Mansion of Osiris rise up.[15]

85 *The messenger replies:* See, I come to you as an equipped spirit. | The wardens
of the gates walk for me, the Powers clear the roads for me, I have fetched the
Greyhaired Ones whom Nenet defied. The Great Ones who dwell in the
horizon fear me, even the wardens of . . .[16] in the sky, who guard the roads.
I make firm the gates for the Lord of All, I have cleared the roads towards
him, I have done what was commanded, for Horus invested me with his shape.
Let my wisdom(?) be granted, for I desire triumph over my enemies. May the
mysteries be uncovered for me, may the secret caverns be opened to me, may
I enter in to the Lord of the Shape, greatly majestic; may I come forth to
Djedu and go all over his mansion, may I tell him the affairs of his son whom he
86 loves, while the heart of Seth is cut out.[17] | May I see the Lord of Weariness,
who is limitless, that he may know how Horus regulated the affairs of the gods
without him.

The messenger attains his aim and addresses Osiris: O Lord of the Shape, greatly majestic, see, I have come, the Netherworld has been opened for me, the roads in the sky and on earth have been opened for me, and there was none who thwarted me.

Be high on your seat, O Osiris; may your breast live and may your buttocks be vigorous. Let your heart jubilate, for you triumph over Seth, and your son Horus has been placed on your throne. Myriads have been assigned to him, the gods have brought him oblations, and the heart of Gēb, who is older than the Great Ones, rejoices. The sky is strong and Nūt jubilates when she sees what Atum has done, whilst he sat among the Two Enneads and gave the authority which is on his mouth to Horus the son of Isis. He has become ruler over Egypt, the gods work for him, he has nurtured myriads and has brought up myriads by means of the Sole Eye, the Mistress of the Enneads, the Lady of All.

1. This spell was studied and translated by de Buck under the title 'The earliest version of Book of the Dead 78' in *JEA* 35, 87 ff. Apart from a few changes, the present translation follows that of de Buck. The underlying idea is that Osiris summons Horus to Djedu to make report on affairs, but that Horus objects and instead sends a messenger, who has to obtain from the Double Lion the passport of the Royal Wig-cover (*nms*) before he can proceed on his journey to report to Osiris.

2. *Bꜣ*, not given an English equivalent by de Buck, here and in several other places in this text has not its common meaning of 'soul', represented by a bird which in later times has a human head, but, as is clear from the context, has the rarer meaning of 'form' or 'shape' (Gardiner's 'external manifestation', *Eg. Gramm.*[3] p. 173).

3. *Wḏb*, lit. 'be turned round'; cf. *JEA* 35, 93, n.1. De Buck's question at the end of this note is surely to be answered in the affirmative.

4. Loc. cit. n.4. Cf. also 'I will be with the Lord of Life', *CT* I, 393*b*.

5. Cf. *sꜣyt* 'chest'(?)', *CT* VII, 452*e*.

6. Reading and meaning alike obscure.

7. *Sšd* here means not 'fillet' (de Buck) but 'flashing', with reference to *iꜣḫw* 'sunlight'; on *sšd* cf. *JEA* 54,41.

8. The text here inserts *nb-r-ḏr* 'Lord of All', apparently without relevance.

9. Lit. 'the Great Moorer'; *mny* 'moor' is a common metaphor for death.

10. See *JEA* 35, 96, n.5. For the obscure word *ḥmꜣtt* cf. *Pyr.* § 373; *CT* III, 22*c*.

11. Cf. *JEA* 35, 96, n.6. I would suggest that the 'special meaning' of *wnwn* here may be rather 'patrol the way in advance'.

12. *Ḫꜣfw*, meaning unknown.

13. Cf. n. 10.

14. Quite obscure.

15. For *ṯn* 'rise' cf. *Pyr.* § 1927*b* (*Pyr. Suppl.* p. 35 = Utt. 666A); *CT* II 224*c*.

16. Cf. n. 10.

17. For *isp* I would suggest 'cut out' rather than 'broken'; *BD* 31,2 has *ḥsk* in a like context.

Spell 313[1]

BEING TRANSFORMED INTO A FALCON. IV, 87

Osiris: Come [in] peace, O my son Horus: so says Osiris. You shall see me in my great *atef*-crowns which Rēʿ gave to me and which Atum and the Enneads made [firm for] me, being pleased about it. You shall see me, my son Horus, seated in front of [. . .] with my uraei on my brow and my *atef*-crowns on my head, my staff in my grasp and my knife in my grip, my image of Truth on my shoulder, and crookedness under my feet. I confirm [powers], I [promote] positions, I obstruct my foes who shall come opposing me, because I have appeared as ruler [of the sky] and king of the earth, and my foes fall through fear when they see me. | I am exalted in my great *atef*-crowns which 88
are in Ninsu, and I indeed am your father, O my offspring upon earth. May you establish my powers, may you increase my rule(?)[2] among those who bestow their powers [on you(?)] and who increase the rule(?) of them for you. Slay and obstruct your foes.

Atum: O Thoth—so says Atum—travel for us upon the Island of Fire, see Osiris for us, for you will find him in Ninsu. I have implanted fear of him, I have created awe of him; regrant his crown for me, for you are the god for the protection(?) of Osiris.

Thoth: Behold, I have come—so says Thoth (to Osiris)—and I have brought

to you truth and joy, I have brought to you authority and vindication. You
are triumphant over your foes, the love of you is in the Bark of Flesh, a fair
89 remembrance of you is in the Castle.[1] I will grant to you the lifetime of Rēʿ,
who is yonder, ⟨. . .⟩ I will place the awe of you in Ninsu, [and also] the awe
of Rēʿ who is in Ninsu. I will grant to you oblations in Memphis, [I] will
repeat your festivals in Ōn, I will open up for you the paths of the Netherworld,
I will put fear of you in Djedu, I will regrant your crown in Abydos, and also
the crown of Rēʿ which is in Thinis.

He who shall come against you in the sky shall be (doomed) ⟨to⟩ the striking-power of your crown.

He who shall come against you on earth shall be (doomed) to the striking-power of your majesty.

Those[3] who shall come against you from the South shall be driven off by Satis, Lady of Elephantine, who will shoot at them with her arrows, which are painful and sharp [against(?)] them.

90 Those who shall come against you from the North shall be (doomed) to
Ḥeḳes [and to] Ḥepḥep.

Those who shall come against you from the East shall be (doomed) to Sopd, Lord of the East, and they shall be driven off with your knives in them.

Those who shall come against you from the West shall be (doomed) to Ḥa, Lord of the West, and they shall be driven off by the striking-power of Atum in his ascendings from the horizon.

I have placed your foes in bonds and the Scorpion in fetters: so says Thoth
to Osiris. I have come that I may do again what is good for you, I will raise up
Truth for you, I will gladden you with what you desire, for I have smitten,
subdued and felled your foes for you, I have driven off for you those who
rebelled against you, I have massacred them, I have obstructed them, again I
have appeared [against them(?)]. I have given you vindication in the Two
Conclaves and joy in the Two Enneads, I have set a fair remembrance of you
91 in the Castle,[1] I have [set] the love of you in the Island of Fire, just as Rēʿ
commanded to be done for you.

Horus: O Thoth, you shall do for me what you did for Osiris, so that I may be triumphant and that you may fell my foes, for I am the offspring of Osiris, I am Horus, son of Osiris, born of the divine Isis. I am king in Chemmis, my face is formed as that of a divine falcon; I created my Eye in flame, I am alert, and my Sacred Eye is united with his Sacred Eye. I made my Eye, a living serpent . . . There shall be done for me more than was done for him; my name is like his name, my form is like his form, my foe is afraid of me,

having fallen on his face; he beholds me with my face formed as that of a falcon. My shape is like that of Rēʿ [. . .] which are in Ōn; Thoth [is he] who makes them firm at my accession | in the shape of Horus because of the shape 92
of [Rēʿ . . .:] so says(?) Rēʿ-Atum of me, because I see my face as his face. My shape is like his shape as a divine falcon, I have smitten the gods with my hands, I have [kicked(?)] them with my toes. I have bruised(?) them with my fingers and I have gripped them with my nails, because my strength [is greater] than theirs in my avatar as Horus great of strength. I am he who spoke to them(?), namely Shu [and Tefēnet], Horus and Nūt, and Thoth and his tribunal; my Eye is stronger than their strength. I departed(?) at my birth and went forth in the manner of kingship with my uraeus on my brow, my great *atef*-crowns on my head, my staff in my grasp and my knife in my grip; |
93 my tress is on my [. . .], the limits of my mouth are those of the head of a vulture, my face is formed as that of a divine falcon, like the shape of Rēʿ [. . .]. I have become ruler of the Two Banks, I have inherited the thrones of Horus, I have taken possession of the horizon of Khopri, I sit on the throne of my father Onnophris by the word of Rēʿ, by the command of Gēb and by the confirmation of Thoth, and the Two Conclaves are pleased at it, the sky is in festival, the earth is in joy, and the Enneads are glad at the sound of the storm of the Blower. I go forth as Horus the vindicated in my avatar as Horus; my name is like his name, my shape is like his shape.

Osiris: I am Osiris, son of Gēb, the successor to Rēʿ; my mother is in the Bark of Flesh, and I will not die, I will not be destroyed, I will not be wiped out, and my name will not be wiped out. I will not be wiped out, for I am in this land for ever.

1. For a discussion of this spell, cf. *JEA* 58, 91.
2. Read *ḥḳꜣt* in a cryptic writing of the word for 'rule'?
3. Note the continued use of the sing. *iw·ty·fy* even though the subsequent pronouns show that the plural is meant.

Spell 314

I am Osiris,[1] Bull of the West, King of those who are not. IV, 94

I am the god of protection(?),[2] I have smitten on your behalf, I have watched over your name.

I am the Unique One in the tribunal of the vindication of Osiris against his foes, I have judged those who are (involved) in your harm,[3] O Osiris.

I am the god whom Nūt bore, who slew the foes of Osiris and imprisoned those who rebelled against him.

I belong to your company, O Horus, (even) you who fight for me and who speak about my name.

I am Thoth who vindicated Horus against his foes on the day of judgement in the great Prince-mansion which is in Ōn.

(I am) a man of Djedu, son of a woman of Djedu; I was conceived in Djedu, I was born in Djedu when I was with the female wailers and mourners for Osiris in the Islands of the Twin Children,[4] when Osiris was triumphant over his foes—so says Thoth to Rēʿ.

May I be triumphant over my foes—so you shall say to Thoth. May I be
95 with Ḥu[5] on the day of the clothing of Teshtesh, | when the jars for the washing[6] of the mysterious Inert One are opened on the day of concealing(?) the mysteries of the deep place(?) in Rostau.

May I be with Horus on the day of greeting the ⌈left⌉ arm of Osiris who is in Khem. May I go in and out[7] with the fiery serpent on the day of expelling the rebels from Khem. May I be with Horus on the day of festival when oblations are repeated in Ōn on the Festivals of the Sixth Day and of the Seventh Day.

I am the priest of Djedu on the day of raising up what is to be high.

I am the prophet of Abydos on the day when the earth is joyful.

I am he who sees[8] the secret thing in Rostau.

I am he who reads the ritual book of the Ram in Djedet.

I am the *sm*-priest, the . . .[9] of the *ḥnw*-bark on its sledge.

I am he who takes his beard[10] on the day of breaking up the earth in Ninsu.[11]

96 O you who cause the perfected souls to draw near to the House of Osiris,[12] give me bread and beer at all seasons, (namely) what pleases the souls who belong to the House of Osiris.

O you who open ways and open up paths for the perfected souls in the House of Osiris, open ways and open up paths for my soul to my funerary estate. It shall enter freely[13] and safely into the House of Osiris, for there is no-one who will turn it away from it. It shall go in favoured and beloved, it shall be vindicated, its command shall be carried out in the House of Osiris, for the heritage of the throne of the Two Banks has been confirmed for the son of the lord thereof.

1. There is no coherent sequence in this spell. First the deceased is identified with Osiris; then he is a champion of Osiris against his foes (94*b* ff). In 94*q* he appears in the role of Thoth,

as in *BD* Spell 1, yet in 94*r* ff. he appeals to Thoth to make him triumphant against his enemies. In 95*i* ff. the deceased appears in various priestly guises, while in 96*a* ff. he appeals to those who look after the perfected souls to do the same for him, and in 96*e* ff. his soul enters the House of Osiris and his commands are executed as for the heir of the throne of Egypt. The whole spell gives the impression of being a compilation of extracts from various sources.

2. For *gs-dpt* cf. 88*k*; *BD* 18,9–10 (later version of this text); *Wb.* V, 200, 14 ff. The suffixes of the 2nd person in what follows appear to refer to Osiris the god rather than the deceased.

3. Read *imyw ḏwt*; *BD* 18,13 has misunderstood this as *wnḏwt* 'company'.

4. Unknown locality.

5. God of authority.

6. Read *iʿw*; the *t* before the det. appears to be an error.

7. Emending as *pr·i ʿḳ·i*; the infinitive is out of place here. *BD* 19,16 has *ʿḳ·i prw·i*.

8. Emending as *mꜣꜣ*, cf. *BD* 20,6.

9. *Wrnw*, meaning unknown. There may have been some corruption here; *BD* 20,9–10 reads: 'I am the *sm*-priest at his duties. I am the Master Craftsman on the day of placing the *ḥnw*-bark of Sokar on its sledge'.

10. Presumably an artificial one as part of his costume. *BD* 20,10–11 has more plausibly: 'I am he who takes the hoe (*ẖbsy*)'.

11. Cf. *BD* 20,11.

12. Here a long passage corresponding to *BD* 20,13–21, 2 has been omitted, see de Buck, 96, n.1*.

13. For *m dndn* 'freely' cf. Pap. Yuya, 2,24; the Ani text *BD* 21,9 has *dnd* with det. . The writing 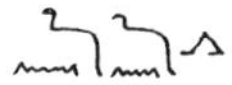 here is a later variant of the stem *dndn*, 'go round about', Pyr. § 2099, and is not to be confused with  'drive off' what is detestable, *CT* III, 393*j*.

Spell 315

The sound of rejoicing is in the realm of the dead, and those who are in the Netherworld have come[1] in peace—so say they to N. Those who are in their tombs are glad because of N, for you (*sic*) are the great god who is in the sky among the gods. Come down to me,[2] O N, for the doors of the paths of the Netherworld are opened for you; I have put the fear of you in Djedu[3] and your oblations in Memphis,[4] I will repeat your festivals in Abydos.[5] I have felled your foes ⟨for⟩ you, I have driven off for you those who rebelled against you,[6] I have warded off Seth for you, I have spat on[7] his confederacy for you, I have given you vindication in the Two Conclaves,[8] I have set a fair remembrance of you in the Castle of the Great Ones who are in the Great Shrine,[9] I have set the love of you in the Netherworld among the spirits, just as Rēʿ commanded me to do it for you. IV, 97

1. *Ḥr* is superfluous before the old perfective.

2. 'Me' presumably is Osiris.
3. Cf. 89*h*.
4. Cf. 89*e*.
5. Compare 89*f*, which has 'Ōn' instead of 'Abydos'.
6. Cf. 90*m*.
7. *ỉsdy·i*; cf. *isd* 'spittle', *Pyr.* §§ 261. 850; 'spit out', § 1628.
8. Cf. 90*p*.
9. Cf. 90*q*.

Spell 316

IV, 98 Becoming the fiery eye of Horus. I am the fiery Eye of Horus, which
went forth terrible,[1] Lady of Slaughter, greatly awesome, who came into being
in the flame of the sunshine, to whom Rēʿ granted appearings in glory,[2] whose
children Rēʿ-Atum made enduring. What Rēʿ said about her: Mighty is the
fear of you, great is the awe of you, mighty is your striking-power, great is
99 your magic | in the bodies of your foes, and the hostile ones[3] have fallen on
their faces[4] because of you; all men have been in the sleep of death[5] because
of you and through your power, and those who shall see you shall be afraid of
you in this vigorous form of yours which the Lord of the Enneads has given
to you—so he spoke of me,[6] so said the Lord of the Enneads of me. I have
become the Eye of Horus—and *vice versa*—I am indeed she who shoots[7]—and
100 *vice versa*— | I am she who triumphs, the companion of Rēʿ.
Behold me, men and gods! Set the fear of me and create awe of me on that
plateau of the Stone of Brightness(?).[8] Behold me, men and gods! I have come
101 into being as the Lady of Glorious Appearings,[9] | I have reappeared in glory,
I have made my being enduring, my flame is behind me, the awe of me is before
me, I have conquered the gods, and there is no-one who can come opposing
me—so say[10] those who are in front of the Great Throne.
What is this[11] on the morning when this god[12] comes? The shades shall
not be judged, the plans of the gods shall not be carried out.[13] Look with
102 your eyes,[14] you elder gods | who aforetime came into existence with the
ancestors, on this spirit who has come here.[15] He has become a flame, he has
come into the Island of Fire. I have betaken myself to him through fear of the
fiery blast of his mouth—so say[16] the elders who are about the shrine. Send
out your soul, that it may see with its eyes; such is Horus when he has re-
103 appeared in glory | and has fashioned his bodily Eye. Behold, it is stronger[17]
than any of the gods, it has taken possession of the Ḥau-nebut, and it is more
. . .[18] than any god.

Behold me, men and gods! I have become the fiery Eye of Horus; it itself
fashioned me, it has knit together *Kḥnḥ* for me, and She whose magic is great
has raised me | before my seat above the gods; Abundance, father of the gods, 104
has clothed me. She[19] has fashioned his bodily Eye, and behold it is stronger
than the gods; there is none who can come opposing me (*sic*) except Atum,
because of his putting me forward(?).[20] I gather together my striking-power,
I control(?)[21] my heat(?)[22]—so said Atum.
Is the Sole Eye stronger than the gods? So say I to my father Atum. Strength 105
has gone forth to me from your mouth, and it means that I have become Her
who is strongest among the gods, and Seth has fallen because of me, I have
made his confederacy slip(?)[23] because of that on account of which he wand-
ered.[24] I have stood on his bonds, the monthly festival was fashioned for me, | 106
the half-monthly festival was celebrated for me, I taste nothing evil, like the
Lord of the monthly festival, the monarch of eternity. I am strong and sharp[25]
of flame, (even) She who closed the house because of the Coiled One, and mine
is the coil of my Eye.
I am Horus who lifted up his Eye, which appeared besouled, high and
mighty; it consumes the river. | Food-offerings are around me, around me, 107
through that spirit(?) who burns up(?) any dead,[26] male or female, who shall
come opposing me.
Behold me, men and gods! I have become the fiery Eye of Horus. The terror
of me has captured for me, the awe of me has taken for me, there has been given
to me everything in the hand of Nu. I am She who is over what is red,[27] | who 108
judges the gods, who is strong and mighty, who protects her father. My
strength resides in[28] the terror of me, the awe of me resides in my wrath(?).[29]
I am he who has experience(?)[30] at the boundary of the Lord of Pe,[31] the
swaying one(?)[32] of the Lady of Unu. I have become Atum, it goes well with
me as Horus, and it goes well with every god of whom I have had experi-
ence(?).[33] | Life and strength have been given to me in the horizon, and every 109
god is under my influence. I am a primeval one[34] of the earth, guide of the
Sole Lord, *ḥknwtt*-serpent of Ḥarakhti. I live the life, I will not be wiped out
nor will my name be wiped out in this land for ever.

1. Lit. 'in fear' in the sense of inspiring fear in others.

2. The det.  of *ḥ3w* in S2P and S1C is apparently an error for . The two signs in question differ in hieratic only by the addition of a tick.

3. Compare *kw* with similar sense in 83*c*; the word may be a derivative of *ky* 'cry out' with the meaning of 'shouters' or 'those who jeer'.

4. Note the det. after *ḥr ḥr·sn* in all three texts.

5. Cf. *Wb.* II, 266,8.
6. The deceased = the Eye of Horus.
7. Or Satis?
8. Compare *ḳꜣḥyt* with det. ⊙ 'bright one(?)', *BD* 355,3.
9. See n.2.
10. Lit. 'in the saying of'. On this view of *m ḏd* we should read *ḫntyw st wrt* in what follows.
11. For the construction *sy pn* instead of *sy pw* see also 110*g*. In the latter instance S1C has the more usual *sy pw*. The nexus of what follows with what precedes is quite obscure.
12. The deceased?
13. Since neuter passive participles make no sense here, *wpyt* and *iryt* have been read as prospective *sḏm·tw·f* forms, but the real meaning is quite obscure.
14. Lit. 'face(s)'.
15. Cf. *Ḥekanakhte*, pp. 111–2. 'Here' suits the context better than 'today'.
16. See n.10.
17. Reading *mk s*(*y*) *nḫt*(·*ty*) with S2P, regarding the following *r·s* as the enclitic particle.
18. *Mḥꜣ*, meaning unknown.
19. The Eye of Horus.
20. *Wdt·f* (with dittograph) appears to be infinitive with agential suffix.
21. Perhaps in the sense of 'hold back, restrain'; cf. *wḫd·i bkꜣt* 'I refrained from the pregnant woman', *Hatnub*, 20,17.
22. For *bḫḫw* see Spell 310, n.1.
23. For *sbn* with transitive meaning see also *Pyr.* § 503 = *Komm. Pyr.* II, 347.
24. For *sbnbn* 'wander' cf. *Pyr.* § 936. The suffix presumably refers to Seth. Note the word-play with *sbn* 'make slip'.
25. Feminine because the 'fiery Eye' is feminine.
26. This passage is very obscure. *ꜣḫt* apparently means 'female spirit' here, representing the 'fiery Eye', but the participle *nsbs* does not show the fem. ending. This verb is not recorded, but seems to be a partially reduplicated form derived from *nsb* 'lap up, lick', *Concise Dict.* 139.
27. At the end of 107*h* read *ṯms* 'what is red', presumably with reference to blood.
28. Lit. 'belongs to'.
29. For *idt* 'wrath' cf. *Hamm*, 114,7.
30. Lit. 'tastes'. Note that the masc. *dp* is used.
31. Assuming ○ in S2P to stand for ⊗; *rpw* of S1C is a *vox nihili.*
32. The uraeus(?). Note the fem. gender.
33. Lit. 'every god of I-have-tasted-him'.
34. Feminine.

Spell 317

IV, 110 Becoming the Nile. The sky trembles and those who are in it bow down; they see the Following as it goes about,[1] the gods[2] give me worship. They say: Who is[3] the god who has come into being[4] today? Khopri has come into
111 the Island of Fire, | the gods come in his bark, he gives a gift[5] to the Lord of

Eternity. They see me when I have appeared as the Nile-god, the unique
Power among the gods. I sit at the head of the Ennead, and the gods[6] come
bowing. I do what I wish, my shape is in the sky, | my rank is Nile-god. 112

Behold me,[7] you gods and spirits who are in the sky and in the desert,
mould my navel-string for me, make my beard for me, for I have appeared as
the Nile-god, his son and his successor (*sic*); I go at my due times and I return
at my due seasons.

I am one who brings food-offerings and provisions to that king, the ruler(?)[8] 113
of the Island of Fire.

I am the Nile-god, the Lord of provisions, who comes with joy, the well-
beloved;[9] he has given me his soul,[10] he has renewed his appearings for me,[11]
he is one who is reborn for me(?).[12] | I have appeared on my throne, I am spirit- 114
ualized with what appertains to me,[13] I am the spirit of Horus,[14] a possessor
of offerings in the lower Netherworld.

I am that Great One who protects the gods regarding their cakes,[15] the
Primeval One of the earth.

I am a *sm*-priest and a noble,[16] one who is in the heart of the Lord of the
Horizon; | I go at my due times and return at my due seasons, in accordance 115
with his command.[17]

I am a noble among the gods,[18] and I do for myself what I wish.

I am the Nile-god, Lord of Waters,[19] who brings vegetation,[20] and I will
not be driven off by enemies;[21] it is he who is exalted, with a satchel at his
side, who has given me this rank of mine. | I have carried out your slaughter- 116
ings, you gods, I have taken those who rebelled against you, I have been
placed in the rank of Nile-god.[22]

Behold me, men and gods, come in my train, give me worship,[23] for I have
appeared as the Nile-god whom men love, protector of the gods; | the *nʿw*- 117
serpents[24] depart from their caverns for me, the bulls who are in their mounds
are disturbed(?).[25] There is no limit to my vision,[26] and there is no oppositon
to my hands.

'How happy is this young god whom Rēʿ made with his power?'[27] say the
horizon-dwellers[28] of me. | They see me in my rank of Nile-god,[29] for indeed I 118
am the young god, I am he who is in the presence of the Primeval One who is
older than the gods, and my seat is prominent in the Bark of Rēʿ in the midst
of the lower Netherworld. I have come[30] that I may make the Two Lands
green; | I go up to the mounds, I climb[31] over the hill-sides just as *Hꜣny* did for 119
himself;[32] I will not be repelled in my shape of Nile-god, and I will not be
restrained in my dignity of equipped spirit; it was Rēʿ who created me as his

120 son, he modelled me in stonework(?).[33] | He exalts[34] my shape above the gods,
he has set me at the head of his Enneads in my dignity of successor to Rēꜥ.

Behold me, you gods, come in my train, give me worship,[35] for I am the
121 Nile-god who is in his year.[36] | I have come here as god of the flat-land and
the hill-country,[37] I have seen the bank of *mꜣṯt*,[38] I have appeared as the Nile-
god,[39] the Elder who protects you (*sic*). My movements are extensive to the
limit of my desire. Here comes the god who guards the land—so say the gods
of the horizon[40] concerning me. They see me when I have appeared as the
122 Nile,[41] | with the sun-folk about me, about me, like Rēꜥ when he was born.[42]
Truth is conducted to me as to Rēꜥ, my women with braided hair[43] are like
the frog-goddesses,[44] I control the cakes for the gods, food-offerings for
123 those who are on earth and invocation offerings for the spirits, I sweeten the
smell of their caverns, the crocodile-gods have been placed in my retinue for
me, and Neith is concerned with(?) my female mourners.[45] I am older than
those seven elder gods, | one hidden of countenance in the presence of the
Lord of Eternity; they are afraid of me and follow me behind the spirits.[46]
My hands are strong(?),[47] I am shaken[48] on my flesh, I resemble those who
(once) existed(?).[49]

124 Behold me, you gods; come in my train, give me worship, | for I am the
Nile-god, older than the Eight;[50] the Entourage rejoice,[51] and those who are
in (my?) train are happy. Acclamation has been given to me by(?) the Two
125 Conclaves, oblations to the gods have been repeated for me, | they see me when
I have appeared as the Nile-god; I have come to the king in my dignity and my
power, and the bark of Rēꜥ sails in the cloudy sky. My hands are strong(?),
126 I shake with my head,[52] | I have cut the dams of the grey-haired ones on which
those who cry aloud stand, against whom action is taken[53] in the Island of
Fire. As for anyone who is (due) to be decapitated[54] who shall oppose himself
127 to me; as for anyone who cries aloud who shall come opposing me;[55] | as for
any god or any rebel who shall oppose me or whom I shall find on my path,[56]
the *ꜣḳdw*-spirits[57] who are before me[58] shall seize him, the *ꜥšmw*-spirits who
are behind me shall devour[59] him, because I am Khopri who created himself,
I have become the essence[60] of Rēꜥ; he has given to me those who are behind
128 his power[61] | and there is no-one who shall come and face me.[62] I am the Nile-
god who acts as he wishes,[63] Lord of the Flood who makes content, and I rest
at the limit of the horizon; I(?) give my water, and Nūt is behind those who
pervade(?) water. My Court is on the mounds,[64] I am one who is exalted over
his Two Lands,[65] I am Khopri ⟨who created⟩ himself.[66]

129 Behold me, you gods; | come in my train and give me worship;[67] see me in

this my very great dignity, with my sceptre (resting) on my divine arm and my
staff in my noble hand.[68] | There are ushered into me the nobles as gods,[69] I 130
am seated in front of the Great Ones[70] like the horned Rēʿ.

Behold me,[71] I shine in the sunrise, I have come into being as the seed[72] of
the Bull of the West, | I have gone forth[73] today in the Bark of Rēʿ, the Un- 131
wearying Stars[74] tremble at me within the Jackals,[75] and the gods give me
worship[76] when they see me in my dignity of a god. | Thoth is in charge of 132
what is carried out for me; his festival-offerings are on his hands,[77] he grants
my power, he makes enduring the awe of me, he sees the children of the gods
in me, he makes my name to endure with him(?) when I appear.[78]

Behold me in my shape,[79] for I am the eldest of the eight Nile-gods, the 133
primeval ones,[80] I appear as a noble, I ascend today from Elephantine, and
they see me as a god equipped with his power and among the gods.[81] | Grain 134
has been given to me and to my suite by the Great One who dwells in his hall,
and provisions belong to me, food-offerings have been prepared for me and
presentation-offerings come down to me. I am one who is vigilant, lifting up
my face,[82] | one older than those who are in the Presence. I have come into 135
being, one whom no vulva made, whom no womb bore.[83]

Behold me, you gods; come in my train, give me worship, for I am the Primeval One of the earth.

1. *Šmsw* is construed as a singular here, presumably the 'Followers of Horus' considered as a unitary whole. This is a long and difficult spell.

2. S1C has 'the gods, they give me', without object. That the plural 'gods' is in fact the correct reading, despite the absence of plural strokes, is shown by the plural suffix in *ḏd·sn*, 110*f*.

3. The rare construction *sy pn* in three out of four texts is confirmed by 101*g*. S1C here has the more usual *sy pw*.

4. Var. S1C *msy* 'who has been born'.

5. In S1C read *dd·f* ⟨*f*⟩*ꜣ* 'he gives what is lifted up' in the ritual gesture of offering.

6. The plural of S1C and S2C is obviously correct.

7. So S1C only.

8. De Buck, n.1*, suggests the restoration  in S1P; the traces suit. The word is lost in S2C and S3C; S1C has *iḳꜣ*, which presumably is a corruption of *ḥḳꜣ*.

9. S3C ends here.

10. Var. S1C *iw rdy n·i bꜣ·f* 'His soul has been given to me'; for the reading *bꜣ* see n.6*; it makes better sense than *sꜣ·f* 'his son' of S1P.

11. Lit. 'he has repeated . . .'; as in the preceding clause, S1C has the passive *sḏm·f* and determines *ḫʿw* with 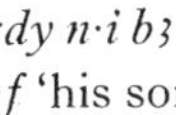 as if it were the word for 'crowns'.

12. S1P reads *i·f iky r·f*, which is quite obscure; *iky* here can hardly be connected with *iky* 'lament', *Pyr.* § 550, or with *ik* 'attack', *Pyr.* § 959. S1C has *i·f mss r·i*, which is equally unintelligible. One could perhaps emend as *i·f* ⟨*m*⟩ *mss r·i* 'he is one who is regularly reborn (imperfective

passive participle) for me', but it is not very convincing.

13. Var. S1C *iw·i ꜣḫ·ky r·f* 'I am more spiritualized than he', which makes less good sense. At the end of 114*a st·i* 'my throne' of S1P seems the best reading.

14.  in S1P is paralleled by  in S1C, which continues 'possessor of offerings who takes possession in the lower Netherworld'.

15. In S1P read *nḏty nṯrw ḥr pꜣkw·sn*, cf. B2L (114*g*), which comes in here with a variant of its own: 'the gods in charge of their cakes. I am Rēꜥ who came into being of himself, I am Nu who does for himself what he wishes'. S1C has obscurely *wḏt-mdw ḥr ḥst·sn*, where the meaning of *ḥst* is obscure, and the plural suffix lacks an antecedent.

16. Following S1P.

17. S1P and B2L omit the reference to times and seasons.

18. So B2L; the other texts are obscure. S1P + S2C appear to read 'a noble whom he knows', while S1C has 'a noble is near me among the gods.' Even B2L is in the 3rd person, with *sꜥḥ pw* instead of *ink sꜥḥ* but what follows confirms the interpretation in the 1st person.

19. So S1C; varr. S1P and S2C 'Lord of Offerings'; B2L 'who brings offerings'.

20. Var. B2L 'who makes vegetation'.

21. For *snṯw* 'enemies' see also VII, 401*a*; *BD* 281,13; cf. also *znṯ* 'hostile', *Pyr.* § 1837.

22. B2L only.

23. Var. S1C 'the gods adore me'.

24. So S1C; the mention of 'caverns' suggests that this is more likely to be the original reading than the colourless *wrw* 'great ones' of S1P and S2C.

25. So S1C; varr. S1P 'I have disturbed(?) the bulls who are in the mounds', with *nẖꜣẖꜣ* for *snẖꜣẖꜣ*; B2L 'I love his bulls within the mounds'. *Snẖꜣẖꜣ* 'disturb(?)' only here; the meaning given to it is a guess.

26. Reading *nn ḏr n ḥr·i*; this accords well with the next sentence.

27. The last clause only in S1C and B2L.

28. Var. 'the Enneads'.

29. S1C and B2L only.

30. Var. S1C 'I have come today'. B2L has 'I have come and the Two Lands are green'.

31. For *ḥfd* 'climb' S1C has *fd* 'pluck' with an indeterminate object. The 'climbing' seems to refer to the rising level of the flood-waters.

32. *Hꜣ·n·i*, lit. 'I have descended', must be a proper name here, as it serves as the subject of the relative form *irt·n*.

33. Cf. *dnj* 'Steinblock o. a.', *Wb.* V, 466,8.

34. The 3rd person in *ṯn·f* (S1P and B2L) is to be preferred to the 1st in S1C, as referring back to Rēꜥ.

35. These two sentences omitted in S1C.

36. A clear reference to the annual inundation. S1C unintelligibly *imy iḥf*; B2L omits.

37. S1C simply 'as god'; for *m* B2L has corruptly 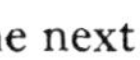.

38. On the plant *mꜣṯt* or *mꜣtt* cf. *JEA* 19, 133. 137; *ZÄS* 96, 12; *BIFAO* 56, 60.

39. S1C unintelligibly 'in accordance with your command'.

40. So S1C; S1P 'so say the spirits and the Enneads'; B2L 'so say the horizon-dwellers'.

41. S1C apparently 'come and see my dignity of Nile-god'; B2L 'they see me in my dignity of Nile-god'.

42. The last clause only in S1C.

43. Omitted in S1C; for *ḥnskwt* B2L has *ḥmswt*.

44. Cf. the Biblical record of the plague of frogs. The next eight sentences are in B2L alone.

45. The significance of this sentence escapes me. For *mꜣṯrwt* > *mꜣtryt*, cf. Caminos. *Lit. Frag.* p. 28; *ZÄS* 96,11.

46. After this sentence the other texts come in again.

47. Cf. *JEA* 57, 18 (31).

48. Emend *wn* into *wnwn*, cf. 125*e*. The basic meaning of *wnwn* is 'sway to and fro', cf. *Concise Dict.* 61. These two sentences appear to describe the condition of a man at the point of death, and they look like intrusions from a funerary ritual.

49. B2L appears to read 'I smooth over my shape at the back of those who follow after', which is most obscure; the translation given above, though not certain, at least suits the immediate context. 123*g*–124*a* are not in B2L, while 124*b–d* (only in B2L) seem out of place.

50. Read *sms r ḫmnw* with S1C. 124*b–d* (B2L only) not translated, see n.49.

51. Varr. 'the Entourage of Rēꜥ'; 'the Enneads of Rēꜥ'.

52. *M tp·i* of S1C seems preferable to *ḥr tp·i* of the other texts. 125*f* (B2L) has been displaced from 125*c*.

53. For *ḫsf ḫt n* 'take action against', cf. *Urk.* I, 101,9. Var. B2L 'it is men who take action', etc.

54. Var. S1C 'As for any foe . . .'; S1C and B2L omit 126*e*.

55. S2C and B2L omit; S1C 'As for any who cry aloud' only.

56. So S1C; var. B2L 'as for any god or spirit who shall oppose himself or set himself against me'. S1C and S2C omit 127*a–c*.

57. Apparently a class of spirits or 'jinn', cf. the *ꜥšmw* below.

58. Var. B2L 'who are on my mouth'.

59. Cf. *Wb.* I, 226, 8–9; S1C has *ḫdw* (unrecorded) and B2L *ḫddw* with an intrusive *f*, which recalls the name of a god of fowling *Ḫdd*, *Wb.* III, 355,15.

60. Lit. 'what is pressed out'.

61. Cf. 123*c*, where, however, *ꜣḫw* is determined with  and lacks a suffix.

62. Cf. *AEO* I, 159*. This sentence only in S1C.

63. 128*b–c* only in B2L.

64. So S1P and possibly S2C, see de Buck, n.1*. S1C 'I have smitten the mounds'; B2L is absent. This passage may be an allusion to the high Nile invading even the 'tells' on which the villages stand.

65. S1C has omitted *kꜣ*; B2L omits the suffix after *tꜣwy*.

66. B2L only, with omission of the verb by haplography.

67. S16C joins in.

68. For 129*f–i*, see de Buck, n.1*. This is not translated.

69. Var. S1P: 'are chosen for me men as gods'.

70. Var. B2L *smsw·sn* 'their old ones'.

71. Two sentences in B2L only.

72. Var. B2L *rḏw* 'efflux'.

73. Var. S1C *iy·n·i* 'I have come'.

74. Var. S1C: 'the Imperishable Stars'.

75. Var. B2L *m-hnw nšwt nt wnš*; the meaning of *nšwt* is not known to me. 'The Jackals'

appears to be the name of a constellation or a part of the sky.

76. S1C adds *m-ḥnw* [. . .]*nwt wnšw*. B2L has 'acclamation is given to me in the horizon'.

77. S1C and B2L differ from the other texts and from each other. S1C: 'his festival offerings are on his hands, what is divine is on his divine hands'; B2L: 'festival is in his divine festival'.

78. B2L only.

79. S1C: 'behold me, you gods, in these appearings of mine'.

80. S1C only.

81. B2L only and ends.

82. Read *ink rs-ḥr⟨ḥr⟩ṯst ḥꜣt·i*, one *ḥr* having been omitted through haplography; *ṯst* is infinitive. *Ḥꜣt* 'forehead' here has the sense of 'face' raised in vigilance.

83. S1C: 'whom no bull fashioned, whom no womb made'.

Spell 318

IV, 136 My magic power came into being in the limits of sky and earth,[1] for I am the
Nile-god, and the Nile came into being in the limits of the earth.[2] I am one
who is in front of[3] the great and mighty gods, I am he who makes offering to
137 Osiris in[4] the great flood, | and it flows upon me. I am the Nile-god in the
great flood which flows for the Nile.[5] I raised up magic in the raising up of the
138 Great One,[6] I apportioned[7] herbage, | I made green the vegetation which
was dried up,[8] I cut the dams of the inundation, I cut the pools of the field-
dwellers while I was in this land, in the limits of all the flat-lands.[9] I the unique
139 one came and joined the Two Brothers, | and it was I who provided for Osiris[10]
on the day when his mother bore him.[11] The threshing-floors[12] have flourished
140 for me upon the ramparts of my paths(?).[13] | The great and small who are in
the Netherworld are pleased with me, for it was I who fashioned the Nether-
world, while the head of Horus remained with that of Seth[14]—and *vice versa*.
141 It was I who inundated the Eye of Horus with the Nile,[15] | which the daughter
of Him who was loosed gave for it.[16] I am Khopri in all my manifestations
and powers, all my spirits and manifestations. I come, and hearts are content;
I make hale, and the Two Lands are nourished. Mine is the inundation-
season,[17] mine is the summer; I am he who created the going forth of this
flame which is on my mouth;[18] the inundation of moisture(?)[19] is my mani-
142 festation, | the winter is the sweat which issues from my flesh, I am he who
celebrates the monthly festival. Such are the Followers of Rēʿ, such are my
messengers of the night, and such am I entirely—and *vice versa*—because this
land prospers for me to the extent of my desire. This sky will be the place of
my heart which nursed me and brought me up,[20] the entire earth is under my
shadow, for I am the Nile-god and I will not become less.[21]

1. B2L and B1P omit the reference to the earth, and write *ḫpr·n·i* without *ḥkꜣ*.

2. 136*b–c* not in S1P–S1Chass.
3. *Ḫnt·i r* in S1P–S1Chass; *ḫnt⟨·i⟩* only in B2L and B1P.
4. B2L and B1P omit *m ꜣgb wr*.
5. 137*a–c* not in S1P–S1Chass.
6. B2L and B1P 'I have knit together the Great One'.
7. For this sense of *šd* cf. *Urk.* IV, 1111, 12.
8. Not in B2L–B1P.
9. S1P omits the final *nb*; S1Chass may have had *tꜣwy* 'the Two Lands'.
10. Lit. 'crossed the mouth of'; the idiomatic meaning of *ḏꜣ rꜣ* as 'contentious' cannot apply here. B2L and B1P omit *rꜣ* and write 'It was I who ferried Osiris on the flood'.
11. Var. 'on the day on which he was born'.
12. B2L and B1P *ḥspw spw* 'the gardens of the . . .'; for the masc. *sp* with det. cf. *Wb.* III, 440, 16 'eine Ortsbezeichnung'.
13. Very doubtful. The only way I can make any sense of this is to regard *ṯbwt(y)* as a word for a path trodden by sandals, but this view may be entirely wrong. Possibly the reference may be to the raised banks of the river.
14. Or possibly 'the head of Horus was made as firm as that of Seth', though in that case one would expect the preposition to read *my* rather than *m*. For *smn* (*zmn*) 'remain', *m* 'with', cf. *Pyr.* §§ 1418; 1420. 'Horus' and 'Seth' in S1P and S1Chass; 'Atum' and 'Seth' in B1P; 'Nu and Horus' and 'Atum and Seth' in B2L.
15. So S1P with for ; *ꜣgb* is almost certainly verbal here. B2L has 'It was I who made the inundation for the Eye of Atum, who was joyful when efflux came into being'; B1P 'It was N. who made considerable the flood for the Eye of Atum, who was joyful when efflux came into being'.
16. So S1P, which ends here. With *wḥꜥ* 'Him who was loosed' compare *wḥꜥ Ḥꜥpy* 'the loosing of the Nile' = the start of the inundation, Dav. *Rekh.* pl. 122, 33(A); the suffix in *r·s* presumably refers to the Eye of Horus. B2L and B1P have 'the son of Him who was loosed is a great and mighty flood', and what is left of B7C is in accord with them.
17. For *mnḫt* read *ꜣḫt*, cf. de Buck's note 3*.
18. The entire expression *ns pw tp rꜣ·i* is determined with ; the reference apparently is to the heat of summer and the rising waters of the river.
19. Apparently a formative of *rḏw* with prefixed *ḥ*; the translation is not certain.
20. These participles are masculine, presumably in concord with *ib*.
21. Lit. 'my littleness will not be'; i.e. the Nile will not fail.

Spell 319

I am this Nile-god who comes and goes[1] at his desire, and there is none who IV, 143
will divert him from what he wishes; Lord of breath(?); Sovereign of eternity, who causes[2] the gods to come bowing to the Lord of eternity; who opens his throat and throws open[3] the caverns of the gods; of whom Atum has taken possession in peace and in . . ..[4] What I have shared[5] with him is all his possessions and all that he makes; I am the flesh of Thoth who defied the Great

Ones; I will come and destroy, I will go and set in order, and that is what my utterance will do, for I am the Nile-god.

1. So B7C; omitted in B2L but a space has been left for the missing words, which may have been in lacuna in the scribe's copy.
2. Reading *dd*, imperf. active participle of (*r*)*dy*.
3. *Ḏbb* with det. . The same verb occurs again 153*a*, where the sense is clear.
4. *St skt im·f* is quite obscure.
5. A superfluous *n*.

Spell 320

IV, 144 I am the Nile-god who provides food, Ḥu[1] who provides what your (*sic*) name desires(?).[2] O you who cross the sky(?),[3] I have heard him who comes. Come into the gate(?) of the plebs in the Banks of Horus, while I am in my dignity of Lord of the *Wtnw*[4] and Sovereign of the Ennead. I am one who is great, a soul at the head of affairs on behalf of the god, one favoured by the Lord of the gods, great of appearance, Lord of the *Wtnw* within the Lower Portal, walking in accordance with my will, which comes at my due times and seasons. I make herbage grow, I nourish the realm(?)[5] of Lower Egypt, I create offerings for the gods, I make Rēʿ content within the flood of the *Wtnw*; a sailor who navigates[6] within the clouds of the sky in company with the Followers of Rēʿ, Satis(?)[7] is in my boat, giving me protection; her son Horus is in the bow of my boat, creating awe of me! in accordance with my dignity of Lord of
145 eternity and Sovereign Lord of the *Wtnw*.

I am he who creates what is and who brings into being what is not. I speak, and Ḥu comes into being; he will come, being multiple(?).[8] One who is in charge of births on behalf of the gods, one favoured by the Lord of the gods,[9] while the seats of the *Wtnw* are within the portal of Khnum[10] and Ḥeḳet; they proclaim me throughout the Two Banks, and also the festivals which are (shared) among(?) the Lords of the sky; they show forth my majesty throughout the Two Lands. I have inundated the Two Banks, and my soul crawls[11] over the sky throughout the Two Lands.[12]

O you plebs, see me, for I am the Nile in charge of births, who creates what is and who brings into being what is not. Implant[13] respect for me, for I am he who will come to you with this shining(?) soul.[14]

1. The god of food here, not to be confused with the personification of 'authority'.
2. Taking *mrw* to be a relative form qualifying *rn·k*, despite the det.
3. Reading *ḏȝ nwt*; there may, however, be some corruption here.

4. For the *Wtnw* cf. 144*h.m*; 145*a.f*; V, 220*b* *Pyr.* § 2037.

5. For the sense given to *ḏr* cf. *m ḏr* 'in the realm of', II, 2*d*.

6. Lit. 'the sailor, he navigates'. The first word appears to be *imy*, a *nisba* formation from *im* 'boat'.

7. Apparently a goddess. The following reference to 'her son Horus' suggests that Isis is meant, but the reference to Khnum in 145*f* hints this may be a writing of the name of Satis.

8. Taking *iwt·f* to be the prospective *sḏm·f* and *ꜥšꜣ* as an epithet of Ḥu in reference to the multiplicity of foodstuffs.

9. These two epithets refer to the speaker rather than to Ḥu; the former is described as *imy-ib n nb nṯrw* above in 144*g* and as *ḫnty mswt* in 145*k*.

10. The association with Ḥeket shows that this is the name of the god, despite the det.

11. No verb *ḥꜣf* is known; read probably as *ḥfꜣ* 'crawl', for which see II, 96*e*; *Wb.* III, 73, 6. The writer has lapsed into the 3rd person here.

12. An allusion to rain-clouds moving across the sky?

13. Plural imperative; for the ending cf. Gardiner, *Eg. Gramm.*[3] § 335.

14. Or 'this soul of the shining one'.

Spell 321

O you gods of the Ennead, come after me and grant 〈me〉[1] my power, create IV, 146
awe of me, for you know him who was aforetime in the region(?) of the sky.[2]
I am the Nile-god who comes in joy, dearly beloved, Sovereign of the Powers,
god, Lord of all that is his(?).[3] Praise and acclamation are given to me, for
there is no-one [who can create][4] what he needs from my food-offerings, there
is no-one who can give himself a meal from my provisions, because[5] I am the
Nile-god, wide-spread of vision, who made the gods; Sovereign of the frog-
goddesses;[6] august god, mysterious of . . .,[7] and all the gods live[8] according to
my decree. I have caused 〈my〉 power[9] to come throughout the lands, and
when it comes, herbage grows, the gods are flourishing(?),[10] the celestial
kine . . .,[11] while my soul comes over the sky[12] to Horus who rules Ōn. Rēꜥ
rejoices over me in company with Him who is in his bark; he acts in accordance
with my nature, which he shows forth(?)[13] to the gods who came into being
before him. | I am . . .[14] for him to the full extent of his goods which have 147
come into being. Indeed I know the Sole One, who is ennobled thereby,[15] and
his soul is more potent than the gods; he has made everything, he has copu-
lated and has grasped orgasm. I have turned myself about . . . you,[16] mine is
he who makes my windings pleasant(?),[17] who takes his place within my wind-
ings. His utterance is what goes forth from his own heart, he has gone round in
the company of Shu upon the circuit of Authority[18] and Perception, who
made enquiry from him.[19] Authority and Perception said to him: Come, let us

go and make[20] the names of yonder winding[21] in accordance with what went out from his heart, even of him who once went round with Shu, for he is his[22] son who fashioned himself. Thus said Atum to the gods: What I say within the sky is: 'Let us make[23] the names of . . .,[24] let us repeat his power together with my own(?)[25] power.' I am Lord of the gods, I am the Nile-god, and I will never grow weary.

1. Read possibly *dy·ṯn ⟨n·i⟩ bꜣ·i*, with merging of *n*'s and omission of the suffix 1st sing.
2. Quite obscure, like much else in this spell.
3. Lit. perhaps 'his all', though one would expect *tm* rather than *tmt*.
4. Restoring *ir* in the lacuna, see de Buck, n.1*.
5. *⟨N-⟩ntt*.
6. Cf. 145*f*.
7. *Ỉdt*, meaning unknown.
8. *ꜥnẖw*; perhaps an instance of Edel's active *sḏmw·f*, cf. his *Altäg. Gramm.* §§ 519 ff.
9. *Bꜣw*; construed as plural in *iww·sn* below.
10. For this sense of *ꜣẖ* cf. III, 6*b*.
11. *Syṯ*, meaning unknown.
12. Cf. 145*i*.
13. A miswriting of ? Cf. 145*g*.
14. *H̱ꜣt·ky*, old perfective 1st sing. of a verb of unknown meaning.
15. By what? The whole passage 147*b* is most obscure.
16. *Pẖr·n·i ẖr·i ṯn* is surely corrupt; probably there has been an omission before *ṯn*. *H̱r·i* also is difficult, but may perhaps be serving as a reinforcement of *pẖr·n·i*.
17. All highly conjectural.  may possibly be a writing of *ꜥꜣb* with transitive sense; for *ḳꜣbw* 'windings' of a waterway cf. *Pyr.* § 2061; *CT* IV, 313*d*. The writer presumably had the river Nile in mind. The suffix in *ir st·f*, which can refer only to *ꜥꜣb*, enforces the interpretation of *ink* in its possessive sense.
18. Ḥu here is not the god of food; the collocation of Ḥu and Sia is well known.
19. The connection of 147*g–l* with what has preceded is by no means clear, and it is possible that there may have been a textual omission somewhere.
20.  is surely superfluous, but occurs again in 147*o*.
21. Singular, despite the plurals *ḳꜣbw* in 147*g* and *rnw* in 147*l*.
22. Shu's.
23. See n.20, so also in *wḥm·n* below. The whole of 147*o* is obscure.
24. *Nw ṯn* is untranslatable and surely corrupt, and the function of the following *ḥm* is quite obscure.
25. The last two words of this passage read *bꜣw·i ḏs·f*, which is nonsense; presumably *ḏs·f* should be emended into *ḏs·i*.

Spell 322

IV, 148 BECOMING KHENTI-KHEM. I am Khenti-khem in control of Khem, one

mightily terrible and greatly majestic. I am the Golden Falcon[1] who snatches
things in the voids of the sky, who eats in the shambles of Horus.[2] | I am a 149
soul[3] who eats his navel-string,[4] who lives on his friends of his foreskin and
who eats of his companions.[5] I am one who travels by night[6] and who hides
by day; I am one alone, | without a companion; I am a wild bull, the fighter 150
of the Crocodile nome,[7] whose hind-quarters are on the mountain and whose
forepart is on the Nile,[8] who smote yonder . . .,[9] | who are placed under my 151
left-hand sandal for me. O you who love Horus,[10] my father fashioned me,
and there is no-one like me . . .[11]

1. *Bik* is spelt out in full in two texts.

2. I.e. the carrion bird which feeds on the offal of the *abattoir*.

3. Written with what appears to be a variant of . The reading *bꜣ* is confirmed by the ram-sign of M24C.

4. *Npꜣ* is the old spelling of *np*, *BD* 391,7, later *npt*, Metternich Stela, 1, where it is named beside *imyw-ẖt* 'entrails', and P. Bremner-Rhind 29,22.23. The Metternich instance speaks against 'Darm' of *Wb.* II, 247,11–12, and *BD* 391,7 points clearly to the translation 'navel-string'. This magically potent object is eaten presumably to obtain the benefit of its powers and to remove it from the reach of the malice of possible enemies.

5. Apparently so in spite of the apparent absurdity. *ꜥnḫ m* in M24C only, but that the initial *m* of the other texts is dependent on *wnm* 'eat' of 149*a* is shown by 149*c*, where S1C[b] inserts = *wnm* before *m*. The reading *ḫnmsw* 'friends' is clear, and is supported by *smꜣy* 'companions' in 149*c*. What these sentences really mean escapes me.

6. for *grḥ* 'night', cf. e.g. 156*a*; 396*b* (five instances).

7. The last two words are a case of honorific transposition.

8. We are reminded of the description of the ox in *Blinding of Truth*, 9,2–4. S2C inverts the order of *pḥwy* and *ḥꜣt* in both versions.

9. Two words of unknown meaning both qualified by *ipf*. All texts agree in reading *šsmw* for the first word, determined with in both S1C texts and with in M24C. For the second word S1C[b] has , S1C[a] has and M24C has det. common to both words; the second word is damaged.

10. Fem. in three texts out of four.

11. Following S1C[b] as the least unintelligible text. The significance of *sp·f* at the end is not clear, but could mean: '(there is none like me) remaining'.

Spell 323

To open what was blocked. O you who extend your arms,[1] O arms, beware! IV, 152
Beware! O you who would harm the Limitless(?),[2] be far from me, for I am
a *tbsw*-plant.[3] Open for me the doors of Him who sees, open up for me the
movements of the great and pure Sunshine-god who is[4] he who makes the
daily shining of Rēꜥ. Open this for me.

1. To hinder the deceased. For *wd*ʿ cf. *Urk.* IV, 339,6, though the reason for the fire-det. does not emerge.

2. Translation doubtful. For *ẖm* 'harm' cf. *BD* 184,16, and with *n ḏr* compare *N-ḏr·f* 'Limitless, epithet of the sun-god, *Pyr.* §§ 1434–5.

3. The *tbsw*-plant is named in *Peas.* R31 as a product of the Wadi Natrun.

4. *ỉmy* of equivalence.

Spell 324

V, 153 TO OPEN WHAT WAS BLOCKED.[1] As for Horus, his forked spear which he uses is employed(?).[2] I am Horus, I have come with my borer(?).[3]

1. *Ḏbb* also in 143*f* above, with det. . The sense is clear and is confirmed by comparison with 152*a*, which uses *wn* 'open' in like context.

2. The interpretation of *ipt* is conjectural and depends solely on the context

3. *Ḏꜣw* is taken to mean a spear-like tool which bores holes (det.) across an obstruction. This too is a conjecture, I can quote no parallel.

Spell 325

V, 154 BECOMING ḤU.[1] The Eye of Rēʿ-Atum appears in the *bbt*-plant,[2] | the Eye of Reʿ-Atum appears in the date-palm—and *vice versa.*[3] He appears in the Opening, a Power who opposed(?) the Powers who were stronger than he.[4]
155 He subdued the Eye when it was angry and fiery, | that he might lead the Great Ones and have power over the gods, that he might make the hour,[5] for Shu has cleansed those who were tousled, he will fetch the hearts of their
156 bulls.[6] | What he has said is what has been done accordingly,[7] and he has made a cleansing in the presence of Rēʿ in the night.[8] To me belongs authoritative utterance; what I say is good, my utterance is good, and what I say is done
157 accordingly. | I am Ḥu, Lord of authoritative utterance.

1. Var. *Ḥkꜣ* 'Magic', showing that here Ḥu personifies authoritative utterance and has nothing to do with food.

2. *Inula graveolens*, cf. *JEA* 20,45–6.

3. A1C + G1T have: 'when the Eye of Atum was high on the date-palm'. These two texts interpolate here: 'He gives Ḥu to Nyw so that he may have power through them'.

4. As the text stands *iṯ·n* can only be a relative form with *sḫm* as antecedent and with the plural *sḫmw* as subject, 'a power whom powers stronger than he overcame', which is contrary to the whole trend of the context. I would suggest that *iṯ·n* may be a miswriting of *itn* 'oppose', to be understood as a participle 'who opposed', which would yield a much better sense.

5. An obscure expression. G1T and A1C add: 'Shu is there to raise up the sky, he subdues the Destroyer'.

6. The prospective form *int* of G1T suggests that the future is intended here. The real meaning of this sentence is quite obscure.

7. *ʾIrw*, perfective passive participle, predicate of a non-verbal sentence with the relative form *ḏdt·f* as subject. Cf. 156*g*.

8. 156*c* (G1T and A1C only) is quite obscure and apparently corrupt. There seems to have been an omission; 'the gods 〈. . .〉 in their presence, having come into being in the night'.

Spell 326

BECOMING HORUS. There is tumult in the sky,[1] | and we see something new,[2] IV, 158
say the primeval gods. Rēʿ shines[3] as Lord of the sunlight,[4] he has put the lords of the terrible ones into dread(?),[5] the Enneads of Rēʿ serve him;[6] | they 160
hear the voice of Rēʿ when he shouts[7] with a voice of great roaring. I have taken possession of the sky, I have divided the firmament,[8] I will show the paths[9] of Khopri, and the dwellers in the Netherworld will follow me. | I shine 162
and am seen in the east of the sky, I go to rest in eternity, and I have acclaim when I have taken possession of the horizon.

1. Var. 'the northern sky'.

2. Varr. 'something new comes into our view'; 'this N has seen what we see'; 'I have seen something new'.

3. Varr. 'N shines', 'N appears'.

4. Varr. 'as Horus'; 'as the sunlight'; 'as Horus Lord of the sunlight'.

5. *Snhḏ*. For the simplex *nhḏ* 'dread(?)' cf. 21*d* above. As object of *snhḏ* read *nbw nrwtyw* with a curious writing in S1C^{b}. From 159*b* to 169*c* Sq6C has a version of its own which reads: 'N has escaped from (*wḥ·n*, with det. of falling wall borrowed from *wḥn* 'throw down') the jackals, N has made the Enneads to vomit, N has subdued the elder gods, N has come that he may stop the tumult . . . N seats himself'. *M kswt* after *ẖnnw* is quite obscure, and there has evidently been some corruption. The rubric in 159*d* belongs to Spell 327.

6. For *dbn* S1C^{b} has *bds* with det. 𓂻, which is a *vox nihili*.

7. Cf. *hw ẖrw* 'loud-voiced'. *BD* 327,13.

8. At this point Sq6C branches off on its own account again: 'N has seized the Sistrum-player, and N will use the Sistrum-player for ever, N will establish Sia at N's feet'.

9. For *sšm wꜣt* 'show the way' cf. *Urk*. I, 127,9; IV, 247,6; V, 75,2.

Spell 327

CAUSING N TO RAISE HIMSELF UP IN THE WEST.[1] | The Nile surges in filling the IV, 163
meadows, the valleys are closed, Osiris is inert(?),[2] N washes himself in it. This bread of his cannot grow mouldy, this beer of his cannot go bad, N raises himself on his left side, being placed on his right side; | he smites with his staff, 164
he governs with his rod, N's arms bring (something) to him in the Great Bark.[3]

1. For this rubric see 159*d*.

2. *Ty* after *wrḏ* probably stands for the particle *tr*; the passive *sḏm·ty* seems ruled out, since this would imply a transitive use of *wrḏ* which has not been recorded. B4Bo[b] inserts an indecipherable clause after this.

3. Var. B4Bo[b] 'N's arms(?) bring [. . .] of the Great One, N is in the bow of the bark of the Great God'.

Spell 328

N appears in front of the *ṯnnt*-shrine, the bark is tied up[1] for N at the stairway, N goes up at the side of the Great East, N goes down at the side of the Great West, N strikes with the sceptre and governs with the staff, N shows the way to the bank of the zenith(?),[2] N brings truth to Rēʿ.

1. For this sense of *gwꜣ* cf. *CT* III, 97*e*.
2. On *iskn* see Sethe, *Komm. Pyr.* II, 338.

Spell 329

IV, 165 BECOMING A SCRIBE OF THE FIELD OF OFFERINGS FOR OSIRIS. My two store-
chests(?)[1] are among[2] the offerings. To me belong[3] the male and female
attendants of Osiris, I am the scribe of the store-chest(?)[4] of the Field of
Offerings beside Thoth among those who make offerings.

1. On *ḥꜣdt* cf. Spell 188, n.6 = *CT* III, 94*a*. B2Bo substitutes *ḥꜣty* (*ꜣḥty*) 'two fields', which suggests that *ḥꜣdty* was no longer understood.
2. *M-m*. B2Bo has three *m*'s.
3. To interpret *ink* as 'I am' yields no sense.
4. Var. B2Bo *ḥꜣwt* (for *ꜣḥwt*) 'fields'.

Spell 330

IV, 166 BECOMING NEPER.[1] I have entered into Ḥu,[2] offerings have gone forth and it
goes well with me,[3] for my sister is in my presence. It is good for the flies
and(?) your father's snakes,[4] my father . . .[5] good offerings[6] in the sky. O
167 Orion,[7] | my father and my mother have been brought to me. I have gone forth
from Ḥu, I have entered into Ḥu, I have gone forth from[8] the Great Smiter,
I have taken away their growth(?)[9] by day and in the evening because of the
noise of the land when it quakes.[10] You[11] shall make to quiver those who are
168 in the bonds[12] of Shu, | and Shu betakes himself to the inert ones(?).[13] I live
and I die,[14] I am Osiris, I have gone in and out by means of you, I have grown
169 fat through you, I flourish through you, I have fallen through you.[15] | I have
fallen on my side, the gods live on me. I live and grow as Neper[16] whom the

honoured ones cherish, one whom Gēb hides, I live and I die, for I am emmer,[17] and I will not perish. | I have entered into truth, I have upheld truth,[18] for I 170
am a possessor of truth. I have gone forth in truth and my shape is raised up, I am he who is pre-eminent in the *ṯnnt*-shrine. | I have entered into truth, I have attained its[19] limit. | I am Ptaḥ, my most joyful path is prepared, I have 171
gone in and out, I have cut off the winds upon earth—four times.

THIS IS TO BE DONE [. . .].[20]

1. The god of grain. This is a most obscure and difficult spell, but it appears that the deceased is identified with grain that lives and dies.
2. In this context certainly the personification of food.
3. So S1C^{a} and S2C; S1C^{b} inserts *m* after *pr·n*. B2Bo and B4Bo have  for .
4. Quite unintelligible.
5. Again entirely obscure.
6. On B2Bo and B4Bo see n.3 above.
7. De Buck apparently regarded *Sꜣḥ* in 166*g* as a vocative introducing 167*a*, but 166*e–g* are totally incomprehensible. In 167*a* B2Bo and B4Bo read at end: 'my mother has been released', *sfr* of B2Bo being clearly a miswriting of *sfḫ* in B4Bo.
8. The texts vary between *pr Ḥw-wr*, *pr m Ḥw-wr* and *pr·n·i m Ḥw-wr*. This last seems to me the most likely version.
9. *Rdw* with det  is not known.
10. 167*d* is entirely obscure.
11. Plural. To whom the pronoun *ṯn* refers is not obvious; also it could equally well be the dependent pronoun as object of *smnmn*.
12. For *ḳꜣsw* S1C^{b} has *ḳꜣw* 'heights'; B2Bo corruptly *ḳꜣswrt*.
13. B2Bo and B4Bo insert *m* before *nnwt*; in the other texts we should perhaps read ⟨*n*⟩ *nnwt*, since *nnwt* can hardly be a direct object of *sb*. In *Wb*. II, 275,13 *nnwt* is given the vague meaning of 'ein Zustand', but here it could be possibly a collective noun derived from *nny* 'be inert'.
14. S1C^{b} omits *ꜥnḫ*. The grain-god Neper is speaking, cf. 169*c*.
15. It is not clear to whom this repeated *im·k* refers. 168*d*–169*a* may refer to the cultivation and reaping of the grain.
16. S2C adds: 'I am Neper'.
17. Varr. *it* 'barley', *it mḥ* 'barley of Lower Egypt'.
18. B2Bo and B4Bo insert *m* before *mꜣꜥt*.
19. *·Sn* is clearly an error for *·s*.
20. A concluding rubric, only in S1C^{a} and S1C^{b}. It is largely lost.

Spell 331

BECOMING ḤATḤŌR. I am Ḥatḥōr who brings her Horus and who proclaims IV, 172
her Horus; and my heart is the lion-god, my lips are the . . .,[1] there is no limit to my vision, there are none who can encircle my arms, every god will take himself off before me. I have appeared as Ḥatḥōr, the Primeval, the Lady

173 of All,| who lives on truth; I am the uraeus who lives on truth, who lifts up the faces of all the gods, and all the gods are beneath my feet. I am She who displays his[2] beauty and assembles his powers, I am that Eye of Horus, the female messenger of the Sole Lord, the like of whom shall not be again.[3]

174 Truly I am She who made his name. I have flourished,[4] | I came into being[5] before the sky was fashioned, and it gives me praise; before the earth was released[6] and it exalts me, while I seek your[7] saliva and your spittle;[8] they are Shu and Tefēnet. I have searched and sought out,[9] and see, I have fetched

175 (what I sought); come with my horns and display my beauty; | come with my face, and I will cause you to be exalted. I have smitten all with my hands in this my name of Ḥatḥōr; I have given my tears.[10] I reduce (them) to order[11] in

176 this my name of She who is over reducing to order;[12] | I make warmth for them in this my name of Shesmētet.[13] Such am I; I am Edjō, I am indeed the Mistress of the Two Lands.

1. G1T + A1C 'my heart and my lips are the lion-god and the *sytyw*'; S2C, both texts, 'my heart is the lion-god(s), my lips are the *sytyw*'. The meaning of this last word is not known.
2. Presumably of Horus.
3. Lit. 'who shall not be repeated'. The reference is to the 'Sole Lord' = Osiris.
4. *Rdt* appears to be a 'complementary infinitive'.
5. Not in G1T + A1C.
6. For this mode of describing the creation of the world cf. *Urk.* IV, 162,6.
7. Horus's.
8. *Ỉš* and *tf* are virtually synonymous; for *iš* cf. P. Ed. Smith, 3, 3–4; for *tf* cf. *Pyr.* §§ 419; 678.
9. *Sẖn* and *ḥḥ* are also virtual synonyms.
10. S2C[a] adds *pt* after *rmwt·i*, by confusion of *ptn* 'these' of S2C[b].
11. For this sense of *syd* cf. *CT* 1, 320*b*.
12. Following S2C; G1T + A1C have more obscurely 'I reduce to order in my name of Her who is over her spittle'; for the sense of *isd* cf. *Pyr.* §§ 261; 850, 1628.
13. 176*b–d* are absent from G1T + A1C and are nearly all lost in S2C.

Spell 332

IV, 177 I am a *nˁt*-snake, a soul in the bark 'Ordainer of power.' I am mistress of the oar in the Bark of Governance. I am the mistress of life, the serpent-guide of the sunshine on fair paths. I am she who strengthens the lashings [on?] the steering-oars on the western ways. I am the third one, mistress of brightness, who guides the great ones who are languid on the paths of the wakeful. I am the mistress of splendour on the paths of the cloudy sky. I am mistress of the winds in the Island of Joy. I am the mistress of strength who guides those who are in their caverns. I am Ḥatḥōr, mistress of the northern sky, who strengthened

the bonds of the wakeful[1] | on that night when the earth quaked(?)[2] and . . .[3] 178
was among the mourners. I am Isis whom Nūt bore, who displays her beauty, who puts together her power and who lifts up[4] Rēʿ to the Day-bark.

1. *Shsw* of A1C is surely an error for *nhsw*.
2. For *nhm* with this det. cf. *nhm* 'dance(?)', *Les.* 79,10.
3. G1T *skswt*, A1C *sytswt*, meaning unknown.
4. For *sšw* 'lift up' cf. *Pyr.* §§ 275; 1101.

Spell 333

I am the soul of Shu who came into being as Rēʿ, and I became Rēʿ—and *vice versa*—the sky was made for me in order that I might be high, I removed my seat from those who came into being before me, and I became very great.[1] I came into being, having become the Lord of All at the head of the Entourage.[2] I live on the smoked grain(?)[3] which is among(?) the living, my soul will not be restrained nor my corpse held back[4] from drinking the water of the flood, for I am indeed a son who wishes, acts and lives, and I live.

1. Adjectival predicate with dative, cf. also 180*c*.
2. The significance of [hieroglyph] | after *šnwt* escapes me.
3. For *npr ḥtyt* see also *CT* II, 95*e*; III, 176*a*; *BD* 165,5.
4. Emend into *ẖ3t·i n šnʿ·t(w)·f*.

Spell 334

BECOMING THE SISTRUM-PLAYER. O you [. . .], the Entourage which is about IV, 179
Rēʿ, see, I go down [. . .]. I am that first seed[1] of Rēʿ; he begot me in the womb of my mother Isis [. . .] powerful in the sky, mighty ⟨on⟩ earth.[2] Such is my condition before my father Rēʿ and my mother [. . .].[3] I will be in this land in company with the living, I desire my [name(?)] to be on their lips as the Sistrum-player, son of Ḥatḥōr. They have worshipped me, and I am brotherly [. . .] the love of me every day. I am the Lord of bread, one in charge of beer, and I hear ⟨. . .⟩.[4] Come, [. . .] male and female providers of the food [. . .] whose hands are what they give to me.[5] They call to me and they open their doors and draw back their door-bolts(?)[6] [. . . they extol] daily this my good
name of Sistrum-player, a child in the speech of those who govern [. . .]. | 180
I am the first(-born) son of Rēʿ, I am a child beloved of my mother.[7] [I am(?)] the son of Nephthys, I have become great, I have become splendid;[8] my side-lock will not perish in the bodies of [my] father or [my] mother [. . .]. I live, I exist in very deed, I protect the patricians from the gods—and *vice versa*.

I am the protector[9] [. . .], I am extolled in this my name of Sistrum-player,
acclamation is given to me in this my name of Khons.[10] I will not perish in the
sky with Rēʿ and with my mother Ḥatḥōr; [I will nor be destroyed(?)][11] on
earth with Rēʿ and with my mother Ḥatḥōr. My name is on earth with the
living; I am the Sistrum-player, the son of [Ḥatḥōr], the sky and what is in it
tremble, bowing down, the Two Lands quake [. . .] at the flash; those who
are in their baskets are watchful, sitting on their coils,[12] who live [. . .] and
who guard the ways of the Eye of Rēʿ-Atum and of the Entourage which is
about Rēʿ.[13] I am watchful for the dangerous ones,[14] the stiff-necked [. . .]
who guard the 'Sandal-of-Rēʿ' bark. Down on your faces! Fear and tremble
at me!

181 |See, I have come as Lord of the Entourage, and those who follow after
the Enneads fear me, the awe of me is before me as the Sistrum-player, the
son of Ḥatḥōr. I am indeed the Great Seed,[15] I have passed between her thighs
[in] this [my name] of Jackal of the Sunshine. I have broken out of the egg,
I have floated(?) on its white(?), I have glided on its yolk(?),[16] I am the Lord
of blood, I am a tempestuous(?)[17] bull, my mother Isis conceived me, and she
swooned under the fingers of the Lord of the gods when he broke into her
therewith on that day of lifting(?)[18] the mat(?)[19] in [. . .] for(?) the Lord of
the gods on that day of tumult before necks were knit on, before the heads
of the gods were cut off, before the sun was firm on the horns, before the face
of *Bꜣt* was knit on.[20] I came into being,[21] I crept, I travelled around, I grew,
I became high like my father [. . . high . . .] he was high. My White Crown
182 of fresh flesh[22] was upon me, my *atef*-crowns were on my brow, | my terrible
one[23] was on my forehead, so that it might put the dread of me into the gods
and the awe of me into the Entourage of Rēʿ, for I am the Lord of dread,
greatly majestic, and it is the god of plenty who raises me up [. . .]. I sucked
from my mother Isis, I tasted her sweetness, and they (*sic*) beweep me,[24] for
they see me not; they mourn me, for they do not hear my voice. I am the child
of my mother,[25] I am a youth, the son of Ḥatḥōr, I am the Inert One who was
in the Abyss [. . .] my name and my place are known. I was seeking the place
where I should be in this my name of Chaos-god, I found myself in Punt, I
built a house there in my birth-place, while my mother was under her sycamore.
I lingered(?)[26] [. . .] children of the great god. I rotted[27] there, I grew brotherly
183 there | in this my name of one brotherly to men and gods. My putrefaction is
myrrh, which my mother Ḥatḥōr places[28] for herself on her head; my smell is
that of incense, [which my mother] Ḥatḥōr [gives to herself] for her censing,
my efflux is *ḥknw*-oil which my mother Ḥatḥōr puts for herself on her flesh;

my head is her bundle which my mother ⟨Ḥatḥōr⟩[29] puts for herself on her arm; my entrails are [her] necklace[30] [which] my mother Ḥatḥōr [puts for herself] on her throat; my hands are her sistrum which my mother Ḥatḥōr gives to herself in order to give pleasure[31] to herself therewith; my thighs are her *ẖn-kt*-garment[32] which my mother Ḥatḥōr gives to herself [in order to clothe(?)] herself therewith; my belly [is her . . .] which my mother Ḥatḥōr [gives to herself] so that she may be knit together[33] by it.

1. Note that *mtwt* 'seed' is construed as a plural like other fluids.
2. Read *sẖm* ⟨*m*⟩ *tꜣ*.
3. Either 'Isis' or 'Ḥatḥōr' could be restored in the lacuna.
4. For this writing of *sḏm* 'hear' see 182*h*. The object of the verb has been omitted.
5. Abnormal word-order, cf. Gardiner, *Eg. Gramm.*[3] § 507.
6. Reading *ḳꜣ* [*rwt·sn* . . .].
7. Written *mwt·f* in accord with regular Egyptian custom.
8. Adjectival predicates with following dative, cf. Gardiner, op. cit. § 141.
9. Read *nḏty*. masculine, despite the woman-det.; a common miswriting.
10. Cf. Posener in *ZÄS* 93, 118, n.38.
11. Restore possibly *n ḥtm·i* or the like in the lacuna.
12. The *tpw nbwt·sn* are serpents coiled and watchful, envisaged in the form .
13. Cf. 179*b*.  is superfluous.
14. Cf. *Wb*. II, 290,15.
15. For *ꜥꜣꜥ* 'semen', 'seed' cf. *Wb*. I, 166,18; apparently used here of the result of the injection of semen, the new-born child, cf. the next clause, which refers to birth. For the writing without the final , cf. *CT* IV, 4*e* (Sq6C). In 181*j ꜥꜣꜥ* is a transitive verb meaning 'conceive'.
16. The verb 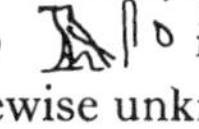 is not recorded, but it could be a specialized use and variant of *ꜣs* 'flow'. *Sfs* is likewise unknown. All of 181*h* is most obscure, but the second clause reads 'I have glided on its blood', where the fem. suffix to *snf* can refer only to *swḥt* 'egg' in 181*g*. If 'its blood' in this context could be the yolk of the egg, then *sfs* (perhaps to be read *sf·s*) might conceivably refer to the white of the egg (cf. *sf*, an unidentified substance, *Wb*. IV, 114,1), making this section an allusion to the embryo in the egg. All this is highly speculative, but the tentative translation that results does fit what has gone before.
17. *Kꜣ ẖnnw*.
18. has been taken to be an unusual writing of .
19. , read here as *tmꜣ* 'mat'; the basic reading *mḏ* 'cattle-hobble' makes even less sense.
20. *Pyr*. § 1096 refers to '*Bꜣt* with her two faces'.
21. In 181*p* and *q* every verb is stressed with a 'complementary infinitive'.
22. The fem. genitival adjective after *tp·i* can refer only to *ḥḏt*.
23. The uraeus.
24. A superfluous *n* in *rmm·sn n wi*, as often with the suffix *·sn* before *wi*.
25. See n.7 above.
26. Reading *sꜣꜣ·i*, see de Buck's note 2*.

27. *Sic*, cf. 183*b*.

28. Note that this text uses the masc. form *ddw* whatever the gender of the antecedent. For a similar fixity of gender in a series see *Pyr.* § 151, where Sothis is referred to with a masc. old perfective, see my *Translation*, Utt. 216, n.4.

29. Omitted in the original text.

30. *T̲ꜣw mnyt* is shown by the context to mean a necklace. The expression is composed of *t̲ꜣw* 'pellets', i.e. beads, since they are worn by the goddess, and of *mnyt*, here written like the word for 'mooring-post', but undoubtedly meaning the '*menat*' sacred to Ḥatḥōr, which would be attached to the string of beads round her neck.

31. *Snn* with det.  is not recorded, but the fact that it gives the reason for Ḥatḥōr taking the sistrum suggests that it means 'give pleasure to' or the like, the tinkling of the sistrum, her sacred instrument, being pleasing to her. The verb appears to be a causative of *nny* 'be inert' with the general sense of pleasant relaxation.

32. *H̱n-kt* is doubtless the original form of the Late Egyptian *ẖn-ky* 'a garment', *Wb.* III, 385,1, quoting P. Harris I, 63*a*, 9. The det.  suggests a connection with *ẖnt* 'hide', 'skin'.

33. Reading *t̲s·tw*, written like *t̲st* 'knot'.

Spell 335

(*a*) *Basic text of Spell without glosses.*[1]

Part I

IV, 184 Going out into the day. There comes into being a speech by me, Atum. I
190 was Rēʿ at his first appearings, I am the Great One, the self-created, | who created my names, Lord of the Ennead, who will not be repelled from the gods. Yesterday is mine, I know tomorrow. The warship of the gods was built in accordance with my command, and I know the name of that great
200 god who is in it. | I am that great phoenix which is in Ōn, the supervisor of what exists. I am Min in his goings out, I have set the two plumes on my head.

While I was on earth[2] I came from my city. I have got rid of my wrongdoing,
210 I have dispelled my evil, | I have removed the falseness which was on me, I have bathed in those two very great lagoons which are in Ninsu, in which the oblations of the plebs are cleansed for the great god who is in it. I proceed on
222 the path which I know in the direction of the Island of the Just, |I arrive at the Land of the Horizon-dwellers in the sky, I go out from the sacred portal. O you who are in the Presence, give me your hands, for I am a soul who has
232 come into being among you. | I restored the Eye after it had been injured on that day when the Rivals fought. I raised up the hair from the Sacred Eye at the time of its wrath. | I saw Rēʿ being born yesterday from the buttocks of
250 the Celestial Cow, and if he is hale, then will I be hale—and *vice versa*— | because I am one of those who follow after Horus.

Hail to you, you Lords of Truth, the tribunal which is behind Osiris, which puts terror into those who are false when those whom it protects are at rest. See, I have come to you so that you may get rid of the evil which is on me, just as you did for those seven spirits who are in the suite of the Lord of the Nomes when Anubis prepared their seats| on that day of '"Come thence!"' (The 260
names of the seven spirits are) *Dḥdḥ*, *ꜣḳdḳd*, 'Bull who was not put to his burning,' 'Black-faced who is in his hour',| 'Bloody one who is pre-eminent 270
in the Mansion of Red Linen', 'Radiant-faced who comes out after having turned back', 'He who sees in the night what he shall bring by day'.

I am his twin souls which are within his two Fledglings. 276

I am that great Cat who split the *išd*-tree on its side in Ōn on that night of 282
making war and of warding off the rebels and on that day in which were destroyed the foes of the Lord of All.

Part II

O Rēꜥ who are in your egg,[3] rising in your disk and shining in your horizon, 292
swimming in your firmament, having no equal among the gods, sailing over the Supports of Shu, giving the winds with the breath of your mouth, illumining the Two Lands with your sunshine, save me from that god whose shape is hidden and whose eyebrows are the arms of the balance on that day of reckoning with the robbers in the presence of the Lord of All, who puts bonds on the evildoers at his slaughter-house, who kills souls; save me from those who deal wounds, the slayers whose fingers are painful. Their knives shall not have power over me, I will not go down into their cauldrons, I will not enter into their shambles, because I know their names, because I am one who proceeds on earth with Rēꜥ and who moors happily with Osiris; their offerings shall not come into being through me for those who are in charge of their braziers and who are in their kitchens, for I am in the train of the Lord of the Ennead and (I am) the scribe of those who exist. I fly up as a falcon, I cackle as a goose. I pass eternity like Neḥeb-kau.

O Atum who are in the Great Mansion, Sovereign of the Ennead, save me from that god who lives by slaughter, whose face is that of a hound and whose skin is that of a man. It is he who is in charge of the interior of the Lake of Fire, who swallows shades, who snatches hearts, who inflicts wounds, who is invisible.

O Lord of Terror who is at the head of the Two Lands; O Lord of Blood 316
who prospers the slaughter-houses, to whom was given the *wrrt*-crown and

joy in Ninsu; O Osiris to whom was entrusted the rulership over the gods on that day when the Two Lands were united in the presence of the Lord of All; potent soul who is in Ninsu, who grants powers and expels evildoers,
320 who shows the paths of eternity, save me from that god who takes souls, | who laps up corruption, who lives on putrefaction, who belongs to darkness, who is in the dusk, of whom those who are among the languid ones are afraid.

O Khopri dwelling in your bark, primeval of body for ever, save me from those who are in charge of examination, to whom the Lord of All gave power to arrest his foes, who put slaughtering into the shambles, who do not relax their watch and ward. I will not fall to their knives, I will not enter into their shambles, I will not sit in their vats, I will not go down into their fish-traps, for nothing is done to me of this which the god detests, because I am one who
325 passes pure through the *mskt*, | to whom is brought an evening meal in the *ṯnnt*-shrine.[4]

1. Spell 335 falls into two distinct sections, clearly originally separate spells. The text of the spell is so heavily glossed that a running translation of the basic text, following T1C^{a}–B1P, here precedes the 'glossed' translation. The notes follow the latter. Part I has been the subject of a monograph by Heerma van Voss, *De oudste versie van Dodenboek 17a*, Leyden, 1963 and of a computerized analysis in two volumes by Gundlach and Schenkel, *Lexikalisch-grammatische Liste zu Spruch 335a der altägyptischen Sargtexte LL/CT. 335a*, Darmstadt, 1970.

2. It is the deceased speaking now.

3. What follows is van Voss's 335*b*.

4. Var. 'an evening meal of fayence in the *ṯnnt*-shrine', but the mention of *ṯḥnt* 'fayence' clearly is dragged in to provide a play on the word *ṯnnt*.

Spell 335

(b) Full version with glosses in italics.

Part I

IV, 184 GOING OUT INTO THE DAY FROM THE REALM OF THE DEAD.[1] There comes into being a speech by me, Atum.[2] I was (once) alone; I was Rēʿ at his first appearings, when he arose from the horizon,[3] I am the Great One,[4] the self-created. *Who is the Great One, the self-created? He is the water of the Abyss.*[5]

190 Who created his names, Lord of the Ennead, who will not be repelled from the gods. *Who is he? He is Atum who is in his sun.*[6]

Yesterday is mine, I know tomorrow. *As for yesterday, it is Osiris; as for tomorrow, it is Rēʿ.*[7]

194 The warship[8] of the gods was built in accordance with my command.[9]

What is the warship of the gods? It is the nšmt-bark.[10]

I know the name of that great god who is in it. '*Praise of Rēʿ is his name.*[11]

I am that great Phoenix which is in Ōn.[12] *Who is he? He is Osiris.*[13]

The supervisor of what exists. *Who is he? He is Osiris. As for what exists,*[14] 200
it is eternity and everlasting. As for eternity, it is day; as for everlasting, it is night.

I am Min in his goings out, I have set the two plumes on my head.[15] *Who is he? What are his two plumes? He is Horus, Protector of his father. They are*
his two great plumes[16] | *which were on the head of his father Atum.*[17] 206

When I was on earth, I came from my city.[18] *What is it? It is the horizon of my father Atum.*[19]

I have got rid of my wrongdoing, I have dispelled my evil,[20] | I have removed 210
the falseness which was on me,[21] I have bathed in those two very great lagoons
which are in Ninsu,[22] in which the oblations of the plebs are cleansed | for[23] 214
this great god who is in it.[24] *Who is he? He is Rēʿ himself.*[25] *What are the two very great lagoons? They are the Lake of Natron and the Lake of Mʿꜣt.*[26]

I proceed on the path which I know in the direction of the Island of the
Just. *What is it?*[27] | *It is the path on which my father Atum went when he proceeded* 220
to the Field of Rushes.[28]

I arrive at the Land of the Horizon-dwellers in the sky,[29] I go out from the
sacred portal. *What is the Land of the Horizon-dwellers?* | *What is this portal?*[30] 224
They are the gods who are about the shrine. As for the sacred portal, it is the double doors[31] *from which Atum proceeded to the eastern horizon of the sky.*

O you who are in the Presence,[32] give me your hands, for I am indeed one
who has come into being among you.[33] *Who are those*[34] *who are in the Presence?*
| *They are Ḥu and Sia who are with my father Atum the whole of every day.* 230

I restored the Eye after it had been injured on that day when the Rivals
fought.[35] | *What is the fighting of the Rivals?*[36] *It means the day in which Horus* 234
fought with Seth[37] *when Seth inflicted a wound on the face of Horus and when Horus carried off the testicles*[38] *of Seth. It was Thoth who did this with his fingers.*

I raised the hair from the Sacred Eye[39] at its time of wrath. *What is the*
Sacred Eye | *at its time of wrath?*[40] *Who raised the hair from it? It is the right* 240
Eye of Rēʿ[41] *when it was wroth with him after he had sent it on an errand.*[42] *It was Thoth who raised the hair from it.*

I saw Rēʿ being born yesterday from the buttocks of the Celestial Cow, and 244
if he is hale, then I will be hale[43]—and *vice versa. What does it mean, the day of being born yesterday*[44] *from the buttocks of the Celestial Cow?*[45] *It means the image of the Eye of Rēʿ in the morning, when he is born every day. As for the*

250 *Celestial Cow,* | *she is the Sacred Eye.*[46]
Because I am one of those who follow after Horus. *What does it mean, one of those who follow after Horus?*[47] *One who speaks on behalf of the beloved of his lord.*[48]
254 Hail to you, | Lords of Truth, the tribunal which is behind Osiris, which
puts terror into those who are false when those whom it protects are at rest.[49]
See, I have come to you so that you may get rid of the evil which is on me, just
as you did for those seven spirits who follow after the Lord of the Nomes,[50]
260 when Anubis prepared their seats | on that day of 'Come thence!' *As for*
'those whom it protected are at rest', it means the fiery serpent.[51] *It follows after*
Osiris[52] *to burn up the power of his foes.*
264 I know the names of the seven spirits | who are in the following of the Lord
of the Nomes, whose seats Anubis made on that day of 'Come thence!' *As for*
the chief of this company,[53] *his name is 'The Great One is not driven away'.*[54]
(The names of the seven spirits are)[55] *Dḥdḥ,*[56] *ꜣḳdḳd*[57], 'Bull who was not
270 put to his burning',[58] 'Black-faced who is in his hour',[59] | 'Bloody one who is
pre-eminent in the Mansion of Red Linen',[60] 'Radiant-faced who comes out
after having turned back', 'He who sees in the night what he shall bring[61] by
day'.
276 I am his twin souls which are within his two Fledglings. *What does it mean?*
As for his twin souls[62] *within his two Fledglings, they are Osiris*[63] *when he entered*
280 *into Djedu and found the soul of Rēʿ there,*[64] *and one embraced the other.* | *Then*
⟨they⟩ became his twin souls. As for his two Fledglings,[65] *they are Horus Protector*
of his father and Horus the Eyeless.[66]
I am that great Cat who split the *išd*-tree on its side in Ōn[67] on that night
284 of making war and | of warding off the rebels, and on that day on which were
destroyed the foes of the Lord of All. *What is that great Cat? He is Rēʿ himself;*
he was called 'Cat' when Sia spoke about him. He was cat-like[68] *in what he did,*
and that is how his name of 'Cat' came into being.[69] *As for the splitting*[70] *of the*
išd-tree on its side in Ōn, it was when the Children of Impotence carried out what
290 *they did. As for the day of making war,* | *it means that they entered into the East*
and war broke out in the whole of the earth and in the sky.

Part II

292 O Rēʿ who are in your egg, rising in your disk, shining in your horizon, swimming in your firmament,[71] having no equal among the gods, sailing over the Supports of Shu, giving the winds with the breath of your mouth, illumining

the Two Lands with your sunshine, save me from that god whose shape is hidden and whose eyebrows are the arms of the balance | on that day of reckoning with the robbers[72] in the presence of the Lord of All,[73] who puts bonds on the evildoers at his slaughter-house, who kills souls. *Who is this god whose eyebrows are the arms of the balance? He is Horus who presides over Khem. Otherwise said: He is Thoth,*[74] *it is he who uses his arm.*

Save me from those who inflict wounds, whose fingers are painful.[75] *As for the slayers who belong to Osiris,*[76] *they are this company which takes action against*[77] *the foes of Osiris.*[78]

Their knives[79] shall not have power over me,[80] I will not go down into their cauldrons, I will not enter into their[81] shambles, because I know their names,[82] because I am one who proceeds on earth with Rēʿ and moors happily with Osiris. Their[83] offerings shall not come into being through me for those who are in charge of their braziers and who are in their kitchens,[84] | for I am in the train of the Lord of the Ennead[85] and (I am) the scribe of those who exist. I fly up as a falcon, I cackle as a goose, I pass eternity like Neḥebkau.

O Atum who are in the Great Mansion, Sovereign of the Ennead, save me from that god who lives by slaughter, whose face is that of a hound and whose skin is that of a man. It is he who is warden of the windings of the Lake of Fire, who swallows shades, who snatches hearts, who inflicts wounds, but is not seen.[86] | *As for this god whose face is that of a hound and whose skin is that of a man, his name is 'Swallower of myriads'.*[87]

O Lord of Terror at the head of the Two Lands; O Lord of Blood who prospers the slaughter-houses, to whom is given the *wrrt*-crown and joy in Ninsu; O Osiris to whom was entrusted the rulership of the gods on that day when the Two Lands were united in the presence of the Lord of All. *As for the Union of the Two Lands, it means that the shroud of Osiris was ordered by his father Rēʿ.*[88]

O potent soul who is in Ninsu, who grants powers and expels the evildoers, who shows the ways of eternity—*He is Rēʿ himself*[89]— save me from the god who takes souls,[90] | who laps up corruption, who lives on putrefaction, who belongs to darkness, who is in the dusk, of whom those who are among the languid ones are afraid. *As for that god who takes souls, who laps up corruption and lives on putrefaction, he is Seth.*[91]

O Khopri, dwelling in your bark, primeval of body for ever, save me from those who are in charge of examination, to whom the Lord of All gave power to arrest his foes, who put slaughtering into the shambles, who do not relax their watch and ward. I will not fall to their[92] knives, I will not sit within their

vats, I will not enter into their shambles, I will not go down into their fish-traps,[93] for nothing will be done to me of this which the gods detest, because
325 I am one who passes pure through the *msḳt*,[l] to whom is brought an evening meal of fayence in the *ṯnnt*-shrine.[94] *As for the msḳt, it is the ḳnḳnt in Ninsu; as for fayence, it is the Eye which conquered the monster;*[95] *as for the ṯnnt-shrine, it is the tomb of Osiris.*

A MAN SHOULD UTTER THIS SPELL WHEN HE ENTERS INTO THE WEST AFTER HE GOES OUT. AS FOR ANYONE WHO DOES NOT KNOW THIS SPELL, HE SHALL NOT GO IN OR OUT, BEING IGNORANT.[96]

1. Several varr. of minor importance. Some texts omit this title; M1NY inserts a *ḥtp-dy-nsw* formula before it.

2. Two texts add 'I am Rēꜥ', anticipating 186*b*. B3C begins the spell with a clause which is indecipherable.

3. In two texts only. BH1Br alone adds the gloss: 'It means that he arose in the east of the sky. Otherwise said: it means that Rēꜥ began appearing on earth'.

4. Varr. 'the great god' in half-a-dozen texts; 'the god' in M1NY; 'Rēꜥ' in T3L.

5. So B9C[a]; BH1Br; 'He is the water of the Abyss, he is the god, the father of the god'; H: 'He is the great god, he is the god of the Abyss (Nu)'.

6. So BH1Br; M57C has briefly: 'he is Rēꜥ'.

7. So BH1Br; M54C and M1C have 'Atum'; fourteen texts have briefly: 'He is Osiris'. BH1Br adds before this: 'What is it? It is that day of "We remain". It is the burial of Osiris and causing his son Horus to rule. Otherwise said: "As for yesterday . . ." ' etc. H reads: 'As for yesterday, it is Osiris; as for tomorrow, it is the Sunshine-god'.

8. Var. 'battle-ground'; BH1Br writes the word as *iḥnt*.

9. Read *wḏ·i* with T1C[a], B1Y and T2Be; most texts have *ḏd·i*, with the incorrect varr. *ḏd·k* Sq4Sq and *ḏd N* B3C.

10. So B1Y and B9C[a]. The former is damaged and has an unusual writing of *ptr*. M8C ff. have: 'As for the battle-ground of the gods, it is the West'; to this two texts add: 'It was built to make the foes of the gods fight' while BH1Br reads 'What is the *iḥnt* of the gods? It is the West. It was built for the power of the gods, according to the word of Osiris'.

11. Corrupted in T1C[b] into *ḥknw pw Rꜥ pw Rꜥ*. Varr. M4C ' "Praise in life" is his name'; BH1Br: 'Who is he? He is "Praise of the soul of Rēꜥ" '.

12. Var. H: 'I am that phoenix which came into being of itself, which is in Ōn'.

13. BH1Br only; T1C[b] briefly: 'He is Osiris'.

14. Var. 'As for the supervision of what exists'.

15. M1NY adds: 'When I was in this land'.

16. So T1C[b]; the other texts have: 'his great uraeus' or 'uraei'.

17. Varr. 'on the brow (*ḥꜣt*) of his father Atum'; 'which was on the plume of his father Atum'; 'which was in the house of his father Atum'; 'of his father Atum'.

18. Var. T3Be: 'I came from my city, I went up from my land, I went down to my nome, and I will be with my father Atum the whole of every day'. The deceased, not Atum, is speaking now.

19. Var. 'his father'; usual confusion of personal pronouns.

20. BH1Br interpolates: 'What does it mean? It means that his navel-string has been cut. Going out into the day'.

21. BH1Br interpolates: 'What does it mean? It means that he was cleansed after his birth'.

22. BH1Br interpolates: 'What are these two very great lagoons which are in Ninsu? They are the Lake of Natron and the Lake of *Mʿȝt*'. T1C^{b} omits the question but has 'The Lake of Natron and the Lakes of *Mʿȝt*'.

23. T1C^{a} has  for  .

24. The suffix presumably refers to the town-name.

25. Var. BH1Br: 'Who is this great god who is in it? He is Rēʿ himself'.

26. M57C inserts between 217*a* and *b* ' "Swallower of the Chaos-gods" is the name of one (lit. 'its name'), "Sea" is the name of the other'. Sq1Sq (216*c*; 219*c*–*g*) has: 'It is the Lake of Natron, its name is "Sea", it is the eastern area(?) in Ōn; it is the Lake of *Mʿȝt*, its name is "Seed of the Seeker(?)", it is the western area(?) in Naref'. B9C^{a} has 'it is the Lake of Natron and the Lake of the Great House'.

27. Varr. B9C^{a}: 'What are the paths?'; M4C: 'As for this path; M1NY: 'Why do I go on the paths which I know?'

28. M1C, which is mostly lost, had a somewhat variant text.

29. Var. 'I arrive at the horizon of the sky'.

30. BH1Br adds: 'It is the gate of the Netherworld', and continues in 227*a* as the other texts.

31. *ʿȝwy ry*; the latter word has a peculiar sign  *et varr.* and could perhaps be derived from *r* 'part', 'fraction' in allusion to the halves of a double door, or alternatively from the dual of *r* 'door', the whole expression meaning perhaps 'door in two parts'. In T1C^{b} the special sign has been read as  and *ʿȝwy ry* corrupted into *ḳrsy*.

32. BH1Br has *imyw sšmw*, apparently 'O you who are among the governors'.

33. Varr. 'I am a soul who has come into being among you (T1C^{a} only); 'I am the One who has come into being among you' (so four texts).

34. Var. 'those gods'.

35. BH1Br has *iḥn* for *ʿḥȝ*.

36. B9C^{a} and T3Be omit *ʿḥȝ* and read 'Who are the Rivals?'; BH1Br: 'What does it mean, that day when the Rivals fought?'; T1C^{b} omits the question, and follows with: 'It means that Horus fought with Seth', see n.37.

37. Varr. T1C^{b} and M1C: 'It means that Horus fought with Seth'; Sq7Sq omits all this except the last two words 'with Seth'.

38. Note in M4C the rare word *insw(y)* 'testicles'. It occurs again in the form *isnwy* in *CT* I, 30*b* (B4C), and *Wb.* II, 205,8 quotes a variant *nyswy*.

39. Sq1C writes *wdȝt* 'Sacred Eye' with 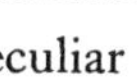, while two texts have . The det. presumably represents the pupil of the Eye.

40. BH1Br has: 'What does it mean, the raising of the hair from the Sacred Eye in its time of wrath?'

41. Varr. T3Be: 'it is the Eye which was punished by Rēʿ'; T1C^{b}: 'it is the Eye of Rēʿ'; BH1Br inserts *ir wḏȝt* before this clause.

42. *M wpwt* 'on an errand' in two texts only.

43. BH1Br has an elaborated version.

44. M7C interpolates meaninglessly: 'the day for his daily birth. As for the Celestial Cow, she is the Sacred Eye'.

45. Var. B1P: 'it means that the image of the Eye of Rēʿ was born in the morning when he was born every day'. M4C adds: 'from the buttocks of the Celestial Cow'.

46. M7C here inserts a repetition of 246*b*.

47. B1P and B5C omit 'one of'.

48. M7C adds 'the name of one of them' with *s* for *sn*. M4C adds: 'It means a man who goes around the sky with *ns* of his mouth, who reports on the Nile, but is not seen'.

49. M4C corruptly *sẖr·s* for *sẖw·s*. Some texts append the town-det. ⊗, perhaps through confusion with the town-name Ḳus.

50. BH1Br omits *nb* before *spꜣwt*. Several texts have this last word in the singular. M57C has 'Lord of the Centipede (*spꜣ*)'.

51. Varr. 'As for the gate (those gates) of "Those whom it protects are at rest", it means the fiery serpent'; 'As for that day of "Come thence!", (corruptly written *mr·k im*) for *m r·k im*), it means pacifying the fiery serpent *n št'* (M4C). BH1Br adds: 'it means the uraeus of Atum'.

52. Varr. 'it was placed behind Osiris': 'Rēʿ gave it to Osiris'.

53. Three texts have *inḏ ḥr* 'hail to'.

54. Several texts omit the negation. M4C and L3Li have *wr pr* 'great one of the house'. 266*a–b* is repeated below, 266*d–e*, in some cases inexplicably after *ky sp ḏd* 'Otherwise said'.

55. The words in brackets are not represented in the original.

56. Varr. *Ḏḥḏḥ, Ndḥdḥ, Nḏḥḏḥ.*

57. Varr. *Nydyd, Nḳdḳd, Ḳdḳd.*

58. Varr. 'Bull whose flame was in front of his burning', 'Bull whose horn was in front of his burning', and various corruptions.

59. So T1C^{a} alone. All other texts have 'He who entered in to him who is in his hour'.

60. *Dšrty. Ḏsr* of B9C^{a} is an obvious corruption.

61. B9C^{a} var. *iṯ·f* 'he takes'.

62. In 276*a–c*, M8C has 'twin sons' for 'twin souls'. 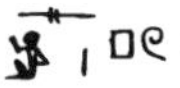 of M4C in 276*b* is a corruption of ; so also 301*b*.

63. Var. M57C 'the great soul of Osiris'.

64. M4C adds *ʿḥʿ m ḫsf* 'standing opposite'.

65. Varr. L1NY: 'his two sons' BH1Br. apparently 'his two souls'.

66. BH1Br adds *ḏd·n·f st r·s* 'He said it about it'.

67. T2Be inserts 'who saw in the night what he brought by day'.

68. *Myw sw*, adjectival predicate with dependent pronoun. In several cases the sentence is introduced by *in*, the full form of *n* 'because'. BH1Br has corruptly *mywy nn ir·n·f*, omitting *sw m*.

69. BH1Br omits *pw* and characteristically has  for .

70. *Pšn, pšsn, pšs, psš.*

71. B9C^{a} adds *psḏ nfr* 'shining well'.

72. Var. 'reckoning with the Great Ones (*ʿꜣw*).'

73. *M-bꜣḥ Nb-r-ḏr* in three texts only.

74. M57C adds: 'Nefertem, son of Sakhmet the Great'.

75. Var. 'Save me from these *ṯnmw* whose fingers are sharp'; M1NY adds at the end 'belonging to Osiris'. The meaning of *ṯnmw*, var. *ṯnmy*, is 'those who boil in vats'—note the det.  in M1NY. A word *ṯnmw* 'vat' for brewing is implied in Blackman's note *JEA* 13, 189–90, and it actually occurs 323*a. c.*; 330*n*.

76. So B9C^a; M4C. The varr. are not significant.

77. For *ḫsf ḫt n* 'take action against' cf. *Urk.* I, 101,9.

78. So four texts. T1C^b has 'of Rēʿ'. L1NY has 'which destroys (*ḥtm*) the foes of Osiris'.

79. *Sn* 'their' of five versions is the better reading, though seven texts out of twelve have *ṯn* 'your'.

80. Var. 'I will not fall to your knives'.

81. Lit. 'your'.

82. In five texts. Three others begin with a gloss which appears to be an addition: 'As for those who deal wounds, it means [. . .] who is among them, belonging to the House of Osiris, who pierces with his eye, who is not seen, who travels about the sky with the flame of his mouth, who makes report on the Nile to the god. He is greatest of the physicians of the *šnw*'. This gloss is present only in three texts out of twelve.

83. Var. 'your'.

84. Lit. 'cauldron-houses'. In B1Y only.

85. B9C^b alone has *nb psḏt*, which appears to be the better reading; all other texts have *nb ḫt* or the like, which would be an easy corruption of *nb psḏt*.

86. For this passage see also 327*k–q* (Spell 336).

87. T1Be and T2Be have 'the sharp-knived one who is gate-keeper of the West'. M1NY has a rubric which has been misplaced; as de Buck points out, it should have preceded 293*b*. It reads: 'As for the day of the Union of the Two Lands, it is the day when Shu buried Osiris'.

88. T1C^b only.

89. So T1C^b and M1NY.

90. Varr. B3C and B1Y: 'the great ones'; M1NY 'the plebs'.

91. This gloss in T1Be only. At the end T2Be has briefly 'He is Seth'; T1C^b 'this Majesty of Seth'.

92. Emend *ṯn* into *sn* as in 323*b.d*, cf. n.79 above. Var. B1Y and T2Be: 'their knives shall not enter into me'.

93. The 'vat' and 'fish-trap' clause seems to have undergone some changes of order and some combining. The translation follows T1C^b.

94. See p. 262, n.4.

95. For *hyw* 'monster' see Faulkner, *Pyr. Transl.* Utt. 226, n.2.

96. So T2Be. T1Be has a much damaged text which refers to 'mooring happily with [Osiris]' (cf. 325*c*, B1Y) and to 'going out into the day, playing at draughts and sitting in a booth after death'. Compare the opening paragraph of BD Spell 17 in Ani, with the accompanying illustrations. The text of M1NY is an elaborated *ḥtp-dy-nsw* formula.

Spell 336

The first portal. What is said about it. The fire is blue(?).[1] It is its flame IV, 327
which drives away on its account(?). Fifty cubits along its side are fire, the

tip of its flame[2] crosses the land from the sky, and the gods have said of it: 'It means blackness(?)'.[3] It has gone forth from the hands[4] of Sakhmet, it has stood upright(?)[5] among those who give.[6] It created itself; afterwards it made the gods into easy prey. It stretches its foot outwards;[7] its name is 'Its horn governs him who is in the hidden place'. A path is opened and prepared for me, and see, I have come. O Atum who are in the Great Mansion, excelling the gods, save me from that god who lives by slaughter, whose face is that of a hound, whose skin is that of a man, who is in charge of the windings of the Lake of Fire, who swallows shades, who snatches hearts, who casts the lasso, but who is not seen.[8]

The second portal. What he (*sic*) said about it. O Long-horned possessor
328 of *ꜣtf*-crowns, ⟨whose⟩[9] ornaments are uraei, | news(?) has come into being for you[10] about . . .[11] As for every god who knows what protects him from Sakhmet, he is one who is hale among you. The mouths of these uraei ⟨. . .⟩.[12] There is the master of this portal, evil is he who does (ill) and his name is 'He who is in the great flame'. A path is prepared for me, and see, I have come. I am he who is in his fiery wrath(?).[13]

O Lord of Terror who is at the head of the Two Lands[14] and is over the waters; O Lord of Blood who prospers the slaughter-houses, to whom is given the *wrrt*-crown and joy; to whom was entrusted the rulership of the gods in the presence of the Lord of All on that day of uniting the Two Lands in the presence of the Lord of All; potent soul who is in Ninsu, who grants powers and expels the evildoers; who shows the ways of eternity: save me from that god who takes the souls[15] of the Great Ones, who laps up corruption
329 and putrefaction, who is in the darkness, who belongs to the dusk, | of whom those who are in darkness are afraid.

O Khopri, dwelling in your bark, primeval of body for ever ⟨. . .⟩.[16]

The third portal. What he said about it. The portal of(?) the persons(?) who approach her;[17] the ornaments(?)[18] which are on her arms are not seen. She descends from the sky, she lays down(?) natron, and no-one at all can approach her, the streams behind her are flames of fire; one is (equal to?) two fires in heat; the third is the fiery blast of the mouth of Sakhmet; the fourth is Nu, whose [. . .] is invisible and they cannot see how to enter into her. Her wishes(?) are proclaimed(?)[19] to Thoth, and it is he who presents himself to the company which is in this portal. Shu and Tefēnet have put their seal on it, and what is under the signet is . . .[20] Great are the distances(?) to these portals and the tribunals which are in this hall . . .[21] who made [. . .] . . . his sides(?);[22] who espied the burning which was in his cavern; who dealt with[23] the evildoer[24] who is with[25] the Lady of Affliction. Evil is the fiery blast, and the door-leaves are broken.[26]

A path is prepared for me, and see, I arrive at(?)[27] this hall. O Lord of the Enneads, save me from those who inflict wounds, whose fingers are painful,[28] who stand guard against foes, who put terror into the mutilators,[29] who do not relax their watch and ward; their knives shall not enter into me, I shall not go into their shambles, I shall not sit within their[30] vats, and nothing shall be done to me of this which the god detests. He speaks about the flesh of the foreskin, for I am one who passes pure through the *msḳt*, to whom is given an evening meal of fayence in the glittering place. There is a chief of this hall whose name is 'For whom is done [. . .] . . . for his face'. A path is prepared for me, and see, I have come; I am the . . .[31] who dwells in Ninsu.

1. For *irtyw* 'blue' see *Concise Dict.* 28.

2. *Ḥꜣt nt tkꜣ* is the subject in anticipatory emphasis of *ḏꜣ·s tꜣ*.

3. *Ḏrbt* is not known. It is guessed to be a corruption of *ḏꜥbt* 'charcoal', 'soot', op. cit. 320; cf. *ḏꜥb* 'coal-black', *Pyr.* § 1105.

4. Note the unusual writing of *ꜥwy* 'hands'.

5. Assuming  to be an error for ; 'knit together' makes poor sense.

6. *Rdyw* must either be corrupt or there must be an omission after it; an object is needed.

7. Or 'backwards', but the det.  favours our rendering.

8. Cf. 312*b* ff.

9. Suffix omitted after *ḫkrw*.

10. Read *ḫpr·n n·ṯn ṯnw-n-rꜣ*; on this last compound word see James, *Ḥeḳanakhte*, p. 114. The plur. pronoun *ṯn* is an error induced by the preceding plurals.

11. *Mḫwt*; meaning unknown, but *Wb.* III, 247,6 quotes  as the name for a gate in the Beyond.

12. *Rꜣw n iꜥrwt* seems quite isolated from the context; presumably there has been an omission of text.

13. *Ḏnḏd* with det.  appears to be unknown, but it could be a corruption of *ḏnd* or *ḏnḏn*, both meaning 'be angry'.

14. Cf. 316*b* ff.

15. Read *bꜣw* with 319*e*. As the text stands it reads *sꜣw* 'sons', which makes poor sense.

16. As in 321*c.d*, but the continuation 321*e* has been omitted, leaving this vocative in the air.

17. Quite obscure; the connection of *ḥꜥw tkn im·s* with *sbḫt* is by no means clear, and there may be an omission or corruption of some kind; 329*f–g* strongly supports this view. The translation of *ḥꜥw* as 'persons' is open to question, but 'flesh' cannot 'approach'. The following phrases enforce the translation of the fem. suffix in reference to *sbḫt* as 'her' rather than 'it'; the portal is thought of as a goddess.

18. For a possible meaning of *srw* cf. *srw* (det. ) *n rdwy* 'anklets(?)' *Wb.* IV, 193,4.

19. For *sꜣr* 'wish' cf. *Urk.* I, 85,8, and *iww* has been tentatively been connected with *iw* 'cry out', *CT* I, 148*a*, but my translation is very much open to question.

20. *Štt·tw*, quite obscure.

21. *Ḏd m bs m rn·f* defeats me, and it is quite obscure to whom the masc. suffix in *rn·f* refers. There surely must be some corruption here.

22. Quite unintelligible.

23. For this meaning of *wsṯn* cf. *Concise Dict.* 69, bottom.

24. *Ỉrrw*; for the implied sense of evildoing cf. *ỉr* 'evildoer', *Pyr.* § 1071; also *ỉrr*, *Peas.* Bl, 193; *ỉrwt* 'evil deeds', *Pyr.* § 298.

25. *Ỉmy* has been taken to be the *nisba* of *m* in its sense of 'together with', cf. *JEA* 25, 166.

26. Reading *ḥsb* (or *sḏ*) *ꜥrty*. For the meaning given to the last word see *RB* 120, 16; 121,1–2.

27. Translation conjectured from the context. The compound *pḏ-ꜥḥꜥ*, here written as a monogram, is known to me only from *Pyr.* §§ 49 + 6, + 9, where it appears to be a term for an archer's mantlet.

28. Cf. 303*a*–*b*.

29. Cf. 322*b* ff.

30. *Ṯn* for *sn*.

31. *Ḥnbꜣbꜣ*, quite obscure.

Spell 337

IV, 331 O Thoth, vindicate Osiris against his foes in:

The great tribunal which is in Ōn on that night of making war and of felling the rebels.

The great tribunal which is in the water of Kher-ꜥaḥa.

The great tribunal which is in Rostau.[1]

The great tribunal which is in the Two Banks of the Kite(?)[2] on that night of the drowning of the great god in 'Andjet.[3]

332 The great tribunal which is in Djedu on that night of the night-offerings.

The great tribunal which is in Khem on that night of erecting the *djed*-pillar in Her-wēr.[4]

The great tribunal which is in Pe and Dep on that night of erecting the two *djed*-pillars.

The great tribunal which is in Abydos on that night of mourning in the Thinite nome.

The great tribunal which is in the paths of the dead[5] on that night of making examination.

333 The great tribunal which is in Ro-areref.[6]

The great tribunal which is in the great[7] ploughing of the land in Ninsu.[8] Horus is joyful, and the Two Conclaves are pleased at it,[9] Osiris is glad, and it is indeed Thoth who will vindicate me against my foes in the tribunals of Rēꜥ and Osiris and of every god and[10] every goddess.

1. 'Which is in Rostau' is misplaced in B3L and B1L.

2. A screeching bird (falcon, kite or crow?), see my *Pyr. Transl.*, Utt. 532, n.1. Edel, *Weltkammer*, I, 235 suggests 'tern', but the cry of that bird can hardly be called a screech.

3. On ʿAndjet see Gardiner, *AEO* II, 176* ff., where it is considered to be an alternative name of Djedu. Here, however, they clearly are distinct, since both place-names occur in close proximity. They may well have been originally two distinct towns, but located so close together that they became merged.

4. On Her-wēr cf. op. cit. II, 84* ff.

5. B3L and B1L have corrupted *mtw* 'the dead' into *mmm* = *mw*.

6. Unidentified locality. Probably an error for Naref, cf. 337*c*; 338*h*.

7. B1Y has a dittograph of *ʿ3* 'great' and B3L omits it.

8. So B3L. Damaged in B1Y, which apparently had *ḥnn-nsw*. B1L has , where  represents *ḥn*.

9. B1L omits *ḥtp* after *itrty*. B1Y stops at this sentence.

10. B1L omits 'every god'.

Spell 338

O THOTH, WHO VINDICATED OSIRIS AGAINST HIS FOES, VINDICATE ME AGAINST MY FOES IN:[1] IV, 335

The tribunal which is in Ōn on that night of making war and of felling that rebel.

The tribunal which is in Djedu on that night of erecting the *djed*-pillar.[2]

ˡThe tribunal which is in Khem on that night of the night-offerings in Khem. 336

The tribunal which is in Pe and Dep on that night of confirming the heritage of Horus in the matter of his father.

The tribunal which is in the Islands of the two Kites(?)[3] on that night of[4] Isis making mourning for her brother Osiris.[5]

The tribunal which is in Abydos on that night of numbering the dead and of counting spirits.[6]

ˡThe tribunal which is in the paths of the dead on that night of making investigation into him who is nothing. 337

The tribunal which is in the great ploughing up of the land.

The tribunal which is in Naref.

The tribunal which is in Rostau on that night when Horus was vindicated against his foes.

The tribunal of him who made the throne.[7]

[. . .] OSIRIS, AND HE WAS GLAD. IT IS THOTH ⟨WHO WILL VINDICATE⟩[8] ME AGAINST MY FOES IN THE TRIBUNALS OF RĒʿ AND OSIRIS AND OF EVERY GOD [AND GODDESS[9] . . .] OSIRIS.

1. Var. T2Be: 'Thoth vindicates Osiris against his foes and N will be vindicated against his foes ⟨in⟩ . . .', in black. The initial *s* of *smꜣʿ·f* in the second clause is written twice.

2. T2Be adds 'in Abydos' and then repeats 335*c*.

3. Perhaps to be read *iww ḥꜣty* rather than *iww rḫty*, compare 331*g*. The locality has not been identified. T2Be has 'the Two Banks'.

4. Note the writing 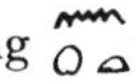 for *n irt* in M8C and M7C. So also 337*a*.

5. M8C has bungled the name of Osiris, writing  for .

6. T2Be has: 'on that night of celebrating the *hꜣkr*-festival in Ōn and counting the dead and the spirits'.

7. In M8C only. The last two words are *ir st*, not *Wsyr*, though de Buck, probably rightly, has taken them to be a miswriting of the name of Osiris, see his n.4*. In T1Be a rubric follows.

8. *Smꜣʿ·f* has been omitted after the name of Thoth, cf. 333*e*.

9. Cf. loc. cit.

Spell 339

IV, 338 O Thoth, vindicate Osiris against his foes in the tribunal of:

Ōn, on that day of the inheriting of the thrones of the Two Banks for the son of the lord thereof.

Djedu, on that day when the Sacred Eye was given to its lord.

Pe and Dep, on that day of the shaving of the female mourners.

Khem, on that day of the night-offerings in Khem.

Rostau, on that day of counting the multitudes and of erecting the two flag-poles.

Abydos, on that day of the *hꜣkr*-festival in the pool(?) of numbering the dead and at the reckoning of him who is nothing.

Ninsu, on that day of ploughing the earth and of making secret the land in Naref.

See, Horus is vindicated, the Two Conclaves are pleased at it, and Osiris is glad. It is indeed Thoth who will vindicate me[1] against my foes in the tribunal of Osiris.

AS FOR HIM WHO KNOWS THIS, HE WILL TRANSFORM HIMSELF INTO A FALCON, THE SON OF RĒʿ. [AS FOR] WHOEVER [KNOWS] THIS [. . .],[2] NEITHER HE NOR HIS
339 SOUL WILL EVER BE DESTROYED. | IT MEANS THAT HIS FOE WILL BE DESTROYED AND THAT HE WILL EAT BREAD[3] IN THE HOUSE OF OSIRIS; HE WILL ENTER INTO

THE TEMPLE OF [EVERY] POTENT [GOD(?)],[4] [. . .] GIFTS [. . .] HE WILL NEVER EAT FAECES [. . .].

1. Read *smȝʿ·f ḫrw·i r ḫftyw·i*.
2. Restore as [*ir r*]*ḫ nb nn*. There follows *tp* [. . .]·*f*, which I cannot interpret.
3. Read *ḫtm ḫfty* ⟨·*f*⟩ *pw iw·f wnm*[·*f*] *t*.
4. Perhaps restore as *ḥwt-nṯr nt* [*nṯr nb*] *mnḫ*.

Spell 340

Spell for entering into the beautiful West . . . . | To me belong all people, IV, 340
and all of them have been given to me.[1] I have gone in as a falcon, | I have 341
come out as a phoenix; O Morning Star, make a path for me, that I may enter
in peace into the beautiful West, | and I belong to the Waterway of Horus.[2] 342
Make a path for me, that I may enter and worship Osiris, the Lord of Life.

A man shall say this spell when he goes in after he comes out from the West. As for him who is ignorant of this spell, together with the knowledge of how to go out into the day, he shall not go in after [coming out . . .].[3]

1. M7C (340*e*) has 'the tribunal of Osiris' before the first clause of the spell; after it B9C has *rdy n·i Rʿ-Itm m rdy n·i my-ḳd·sn*.
2. Var. 'of Osiris'. 'Waterway of Horus' is the Biblical Shihor, on which see Gardiner, *AEO* II, 201*.
3. Restored according to 342*d*.

Spell 341

O door-keeper of the Great House, open[1] to me, for indeed I am Rēʿ in his IV, 343
appearings, and the Nile in its windings(?).[2] Ḥatḥōr laughs at me[3] in the ferry-boat[4] of the sky at my ferrying across. Mine are Isis and Nephthys, the two fair sisters; may your (*sic*) doubles be joined in peace, while those gods who are in the sky stand up.

He is one like to us, he is like a man who has ceased discharging(?).[5] 344

I have come here, having ceased discharging(?), and Anubis is the god cleansing me. There are opened to me the gates of the Netherworld to the fair paths by day in the direction of the Island of Fire which belongs to the just, at the place where the spirits are. I issue thence by the sacred gate and *Iȝȝ* the fair makes report of me[6] in the bark of the Self-created.

O you guardians of the steering-oars, my face is down-turned[7] to the earth; 345
the ruler[8] speaks to Maʿet, and my seat is in the Castle belonging to you, I come to an end happily today.[9]

THIS SPELL[10] SHOULD BE SPOKEN OVER[11] SEVEN SACRED EYES IN WRITING: TO BE WASHED IN BEER AND NATRON AND TO BE DRUNK BY THE MAN.

1. On the position of the particle *my* before the imperative, see Gardiner, *Eg. Gramm.*,[3] 250, last example.

2. *Nnwt* 'inertia' does not convey much meaning here. The word could possibly refer to the state of the river at dead low water, but this seems hardly likely. It is more probable that we have here a derivative of *nny* 'turn about', *CT* I, 306*a*, older *inn*, *Pyr.* §§ 214; 218; 1491, and that the allusion is to the bends in the Nile.

3. Surely in a friendly way, showing pleasure, and not in mockery. For *sbṯ m* 'laugh at' cf. *Sh. S.* 149.

4. Var. 'my ferry-boats'.

5. 343*h–i* appear to be spoken by Isis and Nephthys. *Km bsw* is an odd expression, and one can but choose among unpromising alternative translations. The det. of *bsw* in B2L suggests *bsw* 'morbid discharges', *Eb.* 36, 18–19, where the det. is , and *km* might conceivably refer to the cessation of putrefaction through the embalming operations of Anubis, cf. 344*b*. However, the negation in B1Y and B3L speaks against this interpretation, but see 344*a*.

6. For *smyt·i* B3L has *smy·ṯn*; this may be a corruption of *smyt·i n·ṯn*.

7. Read *ḥr·i hꜣ r tꜣ*; as the verb *hꜣ* is 3ae inf., it cannot be infinitive here, despite the infinitive *mdt* in the next clause. The literal translation is 'my face has gone down to the earth'.

8. Plural in B3L; partly lost in B1Y.

9. So B1L; for the meaning given to *sꜥr* cf. *Pyr.* § 291 (*sic*); *CT* I, 158*d*. B3L has 'it is erected for me', presumably in reference to the castle; B1Y is largely lost, but seems to have had an entirely different text.

10. B1Y had a long rubric of which only a few signs remain; the text which is translated here is common to B3L and B1L.

11. So B1L, which omits *ḥr* 'over'; B3L reads *ḏd s pn ḥr*, having omitted *rꜣ* 'spell' after *s* 'man'. Read in both texts *rꜣ pn ḥr wḏꜣt 7*.

Spell 342

IV, 346 DRIVING OFF A CROCODILE WHICH DRAWS NEAR IN ORDER TO TAKE AWAY A MAN'S MAGIC FROM HIM. Get back! Go away! Get back, you dangerous one![1] Do not come upon me, do not live by my magic![2] May I not have to tell this name of yours[3] to the great god who let you come: 'Messenger' is the name of one, and *Bḏt* is the name of one.[4]

347 *The crocodile speaks:* Your face is toward righteousness. | The sky encloses the stars,[5] magic encloses its settlements,[6] and this mouth of mine encloses the magic which is in it. My teeth are flint, my tusks are the Cerastes Mountain.

The deceased replies: O you with a spine[7] who would work your mouth against this magic of mine, do not[8] take it away, O crocodile which lives by magic.

1. *Swty* has been taken to be a *nisba* of *swt* 'danger', *Pyr.* §§ 652; 1282; *BD* 97,10 has *swy*. Cf. also *sww* or *swy* 'harmful', 'dangerous', *Pyr.* §§ 611; 1335–6; 1931. There is probably no connection with the name *Swty* often given to Seth in texts of the New Kingdom.

2. B2L inserts the rubric here instead of at the beginning of the spell as in B1C, while B1P has a truncated version of it at the end of the spell.

3. *R·k* at the beginning of 346*h* is the enclitic particle reinforcing the negative optative *im·i*.

4. It would seem that two crocodiles are involved, though there is no hint of duality elsewhere.

5. For *wnwt* 'stars' see also *CT* V, 266*d.f*; 267*c*, *BD* 99,11.

6. Presumably in a protective sense.

7. *Ỉ ṯs bksw*; possibly a reference to the dorsal scutes of a crocodile.

8. Note the full writing of the negative imperative *m*.

Spell 343

SPELL[1] FOR AVOIDING[2] THE NET[3] AND OF ESCAPING THE PURSE-NET[4] BY A SPIRIT IV, 348
IN THE REALM OF THE DEAD. Ho N! Hurry, raise yourself,[5] O Lord of shal-
lows(?),[6] Lord of purity, | whom the milk-goddess suckled. He is the prince 350
of those whose seats endure in the sky,[7] one to whom is given those who rest
in the earth. Hurry, raise yourself, grasp the tail of the long-horn, | the com- 352
panion of Anubis, and learn the paths of the West, travel ⟨with⟩ those who
traverse the sky,[8] ferry across the firmament when the Sacred Land is turned
upside down. You shall pass through the place of execution[9] and escape the
purse-net[10] | and the net of the Foremost of the Westerners. (As for) the fish- 354
net, its floats are in the sky, its weights are on earth;[11] it was made for the
spirits who have gone to their doubles.[12] | They perish(?) when his time 356
comes.[13]

You shall take your ease on[14] the firmament; you shall be more starry[15]
than the stars of the horizon as that Lone Star[16] which is in the west of the sky
and the east of the earth.[17] | Your mouth is filled with the plants of the marsh- 358
lands, the bows of Horus Khentikhetef are bent.[18]

May you take possession of the whole of the Two Gardens(?),[19] you shall
stand at that great polar region[20] in front of the zenith(?).[21] | Awaken[22] 'Aḳen, 360
that he may bring[23] to you that ferry-boat in which the equipped spirits ferry
across. May you give command,[24] may they commend you,[25] may they guide
you to the great lake,[26] | may they convey[27] you in the Abyss: may the equipped 362
ones equip you, may you join land to land[28] at the ramp(?)[29] of the Thinite
nome.[30] You shall ascend to the top of the high hill | that you may hear the 364
quiet(?)[31] voice in the eastern gate. You shall travel around the celestial
expanses,[32] the grey-haired ones shall serve you, the silent ones shall follow
you.

1. The rubric translated here is that of T1L. B1C and B2L read 'Spell for not going down into the net and the fish-trap; being vindicated in the presence of Osiris, Bull of the West'; B2Bo has: 'Raising himself on his right side from his left side'.

2. For *šꜣš* 'avoid' cf. *Pt.* (L.II), 4,3; *P. Kah.* 2,15.

3. For *iꜣdt* 'net' cf. *Concise Dict.* 10. De Buck's reading  of the dets. in B2L (see his n.2*) is almost certainly correct. The det.  in T1L and B1C arises from confusion with , cf. *iꜣdt* 'dew', etc., op. cit. 9.

4. *ʾInyt* is not recorded, but the det. represents a net, cf. Gardiner, *Eg. Gramm.*,[3] Sign-list, T24. The word may be connected etymologically with *in* 'cordage', *Concise Dict.* 23. and the translation 'purse-net' rests on the shape of the det. It is clearly a different net from *iꜣdt*. In *CT* VI, 4*f* the word recurs in the form .

5. *Ṯs tw* or *ṯs ṯn* in five texts out of eleven; B1P^b has *ꜥḥꜥ* 'stand up' instead of *wn ṯw* 'hurry'.

6. Cf. *Wb.* IV, 401,9; but the relevance of the word to the present context is not clear. T1L determines the word with the town-sign, but no locality of that name is recorded.

7. B1C–B4Bo show varying degrees of corruption.

8. Again there is some corruption. Either we must supply *ḥnꜥ* after *nmy ṯw*, 'travel ⟨with⟩ those who traverse the sky', or, less probably, regard *nmyw* as a miswriting of the 'complementary infinitive'. T1L reads 'traverse the "lake" *or* "garden"'; B1C–B6C 'who traverse the sky', quite out of context, while B2Bo and B4Bo omit the clause.

9. S1C has *šm* in its transitive sense, cf. *Wb.* IV, 464,22; the other texts have *šꜣs*; note S2C, which conflates *šm* and *šꜣs* into *šms*. For *ḫbt* 'place of execution' T1L has *sbḫwt* 'gates'.

10. For *sn* 'pass by', 'escape' two texts have *syn* 'run', presumably in error. On *inyt* see n. 4 above. B15C–B4Bo have corrupted this word into *int* (*nt*) *iḫ* 'the valley of the trap'.

11. For *ḏbꜣw* 'floats' and *dnsw* 'weights' of a net see also *CT* VI, 10*c*; 17*g*; *BD* 390,13.

12. T1L has: 'those three spirits'. Further, T1L and B15C add *prw nhhn·sn* (var. *nh . . .*) *m P*, which is incomprehensible to me; perhaps one should emend into *prw hꜣw m P* 'who come and go in Pe'.

13. *Tm·sn iw sp·f* is difficult. *ʾIw sp·f* appears to be a virtual adverb clause qualifying *tm·sn*; *iw* cannot be a negatival complement to *tm*, as that would leave *sp·f* in the air. *Tm* therefore is not the negation, and the only meanings that would have any significance here are 'perish' or 'cease'. Even so, the connection with the context is not clear. After this B1P^a inserts 'Ho N!' to introduce the next clause.

14. Read *kbḥ·kꜣ·k r·k r*; T1L and B5C omit the suffix after the verb. S2C seems the better text; 'of the son of Rēꜥ' of the other texts is superfluous.

15. For *sḥd* 'star' cf. *Pyr.* §§ 506; 698; 889; 1583; *CT* II, 117*g*. For *sḥd·kꜣ·k* three texts have *sḥḏ·kꜣ·k* 'you shall make brightness'.

16. Var. 'that great star'.

17. *Et varr.* At this point T1L adds 'may you travel around the great west of the earth, may you tread the limits(?) (*rkrw*) of the earth'.

18. The relation of these two sentences to the context is quite obscure, and before 359*b* T1L inserts 'those who are forgotten are spirit', which is equally obscure.

19. Before this sentence B1P^b inserts 'Ho N!', as if a new section began here.

20. Cf. Sethe. *Komm. Pyr.* III, 393.

21. Cf. op. cit. II, 338. After this clause T1L adds: 'you shall summon (*nis·kꜣ·⟨k⟩*) this god to you when Rēꜥ appears with his soul, you shall summon the celestial ferryman'.

22. Var. *rs·f* in three texts, but the imperative is the better reading. This passage recalls the repeated demand to awaken Aḳen in Spell 397 = *BD* Spell 99.

23. Prospective *sḏm·f*.

24. T1L (360*c*) inserts after 360*b*: 'Ho N! May you be more spirit-like than the spirits of those whom they bring' and omits 361*a*. Note the use of the demonstrative *tw* after a relative form.

25. T1L adds 'in the great lake'.

26. Three texts read: 'the great lake of "Come-to-those-who-come" '.

27. *Nmy* in the sense of 'convey' a person has not hitherto been noted. Var. *sšm* 'guide'.

28. T1L corruptly *ḏꜣ r tꜣ*; B15C omits *smꜣ tꜣ r tꜣ r* and B2Bo and B4Bo have condensed 363*a* somewhat. In B1P^{b} this is preceded by 'Ho N!'.

29. So B1C, B2L and B1P^{b}; for *smꜣ* 'ramp(?)' cf. *Hamm.* 19.

30. B1P^{b} again inserts 'Ho N!' before the next clause.

31. Regarding *bgw* as a derivation from *bꜣgy* 'be weary'.

32. Reading *pḏwt*; for the meaning cf. *Pyr.* §§ 393; 801; 1004; 1486; 1972. The copyists have confused the word with *pḏt* 'bow' or *pḏtyw* 'bowmen'.

Spell 344

I raise myself, I hasten myself by means of this soul of the horned serpent, IV, 366
(even I) whom the milk-goddess suckled;[1] such is he who draws the net[2] for those who dwell in the sky, to whom is given rest.[3]

I raise myself, I hasten myself by means of the tail of that long-horn which supports the bark of Anubis,[4] I know the path of the West, I ferry over the waterway of those who traverse the firmament, I am one who escapes[5] the place of execution. I pass by the Valley,[6] I cross the Sacred Place, I pass through the double doors of the judgement-hall(?),[7] I have hurried over[8] the waterway of . . .[9] in the company of the Foremost of the Westerners. It is what the gods made ⟨for⟩ those who have gone to their doubles,[10] | lest his 367
time come(?).[11] Their net has been fished up, and its floats are in the sky, its weights are on earth; cold water is in the sky with *Ḳbḥ* the son of Rēꜥ . . .[12]

I will summon the celestial ferryman, and he will wake ꜥAḳen,[13] he will bring me the ferry-boat. O equipped spirit,[14] equip me in it. I am more spirit-like than your spirits, I am more equipped than your equipped ones, they come down and they receive me, they ferry me across [. . .], they row me on the Waterway of the Sky-windows, | they join with me on earth, having 368
landed on the hill of the wind. I hear the noise of the flood at the eastern gate of the sky, I travel around on the great western side of the sky, I go all over the great eastern side of the sky; the Great Ones stand up and bow to me, the

grey-haired one fears me, the attendants dread me, the plebs[15] follow me; I have gone around and returned,[16] and afterwards I have gone happily around the corrupt ones(?).[17]

1. Masc., to agree in gender with the speaker.
2. *Srš*, cf. *Wb.* IV, 201,14.
3. For *rdy·n·i* read *rdy·n·f*, cf. 351*a*.
4. Compare 352*a*.
5. Construction of participle as adjectival predicate with pronominal subject. For *nh* 'escape' cf. *Pyr.* § 1453; *CT* I, 284*g*.
6. Cf. Spell 343, n.10.
7. Translation doubtful. *Ḫns*, which is damaged, has been identified with *ḫns* 'double doors', *Pyr.* § 416; *ḥtmwt* may be identical with *ḥtmyt* 'Richtstätte in der Unterwelt', *Wb.* III, 198,9.
8. This transitive use of *wꜥr* is not recorded.
9. *Šnwt*, meaning unknown.
10. Clearly some corruption here. According to 355*a* this clause should follow 367*c*, and itself is defective, since the preposition *n* has been omitted before *sbw*. The fem. gender of the relative form *irt·n* is in concord with *iꜣdt* 'net', further confirming the displacement of this clause.
11. On this obscure clause see Spell 343, n.13, though here *tm* lacks the suffix. All this part of Spell 344 has been garbled, and one can only translate the words as they stand.
12. The last words of 367*d* are incomprehensible; they read 'on earth', 'poverty', 'horizon'. For *snw* 'poverty' cf. *Les.* 79,6.
13. So B9C: B1Y is bungled.
14. The 'equipped spirit' addressed here is probably ꜥAḳen; the sentence is different from 362*b*.
15. *Rtyw* has been taken to be a miswriting of *rẖtyw* 'plebs'.
16. Read *pẖr·n·i iw·n·i*, cf. B1Y.
17. Cf. *iwtyw*, *Pyr.* § 679; perhaps a derivative of *iwtyw* 'corruption', *Urk.* V, 76,9.

Spell 345

IV, 369 SPELL FOR VINDICATION IN THE PRESENCE OF THOTH, THE CHIEFEST OF THE GODS,[1] (AND FOR) NOT TAKING AWAY A MAN'S SHROUD FROM HIM OR A MAN'S
370 COFFIN FROM HIM IN THE REALM OF THE DEAD. | Ho N![2] There will come[3] to you those who come to Horus who dwells in his house[4] on that day when all the
371 gods were clothed | at the burial of Osiris and of that day of interment.

372 Ho N! | Those who wept for Osiris will weep for you on that day of the fourth-day festival.[5]

373 Ho N! | Those who mourned Osiris will mourn you on that day of the sixth-day festival in which the gods swooned.[6]

374 Ho N! Horus himself will cleanse you in that pool of cold water.[7]

375 Ho N![8] Anubis the embalmer[9] will enwrap you with wrappings from the hand of Tayt.

Ho N! Anubis the embalmer has mummified you with his best embalming. Thoth will cleanse for you the fair paths of the West (which lead) to Osiris.

Ho N! Dedwen makes his perfume of what is in you;[10] | Wepwawet will 376
open for you the fair paths of the West.[11] They will guide you to the great land[12] of 'Come-to-those-who-come'. You shall invoke that god whose soul appears by day and Thoth by night.[13] He will be pleased with you just as he was pleased with Thoth, the chiefest of the gods in Ōn.[14]

1. B2L inserts 'by a man in Ōn'.
2. B1P only; so repeatedly in this spell, where it seems more appropriate than elsewhere.
3. *Ỉwt* at the beginning of 370*b* has been interpreted as prospective *sḏm·f*. 370*a* (B1P) shows that 'you' is the deceased.
4. Varr. 'the house of Osiris'; 'his house of Osiris'.
5. Expanded and corrupt in B9C. B1C (372*e*) inserts a dittograph of the 'interment' clause.
6. For *ḫm ḏt* 'swoon' (B9C) cf. *Ch. B.* Text 59, n.2; *ḫm if* of the other texts is an unrecorded variant of this.
7. So B1P. The other texts have briefly: 'Horus will cleanse you'. Cf. 377*b*.
8. At this point S5C interpolates a heading: 'Words spoken by Rēꜥ when opening the paths in the *Wꜣg*-festival, in the *msyt*-festival, in the festival of Sokar, in the festival of Thoth, and on all happy days'. On p. 375 the text followed is the very full one of B1P.
9. So B1P; all the other texts have 'Thoth', but since the sentence refers to 'clothing' the deceased, presumably with reference to the wrappings of the corpse, 'Anubis' seems the better reading; cf. 375*d–i*; 377*c*.
10. Var. S5C *m iḫnt·k* 'from your skin'.
11. B1P adds: 'which belong to vindication on this day against your foes, male or female, in the sky or on earth or in the realm of the dead'.
12. Var. B1P 'the great garden' or 'lake'.
13. Var. S2C: 'who appears in (or 'with') his soul by night, omitting *m hrw*.
14. Varr. S2C: 'Thoth who gives orders to the gods'; B1P: 'Thoth on his *maꜥet*-image, prince of the gods in Ōn'.

Spell 346

Ho N! Horus himself will cleanse you in the pool of cold water; Anubis will IV, 377
enwrap you in his best embalming; Thoth will make clean for you the fair paths of the West (which lead) to Osiris; Dedwen will make his perfume of what is in you.[1] He will open up to you the fair paths of vindication; Nu will
convey you; | it is Wepwawet who will guide you to the fair paths of the West. 378
Acclamation shall be made to him;[2] they[3] shall see him, he having come from the land of the living into the Island of Fire at his places of vindication before Osiris. N has come in the suite of his father Osiris in peace, in peace!

1. Following B4Bo; cf. 375*c*. B15C is corrupt at the end.
2. A switch to the 3rd person. Var. 'the gods shall make acclamation to him'.
3. A confusion of suffixes; B4Bo has in error *ṯn* instead of *sn*.

Spell 347

They go down, they proceed,[1] they conduct me to that day of 'Come-to-the-
IV, 379 *ipt*-on-the-hill-of-the-wind'.[2] I hear that voice of the quiet one(?)[3] who belongs
to the Unwearying Stars which navigate the sky at the station(?) of Him who
is content(?).[4] The great West is joined together at the south of the land and
(at) this polar region which is in front of the zenith(?).[5] See this god . . .[6]
the appearing of Rēʿ with his soul. He will bring my name into being(?),[7]
he will make me as Rēʿ and Thoth[8] on that day and night when they were
380 pleased(?)[9] at it, | Thoth performing the role[10] of Rēʿ according to the
command which Anubis made. I will be there at that northern portal of the
Winding Waterway in which there is no lack of the sky, and I will be beautified,
I will govern the great gods who are at the head of the Enneads.

1. The second *n* between *sḏꜣ·sn* and *sb·sn* appears to be a dittograph. The whole spell is most obscure, and the translation must be regarded as provisional only.
2. Cf. 368*a*.
3. Cf. 364*a*.
4. Obscure and probably corrupt.
5. Cf. 359*b*.
6. *'Isk ꜣ nṯr pw r wi* is unintelligible.
7. Emending *sḫp* into *sḫpr*.
8. *Pw* after the names of the gods seems superfluous and may be an anticipation of *pw* after *rʿ grḥ*. Of the two gods mentioned, Rēʿ represents the sun by day and Thoth the moon by night.
9. *Ḥtpy* perhaps dual old perfective in reference to the two gods above.
10. Lit. 'in the duty of'.

Spell 348

Pe will come to me,[1] I have gone round about Nekhen,[2] I having appeared[3] as a god for ever and ever.

1. Regarding *iwt* as prospective *sḏm·f*.
2. *Nḫn* of B9C^a is the better reading, as counterpart to *P*.
3. Read *ḫʿ·kwy* with B1Y and B9C^a.

Spell 349

IV, 381 NOT LETTING A MAN'S MAGIC BE TAKEN FROM HIM IN THE REALM OF THE DEAD.

Your son Horus has acted on your behalf,[1] and the Great Ones tremble when they see the knives which are in your hands when you ascend from the Netherworld. Hail to you, O Wise One![2] | Gēb has created you, the Ennead[3] has 382
borne you. Horus is pleased with his father,[4] Atum is pleased with his years, the gods of West and East are pleased with the Great One who came into being in the arms of Her who bore the god.

O N! O N! See and behold! O N! Hear and be yonder![5] O N, raise yourself 383
on your side, and do my command.[6] O you who hate sleep but who were made limp, arise, O you who were in Nedit! Your good bread is prepared in Pe,[7] | 384
take your power[8] in Ōn, for it is Horus who commanded that men should help his father. As for the Lord of Storm, the slavering of Seth is forbidden to him(?).[9] He[10] raises you, and it is he who will raise up Atum.[11]

1. Cf. *Pyr.* Utt. 247.

2. So T3Be, in accord with *Pyr.* § 258. This text is closer to the original than the other versions.

3. So T3Be, cf. loc. cit. The other texts have 'Nūt'.

4. So *Pyr.* § 258 and B3C–B1Bo; T3Be has 'his Eye'.

5. T3Be varies slightly in the order of the imperatives, but the other versions follow *Pyr.* § 259. Because the coffin is that of a woman, B3C has attached the very rare feminine ending to the imperatives *sḏmt* and *wnt*.

6. *Ir wḏ* of T3Be is in accord with *Pyr.* § 260. The other texts name Osiris or Rēʿ at this point.

7. Still following T3Be = *Pyr.* § 260.

8. Var. 'your sceptre'.

9. Following my translation of *Pyr.* § 261*a*. The original text reads , and it is easy to see how the corruption *s3ḥ sn·f Isds* of B3C arose. B1Bo is altogether corrupt; the damaged T3Be has *s3ḥ sn·f sd3*.

10. Presumably Horus. B3C has 'raise yourself (fem.)'.

11. So three texts correctly; B1Bo has: 'it is he who will raise you'.

Spell 350

O you bulls who are on the mounds, I will have power over(?)[1] the Vulture.[2] IV, 385
O runner(?),[3] I will break your pen and crumple your papers because of this double harm which you have said you will do to me.

Why?

Because of the property of mine which I have brought[4] from the Field of *N3w* and from the Field of Fire; it is with me at the Field of *D3d3* for the purpose of all business(?).

Acquiring magic power, not[5] taking a man's magic power from him in the realm of the dead.

1. Reading as *sḫm⟨·i⟩ ⟨m⟩*. For the 1st person cf. 385*e*.
2. Cf. Spell 205, n.3.
3. *Ḥpw* appears to belong to 385*c*, since a vocative is needed here.
4. *ʼIšt* here is treated as a masculine, as the relative form *in·n·i* shows.
5. The first words only in B1C; B3C has written the negation *tm* as 'Reʿ-Atum'.

Spell 351

IV, 386 SPELL FOR GIVING A MOUTH TO A MAN FOR HIM IN THE REALM OF THE DEAD SO THAT HE MAY SPEAK WITH IT, AND OF ENTERING TO [OSIRIS.][1] Hail to you, you
387 who make dry,[2] pre-eminent in the Mansion, | in control of darkness.[3] You shall come to me spiritualized and pure, with your arms (clasped) about you
388 and your bowl upon you. | You shall give me my mouth that I may speak with it, you shall guide me to the fair paths of the sky,[4] | for I am in charge of the record of the word of God.

1. This last clause in T1L only. For the second clause see also 389*c* (B3C, B1C, B2L).
2. *Sšr. BD* 85,4 has *nb šsp* 'lord of light'. S14C has *psḏ nfr* 'fair shining one'.
3. *Kkw*; var. *kkw smȝw* 'twilight'. B3Bo adds: 'in control of air'.
4. Var. 'to the stars (*wnwt*) of the sky'.

Spell 352

IV, 390c A MAN DEPARTS AS ONE HONOURED WITH GOD. I have power in my mouth, I have power in my own nose; may I have power in my mouth, may I have
391 power in my nose,[1] | which are complete;[2] so say those gods who are spirits.[3] Be content, O Lord of All. Are you Atum? Are you a green tree?[4] Go up, make summons with your mouths . . .[5]

1. 390*c–d* have adjectival predicate + dative; 390*f–g* have optative *sḏm·f*. L1Li has: 'I have entered that I may, etc.'
2. Reading *ntyw tm* with B3C; the use of the plural is unexpected, and possibly there may have been a textual omission before *ntyw*. This clause is bungled progressively from B1C^{b} to L1Li.
3. Var. B1C^{a}: 'say the horizon-dwellers'; L1Li is quite corrupt.
4. *Sic* B3C: B1C^{b}–B2L^{b}: 'Are you Atum? So says(?) the green tree'. B1C^{a} is unintelligible and L1Li has only *wȝḏ* after *ʼItm*. The whole passage is most obscure.
5. Untranslatable. *BD* 128,13 has *pr m nys m rn·tn ink is ʼItm* 'Go up, make summons with your names, for I am Atum'.

Spell 353

IV, 392 SPELL FOR HAVING POWER OVER WATER.[1] The doors of the Great One[2] are
394 opened for Osiris,[3] | the doors of the firmament are thrown open for Thoth.

O Nile-god,[4] the Great One of the sky[5] in this your[6] name of . . .,[7] | grant that 396
I may have power over water[8] just as Seth had power[9] over the water in the eye(?)[10] of Osiris on that night of the great storm. | May you permit me to 398
despatch for myself[11] the Great Ones who preside over the flood just as their august god | whose name they do not know sent them.[12] I am their august god 400
whose name they do not know,[13] and they are despatched for me.

ACQUIRING . . .,[14] HAVING POWER OVER WATER: EQUIPPING THIS SPIRIT.

1. So B3C. The only significant var. is B1Bo^b: 'having power over water in the realm of the dead; not walking head downwards; sending the soul into the realm of the dead'.
2. The sky, personified as a goddess.
3. So the great majority of texts, but three have 'Isis' and two name no deity.
4. So T1C^a–S1C; also *BD* 312,11. Most texts have *ḥkꜣ* 'magician', but B1Bo^a and B3Ox have a corrupt version of T1C^a ff.
5. Varr. S1C–Y1C: 'the upper sky'; B5C–T1C^b: 'the middle sky'.
6. So most texts, but three have wrongly *rn·f* 'his name'; this clause is a vocative.
7. Untranslatable; the writings vary between *pnḏ*, *pnd*, *pnḏ-tꜣ*, *pd*, *pnn*, *nbḏw* and *ꜥḏ-pt*, showing clearly that this epithet was not understood even in ancient times. Y1C inserts a stock offering formula here.
8. M39C (397*c*) substitutes a damaged passage referring to *isftyw* 'evildoers'.
9. From S1C–Y1C the texts read—with minor varr.—*my Sḫmt ꜥwꜣt Wsyr*, though some omit the name of Osiris; this clause is unintelligible to me, as also B1Bo^a and BH3Ox.
10. *ꜥwꜣt* 'eye(?)' or a part thereof is not recorded.
11. Read most probably *dy·k sb·i n·i wrw*.
12. Read *my sbb sn nṯr·sn pw šps* with T1C^a. 399*c* is an obscure interpolation.
13. Nine texts omit *ink pw* (400*b*), which is superfluous, and T1C^a–B5C omit 400*c*.
14. *ꜥftt* is obscure; for the word see also *CT* III, 329*b*; 376*a*; VII, 278*c*. *ꜥpr* is used here in two distinct senses; for 'acquire' cf. *JEA* 35, 96, n.2.

Spell 354

SPELL FOR A WNWN(?)-PLANT.[1] Your purification is the purification of Horus, IV, 402
Seth, Thoth and *Dwn-ꜥnwy*. Your purification is on your mouth; may you cleanse all your bones, may you provide what appertains to you. *Smyn*, *smyn*, which splits open your mouth! Taste its taste in front of them of the God's booth. Your purification is natron from the cleansing of the Followers of Horus.

1. The two very different readings of this plant-name could both have been derived from an original , through misreading of hieratic, though no such plant appears to be known. See de Buck's note 3*. For what follows see *Pyr.* Utt. 36 and 34.

THE
ANCIENT EGYPTIAN
COFFIN TEXTS

Volume II Spells 355–787

PREFACE

At the time of the publication of vol. I of the present work, it was envisaged as being completed in two volumes, the second comprising vols. V – VII of de Buck's text. When at last the work was completed and in the hands of the publishers, Messrs. Aris & Phillips Ltd., they pointed out to me that the projected vol. II as planned, together with the accompanying indexes, would be inconveniently bulky, and they suggested dividing it. As a result, the present vol. II contains the translations of vols. V and VI of de Buck's text, while vol. III will be devoted to de Buck's vol. VII and to the indexes. The main script of this third volume is already in the hands of the publishers, and it is hoped that its appearance will follow hard on the heels of vol. II.

I am glad to express here my gratitude for the generous help I have continued to receive in the course of the work. I am especially indebted to Mr. C.H.S. Spaull of Cambridge, whose hospitality I have enjoyed, with whom I have read a considerable number of the spells in this book, and whose comments and suggestions have been of great value. I have also had much encouragement from Professor H. S. Smith of University College, London, the general editor of the Modern Egyptology series, from Dr. David Dixon, also of University College, who borrowed and brought to me in Suffolk books from the Edwards Library which my own collection lacked, and to Mr. Adrian Phillips of Aris & Phillips for his helpfulness in coping with the problems of none too easy printing. Lastly, I wish to express my deep gratitude to the Sir Alan Gardiner Settlement for Egyptological purposes and to the Committee of the British Academy for their very generous subventions towards the cost of printing.

R. O. Faulkner.

Spell 355

SPELL FOR HAVING POWER OVER THE WINDS.[1] The mouth of my open nostril[2] is V, 1
in Djedu, my offerings are in Ōn, this house of mine is built by[3] Seshat,[4] Khnum[5]
has sat on its parapets.[6] | If the weather[7] comes as the north-wind, I will sit to the 3
south of it; if the weather comes as the south-wind, I will sit to the north of it;[8] | 5
if the weather comes as the west-wind, I will sit to the east of it; if the weather
comes as the east-wind, I will sit to the west of it. | I blow my nose(?),[9] which is 7
opened up[10] at the place where I wish to dwell.[11]

1. Varr. 'Living on air in the realm of the dead'; 'Going up to Djedu and Ōn, giving offerings in the horizon'. Spell 297 is cognate.
2. *Sic; wnt,* which is the reading of all texts, is a participle qualifying *šrt.*
3. Read *ḳd (ỉ)n* 'built by', slightly bungled in S1C. Compare *CT* IV, 50*d.*
4. Varr. 'Ptaḥ', 'Sakhmet'.
5. Var. 'Horus'.
6. *3a-b* in two texts only, anticipating *4b-c,* and not translated.
7. Lit. 'this sky'; see Spell 297, n.5. Whichever way the wind blows, the deceased intends to sit always on the lee side of his house.
8. B1Bo[a]: 'the south of it' in error.
9. See Spell 297, n.6.
10. Var. B1Bo[a]: 'which the wind opens'. Three texts omit *wbȝ.*
11. B1Bo[a] adds a title in black: 'Going up to Djedu'.

Spell 356

SPELL FOR HAVING POWER OVER WATER AND NOT DYING IN THE REALM OF THE V, 8
DEAD BY A MAN IN VERY TRUTH.[1] The Great One[2] is opened to Osiris, the doors of the firmament are thrown open to Thoth and to the Nile-god, Lord of the horizon in this his[3] name of *Pns.*[4] May you grant that I have power over water as over a limb of[5] Seth the rebellious.

1. In B2L the words *ỉn s m wn mȝʿ* come at the end of Spell 357.
2. The sky, conceived as a goddess. Compare Spell 353.
3. MSS. 'your' in error, except L1Li.
4. Var. *pns-tȝ* in 10*m* (Sp. 358); *BD* 132,12 has *pdsw.* In 8*d* L1Li reads: '[. . .] flood of the Nile-god, Lord of the horizon, in this his name of *Sw-dy-tȝ*'.
5. Note the use of *m* for the genitive; so also 24*b*; VII, 14*p, ỉm.ỉ* 'belonging to me' in VII, 242*i,* again after *ʿt* 'limb'; sim. *ỉm.f* in VII, 451*e.*

Spell 357

V, 9 I am he who crosses the sky, I am the Lion on the day of butchery. I have separated[1] the fore-leg, I have crossed the Two Lands with the limb, I have gone all over the banks north of the Field of Djeret.[2] Eternity has been granted to me, and I will not die;[3] I have no end,[4] because I am the heir.[5]

1. Lit. 'opened'.
2. Cf *Sḫt Ḏryt,* 126*b* below; *Sḫt Ḏr* in *Pyr.* §1314.
3. B1C only; probably no room in L1Li, see De Buck, n.3*.
4. Reading as 1st person. Both *pḥwy* (B2L) and *ḏr* (B1C) mean 'end'.
5. L1Li reads: 'because N is the heir of eternity and [everlasting has been given to him]', cf. de Buck, n.4*. On the rubric in B2L see Spell 356, n.1.

Spell 358

V, 10 The great One[1] is opened to Osiris, the doors of the firmament are thrown open to Thoth and to the Nile-god in this his name of 'He who turns the land upside down'. May you grant that N have power over water today as over the food(?)[2] of Seth the rebellious on that day of the storm over the Two Lands. It is the Great Ones of the sky who bring those who are in the west of the firmament who would draw near to you,[3] and you will not be disturbed, you will not be flooded, you will not be scorched, for you belong to Rēʿ; you are the good oar[4] of Rēʿ with which he rows his old ones and his female kindred(?).[5]

The efflux of Osiris is lifted up ⟨to⟩ the Island of Asyut, the Great One is opened to Osiris, the doors of the firmament are thrown open to Thoth, a path is prepared for the Nile-god of seven cubits over the land in this his name of *Pns-tꜣ.*[6] May you grant that N have power over water today as over the food(?)
11 of Seth the rebellious on that day of the storm over the Two Lands.|The Great Ones are brought ⟨to⟩[7] him at the Bend of the Westerners, and they know the god, the equipped and worthy spirit. Men bring to him for the meeting(?)[8] of his needs, men approach him for the quenching(?) of his thirst.

Ho N! Your . . .[9] are opened by Neper, water is measured out to you by the Nile-god, Neith will come[10] to you with her attendants.

Ho N! Your breakfast(?)[11] is fashioned [. . .] up above [. . .] this day.

1. The sky, as in 8*c*.
2. Cf. 8*e*, which has *ʿt m Stš* 'a limb in Seth'.

3. The 2nd person here and in what follows refers to the deceased.

4. Read *mywḥ<mʿwḥ*, see also 12*c.*

5. *Hꜣhꜣt* is not recorded. It could perhaps be a reduplicated fem. of *hꜣw* 'kindred'.

6. Cf. Spell 356, n.4. *Pns-tꜣ* may be a corruption of *Pnʿ-tꜣ* in 10*b*, or *vice versa.*

7. Read *ỉnn.t(w)* ⟨*n*⟩*.f wrw,* cf. 11*c.*

8. Lit. 'numbering', but presumably the needs are numbered in order to be met. The same comment applies to 'thirst' in 11*d.*

9. *Ḏrrw* is untranslatable; the spelling is odd and the det. indecipherable.

10. Prospective *sḏm.f.*

11. *'Iʿʿ* is not recorded, but the dets. suggest a var. of *ỉʿw* 'breakfast'.

Spell 359

[SPELL FOR] HAVING POWER OVER WATER IN THE REALM OF THE DEAD.[1] V, 12
|I am that oar of Rēʿ with which he rows his old ones, and I will not be destroyed nor scorched.[2] I am Babi, the eldest son of Osiris,[3] |who assembled every god 13
within the circuit of his eye in Ōn;[4] I am the heir of Osiris, the despoiler of the Great One[5] who himself grew weary; I have despoiled the Great One[6] who himself grew weary; I have power through him, |and I have taken away the power 14
of the other one[7] from him.

1. At the beginning of this spell TIL[a], which lacks the rubric, inserts 'Ho N! You will not be scorched, for you belong to', or possibly 'you are Rēʿ'.

2. Reading *n ʿḫm.ỉ n nwḫ.ỉ* with B1C and B2L. *ʿwḫ.ỉ* of G1T and A1C appears to be a conflation of *ʿwg* 'be scorched', 12*a,* and of *ʿḫw* 'be over-heated', Dav. *Ptah.* II, 14. In any case a second word for 'scorching' is superfluous.

3. Var. TIL[a]: 'you are that eldest son of Nūt'.

4. A1C interpolates, somewhat superfluously! 'I am the son of Osiris'.

5. *'Ink* of G1T is erroneous; this epithet, as well as that of 13*a,* refers to Babi and not to the deceased, as the following context makes clear.

6. B1C and B2L omit *wr,* perhaps by haplography. The significance of 'despoiling' is that the heir of Osiris takes over all his father's attributes.

7. Presumably Seth, the enemy of Osiris.

Spell 360

BEING INTERRED IN ŌN. These are the oars[1] of Rēʿ with which he rows the old ones, and he will not be flooded, he will not be scorched.[2] I am those oars[3] of Rēʿ with which he rows the old ones.

1. Note the archaic use of the plural *ỉpw* as subject of a sentence with nominal predicate. Middle Egyptian would have used *ḥmw pw* or *ḥmw nn*.

2. 'He' can only refer to Rēʿ.

3. Shown to be plural by the demonstrative *ỉpw* and by the resumptive pronoun *sn* in 14*i*. This clause is repeated by dittograph in 14*h-i*. This is the only instance known to me of *ḥmw* being used of rowing-oars. Here it is parallel to *mʿwḥ* in 12c.

Spell 361

V, 15 HAVING POWER OVER WATER. I am that oar of Rēʿ with which he placated the
16 Beauteous One,[1] which is not wet because of water, which is not scorched because of fire.[2] I am[3] Babi, who has power over water.[4]

1. Var. 'with which he caused the Beauteous One to appear'. After this, B1C and B2C anticipate 16*b*.

2. Cf. *CT* II, 54*j-p*. B1C and B2C invert the order of 15*d* and 16*a*.

3. B4Bo—B1BY omit 'I am' before the god's name, presumably referring back to *ỉnk* in 15*b*.

4. Var. B9C: 'Babi: Who is the one who has power over him?' (see 16*e*), presumably a rhetorical question. The name of the god is written with a sign which combines  and the standing king wearing the White Crown in one ideogram. The rubric in B1C (16*f*) belongs to Spell 387.

Spell 362

V, 17 HAVING POWER OVER WATER, BATHING IN THE FLOOD, BEING INTERRED IN ŌN.[1]
I wash my hands, I appear as Horus, I wash my face,[2] I am exalted in Ombos,[3]
18 I bathe in the pools of Ḥetep;| I have wiped my face with what belongs to him who is at the side of Rēʿ; see, I have appeared as Horus who issued from Gold.[4] Praise is given to me by those who are in the West, and the earth is kissed before
19 me by the sun-folk.| I will not be thirsty, my lips will not be dry, I have quenched my thirst with that great efflux of my father[5] Osiris.
20 I am that oar of Rēʿ[6] with which he rows those old ones who belong to Rēʿ, who are in the horizon,[7] who live on water, who have power over the starry sky,[8]
21 and who quench their thirst with the great efflux of my father Osiris.[9] As for her who is saved today (?), I go down to drink these waters.[10] I will guard[11] the great female falcon on earth, who dwells in Ōn, while Rēʿ stands in the middle of the
22 sky.[12] |He breaks my knife, he splits my shield (?).[13] I will not be thirsty, my lips

will not be dry. I have quenched my thirst with the efflux[14] of my father Osiris. O Isis, [I have quenched] my thirst with the high Nile, with the flood of Osiris.[15]

1. So T1C (in black). B3Bo (in red) omits *wꜥb* 'bathing', and S1oC (in black) contents itself with 'having power over water' and omits everything up to and including 20*b*. In Sq11C the rubric is at the end of the spell.

2. 17*d-f* in Sq11C only. For the 1st person see T1C and B5C.

3. S1oC inserts here: 'I will go down' (*hꜣy.ỉ*).

4. This is the well-known epithet of Ḥatḥōr, whose son Iḥy is sometimes equated with the young Horus. For *ỉsṯ* at the beginning of this clause, Sq11C has *sšw;* after it this text interpolates *wꜥb N pn.* In 18*c* Sq11C inserts 'N is pure'.

5. After *it.ỉ* Sq11C inserts an obscure phrase (19g).

6. B5C here inserts 'with which he placated the Beauteous One' (cf. 15*c*) and follows this with a passage which is nearly all lost, but which the surviving traces show to have read: 'which is not scorched with fire nor wet with water', cf. *CT* II, 54*j-p*.

7. Following S1oC. The other versions have interpreted the fem. collective *ỉꜣwt* 'old ones' as a dual, and all texts except S1oC are confused; even this last has *ẖnn.ỉ* instead of *ẖnn.f.* Why it appends *ḫnt* 'former' to the end of the passage is not clear.

8. Read *ḫꜣbꜣs.*

9. S1oC inserts here: 'I will not be thirsty, my lips will not be dry'.

10. *'Ir myn nḥmt* is quite obscure. At the end of 21*c* read *swr nn n mw.* S1oC is quite incomprehensible: 'As for her who drove her husband away, I go down to the *Sꜣ*-water'.

11. So S1oC, reading *sꜣ.kꜣ⟨.ỉ⟩ r.f.* The other texts have 'I will await', which seems poorer sense; in them *sꜣ* is determined with 𓂻 .

12. For *ỉsṯ* Sq11C has *sr* and B5C has *ỉsš*. S1oC inserts: 'on the bonds of the Outcast.'

13. For *pšn* 'split' B5C has *whn* 'throw down' and S1oC has *snsn,* a reduplicated form of *sn* 'cut off', 'sever'. *Šnṯw* is unknown, but the context suggests that it may refer to a kind of shield. These two clauses appear to have no relevance to the context, and they may be intruders from elsewhere.

14. T1C and B3Bo read *rḏw wr* 'great efflux', and Sq11C has a dittograph of the genitive *n* on passing from line to line.

15. So S1oC, which omits 22*e*.

Spell 363

SPELL FOR[1] 'THE BEAUTIFUL WEST IS JOYFUL AT MEETING THE MAN'. I have V, 23
come to you, O son of Nūt; may you reach Rēꜥ on the day of his festival, while the gods are in mourning, for they have seen the terror of the Broad Hall.[2] May you reach Nūt, may you see the hidden things, may you rescue(?) Shu, may you extend your vision, for they[3] have seen those who are in the limits of the horizon. Those who are in the sky have come[4] to you on the day when

24 the long-horn is lassoed, |while the beautiful West is in joy, for they have seen the limb of the god.[5] Such am I.

1. *Rꜣ n* seems superfluous, cf. 28*c*.
2. Var. B1C: 'the sky'.
3. The gods of 23*d*.
4. So three texts; B2L^{b} has the prospective form *ỉwt*.
5. See Spell 356, n. 5.

Spell 364

I am the uncircumcized one (?)[1] who came forth from Rēʿ, I have issued from between the thighs of the Enneads; Shesmet conceived and bore me.

V, 25 I am the falcon which came forth from Rēʿ, I am the living uraeus which came forth from the Eye of Rēʿ, |I fly up and alight on the bark[2] of Khopri, on the bow of his bark which is in the Abyss.

1. For *ʿmʿ* cf. Piankhi Stela, 150.

2. B2L^{b} has: 'I fly up from the vertex of Khopri in the bow of his bark'; *BD* 148,12 has 'I fly up and alight on the vertex of Rēʿ in the bow of his bark', and what remains of D1C is in accord with this.

Spell 365

V, 26 I have gone down into the land of the Silent One, I have been equipped[1] because of the vulture, I have been vested because of the . . .[2] of the birds, my cloak[3] is on my back, the Great West is he who stretches out my bones and extends my limbs, so that I may walk on my feet like Osiris, my two kites[4] being in the east of the sky. My bones are stretched out and my limbs are extended, and I walk on my feet like Osiris.

1. 1. Read *šṯ.ky* with B2L and B1C rather than *sṯ.n.ỉ*, which would need an object (*wỉ*). For the verb cf. *CT* I, 280*h*.

2. *Ptḫt*, determined with a bird. Meaning not known.

3. From B2L it is probable that the garment  is meant. Since it is on the speaker's back, it is likely that it is a cloak.

4. Isis and Nephthys in bird-form.

Spell 366

My brow is raised up by Shu with his left hand with which he supports the sky. V, 27
If my brow should fall to the ground, then will Nūt's brow fall to the ground.
The soles of my feet are made firm on the earth by Isis, and she makes me firm,
does Isis,[1] on the earth as a living god.[2] | I am raised up[3] by Isis, just as she 28
established her son Horus in the bow of the bark of Rēʿ which he raised up.[4]
THE BEAUTIFUL WEST IS JOYFUL AT MEETING THIS MAN.

1. *ʾIn ꜣst* is omitted in B2L.
2. B2L, B1C and B2P insert here *Wḏʿ* = Seth after *ꜣkr,* but this destroys the sense of the passage. Sq6C, which omits this, gives the obviously correct reading.
3. Var. Sq6C: 'N's brow is raised up'.
4. Sq6C ends with *ṯs.f* as against *nss.f* of the other texts. *Ṯs.f* is the better reading.

Spell 367

SPELL FOR NOT WALKING UPSIDE DOWN. If I am upside down, then will he[1] be V, 29
upside down. | I am a god who lives on men, I am one who goes up from the
Nile. I am a . . .[2] in the tribunal. The Great One stands up, and he does not beg;[3]
I will walk upright, I will not walk upside down.[4]

1. The person or being to whom 'he' refers is not specified. In B2P we read 'I . . . you . . .'; in Sq6C we have absurdly 'N . . . Osiris N . . .'.
2. See de Buck, notes 2*, 4*, and 7*. In three texts the word reads *snt* 'sister', which makes no sense; in the other two an indecipherable sign is used.
3. Var. Sq3C: 'he is [not] afraid'.
4. Sq6C and Sq3C place the rubric at the end of the spell.

Spell 368

'Get back, Faeces!' 'But Faeces is not my name.[1] My name is Rēʿ, my name is V, 30
ʾIḥy, Rēʿ on my[2] two thrones. If you say "Eat this", Rēʿ[3] will eat tortoises'.

1. *Rn.k* yields poor sense and should almost certainly be emended into *rn.ỉ.* If this emendation be accepted, then 30*b-c* will be the rejoinder to the insult of 30*a.*
2. Emending *nsty.f* into the 1st person, as suggested by the omission of the suffix in B2L.
3. B2P has corrupted *wnm.kꜣ Rʿ* into *wnm ꜣkr* 'the earth-god will eat'.

Spell 369

V, 31 Go forth, O snake, at the movements of Shu (?).[1] You have eaten a mouse, which Rēꜥ abominates; you have chewed the bones of a putrid she-cat. DRIVING OFF A SNAKE IN THE REALM OF THE DEAD.

1. 31*a* is unintelligible as it stands, and is evidently a garbled version. *BD* 100,12 has *ỉ rrk m šm mk Gb swỉ* (read *wỉ*) 'O snake, go! Gēb protects me', where *m* is taken to be the particle of *Eg. Gramm.*[3] §250 in its less common use as a non-enclitic. In the *CT* passage *pr* 'go forth' appears to be an imperative addressed to the snake to tell it to go away, so that possibly the archetype may have read: *pr r.k rrk m šmwt Šw*: such a concatenation of *r*'s and *k*'s would invite corruption. *Rrk* is a common word for 'snake' in funerary texts, cf. e.g. *CT* V, 41*c*; *BD* 100,12, which could even have originated in a misunderstanding of the imperative *pr r.k* 'get out!' when addressed to a snake.

Spell 370

V, 32 O *Nk* and *Ḳd*(?)[1], I am indeed *Ḥty* on the night[2] of perishing (?).[3] I am indeed one who comes when summoned,[4] and you shall come to me (prostrate) on your face,[5] your . . .[6] on your left eyebrow, and baldness is what is on it. I am this one who comes of his own accord, and nothing is taken ⟨from me(?)⟩.[7]

'O Shu', says He of Djedu—and *vice versa.* 'Neith is wearing her headcloth, Ḥatḥōr makes Osiris glad,[8] and who is he who will eat him or eat me? You are he whom he placed in the marshlands (?);[9] I do not know who will let me speak'.

33 THE MAN SHOULD RECITE THIS SPELL over it,[10] not letting these snakes eat him in the realm of the dead, but he will eat all these snakes.

1. Both reading and meaning of 32*a* are doubtful, except that it appears to be a vocative addressed to two enigmatic beings. The spell gives the impression of having been made up of a motley of odd sentences culled from various sources without regard to context, like e.g. *BD* Spell 1B.

2. 𓐍 after *grḥ* in B2P is an obvious slip for 𓇳 .

3. Reading simply *tm* with B1C, but the meaning is doubtful.

4. Lit. 'at his summons'.

5. 𓋹𓋹 of B1C is another obvious slip.

6. Meaning unknown.

7. With *ḫ̮ḫ̮mm*, var. *ḫ̮ḫ̮mw*, compare *ỉḫ̮ḫ̮m* 'take away (?)', *Pyr.* §§ 61; 89. At the end perhaps *ỉm.ỉ* may have been omitted by haplography.

8. For *ḫ̮nms* read *ḫ̮nm.s*.

9. 32*l* is certainly corrupt. The simplest emendation is to supply the *m* of predication

after *ỉw.k*, regarding *ddy.f* as a relative form, but even so the sense is quite obscure.

10. Over the written spell?

Spell 371

SPELL FOR EATING BREAD IN THE REALM OF THE DEAD. I have come as Neper, I have stood up as Wepwawet, my plumes are on my head like Min of Coptos, | I V, 34
have entered into the house of Ḥu,[1] what has been given to me is what I require from it.[2]

1. Misread in B1P as *Šw*.
2. Corrupted in B2L into *dbḥt.f wỉ ỉm.f.* In all texts the suffix in *ỉm.f* refers to the 'house' of 34*a*.

Spell 372

O *Hty*, may the tower of 'He arranges (?)[1] the air which restores (?)[2] the nostrils' endure (?). A MAN SHOULD SAY THIS SPELL OVER IT,[3] not letting the snakes eat him in the realm of the dead, but he shall eat all the snakes in the realm of the dead. This is useful and effective (?)[4] for N.

1. 34*c* is incomprehensible to me. No recorded meaning of *sk* seems applicable to the context, and the sense given to it here is a guess based on the known word *skw* 'ranks'. The whole clause beginning with *sk.f* seems to be a noun clause dependent on genitival *n*.
2. The translation of *ỉdn* is doubtful; normally it means the replacement or substitution of a person or article. B1C omits *ỉdn* and reads *sk.f ṯȝw r šrwt* 'he arranges (?) the air for the nostrils'.
3. Over the written spell?
4. For *ỉtp* see also *CT* I, 4*a*; III, 270*d*.

Spell 373

BREATHING AIR AMONG THE WATERS.[1] 'Hidden are the ways for those who pass V, 35
by;[2] light is perished and darkness comes into being'— so says Nephthys.

'Why is it said?'— so says the Outcast.[3]

'*D.f-ȝw*[4] is upon (?) the Outcast . . .[5] It means that the Outcast, the son of Nūt, has fallen on his side and that his breath has been taken away'— so says[6] *D.f-ȝw*, and the arm of Him who rests wearily is uplifted.

The doors of the *ḫns*-water are opened, and the winds pass out; its *Nt*-crowns are parted, and the air goes in. I have gone down in order to present Maꜥet with water, for breath is in my nose; I will go forth[7] and open the Eye of Rēꜥ upon earth, for breath is in my nose. It is the Outcast who speaks to me and informs me that life is provided[8] and that air is breathed among the waters.
36 BREATHING AIR AMONG THE WATERS. THE OFFERING OF THIS WIFE OF HIS IS PUT INTO A NEW BOWL IN THE EARTH, AND THE MAN SHALL TAKE IT[9] ON THE DAY WHEN THE EARTH QUAKES, AND THE MAN SHALL ANOINT HIMSELF WITH IT . . .[10] THE MAN SHALL BREATHE IT.

1. B2L only.
2. B2L omits *wꜣwt* 'ways'.
3. *Wḏꜥ*, i.e. Seth.
4. Lit. 'his hand is extended', apparently an epithet of a god.
5. *Nbḫ*, meaning unknown.
6. As the text stands it makes no sense; it is taken to be a miswriting of *ỉ.ỉn* 'so says', cf. 35*d.f.*
7. The full writing *pry* in B2L suggests the prospective *sḏm.f.*
8. Or possibly 'destroyed'; in B2P the det. is [hieroglyph], but this meaning seems unlikely.
9. The imperfective here stresses the adverbial adjunct.
10. The blank space in 36*d* presumably indicates a lacuna in the scribe's source. Except for the last sentence, I find 36*d-e* incomprehensible, and it is possible that the scribe may have lumped together odd words on loose fragments, some of which may indeed have belonged to this text.

Spell 374

TO BECOME A BULL-SNAKE AND A NꜥW-SNAKE.[1] I am a *nꜥw*-snake, a bull-snake
V, 37 who leads,[2] who swallowed his seven uraei, and his seven neck-vertebrae |came into being;[3] who gave orders to his seven Enneads which hear the word of the monarch.[4] My mother is the Pelican, and I am her son;[5] I have come that I may inhale myrrh[6] and accept myrrh; my nostrils (?)[7] are (full of) myrrh, my finger-nail[8] is (full of) myrrh. I have taken away your divinity, you gods;[9] serve me when I confer your powers.[10] I am Neḥebkau (=He who confers powers).[11]

1. This spell is a copy of *Pyr.* Utt. 318, §§ 511-12, see p. 100 of my translation. For the 1st person, which may have been original, see B2L.
2. Sq1Sq is the best text of the three, and it follows the W-text of the Pyr. B2L and B2P favour the T^1-text but have suffered some garbling.
3. B2L and B2P: 'I became these neck-vertebrae'; the strokes following *nḥbt* indicate

the plural, and are not to be taken as the numeral 'four'.

4. B2L and B2P: 'which these Enneads commanded'; the fem. *wḏt-mdw* can refer back only to *nḥbt.* Sq1Sq has misread  of *ỉtw* as .

5. So B2L and B2P, as T^1; following W, Sq1Sq omits this clause.

6. The clause *ỉꜥm.f ꜥntyw* in Sq1Sq = *Pyr.* §512*a.* B2L and B2P follow T^1 in omitting it.

7. *ꜥny* with snake det. in all three texts, having misunderstood the suffix in *ꜥny.f, Pyr.* §512*b* (W), as a snake-det. B2L and B2P here favour W.

8. Plural in B2L only, probably wrongly, see my translation of *Pyr.* Utt. 318, with n.2. Sq1Sq and B2P agree with W in having the singular.

9. Sq1Sq only, as W, but with *nṯrt* 'divinity' instead of *wsrt* 'power'.

10. Cf. *Pyr.* §512*d.*

11. Not in Pyr. nor Sq1Sq.

Spell 375

NOT EATING A MAN BY A SNAKE IN THE REALM OF THE DEAD. 'O Shu', says He of V, 38
Djedu[1] – and *vice versa.* 'Neith is wearing the head-cloth, Ḥatḥōr cares for[2] Osiris, and who is he who will eat her[3] or will eat me?'

1. This spell repeats 32*h-k.* All three spells 375-7 are included in the single spell *BD* 35.

2. Read *ḫnm.s n* in B2Bo. The usage with the dative is not recorded, but may bear the sense of 'care for', cf. *ḫnmtt* 'nurse', 'attendant'.

3. 32*k* has *sw* 'him' in reference to Osiris; *s* here apparently refers to Ḥatḥōr, and is so translated, but emendation into *sw* 'him' may well be considered.

Spell 376

The bleared eyes[1] of the Great One fall on you and Maꜥet will examine you[2] V, 39
for judgement.

1. The blearing of the eyes of the Great One may be an allusion to the damage done by Seth to the Eye of Horus.

2. For *sypt* of B2Bo and B7Bo read *syp* with M23C.

Spell 377

O lotus-bark,[1] loose me,[2] let me escape[3] – and *vice versa.* O *sksk*-snake which are in your *smꜥ*-plant, beware of the gardener![4] It is Osiris who will demand

V, 40 burial.[1] The fire goes up against Gēb; O you who burn Neḥebkau,[5] the Bull goes forth, the mottled snake is he who shakes (?)[6] for him the bones of [. . .] Beware of the leaper (?).[7]

1. Cf. *sšnt* 'lotus-bark' *CT* VII, 259*a*, with varr., i.e. a vessel with carved or painted lotus-flowers at bow and stern.

2. Read *sn wỉ*. For the verb cf. *sny* with rope-det, *Pyr.* §1100.

3. Restore the det. after *nh* in B2Bo; the sense seems to be an extension of the original meaning 'escape' death, *Pyr.* §1453; *CT* I, 284*g*. *Nht* 'shelter', 'magical protection' is cognate.

4. *Kꜣny;* for the writing cf. *BH* I, 29. So B2Bo and originally S2C; M23C has the apparently meaningless 'beware of the leek', where *ỉꜣḳt* 'leek' is dragged in to provide a pun on *ỉꜣḳ* 'leaper(?)' in 40*d*. Note after *sꜣ* the dependent pronoun *ṯn*, although this is a man's coffin; in 40*d* the text has the correct pronoun *ṯw*.

5. Neḥebkau is a serpent-god, which in a spell against snakes might account for the reference to burning him.

6. Doubtful, but cf. *ꜥꜥw* 'flutter' of the heart, *Eb.* 41, 21; 42, 9.

7. Cf. *ỉꜣḳ* 'leap(?)', *Concise Dict.* 9. In 44*b* below, *ỉꜣḳ* has the snake-det., and the *f*-sign here clearly has the same function. 'Leaper', if that be the correct translation, could refer to the swift stroke of an attacking snake. At this point, where B2Bo comes to an end, S2C and M23C go off into a long but badly damaged variation which seems largely to have repeated what has gone before.

Spell 378

V, 41 To drive off a snake and not to take a man's head from him. O snake, the movements of Shu are what Bastet opened up,[1] and I will not be given to him who eats those things which are cut off.[2] I am Horus,[3] I have come here from the limits of the sky and of the Netherworld, I have passed by the soul-chapel of Ḥatḥōr, on which are fixed the four supports of the sky, I have seen the expulsion[4] of the Destroyer[5] and the destruction of the doubles in the house of those who suffer beatings, and I will tell what I found there.[6]

42 O you snakes, fall[7] on your faces! Their heads shall be cut off and their vertebrae severed. They shall not associate nor unite against me,[8] for I have come that I may expel the Destroyer and destroy the doubles. DRIVING OFF A SNAKE AND DESTROYING THE DOUBLES.[9]

1. A sentence with nominal (relative form *wpt*) predicate.

2. Butcher's offal? At any rate, something ritually unclean.

3. Var. 'the Great One'.

4. T1C has a superfluous *f* in *ḫsf*.

5. B1C has corrupted *nbḏ* 'the Destroyer' into *nb r ḏr* 'the Lord of All'.

6. 41*i-j* is omitted in B1C.

7. The rare fem. imperative, in concord with the fem. collective *ḥfꜣt*.

8. 42*a-c* omitted in T1C.

9. Not in T1C, which has its title in 41*a*. In 38*f-g* is recorded what remains of the title in M23C.

Spell 379

To drive off a snake. Come, raise yourself, O Lord of walls,[1] seek out the Lady of Dep, stir up the living body,[2] | go to and fro in the sight of the plebs, see me V, 43
in your sight as a panther.[3]

Your tail is the bull *nʿw*-snake, your hinder parts are . . .[4] Come to me, O Horus,[5] for your phallus.[6]

May he come.[7]

1. I.e. the occupant of the walled tomb-chamber.

2. Not 'the flesh of the living'; it is the deceased himself who is being roused to activity.

3. Or possibly 'elephant', the det. is noncommital.

4. The deceased speaks. For *pḥwy.k* 'your hinder parts' B1C has *pḥ.k* 'you reach'. I can make nothing of *bsb m wnm*.

5. Corrupt in B3L, which omits 'Come' and the suffix 1st sing. after *n* 'to'.

6. *Sic*, but the allusion is obscure.

7. *Ỉwt* is prospective *sḏm.f* in a wish-clause, 'he' being Horus. B1L and B3L add *ỉm.ỉ* 'as me'.

Spell 380

Be far off, O *ḥty*-falcon; be far off, O *ḥty*-bull. It means . . .[1]

1. This short spell is most obscure. The meaning of *ḥty* (see also 32*b*) escapes me, and I cannot translate 43*j*.

Spell 381

Get back . . . from (?) the sounding-pole.[1] Beware of the leaper (?).[2] | IT MEANS V, 44
DRIVING OFF A SNAKE AND DESTROYING THE DOUBLES. If a man recite this

spell against a snake, it means that it will be driven off.

1. *Tꜣš sn ꜥnḫ* is untranslatable. For *smꜥ* 'sounding-pole' cf. *Pyr.* §1176, *CT* I, 267*f*; V, 147*a*.
2. See above, Spell 377, n. 7.

Spell 382

My father is besouled (?), my mother is . . . ,[1] and the snake is driven off in the realm of the dead.[2] IT MEANS THAT THE SNAKE IS DRIVEN OFF.

1. The translation of *bꜣꜣw* is uncertain and *ppw* in 44*g* is quite obscure.
2. B1L adds *ḥr ỉf(?) N pn* 'from upon the flesh (?) of N'.

Spell 383

V, 45 NOT LETTING THE HEART BE WEARY[1] IN THE REALM OF THE DEAD.[2] 'I am the torch of the Milky Way (?), the gate-keeper of the Double Lion, and a path is prepared for me'.[3]

'Who are you?'[4]

'I am the heron (?), the lotus-bird which is on the limitless plain.'

46 'What do you want?'[5]

'I am going to spear fish in the lakes of the Abyss'.

'Do you know the path on which you should go?'

'As the Sole Lord lives, I know the sky in all its coasts'.[6]

47 'Tell me the particulars[7] of the House of the Double Lion which is there.

'The Mansion of the Double Lion is on the north of the House[8] of the Morning at the House of *Dwn-ꜥnwy*,[9] and I will be there.[10] I see and I know
48 the spell for[11] coming into being; If I wish[12] to be there, I will be there.[13] I have asked of my father the Sole Lord[14] that I may eat with my mouth and defecate with my hinder parts'.

'Come, betake yourself to the god'.[15]

1. Var. B1Bo: 'not letting a man's heart sit down'.
2. After the rubric G1T adds in black '(but) to be alive in the West'.
3. So B1Bo and B4C only.
4. For this interpretation of the enigmatic 45*f*, see de Buck, *Archiv Orientálni*, 20, 399.

5. Lit. 'you are for what?'; *sb* is a hitherto unrecorded fuller writing of the interrogative normally read as *sy*; cf. also *CT VI*, 57*f*; 338*q*; Spell 397, n. 40.

6. T3L adds *m sb(ꜣ)t.s nb* 'in all its stars' in an abnormal writing.

7. *Šsꜣw ỉpn* 'diese Anweisungen', *Wb.* IV, 544,14. The demonstrative, as often, plays the part of the definite article.

8. B1Bo omits *pr* 'house'.

9. Var. B1Bo: 'at the side of *Dwn-ꜥnwy*'. Note that A1C and T3L write the name of the god with the falcon with closed wings. B4C omits the reference to this god.

10. *Wn.ỉ* possibly a slip for *wnn.ỉ*, cf. 48*a*.

11. Reading *rꜣ n* with B1Bo; it makes better sense than *rn n* of the other texts. A1C has combined both readings.

12. Three texts have the infinitive *mrt,* while T3L has the *sḏm.f* form; in either version the sense is much the same.

13. In B1Bo only, but the clause is needed. Probably the omission in the other texts is due to avoiding a repetition which looked like a dittograph.

14. So B1Bo; G1T and T3L have *nb šmꜥw* 'Lord of Upper Egypt'; A1C has *nb šmsw* 'Lord of the Suite'.

15. The interrogator of the deceased is now satisfied and lets him pass on his way. The imperative *m ir.k sḏꜣ ṯw n* 'Come and betake yourself to' gives a better sense than *mk sꜣw n* 'See, wait for' of B1Bo.

Spell 384

NOT TO TAKE A MAN'S SOUL FROM HIM. O Mighty One, go, speak to him who V, 49
sent you,[1] because[2] my utterance is indeed more powerful than his knife.[3] O you
whose movements are vigorous(?),[4] says the angry one whose names are wide-
spread(?),[5] | take possession of your soul, arrest him who would rob you; make 50
acclamation and come for me; let me not assign you[6] to your mother who is over[7]
the Mansion of the Two Sisters. She who is attached to you has taken possession
of you in my presence(?).[8] | Your blood is drunk among those who rage; tread on 51
the earth, for I have spoken your name; I was primeval before you came into
being(?)[9] ⟨in?⟩ [10]this your name of 'Swallower'.[11] O you who carry off the powers
of the elders, do not take away my power,| but have respect for my soul. Behold 52
my magic power! My sacrificial bulls are within the holy places,[12] the remem-
brance of me is yours. I am an Upper Egyptian(?) and the plume of the standard
is by me(?).[13]

1. B6C adds *r N pn* 'for N'. This is a difficult spell, and the first part of it is most obscure.

2. B4C introduces 49*c* with *ntt,* presumably for *n ntt.*

3. Apparently the deceased is sending *Sḫm* back to 'him who sent him' with a message of defiance.

4. Lit. perhaps 'O you who are mighty in movements'.

5. Translation by no means certain; at the end *rnw* 'names' of B6C is certainly to be preferred to *rn.n* 'our name(s)' of B2Bo and B4Bo, because there is no antecedent for the suffix.

6. Reading *ỉm.ỉ sypw* as B6C etc.; S2C has the affirmative *syp.ỉ* 'that I may assign you', which in fact would seem the more probable reading if it were not in a minority of one to four.

7. Read *ḥrt ḥwt* with S2C; in B6C–B4Bo the *-t* of *ḥrt* has been omitted by assimilation in the script with the *-t* of *ḥwt*. B4C has *ḥrt-ỉb ḥwt* 'who dwells in the Mansion'.

8. *'Irt.k* is certainly the subject of *ḫnp.n,* but the word-order is abnormal and the meaning obscure. The suffix in *gs.k* must be emended to the 1st person.

9. 51*d* in B6C–B1Y is quite obscure. The meaning of *pꜣt.k* is itself uncertain, for the word is written like that for 'offering-cake', *Pyr.* §§34, 35, and it is followed by *ny.ỉ ḫprt.k* or *N (pꜣt ky n.ỉ* in B2Bo), which is unintelligible. I know of no instance where the negations *n* or *ny* are followed by a suffix pronoun. The explanation may well be that we have here a corruption of *pꜣy.ỉ n ḫprt.k* 'I was primeval before you came into existence', see the damaged texts of S2C and B4C.

10. *Rn.k pw* of 51*e* suggests that *m* may have been omitted before *rn.* B4C has simply *ꜥm.k* by itself.

11. The speech of 'the angry one' seems to end here.

12. Reading *m-ẖnw ḏsrw* with S2C and B4C; in B6C–B4Bo [hieroglyphs] is probably a miswriting of *dsr.*

13. The translation of 52*e* is very doubtful. B4C is certainly corrupt.

Spell 385

V, 53 I am purified with natron, I have lain down in *Sꜣṯw*[1] as one who is favoured thereby in sky and earth. Hearken!

1. Hardly *sꜣṯw* 'ground', since all texts show the town-det.

Spell 386

CROSSING THE RIVER AS AN IBIS. I have flown up as an ibis, I have surpassed my limit of height(?)[1] so that I might see *Dꜣfy(?)* the son of Ḥatḥōr.

1. *Sḳꜣy* lit. 'my making high'. The sense appears to be something like 'I have soared into the empyrean'.

Spell 387

NOT TAKING A MAN'S HEART FROM HIM IN THE REALM OF THE DEAD.[1] Get back, V, 54
you messenger of any god![2] Have you come to take away this heart of mine
| which belongs to the living? I will not give this heart of mine to a stranger.[3] 55
The gods have judged the blessed ones,[4] | and they fall flat(?)[5] on their faces. 56

1. Two minor varr. B3L and B4C have the rubric at the end, and B1C inserts it at the end of Spell 361.

2. T1C has *n.ỉ nṯr* for *n nṯr*; for 'any god' B1C and B2L have the plural 'all the gods'.

3. So B9C; for *ḫpp* 'strange' cf. *GAS* 97. T1L and B3L have the plural 'strangers', so also T1C, which reads simply *m ḫppw*. S14C, B1C and B2L have substituted *ḫpw* 'those who have gone' = 'the dead' for *ḫppw*; S14C reads: 'I will not give you this heart of mine which belongs to the living and the dead'; B1C and B2L have inserted *nb* between *ꜥnḫw* and *ḫpw*.

4. For this usage of *sḏm* with direct object of the person cf. *Wb.* IV, 386,10; for *ḥtptyw* 'the blessed' cf. *Pyr.* §910; *D. el B.* IV, 114. T1C reads: 'I judge the gods of the offerings', which does not make sense, while B1C and B2L read, quite corruptly: 'who control the god's-offerings' with *ḫpw* as apparent antecedent. S14C has *ḥtpw* without det. for *ḥtptyw*.

5. The final word *ṯmṯmy* is unrecorded, and my translation 'flat(?)' is a guess. S14C–B2L show varying degrees of corruption; *ṯmṯmy* of B9C–B3L was clearly as obscure to them as to us.

Spell 388

NOT TAKING A MAN'S HEART FROM HIM. O Lion, I am the Hare; the shambles of V, 57
the god is what I abhor, | and this heart of mine shall not be taken to him who 58
fights against Ōn.[1]

1. The preposition before *ʾIwnw* is omitted in M22C, B4Bo[a], and B1Bo, while B2Bo[a] omits both the preposition and . B2L has *smsw ʾIwnw* 'the Elder of Ōn', while M6C reads: 'this heart of mine shall not be taken from me'. Before 58*b* B1Bo inserts (58*a*): 'this heart of mine shall not be taken to the shambles of the god'.

Spell 389

NOT TO ENTER INTO THE SHAMBLES OF THE GOD.[1] I am the Lion;[2] entering V, 59
into the shambles of the god is what I abhor. The leg[3] is covered, is covered;
guard it! The leg is covered, and what they have found, they will bury.[4]

1. 'Of the god' omitted in B2Bo, which writes the heading twice.

2. Varr. 'Anubis' (B2Bo, B4Bo); 'Seth' (S10C). On the writing in Y1C see de Buck's note 1*.

3. On *ḫnd* see *AEO* I, 17–18.

4. Is this an allusion to the burial of a dismembered leg of Osiris? All texts omit the resumptive object-pronoun after *ḳrs.sn,* but it is difficult to see how else to interpret 59*g*.

Spell 390

V, 60 NOT TAKING A MAN'S HEAD FROM HIM.[1] I am a Great One, the son of a Great
61 One; I am He of the *nsr*-shrine, son of Him of the *nsr*-shrine,[2] | to whom was
62 given his head after it had been cut off. His head was not taken from him after
64 he was decapitated,[3] and my head shall not be taken from me | after it has been cut off.[4]

1. Ḳ1T: 'Giving a man's head to him'.

2. None of the varr. are important, except that B3L has simply 'son of Him of the *nsr*', without context.

3. T1C ^{a} ff. omit the negation *n* before *nḥm,* doubtless originally a case of haplography, but an error which, once committed, was perpetuated by later copyists.

4. B2L adds: 'I am an equipped spirit'; similarly B1C ^{c}.

Spell 391

V, 65 SPELL FOR BEING INTERRED IN ŌN.[1] I am this one who belongs to *Šȝyt,*[2] one who acts as pilot in the *ỉwt*-bark of the Great Ones,[3] thrusting aside[4] those who are in the horizon on that night of stopping[5] movements.

1. M2NY has a minor var. of this rubric at the end of the spell.

2. Var. *Mnwy* T1C ^{b}. The meaning of neither word is known, but they appear to be names of divinities.

3. The *m* which precedes *sšm* in T1C ^{b}, T1L and M2NY appears to be the *m* of equivalence, referring back to *ỉnk*. P. Gard. II refers this clause to *šȝyt* with the fem. *ḏȝt,* reading: 'who ferried over as pilot(?) (*sš* for *sšm*?) in the *ỉwt*-bark of the Great Ones'.

4. For *snwḏ* 'thrust aside' cf. *BD* 138,12.

5. Or 'averting'.

Spell 392

V, 66 NOT TAKING A MAN'S MAGIC POWER FROM HIM IN THE REALM OF THE DEAD.[1] O you straightforward ones, you of the mounds, you mighty ones; O you son of the sailor, make your rope fast,[2] for I have come to you, I have broken your pens, I have torn up your papers because of this double ill which you have worked[3] against me because of my affairs. My head has been brought to me, my bones[4] have been gathered together, my members have been made hale for me, and my great magic power has been brought to me with it,[5] I being hale;[6] the offerings for the mouth have been made again, the hair has been put together.[7]

1. The final qualification is omitted in B2C[a]. B1C has: 'Not taking a man's head from him' at the end of the spell, but see de Buck's n.3*.

2. On *hy (m) nwḥ* see *JEA* 57,202. Another instance not quoted there, beside the present one, is *CT IV,* 15*e*.

3. Var. 'said and worked.'

4. Var. *k3w.i* 'my powers', but *ḳsw* 'bones' is more likely to be the original reading as the semantic object of *s3ḳ*.

5. This appears to be where the original spell came to an end, but B1C continues as in the translation above. The reference of the suffix in *ḥnʿ.f* is uncertain, but it may possibly go back to the 'bringing' of the head in 66*i*.

6. Emending into *sḏ3(w),* old perfective 3rd sing.; B1C is in the 3rd person throughout, but the 1st person has been retained in the translation for the sake of continuity.

7. The following *iʿnw n.k* appears to be a dittograph of the first words of Spell 452, see de Buck's n.2*. On the rubric in 66*n* see n. 1 above.

Spell 393

The Bull of . . .[1] is caught in the presence of Him who is in his . . .[2] at the front of the northern sky. I receive the fillet in the Winding Waterway, I am inducted into the House of *Bḥw* on the Bank of the *3hrw,* I judge the Entourage in the Ennead(?)[3] as when the Warm One(?)[4] goes in and as when the Warm One(?) goes out. V, 67

1. I can neither read nor interpret this group, but the det. suggests a celestial being. All this spell is most obscure.

2. *Wnd.f* or *wndn.f* is equally untranslatable.

3. Or 'as the Shining Ones'.

4. Cf. the det. in B2L[b]. Who this being may be is quite uncertain, but the epithet could perhaps refer to the revivified Osiris, warm with new life. An allusion to the sun-god is also a possibility.

Spell 394

NOT TAKING A MAN'S HEAD FROM HIM. My blood is drunk, (even) my redness.[1]

1. *Dšrw,* another name for blood. It appears to be in apposition to *snf.*

Spell 395

V, 68 SPELL FOR GOING ABOARD THE LOTUS-BARK.[1] 'O Soul of Shu,[2] open to me!'

'Where are you going?'[3]

'I am going to *Wrs.*[4] Open to me!'[5]

'Who are you? You are . . . Where ⟨did you come into being?'⟩[6]

69 'I am one of you'.[7]

'Who are those who are with you?'[8]

'They are the two black storks;[9] open to me!'

70 'Before whom do you go?'[10]

'I go before him who is near the Milky Way(?),[11] and the seated one rejoices(?)[12] . He it is who will have me ferried over[13] to the Mansion of the Ibis-faced ones:[14] I know the name of her ferryman'.[15]

71 'I ask for the name of the ferryman'.[16]

' "He who is wary"[17] is the name of her ferryman, and "The Two Baboons" is the name of her steering-oars'.[18]

'I ask for the name of her rowing-oars'.

' "The Two Locks of Hair" is the name of her rowing-oars'.[19]

'I ask for the name of her bow-warp'.

' "The Two Wakeful Ones"[20] is the name of her bow-warp'.

72 'Where are you making for?'[21]

'To cross over, to put myself in the lotus-bark.[22]

'Why?'[23]

'To give to myself *šns*-bread and a jug of milk'.[24]

73 'Open to him, for he knows us'.[25]

⟨ TO BE SAID ⟩ BY A MAN IN THE REALM OF THE DEAD.[26]

1. Var. 'Spell for fetching a ferry-boat'. What follows is a dialogue between the Soul of Shu and the deceased, who needs a boat to cross to the Beyond.

2. Following B2L[b.c.] There are many omissions in the parallel versions; thus B9C begins at 68*d* and omits 68*e-i*, while all the other parallel texts except L1Li start at 68*j*. This last text starts at 68*h* but is damaged; it can be restored as 'Open [to me! So say] the spirits who are in the realm of the dead'. This latter sentence is repeated in 69*e.j*.

3. Lit. 'You are for where?'

4. The region *Wrs* is unidentified.

5. Here L1Li begins.

6. *ʾIbw* in 68*k* is quite obscure, and this passage, present in all texts except L1Li, is untranslatable. L1Li omits both 68*k* and 69*a*, and de Buck points out that the passage in this text corresponding to 68*k* is the damaged 69*b*, which indicates that *ḫpr.n.k* should be supplied after *ʾỉbw* in 68*k*.

7. 69*a* is unintelligible as it stands, but *ỉm ṯn* in three texts shows that this is a corrupt version of *ỉnk wꜥ ỉm.ṯn* 'I am one of you', L1Li's answer in 69*d* to the question 'Where did [you] come into being?' This text continues with the sentence 'so say the spirits', etc., quoted above in n.2.

8. All texts except L1Li and B5C have the fem. *ntt,* anticipating *mrwrwty* (fem. dual) in 69*h*; L1Li has *nty* and B5C corruptly *ntk. Ḥnꜥ.ỉ* of three texts is in error.

9. The *mrwrwt*-bird (*mrwryt* at Beni Hasan) is identified by Mrs. N. de G. Davies as the black stork, *JEA* 35, 16; Pl. 2. L1Li determines the word with two *nṯr*-signs, omits 69*i* and inserts 69*j*: 'so say the spirits', etc.

10. Var. B9C: *ỉr.k ỉr.f tp m m* 'For whom are you making?'.

11. So B1C–B2L^{a}; B9C and L1Li omit the initial *rwy,* as B2L$^{b.c.}$, but these two last read simply 'before *Tkš*' with an obscure det., cf. 197*f* (B5C) and *JEA* 58,109.

12. Only in B1C–B9C. For *rnn* 'rejoice' cf. *GNS* 37.

13. So B2L$^{b.c}$; B1C and B2L^{a} have corrupted *ntf rdy.f* into *ntf rn.f,* while B5C has *ntf rnn.k.* B9C has turned this passage into a question: [*n*] *tf dd.f ḏꜣ.ỉ r ṯn* 'Where will he have me ferry over to?'; L1Li reads: 'He will cause me to ferry over'.

14. For *gm* 'ibis' cf. *Adm.* 2, 8; for the fem. *gmt* and the identification of the bird as the black ibis see *Eg. Gramm.*[3] Sign-list G 28. B1C and B2L^{a} have misread the ibis *gm* as the cormorant *ꜥḳ* and thus have made nonsense of the name of the mansion.

15. In B2L$^{b.c}$ only. Note the use of the fem. suffix after *mḫnty* to agree with the unmentioned *mḫnt* 'ferry-boat'.

16. In 71*a* B9C interpolates *šn*⟨.*ỉ*⟩ *r rn n mḫnty* 'I ask for the name of the ferryman'. This could well have been present in the archetype; so too 71*d.f.*

17. For this sense of *sꜣḳ* cf. *Mill.* 1, 3; *Les.* 80, 19. B1C–B2L^{a} have *mḫnt.f* 'his ferry-boat' for the correct *mḫnty.s* 'her ferryman'; L1Li omits the suffix, as also B9C.

18. The dual *bnty* 'two baboons' shows that two baboon-topped steering-oars are envisaged; pairs of such oars are common on ceremonial boats, cf. e.g. the frontispiece to *Cat. Egn. Antiq. Brit. Mus.* II: *Wooden Model Boats,* where the steering-oars are falcon-headed; see also Pl. XII, no. 30, where a pair of such oars have jackal-heads.

19. The projecting banks of oars on either side of a boat are likened in B2L$^{b.c}$ and B9C to spreads of hair. *Nšy šn* in L1Li may be a corruption of a double writing of *šn* to indicate the dual, while *wšy* of B1C–B2L^{a} means 'him whose hair has fallen out'(!), perhaps in allusion to the resemblance of the oars to scanty straggling locks. Note that four texts have the masculine suffix, '*his* oars'.

20. So L1Li, almost certainly corruptly, since it is hard to see the connection of 'the two wakeful ones' with a rope; in the other texts complete confusion reigns as regards the name of the warp. Here also B1C–B2L^{a} have *ḥꜣtt.f*; B2L$^{b.c}$ have correctly *ḥꜣtt.s,* while L1Li omits the suffix. This last text is alone in adding in 71*h*: '*Ḏwstt* is the name of her steering-oar', and in 72*a*: ' "Exact and accurate" is the name of her bailer and also her. . .'. These two epithets would be more appropriate to the steering-oar than the bailer, and it seems certain that some confusion has occurred. I suspect that 71*h* and 72*a-b* were not present in the archetype of this spell.

21. 72*c* is in B9c only, but probably it is original, as it supplies the question to which 72*d.e* is the answer.

22. No two texts are exactly alike, but most show corruptions of *ssn̆* 'lotus-bark' in B2L^{c}. L1Li is completely garbled.

23. Again B9C only.

24. *M ỉrytt* of B2L^{b} is obviously corrupt. B2L^{c}–B9C are essentially in agreement, except that *ds* in B2L^{c} is superfluous. L1Li has its own version; 'so that there may be given (*r rdy.t(w)*) a jug of milk and this *šns* of meat to N in the temple of Anubis'.

25. B9C only.

26. So B2L^{b}, omitting *ḏd*. B2L^{a} has: 'Bringing a ferry-boat'.

Spell 396[1]

V, 73 'O you who can count,[2] may you not go down, for you are young. Count your fingers [for] me[3] [. . .][4] one, the second, my companion who is before me. He has torn out and ejected for himself what was to be ejected(?),[5] he has awakened him who slept(?)[6] on the north of the Oldest One'.[7]

'O Ferryman, bring Horus to me for his Eye and the Outcast to me for his testicles; there leaps up the Eye of Horus which fell in yonder eastern side ⟨of the sky⟩,[8] and there rise on high the wings of Thoth which fell in yonder eastern side of the sky. O Maḥaf,[9] awaken ⌈Aḳen[10] for me and bring me this,[11]⌈for see, I

74 have come'.

'Who are you?[12]

'I am a magician'.

'Whence have you come?'

'I have come from the Island of Fire'.

'What has happened? . . .'[13]

'The shades stand, the ribs(?)[14] of the boat are broken,[15] pleasing . . . the sound of my affairs(?).[16] O Maḥaf, awaken ⌈Aḳen, so that he may bring me this, as you are endowed with life. See, I am a Great One, and I have come'.

'Who are you?'

'I am a magician'.

'Who is concerned with her, the [. . .]-boat?'

'She is put together for me . . . darkness, but not going about in it(?)'.[17]

'She is taken to pieces [. . .] she [has no] "reeds"[18] or finials(?),[19] she has no oar-loops(?) or lacings(?),[20] she has no *mrkt*,[21] she has no *ḫsf*,[22] she has no decking(?)[23] or ribs(?).

'Bring me her mast-crutch,[24] for the "reeds" are the bands(?) [which are under(?)] the bright hair of Seth; her finials(?) are the slaver which is on the lips of Babi, her oar-loops(?) are the hands of the magic image of the Great One who guides them; her cable(?) is the backbone of Him who is in the sunshine; her *mḫsf*[25] is the sweat(?)[26] of the ribs of Babi, her decking(?) is . . .'[27]

1. This spell represents in a shorter variant form the dialogue, much more fully developed in Spell 397, between the dead man who needs a boat to ferry him over the Winding Waterway and the ferryman Maḥaf who is reluctant to provide one.

2. *Ṯn* in this epithet is taken to have the same root meaning as *ṯn* 'count' in 73*f-g*, where there is certainly an allusion to the finger-counting riddle(?), on which see Sethe, 'Ein altägyptischen Fingerzählreim' in *ZÄS* 54, 16; Gunn, 'Fingernumbering in the Pyramid Texts' in *ZÄS* 57, 71. Cf. *CT* V, 115*h* ff. The ferryman Maḥaf is speaking.

3. Restoring *n* in the lacuna after *ṯn*; the presence of *r.k* suggests that *ṯn* may be an imperative.

4. On the analogy of 115*h* one would expect the lacuna after *dbꜥw.k* to have read *ỉṯ n.k*, imperative with reinforcing reflexive dative, as there is sufficient space, but de Buck's positive identification of in the middle of the lacuna (n.4*) precludes this restoration. I can suggest no alternative.

5. The jingle *fd.n.f wd.n.f n.f wd.n.f n.f wdyt* seems unintelligible. The second *wd.n.f n.f* may well be a dittograph, while *wdyt* at the end of 73*h* has the look of a passive participle, but even so the translation offered is merely a guess. 'He' is presumably the 'companion' of 73*g*.

6. Reading *sḏrr* on the assumption that is an error for . Compare 73*n* and the demands for the awakening of ꜥAḳen in Sp. 397.

7. The three words *m mḥty smsw* have been translated literally, but they make such poor sense that it seems almost certain that something has been omitted before *smsw*.

8. Cf. 76*a-c*. The text has omitted *n pt* 'of the sky' at the end of 73*l*.

9. The ferryman. The *n* which here exceptionally follows *mꜣ* in this name is presumably that which occasionally appears in writings of the stem *mꜣꜣ* 'see', cf. *Eg. Gramm.*[3] §§299. 439. 448.

10. 'Aḳen is the custodian of the ferry-boat, see Spell 397, *passim*. He occurs already in *CT* IV, 360*a*; 367*f* (misspelled in one text).

11. The regular form of request for a boat in funerary texts.

12. On the interpretation of this group, see de Buck, *Archiv Orientální*, 20, 399.

13. *Ỉw r.k ꜥwꜣ* seems to be a comment by the questioner, but I can make nothing of it. What follows is presumably the answer to the question.

14. The word *wg* in 74*g* may be identical with *wgyw*, lit. 'jaws', of 134*b*; var. *wgꜣyw n ỉmyw ḥtw.s* 'the jaws of what is in her timbers', *BD* 206, 14–15. This indicates that the 'jaws' are part of the woodwork of the hull, perhaps a framework of ribs round it. The description of the *wgyw* in 134*b* as 'the ribs of Nephthys' certainly suggests that they radiate from a central timber just as the ribs spring from the breastbone. But that central timber is not a kelson, which was not known to the Egyptians.

15. Or 'counted'; either interpretation is possible.

16. I can make nothing of *hry rn ḫrw ḫt.ỉ*.

17. I do not understand these last two clauses. What follows in 74*q* appears to be spoken by Maḥaf, cf. 84*a*.

18. I.e. the bundles of reeds with which the primitive canoe was built, used here perhaps as a figurative term for the planking of the hull. It is clear from the next spell that a sophisticated type of boat was envisaged. Cf. 85*c* ff.; the ferryman is trying to make out that the boat is not in a serviceable condition.

19. *Šꜣ* with plant-det. probably refers in a similar manner to the bow- and stern-pieces, representing the ends of the reeds lashed together at either end of the boat; cf. *šꜣy* 'bundle', *Westc.* 12, 17.

20. *Dḥꜥw,* lit. 'leathers', may well be leather grommets used as rowlocks; in 74*q* they are likened to hands, perhaps because they 'hold' the oars. *Mdꜣm,* with skin-det. here and rope-det. in 129*a*, may be leather lacing for the hull; in VI, 39*o* it has both determinatives.

21. *Mkrt* is unrecorded, but cf. the late word *mkr* 'Art Schiff', *Wb.* II, 163, 2.

22. Unidentified.

23. *Pd* 'decking(?)' may possibly have a similar derivation to *pḏt* 'celestial expanse', *Pyr.* §§393; 801; 1443. On *wg* see n. 14 above.

24. Apparently a forked rest to support the mast when lowered. Here the deceased is speaking again.

25. Written *mḫsf* here, *ḫsf* in 74*t*.

26. Note the det., but cf. 88*a* and n. 18 thereon.

27. Reading *pd.s* as 74*u*; otherwise the word is meaningless. The spell breaks off here.

Spell 397

V, 75 SPELL FOR BRINGING A FERRY-BOAT IN THE REALM OF THE DEAD.[1] 'O Ferryman, bring me this; bring Horus to me for his Eye, bring Seth to me for his testicles.[2] There leaps up[3] the Eye of Horus which fell in the eastern side of the
77 sky | so that it may protect itself from Seth. O Maḥaf, awaken ꜥAḳen for me, as you are endowed with life;[4] see, I have come'.

'Who are you who have come?'[5]

79 'I am one beloved of my father, whom my father greatly loves. | I am he who awoke my sleeping father.[6] O Maḥaf, awaken ꜥAḳen for me, as you are endowed with life; see, I have come'.[7]

'Do you say that you would cross to the eastern side of the sky?[8] If you cross, what will you do?'[9]

81 'I will lift up his head, | I will raise his brow, so that he may make a decree for you,[10] and the decree which he will make for you shall not perish nor become void in this land for ever. O Maḥaf, awaken ꜥAḳen for me, as you are endowed with life; see, I have come'.

83 'Why should I awaken ꜥAḳen for you?'

'So that he may bring[11] me this boat[12] which Khnum put together from

out of the Lake of the shanks; she has been taken to pieces and placed in the
dockyard. | Take her starboard side and fix it to her bow; | take her larboard side[13] 85
and fix it to her stern'. [14]

'But she has no "reeds", she has no finials(?), she has no *ḫsfw*, she has no
oar-loops(?)'. [15] 86

'Her finials(?) are the tuft which is on the tail of Seth; [16] her "reeds" are 87
the slaver(?) [17] which is on the mouth of Babi; her *ḫsf* is the sweat(?) [18] which is
on the ribs of Babi; her oar-loops(?) [19] are the hands of the magic image of Horus
who made her. [20] It is the Eye of Horus [21] which will guide her to me. [22] O Maḥaf, 89
awaken ᶜAḳen for me, as you are endowed with life; see, I have come'.

'Who will guard this boat for us?'

'Fetch the tail of the *snmmty*-animal [23] and put it in her stern. | It will 90
guard her. O Maḥaf, awaken ᶜAḳen for me, as you are endowed with life;
see, I have come'.

'Who shall bring her and me to you?' [24]

'Bring her to me with the best of the gods, [25] (namely) | Imsety, Ḥapy,
Duamūtef, Ḳebḥsenuf, and he will command her, [26] the *ttwy* being placed in her 91
bow, and he shall steer her to the place where you are'. [27]

'What is she?' [28]

'She is the wings of the *ttwy*'.

'The weather is windy and she has no mast'. 92

'Fetch the phallus of Babi which creates children and begets calves'.

'To what shall I fasten it?'

'To the haunches which separate the shanks'. [29]

'(What about) her cable?' [30] 93

'It is the *nᶜw*-serpent which is in the hand of Ḥemen'. [31]

'Where shall I put it?'

'Put it in her bilge-water'. [32]

'(What about) her sail?

'It is the cloth which issued from the *swtyw*, [33] which Horus and the 94
Ombite [34] kissed on New Year's Day'.

'(What about) her gunwales(?) [35]

'They are the sinews of him of whom all these [36] are afraid.

'Who is he of whom all these are afraid?' [37]

'It is this one [38] who is alive on the night of New Year's Eve. | O Maḥaf, 95
awaken ᶜAḳen for me, as you are endowed with life; see, I have come'.

'Who are you who have come?'

'I am a magician'. [39]

'In what manner have you come?[40] In what manner have you gone up?'

96 'I have gone up upon those . . .'[41]

'What have you done for her?'[42]

'I have trodden on her spine,[43] I have directed her . . .[44] aright'.

'What else have you done for her?'

97 'My right is toward her starboard,[45] my left is toward her larboard,[46] my
front is toward her bow,[47] and my back is toward her stern'.

'What else have you done for her?'

'In the night her bulls were slaughtered and her geese cut up.'[48]

98 'Who stands upon her?'

'It is Horus of the rulers'.[49]

'Who takes her cordage?'[50]

'He who is before the oldest ruler'.

'Who controls her bowls?'

'It is Horus of the rulers'.[51]

'What else have you done for her?'

99 'I went to Min of Coptos and Anubis the Controller of the Two Lands.
I found them[52] celebrating their festivals and reaping their emmer, and the ears
100 of corn . . .[53] with their sickles between their thighs, | and I will make[54] loaves
for you therefrom. The Ascender directed me to the Ascendress,[55] The Mistress[56]
of Pe directed me to the Mistress of Netjru,[57] to the gods who are in front of
their houses. I found them washing their headcloths; | they will come bearing
101 the loaves of the gods, and they will make loaves for you when going down-
stream and round cakes when going upstream. O Maḥaf, awaken ⸢Aḳen for me,
as you are endowed with life; see, I have come'.

102 'Who are you who have come?'

'I am a magician'.

'Are you complete?'

'I am complete'.

'Are you equipped?'

'I am equipped'.

'Have the limbs been restored for you?'

'The limbs have been restored for me'.

103 'What are those two limbs?'[58]

'They are the arm[59] and the leg.[60] . . .[61]

'Do you say that you would ferry over to the eastern side of the sky? If you ferry over, what will you do?'[62]

104 'I will rule the towns, | I will govern the villages, I will know the rich and

give to the poor,[63] I will make[64] loaves for you when going downstream and
round cakes when going upstream . . .[65] O Maḥaf, awaken ʿAḳen for me, as
you are endowed with life; see, I have come'.

'(As for) this which you say, that you would ferry over to the eastern side
of the sky,[66] | if you ferry over, [what will you do?][67] Do you know the path on 105
which you must go, O magician?'[68]

'I know the path on which I must go'.[69]

'What is the path on which one must go?'[70]

'It is "Power of the Earth",[71] I will go to the Field of Rushes'.

'Who will guide you?'

'It is the Royal Twins[72] who will guide me'.

'Who will tell your name to this august god?' 106

'It is the Announcer,[73] that eldest brother of Sokar. O Maḥaf, awaken ʿAḳen
for me, as you are endowed with life; see, I have come'.

'He will not wake for me'.

'Say to him: "O vulture-god,[74] I will build up your courtyard,[75] I will smash 107
your box, I will break your pens, I will tear up your papers, for my face is that of
Nu;[76] if I see, Shu will see, and if I hear, Shu will hear. I will give orders to the
Imperishable Stars, and it will be well with me on earth" '.[77]

'What is it?' says ʿAḳen, 'I was asleep'. 108

'O ʿAḳen, bring me this,[78] as you are endowed with life; see, I have come'.

'Who are you who have come?'

'I am a magician'.

'Are you complete?'

'I am complete'.

'Are you equipped?'

'I am equipped'.

'Have the limbs been restored for you?'

'The limbs have been restored for me'.

'What are the limbs?'[79] 109

'They are the arm and the leg . . .[80] O ʿAḳen, bring me this, as you are
endowed with life; see, I have come'.

'Have you power over what is not brought to you,[81] O Magician, namely
this boat?[82] She has no bailer'.

'Bring me that . . .[83] of Khnum which brings to life what is in her; | put it 110
in her.[84] O ʿAḳen, bring me this, as you are endowed with life; see, I have come'.

'Have you power over what is not brought to you, O magician, namely
this boat? She has no spars(?)'.

'What is missing from her?' [85]

111 'She has no beams, | she has no rigging, she has no mooring-post, she has no warps'. [86]

'Go to that god who knows you [87] and all that you would mention to him in respect of her spars(?), and what he has given to you will come'.

'Who is that god who knows me [88] and all that I would mention to him in respect of her spars(?), and what he has given to me will come?'. [89]

112 'He is Horus with whom is a seal-ring. | O ʿAḳen, bring me this, as you are endowed with life; see I have come'.

'Have you power over what is not brought to you, O magician, namely this boat? She has no cable'.

'Fetch that *nʿw*-snake which is with the Controller of the Two Lands [90] and put it in her, with its head in your hand and its hinder-part in my hand,
113 | and we must pull it tight between us ⟨in⟩ its name of 'Pain(?)' ⟨. . .⟩ the lakes which are in those two towns. [91] The river is in good order(?) [92] and the *ḥtpt*-waterway is in good order(?) at that river. [93] O ʿAḳen, bring me this, as you are endowed with life; see, I have come.

'What are those two towns, O magician(?)'

'They are the horizon(?) and the malachite-place, or so I believe'.

114 'You know those two towns, O magician?' [94]

'I know'.

'What are those two towns, O magician?'

'They are the Netherworld and the Field of Rushes. O ʿAḳen, bring me this, as you are endowed with life; see, I have come'.

115 'Have [95] you power over what is not [96] brought to you, O magician? | (As for) what you have said, that you would ferry over to the place where this august god is, [97] this august god will say: "Have you ferried over to me a man who does not know the number of his fingers?" '.

'I will say: [98] "I know the number of my fingers" '.

'Count, so that you may let me hear'.

'Take [99] the one, take the double one, [100] quench it . . ., [101] remove it, [102] give
116 to me; [103] what is well disposed toward me, [104] | do not let go of it, [105] have no pity on it, [106] brighten the Eye, [107] give the Eye to me. [108]

1. Rubric according to Sq1C. There are four varr., none of major importance. On this spell see Sethe, *ZÄS* 54, 1 ff.

2. Read *ỉn n⟨.ỉ⟩*, not *ỉnn*; 3ae inf. verbs do not normally geminate in the imperative. Sq7Sq shows a curiously abbreviated writing of 76*b*.

3. Sq7Sq has not completed the writing of *stp*.

4. T3L omits *m ꜥnḫ* and Sq7Sq has misread *ḥn.k* as *ḥw.n.f*, which makes no sense.

5. On the varr. cf. de Buck, *Archiv Orientální*, 20, 398.

6. The 'father' presumably is Osiris, who is resurrected.

7. *79b–80a* omitted in three texts. T2L omits *79a* and *80a* and bungles *79b*; T3L omits *m ꜥnḫ* after *ḥn.k* in *79c* as in *77c*.

8. The interrogative particle only in T1C, but a question seems needed here. Sq1Sq and Sq2Sq have *ỉḏd.k r.k* 'you shall say'; T3L and Sq7Sq omit the prothetic *ỉ* but are otherwise the same. T1Be has *ḏd r ḏꜣ.k* 'speak so that you may cross'. T2L omits *80b*.

9. Three texts have simply *ỉr ỉšst* 'to what purpose?'.

10. Plural. Sq1Sq has *n.ṯ* for *n.ṯn*, and Sq2Sq omits the suffix. Sq7Sq begins *81b* with a superfluous *ỉr.n*.

11. Prospective *sḏm.f* used to express intent.

12. *Dp(t) tn* 'this boat' inserted in Ab1Ph before *dmḏt*.

13. Note the variant writings of *tꜣ-wr* in *85a*; Ab1Ph has *smꜣ* for *wꜣḏt* in *84c*; M2C has *ỉmy-wrt* in *85b* for *ỉmy-nḏst*.

14. These directions are curious; one would expect the sides to be attached to both bow and stern. However, this is not a treatise on boat-building, and the obvious demand of the deceased is that the hull should be put in order.

15. Maḥaf starts to affirm that the boat is not fit for service. On the nature of the items alleged to be missing see Spell 396, nn. 18 ff. Sq1C once had a question in *86b*.

16. In three texts this clause is found in *87b*.

17. For the translation of *ssd* (*šsd* in T1C) cf. the det. in Sq7Sq. After *87b* Ab1Ph inserts in *87c-d* a 'bring me this' formula, much damaged.

18. *'Išdd* in T1C, with five varr. Judging by the dets in *74bb* and here in T1C, 'sweat' seems a probable translation, that being the moisture proper to the ribs and a counterpart to the 'slaver' on the lips.

19. T1C and Sq1C have the alternative spelling *ḏḥr*.

20. Sq1Sq and Sq2Sq omit *rpyt*.

21. So four texts out of six. T1C omits *ỉn*, and Sq1Sq has *ỉr* for *ỉrt Ḥr*.

22. Reading in *88d sšmt s(y) ⟨n⟩.ỉ* 'which will guide her to me'; to take the final group as the plural suffix *.sn* makes poor sense, despite the plural strokes of T1Be.

23. Var. *smsmty* (M2C). Species unknown.

24. So T1C; garbled in the other texts.

25. In *90f* read *ỉn n.k n.ỉ sy* with Sq1C and T1Be. At the end the various readings are *mst ḏs.f* (Sq1Sq and Sq2Sq); *mst mwt ḏs.f* (Sq1C, sim. T1Be); and *msw mwt ḏs.s* (M2C). These yield no coherent sense, and the words have been omitted from T1C, as if not understood, as also in the translation. It is conceivable that in these obscure words we may have a corruption of *msṯw.f* 'his offspring', which would fit well into the context.

26. Apparently regarding the familiar quartette as a single god.

27. The *ttwy* is a winged animal, cf. *91e*, not a bird, for it takes the skin-det. In *91c nty.f* of T1C is an error for *nty.k* of the other texts.

28. Var. Sq1Sq: 'What is she like?' M2C has corrupted *ỉ.s* into *šm*. The fem. suffix refers to the boat, cf. *92a*. Sq7Sq (p. 117) has the masc. suffix, which can refer only to the

ttwy. This reading is rendered unlikely by the fact that the next sentence also employs the fem. suffix.

29. Mr. Spaull plausibly suggests that the mast-step is meant here.

30. A virtual question, without interrogative word, only á noun and the enclitic *ỉr.f*. *ʾIbw* is clearly a rope of some kind and of some thickness. That it is in the singular is shown by the reply to the question, where it is likened to *a* snake, see n.31. T1C has *tȝwt* 'sail', cf. 93*e*.

31. T1C and T1Be have less well: 'Fetch the *nˁw*-serpent', etc. *Nˁw* is singular in all texts.

32. Lit. 'urine', but it is not obvious why a rope, *alias* a snake, should be immersed in the bilge.

33. *Wȝb*, here translated by 'cloth', occurs again in *Siut*, pl. 11, 13, there apparently with the sense of swaddling-clothes'. The det.  in Sq7Sq (p. 117) is taken from the homophonous word for 'root', which makes no sense in this context. At the end of the sentence *swtyw*, var. *swm*, with hair-det. or town-det., is of unknown meaning. 'Reed-dwellers' is a possibility, cf. *CT* VII, 265b.

34. I.e. Seth, whose name is appended to this epithet in Sq1Sq; see also Sq7Sq (p. 117). At the end of the clause, note the odd writing of *hrw tpy rnpt* in Sq1Sq. T1C lacks 93*e*-94*a*.

35. *Spty* 'lips' in three texts'; perhaps 'gunwales' are meant. Sq1Sq has *sprw* 'ribs'; Sq7Sq (p. 118) has the sing. 'rib'; T1C has *byw*, with wood-det. and plural strokes, meaning unknown.

36. According to Sethe, *ZÄS* 54, 14, an expression for 'the whole creation'.

37. Following T1Be and M2C. Sq1Sq has *sy ȝ p(w) pfȝ* 'who is that one . . . ?', and T1C has the same, but with a superfluous *n* before the enclitic *ȝ*; similarly Sq7Sq without the enclitic.

38. Read *pȝ pw* with T1Be and M2C.

39. 95*d.e* in T1C only.

40. Note the use of the infinitive as a genitive after *my sy* 'like what?', lit. 'like what of coming', as also in 95*g*. Sq1Sq and Sq2Sq turn *my sy* into *my s*, var. *my m s* in 95*g*, which indicates that here at any rate the reading of the interrogative word was *sy*, despite the occasional reading *sbw* as in 46*a*. In 95*g* T1C omits *my sy*.

41. *ʾIkt sfryt*, var. *ỉkn sfry*, meaning unknown. A word *ỉkt* with a different det. occurs in *Pyr*. §423, and *sfrt* in §517, but in neither case is it possible to allot a meaning.

42. So T1C; var. Sq1Sq: 'To what purpose have you acted for her?'; T1Be 'What have you done?' with a superfluous *m* at the end; M2C has a superfluous *r* after *ir.n.k* but is probably intended to mean 'How have you acted?'. Sq7Sq expresses the same meaning as T1C, but words it differently: *ir.n.k n.s ỉšst*.

43. Hogging-beam? A longitudinal beam running the length of the boat at deck level, and thus readily comparable to the spine.

44. For *ỉkt*, see n.41 above. The plur. suffix *.sn* in T1Be and M2C is an error for the fem. sing. *.s*.

45. 96*e*-97*e* are omitted in T1C.

46. In 97*b*, M2C only, though this is the logical place; T1Be and Sq7Sq have it in 97*d*. Sq1Sq omits; lost in Sq2Sq and Sq1C.

47. Quite muddled in Sq1Sq, which here comes to an end.

48. I.e. sacrifice was made to the boat. Note the use of *sḏr.n* as an auxiliary verb 'did (something) in the night, cf. *Eg. Gramm.*[3] § 483, 1, third example. At the end of the clause

M2C has *nbḏ* 'destroyed' instead of *npd* 'cut up'; although the recorded meanings are not identical, they are cognate, and the two words may in fact be variants the one of the other.

49. Var. T1Be:'He who is at the head of the rulers and the elders', similarly Sq1C and T3Be. Sq7Sq has *in Ḥr ḫnty* [. . .].

50. For *ssšnw* 'cordage' Sq7Sq has *nšnw* with 'bowl' det., certainly a corruption of *sšnw,* for bowls (*pgꜣw*) are named in the next question. Sq2Sq likewise has the bowl-det., and T1Be appears to have *nšn* 'storm'!

51. So T1Be; the plural *ḥkꜣw* is preserved in Sq2Sq and Sq7Sq. T1C has: 'he who is in front of the ruler of *Bꜣt*', which makes no sense.

52. Sq7Sq omits *.sn* after *gm.n.ỉ.*

53. Sethe, *ZÄS* 54, 14-15, thinks that because the words *bty kꜣmwtt* are written in red in T1Be they are an interpolation by Maḥaf, but *bty* 'emmer' is clearly the object of *ꜣsḫ* 'reap', and *kꜣmwtt* 'ears of corn' comes into the same context, whatever may be the meaning of the following *ḏrk ḫtw* and varr. In 99*e* no two texts are exactly alike, showing that the ancient editors were themselves at a loss; T1C is the most intelligible.

54. The writing of T1Be indicates the prospective *sḏm.f* form. This sentence is not in T1C, and M2C lacks 100*a*–101*a.*

55. Two quite obscure beings, the *ʿr* and the *ʿrt,* male and female. T1Be with the writing *ỉʿ* confirms the reference to ascension, but in that text both words are masculine. I cannot guess what this passage means.

56. Written *ḥnt* in T1C, *hwnt* in Sq1C (with bird-det.) and T1Be; probably intended for *ḥnwt* 'presiding lady, mistress' of a place.

57. *Nṯrw,* Iseion, Gauthier, *Dict. géogr.* III, 107.

58. Sq1C and T1Be add the vocative 'O magician'.

59. Thus rather than the alternative meanings 'elbow' and 'shoulder'; a good example of the loose way the Egyptians tended to use their terms for the limbs.

60. For *wʿrt* 'leg' Sq2Sq has *ʿrt* with an unusual det.; this must be an error, for no known word *ʿrt* will fit this context.

61. Sethe, *ZÄS* 54, 7 would translate 103*d* as 'look out!', 'beware!', but neither of the texts he quotes in support will bear that meaning. In Pyr. §1252*b* the passage runs: *ỉr ṯw ỉr wpty pw n nṯr* 'take action against that god's messenger', with the well-known idiom *ir r* 'act against'; in Lacau, *Textes rel.* 17, 23 = *CT* II, 216 we read: 'He is the god, lord and heir of the Ennead *ỉr ṯn r.f m ḫnw swḥt* who made you within the egg', *r.f* being the enclitic particle. I have, however, no alternative to offer; 103*d* defeats me as it defeated Grapow in the translations accompanying his *Religiöse Urkunden,* and as apparently it defeated the ancient editors, to judge by the varr. T1Be puts it in red, but it can hardly be part of the speech by Maḥaf, which begins in 103*e*, and M2C omits the interpolation. A warning to beware seems quite out of place here, no matter who is supposed to utter it. See also n. 65 below.

62. Sq2Sq has: '(As for) this which you say' as in 104*j*, and then a lacuna; T1Be has *ỉrr.k* for *ỉr.k* of T1C; M2C omits 103*f*–105*c*.

63. *Nty n.f. . . ỉwty n.f,* lit. 'him who has . . . him who has not'.

64. An admirable example in T1C of the 1st sing. of the prospective *sḏm.f* of a 3ae inf. verb, showing the suffix as 𓇋 beside the third radical *y*.

65. Sq2Sq and T1Be repeat between this sentence and the next their versions of the

enigmatic group discussed in n.61. There can be no question here of its being an interpolation by Maḥaf, as it precedes the usual appeal to him, coming within a speech by the deceased. It is omitted in T1C.

66. 104*j*–105*a* omitted in T1C.

67. In T1Be only; damaged but restored as [*ỉr.k ỉ*]*šst* as 103*f*.

68. The vocative 'O magician' only in T1C. For 105*b-c* M2C substitutes: 'Where will you go?' (105*d*).

69. So T1Bc; T1C omits; Sq2Sq: 'I know'; M2C: I know it'.

70. So T1Be; Sq2Sq shortly: 'What is the path?' in a slightly corrupt form. Note that the interrogative word has a fem. form *syt* in both texts, presumably in anticipation of the fem. noun *wꜣt*. 105*f* is omitted in M2C, which has *šm.k ṯn* 'where will you go?' in 105*d*.

71. So T1Be, the most intelligible of four different versions of 105*g*, suggesting that we have here a passage which was obscure already to the ancient editors; T1C appears to read: 'it is on the face of him who is still(?)'; Sq2Sq: 'it is on the face of the power of the lake(?)'; M2C: 'it is those who are over the powers'.

72. Cf. Sethe, *ZÄS* 54, 15.

73. *Wḏꜣ-ỉb* 'he who is informed'; for this sense of *wḏꜣ-ỉb* cf. *Pyr.* §1444; *P. Kah.* 22, 5.

74. For *gbgꜣ*='vulture' cf. *CT* III, 144*d* (B1Bo), where the word is determined with Gardiner, Sign-list, G1 (*Neophron percnopterus*).

75. Apparently so; since the context shows this to be a threat, the implication appears to be that the vulture-god is to be imprisoned by having the exits from his courtyard built up. The suffix 1st sing. appears in T1Be, which otherwise is corrupt; it and M2C have *hn* 'chest', 'box' instead of *h* 'courtyard'. *Hn* is correct in 107*b*.

76. Sq2Sq here comes to an end with a stock funerary formula (107*j*).

77. So T1C, clearly correctly; the clause is bungled in both T1Be and M2C.

78. The boat.

79. T1Be adds the vocative 'O magician'. M2C omits everything down to 110*e*.

80. See n. 61 above.

81. I.e. 'can you do anything about it if I do not comply with your request?'. My interpretation of this passage in *Concise Dict.* 299, top, s.v. *Urk.* V, 172, is to be deleted.

82. Lit. 'it is this boat'.

83. Hardly 'fire-drill' as suggested *ZÄS* 54, 15, as that word is masculine. In any case, it is hard to see what role a fire-drill could play in this context. I cannot translate *ḏꜣt*.

84. Read *ỉmy n.k sy ỉm.s*; only in T1C.

85. T1Be omits the final suffix.

86. Var. T1C *ꜣḳꜣ*, determined with knife and wood; meaning unknown.

87. So T1Be, making the best sense. Varr. T1C: 'whom you do not know'; M2C: 'whom you know'.

88. So correctly M2C. T1C and T1Be have thoughtlessly repeated 111d and have left the text in the 2nd person.

89. For the 2nd person read the 1st in T1C only; the other texts omit 111*g*.

90. So T1C;; T1Be has 'Hemen and Anubis, the Controller of the Two Lands'; var. M2C: 'which is in the hands of the Controller of the Two Lands'.

91.  in T1C is surely a misreading of original  ; after *mrt* there seems to have been an

omission, for the reference to 'the lakes which are in those two towns' is in the air. T1Be is unintelligible; M2C has 'it will serve me as those two who are in Ōn would wish'; Sq2C is damaged. Note that in four texts there are four versions of this passage; hereafter T1C is the sole text down to 114*d*.

92. *ʿpr*, lit. 'equipped', but one cannot 'equip' a river. The significance of 113*b-d* escapes me.

93. 113*c* - 114*c* are in T1C alone, as are 114*g-k*.

94. A 'virtual' question, cf. *Eg. Gramm.*[3] § 491.

95. Read *ỉn ỉw*, not *ỉn ỉw.ỉ*; cf. 109*h*; 110*e*; 112*d*.

96. The apparent suffix 1st sing. in T1C after *tm* is an error, as in *ỉn ỉw*.

97. Not in T1C.

98. In T1Be and M2C, for *kꜣ.f* read *kꜣ.ỉ*; the deceased is speaking. 115*e-g* are omitted in T1C. For what follows cf. Sethe in *ZÄS* 54, 16 ff.

99. *ʾIṯ n.k* interpreted as imperative with reinforcing dative rather than *sḏm.n.f* as Sethe. The imperative *ỉmy* in 115*l* seems conclusive on this point.

100. I.e. number two, dual of *wʿt* 'one'. T1Be has 'take two, the double one'.

101. The reading and sense of *ỉk*(?) at the end of 115*j* in T1C are alike obscure; Sethe would emend 115*j* as *ʿḫm n.k s(y) ỉr.f.* T1Be has *ỉḫm.k (sy) m tp n Ḥr* 'you shall annul (it) in the head of Horus'; so too M2C, which has *ỉʿḫm* for *ỉḫm.k*. Whichever version is chosen there is in the first word a remote pun on *ḫmt* 'three'.

102. *Fd* puns with *fdw* 'four'. 115*k* is omitted from T1Be, 115*k* and *l* from M2C.

103. Pun with *dyw* 'five'; rather far-fetched, as the imperative of *dy* is *ỉmy*, which is what we have here in T1C; T1Be is indecisive.

104. *Snsnt* is a far-fetched pun on *srsw* or *sysw* 'six'. The fem. ending is common to all three texts and presumably is authentic; it seems that we have here a participle instead of the imperative. T1C has the best text. For *r ḥr.ỉ*, 'lit. 'to my face', T1Be has *ḥr.k m* and M2C *ḥꜣt.f.*

105. A good pun on *sfḫ* 'seven'; this is a well-worn phrase which goes back to *Pyr.* § 16*c*. M2C has misplaced the next sentence to precede 'seven', see 116*a*.

106. A very remote play on *ḫmn* 'eight'; only the initial consonant is common to *ḫꜣtb* and *ḫmn*. For the phrase cf. *Pyr.* §§ 635; 1336.

107. *Sḫd* represents *psḏ* 'nine'. T1Be has absurdly: 'Break (*sḏ*) the Eye'; M2C omits.

108. *ʾImy*, written as *dy*, represents *mḏ* 'ten'. M2C has: 'I give you your Eye, you give me my Eye'.

Spell 398

'O Ferryman, bring Horus to me for his Eye,[1] bring Seth to me for his testicles, V, 120
bring me the Eye of Horus[2] which fled and fell | in his garden[3] and which was 121
rescued from Seth. O Ferryman, bring me this.[4]

'Who[5] are you?

'I am one who loves his father'. 122

'Your father loves you. What will you do for him?'[6]

123 'I have knit together his bones, | I have gathered up his members, I have given him bread at my will; it goes well with him and it goes well with his
124 survivors. Complete the barge; | see, she is at the wharf'.[7]

'She has not been cut out'.[8]

'Cut her out, frap her, assemble her in company with Sokar, Lord of the *ḥnw*-bark.[9]

125 'Her bow-piece is the brow of Ḥa, Lord of the West.[10]

'Her stern-piece is the brow of Sobk,[11] Lord of *Rꜣ-mꜣḳw*.

126 'Her *wꜣmyt* is the backbone (*sic*) of the Field of the Kite.

'Her four[12] openings are Imseti, Ḥapy, Duamūtef and Ḳebḥsenuf.

127 'Her steering-posts(?)[13] are the elder gods who preside over Nedit.

'Her *ḫsfwt* of the gunwale(?)[14] are the great gods who are in the Abyss.

128 'Her bulwarks(?)[15] are Horus wrestling[16] with Seth on the plain of Nedit.[17]

Her *wrm* are the lips of the Lord of Dep.

129 'Her gunwale lashings(?)[18] are the ropes which are in the bonding of the *ḥnw*-bark.

'Her *ḫsfw* are the strong arms of the Lord of the Plebs.

130 'Her *ỉnt* of the gunwale(?) is the knee-cap of Atum.[19]

'Her finials(?)[20] are the beard[21] of the Ram of Kenzet.

131 'Her masthead-eyes[22] are the eyes of the spirit when he sees the Great One.[23]

'Her spars(?)[24] are the entrails of Isis and of Osiris.

132 'Her masthead[25] is the phallus of Babi.

'Her "cordage-smiter"[26] is the two fingers of Osiris.

133 'Her cordage[27] is the slaver(?)[28] which was on the mouth of Osiris.

'Her *mḏꜣt*[29] are the teeth of Osiris when he fell and embraced the earth in Nedit.

134 'Her *smꜣḏyt* are what divides the thighs of the Great One.

'Her ribs(?)[30] are the ribs of Nephthys.

135 'Her *msrt*[31] are the ribs of Isis and Osiris.

'Her *ỉnṯw* are the armpit[32] of Babi.

136 'Her *mꜣʿw* are the *ḥsmt*-monster which eats the Libyans.[33]

'Her bow-timbers(?) are the demons which are in the Abyss.[34]

137 'Her looms(?) (of her steering-oars) are the hide of the Ram who is with Horus and Seth.[35]

'Her bent timbers are the seats of Horus the sandalled(?).[36]

138 'Her *sḫt* are the offerings of him who is in *Ṯmꜣt*.[37]

'Her bailers are the frog-goddess in the mouth of her lake.[38]

'Her *snbw* are what separates the thighs of Babi when he goes around the 139
land.

'Her steering-oars are the god and goddess of Netjrw.[39]

'Her columns are the jaws of Isis and Osiris.[40] 140

'Her mast is the Lone Star which has severed the storm from the sky.[41]

'Her *nfw*[42] are the weakness of the arms of Babi. 141

'Her forestay is the great star of Rēʿ.[43]

'Her backstay is the braided tress of Mafdet.[44] 142

'Her *kꜣ-šspt* are the gods and souls of Pe.

'Her braces(?)[45] are the backbone of Neḥebkau. 143

'Her starboard side is the right arm of Atum.[46]

'Her larboard side is the left arm of Atum. 144

'Her stern-post is Sakhmet when she dances.[47]

'Her tiller is Sakhmet when she protects.[48] 145

'Her cabin is Nūt the equipped.

'Her sail is Nūt who is spread out.[49] 146

'Her oars[50] are the movements which are in the hand(s) of Horus when he
travels.[51]

'Her sounding poles are the Souls of Pe and Nekhen for her guide-lines[52] 147
to the horizon.

'Her "sandals" are the movements which are in the hand(s) of Horus when he travels to the guide-line to the horizon.[53]

'Her bow-warp is the beard of the Ram, the Lord of *Ḥnw*.[54] 148

'Her stern-warp is the White Crown when it supports Edjō.[55]

'Her forward mooring-post is the tail of the great Wild Bull.[56] 149

'Her after mooring-post is Nekhbet[57] with her arms about Horus.

'Her mallet is the backbone of the Ram.[58]

'Anything which I have forgotten in this ferry-boat is what is invoked on 150
my behalf for it by those gods who are in them;[59] it is they who will take them
from the storehouse; they took (something) thence for Horus the Lord | when he
ascended to the sky angry with men. Indeed ⟨ . . . ⟩ are put for you among her 151
gear(?)[60] for going to *'Imyt'*.[61]

'What are these two *ỉmyt* from which you have come?'[62]

'The Field of Offerings and the Field of Rushes'.[63]

'Your warrant indeed comes to you'.[64] 152

'I have come ⟨from⟩ the two *Ww*-towns,[65] being in their hands, (namely)
the gods; may they not take away[66] this which they have given to me at the
waterway of the Field(?)[67] of Rushes. | (As for) these seven gods, I found them 153

bowed down [68] reaping emmer . . . ;[69] I gathered together what was between their
thighs [70] for invocation offerings for them there when travelling downstream to
Khem or upstream – may he see'.[71]

154 'Bring him a boat,[72] for he is an equipped spirit; the fare[73] for it has been
brought to him. May you go aboard [74] the ferry-boat, because[75] you know the
number of your fingers'.

'One alone; [76] he has inherited from you [77] because I am content.

155 'Two, two; he has passed by the second of two.[78]

'Three, three; he has become three because of the second of my two.[79]

'Four; one is plucked out and two are in pain.[80]

'Five; the second is placed for him and my(?) one is among the sealed
documents'.[81]

156 How good it is to go down after *'Iw3wt*;[82] indeed I will go after her when
the fire has gone up.[83] Hail to you, Eye of Horus, uniting the gods to yourself![84]
157 The sky and the earthlings tremble at me, | the gods remove them from their
seats, and they say: 'It is an equipped spirit who has come to this land,[85] and he
is the spirit [86] whom the southern, northern, western and eastern gods equipped
for his benefit.'[87]

158 Come, that you may see me adorned with a fillet and wearing the royal
head-cloth.[88] Joy is given to me by means of it, and the Lakes of Rushes are
159 filled.[89] | Their thickets (of rushes) and pools are in my possession, and I ferry
across. O Ḥatḥōr, may your hand be given to me, and may I be taken[90] to the sky;
may I sit between the two great gods to give judgement, and I will say what is
160 true, | I will control[91] the patricians and the plebs, who will come to me bowing.
It is well.[92]

1. Var. T3L: 'bring me the Eye of Horus for him'.

2. Varr. 'the boat of Horus', 'the boat of the Eye of Horus'; the common phrase 'which was rescued from Seth' in 121*b*, with the fem. participle *nḥmt*, shows that the reading *ỉn n.ỉ ỉrt Ḥr* of M3C, M6C and M5C is correct.

3. So G1T–T3L (*ḥsp*); M3 ff. 'in the east of his garden (*š*)'; M2NY: 'of his garden (*š*)', with 'in the east' omitted.

4. The boat. G1T–T3L have omitted *nw* 'this'.

5. G1T–T3L have an unexplained *w* following interrogative *m*; M2NY has *wy* without *m*.

6. The writing *ỉry.k* of M5C suggests the prospective *sḏm.f*. This text has already put this question, with *m* instead of *ỉšst*, in 122*c*.

7. These two clauses obviously belong together, but the first appears in G1T ff., and the latter in M3C ff.; only T3L has them both, and that text has 'fill her', without *wsḫt*.

8. Lit. 'what should be cut out for her is not', i.e. she has not yet been built.

9. A superfluous *ḥnꜥ* has been inserted between *Skr* and *nb ḥnw* in G1T-A1C.

10. Here begins a long catalogue of the components of a ship, each entry being accompanied by a mythological description; many of the items named are of unknown identity, and others can be identified but tentatively. Cf. Jequier, *BIFAO*, 9, 37ff, but I do not agree with his 'solar bark' view; this is a list of the parts and gear of a normal sailing-boat.

11. Var. G1T, A1C: 'Min', see de Buck's n. 1*. The following place-name is not identified.

12. *Ḏdw* of A1C is an obvious corruption of *fdw*.

13. *Wḏ* appears to be a variant of *wḏwt, Urk.* V, 205, 6; *CT* V, 189*d*; these terms may be related etymologically to *wḏ* 'act as pilot', *Concise Dict.* 74, and so be associated with the steering-gear of a vessel; since there is a pair of *wḏ,* the translation 'steering-posts' seems possible. *Wḏyt* of VI, 264*m* seems to refer to the steering-gear itself, the 'helm'.

14. G1T *ḫsfwt spt,* A1C and M3C *ḫsfwt* alone. The M21C group of texts has mostly the same items as G1T, but in reverse order in pairs; the G1T group is followed here. The fem. *ḫsfwt* is distinct from the masc. *ḫsfw,* compare 127*b* and 129*b*; both are items in this list. Its meaning is not clear. M21C ff. read *sprwt* 'ribs'.

15. *Sꜥꜣ* is rendered as 'Bordbrett' in *Wb.* IV, 43,1. Caminos, *L. Eg. Misc.* 161, translates as 'gunwale', but we have allotted this term to *spty* 'lips' of the boat, see Spell 397, n. 35. 'Bulwarks' seems a possible interpretation.

16. *Ḳmꜣ*, determined in G1T and A1C with two grappling men.

17. So G1T; A1C: 'on the plateau of . . . '; M3C: 'in the high place of the land, in Nedit'; M21C: 'on the plain in the high place of the land in Abydos': M2NY and M5C have 'Nedit' for 'Abydos'.

18. *Šspt nt spt* is determined with the wood-sign in G1T and A1C, but with cords in M13C and (in 129*b*) in M21C ff.; the description as ropes in what follows favours the latter reading. M21C here has *mdꜣ(m)* 'lacing(?)'.

19. Var. M6C: 'Neḥebkau'.

20. On *šꜣ* see Spell 396, n. 19.

21. 'Beard' rather than 'tail', cf. 148*a*, where *ḫbsyt,* certainly meaning 'beard', is named beside *sd* 'tail'. The allusion may be to the curved beard of a god.

22. Cf. M2NY in 131*b*, which reads clearly *irwt ḫt* 'eyes of the wood', i.e. of the mast; also the items which follow are concerned with the masthead and the mast. The expression appears to refer to the holes or 'eyes' in the metal(?) masthead through which the stays and halliards passed, see n. 25 below. The use of the plural here rules out the 'oculi' painted on the bows. The writings *rrt, rrwt* of G1T and A1C are *voces nihili* and are assumed to be merely corruptions of *irwt* 'eyes'.

23. Varr. M21C: 'the eyes of the female spirit who sees Horus'.

24. *Ḫmt*, lit. 'three', is in some way connected with the mast, as is shown by the context in which it occurs, and I would suggest that it may refer to the three spars, i.e. the mast and two yards. It would seem as if *ḫmt* and *bḏꜣ* 'masthead' in 132*a* have been transposed, because the description there of *bḏꜣ*, 'the phallus of Babi', is applied to the mast in 92*b*. If this transposition be accepted, we would have the natural sequence 'masthead eyes', 'masthead', 'spars'. However, the text has been translated as it stands, rather than venture on emendation, though M21C ff. have their own version.

25. *Bḏꜣ* 'masthead' is determined here with the rope, but in *Urk.* V, 207, 13 the det. is clearly intended to represent the flanged and perforated appendage at the head of the

mast through which passed the stays and halliards, see *D. el B.* III, 72–5. It is the holes for the ropes in the flanges of this object which I have taken to be the 'eyes' referred to above.

26. Just possibly a reference to the two flanges of the masthead gear, see n. 22 above. Although no writing of this term shows the dual, its essential duality is suggested by the reference to 'the two fingers' in seven out of nine texts.

27. For this word cf. *Les.* 68, 7; *Urk.* V, 173, 14; 174, 14.

28. The association of *ḥngw* with *ỉnw* 'rigging' suggests strings of slaver hanging from Osiris's lips.

29. *Mḏ3bt* of G1T and A1C is an error, that word belongs to 138*b*. The true reading here is *mḏ3t*, cf. M21C ff. in 134*a*. According to *Wb.* II, 187, 3 the meaning is a wooden tube.

30. See Spell 396, n. 14.

31. Written *msprt* in 135*b* (M5C).

32. Cf. Caminos, *Lit. Frag.* p. 15, n.1.

33. Meaning unknown; in *Adm.* 3, 11 *m3ʿw* is a term for a kind of wood. *Ḫsmt* is also unknown, but from the det. in G1T and its description it would appear to be a man-eating monster.

34. *'Ibsw*, var. *ỉbsyt*, *BD* 207, 5, may be derived from *ỉbs* 'introduce', with the significance of 'inducting' the boat into the waters, the function performed by the bow. For the *šm3w* as demons, cf. Breasted, *Ed. Smith Pap.* 385. In G1T and A1C *ỉmyw* is corrupted into *wnm*.

35. On *ns3w* see Spell 404, n. 48. *'Imy* here must surely mean 'who is with'; no other interpretation makes good sense.

36. *Ḫ̆ndw* is taken to be a derivation of *ḫ̆nd* 'bend' wood, *AEO* I, 66; *wḫ̆3ty* is presumably connected with *wḫ̆3ty* 'pair of sandals', Cairo 28083; 28091; *Pyr.* §219.

37. *Mšʿt* is not recorded, but has been regarded here as synonymous with the familiar word *šʿt*. In all texts except G1T and A1C *mšʿt* is followed by three rectangles as if to read 'the offerings of the lakes'. In all texts *ỉmy* is masculine and therefore in G1T and A1C it cannot qualify *mšʿt*, and is presumed to be a direct genitive in these two texts. *Ṯmt (et varr.)* is unknown, and the absence of any determinative of place is noteworthy.

38. *Mḏ3bt* 'bailer' occurs also in *Urk.* V, 172, 15; *BD* 206, 11; 454, 3; the bowl-det. in G1T and A1C, also in M5C in 139*a*, indicates its function. In the description, *Ḥḳt* of M46C ff. is certainly to be preferred to *ḥḳ3* of G1T and A1C, which not only makes poor sense, but fails to account for the fem. suffix in *r3 š.s*. That suffix makes it unlikely that *r3 š* can be a place-name.

39. *Ḥmw* 'steering-oars' in G1T and A1C; varr. *šwt*, *ḥḏwt*, *snbw*, all obscure as components of a vessel; *nṯr nṯrt* 'god and goddess' in G1T and A1C; *nṯrty* 'two goddesses' in the other texts.

40. The reference of *ʿ3w* 'columns' is presumably to vertical timbers supporting deck or half-deck. The det. ⁰ı̣ı of *ʿrt* in G1T is an error, presumably for the flesh-sign; *ʿrt* determined with o in *Pyr.* §505 means 'death'.

41. We have already had *ḫ̆mt* in 131*b* apparently meaning 'mast and yards'; *ḫt ṯ3w*, lit. 'wood for the wind; occurs elsewhere as a phrase for 'mast', e.g. *Siut*, 11, 25; *BD* 205, 15, but with *n* inserted as in M3C and M13C perhaps only here. For the description as translated see G1T, A1C, M3C and M6C, also probably M46C; M13C ends with *wḏʿ mdw*, the rest of the passage being lost; M2NY adds *wḏʿ mdw m sḫ̆m* (or *ḫ̆rp*) 'who gives judgement with a sceptre';

similarly M21C, M4C, where in both cases the final sign could be a corruption of .

42. Hardly 'sails', as the word is dual and is determined either by the wood-sign or the rope. No contemporary Egyptian ship was rigged with two sails; also the sail (*ṯꜣwt*) occurs in 146a.

43. *Ḫft-ḥr,* here translated by 'forestay', is lit. 'the before-the-face rope.' In what follows I have preferred the concrete noun *sḥd* 'star' of most texts to the vague *sḥḏ* 'shining' of G1T and A1C.

44. *Ḥꜣ-ṯꜣw* is lit. 'the behind-the-wind rope', translated as 'backstay.' 'Mafdet' only in G1T and A1C; all other texts have *ḥddt* 'the scorpion'. *Ḫsft-ḥr* of M2NY ff. is probably a corruption of *ḫft-ḥr* of 141*b*.

45. On *îbw* see Spell 397, n. 29; *fꜣt ṯꜣw* 'sailing' is bungled in G1T. The expression could perhaps refer to the braces controlling the yards.

46. Omitted in G1T and A1C. *Ḥr.s îmy-wrt-ꜥꜣ,* lit. 'her starboard face', could perhaps refer to the broadside view of the starboard side, and this possibility receives support from the reference to 'her larboard' in 144*a*; the writing 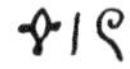 in 144*a.b* (M5C) is perhaps due to confusion with the *ḥrt*-rope of 169*g*.

47. For *îmy-tp* 'stern-post' see also *CT* III, 77*g*; V, 169*e*. At the end of 144*b, rw.s* occurs only in G1T and A1C; the other texts have *ḫw.s* as in 145*a.*

48. For *ẖr-ꜥ* 'tiller', lit 'what is under the hand' cf. *CT* III, 77*f*; V, 169*c*. Not much weight can be attached to the cord-det. of 145*a*; this sign is used quite loosely, and the wood-det. recurs in 145*b*. Note that *ẖr-ꜥ* 'tiller' and *îmy-tp* 'stern-post' are paired in V, 169*e*. *Ḫw.s* has been corrupted into *ꜣḫ r.s* in G1T and A1C.

49. In M21C only, referring metaphorically to the expanse of the sky. M5C refers to 'Nūt who rests [. . .]', while M2NY refers to 'the runner of Horus'.

50. M3C and M6C combine this with 147*a.*

51. So G1T and A1C. All other texts except M21C have 'the gods and souls of Nekhen'; M21C substitutes Pe for Nekhen.

52. For *mꜣꜥ* 'guide-line' cf. *CT* II, 135*d.e;* 137*c*. The varr. omit the allusion to *mꜣꜥ*.

53. Lost in G1T. A1C corruptly: 'the day of guide-lines to the horizon', having apparently been led astray by the circular town-dets in 147*a*. The rest have the 'movements' passage, with minor varr., except that M4C has badly corrupted the end.

54. So G1T; M6C omits *nb ḥnw.* All the other texts combine 148*a* and *b* and for *nb ḥnw* have mostly *ḥnbwt;* the exceptions are M3C, which reads *m ḥnbwt,* and M4C, which is quite corrupt.

55. Var. M6C: 'the hair of the plebs'(!). The combined texts in 148*a* have 'the tail of the Wild Bull', which is fact more appropriate to a warp than either version of 148*b*.

56. See the last note; 'The tail of the great Wild Bull' is in G1T only. The other texts, except M6C, use G1T's description in 148*b;* M6C has 'Sakhmet when she protects'.

57. M6C has *Sḫmt m ꜣw.s;* with this untranslatable expression compare 145*a* (G1T, A1C). 149*b* is absent from A1C.

58. Var. A1C: 'of Babi'. M2NY and M5C have *bꜣ* 'the soul', a homophone of *bꜣ* 'ram'. The catalogue of ship's components ends here.

59. The forgotten components.

60. The subject of *dy* (*d* in M2NY and M4C, corruptly *dr* in M5C) has been omitted in all texts, and G1T–T3L omit *sšsšt.s*. The translation of this last word as 'gear' is only approximate; the precise meaning of the word is not known.

61. A dual place-name, cf. 151*e*.

62. Presumably the question is asked by the ferryman Maḥaf, the very long speech by the deceased having come to an end at last. Note that in G1T–A1C the demonstrative qualifying *ỉmyt* is masculine, whereas M2NY–M4C have the correct feminine.

63. G1T–T3L omit *ḥtp* after the first *sḫt*, evidently following an error in a common ancestor.

64. Apparently spoken by Maḥaf; the 'warrant' (ꜥ) is presumably the deceased's ticket for the crossing of the river, but the plural suffix *.ṯn* is surely an error for *.k*. T3L has *ꜥ n Ḥr* 'warrant of Horus'.

65. In all texts except A1C the expected preposition *m* is absent, and in that text we have *ỉm.s*, which does not make sense; there has certainly been some corruption here, for T3L has only a repeated group of indecipherable signs. It would be possible to translate as 'the two *ww*-towns come to me'; but the rendering actually adopted seems the more probable; in either case it is the deceased who is speaking. A single place-name *Ww* occurs in *CT* IV, 41*c*.

66. Reading as the negation *ỉmy* with T3L ff.; imperative *ỉmy* makes poor sense.

67. All texts are surely corrupt here; *rꜣr* and *šꜣr* are *voces nihili*. The emendation *sḫt* 'field' is probable.

68. Reading *gm.n⟨.ỉ⟩sn ksw* with T3L.

69. This is an echo of 99*d*, but what follows *kꜣmtt* 'ear of corn' is incomprehensible. It is clear that the original editors were quite at a loss with the words following *bdt*, and M2NY–M4C have not understood even that common word; only G2T and T3L have *kꜣmtt* more or less correctly, and *ks.k* which follows makes no sense at all.

70. Compare 99*e*.

71. Compare 101*b*. The reading of the place-name as *Ḫm* (Letopolis) is confirmed by M2NY and M4C and the corrupt *ḫnmty* of M5C, though the suffix *sn* following the name in M2NY and M4C is superfluous. The significance of the final clause *mꜣ.f* common to all texts is quite obscure.

72. Maḥaf speaks.

73. For *hmt* 'fare' for conveyance, cf. *Pyr.* §334; *Peas.* B1, 172. M2NY ff. are corrupt, apparently thinking of *hy* 'husband', to judge by the dets.

74. T3L has corrupted *hꜣ.k* into *ꜥꜣ.k*.

75. Read *n* 'because'; the negation does not make sense.

76. Compare 115–6. This numbering differs from the other in that it runs only from one to five; G1T–T3L omit numbers one to three. This version is even more obscure than the other, and the translation can be regarded only as tentative to a degree. It is doubtless the deceased who is supposed to be speaking, to clear himself of the charge of ignorance.

77. For this sense of (*ỉ*)*wꜥ* cf. Cairo 20543, *a*, 9; *RB* 111,4.

78. A totally obscure play on *snwy* 'two'. *Snnt* has been taken to be intended for the fem. *snty* 'two'; the doubling of *n* recurs in *snn.n.f* 'he has passed by(?)' next below. On the other hand, *snt* at the end of 154*a* has but one *n*.

79. Note here also the doubled *n* in *snnwt* and *snnwy*.

80. Here the verb *fd* 'pluck out' replaces the repetition of *fdw* 'four'. M2NY and M5C have *m fd.n.f* between *fdw* and *wꜥ*. *Mr* after *snt* can hardly be other than the old perfective, but the fem. ending is lacking. Possibly because of the notion of duality inherent in *snt*, the common (masc.) gender 3rd plur. is used, but even so the det.  is missing.

81. Here *dy* 'is placed' is substituted for the repetition of *dw* 'five'. *Snt nw* of T3L is a corruption of *snwtt*.

82. *ꞽIs* at the beginning of 156*a* is clearly a non-enclitic particle, presumably a variant of *ỉsw*, cf. *Eg. Gramm.*[3] §232. *ꞽIwꜣwt* is apparently a female spirit.

83. *Sb*, on the evidence of the varr. *sbw, sby*, has been taken as prospective *sdm.f* with omission of the suffix 1st sing. *R.k* can hardly be other than the enclitic particle; T3L and M2NY have transformed it into *m rkrk* 'creeping', as probably M5C. Notable in M2NY is the sportive writing of *sḏt* 'fire' with a broken pot for *sḏ*. The real meaning of all this remains enigmatic.

84. 3rd person in the original, in accord with regular Egyptian usage.

85. In M5C read *mk* [*ꜣ*]*ḫ pw*. G1T and G2T omit *pn* after *tꜣ* and A1C omits everything after *ỉw*.

86. Var. T3L: *ꜣḫ n.f* 'with whom it goes well'. *ꜣḫ* is determined with  only in M5C, but that indeed we have here the word for 'spirit' can hardly be doubted.

87. 157*e* only in M5C. It is almost entirely lost.

88. Note the additions in M2NY and M5C, which can scarcely be part of the original text. M2NY reads *r rmn nst.ỉ* 'in order to support my throne'; M5C could have read *n r*[*krkt*] *r rmn* [*nst.ỉ*] 'because of the [creeping] snake in order to support my [throne'].

89. Reading *šw ỉꜣw* with M2NY and M5C rather than *ỉww ỉꜣrw*; one cannot 'fill' islands. *R.sn* is apparently the enclitic, despite the writing of A1C; a mention of 'their (whose?) mouths' would be meaningless here.

90. Reading *šd.tw.ỉ*; G1T and A1C reads *šd.ṯn wỉ* 'may you (pl.) take me', but there is no antecedent for a plural suffix. G1T has *šd.nṯ* for *šd.ṯn* of A1C.

91. T3L strangely *mꜣ.sn* 'they will see'.

92. So S1C. What remains of M2NY differs from the other four texts, and M5C is lost.

Spell 399[1]

A boon which the king grants (to) Anubis[2] who is on his mountain, who is in V, 165
the place of embalming, Lord of the Sacred Land, in all his pure and fair places, (namely) invocation offerings for one who is honoured with the great god, Lord of the sky, for N,[3] the worthy and vindicated; a thousand of bread and beer,[4] a thousand of cattle, poultry, wild game,[5] alabaster, clothing, the funeral meal, and a thousand of all pure and good things of which the spirits
wish to eat, for N [. . .]. [1]May he cross the firmament, may he traverse the sky, 166
may he travel safely on the fair paths on which the blessed travel, may hands be given to him in the *nšmt*-bark among the blessed.

Orion and the Great Bear are ready(?) as stars, the land is placed in(?)[6] the side of the great West at the stairway of the lotus-tank at the place for travelling upstream in the Lake of the Favoured Ones in the River of Food-offerings to the place where N is, so that he may live. It is the river of the Lord of All when he was in the flood in the Abyss with the inert ones, when he was weary in the Great Hall. The worthy and vindicated N is interred in it at the place where Osiris is.

Captions of the boat-diagrams.

167 A. Ptaḥ-Sokar.

B. Incense on the fire.

C. The guiding-serpent[7] of the [Field of] Offerings.

D. The equipped spirit will go down safely to the lotus-tank in front of Orion in the southern sky on every occasion[8] at the place where Osiris is, at the stairway.

E. This bowl[9] is the mistress of drink-offerings[10] in the rank of flood, which controls[11] the *wtnw* of the inundation.

F. Musician-goddess.

G. This[12] is the mistress of the bow (of the boat).

H. The Souls of Pe.

I. Musician-goddess.

J. The stern(?).[13]

K. Orion and the guiding serpent set the streams in order on every ⟨occasion⟩[14] at the place where Osiris is [. . .].

L. The equipped spirit descends safely into the southern sky.[15]

M. The bow.

N. He who opens the mouth.

O. The weary one.

P. The Great Bear.

Q. He who opens N's mouth.

R. The two eyes.

S. He who flies up is he who sits at the place where Osiris is.[16]

T. The Souls of Nekhen.

1. See de Buck's remarks, p. 165, n. 1*.
2. Following GIT[a]. *'Inpw* is misspelt.
3. In 165*c* GIT[a] inserts a superfluous *n* before the name of the deceased.

4. The catalogue of offerings is omitted from GɪT[a], here GɪT[b] is followed.

5. Represented by the head of an oryx(?).

6. Obscure; *tꜣ dy r ỉm* of the text should perhaps be emended as *tꜣ dy m*; otherwise *gs ỉmy-wrt* is left in the air.

7. Restoring *sḫt* in the lacuna; the remaining trace would suit.

8. *R ṯn sp 2 (sic)*, var. *r ṯnw* in K.

9. The translation of *wsḫt* as 'bowl' is certain, but there is a hidden pun on *wsḫt* 'barge', see the position of E in the diagrams.

10. Lit. 'What is lifted up' in offering, with det. 𓈗 in AɪC.

11. Fem., in concord with *wsḫt*.

12. Assuming *ỉtn* to be the fem. sing. demonstrative in a rare spelling and independent use.

13. See de Buck's n. 2*.

14. *R ṯnw* without *sp*, see n. 8 above. From here on we depend on AɪC.

15. Compare D above.

16. Translation doubtful; the reading is not certain, see de Buck's n.4*; if we really have here 𓁹 as an auxiliary verb, *ḥms* should be the infinitive *ḥmst*.

Spell 400

SPELL FOR [JOINING(?)][1] THE FERRY-BOAT TO THE REALM OF THE DEAD, TO V, 168
THE PLACE [WHERE OSIRIS IS(?)][2].

The boat is the lotus-bark which put into the land of the god.[3]

The mooring-post is . . . west of the seats of *Rrwt*.[4]

The bow-warp and the stern-warp are the claws (?) of the scorpion-goddess.[5]

The 'sandals' are like the thigh of the Great Lady.[6]

The mast is the day of destroying(?) the shining sky.[7] 169

The cable is the flame(?) making rejoicing for the Destroyer.[8]

The *kꜣw* are they who restrict the influence of the sunshine.[9]

The sail is the red one who . . . those who are brought content.[10]

The stern-post and the tiller are the Great One when he is with those who pray.[11]

The *ḥrt*-ropes are the bowstrings of those who are about the Abyss.[12]

The bailer is the pit[13] which is in the realm of darkness.[14] 170

The oars are the staves(?) of Ḥapy.[15]

The steering-oars are those who stand before Anubis the great.

The sounding-pole is the ferryman whom they cannot see.[16]

O you seven spirits,[17] the ferrymen of the sky;[18] O Maḥaf,[19] come and bring 171
me the ferry-boat in its name of *kꜣyt*-boat[20] and in[21] its power of *kꜣyt*-boat,

which is sent from [22] the mountain . . . [23]

172 O you gods beside(?) the god, [24] a message has come for me;| the Night-bark and the Day-bark are built.[25] He leans on me [26] and relies on me, and Rēꜥ is at peace. I sit beside him, and the Soul which is in the horizon gives judgement; I have extended my arm over the arm of Horus and the sandal of Seth; [27]|I am the
173 twilight which is over the approach of the storm; [28] I travel around . . . [29] May (something) be brought to me that I may see the bull-snake, may the warrant [30] of the bull-snake be brought to me . . .[31] Those who ferry over are those who open my paths ⟨ to ⟩ the Lake of the Shanks.[32] She[33] brings and takes away, for she has knelt at the stairway, [34] she crosses over to the Field of Rushes.[35]

1. For the restoration see de Buck's n. 1.*
2. Restoration conjectural.
3. Following S1C. This spell is most obscure.
4. Restored with the aid of M2NY. I cannot translate *nḳꜣw*.
5. M2NY has the clauses in a different order from S1C. *Mnyꜣ* is not recorded, but from the duality implicit in 168*e* (S1C, M5C), it could refer to the scorpion's pair of claws; the sting in the tail is the only likely alternative. M2NY (168*e.f*) corresponds in S1C to 168*g* and 169*a*.
6. For *ṯbwt* 'sandals' as a technical term for part of a boat cf. 147*b*. In S1C, for *ỉs* 'like' cf. *Eg. Gramm.* [3] §247,5; for *m* instead of *n* in an indirect genitive cf. Sp. 356, n. 5. On the reading of M2NY see n. 8 below.
7. Restoring the lacuna in 169*a* (S1C) with the aid of 168*f* (M2NY). 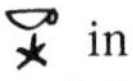 in 168*f* may have borrowed its det. from *ỉḫmw-sk* 'the indestructible stars' like *sk* 'flour' in *Pyr.* §1065; in §785(P) *sk* seems to be an error for *sbꜣ*. M2NY appears to be corrupt; it anticipates 169*c*.
8. Reading *mrr ḥr sḥꜥ n ḥtmw*, cf. 168*g* (M2NY), where the text reads *mrr ḥr ḥꜥ n ḥtmw.' Mrr* 'flame(?)' is not recorded.
9. With *kꜣw* compare *kꜣw-ššpt* in 142*b*, there preceding *ỉbw* 'cable' in 143*a*.
10. Read *ṯmsst sḫwꜥt ỉnw*; the reading *ṯmsst* is confirmed by the palette sign, cf. *Pyr.* §1460. It is distorted in M2NY, which for *sḫwꜥt* has *sḫꜣ ꜥ*; I can translate neither. For *ỉnw* of S1C M2NY has *ỉnw hrw*, which seems an improvement.
11. For *ỉmy-tp* cf. *CT* III, 77*g*; V, 144*b*. For *ḥry-ꜥ* cf. III, 77*f*; V, 145*a. b.* For *wr* of S1C, M2NY has *Ḥr* 'Horus'; *im.f* of S1C is clearly an error for *ỉw.f* of M2NY; and *ḥnꜥ* following it in both texts indicates that *dbḥw* is an active participle describing persons. M2NY splits this sentence into two: 'the stern-post is Horus when he is with those who pray; the tiller is the bow-strings (*or* 'sinews') of those who are about the Abyss', anticipating the description in 169*g*.
12. The *ḥrt* (upper) ropes may possibly refer to those used to hoist the yard, and the identification with *rwḏw* 'bowstrings' or possibly 'sinews' is not inapt.
13. *Šꜣdt*, lit. 'what is excavated', determined in S1C with .
14. Var. M2NY *snk(t) nt hrw* 'the darkness of the day'.
15. The translation of *gbw* as 'staves' is doubtful; in *BD* 400, 15  is a place

which harbours slayers, but that can hardly be the sense here. Note again *m* for genitival *n*.

16. The man-det. after *smꜥ* in S1C is superfluous. For *mꜣ.n.s* of S1C read *mꜣ.sn* of the other two texts (170*e*). In M2Ny the initial *m* of *mẖnt(y)* is cryptically written with 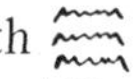 , as also in 174*a*. Here the catalogue of boat-parts comes to an end. 170*f* is apparently a title, see de Buck's n.8*, and it has been included as a restoration in the translation of the title at the head of this spell. The text continues with an address to the ferrymen-spirits.

17. Some new texts come in here; beside M5C^{b} we have M2NY^{a} and M5C^{a}. The number 'seven' is in S1C alone; the intact parallels have 'four'.

18. M2NY^{b} and M5C^{b} have: 'the ferrymen of the West, the ferrymen of the sky'.

19. Corrupted in the same two texts into *Mꜣ-ꜣḫ.f.*

20. Written variously as *ḳꜣt, ḳꜣyt* and *ḳꜣytt.*

21. S1C omits *m*.

22. A dittograph of *m* in M2NY^{b}.

23. After *ḏw* S1C has *ḥr ṯrrf,* as apparently M2NY^{a}: M2NY^{b} has *ḏw ṯnrf.* Both readings are equally obscure.

24. So S1C, taking *ḏr* in its archaic sense of a preposition of place. Var. 'O you gods who are in the presence of the Houses(?)'.

25. So M2NY^{a} and M5C^{a}; this version seems more plausible than 'have been buried' of S1C; *ḳsn n* 'it goes ill with' of the other two texts is likewise unconvincing.

26. There surely must have been a textual omission in the scribal source; this sentence and what follows have no nexus with what precedes. Who is 'he'?

27. Following M5C^{a}; this text seems superior here to S1C and M2NY^{a}. The sense is that the deceased exercised some kind of restraint over these two contending gods.

28. Following M5C as the only translatable version of the three, though it may be an ancient emendation. The meaning of  *n pt* of M2NY is obscure; S1C is damaged.

29. Incomprehensible. All three texts differ materially, which suggests that the copyists themselves were all at sea.

30. Hardly 'arm' as S1C, since snakes are limbless.

31. I do not understand *m dmḏt H̱nm* (var. *ỉb*).

32. Following M5C; the other two texts are incomprehensible.

33. There must have been another omission after 173*e*, for the fem. suffix has no antecedent.

34. Reading *mꜣs.n.s* ⟨ *r* ⟩ *rwd,* the preposition having been omitted through haplography. *Mꜣꜥ.s dy.s* of M5C yields little sense, but this preserves *r* before *rwd.*

35. Var. S1C: 'she travels to the [. . .]' with fire-det.; M2NY 'she travels to *ỉw',* with plant-det.

Spell 401

SPELL FOR A FERRY–BOAT.[1] O you [seven(?)][2] spirits, ferrymen [of] the West, bring me[3] the ferry-boat when I call out,[4] [because(?)][5] I know you and I know your names. O *Mꜣ-ꜣḫt-n.f,*[6] bring me the ferry-boat in [its name of *ḳꜣyt*-boat and in][7] its power of *ḳꜣyt*-boat [. . .] I will go down in it to the West, I will reach[8] the god who is in(?) [. . .]. V, 174

1. On the writing of *mḫnt* see Spell 400, n.16.
2. Restored from 170*g*.
3. Restore  in the lacuna, cf. 174*g*.
4. Cf. *ỉw* 'cry out', *CT* I, 148*a*.
5. Restore *ḥr* in the lacuna, see below.
6. Corruption of *M3-ḥ3.f*, cf. 171*a*.
7. Restored from 171*b*.
8. Read 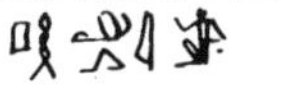

Spell 402

V, 175 Not dying again and giving a man's magic to him. I am Khopri who came into
being of himself upon his mother's lap,[1] who gave the she-jackals to those who
are in the Abyss[2] and the predators(?)[3] to those who are in the tribunal; see,
this magic of mine has been brought to me;[4] gather together this magic of mine
176 for me[5] wherever it may be;|be quicker than a hound, be speedier than Shu.[6]
O you who bring the ferry-boat to Rēʿ, strengthen your warp, launch[7]
your ferry-boat, ferry over to the Island of Fire, for see, I have gathered together
this magic of mine[8] wherever it was. Now anyone with whom it is, be quicker
than a hound, be speedier than Shu.
The heron is in distress[9], the gods are silent, having caused the heron
177 to cry aloud(?),[10] so that it may make announcement[11] to the gods.|See, I have
gathered together this magic of mine wherever it was. Now anyone who is
with it, be quicker than a hound, be speedier than Shu, for I am a festal bull,
pure of mouth, living on milk of the god's mother.

1. Lit. 'leg', but the context demands the rendering 'lap'.

2. Var. M2NY: 'the jackals (masc.) of the interior of the Abyss.' L2Li appears, from which is left of 175*e*, to have had a different text.

3. Lit. 'killers', with skin-det. in M2NY; a hunting quadruped of some kind seems required as a counterpart to 'jackals' in 175*e*.

4. So T1C; M2NY attaches *ỉsṯ* to *dmḏ.n.ỉ* below and omits 175*g*. On L2Li see n. 5 below.

5. M2NY interpolates here *dy n.ỉ* 'which was given to me'; in 175*g-h* L2Li reads: 'see, magic has been brought and collected for N for him (*sic*) wherever he is.' M2NY adds: 'I know wherever it is'.

6. So T1C; M2NY omits *tbn r* at the beginning of the clause. L2Li agrees with T1C except in writing  after [*tb*]*n*, but de Buck's text here is of necessity a copy of a copy, so that the published text may not be in accord with the lost original. L2Li ends the spell here.

7. The negation of T1C is surely contrary to the sense required; one may guess that the initial *m* in *mḥ* (written out in both texts) was at some stage confused with the negation *m*,

and that the latter in its turn became  . For *mḥ* 'launch' a vessel cf. *Urk*, I, 109, 4.

8. Var. 'gather together this magic of mine for me', optative *sḏm.f.* In T1C the non-enclitic *ỉsṯ* rules out the imperative with dative.

9. For *ḳmw* see also *CT* I, 26*c*; VI, 157*i*; T1C has *bꜣw* 'power'.

10. *Wgb*, var. *wbg*, with this det. is not recorded. The meaning given to it depends entirely on the context.

11. M2NY has corrupted *sr.f* into *srfw* 'warmth'.

Spell 403

Spell for bringing a ferry-boat to N and for crossing into the realm of the dead.[1]
O you who come from the Abyss | as ferryman of the sky, who are in charge of V, 178
the field of irrigated land(?),[2] bring me this, which is light(?)[3] but is not frapped.
You shall frap it[4] with clay(?)[5] and with the double cord which is on the tomb of
the lip of Osiris,[6] without the descending of the spars(?) on her;[7] | I will cause the 179
spars(?) to descend on her by means of the plumes of the wings of the two falcon-gods.[8] I have come that I may raise up my seat and make the ferry-boat ready,
my fire being on the quays[9] of the 'Great-White' bark.

Bring me this; | O you who go and come, bring me this, for I am *'Itty*,[10] I 180
have come into the Island of Fire,[11] I will slay thousands, I will adjudge hundreds(?),[12] I will live on the brains(?)[13] which are on (*sic*) the heads of the Souls of Ōn.[14]

1. So BH1C.

2. Varr. *ꜥꜣḏw*, *ꜥꜣww*. For the meaning of *ꜥꜣdw* cf. *Wb.* I, 168, 12. M21C omits all from 177*l* to this word in 178*b*.

3. *'Isyst*, var. *ỉst*, is apparently a fem. participle to agree with the implied *mḫnt*. The meaning is quite uncertain, and the suggested derivation from *ỉs* 'be light', of weight, may not be right.

4. There is much confusion in the texts; Sq5Sq seems the most intelligible.

5. The context suggests some substance used for caulking.

6. All texts agree in reading *spt* 'lip', but it is possible that the archetype may have read *spr* 'rib'. In 178*f* Sq5Sq inserts: 'bring N this'.

7. Apparently the deceased is asking for an unrigged hull, which he will rig himself, cf. 179*b*. For *ꜣḫꜣḫ r.s* Sq5Sq has *ꜣḫꜣḫ.s* 'her spars(?)' both here and in 179*b*. *Ḫꜣḫꜣt* of M21C is clearly a corruption.

8. Again Sq5Sq interpolates 'bring N this'.

9. For this sense of *dmy* cf. *JEA* 22, 104.

10. Unknown.

11. So Sq5Sq; for *nsrsr* M18C and M21C have a writing with two cows(?).

12. *Nṯnwt*, varr. *snṯwt* Sq5Sq, *nṯwt* BH1C, is quite obscure, but the context suggests that

šnwt 'hundreds' may originally have stood here but has been unrecognizably corrupted.

13. Lit. 'entrails', but in this context that rendering is meaningless. 'Brains' seems the most likely alternative, though in that case it is not clear why *ḥryw tp* rather than *ỉmyw tp* should be employed.

14. The spell ends here. Sq5Sq adds once more 'bring N this' and ends with a rubric: 'Bringing N's ferry-boat to him in the realm of the dead'.

Spell 404 [1]

V, 181 SPELL FOR ARRIVING AT THE FIRST PORTAL OF THE FIELD OF RUSHES. WHAT IS TO BE SAID TO THE GATE-KEEPER:[2] 'Open, O *Gšgš*, for your name is *Gšgš*'.[3] Hail to you, You of the Netherworld, my lord;[4] make ready your place for me'.

182 'Come, be a spirit, my brother;[5] proceed to the place of which you know'.

He will arrive at another portal.[6] He will find the Sisterly ⟨Companions⟩[7] standing there; they will say to him: 'Come, that we may kiss you', and they will

183 cut off the nose and lips of whoever does not know their names.| When he reaches [them], the man shall say: 'Hail to you, Sisterly Companions who comfort the Well-beloved![8] I have come between you[9] with my magic, I am he who shines in the Night-bark, I am Horus son of Isis, I have come to see my father Osiris'.

'Come, be a spirit, my brother;[10] proceed to the place of which you know.'

184 He will arrive at another portal by which the air enters and is cut off. It shall be said to it: Hail to you, Runner, whose name is "Son of a Runner!"'

'Come, be a spirit, my brother; proceed to the place of which you know'.[11]

He will arrive at another portal; he will find its gate-keeper standing with

185 the satchel[12] of a corn-measurer| and with a corn-measure in his hand, wherewith to measure a man's excrement. THE MAN SHALL SAY TO HIM: 'Hail to you, *Twt*, whose name is *Twt*![13] "What is to be filled" is the name of your corn-measure'.[14]

'Come, be a spirit, my brother; proceed to the place of which you know'.[15]

'Hail to you, Striker of the pillar-amulet,[16] whose name is "Striker of the pillar-amulet"'.

'Come, be a spirit, my brother; proceed to the place of which you know.

186 'Hail to you, you two throwsticks, whose name is ⟨"Throwsticks"⟩'[17]

'Come, be a spirit, my brother; proceed to the place of which you know'.[18]

He will arrive at these grounds[19] and these grounds will say to him: 'We will not let you tread on us'.[20] HE SHALL SAY TO THEM: 'Hail to you, you backbone

187 of Rēʿ| which repels the Serpent, which Neith sends down to the crocodiles'.[21]

'Come, be a soul, my brother; proceed to the place which you know'.

WHAT IS TO BE SAID TO THE FERRYMAN OF THE FIELD OF RUSHES[22] so that

his regard may be on those gods who are on yonder side of the river. He[23] shall say to [them][24] when he calls: 'O[25] Cut Rush, Tongue of Rēʿ! . . . ;[26] leader of 188
the Two Lands, do not go back to them; O Power in the sky who reveals the sun-disk, O Rēʿ, Lord of the dawn-red,[27] bring to me,[28] do not leave me boatless'.

'Tell my name' says[29] the bow-warp. 'O Braided tress of Isis which Anubis has affixed by means of the craft of the embalmer'.

'Tell my name' says the mooring-post. 'Your name is "Lady of the Two 189
Lands in the Shrine" '.

The name of the mallet[30] is 'Buttock of the Bull of the Wind'.[31]

The name of the steering-posts[32] is 'Reeds[33] of the Field of God'.

The name of the hull(?)[34] is 'Earth-god'.[35]

The name of the mast is 'He who fetched the Great Lady after she had been far away'.[36]

The name of the *mhnnw* is 'Standard of Wepwawet'. 190

The name of the yards(?) is 'The staffs of Rēʿ which are in Unu'.[37]

The name of the *dbḥw* is 'The staffs of Rēʿ which are in Unu'.[38]

The sail: 'Your name is Nūt'.[39]

The lacings(?), halliards(?) and *ỉwt*:[40] 'Someone has made you from the skin 191
of the Mnevis bull and the sinews of the Ombite.'

The name of the oars is 'The fingers of Horus the Elder'.

The bailer is 'The hand of Isis when she swabbed up the blood from the Eye of Horus'.

The bailer (*sic*)[41] is 'The gullet of Imsety.

The ribs(?) in her hull[42] are Imsety, Ḥapy, Duamūtef and Ḳebḥsenuf, (that is to say) "He who plunders", "He who acts as a robber", "He who sees his father", and "He who makes his own name".'[43]

The hogging-beam(?):[44] 'Your name is "She who presides over the gardens".'

The butt(?) (of the steering-oar):[45] 'Your name is *mrw*-wood'. 193

The steering-oar:[46] 'Your name is "Accurate", and the name of your blade is "Sunshine which cuts through the water".'[47]

The name of its loom(?) is 'Nose of Ptaḥ'.[48]

The name of this boat is 'Leg of Isis which Rēʿ cut off with a knife when she brought the Night-bark to him'.

The name of the skipper: His name is . . .[49] 194

The name of the pilot(?): His name is . . .[50]

The name of the helmsman: His name is 'Two Baboons'.[51]

The name of the wind[52] is 'North-wind which came forth from Atum to the nose of[53] the Foremost of the Westerners, the Lord of Abydos.

'Tell [54]my name' says the river. 'Your name is "Those who see their lord." ' [55]

195 'Tell my name says the river-bank. [56] 'Give me your hand, O lips of Isis, on the day of the supper-festival; "He who eats putrefaction in darkness," and "She who puts an end to him who would extend his hand against the waters".' [57]

WHAT SHOULD BE SAID TO THOSE GODS WHO ARE IN THE WRITING;[58] 'Hail
196 to you, you whose attributes are good, your lords of possessions,[59] who will exist for ever and ever! I shine for you that you may please me and that you may put truth in this mouth of mine for me so that I may speak with it. My
197 bread is in Pe, my beer in Dep,[60] my cake is baked,| and my seat is spacious in the presence of the great god; I know the name of that god for whom provision is placed before him,[61] his name is *Tkm.* He opens up the western horizon, he
198 knows the eastern horizon, and his name is *Tkm.*[62] | If he depart, then will I depart when he is expelled from his *msḳt.* Those who rebel will have no power over this flesh of mine, for my bread is in Pe and my beer in Dep, and this power of mine belongs to me. My power is bread and beer,[63] my power is life, prosperity and health.

199 Going out into the day in any shape that I may desire, and going out thence into the Field of Rushes.[64] As for anyone who knows this spell, he will go down into the Field of Rushes, and there will be given to him a *šns*-loaf, a beer-jug, a *psn*-cake and an aroura of land, with barley of seven cubits and likewise of
200 emmer,|and it is the Followers of Horus who will reap it. He shall chew this barley and this emmer and he shall rub his flesh with it, and his body will be [hale] like that of these gods, and he shall go out into the Field of Rushes in any shape that he wishes to assume.

1. For a detailed study of spells 404-5 see D. Mueller in *JEA* 58, 99 ff. He has dissected the spells into parts which he has rearranged in accord with his view of the text, but I am not entirely convinced that this rearrangement is valid. In this translation I adhere strictly to the text as presented by de Buck. In Spell 404 there are two clearly marked versions, B5C+B7C and B9C+B10C, with the abbreviated texts M2C and L1Li as their respective supporters.

2. Var. B7C: 'Spell for going down to the Field of Rushes. They will say: "Here is a man spiritualized [. . .]" '. M2C has: 'He shall reach the keeper of the first gate and shall say to him:'; what remains of Ab1Ph suffices only to show that the sentences occurred in a different order.

3. So B5C and B7C. The reduplication mark *sp 2* has given rise to the varr. of M2C-B10C; L1Li is slightly garbled. See *JEA* 58, 112.

4. Cf. op. cit. 112-3, but *ỉmḥty* could be an epithet of *Gšgš. Nb*, which follows in all texts, both here and in Spell 405 (200*f*), is best interpreted as *nb⟨.ỉ⟩* 'my lord'; no other plausible explanation is available. Mueller's translation 'whatever *ỉmḥty* (you are)' would have been expressed by *ỉmḥty m rn.k pn* (or *pw*), see my *Pyr. Transl.* Utt. 249, n. 2.

5. In red in B5C and B7C, because of the change of speaker, who is now the gate-keeper. Here and in M2C we should read *ỉy ꜣḫ sn.ỉ wḏꜣ r.k r bw*, etc., as in B9C, B10C and L1Li, and as also in 183*g* (all texts), 185*e.g* and in 186*b* (B9C and B10C) and also in Spell 405; *wḏꜣ r.k* here and in 184*e* and 185*e* in B5C and B7C is clearly misplaced from its natural position before *r bw*, and even in these two texts 183*g* conforms to the normal order of the words. Mueller, *JEA* 58, 112-3, translates *ỉy ꜣḫ* as 'you who come spiritualized', but then one would expect 'spiritualized', which on this view is adverbial to 'come', to be expressed by the old perfective *ꜣḫ.ty*; a better sense is obtained by regarding *ỉy* and *ꜣḫ* as imperatives. For the old imperative form *ỉy, ỉw* 'come!' cf. Edel, *Altäg. Gramm.* § 609; Gardiner, *Eg. Gramm.*[3] §336. L1Li ends here.

6. A new episode; incomplete in M2C, which ends here. B9C and B10C omit 182*b*–183*a*.

7. Cf. *JEA* 58, 113. I take the Sisterly Companions to be Isis and Nepthys, despite op. cit. 114-5; see n. 8 below.

8. Mueller's rendering of *tty-ỉb mrwty* as 'love-makers' (op. cit. 113–4) seems to me altogether far-fetched. If indeed the Sisterly Companions are Isis and Nephthys, as seems probable, then *mrwty* 'the Well-beloved' will surely be Osiris, and *tty-ỉb* will mean something like 'comfort' or 'put at ease'; I can see no reason for giving this expression a sexual connotation. In *Pyr.* 26.488 *tt-ỉb* means 'reconcile', and in *Leb.* 40 it means 'be in accord with' (*ḥnʿ*).

9. *Wp.n.ỉ* seems to imply that the deceased separates the two goddesses by standing between them. B5C omits the object-pronoun *ṯn*.

10. See n. 5 above. In each case this is deemed to have been said by the warden of each portal in turn.

11. In B5C and B7C *wḏꜣ r.k* is displaced as in 182*a*; see n. 5 above.

12. For *šṯ* 'satchel' cf. *CT* I, 71*h*, IV, 115*g*; B7C reads *šṯw* (old perfective) *m šṯ n ḫꜣw* 'girded with his corn-measurer's satchel'.

13. Cf. op. cit. 118.

14. For *mʿḏt* cf. op. cit. 301. The word is omitted in B9C and B10C, possibly, as Mueller conjectures, because of a lacuna in their common original. He also calls attention (op. cit. 118) to the use here of the possessive adjective, which is exceptional at so early a date.

15. After this passage B5C and B7C omit 185*f*–186*b*.

16. Mueller: '*ḥy* of green-stone'.

17. Both texts are garbled; read *ỉnḏ ḥr.ṯn ʿmʿꜣwy, ʿmʿꜣwy rn.ṯn*.

18. B9C omits *r bw rḫ.n.k ỉm*.

19. In view of the persistent det. 𓇿 in 186*c.d.f* I translate *sꜣwt* as 'grounds', i.e. 'areas', rather than 'planks' (Mueller); his idea of 'boarding-planks' does not fit well with the fact that in the original there has so far been no mention of a boat; 'grounds' may well be sacred and desirable places to reach. For a related fem. word for 'ground' cf. *sꜣṯt, Siut,* 13, 20. 186*c-e* are omitted in B9C and B10C.

20. B10C interpolates here: ' "Tell my name" says the ground, "since you would tread on me" ', and both B9C and B10C omit the rubric in 186*h*.

21. My interpretation of 186*i*–187*a* differs widely from Mueller's (*JEA* 58, 122). I take *šnʿw* to be an active participle of *šnʿ* 'repel', deriving its flesh-det. in B5C and B7C from *psḏ* 'backbone', and its object being the serpent-deity Nehebkau; it is he whom Neith hands

over to the crocodiles. For *psḏ* 'backbone' B9C and B10C have *psḏ* 'the shining one'. For the association of Neith with crocodiles cf. *Pyr. Transl.* Utt. 308, §489, with n.6; §510; *BD* 158,3.

22. B9C and B10C omit 187*b-f*; in 187*f* B10C inserts a passage of its own: '[Spell] for calling to the ferryman of the Field of Rushes'.

23. The deceased.

24. *Sic; s* of *sn* is preserved in B7C. The speech which follows is really addressed to the ferryman, but the scribe has been led astray by the plural 'gods' in 187*d*.

25. *Wnm* of the varr. is corrupt, cf. *JEA* 58, 104.

26. *'Indbw,* meaning unknown.

27. 188*d.e* are absent in B9C and B10C, but in 188*f* they insert: 'may the sunshine be opened up by Rēʿ, Lord of the dawn-red', confirming the reading *dšrw* at the end of 188*e*.

28. I.e. the boat; the usual *nw* after *ỉn n.ỉ* has been omitted.

29. Here and in 189*a* B5C and B7C for 'so says' have *ỉt.ỉn,* a combination of *ỉ.ty* and *ỉ.ỉn*; they also consistently use red for the 'name' clause.

30. B9C and B10C regularly have: ' "Tell me my name" says . . . '.

31. B7C adds *.f* at the end of 189*c*; 204*h* reads *ṯꜣw-sp.f.*

32. Cf. Spell 398, n. 13. The det. of *wḏwt* in *Urk.* V, 205,6 could well represent a vertical post. *Wḏyt* in VI, 264*m* appears to stand for the steering-gear and has been translated with 'helm'.

33. For *ʿꜣʿw* 'reeds' cf. *CT* IV, 3*b*; 4*e*.

34. *Ḥʿt* with boat-det. As suggested in *JEA* 58, 106, the var. *ḥpt-ḫt* may mean the mast-step.

35. *ꜣkr.*

36. *'I.ỉn* (B5C) and *ỉnt.ỉn* (B7C) are superfluous; in 189*i* at end, *pw* is to be preferred to *pf.*

37. B9C and B10C substitute: ' "Tell my name" says the masthead" '. 'It is the gullet of Imsety'. B5C and B9C allot this description to the bailer in 191*h*.

38. As Mueller points out, op. cit. 106, the repetition of the description of the preceding item is suspicious; it looks very much as if the scribe's eye had strayed to the preceding section.

39. So B5C; lost in B7C. B9C and B10C have Nu for Nūt, but since the word for 'sail' is fem., 'Nūt' is doubtless the better reading.

40. *Šdw* is guessed to be lacing or frapping cut from leather; in *BD* 206, 6 it is determined with  and in *Urk.* V, 208,17 with 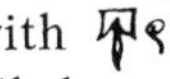 ; *ʿt* occurs in *ʿt nt ẖrt, Urk.* V, 207, 3. 10, where the det. in 207, 3 suggests coiled rope. *'Iwt* defeats me.

41. The only likely reason for the inclusion of two words *mḏꜣbt* is that we have here a dittograph, the second instance taking the place of another component of the boat. The name of the first *mḏꜣbt* recurs in 205*a*.

42. On *wgw* see now Spell 396, n. 14; *m ḫt.s* 'in her belly' surely refers to the hull; I cannot accept Mueller's 'innards'. *BD* 206, 14–5 refers to the *wg(ꜣ)yw n ỉmyw ḫtw.s* 'the ribs(?) which are in her timbers'. The fem. suffixes in 192*c* refer to the ferry-boat. For *wgw* B9C and B10C have *wgsw* or *wgsy,* surely in error.

43. The last epithet could also be read as *ỉrr n.f ḏs.f* 'he who acts on his own behalf'.

44. Lit. 'that which unites', suggesting the hogging-beam which ran the length of

riverine boats at deck level and lent rigidity to the hull. Mueller translates as 'dovetails', quoting Allen and Jéquier, but in that case we would surely have had the plural; the insignificant size of dovetails also makes it unlikely that they would have been included in this list.

45. Mueller, following Jéquier, translates *ỉbꜣyt* as 'rower's seat', where *BD* 207,5 has *ỉbsyt*, but in 230*e* it is part of the steering-oar; since we have *ḏnḥ* 'blade' of the oar and *nsꜣw* 'loom(?)', see nn. 47. 48 below, as well as *ḫry-ꜥ* 'tiller', there is only the 'butt' left for *ỉbꜣyt*.

46. I have pointed out in the glossary to the *Brit. Mus. Cat. Egn. Coll.*, II. *Wooden Model Boats* that the term 'rudder' is a misnomer; that form of steering-gear was not in use until the twelfth century A.D.

47. B9C: 'the name of your blade is "Sunshine in summer" '; B10C: 'Sunshine in the water in [heat(?)]'. All versions seem to be derived from the flashing of the wet blade in bright sunshine. Note that B5C, B7C and B10C have the dual *ḏḥnw(y)*, as if the boat had two steering-oars, but only one such oar is indicated in 193*c*, and *nsꜣw* 'loom'(?) of the oar in 193*f* is likewise singular.

48. Read *rn* ⟨*n*⟩ *nsꜣw.f*, which one *n* suppressed through haplography; for the reading *nsꜣw* with initial *n* cf. 137*a.b*. It is not likely to be the tiller, because that appears to be represented by *ḫry-ꜥ*, lit. 'what is under the hand', cf. *CT* III, 77*f*; V, 145*a.b*; 169*e*. *Nsꜣw* may mean the loom of the steering-oar, to the end of which the blade is attached. Mueller's *sꜣw* 'handle' falls to the ground.

49. The name is indecipherable. B9C has *rn.k* for *rn.f*, 194*b* is lost in B10C.

50. *Nfw* in 194*c* is surely a dittograph, as there cannot be two skippers on a vessel; possibly what is displaced is a word for 'pilot'. Again the name is indecipherable. 194*c-f* are omitted in B9C and B10C.

51. Perhaps in reference to two baboon-topped steering-posts.

52. Elsewhere the word is *nfwt*, cf. *CT* II, 44*f*.

53. In B10C *fnḏ* 'nose' has been corrupted into *nḏnḏ* 'burn up(?)', for which see also *CT* II, 150*k*; the word is damaged in B9C but has 𓂉 for det.

54. *Ḏd* has to be supplied in B5C and B7C, cf. 189*b*; 190*a*; 193*f* ff; followed by *rn.ỉ*, written as *rnn.ỉ* in B5C and B7C.

55. Pl. *nbw* 'lords' in B9C and B10C. After this they insert a corrupt version of 193*f.g*.

56. See n. 54.

57. See Mueller in *JEA* 58, 107-9. In *sytmt* the participle is feminine. These are the names of the lips.

58. I.e. who have been named in what precedes.

59. See op. cit. 108-9.

60. Omitted in B9C and B10C.

61. Lit. 'at his nose'.

62. Var. B5C: *Tkš*. Cf. op. cit. 109.

63. I.e. 'my power lies in bread and beer', etc.

64. In B5C read *prt ỉm m Sḫt 'Iꜣrw*; minor varr. in the others with a cryptic writing of *'Iꜣrw* in B3L.

Spell 405[1]

'Open, O *Gšgš*! Open, O *Gšgš*![2] Hail to you, Imsety, my lord;[3] make ready your place for me'.[4]

V, 201 'Come, be a spirit, my brother; | proceed to the place of which you know'.

'Hail to you, Sisterly Companions who comfort the Well-beloved;[5] I have come between you in the Night-bark'.

'Come, be a spirit, my brother; proceed to the place of which you know'.

'Hail to you who come from the Two Regions; "You who come from the Two Doors" is your exact name'.

'Come, be a spirit, my brother; proceed to the place of which you know'.

'Hail to you, District of the Runner: "District of the Runner" is your exact name'.[6]

'Come, be a spirit, my brother; proceed to the place of which you know'.

202 'O Cut Rush, Tongue of Rēʿ[7], | . . .[8], Leader of the Two Lands in Nekheb,[9] do not go back ⟨ to ⟩ them.[10] O Great Power who reveals the sun-disk with Rēʿ, who is in charge of the dawn-red, grant that the ferry-boat be ferried across for this spirit, for see, he has come clothed and put together;[11] may he go down to the river-bank as a messenger of the great god; grant[12] that the ferry-boat be ferried across for the spirit, for see, here he is'.

The skipper of the ferry-boat of the District in Khemennu[13] shall say: 'If the one there be indeed this spirit,[14] let him pronounce the name of the ground on which he has arrived'.

203 This spirit shall say to the skipper of the ferry-boat of the District in Khemennu: 'I know the name of the ground [on which] I have arrived; its name is "Backbone of Gēb and ribs of Isis on which are the repellers of the Serpent,[15] Destroyer with outstretched arm in the Pure Place" '.

The skipper of the ferry-boat of the District in Khemennu shall say: 'If he go aboard at the bow of the ferry-boat, his soul will destroy him, but if he [go aboard] at the stern of the ferry-boat, this spirit will be one of them'; and the skipper of the ferry-boat of the District of Khemennu shall say: 'Pronounce[16] the name of this boat when you go aboard her'.

204 This spirit shall say to the skipper of the ferry-boat of the District in Khemennu: 'I know the name of this entire boat, and I know the name of her bow-warp; its name is "Braided tress of Isis which Anubis has affixed by means of the craft of the embalmer".

'I know the name of her mooring-post; its name is "Mistress of the Land in the shrine".

'I know the name of her mallet; its name is "Buttock of *Ṯꜣw-sp.f.*"

'I know the name of her steering-posts(?);[17] they are "Serpents of the Field of God".

'I know the name of her oars; they are "Fingers of Horus the Elder".

'I know the name of her bailer; it is | "The hand[18] of Isis which swabbed V, 205
up the blood from the Eye of Horus".

'I know the name of [her] ribs(?); their names are Ḥapy and Duamūtef".

'I know the name of her mast; its name is "He who fetched the Great One after she had been far away".

'I know the name of her mast-head: it is "Gullet of Imsety".

'I know the name of her *mhy*; it is 'Back of [. . .] who passed by".[19]

'I know the name of her lacings(?), her halliards and her [. . .]; they are "It has been made from the skin of the Mnevis-bull and from the sinews [of the Ombite]".[20]

'I know the name of her yards(?); it is "[. . .] lands of the Field of the God which is in Unu".[21]

'I [know] the name of her sail; its name is Nūt. 206

'I know the name of [her . . .]; it is ⟨Imsety⟩, Hapy, Duamūtef and ⟨ Ḳebḥsenuf ⟩; their names are "He who acts as a robber", "He who makes his own name", "He who plunders" and "He who sees his father".[22]

'I know the name of the butt(?) (of her steering-oar);[23] its name is "Mistress of the Land in the garden".

'I know the name of her steering-oar; [its name is] "Accurate", and the name of its blade is "Sunshine which cuts through the water".

I know the name of the whole of this boat; it is "Buttock of Isis which Rēʿ cut off with a knife for his Eye on his own behalf in the Bark of [. . .]" '.

The skipper of the ferry-boat of the District in Khemennu shall say: 207
'Pronounce the name of the river, since you (pl.!) go down to it'.

This spirit shall say to the skipper of the ferry-boat of the District in Khemennu: 'Its name is "He who looks at them" '.

The skipper of the ferry-boat of the District in Khemennu shall say: 'Pronounce the name of the wind, since you sail by means of it'.

'Its name is "The north-wind which went forth from Khemennu to the nose of the Foremost of the Westerners, the Lord of Abydos." '

The skipper of the ferry-boat of the District in Khemennu shall say: 'Pronounce the name of the river-bank, since you go down on to it'.[24]

'Its name is "Backbone of Gēb and ribs of Isis which repel the Serpent 208
from it" '

It means going forth into the presence of the Great Ennead which is in Ōn, which comes joyfully to meet this spirit. This spirit shall be prostrate[25] on his belly among them, and he shall say to them: 'I have come here to greet you, you lords of possessions who are [in] eternity, (who are within) the limits[26] of everlasting. [I have] moored(?),[27] my cake is baked, my bread is in Pe, my beer is in Dep, I possess offerings, and my offerings are bread and beer, life, welfare, health and a clear character;[28] (also) going forth in any shape which I desire within the Field of Rushes'.

209 The Great Ennead which is in the Field of Rushes shall say: 'Give him a *šns*-cake, a beer-jug, and a portion [of meat], and he shall eat of it, and he shall not go forth for ever and ever'.

The [Great] Tribunal which is in the Field of Rushes shall say: 'Give him an aroura [of land] with barley three cubits [tall]. The Followers of Horus shall cut it for him for the first year, and he shall chew on it and rub his body with it, and his body will be hale [29] like all of them'.

The Great Tribunal which is in the Field (of Rushes) shall say: 'Give him the . . . [30] of a washerman and a washerwoman; let him drink water at the eddy and grant that he achieve orgasm'. [31]

The Great Tribunal which is in the Field (of Rushes) shall say: 'Let him
210 sing and dance and receive ornaments, | let him play draughts with those who are on earth, may his voice be heard even though he is not seen; let him go to his house and inspect his children for ever and ever.'

This spirit shall say: 'I have come here in order to inspect my children and to receive for myself the garment(?),[32] for I am the Biter in his coil; I am the Baboon with the strong name; I am the . . . [33] which fights stubbornly(?) [34] and fells the confederacy of Seth. I have come here speaking and reciting the Book of the Divine Words'.

1. See Spell 404, n.1; 405 is a somewhat corrupt and altered version of 404.
2. Compare 181*i*.
3. See Spell 404, n.4. 'Imsety' is a corruption of *ỉmḥty* in 181*j*.
4. M1C has 'make a spell'.
5. See Spell 404, n.8. Here *mrwty* is given a plural form; in both versions the bird-sign *tyw* has been misunderstood.
6. A garbled version of 184*d*.
7. Cf. 187*g*.
8. *ꜥnḏ nb* is unintelligible; it corresponds to the obscure *ỉnḏbw* in 188*a*.
9. Written as *ẖꜣbt* in M1C.
10. Here *.sn* is without antecedent, but in 188*b* it refers back to 'those gods who are on

yonder side of the river' in 187*d*; in 202*a* both texts are somewhat corrupted and we should read *m ḥmw n.sn* as in 188*b*.

11. Mueller, *JEA* 58, 104-5, translates *sꜣḳ* with 'wrapped', which is dubious, since it does not seem to correspond to the root meaning of this verb, and I take it to mean 'put together', 'reassembled', of the corpse of the deceased, cf. *Pyr.* §§ 654; 735 and often; here the deceased is not only properly dressed, but all present and correct in person.

12. *Ḏd* before *ỉmy* 'grant' in MIC seems superfluous; this clause is in continuation of the prayer beginning in 202*d*.

13. We appear to have here a direct genitive with honorific transposition, to be read *nfw-n-mẖnt-tn W-m-H̱mnnw;* Mueller favours a *badal* apposition.

14. An odd construction, see Mueller, op. cit. 105. My own view is that in this particular case *pw n* is equivalent to *nn n* and that *pw n ꜣẖ* means simply 'this spirit', but the significance of such a construction escapes me, and I am not certain that this interpretation is correct.

15. Cf. 186*i*.

16. Read *dm,* cf. 202*b*.

17. Cf. Spell 404, n. 32.

18. Read *ḏrt tw,* cf. 191*f*.

19. Read [*s*] *wꜣyt* by virtue of the cross sign.

20. Cf. 191*a-b,* but corrupted here.

21. A corrupt version of 190*d*.

22. Cf. 192*d-e*; clearly all four Children of Horus were originally named here. One would expect the ribs to have been included here, but they are already accounted for in 205*b*.

23. On *ỉbꜣyt* see Spell 404, n. 45.

24. Var. MIC: *prt.k* [. . .]. MINY ends here with the designation of the deceased (208*o*).

25. Cf. Mueller, op. cit. 110, though 'spread out' does not seem the happiest possible translation of *sẖ*.

26. Taking *ḥntyw* to be a plural *nisba* of *ḥnt* 'space' of time, *Concise Dict.* 171. See also *nḥḥ ḥnty ḏt* 'for ever and ever', 196*a*.

27. Restoring as *mny* [*.n.ỉ*].

28. For this translation of *bꜣkt* cf. *Letters to Dead,* n. on I, 3; *JEA* 28, 19(*l*).

29.  is presumably a substitute for .

30. Reading and meaning alike obscure.

31. Cf. Mueller, op. cit. 110-11.

32. The precise meaning of *ʿmʿm* is not known. I have translated it with 'garment(?)' because the det. resembles that of *snd* 'cloth' in *CT* I, 109*a*; III, 82*a*. Mueller suggests 'basket(?)'.

33. *Ḥwnt,* meaning unknown, apparently a fighting animal; again *CT* VII, 163*j*. Compare *ḥwnw* VI, 328*n*.

34. *Mnty* appears to be old perfective 3rd fem. sing. of *mn* 'be firm', 'endure', hence by extension 'be stubborn', referring to *ḥwnt*.

Spell 406

V, 211 SPELL [FOR] THE SEVEN KNOTS OF [THE CELESTIAL KINE][1]. Get back, you watchful one, who changes shape, who conveys away souls, who drags away hearts; go away from me, for I am Gēb, chiefest of the gods, and Atum, Lord of being.

1. Restored as 212a.

Spell 407

V, 212 SPELL FOR KNOWING THE SEVEN KNOTS OF THE CELESTIAL KINE.[1] O you who
213 knot your[2] rope and frap the ferry-boat, O ferryman of the Souls of Ōn,| knot your rope and frap your ferry-boat; pilot[3] me to the southern sky and row
214 me to the northern sky,| so that I may set the Longhorn in the northern sky, for mine are the celestial kine.

O Seth,[4] possessed of your power, great Longhorn[5] dwelling in the northern
215 sky,|give me air among the *wtnw* who give rest to the celestial kine.[6]

216 O you who are loud-voiced, |greatly majestic, sitting in the midst of darkness, give me air among the *wtnw*[7] who give rest to the celestial kine.

The river is still for the Lord of splendour; the *nt*-crown attacks(?) the
218 *wtnw*[8] |who give rest to the celestial kine.

The crocodile[9] goes forth from under the Heights of Neith[10] and from under the river banks.

219 Rest(?),[11] O Earth-god; grant rest to the celestial kine, for a cry goes forth and tumult[12] starts up.

220 O Neith, Mistress of . . .,[13] come under my feet[14] among the *wtnw* who give rest to the celestial kine.

221 O Lord of the seed of the Five Bulls,[15] yours are the bonds of the strong bull.[16]

222 O you seven knots of the celestial kine, I know you and I know your names; may you make me hale, may you make my flesh hale, may you make my members
224 hale, may you grant supports for my bones,[17]| may you save me from all things evil,[18] may nothing evil happen to me, because I am a worthy spirit who does not listen to magic; I will not be taken to the shambles by him who is in charge of the butchers(?), their desires[19] shall not come to pass through me. I will not go upside down, I will walk on my feet, and I will be enduring in my place.

1. So B2C; minor varr. in the other texts.

2. In the 3rd person in the original, as is usual in vocatives of this kind.

3. For this meaning of *wḏ* > *wd* see *Urk.* IV, 1847, 13. Three texts omit the object.

4. B1C and B2L add *wr* 'the great' after the name of Seth.

5. B3Bo has a superfluous *ꜥꜣ* 'great' before *ngw*.

6. is probably to be preferred to , but the sense will be the same; its object *ṯꜣw* has been omitted in three texts, but cf. 216*c*; 225*g.l.*; 226 *a.d.h*; S1C has: 'give me my heart'. On the *wtnw* see *Pyr. Transl.* Utt. 681, n. 3.

7. Note that four texts omit *d n.ỉ* before *ṯꜣw*. Var. B2Bo: 'in the darkness of the *wtnw.*'

8. For *ỉd* 'attack(?)' cf. *CT* III, 365*b*; 387*d*. Var. B2Bo: *ỉd ꜣt.ỉ wtnw* 'my power attacks(?) the *wtnw*'. In B1C and B1L this passage follows 221*c*, see de Buck's n. 3*. The water det. after *nt* in several texts is probably borrowed from *wtnw*.

9. The common noun rather than Sobk the crocodile god; note the plurals in B2Bo and S1C and the var. *msḥ* in B3Bo.

10. B2Bo, S2C and S1C read: 'the crocodile of the Heights of Neith', omitting *ẖr*. The 'Heights of Neith' could refer to her breasts, since she was the mother of crocodiles, cf. *Pyr. Transl.* Utt. 308, n. 6. B1C and B2L (218*c*) strangely have *ḥnꜥ* 'together with' after *sbk*.

11. The verb in 219*a* is written *sḫnš* three times, *snḫš* twice, *sḫn* once, and is determined mostly with , while B1C and B2L (219*d*) have *ḫšy* with det. . Of all these varr., the only intelligible one is *sḫn*, but it is very doubtful if that were the original reading. The use of the enclitic *r.k* shows that this enigmatic verb is in the imperative.

12. Var. M6C: *ỉꜥnw* 'woe'.

13. *Nṯst*, meaning unknown; S1C substitutes *ṯnnt*.

14. Meaning perhaps 'support me'.

15. B1C and B2L have: *ỉ nb kꜣw khꜣ dwt.f* 'O Lord of the bulls who bellow his cry'.

16. So B1C and B2L, which add the refrain *sḫn n mḥt-wrt; nttyw* of the other texts is a variant of *nṯṯ*, though they do not show the possessive dative; S1C has *nb nttyw*. Note that the clauses starting with 214*c* and ending with 221*b* are eight in number, and thus correspond to the seven cows and the bull of the *mḥt-wrt*. 212*a*-214*b* form an introductory paragraph.

17. Var. B3Bo: 'may you make my bones and my members hale'. For 222*a-d* and 233*a-c* B1C and B2L have (222*e-i*; 223*d-i*): 'O you seven knots of the celestial kine, make me hale, nourish me, give strength to my bones and life to my members. Make my flesh hale for the whole of my life, for I know you and I know your names; I will not die, I will not be poor, I will not go blind, I will not be deaf, for indeed I am one of the gods, and I know your names'. The following 224*a* (M6C) is a repetition of 223*b*, except that it has *ḥꜣty* 'heart' instead of *ꜥwt* 'members'.

18. What follows (224*d-f*) is in M6C alone.

19. Lit. perhaps 'their what-is-desirable'; the writing is that of *ꜥꜣbt* 'food', but that sense hardly fits the present context.

Spell 408

V, 225 SPELL FOR THE SEVEN KNOTS OF THE CELESTIAL KINE. O you who knot your rope and frap your ferry-boat, O ferryman of the Souls of Ōn, knot your rope and frap your ferry-boat; act as pilot in the southern sky, row in the northern sky, go down into [. . . see, you] have come under my feet;[1] give me air among the *wtnw* who give rest to the celestial kine.

O you bulls who bellow [. . .], yours are your [bonds]. O Strong Bull, come under my feet, give me air among the *wtnw* who give rest to the celestial [kine].

O Seth, [possessed of your] power,[2] Great Longhorn dwelling in the northern sky when(?) the Longhorn is caused [to ascend(?)] to the northern
226 sky, [see, you] have come under my feet; give me air among the *wtnw* who give rest to the celestial kine.

O Lord of Peace at the head of Neith,[3] who gives air to those who are in her company, see, you have come under my feet; give me air among the *wtnw* who give rest to the celestial kine.

[The crocodile(?)][4] goes forth [. . .] Mistress of Mendes, see, you have come under my [feet]; give me air among the *wtnw* who give rest to the celestial kine.

O you seven knots of the celestial kine, I know you and I know [your] names; make me hale.

1. For this expression see Spell 407, n. 14.
2. Cf. 214*c*.
3. The name of the goddess rather than that of the crown, cf. 220*a*.
4. Cf. 218*b*.

Spell 409

V, 227 Hail to you, you *nšmt*-bark of Osiris, the first [boat][1] which Rēʿ built and which you shall bring to N's soul for him and for his body. May he go aboard the *nšmt*-bark, may he go down on the starboard side and go up on [the larboard side]; may he strike with his sceptre and govern [with his staff]; may you[2] vindicate N's [soul] against his foes in the sky, on earth, and [in] those seven tribunals, the tribunals [of Osiris].

Hail to you, [you] two great and mighty [gods(?)] who are in the [*nšmt*]-
228 bark! N knows you by your names and by your [shapes] in which you came into

being; may you grant that N's soul [may go down] to his body aboard the
nšmt-bark; may he go down on the starboard side and go up on the larboard
side; may he strike with his [sceptre] and govern with his staff; may you
[vindicate] N's soul against his foes in [the sky, on earth], and in those seven
tribunals [of Osiris].
Hail to you, steering-oar of the [*nšmt*]-bark! N knows you by your name
and by your shape in which you came into being; [you are] the support of Thoth[3]
which Rēʿ set up on the day of the great [. . .]-bark[4] which came into being in
the Netherworld.[5] May you bring[6] N's [soul] to his body for him; | may he go 229
aboard the *nšmt*-bark [of Osiris]; may he go down on the starboard side [and go
up on] the larboard side; may he strike [with his sceptre] and govern with [his]
staff; may you vindicate N's soul [and body][7] against his foes in the sky, [on
earth], and in those seven tribunals [of Osiris].
Hail to you, blades of the steering-oars[8] of the *nšmt*-bark! N [knows] you
by your names and by your shapes in which you have come into being; you
are the[9] tongue of Rēʿ. May you [bring] N's soul [to his body for him]; may he
go aboard the *nšmt*-bark of [Osiris];[10] may he go down on the starboard side [and
go up on] the larboard side; | may he strike [with his sceptre, may he govern] with 230
his staff; [may you vindicate] N's soul against [his] foes [in the sky], on earth,
and in those seven tribunals ⟨of Osiris⟩.
[Hail] to you, butt(?) of the steering-oar[11] of the *nšmt*-bark of Osiris!
N knows you [by your name] and by your shape [in which you] came into
being. May you bring N's soul to his body for him; may he go aboard the *nšmt*-
bark of Osiris; may he go down on the starboard side and go up on the larboard
side; may he strike with his sceptre and [govern] with his staff; [may you]
vindicate N's soul against his foes [in] the sky and on earth and in [those seven]
tribunals of Osiris.
Hail to you, [helmsman(?)][12] of the *nšmt*-bark of Osiris!. | N [knows] you 231
by your name and by [your] shape in which you came into being; [you are that]
Horus, son of Osiris. May you bring N's soul to his [body for him]; may he go
aboard the *nšmt*-bark [of Osiris]; may he go down on the starboard side [and go
up on] the larboard side; may he strike with [his sceptre and govern] with his
staff; may you vindicate N's soul against his foes [in the sky and on] earth and
in those seven tribunals [of Osiris].
Hail to you, staff of the *nšmt*-bark of Osiris! N knows you by your name
and by ⟨your⟩ shape[13] in which [you came into being]; you are that being
[. . .] who carried off his soul and took away his shade.[14] [May you bring]
N's soul to [his] body for him; | [may he go aboard] the *nšmt*-bark of Osiris; 232

may [he] go down [on the starboard side], may he go up on the larboard side; [may he strike] with his sceptre and govern with [his staff]; may you vindicate [N's] soul [against his foes] in the sky and on earth, and in those seven [tribunals] of Osiris.

[Hail to] you, bulwarks(?) [15] of the *nšmt*-bark of Osiris! N knows you by your names and by your [shape] in which you came into being; [you are] these(?) [. . .] of the First Company of Rēʿ.

Hail to you, [. . .] of the *nšmt*-bark of Osiris! N knows you by [your name] and by your shape in which you came into being; you are that [. . .] which is in front.

233 [Hail to] you, sail and mast of the *nšmt*-bark! N knows you | by [your names] and by your shape in which you came into being; you are that [. . .] which was made into that kite [16] of the sky [. . . Gēb] and Nūt when he[17] protected(?) [. . .].

[Hail] to you, rigging of the mast of the [*nšmt*]-bark! N knows [you by] your names and by your shape [in which you] came into being; [you are] the Children of Weakness [. . .] who made a great slaughter of [. . .] Nūt.

Hail to you [. . . of the] *nšmt*-bark of Osiris! [18]

1. See de Buck, n. 6*.
2. Masculine!
3. Perhaps in reference to the perch on which the sacred ibis stands; on the repeated *pw* as restored see n. 9 below.
4. The masc. adj. *ʿꜣ* precludes the restoration *nšmt* in the lacuna.
5. *Dꜣt* is surely the better reading, see de Buck's n. 2*.
6. Prospective *sḏm.f.*
7. Restore *ḏt.f* rather than *n ḏt.f* as de Buck.
8. There is no mention of a pair of steering-oars, but in what follows, the idea of duality is pursued.
9. Of the two successive demonstratives *pw* the first appears to represent the definite article.
10. For 229*k*-231*l* T1C*a* has a text which is almost entirely lost, cf. 229*m*.
11. See Spell 404, n. 45.
12. Restoration suggested by de Buck, n. 3*.
13. Suffix omitted, see de Buck, n. 3*.
14. 'His' here refers to the 'being' and not to the deceased.
15. See Spell 398, n. 15.
16. I.e. the bird.
17. *Scil.* the kite.
18. T1C*b* ends here; T1C*a* (233*i-j*) is almost totally destroyed.

Spell 410

A MAN SHALL REMEMBER HIS NAME IN THE REALM OF THE DEAD.[1] I have V, 234
spoken[2] my name in the *pr-wr*, | I have remembered my name in the *pr-nsr*[3] on 235
the night of reckoning years and numbering months.[4]

1. B2L^{a} omits *m ẖrt-nṯr*; B4C has: 'Not to let a man forget his name and his magic in the realm of the dead'. Note in B2L^{b} *rnn.f* for *rn.f*.

2. Var. S14C etc.: 'Remembrance is given to me in the *pr-wr* and the *pr-nsr*', combining 234*c* and 235*a*; L1Li and probably B6Bo^{b}: 'A name is given to me in the *pr-wr*'. B2L^{b} and T1C have corrupted *ḏd.n.ỉ* into *d.n.ỉ* and *nn.ỉ* (*sic*).

3. T1C follows this with (235*d*): 'if a man remembers his name, then will I remember his name', and ends.

4. So B6Bo^{b} ff., with a minor var. in L1Li; four texts (two damaged) add 'in the presence of the Master of Navigation'.

Spell 411

O Thoth, I am a great one,[1] I have appeared in glory.[2] Such am I; I am in my V, 236
name, and my name is a god; I will not forget it, this name of mine.

O *Bꜣt*, my name is 'Isis in the sealed place';[3] I am [in my name]. and my 237
name is a god;[4] I will not forget it, this name of mine.

O Rēʿ-Atum, O Khopri, I am one who was born on the First of the Year,
and I know my name;[5] | this name of mine is a god[6] who is in this body of mine,[7] 238
and I have driven off him who would carry away for himself[8] my name and my heart[9] in his hand. I will not forget this name of mine in the presence of the Lord of Judgement.

1. Three texts are damaged, but M19C yields a probable reading. B1Bo omits.

2. For 236*c* (S14C); B1Bo substitutes: 'If N's soul appears in glory, then will he appear in glory'. The other texts are mostly destroyed.

3. So M23C. B1Bo has *ỉ ṯꜣw* 'O wind', surely a misreading of *ỉ Bꜣt*, and also omits *ꜣst* 'Isis', thus destroying the sense of the passage. The doubtful sign in S14C is probably intended for *Bꜣt*. M23C follows the Isis clause with *ỉw.ỉ* [. . .], to be restored as *ỉw.ỉ m rn.ỉ* as in 236*e*; B1Bo has *m rn.f pn*; omitted in S14C.

4. S14C only.

5. S14C only. In 237*h* B1Bo and B6Bo^{b} substitute 'he is in his name'; following this the two B6Bo texts added in 238*a* a clause which is mostly lost.

6. S14C only.

7. M23C has: 'I will not forget this name of mine which is in this body of mine'; B1Bo: 'he will not forget this name of his which will expel the forgetfulness which is in the body of N'; similarly B6Bo*b*.

8. B1Bo omits the *n* of *n.f.*

9. *Ḥꜣty.ỉ* 'my heart' in S14C only.

Spell 412

V, 239 A MAN SHALL REMEMBER HIS NAME IN THE REALM OF THE DEAD. I am this builder who sits in the great place of the sky,[1] and as for any god who will not come following me, I will speak my name.[2]

1. *Bw wr n pt*; L1Li has *wrt ꜥꜣt nt pt.*

2. Conforming to T1L, which seems the text most likely to be original, in view of the opening rubric; L1Li has: *r ḏd rn.ỉ m-ḫt* 'in order to speak my name afterwards'; P. Gard. III: *ḏd.ỉ m-ḫt* 'I will speak afterwards': Y1C: *dy d.ỉ m-ḫt.ỉ*, which could well be a corrupt version of P. Gard. III; it is followed by both S10C texts.

Spell 413

V, 240 A MAN SHALL SEND HIS SOUL INTO THE REALM OF THE DEAD.[1] Anubis is at
rest, and it goes well with the son of Rēꜥ[2] in peace through my sacred Eye;
may you glorify[3] my soul and my shade; may they see Rēꜥ by virtue of what he
241 brings. | I ask that I may come and go,[4] that I may have power in my foot so
that this person may see him in any place where he may be by means of my
242 nature and my wisdom | and in my true spirit-shape, which is equipped and divine;
it shines as Rēꜥ,[5] it travels as Ḥatḥōr.[6] Therefore you have granted that my soul
243 and my shade and my shape may walk[7] | on their feet to where this person is so
that he may stand, sit, walk and enter[8] into his funerary estate, because I am
one in the entourage of Osiris, one who goes by night and returns by day, and
no god can be created when I am silent.[9]

1. Var. 'to send a soul into the realm of the dead'.

2. *ꜣḫ n* of M5C seems the best version; see also *BD* 491, 9 (*ꜣḫ n.k*) B2Bo has *ꜣḫ Rꜥ* (sic) *sꜣ Rꜥ* 'the son of Rēꜥ is a spirit'; so too probably B1Y; B4Bo inserts the name of the deceased before *Rꜥ*; B1Bo has *ꜣḫ.k sꜣ Rꜥ* 'may you be a spirit, O son of Rēꜥ'; *ꜣḫt* of S2C could be interpreted as a hortatory old perfective; S10C omits 240*c*.

3. Since the verb is transitive, *sꜣḫ* of four texts is a better reading than *ꜣḫ* of S2C and S10C; see also *BD* 491,10.

4. For the 1st person cf. 240*c.d*; 241*e*.
5. S1oC, which omits 242*a*, has here: 'I have come, my soul being as the soul of Rēᶜ'.
6. S1oC: 'my being is that of Ḥatḥōr' and ends.
7. 413*e* is in S2C only.
8. B1Y and B2Bo have misread *ᶜḳ* 'enter' as *bꜣ* 'soul'.
9. Var. B1Bo: 'no festival of those who rebel against N will be celebrated'.

Spell 414

DRIVING ᶜAPEP FROM THE BARK OF RĒᶜ.[1] Woe to you, *'Imy-nhd.f*,[2] O you of V, 244
whom the Double Lion is afraid;[3] see, burning[4] has gone out from the sky into
the interior of the Cavern of the Rebel. He has uttered his rebellion against[5] Rēᶜ,
he has committed robbery against him | and his head[6] is guarded by the Great 245
Demolisher.[7] A light has been kindled against him in the Mansions of Sepa, his
fetters have been made firm by the gods . . .[8] May you be protected![9]

I have fallen down and have crawled away, because I am he of the *wꜣs*-
sceptre, the Great Power at the neck of Gēb.[10] | O you entourage of Rēᶜ of 246
the right-hand and the left-hand,[11] regard me as one wholly unique, for Rēᶜ
has spoken to me, I have driven off the rebel, I have made ᶜApep impotent, | I
have withdrawn(?),[12] and burning goes out from the sky into the interior of the 247
Cavern of the Rebel.[13] He has uttered his rebellion against Rēᶜ, he has committed
robbery against him; may Rēᶜ go down in the Bark of Goodness,[14] may he travel
beneath the Fire-goddess,[15] may those who are on the thrones of the West
rejoice.| May I[16] travel in safety, O Rēᶜ; may you find me and meet me.[17] 248

1. So B2L and B1C, the latter at the end of the spell; B2Bo and S2C stop at 'ᶜApep,' while B4Bo omits the rubric.

2. On *iᶜnw n.k* see James, *Ḥeḳanakhte*, p. 109; a threat against the serpent *'Imy-nhd.f* is surely implied here. For this mythological serpent cf. *Wb.* II, 288, 5.

3. So B2Bo; varr. B1C: 'of whom Horus and the Double Lion are afraid'; B2L: 'of whom the Many-faced and the Double Lion are afraid': B4Bo substitutes the name of the deceased for the suffix in *n.k* and apparently reads: 'the Double Lion is afraid of N', which is not only poor sense in itself, but also makes nonsense of the interjection *hꜣ*.

4. For *hwt* 'burning' cf. *Siut*, pl. 13, 14; *CT* II, 73*a*.

5. The preposition *r* before *Rᶜ* is omitted in B1C and B2L; the latter has a dittograph of *Rᶜ*.

6. Var. 'his mouth'.

7. For *snš* of B4Bo, B2Bo and S1C read *sšn* with B1C and B2L; for the meaning 'demolish' cf. *Pyr.* §1121; *Urk.* I, 103, 12; 219, 2.

8. Here appears in all texts an incomprehensible word *ᶜftt*; see Spell 1034, n. 1.

9. The suffix *.k* is shown to refer to the deceased by B4Bo, and the absence of an object points to the interpretation as a passive. The  of S2C is apparently a kind of determinative here. In what follows, the deceased is speaking.

10. Var. 'the Great Power of the West'.

11. I.e. standing on both sides of Rēʿ. B1C and B2L insert *bnrt* 'sweet' among the qualifications of the entourage; B2Bo adds at the end *n pt tꜣ* 'of sky and earth'.

12. For *nḥm* 'withdraw' cf. *Pyr.* §1098, where *nḥm ḏt.f* is better translated 'who withdrew himself; here the verb is used without expressed object.

13. Var. B4Bo and B2Bo: 'who rebelled against Rēʿ'. These texts and S2C omit 247*b*.

14. The name of Rēʿ is omitted in B4Bo and B2Bo, which are shown by the enclitic *r.f* to be in the imperative, but the optative *sḏm.f* form of B2L better fits the context. B1C has substituted 'Rēʿ rejoices in his beauty'.

15. Again B4Bo and B2Bo present us with an apparent imperative as against a *sḏm.f* form in B1C and B2L; the latter is to be preferred. *Ḫt-wtt* 'fire-goddess' is best presented in B2Bo; B1C has *ỉrt Wtt* 'the eye of the goddess'. For *Wtt* as a serpent deity, cf. *Pyr.* §§900; 902; *CT* I, 186*e*; but more commonly the name is attached to another word to yield a deity; *'Iḫt-wtt,* e.g. *Pyr.* §§198; 791; 1503: *CT* I, 280*i*; 285*g*; 294*d*; *Rnn-wtt, Pyr.* §§302; 454; 1755; *BD* 443, 1; *Ḥkn-wtt, Pyr.* §288; and now *Ḫt-wtt* here.

16. Note the miswriting of the suffix 1st sing. in B2Bo, which has been assimilated to the det. of *ḫpy* 'die'.

17. Three texts out of five insert 'as Rēʿ' here, but the insertion seems alien to the text of 248*b.c*, and following B1C and B2L, it has been omitted from the translation.

Spell 415

I have gone up into Pe, I have gone down in Dep, and Ḥemen is he who has done this work with me.

Spell 416

V, 249 SPELL FOR BURIAL. I have gone to and fro, I have sung what I should sing, what I have made is a cord(?)[1] The two portals are opened for me, and I have gone up
250 on the stairway, I have received . . . ,[2] | I have stood on the sky with the Truth-goddess, I have found the crew of Rēʿ-Atum, and they said: 'Welcome! You say what is true, you see what is good, so go up on the Stairway of Vindication, for you are he who said that he would come'.

1. Regarding *ỉrt.n.ỉ*, like *ḥst.n.ỉ* above, as a perfective relative form. *'Ihmst* seems to be a var. of *hms* 'cord' in 280*f*.

2. *'Iṯnw-sw,* quite obscure. It may be a corruption of *ỉṯnws* 'a tree', cf. Sp. 1029, n. 8.

Spell 417

NOT TO GO UPSIDE DOWN. The two *ḏd*-pillars of Rēʿ stand up, and I go and V, 251
come between them. My two Fledgelings are upside down, my hair stands up, and I cannot eat meat.[1]

1. *Sfꜣw* is not in *Wb*, but the det. and the context leave little doubt as to the meaning.

Spell 418

TO WARD OFF THROWSTICKS.[1] Get back, you throwstick[2] which runs and speeds, V, 252
you female messenger of the gods, whom the gods send on to the banks of the
Winding Waterway to meet their children,[3] | as a magician[4] who knows their 254
spells, in order to take away[5] their magic and to remove their power.

Go down,[6] | you throwstick which runs and speeds, you female messenger 255
of the gods whom the gods send.[7] You shall fall, | you shall creep away, for I have 256
taken my body from you.

1. In four texts only, with four different spellings of *ʿmʿꜣt*.
2. Plural in M3C and M5C.
3. S2C substitutes '[their] fathers'.
4. So S14C; the other texts omit *m* before *ḥkꜣw*.
5. In B1C ff. the fem. ending of the infinitive *ỉṯt* is not written, but see B1Y ff.
6. The enclitic *r.ṯ* is repeated after *hy*. *Nhy* in M3C is corrupt.
7. This last clause in M3C only.

Spell 419

Hail to you, Osiris, august father of the gods, in your happy day of the festival of Sokar! Hail to you, N, in this happy day of the festival of Sokar! May men behold you, may all the plebs serve you, may all the patricians worship you.

Spell 420

I have entered into the zizyphus-tree of the Mound[1] of the Double Gate of V, 257
the . . . ,[2] I have gone down so that I may wash myself in the Lake of Natron, since I have entered into the pillared hall so that I may see the god, the Lord of the gods, (even) Arsaphes, Lord of Ninsu, exalted of jewels(?),[3] fair of

plumes; Bull who copulates with fair ladies; Lord of blood, flourishing of shambles; potent spirit who dwells in Ninsu, on whose vertex are the plumes of Sopd and the *ꜣtf*-crowns of Rēꜥ.[4]

1. *Ꞽꜣw* is probably a var. of *ꞽꜣꜣ* 'mound', *Rec. trav.* 29, 164, 7; cf. also *ꜣꜣ* 'mound', *JEA* 34, 15.
2. Quite obscure.
3. Reading uncertain, see de Buck, n. 4*.
4. 'Of Rēꜥ' only in B1Y.

Spell 421

V, 258 TO GO[1] TO ŌN AND RECEIVE OFFERINGS THERE. I am the three baboons;[2] see, my hinder parts are at my back, my leg(s) are at my shoulders,[3] my spinal cord is in the nest of children, I sit among the gods, and I act the baboon among the waters of children.

1. *Šm* is surely infinitive, despite the absence of the fem. ending; compare the similar omission in *ꞽt(t)*, 254*b*.
2. For these three words for baboon' cf. *Pyr.* §505. My translation there of *hṯt* as 'hyaena' was a slip of the pen.
3. *Ḫpdwy* of S10C is clearly an error. We have here a picture of an ape or man squatting with his knees drawn up to his chin.

Spell 422

V, 259 RECEIVING BREAD. I am he who made his seat in Ōn – four times – within the shining(?) Mansion of Sunrise.[1] I am with my foot on the sky and my hand on the earth,[2] I am he who dwells in the shining(?) Mansion of Sunrise in Ōn, I am
260 he who rises, I am he of the Pyramidion,[3] I am he of the *bulṭi*-fish, I am the fruitful female(?), I am the fruitful male(?),[4] I am the messenger, *Pꜣšt* the great is my protection(?).[5]

1. Var. B3Bo: 'in the Mansion of the Pyramidion in Ōn'. B4Bo has *wbn Rꜥ wbnbn*. The reading *ḥwt wbn Rꜥ* 'The Mansion of Sunrise' is straightforward, but the significance of the following *wbnbn* is by no means clear, and it seems probable that it is faulty, for the reduplicated verb has not been recorded, the fem. ending is lacking, and it has the appearance of being confused with the word for 'pyramidion', see the variant of B3Bo quoted above and also 260*a*. 'Shining' seems a possible translation.

2. So B2Bo, B4Bo and B1Y. *Snk,* var. *sn,* at the end of the first two texts may be a direction to the reader, compare the similar notations recorded in Spell 76, n. 26; this notation is lacking from B1Y. The other three texts have: 'I am he who destroyed (*sic*!) his arm in sky and earth – and *vice versa*'.

3. 259*e*–260*a* are only in the S1C and S2C texts.

4. Taking  in each case as standing for , cf. *Wb.* II, 308, 15–309, 1.

5. Following S1C and S2C^{b}; B2Bo and B4Bo are obscure. *Pȝšt* could perhaps stand for *Pȝḫt* of Beni Hasan, e.g. *BH* I, 25, 18.

Spell 423

NOT DYING A SECOND DEATH.[1] I am Atum, I have power[2] as the Double Lion, V, 261
I am helped(?)[3] by the eldest god, my face is made bright(?)[4] by the eldest god.
I eat life, I live by air, | I will make[5] offerings to the *hnhnw*-bark, I will be raised 262
up from the *hnhnw*-bark to the bark of Khopri, he will let me enter to see what
is there, I will recite his words to the judges, and he will let me converse with
those four mighty spirits who move to and fro[6] and live after they have died. | May
I live after death like Rēʿ every day,[7] who lives after death. As for any god or 263
goddess, any spirit or dead person, or any snake in heaven or earth who shall go
to and fro,[8] my magic will drive them off. | The fire will go up, the flame will go 264
up from the bellies of those who creep, and the fiery one will be against them as
the Eye of Rēʿ. I have butchered and eaten[9] herds black and white, and I live on
their hooves; in fact(?)[10] I will not die, and in fact(?) I will not die a second time
on earth.

1. Var. 'not dying another time'.

2. So B1Y; var. B2Bo: 'may you have power, O N' with *ȝḫ.k*; B4Bo has *ȝḫ* as adjectival predicate with the fem. dependent pronoun (woman's coffin) with much the same meaning.

3. Guessing *smt* to be a writing of the passive of *sm* 'help', *Concise Dict.* 225.

4. The leg-det. suggests the reading *sbḳ.t(w)* while *sbḳ* in its turn could be a miswriting of *sbȝḳ* 'make bright', *Pyr.* § 457; *CT* IV, 155*f.*

5. Prospective *sḏm.f.*

6. Read *ḫnsw* with B1Y.

7. B2Bo has a dittograph of *N m-ḫt mt.* B4Bo omits 'after death'.

8. For this sense of *nn(y)* cf. *Pyr.* §310.

9. The original reverses the order of these two verbs.

10. Regarding *sp.f* here and in 264*c* as adverbial; '(in) its fact' does not seem an impossible translation.

Spell 424

V, 265 SPELL FOR DRIVING AWAY THE CROCODILES WHO STEAL MAGIC.[1] Get back,
you crocodile of the West, living on the Unwearying Stars.
266 Get back, you crocodile of the East, living on mutilations.[2]
Get back, you crocodile of the South, living on stinking faeces.[3]
Get back, you crocodile of the North, ⟨ living on ⟩ the twilight in the midst
of the distant stars.[4]
267 Abhorrence of you is in my body, and I have absorbed the powers of Osiris;
268 I am Seth,[5] | and I have trodden down her who was pregnant by you, O Osiris.
There is no wrath which is in me,[6] my seed is in my head and my belly,[7] for I am
Sopd and I am Atum.

1. Var. S1oC: 'Spell for driving off the four crocodiles of the realm of the dead'. In what follows B1Bo seems the most intelligible text.

2. *ꜥfꜣwt,* a derivative of *ꜥfꜣ* 'tear out' testicles, *CT* I, 30*b*.

3. For the sense given to *ỉꜣbty* in B1Bo cf. *ỉꜣb* with similar meaning in *Pyr.* §§1790; 1931. Of the other versions S1oC is close to it: 'living on stinking and constricted faeces' (267*b*), where the fem. form *gwꜣt* has doubtless been influenced by the writing of *ỉꜣbt(y)* just above it; the double columns covering both South and North in 266*d* appear to read: 'living on faeces of this region of the lesser (*twꜣt*) eastern stars' (B2Bo and B4Bo); S14C has an even less intelligible variation.

4. B1Bo omits *ꜥnḫ m* 'living on'. S1oC (267*c*) has: 'living on this one above the stars'. On the obscure texts of 266*d* see n. 3 above.

5. Var. 'the Outcast'.

6. Var. 'in his head'. in 268*c* S1oC has 'I am Sopd', having misplaced it from 268*e*.

7. B1Bo omits 'head' and S1oC omits 'belly'.

Spell 425

V, 269 SPELL FOR DRIVING AWAY A VULTURE. Hail to you, Bull-of-bulls and Searcher-
out-of-truth, you two vultures who are on the booths of the Potter! I have come
270 to you that I may break your water-pots | and smash your inkwells,[1] for a path is
prepared for me to the place where the great god is.

1. For *wḏꜥwt* 'inkwells' cf. *Pyr.* §2030, where the det. suggests the original use of a mussel-shell or the like as an ink-container. The absence of the fem. ending in B2Bo and B4Bo may be due to a faulty archetype.

Spell 426

O starry youths(?),[1] I will not give you this magic of mine.[2] | I sit with my back V, 271
to the sacred place[3] in Ōn. Who is this magician[4] who will take me to the sky?
NOT TO TAKE AWAY A MAN'S MAGIC FROM HIM IN THE REALM OF THE DEAD.

1. The correct reading here is doubtful. B1Bo has *ỉ ḥwnw sḥd* 'O starry youths'; three texts have *ỉḥm sḥd* and S1C has *ỉḥw sḥd.* The plural number of the noun is indicated by the suffix *ṯn* in 270*d*.
2. So all texts except B1Bo, which has: 'you do not know N's magic'.
3. Var. S1C: *ḏsrt wrt* 'the great holy place'.
4. B1Bo omits this clause.

Spell 427

TO EAT WITH THE MOUTH, TO DEFECATE WITH THE HINDER PARTS, TO BE
EQUIPPED . . . ,[1] TO HAVE POWER OVER WATER [. . .].[2] | He grants that my shade V, 272
shall go to me,[3] and I have traversed the storm, I have hurried over the sky, | I 273
have reached the . . .-region.[4] It is Ḥatḥōr who raised me up,[5] an obstacle is
smitten down for me,[6] and I am placed in the presence of Atum.[7]

1. On the obscure word *ꜥftt* see Spell 1034, n. 1.
2. P. Gard. II has a variant rubric: 'Spell for raising a man up to the god [. . .].
3. So B2Bo and apparently B4Bo. All the other texts have the name of the god Shu instead of *šwt* 'shade'. *D.ỉ n.f šꜣs.ỉ Šw* of S1C is quite obscure, for I know of no instance of *šꜣs* taking an object of the person; S2C appears to read: 'he grants that I go [to] Shu'; P. Gard. II, S10C and B4C omit *dy.f* in 272*a* and read: 'Shu goes to me'.
4. *'Iꜣdt* with det. 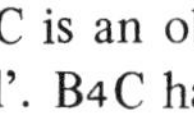 , except as a word for 'net', is not recorded; *ỉꜣdt* 'tract of land', *Peas.* B1, 143, is probably related, but is too imprecise in meaning, for here the word seems to refer to an exact location. An echo of this spell, much changed, occurs in *CT* VI, 330*i* ff., where *ỉꜣdt* becomes the *ỉꜣd*-star.
5. Read *in Ḥwt-ḥr syꜥt wỉ* with P. Gard. II; all the other versions seem to have gone slightly wrong except perhaps B4Bo.
6. For *ḫw sḏb* in a favourable sense cf. *Wb.* IV, 382, 5.
7. *Wd.n.ỉ* of S1C is an obvious error. S10C reads: 'I have been placed among the Followers of the Lord of All'. B4C has: '[. . .] of the Lord of All in the presence of the august god'.

Spell 428

V, 274 TO GO TO THE GREAT GOD.[1] I have seen the doubles, and the fire goes forth; it guides[2] me on a fair path[3] to the place where the great god is.

1. The rubric in P. Gard. II only.
2. S2C has the fem. participle *sšmt* instead of the *sḏm.f* form of the other texts.
3. Var. P. Gard. II: 'a fair inherited path'.

Spell 429

V, 275 Hail to you, you Lords of fishing and fowling! You have given me a catch of fish and fowl, you have divided up the Field of Offerings for me. May you be well-disposed to me as regards your own bodily members,[1] for you have granted to
276 me to outsoar[2] the falcon with ruffled plumage.[3] | O you gods, you gods, who are[4] the plumed ones who row[5] in the horizon when Rēꜥ sails in the firmament? Offspring(?)[6] of Shu! Offspring(?) of Shu! May you not speak, O offpsring of Shu!

1. The words *ꜥwt ḏt.tn* seem to be adverbial to *i͗mꜣ* in the same manner as *i͗b* in the well-known expression *i͗mꜣ i͗b*.
2. Read *sn* in its sense of 'surpass', cf. *GNS* 72. 160. The writing of B2Bo shows confusion with *šm*.
3. S1C and S2C are perhaps to be understood as 'the wind-falcon with wind-ruffled plumage'.
4. For this writing of *i͗n-m* 'who?' cf. de Buck, *Archiv Orientalní*, 20, 399.
5. Var. S1C: 'the plumed ones, the gods who row'.
6. *Ḫnm* with child-det. seems not to be recorded, but *ḫnm* 'wild-fowl' and *ḫnmw* 'herd', *Wb.* III, 381, 14.15, suggest 'offspring' as a possibility, though the sense of the passage remains obscure.

Spell 430

V, 277 TO DRIVE AWAY THE VULTURE.[1] O you who are greatly poisonous on your mounds, fair noble, son of a *i͗hm*-bird, I have come for you, O greatly poisonous,[2] that I may break your pens and tear up your papers because of these double ills which I have brought in my hand from the Island of Fire, which were in my hand in the Field of *Ḏꜣdꜣ*.[3] So said the god to him.

1. Dual in B2Bo and S2C.

2. Var. S1C: 'you who act the greatly poisonous'.

3. For this obscure locality see *CT* IV, 385*j* (Spell 350), with which the present spell has something in common.

Spell 431

TO RECEIVE GIFTS, TO BE . . . ,[1] TO HAVE POWER OVER WATER, [TO RECEIVE] WHAT IS BENEFICIAL. I am the devourer[2] of the Inert One, who ascended from the Abyss, who went forth from Unu,[3] and every soul belongs to me; I live on the entrails of the Baboon.[4] V, 278 279

1. *ʿpr ʿftt*, see Spell 1034, n. 1; in B1Bo^{c} it constitutes the whole of the rubric.

2. *ꜣfʿ*, here translated 'devourer', surely belongs to the stem *ꜣfʿ* 'glutton', 'gluttony', *Concise Dict.* 3. B4C transforms *ꜣfʿ* into *ʿfꜣ ʿwt* 'who tears off limbs'. Most texts start this clause with an independent pronoun or the name of the deceased, but B1Bo^{b} appears to be a vocative, and B1Bo^{a} has *ꜣfʿ* alone, perhaps as a vocative also.

3. Three texts omit the reference to Unu and four the reference to the Abyss; one alone (S1C) names both places, though probably S2C once did so also.

4. S1C omits the reference to the Baboon.

Spell 432

NOT TO ROT AND NOT TO DO WORK IN [THE REALM OF THE DEAD].[1] I eat and I swallow[2] and I sit as Horus(?);[3] the *ḥms*-cord is spun for me(?).[4] V, 280

1. In M22C only. Restore [*ẖrt*]*-nṯr* at the end as in 281*a*.

2. Following S1C, which alone has *sʿm* 'swallow' and presents the *sḏm.f* form as against the *sḏm.n.f* of B2Be and B1Bo.

3. Quite unintelligible unless 𓁷 be taken to be a writing of *Ḥr* 'Horus' followed by the enclitic *ỉs* in the sense of 'as', 'like', Edel, *Altäg. Gramm.* §828; *Eg. Gramm.*^{3} §247, 5. *'Is* corresponds to no noun upon (*ḥr*) which one could sit.

4. Reading *ḥs.tw n.ỉ ḥms*; for *ḥs* 'spin' cord cf. *BH* II, 13. *Hms* is not otherwise known, but the det. indicates a cord or rope; *ỉhmst* of 249*d* may be a variant. S1C has *hmst* without det.

Spell 433

Not to rot and not to do work in the realm of the dead.[1] The louse comes, the louse comes dead,[2] the louse is chewed. I have traversed the cataract,[3] V, 281

282 those who are in the gates[4] open their arms to me, | one who is conceived and born – and *vice versa.*[5] What Osiris himself said to me: 'You shall go down[6] into the earth, a portion shall be prepared for you(?).[7] Those who should draw near to you will draw near(?) . . .'[8]

1. In B1Bo*b* only.

2. For *ktt* 'louse' see *CT* II, 94*a*. How the opening clauses are to be read is made plain by S1C, but the numeral 2 after *ktt* in this MS and in S2C and B4C is probably to be regarded as an echo of *sp 2* in B2Be and B1Bo*a, b*.

3. The most intelligible text again is S1C, but its relevance to what precedes is not obvious.

4. Var. 'their gates'.

5. The writings of B2Be suggest that *sywrwty* and *mswty* may be formations akin to *mrwty* 'the well-beloved', *Concise Dict.* 111, and *k3wty* 'workman', op. cit. 283. The texts of S1C, etc., are unintelligible as they stand, but they suggest that for *sywrwty* we should read *ỉwrwty*; the former means 'make pregnant' (op. cit. 212), which does not make good sense.

6. For the 1st person in 282*b*, see the foregoing text of S1C, and for the 2nd person here, cf. 282*d*. A clear case of the oft-noted confusion of pronouns.

7. A guess prompted by the dets. of *ỉknt* in B2Be and in B1Bo*a* and by the variant *ỉšt* in B1Bo*b*. The precise meaning of *ỉkn* and *ỉknt* here is not clear.

8. 282*e* and *f* are mostly unintelligible, and B1Bo*a* ends with the obscure rubric *ꜥpr ꜥftt*.

Spell 434

V, 283 TO PASS BY THE PRIMEVAL ONE[1] AND TO DRIVE OFF A SNAKE.[2] I have gone up
284 from the Poor Woman to the house of the Poor Woman, | I am he who is with
285 the face-measurer,[3] for I am seeking Osiris in Ōn, | I have been sent by that Great One, the Lord of All, who cannot die.[4]

1. A variant in 285*b* (B1Y).

2. In B1Y only.

3. The meaning of these two clauses escapes me.

4. B9C and B1Bo*a* follow 285*a* with additional texts, 285*e* (B9C) reads: 'N will [never] die'; 285*d* (B1Bo*a*) has: 'N is his successor in On,' followed by the *ỉm3ḫy ḫr* formula.

Spell 435

V, 286 TO DRIVE OFF [A SNAKE][1] AND DESTROY ITS VENOM. I have warded off your (power of) making to tremble, O great Bull-snake, whose venom is this which is within your skull, whose breath is for your slaying – and *vice versa*; [. . .][2], give me what is on your mouth, for I am one of you after . . .[3]

1. See de Buck, n. 11*.
2. Lacuna with incomprehensible remains.
3. Untranslatable; compare 289*b*.

Spell 436

TO DRIVE OFF A SNAKE AND DESTROY ITS VENOM.[1] O you who cut off the heads V, 287
and sever the necks of the foes of Osiris;[2] O you *ḥnbꜣꜣ*-snake which has neither 288
arms nor legs,[3] are you proud because of this which is on your mouth,[4] which
your mother[5] has given to you? Your mother goes up to you;[6] go off to her who 289
regards you as weak'.[7]

1. Var. B2Bo[a], second heading: 'to drive off and destroy the *kꜣw*-snake'. :'.

2. An obscure passage, complete only in B2Bo[b]. *'In* 'sever' (var. *ỉnn*) is not in *Wb.*, but in I, 92, 20 is a similarly written word for 'knife'; a reduplicated form *ỉnỉnt* is in I, 94, 11, and a verb *ỉnỉn* 'cut down' a foe is discussed in Sethe, *Komm. Pyr.* III, 241. between *nḥbt* and *ỉpw*, which is found also in three damaged texts, is incomprehensible as it stands, and must surely arise from a corruption of long standing. It seems not unlikely that the archetypal reading may have been *ỉ šꜥ tp ỉn nḥbt ỉpw nw ḫftyw* with *ỉpw* in its exclamatory sense reinforcing the initial interjection *ỉ* (once written *ỉn* in error), and the passage has been translated in this sense. Quite incomprehensible is the mention of a 'third neck' in M23C[b]. *'Ipw* is masc. plur. and ejaculatory in force, referring to 'you who cut off'.

3. Only in B2Bo[b] ff. There has clearly been an omission after 287*c*, as that vocative, addressed to the enemies of the snake, has been left in the air; 288 is addressed to the hostile snake itself. The writing of *ḥnbꜣꜣ* recalls the obscure word *bꜣꜣ* in *Pyr.* §432, also a snake-spell.

4. A reference to the snake's venom?

5. B2Bo[a] and B7Bo[b] omit the suffix after *mwt* and append an illegible name; so too S2C[a], which, however, retains the suffix in *mwt.k*.

6. Only in B2Bo[a]–M23C[b].

7. Lit. perhaps 'her who looks at you who are weak' or 'the weak one'; the snake-det. at the end may possibly determine the whole phrase.

Spell 437

N is Atum who issued from the Abyss into the *Hnhnyt*-water of the sky, N [has received] a fair place which is in [the West].[1]

1. For the restorations see de Buck's notes; in BD Spell 38A (ed. Budge, pp. 102,17–103,3) the text is in the 1st person.

Spell 438

V, 290 SPELL FOR LIVING AFTER DEATH.[1] I am the Double Lion, older than Atum,[2]
having received the throne of the West, king in Chemmis.[3] Those who are in
their booths have taken me, those who are in their booths and in their shrines
have guided me; those who are in their caverns have taken me, those who are in
their holes have guided me,[4] and I have performed the voyage of the *hnhnw*-
bark because(?) the *hnhnw*-bark travels [. . .],[5] it guides me on the way of
291 Khopri. | I stand on [. . .], I recite his words to the living, I repeat his words to
those whose throats are constricted,[6] I give orders to the crew of Atum, and
those who are in their shrines fear me,[7] I give orders to those strong winds which
strengthen the Double Lion in the evening, I open my mouth, I eat [. . .] and I
[breathe(?)][8] the winds, I live again after death daily like Atum. May I be one
alive among those who have died again;[9] I daily come into being as Rēʿ, and I
live after death.

1. See de Buck, n. 1*. This rubric only in B3Bo.

2. B2L inserts in 290*d* a rubric 'Not dying again in the realm of the dead'. *Šsp* in black which precedes it in 290*c* belongs to 290*e*; the scribe had started to write this sentence when he realized that he had forgotten the rubric.

3. So B3Bo; B2L reads: 'I have received my throne of the Two Lands in the West, my vision is in Chemmis', with an altogether abnormal writing of the place-name. On the displacement of *šsp* see n. 2.

4. B2L omits 290*h-j*.

5. B2L omits 290*l*.

6. I.e. the dead; despite the writing, the context demands that *g3 ḥtt* be translated as a plural. B2L omits 291*a-c*.

7. Note the uncommon use of *snḏ* with direct object; the sense demands that *s* (for *sy*, woman's coffin) must stand for the object of the verb. The spell has been interpreted in the 1st person, as is B2L, which omits 291*e-g*.

8. Restore *sn* 'breathe' at the end of the lacuna? B2L omits 291*j-k*.

9. 291*l-n* only in B2L. Between 291*l* and *m* the copyist has left an empty space which suggests the presence of a lacuna in his original.

Spell 439

V, 292 SPELL FOR DRIVING OFF THE (FEARSOME) COMPANIONS.[1] Go in peace, O N, go in peace! The earth is ploughed up for you, offerings are presented to you, the night-ritual is performed for you in Khem. You shall go round the wall with *Ḥnw*, you shall occupy[2] the castle beside Him who is South of his Wall on that day of judging cases. Wash yourself in the swamp-waters of the inundation and in the waters of the Nile which are in the Broad Hall, for I have brought to you the Eye of Horus so that you may feed on it just as Horus fed on it.

1. *Rḥty* with 'monster' det. Cf. de Buck's n. 1*.
2. For this transitive use of *ḥms* cf. *Pyr.* §1182; *Urk.* IV, 1849,2.

Spell 440

SPELL FOR DRIVING OFF PIGS.[1] I am Rēʿ who is hale for ever, I am Atum, more V, 293
of a spirit than the spirits, I am the Lord of Eternity, worthiest of the worthy, I
am the Lord of these two *mrwt*,[2] the companions of Rēʿ, |who take the throne of 294
Khopri from him in the presence of the Lord of Eternity, the Spirit unique of
power(?), bearded of face(?)[3]. O *Tbtb* and *'Isṯṯt*, you noble companions of Rēʿ[4] 295
who make Rēʿ hale, |you possess what you have requested,[5] you possess your joy.
O you two *mrwt* of Rēʿ, approach the god on his throne, that my being may be
protected from the Quivering One,[6] and you will possess your joy. The knife of
Mut[7] has been placed in my hand[8] against you, |my eyes are opening(?)[9] [. . .], 296
my heart itself protects itself, alone in the middle of *ʿwʿ*-bird(s).[10] I am a pure
one, I have discarded [my body],[11] I have eaten the *ḳny*-garment,[12] I have
demolished [my] portal.[13]

1. Var. 'the *mr*[*wt*]'. This begins a sequence of spells concerned with the *mrwt* which could be more or less corrupt versions of a common original.

2. *Mrwty* here is not the word for 'well-beloved', since that interpretation would be entirely inappropriate in 294*a* (but see 298*a*), 297*a*, 301*a* and 302*a*. In 297*e* *mrwty* is determined with a pair of birds, and is in fact regularly construed as a dual. It is possible that it may be the original form of *mrwytt*, quoted in *Wb.* II, 104,15 as an epithet of Sakhmet, in which case it might well carry a connotation of something to be dreaded.

3. On B6C and B2Bo see de Buck's notes 2*, 3*, and 6*. B12C has read the obscure group as *pn*, while S1C substitutes *kȝ ʿpr ḥr*. This suggests that the original reading may have been *kȝ spȝ ḥr*. The meaning of this is not clear, but *spȝ ḥr* occurs in *Pyr.* §1098, where the reference may perhaps be to a bearded face.

4. Following S1C; the other versions are confused.

5. Regarding *dbḥt.ṯny n.ṯny* as a clause of possession with the verb in the relative form; B12C lacks the ending *-t*. S1C appears to be corrupt.

6. On *ȝhd* see *GNS* 30. B12C has *Hḏ* here.

7. Or '⟨my⟩ mother'.

8. Read *m ḏr⟨t⟩.ỉ* with 310*c*.

9. On sš (*sn*?) see *GNS* 72. 160.
10. S1C has *ḥr-ỉb wꜥ ꜥwꜥ*, which appears to be meaningless. For the plural cf. 314*k*.
11. Emended in accordance with 299*g*, cf. Spell 441, n. 13.
12. See also 300*c*; on this garment see *SDT* 211.
13. The reading *sšn* 'demolish' of S1C is to be preferred, cf. 300*d*.

Spell 441

V, 297 TO DRIVE OFF THE TWO *MRWT*[1] WHO COME TO TAKE AWAY A MAN'S SOUL FROM
HIM.[2] I am a Chaos-god, I am Rēꜥ the Lord of Life, I am the beam which upholds
eternity,[3] Lord of those two *mrwt* who bring faculties(?) and unite powers; who
298 put the love of them[4] in the hearts of the spirits, who drag the throne of Khopri
into the presence of the Lord of Eternity, who control(?)[5] this new-formed[6]
spirit when he comes into being in the *ẖns*- and *ḥtm*-waters.[7] Go,[8] you two *mrwt*,
the noble ones of Rēꜥ, the companions of Osiris. Go, for I do not desire ⟨. . .⟩.[9]
299 You possess what of yours is good, you possess what of yours is bad; you possess
your back,[10] you possess your plumes. I have brought away my soul, I have
rescued my magic,[11] I will not give away my powers,[12] for I am a pure one who
300 has discarded[13] his body, I am a child[14] and I am inert; I have smitten Seth and
I have fettered him on the bank of those who are constricted.[15] I have eaten the
ḳny-garment,[16] I have demolished my portal,[17] I possess my power of motion,[18] I
have received my panoply.

1. See Spell 440, n. 2.
2. B1Bo adds: 'in the realm of the dead'; B3Bo has: 'Not to take a woman's heart from her' (woman's coffin) in 297*b*.
3. Lit. 'the beam of eternity.'
4. *Mrwt.sny*; pun on the name of the objects of the spell.
5. For this sense of *ỉtḥ* cf. 160*a*.
6. For *snṯ* in the sense of 'forming' cf. *M.u.K.* 1, 8.
7. For the *ẖns*-water cf. *CT* III, 3*a*; V, 35*k*; 308*b* and with *ḥtm* compare the *ḥtmyt*-water, III, 3*b*; V, 308*b*.
8. Note the double enclitic after the imperative here and in 298*g*.
9. The object of *n mr.n.ỉ* has been omitted.
10. So B3Bo; *wꜣ* of S14C is unintelligible, and both readings seem doubtful.
11. B3Bo inserts here: 'she possesses her magic'.
12. B1Bo and presumably M22C add: 'to the strong-armed one who is behind the slayers', and M22C alone continues with what appears to be a damaged repetition of 299*b* and *d*.
13. Lit. 'who has demolished'.
14. Probably a mistake for *Nw*, god of the Abyss, cf. 312*e*; 316*f*.

15. So B3Bo and M22C; S14C has *psḏntyw* 'dwellers in the new moon', and B1Bo has *nꜣwy* determined with a bird, which looks like a miswriting of *nyw* 'ostrich'.

16. See Spell 440, n. 12.

17. The entrance to the tomb?

18. Lit. 'my movements'.

Spell 442

TO DRIVE OFF THE *MRW*[*T*]. I am Rēʿ, I am Atum, I am the Lord of Everlasting, V, 301
I am the beam which upholds eternity.[1] To me belong[2] those two *mrwt*, the
possessors of a soul who unite powers and | who take away the powers of the 302
worthy.[3] They shall come[4] bowing to the Lord of Flame, whose plumes are
tall, (even they) who took the throne of Khopri from him in the presence of the
Lord of Eternity.[5]

1. So B1Bo, see Spell 441, n. 3. S14C^{a} has *wḏꜣ ḏt* 'who is eternally hale'; S14C^{b} omits *ỉnk nb nḥḥ* and reads *swḏꜣ.ỉ ḏt* 'I make eternity hale'; in S2C$^{a.b.}$ the second clause of 301*c* is lost.

2. To translate *ỉnk* as 'I am' would not make sense here.

3. So B1Bo; S14C^{a} has: 'who take away the powers of the worthiest of the worthy'; S14C^{b} reads: 'who take away the powers of the spirit, who take away the worthiness of the worthy one', with plays on *ꜣḫ* and *ỉḳr*. The second clause is de Buck's 302*d*.

4. *'Iwt.sn* here is prospective *sḏm.f*; the *mrwt* are to be subjected to *nb nby*. I cannot account for *n* before *ḳꜣ* in B1Bo and S14C^{b} does not have it.

5. Compare 294*a* and contrast 298*a*.

Spell 443

TO DRIVE OFF THE *MR*[*WT* . . .].[1] I am that lone spirit with bearded(?) face,[2] V, 303
my eyes are opened, my ears are drilled open,|a cavern has been dug for me by 304
my fathers.[3] I have come to this land in which I am,[4] spiritualized and equipped
with magic, | and I will not be harmed in sky and earth, I will not be harmed in 305
water and the Nile;[5] | there is nothing which I do not know of what Thoth does 306
not know,[6] there is nothing which I do not know of what Thoth knows, and
there is nothing which I do not know in my abode.[7] | I am the Morning Star, I 307
know the names of those two Sisterly Companions who put the love of them in
the hearts of the spirits; | the spirit thrusts aside the enemy,[8] and he falls into 308
the *ḫns*- and *ḥtmt*-waters.[9] O *Tbt*, O female enemy,[10] | limpness(?)[11] is yours, 309
being entrapped [12] is yours, apprehension is yours, your heart is not yours,[13] you
mrwt.

O you *mrwt,* you companions of Rēʿ, whom Rēʿ sees daily, who make
310 health for Rēʿ daily,[14] | who govern souls, do not (*sic!*) quiver,[15] for my knife is in my hand against you;[16] I possess my eyes, and they are firm in my face, my heart itself protects itself, and I am a pure one who demolishes his castle.[17]

1. A long rubric of which only fragments remain. B1Bo^{b} has briefly: 'To drive off *rḥty*'; compare 292*a*.

2. Cf. 294*b*, with n.3.

3. My translation of 304*d* is by no means certain. Judging by the many varr., the ancient editors were also at a loss.

4. So S14C^{b}; the absence of *pn* in three of the well-preserved texts is curious.

5. So B1Bo^{a}, which seems to me to have preserved the true reading; 'There is nothing which I do not know' of the other texts seems weak and unconvincing. Probably they are anticipating 306*a*.

6. B1Bo^{a} omits 306*a* entirely; two texts have shortly *m Ḏḥwty* 'as Thoth', carrying on from 305*c*, but S14C^{b}, the only one of the remaining texts which is intact, goes on with *nn ḫmt.n.ỉ,* etc., here quite plausibly.

7. These last two clauses in 306*d*.

8. For the stem *snṯ* with 'hostile' significance, cf. *Pyr.* §1837; *CT* IV, 115*f*; VII, 401*a*; *BD* 281, 13.

9. Cf. Spell 441, n. 7.

10. So B1Bo^{a}, *Tbt Sṯṯ* in S14C^{a}, lost in S2C$^{a.b.}$ and B4C^{b}, and absent from the remaining texts, compare 294*c*. These names clearly are corrupt. S14C^{b} in 308*d* substitutes: ' "Pass by, O worthy spirit, and be joyful; sit on the thrones of the gods"; so say they to me', and ends. This passage appears to be an interpolation from another source.

11. There is nothing to decide between *bg* of B1Bo^{a} and *gbg* of S14C^{a}; since *bg* could stand for *bꜣg* 'be weary' and *gbg* be related to *gbgb* 'fell' a foe, *Pyr.* §678, I have guessed 'limpness' as an approximation, but it is clear from the variations in the text that its meaning was not really understood even in ancient times; these passages seem to be ill-wishing the hostile beings named in 308*c*. Here B1Bo^{a} is followed; B4C^{b} omits everything from 309*a* to 310*c*.

12. For *ỉbṯ* as a verb 'entrap', cf. *CT* VII, 254*b*; *BD* 289, 3.

13. Regarding *nfr* here as the negation of *Eg. Gramm.*^{3} § 351; to take *nfr ỉb* as meaning 'happiness' would be to contradict what has preceded.

14. B1Bo^{a} in 309*f*; S14^{a} and S2C$^{a.b}$ in 309*e*.

15. Compare 295*d*.

16. 310*b* and *c* are omitted from B1Bo^{a}.

17. B4C^{b} adds a couple of lost or damaged clauses in 310*h-i*.

Spell 444

I am a glad-hearted spirit,[1] I have swallowed the *ḳny*-garment, I have demolished V, 311
my portal, I have smitten Seth on the bank of the ibis-gods.[2] I will not give away
my power, I will not give away my magic to those two *mrwt,* the companions of
Rēʿ;[1] they have found me[3] equipped with my magic in front of the great ones, I 312
have taken the panoply of the Lord of Eternity.[4] I am Nu,[5] I was inert when the
Two Lands were complete, (but) I was not gripped and my magic was not
attacked; I was not gripped and my foot was not repelled,[1] those two *mrwt,* the
companions of Rēʿ, did not control me. I passed upon the way, I controlled my 313
appearing, and praise was given to me in front of Khem by the great ones of the
First Generation. The fear of me is in the bodies of the *mrwt,* and I am the Lord
of Eternity.

1. S2C[b] writes  for  .
2. *Gmtyw,* a plural nisba of *gmt* 'black ibis'.
3. BIBo[a] inserts *ȝḫ m kȝ.f* 'empowered with his double' in 312*b*. Compare 315*d*, but with *ḥkȝ* 'magic'.
4. BIBo[a] appears to read  for  , see de Buck's n. 1*.
5. Written *nwt* in BIBo[a]

Spell 445

[I am a] glad[-hearted] spirit,[1] who sits [. . .][2] those two crews[3] of Rēʿ V, 314
[who see (?)] Rēʿ daily, who entrap you(?) [. . .] who approach him who
sits[4] [. . .] his throne. My double is protected from the Quivering One, and
you are glad. My knife is in my hand against you[5] [. . . alone][6] in the middle
of ʿwʿ-birds [. . .] I have eaten the *ḳny*-garment, I have demolished the portal,
I have smitten Seth on that bank of [. . .] I am [. . .] the two *mrwt,* I am a
spirit [. . . who passes][7] on the way, my panoply has been given to me, [I have]
received my panoply.

1. A badly damaged variant of Spell 444. The suffix 1st sing. is not written consistently.
2. The obscure hieratic group at the beginning of 314*b* may have been a dual det. of *mrwt.*
3. Surely a misreading of *smrty* 'female companions'. In 315*l* the error is further developed into *sḳdwt* 'sailors'.
4. See de Buck, n. 7*.
5. Cf. e.g. 310*c.*
6. See de Buck, n. 9*.
7. See nn. 13*, 14*.

Spell 446

V, 315 N is an equipped spirit, the Sole One at your head. The eye is opened, the ears are drilled open, she removes the Companions,[1] the *mrwt*. N has come empowered with her magic[2] and equipped with her magic; she will not be remembered (*sic*) yonder by reason of her magic. O Thoth, N will not be forgotten[3] yonder at the Gate[4] by reason of her magic. The names of those Companions who sent(?) out their *mrwt* against the hearts of the spirits who move along have been accused, and the enemy has fallen into the *ḫns*-water of *Ḥtmy*. O glad-hearted spirit, sit on the thrones of the gods. O *Tb*[*tb*], O *Sṯṯty*, you sailors[5] of Rēʿ who daily make Rēʿ hale, you have your . . . [6] A knife is in N's hand against you, her eyes are
316 opened,[7] her heart itself protects itself. O you two lone ones (fem.) who dwell in the bark of Rēʿ, N has eaten the white bread, she has eaten ⟨ . . . ⟩ [8] she has made her portal firm,[9] she has smitten Seth upon the bank of 'I-have-found-him-on-it'.[10] N is Nu, she is inert, (but) her hand and her foot are not repelled, for N is a glad-hearted spirit, she has passed by, and she has received her fair panoply this day.

1. Read *šdd.s r.s rḥty, r.s* being the enclitic. This is a woman's coffin.
2. For *ḥkȝ* 'magic' read perhaps *kȝ* 'double', cf. 312*b*.
3. See de Buck's n. 1*. Was this text once in the 1st person?
4. Presumably of the Netherworld.
5. An error for *smrty* 'companions', see Spell 445, n.3.
6. *Nḥʿ* with water det., meaning unknown; perhaps a corruption of 309*c*.
7. *Nš wy* is meaningless, but may be a corruption of *snš* 'unstop', usually of ears, cf. *Pyr.* §§712; 1673; *CT* III, 13*b*; 14*a*.
8. Object omitted.
9. *Smn.n.s* is in fact an error for *sšn.n.s* 'she has smashed', cf. 296*f* (SIC); 300*d*; 314*n*.
10. Compare 311*d*.

Spell 447

[. . .] WHO TAKE AWAY MAGIC. N has travelled [. . .] the Companions who sit by *Tb*[. . .].

Spell 448

V, 317 I have presented a calf[1] of my north land,[2] I have passed by and I have travelled, I have recognized those two pellets of wax which Rēʿ and Khopri made for the god in order that I might live through them; I found the Companions sitting with your (*sic*) faces downcast – and *vice versa* – with *Tbtb* and *Sṯṯy* behind you, who overturned your altars and revealed your shapes.

1. See de Buck, n. 4*.
2. Apparently so; a suffix cannot be attached to an attributive adjective.

Spell 449

N is a shape[1] in which is its blood, and Thoth who is with offerings. N has gone V, 318
between them, she has sat between them,[2] she has presented a calf of the north, she has passed by and has travelled, they have asked her name[3] . . . [4], they have asked the name of Atum from her. The Eye of Horus stands up, and N her very self stands up, because[5] 'her very self' is the name of her feet (*sic*!), and she spears fish, having attained vindication.

1. See Spell 312, n. 2.
2. Dual, the *mrwt*?
3. For *nḏ rn* 'ask someone's name', see also *Pyr.* §1940*a* = *Pyr. Suppl.* 40.
4. *M mgwn* or *m-m gwn* is quite obscure; to ask a name 'from' someone requires the preposition *m-ʿ*, cf. loc. cit. and 318*h* below.
5. Read ⟨*n-*⟩ *ntt.*

Spell 450

TO DRIVE OFF THE *MRWT* of Rēʿ who come to take away N's magic from him.[1] V, 319
Get back, you flame, get back, *'Isṯṯt*, you Companions, you *mrwt*! I will not give you this magic of mine, and your faces are downcast – and *vice versa*.

I have travelled the northern parts(?)[2] of the sky; I have travelled and I have passed my[3] . . . [4] *pꜣḳ*-cakes which were made and came into being[5] in the realm of the gods. I found the Companions seated, [namely . . .] and *'Isṯrt*;[6] get back, you Companions, you *mrwt*! Your pillars are overturned, your shapes are revealed, your faces are downcast – and *vice versa*.

1. The title of this spell is culled from 319*c* + *n*, see de Buck's n. 1*.
2. The precise meaning and reading of *srwt mḥtwt(?)* is not clear; see de Buck's n. 2*.
3. Lit. 'his'.
4. *Šꜣ* is obscure, but appears to be an adjective qualifying *pꜣḳw*.
5. Possibly corrupt for 'which Khopri made', compare 317*f*.
6. Doubtless an error for *'Isṯṯt* above.

Spell 451

V, 320 SPELL FOR ENTERING TO OSIRIS IN THE WEST THROUGH HAVING POWER OVER WATER IN THE REALM OF THE DEAD. O Shu, make a way for me, for I am he who restored Osiris. I have come and I have seen what was restored for me as Osiris;[1] may there not be distension(?)[2] in my flesh.

1. So B9C and B2Bo; var. Sq1C: 'I have come and I have been restored'. So too probably Sq7C.
2. Lit. 'height', perhaps in reference to the distension of a decaying corpse. Sq1C appears to be slightly corrupt; Sq7C probably read likewise. For *if.f* read *if.i.*

Spell 452

V, 321 Greeting to you, O Rēʿ! Guard N when he waits[1] in the gates of the *wꜣs*-staff on the neck of Gēb, for N is the balance of Rēʿ in which he weighs Truth,[2] and N proclaims eternity(?).[3] You have a soul, you have[4] *bꜣt*-grain, and N has come to you, for you are old.[5]

1. BH4C reads *mkw štꜣ[w]* . . . 'guardian of the secrets [of the portals]', cf. *BD* 33, 4 (Spell 12), see de Buck's n. 5*. The *BD* text is in the 1st person.
2. So B1C; var. BH4C: 'on which Rēʿ weighs Truth'; B3Bo: 'which weighs Truth for you'.
3. Lit. perhaps 'N proclaims both ends' (B3Bo); on *ḥnty* cf. *Concise Dict.* 171. BH4C and *BD* Spell 12 omit this passage, while *ḥnnk sp 2*(?) *N pn* of B1C appears to be corrupt; the passage is almost entirely lost in M2NY, which ends here.
4. The second *n.k* only in B1C. BH4C had a different text, now partly lost; *BD* has *mk wỉ bꜣ.i tꜣ.*
5. So B3Bo, with the old perfective 2nd sing.; B1C has the 3rd sing., 'being old'.

Spell 453

V, 322 TO REPEL HIM WHO WOULD PLACE (ILL) REMEMBRANCE[1] IN THE REALM OF THE DEAD AND HIM WHO WOULD COME TO CLOSE A MAN'S MOUTH IN THE REALM OF THE DEAD. O you who cut off heads and sever necks, and who place (ill) remembrance in the mouths of the spirits, and who close the mouths because of the magic which is in their bodies, you shall not cut off my head nor sever my neck, nor place (ill) remembrance in this mouth of mine nor close my mouth because of the magic which is in my body, as you are wont to do to the spirits because of the magic which is in their bodies. Go away because of those two sentences which Isis spoke against you, do not come[2] to place (ill) remembrance in the mouth of Osiris at the will of his foe Seth when she[3] speaks against you.

May your face be downcast, O Lion-face; the great fire has gone forth against you from within the Eye of Atum,[4] the injured Eye, Mistress of the Night.[5] She cast you forth when Osiris turned back, and the detestation of you is in him – and *vice versa.* I have turned back, and the detestation of you is in me – and *vice versa.* If you come against me, I will speak against you; if you do not come against me, I will not speak[6] against you, and the executioners[7] of Shu will go away. 323

1. The significance of *sḫꜣ* here is not altogether clear; one would imagine that the deceased would welcome the perpetuation of his memory. To make the spell comprehensible a nuance of ill-repute has to be attached to *sḫꜣ*.

2. Surely so, despite the writing, cf. 325*f.*; *m ỉwt.k* appears to be a construction of the type *m sfḫḫ.k* do not let go', *Pyr.* §16, cf. Edel, *Altäg. Gramm.* §1104. *'Iwt.k* is presumably prospective *sḏm.f* dependent upon the negative imperative *m* 'do not'.

3. Reading *s* rather than *sn,* cf. 325e.

4. Var. 'from the mouth of the Great One within the Eye of Atum; B2L has clearly the better text.

5. The waxing or waning moon.

6. B17C omits *nn* before *dd.ỉ.*

7. Reading *syftyw* with B2L; *ỉsftyw* of B17C means 'wrongdoers'. See also 324*f.*

Spell 454

O you who cut off heads and sever necks, | who put (ill) remembrance in the mouths of the spirits and close the mouths of the spirits because of the magic which is in their bodies, you shall not see me with your eyes, by means of which you shall see with your knees, your face shall be turned backward, the executioners[1] of Shu who pursue you can see to cut off your head and to sever your neck on an errand of bringing back into his Eye, because of this which you have said you will do to me of cutting off my head, | of severing my neck and of putting (ill) remembrance in this my mouth, closing my mouth because of the magic which is in my body, as you are wont to do to the spirits because of the magic which is in their bodies. V, 324 325

Go away because of those two sentences which Isis said against you; do not come[2] to put (ill) remembrance in the mouth of Osiris at the will of his foe Seth when Isis speaks against you. O Lion-face, the great fire goes forth against | you within the Eye of Atum, the injured Eye, Mistress of the Night.[3] She swallowed you when Osiris turned back, and the detestation of you is in ⟨him⟩[4] — and *vice versa.* I have turned back, and the detestation of you is in me – and 326 *vice versa.* If you come against me, I will speak against you, but if you do not come against me, I will not speak against you, and the executioners of Shu will go away.[5]

REPELLING (ILL) REMEMBRANCE FROM THE MOUTH IN THE REALM OF THE DEAD AND HIM WHO COMES ⟨TO⟩[6] CLOSE THE MOUTH OF A MAN.

1. Following B4C, see spell 453, n. 6. Here the *f* in *syftyw* has been omitted.
2. See Spell 453, n. 2.
3. See Spell 453, n. 5.
4. See de Buck's n. 1*.
5. In English the sense demands the future tense, despite the *sḏm.n.f* form *ḥm.n* of B4C, which in B2L could be interpreted as 'will go away for me'; cf. 323*j* (B2L), where the simple *sḏm.f* form occurs.
6. Cf. 322*b*.

Spell 455

V, 327 The path from the gates which are in the tombs. Going out into the day so that a man may have power in his feet in the realm of the dead ⟨on(?)⟩ the path from the gates which are in the tombs.[1] See me, O men, gods, spirits and dead,[2] when I go out into the day. My eyes are opened and my ears are drilled open by the Eyeless One; the cords which are in my mouth have been opened and what is in my hinder parts put right by the Eyeless One.[3] I have gone out into the day, I
328 eat with my mouth, I defecate with my anus. I have gone out into the day, I have power over my foes, and I am protected from him who would harm me. GOING OUT INTO THE DAY.

1. This exordium in S10C alone; in the other two texts it is represented by the brief rubric at the end.
2. The other two texts have 'men and gods' only.
3. 327*i*-*j* are absent from S10C.

Spell 456

My bones have been given[1] to me by those who are in Djedu, my members have been strengthened[2] by those who are in Khem, my bones[3] have been brought to
V, 329 me, my members have been conveyed[4] to me. Shu issues[5] from this flesh of mine, and I am guided on the path[6] of the spirits; so says Anubis, Lord of the West, of me. I go out into the day so that I may have power over the dead,[7]

and I am protected from him who would harm me by command of the Bull of the West.[8]

1. Var. 'brought'.
2. Var. 'my sinews have been brought to me'.
3. *Ḳsw* omitted in S10C.
4. Var. *sṯnn* 'have been raised up'.
5. B3L and B1L appear to read: 'Shu issues empty'.
6. Var. B3L: 'the land'.
7. Var. 'my foes'.
8. In S10C alone. After 329*f* B3L and B1L have only the rubric 'Going out into the day'.

Spell 457

The fly is ushered into Ōn for the Sistrum-player,[1] I have entered to Him who is V, 330
dreaded(?), (even) this god,[2] (someone) is ushered into me at Abydos for Ōn,[3] and I enter to the Lord of All. ENTERING TO THE GODS TO WHOM A MAN DESIRES TO ENTER.[4]

1. Var. B1L: 'for *Sny*' or perhaps 'for *Ḥy*'; L1Li appears to read: 'He raises up a sweet savour in Ōn, for the god is not'.
2. For *nhd* cf. *Pyr.* §397; *CT* IV, 21*d*. *Nṯr pn* only in L1Li; the other texts omit *nṯr*.
3. Quite obscure. L1Li has *sṯꜣ m ꜣbḏw n ꞽIwnw* 'someone is conveyed from Abydos to Ōn'.
4. At the end of the rubric *ḫr.s* stands for *ḫr.sn*.

Spell 458

O you who take away years and bring days to an end, do not take away my years or bring my days to an end, for I am Horus, Lord of the Netherworld, Monarch of the Western Horizon.

I will not die in the West,[1] and the messengers of Osiris have no power over me, for I am Horus, son of Osiris.

I will not die in Ōn, Kherʿaḥa or the East,[2] and the messengers of Sopd have 331
no power over me, for I am Horus, son of Osiris.

I will not die in the South, and the messengers of Horus have no power over me, for I am Horus, son of Osiris.

I will not die in the North, and the messengers of the Outcast have no power over me, for I am Horus, son of Osiris.

I will not die in the waters, and the messengers of those who are in the waters have no power over me, for I am Horus, son of Osiris.

I will not die in the Abyss, and the messengers of those who are in the Abyss have no power over me, for I am Horus, son of Osiris.

332 I will not die a second time,[1] and the dwellers in the Netherworld have no power over me. I will not eat their fish, their fowl shall not scream[3] over me, for I am Horus, son of Osiris. NOT TO DIE A SECOND TIME IN THE REALM OF THE DEAD.

1. The tabulated text, see de Buck, nn. 1*; 3*.
2. In 331*a* B1L, 1. 160 mentions these two towns, which presumably precede the reference to the East in 1. 160*a* (331*l*). In B3L (331*e*) the allusion to the towns is both misplaced and obscure, see de Buck, n. 2*.
3. Read *n ḥꜣ ꜣpdw*; B3L has omitted the *d*.

Spell 459

Hail to you, O heart of mine (*ỉb* and *ḥꜣty*) of my bodily essence; it will not forsake me. GIVING A MAN'S HEART TO HIM.

Spell 460

V, 333 Hail to you, Khopri within my body, who are at the head of those who are in their tombs, whose faces are hidden, whose bandages are firm. Commend me to that baboon, sharp-haired and with hair on end, in whose presence is spoken the great word which will not repeat itself. May he commend me to the door-keepers of the District of Silence, may they not oppose me, may they let me go out in company with men, may I kiss the ground to the Lord of the gods; may I eat bread with them, may I drink with them, for I know them by their names,[1] He-who-acts, He-who-takes-names, Crocodile-faced, . . . ,[2] Angry One. WHAT A MAN SHOULD SAY WHEN HE GOES OUT; IT MEANS THAT MEN ARE FORGETFUL OF HIM.[3]

1. 333*n-o* appears to consist of a series of epithets in apposition to *rn.sn* in 333*m*.
2. *Dfdy,* var. *Dfḏy,* meaning unknown.
3. With *smhy ỉb* 'be forgetful' compare *smhy* 'forget', *CT* II, 93*f.* B1L has *smh.f ỉb* instead of *smhy ỉb pw* of B3L; the latter makes better sense.

Spell 461

O men and women, I pull out[1] the brick which is in my father's tomb, and I stop up[2] your mouths with it.

1. *'Iš* is probably connected with *išš* 'spit out', *Pyr.* §§1652; 1871, and *išw, Pyr.* §246. The particle *tr* appears to convey emphasis.

2. *Tm̆* (B3L) snd *dbb* (B1L) are virtual synonyms, meaning respectively 'close' and 'stop up'. The reason for this action is not obvious.

Spell 462

I have come to the place ⟨ where ⟩[1] is *'Ib-wrt,* keeper of the war-boat of the gods. V, 334
Let me go out into the day, may my foes be brought [to] me, even as He whose shape is invisible commanded. It was the Many-faced whom I sent for him, and [he] will judge them;[2] he will bring me to this house . . . ,[3] for he has brought my years to an end [. . .] upon earth.

1. *'Im* appears to have been omitted from the end of the clause.
2. The foes of 334*f.* On *ny* 'them' cf. *Eg. Gramm.*[3] §§34, Obs. 3; 486, Obs. 2.
3. *Wn*?, *wnḫ*? Meaning and reading uncertain.

Spell 463

TO CAUSE A MAN TO APPROACH THE TRIBUNAL OF THE WEST.[1] O *Iṯn-wr*[2] in V, 335
your power, guiding Rēʿ on the hidden paths, bring this being to[3] the lower part of the sky, the Netherworld. I have come that I may give great abundance, being what they allot in the presence of the Bull of Watchfulness(?).[4]

1. So B4C. The insertion of *imntt* 'the West' as the first word in the rubric appears to be intended for honorific transposition, since it is meaningless as it stands, and it has been translated as a genitive referring to *ḏ3ḏ3t* 'tribunal' at the end of the rubric. In B1Y the rubric, now mostly destroyed, began with *sʿrt* 'causing to approach'; P. Gard. II substitutes: 'Guiding a god in the tribunal', while B9C has no rubric.

2. B9C and P. Gard. II agree in reading *iṯn,* meaning obscure, but probably original. B4C has turned it into *itn* 'sun-disk'.

3. So B4C; P. Gard. II substitutes *sd3 wn pw prr m ḫry-ḫt pt dw3t* 'Conduct this being who has gone up from the underside of the sky, the Netherworld'.

4. The meaning of *rswt* here is not clear; 'dream' hardly fits the case.

Spell 464

V, 336 TO BECOME HETEP, LORD OF THE FIELDS OF OFFERINGS.[1] The Falcon is taken
337 by *Sty*,[2] and I see what you[3] consume, you Field of Offerings. | Release[4] the Falcon from *Sty* for me, open for me the paths of Rēᶜ on that day of choking(?)[5] and stifling the sky because of the anger of Seth at the air because of its vivifying
338 Him who is in his egg.[6] | He has taken away Him who was in my womb[7] from the Silent Ones while I[8] rowed in the bark on the waterways of Ḥetep. It was I who took him from the members of Shu;[9] his northern stars and members[10] are in due season(?).[11]

339 I row on its waterways, I arrive at its towns,[12] I am more prominent than the
340 god who is in it,[13] because I am Ḥetep who is in his field.| He guides[14] his Enneads[15] whom he loves,[16] he pacifies the Combatants[17] for those who belong to
341 the West,[18] he creates what is good, he brings content,[19] | he drives away mourning from their elders, he suppresses uproar for their young ones,[20] he entraps those, male or female, who would harm Isis,[21] who would harm the gods, he removes
342 uproar from the Rivals, | he shares(?) Ḥu for his light(?),[22] he gives abundance to doubles and spirits, and I have power over them.

I am one whom Ḥetep knows;[23] I row on its[24] waterways, I arrive at its
343 towns, | I am stronger and more acute than the spirits,[25] and they have no power over me. I acquire this field of yours, O Ḥetep, which you love, the Mistress of
344 the Winds;[26] | I eat and carouse in it,[27] | I drink in it, I plough in it,[28] I reap in it,
346 I am not destroyed in it, I copulate in it,[29] my magic is strong in it,[30] | I will not be aroused in it,[31] I will not be apprehensive in it, I will be happy in it.[32] I know
347 the jackal-headed post of Ḥetep;[33] | its name is 'Bright Goddess'.[34] It was made firm on the blood[35] of Shu and it was lashed[36] with the cords of the years on that day when the years were divided and the utterance of Him whose mouth is silent was
348 made enduring.[37] | What I say is mysterious;[38] | I complete eternity and pass everlasting.

1. The rubric is in B1Bo alone; 'fields' is in the dual. On the Ḥetep spells 464-8 see Lesko in *JARCE* 9, (1971-2), 86 ff.; his translations differ somewhat from mine.

2. For *Sty*, *BD* 224, 5 has 'Seth'.

3. Suffix 2nd fem. sing. in B9C–B6C, with reference to *Sḫt-ḥtp* below. B1C–B1L read: 'Rēᶜ looks at me when I consume', cf. *ḫmy.ỉ* in B1C. B1Bo: '. . . when you (fem.) consume'.

4. B9C–B6C have optative *sḏm.f* with fem. suffix; the others have the imperative.

5. *'Imt*, not recorded with sail-det. as in B9C, B5C, B1C and B1L (337*c*). B6C has *ỉmt*  and B1C has 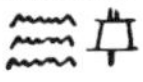. The context and the sail-det. suggest a near synonym of *ỉtm* 'stifling'; *ỉmt* 'groaning' seems unlikely.

6. The young Horus, cf. e.g. *CT* II, 212*b*. B9C has *št* for *špt* and *ỉb* for *ḥr*, clearly in error. For 'Him who is in' the texts vary between *ḫny* and *ỉmy*; B1L has *ḫnw m* only. Following *ṯꜣw* B1Bo has corruptly *ḥr sḫm*.

7. *Sic* B9C–B1C, as if Isis were speaking; B3L omits the suffix after *ht*. *Nḥm.n.f* only in B9C; B1L has an odd writing of *nḥm.f* and continues with *m ỉgrw*. B1Bo omits the verb and writes *ỉmy ẖt.f* 'who is in his body'.

8. Apparently the deceased. For *m wyꜣ pw* B1Bo has *m š.f pw*.

9. For *Šw* B1Bo has *Ḥw*, surely a misreading.

10. Read *sbꜣ t.f ʿwt.f mḥwt*.

11. B9C: *m hrww rnpwt* 'in days and years'; B5C–B1L *m trw rnpwt* 'in (due) seasons of years'; B1Bo is slightly corrupt.

12. The fem. suffix refers to the *Sḫt-ḥtp*.

13. B9C has misplaced the preposition *r*, see B5C and B6C; the other texts omit the *r*, which seems necessary to the sense. B5C adds at the end the adverb *twt* 'utterly'. B1Bo has *ḫnt.f ỉm.s* 'he sails upstream in it' and adds in 339*c*: 'N is stronger in it than the gods who are in it'; in 339*d* it omits *m* before *sḫt.f*. In 339*b* B3L is corrupt.

14. Var. B9C: 'who guides'.

15. Var. '*the* Enneads'.

16. The masc. *mrrw.f* is due to the Ennead being predominantly male. B1Bo ends with an obscure *n mrwy.f*.

17. B1Bo: 'the great ones'.

18. So B9C–B6C; the other texts have *ỉrw.sn* 'who belong to them'. In 340*c* B1L adds *bḥn.f ỉꜣkb*, anticipating 341*a*.

19. 340*f* is a virtual dittograph of 340*b* and has therefore been omitted from the translation.

20. B1Bo omits *dr.f*, leaving 341*b* without a verb.

21. B9C repeats *ỉḥ* in error after *nknt*; B1L has *ḥw* 'smite instead of *ỉḥ* 'entrap'; so also in 341*d*. B1Bo omits the name of Isis and has corrupted *nknw nknwt* into *nknwyt* with det. [hieroglyph] .

22. Meaning doubtful, but the next clause suggests that *Ḥw* may represent 'food' rather than 'authority'; B9C and B5C omit the suffix after *šw* 'light'. B1Bo reads *sḥtp.f Ḥw n rḫ sw* 'He makes Ḥu gracious to him who knows him'.

23. Or 'who knows Ḥetep'.

24. The distinction between the god Ḥetep and the region *Sḫt-ḥtp* is not always strictly observed; there is clearly a confusion of this nature here. See also Spell 467, n. 16.

25. This reading (B5C, B1C, B3L, B1L) seems preferable to *wsr rꜣ.ỉ* 'my speech (or 'mouth') is stronger' of B9C, B6C and B1Bo; this last reads 'N's mouth is stronger and his teeth sharper than (those of) the spirits'.

26. B5C omits the suffix after *sḫt*. Var. B1Bo: 'It means that N knows what is peacefully acquired in this field of yours which you have loved: the field is Mistress of the winds and Mistress of vegetation'.

27. So B9C; B5C: 'I carouse and eat; B1C and B3L: 'I carouse and am strong'; B1L: 'I carouse, copulate and rouse up'; B1Bo: 'men carouse and N carouses'.

28. B1C and B3L: 'I eat and drink in it'; B1Bo: 'men eat and N eats in it; men drink and N drinks in it; men plough and N ploughs in it'.

29. So B9C; the negation before *nk* is certainly in error, having been derived from an arrangement such as that in B6C, where again the negation surely cannot apply to *nk,* while B5C has it both ways, which makes no sense: B1C, B3C and B1L are correctly in the affirmative; B1Bo has obscurely *nhpt n sk.*

30. B1Bo adds: 'N shouts in it'.

31. For the interpretation as a future cf. *nn snhs.ỉ* in B5C; B6C has the simplex *nhs.* B1C and B1L have *n sk.ỉ* 'I will not be destroyed'., var. B3L: *n sk ỉb.ỉ* 'my heart will not be destroyed'. B1Bo goes straight to the *n ḥwꜥ ỉb* clause, and omits the following sentences of 346*a.*

32. So B1C. B9C, B5C, B3L and B1L have simply *nḏm*; B6C omits *nḏm.* On B1Bo see n. 31 above.

33. Var. B9C: 'I know Ḥetep'; B5C: 'I am the *wsrt*-post of Ḥetep'; B1Bo: 'as one who knows the strong one (*wsrt*) of Ḥetep', continuing in 346*c*: 'N has departed, knowing the strong one of Ḥetep; the goddess (*wtt*) is superior to him who slips away (*sbnw*)'. This last clause corresponds to 347*a.* For *wsrt* as a term for a jackal-headed wooden post see *CT* II, 138*e.*

34. For names compounded with *wtt* 'goddess' cf. *Rnn-wtt,* passim; *'Iẖt-wtt, Pyr.* §§ 198; 791;*CT* I, 280*i*;285*g*; other exx. in Index I, s.v. *Wtt. Bḳ* is taken to be a writing of *bȝḳ* 'bright'. *Ts* at the end of B1L is a corruption of *rn.s.*

35. For *ṯr* 'blood' cf. *Pyr.* §§451; 1263; see also Harris, *Minerals,* 154.

36. Read *ḳȝs.t(w).s* with B1C.

37. Or 'was hidden'. for *ỉgr rȝ.f* B1L has *ỉgr rn.f* and B1Bo *ỉgrw ẖr.*

38. Lit. perhaps 'mysterious is I-say-it', interpreting *ḏd.ỉ sw* as a noun-clause acting as subject of a sentence with adjectival predicate *sṯȝ.*

Spell 465

TO BE ḤETEP,[1] Lord of the Field of Offerings. This is Horus of the Tree(?);[2]
V, 349 he is a falcon, he is a thousand cubits long, | life and equipment[3] are in his hand, he comes and goes at will in its waterways and towns, he rises[4] in the birth-place of the god and he sets in *Ḳnḳnt,* he does everything in it as is done in the
350 Island of Fire, and there is no shouting at all in it, | there is nothing evil in it.[5]

This is Ḥetep who walks through this field of his, and he partakes of a meal in the birth-place of the god. If he goes to rest in *Ḳnḳnt,*[6] he will do
351 everything in it | as is done in the Island of Fire, there will be no shouting at all in it and there will be nothing evil in it.[7]

1. Omitted in B9C.

2. An obscure expression; for some conjectures cf. Lesko, *JARCE* 9, 93, n.*b.*

3. Var. B1C: *wȝs* 'dominion'. By 'equipment' presumably magical powers or amulets are meant.

4. Read *wbn.f* with B6C–B1L. B3L shows clearly how the double columns of 394*c.d* are to be read; *wbn.f m msḫn nṯr ḥtp.f m ʿnḫ m Ḳnḳnt,* though B3L has written *msḫn* as *msḫ*.

5. B9C omits the negation , making this clause dependent on *n wnt* in 349*f*.

6. *ʾIr* 'if' only in B9C–B6C. B9C omits *m ʿnḫ* after *ir ḥtp.f*.

7. In 351*d*–352*f* B6C repeats the spell and B5C repeats the rubric.

Spell 466

The roman numbers refer to the compartments in the plans of the Field of Offerings, see de Buck, pp. 359–62.

I. *Ḳnḳnt,* 7.[1]

II. Offerings, 9.[2]

III. Great Ladies, 7.[3]

IV. TO BE ḤETEP, LORD OF THIS FIELD[4], WITH BREATH IN HIS NOSE; V, 353
HE WILL NEVER DIE.

V. It is a thousand *schoeni* long and a thousand wide; its name is 'Horns of the Mistress of Purity'.

VI. Offering-bowls(?), 4.[5] 354

VII. Red cloth, 3.[6]

VIII. Vegetables,[7] 3

IX. Mistress of the Two Lands, 3.[8]

X. The Waterway of the White Hippopotamus; it is a thousand *schoeni* long, but its width is not told; | there are no fish or snakes in it. 355

XI. The length of the sky is the length[9] of the Waterway of Ḥetep[10] opposite Upper and Lower Egypt.

XII. The Mighty Lady.

XIII. She who unites.

XIV. Ploughing and reaping barley and emmer of the god's estate; 356
there are no snakes in it.[11]

XV. Mistress of the winds.

XVI. It is a thousand long, but its width is not told;[12] its name is 'He who raises the storm'.[13]

XVII. Those who row him[14] are ʾImsety, Ḥapy, Duamūtef and Ḳebḥsenuf. 357

XVIII. Food-stuffs, 3.

XIX. . . . ,[15] 4.

358 XX. It is the sea of the gods, who put coolness into it[16] for every god. Its length and its breadth are not told to Osiris.

XXI. The birth-place of the gods is *Ḳnḳnt*.

XXII. Milk, 3.

XXIII. The great field.

XXIV. Baskets, 4.

XXV. Serpent-boat(?).[17]

XXVI. Lapis lazuli.

XXVII. The women in it, 4.

XXVIII. Imsety, Ḥapy, Duamūtef, Ḳebḥsenuf.

1. Varr. 8; 6. The reference of the numerals is not always clear.
2. Var. 8.
3. Var. 8.
4. The demonstrative *tn* only in B9C and B5C.
5. Var. 3.
6. Varr. 4; 2.
7. For this sense of *wꜣḫ* cf. *CT* II, 157*e*.
8. Var. 2. B9C writes *nb* for *nbt*.
9. Lit. 'its length'.
10. Corrupted into *ꜣw.f pt šm.f Ḥtp,* etc., in B1C and B2P; *ꜣw.f pt ꜣw.f pt Ḥtpt.f*, etc., in B3L; *ꜣw.f pt ḥbs Ḥtp*, etc., in B1L.
11. In the oval representing the estate; B9C has the numeral 3 and B5C and B6C read 4; B3L lacks the numeral. For *št* (*spꜣt*) *nṯr* B1C, B1L and B2P have *ẖrt-nṯr* 'realm of the dead.
12. Masc., though the word for estate is fem.
13. B3L omits the 'name' clause. B1L has *wṯs šnyt.ṯ* (sic) *rn.f.*
14. Presumably Hetep.
15. Meaning unknown. Lesko, *JARCE* 9, 95, n.*m*, suggests 'steps'.
16. B5C and B6C insert after *wꜣḏ-wr pw* an oval sign interpreted by Lesko as 'isle'. To me it seems more likely to be a general 'phrase-determinative'. The reference to 'coolness' only in B9C–B6C.
17. So B5C, probably in reference to the serpent-ended boat depicted on the plans. The dets. of *ḏt* in B9C and B3L are obscure; B1C and B2P appear to read 'son of the serpent'; B1L 'daughter of the serpent'.

Spell 467

I live as Ḥetep, my bag and my bowl are upon me,[1] which I have filled[2] in the V, 363
isles, (being) one whom the spirits of the Lords of Plenty guide. I depart so that
I may ascend to him who brings it,[3] so that I may have power through him; he
will accept on my behalf, for I am he whom Ḥetep equips.[4] | This great magic
of mine is powerful within this body of mine and these[5] places of mine; I recall 364
to myself that of which I have been forgetful. I plough and I reap,[6] for I am
Ḥetep in the abode of the god. I know the names of the towns, districts and
waterways within the Field of Offerings | in which I am,[7] I am strong and a
spirit in them, I eat in them and move about in them,[8] I plough in them and 365
reap in them, I rise early in them and go to rest in them,[9] I am a spirit in them as 366
Ḥetep, | I sow in them and move about in them, I row on its waterways and
arrive at its [10] towns as Ḥetep according to my utterance. [11] My horns are sharp,
I give abundance to the doubles and spirits, I allot authority to him who knows
(how to use) it.

I arrive at its towns, | I row on its waterways, I traverse[12] the Field of 367
Offerings as Rēᶜ who is in the sky, and it is Ḥetep who makes their contentment.
I have gone down to the earth and have made 'Corn content; I have gone up,
and there has been given to me [13] what makes joy.[14] I have taken strength,[15] and
peace has been promised to me.

BEING IN ḤETEP. O Field, I have come into you[16] with my soul behind me 368
and authority[17] before me. O Lady of the Two Lands,[18] confirm my magic for
me, so that I may recall what of it I had forgotten. I am alive, and there are none,
male or female, who can harm me, and joy has been given to me; your[19] peace is 369
mine. I create[20] seed and I have received breath.

BEING IN ḤETEP, LORD OF THE WINDS. I have come into you,[21] having
opened up my head and having aroused my body. I close my eye, (yet) I shine
on the day of the Milk-goddess; I have slept by night, | I have restored the milk 370
to its proper level, and I am in my town.

O TOWN OF THE GREAT LADY,[22] I have come into you so that I may reckon
up abundance and cause vegetation to flourish; I am the Lone Bull, high-piled
with lapis lazuli, | Lord of the Field of the Bull of the Gods, and Sothis speaks to 371
me in her good time.[23]

O VEGETABLE-TOWN,[24] I have come into you, I have taken the Grey-haired
One to the roof, for I am the moon, I have swallowed the darkness.

O (TOWN) FAIR OF OFFERINGS,[25] I have come into you, I eat my meal, I 372
have power through choice pieces of my fowl and cattle,[26] the poultry of Shu

which attend on my double have been given to me.

373 O PROVISION-TOWN,[27] I have come into you,[28] | I have knit up the six-weave cloth, I have donned the fringed cloak as Rēʿ in the sky whom the gods who are in the sky serve, and I am Rēʿ whom those who are in the sky serve.

BEING IN ḤETEP, LADY OF THE TWO LANDS.[29] I have come into you, I
374 have immersed the waterways | as Osiris, Lord of corruption, Lord of vegetation, as the Oldest One, Bull of vultures;[30] I am a flamingo,[31] who has eaten the like.[32]

O *ḲNḲNT,*[33] I have come into you, I have seen my father, I have recogniz-
375 ed my mother, I rise early,[34] I catch fish. | I know the deep holes of the snakes, and I am saved. I know the name of this god; He whose mouth is joined together,[35] Lord of holy things, whose hair is in good order, whose horns are sharp. If he reaps, I will plough and will reap.

376 O MILK-TOWN,[36] I have come into you, those who would oppose me and | drive me off[37] and follow after me are the Followers of Horus; heads are given to me, and I knit on the head of the Blue-eyed[38] Horus, one who acts according to his desire.

O UNION-TOWN,[39] I have come into you; my head is whole and my heart is
377 awake beneath the White Crown; | I am guided above and am made hale below, and I give joy to the bulls which are in charge of the Enneads, for I am a bull, Lord of the gods, who travels with turquoise.

O MIGHTY LADY,[40] I have come into you, I have taken the Grey-haired
378 One | to the roof, I have fashioned Ḥu, I am in the middle of my eye (*sic*).

O BARLEY AND EMMER OF THE GOD'S ESTATE,[41] I have come into you, I have travelled upstream, I have sailed on the Waterway of the Horns of the Mistress of Purity,[42] I have driven in the mooring-post in the upper waterways.[43] | I have borne aloft the storms of the Disturber,[44] and I have upheld the supports(?) of the Old One.

SEEKING THE FIELDS, TOWNS AND WATERWAYS,[45] PLOUGHING, REAPING, SEEING RĒʿ, OSIRIS AND THOTH DAILY, HAVING POWER OVER WATER AND AIR, DOING ALL THAT HE WISHES LIKE ONE WHO IS IN THE ISLAND OF FIRE WITH LIFE IN HIS NOSE, WHO WILL NEVER DIE,[46] WHO IS IN THE FIELD OF OFFERINGS IN WHICH ARE HIS FIELDS AND HIS GIFTS FOR EVER AND EVER.[47]

1. B9C writes *ỉwnt* 'bag' as *ỉwt.* B3L writes *tp* with the feather .

2. Reading *mḥt.n.ỉ*: B5C and B6C have *m mḥt* 'being filled'; B3L has *mḥ* and . The fem. gender is in concord with *ỉwnt.*

3. Or 'himself'; to what *sw* refers is not clear.

4. B3L omits *ỉnk.*

5. Masc.; one would expect the fem. *ptn* as in B1C alone.

6. So B5C and originally B9C. Var. B6C: 'N travels (*sḏꜣ*), ploughs and reaps'; similarly B1C. For *sḏꜣ* of these two texts B3L has *sꜣ* 'I am wise(?)'.

7. Var. B5C: 'in which I travel'; B3L: 'in which I am great'.

8. *Wnwn.ỉ ỉm.sn*; B9C has *wn.ỉ* without a predicate.

9. The Field. The correct writing of *nhp* is in B3L alone; the other texts write it as the like word for 'copulate'. *Ḥtp.ỉ ỉm.sn* 'I go to rest in them' confirms the translation of *nhp.i* as 'I rise early'. From here on B5C alone preserves the plural suffix; the other have *.s* for the plural, cf. *JEA* 16, 64(5). We are still dealing with the 'waterways', etc.

10. In 366*b* the suffix *.s* refers to the *Sḫt-ḥtp* and is common to all texts, being used rightly for the sing.

11. Var. B1C *r ꜥ.ỉ* 'according to my condition'; B5C omits this phrase.

12. Var. B3L: *sḫs.ỉ m* 'I run in'.

13. Read *hꜣ.n.i r tꜣ, sḥtp.n.ỉ ššr, pr.n.ỉ rdy n.ỉ ꜣwt-ỉb. Šsr* is the deified corn, cf. *BIFAO* 30, 179. B5C and B6C substitute 'Rēꜥ' and B6*C* has 'Gēb'.

14. B9C has corruptly *r ꜣw ỉb.*

15. Var. B3L: *ḥtp* 'peace', 'content'.

16. Var. B3L: 'I have ruled in you'. The distinction between the god Ḥetep and the *sḫt-ḥtpw* has been blurred, and in what follows Ḥetep refers to the Field. See especially 373*d.*

17. For *ḥw* B6C has *ḫrp.*

18. Cf. Spell 466, IX.

19. Masc.

20. Lit. 'knit up'.

21. I.e. the Field.

22. Cf. Spell 466, III. B9C and B6C have omissions.

23. Perhaps a reference to the regular heliacal rising of the star.

24. Cf. Spell 466, VIII.

25. Cf. ibid. II, VI.

26. B9C: 'I have power through fowl and cattle'. B3L reads: *nwn.ỉ m spꜣw.ỉ* 'I am dishevelled through my made-to-fly birds'; the last word links this version with Spell 466, XIX.

27. Cf. ibid. XVIII.

28. B3L omits *ỉm.t.*

29. Cf. n. 16 above; note the det. of *ḥtpt* in B1C. Cf. Spell 466, II, VI.

30. Cf. *Orientalia,* 7, 67.

31. *Šbdd, šbd, šbd dšr, dšr*; this last, in B3L, is the clue to the sense.

32. It is not clear to what *mytt* refers.

33. Cf. Spell 466, I.

34. The meaning of *nhp* is indicated by the star-det. in B3L; three texts write the word as if it meant 'copulate', which makes no sense here; B6C, with det. of the striking man, could mean either. Compare 365*e* and n. 9 above.

35. With det. of the pitchfork in four cases, borrowed from *ꜥbwt* 'forked staff', cf. *Concise Dict.* 41; B1C has the normal det. of the bowl.

36. Cf. Spell 466, XXII.

37. For the second word read *ḫsb* 'drive away', 'oppose', cf. *Pyr.* §§ 334; 336; 448; 492;

the serpent-sign is borrowed from *ḫsb* 'snake', *CT* III, 347*e*.

38. cf. *ḫsbḏ* 'lapis-lazuli', Spell 466, XXVI.
39. Cf. ibid. XIII.
40. Cf. ibid. XII.
41. Cf. ibid. XIV.
42. Cf. ibid. V.
43. Var. B3L: 'the golden upper waterways'.
44. Cf. Spell 466, XVI.
45. Var. B5C: *spꜣwt* 'districts'.
46. Cf. Spell 466, IV.
47. B1C adds the colophon *ỉw.s pw* 'it is finished'.

Spell 468

V, 381 I have entered into you[1] in peace, I share out(?) what is on me for the isles;[2]
I guide my spirits to those who know me,[3] I make my magic hale for him who
brings it,[4] and I have power through it;[5] he gives to me and I give to him,[6] for I
am he who equipped Ḥetep,[7] and I have power through it, this very great magic of
mine which is in this body of mine and which made these seats of mine for me;[8] I
have recalled what I had forgotten of it.[9] I proceed with Ḥetep into the abode of
the god, I plough and I reap with Ḥetep in the god's estate,[10] because I know the
382 names of the towns and districts which are in the Field of Offerings,[11] and I am
strong in them,[12] I move about in them,[13] as ⟨in⟩ the Field of Offerings.[14] I am
strong and sharp-toothed,[15] I put the dread of me into souls and spirits,[16] I allot
authority to him who knows me.[17]

I arrive at their towns,[18] I row on their waterways, I run in[19] the Field of
Offerings as Rēʿ who is in the sky and Atum, Lord of Offerings. I have gone down
to the earth, and have propitiated Gēb;[20] I have ascended to the sky, and joy is
383 given to me.[21] I have taken strength and peace has been promised to me.[22]

ENTERING[23] ⟨into⟩ the abode of the Great Lady and the Mistress of the Two
Lands. I have come into you[24] with my soul behind me and authority before me,
I make my magic endure, for I have recalled what I had forgotten of it, and I will
384 neither forget nor be harmed;[25] I have taken possession of sky and earth,[26] and
joy has been given to me; I am at peace, and I have created my seed.[27]

O Milk-goddess, Lady of the Winds, I have come into you, my eye is opened, my eye [is closed][28] I shine by day, I sleep by night,[29] I restore the milk to its proper level.[30] A Chaos-god is in me, two Chaos-gods are in me.

O you who were born among them; O you who flourish,[31] I have come into you, I reckon up my abundance[32] and cause vegetation to flourish, for I am a

long-horn,[33] thickly eye-painted, | Lord of lapis lazuli, Lord of the Field of the 385
Bull of the gods; I copulate with my sister Sothis in her hours.[34]

O Ḥetep [. . .], I come into you, I eat a meal, I have power through my choice joints and [my] poultry,[35] he[36] propitiates for me those who attend on my spirits.

O Ḥetep, O Lord, I have come into you,[37] I take the Grey-haired One to the roof, I am Ḥu, I am in the middle of my strong eye.[38] I have come into you, I immerse the waterways as Osiris, Lord of corruption, as ʿAndjety, Bull of vultures.[39] I am indeed the *šbd*-fish which [I(?)] have eaten.[40]

O food-goddess and water-goddess,[41] I have come into you, I don the six-weave cloth, I knit up the fringed cloak of Rēʿ who is in the sky, and the gods who are in the sky serve me.[42]

Variant text of BIBo

N is the head of the Great One, blue of eyes, who acts at his desire;[43] his
mounds are there before him. | He makes the upper ones hale, he makes the lower 386
ones to flourish, he gives joy to the Bull who is in charge of the Ennead, for N is the Bull of the gods, Lord of turquoise,[44] Lord of electrum(?)[45] within Ḥetep.[46] N has fared downstream in Ḥetep and (also) upstream; he has sailed ⟨in⟩[47] (the region called) 'The Horns of the Mistress of Purity',[48] his wind is in the waterway of the great gods, he has driven in the mooring-post in the upper waterways, and the storm is borne aloft;[49] he has made disturbance on account of his mouth, (even he) the Sole One, for he cannot speak, he cannot lift his head.

1. I.e. the Field of Offerings. This spell is a variant version of 497.

2. A distorted version of 363*b-c*. *Dny* has been tentatively identified with *dny* 'share out', *Concise Dict.* 314.

3. Cf. 363*d*. BIBo is closer to it and has been followed here.

4. Cf. 363*e*.

5. Cf. 363*f*. The suffix in *sḫm.f* in B3L appears to be a later erroneous insertion; this text is in the 1st person.

6. Cf. 363*g*.

7. Cf. 363*h*. The masc. suffix in the BIBo insertion *sḫm N pn im.f* 'N has power through it', apparently refers to *ḥkꜣ* 'magic' next below. This has been omitted in B3L, but could well be original.

8. Cf. 364*a*. In 381*i* read *ḥkꜣ.i pn wr.i ꜥꜣ.i*, the suffixes after the adjectives apparently serving for emphasis. In 381*j* BIBo is followed, as it has some relationship with 364*a*, whereas B3L is unintelligible after *ḫt.i*.

9. Cf. 364*b*. BIBo has: 'what he knew and what he did not know are what he has recalled'.

10. Cf. 364*c-d*. In 381*l* BIBo omits *sḏꜣ.f*.

11. Cf. *364e–365a.* BɪBo is corrupted, but perhaps may be emended as ⟨*n ntt*⟩ *N*⟨*rḫ*⟩ etc., '⟨ because ⟩ N ⟨ knows ⟩ the names of the towns and estates which are in them, the Fields (*sic*) of Offerings', continuing in 382*a*: *ntt N pn ỉm.s* 'in which N is'.

12. Cf. 365*b*. BɪBo expands this into 'He is strong in it (the Field), being strong; he is at peace in it, being peaceful'.

13. Cf. 365*c*.

14. So B3L. English usage requires a preposition before the mention of the Field. BɪBo has (382*e-f*): 'I row ⟨on⟩ (*m* omitted, cf. 366*b*) its waterways, I arrive at its towns as Ḥetep'.

15. Cf. 366*c*. Var BɪBo: 'his magic is strong and sharp in it'.

16. Cf. 366*d*. Var. BɪBO: 'he gives abundance ⟨to⟩ souls and spirits'.

17. Cf. 366*e*. BɪBo has *psš* 'share', 'divide' for *ỉp* of B3L and omits the preposition before *rḫ*.

18. Cf. 366*f*, etc. Here B3L has miswritten *spr.ỉ* 'I arrive' as *spt.ỉ* 'my lips'.

19. Cf. 367*b*. B3L has *sḫn.n.ỉ* for *sḫn.f* of BɪBo, but the presence of the preposition *m* in 382*j* shows that *sḫn* of B3L is a miswriting of *sḫs* as in 367*b* in the same coffin. BɪBo has adopted *sḫn* entirely, and reads 'I seek the towns and waterways of the Field of Offerings'.

20. Cf. 367*e*; BɪBo adds in 382*m*: *syp n.f Gb* 'Gēb makes inspection for him'.

21. Following BɪBo here, cf. 367*f*. Var. B3L: 'I have done my will'.

22. So also 367*g-h*.

23. B4C comes in here with *ꜥḳ* 'enter' in red, without following preposition.

24. 2nd plur. in B3L and B4C, as if two entities are invoked; i.e. *Nbt tꜣwy* and *Nywt wrt.*

25. Cf. 368*b* ff. BɪBo has transferred *nbt tꜣwy* 'Mistress of the Two Lands' to 383*g*; In 383*h* it has for  (=*nn*) and continues: 'there is nothing which he has forgotten of it, and he will not be harmed, he will have no wound (*nkt*, with knife det. cf.,*nk* 'suffer harm', *Pyr.* §1468) there, he will have no hindrance (*imy-rd*)'. Note that in 394*a* (Spell 469) *nkt* appears to be used of 'cuts' of meat. B4C has: 'There is none who will forget, and she will not be harmed'.

26. So B3L. BɪBo: 'sky, earth and joy have been given to him'; B4C starts incomprehensibly with *n.ṯn*.

27. B4C ends here. BɪBo omits 384*a-b*, and substitutes: 'he receives breath and assumes more power than those who promise contentment'.

28. So B3L which presumably read originally: *ỉrt.ỉ wnty ỉrt.ỉ ꜥẖnty*; cf. 369*e-f*. BɪBo is corrupt, but could perhaps be emended to read: *ỉrt.f wnty, tp.f rs, ỉrt.f ꜥẖn.ty* 'his eye is open, his head is wakeful, his eye is closed'.

29. Cf. 369*g-h*.

30. Cf. 370*a*.

31. *Mst* is fem., *wꜣḫ* is masc. The double bar at the end of 384*j* shows that a section ends there and that in 384*k* we have two vocatives ushering in a new section; *ỉw* of BɪBo is superfluous.

32. Mostly lost in B3L, but see BɪBo, which adds a suffix to *bꜥḥ* which is lacking in 370*e*; it omits 384*n*.

33. Var. BɪBo: 'I am the Lone Bull' as in 370*f*, but with *wꜥt* for *wꜥ*, surely in error.

34. Cf. 371*a-b*. BɪBo omits *Spdt* and for *m wnwt.s* of B3L, BɪBo has simply *rnpt* 'year' without either preposition or suffix, and from here on in 385*v*–386*m* a text quite different

from B3L, see n. 42 below.

35. Cf. 372 *a-d.* The suffix 2nd plur. in 385*d* shows that a second entity was invoked, but it has been lost in the lacuna.

36. I.e. Ḥetep.

37. Plural.

38. Cf. 377*g* – 378*b.*

39. Cf. 373*f* – 374*b.*

40. Cf. 374*c-d.*

41. *Dfꜣt tꜣḥt,* ‘lit. ‘provision-goddess and immersion-goddess’.

42. Cf. 373*a-c.* B3L ends here, and the continuation is from B1Bo in the 3rd person. The two texts part company at 385*c,* and therefore overlap a little.

43. Cf. 376*d-e.*

44. Cf. 377*a-d.*

45. This identification of *sꜣꜣwy* is conjectural; on this substance see the one hand Sethe, *Zahlen,* 95, and on the other Harris, *Minerals,* 38.

46. Another clear instance of confusion of Ḥetep the god with *Sḫt-ḥtp.*

47. A preposition omitted.

48. Cf. 378*f.*

49. Cf. 378*g*–379*a.*

Spell 469

MY SPIRIT IS EQUIPPED [FOR(?)] A GOD WHOSE NAME IS HE OF THE DAWN;[1] HE V, 387
IS EVER BETWEEN THE TWO GREAT[2] GODS WHEN THEY ARE IN THE SKY, ONE OF
THEM IN THE WEST OF THE SKY AND ONE OF THEM IN THE EAST OF THE SKY; THEY
LIVE ON ALL[3] THE GOOD THINGS OF THIS LAND. HE, (NAMELY) HE OF THE DAWN,
WILL COME FOR IT, FOR HIS HOLOCAUST, AND HE WILL EQUIP EVERY SPIRIT
BELONGING TO HIM[4] IN THE SKY AND IN THE WEST, | AND IT IS HE WHO WILL 388
PLACE A SPIRIT IN THE REALM OF THE DEAD.[5]

O You of the dawn who wake and sleep; O you Limp One who are in Nedit
before me, I have appeared as the great Primeval One – so says to me He who is
limp, (even) he who is in Nedit. He has cleared[6] the sky, he has joined the land
together, he has cleared[7] Nūt the Great before the great primeval goddess | who 389
has granted appearings to me. The great primeval goddess guides me, (even) Nen-
mut who is in the booth of the Great One,[8] whose eyes are keen(?)[9] whose claws
are sharp, the ferocious lioness(?),[10] Mistress of those who see, the lioness[11] who
sees and catches by night. My mother is Sothis, and she prepares my path, she
sets up a stairway to this very great plain of Nenmut for my ascent from the
Valley of the Mountain of the *Seḥseḥ*-bird [12] on the north within my river-banks,| 390
at the place whence Orion issues. I find Orion standing in my path with his staff

of rank(?) in his hand; I accept it from him and I will be a god[13] by means of it. He gives me his staff which is in his hand, and I will cause the strong ones(?) to tremble by means of it,[14] I will spit on(?) [15] the great ones by means of it, it will make me noble in the presence of Sothis, it will make me secure [16] in the Mansion of Orion. I ascend and appear as a god, [17] my signs of rank are on me, and I will
391 make the lands of the Fenkhu impotent through them. I sit on a throne within the shrine and make summons to Orion that he should come to me:[18] O Orion, come and see me! I have come manifest and besouled, exalted, divine and enshrined[19] in these divine dignities of mine. My soul gives me power over authority, and I have absorbed the perception of every god.[20] I have taken away the powers[21] of the spirits and I have gripped their spirits. See, I have come that I may eat their magic, for I am one alone, without an equal; the Red Crown is in my body, I have gathered their [22] children together, I have fetched them all, and none ever
392 strayed [23] from the company [24] of the spirit of Sia. I have brought these two Ḥu-gods; they eat the food of magic in the barks which assemble their magics and their powers.[25] My soul has taken possession of the *Ḥꜣw-nbwt,* I have brought the dread of me into my body, the awe of me is on my lips, my strength is in my gullet. I am high-handed,[26] and the dread of me is in my flesh; my strength is in my arms, my powers are in my legs; I am a god whose arms rule and in whose heart is power.

393 Anubis brings to me, and his phoenix ushers in to me; I have taken possession of their souls, I have smitten their spirits, my *ꜣtf*-crown[27] is on me and its plumes are on my vertex; I am enshrined[28] as Lord of shrines, I have assumed the Sole Lordship. Come, Orion, and see me; again I have appeared with the *wrrt*-crown, and Shu the Great has given me a throne; I have seized those who would take possession[29] of the gardens by their power and strength, [30] my titulary is my warrant which backs me up. [31]

394 Come, Orion, and bring me these two shares of mine of the cuts of meat [32] which are in the shambles of *H̱rsw*. I will act as him who would destroy(?) these two who approach them,[33] I bring to you these two gardeners(?),[34] they will bring the two Ḥu-gods in their hands and I will eat magic in the Barks of Assembly. The weary Sia sends to them, [35] for he is not equipped with what he needs, [36] and they two have done what had to be done for me in the matter of my daily holocaust;[37] one of them [38] is for my food-offerings and one of them for my night-ritual. It is said to you: [39] 'Come, be a spirit, be equipped' – so says Orion
395 to me. What shall we plan for these two noble ones,[40] from whose souls myriads absorb life, who feed on authority? They shall have power over Sia the weary, who is not equipped with what he needs; they shall assemble the Children

of the Red Crown, being noble in the House of the Two Souls; who were given suck [41] in the Mansion of Orion. They sit on the throne, they see the secret holy things, when their sight falls on the exclusion(?) of . . . , [42] they have partaken of [43] the offerings, in which a holocaust is made daily for the two goddesses(?).[44] Let me hear;[45] I am more of a spirit than they, and what is right to my mind is what they bring.[46]

Those who are in charge of cutting [47] will not come to me, they shall not 396
give ⟨to⟩ [48] the gardeners(?); the dread of you[49] shall be put on those who are in charge of cutting, the gardeners(?) shall fear you, and also their gods and their nobles (*sic*). O you gods who appear because of your [50] nobility, dark ones(?) [. . .], see, it is at your head and at your tail. Come to me bowing down, tremble at me and fear me and give me praise, for I have appeared as a god, I have seized your brows, I have grasped your necks, I have taken possession of what is mine,
namely the other two; I have fetched them all. | You shall not leave me out,[51] O 397
son of *'Iḥst* who dwells in the fire(?), for I am the owner of shrines.

Orion speaks. You have spoken truly – so says Orion to me. Let me hear you summon those noble helpers who remove and re-grant power; [52] they will hear your voice and fear and tremble and do what you order them.

The deceased. Trembling at me is in their flesh, the dread of me is in their hearts, they fall on their faces. [53]

Or. You have come, being a spirit and equipped, and you know their names. Tell them that I will absorb the Red Crown for you.

Decd. I will make your holocaust for you of the magic food which is collect- 398
ed in the Barks, I have committed no robbery, and it is Orion who tells me their names.

Or. You shall make summons for me to them by their names which they know in their hearts, for you have come, being a spirit and equipped, and you know their names. [54]

1. So S2C; B2L is corrupt.
2. B2L omits *ꜥꜣwy* 'great'.
3. *Nbw* only in B2L.
4. Reading *ꜣḫ nb n.f ỉmy m pt* with B2L.
5. B2L adds: 'this is a spell for passing by it'.
6. For this sense of *ḏsr* cf. *CT* I, 223*a*.
7. *Ḫsr nwt* is virtually synonymous with *ḏsr pt* above. For *ḫsr* B2L and B1P write *ḫrsr*.
8. Masc. B2L and B1P have shortly *nn wr*; the blank space between these two words in B2L suggests that once there was a lacuna in the original copy at this point which apparently

was forgotten when B1P was written.

9. *ȝšt* appears to be a fem. adjective referring back to *nwt*, but the word is not recorded, and the meaning given to it is a guess.

10. *Mȝ-sḥwt* appears to be a compound analogous to *mȝ-ḥsȝ* 'fierce lion', but it does not seem to occur elsewhere. Both 389*e* and *g* point to *mȝ-sḥwt* being a designation of a lioness-goddess, but its precise meaning remains obscure; the knife-det. suggests ferocity. Compare 399*a* ff., where the goddess is the lioness Pakhet.

11. Note the cat-det. in B1P and the absence of a qualifying suffix.

12. Cf. *Pyr.* §§389; 1118.

13. The writing out of the final weak radical in *nṯry.f* points to the prospective tense. By analogy it has occasioned the writings with final *-y* of the 3 lit. verbs *sdȝy* in 390*f*, *ỉsdy* in 390*g*, *snby* in 390*h*, and *sydy* (B2L) in 390*l*, where the tense likewise seems to be prospective.

14. *Sdȝ* is used here in its original sense of the causative of *dȝ* 'tremble', *Concise Dict.* 309.

15. For *ỉsdy* 'spit on(?)' a foe (B2L) cf. *CT* IV, 97*k*; S2C omits the initial *ỉ*.

16. *Snb* with transitive sense; for the implication of security cf. *mrw snb* 'the terrain is secure', *Urk.* IV, 656, 15.

17. S2C has the sing. 'god', but at the end of 390*l* refers back to it with the plural suffix *.sn*.

18. S2C omits the prospective clause *ỉwt.f n.ỉ*.

19. *Kȝr.ky*, old perfective 1st sing. of a denominative verb derived from *kȝr* 'shrine'.

20. The deceased is assuming the attributes of the regular pair Ḥu and Sia.

21. Or 'necks'? Cf. 396*n*.

22. The plural suffix presumably refers back to the *ȝḫw* of 391*i*.

23. Note the use of subjectless *sḏm.f* after *n sp*.

24. Surely so; neither 'body' nor 'womb' fit the context.

25. *Ḥkȝw.sn ȝḫw.sn* in B2L; S2C has *sḫmw.sn ȝḫw.sn* 'their strengths and their powers', omitting the reference to *ỉmwy* 'the two barks'.

26. Lit. 'I am great in my heart'; the sense seems to be 'high-handed' or 'oppressive'.

27. Shown to be singular by the suffix in *šwt.f* below.

28. See n. 19 above; in 393*f* *kȝr.ky* has the prothetic *ỉ*.

29. Reading *iṯ.t(y).sn* with S2C.

30. B2L: 'by their spirits and gods'; S2C seems to have the better text.

31. So S2C. B2L has: 'I am placed with protection about me'.

32. See Spell 468, n. 25.

33. The two versions of 394*b* are not in accord, nor do they fit into the context. S2C appears to say: 'I will act as him who would destroy (read *ꜥḏ.ty.fy*?) those two who approach them' (who are 'them'?). B2L has 'destruction of those two who approach them', reading *ꜥḏt ⟨t⟩knw.* Both versions seem so remote from the context that either there must have been an omission of text after 394*a* or this clause has been interpolated from elsewhere.

34. Reading *kȝnw*(?) here and 396*b.d*; there is a reference to 'gardens' (*ḥspw*) in 393*k* above.

35. B2L has a dittograph of *n.sn.* The plural pronoun appears to refer to one of the pairs of gods named in 394*c-d*.

36. Lit. 'with what appertains to him'. For *ỉrt.f* B2L has wrongly *ỉtrt.f.*

37. So B2L; S2C inserts a damaged clause starting with *r ꜥḥꜥ* before *ẖrt hrw*.

38. Emending as *wꜥ ỉm.sn* in both texts, cf. 394*k* in S2C.

39. Apparently impersonal *sdm.f* + dative, followed by three hortative old perfectives; 394*m* indicates that these instructions emanate from Orion.

40. S2C has a superfluous  after *kꜣ.n*; B2L has *sr* 'prince' for *sꜥḥ* 'noble one'.

41. For *sbn* 'give suck' cf. *Pyr.* §716, of cattle; *Peas.* B2, 120, of woman.

42. *Bst* is recorded in *Wb* I, 172, 18. 19 as occuring in an official title *wr bst* and also as a town-name, but there seems no clue to its meaning here, where it has the woman-det. This passage defeats me. B2L omits *ḥr* before *ḫm*.

43. Apparently so, though the preposition is *r*, not *m*. To read *smꜣ rḫt* yields poor sense.

44. Both texts seem incorrect as they stand; perhaps we should emend into *m ẖrt hrw n nṯrty*.

45. 395*m* shows unusual writings of the enclitic *ỉr.k*.

46. *Int.s* for *int.sn*; the pronoun presumably refers to the two goddesses of 395*l*. It is difficult to see what can have stood in the small lacuna in 395*o* (S2C); [*n*.]*k* or [*r*.]*k* do not fit the context.

47. Cf. *kft*, *kf*, *Wb.* V, 120, 1–2; *kf* 'knife', *CT* II, 133*f*. The deceased is not to be a victim in the Beyond.

48. Suppression of *n* by haplography, read *n rdy.n.sn* ⟨*n*⟩*kꜣnw*.

49. A change to the 2nd person; the deceased must surely be meant.

50. English demands the use of the 2nd person here.

51. Read *n sp.k wỉ* with B2L; S2C omits *wỉ*. For the sense of *sp* cf. *Urk* IV, 84, 5.

52. B2L omits *ꜣḫ* 'power'.

53. To be read as *nrw.ỉ m ỉbw.sn ḥr.sn m ḥrw.sn*. The trace in the lacuna of S2L is uncertain, but *ỉb* is superior to *ḥr* of B2L. and resemble each other, and confusion could easily arise. In 397*l* we should certainly read *ḥr* for *ỉb* in both texts.

54. It is clear that we have here a dialogue between Orion and the deceased, but it is by no means certain who is speaking at a given moment, and my apportionment of the speeches is only provisional.

Spell 470

SPELL FOR REACHING ORION.[1] O You of the dawn who wake and sleep, O You who are in limpness, dwelling aforetime in Nedit, I have appeared as Pakhet the V, 399 Great,[2] whose eyes are keen(?) and whose claws are sharp, the lioness who sees and catches by night. O Sothis my soul, make my path ready, set up a stairway to the great plain, for you are my mother(?),[3] and Ḥu is at (the place) whence Orion issues.[4] I find Orion standing on the path with the staff in his hand, and I set up the staff and receive it, and I am a god by means of it. He gives me the 400 staff which is in his hand, and he says: 'Give me my son, for it is he who rises in peace; you shall be ennobled before your throne, for you are[5] my son, the lord of my house'.

1. A shorter variant of Spell 469.
2. In 389*b* the word seems to be *pꜣwt* 'the Primeval One', though there the writing in B2L is ambiguous. In 389*c* the following description is applied to Nenmut.
3. See de Buck's n. 1*.
4. A corrupt version of 389*j* – 390*a*.
5. Read *ṯwt* with B1C.

Spell 471

A MAN HAS POWER THROUGH HIS MAGIC. I have stood up as a holy woman,[1] I have sat down as [. . .] the sky, because you[2] know my magic which I take to the sky.

1. Man's coffin.
2. Plural, but the beings addressed are not specified.

Spell 472

VI, 1 SPELL FOR CAUSING SHABTIS TO DO WORK[1] FOR THEIR OWNER IN THE REALM OF THE DEAD. See him,[2] you gods, spirits and dead who are in[3] sky and earth, he has taken possession of his strength and his power,[4] he has taken possession for himself of his thrones, he has come to rule among the (human) herds[5] who were made for N in accordance with the command of the gods. If N be detailed for the removal(?) of a block(?) to strange sites(?) of the desert plateau,[6] to register the riparian lands, or to turn over new fields for the reigning king, 'Here am I' you[7] shall say to any messenger who may come for N when taking his ease(?).[8] Take your picks(?),[9] your hoes, your pegs[10] and your baskets[11] in your hands, just as every young man does for his master.

2 O you shabtis which have been made for N, if N be detailed [12]for his task, or an unpleasant duty in it be imposed on N as a man at his task, 'Here we are' you shall say. If N be detailed to keep an eye on[13] those who work there at turning over new fields, to plant the riparian lands or to convey sand to the West which was placed on the East – and *vice versa* –[14] 'Here we are' you shall say about it.

TO BE SPOKEN OVER AN IMAGE OF THE OWNER AS HE WAS ON EARTH, MADE OF TAMARISK OR ZIZYPHUS WOOD AND PLACED ⟨ IN ⟩ THE CHAPEL OF THE DECEASED.

1. Plural as written, despite the sing. suffix in *nb.f,* note the plur. suffixes in 1*k-l.*

2. The deceased.

3. *Sw* here is clearly corrupted out of 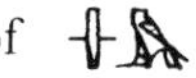 , though it is certain that *sw* is what stands in both texts, see de Buck's n. 1*.

4. Reading *pḥty.f ꜣt.f* with BɪP.

5. For *ꜥwt* 'herds' used figuratively for 'men' cf. *Westc.* 8, 17; *CT* I, 155*b.*

6. 1*f-g* has some obscure terms. *'Iwꜣw* is followed by the plural genitive *nw,* presumably on account of the ending *-w* of the noun; it has been regarded here as a derivative of *ꜥwꜣ* 'steal' in what seems to be its basic sense of 'forcible removal', compare *ꜥwꜣy* 'reap'; for initial *ỉ* instead of *ꜥ* cf. *ZÄS* 59, 27. BɪP has *wꜣwt* at this point, which I cannot interpret except as a corruption of *ỉwꜣw.* For *ḏbꜣt* 'block(?)' see also *CT* III, 90*d. Drdrw* in 1*g* is perhaps to be understood as a derivative of *ḏrḏr* 'strange'.

7. The shabtis are here addressed in the singular despite the plural suffixes of 1*k-l.* The singular probably represents the original form of the spell, of which the author of the present version does not seem to have become fully free. It is worthy of note that the version of *BD* Spell 6 (Nebseni) still addresses the shabti in the singular, so it would seem that the provision of a gang of shabtis was a novelty at the date of this coffin, hence the confusion of number.

8. Lit. perhaps 'in his pleasure'; for *snw* 'pleasure(?)' cf. *CT* III, 82*d* – 83*a.*

9. *Išrt*; the translation as 'pick(?)' is a guess.

10. Presumably for demarcation of plots of land, cf. the late word *nbꜣt* 'Pfahl', *Wb,* II, 243, 10.

11. Certainly containers of some kind, cf. *ḥnkw* 'scale-pan' of balance, Peas. Bɪ, 323; *BD* 264, 8; 'jar' for wine, ibid. 11. Doubtless identical with *ḥnkw* in *CT* II, 203*a,* again associated with hoes. The det. indicates a basket.

12. 2*b* appears to be a conflation of three versions of the text, i.e. *ỉr ỉp.tw ṯw* 'if someone detail you'; *ỉr ỉp.tw wỉ* 'if someone detail me', lastly *ỉr ỉp.tw N pn* 'if N be detailed'. The last is to be preferred here.

13. The eye-sign here appears to do double duty as the det. of *nw* 'see', 'look', *JEA* 31, 113, and as the phonogram for *ỉr* in *ỉrrw.*

14. On the transfer of sand from East to West and inversely by the shabti on behalf of the deceased, cf. H. von Voss in *Phoenix,* 9 (1963), 53. He is of opinion, with Petrie, that the purpose of the work was to remove encroaching sand.

Spell 473

SPELL FOR THE NET[1] AND THE FISH-TRAP[2] AND OF ESCAPING FROM IT. O you who look backward (*Ḥr.f-ḥꜣ.f*), fisher of the canals,[3] the aggressive one, son of Gēb and her who opened the earth;[4] O you fishers of the dead, O you children of your fathers who catch the dead,[5] you may trap[6] those who are all over the land, but you shall not catch me in your nets in which you catch the dead; trap[7] (only) those who are all over the land, because I know your names;[8] the net of the gods is a purse-net(?).[9] VI, 3 4

Because I know the name of its . . . ;[10] it is this open space(?) when he placed
his White Crown of lapis lazuli on his head.[11]

5 Because I know the name of its field;[12] | the wig(?)[13] which is on Osiris the
fortunate.[14]

Because I know the name of its flax; the staff of Horus which is in the hand
of Rēʿ.

Because I know the name of its netting [15] and plaiting; [16] it is She of the
taping(?) and She of the coiling.[17]

6 Because I know the name of its drag-rope and its *ḳmꜣt*-rope; [18] they are Isis
and Nephthys.

Because I know the name of the reel in it, it is the big finger of Osiris.
I know the name of its knife (*šʿt*) [in] it; it the cutter (*ḥsbt*) of Nephthys.[19]

Because I know the name of the guard-beam(?) in it; it is the shank of the
Winepress-god.

7 Because I know the name of the roller(?) [20] in it; it is the finger-nail of
Osiris.

Because I know the name of its four tufts; they are the tufts which are in(?)
the bird-trap of Sobk, which is behind the coiffure(?) of ʿAnti.[21]

Because I know the name of its ropes; they are the sinews of Atum.

Because I know the name of the man who goes down and receives the fish in
8 it;[22]|it is the containers(?) of the gods.[23]

Because I know the name of the man and the knife (*sfṯw*) in it; it is the sharp
knife (*mds*) which is in the hand of the Winepress-god.[24]

Because I know the name of the 'woman' in which he cooks it; it is the
cauldron in the hand of the Winepress-god.[25]

9 Because I know the name of [the man] who cooks it on it;|it is the brazier
of the great-breasted one who sits with every god about him.[26]

Because I know the name of the man and what he has laid upon it; it is the
offering-table with which the land is pleased, (even) the ear which listens to
Ḥatḥōr.[27]

10 Because I know the name of the place in which it is drawn tight after it has
been used; it is the celestial plain on which every god dwells.[28]

Because I know the place where it was put after fishing; it is the papyrus-
wand which is in the hand of Isis.[29]

Because I know the names of the floats which are above and the weights
which are below; they are the kneecaps of Osiris and the fingers of Gēb.[30]

Because I know the name of the boat from which it fishes; it is the *nšmt*-
11 bark | in which [31] things are conveyed to the Souls of Ōn.

Because I know the name of the steering-oar; it is the corner which is between the platforms(?) [32] of the *nšmt*-bark.

Because I know the name of her mast; it is the phallus of Babi.

Because I know the name of her oars; it is the shank of Gēb and the thigh of the Winepress-god.

Because I know the name of her sounding poles; [33] they are the oarsmen[34] who navigate the *nšmt*-bark for the Souls of Ōn.

Because I know the name of her bailer; it is the bailer of those who bail out 12
and who drive off those who are not.

Because I know the name of her 'reeds', her rigging, her finials and her masthead; [35] the earth-hair which the earth yields. [36]

Because I know the name of her bow-warp; the *sḏf*- and the *tmm*-cords which are about the tomb of Osiris.[37]

Because I know the name of the man who goes aboard her; he is a Great One 13
and I am a Great One; I will appear as a Great One and will go aboard the
boat [38] and sow the land to the northern sky, and I will join up there with the
gods, for my bread is in the Field of Rushes,[39] my supper is in the Field of
Flood; [40] | I will not eat faeces for you,[41] I will not drink urine for you, I will not 14
walk upside down for you, but I will live there on red emmer, I will eat there of
white emmer. [42] It is Isis who will give me water, it is Sokar who will bend down
on my behalf.[43] I know you, O *Ry*, [44] | I will make a break in your *sḏf*-cord,[45] , I 15
will loose the *sḏf*-cords [46] which go up from the . . . ,[47] and I will be well [by
means of(?)] it with Her who is over the spirits of the gods. I will ascend to the
sky among the gods, I will bring and repeat [48] the words of the gods. Such is my
magic; you have given to me [49] the Winding Waterway for my eternity with the
god and his *wtnw*. [50] | I will eat of its [51] fish, I will take its abundance, I will go 16
down on to its riparian lands, I will fell ʿApep, and I will glitter there; [52] I have
glittered as Sobk on its top, [53] I have glittered as [54] ʿAnti on its middle, I have
glittered as ʿAnti on its top, [55] I have glittered as a Great One.

1. See Spell 343, n. 3.
2. Cf. 34*a*, where *ỉssyt* appears to be determined with a fish-trap.
3. *Wḏʿw*, lit. 'something cut away, of earth, i.e. artificial channels.
4. *Wbꜣt tꜣ* appears to be the name of a net, cf. 21*b* and Spell 474, n. 17. Here it is identified with the spouse of Gēb.
5. Not in B9C or B1Y.
6. Written 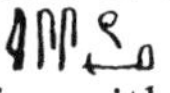 in *BD* 390, 11. 12; cf. *ỉsst* 'fish-trap' in 3*a* above.
7. Imperative with reinforcing enclitic.
8. Read *n-ntt* 'because'; also 4*d* (B6Bo) and 4*e* (B1C). B9C and B1Y have considerable

omissions at this point. B6Bo (4*d-e*) reads: *⟨n-⟩ntt N rḫt sn rḫt rnw.sn* 'because N knows them and knows their names' – the fem. *rḫt* is because N is a woman. B1C (4*e*) has: *⟨n-⟩ntt wỉ rḫ.kw rn.s* 'because I know its name', i.e. of the net.

9. Probably a var. of *ỉnyt* 'purse-net', cf. Spell 343, n. 4. This spell regularly uses the vine-frame as a determinative for 'net'.

10. *Mm,* meaning unknown, but apparently a part of the net.

11. This passage is quite obscure. For the meaning assigned to *pḏw* cf. *pḏt* 'expanse' of sky, *Pyr.* §§393; 801; 1443. The fem. genitive adjective following *tp.f* (B1C) must refer back to *ḥḏt*, as *tp* is masculine, so that we have the anomaly of a White Crown made of a blue substance. B6Bo, which is damaged, omits the preposition before *tp* and has 'her head'; as this is a woman's coffin, it follows that the person crowned is the deceased.

12. Presumably meaning the area of the net when spread out.

13. *Ḫ3w,* translation uncertain.

14. So B1C; between *Wsyr* and *mꜥr* B9C has a damaged word which is lost also in B1Y, but which may have been absent from B6Bo.

15. Cf. *sšnw* 'ropes', 'cordage', *CT* V, 98*c*; *sšnt* again VI, 221*l*, in a 'clothing' context.

16. Cf. *msn* 'spin(?)', 'plait(?)', *Concise Dict.* 117.

17. *3yt* may be connected with *3y, 3yr* 'strip' of tape, Breasted, *Ed. Smith Pap.* 512; and *mḥnt* appears to be a derivative of *mḥn* 'coil', *Concise Dict.* 114-5. The reference may be to the binding and whipping of the roped edge of the net. For *3yt* B6Bo has *st3y* [*t*] 'the mysterious one' and B1C has *T3yt,* the name of the goddess of weaving; it is clear that the copyists of these two texts did not understand *3yt* of B9C and B1Y and emended it as seemed to them best on the assumption that the beginning of the word had been lost. B1C has also misunderstood *mḥnt.*

18. B9C and probably, B1Y omit *km3t.s,* but the following 6*a* points to a pair of ropes being named here.

19. B6Bo only.

20. Written and read exactly like *mḏ3t* 'roll' of papyrus; in 22*i* it is spelt out with the wood-det., so I have guessed the meaning to be something like 'roller'. In 25*o* it has the knife-det.

21. For *g3bt* see also *CT* III, 289*b*, but the meaning of 7*c-d* escapes me. Note the writing of the *n. div.* ꜥAnti in B1C; so also in 16*g.h.*

22. We proceed here from the parts of the net to the handling of the fish. They are apparently stacked in baskets.

23. *Gnmy(t)* is not recorded, but the det. in B1C suggests a basket. At the end of 8*a* B9C reads 'the brothers of the gods'.

24. The fish are now being gutted. This passage in B1C alone.

25. 'Woman' in 8*d* is clearly a term for a kind of cooking-pot, perhaps deriving from a comparison of a large round pot with a pregnant female.

26. B1C seems to have the better text; *ḥr.f* 'on it', referring to the brazier mentioned in 9*a*, is more factual than *ỉm.s* 'in it'.

27. The cooked fish now comes to table, but why the table should be likened to an ear is not easy to grasp; is it envisaged as oval in shape?

28. The text now deals with the disposal of the net after the removal of the fish.

29. Var. B9C 'Osiris', but a papyrus-wand is usually borne by a goddess.

30. This suggests that the floats were wooden discs and that the weights were narrow strips of metal or stone. The function of *ḥrw* 'upper' in 10*e* is presumably to make it clear that the preceding ideograms are really fingers and not toes; it has been omitted from the translation because 'upper fingers' makes no sense in English.

31. B9C has inserted a superfluous *n* after *ỉm.s*.

32. *Wꜥrt* as part of a vessel is obscure; the use of the preposition *ỉmyt(w)* 'between' implies that there were two of them, and the normal meaning of *wꜥrt* suggests raised portions of deck on which the helmsman could stand.

33. So B9C and B1Y; B1C has *ꜥḏw* 'reels', presumably in error. We have had this word already in connection with the net.

34. B9C and B1Y originally read *msḥty*, meaning unknown; B1C has *ḥpwty* 'oarsmen', cf. *CT* VII, 401*a*; 408*c*.

35. For *swt* 'reeds' cf. Spell 396, n. 18; for *ỉn* (det. 𓍢) 'rigging' cf. *Concise Dict.* 23; for *šꜣw* 'finials' of boats cf. Spell 396, n. 19; for *bḏꜣ* 'masthead' cf. Spell 398, n. 25.

36. It is not clear in this context what is meant by 'earth-hair', which is the name of a plant; it may be a figure for a fringe of cords on net or rope, cf. *šnw* in 23*k*, Spell 474, n. 28.

37. *Sḏf* 'cord' does not seem to be known; *tmm* recalls the *tm*-cord of *CT* V, 178*e*.

38. Note that B1C here preserves the older usage *hꜣy m* for boarding a boat, whereas B9C and B1Y use *hꜣy r*, which is normal for Middle Egyptian.

39. Note the variant *ꜥꜣrw* for the usual *ỉꜣrw*; in B1Y *ꜥꜣrw* has actually been corrected over original *ỉꜣrw*, see de Buck's n. 3*.

40. Here in 13*j* B9C anticipates 14*b* and is translated there.

41. Plural, presumably in reference to the gods of 13*g*.

42. 14*f* is a dittograph of 14*c* and has been omitted from the translation. B9C omits all 14*d-f*.

43. Presumably to help the deceased; hardly to do obeisance!

44. So B1Y; *Rwy* in B9C; *Ry-sḏ*(?) in B1C. Quite obscure.

45. Lit. 'I will break a breach of your *sḏf*'. B1C has 'I will breach your *sḏf*.

46. Var. B1Y: 'I will loose the *sḏf*, I will make a break in the *sḏf*.

47. *Sꜣt*, meaning obscure, as is all of 15*c*.

48. For *wḥm* 'repeat' B1C has *wꜥb* 'purify', which yields poor sense.

49. Var. B1C: 'there is given to me'.

50. For the *wtnw*, here miswritten, cf. Spell 320, n. 4, where the reference V, 320 should read V, 220. The use of the sign of the Red Crown with the water-sign in B1Y assures the reading.

51. Of the Winding Waterway.

52. B1C has bungled the writing of *ḫꜣbs* here and in 16*f* and for *ỉm* has *sm*; see n. 54 below.

53. Both versions are faulty; read *ḫꜣbs.n.ỉ m Sbk tp tp.s*. The fem. suffix at the end presumably refers to the net *ỉꜣdt*.

54. B1C inserts a superfluous *s* (for *ỉs*?, cf. 16*h*, B9C) before *m* 'as' here and in 16*h.i*.

55. B9C omits *ḥr-tp tp.s*, and inserts the enclitic *ỉs* before *m*.

Spell 474[1]

VI, 17 O you who look backward (*Mꜣ-ḥꜣ.f*), aggressive one who fishes with the spear,[2] the fisherman of the *wꜣḏt-tꜣwy* net;[3] O you fishermen, you children of your fathers, who fish round about within the Valley, you shall not catch me in [your] net[4] in which you catch the dead, you shall not trap me in your fish-trap in which you trap those who are all over the land, the floats of which are in the sky and the weights of which are on the earth. I have escaped from it, from the bight(?)[5] of it; I have appeared as *Ḥnw*. I have escaped from its clutch; I have appeared as Sobk and I have used ⟨my⟩ arms ⟨as⟩ one who flies from you.[6]

O you who fish and net whose fingers are hidden, I know the name of my[7] reel in it; it is the big finger of Sokar.

18 I know the name of my guard-beam(?) in it; it is the shank of the Winepress-god.

Because[8] I know the name of my roller(?)[9] in it; it is the hand of Osiris.

Because I know the name of my knife in it; it is the cutter of Isis with which she cut the navel-string of Horus.

I know the name of its floats and weights; they are the kneecaps of the Double Lion.

I know the name of the ropes which pull it up; they are the sinews of Atum.

I know the name of the fishermen who use it; they are the earth-gods, the forefathers of those who swallow(?).

I know the name of my hands which receive it; they are the hands of the great god Rēʿ who gives judgement in Ōn on the night of the half-moon festival.

19 I know the name of the plain on which it is drawn tight; it is the great celestial plain on which the gods stand.

I [know] the name of the servitor who receives the fish from it; it is *ꜣbd-ms* the servitor of the gods.

I know the name of his table on which he lays it;[10] it is the great table which satisfies every god, about which every god sits.

I know the name of 'He-sets-it-down-for-himself'; he is the Great One who sits alone in darkness and who cannot be seen, of whom those who have not given him praise are afraid.[11]

I have come, having appeared as a Great One, and I exercise governance in the land; I have gone down ⟨to⟩ my land in my two great barks; it is the Great One who will grant [bread(?) to] me within the mansion of the Great One.

20 I have come to you, O you who fish with the *ʿryt* net;[12] my reel is in my hand, my knife is in my hand, my cutter is [in] my hand, my knife is in my hand. I

go up so that I may go about and catch with my net.

O you four who fish with the purse-net; O you [fair(?)] one; O you contented double; do not oppose me with this net of purse-net (type). I [know(?)] this Eye of Horus which is speedy and effective, I rise by means of it as a cobra, I ascend upon its peg(?)[13] [. . .]. The arrow(?) of Neith flies[14] when she shoots, Nephthys inflicts(?) this wound. I have gone up by means of it because[15] I am the son of my worthy father whom you know, and whose utterance the fisherman and the netter know, (even) they whose fingers are hidden.

O *Mn-ḥꜣ.f,*[16] | you who fish with its spears, the strong-voiced, the fisherman 21
of the *wbꜣt-tꜣ* nets,[17] I will not go to you, I will not come [to you], for I have escaped from the bight(?),[18] having appeared as Sobk.

I have gone up, having appeared as *Ḥnw* . . .[19] [. . .] because I am the son of my worthy father, whom you know, and whose utterance the fisher and the netter know, (even) they whose fingers are hidden.

O you who [. . .] this net of yours, this secret thing of yours which catches living things under the fish-traps of Reʿ, under the bights(?) in front of the Great One, I have escaped from it,[20] having ended up as the Baboon of a myriad, the Messenger from Abydos.

I escaped from the wounds when Rēʿ [went forth] on that night of uproar,
because I know the name of the reel and cord of the mouth of the opening in 22
it;[21] it is the big finger of Osiris.

Because I know the name of the fingers which grasp it;[22] they are the first fingers of the hands ⟨of Rēʿ(?)⟩[23] and the first nails of the hand of Ḥatḥōr.

Because I know the names of the ropes which are on the reel; they are the sinews of the Lord of the plebs.

Because I [know] the name of its guard-beam(?); it is the shank of the Winepress-god.

Because I know the name of its roller(?);[24] it is the hand of Isis.

Because I know the name of its cords; they are the cords of the oldest god.

Because I know the name of its lines; they are the light-rays(?)[25] of the daytime.

Because I know the name of the fishermen who use it; they are | the earth-gods 23
who preceded all the world and who preceded Gēb.

O you who have brought food for yourself, bring me food for myself.

O you who swallow for yourself, swallow for me.

O you who look backward (*Ḥr.f-ḥꜣ.f*), who fish with the spear;[26] O you who are aggressive; O you fisherman of the *wbꜣt-tꜣ* net; O you fishermen, children of your fathers, who establish trappers in the Valley, you shall not[27] catch me in your nets, you shall not trap me in your pendent cords,[28] you shall not catch me in this your net in which you catch the dead, in which you trap those who are all over the land, because I know it concerning the floats which are above and the weights which are below.

24 I know it concerning its floats which are above; they are the iron on the hands of Rēᶜ.

I know it concerning ⟨its⟩ weights which are below; they are the kneecaps of Osiris.

I know it, the peg(?)[29] which holds it still; it is the sinew of Atum on the day of burial.

Because I know the name of the fishermen who use it;[30] they are those who swallow(?) and the fiery ones, the most primeval of the gods.

I know its rope[31] which pulls it; it is the navel-string of Horus on the day when his mother gave him birth.

I know the plain on which it is drawn tight; the great celestial plain on which the gods rest.

25 Because I know [the name of] the cover[32] of my knife on it; it is the offering-table which is the offering-table of the gods.

I know the name of the altar at which I eat; it is ⟨. . .⟩[33] of the moon on the day of the festival of the half-moon.

See me, see me, a living soul, who releases the willow; see, I have come with my guard-beam(?) in my hand and my roller(?) in my hand.[34] I have come that I may enter, I have come that I may enter, I have come that I may cut, I have come that I may catch it and put it in its place; I break the bow and I allot it into its place.[35] As for its guard-beam(?), it is the shank of the Winepress-god.

I know its reel; it is the finger of Sokar. As for its roller(?), it is the finger-nail of Isis; as for this its knife which is in my hand, it is the cutter of Nephthys.

See, I have come, see, I have come, a living soul who releases the willow. See,
26 I have come, having sat down as Rēᶜ;[1] I cross the Winding Waterway to the north of the sky, I hear the speech of the gods and I do what they do. Acclamation to my double; may I live as those who shall live there.

1. This spell is clearly the source of *BD* Spell 153A. There is a single instance of the 1st person in 25*k*, and the *BD* text is in the 1st person. As it stands Spell 474 is a composite text made up of three variant versions of the same text, and this holds good also of the *BD* text.

2. For *ḏᶜw* 'fish-spear' cf. *ḏᶜ* 'spear fish', *P. Kah.* 33, 16. The vine-frame is a regular det. of fishing implements in these texts.

3. Shown to be a net by the vine-frame det.

4. Read *ṯn ntw*; one *n* has been dropped through haplography. So also in 17*f*.

5. *Ỉby* with bowl-det. may perhaps mean the bag or bight of the net; in 21*d* it takes the wood-det., as also in *BD* 390, 14.

6. Reading *ir.n.f ꜥwy ⟨.f m⟩ pꜣy r.ṯn,* cf. *BD* 390, 16. The figure is that of a bird flapping its wings in flight.

7. The deceased appears as the owner of the parts of the net. Cf. 20*a-d.*

8. *N-ntt* instead of *ỉw* is probably due to the influence of Spell 473, 4*c* ff. So also below, 22*a* ff. In 18*e* we have both *n-ntt* and *ỉw.*

9. On *mḏꜣt* 'roller(?)' cf. Spell 473, n. 20. *BD* 391, 4 substitutes *ꜥꜣ* 'valve' (lit. 'door'), and at the end of the clause, for 'Osiris' has 'Isis'.

10. The fish.

11. Both here and in *BD* 392, 7–8, which inverts the order of *ntyw* and *ỉwtyw,* the text appears to be corrupt. I suggest emending 19*k* into *snḏw n.f ỉwtyw ddw n.f ỉꜣ* 'of whom those who have not given him praise are afraid'.

12. Possibly a type of purse-net, in view of the determinative.

13. Reading uncertain, see de Buck, n. 4*. It may perhaps be identical with  'peg(?)', 24*e* below.

14. Read *pꜣ ꜥrt ⟨t⟩w nt Nt, ꜥrt* 'stem' of plant, *Wb* I, 208, 8-9, being possibly figurative for the 'shaft' of an arrow, hence by extension being used for the 'arrow' itself. The translation of 20*k-m* is almost all doubtful.

15. *N-ntt* is followed by an obscure concatenation of particles.

16. *Mn-ḥꜣ.f* appears to be a corruption of *Mꜣ.ḥꜣ.f.*

17. *Wbꜣt-tꜣ* is determined with the signs for both kinds of net. See Spell 473, n. 4.

18. See n. 5 above.

19. I cannot translate *dḥn.f ꜥ.*

20. The net; cf. *BD* 391, 2.

21. In 20*m* and 21*p wbnw* may well have its usual meaning of 'wound', but that makes no sense here, where it seems to refer to an opening in the net; *ỉm.f,* having the masc. suffix, presumably refers to the *wbꜣ-tꜣ* net of 21*b* or the fish-trap of 21*k.*

22. Presumably the reel.

23. For the insertion see de Buck's n. 1*; *BD* 393, 1.

24. Written  above, cf. 7*a*; 18*c*; Spell 473, n. 20.

25. Unknown word; the translation is a guess, but cf. *nw* 'time', *Concise Dict.* 127.

26. See n. 16 above.

27. Note the rare enclitic negation *w.*

28. Thin cords attached to a net or to a rope like a fringe of hair? In 12*e* we have *šnw-tꜣ* the plant 'earth-hair'.

29. Lit. 'column', 'pillar'. The fem. pronoun after *rḫ* is reproduced automatically from the preceding clauses, but should be the masc. *sw* to agree with *wꜣḏ.*

30. The net.

31. The sense demands the singular, despite the plural dots; cf. *npꜣw* below.

32. Cf. *šṯ* 'satchel', *CT* I, 71*h*; IV, 115*g*; the stem seems to carry the general sense of 'covering up', cf. Sp. 310, n. 2; 1043, n. 1. Here the word is strangely written *šṯtw,* probably to be read as *šṯwt* or *šṯt tw.*

33. In 25*c* there is an omission between *ỉsṯ* and *ỉꜥḥ*.

34. Here *mḏꜣt* 'roller' is given the knife-det.

35. Note the single occurrence of the original 1st person in *wḏ.ỉ*. It is not clear to what the pronoun *sw* in 25*h-k* refers, nor is the masc. *pḏ* the usual word for 'bow', which is the fem. *pḏt*, but the fact that it can be broken supports the translation as 'bow'.

Spell 475

SPELL FOR THE NET FOR FISHING. [I] know[1] [the name of . . .].

VI, 27 O you anglers(?)[2] of the god, its name [. . .].[3]

Trappers; its god [. . .].

Fishermen, its god [. . .].

Underlings; its god [. . .].

They whom their fathers brought into being; its god [. . .].

[I know the name of] its ropes; they are the sinews [of Isis].[4]

[I know the name of] its guard-beam(?); it is the shank [of Atum].

[I know the name of] its reel; it is the finger [of the Winepress god].

[I know the name of] its roller(?); it is the fingernail [of Ptaḥ].

[I know the name of] its knives; they are the cutter of [Isis].

[I know the name of] its floats(?);[5] they are the plume of [the Falcon].

[I know the name of] its weights; it is the iron [in the midst of the sky].

[I know the name of] its fishermen; they are baboons.

[I know the name of] the plain on which it is drawn tight; [it is] the middle of the Mansion [of the Moon].

28 [I know the name of] | him who fishes for himself; he is the great and mighty one [who dwells in the eastern side of the sky].

I know the name of that [very] great net;[6] Provider of [fish(?)] is its name.

I will not eat, O great and mighty one;[7] I will not be prostrate,[8] O great one; I will not sit, O great one, on my haunches by the water, for I have eaten and have swallowed his heart(?); my soul gulps down(?) the [food] of the dead which is in my [belly](?).[9]

1. Cf. *ỉw.i rḫ.ỉ* in 28*b*. Comparison shows that this spell was the original source of *BD* Spell 153B, so that the lacunae can be restored.

2. *Wsf*, here without determinatives, appears in fuller form in *BD* 395, 11, meaning a class of fishermen. The translation 'anglers' is a guess, but shows it to be a word distinct from the other classes of fishermen already encountered. In its *BD* spelling it closely resembles the word for 'sluggard', and indeed it could perhaps be that word used as a nickname for the angler, who does not appear greatly to exert himself.

3. The lacunae all occur in the lower part of the text, see the plan on de Buck's p. 26. The regular fem. suffix refers to the net *ỉꜣdt*.

4. Cf. *BD* 396, 6. The restorations follow *BD* Spell 153B.

5. *Sẖpw,* var. *sẖpwt* in *BD* 397, 1 is an alternative name for 'floats' of a net to *ḏbꜣw,* the term met hitherto. See Spell 477, n. 9.

6. Restoring *ỉꜣḏt tw ꜥꜣt* [*wrt*], which seems to fill the lacuna; cf. *BD* 396, 3-4.

7. What follows suggests that *ꜥꜣ wr* is a vocative. The god-sign in 28*d-h* appears to be a determinative, since it lacks the stroke, compare 27*b-e*. With 28*d* ff. compare *BD* 397, 9 ff.

8. For *sẖy* 'be prostrate' cf. *CT* V, 208*d*.

9. *Sꜥꜣb* of 28*h* is not known. *BD* 397, 11–12 reads *ỉw ỉẖbw mt m ẖt.ỉ* 'the food(?) of the dead is in my belly', which to me has the appearance of an emendation of a passage not understood. That there is corruption here in *CT* seems certain; note the repetition of *mt* 'the dead'. A possible emendation is to regard  as an error for  (cf. *ỉẖbw* of *BD*) and the second *mt* as an error for *ỉmt* 'which is in', yielding the emendation *sẖb bꜣ* ⟨*.ỉ* ⟩ [*wnmt*] *mt ỉmt* [*ẖt*] *.ỉ* 'my soul gulps down [the food] of the dead which is in my [belly]', but it does not carry much conviction.

Spell 476

O you who look backward,[1] you fisherman who opens the net,[2] aggressive one, fisherman of the *ỉbꜣt-tꜣ* net,[3] I have come to you that I may release Him of the willow for men and underlings and for yonder children of their fathers. O you who fish, O you who provide for those who fish, the fish-trap of those who are all over the land, you shall not catch me in this net of yours with which you catch (fish), you fish-trappers, and in which [you] trap those who are all over the land;[4] | you shall not lash me tight in it on either its middle or its sides. I will appear from it as *Ḥnw* the great, I will use my arms as one who flies from it as the Small Lad,[5] voracious(?) are my fingers which close around my knife(?).[6] My netter nourishes me [. . .]. VI, 29 30

The guard-beam(?); it is . . . ,[7] it is the shank [of the Winepress god].

The reel; it is . . . , it is the big finger of Osiris.

The knife; it is . . . , it is the cutter of Nephthys. 31

The roller(?);[8] it is . . . , it is the fingernail of Osiris.

The floats; they are . . . , which are in the sky, they are the plume of the divine Falcon.

The weights; they are . . . which are on earth, they are the kneecaps of the Double Lion.

The ropes; they are . . . of your fishing, they are the fiery ones and [. . .].[9]

The plain on which you[10] are drawn tight; it is the plain at which the gods moor. 32

Such is the man who receives the fish from you; he is the Fiery One, the servitor of the gods.

Such is the knife with which he cuts it; it is the sharp knife which is in the hand of [11] the Winepress god.

Such is the bowl in which he cooks it; it is the cauldron which is in the hand of the Winepress god.

Such is the table on which he eats it; it is the table which makes the Two Lands content [. . .].[12]

33 [. . .] it is the Great One who [. . .].

O Great One, I am not carried off, I am not eaten, I shall not be for eating [13] [. . .] yesterday or for fishing today. You shall not catch me,[14] its . . . [15] shall not entrap me, . . . shall not sit,[16] . . . I shall not enter into . . .(?)[17] I have flown up in flight(?),[18] I have gone down from it as(?) . . .[19] the Great . . . who is in it who is(?) a fish of the waterway of *ꜣšt*(?),[20] I have gone down that I may cut, I have gone up that I may net, because I am . . . who releases the willow(?) . . . [21]

1. S2C apparently had a rubric which is now lost.

2. Corruption of *wḥꜥ m ḏꜥw* 'who fishes with the spear', 17*b*.

3. Var. of *wbꜣt-tꜣwy* of 17*b*.

4. A clumsy sentence. *Ỉssw* seems out of place in 29*g*; one would have expected 29*f* – 30*a* to read somewhat as *n ḥꜣm.ṯn wỉ m ỉꜣdt.ṯn tw ḥꜣmt.ṯn ỉm.s, ỉsst tw ỉsst.ṯn ḫtyw tꜣ ỉm.s* 'you shall not catch me in this net of yours in which you catch (fish), or this fish-trap in which you trap those who are all over the land'. Compare 17*e-f*.

5. Compare 17*l*.

6. Emend into *ḏbꜥw.ỉ pẖrw šꜥt.ỉ*?

7. *Ṯ pw*; a horizontal line (279a in S1C, 366*a* in S2C) crossing the vertical lines 279–81 and 366–9 respectively. Its meaning escapes me.

8. S1C determines *mḏꜣt* here with the bowl.

9. See de Buck, n. 1*.

10. Fem. sing., addressing the net.

11. A superfluous *n* follows *pw* in S1C; it is lacking in the like phrase 32*h*. S2C omits 32*e–f*.

12. Cf. 9*c*: *msḏr sḏm n Ḥwt-ḥr* 'the ear which listens to Ḥatḥōr', but here in S1C the space is altogether inadequate and the trace after *sḏm* does not suit, while in S2C the space in the lacuna seems too much.

13. Reading *nn tw.ỉ r wnm*; if this be correct it must be the earliest recorded example of *tw.ỉ*.

14. Emend into *n ḥꜣm.k wỉ*.

15. *Ḥꜣytyw*, meaning unknown.

16. *33g* is a very corrupt version of *28f*.
17. Reading uncertain, see de Buck, n. 7*.
18. See de Buck, n. 8*.
19. See de Buck, n. 9*.
20. Translation all very uncertain. If *wnw* really means 'who is', the *m* of predication is missing.
21. See de Buck, nn. 10*. 11*. *Wḥꜥ ṯrn* presumably is a corruption of *wḥꜥ ṯrt* in *25s*, see also *29c*.

Spell 477

ANOTHER SPELL FOR escaping from the fish-trap. O you who look backward, VI, 34
O you cutter of(?) him who cuts his flesh; O you fisherman of theirs;[1] O you children of [your] fathers;[O you who have power [2] over what they desire in respect of the net for catching the dead[3] in which you catch the dead; O you trappers of the fish-trap in which you trap those who are all over the land, being those who fish with the dead-net[4] in which you catch the dead; I will escape[5] from this very great fish-trap in which you trap those who are all over the land. Do not catch me, O men, as those who would do what is secret against me, O gods and dead, etc., when the benighted traveller(?)[6] sleeps and the . . .[7] of the day have come into being in the very great net of Osiris, the weights of which are in the sky and its floats are on earth.[8]

What is to be said to men, gods, spirits, those who are among the dead, uraei, 35
powers and all dead, etc., from whom I do not escape: O men; O gods; O spirits; O you who are among the dead, uraei, powers and all dead, etc., do not(?) [. . .] it is Sobk who fishes and nets; it is he whose fingers are hidden. I know it, I know the name of its parts.

As for its guard-beam(?), it is the shank of the Winepress-god.

As for its reel, it is the fingers of Sokar.

As for the knife, it is the cutter ⟨with which⟩[9] they cut the navel-string of Horus.

Its roller(?) is the hand of Nephthys.

Its floats (*sḫpw*) are the plumes of the divine Falcon.

Its weights are the iron which is on the hands of Reꜥ.

Its floats (*ḏbꜣw*) [are] the Children of Weakness.[10]

Its rope is the navel-string of Horus who is on his papyrus-plant. 36

Its cord is the navel-string of Nephthys.

Its fishermen are the swallowers(?) who are with the fiery ones.

These fishermen who fish with it are they of Abydos.

The plain on which it is drawn tight is the plain on which the gods stand.

The god who looks [backward] and fishes with it[11] is the Great One who sits in darkness.

Hail to you, [Twice] Great! I have wished(?)[12] for you, I have given you praise; may you grasp this Great One of yours for me. I will escape from him just as Horus escaped from upon the hands of his maternal brother the Outcast[13] when he conjured him on the river-bank of the gods.

See me,[14] men, gods, spirits, you who are among the dead, uraei,[powers], all dead, etc.; see me, I [have gone down] from it,[15] I have gone up from it [. . .] the face is knit on, the plume is . . .[16] I have gone up ⟨ . . . ⟩[17]

1. Of 'the children of their fathers'? Cf. 34*d*; 37*d-e*.
2. Restoring the lacuna as 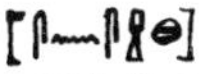 , see de Buck, n. 3*.
3. *Nnnnt* is corrupt for *nnwt*; the vine-frame det. to the compound *ḥꜣm-nnnnt* denotes the net for catching the dead, more briefly *nnwt* with the same det. in 34*i*.
4. *Nnwt* alone in the sense of 'net', see n. 3.
5. The group before *ỉwy.ỉ* in 34*j* is a blundered dittograph of *ỉm.s* above.
6. *Wḏty* is obscure. It has been guessed to be connected with *wḏyt* 'expedition'.
7. The reading *sḫtt* is not certain, see de Buck, n. 6*.
8. Reversal of the usual order, in which 'floats' are above and 'weights' are below, which corresponds to the natural state of affairs.
9. *Ỉm.s* omitted from the end of the clause.
10. On *sḫpw* 'floats' instead of the more usual *ḏbꜣw* see Spell 475, n. 5; VI, 38*n*; in this text the latter term is given second place in 34*p*, while here it is not only given second place but named in addition to its synonym *sḫpw* and given a most unlikely description. There has surely been some confusion here; it looks as if a copyist, having used *sḫpw* 'floats' in the proper place, recalled *ḏbꜣw* and did not know what to do with it. He seems, therefore, not only to have inserted it unnecessarily in the wrong place, but to have given it a name which seems quite nonsensical, being an epithet of enemies of the sun-god.
11. Read probably *nṯr mꜣ ⟨ḥꜣ.f⟩ ḥꜣm ỉm.s,* a case of haplography.
12. *Mr* with det.  ; meaning doubtful.
13. Read *sn mwt.f.*
14. Read *mꜣ(ꜣ) wỉ* shown to be imperative by the following *ỉn.ṯn.*
15. The net.
16. *Ḫnfꜣ*, meaning unknown.
17. The spell stops short at *pr.n.ỉ*, see de Buck, n. 7*.

Spell 478

O you who look backward, O you who divide; O you who sever your ropes; O you VI, 37
fishermen of theirs; O you children of your fathers, this is the net for catching the dead.

Spell 479

SPELL FOR[1] ESCAPING FROM[2] THE *'IꜢDT* AND *'IBT-TꜢ* NETS AND THE *'ISSWT* AND *ḎSF* FISH–TRAPS, BECAUSE I KNOW IT[3] AND I KNOW ITS NAME. O you who look backward, you who fish with the spear,[4] aggressive one, fisherman of the *i͗bt-tꜣ* net, you shall not catch me in this net of yours in which you catch those who are all over the land, you shall not trap me ⟨ in ⟩ this fish-trap of yours in which you trap the dead, because I know it, and I know its name,[l] I know the name in
which it came into being; it is the temples(?)[5] of the head of Isis; those waters VI, 38
in which it is dragged are the final(?)[6] putrefaction from under the ribs of my father Osiris.

Its guard-beam(?)[7] is the shank of the Winepress god.

Its reel is the big finger of the great god.

Its roller(?) is the hands of Isis.

Its knife is the cutter of Nephthys.

Its floats which are above, which are in the sky, are the iron which is on the hands of Rēʿ and the plumes of the divine Falcon when he ascends to the horizon,[8] to whom those who are yonder give praise.

Its weights, which are on earth, are the kneecaps of Atum, he in whom is a foot, messenger of the god.

Its lines, its ropes and its cords[9] are the line of Atum and the sinews of Horus who is on his papyrus-plant.

This boat from which it catches fish is the great barge which ferries the seven[10] gods who are north of the horizon of the sky.

Its doors, ribs(?),[11] 'sandals'[12] and mooring-post are the calves and thighs of Horus pre-eminent in Khem on that night of the greatest of those who are inert(?).[13]

Its 'reeds', tow-rope(?),[14] mast-head, finials(?),[15] and cable(?)[16] are the hair (*sic*) of the sky which fashioned the earth and the fillet of Horus who is on his papyrus-plant.

Its adze, chisel and saw are what is on the mouth of Ḥa and the . . .[17] of Nephthys.

39 Its lashing[18] is the hands of Isis and the fingers of Nephthys.

Its . .[19] is the great shank of the Winepress god.

Its . . . [20] is the kneecap of Osiris.

Its steering-oar is that which causes the fair staff which is in the grasp of Rēʿ to pass by(?).[21]

The sounding-pole is that which causes the fair tree[22] which appeared in front of Nehebkau to pass by(?).

The oars which row it are the hand of Mafdet which rescued the leg(?)[23] from the rage of those who ate the Great Ones.

Its drag-rope is the intestines of Isis.

Its bailer is the hands of Isis.

Its lacing(?)[24] is the big finger of Rēʿ.

This waterway of malachite(?)[25] in which it catches fish is the name of the pleasant water of Her who is in the Two Cities.

This great plain from which it catches fish is the great plain of iron on which your (pl.) gods stand to receive the god's-offerings.

The fishermen who catch fish are the swallowers(?)[26] who are before the fiery ones — and *vice versa.*

40 The servitor is he who comes that he may receive the fish from upon it; his name is[27] *ꜣbḏ-wr,* the servitor who satisfies the Great One. O *ꜣbḏ-wr* servitor who satisfies the Great One, you shall not grasp me, you shall not seize me, you shall not work your will against me, because I am the *ỉby*-plant which fish detest, I am the small one which the gods detest.

That brazier on which you cook is the Great-breasted one, nurse of the Eye of Horus.[28]

That vessel(?)[29] in which you cook is the contentious shooters(?)[30] of Seth of Ombos.[31]

That great table on which you cook it and place it is the great 'table of satisfaction' around which all the gods eat bread.

That Great One is he in whose presence you cook it and place it. He is the Double Lion who is not seen[32] nor is his voice heard; those who exist see me, those who do not exist worship me,[33] for I am the Double Lion who is not seen[34] nor is his voice heard. Those who exist see me and those who do not exist worship me,[35] those who are yonder give me praise.

41 See me, you fishermen of the gods; look at me, you fishermen of men. You shall not seize me, you shall not grasp me,[36] you shall not work your will against me, because I have gone up from its heart,[37] I have escaped[38] from its clutch as a falcon of seven cubits along its back, I eat with my mouth, I defecate with my

anus. Those who exist see me, those who do not exist worship me, those who are yonder give me praise.

See me, you fishermen of men; look at me, you fishermen of the gods. You shall not seize or grasp me, you shall not work your will against me, because I have gone up from its heart, I have escaped from its clutch as Sobk and Horus the Northerner. Those who exist see me, those who do not exist worship me, those who are yonder give me praise.

See me, you fishermen of men; look at me, you fishermen of the gods. You
shall not seize or grasp me, you shall not work your will against me, because I
have gone up from its heart, | I have escaped from its clutch as Sokar of the Two 42
Truths. I eat with my mouth, I defecate with my anus. Those who exist see me,
those who do not exist worship me, those who are yonder give me praise.

See me, you fishermen of men; look at me, you fishermen of the gods. You shall not seize or grasp me, you shall not work your will against me, because I have gone up from its heart, I have escaped from its clutch as the great heron, the lotus-bird which catches fish; it eats on the banks of the Winding Waterway. I eat with my mouth, I defecate with my anus. Those who exist see me, those who do not exist worship me, those who are yonder give me praise.

See, I have come to you, you seven bald-heads. Hail to you, you seven bald-
heads, who meet(?) the broken Eye of Horus; IF YOUR REEL, ROLLER(?) AND
KNIFE ARE IN YOUR POSSESSION, THEN WILL MY REEL, ROLLER(?), *ꞽŠꜤT-KNIFE* 43
AND *ḎSF*-KNIFE BE IN MY POSSESSION.

See, I have come to you, you seven bald-heads, who meet(?) the broken Eye of Horus. I have cut the trap-rope for you, I have trapped my chopper[39] in the net of men and gods. Those who exist see me, those who do not exist worship me, those who are yonder give me praise.

1. Corrupted into *rn n* in the original.

2. Preposition *m* omitted.

3. 'It' applies to all the fishing apparatus collectively; the terms are all of fem. gender except *ḏsf*.

4. *Ḏw* is a miswriting of *ḏꜤw* 'fish-spear'.

5. *Šswy* seems a more probable reading than *ššw.s* as suggested by de Buck in his n. 2*. The det. seems to indicate either 'cheeks' or 'temples' of the head, more probably perhaps the latter; the context shows that we have here a part or parts of the head. But why they should be likened to a fishing-net remains obscure.

6. Connecting *nfrt* with *nfrw* 'end', cf. *JEA* 4, 110, n. 1; 22, 178; the usual sense of *nfrt* as 'good' or the like makes no sense as a qualification of *ḥwꜣꜣt* 'putrefaction'.

7. *Ḥsw* here takes the place of *mḫsf* or *ḫsf* in the sense of 'guard-beam(?)'; it is identified

by the following description and by its position at the head of the catalogue of the parts of a net, regularly followed by the reel.

8. *Nṯr* after *byk* is misspelt. In the following *m pr.f n w ꜣḫt* the *w* is apparently intrusive, for it seems to yield no sense, while the rest of 38*o* reads *ddw n.f ntyw ỉm ỉꜣ.*

9. The precise differences between these variously named ropes and cords are a technical matter to the understanding of which we have no clue.

10. One unit-sign is lost.

11. See Spell 396, n. 14. From here on we are dealing with the parts of the fishing boat.

12. This term is found also in *CT* V, 147*b*; 168*g*; to what part of the boat it refers is not clear.

13. Read *wr n wrḏ-ỉb*? Lit. perhaps 'the great one of inertness'.

14. *Swt* could represent the word translated 'reeds' as part of a boat, see Spell 396, n. 18; *sšt* could perhaps be a writing of *sšꜣt* 'tow-rope', Fischer, *Dendera,* p. 5, n. 22.

15. Cf. Spell 396, n. 19.

16. *Nyn* appears to be an unfinished writing of *nynṯ* 'cable(?)', *CT* V, 74*aa.*

17. *Grḥ* 'night' clearly is not meant here; the definite article *tw* which follows shows that the word intended was feminine, though the noun lacks the fem. ending. The determinative after *pw* is superfluous unless something has been omitted.

18. Cf. *CT* V, 129*b*.

19. See n. 7 above. Here *ḥsw* is substituted for *mḫsf,* an unidentified part of a boat. Spell 396, n. 22.

20. *'Inyt*; not the word for 'purse-net' here; it is an unidentified part of the boat.

21. The translation of *sn* as 'pass by' is by no means certain.

22. *Snt*; not recorded.

23. *'Ibṯt* with leg-det.; not recorded thus.

24. See Spell 396, n. 20.

25. *Šst*; possibly a var. of *šsmt* 'malachite', cf. *Urk* IV, 875, 15.

26. Var. of *ꜣḫbw,* 18*l*; 24*h*; *BD* 391, 13.

27. 'His name is' has been omitted by inadvertence.

28. The det. of *ꜥḫ* looks like a chest, but is probably intended for a rectangular brazier on feet. For *ss* 'burn' cf. *Urk.* IV, 1437, 10; here the word clearly means 'cook'. For the association of *wr mnḏw* and the brazier see also 9*a*.

29. *Nw* looks like an incomplete writing, compare *nyn* for *nynṯ,* cf. n. 16 above. The adverb *ỉm* indicates that some kind of cooking vessel is meant.

30. Written with three arrow-heads and final *-t.* Possibly a collective noun.

31. An unusual writing of *Nbt* 'Ombos'.

32. The sense demands that *mꜣ* here and its variant *mꜣn* in 40*a* be interpreted as passive *sḏm.f.*

33. Read *dwꜣ wỉ ỉwtyw* here and in 40*s*; for the correct writing see 41*h*, 42*n* and 43*f.*

34. See n. 32 above.

35. See n. 33 above.

36. Note the liaison between the suffix *ṯn* and the dependent pronoun *wỉ*, expressed by the linking *nw*-sign.

37. I.e. from the middle of the net.

38. The translation of *snšnš.n.ỉ* as 'I have escaped' seems enforced by the context; it would seem to be distinct from *snšnš* with det. 'inspire fear(?)', *CT* IV, 59*c*. Here the det. suggests a man in hiding.

39. This obscure sentence has the look of a literary device to provide an antithesis to 43*c*.

Spell 480

O you who look backward, you who fish with the spear, aggressive one, you who fish with the *wbꜣtt-tꜣ* net; O you fishermen, children of your fathers, who fish all round the valleys, you shall not catch me in this net of yours, you shall not capture me in this fish-trap of yours in which you catch the dead[1] or in which you fish up those who are all over the land, BECAUSE I KNOW THE NAME OF VI, 44
THE GUARD-BEAM(?), THE REEL, THE ROLLER(?) AND THE KNIFE IN IT; they are the shank of the Winepress god, the finger of the great god, the fingernail of Isis, the cutter of Isis ⟨with which⟩[2] she cut the navel-string of Horus the young child:

BECAUSE I KNOW THE NAME OF its weights; they are the iron of the One,[3] (they are) what belongs to the throat of the great god.[4]

Its floats are the kneecaps of the Double Lion on the day of appearing in gold.

Its planking(?)[5] is the intestines of Isis when she . . . which is in her.[6]

Its drag-rope is the intestines of Atum on his day of burial.

The fishermen who use it are the swallowers(?)[7] who are before the earth-gods.[8]

This 'ear' and what it lays on it[9] are the ear of the great god who is in charge 45
of judging cases in Ōn at the monthly and at the half-monthly festivals of the moon . . .[10]

He who receives the fish from upon it is the servitor *ꜣbḏ*, the servitor of the gods.

The table and what he lays on it is the table which satisfies the gods, around which the gods sit.

The great god who will take you to himself is the Great One who sits in darkness, who is not seen nor is his voice heard, for whom all men stand up, to whom all men give praise.[11]

I come to you, O fisherman, you of the willow, with my reel in my hand, my *dsft*-knife in my hand, my roller(?) in my hand, my *ỉsšꜥt*-knife in my hand. I spear, but the fish-trap of Isis diverts me; I rise and ascend by means of it to the sky among the gods. I come that I may appear and go aboard the bark, for I am the spearer among you.

1. This text uses the pronouns of the 2nd fem., as if it were the net which is invoked; in 43*m* read *ỉn.ṯn.*
2. *'Im.s* omitted at the end of the clause.
3. Feminine.
4. The weights of the net are likened to the beads of a necklace.
5. *Sꜣꜣ*, without det., is of obscure meaning; it may be a derivative of *sꜣw* 'beam', 'baulk', *Concise Dict.* 209; compare *sꜣyw* 'planking', *CT* II, 304*a*.
6. Or 'in it', meaning the net. I cannot translate *ḥnn.s r sḏfw.*
7. Cf. Spell 479, n. 26.
8. *ꜣkrw.*
9. The reference to the 'ear', together with that to the 'table' in 45*e*, recalls the association of the 'ear' and the 'table' in 9*c*. The suffix in *wꜣḥt.s* presumably refers to the net.
10. I am not at all sure that de Buck's sentence-division is correct here, for the mention of *ỉꜥḥ* seems to me rather to belong to 45*b*. I cannot translate the word *sꜣbt* which follows, and which appears in *BD* 392, 1 as 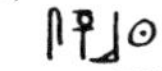 ; here too the words *ỉꜥḥ sꜣb* come at the end of their clause. With 45*a-c* compare 18*m-n*. The variations of the several 'fishing-net' texts show progressive corruption, and the texts of P. Gard. II seem to be among those furthest removed from the archetype.
11. *Tmw*, despite the det., is not the name of the god Atum, but a writing of the word for 'everyone', *Concise Dict.* 299.

Spell 481

VI, 46 ESCAPING FROM THE NET. Mine is the *ꜥbꜣ*-net, the slayer(?)[1] who came forth from the Eye, and I spear and trap in this place[2] from which I have escaped; the rope is not set down against me . . . ,[3] I am not held by the earth-gods. O you
47 four who speak the anger of the Great Lady, be apprehensive, for the heart of him whose neck[4] was broken is cut out. O Anubis, Lord of Asyut(?), who spears and traps[5] in the place of the wounded one, I have escaped from it.

1. Cf. *sẖw* 'slaughter-house', *CT* II, 306*b*; *Urk.* IV, 506, 16, here determined in two texts out of three with 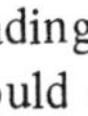 .
2. So S1C; var. S2C$^{a.b}$: 'in the place of the wounded one', cf. 47*c*.
3. The reading *ỉꜣḥytyw* at the end of S1C (the other texts are damaged) is manifestly corrupt; one would expect *ỉn* 'by' and the name of an agent, on the model of 46*g*. Compare *ḥꜣytyw* in 33*f.*

4. Lit. 'throat', but we do not speak of 'a broken throat'.

5. The reading after *nb* is uncertain, see de Buck, n. 1*, and the suffix after *sty ḏsf* is superfluous.

Spell 482

TO BE CLAD [. . .]. I[1] greet the Retinue, and the gods rejoice. I foretell the VI, 48
festival of the coming into being of the Protector of the land. Ḥatḥōr[2] rises
within the horizon, and I control[3] the sky, I make the Two Lands content,[4] 49
while her entourage is about her.[5] | It is he who should go down who goes down
therein,[6] and I am alone as he who goes down therein.[7] 'Go and grasp' say the
crocodiles.[8] Those who are about the entourage of the tomb,[9] they see me when
I have conquered(?) with my staff.[10] | I have removed the fire [11] which was about 50
the entourage of Rēʿ by means of my power, my dignity, my great *atef*-crown
which is on me and my god-like rank.[12] It is Orion who has given me his warrant; 51
it is the Great Bear which has made a path for me to the western horizon;[13] it is
Sothis who greets me as[14] the birth of a god. | 'Here comes the god whom the Red 52
Crown bore' – so say those who are in the Retinue concerning me. O you who
come in joy, cause my requirement to be despatched.[15] What is it? See, I am at
my duty, and I am one who knows my way.[16]

1. For the 1st person cf. 48*c.f*; 49*b.f.*

2. 'Ḥatḥōr' three times, 'Reʿ' twice; that the former is correct is shown by the fem. suffix in *sšm.s* in 48*e* in three texts out of four.

3. Three texts refer this to Ḥatḥōr, but S1C^{a} retains the 1st person, see 48*f*, where it certainly has the best text.

4. *Shrr.ỉ tꜣwy* makes better sense than *sr.s tꜣ* or *sr tꜣ* of the varr.

5. Var. S1C^{b}: 'the entourage is about me'; in B2L the final suffix is lost.

6. Into what? The entourage?

7. Not in S1C^{a}.

8. Varr. 'lions', 'jackals', 'the Double Lion'.

9. S1C^{b} omits the final *ḥꜣt.*

10. *Mm* in S1C^{a}; *ptpt.n.i* in S2C^{b}; similarly S2C^{a} and S1C^{b}. *Mm* is obscure, and *ptpt,* which usually means 'tread under', 'trample', here seems to mean 'conquer' with a weapon. See also 50*e* (B2L only).

11. For *wḏʿ.n.ỉ sḏt* B2L has *wḏʿ ḫt,* which yields no sense here.

12. 50*b-d* are omitted in B2L, which now comes in with the *ptpt*-clause, see n. 10 above. The next sentence (51*a*) is absent from S1C^{a} and indeed seems irrelevant and corrupt, so it has been omitted from the running translation.

13. The allusion to the western horizon is in S1C^{a} alone, and may be in error; one would

expect the Great Bear to clear the way to the circumpolar stars rather than to the western horizon.

14. Var. *m-m* 'among', which is an odd preposition in this context.

15. *Sḫꜣʿ* is a hitherto unrecorded causative; for the simplex *ḫꜣʿ* 'despatch' a message, see *Pyr.* §400. The following *ỉššt pw* 'what is it?', though common to all texts, seems entirely irrelevant.

16. In S1C only.

Spell 483

VI, 53 I am one who followed[1] the sole musician of Ḥatḥōr,[2] I have come to the place
where my mistress is so that I may see her beauty and give her the dress.[3]

1. S1C omits *šms,* which four other texts have in common.
2. 'Ḥatḥōr' in three texts. B2L: 'my sole musician'; B1Bo: 'the sole musician of this day'.
3. *Ṯstn,* var. *ntstn,* is the name of a feminine outer garment, cf. *Pyr.* §1426.

Spell 484

The Pelican prophesies, the Shining One goes forth, THE DRESS OF ḤATḤŌR IS
VI, 54 WOVEN, a path is prepared for me that I may pass by.[1] I know his path, (even
of) him who is skilled in his movements,[2] one whose face is hidden from those
who see him. The Sistrum-player[3] is in my body,[4] the pure flesh of my mother,
55 and the dress will enclose me.[5] | I don the dress of Ḥatḥōr,[6] my hands are under
it to the width of the sky, my fingers are under it as living uraei, my nails are
56 under it as the Two Ladies of Dep, and I kiss the earth,[7] | I worship my mistress,[8]
for I have seen her beauty; I give praise to Ḥatḥōr, for I have seen her beauty. I
give her the dress, her shape is distinguished above (those of) the gods, and I see
her beauty. She creates the fair movements which I make when the Protector of
of the Land comes; the gods come to me bowing and praise is given to me by the
57 gods,[9] | they see me[10] at my duty,[11] and I am initiated into what I did not know;
I cross with the retinue of this Great Lady to the western horizon of the sky, I
speak in the Tribunal.

'This path of yours; whence is this path of yours?',[12] say the horizon-dwellers to me.

58 'I have come here[13] | from the river-bank of Ḥu on my ascents of the
Mountain of the *sḥsḥ*-bird,[14] so that I may don the cloak[15] of this Great Lady
who is in the bow of the bark of Rēʿ and in the middle of the bark of Khopri.[16] I
59 found her when she repeated her manifestation[17] | and trebled her faces,[18] her

Serpent of Terror being on her brow, and her shape is distinguished above (those of) the gods'.

'The god who protects the land comes',[19] say they of the South-land concerning me when they see me having taken my seat and occupied my throne,[20] and
having acquired [21] what I found there. I am one wide-awake and not weary, I am 60
in the retinue of the king[22] of the sky.

'The god who protects the land comes', say the horizon-dwellers concerning me. 'The god comes, having gone aboard the bark', say they who are about the
shrine,[23] who sit in the sides of the bark, who eat their food.[24] They see me as 61
the Sole One with the secret seal. I don the dress, I wear(?)[25] the robe, I receive the wand(?),[26] I adorn [27] the Great Lady in her dignity. Her Sistrum-player[28] is on her lap, and he has built mansions among your great ones, he has presented
offering-cakes, [29] so that he may live thereon and that he may celebrate the 62
monthly festival in his hour in company with those who are in linen, for he has looked as his face. [30] So says the occupant [31] of the throne of the Great Lady concerning me.

1. BıBo only. The varr. omit the rubric and the 'passing by'.

2. BıBo has corrupted *m šmwt.f* 'in his movements' into *m ḫmt.n.f* 'as what he did not know'.

3. The young son of Ḥatḥōr.

4. Meaning apparently that the speaker is the embodiment of the Sistrum-player.

5. 54*i*, in BıBo only, is in effect only an anticipation of 55*a*, and therefore has not been included in the translation.

6. Var. B2L: 'my mistress'.

7. B2L precedes this last phrase with 'I have come' (55*e*).

8. So SıC; B2L has: 'I praise the gods for my mistress'.

9. 56*k* only in B2L.

10. Note the liaison between *.sn* and *wỉ*; so also 59*e*; 61*a*.

11. B2L inserts *ỉy.kw* 'I have come' before *m ỉrt.ỉ*.

12. This question really amounts to 'Where have you come from?'. B2L has lit. 'whence is it, this path' and BıBo has even more briefly 'whence is your path?'. In 57*f* B2L amplifies this question with 'whence have you come?' and BıBo has 'what are you making for?', with the var. *sbw* for the interrogative *sy* already noted in *CT* V, 46*a*. BıBo also substitutes *ỉmnt* 'the West' for *ꜣḫtyw* 'the horizon-dwellers'.

13. *Myn* clearly means in this passage 'here' rather than 'today'; note the variant *ꜥꜣ* 'here' in BıBo.

14. S2C[a.b] and B2L read *ỉdb Ḥw,* and SıC is probably to be read likewise. BıBo seems quite corrupt and unintelligible. *Pryt* has det. Λ in SıC and strangely [hieroglyph] in B2L, which also misspells *sḥsḥ* at the end of the sentence.

15. Var. B2L: 'the dress and the cloak'.

16. B2L and B1Bo omit the second qualification.

17. B2L and S2C^{a} have both misread *wḥm.* The latter text is damaged beyond this point; B2L omits the suffix after *ḫꜥw,* while B1Bo adds *r.f* at the end for some reason which is not clear.

18. B2L has apparently *ḥrw.sn* 'their faces', which clearly is an error.

19. Var. B2L and B1Bo: 'the god comes, having gone aboard his bark'.

20. For *ḏbꜣ* 'occupy' a seat, cf. *Pyr.* §§906; 1171; 1325; *CT* VII, 413*e.* B2L has *ꜥpr.n.ỉ swt* 'I have acquired seats' and B1Bo, omitting 59*e,* reads: *ỉw ḏbꜣ.n N pn st.f.*

21. For *ꜥpr* B2L has *ḏbꜣ.*

22. So B1Bo; *n sꜣḥtny* of S1C is simply a corruption of *n nswt* of B1Bo in S1C.

23. *'Iꜣbtyw ḥrw,* only in S1C, is clearly an interpolated corruption, for it does not make sense. Read *ỉn.sn ḥꜣw kꜣr.* S2C$^{a.b}$ follow this with broken versions of 61*c.*

24. *ꜣbgbg* is an unidentified foodstuff, apparently not recorded elsewhere.

25. *Sꜣ,* meaning doubtful. For the garment *sfḫ* see *CT* I, 258*f.*

26. An object made of wood. Cf. *tbꜣw* 'Art Holz', *Wb.* V, 261, 7.

27. For *sšr* 'adorn' cf. *Pyr.* §§56; 198.

28. I.e. the deceased himself in this role.

29. After 60*b* B1Bo diverges into a text of its own (61*j*) which runs: 'The *sfḫ*-robe and the *syꜥr*-garment are received by Sia for N when he celebrates the monthly festival in the course of his duty among those who are attached to the seal'.

30. I.e. the deceased has appeared as the Sistrum-player, and therefore has a face like his.

31. *Ḥry* 'who is on', strangely in masc. gender. The absence of the fem. ending may be due simply to inadvertence.

Spell 485

I am in the retinue of Ḥatḥōr, the most august of the gods, and she gives me power over my foes who are in the Island of Fire. I have put on the cloak of the
VI, 63 Great Lady, and I am the Great Lady.[1] I am not inert, I am not destroyed, and nothing evil will come to pass against me. I am the Great One who came forth from Rēꜥ, I was conceived and borne by Shesmētet, and I have come that I may weave the dress for my mistress. The dress is woven by Horus and Thoth and by Osiris and Atum, and indeed I am Horus and Thoth, I am Osiris and Atum.

Spell 486

WEAVING THE DRESS FOR ḤATḤŌR. The mountain is broken, the stone is split,
VI, 64 the caverns of Ḥatḥōr are broken open;[1] she ascends in turquoise and is covered[2] with her royal wig-cover. She has found me standing in her path, for I have appeared as a god, and my hands support Tayt.[3] Those who are above are brought to me, I watch over those who are below,[4] the two spells are joined together for

me,[5] I have woven the dress for Ḥatḥōr,[1] the western and eastern, upper and lower horizons rejoice,[6] and she favours and loves me[7] and has woven the dress for me.[8] 65

1. B2L omits 'of Ḥatḥōr' and adds (64*a*) 'the eastern horizon is opened for Ḥatḥōr'. This text appears to be somewhat corrupt, and it contains an amount of apparently secondary matter that is not included in the other versions. This additional matter is dealt with in the notes.

2. B2L misspells the old perfective *nms.ty*. S1C employs the *sḏm.f* form *nms.s,* thus making a perfect word-play with the noun *nms.s.*

3. The goddess of weaving. B1Bo follows (in 64*g*) with a clause more in place in 64*n*, while B2L has the var. 'I raise up the hands of Tayt to her', and continues with a long and not very intelligible insertion: 'Her satchel on her left arm is of falcon-skins; I knit up her right side with turquoise, I touch the faces'. The reference to turquoise could apply to a blue garment, for the verb *šfn* 'touch' cf. *CT* III, 47*i.*

4. B2L has: 'I will bring those who are above on the fair days of Ḥatḥōr'.

5. Varr. 'for her', 'for Ḥatḥōr'; the allusion is quite obscure. After this B2L inserts *ḥs n Ḥwt-ḥr* 'Ḥatḥōr is pleased(?)'.

6. So B1Bo, not in S1C. B2L has: 'the upper horizon rejoices, the lower horizon rejoices in Ḥatḥōr'. It then continues alone (65*b-h*): 'she ascends in turquoise, being covered with her royal wig-cover. She has found me in her path, for I have appeared as a god, and I raise up the hands of Tayt to her. The god sees and is aware, the god is well pleased(?), and the festival is put together for Ḥatḥōr'. All this is but a variant of 64*b* ff.

7. So S1C; B1Bo has: 'Ḥatḥōr is pleased(?), the love (on the part of) Ḥatḥōr is on account of it'; B2L shortly: 'Ḥatḥōr is pleased(?)'.

8. Var. B1Bo 'the dress is woven for Ḥatḥōr'; this may well be the better version.

Spell 487

The portals(?)[1] of them of the firmament are opened, the portals of them of the VI, 66
firmament are thrown open, and those who are in the gates before them, who are the Primeval Ones, depart to them. The firmament is open, the Mansion is thrown open, the Great One raises[2] my members, I support the Great Lady, and the eastern powers(?)[3] go up to them. They send me to the . . . ,[4] they raise me, and I am he who clothes the Great One, my members support the Great One, I am the Sole One who crosses the Abyss, whose name men do not know, I receive the staffs, I govern the Conclave, I tread the earth,[5] the throne of Gēb is given to me,[6] the whole of sky and earth (depend?) on my movements. I pray to(?) the hippopotamus:[7] 'May you be content with navigating the *hnhnw*-bark'.

1. *Bṯꜣw* is not recorded and its meaning is obscure. Its connection here with *wn* 'open' and *sn* 'throw open' suggests 'doors' or 'door-bolts' as the meaning, but the flesh-det. speaks against this; however, it might be an error for a sign representing a lump of metal.

2. For *sšw* 'raise', 'lift up' cf. *Pyr.* §§275; 1101.

3. For the rare and obscure stem *kꜣꜣ* cf. *Pyr.* §§2087; *CT* IV, 8*e*, where in both cases it occurs in an 'eye' context; the use of the lion-head determinative suggests power. In *CT* IV, 8*e*, Sq6C has the lion-head det. as in the Pyr. and here, but T1L has a louse(!) and Sq3C a small circle. It looks as if the copyists themselves did not know what the presumably archaic word meant.

4. *Bhṯw wsrwt nfrw wsrt.* I can make nothing of this.

5. Gēb, personification of the earth.

6. Reading *rdy n.ỉ*; the duplicate *n* appears to be in error.

7. With *nḥḥ* as a word for hippopotamus compare *dbt nḥḥwt* 'immortal hippopotamus', *Pyr.* §522. For the preceding *m* one would have expected *n*, but the suffix of the 2nd person in *ḥtp ỉb.k* following shows that the prayer is addressed to the hippopotamus. The relevance of 66*s-t* to the rest of the spell is not clear.

Spell 488

VI, 67 O my soul, O my spirit, O my shade,[1] open the shutters of the sky-windows within(?)[2] the horizon; may you have power over your legs as a living soul, a possessor of majesty among the gods like Osiris. Go, O my soul and my shade, so that you may see Rēʿ within his shrine, and so that he who is in charge of their (*sic*) hearts and who watches over hearts may not be driven away from the inundated land.[3] O you who are in charge of the gates of the upper sky, open the ways for my soul, my spirit and my shade, so that it may support Right for Rēʿ.[4]

1. These three entities are referred to with a singular suffix in B9C, as if they made up together one individual, so too 67*e* and 67*k* (both texts).

2. *M snw* is obscure, but may be a compound preposition, lit. 'in the two', referring to the space between the peaks of the horizon-sign usually occupied by the sun.

3. So the text, though *ỉꜣḫw* 'sunshine' is what one would expect.

4. An allusion to the ritual gesture of offering an image of Maʿet to the god.

Spell 489

VI, 68 O Osiris, Osiris, see, my soul has come to you in order to improve affairs for you and to set your movements in order. Make a path for me[1] on this day of covering the lips,[2] for I am one who surpasses[3] mortal men.

1. The text of *68d.e* can be spoken only by the deceased and therefore should be in the 1st person.

2. This may be a reference to the wrapping of the mummy.

3. *Swꜣ* is a participle serving as an adjectival predicate.

Spell 490

SPELL FOR GIVING A SPIRIT POWER OVER HIS LEGS IN THE REALM OF THE DEAD.[1] Your bread is with those who are in the sky, your beer is with those who are on earth; go, go, O soul of N, may you not come to them, for you have power in your legs.

1. TıBe is entirely in red; the damaged B4C, which is in black except for the introductory rubric, has on the whole the better text.

Spell 491

A path is opened for my soul, my spirit, my magic and my shade, and it will enter VI, 69
to Rēʿ[1] within his shrine, it will see the great god in his true shape, and it will
repeat the words of Osiris to those whose places[2] are secret, who are in charge of
the members of Osiris.[3] | O you who watch over all souls and constrain the shades 70
of all who are dead,[4] may you not have power to constrain me or to watch over
my soul, my shade, my spirit or my magic.[5] It possesses the ritual which is for
bringing Right to Rēʿ,[6] and it has asked that it may live by means of it. | Go, go, 71
my soul, my spirit, my magic and my shade, open the shutters of the sky-windows, throw open the Great Mansion, so that you may go to and fro and have power in your legs; you shall not be restrained by those who are in charge of the members of Osiris, who watch over all souls and who constrain the shades of all the dead. Go, go, my soul, my spirit, my magic and my shade, so that you may have power in your legs and that you may bring Right to Rēʿ.

1. Following in general the B3L texts, but in *70b*, *Rʿ* of the parallel texts is to be preferred to *r.k* of B3L.

2. *Swt* 'places' of the parallel texts is to be preferred to *ḥrw* 'faces' of B3L.

3. Note the curious 'squiggle' used by B3L to write the name of Osiris.

4. *Sꜣꜣw* 'they who watch over' is to be interpreted as guarding prisoners. *Ḫnr* is translated both as 'constrain' and as 'restrain' according to the immediate context.

5. For *ḥkꜣ* 'magic' of B3L^a, B3L^b has *kꜣ* 'double', surely a slip of the pen.

6. B4C is a confusion of *ỉw.f ḥnʿ Rʿ ẖrt hrw nt rʿ nb,* cf. Spell 495, n. 6.

Spell 492

O my soul, my spirit, my magic and my shade, open the doors of the sky,[1]
VI, 72 throw open[2] the gates of heaven, | may your ornaments be secured on yourself so that you may enter to the great god who is in his shrine[3] and see Rēʿ in his true shape. O you who are in charge of the secrets of Osiris,[4] be far from this soul of mine; do not restrain it, for it is the soul of the Bull of the West, to whom is granted procreation upon earth.[5]

1. Var. B9C and probably B1Y: 'open the sky-windows for my soul'.
2. For *n.k* of the B3L texts, B9C has *n.f.*
3. So the B3L texts (72*b*). B9C and B1Y substitute (72*c*): 'the house of his soul which is over me is within his shrine'.
4. Var. B9C: 'you who are in charge of the soul'.
5. 72*i* only in the B3L texts.

Spell 493

VI, 73 Not to restrain a person's soul from going out or coming in as he wishes in the realm of the dead.[1] Shu has wept at what is hidden from him; O my soul, be far from the corpses[2] which my father has slain. O Old One, prepare a path for me, may my soul be saved from the trappers who take away souls and constrain shades, who are put in the shambles of the Chaos-gods, who witness its arrival.[3]
74 Be far from this soul of mine, | do not restrain it,[4] for I am that Old One who is wept for in the place of the mourners,[5] at the time of the wailers.[6] I possess my soul, I procreate by means of it, for I am a man of Djedet,[7] and what I say is done for me.[8] My corpse will neither be wrested away[9] nor constrained, for I am that corpse for which Atum wept and which Anubis buried. [My] soul, my body and my shade are at its side, for I am indeed the guard of the prisoners after the secret matters of the Coiled One.[10]

I will not be seized,[11] nor will my corpse be constrained; the Eye has wept for me in the presence of the *fnṯ*-snakes.[12] I have not [. . .] my fiery blast, I have not attained my heat,[13] (yet) my foe has fallen to me and I have restrained
75 his confederacy. | I am an Old One, my soul is in Djedet and in Ninsu, I am not restrained by those who are on earth, who massacre the Old Ones, my protection[14] is in the realm of the dead, and my soul and my body belong to it, and I am the guard of the prisoners after the great battle.

1. This title only in B3Bo. Although this is a woman's coffin and the deceased is referred to as *st* 'woman', the masculine suffixes are used in the rest of the title.

2. Var. B3Bo: 'foes'.

3. I.e. of the soul.

4. B3Bo omits 74*a*.

5. B3L^{a} ends here.

6. *ꜣt* 'time' only in B3Bo. *Sḥꜣw* 'wailers' is the masc. form of *sḥꜣwt*, for which see *CT* IV, 94*o*.

7. Var. B3Bo: 'I am the soul of Djedet'.

8. Here the texts of B3L and B3Bo diverge completely. B3Bo being represented by 74*k*. ff. B3L (74*f-j*) is translated first.

9. For *hp* 'wrest away' cf. *Pyr.* §§36; 39.

10. Compare 75*g*.

11. The B3Bo text, 74*k* ff. In order to accord with what has gone before, it has been transposed into the 1st person.

12. The det. of *fnṯ* is the headless snake.

13. Apparently a bungled version of 76*d*.

14. Read *gs.s dpt*, cf. Spell 783, n.8.

Spell 494

The sound of greeting(?)[1] is in the horizon, Sia goes up into the shrine,[2] for he
has heard the sound of my soul saving itself from the trappers who carry off
souls and constrain shades,[3] which are put in the shambles | of the Chaos-gods, VI,
who witness its arrival.[4] Be far from this soul of mine, your[5] fiery blast shall
not reach it and your testimony shall have no power over it.

1. On *iꜥnw* see James, *Ḥeḳanakhte*, p. 109.
2. B3Bo adds: 'on business of Him whose name (*sic*) is covered'.
3. B3Bo omits 75*n* and substitutes 76*a*: 'which are imprisoned in caverns'.
4. Cf. Spell 493, n. 3. B3Bo omits 76*b*.
5. Plural, referring to the Chaos-gods.

Spell 495

I extend my arm in company with Shu, I am released in company with *Wnwt*.[1]
I have fled[2] with the Sistrum-player, I have reached the horizon as a great falcon,
I have got rid of my impediment in the horizon,[3] | I have saved myself from the VI,
slayers,[4] the carvers[5] strong of arms. Be far from this soul of mine, which is with
Rēꜥ daily.[6] My soul belongs to my[7] body, my shade is at my side,[8] I am the guard
of the prisoners after the secret affairs of the Coiled One.[9]

1. Generally following B3L; for the 1st person see *77d.e.* *76h* is in B3Bo only, and is damaged; in B3L the corresponding passage is *76k.*

2. B3Bo has *wsr n.s* 'she has become strong'.

3. B3Bo (*75h*): 'in the Netherworld'.

4. *Ḫꜣtyw* 'the slayers' of B3Bo is to be preferred on grounds of sense to *ḫbntyw* 'the prisoners' of B3L.

5. So B3Bo; *ḥnṯw* with knife-det. appears to be identical with *ḥnṯyw* 'carvers' of meat, *Pyr.* §966, and accords with the preceding *ḫꜣtyw.* The addition of *rw* 'mouths' in B3L suggests confusion in this text with *ḥnty* 'greedy', *Concise Dict.* 173.

6. *77b.c* is not in B3L. *77c* is confused, but is doubtless to be read as *ỉw.f ḥnʿ Rʿ ẖrt hrw nt rʿ nb.* A somewhat similar confusion in *70d* (B4C), see Spell 491, n. 6.

7. Read surely the 1st person here.

8. Of the body (*ḏt*).

9. Cf. *74j.* B3Bo reads in *77f*: 'after the great battle' as in *75h.*

Spell 496

The vision of the god is cleared,[1] the worship of him is on high,[2] great is the soul
VI, 78 and mighty is the majesty[3] | of him who puts the fear of himself into all the gods, who is on his pedestal.[4] May he prepare a path for the equipped spirit in me,[5] I indeed have prepared a path to the place where Rēʿ is,[6] to the place where Ḥatḥōr is.

1. Read *wn ḥr (n) nṯr* in B3L, cf. B4C; B3Bo has *wn ḥr Rʿ.* The writing of *ḥr* in B3L is due to confusion with 'Horus'.

2. Minor varr. in B3Bo and B4C.

3. So B3L and Sq12C; var. B3Bo: 'Lord of terror, greatly majestic'.

4. Lit. 'his great block'; for *ḏbꜣ* 'block' cf. *CT* III, *90d*; VI, *1f.* Var. B3Bo: 'who appears more gloriously than the gods on his pedestal'. For the reading *ḫʿw r* see de Buck, n. 7*; because this is a woman's coffin, *ḏbʿ wr* has been wrongly 'feminized'. B4C has *wrw* 'great ones' after a short lacuna and there ends.

5. Here B3Bo ends, and B3L adds, somewhat tautologically (*78d*): 'a path is prepared for me and for the equipped spirit in me'. This sentence is omitted in Sq12C and probably is not part of the original text.

6. B3L has inserted the suffix 1st sing. after *ỉm* in error, probably influenced by *ỉm.ỉ* in *78c.d.* Sq12C, which is damaged, omits *wꜣt* 'path'.

Spell 497

O all you gods who are in sky and earth, in the waters and in the horizon,
VI, 79 prepare a path for my soul, my spirit and my shade in the retinues of Rēʿ and of Ḥatḥōr for all eternity.

Spell 498

O Rēʿ, great in[1] your shrine, exalted on your pedestal,[2] may you fare southward
to the Great Place,[3] may you moor at the very great plain to the south of the VI, 80
horizon of the sky,[4] may you take your seat on it,[5] may praise be given to you
by all the gods who are in the sky, the lords of the horizon of the sky, who are
upon the upper sky,[6] may they please you with it every day.[7] You have taken
my soul and my spirit, my magic and my shade with Rēʿ and Ḥatḥōr[8] to the
place where Rēʿ is every day, to the place where Ḥatḥōr is every day, for all 81
eternity.[9] Those who are in charge of the members of Osiris[10] shall not constrain
me; those who are in charge of the members of Osiris[11] shall not have power to
constrain my soul or my magic or to watch over my spirit or my shade at the
time of all eternity.[12]

1. Two texts omit *ḥr ỉb*.
2. For *ḏbꜣ.f wr* B4C has *ʿprw.f wr* 'his (i.e. 'your') great equipment'.
3. Var. B3Bo: *st.k nt ḏd ḫt* 'your place of saying things'.
4. So B3L; Sq12C: 'may you appear on the very great plain', etc.; B3Bo: 'may you be exalted on the plain of the horizon'; B4C: 'may you be exalted on the pedestal'.
5. Sq12C: 'on which you sit'; B3Bo: 'may you sit ⟨on⟩ this its throne'.
6. B3Bo and B4C omit 80*c.d.*
7. Var. B3Bo and B4C: 'may it (i.e. the praise) please you every day'.
8. B3Bo: 'you have taken the soul of N with you'; Sq12C omits the particle *ỉsṯ* and mentions only N's soul, but otherwise accords with B3L, the lacunae being minor. B4C is incomplete.
9. B3Bo and B4C omit 80*g*–81*a*.
10. In 81*b* B3L has lapsed for once into the 3rd person; for *ʿwt Wsyr* 'the members of Osiris' of B3L and Sq12C B3Bo has *ʿrrwt Wsyr* 'the courts of Osiris' and B4C has *ʿwt* (det. □) *ʾItm* 'the chambers of Atum'.
11. B3Bo: 'the chambers of Osiris'.
12. For 81*c*–*e* in B3L, Sq12C has: 'those who are in charge of the members of Osiris shall not have power to watch over or constrain my soul or my shade, the possessor of eternity'. B3Bo omits the references to constraint and supervision and states that 'those who are in charge of the chambers (*sic*) of Osiris shall not have power over the soul or the shade of N'.

Spell 499

TO OPEN A PATH FOR MY SOUL, MY MAGIC AND MY SHADE, SO THAT IT MAY VI, 82
HAVE POWER IN [ITS] LEGS and that it may go up[1] and see the great god Rēʿ[2]

within his shrine on the day of reckoning up all souls, all spirits, all shades and all [magic(?)].[3] My soul is there to be chiefest among those who allot years.[4]
83 O Rēʿ and Ḥatḥōr, take my soul, my spirit and my shade with you,[5] | may I establish your[6] ornament on the vertex of Rēʿ. O you who are unaware of your faces, who are in charge of the members of Osiris,[7] you shall not have power to watch over me or to constrain my soul, my spirit or my shade[8] at the time of all eternity, for I am one who has power in his legs for ever and ever, who serves every god.

1. So B3L; the other texts have (82*c*): 'Opening a path to have power in its legs.
2. T3Be omits 'Rēʿ and after *kꜣr* B3Bo adds *rʿ nb*, replacing *rʿ* 'day' in 82*e*.
3. So B3L; in the lacuna at the end of 82*e* *ḥkꜣw* seems a much more likely restoration than *bꜣw* as suggested by de Buck, n. 1*, for *bꜣw* has occurred already in this clause, compare 69*e*; 70*b*; 71*a.h*; 80*f* and 82*a*. B4C and T3Be have: 'the day of reckoning souls'; B3Bo: 'reckoning all souls'.
4. Var. B3L: 'among the crew' (of Rēʿ), but according to de Buck's n. 2* the reading is doubtful. T3Be alone adds (82*g*): 'allotting my soul in the path'.
5. Varr. B3Bo: 'take the soul of N with you, O Eye of Horus' and ends; T3Be: 'place my soul with you and act'.
6. I.e. Ḥatḥōr's, as the suffix 2 fem. sing. shows. T3Be omits the suffix.
7. T3Be corruptly *ỉw ḥrt ʿwt Wsyr*.
8. Varr. B4C: 'you shall not constrain N's soul'; T3Be: 'I will not be afraid of your constraining my soul'.

Spell 500

O my soul, my spirit, my magic and my shade, go, reach[1] the path toward them, your qualities, which are in every god, being with you – so say those seven gods
VI, 84 who are equipped daily. May they guide[2] you on the paths of every god, | may you sit there at the head of the Great Ones who are in front of the seats[3] in the horizon in the retinue of Rēʿ and Ḥatḥōr for all eternity. It[4] shall not be constrained, nor shall either my soul or my spirit, either my magic or my shade be watched over by those who guard the members ⟨of Osiris⟩[5], together with those who watch over souls and constrain the shades of the dead.

You shall not be seized or constrained by any of those who are in sky and earth; be far from your corpse which is in the earth. May you not be among those who use the pitchfork or among the watchers who are in charge of the members ⟨of Osiris⟩[6]. You are one having power in your legs, the son of a god who has power in his legs.

Be far from your corpse which is in the earth, for you are a Power, the son of a god who has power in his legs; they shall not have power to constrain or watch over either my soul or my spirit, my magic or my shade, at the time of all eternity.

I am one having power in my legs, who serves Rēʿ and Ḥatḥōr and who
serves every god who is in sky and earth for all eternity. O both my soul and my
spirit, both my magic and my shade, all my bread and beer, you are for all those
who are in sky and earth, and every fair path of yours which Ḥu has prepared 85
for you . . .[7] Go, [. . .] be far from them, for you are one having power in your
legs, the son of a god who has power in his legs.

My soul, my spirit, [my magic] and my shade shall all be in every place where it[8] wishes to be.

1. For *sb* with the sense of 'reaching' or 'attaining' cf. *Urk.* I, 222,10; IV, 1845,16, there with good repute as the objective.
2. *Sšmw.sn* appears to be an authentic case of the *sḏmw.f* narrative form, cf. Edel, *Altäg. Gramm.* §§511 ff.
3. The det. of *swt* 'seats' seems to have been carried over from *wrw* above.
4. The singular suffix refers to the soul, etc., regarded as a single entity, as regularly in this group of spells.
5. The name of Osiris appears to have been omitted after *ʿwt,* as also in 84*h.*
6. See n. 5 above.
7. I can make nothing of *py ḥr ỉb gwst wrt.*
8. See n. 4. above.

Spell 501

I have made presentation of pyramidion-loaves in the East, my face is two faces
in . . . ,[1] with one face behind me ⟨ and one face ⟩ in my front,[2] I have trodden
in my . . .[3] of my sandals, I conduct *Hpnn*(?),[4] I present Right[5] to Rēʿ that he
may loosen my knots. The Lord of the *wtnw,* he has prepared a path for me, for VI, 86
I am *Wtwt,* the scribe of Him who departs and returns. What I detest is going out
into the night, I will always go out by day. I was conceived in the night, I was
born in the daytime; I departed yesterday and returned today, seeking my foes;
fulfilment(?) has been put in my possession for me in the Tribunal.

1. *M srḫ* defeats me; 85*i-j* is a corrupt version of 87*e-g*.
2. Reading *ḥr m-ḫt.ỉ,* ⟨ *ḥr* ⟩ *tp-ʿwy.ỉ,* cf. 87*f-g*.
3. *Bꜣḏy,* also in 88*a*, appears to be some part of a sandal; the strapping?
4. For *Hpnn,* var. *Hpy,* see 88*b*.
5. *ʿ* of *mꜣʿʿt* has been duplicated on passing from line to line.

Spell 502

Departing today, returning tomorrow, a man goes forth against his foes in the
VI, 87 realm of the dead. O you who ascend, fold your arms;[1] | O you who are afar, the god(s)[2] assemble for me.[3] I am the attendant of Rēʿ in the West,[4] and pyramidion-loaves are presented in the East; my face is two faces, with one face behind
88 me and one face in my front,| and my shank is in the . . .[5] of my sandals.[6] I bring down *Ḥpnn,*[7] I go down to my survivor,[8] Right follows me,[9] and it is *ʾIꜣpy* who will prepare a path for me,[10] for my abode is in the Field of Offerings. My head is combed,[11] for I am *Mty*(?) who is the scribe of Him who departs and returns,[12] I
89 spend the night being born and being conceived every day;[13] | I departed yesterday, I returned today, and that there is no god who shall oppose himself[14] is what I wish.

1. S10C^{b} adds at the end of 86*k*: *ḥr.ỉ* 'on my account'. M22C seems to read: 'O you who ascend, I have bound(?) your arms'. S10C^{a} and Y1C insert this passage in 87*b*. They read respectively: 'your arms go out to me'; 'your arms are folded(?) for me', cf. de Buck, p. 87, n. 2*.
2. Var. M22C: 'both the rulers'.
3. On 87*b* see n. 1 above.
4. Var. S10C^{b}: 'the East'.
5. See Spell 501, n. 3.
6. Corrupt in Y1C.
7. Omitted in B1Bo and S10C^{b}. For *Ḥpnn* M22C has *Ḥpy*.
8. The suffix 1st sing., which is all that is left in M22C, supports *r tp-tꜣ.f* of B1Bo against *r tꜣ* of S10C^{b}. S10C^{a} and Y1C omit 88*c*.
9. S10C^{b} and Y1C are both corrupt. *ʾIn ʾIꜣ* of 88*e*, in B1Bo alone, seems superfluous.
10. So B1Bo and M22C; S10C^{b} has *ỉn ʾIꜣḥy* alone, and the other two texts omit 88*f*.
11. For *ḥt* 'comb' hair, see *Westcar* 5, 15 = Simpson in the Yale Univ. Press *The Literature of Ancient Egypt,* p. 20. The preposition *m* after *ḥt.n.s* in Westcar is presumably that which sometimes intervenes between a transitive verb and its object. 88*h-i* are in B1Bo alone. All the other texts except S10C^{b} come to an end in 88*g*.
12. Compare 86*b*.
13. Compare 86*e*. S10C^{b}: 'I spend the night and am conceived every day'.
14. Read *ḏꜣ.ty.fy sw* with S10C^{b}.

Spell 503

I have gone up on Shu, I have climbed[1] on the sunbeams; it means that my feet and my hands have attained . . . (?).[2] TO BE RECITED BY HIM WHO KNOWS THIS

TEXT WHEN HE GOES FORTH SO THAT HIS HEART MAY ENDURE IN EVERY SHAPE IN WHICH ONE WISHES TO GO FORTH, AND THAT HE MAY EJACULATE HIS SEED SAFELY[3] ON EARTH, HIS HEIR EXISTING FOR EVER. HIS SOUL SHALL NOT BE SEIZED[4] NOR SHALL HIS SHADE BE SNARED. A MATTER A MILLION TIMES TRUE.

1. Var. B3L and B1L: *hꜣ.n.ỉ* 'I have descended'.

2. A most obscure passage which is almost certainly corrupt. For the sense given to *ḏr.n* cf. *ḏr.ỉn.f mḥ 24* 'it amounted to 24 cubits', *Westcar*, 6, 11, where *ḏr* certainly has the sense of attaining a limit. The object of the verb in the second clause varies here with each text, but in no case does it make intelligible sense. B1L alone continues with: 'it will go well happily with N for ever and ever'.

3. Reading *ꜥḏ* with de Buck, n. 2*.

4. Read *n nḏr.n.tw*; so also *grg.n.tw* in 89*n*.

Spell 504

I am[1] the hair of the son of the Old Woman; pray come and go forth,[2] that I may be exalted[3] above your soul. VI, 90

1. *N pn* of B1Bo shows that identity, not possession, is meant, but its real meaning remains obscure. For *sꜣ* 'son' S10C^{b} has *Gb*.

2. Imperative in S10C^{a} and T1C; prospective *sḏm.f* in B1Bo.

3. Prospective *sḏm.f* in B1Bo and S10C^{b}; in Y1C the final radical is not written. In S10C^{a} *ḳꜣy.ỉ* has been misread as *ḳꜣw* 'heights'.

Spell 505

[TO COME INTO BEING(?)] BY DAY, THAT I MAY HAVE POWER [. . .] EARTH. I am the lord of myriads, I have extended my arm as Rēꜥ, I have stretched out my arm as [. . .], I am the scribe of [Him who departs] and returns. I departed [yesterday, I returned] today, [I was] conceived [in the night], I [was born] on this day.[1]

1. For the restorations cf. 86*b.e.f*, except for the rubric, see de Buck, n. 2*.

Spell 506[1]

VI, 91 [. . .] whom Shu begot. Shu is he who loosed [my knots],[2] Lord of the *wtnw*, [. . .] he has bound up[3] my face for me which my father bandaged(?). I am Horus, whose face [. . .] in his mouth,[4] the scribe of Rēʿ. I departed yesterday, I returned today, [I] was conceived [in the night, I was born][5] in this day, I go hither and yon against that foe of mine, and he has been given to me [completely(?)][6] into [my] possession. I turn(?) my face to Rēʿ and Ḥatḥōr [. . .] upon her [. . .] who is in the Tribunal and everyone who will oppose himself to me. He who would repel me is given [. . .] Osiris, and departing is like returning – and *vice versa* – like Rēʿ. In the night he has turned himself about in the sky(?)[7] [. . .]. O Sole One [. . .] the sunshine, for I have broken open the Netherworld. O Sole One [. . .] I go up [to Rēʿ] so that I may present [Right to him[8] . . .] the sunshine, for I have broken open the Netherworld.

1. A badly damaged spell in which a few of the lacunae can be restored from the preceding texts.
2. Cf. 85*n*.
3. Read *ḥtr.n.f*.
4. Probably nothing lost after *rꜣ.f*, see de Buck, n. 8*.
5. Cf. 86*e*.
6. Restore *km* in the short lacuna? Cf. 86*h*.
7. Taking *ḫw* to be an error for *nwt*.
8. For the conjectural restorations cf. 85*m*.

Spell 507

VI, 92 [. . .] AT THE REALM OF THE DEAD. This is Osiris who used the hoof(?) as Osiris. You have looked behind you, and such is your face which went out from the shrine. Atum has pulled himself together as the protection of his two primeval Enneads who came into being with him. O you two Primevals, spread protection over me[1] with him in front of the horizon of the sky, prepare(?) protection over me, for I have lifted up my face before them.[2] I know how to oppose his[3] power over me . . . Atum himself[4] who watches over the many faces which are in the sky, (even he) whose shape is invisible, who wards off the Tribunal on my account. May you[5] prevent any evil opposition from issuing from the mouth of any god
93 or goddess, | or what men, gods, spirits or the dead may say they will do against me in this year, in this month,[6] in this night or in this day, indeed for ever and ever, in the presence of those who are in the sky, (even) those who should do

something(?) good[7] while in attendance on me. He[8] will save me from the evil slaying which men, gods, spirits, or the dead say they will do against my soul. [. . .] A TRUE MATTER.

1. For the 1st person cf. 92*k*; 93*d*.
2. For the sense given to *m-ḏr* cf. *rdy.ḫr sw Stš m ḏry.f* 'Seth will place him before him', *BD* 219, 12–13. But who are 'them'? Perhaps the Primevals, but in that case we would have expected the 2nd person plural.
3. Seth's?
4. I can make nothing of 92*l-m*; the name of Atum survives in B1Y.
5. Plural, presumably referring to the Primevals of 92*h*.
6. So B1Y.
7. Reading *ỉrty.s[n ḫt] nfr*? The restoration *ḫt* is suggested by the remains of B1Y.
8. Atum?

Spell 508

The apertures[1] of the sky-window are opened for Rēʿ, and it shows the burial of Osiris; woman and man as female and male[2] will go down to me. My possessions are mine; these are warmth[3] and offerings. 'Come, bring my possessions', say Atum and the Double Lion, 'warmth and offerings of burial and interment. He is one of the[4] children of their fathers who make the spell for the burial of Osiris on the path of Anubis, Lord of burial. The West is yours'. TO BE RECITED OVER THE WEST . . . A *'IMȝ*-TREE, TO BE PUT FOR A MAN [ON] HIS NECK. VI, 94

1. B9C: *pḫw*, a word not recorded; B1Y certainly [*ṯ*]*pḫwt*. Although these words are both plural, *ptr* 'sky-window' is singular; note the suffix in *sr.f*. The translation of this word as 'show' makes better sense than its homophone *sr* 'foretell'; in the latter case the suffix would refer to Rēʿ.
2. B1Y reads *ḥmt m ḥmt ṯȝy m ṯȝy*, but the meaning is the same.
3. *Sic*, surely not 'dust'! It appears to be a miswriting of the homophone *ḫm* 'warmth', which should have the fire-det.; 'dust' makes no sense. See Spell 509 below.
4. *Nw n* here is better translated as the definite article than as a demonstrative.

Spell 509

Rēʿ rises up, (even) he who warms[1] the two Enneads. Come to me, all of you, for everything is mine; I am the Sole One of the woven stuff(?),[2] I fare upstream to Elephantine,[3] and what you find, they will bring to me.[4] VI, 95

1. See Spell 508, n. 3.

2. *Sḫtꜣ* or *sḫtyw* is obscure. I have tentatively connected it with *sḫt* 'weave', with reference to the wrappings of mummies.

3. Var. 'Abydos'.

4. Var. B1Y: 'what you find, I will bring it'. This may perhaps be the better reading, as there is nothing to show to whom the plural pronoun *sn* of B9C refers.

Spell 510

The earth opens its mouth, Gēb throws open his jaws on my account, and I will raise up Horus pre-eminent in Pe[1] on to his lotus-flowers,[2] I will receive abundance, I will travel to the great stairway because of the Great Lady, the earth-god[3] will not oppose me, Shu the Lion[4] will not grasp me, I have shot and killed my
VI, 96 obstructor(?),[5] the dead have lost me, and I will live in the sight of Rēʿ and Rēʿ-Atum, I will depart and return[6] between them. My wig[7] is what is on me, I am the owner of offerings, and what I detest is wrong-doing.

1. B9C inserts an unnecessary suffix *.f* after *P.*

2. For *sꜣpt* 'lotus-flower' see also *CT* III, 286*c*.

3. *ꜣkr*.

4. Var. 'the Double Lion'.

5. The meaning given to *st.n.i.* 'I have shot' is indicated by the following *npd.n.i* 'I have killed'. *Ḥnty* is obscure in this context, which suggests an undesirable being, but it could possibly be a derivative of *ḥn* 'obstruct', *Concise Dict.* 171; it clearly is not comparable in sense to *ḥnt* in 102*i* or to *ḥnty* in 102*o*.

6. Reading B9C as *šmy.ỉ ỉy.ỉ*; *ỉṯy.ỉ* is an obvious corruption. B10C has the var. *šm.ỉ wỉ* 'I will take myself off'.

7. Lit. 'hair', but it seems unlikely that the deceased is referring to natural hair.

Spell 511

Spell for entering into the beautiful West and going out by day in the realm of the dead. Hail to you, you who are at the head of your rams;[1] I have come here to be in the field,[2] to rule the riparian lands in the middle of it, so that it may be at peace and protected.[3]

1. *Bꜣw* with det. of an animal's head; 'leopards' is a possible alternative.

2. Var. 'the island of the field'. Although in B9C *sḫt* has the plural strokes, yet it is referred to by a singular suffix in 96*j.k.*

3. The town-det. at the end of both texts of this spell is perhaps meant to indicate that it is concerned with a locality. Otherwise it is hard to account for it.

Spell 512

DIGGING A POOL. I am a Power, a Great One mightily strong, to whom is given VI, 97
power over you(?),[1] while Nu is . . .[2] 'Do not take away the cows', says *ꜥnḏ-ḥr,*
'do not suck the milk of the cows'. See, the Eye has gone forth over the waters
which I have found as an ibis;[3] see, the Eye has gone forth over the waters in the
presence of the Great One. 'Stand up!' says the Great One who has permitted
me to speak.

1. Read *sḫm* ⟨*m*⟩*.ṯn*?.
2. *Ḫrꜣ* is quite obscure.
3. This sentence seems to have been brought in for the purpose of the pun on *gm* 'find' and *gmt* 'black ibis', *Eg. Gramm.*³ p. 470, G28.

Spell 513

My dissolution[1] was caused yesterday, | I have returned today, a path has been VI, 98
prepared for me, and I will go up and take possession of the shape of Anubis.[2]
I am one who is tousled(?),[3] | who went up into his horizon;[4] I am one who is 99
dishevelled, who went up with his sceptre;[5] I am Lord of my *wrrt*-crown;[6] I am
the third of the magicians, | being one whom Maꜥet protects; I am the Red One,[7] 100
the protector of his Eye. I died yesterday,[8] I raised myself today, | I returned
today,[9] and a path has been prepared for me, (even me) the door-keeper of the 101
great warship.

1. *Wsṯ,* lit. 'dilapidation'. For this word cf. *Pyr.* §§1929; 2233 (both in *Pyr. Suppl.*); Caminos, *Lit. Frag.* pl. 1, 1, 2. Compare 100*e*.
2. So B9C and B1Bo. The other texts have made nonsense of this passage by misreading *pry* as *ḥry* and *ỉṯy,* var. *ỉṯ,* as *šm.*
3. For *sps* 'be tousled(?)' see also *CT* IV, 155*f*; VI, 240*k*.
4. Var. B1Bo: *m ỉꜣt.f* 'on to his perch'.
5. Var. B1L: 'his mace'.
6. Var. B9C: 'White Crown'. B2L and B1L omit the final possessive suffix.
7. Omitted in all texts except B9C and B1Bo.
8. So B9C and B1Bo. The other texts all have *mšd,* which is unintelligible. At this point B9C alone inserts *ỉy.n.ỉ bkꜣ* 'I returned on the morrow', contradicting 98*a* and 101*a*. In view of the lack of coherent sense which results, 100*d* has been omitted from the translation.
9. In B9C only.

Spell 514

Almost entirely destroyed.

Spell 515

VI, 102 The earth has opened its mouth for me,[1] Gēb has loosened[2] his jaws on my account, I have risen up as Horus pre-eminent in Pe,[3] I am on high on the lotus-flowers,[4] I eat bread,[5] I receive abundance,[6] I travel to the great city, I am immersed in the lake,[7] I have died the death, (yet) I am more alive than the Ennead, and am hale because of the Sole Lord.

I have received a stairway,[8] I have gone up to the day of . . . ,[9] I have died the death, I have returned alive,[10] I have sown in your presence(?),[11] I have more warmth than the uttermost parts.[12]

1. For 'opened' B3L has *wp.n*, the other two texts have *wn* ⟨*.n*⟩.

2. Reading *snfḫfḫ.n* with B3Bo; the other two texts have *sn.n* 'has thrown open'.

3. B3Bo (woman's coffin) reads: 'she has raised herself (*ts.n.s s*⟨*y*⟩) to you (pl.) as Horus', etc.

4. Plural in B3Bo, dual in the other texts.

5. Between *wnm* and *t* B3Bo inexplicably inserts *šm N tn*, which appears to be an anticipation of the beginning of 102*f*.

6. B3Bo, reverting here to the original 1st person, reads: 'I walk afoot to abundance'; *bcḥ* 'abundance' has lost its *ḥ* in this text. At this point B3Bo and B3L + B1L diverge, the former occupying 102*h-k* and the latter 102*l-o*. These are translated in order as printed in de Buck.

7. Surely so in this context, despite the det.

8. Here we turn to the text of B3L + B1L.

9. *3rt*, meaning not known.

10. Taking *r.ỉ* to be the enclitic particle.

11. An obscure clause; the translation is doubtful. Compare 95*n*, where, however, *st.n.ỉ* seems to have a different meaning.

12. Lit. 'the two ends', probably of the sky. Cf. *Pyr.* §1174 ; *BD* 166, 14.

Spell 516

VI, 103 Awake, you sleeper![1] Awake, N, sleeping on your side! [. . .]. Ho N! Raise yourself for those who are greater than you! You shall eat figs and drink wine, for your face is (that of) the jackal of Anubis; be covered[2] with it. The spines

of the nails which are on your fingers are like the spines which are on the fingers
of Thoth.[3] | May you cross over [as] a goose,[4] may you open the double doors 104
of the Foremost of the Westerners[5] which keep out the plebs. May those who
are in the nomes come to you,[6] may those who are in[7] the realm of the dead
serve you, may the foremost ones be pure for you, may the Great Mooring Post
call to you,[8] may [your] mother [the White Crown(?)] nurse you, may your
two mothers[9] kiss you, [may] the stairway of the river-bank [be firm(?)] under
you, may you ascend to the sky, may you do the snake-crawl behind Shu, | may 105
you ascend and go up to your house[10] as a star over your house, may you save
your children from mourning, may you make the . . .[11] to flourish on earth for
ever.

1. For *wrš* in the sense of 'wake' cf. *Pyr.* §875; *Rec. trav.* 39,108; for *ỉbꜣn* 'be drowsy', 'sleep' cf. *Pyr.* §§735; 894; 1901; 2224; 2240. This latter verb often takes the det. O, i.e. the closed pupil of the eye, and with only one exception (*Pyr.* §1901 = Nt 661) is followed by the enclitic *r.f.*

2. Alluding to a jackal mask 'covering' the face; for *šṯ* 'cover' cf. *CT* IV, 66*a*; 67*a*.

3. The 'spines' of the finger-nails are presumably their sharp outer edges which can scratch; in the case of Thoth the god may have been envisaged as a baboon. If he were thought of as an ibis, the 'spines which are on the fingers' would refer to the claws on the bird's toes. Elsewhere the word *my(ꜣ)sw* seems to refer to the shafts of feathers, cf. *Pyr. Transl.* Utt. 674, n. 13.

4. Restoring 104*a* as *ḏꜣ.k m smn.*

5. Reading *ḫnty ỉmntyw* as B10C^b; B10C^a has omitted the *ỉmn*-sign.

6. B10C^a has omitted *ỉmyw,* the second omission in a short space.

7. Probably to be interpreted as a plural, despite the absence of the ending.

8. *Ḏsr* of B10C^b is a corruption of *ḏsw* 'call'; compare *ḏsryt* as a var. of *ḏsyt* 'shout' (n.), *CT* I, 82*b*. For *Mnyt wrt* 'Great Mooring-post' as a goddess, cf. *Pyr. Transl.* Index I, p. 321.

9. Nekhbet and Edjō?

10. 105*a* is somewhat confused; B10C^a seems nearest the mark. The appearance of an imperative in this long series of optative *sḏm.f* forms appears incongruous, and I would suggest emending as *šw.k pr.k r pr.k*; the pun on *pr.k* is closer as emended.

11. *Ḫnt(y)-š,* which occurs in the plural in *Pyr.* §1348, is of unknown meaning; its relation to *ḫntyw-š* 'tenants(?)', *Concise Dict.* 194 is obscure.

Spell 517

[. . .] the Great Wild Cow;[1] may she guide you. Go,[2] O Gēb who are at the
head of the Ennead, as *Wpw* who is pre-eminent in Ōn; | fill the lake,[3] arrive at VI, 106
the Great Stairway, stamp[4] the feet and extend the arms; call [the Great Mooring-
post];[5] the sun-folk have burned(?) for you;[6] so says your mother. Yours is the

White Crown[7] of Nekhen; yours is the White Crown and headcloth within Nekheb.[8] She who is long of plumes and prominent(?)[9] of breasts, she has lifted you to the sky, she will not instal you on earth, she will take her breast to your
107 mouth,[10] | she will suckle you and will not wean [you],[11] Thoth will not upset what he has done for you, you shall sit on the iron throne, you shall summon the slayers and shall rule the Imperishable Stars.

1. Restore as *smꜣt wrt,* confirmed by the trace of the knife-det in B10C^b.
2. The translation of *šm* as an imperative seems enforced by those which follow on p. 106.
3. B10C^a has lost the *r* of the enclitic *r.k* in B10C^b; judging from the size of the lacuna, B9C has no space for it.
4. I.e. in a ritual dance.
5. Restored from 104*f.*
6. Reading *ỉns ṯbs n.k ḥn*[*m*]*mt* with B9C. For *ṯbs* 'burn(?)' cf. *Pyr.* §396; similarly *BD* 369,9; 378, 6–7.
7. Read *ỉn mwt.k ỉs ṯwt ḥḏt,* cf. 106*g*.
8. Written as *ḫꜣb,* but the identity of the place is assured by the association with *Nḫn.*
9. The translation of *wḫꜣt* is not certain but is suggested by the context. The word could perhaps be connected etymologically with *wḫꜣ* 'column', 'pole', *Concise Dict.* 67, with the literal sense of 'columnar' of breasts.
10. Restore 106*k* as *ḏꜣ.s mnḏ.s r* (var. *ḥr*) *rꜣ.k,* cf. *Pyr.* §§381; 1119; 1427, where the preposition is *tp.*
11. Restore 107*b* as *n wḏḥ.n.s ṯw,* cf. *Pyr.* §§729; 1344; 2003; the *sḏm.n.f* form is suggested by *ḫn.n* of 107*c* and is appropriate to a future negative clause. B10C^b apparently originally read *wḏḥy.s ṯw.*

Spell 518

O you who are vindicated and who see [. . .] N comes. O N, begone, begone(?),[1]
VI, 108 [. . .] in the day,| you shall tell him of the true matter . . .[2] do not drive him away.[3]

1. Translation doubtful; the words have been regarded tentatively as hortative old perfectives.
2. I cannot translate *ḳꜣḳꜣ.*
3. For *ỉw* read *sw.*

Spell 519[1]

Ho N! Raise yourself upon your iron bones and [golden] flesh,[2] for this [body] of yours[3] belongs to a god; it will not grow mouldy, it will not putrefy, it will not

be destroyed. [The warmth which is on your mouth is][4] that which issued from the nostrils of Seth, and the winds of the sky will be destroyed if the warmth which is on your mouth is destroyed; | [The sky] will be deprived [of] the stars[5] VI, 109
if the warmth which is on your mouth is lacking. May your flesh be born to life, and may your life be [more than] the life of the stars in their season of life.[6]

1. This spell is a version of *Pyr. Suppl.* Utt. 723, §§2244–5.
2. Read *ỉf.k* [*nbw*] = *ꜥwt.k nbw* of §2244*a.*
3. Read [*ḥ*] *ꜥw.k* or possibly *ꜥw* [*t*] .*k*; the suffix of the 3rd person is in error, for it makes no sense. The deceased is addressed directly, see also 108*l*; 109*b.c.*
4. Cf. §2244*d*, but there is hardly room in the lacuna for *ṯꜣw* 'breath'.
5. Cf. §2245*b*, which reads *ỉtm pt m ꜣḫꜣḫw.s.*
6. 109*e* agrees with the fragment JPII, 1055 + 32, cf. §2245*d*, nn *a-b*.

Spell 520

O N,[1] I am Imsety, and my father Horus said to me: My son,[2] come, betake yourself to my father N[3] in your name of Imsety. | You have come that you VI, 110
may gather my father N together; join him up, smoothe(?) him,[4] and you will be his good fortune, for you are my[5] son, a child of Horus. You have come to N; betake yourself beneath him and lift him up, do not be far from him, (even) N, in your name of Imsety.

1. In B2C only. This is the first of a group of four spells spoken each by one of the Children of Horus and linked with the drawings of 'Canopic' boxes on de Buck's p. 117.
2. In B2C only.
3. This clearly was originally a mythological text dealing with the restoration of the body of Osiris, but the automatic insertion of the name of the deceased tends to obscure the issue, which is further darkened by much confusion of suffixes, see n. 5 below.
4. Lit. perhaps 'use the adze on him' to smoothe down the roughness arising from putting the fragments of the body together. The writer seems to have had a figure of stone or wood in mind.
5. The suffix-pronouns have become thoroughly confused in the latter part of this spell; thus in 110*e* we should read *sꜣ.ỉ* 'my son', since Horus is speaking; in 110*f* *ỉw.n.k* should be read, following 110*a*, for Horus is still speaking to Imsety; 110*g* is correctly in the 2nd person singular; in 110*h* (B18C only) the text starts off wrongly with the 2nd person plur. in *fꜣ.ṯn* but changes into the correct sing. in *ỉm.k*; in 110*i* *rn.f* should read *rn.k* in all texts, as in 109*k.*

Spell 521

VI, 111 O N, I am Ḥapy,[1] and I have come to you. My father Horus said to me:ǀ Run after my father Osiris[2] and split open his mouth.

I am Ḥapy and my father Horus said to me: You are the great runner;[3]
112 come,[4] that you may join up my father Nǀand not be far in this your name of Ḥapy, for you are the greatest of my children – so says Horus.

You have come, O Great Runner, for you are my father N. (*sic*).

1. B5Bo has: 'N is Ḥapy', which makes nonsense of what follows; so too 111*g*.
2. So B18C; surely the original version.
3. Note the paronomasia between the name of Ḥapy and *ḥpy* 'runner' in 111*e.i*; 112*e*.
4. *M* 'come!' in two texts out of five.

Spell 522

VI, 113 O N, I am Duamūtef, and my father Horus said to me: Come and worship my father N for me,[1] just as you went that you might worship my mother Isis[2] in your name of Duamūtef. Join up my father N and do not be far from him, for you are my[3] son, a child of Horus. You have come beneath N in your name of Duamūtef, for you are his beloved son.

114 I am Duamūtef,[4] and my father Horus said to me: Come to N.

1. So B19C, but with a superfluous *n* before *ỉt.ỉ* 'my father'.

2. B2C and B5Bo have *mwt.k* 'your mother' in error; Horus is referring to his own mother Isis.

3. Again confusion of pronouns.

4. B5Bo: 'N is Horus', but this MS is apt to be confused, cf. Spell 521, nn. 1.2. B2C and B18C have: 'N is Duamūtef'.

Spell 523

O N, I am Ḳebḥsenuf, and my father Horus said to me: Come, refresh my father;
VI, 115 betake yourself[1] to him[2] in your name of Ḳebḥsenuf. You have come that you may make coolness for him after you,[3] and do not be far from him; join him up, put him together, knit him up as regards his bones. O N,[4] do not be far from him; O Ḳebḥsenuf, come, betake yourself[5] beneath N and refresh him.

116 You are my father in your name of Ḳebḥsenuf.[6]

1. Read *ms kw* with B18C.

2. All texts have *ḫr.k*, but *ḫr.f* is certainly to be read; no-one can betake himself to himself. Conversely, in 115*b* for *m-ḫt.f* read *m-ḫt.k.*

3. See n. 2 above.

4. All texts agree in heading 115*f* with *Wsyr N pn,* but it looks like an intrusion; in the preceding three spells it is the god who must not be far from the deceased.

5. Again read *ms kw* with B18C.

6. Presumably these words are spoken by the deceased; B19C alone adds: 'you are N's protection'.

Spell 524

O N, I am Horus who went forth as Horus and Seth,[1] and my father said to me: Come, betake yourself to my father N and do not let him be subdued[2] at the hands of his foes in your name of Horus. You have come that you may join him up, (even) N; do not be far from him. Place yourself and your father in his embrace,[3] | do not ever let go of him,[4] and smite his foes from him,[5] (even) N. VI, 117

1. For 'Seth' B11C has *Wḏꜥ* 'the Outcast'; B5Bo shows the *s* of *Stš* but reads: 'N is he who went forth as Horus and S[eth]'.

2. *Rdy* has been omitted in B11C; for once B5Bo has the better text.

3. I.e. in a mutual embrace.

4. Both texts of 117*a* are slightly corrupt; emend as *ỉm.k sfḫḫw ỉm.f ḏt,* cf. *Pyr.* 16*d.*

5. Both texts strangely: *ḫftyw.f sn.*

The remainder of de Buck, p. 117, is taken up with drawings of chests depicting various gods. Besides the four Children of Horus we meet Neith, Nūt, Selket, *Mnkrt, Rnnwtt, Snḏt* and *Dwn-ꜥnwy.*

Spell 525

Horizontal line: Your mother Nūt spreads herself over you. VI, 118

Four vertical lines: A boon which Imsety gives to the blessed N.[1]

" " Ḥapy " "

" " Duamūtef " "

" " Kebḥsenuf " "

1. The first vertical line (Imsety) begins with a reversed *w* instead of *nsw.*

Spell 526

I am Nephthys, and I have come that I may lay hold of you and that I may place your heart in your body for you; I bring you Horus and his Great-of-Magic, I bring you Seth [and his] Great-of-Magic.[1]

I am Isis, and I have come that I may lay hold of you and that [I] may
VI, 119 place your heart in your body [for] you; I bring you | Horus[2] and his Great-of-Magic, I bring ⟨ you ⟩ [Seth and his] Great-of-Magic.[3]

1. S2C*b*, which is all in red ink, ends here, but S2C*a*, all in black, continues with a counterpart in the name of Isis; compare *Pyr.* §4*c.e.* The 'Great-of-Magic' is the god's crown.
2. A scribal omission, see de Buck, n. 1*.
3. Illegible traces in 119*g*, see de Buck, n. 4*.

Spell 527

O Rēꜥ-Atum, my purification is the purification of the two great and mighty gods who are pre-eminent in Upper Egypt; my purification is the purification of the spittle which issued from the mouth of Rēꜥ-Atum. I am pure, for my purification is the purification of Horus when he bound his foes and was vindicated against whoever would dispute with him. My purification is the purification of the Great One who is high on the dais [. . .] my purification is the purification of sky and earth which were purified[1] for Rēꜥ and for Gēb; my purification is the purification of Anubis whose body is warm(?).[2]

1. *Wꜥbt* is fem. to agree with *pt.*
2. Assuming the reading *tꜣ ẖ*[*t*]*.f* with omission of the fire-det. after *tꜣ*.

Spell 528

VI, 120 Ho N! Wake up, raise yourself, so that you may be pure and that your double may be pure! Your purification is the purification of Horus and Seth,[1] your purification is the purification of Thoth and *Dwn-ꜥnwy*, your purification is the purification of your double, your purification[2] also is among your brethren the gods. Be silent [. . .].

1. With this and the following sentences compare *Pyr.* Utt. 36.
2. For read . Note the writing *dyṯw* for *ḏdṯ* 'you also' in 120*e.*

Spell 529

N recites and says: I have entered into a dust-devil,[1] I have gone forth pure, I have travelled on the fair road which I desired and favoured . . .[2] I have gone up and down ⟨ to ⟩ my house, favour is mine, and a rope is made for me.

1. For *ssw* 'dust-devil' cf. *Pyr.* §308; , the deceased is supposed to ascend in one as it whirls upwards. The word is distinct from *ssw* with sky-det. in *CT* IV, 46*b*, which seems to refer to celestial waters.
2. The meaning of *ỉḥh* in 120*n* is quite obscure.

Spell 530

Purity, purity for your[1] double! You are pure for your double, your head is VI, 121
censed with sweet-smelling incense, you are made strong[2] by means of incense, the fragrance of a god is on your flesh, the two Great Ones, the Lords pre-eminent in Upper Egypt,[3] cleanse you. The incense comes, | the incense comes;
the ear of corn comes, the ear of corn comes; there comes the spinal cord which 122
issued from the backbone of Osiris,[4] there comes the marrow,[5] there comes the marrow, there come the limbs which issued from Osiris, and Horus censed him because of his Eye. O N, I cense you because of the Eye of Horus, I make a god of you because of the Eye of Horus, I equip you as a god, it[6] equips you as a god, its [perfume] diffuses over you, and the perfume of the Eye of Horus is on you.[7]

1. This spell was originally addressed to the deceased in the 2nd person, note the appearance of the pronouns of the 2nd person sing. in 121*c.e.f*; 122*h.j-n*, and it has been translated accordingly.
2. Reading *srwd* rather than *srd* as written; the meaning of the latter 'make to grow' yields poor sense.
3. Two texts read: 'Horus and Seth, the two Great Ones'; T1C has omitted *šmꜥ* at the end of the sentence.
4. Sq10C transfers this clause to 122*d* and substitutes the name of Gēb.
5. Lit. 'great firmness'; for this term see also *Pyr.* §116.
6. The suffix *.s* refers to the Eye of Horus.
7. Written *ḥrr.k*.

Spell 531

VI, 123 Hail to you,[1] You who are kindly of countenance,[2] owner of eyes which see, whom Anubis knit together, whom Ptaḥ-Sokar exalted, to whom Shu gave the Supports,[3] kindly of countenance among the gods, whom Rēʿ gave to Osiris for the secret thing which was done against him in order to end the injury by Seth against him. Your White Crown is that of Thoth,[4] your vertex is that of Wep-
124 wawet,[5] your eyebrows are those of the two Enneads,[6] | your eyes are those of the Night-bark and the Day-bark, your tresses(?)[7] are those of Isis and Nephthys, the back of your head[8] is that of *Dwn-ʿnwy*, your braid is that of the scorpion,[9] your linen is that of *Ḥḏ-ḥtp*; you are in front of N, and he will see by means of you.

125 May you make him to be a spirit, may you subdue his foes for him,[10] may you guide him to the fair places of the realm of the dead, may you smite the confederacy of Seth for him.[11] The king has commanded [12] that N be made triumphant over his foes before Horus, Lord of Patricians.

That I be one who is enduring, enduring, is what has been commanded, (even) enduring like Rēʿ for ever.[13]

1. M16C begins this spell with a stock *pr-ḫrw* formula.
2. For the significance of *nfr ḥr* cf. *ZÄS* 53,115; *JEA* 39, 53.
3. Of the four corners of the sky.
4. For this sentence in M16C and M1Ann, see 124*f*.
5. See also 124*c*.
6. See also 124*b*, which shows clearly that at the end of 123*k* we should read *psḏty* 'the two Enneads'; *rʿty* 'the two female suns', as written in M36C and M35C, makes no sense.
7. *Swty*; precise meaning unknown.
8. M36C and M35C have the abnormal spelling *mkḥ3*, while M16C omits the word, presumably by inadvertence. It is spelt correctly in M1Ann.
9. The braided lock of hair is likened to the jointed tail of a scorpion.
10. The counterpart of this clause in the other texts is 125*e*, where M35C has: 'may you make his foes impotent for him'; M16C: 'may you accuse his foes for him at every dais'. M1Ann. begins with *srḫ* 'accuse', but otherwise is lost except for a single sign  at the end; in M2Ann. only  is extant, apparently the determinative of a name, see de Buck, p. 124, n. 4*.
11. M1Ann. is largely lost, but may have had a different text; it appears to read *ḥy.k gs* [. . .] 'may you smite the side of [. . .]. M2Ann. has omitted the verb and has *nb* for the suffix *.k*.
12. Var. M2Ann. 'the king has said'.
13. Apparently spoken by a son of Horus, see de Buck, n. 2*.

Spell 532

SPELL FOR GIVING A MAN'S HEAD TO HIM IN THE REALM OF THE DEAD. My head VI, 126
is knit on for me by Shu, my neck is made firm for me by Tefēnet on that day when the heads of the gods were knit on to them. My eyes have been given to me that I may see with them, I have received my spinal cord through[1] Ptaḥ-Sokar,[2] my mother has given me her hidden power, my son has extended his arms over me,[3] in order to put an end to the injury which Seth did in the secret thing which he did against me in this my name of N.

126m (T2L) reads: My tresses(?)[4] have been knit together for me in Ōn on the day of cutting off the lock of hair.

1. Read *ḥr* with T2L.
2. The two texts diverge at this point; T1Be has 126*i-l* and T2L has 126*m*.
3. The text seems confused in 126*j*. I suggest reading *ỉw rdy.n mwt.ỉ ꜣḫ.s sštꜣ, dwn.n sꜣ.ỉ ꜥwy.f ḥr.ỉ*, dividing *i* and *j* at a different point from de Buck.
4. *Sty* may be a var. of *swty* in 124*d*.

Spell 533

TO BECOME [. . .]. I am he who makes presentation with his head,[1] one promi- VI, 127
nent of horns whose arms are folded; a lector, a writer of fair words attached
to Sia | in the hidden mansion in the tribunal[2] of Him who guards the Great 128
Lady; scribe of what is in the record[3] in respect of offerings; one who is with
Sia; I make the spell for their offerings | within the horizon of Ḥatḥōr; I guide 129
the *wḫ*-symbols[4] to their places on the day of allotting justice. Ḥatḥōr lays her
hands on me, | for I am a scribe whom she loves and who daily does what she 130
wishes. I have come playing music to Ḥatḥōr,[5] I set down[6] bread for Atum, I
institute offerings for Ḥatḥōr, I open the gate, I throw open the gate,[7] I traverse[8]
the great house of Ḥatḥōr. | How good is the acclaim of me in it! I control [. . .] 131
in company with the Lord of the Suite, I remove Shu, I traverse[9] the earth,[10] I spend the night in their priestly service, my hair ⟨is parted⟩.[11] The face of Ḥatḥōr is bright for me, Ḥatḥōr lays her hands on me.

1. M22C reads: 'who makes presentation in his chapel of the Eye'.
2. Var. M4C: 'overseer of the tribunal'. M22C in 128*e* substitutes at this point: 'I have come to my place at the head of the great house, which belongs to (the place, not the house, the genitive is fem.) Him who guards the Great Lady'.

3. For the position of *sš* in this phrase cf. 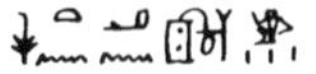 'scribes of the king's records, *P. Kah.* 14,47.

4. On the *wẖ*-symbol cf. Blackman, *Meir,* I, pp. 2–4. Var. 'I guide to (*r*) the *wẖ*-symbols'.

5. For *n Ḥwt-ḥr* of M6C, M3C has inexplicably *ỉknst sp 2* and M12C is in accord with it; M3Ann. ends at *ỉy.n.ỉ ỉmꜣḫt.*

6. M3C repeats *ỉy.n.ỉ* 'I have come' in 130*c.*

7. M6C has later inserted 'to these three', who presumably are Sia, Ḥatḥōr and Atum. M3C has: 'I open the gates to N', and ends the spell.

8. M12C: *pr* [. . .].

9. *Šꜣs* of M23C yields a better sense than *smn* of M6C.

10. M6C omits 131*e*, which is damaged and obscure in M23C.

11. Read ⟨*wp*⟩ *wprty* with haplography; for *wprt* 'die Seitenlocke des Kindes' cf. *Wb.* I, 305,6, here apparently used of the hair of an adult man.

Spell 534

I will[1] see Right in the presence of the Lord of All, I will raise up Right to the Lord of Everything, I will be with the Lord of Life, I will act according to his command, I will go to and fro in the Night-bark in company with those who are in the Suite, ⟨even I⟩, N.

1. For the translation in the future tense see the prospective forms *wnn, pry.ỉ* and *hꜣy.i* below.

Spell 535

VI, 132 I am Shu the equipped; I will not be taken to the shambles of the god, for I am covered with the *ḳny*-garment, food-offerings will not be placed away from me[1] by those who are in charge of the chambers of Osiris, who put slaughter into the shambles, I will not enter into their shambles, I will not be made to enter into the shambles of the god, for I am covered with the *ḳny*-garment; I will not be watched by those who watch souls, my soul and my shade will go up because of it[2] on the day of [. . .]. I live and my eye has power over water(?)[3] and wind, because I am this equipped spirit who knows his spell, and who will not enter into the shambles of the god; I will not listen to magic.

1. *Ỉm.ỉ,* apparently meaning 'out of my reach'.
2. The wearing of the *ḳny*.
3. Read *ꜥnḫ.ỉ sḫm ỉrt.ỉ m mw*? See de Buck's notes 8* and 9*.

Spell 536

[. . .] I am [covered][1] with the *ḳny*-garment, [. . .] I will [not][2] enter into VI, 133
the shambles of the god [. . .].

1. Restore as *ʿfn.ky*, cf. 132*c*.
2. The negation restored from 132*g*.

Spell 537

To become Neḥebkau. [. . .] as Neḥebkau; I am [. . .] your [spirits, I][1] am Neḥebkau.

1. See de Buck, nn. 3* and 4*.

Spell 538

To become the scribe of Rēʿ-Atum. [. . .] of Rēʿ-Atum, who spent the day [. . .]. VI, 134

Spell 539

I am the son of the Lord of All, the scribe of Ḥatḥōr, who will never die, who will never perish, who will never fall, who will never suffer.[1] I will not fall, perish, suffer or die.

1. Read *nsns* with 134*i* (P. Gard. III). For the verb see also *Pyr.* §903.

Spell 540

TO BECOME THE SCRIBE OF ḤATḤŌR. Sky and earth come to me, and their VI, 135
great ones come to me, (even) the gods who are above; they open the sacred paths for me [. . .]. O Gēb, [chiefest][1] of the gods, see me and make me grow and break out from within my egg. The two barks come to me, I have received my thrones in the bark, I have protected my thrones in the bark, [. . .] those who control the rowing. Their thrones have been given to me, and it means that I have been raised up to be her scribe, the possessor of a seat[2] at the head of their great

ones and at the head of their mighty ones[3] and their women. I am [. . .] their two who have power and [. . .]. I do not use my hand[4] on them, while my scribes are on their haunches with my palette(s) in their armpit(s).[5] I am greater than their great ones, I am [more] to be dreaded [than] the great [. . .] of her[6] tribunal. I have received the four[7] reed wands and the reed pens of Maʿet.[8] | I
136 receive them from her fingers, I moisten(?)[9] them [. . .] . . .[10] It is the gods who are in their tribunal who will see; it is he who is faint[11] who bears the four reed wands and reed pens [. . .] . . . the Lord of endowments. It is the great ones, the Lords of their tribunal, who know the names of the wands and pens of Maʿet; I know them by their names. I bring what is good[12] [. . .]; I cause Right to enter in, I reduce the two Warriors to order,[13] I detest him who will not see wrong,[14] whom the crew of Rēʿ, the Eldest in sky and earth, make impotent;[15] to whom come the gods [and to whom those who dwell(?) in][16] the horizon bow down. I know you and I know your names; I have gone forth pure with my plume on my [head(?)], the gods come joyful in honour [. . .] I will not perish nor be destroyed[17] in this land [for ever]. I am the scribe of Ḥatḥōr, the writing materials of Thoth are opened for me, and I am his helper.

1. Restore [*rp*]*ʿ*.
2. Compare *Les.* 74,18.
3. Both fem.
4. For a similar use of *gm* cf. *RB* 61,12.
5. *Gsty* and *ḥṯṯ* are both written as sing. because each individual bore but one palette and has only one armpit in use; the palette is envisaged as carried between upper arm and side. The suffix *.s* after *ḥṯṯ* stands for *.sn*; so also in 136*a*.
6. Ḥatḥōr's.
7. Read *fdw* 'four', cf. 136*c*.
8. *wrw sp 2 wrw r pt tȝ* is most obscure, and seems to be an interpolation from elsewhere which has no business here; the passage 136*a* seems to follow naturally on the reference to the wands and pens of Maʿet. The *wrw* clause has therefore been omitted from the translation.
9. *ʿwḥ* is not recorded, but appears to be a var. of *ỉwḥ* 'moisten'.
10. I can make nothing of what follows the lacuna, down to *pss*.
11. On *ʿm-ỉb* cf. James, *Ḥeḳanakhte*, p. 110, with n. 2.
12. Despite the absence of suffixes in *ỉnn* and *sʿḳ* and the 3rd person thereafter, I believe all this to be spoken by the deceased and to have been originally in the 1st person, and I have translated accordingly. The 1st person is resumed in 136*n*.
13. For this meaning of *syd* cf. *CT* I, 320*b*.
14. There is surely some corruption in what follows *bwt.f.* I suggest the emendation *ỉwty mȝȝ.f.*
15. For this alternative meaning of *syd* cf. *JEA* 4, pl. 9, 2; *CT* V, 246*e*.

16. A possible restoration of the lacuna is [*ḫmsw m*]; I cannot believe in Lacau's restoration as quoted in de Buck's n. 10*.

17. Restore the second verb as [*ḥ*] *tm. ỉ.*

Spell 541

[...] Ḥatḥōr [...]. The doors of *Pndnd*[1] are opened for Ḥatḥōr, [the gates(?)] VI, 137
of the horizon [are thrown open(?)] for Ḥatḥōr.[2] I eat the hidden things, I chew *nšnw* in the suite of Ḥatḥōr.

1. *Pndnd* of M22C and *pdndn* of P. Gard III may be variants of *pndn*, an epithet of the sun-god, cf. *Pyr.* § 200.

2. M22C ends here; the continuation is in P. Gard. III alone.

Spell 542

I am one of your sacred cattle,[1] O my mistress Ḥatḥōr; one who eats the hidden things and chews [*nšnw*] and who spends the night doing their[2] priestly service.
Ḥatḥōr has put her hands on me under the branches of the *ỉtnws*-tree.[3] VI, 138

1. On *ṯntyw* 'sacred cattle' of Ḥatḥōr, var. *ṯntt*, see Blackman, *Meir*, I, p. 2.

2. Presumably of the gods in general.

3. M22C ends this spell with *ḏd m r3*, lit. 'enduring in the mouth', which may be a kind of editorial comment. It is lacking in P. Gard. III.

Spell 543

[To be] in the suite of Ḥatḥōr. [...] bright is the horizon. [...] a boon which is given. Opening [a gate] in the horizon. I will be in your suite. [I will chew] *nšnw*, I will be in your suite.[1]

1. These last two sentences have been written twice, though the right-hand text has been much damaged.

Spell 544

VI, 139 O Arm[-swallower(?),] [1] prepare a path [for me], for I am the son of a Great One
whom Rēʿ has daily equipped, possessor of good protection from upon the hands
of Thoth. I have come [for you at(?)] [2] the Mansion of the Sistrum-player; I am
one [. . .] his hinder parts; the Great One goes forth [. . .] the Sole One of
Ḥatḥōr, he who rejoices in the Abyss – four times.

1. Restore [*ỉ ꜥ*]*m-ꜥ* with de Buck, n. 1*.

2. On the basis of de Buck's text, it is difficult to fill the lacuna. If de Buck's *ṯ* were in fact *r* one might read *r*[*.ṯ*] *r* 'for you at', which makes good sense.

Spell 545

I am the scribe of [Ḥatḥōr], many of rowings in Dendera, upraised on my Maʿet-
symbol; I am this one whom you[1] protected from the djinn[2] who is in his jar,
VI, 140 though he did not speak ⟨ to ⟩ me(?)[3] [. . .]. [The doors of the sky(?)] [4] are
opened to me [. . .] to(?) these three or four gates of Rēʿ;[5] how good is what
I will proclaim there in the suite of Ḥatḥōr![6] I will be there with my mistress
Hathor under the branches of the *ỉṯnws*-tree.[7] I climb the air, I traverse the earth,
141 I travel the air, I traverse the sunshine,[8] I travel and climb the *ỉꜣd*-star,[9] I eat the
hidden things, I chew *nšnw* in the suite of Ḥatḥōr,[10] for joy is widespread, honour
is widespread, my hands are performing rites,[11] [. . .] I reach the horizon.
I will be the scribe of Ḥatḥōr, the Sole One, the third, fifth and seventh of
the sistrum-players, [12] a sistrum-player in the fair sky and the Abyss [. . .] . . .
142 every(?) day. [13] He who conceals the Great One sees me . . . [14] . . . you[15] save
me from the constriction[16] of Ḥa and Ḥu. I know the name of the ink[17] [. . . I
know] the name of the reed pens which [I] put [in(?)] water for her . . . I know
the name of the water-pot.

1. Masc.

2. *Bkꜣ* is apparently a harmful spirit who lives in a jar.

3. M22C is at least in part corrupt, and the damaged state of the texts prevents us from being certain whether *tm.f* of M22C or [*t*]*m.n.k* of P. Gard. III is to be read. Perhaps the least unlikely solution is to emend M22C to read *tm.f ḏdw* ⟨*n*⟩*.ỉ* [. . .].

4. The restoration *ꜥꜣwy n pt* at the beginning of the lacuna receives some support from de Buck's n. 3*, where Lacau's *pn* could, in the state of this manuscript, easily be a misreading of *pt*.

5. P. Gard. III must have had a different text, for the long lacuna ends in the Ḥatḥōr sign.
6. *M šmsw n Ḥwt-ḥr* is omitted from M22C.
7. Not in P. Gard. III or IV; compare 138*a-b*. The following 140*e* seems better placed in 141*b*, where P. Gard. III and IV have it.
8. P. Gard. IV reads *ỉpḥ.ỉ 'Iꜣsw* 'I reach *'Iꜣsw*'.
9. Cf. *Pyr.* § 280.
10. See n. 7 above.
11. 141*c*, only in P. Gard. III and IV, seems to be slightly corrupt. Read perhaps as *ꜣwt-ỉb ꜣw.ty, ỉmꜣḫ ꜣw ꜥwy⟨.ỉ⟩ m ỉrt ḫt.* From here on we depend on M22C alone.
12. *Sic*; there must have been a textual omission, for this does not make sense as it stands,
13. I can make nothing coherent of what remains of 141*i-j*.
14. Another obscure passage. *Tꜣ* as it stands means nothing; *ḥnṯw* may be a variant of *hnṯw* in 141*m*, of unknown meaning. The rest of this spell is too much damaged to yield a coherent text.
15. Fem., i.e. Ḥatḥōr.
16. Or 'deprivation'.
17. Cf. Harris, *Minerals*, 147.

Spell 546

[TO BECOME] ANUBIS. I am [. . .] the Milk-goddess; I am at the foot of the Great Lady; I am Lord of the Tower; I am Anubis, Lord of the Wand in Abydos [. . . I am] Anubis, Lord of the Sacred Land, the Great One; I assume my rank, I assume the eldership of my rank.

Spell 547

TO BECOME THE NILE-GOD. [I heap up the waters(?)],[1] I become [. . .] of the VI, 143
Coiled One, [. . .] I speak [about] it, I go forth in my strength(?),[2] I am a flood [. . .] as what appertains to him. One [. . .] whom his mother bore [. . .] of the path. I brought into being for him the gods in this land of what is hated,[3] and he will be [. . .]; I have filled the water [. . .] pastures [. . .] for it behind Horus in the flood. Osiris has placed his efflux in[4] his coffin; I [. . .] to myself for life, well-being and health.

1. Restoring as *wbs mw*; for *wbs* see de Buck, n. 1*. This restoration might just fit the lacuna. This spell is damaged too badly to yield a coherent sense.
2. *Ḏryt* is perhaps a derivative of *ḏry* 'fest', etc., *Wb.* V, 599.
3. I.e. the land of death.

4. It is hard to see what can have stood in this short lacuna; Lacau's ? (n. 13*) is impossible, following as it does on a preposition. Since the damage extends to the following signs, it is difficult to estimate its exact extent, and it seems quite possible that nothing has been lost; on this basis the passage makes sense.

Spell 548

VI, 144 NOT TO FERRY A MAN TO THE EAST IN THE REALM OF THE DEAD.[1] O you phallus of Rēʿ which goes awry for him in uproar, the inertness of which comes into being through Babi, may I be[2] stronger thereby than the strong ones, mightier
145 thereby than the mighty ones. If I be taken and ferried over to the east | in order to carry out wrongful slaying on me in the festival of those who rebel against me[3] by smiting[4] my horns,[5] I will swallow[6] for myself the phallus of Rēʿ and the head of Osiris when I have been guided to the tomb of the decapitation of the
146 gods[7] | that they may make answer there. I will bind[8] the horns of Khopri, I will create a stone in the eye of the Destroyer,[9] if[10] I be taken,[11] and if I be ferried across to the East and if the festival of those who rebel be celebrated over me.[12]

1. T2L substitutes: 'Spell for not dying again in the realm of the dead'.

2. For the 1st person see 144*h* ff.; *BD* 196, 15 ff.

3. M2NY, now largely lost, had a different text after *šʿt r.ỉ*. T2L and T2Be: 'in order to celebrate the festival of those who rebel against me by means of wrongful slaying'.

4. For *ḥwt* of M18C, M2NY has *ḥ3t* and T2L *ḥ3tḥ3t*, both certainly being corrupted from *ḥwt*.

5. 145*c* (T2L and T2Be) is out of place here; in M18C and M2NY it comes in 146*c*, see also *BD* 197,7.

6. Read *ʿm.k3.ỉ* with M18C and *BD* 197, 3.

7. T2L is nearer to *BD* with *sšm* than is T2Be with *šm*, but there is a superfluous *r* before *sšm* in T2L. *Ḥ3t* 'tomb' of T2L and T2Be yields better sense than *ỉḥw* 'cords' of *BD* 197, 5.

8. Read *ndb* with M18C and *BD* 197, 6.

9. Var. 145*c* (T2L, T2Be) 'in the eye of *Ṯb*'; *BD* 197, 8: 'in the eye of Atum and the Destroyer'.

10. The repeated *ḏr* in the remaining clauses seems to have the force of a conditional particle.

11. *BD* 197, 8 has *nḏr* here.

12. *BD* 197, 10–11 adds *ḏr ỉr.tw šʿt ỉm.ỉ ḏw* 'if a slaying be executed on me wrongfully'.

Spell 549

VI, 147 TO ASSEMBLE A BURIAL. O N, you are one of those who spear (fish), who are over the netters, who have gone to the *tnnt*-shrine and have found a coffin for themselves. TO ASSEMBLE A MULTITUDE FOR BURIAL.

Spell 550

The rope-ladder is knotted, the ladder is erected, its front ropes are loosed VI, 14
⟨by⟩ the jackal-gods, its back-ropes by the gods of Nekhen,[1] until N goes up on
it to the sky, and it will be firm under N ⟨at⟩ the great threshing-floor of the
sky. O . . .[2] who ascended from the Abyss, give your hand[3] to N, for N has gone
up from the place of darkness. TO KNOT A LADDER TO THE SKY IN THE REALM
OF THE DEAD.

1. In 148*b-c* read *ḥ3twt.s ỉn 'Inpww, pḥwt.s ỉn nṯrw Nḫn.* In 148*b* the suffix *.s* after *ḥ3twt* seems needed, but in B1Bo and BH2C there has been haplography of *ỉn* 'by' and *'Inpww,* lit. 'Anubises'. In 148*c* B2Be has *ʿprw* 'equipped ones' instead of *'Inpww.* In 148*c* in B1Bo read *.s* for *.sn,* since only one ladder is involved; B2Be has *.sn* like B1Bo and omits *ỉn* 'by'; BH2C omits the suffix after *pḥwt.* The terms for the ropes cannot be interpreted as 'bow-warps' and 'stern-warps' here, because we are not concerned with boats; these words must refer to ropes forming part of the ladder.

2. *Swš* of B1Bo is written like the word for 'surgical swab' in P. Ed. Smith 5,18; 6,10; cf. also *Wb.* IV, 75,16–76,3, but its meaning here is quite obscure, except that it looks as if it were meant for a *nomen divi.* B2Be writes the word as *sšw* and BH2C as *sw.* Both these texts have *nwt* instead of *nw* and BH2C omits the preposition *m* after *pr.*

3. B2Be has the not uncommon miswriting of  as .

Spell 551

I have come to you, my father Rēʿ; I have traversed the air, I have swallowed the VI, 149
Great One,[1] I have gone around the watery Chaos four times, I have passed by
the water-pourer(?)[2] who is in the Abyss, I have passed by the angry one who is
in the limits of the horizon, who smites[3] every god, I have bathed in the Lakes 150
of the Netherworld, | I have washed in the Lakes of the Jackals, I have . . .[4] the
bark, I have descended the ladder,[5] I have received[6] Her of the Great West, the
helper[7] has raised me up, I have entered among those who follow me, I grip the
Mighty Lady, I grip your[8] terrible one, the Lord of the Sunshine, I dwell in the
awe of you; She who is over the flame is bound for Him whose face is hidden | and 151
who cannot see Him who conveys Osiris within[9] Orion. I am one who gives
commands for Rēʿ in the whole of the sky; I knit up the full Eye[10] and replace
the empty Eye.[11] GOING ABOARD THE BARK OF RĒʿ.

1. Barguet, *Livre des Morts,* 173, n. 4, considers the 'Great One' to mean celestial space.

2. Cf. *ḥnᶜ* 'Gefässe änfullen', *Wb.* III, 127,7–9. G1T reads *ḥnb.*

3. Var. *ḫsf* 'who repels'.

4. In B1Bo written like *syf* 'insult', *Wb.* IV, 37, 3; in B2Be the det. is borrowed from *ỉf* 'flesh'; in G1T there is no det. What the word means here remains obscure.

5. G1T has the best text. *Ḳmꜣw* of the other two texts, meaning doubtful, is in origin apparently a metathesis of *mꜣḳt* 'ladder' in G1T.

6. G1T again has the best text. The versions of neither B1Bo nor B2Be yield good sense.

7. Plural in B2Be; B1Bo: 'his brethren who are the helpers'.

8. All texts show the suffix *.k,* but there is no clue to whom it refers.

9. *M-ḫnw* in G1T. The other texts write *m ḥnt* as if *ḥnt* were a place-name, which makes no sense in this context; it could perhaps be an eccentric writing of *ḥnt* 'swamp', 'water-course'.

10. So G1T, certainly correctly; the other texts refer to 'lifting up (*ṯs*) their fullness'.

11. Here G1T has *šwt* 'the empty eye', with det. of a blank eye, where the other texts have the name of Shu. The rubric of G1T in 149*h* belongs to Spell 550.

Spell 552

O my[1] seat, ⌈my stool(?)⌉[2] and my throne, come and serve me, for I am your lord.[3] O you gods, come in my train, for ⟨I am⟩ the son of your lord;[4] [you are mine],[5] and it is my father[6] who will create you.

1. The corresponding BD Spell 47 is in the 1st person, which presumably is original.

2. Not in BD, which mentions only *st* and *nst.*

3. The *nṯr*-sign is a det. of *nb,* as commonly in the Lisht texts.

4. Reading ⟨*ỉnk*⟩ *sꜣ nb.ṯn,* cf. de Buck, n. 5* and *BD* 121,6.

5. Restored from *BD* 121,7.

6. In L2Li read *ỉn ỉt N pn* = *ỉn ỉt.ỉ* of *BD* 121,7.

Spell 553

VI, 152 Not to take a man's soul to the shambles of Shu.[1] Make offering before him, the Lord of conjuration(?),[2] who is on his throne, whom Maᶜet does not know, who is in charge of the affairs of his father's father, the Bull who attends(?)[3] his mother, who is on his standard, who makes the Great One hale.

O you four spirits who are in the shambles[4] whom my mother does not know, I know you, and I am not unaware of your names. If you do obeisance to me and

153 do this for me | which you do for those great ones who know you, there will come to me the great throne which Rēᶜ accepted for me and which the Lord of

the horizon founded for me.[5] I have come there so that I may get rid of what is wrong and save the thing which is right.

1. Var. B4C, in red: 'Not to fall into the shambles of Shu'.
2. A conjecture; cf. *šnt* 'conjuration, *Concise Dict.* 268; *šny* 'dispel' strife does not seem to fit the context.
3. The meaning of *hn* is not certain, but I have connected it with *hnn* in the sense of *Wb.* IV, 494,14.
4. Var. B1Bo: 'O you four who are in the West'.
5. See de Buck, n. 1*; *ṯ* and *t* appear to have been merged by haplography, the distinction between the two sounds having been lost. Read *šnṯt.n.*

Spell 554

Protection is [in] Shu, the great ones rejoice, those who are in the Presence are
content. Not to stir up fighting(?)[1] in Ōn, | for they have seen Shu bearing the VI, 154
mace;[2] he leads appearance in glory to him whom he wishes, he grants length
(of time) to the Enneads; he mixes[3] the voices(?) of those who are to come; he
divides the hours[4] and the dawns; he makes Rēʿ content with Right, and Shu,
the father of the gods, appears in glory with the river behind him in the flame of
the sunshine.[5]

I am strong as Shu is strong,[6] I am hale as Shu is hale,[7] I am beneath the
sky,[8] I strengthen its light, I command the bulls to be forgetful of the cows. Nūt
has lifted up every god on to my hands, and the masses are hale, the myriads are
content,[9] | they make life, welfare and health for me, for I am Shu of the 155
gods,[10] mine are sky and earth, mine are those who are in them, mine is God's-
land and I am the ruler, I am at my desire.[11]

1. *Tm* appears to be infinitive. *Ḫrwrw* is not recorded, and the translation of this passage rests on the context.
2. B2Bo less probably: 'the White Crown'.
3. *Sic,* but the real meaning is not clear.
4. B1Bo inserts a superfluous *n* before *wnwt.*
5. Following B2Bo; probably nothing is lost in the lacuna. B1Bo omits *ḥȝ.f m,* reading 'the river is the flame of the sunshine'. This may be an allusion to the Nile glittering in the sun.
6. B2Bo adds 'and *vice versa*'.
7. In B1Bo only.
8. B1Bo *ỉw nwt tn* only.
9. B2Bo adds obscurely *m ʿḏḏ ȝst.*

10. So B2Bo; B1Bo has here *ḥw nṯrw py N pn* 'it means that the gods proclaim N'.
11. Lit. 'upon this my heart'.

Spell 555

To be beside Thoth. I put dread into him who rages, I ward off[1] her who is warlike, I have struck with a knife, I calm him who is proscribed,[2] I have made an
VI, 156 amulet against[3] her who is warlike, | I have made the sharp knife which is in the hand of Thoth strong in him who rages.[4]

1. Surely so, despite the det. in B1Bo; 'satisfy' makes poor sense.
2. For *n3š* 'proscribe' cf. *Pyr.* §1279.
3. Lit. 'of', direct genitive.
4. B1Bo puts the title of the spell at the end.

Spell 556

O Osiris, Bull of the West at the head of the Great Ennead! Go down, N, and put the fear of you in the land, (even) your strength which is in the Netherworld. O N, go forth as Gēb, the chiefest of the gods; assume the White Crown of Horus,
VI, 157 for Thoth is at the head of the Conclave, the god himself is the spokesman(?).[1] | Osiris shoots at his foes, the Imperishable Stars will acclaim[2] him when they see the strengthening of N when he goes down into the Sacred Land as the god himself within . . .[3] 'Go to my father Osiris', says Horus ⟨who is over⟩ the blood(?) of the red bulls. The fledgeling(?) goes down,[4] and those who have gone to their doubles are in joy; the foes of Osiris are in confusion.[5] 'My son', says Osiris joyfully to Horus when he follows his father Osiris to the seats of the weary, according as the gods who are in the Presence commanded him[6] in the matter. May your sight be clear, O you who receive your head-cloths, may your garment
158 be donned when your sight is clear, | may you be anointed when meeting N;[7] may he go out from his house. Recite four times: O you who are vindicated against your foes, to whom someone comes preparing food-offerings, come in all your aspects; there is no member which will oppose you.[8]

1. *R3 rpˁ*, lit. 'mouth of the chief'.
2. Eccentric word-order; the object *hny* precedes the subject *ỉḫmw-sk* so that the stock expression *ỉr hny* should not be further split up, only the dative *n.f* intervening.
3. *ˁftt*, meaning unknown; I have collected examples of it in Spell 1034, n. 1 in Vol. III.

4. B2Bo adds obscurely *šm.n n.f* before *sbw*.

5. For *ḳmw* 'distress', 'confusion' cf. *CT* I, 26*c*; V, 176*j*.

6. *Wḏ* 'command' with direct object of the person is rare; the dative is the usual construction.

7. So B4Bo; the suffix *.ṯ* is probably a miswriting for *.ṯn*, carrying on the preceding sentences, though this is a woman's coffin. B2Bo has apparently, 'N smears on his ointment'.

8. Lit. 'approach you' with a nuance of opposition.

Spell 557

Ho N! Come, that you may see Osiris; the earth is hacked up for you, the offering is presented to you, reverence[1] is paid to you; it means that the king will come down.[2] O N, live and be a spirit[3] for ever in these your six festivals of eternity, that is (to say) the fourth-day and the eighth-day festivals, the *msyt* and the *wꜣg*, | the shouting festival and the festival of Sokar. VI, 159

Ho N! Come, that the diurnal ritual may be celebrated for you every day.

Ho N! The gods who are in the Netherworld and the august spirits[4] will ennoble you.

Ho N! The patricians will worship you and the plebs serve you.

1. For *sꜣ-tꜣ* 'reverence' see also *D.el B.* 114.

2. After *nsw* there is inserted a word *ṯn*, as also after *ꜥnḫ* in 158*l*, after *ꜣḫ* in 158*m* (B4Bo only) and after *špss* in 159*d*, which seems to have no bearing on the context and which is altogether obscure. Possibly it may be a notation for the use of a reciter.

3. See n. 2. above. *Sp sn* presumably refers to the obscure *ṯn*.

4. On *ṯn* see n. 2. above.

Spell 558

O Bull who are on your standard, O potter who are at your kiln,[1] do not come down on N, | for this is the Eye of Horus[2] which is within your grasp. VI, 160

1. Lit. 'tower'.

2. Var. BH2C: 'I am the Eye of Horus'.

Spell 559

TO JOIN THE RIVER-BANKS TOGETHER. Bring the Great One to the Great One,[1] join spirit with spirit,[2] bring the west bank that it may kiss the east bank, bring the east bank that it may kiss the west bank,[3] for it is the *îm3*-tree which joins the ascent to them.[4]

1. Presumably the two fem. 'Great Ones' refer respectively to the two banks; *n N* of B1Bo looks like an interpolation. Compare Spell 171.

2. *3ḫ* 'spirit' is masc. in three texts, but is fem. in BH1Ox, which is a woman's coffin. This text also has the var. 'bring spirit to spirit'.

3. 160*f-g* in BH1Ox only.

4. B1Bo omits the *n* of *n.sn.*

Spell 560

VI, 161 N is the dishevelled one, the son of Rēʿ who steers his bark. O Rēʿ, ⟨he⟩ is ferried across,[1] and he will neither perish nor be head downwards nor be destroyed, for N is Babi.

1. Read *d3.t⟨w.f⟩* with the suffix inadvertently omitted. BH3Ox has lost nearly all 161*d*, but appears to have had a somewhat different text.

Spell 561

N is *Rrt,* mistress of the *3tf*-crown, the one[1] who went to and fro on the folded cloth,[2] who purified himself on the folded cloth, to whom was sung loud-voiced acclamation,[3] because N is *Rrt,* mistress of the *3tf*-crown; to him belongs acclamation and reverence, to him is sung acclamation and reverence. JOINING THE FERRY-BOATS IN THE REALM OF THE DEAD.

1. This refers to the deceased; the gender is masculine.

2. Cf. *Eg. Gramm.*[3] Sign-list S29; hardly the objects of *Urk.* IV, 631, 13.15.

3. So B1Bo, lit. 'acclamation by shouting'; the *m* is doubled, surely in error. BH3Ox has *hny m s3-t3* 'acclamation by reverence.

Spell 562

The hair of Isis is knotted to the hair of Nephthys, the myriads who fled(?) are united,[1] and he who reaches the *ḫns*-water has taken possession of the union of the Two Lands. The western bank is joined with the eastern, and they are closed together and (then) divided, while I have passed by so that I may take what belongs to the west to the east, and that I may bring what belongs to the east to the west. I have come so that I may be joined to the two Sisters and be merged in[2] the two Sisters, for they will never die.[3] I am he who joins the river-banks together. JOINING TOGETHER THE RIVER-BANKS BY A MAN AT WHICHEVER PLACE HE WISHES. VI, 162

1. Reading *dmḏ ḥḥw bṯw; dmḏ* is miswritten.
2. For *ꜣbḫ* as a transitive verb cf. *CT* III, 294*g*; VII, 275*c*; the latter is closer to the present meaning.
3. *Mn* is taken as a writing of *mny* 'die'. The det. is borrowed from varr. of *mny* 'jar', *Concise Dict.* 107.

Spell 563

I am a Great One whose name is unknown; the ram-gods are my soul, the Khnum-gods are my shades, I am the Lord of Right who loves what is good. I will not be head downwards among those who are head downwards, I will make marches afoot like Nefertum, I will snuff the air with my nose like Khons the ruler of provisions,[1] I will see a path with the vision of my eye[2] like the Sistrum-player, the son of Ḥatḥōr, her beloved.

1. Cf. Posener, *ZÄS* 93, 118, n. 38.
2. Read probably *m mꜣw ỉrt.ỉ.*

Spell 564

NOT TO FALL INTO THE SHAMBLES OF THE GOD. This is Osiris, the West [. . .] if he knows his name, Osiris will know his name. Not [. . .] I will [not] be in it, for I am Seth who is among the gods, and I will not perish. VI, 163

Spell 565

NOT[1] TO PERMIT A MAN TO BE JUDGED WITH A FOE IN THE REALM OF THE DEAD.
VI, 164 I will not be judged in the lower year(?)[2] which Thoth has fostered. | The . . .[3] the Ennead are in my power(?). As for the judgement with me by Gēb,[4] you shall tread (the steps of) the two thrones[5] and the donkey(?)[6] shall plough. You shall not strike at me, you shall not give orders against me, for it is Gēb who hears this case. I have crossed *'Iȝsw,*[7] and I am the finger[8] of Thoth, the Lord of All. HAVING JUDGEMENT BY A MAN WITH A FOE IN THE REALM OF THE DEAD.[9]

1. *Sic*; the exact opposite of the rubric at the end of the spell in B1Bo. Here in B4C only.
2. An obscure expression, perhaps referring to the year to come.
3. *Ttḫ*, meaning unknown.
4. A miswriting of the name of Gēb; again in 164*f.*
5. Read *hb.kȝ*⟨*.ỉ*⟩.
6. See de Buck, n. 1*.
7. So B1Bo. *'Iȝsw* is a part of the sky, cf. *Komm. Pyr.* III, 303. BH3Ox has *'Iȝsw-ḫw* with det. of a pillared hall(?).
8. Dual in BH3Ox, probably a misreading of the finger-sign with following stroke.
9. In B1Bo only.

Spell 566

NOT TO LET A MAN'S HEART SIT DOWN AGAINST HIM IN THE REALM OF THE DEAD.
VI, 165 I stand up[1] in the Island of Fire[2] so that I may be vindicated; | those who examine are under me,[3] so that your two columns and your two pillars do not watch me, O Rēꜥ. I raise myself between them,[4] they stand up and my hair stands up,[5] and my two Fledgelings are upside down.[6] I am one who does what is right, and what I detest is wrongdoing to Atum, There is no obstructor[7] who will harm me, there is no obstructor who will pursue me.[8]

1. B4C has the *sḏm.n.f* form; B1Bo is probably *sḏm.f,* as is BH2C.
2. So B4C; the other texts have 'in the horizon'.
3. So B1Bo; BH2C: 'I examine myself for my double'; BH3Ox: 'He examines himself for the doubles'.
4. 165*c* and *d* are manifestly corrupt and have been emended to agree with *CT* V, 251*c-e,* of which they are a bungled version. For the first part of 165*c* read *wṯs.ỉ wỉ ỉmt.sny,* cf. V, 251*c.*
5. Emend into *šn.ỉ ꜥḥꜥ* as V, 251*e.*
6. Emend into *ṯȝwy.ỉ sḫdḫd,* cf. V, 251*d.*
7. For *ỉmy-rd* 'obstructor' cf. *Pyr.* §§2232; 2291.
8. This full version in B1Bo only.

Spell 567

The god has gone forth against his foe in the realm of the dead.[1] O Arm-swallow- VI, 166
er, prepare a path for me, for I am Rēꜥ; I have gone up from the horizon against
my foe. He has [harmed(?)][2] me, but he will not save himself from me.[3] I have
directed my arm as the Great Lord, I have extended my feet as one who is ever in
glory, I will not be allowed to fall.[4] He[5] has been given to me, and he will not be
taken from me. I have given greetings here to Him who dwells in the sky [and(?)][6]
greetings to the great *ḫꜣyt*-tree,[7] and He who is in his *ḫꜣyt* hears this plaint of
mine,[8] and he who is in [the sky(?)] is commanded to permit me to go out 167
against my foe; he has been given to me, and he will not be taken from me.

1. B4C has a damaged rubric; '[Causing] a woman [to go forth] against her foe by day in the realm of the dead'.

2. It is difficult to complete the lacuna owing to the small space; *ỉw.f ỉr.f r.ỉ* 'he has acted against me' would make sense but would take up too much room.

3. Clearly omission of negative and confusion of pronouns here; read ⟨*n*⟩ *nḥm.f sw mꜥ.ỉ* 'he will not save himself from me'; *mꜥ.ỉ* at the end is confirmed by *mꜥ.s* of B4C, which has lost the preceding text. Compare 166*k*; 167*b*.

4. B4C had a longer text (166*h-k*) of which a good deal is lost.

5. The foe.

6. Restore *ḥnꜥ* in the lacuna? There is room enough, though the traces shown by de Buck, n. 4* do not suit.

7. 'Tree' of S10C seems more likely than 'garment' of B4C.

8. S10C has only *ỉwꜥ.ỉ pn* 'this heir of mine' in 166*m*, which does not make sense. The copyist in the scriptorium appears to have been misled by *ỉw* 'plaint' of B4C.

Spell 568

Stand up, O Power, and meet Gēb,[1] for your faces are spirits, and the power of Seth is brought to naught.

1. So S10C and B1Bo; B4C less intelligibly: 'Shu stands with his face as Gēb'.

Spell 569

THAT A MAN MAY HAVE POWER OVER HIS FOES. The power of the Hidden One VI, 168
acts as proxy for me, Ptaḥ stands up for me,[1] my champion is Thoth, his strength

is in my arm,[2] his might is in my mouth,[3] I have taken possession of the might of
169 Atum;[4] | I go on my feet, my speech is in my mouth when I smite[5] my foes, I
have come against yonder foe of mine,[6] who has been given to me,[7] and he will
not be taken from me; I have power over him.[8]

1. Var. B4C: 'N [has stood up] as Horus, she has sat down as Ptaḥ'. Compare *BD* 32, 10–11. For the 1st person see S10C.

2. B1Bo[b] alone inserts *šm.f* 'he goes' before this clause, which is lacking from three versions.

3. Var. B4C: 'her might is in her hand'.

4. B4C has *nḥm* for *i͗ṯ*; S10C has *wsr.i͗* for *wsr 'Itm*; B1Bo[b] is corrupt. B1Bo[c] has *nb tm* 'Lord of All' for 'Atum'.

5. B4C has *ḥḥ* 'seek' for *ḥw* 'smite'.

6. Only in S10C and B1Bo[c].

7. B1Bo[a] adds 'in the tribunal'.

8. So B1Bo[b]; B1Bo[a] has: 'what he has given to him is the strength of N'. For 169*e-h* S10C and B1Bo[c] substitute in 169*i*: 'he has come to an end under me'.

Spell 570

VI, 170 The door of the cavern of those who are in the Abyss is opened,[1] the cold waters
of those who are in the sunshine are thrown open for you,[2] O Far-Strider, whose
legs fare far.[3] Prepare a path for him who trembles.[4]

1. B1Bo omits *ꜥꜣ* 'door' and substitutes a superfluous *ṯ*.

2. B1Bo: 'the movements of the sunshine are thrown open', possibly under the influence of 170*c*. In S10C, for *n.ṯ* after *sn* read *n.k* (man's coffin).

3. Lit. 'whose knees are extended'; S10C has omitted the *d* of *dwn*.

4. B1Bo adds: 'he will fall, having trembled', forgetting that here the trembler is the deceased himself and not a foe of the deceased.

Spell 571

TO BUILD A MANSION AMONG THE WATERS. The Nile is uncovered, those who
are on the river-banks are joyfully united, the crocodile-gods are happy, Neith is
VI, 171 content, | the Wine-press god and Sokar foremost in *Pḏw-š* are over the distribution
of offerings, and they are happy and content when they see that this mansion of
mine[1] is founded among the waters and among their mansions, that their pools
are dug and their trees planted, while Sokar belongs to Rostau.[2] Thousands are

their houses,[3] tens of thousands are their trees, hundreds of thousands are their
plots.[4] It is the Nile-god who brings it[5] barley, it is the Fen-goddess who brings
it fowl, it is the crocodile-gods who catch fish for it, it is Sakhmet who is in her
year who brings it herds for this mansion of mine, | it is Donkey-face who is upon 172
the polar sky[6] who brings ships to this mansion of mine. The Winepress god is in
its garden, Sokar foremost in *Pḏw-š* is its treasurer, Sokar of Rostau[7] is my
steward, and he has reckoned up the property in it; he has brought good things,
and he has heaped up the altar-chambers for this mansion of mine.

O men, O spirits, O dead, rejoice and be glad when you[8] see this mansion of
mine which is among the waters. O sheriff, [. . .] are brought for it and riches
heaped up for it by *Fnfn* the ferryman who puts ashore for me at this mansion of
mine among the waters, and he has found Seth in it with his staff in his hand
subduing the patricians [for] me; the Winepress god tells him the names,[9] and the
gods see me when giving me praise. It means that he is pleased with me when I
enter to him, and it means that he is vexed with me if I do not enter into him. The
Nile-god has given me my villages and the sea is for my seat | on which I sit, and a 173
thousand men are seated on the river-banks of Sais. (As for) the scribe of the
mansions among the waters, if it be that what goes out from [my mouth(?)
is][10] what goes out from the mouth of the scribe of your (*sic*) tribunal, this man-
sion of mine will be built and my voice will pass through it, so that they will bring
to me fields, people, barley of Upper Egypt, emmer and herds; its trees will be
planted, its pools will be dug and its towers set up. But if I be forbidden and my
desire to build it be not granted,[11] the mansions will be burned down,[12] the
lower mansions will be wholly thrown down, [. . .] will be trampled under
foot(?)[13] on the great plain. If something be said over the waters, or if something
be broken over the Nile,[14] this mansion of mine among the waters will be thrown
down, but you shall turn back your hand when I announce the building to you.[15]

As for these mansions among the waters of sky and earth, if my wish to 174
come to them[16] be not granted, sky and earth will be trodden down,[17] the
ḥbnnt[18] which is in front of the house of Nefertum will be trodden down, the
hands of . . . the daughter of *Ḫꜥkws* will be trodden down,[19] the . . .[20] of Neith
will be trodden down . . .[21] . Haste you about it, stop it; see, I have told you.

1. For the 1st person cf. 173*r*; 174*g*.

2. [hieroglyph] of B1Bo is an error for [hieroglyph] of S10C; so also 172*d*; 291*l*.

3. S10C has *ỉw snwt m pr.sn* 'the sisters are in their house', a corruption arising from confusion of hieratic [hieroglyph] and [hieroglyph].

4. Var. S10C: *šnwt* 'hundreds'.

5. The mansion of the deceased.

6. Cf. *Komm. Pyr.* III, 393; For the det. 𓈋 cf. *BD* 284, 7; 'necropolis plateau', *GNS* 30, is less likely in a 'ship' context.

7. See n. 2 above.

8. Note the use of the suffix of the 3rd person plural in referring back to a vocative; in English the use of the 2nd person is unavoidable.

9. Whose names? Perhaps of the gods next to be mentioned.

10. Restoring as *ỉr wn pr m* [*rꜣ.ỉ*].

11. For *n wḏ.tw* 'be forbidden' cf. *Westc.* 8, 17. *N wḏ.t⟨w⟩.f* and *n rdy.t⟨w⟩ ỉb.f* are virtual conditional clauses in the negative, but lacking the particle *ỉs* (*Eg. Gramm.*[3] §216, end) so also 174*a*.

12. Cf. *znznt* 'conflagration', *Pyr.* §§292; 1876, in the latter case determined with a town in flames.

13. The verb *sḥsḥ* is not recorded. The absence of the passive ending *.tw* may be due to damage. *Wꜥrt* at the end of 173*o* can hardly refer here to the polar region.

14. *Ḏd* and *sḏ* seem to be impersonal passive *sḏm.f* in virtual conditional clauses.

15. I.e. you shall cease your damage when I announce the building of the mansion, but it is not clear who 'you' may be.

16. For *r.s* read *r.sn*; the pronoun refers to the 'mansions' of 173*r*.

17. Read *hb.kꜣ⟨.tw⟩*; the passive ending has been omitted; so too in 174*b*.

18. The name of an offering-cake, cf. *Pyr.* § 94; *CT* I, 169*i*.

19. On *hb.kꜣ* see n. 17 above. The beings named are quite obscure, and I cannot read the first name.

20. The loss of the determinative makes the meaning obscure.

21. I can make nothing of the end of 174*e*.

Spell 572

SPELL FOR BRINGING A MAN'S [MAGIC] TO HIM IN THE REALM OF THE DEAD. O you porters of Horus who bring the magic of Horus to him as his great protec-
VI, 175 tion,[1] | bring[2] the magic of Horus to him as his great protection, and bring this magic of mine to me wherever I may be;[3] tell me what I should know and what I should forget; examine and heal(?),[4] so that you may bring the Eye of Horus to him,[5] the foes of which[6] fell into the fire, the foes of which[7] were firmly fixed [on] the fire, the foes of which were firmly fixed[8] by reason of its cords.
176 'O magic of mine, come to me!' | My mouth is aware and my lips have said, 'Come at this my wish!' See, this mouth of mine is concerned with my desire,[9] and my hand is pure when it receives it, (namely) what should be in it; my heart is not ignorant of its place, and it is firm on its base(?).[10] I know my name, I am not ignorant of it, I will be among those who follow after Osiris, together with those

who are in the Suite, those who are attached to the chambers of Osiris, and those who are on (the steps of) the throne in the secret chamber.

For 176a ff. (M9C) BIBo substitutes (176k ff.) the following much damaged text, of which the first part (176k-n) continues the 'magic' theme, while 176o-p seems to be part of a spell copied from a woman's coffin; note the fem. suffixes. 176q perhaps reverts to the original theme, but the traces are few and doubtful.

[. . .] he will give you to Rēʿ, for he knows [you],[11] and the Great Lady who is in [. . .]; I [will put(?)] my magic and [my] power in the heart of [. . .]. You (*fem. sing.*) shall not turn back[12] the Great Lady who is with the Angry One(s) [. . .] you (*fem.*) shall fare upstream [to the mansion of][13] the Great Lady. [. . .] magic(?) to me [. . .].

1. For 174*i-j* M28C has *ỉnw ḥkꜣw ỉpw n Ḥr*, etc., 'O you who bring this magic of Horus to him as his protection'.
2. Reading *ỉn n.ṯn*, imperative with reflexive dative, cf. 175*b* (BIBo).
3. In 175*b* both M9C and M28C are introduced by *sk*, which here appears to serve as a simple conjunction. M28C has *n.k* instead of *n.ṯn*, and has moved the dative *n.ỉ* to its normal position, incidentally with the suffix of the 1st person, which is confirmed by 175*e.f.k*; 176*a* ff. On the other hand, it puts *bw ntf ỉm.f* in the 3rd person, thus displaying that confusion of pronouns endemic in the Coffin Texts.
4. The interpretation of *ỉp sḏꜣw* is doubtful; I have taken them as further imperatives addressed to the porters of Horus and have guessed *sḏꜣw* to be a bungled writing of *swḏꜣ* 'make healthy'. M9C omits 175*c* and after *ỉp sḏꜣ* reads in 175*e-f rḫ.n.ỉ [rḫt.n.ỉ(?)] sḫꜣ.n.ỉ smḫ.n.ỉ* 'I know [what I should know(?)] and I recall what I had forgotten', which is a substitute for 175*c* (BIBo). M28C has (175*f*) *d.n.ỉ sḫꜣ n* [. . .] 'I have placed the memory of [. . .]' and stops.
5. M9C: *my ỉp [sḏꜣ ỉrt Ḥr(?)] n.f*; the suggested restoration is by no means certain.
6. Of the Eye.
7. Restore as *smnt nkyw.s ḥr sḏt*.
8. Read *smnt nkyw.s*, cf. M9C.
9. For *šsp n ỉb* 'wish', 'desire' (n.) cf. *CT* III, 199*h*.
10. Cf. *mkꜣt* 'basis', *Wb.* II, 162, 13. The det. looks like a stela standing on a foundation slab.
11. Restoring as *sṯ rḫ.n.f ṯw*.
12. For *sḥn* 'turn back' cf. CT I, 310*g*; *Wb.* IV, 219, 3. The construction is *n sḏm.n.f*.
13. See de Buck, n. 12*.

Spell 573[1]

VI, 177 TO TAKE SHAPE [. . .].[2]

The sky is overcast,
The stars are darkened,
The celestial expanses quiver,
The bones of the earth-gods tremble.
The planets(?) are stilled,
Which see me ascending and exalted
As this god, Lord of myriads,
Who lives on offerings,
Whom Osiris has equipped.
I am Rēʿ, the sole jackal in the sky,
Whose mother knows not his name.
My power is in the horizon,
My glory is in the sky,
Like Rēʿ-Atum my father who begot me;
He gave me[3] his soul,
He [gave] me his power,
And I am indeed a spirit.
178 My magic is about me,
My . . . are under my feet,[4]
The gods are on me,
My uraei are on my brow,
My guiding serpent is on my vertex,
My soul has looked in the flame,
And it is licked up.
It is I who have acquired his powers,[5]
I am the Bull of the sky
Who conquers(?) at will,[6]
Who lives on the beings of the gods,
And who feeds on hearts and magic;
(Even of) those who come ⟨with⟩ their bodies full of magic
From the Island of Fire.
Those who are in the celestial expanses serve me,
And I have appeared among them as a god,
A possessor of helpers.
I sit with my back to Gēb
At the head of the Two Conclaves,[7]
For it is I who will give judgement
In company with Him whose name is hidden
On that night of slaying the Oldest Ones.
179 I am a Lord of men who lives on the gods,
I am one who himself prepares his meal.
It is Destroyer-of-messages who resides in *Kḥꜣsn*

Who lassoes their magicians for me;[8]
It is He who uses his hand
Who binds them for me;
It is He who is over the blood-offering(?)
Who guards them for me,[9]
And extracts for me what is in their bodies;
It is my messenger Khons
Who is sent against him who would oppose;
It is the Winepress god, red of timbers,[10]
Who slaughters them for me
And who cooks for me a portion of them
On his evening hearth-stones.
The Chaos-gods are chewed,
The sun-folk are swallowed,
The new moon circulates under them.[11]
It is the Great of heart in the north of the sky
Who makes ready the cauldrons for me against them
On account of the legs of their women.[12]
The fire is put to the cauldrons for me,
And a portion of them is cooked for me 180
From the thighs of the spirits which are among them.
Their big ones are for my night meal,
Their little ones are for my morning meal,
Their middle-sized ones are for my supper,
Their old ones are for my hearth-stones.
I am a Power more powerful than the gods,
I have circumambulated all the two skies,
I have gone all over the sky, the earth and the river-banks,
I have appeared among the Powers who are in the horizon,
And him whom I found in my way,
Him I devoured piecemeal(?).
See me, men and gods![13]
I have appeared as one older than the Old Ones,
I have reappeared in the sky,
I am crowned in the realm of the horizon. 181
Men offer to me with myriads of caught fish(?),[14]
I have eaten of the hearts of the gods,
I have cut off the baboons(?) and their vertebrae,
I have eaten of the Green One,
I have gulped down the Red One,[15]
I have become a spirit by means of the . . . of the Red Crown,[16]
And there are no potentates who shall act by destroying
My favourite place in the whole of the Two Lands.[17]
I eat of their magic,
I gulp down their powers,
My strength in me is more than theirs.
Their powers are within me,
Their souls are with me, 182

Their shades are with their lords,
Their magic is in my belly,[18]
The Great Lady who dwells in the plain of the Silent Ones stands firm for me,
And I have fished them[19] up.
It is the star which rules[20] in the east of the sky
Which brings to me;
. . . of their catch-nets,[21]
My father's daughter being among them;[22]
Skilful is he who knows
How to cut up caught fish,[23]
Being what went forth from it.[24]
183 The meat for me is for my breakfast today,[25]
The meat of the morning's slaughtering.[26]
I am Rēʿ of this day;
My father Rēʿ is [. . .].[27]

TO EAT THE MAGICIANS, ALL OF THEM.

1. This spell is a later version of the so-called 'Cannibal Hymn', *Pyr.* Utt. 273–4. It is a classic example of what can happen to a text in the course of transmission, and it is translated here as it stands in CT.

2. So S1C; S2C has 'Spell for magic [. . .].'

3. The dative *n.ỉ* only in S2C.

4. With 178*a* compare *Pyr.* §396*a*; *kꜣw* 'powers' has become *ḥkꜣw* 'magic', and the obscure word *ḥmwst* has been distorted into the meaningless *ḥnwt.s* 'her mistress'.

5. Not in Pyr. The antecedent of 'his' is not clear, it can hardly refer to the deceased's own soul.

6. Reading *kꜣ pt nhd m ỉb.f* with *Pyr.* §397*a*. *Nh m ỉb.f* 'who escapes in his heart' of S1C makes no sense, and [*n*]*hm ỉb.f* 'whose heart shouts' of S2C is not much better.

7. Not in Pyr.

8. Corrupted out of *Pyr.* §401*a*.

9. With 179*d-e* compare Pyr. §401*b-c*. *Ṯrwt* is perhaps better translated 'blood-offering' than 'reddening' of my published translation, cf. *ṯr* 'blood', *Pyr.* §§451; 1263.

10. With the pressed-out grape-juice? This epithet of *Šsmw* is not in Pyr.

11. 179*j-k* are a substitute for *Pyr.* §§403*c*-404*d*.

12. 179*l-m* is a thoroughly corrupted version of *Pyr.* §§405*a*-406*b*.

13. Not in Pyr.

14. *Wdn* in 181*b* is perhaps impersonal *sḏm.f*; taken thus it yields a better sense than would the *sḏm.n.f* form *wdn.n.ỉ*. The last sign in 181*b* is perhaps a bungled version of the skeleton of a fish, cf. 182*h* and n. 23 below. This passage is not in Pyr.

15. With 181*a* compare *Pyr.* §§409*a*-410*a*.

16. Here a new text G2T appears. 181*g* is a garbled version of *Pyr.* §411*a*. *Šbw* with these dets. is not recorded.

17. Cf. *Pyr.* §414*b-c*.

18. With 181*k*-182*b* compare *Pyr.* §413*c*; 182*c* = §411*b*, , second clause. The rest of the

spell has no connection with Pyr.

19. The Silent Ones?

20. For the verb *srỉ*, derived from *sr* 'magistrate', cf. *CT* I, 324*b*.

21. Incomprehensible; *wꜥw*, var. *ꜣꜥw*, apparently with fish-det., is entirely obscure, as is the reference of the suffix *.sn* after *ỉꜣdt*; that this last is indeed the word for 'net' is indicated by the curl imposed on the det. in G2T, which implies something of cord. See also 182*h* below.

22. *Sic.*

23. Reading *ỉḳr ỉrḫ ḥsḳ ḏsf* with S1C; *ḏsf* with det. of fish-skeleton(?) appears to be connected with *ḏsf* 'catch' fish, *CT* VI, 20*d*; *BD* 392, 13; 394, 10.

24. I.e. what was taken from the net; *ỉꜣdt* is the only available antecedent for the fem. sing. suffix in *ỉm.s*. *Prt* appears to be a vague neuter.

25. Reading *ỉf n.ỉ n ỉꜥꜥw.ỉ nw hrw pn* with S2C.

26. So S1C.

27. S2C only.

Spell 574

[NOT] TO GO HEAD DOWNWARDS, SO THAT A MAN MAY HAVE POWER IN HIS LEGS.[1] VI, 184
I have hacked up the sky,[2] I have opened up the horizon, I have passed through[3] the sunshine, I have trodden out its movements, I have taken possession of the powers of those who were older than I,[4] because I am a spirit whom his myriad equipped.[5] I eat with my mouth, I defecate with my hinder parts, because I am a god, Lord of the Netherworld, and there have been given to me those things which were established in the past.[6] GOING YESTERDAY, RETURNING TOMORROW, SO THAT A MAN MAY HAVE POWER IN HIS LEGS IN EVERY PLACE WHERE HE DESIRES TO BE.[7]

1. So S1C; var. B4C: 'Going out into the day, so that a man may have power'.
2. B4C: 'the sky is hacked up'; *BD* 31, 2 has *šd.n.ỉ pt.*
3. Read *šꜣs* as in the next clause.
4. B4C: 'of the Old Ones'.
5. B4C: 'because it was she whom her myriad equipped with magic'.
6. Cf., however, de Buck's n. 3*.
7. S1C only.

Spell 575

O Gēb, Bull of the sky, prepare a way for me[1] on this path of yours, for I am VI, 185
Horus, the heir of my father Osiris. I am one who goes and returns,[2] I am the

fourth of the spirits who bring water,[3] who administer purification, who have
186 rejoiced in the strength of their fathers; I desire to be vindicated by what I have done.[4] I the orphan have had judgement with the orphaness,[5] Maᶜet has ⟨judged⟩,[6] Shu was witness.[7] I have collected the thrones of Gēb for him, and
187 his souls which were in the Abyss are united. I put a stop to the affair in Ōn, for I go forth today in the real form of a living spirit, so that I may break up the fight, cut off the turbulent ones, and search out [Maᶜet], who is with those who bring the sunshine.[8]

188 I inherit from[9] Atum the throne of Horus the Elder; my refuge is my Eye, my protection is my Eye, my strength is my Eye, my power is my Eye,[10] and I have seen the gods bowing in the haze(?)[11] of the fiery breath of my mother
189 Ernūtet, and she has struck(?) their hearts.[12] Come to me, my mother, my mother, for I am the *alter ego* of my father,[13] the toothless one of my mother;[14] I detest travelling in darkness, for then I cannot see those who are upside down.
190 I go out into the day in my true shape of a living spirit, so that I may bring Maᶜet, and she will be with me; I will not be given to my shroud(?),[15] for I am with you,[16] you gods.[17]

[. . .] I turn[18] to you, you gods, at [. . .] I go out into the day, I come and go, and he who is in [. . .] as the lower . . .[19]

1. For the 1st person see various passages below. Compare *Pyr.* Utt. 260.

2. B4C: 'I am your son [. . .].

3. For 'water' B3Bo^b has *ntt,* an error for the old word *nt.*

4. Compare *Pyr.* §316*d,* which also was originally in the 1st person. The two B3Bo texts have unaccountably introduced the 2nd person here.

5. Reading *wḏᶜ.n.ỉ tfn ḥnᶜ tfnt,* cf. *Pyr.* §317*a.* All three extant CT texts have misunderstood *tfn,* the two B3Bo texts reading respectively *rn.f* and *rn.s* and thus making nonsense of the passage; B4C has read *dfn dfnt,* omitting *ḥnᶜ.* On this passage cf. Sethe, *Komm. Pyr.* I, 398 ff.

6. The B3Bo texts have both omitted *sḏm,* cf. loc. cit. The traces in S2C come from a different text.

7. Certainly so here, though in *Pyr.* §317*b* the absence of det. has led to a different translation of *šw.*

8. Var. B4C: 'and bring Maᶜet who is with those who are in the sunshine, for she is with [me]'.

9. For this sense of *ỉwᶜ* cf. *ỉwᶜw Gb nsyt tꜣwy* 'who (i.e. Osiris) inherits from Gēb the kingship of the Two Lands', *RB* 111,4–5. 187*e-f* is not in Pyr., and after it there comes a long insertion in S2C which is almost entirely destroyed. Since this appears not to be part of the original spell, which resumes at 188*c* = *Pyr.* §320*a,* it is assumed to be an interpolation. All that can be made of it is: 'I go out into the day in my [true] shape [of a living spirit]' in 187*h*; cf. 190*a*.

10. Of the four texts only B3Bo is intact, and that is corrupt; moreover, none of the four are in agreement with each other, but all descend from *Pyr.* §320. To make sense of the passage I have used the Pyr. text in the translation.

11. Lit. 'bleariness' of vision, *Concise Dict.* 163, here perhaps thought of as 'haziness' induced by the fiery breath of the goddess. With this clause and the next compare *Pyr.* §321*b.c.*

12. Here follows a damaged interpolation in B4C which reads: 'do not go down [. . .] from whom he saved N'.

13. With 189*d* compare *Pyr.* §322*b,* which confirms the reading *ḏsḏs* (lit. 'self self') of B4C; *ḏḥḏḥ* of B3Bo is a misreading of *ḏsḏs.*

14. For *ḫ3bw* 'toothless' cf. *Pyr.* §225; apparently the deceased sees himself as a newly born baby. *Byby* of S2Chass. cannot be explained; for the stem cf. *Wb.* I, 442, 9.10.

15. Cf. the textile *mnyt* in *Urk.* I, 294,16; 296,9.

16. With the last two sentences compare *Pyr.* §323*b.c.*

17. 190*d-e* only in B3Bo and B4C, which ends the spell. The two S2 texts substitute the damaged 190*f-h,* which is not represented in Pyr.

18. For *ỉnn* 'turn about' cf. *CT* I, 306*a.*

19. Quite obscure.

Spell 576[1]

Copulating[2] by a man in the realm of the dead. My eyes are the lion, my phallus is Babi, I am the Outcast,[3] seed is in my mouth, my head is in the sky, my head is on earth. I am one having power in my heart, mine is . . . , mine are . . . ;[4] I am one who ejaculates when he knits together(?),[5] I ejaculate seed as that one and this one.[6] AS FOR ANY MAN WHO SHALL KNOW THIS SPELL, HE SHALL COPULATE IN THIS LAND BY NIGHT AND BY DAY, AND DESIRE SHALL COME TO THE WOMAN BENEATH HIM WHENEVER HE COPULATES. TO BE RECITED OVER A BEAD OF CARNELIAN OR OF AMETHYST, TO BE PLACED ON THE RIGHT ARM OF THE DECEASED. VI, 191

1. Cf. Müller, *Orientalia,* 35 (1966), 260 f.; Zandee, *ZÄS* 90 (1963), 153f.

2. Despite the det., the context makes the meaning of *nhp* quite clear.

3. I.e. Seth. The name is omitted in B1P.

4. The strange sign may read not *b3* (Müller) but *ỉdr,* cf. *Eg. Gramm.*[3] Sign-list V37. In 403*f* below it seems not to read *b3,* cf. 403*k.* Zandee translates as 'die Macht', 'die Mächte'; I do not venture on a translation, for to me the word is quite obscure.

5. The meaning of *ṯs.f* is not clear; I have taken it as referring to the union of man and woman. Müller translates as 'Ich bin ein Erzeuger'; Zandee as 'Ich ergeisse meinen Sprüch aus'.

6. B1Be omits the *m* of B1P before *pf pn*; since these are both masculines, *m* can hardly mean 'into', and I take it to imply similarity.

Spell 577

VI, 192 I will go out into the day against my foe and I will have power over him, for he has been given to me and he will not be taken from me, he will be put to an end under me in the Tribunal. The Great Mound (*sic*) which is on the sceptre of the gods has given him to me;[1] he is (doomed) to my finger-nails as to a fierce lion,
193 he is (doomed) to the palm of my hand as to a crocodile; prepare a path for me so that I may fetch my foe. I am Osiris as one who covers up his seat[2] while the Foremost of the Westerners is giving heads; I am a possessor of blood[3] in the days which have come into being; I am the Lord of them of the sharp knives, and I will not be robbed.

A path is prepared for me in front of the temple; I will enwrap those who are in the date-palm(?)[4], there will be brought to me what appertains to the great Red Crown and the great Red Crown will be given to me; it will be granted that I go out into this day against my foe[5] so that I may fetch him and have power over him.

THIS BOOK WAS UNDER THE FLANK OF KHNUM.[6]

It is at an end.

1. So B1Be, B5C and B1P^b. Var. B1L: 'the path of the greatest of the gods has given him to me'; B2L: 'the path of the Great Lady has given him to me'. Both these texts end here; B1P^a ends in 192*a*.

2. Possibly in the sense of occupying it.

3. Or 'of wrath'.

4. Cf. *CT* VII, 355*h*.

5. Singular, despite the plural strokes, cf. the sing. pronouns in 193*l.m*.

6. An indication of the miraculous origin of the spell. On the reading of the god's name see de Buck, n. 4*.

Spell 578

VI, 194 WHAT IS TO BE WRITTEN ON THE FACE. . . .[1] the inertness of this face of yours. How mysterious is he whom you see when he glances to and fro![2] I am Horus, I have come that I may speak on your behalf, O my father. I am[3] a Great One, the son of a Great one. THIS SPELL IS TO BE WRITTEN WITHIN (*sic*) THE FACE OF THE HIDDEN ONE,[4] BEING A SECRET OF THE GREAT LECTOR.

1. *Ḥw* with this det. is obscure; the whole of this spell is difficult to understand.

2. In *M.u.K.* 1, 9.10 *ḥnmnm* with 'legs' det. means 'creep'; used of eyes it may refer to 'looking about'. The stem *nmnm* implies to-and-fro movement, cf. *Pyr.* §§1120; 1771; *BD* 289,5.

3. The deceased.

4. The deceased again.

Spell 579

Sky and earth are cleared, the . . .[1] tremble in sky and earth, for it is you[2] who speak to me, O Repellent-of-visage.[3] Get back! Go away because of this White Crown who herself caused the Nubian(?) to be born, (even) he who raised up the gods in . . .[4] Who is he who will complete a coil and ennoble the god in the morning? I will break[5] the stranger who will come to meet me. TO DRIVE OFF 'TAKER-OF-FACES'.

1. *Šwrwrw ty*; reading uncertain and meaning unknown; *ty* could perhaps stand for *ỉty* 'father' as in 194*f*.
2. Apparently *ḥsf-ḥr* below.
3. The translation of this epithet is not certain.
4. 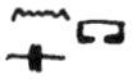; possibly a miswriting of *pr-nsr*.
5. Reading *sḏ⟨.ỉ⟩ ỉr⟨.ỉ⟩*.

Spell 580

NOT TO WALK HEAD DOWNWARDS. Get you back, you who are made to fly and VI, 195
you who are made to grow! – and *vice versa*. [Do not] descend[1] upon me.[2] The house of Ḥemen is sealed(?)[3] and I will not eat faeces or drink urine for you;[4] I will live on the two *ḫnmt*-loaves which are issued from upon the altar of Rēʿ. It is this she-monkey[5] who will take to me what is in the house of the she-tortoise(?);[6] it is the god of the flood who will set it down for me, for Khnum, for Rēʿ-Atum and for the Enneads, and I will not eat faeces, I will not drink urine, I will not receive with my hands, I will not stamp[7] for you with my feet, I will live[8] on what Horus of the earth lives on, I will not walk head downwards for you.

1. See de Buck, n. 1*.
2. For the original 1st person cf. 195*j*, where we must read *wnm ⟨.ỉ⟩ ḥs swr ⟨.ỉ⟩ wsšt*.
3. Miswriting of *sḏꜣy*? *Stꜣy* with this det. is not recorded.

4. Plural, referring to the beings named in 195*b*.

5. On the monkey *gf* cf. Caminos, *L.-Eg. Misc.* 442.

6. *Štṯwt*; possibly a miswriting of *šṯwt* 'female tortoise'.

7. For *tyty* 'stamp' see also *BD* 436,1; the word is used also of a trotting horse, Caminos, op. cit. 602.

8. The negation in 195*m* is clearly in error and has been ignored in the translation.

Spell 581

VI, 196 NOT TO EAT FAECES. I have flown up as a swallow, I have cackled as a goose, I
have alighted[1] on the great northern plain of the Great One. See,[2] I will not die,
standing on you[3] when I appear as a god; I see you when I seek out your
riparian land.[4] I glitter as a glitter-bird on your vertex, my water-sources are the
marshes of the Mansions of the Red Crown, my eye is the pupil(?)[5] of the Eye
of Horus. I will make a descent to the riparian land of *Sk*; I will eat and gorge[6]
in the Field of Offerings, I will land in the northern sky, I will open the doors of
the horizon, I will attain to the limits of the horizon, I will travel to the northern
limits. I am bound for the northern sky and I will dwell in it with Seth.

'What will you live on?' say the gods to me.

197 'I will live on what you live on, and I will carouse on what you carouse on.
My detestation is faeces, and I will not eat what [I] get rid of,[7] I will not tread in
it[8] with my sandals'.

My bread is of white emmer, I carouse on bright emmer, for I am the Child, the son of Rēꜥ-Atum, and I will live on that pleasant tree which is in the Shrine. I am *Pny* the Bull of offerings, Babi of the horizon, possessor of seven portions in Ōn; three are in the sky with the Two Falcons, and I am on their wing-tips; four are with the Two Snakes, and I am on their coils. It is the Night-bark and the Day-bark which will take warmth to me daily from the storehouses of every god.

My detestation is faeces, and I will not eat it, I will not drink urine, I will
not walk head downwards, because I am indeed he who sees him, the son of
198 Rēꜥ, who will bring his meal and eat his meal on earth – four times – while Rēꜥ
is in the sky, the sky. I am the *wnb*-flower which issued from Rēꜥ, the *ꜥꜣꜥ*-
flower which issued from the horizon, I am the *ꜥꜣb*-flower which issued from the
garden, I am the uraeus which issued from Chemmis. I am guarded, O faeces; I
am cleansed, O urine,[9] just as Horus and Thoth guarded her who is with the
Two Falcons. I will cross over to the sky, I will live on what they live on, I will
eat of what they eat of, my booth is in plenty, my abundance is in the Field of
Offerings, and I am well-supplied[10] in company with the gods, for I am one

of them, I am the Bull of the Great One, I am the Bull of *Ḥnnt.*[11] My detestation is faeces, I will not drink its sister urine, (even though) every god has said that if I will eat what I detest he will eat with me. I am the possessor of five portions; three are in the sky with Rēꜥ and two are on earth in the temple. It means that the head is cut off,[12] and that I have received the service due to me(?);[13] I travel on the path of the owners of doubles, and see, I have come. I have received the service due to me(?), I have appeared in glory, and I am exalted on high as Ḥapy.

1. So BH3C. P. Gard. II has *ỉr.n.ỉ ꜥḥꜥw* 'I have made a standing'. On this spell see also Zandee, *ZÄS* 90, 150.
2. P. Gard. II has *mꜣꜣ ṯn,* imperative with reinforcing fem. dep. pron.; the fem. gender indicates that *wꜥrt ꜥꜣt* 'the great plain' is addressed. BH3C has *mꜣꜣ sy* 'see it'.
3. Fem. referring to the plain.
4. BH3C ends with a lacuna and a rubric: 'Becoming a goose'.
5. *Ṯpṯt,* not recorded and translation not certain.
6. For *ꜣf* 'gorge' food cf. *CT* II, 394*a*; IV, 23*i*, VII, 227*o*.
7. Restoring as *drw*[*t.ỉ*] ; cf. de Buck's n. 1*.
8. A superfluous *m* has intruded before *ḥr.f.*
9. An unnecessary suffix follows *wsšt.*
10. Reading *ꜣgbw.ỉ,* passive *sḏmw.f.*
11. An unidentified locality, Gauthier, *Dict. geogr.* IV, 30.
12. The relevance of this clause is not clear; perhaps it refers to the butchery of an animal for food.
13. The meaning of *ḥnty.ỉ* is not certain. I have provisionally identified it with *ḥnty* 'service', *Pyr.* §§1452; 1470, regarding *ḥnty.ỉ* 'my service' as meaning 'the service due to me'.

Spell 582

N has flown up as a swallow, N walks as a pigeon, N alights on that great standard VI, 199
of Osiris, on which he who falls cannot remain(?).[1] O you who look on N when he is made manifest as a god, let N go down to the Winding Waterway so that he may stop poverty(?),[2] because N is the amulet which is at the throat of Horus, and he will land at the northern sky.

1. Translation uncertain. *N* before *mn.n.f* has been regarded as a writing of the negation. That the clause refers to the standard is shown by the fem. suffix in *ḥr.s.*
2. *Snšy.f ḥwrr* is obscure; *snšy* may be a metathesis of *sšn* 'stop', 174*f,* and *ḥwrr* appears to be a derivative of *ḥwr* 'poor'.

Spell 583

N has gone up as a swallow,[1] N has walked as a goose, N has made a descent into [. . .] a star when this fair abode descends. He who sees it will never die, but will stand up.[2]

1. *Wr pn* is an error for *wr* 'swallow' as in 199*a*.
2. *ꜥḥꜥ* could perhaps be the old perfective, but it seems more likely that the suffix *.f* and possibly some more has been omitted; the text as it stands looks unfinished.

Spell 584

VI, 200 SPELL FOR BECOMING A MALE . . .[1] I(?) spent the night and a path was shown [. . .]. O Great One who dwells in hidden places; O Great One who is yonder; O Great One who dwells in darkness; O Great One who is on his side asleep, whose head is on the sky,[2] whose face is to the east, [. . .] me, for I am noble, I am a spirit, I am equipped, I am noble (*sic*), I am a god.[3] My birth will be tomorrow, I will break out from the egg[4] on the day when men bring[5] to me.
201 I have taken possession of everything completely which my head has brought to me,[1] I have knit together the backbone of Osiris after [. . .],[6] and the Entourage has cut off the inner[7] evil of Osiris.

1. The term *bꜣsty* is not recorded. It recurs, always followed by *ṯꜣy* 'male', in Spell 585 in 203*b*; 204*g*; 205*e.g.* It is written *bꜣt* in *CT* VII, 232*g*. Its meaning is not known; it seems to have no connection with *bꜣs* 'devour', *CT* I, 293*b*, with *bꜣs* 'ointment jar', *Wb.* I, 423,4, or with the name of the goddess Bastet.
2. S2C omits *ḥr* before *pt tn*.
3. The writing of *ꜥpr.kỉ* suggests that all the words with final *k* are old perfectives 1st sing.
4. So B2Bo; it is difficult to see what can have stood in the lacuna in S2C.
5. Impersonal *sḏm.f*; one would have expected the infinitive.
6. B2Bo omits the word after *m-ḫt*, which is lost in the lacuna in S2C.
7. For *ḫnwtt* 'inner' see also *Pyr.* §1961.

Spell 585

O men, gods, spirits, powers, uraei,[1] see me and be afraid of me, for I have come in company with Ptaḥ, I [have come in company with(?)] the Ennead,[2] and I

have sat between them.[3] The great ones[4] of the horizon bring to me, and they VI, 202
have written down what I have said to them.[5] I am one having power [over] those who would smite the great ones and their nobles,[6] I live by means of falcon-knives for ever.[7] I have come [. . .] after me, who judge as the gods; I consult their wisdom when going out from my [abode(?)].[8] Mine is the incense-smoke which conceals the plebs; I am indeed he who is in charge of exhalation, living on blood.[9]

See me, O men, gods, spirits, the dead [. . .] a male . . .[10] I have gone down 203
[to him,[11] I] establish [him],[12] and he sits on that [seat] which is north of the sky[13] [. . .] for N on account of(?) it. My flesh is in [. . .] who encircle [. . .]. He whose face is hidden [. . .]. O men, gods, spirits, the dead [. . .], I know
the names of those gods of theirs [. . .] who go down [. . .]. My bow[14] which 204
I stretch with my grasp belongs to me, my arrows are in my grip.[15] I give life to the men whom I guide [. . .], because what I have found is . . .[16] a male . . I [have] gone down to him, my company follows after me, and they write down the wisdom of the gods.[17]

O all you men,[18] gods, powers, spirits, the dead, who shall see[19] me in 205
[. . . I pass over(?)][20] the land on foot, and it gives me praise; my seat [. . .].[21] I go down [to him],[22] to the male . . . [TO BE SAID(?)][23] WHEN EQUIPPING A SPIRIT IN THE REALM OF THE DEAD.

1. For *ỉʿrwt* 'uraei' Sq6C has *mtt* 'the dead'. Throughout this spell the two versions vary considerably; in addition Sq6C is badly damaged. In the translation S2C is followed where available.

2. Restoring the lacuna in S2C tentatively as *ỉy.n.ỉ ḥnʿ*, following 201*g*. Not in Sq6C.

3. 202*b* is not in S2C, and in Sq6C is all in lacuna.

4. Sq6C: 'the great ones of the sky and the horizon'.

5. In Sq6C between *sš* here and *ḥw* in 202*e* everything is in lacuna.

6. 202*f* is not in S2C, and except for the name of the deceased is lost in Sq6C.

7. Sq6C: 'who live on blood for ever'; since this text is in the 3rd person *ʿnḫ* must be a participle. *Bykw* of S2C, with knife-det., may possibly mean knives with a figure of a falcon on the hilt, though one would expect the name of a foodstuff here. After this Sq6C omits 202h–203*c*.

8. I suggest that  or possibly  be restored at the end of 202*i* as against de Buck's n. 4*.

9. Surely so, despite the det., cf. 202*g* (Sq6C).

10. Cf. Spell 584, n. 1.

11. For the restoration cf. de Buck, n. 3*.

12. Restoring as *smn*[⟨*ỉ*⟩ *sw*], assuming omission of the suffix 1st sing. Sq6C appears to read *smn.t⟨w⟩.ṯn* 'you (plur.) are established.

13. It seems necessary to restore a word for 'seat' or the like in the lacuna, but it is not clear what the word could have been, cf. de Buck's n. 4*. S2C omits 203*e*–204*a*, and we have to fall back on Sq6C, which is nearly all in lacuna.

14. *Ḏt* 'body' makes no sense in 204*b*, and is surely an error for *pḏt* 'bow'; note the reference to arrows in 204*d*. This may perhaps be a case of misheard dictation. Sq6C omits 204*b* and for 204*c* has: 'the winds are in N's grasp'.

15. Sq6C has 'his [. . .] are in [his] grip' and continues with a lacuna which has no counterpart in S2C. Thereafter Sq6C omits 204*f–i*.

16. I can make nothing of *dw ỉs pw ỉnp* [. . .].

17. 204*k* is not in S2C and is almost all lost in Sq6C.

18. Supplied from Sq6C.

19. Restore as *mꜣꜣ.t(y).f(y)* in S2C; there is no space for *.sn*. Sq6C has: 'they see N [. . .]'.

20. The damaged first word in 205*b* (S2C) could be *swꜣ.i* or *sḏꜣ.ỉ*. 205*b–c* are entirely lost in Sq6C.

21. In 205*d* Sq6C has: '[. . .] a seat here' (or 'today').

22. Cf. de Buck, n. 5*. Sq6C has 'the male . . . goes down to him'.

23. Conjecturally restoring *ḏd* or *ḏd mdw*. In Sq6C the rubric reads: 'Becoming a male . . .'.

Spell 586

TO REPEL A SNAKE AND TO REPEL CROCODILES [. . .] MAGIC. Get you back, black-face, for you have not been named;[1] when your power is against me, I am inside my body,[2] I am placed within my body, for I am one who goes about
VI, 206 reaching out the mouth[3] | (as) a man in need.[4] You have done nothing to me, the earth-god has not transgressed against me.

O cauldron, you are[5] a cauldron; you have cooked in a brazier, (but) there is complaint against you[6] in the Netherworld; as for(?) those who watch my mouth, may the water-runnels not be filled on account of their brethren.[7]

Hail to you, O Rēʿ, wearing your circlet![8] May you proceed to the council-chamber and reckon up your fathers who watch for him who destroys[9] doubles. O Blue-eyed one who freshens eyes, whose power is severe, whose soul will never be opposed, rouse the Great Lady who is inert, so that she may see[10] him who destroys the doubles, whose heads are injured and whose faces are afraid.[11]

207 O Blind of vision who are on your face, | lift up your arm, put him on your strong arm. As for(?) [12] him who destroys doubles, may he not harm(?)[13] Rēʿ in his circlet . . .[14] I am their . . . , the father of *Tn* is awake,[15] the waters are uncovered,[16] their snakes are executed; this strong arm of yours is in the realm(?) of Atum. Receive your weapons in your hand(?); [17] speak on behalf of Rēʿ, and Rēʿ will speak on my behalf and your behalf.[18] Smite this killer of his doubles and destroyer of his doubles [19] with this strength and might of yours, with this

power of yours. May Rēʿ who sends out his double not fall; then I will not fall when I send out my double, for I am Atum equipped with my weapons.[1] I have 208
stolen the strength of him who destroys his doubles, and if I grow weary, Rēʿ will grow weary; if I stand up, Rēʿ will stand up, for I have(?)[20] my circlet which is in my hand. Stand up!.[21]

1. So 205*j* (S1C); on the construction *n sḏm.n.f ỉs* cf. Sethe, *Komm. Pyr.* I, 2. S2C has the var. 'it is [not] I who name [you]'.

2. Note the unusual writing of *m-ẖnw*. For *ẖt.f* read *ẖt.ỉ* as in 205*m*. The point of the sentence seems to be that concealed within his body the dead man is inaccessible to snake or crocodile. One might ask whether *ẖt* 'body' refers to the embalmed corpse or to the statue of the deceased.

3. In search of sustenance, cf. *Peas.* B2, 119; *Urk.* IV, 240, 1.

4. *Sꜣš* in S1C; *sꜣry* in S2C; the latter is the usual term, *Concise Dict.* 210, *Sꜣš* is not recorded.

5. Note the use of the masc. form *ṯwt* for the fem., cf. *Eg. Gramm.*^{3} §64, Obs.

6. With *ṯryt.ṯ* 'complaint against you' compare *nn ṯryt.ỉ* 'there is no complaint against me', *CT* I, 173*c*. The 'cauldron' clauses 206*d-f* appear to bear no relation to what precedes or follows, and may be intrusive.

7. The relation of 206*g-h* to the context is also not clear; the suffix in *snw.sn* must refer to *sꜣꜣw*, for there is no other antecedent available. *Tꜣḥt* is clearly related to *tꜣḥw* 'springs' or 'sources' of water, cf. Spell 190, n. 6; *CT* III, 145*f*; VI, 196*l*, where the word is unquestionably plural; perhaps 'runnels' for irrigation is the best rendering of *tꜣḥt*. S2C has corrupted this rare word into *tꜣ ḥs* 'land of faeces'!

8. *Nws*, better written in 207*d*, and determined with a crown, appears in fact to have been a head-band or circlet, cf. *Pyr.* §2274 (Nt 43); one may imagine a circlet such as that from Lahun, cf. Aldred, *Jewels of the Pharaohs*, pl. 39, which certainly is of the nature of a crown. Cf. Jequier, *Frises*, 6. The suffix of the 3rd person here must be rendered in English by the 2nd person.

9. Singular, cf. 207*c-d*.

10. *Mꜣn.s* is taken to be a writing of the *sḏm.f* form, cf. *Eg. Gramm.*^{3} §445.

11. I.e. the distressed doubles.

12. *'In* appears to be a slip for *ỉr* 'as for'.

13. *Ssw* may well be the negatival complement of *zz*, var *ỉzz*, with the sense of 'punish' in *Pyr.* §§173; 271; 643; the basic meaning may be 'do harm to'.

14. 207*e* is surely corrupt, with a material omission. *Tms* can hardly bear any relation to *tms ḥr r* 'turn the face to', *Urk* IV, 971, 4 and we should read *tm s . . .* , with the rest of the second word omitted. The idea of an omission, perhaps considerable, is confirmed by the suffixes 3rd plur. in what follows, which lack any antecedent.

15. *Rt* is a *vox nihili*; no god *Ṯn* seems known, while the relevance of 207*f* to the context is quite obscure.

16. Lit. 'naked'.

17. I differ here from de Buck's division of the sentences. It seems to me that his *mk*

at the beginning of 207*j* is a miswriting (or possibly a misreading) of *m-ʿk* 'in your hand' as an adjunct to *šsp n.k ʿḥʿw.k,* meaning 'take your weapons in your hand', and the imperative *mdw* 'speak!' should begin 207*j.*

18. S2C has a longer text in 207*l*, now mostly lost.

19. The suffix *.f* probably refers to Rēʿ.

20. A preposition has been omitted after *ỉw.ỉ*; perhaps even more.

21. De Buck, p. 208, n. 1*, thinks that the spell may have been cut short. Compare the same end to Spell 583.

Spell 587

I am the Bull of Offerings, possessor of five loaves in the temple; three loaves are in the sky and two loaves are on earth. I bathe in the pools of the Netherworld, I ascend to the place of Shu belonging to the sky. What Seth detests is the Eye of Horus, and I will not eat faeces; what I detest is urine, and I will never drink it, just as Seth detested the Eye of Horus after the judgement in the great Prince-mansion which is in Ōn. If one gives him to you,[1] fighting will not be stopped,
VI, 209 uproar will not be suppressed, the mottled cattle will not move about for themselves,[2] | Seth will swallow the Eye of Horus for himself after the judgement in the great Prince-mansion which is in Ōn, and if you give this to me, there will be no coming into being or existing.[3]

Hail to you, Thoth, creator of the Two Brethren, whose utterance Rēʿ accepts when the Great Tribunal sits to give judgement; you shall sit for me before them, for it was not I who received the heads of the mottled cattle for them after the judgement in the great Prince-mansion which is in Ōn.

1. *'Ir dy n.k sw* has been regarded as a conditional clause with impersonal *sḏm.f,* the object *sw* referring to Seth and the dative *n.k* being the anonymous person to whom these words are addressed. In 209*c* the possibility is envisaged that the unknown person may foist the troubles resulting from this gift on to the speaker, with further disastrous results.
2. Perhaps meaning 'will stop grazing'.
3. See n. 1 above.

Spell 588

[SPELL FOR BEING IN THE PRESENCE OF ḤATḤŌR].[1] I am [one who passes by] bald;[2] O Sistrum-player, Sistrum-player, I will be in the suite [of Ḥatḥōr].

1. Restored from *BD* Spell 103, where the 1st person is probably original.
2. Restore [*swꜣ*] *iꜣ*[*s*] ; there is not room for *swꜣ wʿb ỉꜣs* of BD.

Spell 589

SPELL FOR PRAISES. Rēʿ has praised my father Osiris; O Thoth, recite his virtues! VI, 210
Down on your face, O you who would slay my father Osiris!

Spell 590

SPELL FOR AN ʿ*PRT*-JAR. O lector of mine, it is Thoth who has brought a lector[1] who reads it when walking[2] on the morning of the *ʿprt*-jar. Horus has equipped his father Osiris with the gold collar of Sokar himself; Rēʿ has commanded that he make it, Thoth having received his wealth and the craftsmen of Sokar being assembled.

1. Following the singular of S1C rather than the plural of S2P; so too *šmwt* and *dwꜣwt* in 210*g*.
2. Reading of S2P not quite certain. S1C has: 'in the night and in the morning'.

Spell 591

SPELL FOR A TABLE OF OFFERINGS. My father Osiris is content with his mouth- VI, 211
fuls of natron, and he has become a god[1] in Nekheb.

1. S3C omits *nṯr.n.f.*

Spell 592

SPELL FOR A CHEST OF NATRON. O all you gods who are in the *snwt*-shrine, come, that you may see this foe; he is one trodden down and bound in the presence of my father Osiris, for I have killed his foes, whose slaughtering has been effected, and my father Osiris is triumphant. O lector, O *sm*-priest, bring a chest of natron and let the god's-offerings be issued.

Spell 593

SPELL FOR A *TNHR*-CHEST. Where is he,[1] that loud-voiced caller, Horus[2] in the VI, 212
midst? He has reached the garden,[3] he has crossed[4] the sea; the Destroyer has made strife, he has repeatedly plundered, he has created uproar.

1. Read *ỉ.f ṯn*. S2P and S3C have combined two distinct constructions, namely *ỉ.f ṯn* and *ṯn sw*, cf. *Eg. Gramm.*[3] § 503, 1.4.

2. Reading doubtful, see de Buck's notes 2*. 5*. 7*.

3. So S1C. In S2P and S3C the lost verb of motion had no object.

4. So S1C and S11C; S2P: 'he has encircled'.

Spell 594

SPELL FOR TWO WIDTHS OF KILT. Extensive are the movements of my father
VI, 213 Osiris [. . .] to whom are brought gold of the deserts, | myrrh of God's-land, costly stones of the isles, by Horus the Elder; fayence of Libya; lapis lazuli of the Blue Land, haematite(?) of *Hbks*; turquoise of Sinai; [costly stones(?)][1] of *Rꜣ-ꜥḏyt*, carnelian of *Šꜣyt*.

1. Conjecturally restored after *ꜥꜣwt nt Ḫꜣw-nbwt* in 213*a*.

Spell 595

SPELL FOR *TꜣFSYT*-JARS. I have set a limit to the confederacy of Seth, I have effected their slaughtering, I have put them in the place of execution south of Sepa and north of *Ḥnn*(?).

Your father is their master, (even) Anubis, Lord of Sepa, and Horus, Lord of *Ḥnn*(?).

Spell 596

VI, 214 SPELL FOR AN ARM-BAND. 'How good is the favourite place of my son!' says Gēb, the chiefest of the gods, concerning his son Osiris. There are brought to him gold of the deserts, malachite[1] of God's-land, jasper(?)[2] of Punt. How joyful is he in triumph! Driven fowl(?) are for [my(?)] son.

1. Assuming *sšmt* to be a metathesis of *ššmt*.

2. Cf. *h̭nmt* 'red jasper', Harris, *Minerals*, 113.

Spell 597

I am your son Horus; I have come and I bring you incense, clothing in bundles, and sandals in my hand for my lord,[1] and he will give to me.[2]

1. Read *nb. ỉ* ⟨*ỉ*⟩*r.*⟨*ỉ*⟩, this last being the enclitic particle?
2. Read *ntf r dy*⟨*t*⟩ *n. ỉ*?

Spell 598

SPELL FOR THOSE WHO POUR[1] WATER. Hail to you who pour water,[2] who bring VI, 215
water of the Nile to Osiris; may you bring[3] water of the Nile to me, for I am a follower of Osiris.

1. Feminine plural.
2. Var. 'possessors of water'.
3. Prospective *sḏm.f* in optative use.

Spell 599

SPELL FOR THE FUNERAL MEAL. I am Osiris, son[1] of Gēb, born of Nūt; the funeral meal is before me, and it will not be far from me.[2]

1. Omitted in S1C owing to the close conjunction of two identical bird-signs.
2. So S9C; S1C adds *ḥr Wsyr* 'with Osiris', S5C adds *ỉm3ḫy* 'the blessed one' in apposition to the preceding suffix, and S11C follows *r.ỉ* with a lacuna ending in *N ỉḳ*[*r*] 'the worthy N'.

Spell 600

[. . .] I am your son Horus who protects his father from those who would rob VI, 216
him; I have come and I will bring to you her who wronged you.

Spell 601

I am Rēʿ-Atum who himself moulded himself; I groaned at the matter of my birth. They (*sic*) come to my offerings in this my name of cedar-wood; they have loved me because what they have given to me is praise in this my name of *mrw*-wood. The *wrrt*-crown has gone up, having been placed upon me, because so great was their good-will towards me in this my name of Him of the *wrrt*.

Spell 602

VI, 217 See, I bring to you your children who support you; do not yield(?) to your foes, but pull yourself together.

Spell 603

See, I bring to you those who slew your father Osiris in those names of theirs of 'Wild Bulls'. May you breathe and exchange greetings;[1] raise yourself, O my father Osiris, so that your foes may fall to you beneath you.

1. The suffix *.k* is common to both verbs.

Spell 604

VI, 218 TO BRING[1] AN OFFERING OF BREAD AND BEER IN THE REALM OF THE DEAD. Hail to you, you lords of food-offerings, who grant provisions, who bring food and convey provisions; may you bring me food and convey provisions to me, for I am a living soul, a follower of Osiris. Come to me[2] and bring me the food-offerings and provisions of Osiris, for I am a 'son-who-loves'.

1. Reading *ms* 'bring' at the beginning of the lacuna.
2. Imperative with dative; so also *ỉn n.ỉ*.

Spell 605

SPELL FOR A BED. I am a son of the Milk-goddess, and I have come here to the place where Osiris is, for I am vindicated. My bed is in my possession, my seat is beneath me, my weary soul is at rest.[1]

1. 218*p.q* consist solely of stock epithets of the deceased and are not translated.

Spell 606

SPELL FOR A *SNBT*-JAR. Nourishment[1] . . . because my father is becoming VI, 219
weary(?);[2] the Destroyer is driven off from within the secret places.

1. Cf. *Wb.* IV, 165, 1.
2. 219*b* defeats me, and the translation of 219*c* is far from certain; *m* before *b3gg.f* in S1C seems superfluous.

Spell 607[1]

Take the Eye of Horus which he has sent into your[2] mouth; I bring it to you, I put it in your mouth for you. O N, take the . . . of Osiris — . . .[3]

This is the Great One who went forth from the earth, who was loosed from the Abyss, who went forth from Nūt;[4] the great Power, born of Gēb,[5] who VI, 220
repelled Seth in his rage and who was set over the foreign lands, when they departed.[6] The Ennead cried aloud at knowing his name, which grew from the body of that noble Fen-goddess, who is the flesh of the East-land,[7] the assistant of ⌜ʿAnti, the guardian of Sopd, Lord of the East, and she who is the protection of Osiris.[8] The two Lords of the East have knit their arms on him, (even) him who cut off the hands of the children of their fathers when he plucked (plants) in the field.[9]

'See, I bring everything to you completely, assembled on the Mounds', says your mother Isis,[10] 'and I have desired that you protect your Eye from him who would harm you.[11] Get to know this one for us, so that he may bring this to Horus for this year;[12] there are brought to him the sky in cloud and the earth in mist, with quiet foot and hidden sandal;[13] may the Destroyer, the son of Nūt, not find a way against him'.[14]

As for him who would harm your father when weak, he will be against you, O Horus-Eye, and you will be against him, O Horus-Eye. Your right Eye is the Night-bark, your left Eye is the Day-bark; your two Eyes, [O Horus], which issued from Atum, are Shu and Tefēnet.[15] What revolts them is that the hand of the god should misuse them, and the emission of the god's shade should be behind them, and his semen shall not enter into them.[16] I have removed the Day-bark because of your Eyes, O Horus, I have put them in the Night-bark and I have put them in the Day-bark for Horus of Manu.[17] The Blind Ones, rich in fluid(?), bleary-eyed, shortsighted, are at the feet of Horus of Manu, and they will neither be swollen(?) nor wobble(?) under the fingers of Horus of Manu.[18]

1. The translation of this spell depends largely on the article by Kees, 'Ein altes Gotterhymnus als Begleittext zur Opfertafel' in *ZÄS* 57 (1922), 92 ff., see de Buck's note 8*. The L2Li text is both damaged and corrupt.

2. For *rꜣ.s* read *rꜣ.k*; the fem. suffix is due to the influence of the fem. *i͗rt.*

3. The substance *škw* = *šyk* of *Pyr.* §31*c* is not identified.

4. Read *wr pw nn pr m tꜣ snw m nw pr m Nwt,* Kees, pp. 96–7, whose translation begins here.

5. Note the writing in L2Li of the name of *Gb(b)* with *ḳ* for *g.*

6. Read *ḫsf Stẖ m nšn.f wdy ḥr ẖꜣswt rw.sn,* id. p. 97.

7. Read *ky.n psḏt ḥr rẖ rn.f rwd m ḥꜥw sẖt tw špst i͗myt ḥꜥw i͗ꜣbtt,* id. pp, 98–9.

8. Read *ẖrt-ꜥ ꜥnty sꜣꜣt Spdw nb i͗ꜣbtt ntt m gs-dpt nt Wsyr,* id. p. 99. On *gs-dpt* see Kees p. 100, n. 11. He takes this expression at the foot of the letter, 'an Bord des Schiffes', but here its secondary meaning of protection seems more appropriate; a reference to a ship is a little out of place; other *CT* examples are IV, 88*k*; 94*b*.

9. Read *ṯs.n nbwy i͗ꜣbtt ꜥwy.sn ḥr.f šꜥꜥ ḏrwt nt msw i͗tw.sn ḥr fd.f m sẖt,* Kees, p. 101.

10. Read *mk i͗n n.k my-ḳd tm sp 2 dmḏ ḥr i͗ꜣwt i͗t i͗n mwt.k ꜣst,* id. pp. 102–3. Kees renders *i͗t i͗n* ff. with ' "O König" sprach deine Mutter Isis', taking *i͗t* for 'König' and *i͗n* for 'sprach'. It was not until some years later than his article that it was pointed out (cf. *ZÄS* 64, 3; *JEA* 21, 182–3) that *i͗t i͗n* means literally 'says she, namely' after quoted speech, *i͗t* standing for the old perfective 3rd fem. sing. of the verb *i͗* 'say' and *i͗n* being the agential particle.

11. Read *i͗mr.n ⟨i͗⟩ nḏ.k i͗rt.k m-ꜥ i͗r r.k,* Kees, p. 103.

12. Read as de Buck, 220*k*; the L2Li text has *nn* 'this one' after *rẖ m n.n* where the later versions have *sẖm ꜥnẖ,* id. p. 104.

13. Read *i͗nt.f n.f pt m i͗gp tꜣ m sym rd ḳb tbt ḥꜣpt,* loc. cit.

14. Read *i͗m grḥ nbḏ sꜣ Nwt wꜣt r.f,* loc. cit.

15. Read as 220*o-r* in de Buck, restoring *f* in the small lacuna in 220*o* and *Ḥr* in the lacuna in 220*r*. Cf. id. 107–8.

16. Read *bwt.sn i͗ẖr ꜥ nṯr ḥr-ẖt.sn mnsꜣ šwt nṯr ḥr-ẖt.sn n ꜥḳ mtwt.f i͗m,* id. 100. As Kees has seen, this passage refers to the insulting sexual misuse which the Egyptians considered fitting treatment for those they disliked, cf. e.g. Seth's treatment of Horus as described in *P. Kah.* 3, 32 ff. and in *Horus and Seth,* 11, 3.

17. Read as de Buck, 220*u-v,* restoring  in the lacuna; cf. Kees, p. 111. Note the unusual form of the *sk*-sign in the name of the *(M)sktt*-bark in 220*v*.

18. Read *špw ẖwd ꜥꜣꜥw ẖꜣtyw ḥwꜥ mꜣꜣ [tp rdwy] Ḥr Mꜣnw n bn.sn n dꜣ.sn ḥr ḏbꜥw Ḥr Mꜣnw,* id. p. 111; for *n dꜣ.sn* L2Li has *n i͗rw.sn. Ḫwd ꜥꜣꜥw,* as Kees would interpret the words following *špw,* could well refer to a copious discharge, even if only of tears, from eyes which are diseased. *N bn.sn n dꜣ.sn* are interpreted by Kees as 'nicht kommen sie heraus, nicht kommen sie davon', i.e. from under the fingers of Horus, but *bn*> *bnb*> *bnbn* stands basically for what is stiff and upright, cf. *Concise Dict.* 82, while *dꜣ*> *dꜣdꜣ* stands for to-and-fro movement, cf. the various meanings attached to the stem in op. cit. 309. My assumption is that the passage refers to lumps and soft swellings caused by disease, which disappear under the fingers of Horus.

Spell 608

Ho N! You are clad in the Eye of Horus which belongs to your body.[1] Ho! I VI, 221
have given it to you, it having appeared and having been seen[2] on your flesh and having been joined to your flesh in this its name of 'Red Linen'.

You are clad in it in this its name of 'Cloth'.
You are great in it in this its name of 'Great One'.
Your face is bright by means of it in this its name of 'Bright One'.
It is joined to your flesh in this its name of 'Red Linen'.
Here comes Tayt.
Here comes Taytet.
Here comes the Eye of Horus which issued from the earth.
Here comes the netting[3] of Isis.
Here comes the cloth[4] of Nephthys.
Here comes the plaiting[5] of Neith.
Here comes the woven stuff of the two Sisterly Companions.
Here comes what Ptaḥ has worked in.[6]
Here comes what Horus gave to his father Osiris to clothe him in it.
Ho N! Provide yourself with the Eye of Horus which belongs to your body.
Provide yourself with the woven Eye of Horus.

1. Surely so, despite the det.; this spell is concerned with clothing the body of the deceased.

2. The second *mꜣty* is a dittograph, cf. de Buck, n. 2*.

3. Cf. *sšnt* 'netting', CT VI, 5*d*; Spell 473, n. 15. This and the four following sentences refer to the materials for garments.

4. Cf. *sṯy* 'weave', *Pyr.* § 1202; *sṯꜣ* 'cloth', *Wb.* IV, 355, 6.

5. Cf. *CT* VI, 5*d*; Spell 473, n. 16.

6. Cf. *sʿm* 'inlay', *Urk.* IV, 669, 15, here apparently referring to a pattern worked into the material of the garments by Ptaḥ.

Spell 609

'There speaks the voice of this blessed one who has come', says Osiris to the VI, 222
beautiful West. 'I have come here from the Island of Fire;[1] bow down to me on your bellies and kiss the earth[2] to me at my feet, make acclamation to me, create reverence[3] for me'. Such is Osiris;[4] he is your king to whom worship is given,[5] at
seeing whom men rejoice. 'I have come here from the land of the living to my 223
place of vindication',[6] says Osiris the Bull of the West[7] concerning N,[8] who has

come safely in the retinue of his father Osiris;[9] so say the blessed ones,[10] so say the august desert and the spirits which are in it, concerning N.[11]

1. S12C adds: 'to his place of vindication', anticipating 223*e*; S11C reads: 'I have come here safely from the land of the living', anticipating 223*d*; S10C omits 222*c.d*.
2. S10C and S12C omit *tꜣ* 'earth'.
3. *Sꜣtꜣ*; cf. *CT* VI, 158*j*; *D. el B.* 114.
4. The deceased and Osiris are completely identified.
5. S11C being a woman's coffin, it has the fem. dative *n.s*, despite the anomaly of the fem. in reference to *nswt* 'king'; so also *mꜣ.s* in 223*c*.
6. The multiplicity of short strokes found in S5C, S6P and S12C, and in S5C a repeated *t* and strokes in *st.f*, obscure the fact that *st.f nt mꜣʿ-ḫrw*, in the singular, should be read in S5C and S6P. S10C and S11C omit 223*d-f*.
7. S12C omits 223*e* and has a version of its own (223*i-k*): 'he has got rid of his dust and has nourished his body, (even he) N'.
8. Only in S5C.
9. S10C adds 'to his place of vindication'; *st* is to be regarded as sing., see n. 5 above.
10. So S6P; S5C omits *ḫr imꜣḫy*; S11C has *imꜣḫt* without preceding *ḫr*.
11. *R* 'concerning' only in S6P.

Spell 610

VI, 224 N is Shu upon the river-banks, who exhales[1] and is on high, on high. N belongs to me,[2] N greets Atum, with his tongue in the water (*sic*), N is the pair of . . . of the killing-knives,[3] N is *Hdd* in the middle of his eye who goes in and out of the fire. O you great and mighty ones who belong to N, he desires the power of the great and mighty ones so that he may strengthen(?)[4] himself thereby; N brings to himself the power of the mansion of the great ones, and it[5] brings and unites Shu and Atum, who desire that it should judge. A path is made for N by means of it, and N spits on the scalp of Atum[6] so that he may calm *Hdd*, Shu and Thoth, whom he loves and who are united behind the great god . . .[7] It has been commanded to N that N spit on his scalp and that N comfort his backbone, for a portion (of food) is in N's belly, and N will not refuse the life of the Lord of Eternity.

1. For this meaning of *bš* cf. *CT* II, 12*h*; the literal 'spit' is represented in this spell by *psg*. The difficulties of translation may be due in part to textual omissions.
2. Who is this?

3. *ꜥꜣt* is quite obscure; as this is a man's coffin, the fem. *ꜥꜣt* cannot refer to a personal attribute of the dead.

4.  may stand for the causative *snḫt*; the pronoun *sw* indicates that a transitive verb preceded, of which only the determinative has been written.

5. The mansion.

6. To heal it, cf. *JEA* 16, 171, n. 4.

7. The words *šw smꜣ* appear in isolation, without nexus with what precedes and follows, and they may well be the survivors of an omitted passage.

Spell 611

The shutters of the sky-window are opened, the doors of the movements of the sunshine are thrown open, the *twn*-plant is cleansed;[1] it means that it is the shining of Rēꜥ which he will open for N.[2] VI, 225

1. For the *twn*-plant cf. *Pyr.* §§513; 557. BIC repeats *twr twn*; TIL follows it with *ṯs pẖr* 'and *vice versa*', which makes no sense here.

2. So TIL; BIC has instead of *psḏt Rꜥ* the obviously corrupt *rrp* with snake(?)-det., and omits the suffix *.f* after *wn*. The final *nw* in both texts appears to be an equivalent of the more usual *pw* in the sense of 'it means that'.

Spell 612

TO BECOME ḤATḤŌR. How happy are those who see the festival in this place of mine! I am seated on the throne of Khopri, I give judgement in company with the seven cobras, I see the eight . . . ,[1] I have swallowed the seven uraei, because I am Ḥatḥōr, Mistress of rams, the serpent who laughs with Edjō, | the great wild cow[2] of the Mansion(?)[3] of the heads. Here am I; may you[4] not kill the Great VI, 226
One who has appeared in her proper shape.

1. *Sꜣsꜣ*, entirely obscure.
2. Read *smꜣt wrt,* since this alludes to Ḥatḥōr.
3. Reading doubtful, see de Buck, n. 1*.
4. Plural.

Spell 613

GIVING GIFTS IN ŌN. N is . . .[1] the falcon Horus, the third of . . .[2] My face is that of a fierce lion . . .[3] water in my hand; that is . . . of the *Ḥnw*-bark;[4] I travel away.[5]

1. Reading in both texts uncertain, see de Buck, nn. 4* – 6*.

2. *Ṯ3m sp.* B2 L omits 226*h*.

3. *Gps.*

4. B1C: *gps pw n ḥnw*; B2 L: *gps 9 ḥnw*; both are quite obscure.

5. For *skr (zkr)* as a verb of motion cf. *Pyr.* §§241; 1847; there is a play here on the name of the *Ḥnw*-bark, which is the bark of Sokar. The final *skrt* is a 'complementary infinitive'.

Spell 614

VI, 227 NOT TO LET A MAN'S HEART SIT DOWN AGAINST HIM IN THE REALM OF THE DEAD. My bread indeed is in an ear of corn(?)[1] in this my name of Him of *Ḥnbt*(?),[2] while a star-god is acting against me, and my brother is ill.

1. Read *ḥms*? An abnormal writing, and there is no determinative, but no other interpretation seems plausible.

2. Reading *Ḥnbty*(?), cf. B2 L^b. For the town *Ḥnbt* cf. *CT* I, 272*g*; 289*a*. B2 L^a has *n Ḥnᶜty*.

Spell 615

ASSOCIATING WITH THE GOD. I am one who gives pleasure[1] to the god's heart, who distracts the heart of him who brings weeping; in the night[2] I warded off the tears of the gods and made contentment.

1. On *syn* cf. Spell 334, n. 31.

2. *Sḏr* appears here to be an auxiliary verb akin to *sḏr.n* of *Eg. Gramm.*^{3} §483, 1. It is omitted in B2 L^b.

Spell 616

VI, 228 Spell for navigating to Ōn. O Atum, may you place ⟨ . . . ⟩ on me,[1] for I have navigated myself(?) in the time of us two(?);[2] may we both speak[3] with *Dw3-wr.*

1. The object of *dy.k* has been omitted.

2. In 228*c* the lacuna in B3 Bo^a is too small for more than one full-sized sign, and the most probable restoration is *w* of *wỉ*, reading *sḳd.n⟨.ỉ⟩ [w]y* 'I have navigated myself'. *M sp.ny* is obscure, and the translation uncertain; the man-sign following *ny* seems superfluous. *Ny,* without the man, occurs again in *mdw.ny* in 228*d*, which suggests that it may be the

suffix 1st dual, referring to Atum and the deceased.

3. B3Bo[b] omits *mdw.ny*.

Spell 617

O Thoth,[1] open those wings of yours to me, for I am one of those nine spirits of
yours[2] | who live on the fluid[3] of your eyes and on the hair which is in your arm- VI, 229
pits. *Ḥkk* goes up to the bow of the Bark[4] and gives orders to Ḥu,[5] and you shall
commend me to Ḥu.[6] Here am I, one who has been commended to you[7] by the
Great Wanderer.

1. So B2L; B3Bo[a] has 'O Rēʿ', but the opening of wings is an action more appropriate to the ibis Thoth than to the sun-god.

2. So P. Gard. III; B2L omits *ỉnk wʿ ỉm* and B3Bo[a] has completely distorted *wʿ*.

3. So B3Bo[a]. *'Iꜣfw* is not recorded, but the det. and the context make its meaning clear. The reading *ỉꜣfw* is confirmed by P. Gard. III. B2L has *ỉꜣꜣ* 'reed', which makes no sense.

4. B3Bo[b] adds 'of Rēʿ'.

5. So B3Bo[a]; P. Gard. III has *wḏ.n.f wỉ n Ḥw* 'he has commended me to Ḥu', a sentence which B2L puts into the 2nd person: 'you have commended', etc. This unexpected switch over to the 2nd person holds good for the rest of the spell in B3Bo[a] as well as in B2L; B3Bo[b] does not go beyond 229*c* and the latter part of P. Gard. III is lost.

6. B2L: 'you have handed me over to Ḥu'.

7. B2L omits *wḏt*.

Spell 618

Spell for vindication. 'O! This is the slayer!' says Atum; 'Here is truth'. N is a VI, 230
slayer, and his sharp knife is against you, you gods [. . .] powers. N sits at the
head of the Conclaves, and he puts dread [. . .] the Enneads. 'Travel here,[1]
that men may give you the powers that belong to you', says Atum to N.

1. Note the double enclitic stressing the imperative; on *mynn* 'here' cf. James, *Ḥeḳanakhte,* p. 112. This is a further instance of a rare usage.

Spell 619

The Great Lady is censed[1] for her bull at the houses, the flame of the Chaos-gods VI, 231
is on your faces, O you who are behind the shrine. Make a path for me, and I will
indeed pass by. If you do not make a path for me so that I may indeed pass by, I

will strike the Westerners as Gēb,[2] father of the gods, the phoenix will prophesy,
the shining one will go forth, the Great One will arise,[3] the Ennead will speak, the
earth will not open, Gēb will not speak, Rēʿ will not be on high, the skins of the
scorched ones(?) will be laid bare,[4] the water-springs(?)[5] will be dammed off, the
. . . will be joined,[6] and they will unite the river-banks,[7] ropes will be cut, the
Milky Way(?)[8] will be flooded, something unpleasant(?) will be put in the Meadow
232 of Apis.[9] *Rꜣmdw* is he who will watch the paths against those who pass by[10] | in
order to bar the gates(?)[11] against those who would go forth in front of me to the
Pillar[12] of Kenzet, and I have appeared at the Pillar of the Stars;[13] I put the fear of
me into the slayers[14] on that day when I desired to come there.

O Greatest of the cultivators who dwells in the Netherworld, make a path for
me, and I will indeed pass by. See, she has come to meet me; the Beautiful West
has come to meet me, and she says: 'Here comes my son the Bull to the sky, the
Bull of the eye-painted bulls, Lord of the West! Here comes my offspring;[15] I
brought you up, I bore you[16] and brought you up. You shall depart pure to the
233 Field of the Netherworld, you shall travel to Him who is on the *ḳꜣdt*-plant and
to Him who is on top of his height. | You shall go forth from the earth, his number
three over and above his children, over and above those female apes of his who
cut off heads, whom . . .[17] has seen in his fetters, whom they worship in his
peregrinations in protection of Him who is in his red linen'.

I have gone in to you, my head is knit on, and I have knit on your[18] own
heads in this function of mine of him who knits on your heads. I grant your
meals, being your food and your drink beside(?) you. I am protected by those
who see your provisions in front of the great ones in their presence, (even of)
the two Brotherly Companions who hold judgement concerning the celestial
kine,[19] who watch over the happy-hearted one. I have become heir to the Bull
of the sky, I have attacked his foe[20] who would take my meal from me, and my
234 heart is against him; | who would take away my copulation with my wife from
me[21] while he is in being; who would bring my days to an end in death;[22] who
would lessen my days of life. His blood shall belong to those who are in the sky,
his gore shall belong to those who are on earth in their presence, (even of) the
two Brotherly Companions who hold judgement concerning the celestial kine;
who save me and who give me[23] this food which my father has given to me and
which my father Osiris has adjudged to me. Him whom I find in my path, him
I will devour piecemeal(?)[24] . . . his head will be cut off.

1. *Syd* is the causative of *ỉd* 'cense', but here displays no perceptible difference of meaning from its simplex; 235*i* (Spell 621) has *ỉd* and 236*a* (Spell 622) has *ỉdy*. Spells 619

and 622 both largely consist of much altered versions of *Pyr.* Utt. 254.

2. The threats here vary a good deal from and are more extensive than *Pyr.* §§278–9.

3. *ꜥḥꜥ wr* is omitted from B3L. Cf. *Pyr.* § 278*b.*

4. *'Inmw* 'skins' is not in B3L. *ꜥgw* may well be a writing of *ꜥwgw* 'scorched one'; for *ꜥwg,* var. *ꜥg,* cf. *CT* V, 10*g*; 12*a; BD* 133, 5.

5. *ꜣḫ, ꜣḫy* are not recorded, and may be corruptions of *tꜣḥw, tꜣḥy* 'springs' of water, *CT* III, 98*n*; 145*f*; VI, 196*l*, cf. Spell 190, n. 6.

6. Quite obscure, compare 236*k*. Pyr. § 279*a* has *dmḏ ṯnwy* 'the borders will be joined together'.

7. With the result that the river itself will vanish. Cf. *Pyr.* §279*a.*

8. *Msḵt* with water- or bowl-det. is not known to me, but it may well be a writing of *msḵt* 'Milky Way(?)', *Concise Dict.* 118, cf. 236*l.*

9. *Bḏnw,* var. *ḏbnw,* is of unknown meaning, and in fact this clause is a corruption of *Pyr.* §279*d*, but an obscure verb *bḏn* or *bnḏ* apparently descriptive of an unpleasant human condition occurs in *CT* III, 60*i.*

10. A corruption of *Pyr.* §279*b.*

11. In the first part of 232*a* neither version seems to be entirely correct; *r šnꜥ* of B3L is preferable to *šnꜥꜥ r* of B1L, but *rwwt* 'gates' of B1L is perhaps a better reading than *rwdw* 'stairway' of B3L. For *šnꜥ* 'bar' gates cf. *Urk.* III, 24, 9 = Piankhi Stela, 78.

12. For the reading *ḏbꜣ* or *ꜥpr* see de Buck's n. 1*, but there can be no doubt that this is an error for *i͗wn* 'pillar', see n. 13 Below.

13. B3L had originally 'the Pillar of Kenzet', but 'Kenzet' has been cancelled. The 'Pillar' of Stars' and the 'Pillar of Kenzet' are named in close proximity in *Pyr.* § 280.

14. B3L has a dittograph of *mds*; B1L likewise, except that the initial *m* of the second *mds* has been moved to follow *snḏ,* so that it reads *snd m mds dsw.* Compare *Pyr.* §281*a.*

15. In 232*k* we have two bungled writings of *msṯw* 'offspring'; read *i͗w msṯw.i͗. Pyr.* §282*c* has *i͗w ms.n.i͗* 'here comes he whom I have borne'.

16. In 232*m* read at the beginning *ms.n.i͗ tw*; B1L has inserted a superfluous *n* after *ms.n.i͗.*

17. Indecipherable, see de Buck, n. 1*. With 232*o*–233*b* compare *Pyr.* §§284*c* ff. Note the distortion of *Pyr.* §285*b* in 233*a.*

18. The pronouns have changed from 2nd fem. sing. to 2nd plur., note also the plur. 'heads', which suggests a textual omission. In the first place the being addressed is apparently the Beautiful West.

19. Read *wḏꜥ-mdw ḥr mḥt-wrt* as 234*f.*

20. Sing., despite the plural strokes, cf. the sing. suffix in *r.f* below.

21. *M-ꜥ.i͗* only in B1L.

22. Reading *m mt* with B1L; B3L has: 'My days *nw mt* of death', which yields poor sense.

23. Read *dy n⟨.i⟩* with B1L; B3L omits *n.*

24. Compare Pyr. §278*a,* but in this text the adjunct *mwmw* is postponed to the last word in the spell, where it is out of place. Note the writing of *mwmw* here and in 236*h.* B3L inserts a superfluous dative after *wnm.i͗*; note that 234*i* is far removed from its proper place. It should precede 231*f*, cf. *Pyr.* §278. I can make nothing of *n wꜣ* at the beginning of 234*j.*

Spell 620

VI, 235 O Atum, see,[1] your name is 'The Sole One shines, (even) he who goes forth among his multitudes'. The Eye of Horus is pleasant, and I take it; it makes me go up.[2] Those who are in the sunshine suppress them[3] when I have opened the Netherworld.

1. *Mk* 'see' only in B1L.
2. *Sʿr.s wỉ* is not in B1L.
3. Or: 'they suppress those who are in the sunshine'. In neither case is the reference of the plural pronoun clear.

Spell 621

The Great One is censed for the Bull ⟨ . . . ⟩[1] on the throne [of] the Sole Lord; the flame is on the land. Get back, you shining one, Lord of the horizon![2] Make a way for me ⟨ . . . ⟩[3]. Gēb will raise aloft, Gēb will weigh(?).[4]

1. A blank space, perhaps indicating a lacuna in the scribe's copy. Restore perhaps 'of Nekhen', cf. *Pyr.* §276; but cf. 236*a* below.
2. The second *nb*-sign is a dittograph.
3. Another blank space.
4. Reading as *wd⟨n⟩*.

Spell 622[1]

VI, 236 The Great Lady is censed for the Bull of the Island of Fire; the fiery blast is on you, you gods who are behind the shrine. O unknown god, what is allotted is in every place of the Sole Lord.[2] O ⟨ Lord of the horizon ⟩,[3] make a path for me,[4] for if you do not make a path for me, I will command a curse on my father Gēb,[5] the earth will speak no more, Gēb will speak no more, he will be unable to protect(?) himself,[6] and him whom I find in my way, him I will devour piecemeal(?).[7] The pelican will prophesy, the shining one will go forth,[8] he (*sic*!) will join the . . . ,[9] the river-banks will unite. Set the rope aright, so that the Milky Way(?) may be crossed;[10] the roads will be made impassable to travellers,[11] the names will be changed for those who go and those who return, *Sḏnw* shall be struck down in the Meadow of Apis.[12] O! your fields will pass away when the *ỉꜣd*-star is before me.[13] I am the Pillar of the Stars and they see me as the Pillar of Darkness (*sic*),[14] the Bull of the sky, the Shining One, the Ox-herd who is on his pool, and the woman endures (*sic*).[15]

Lift up your face[16] and look at your mother the Beautiful West bowing
down, | having come rejoicing at meeting you. O N, spit on her head and her 237
hair,[17] on her arms[18] and her legs, and she will say: 'My son whom I bore is one whose horn is upstanding and whose eye-painting is green.' 'You are he who made proclamation for me concerning what is yours'[19] says my mother the West of me. Ho! Fear and tremble, you violent ones who are on the storm-cloud of the sky which he split open safely on the day when he desired to come thence' – so says the cultivation-ass which dwells in the Netherworld.[20] Your uproar will pass to the Field of Rushes, and you shall travel therein to Him who is on his *kꜣdt*-plant, having appeared as *Ḫnty-mnyt.f.*[21] You sink into the earth to your thickness, to your middle, to ⟨your⟩ full span(?), you see Rēʿ in fetters, you worship Rēʿ in the loosing from fetters by means of the amulet of the Great One who is in red linen, the Lord of offerings.

O you female apes of the sky, cut off (*sic*) your heads until I have passed by you safely;[22] I have affixed my head to my neck and my neck is on my trunk in
this my name of Affixer-of-head(s), | by means of which I affixed the head of the 238
Pelican on the day of the head-festival of the Bull. I have seen Rēʿ in fetters in your loosing from fetters,[23] and I will be honoured[24] by those who see me. The Serpent of Praise on her sceptre is Tefēnet whom Shu supports;[25] He makes spacious my place in Djedu, in Djedet and in Djedyt, I excavate my pool in the Field of Rushes,[26] I confirm my land in the Field of Offerings, I set up my standard in front of the Great Ones, and I give judgement in the heavens[27] between the two Contestants. My strength is the strength of *Tb,* my power is the power of *Tb,* I am protected from him who would harm me, from him who would interfere with me, for there are none who will take my meal away from me, and there are ⟨none⟩ who will take away my supper ⟨from me⟩.[28]

1. This spell, like 619, is an altered version of *Pyr.* Utt. 254, and is closer to the original than 619.
2. Cf. *Pyr.* §276*c*.
3. So *Pyr.* §277*a*; clearly the name of a god has been omitted after the interjection.
4. For the original 1st person cf. *wḏ.kꜣ.ỉ* in 236*e*.
5. Cf. *Pyr.* §277*b*.
6. Cf. *Pyr.* §277*c*.
7. Note the writing of *mwmw* with cat-det.; in 234*j* it has the skin-det.
8. Cf. *Pyr.* §278*b*. *Psḏt* 'the shining one' (N.B. fem.) stands for Pyr. *psḏt* as a word for 'pelican'.

9. *Rpꜣty,* meaningless. *Pyr.* §279*a* has *ṯnwy* 'borders', cf. *Pyr. Transl.* 254, n. 7. The masc. suffix in *dmḏ.f* is itself a corruption.

10. Cf. *Pyr.* §279d.

11. Cf. *Pyr.* § 279*b*.

12. A corruption of *Pyr.* §279d. 236*l* should have preceded this clause, which in its original version was not a threat.

13. Cf. *Pyr.* §280*a*.

14. *Knm* is a corruption of *Knst,* cf. Pyr. §280*b*. The pronoun *ṯn* after *mꜣ.sn* is superfluous; this passage is not in the 2nd person.

15. A corruption of *Pyr.* §280*c*.

16. The deceased is now being addressed.

17. For *nꜣbwt* 'hair', 'tresses' cf. *Pyr.* §282*b*. The spitting is a healing operation.

18. The preposition *r* in *r ꜥwy.s* is repeated on passing from line to line.

19. Reading *n ṯwyt.* The passage 237*f-g* appears to have little relation to the context, and may be an interpolation; there is also some confusion of persons.

20. With 237*h-j* compare *Pyr.* §§281*a*–282*a*.

21. With 237*k-m* compare *Pyr.* §§284*b*–285*a*.

22. With 237*s* ff. compare Pyr. §286. The somewhat nonsensical translation of 237*t* is unavoidable, *sn tpw.tn* being a main clause in the imperative qualified by an adverbial clause of the type *r sḏmt.f.*

23. Compare 237*o-p*.

24. Cf. *Pyr.* §287*c*; *ỉẖ mk.t(w) W ỉm* has been distorted into *ỉḫm N tn* 'this N knows nothing', which makes no sense at all.

25. So *Pyr.* §288*a*; 238*d-e* are utterly garbled.

26. Compare *Pyr.* §§288*b* ff.. The personal pronouns have become confused in transmission, cf. 238*f*, where we have the masculine instead of the feminine of Pyr.; here it seems likely that the fem. suffixes were thought to refer to the woman owner of the coffin, and accordingly they have been translated in the 1st person.

27. 238*j* should read: *wdꜥ.s ⟨m⟩ mḥt.wrt.*

28. 238o-q correspond to *Pyr.* §§290*c*–291*a*. 238*o* is a perfectly intelligible adaptation of *Pyr.* §290*d,* but 238*p-q* is an exact copy of *Pyr.* §291*a,* with the exception of the final *m-ꜥ.ỉ,* which has been omitted because of the line of text coming to an end. The scribe has forgotten that because 238*o* has been put into the negative, therefore 238*p-q* should also be in the negative, or alternatively both clauses should be in the affirmative. In fact the latter would more strictly follow the archetype, but putting *both* clauses into the negative also makes good sense.

Spell 623

VI, 239 Spell for going aboard the bark of Ḥatḥōr. I will wash[1] my hands, I will go all over the horizon, I will travel in[2] the bark which is in the charge of *'Iḫt-wrt,* I will gather together the Golden One in the isles[3] of the sky, I will gather together the god with[4] his brethren, I will make the light bright, I will go aboard your (*sic*) bark,[5] I will acquire the thrones,[6] I will ply my oar in those happy monthly festivals of yours[7] of the summer,[8] of the inundation season and of the winter, Sothis will convey me upstream at the First of the Year, and how good it will be when I am proclaimed there!

1. Prospective *sḏm.f.*
2. T1C^{a} omits the preposition.
3. T1C^{a} interpolates *nbw* 'gold' before *ńbwt* 'isles', perhaps as a combined phonogram and pun.
4. T1C^{a} omits the preposition.
5. *Hꜣy⟨.ỉ⟩* is prospective *sḏm.f.* Note the older usage with *m* here; the more common usage with *r* is in 239*a.* The fem. suffix after *wyꜣ* is only in T1C^{b}; presumably it refers to Ḥatḥōr.
6. So T1C^{b}; T1C^{a}: 'I have adorned the long-horn'.
7. T1C^{a} is much abbreviated and lacks the verb.
8. In 239*k* T1C^{b} inserts 'Ḥatḥōr', where it seems out of place.

Spell 624

Being a spirit in the sky. I am one who crossed the Broad Hall in my sandals, the VI, 240
sunshine-god sharp of power. My power is in the sky, the terror of me is on earth, for the sky is mine and the earth is mine, it is my might which has made [my] strength – and *vice versa.* Men have acted on my behalf, and the length of the sky is my stride, the breadth of the earth belongs to my settlements. He who departs is red and smeared, he who departs is tousled and dishevelled;[1] I seek out the Wakeful Ones [who are in][2] the shrines. The god(s) are ejected[3] from their paths, but I do not know the sky, [I do] not [know the emerging earth or][4] the Abyss. Ḥa does not listen to me, though I bring the horn to him, unless indeed [they(?)] have fashioned[5] [. . .] words of wrath. | I am a *mꜣsw*[6], red and 241
smeared, which is under [. . .] under the fingers of the great god who departs red and smeared, tousled and dishevelled. [Thus said][7] the gods when they lamented: 'Yesterday is past! Down on your faces!' He has come to me while [the dawn] was without you (pl.), the three are my protection for you(?).[8] My deed(?) is in my belly, and I have not spoken to . . . ,[9] I speak . . .[10] I have stood up on the day of eternity and the year of everlasting; I know it, though none have told it to me. Falsehood is of yesterday; O Maꜥet, I have attained Truth.

1. Reading *šmw* as a participle; compare 241*c*, where [hieroglyph] is lacking. The *m* before *dšr* in 240*k* is lacking in 241*c*, but the latter has *m* before *sps* and before *nwn*, where it is lacking in 240*k*. Perhaps we should read *m dšr m ṯmsw m sps m nwn*, with the *m* of predication before a succession of participles. For the reading *ṯmsw* rather than *ṯmss* cf. 241*a*. *BD* 183,1 has transformed 240*k* into *šm.ỉ spḥ.n.ỉ m Wnw* 'I have departed and have reached Unu'.

2. See de Buck, nn. 4*. 5*. *BD* 183,2–3 reads: *sḫ.n.ỉ nhsw ỉmyw kꜣrw.sn* 'I have struck down those who are wakeful who are in their shrines'. *Sḫn* 'seek out' of CT could also be translated as 'embrace'.

3. *Ḫꜣḫꜥ* is a confusion of *ḫꜣꜥ* 'throw', etc., *Concise Dict.* 183, and *ḫꜣḫ* 'be speedy', etc., op. cit. 185. According to *BD* 183,2 the former is meant.

4. Read perhaps *ỉ*[*rḫ.ỉ tꜣ-ṯnn*] *Nw*, cf. *BD* 183, 3–4.

5. Regarding *ms* in *n ms ỉs* as the enclitic particle, but 240*r* is not really intelligible.

6. *'Ink* does not stand here for 'to me belongs', for which this text uses *nnk*, cf. 240*f*. It follows that *mꜣsw* is singular, despite the plural strokes in the writing of the word. For this unidentified animal cf. Caminos, *Lit. Frag.* 32; the fem. *mꜣswt* occurs in *Urk.* IV, 1304,6.

7. Restoring *ḏd.ỉn* 'thus said' in the lacuna, following *BD* 183,7.

8. The real meaning of 241*g-h* escapes me, apart from the pun on *ḫmt*. For the restoration of *nhpw* in 241*g* see de Buck, n. 3*.

9. *Ḥwꜣn* in 241*j* is quite obscure. Unless there has been a textual omission, it cannot stand for the old perfective 2nd plur. *ḥw.tywn*, for as the text stands, a noun is required here. 241*k*, apart from the omission of *n*, is a dittograph of 241*j*, and as such has been passed over in the translation.

10. I am unable to translate *ꜣw šw*. All the latter part of this spell from 241*g* onward consists of various clauses without discernible nexus with what has gone before; it would seem either that there is deep-seated corruption at this point or else that a series of sentences of various origins have been inserted without regard to their meaning, a phenomenon not unknown in BD.

Spell 625

VI, 242 O Great Tribunal of the sky, you have brought me[1] among[2] you as one of you, and I will not give these utterances of mine which I know to those who are ignorant. O evil-doers, open the doors to me; O tamarisk people,[3] open the flood(?)[4] of the Great One; he supports the comfortable(?) wing which is in his body.[5] May the two boats of Him who is tied up be bright for me, may the paths of the dark place be broad for me, so that I may protect the branches of the tamarisk people,[6] and so that I may go forth and receive white bread.

1. A 'liaison' *n* is between the suffix *.ṯn* and the dependent pronoun *wỉ*.

2. S14C: *m-m* 'among'; L1Li: *ḥnꜥ* 'with'.

3. *'Isrtyw*, so S14C; L1Li repeats *ỉsftyw* 'evil-doers'.

4. A guess; none of the normal meanings of *ḥsꜣ*, i.e. 'milk', 'mucus', 'dough', *Concise Dict.* 177, is suitable here.

5. So L1Li. S14C appears to be garbled, with *rn.f n* for *rmn.f* and with repetition of *ḥtp*.

6. See n. 3 above.

Spell 626

To assemble a coffin. Come to your house which Isis has made for you, which VI, 243
Ptaḥ has erected for you ⟨in⟩ his corner; the cavern of the sky-window of the house of Atum will be opened;[1] and the chest which the patricians drag to the Double Lion will be drawn from Ōn, but it is a woman who will weave his shroud(?).[2] To me belongs the flood of Osiris as the Double Lion; to me belongs the House of Cloth in the flood-waters. May I be exalted above the Guardian, for I am Lord of the West.

1. Read *wn tpḥt ptr n ’Itm*; S10C^a inserts a superfluous *r* after *tpḥt*, and S10C^b repeats the genitive before *’Itm* on passing from line to line.

2. In 243*g* both texts seem defective; I have provisionally combined them into *ḥmt ḥm stꜣy(t) tꜣm.f* 'but it is a woman who will weave his shroud' (of the deceased) or 'his cloak' (of *Rwty*), taking *ḥm* to be the enclitic particle.

Spell 627

Gēb has appointed himself to be the chiefest of the gods.[1] I come among them, VI, 244
the dignitaries of God, who act so that Maʿet may sit; who seat themselves in the tribunal of the Lord of all things in (this) place.[2] I give an order concerning the two kilns(?),[3] for I have ruled their places.[4]

The great name.[5] Uplifted of face. He who is triumphant(?).[6] He of the ear of corn. He who goes afoot. She of the frightening fire. He whose mouth is his [. . .]. Beneficial of action. Great of shape. *Ḏnr*.[7] He who has two knees. Growing flower. He who glitters. He of the depths. She of the fringed cloth. Primeval spirit. Leader of those who act. He whose face is double.[8] He who is on his *dom*-palm. His two plumes are on him. *Ṯnh*.[9] He who is on the top of the throne.
Hidden of face. Spirit with imitation body.[10] | Upstanding of name. Wailer with 245
dummy face.[11] Crocodile-face.[12] Heart-swallower. He who is honest.[13] He who has two phalli. Spirit whose mouth is wide.[14] *Ḏꜣty*. Two who are content. His pole. Weighty of power. *ʿbꜣꜣ*-fish. Growing ear of corn(?).[15] *’Ingy*. Spirit who slew his father. Various of faces. Many of likenesses. She who is wary(?). Scribe of the

two crowns. *Sꜣyw*-fish. She of green and red herbs. Hot-hearted anointed one. Spirit who made it. [16] He who rises. *Hꜣrr-ḥꜣr*. Greatly strong. The two Conclaves. Content of name. The name is prominent(?). Detestable concerning water. Hidden spirit. Spirit who created his double. Living traveller. Plunderer. Resting-place. [17] Foremost one who sits. He whose heart is fortified. He whose bread is lotus. Equipped spirit. Spirit who is *ḥbny*. He who is pleasing. He whose faces are
246 dummy.[1] He who put his heritage together. Great of name. He who cuts open. [18] Overweening. Spirit with outstretched arm. His five spirits. Great One of the Curtain(?). Heart-puller. Lion who is fruitful(?). [19] He who gathers together his property. Upstanding of face. Divine spirit. Spirit who acts at his desire. Spirit who partakes of his desire. Ennobled spirit.

I am he whom he recognizes, having spent the day in order to knit (things) together: [20] who bears witness to this [21] time; *Pꜣr* is he who opens the chest, and he will make presentation of bread to the hand of Thoth[22] who opens the books of the gods as he who proclaims their utterance.[23] I am he who will seek an end of words. [24]

1. So S1oC; B1BO has merely 'Gēb'.
2. So B1Bo, which omits the *m* before *ḏꜣḏꜣt*; S1oC has: 'your tribunal daily in [. . .]'.
3. Cf. *Concise Dict.* 293.
4. Presumably of the 'dignitaries' of 244*b*.
5. The epithets which follow presumably refer to the members of the tribunal, the 'dignitaries' aforementioned.
6. *Tpy dwnt.f.* Cf. *Wb.* V, 433,6–9.
7. Quite obscure. The hoe-sign suggests that this word may be derived from the stem *ḏny*, with *r* for final *y*.
8. Perhaps looking fore and aft, a Janus-spirit.
9. Meaning unknown. The only *ṯnḥ* on record is a late word with eye-det. meaning 'glance at', *Wb* V, 384, 10. 11.
10. Lit. 'substituted of body'. Compare *ỉdnt* 'imitation woman', *Pyr.* §1273.
11. For *sḥꜣw* 'wailer' cf. *CT* IV, 94*o*; VI, 74*b*. On *idn* see n. 10.
12. For *ꜥšm-ḥr* see also *CT* IV, 4*d*; V, 333*n*.
13. For *pgꜣ-ḥr* 'honest', cf. Barns, *Ram.* p. 9.
14. Lit. 'long', presumably from corner to corner.
15. Assuming *šm* to be a miswriting of *wšm*, cf. 244*j*. A miswriting of the synonymous *šms*, *CT* II, 369*c*; 388*f* is also a possibility.
16. Or 'her'. The rather large space following *s* probably marks a separation between two epithets, even though the usual determinative is lacking. cf. de Buck, n. 2*.
17. Cf. *CT* V, 349*d*.
18. For *wgs* 'cut open' fish cf. *Concise Dict.* 71.
19. Assuming to be a mistake for , as in *Nḫbwt*, *Pyr.* §§123*b*; *nḫbt* §1451.

20. So possibly 246*q* in B1Bo, regarding the final *r.f* as the enclitic particle. *Ṯs pẖr* of S10C makes no sense. The clauses 246*q-s* are all obscure.

21. S10C has misread hieratic *p* as plural strokes.

22. So S10C; B1Bo has *iꜥ.f t*, perhaps an error for *iꜥb.f t*.

23. B1Bo simply 'as Ḥu'.

24. So B1Bo; S10C: 'I am he who will make an end of words'.

Spell 628

TO CAUSE THE WEST TO GIVE HER HANDS TO A MAN. IT MEANS BEING HALE. VI, 247
Hail to you, Beautiful West! See, I have come safely to you, you Great Lady; the Mighty One has been passed, and true is Isis who has acted on my behalf; I have uncovered those wings of yours.[1] It means that Thoth(?)[2] will not destroy me, while Atum(?)[3] is in Ōn with Yusas. O you Lady of the north and west, be hidden(?).[4] Take[5] me on your lap and give me that breast of yours which you gave to him;[6] may you nurse me with it, for I will come on to the lap of Him who cares for(?) the young child. I have not placed you ⟨. . .⟩.[7]

1. Masc. suffix.

2.  an error for  ?

3. A miswriting of *'Itm*? Note the association with Ōn.

4. Hortative old perfective? Hardly imperative plural; the sing. suffix *.ṯ* below shows that *mḥtt* and *imntt* refer to one and the same person.

5. Imperative with reinforcing dative.

6. To whom? Hardly for 'to me' here. Perhaps Horus is implied.

7. The text has clearly been left unfinished.

Spell 629

To lash together a ladder for the sky. I have seen those who have achieved their desire[1] for themselves in the Island of Fire, I have seen my face (*sic*). A fair path has been made for me to those two fields of . . .[2] of the *dom*-palm, and the Bull removes himself(?).[3] I have come so that I may receive the two fields, and what belongs to me is made for me. The windings[4] of ꜥAndjet have been put in order for me, so that I may give accuracy and set the plumb-line in order. The hot weather[5] has been set in order for me at the two Fields of Offerings which belong to Osiris and which give bread thence to the owners of food-stuffs(?).[6] I will prepare[7] what belongs to me, and I will receive my two fields; I will prepare what VI, 248 belongs to (each) one of them, and those who watch over them will be established for me.[8]

249 'Who are you?'[9]

'The messengers[10] of the Bull of the flood come to me, for I am the trampler'.

'Why have you come here for me?'[11]

'I have come in order to give what belongs to (each) one in the two Fields of Offerings which belong to Osiris'.

'Who is he who will put the windings of ʿAndjet in order for you so that you may set the drag-ropes aright and establish the fishermen of the land who made the landmarks[12] of the king for you?'

'Open the cavern in order to go forth to Djedu; go and put in order the winding of ʿAndjet for me, set the drag-ropes aright[13] for me, establish for me the fishermen of the land who made the landmarks of the kings for me'.

'Who will act with you?'

'It is Anubis, Lord of the desert'.

'Who will let you go forth?'

'It is *Bswr*'.

'Who will conduct you?'

'It is the Great Bull'.

'Why will you go forth?'

250 'I will go forth because of Shu, I will climb on the sunbeam'.

'Where will you travel to?'[14]

'I will travel on that great causeway on which those whose shapes are great travel'.

'Who will present you to the monarch who is yonder?'

'It is she who mounts up and she who is combed'.[15]

'What is it that you will do for me as a reward for it?'

'I have set aright . . .[16] for them at my cauldron which you have made with me. I have filled their fists with flowers belonging to the goddess'.

'Where will you go in and in what shape will you go out?'

'I will go in as a hare and I will come out as a falcon'.

'What will you live on?'

'I will live on lapis lazuli, I will live on carnelian'.

'With what will you be clad?'

'With the tresses(?) of the Great One, with what issued ⟨from⟩ Shu, for he is a true god, to whom everything is given, and he has put the windings of ʿAndjet in order in the realm of the dead.

1. Lit. 'those who have acted on behalf of their hearts'.

2. *'Ikwy*, var. *ỉwkwy*, meaning unknown.

3. It is not clear how the verb following *kꜣ* is to be read; neither spelling corresponds to a known word. The fish-det. in S10C[b] suggests the possibility that the original word may have been *sbn*, with a general sense of 'go', 'crawl away', of snakes and other pests.

4. So S10C[a]; presumably of the ⸢Andjetian waterways. S10C[b] has *mꜣʿw* with det.  almost certainly a misreading of 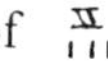 ; for this word see *Concise Dict.* 102.

5. Lit. 'summer'.

6. *mḫꜣdt*, not recorded.

7. Read probably *ỉry⟨.ỉ⟩*, prospective *sḏm.f*, as in 248*o*.

8. 248*p*–249*e* are absent from S10C[b].

9. There is no indication of the identity of the questioner.

10. Perhaps to be equated with *ỉnw* of *Pyr.* §§140; 535, 660; etc., the preceding  is surely for *ỉy* 'come'.

11. The text has: 'Why have I come here for you?', but this is obviously an inversion of the sense; the reply in 249*e* 'I have come' confirms this view.

12. For *ỉst* 'landmark' cf. *Pyr.* §§1142; 1236; note the det. in S10C. S10C[b] ends the spell here.

13. For *mꜣʿ* read *smꜣʿ* with 249*g*. Note that the deceased does not answer the preceding question 'Who is he', etc., but issues orders to his interlocutor.

14. The function of *sp.f* at the end of this clause is not clear to me, since it does not seem necessary to the sense.

15. Cf. the verb *ʿʿb* 'comb' the hair, *GNS* 111.

16. *'Ikwt* is of unknown meaning; compare perhaps th equally unknown *ỉkw, ỉkt* of *Pyr.* §§423–4.

Spell 630

O N, you are the companion(?)[1] of Horus of the north of the sky. I have consid- VI, 25
ered(?)[2] a matter in the House of the Two Souls, and water of the Eye was given to me before I descended. I have not made a bundle of woe(?)[3] because of Gēb, though woe(?) has been placed in the midst of the sky because of Gēb, (even) he who gives air and takes away air, and he who is deprived of air dies. But it is not I who speak; it is he who is just who utters the reckoning[4] because of breathing air beside him.

O N, you are one who guides himself to him who possesses a voice.[5] 252

Judgement has been made in the presence of Neith, and air has been given to me, since I know it.[6] I do not speak about this air the name of which men know, I speak about the lone air which is in the Mansion of Seth; its name is . . .[7]

O N, . . .[8] is the Lord of the air.

253 I know the air by this its name of Seth . . . ;[9] | see, I know it and I have said: 'My air is mine, and eternity is mine'. GIVING AIR TO A MAN IN THE REALM OF THE DEAD.[10]

1. *Ḏrw*, lit. perhaps 'who are at the side of'.
2. *Nkꜣ* of Sq3C may be identical with *nkꜣ* 'think about', *Concise Dict.* 141, though the det. here is not recorded for that verb. *Skꜣ* of Sq6C is not known, and would be a very easy corruption of *nkꜣ*. For the use of the 1st person in the translation cf. 251*i* (Sq3C); *.f* in *skꜣ.n.f* (Sq6C) must refer to Horus, not to the deceased, who is addressed in the 2nd person in the preceding sentence.
3. Quite obscure; for *ỉꜥnw* 'woe' see James, *Ḥeḳanakhte*, p. 109. Possibly the sense may be that the deceased is disclaiming having collected troubles for somebody.
4. Reading *ḏd ḥsb*; the passage seems to imply that only those of good record will be allowed to breathe. In 251*i* the deceased disclaims any responsibility for the judgement.
5. The unmistakable 2nd person of 252*a* and the parallelism with 251*a* speak against accepting *ỉnk*(?) of Sq3C, which could have been substituted thoughtlessly for the personal name, which is certainly original here.
6. Sq6C has *ḥr.f sw* for *rḫ sw N.*
7. I cannot interpret the name of the air.
8. *'Isṯ.ty*, meaning unknown.
9. *'Isṯ.ty* again.
10. Sq4C adds: 'entering(?) into [. . .]'.

Spell 631

To exist by air, to breathe the air in the realm of the dead in the Field of Rushes.[1] The sound of woe is in the horizon, fear falls on the Netherworld, uproar is in the Field of Rushes, the gods on their thrones go to them, the Sole Lord has collected his wits, for he has seen storm in the upper sky,[2] [he has] foretold

254 [cloudiness][3] in the lower sky on the hands of Him who is greatly strong, | he has foretold him who is stronger than he to those who are in the Presence,[4] the dread of whom is put for him into the primeval ones.[5] O Lord of the two *ptḥy*, implant an obstacle against them;[6] cry out ⟨to⟩ the Destroyer who treads the battle;[7] send to the Sole Lord,[8] cry out to the two great Enneads, listen to them in the land. The two Conclaves have appeared at it(?), the festivals are . . . ,[9] the Servitors have gone all over the fields of them of turquoise;[10] the pure one takes possession of the Mansion as Gēb with the power and voice of a god. See, he comes, having immersed the sky and disturbed the earth, one who satisfies himself thereby; he shall not be named among you – so says the Eyeless One. N has

spoken to you, you gods; O N, you are . . . [11] who dispersed[12] the storm. N sets his power in (the place) where it was extended, N hears the matter of what is brought to him – so say Thoth and the Eyeless One. N knows the Lord of the two *pḥty* as one, and the gods who are in them are made content. Such is N.

1. Sq6C lacks 253*g.h,* while B3Bo lacks 253*i.j.*
2. Var. 'he has seen Seth in the upper desert'. The next sentence is lacking in Sq6C.
3. Restore as *sr*[*.n.f ḥꜣ*]*ty.*
4. Both texts are somewhat garbled; read *sr.n.f wsr r.f n ỉmyw-bꜣḥ* 'he has foretold him who is stronger than he to those who are in the Presence'.
5. So Sq6C, with a superfluous *s* at the end; var. B3Bo: 'he puts the dread of him into those who are among the primeval ones'.
6. Not in B3Bo. From here on the spell becomes most obscure, and in some places I translate the words without grasping their real meaning.
7. Note the loss of the preposition *n* before *nbḏ*. Not in Sq6C.
8. B3Bo adds *mrt Rʿ* 'what Rēʿ desires'. This text ends here.
9. I do not understand *dmy* with boat-det.
10. The sign [hieroglyph] inserted between *šmsw* and *sẖwt* seems to have nothing to do with the sentence and to be intrusive; *pẖr šmsw* demands a direct object.
11. *Ḫrr* with det. of Seth-animal.
12. Lit. 'who split up'.

Spell 632

N has gone down, he has breathed the air, he has smelt Truth,[1] N has smelt the air, N [has gone forth(?)][2] in order to open the Eye of Rēʿ, N has gone down in order to ease the Weary One, Khons opens (the doors),[3] and [the winds] pass out;[4] the *Nt*-crowns are parted and the wind enters into N's nose. TO BREATHE THE AIR IN THE REALM OF THE DEAD. VI, 255

1. Var. Sq3C: 'he has breathed Truth'.
2. Cf. de Buck, n. 1*, but apparently [*pr*]*.n* is to be read rather than *pry,* though in that case the space available suggests that something else is lacking between *tꜣw* and *pr.*
3. Compare *CT* V, 35*k*; de Buck, n. 2*. Not in Sq6C.
4. Cf. de Buck, n. 3*.

Spell 633

The air is in N's nose like Seth, N has spoken to Seth, N has been informed. AIR SHALL BE IN A MAN'S NOSE IN THE REALM OF THE DEAD.

Spell 634

VI, 256 Recitation [. . .].[1] Hail to you, Mighty Lady! N has come [. . .] N. N is Maʿet [. . .] you, O Mighty Lady, when pleasing Shu who is in the horizon. N has breathed [the air . . . .].[2] [O N], you are that Maʿet whom he (*sic*) desires and by means of whom he lives every day [. . .] N [. . .] the desert [. . .] Maʿet the riparian lands; the terror of the *Nt*-crowns [. . .] the *Nt*-crowns [. . .]. N is Maʿet in [. . .].[3]

1. The heading is absent in Sq6C.
2. The lacuna is considerably longer in Sq6C than in T1L.
3. If de Buck is correct in restoring *ṯwt* in 256*h* at 9*, the text of Sq6C may have differed somewhat from that of T1L.

Spell 635

VI, 257 O you of the seasonal festivals who cut off the foreleg; O you who are upon the mountain who see the wounds; O you who acclaim the horns which keep the pallid one(?) away; O you who make the Two Warriors content with wisdom; O you who are in charge of your shrine,[1] who see your two spirits; O you who are united within your two mansions; O Orion who loosed the cord, I have come that I may see the shrine; O you who are above and you who are below, the iron of the west ⟨is in⟩[2] the mansion; O you who spend day and night on your left side, I have gone in and out and have absorbed it.

O you hidden one who are in the mansion of Neith and Ptaḥ . . .[3] bearing foodstuffs, I am content ⟨with⟩ what you have taken, the funeral meal which is with(?) me, the secret thing which is in the mansion of Him who cries out,[1]
258 because my breath is mine[4] and my breath has been given to me by *ʾIny*, father of the four heralds(?) [. . .] Lord of Offerings, herald(?) of the Lord of All [. . .]. Rēʿ has no power over me, and it is I who take away his breath; Atum has no power over me, and I violate his hinder parts; the oppressive agents(?)[5] of the gods have no power over me [. . .] I have released *ʾIꜣst*,[6] I have eaten the bread[7] of the falcon in his mansion,[8] I have warded off [. . .].

1. Cf. 257*h*, where this word has the house-det.
2. The absence of a preposition is inexplicable, unless there has been an error of omission.
3. *ʾIk wꜣtys*; unintelligible.
4. The construction is obscure, and I am by no means sure that I have understood it.

5. *ꜣꜥbw*; for the meaning cf. *ꜣꜥbt* 'oppression', *Concise Dict.* 1.
6. Perhaps the presiding goddess of *'Iꜣsw* 'part of the sky', *Pyr.* §709.
7. For *pyt* 'bread' cf. also *CT* III, 349*l*.
8. The name of the deceased is superfluous here.

Spell 636

SPELL FOR A MAN TO HAVE POWER THROUGH HIS MAGIC IN ORDER THAT HE MAY ESTABLISH(?)[1] HIMSELF IN THE REALM OF THE DEAD. Sobk in the water, Dedwen in Zety-land, Ḥa in the west, Sopd in the east, they bring me my double for my body, and it will be in the water with Sobk. Bring it to me, so that it may be in the sky escorting the great god. Bring it to me, so that it may remember me and act so that I may live. VI, 259

1. The sense of the four signs following *ḥkꜣ.f* is not clear. The reading is *r ddr.f,* a clause of purpose with *r* and *sḏm.f,* but no verb *ddr* is known, and the translation 'establish(?)' is a guess.

Spell 637

TO OPEN [THE DOORS] OF THE SKY. These are the two doors which belong to Him of the sky-window[1] and which belong to Him who is under the tree[2] in front. O Keeper of his mooring-post, prepare a path for N so that N may pass, he being alive, prosperous and hale, for there are none who will do anything evilly against N.

1. Read *ꜥꜣwy ỉpw(y) nn nwy Ptr.*
2. *Wb.* III, 395,12 records a late deity *ẖry-ḫt.*

Spell 638

SPELL [. . . AND FOR] NOT PERISHING IN THE REALM OF THE DEAD. I am the Destroyer, because I know that I will go down,[1] for I have appeared and am mighty. O [. . .], I am one who calls out, who is excluded(?)[2] when he adorns[3] the two Enneads. I have appeared and am swift, I am indeed one who exists. VI, 260

1. *N* before *rḫ* appears to be the conjunction 'because', not the negation.
2. The meaning of *ḫm* is not certain, but 'debar' or 'exclude' seems the least unlikely equivalent.
3. It is not clear whether the suffix in *ššd.f* refers to the being addressed in 260*e* or to the deceased.

Spell 639

[SPELL FOR SITTING AMONG THE GREAT GODS]. N [has sat] among the great gods, [N has passed] by the House of the Night-bark; it is the *bꜣt*-bird which brings you, O N.[1]

1. The rubric is restored from *BD* 215,16; the other lacunae from *CT* Spell 309; cf. de Buck, n. 5.

Spell 640

VI, 261 SPELL FOR NOT ENTERING INTO [THE SHAMBLES][1] OF THE REALM OF THE DEAD.[2] My word is spoken, the knot is tied[3] behind me in the sky, the earth is guarded by Rēʿ every day.[4] I have made the knot firm against the inert ones at my feet on that day of cutting off the tress.

The knot is tied behind me by Seth, in whose power the Ennead were at first, before uproar had come into being, so that you[5] might make me hale as this one who slew my father, for I am he who takes possession of the [Two] Lands.

The knot is tied behind me [by] Nu[6] who saw [the First Occasion],[7] before the gods were born, [. . .].[8] I am *Pnty,* I am the heir(?)[9] of the [great][10] gods.

1. For the restoration *nmt* cf. *BD* 121,14; 122,8. The Nu text of BD (Spell 50B) is closer to CT than Nebseni (50A).

2. M2NY has the alternative rubric 'Driving away a snake'.

3. So M2NY and *BD* 122,9; the reading of T2Be is not certain, but appears to be '[the knot] is behind me'.

4. T2Be has a dittograph of 'Rēʿ'; M2NY appears to be corrupt, while *BD* 121,16 is much altered at this point. For *sꜣw tꜣ* BD 122,9-10 has *ỉrt tꜣ*.

5. Plural suffix, but it is not clear to whom it refers. Note the 'liaison' *n* between *ṯn* and *wỉ*.

6. M2NY probably read 'Nūt', see the fem. participle in 261*l*; so also *BD* 122, 2. 16.

7. Restored from *BD* 122,16.

8. Passalacqua's copy (see de Buck, n. 16*) of the text in the lacuna is incomprehensible; *rmt* is clear, but not what precedes; one might expect *n ỉrt rmṯt* 'before men were made', but the traces cannot be so read. *BD* 122, 3–4; 123,1 read *n ms(t) nṯrw ʿšmw.*

9. Restoring as *ỉwʿ; ỉwt* of *BD* 123,2 does not yield good sense.

10. *ʿꜣw* restored from *BD* 123, 2.

Spell 641

TO BE A GREAT ONE IN THE REALM OF THE DEAD.[1] I am Rēʿ in the midst of his VI, 262
Eye; a lament goes out, a cry of woe is given in the horizon, the . . .[2] of the god is withdrawn, this one comes because of you[3] and of the two blood-offerings.[4]

I am Rēʿ in the shrine of Maʿet,[5] I surpass the great ones who are on the path of the Foreleg,[6] I sit on my stool(?), I judge the retinue of the Ennead, for I am their ruler, and their gaze has gone forth.[7]

1. Var. 'Spell for [being] in the tribunal of the god'.
2. *Ššt.*
3. DɪC omits *ḥr.k.*
4. *Ṯrwty*; for *ṯrwt* cf. *Pyr.* §401; *CT* III, 285*a*; VI, 179*e*. The god-dets. seem superfluous.
5. For *ḫm* 'shrine' as written in M2NY cf. 257*e.h*; *ḫm* 'not know' of DɪC is a corruption.
6. Reading in 262*i* *ḥr w3wt ḫpš.*
7. Reading *pr.n ḥr.s[n]* with M2NY. 262*l.m* are not in DɪC, which substitutes 262*n*: 'I am a god'.

Spell 642

The festival is brought about,[1] the servitors go round about, the paths are made VI, 263
known, the servitors make presentation, the great ones are protected,[2] he who has come is made ready(?).[3] The coming forth of the Bull, the Lord of the West; the sceptre is on high, the spirits of . . .[4] are caused to circle round(?).[5]

1. Var. GɪT: 'the abode of the festival is brought'. It would not be impossible to interpret 263*a-e* as a series of imperatives.
2. Despite the writing, *mk* can hardly be the particle.
3. Reading *ḥr.t(w)* 'is made ready'; no other interpretation seems plausible.
4. *Smt.*
5. *Ššny* may be the causative of *šny* 'encircle', etc.

Spell 643

. .[1] I open up the obstacles, I split open the Netherworld, I go out among the retinue of the Lord of . . . ;[2] he makes me into one who goes to and fro, and it means that I am he who opened the obstacles and split open the Netherworld, having power in my feet;[3] who broke open the firmament and lightened the darkness(?).[4] I go to and fro in contentment,[5] I am strong, and my mark of distinction is on my head.

1. The opening words of this spell in 263*i* are meaningless as they stand, and are obviously corrupt.

2. *Ḥknwt.*

3. 263*m-o* seem to be badly confused in A1C, and even in G1T we must surely emend *rdwy.sn* into *rdwy.ỉ.* I have the impression that originally, in an earlier MS that has not survived. *wn pw srt* and *wbꜣw dwꜣt* will have been written side by side and then followed by *sḫm.ỉ m rdwy.ỉ,* and I have translated the passage in that sense.

4. Read *sšpw grḥw*?

5. Reading *hꜣr* in G1T as well as A1C; the *ꜣ* appears to have been added as an afterthought in G1T. I have taken *hꜣr* to be but a variant of *hr* 'be content', as at times in later texts.

Spell 644

VI, 264 O Nūt, spread yourself over me when you enfold me with the life which belongs to you;[1] may you fold your arms over this seat of mine, for I am a languid Great One. Open to me, for I am Osiris; do not close your doors against me, so that I may cross the firmament and be joined to the dawn, and that I may expel what Rēꜥ detests from his bark.

I have come that I may drive off ꜥApep and that I may make known the course[2] to the northern sky; I am he who takes the helm in the Bark of Governance and throws out the bow-warp from the god's bark, and vindication is granted to me in the tribunal of Rēꜥ-Atum. I am one who is joyful[3] in the coffin, and the Decapitator will have no power over me.

I have come that I may conduct the funeral meal and propitiate those who
265 are in the upper houses; I am Anubis as one who fosters the place of embalming, who embalmed the god[4] in the hidden place.

I have come that I may cover up corruption and deal with the mummy-wrappings, and that I may pour away the putrefaction after death.

I have come equipped with my power, I have quenched my thirst with it, I am a possessor of provisions.

1. Read *ẖnmt.ṯ wỉ m ꜥnḫ ḫry.t,* the verb-form being *sḏmt.f.* G1T has confused the text writing *ẖnmt ṯw n,* etc.

2. *Sḳdwt,* lit. 'navigations'.

3. *Ḥꜥw* in A1C; *ḥꜣw* 'who wail' of G1T is surely an error. For *mm* of A1C read simply *m.*

4. Reading *w[t] nṯr.*

Spell 645

The door into the Netherworld is opened for N; O you of the expanses of Shu who are in the sunshine, prepare a path for N, open for him a portal in the land of the Netherworld; (as for) N, to him belongs the entire land.[1] TO OPEN THE DOOR FOR [A MAN][2] IN THE LAND OF THE NETHERWORLD.

1. *Wnt* is a particle. Note a superfluous *n* at the change of line in 265*m*.
2. See de Buck, n. 4*.

Spell 646

SPELL FOR THE STAFF WHICH OPENS(?) [. . .]. Stand up, stand up behind Osiris, stand up, O staff, behind Osiris, that he may smite the contentious ones, the confederacy [of Seth(?) . . .] penetrating of visage, greatly strong, who cuts down the foes of Osiris. [May] you [put][1] your arm about me as a *wtnw*, so that I may be vindicated. If the heart of Osiris be [at peace][2] in the West, then will my heart be at peace at the place where he is. I am his child, I am pure, [I am a god—so says(?)][3] the well(?) of Abydos. VI, 266

May you receive natron from before the god, may you clothe yourself in your fringed cloak; I [am][4] with you as one who is in front.[5] I am pure, I am a god[6]— so says the flood in which there is cleansing for you, and I am your successor.

1. See de Buck, n. 4*.
2. See n. 5*.
3. See nn. 6*; 7*.
4. See n. 8*. This part of the spell appears to be uttered by the son of the deceased as officiating priest; cf. 266*q*.
5. Determined with a strange creature.
6. See n. 9*.

Spell 647

PROTECTION THROUGH PTAḤ. I am a high Power, headman of the Two Lands, VI, 267
Lord of justice, scribe of all the *pr-wr*; [I am[1] the . . . of] Isis, the sweat of Gēb,[2] the Lord of herbage, green of fields, nourishing the grain of the Field of Offerings and knitting the seed together – so says Atum. My spine is enduring, my egg is

firm on the spines of the celestial kine. O my son, how fair is your face! My likeness(?) is created,[3] and that is how this my name of Ptaḥ came into being; one fair of face, mighty of strength, to whom men appeal(?)[4] within the castle of the Lord of life, to whom his places appeal(?); his nobles are in front of him, in front of those who are greater than he – so says Sia concerning me. That is how this my name of 'Succourer, Lord of justice, scribe at the head of the *pr-wr*' came into being. Maʿet is joyful when I am strong [for] life and dominion; Thoth is on my great flood; as for the repelling of my pen concerning it, there is nothing which the gods have done.

I am one who succours(?)[5] his place, a favourite of the Lord of the shrine;[6] I have gone in and out of the interior of the shrine of the Lord of All, I have lifted Maʿet on to the altar of Shu who is in the coffin. I have brought in the Sacred Eye, I have destroyed falsehood in the tribunal, I have expelled what Rēʿ
268 detests from his bark,[7] | and every god is in it. I am exalted, and every spirit is possessed with the awe of me, and the plebs worship my goodness. I make the herbage to grow, I make the riparian lands of Upper Egypt green, (I) the Lord of the deserts who makes green the valleys in which are the Nubians, the Asiatics and the Libyans. I have entrapped the Nine Bows, and everything is given to me by Rēʿ, the Lord of All.

I am He who is south of his wall, monarch of the gods; I am king of the sky, (even) Neḥebkau who rules the Two Lands, Neḥebkau who grants souls, crownings, doubles and beginnings. I am Neḥebkau, and their lives are at my hand; when I wish, I act, and they live. There are none among them who speak to me apart from [. . .] this my sole name, because I am Ḥu who is on my mouth and Sia who is in my body; it is my *wrrt*-crown which twists the *nʿt*-snake(?)[8] into my back and which incites against those who are disaffected against me when their hearts are cast against me. My dignity is on my hands, and my face reduces to order him who is in the waterway(?);[9] headman of the land who is in the hearts[10] of the headmen who are those who are seated(?).[11]

269 I am Lord of the *wrrt*-crown at the head of the firmament, and the earth is ploughed up for me; I have presented [offerings],[12] and the firmament has been created for me by the turquoise-folk, I have steered the Night-bark[13] and the sailors of the bark are in joy, while [the crew][14] of Rēʿ guards the land. Ḥu is joyful, Sia-Rēʿ is happy, the Ennead is cheerful, the uraei [. . .] when Ptaḥ who is south of his wall comes in front of the thrones for the gods. I have tied up the bark at the Island of Herbage, I have gone in and out of [. . . the Lord] of All. I tell him the governance of the Two Lands when I make them live thereby, while he speaks to me. It is Rēʿ, Lord of the Ennead, who comes; the Lord [. . .]

while those who give are about him, about him, and it means that I have come into being for the Lord of lords.

I am He who is south of his wall, the protector of the gods; neither men, gods, spirits nor the dead have power to turn [me] back to harm me. I am He who is fair of face, whom the Lord of Life and She who rules the gods love. I give life, controlling offerings for the gods the lords of offerings; I am the Lord of Life, ruling in the sky, while Seth is my protection because he knows the nature of what I do; I am the Lord of Life.

1. Cf. de Buck, n. 2*.
2. *Ḳysw*; cf. *CT Transl.* Spell 101, n. 6.
3. For *ptḥ* 'create' cf. *JEA* 35,64 (4). *Ṯw* . . . may perhaps stand for *twt* 'image', 'likeness'.
4. Assuming an extension of the meaning of *smy* 'succour'.
5. *Sym* as written is meaningless; it has been taken here to be a miswriting of *smy*, cf. 267*k.l.*
6. Assuming that  here and in 267*u* stands for *k3r* 'shrine'.
7. Read *dpt* rather than *ỉm* or *wy3* because of the fem. suffix in *ḥr.s*, 268*a*.
8. *Nʿʿt* with snake-det. is not intelligible as it stands; I suggest emending to *nʿʿt nʿt* 'which twists the *nʿt*-snake' as a rope to serve as the speaker's spinal cord; for *nʿy* 'twist' a rope cf. *CT* III, 97*g*; 113*n*; *Rev. d'ég.* 24, 61, n. 13.
9. *Šmw*, cf. *Pyr.* §§1049; 2175. Or should we read *mr*?
10. Read *ỉmy ỉbw* only, the space in the lacuna is about right for *m*.
11. Regarding *ỉmyw* here as being of predication; for *ḥfd* 'sit' cf. *BD* 212,8.
12. For the restoration cf. de Buck, n. 2*.
13. For *ḏsr ḥpt m* cf. *JEA* 20,162; the sense appears more precisely to be 'steer'.
14. For the restoration *ỉswt* cf. de Buck, n. 1*.

Spell 648

The sky was pregnant on the day when Nūt bore him and the arms were given.[1] VI, 270
[The Servitors][2] go round about [. . .] Lord of the horizon on the day of eternity. He rises as Nu, his entourage is serpents, his Ennead displays(?)[3] itself behind him, his powers put fear into the gods who come into being after him, his myriad of spirits is within his mouth. It was magic which came into being of itself, at seeing which the gods rejoiced, and through the sweet savour of which the gods live; who created the mountains and knit the firmament together.

O you Souls of Pe and Nekhen, come behind and before me; O you gods of the south, dread me; O you gods of the north, fear me; O you gods who are on earth,[4] fall to me, for I am Rēʿ the self-created, I have gathered together the fluid of my egg,[5] and I have power over you in this my name of Sakhmet; I am far from you in this my name of Horus at the head of the Ennead. Beware of me, you *ꜣkrw* of the sky;[6] beware, O you who guard the ways in the northern sky; prepare a path for me so that I may pass on it, for I am your lord and your headman. My magic spells are on my mouth, and I have power over my foes who are in the Island of Fire, so that I pass unharmed.

1. The sections 270*a–i* are descriptive of the sun-god, with whom the deceased presumably was identified; the rest of the spell is spoken by the deceased. The clause 'the arms were given' probably means 'her arms were extended' in embrace.
2. Cf. de Buck, n. 3*.
3. *Nṯb*; unrecorded and meaning uncertain.
4. Lit. 'on the back of Gēb'.
5. Note the masc. *ḥbb* instead of the normal fem. *ḥbbt*. The suffix in *swḥt.f* surely refers to the deceased speaker, and therefore must stand for an original 1st person.
6. An unusual attribution of the *ꜣkrw*, who elsewhere are earth-gods.

Spell 649

VI, 271 O you Ram-man,[1] open a path for me, for I am the young child; let me pass unharmed.

O Crocodile-man of his,[2] open a path for me, for I am a magician whose names are pure.

O Lion-man of his, open a path for me, for I am Thoth, and the Eye of Horus is in my body.

O Lion-man of his, open a path for me, for I am Seth about to sail the bark.

O Lion-man of his, open a path for me, for I am Maʿet at the nostrils of Rēʿ.

O Lion-man of his, open a path for me, for I am Horus seeking his Eye.

O Lion-man of his, open a path for me, for I am Gēb about to give judgement.

O Lion-man of his, open a path for me, for I am a fire about the shrine.

272 O Snake-man of his, open a path for me, for I am Min seeking[3] women.

O Jackal-man of his, open a path for me, for I am ʿAnti perambulating the *ḥnw*-bark.

O Messenger of his, [open] a path for me, for [I] am Khons about to write what is true.

1. The man-sign is to be read as a determinative; in 271*b-h* and 272*a-c* it is followed by the suffix *.f.*

2. Perhaps of the Ram-man, but in Spell 653 the suffix has no obvious antecedent; so also 274*a*.

3. Lit. 'in the seekings (for)' or 'embracings of'; the det. of *sḫnw* points to the former meaning.

Spell 650

Hail to you, River of Fire, Lord of Souls, great of power, mightier than your lord, great of wells(?),[1] Lord of rivers, greater than Nu: Let me pass, for I have come from the Island of Fire and I have filled my body with magic. You shall say:[2] 'You may pass unharmed when travelling (on) one of these paths'.[3] It means that you shall tell what is in the heart of Maʿet. You shall say:[4] 'Pass on the one of them which you wish'. I am one who walks; attend to what I say[5] to you truly about it.

1. The reading and meaning of  is not clear; it is suggested that, in view of the context, it may be an ideographic writing for *ẖnmwt* 'wells', though the significance of the apparent dual ending remains obscure.

2. Emending to *ḏd.ḫr.k* as 272*k*; there is no antecedent for a suffix of the 3rd person.

3. Lit. 'a path among these paths'.

4. Emending to *ḏd.ḫr.k* as in n. 2.

5. Emending *ḏdt.f* to *ḏdt.ỉ*. This short spell well exemplifies the confusions of pronouns so often found in CT.

Spell 651

Hail to you, Sakhmet among the great ones, Lady of the sky, mistress of the Two VI, 273
Lands; what you wish is what you do among the gods who are in their shrines. All men are possessed with the awe of you, Lady of life who is with the Green One. As for him who knows this word of God, he shall be in the sky with Rēʿ among the gods who are in the sky, and vindication shall be given to him in every tribunal into which he goes down. He shall eat bread in every place to which he goes, and he shall achieve transformations into anything he wishes. It is a matter exactly true.

Spell 652

This is the allotting of the field of the gods, the grapes from which Rēʿ and his retinue eat.

These are the shrines of the knife with the air thereof.

This is the field of Thoth which is in it; everything in it is in the hand of whoever knows this magic spell.

This is the field of garden plots in the hands of the gods.

This is the field of garden plots in the hands of the spirits.

274 This is his man who eats what he sees; his name is 'Slayer'.

This is the Lord of offerings.

The man who is attached to all this; his name is 'Lord of Spirits'.

These are the Corn-goddess, Bastet, Thoueris and the six ladies.

Spell 653

This is this man of his, whose name is 'Loud-voiced', and this is his stream.

This is this man of his, lord of robbery, who lives on what he has seen; do not pass by him.

This is this man of his, lord of turmoil, with face of fire and eyes of flame; pass by him.

This is this man of his, whose name is 'He who takes the oar'.

This is this man of his, whose name is 'Vindicated'.

Ḥatḥōr.[1] Shesmētet. Bastet. Eye of Horus. Eye of Rēʿ. Edjō. Sakhmet. The Sacred Eye. Khons. Ḥu. Sia. Nefertem. Thoth.

1. A list of deities from the lower left of the plan on p. 271 of de Buck.

Spell 654

VI, 275 I have come rejoicing, a scribe of Maʿet. The birds are in the sky, the fish are in the river, the herbage is in the fields, the *ḫbꜣt*-barks of Ḥatḥōr and the *nšmt*-bark are in the god's lashing together.[1]

1. I.e. are lashed together, built, by the god.

Spell 655

TO GO TO AND FRO AMONG THE SERVITORS, TO ISSUE FROM THE NETHERWORLD, TO KNOW [. . .]. [O] Sakhmet, I assemble the spirits, I go out, I have power over [. . .] word, I do not reveal the word of my . . .[1] Protection is in my hand [. . .] to whom [. . .] goes down; so say they, the offerers and servitors, concerning me. O you powers and gods, help me[2] in [. . .] for me; burning(?) [. . .] water; it quenches the fire of his breath. His soul is the Demolisher who comes(?)[3] [. . . in peace],[4] an equipped spirit; so say they, those whose sanctuaries[5] are secret, concerning me, after him who is weak [. . .].

The obstacles are opened up and the darkness is lightened; may you go out VI, 276
into the day, may [you] have power over your foes, may you have news of(?) the . . .[6] Proceed on your journeys, go to and fro, may you [go forth][7] among them, the living. Do not reveal the word of those who are on earth as to the shape of a living spirit; may you astonish those who see you and may your sceptre be in [your] hand against your foes. O you god, going to and fro among them, the living, do not reveal the word of those who are on earth who recall for you the coming.[8]

1. *Ṯnby.ỉ*, meaning obscure. *Wb.* V, 380, 9 shows a word *ṯnb* with legs det., also of uncertain meaning.
2. The position of the dative is abnormal.
3. The translation of 275*s* is most uncertain.
4. Cf. de Buck, n. 9*.
5. Equating *sṯwt* with *sṯyt*, which occurs as the name of the sanctuary of Sokar.
6. *ꜥ3hw-ỉb*.
7. Restoring as *pr.k*.
8. Apparently so, but it is not clear what is meant; the sentence appears to have been left unfinished.

Spell 656

O Swallower of [myriads], O [Ass], may you oppose yourselves to yonder foes of Osiris. (As for) N, those who will come are [those who would oppose her][1] in order to take away her bread from her; he who is in [. . .] tomb, she who is in the burial chamber(?) in order to drive back to you those who show respect[2] to
you, and [you are driven back(?)][3] with your fat(?) in your mouths,[4] you have VI, 277
defecated with what is on your hinder parts,[5] your [. . .] is upon your heads, [. . .] your heads for Rēꜥ [. . .] Horus has challenged(?) yonder foes[6] among them, (even he), the distinguished of shape(?).[7] [. . .]. None will make

rejoicing for you when meeting [you, . . .] in your . . .[8] in the place of execution. There will be no [. . .] the West, there will be no going forth at the festivals of Ḥatḥōr for [. . .].

O Swallower of myriads, O Ass, [. . .][9] N's foes [who shall come][10] to meet you in order to oppose [the Swallower(?)].[11] She has ploughed and she has reaped with her servants, she has [drunk][12] the water which the Nile made for her. O Rēꜥ, [yonder foes][13] of N have said that they will take away the great
278 White Crown ⟨which is on⟩ your head[14] and the *ꜣtf*-crown which is on your vertex; they have said that they will smash heads so as to disturb [. . .] in the Presence; they have said that they will disturb truth in order to [foster][15] falsehood at the Throne. O Rēꜥ, vindicate N!

1. Restore as *ḫsf.ty-sn ỉm.s*; cf. de Buck, n. 7.
2. Note the absence of determinatives from *try*.
3. Restore as *ỉw.ṯn sḫt.tywn*?
4. Apparently so; there is no other word *ꜥḏ* that could possibly fit here.
5. Read simply *tpyw* (or *tpyt*) *pḫty.ṯ*.
6. Restore as *sr.n Ḥr ḫftyw ỉpf ỉm.sn*; for the translation of *sr* as 'challenge' cf. *sr ꜥḥꜣ* 'challenge to battle', *JEA* 21, 222.
7. Regarding *ṯn* as the word for 'be distinguished', written without determinatives.
8. *Bꜣwt*.
9. The surviving *f* at the end of the lacuna shows that its content differed from 276*m*.
10. Restore *ỉw.t(y).sn* in the lacuna, cf. de Buck, n. 7*.
11. There is enough room to restore *ꜥm*, see 277*h*. The abrupt change of topic after the lacuna suggests that there may have been a textual omission.
12. Restore *swr*.
13. Restore *ḫftyw ỉpf* with 276*m*.
14. Read ⟨*tpt*⟩ *tp.k*.
15. Read *r s*[*ꜥnḫ*] *ỉsft*.

Spell 657

To call magic to mind. I am one to whom (things) were given, a son of Rēꜥ and a son of Thoth; I sought[1] this which I found in my mouth; what I picked up, I found under my . . . ;[2] a tress and a pigeon(?)[3] – and *vice versa*. He[4] grants to me that I receive what has been allotted to me, and I have been watchful with my mouth and my belly so that I may receive this which my lips give. O my heart, raise yourself on your base that you may recall what is in you; the letter goes out from the house of Rēꜥ, having been sealed in the house of Thoth, and I have called to mind all the magic which is in this my belly.

1. Read probably *sḫn.⟨n.⟩ỉ*, with merging of successive *n*'s.
2. *Nḏḏ*; an unidentified part of the body.
3. For *ḏꜣꜣ* 'tress cf. *CT* III, 288*a*; *Siut,* 15,21; the bird *ꜥbw* may be identical with *ꜥb(ꜣ)* 'a pigeon or dove', Edel, *Weltkammer,* I, 227. This association seems inexplicable.
4. Rēꜥ or Thoth?

Spell 658

To raise up a man to the great god; to go aboard the bark of Rēꜥ. Hail to VI, 279
you, great god, Bull of the West! Endure and know no weariness! I will go aboard your bark, which I have tied up at the stairway, and I will make descents into the riparian land . . . ;[1] I will come to land in the western sky, having appeared as Rēꜥ. I will take shape as Khopri, I will fly up on to your thrones as a divine falcon,[2] I will fare upstream at the bow, I will guide the voyages, and the starboard watch will hearken to my voice, your larboard watch . . . ;[3] he who bears a sceptre speaks to me, the wand-bearers attend on me, your rope is made fast.[4]

1. *Skw.*
2. Reading *byk nṯr,* regarding  not as *sꜣ* 'son', but as an additional general bird-determinative.
3. I can make nothing of 279*o*. 280*f* (Spell 659) has *ḥy.n.i tꜣ-ꜥꜣ.f sḏb* 'I have removed the trouble of her larboard watch'.
4. The end of the spell in 279*r* is corrupt; what should stand here is *hy nwḥ.k* 'your rope is made fast', cf. 280*l* (Spell 659). On this expression see my note *JEA* 57,202.

Spell 659

SPELL FOR LANDING. Hail to you, Bull of the West, Lord of fayence in the VI, 280
festivals of the two Maꜥets! I go aboard your bark, which is tied up at the stairway, like Ḥemen who knows no weariness, I have screeched as a falcon on his tree, I have removed the trouble of her[1] larboard watch, and her starboard watch is in my charge. I have acted and I have gone down ⟨into⟩[2] the riparian land so that I may land at the northern sky, in order to serve(?)[3] Rēꜥ every day. The attendant speaks, the wand-bearer stands up, your rope is made fast, and I am a possessor of praise in the *ṯnnt*-shrine.

1. The bark's; feminine in English. Note that *tꜣ-ꜥꜣ.f* has been given honorific precedence over *sḏb*.

2. Supply *m* after *hꜣ.n.ỉ*, cf. 279*h*.

3. The word following *mḥtt r* is corrupt and unintelligible. 279*j* has *ḫꜥ.ky m Rꜥ* 'having appeared as Rēꜥ' at this point.

Spell 660[1]

I will cut off your heads, O you who oppose my path; I will lift up your heads on my hands, for my birth was the birth of a god on that day when the *hdn*-plant was fashioned, before sky and earth had come into being, before water had come
VI, 281 into being, before the Abyss had come into being, | before Gēb and Nūt had come into being, before Osiris and Isis had come into being, before Seth and Nephthys had come into being. I was born at the birth of Isis, and those who are on their *kꜣkꜣ*-plants[2] and who are in their irrigation ditches(?)[3] come that they[4] may guide the bark of Sokar in order to wipe the eyes of . . .[5] They prepare a path for me, (even I) who moor with those who are in sky and earth. I will[6] sit down, turn round,[7] take my seat, and appear in my flaming glory; I will acclaim my sceptre and will flourish by means of my rod. I have tied my ornament to my neck, the Red Crown is my strength, I will receive water at the streams, and there is nothing which you[8] will find so that you may speak against me who am in the sunshine. I have seen my father face to face,[9] and He who is in front of his shrine will bring to me; I am the sole flower of my mother, the third of those whose faces are terrible;[10] I am the eldest son of *'Imtw*, the second of the Pair, the third
282 of *Kꜣ-sp.f.* | I came into being before the sky had come into being and before the earth had come into being; I am the *hdn*-plant of the aftermath,[11] which I prepared,[12] over whom the Flaming One has no power. I am a king who probes(?),[13] and the two Truth-goddesses have laid their hands on me,[14] being hungry on the day of . . . [15]in the Sokar-bark of the two Truth-goddesses.

I am a lion in the Nile, I am the snake of Upper Egypt in the tribunal of *ꜥḥꜥ-wr*, and I will never feed(?).[16] I will walk upright, I will not walk upside down, and I will go aboard[17] the bark which is tied up at the stairway. I have removed the trouble of the larboard watch,[18] and the starboard watch is under my command. There is praise in the *tnnt*-shrine, and I am the keeper of five portions in Ōn; three portions are in the sky with Rēꜥ, two portions are on earth with Gēb, and it is the Night-bark which brings[19] to me, it is the Day-bark which gives in my presence. I will not travel upside down; I detest filth and will not eat it, I will not
283 go up to it with my hand or tread on it with my sandals, | because[20] I am indeed a great heron on the battlements of the sky.

O knife which is on Nūt, O flattener(?) [21] of faeces, do not use your hand against me, do not kiss the backbone(s) of the souls at the front of the sky, because they have indeed flown up to the sky as falcons, and I am on their wings; because they have indeed gone down to the earth as snakes, and I am on their coils. My breakfast and supper [22] belong to the seventh-day festival, because I have heard the shout in the mouths of the shorn priests of Ōn.

'What is this? On what will you live?' say the gods to me.

'I will live on bread of white emmer ⟨on which⟩ [23] the gods live, because I know the name of the mortar in which it was pounded; it is the acacia of Yusas-town north of Souls-of-Ōn'.

'I know the name of the basket in which it was sifted; [24] | it is the skin[25] of 284
Sokar which belongs to his own fire-blowing; [26] it means that there will no fire-blowing by [27] his craftsmen'.

'I know the name of the cooking-vessel in which it is cooked; it is the vessel [28] of Ḥatḥōr'.

'I know the name of the pot in which it is cooked; it is the jar which belongs to Rēʿ'.

'I know the name of the [29] bowl in which it is cooked; it is the base(?)[30] of the acacia north of Yus(as)-town and south of Souls-of-Ōn'.

'I know ⟨the name of⟩ [31] the fire which is put to it; it is the tears of Ḥemen'.

'What is this? On what will you live?' ⟨say the gods to me⟩.

'I will live on the *sšt*-fruit of the leather bowls(?) [32] on which Ḥatḥōr and Horus live'.

'What is this? On what will you live?' say the gods to me.

'I will live on the myrrh and incense on which the gods live | when I have tied 285
this bark of yours to the land at the stairway. O you who glitter,[33] I am one who glitters; I screech as a heron [34] and as a divine falcon, I fare upstream at the bow (of the bark). I will control the navigation when I come to the after-part, I will use the steering oar. When I enter into . . . , [35] I will act as a noble, and the larboard watch and the starboard watch will be in my charge.[36] I will cast the rope of the great bark; it will be loosed, and what I loose is good in this day'. [37] My years are (those of) Maʿet, of whom I take possession. [38]

The waters are made to flourish, the waters are made to flourish, and my property comes ⟨to me⟩.[39] O Maʿet, bring it to me, for it is I who allot business.

I am pure in the Presence, in the pools of Shu; never will I wash my foot in my . . . [40]

What is detested is the rejection(?) of an offering-table; my offering-table is in *Wr-ỉṯ-sw*.

He has brought you [41] to me, while the goods of Osiris are in Djedu; it is he [42] who has gathered together for them what he has received.

Hail to you, Serpent! What you will receive is your place on my head. |‘In
286 very truth it means that he has commended you to her who bore you’ [43] – so says Thoth. ‘Give him what is in your hand, the wig-cover which should be on him’.

I have placed my eye(?) [44] in my bush, and it is what is commanded to you [45] that your hand shall move to and fro(?) [46] because of what is non-existent.

I have made an offering which is shared; it means that my offering is something more wonderful than the sun-folk.

Tefēnet is she who allots what is to be allotted by eternity; you [47] shall adore her upon the waters which are in her, (even) you who follow after the Eye of Horus, and I will adore her waters.

The god stands up, and his Eye is strong above the sky and beneath the Mansions of the Red Crown; I am strong, having appeared ⟨ in ⟩ my purity, [48] and strong am I who have appeared, Lord of the great city.

You [49] divide it ⟨for(?)⟩ the retinue of the mistress of your bull-snakes.

The . . . [50] is like those who are in the fire; it is I who tread my Two Lands, . . . [51] being behind me.

O Rēʿ, prepare a path for me which the phoenix will allot.

1. Cf. M. Münster, *Untersuchungen zur Göttin Isis,* 81. For the 1st person cf. 283*l*–284*r,* where the gods question the deceased; his replies must of necessity have been originally in the 1st person.

2. Cf. *JEA* 29,10, n.*b.*

3. Cf. *CT. Transl.* Spell 140, n. 1.

4. *S* for *sn.*

5. An obscure sign resembling *ḏr*; the context calls for a direct genitive of either a god or the deceased, so that the conjunction *ḏr* can hardly be intended here, while the phonetic complement *r* is lacking.

6. The translation in the future tense is indicated by the prospective *sḏm.f* form *ḫʿy.f* in 281*j.*

7. The spelling of *wḏb* is due to calligraphic reasons.

8. Plural.

9. To be emended into ⟨ *ḥr ḥr* ⟩ *ḥr.f*?

10. *Nḥꜣ-ḥr*; for *nḥꜣ* ‘terrible’ cf. *Concise Dict.* 136.

11. I.e. of the concluding rite of the ceremonies, when the floor is swept clear of footprints. The reference may perhaps be to clearing up after the act of creation.

12. Lit. ‘cooked’.

13. Lit. ‘forthgoing of nose’, i.e. pokes his nose into affairs.

14. The verb-form is fem., but as BiBo is a man’s coffin, it would seem that the verb refers

back to Maꜥet. It has been translated in that sense, but it is at least possible that there has been an error in the gender and that the reference is to the deceased.

15. *Skrkr,* not recorded and meaning unknown. It can hardly be connected with *skr* in *Pyr.* §§241; 1847, for that is an intransitive verb of motion.

16. No word *synm* is known, and as written it looks very like a variant of *snm* 'feed', but that does not make much sense.

17. The preposition *r* has been omitted, cf. e.g. 279*f.*

18. Cf. Spell 659, n. 1.

19. Note the lack of concord in the participle *ỉnn,* the fem. ending having been omitted; it is present in *ḏdt* below.

20. Note the writing of *n ntt* 'because', as also in 283*h*; in 283*f* the normal writing is used.

21. Cf. *ỉdꜣ* 'smooth' a new-made pot, *MDAIK* 3,82; perhaps the deposited faeces are beaten flat.

22. Cf. de Buck's n. 2*.

23. The preposition and resumptive pronoun *ỉm.s* have been omitted after *nṯrw.*

24. For *ꜥḏy* 'sift' grain cf. also *BH* II, 6.

25. Cf. *ḫꜣwt* 'hide' of animal, *Concise Dict.* 184.

26. The strangeness of the words following 'Sokar' leads one to suspect corruption of the text. Perhaps the 'fire-blowing' sentences (hardly gold-smelting here) may have come from an omitted allusion to preparing the fire for baking, though the reference to a skin hardly fits this suggestion, nor does the mention of craftsmen in 284*b.*

27. Lit. 'of', direct genitive.

28. *Nbt* here and in 284*d* cannot mean 'basket', which would be useless for baking.

29. *Pw* is out of concord; so also *pssw ỉm.f* which follows; it looks as if the copyist had skipped from a feminine entry to a masculine, omitting the masculine object.

30. Or possibly 'covering' of a tree, referring to the foliage. *Kfꜣ* is used of the bottom of a jar in *Eb.* 54,22.

31. *Rn n* 'the name of' is omitted.

32. A guess based on a possible connection of *ẖnw* with *ẖnt* 'skin'.

33. Note the cormorant-sign as det. of *ḫꜣbs,* which has a bird-det. also in 16*e.h.*

34. Cf. Gardiner, Sign-list, H2, n.1. The dual strokes after the word are due to confusion with the two truth-goddesses, cf. 282*e.f,* end. The suffix after *mꜣꜥ* is in error.

35. Perhaps 285*f* should be emended to read *ꜥḳ.f r.f r . . .* ; the reading and locality of the place-name are not known.

36. Read *ẖr st-ḥr.*

37.  here is taken to be an ancient error for  as det. of *fḫt.*

38. From 258*k* onward the text gives the impression of being a sequence of unrelated extracts from another source or sources.

39. Assuming *rr* to be the enclitic particle; the dative *n.f* is absent.

40. *Snnw* with leg-det., meaning unknown.

41. Feminine or plural, but who?

42. Regarding *ỉntf* as a writing of *ntf*; cf. *ỉntsn,* Edel, *Altäg. Gramm.* §173.

43. Doubtful. *'I* before *mst* has been taken to be prothetic.

44. Cf. de Buck, n. 2*.

45. Masc. sing.

46. *ʾIt̲ ỉy,* perhaps meaning purposeful motion; compare *ỉt̲ ỉn, Concise Dict.* 34, used of random motion.

47. Plural, perhaps referring to *ỉmyw-ḫt ỉrt Ḥr* of 286*k*.

49. 'You' is plur. The reference of the masc. pronoun *sw* is obscure; not to *nywt wrt,* which is fem. A preposition has been omitted after *sw*.

50. *Mspr,* meaning doubtful; of the three words *mspr* recorded in *Wb.* II, 144, 3–6, none fit here.

51. *Nmʿ* with an obscure det.

Spell 661

VI, 287 SPELL FOR RECEIVING BREAD IN ŌN. I am he who offers, I decapitate in Ōn; my bread is in sky and earth, my bread is in the house of Horus and Thoth. It is the Night-bark and the Day-bark which bring to me from the shrine of Horus, and I will not eat faeces, I will not drink urine, I will not walk upside down. It is the Servitors who will adore me,[1] for I am a Great One in Pe, a possessor[2] of bread in Ōn, one great for Osiris. My bread is in sky and earth, and is what goes forth for me from the shrine of the gods; it is the Night-bark and the Day-bark which lift (things) up to me.

1. A 'liaison' *n* before *wi.*
2. Feminine; woman's coffin.

Spell 662

Get back, down on your faces, you two asses[1] of Shu, you two extensions of the Eye, you two whose knees are high[2] in front of the two Conclaves of Rēʿ, whom
VI, 288 Shu takes to the sky, who navigate[3] Rēʿ in the Day-bark! | Prepare a path for me, so that I may come and go on it, for it is you who will guide(?)[4] me on it. I am(?)[5] he who comes to you[6] in due season(?) . . .[7] I have come so that I may cut a skin(?) for you,[8] O you who were fashioned by the hands of the Ennead(?),[9] ⟨ . . . ⟩ who worship(?)[10] Rēʿ when he flies up from the Abyss. I am he who takes the bow-warp, I am the Bull of *Ḫnst,* a possessor of seven portions in Ōn; four of them are in the sky with Rēʿ and three of them are on earth with Gēb. Two portions are in the House of Rēʿ-Atum, so that I will not eat faeces for you, I will not drink urine for you, I will not come to you all astray, I will ⟨not⟩[11] go

down to you upside down, your mighty ones will not have power over me. It is the Night-bark and the Day-bark which will take my meal to me [12] from the shrines of the gods, the Souls of Ōn.

1. What follows suggests that the reference is not to quadrupeds but to ass-headed spirits.
2. Possibly an allusion to the asses standing on their hind legs.
3. For the det. of three boats see *ẖnyt* 'rowing', 313*j*, also BiBo.
4. The signs  following *ṯwt* are incomprehensible as they stand, and there must be some corruption here. Conceivably they might be a bungle for the last two signs of *sšm* 'guide'. A verb with some such meaning could be expected here.
5. 288*c-e* is most obscure, and any attempt at translation is hazardous, to say the least. In 288*c* *ỉntk* makes no sense as it stands, but it may be a corruption of the pronoun *ỉnk,* see 288*g.h.*
6. Singular.
7. *M-ꜥ* or possibly *m* 'who?'; there appears to have been an omission after this.
8. For the verb *sš* (or *sn*) cf. *JEA* 37,51(*o*); 'you' is plural, probably for dual. *Nt* with skin-det. is not recorded and its meaning is doubtful.
9. *Ḳd m-ꜥ psḏt* again is difficult, and I am by no means sure that I have understood it.
10. *Wyꜣ Rꜥ* is meaningless as it stands, and the initial *w* may well be the last remnant of a considerable omission; in that case *ỉꜣ* could be a participle of *ỉꜣ* 'worship'. If, on the other hand, the reference were to the solar bark, despite the absence of determinative, there must certainly have been loss of the main part of the sentence.
11. The negation *n* has been omitted before *hꜣy.f* through haplography with the final *n* of *dbnbn.*
12. See de Buck, n. 2*; the dative, if such it be, is out of normal place.

Spell 663

N breathes the air, and there is none who will take it from him; She who shines in VI, 289
Ombos is she who gives air to his Ennead.[1] Alone he has taken possession of all strength, he traverses [. . .] as the Soul[2] of Djedet, he lassoes him who would escape him,[3] and he eats and drinks. N has abundance through the offspring[4] of Mafdet, N has abundance and has carried out for himself what he wishes, and it is N who has done his will. His foes are his butchered cattle, the foes of his double are butchered cattle, inert on the night of those who sail. He has power in himself over him who fashioned him (and over) him who escaped from(?) those who follow him. N is in the middle of the faces of those who are loud of speech, mighty of stroke and strong for Rēꜥ, whom he knows. The mother comes to N bearing life; Neith comes to him bearing[5] her loin-cloth;[6] N's soul and shade 290

are made to appear[7] by Ḥatḥōr. | He has achieved it as Lord of the Field of Offerings, as Rēʿ bearing *snt*-bread. N has supported Nūt, and it is N who supported his (*sic*) Isis; (as for) the Lord of the Field of Offerings, N knows his name, and N comes as he desires; he decapitates the living[8] who are in *Tnn*.

1. The reference to *psḏt.f* 'his Ennead' seems to have been dragged in to provide a pun on *psḏt* 'she who shines'. *Psḏwt.f nbt* 'all his Enneads' is perhaps not to be taken literally.
2. Reading *bȝ*, cf. *Eg. Gramm.*[3] Sign-list, W10*; it is quite distinct from V37 (*ỉdr*).
3. Lit. 'his escaper'; for *nhp* 'escape' cf. *Pyr.* §§582; 652; 1855.
4. Lit. 'fledgelings', but Mafdet is a mammal, probably a mongoose.
5. *Ḫr* is repeated on passing from line to line.
6. As her gift to the deceased.
7. An unrecorded transitive-passive use, note the following *ỉn* 'by'.
8. *ʿnḫ* is repeated on passing from line to line.

Spell 664

N is one of you, the fourth of those who offer blood(?),[1] the reddest of those who are ruddy, who . . .[2] the sky with him who supports it, since the time when N . . . his being announced;[3] N is the janitor of the two mansions of Nu.

1. Connecting *ṯrw* with *ṯr* 'blood', *Pyr.* §§451; 1263; *ṯrwt* 'blood-offerings', *Pyr.* §401; *CT* III, 285*a*. This conjecture receives some confirmation from the allusion to redness in 290*j*.
2. *Ṯyt*.
3. *Ḫȝwt* is obscure; *sḥnt* has been taken to be a derivative of *sḥn* '(Worte) verkunden o.ä.', *Wb* IV, 218, 8.

Spell 665

VI, 291 Gēb has sat beside him,[1] the Chaos-god goes forth, having appeared in[2] the wig-cover, worship is given, trembling[3] is put into the two Conclaves, the strife-makers are execrated(?),[4] for they cause plundering and they foretell the flood, they see what is allotted when strife comes;[5] Seth comes, one who provides shares whenever food is provided(?). Horus comes equipped and clad as king[6] so that [he] may establish Osiris in his place on this his day of accession; the southerners are for the great levy, the northerners are for the great levy of Rostau.[7] N is his scribe, *Ḳnḳnwy* by name, and *Ḫṯȝt*[8] is the name of ⟨his⟩ mother; N's pen is a spool(?), his pen is a wand which lets him surpass; he will perform deeds and
292 achieve governance – so says Osiris of N. | One who has recourse to the storm, with

protection in his hand, he speaks in their[9] places about their duties in their dignities.

'O Rēʿ-Atum, open your hand',[10] says Osiris, 'so that my son may pass at the head of all the gods in their places, in their duties [11]as nobles of the south(?) concerning the sanctuary and the robing-room in ʿAnpet, the Westerners being at peace in their hills, while you are enduring in respect of your soul and great in respect of your dignity'.

'Receive bread,[12] receive beer, receive water, discharge your efflux in life, your progeny being on earth; let their baskets pass' [13] – so says the scribe of Osiris, (who is) at peace by means of what is done for him.

'O you who go to rest in life, open your hand, let the god pass with his soul, for he will have no injury, he will be unharmed' – so says the complete[14] Osiris.

1. For *ỉm* 'side' cf. *Pyr.* §1114. Cf. *ZÄS* 64, 9.
2. *M* is repeated on passing from line to line.
3. For *ꜣwr* cf. *Pyr.* §924; *Eb.* 38,5.
4. Lit. 'woe to'; the alternative translation 'was greeted' is improbable.
5. Perhaps meaning 'they see that they get their share of plunder'.
6. *Byty* stands here for 'king' in general; note that the det. has the White Crown.
7. For this writing of the name of Rostau cf. *CT* VI, 171*f.*
8. Apparently deified bread, for *ḥṯꜣ* 'bread' cf. *BH* I, 18; see also *ḥṯ, Pyr.* §73.
9. The plural suffix *sn* has no antecedent, which points to a textual omission between 292*a* and *b.*
10. Read ʿ 'hand' with 292*o*. This is a common corruption.
11. Emend *.k* into *.sn,* cf. 292*b.*
12. 292*i-l* appears to be addressed to the deceased.
13. *Swꜣ nbwt.sn,* meaning perhaps 'be prosperous'.
14. Or 'black'.

Spell 666

'O you who flourish(?),[1] go down into the earth, go up as one who lives'[2] – so VI, 293
says Osiris to you.

N is a spirit;[3] as for N, Osiris is abandoning the . . . of the Silent One.[4] N has gone down into the earth,[5] N has gone up spiritualized, N is lifted up.[6] N is pleased with his double, and N's double is pleased with him; a hand is full of this barley of his,[7] and N will not disturb the filling of a hand with this barley of his – so say yonder . . .[8] who come with oppression(?).

O you who are non-existent, N comes, having destroyed those who pray for a place in . . . for ever,[9] and his death shall not be.

Get back, Black-face, skilled(?) with your smell, dweller in the Mansion of the Desert, disturber who is sent in storm! O you who live by your thefts, get back, go away, get back! N shall not speak[10] this name of yours to you, and your
294 barley shall be totally destroyed.[11] | It means that you shall be empty, you shall depart empty. Your bread is faeces which issued . . . fire, . . .[12] which went forth to you from it, which came to you from it, and which the fire gave[13] to you in the place from which you have come forth. Go, turn yourself about and extinguish it! It is said to N: 'It is you who shall extinguish it'. N has brought his soul, N has brought his magic, and N has taken possession of his soul, N has taken possession of his magic, N will not give his powers to the messengers of Seth who live by their thefts. [14]

O you mighty one who are behind those who are concerned with corpses, N has brought his magic, it being placed in his body, and N has . . . ,[15] having it as(?) electrum(?), N's teeth are closed having it as(?) stellar iron,[16] N's lips are closed because of it as(?) . . . of *Ḥrrt*.[17] N has brought his magic, N has taken possession of his soul, and he will not give away his powers.

1. Read *ỉn twt*; the masc. dative of the 2nd person in 239*b* shows that the verbs of 293*a* are imperatives, and suggests that we have to read *ỉn twt* rather than *ỉ ntwt*, which presumably would be feminine. It seems necessary to interpret *ỉn* as an interjection, since none of the normal uses of this particle are applicable; *twt* with this det. is not recorded, but compare the det. of *nḫbt* 'fruitful one' in *Pyr.* §4. This spell is full of difficulties, and gives the impression of having been compiled from several different sources, a characteristic of BiBo.

2. *M ʿnḫ.ty* looks like a confusion of *m ʿnḫ* 'as one who lives' and *ʿnḫ.ty* 'being alive'.

3. An abrupt change of person, which suggests a change of source.

4. For a bird *ʿwʿ* cf. *CT* V, 296*c*; the last word appears to read *ỉgr*, but see de Buck's note n. 2*.

5. An abnormal writing of *gb* 'earth'; see also VI, 300*c.d.*

6. There is a dittograph of *šwy*.

7. Emend *ỉtfty* into *ỉty.f* as 293*j*. There is no det., but presumably barley is meant.

8. De Buck reads *ȝhtw*, but his *t* appears in fact to be a small *r*, for this passage is a bungled version of *CT* III, 358*b-c*, which reads *ȝhrw ỉpw ỉww m ȝrwt*. Who the *ȝhrw* may be remains obscure.

9. The translation of 293*m* is by no means certain, and something has certainly been omitted between *m* and *n.f.*

10. *Ḏd* is repeated after *N pn*.

11. Reading *nk.t(w) ỉtw.k twt*.

12. There is corruption here. After *pr* one might expect *m* 'from' and a mention of the source of the faeces; instead we have a reference to fire (*sḏt*) which is unintelligible as it stands. After *pr* there must be a textual omission which includes not only its expected adverbial

adjunct but also a change of topic. I can make nothing of *rḥyt smyt* following *sḏt*, but they may well be the antecedents of the participles *prì* and *ìyt* in 294*d*.

13. Reading *dy*⟨*t*⟩, assuming omission of the fem. ending.

14. For *ꜥw3.f* read *ꜥw3.sn*, to agree with the certain plural *wptyw*.

15. *Nḏd* is quite obscure; it has no connection with *nḏd* of *CT* II, 50*b*, which appears to be a corruption of *ḏnd* 'be angry', and probably not with *nḏd* 'a part of the body', *Wb* II, 386,5.

16. Lit. 'iron of a star'; for the fem. *sb3t* 'star' cf. *Pyr.* §2061; here the word has taken over the det. of *sb3* 'teach'.

17. *Ḫsmt* or *ḫmt* appears to be a term for a metal, parallel to *s33* and *by3*; *Ḥrrt* is the name of a goddess with a Seth-like determinative in *Siut,* pl. 11,33.

Spell 667

O Vulture! O Sailor-bird! O You who are on the mounds, brother of the *sḳdmw*- VI, 295
bird! This name of yours [is the name of(?)] [1] N, whom you know, and you shall not tell it to those who are above, you shall not tell it to those who are below, who dwell in the Island of Fire. N shall not come for you, for he will break your bowls and smash your offering-tables and strew your water-pot(s) on the ground; your dues are faeces, and N will not give you this which he brings into the Island of Fire. N's warrant is concerning the Island of Fire for the tribunal of(?)⟨ . . . ⟩ [2]. The detestation of N is efflux, and N will not eat what N's lips spew out, he will not drink from this watery(?) pool[3] of theirs. N is one who prepares five meals in the presence of Osiris; three meals are in the sky with Rēꜥ and two are on earth
with Gēb. N has flown up as a falcon, N is a crocodile, N has screeched as a falcon, 296
N is a crocodile, N has flown up[4] as a vulture, N is Anubis, Lord of burial. He has cut out their[5] tongues, he has fingered their . . . ,[6] he has landed above them, having flown up among his brethren the gods who are in the horizon, he spits on the scalp,[7] he sends out the leg (of beef), he gives breath to him whose throat is constricted, N has brought his soul, he has taken possession of his magic and his powers.

1. The traces in the lacuna as shown in de Buck's n. 2* look like *rnrn* or *rn r.f,* either of which could stand for a corrupted *rn.n.* Note that the epithets of 295*a-b* all refer to the same being.

2. *N ḏ3ḏ3*; the latter word lacks a determinative and the clause clearly is incomplete.

3. Read *š.sn pw* ⟨*n*⟩ *nwnwt;* the last word, if not a miswriting of *nwyt* 'waters', must be an intensive reduplication of that word, but it is difficult to see what such an inflection could convey. To me a dittograph of *nw* seems the more likely explanation.

4. Note that the causative *sp3.n* has lost its causative meaning here, and is used with

exactly the same meaning as the simplex *pȝ.n* in 295*s*.

5. Whose? The lack of an appropriate antecedent to *.sn* here and in what follows points to an omission between *ḳrst* and *šʿ.n.f.*

6. *Ḫȝʿʿ.*

7. An act of healing.

Spell 668[1]

To become Babi in the realm of the dead. N has cleared the night, the midnight[2] stars tremble at him, he having appeared mighty and equipped as Babi, the soul of the . . .[3] of Him who is in darkness, the . . .[3] of N in his hand, it belongs to the
VI, 297 Lord of the night sky.| The lords are afraid of him, men tremble at him, because N is Babi, Bull of the baboons, and he who shall see him shall not live. The . . .[4] are afraid of N, those who are on earth tremble at him in their time, because N is Babi who is among you.

1. On this spell cf. Hornung in *ZÄS* 86,112; Derchain, *ZÄS* 90,23; It is a garbled version of *Pyr.* Utt. 320.

2. *Wšȝw* refers to the middle four hours of the night according to Parker, *Egyptian Astronomical Texts,* p. 35. I owe this reference to Mr. Spaull.

3. *ʾIknt.*

4. Reading and meaning alike obscure.

Spell 669

N is Neith in the marshlands(?), Ḥatḥōr in the riparian lands, so worship![1] He has traversed Standard-town, he has travelled the Circuit,[2] he has sat on the dam of *ʾIṯnwsw.* TO BECOME NEITH IN THE REALM OF THE DEAD.

1. *ʾIȝ* stands without context, and it has been taken to be an imperative addressed to the world at large. It seems to have been dragged in to make a pun with the place-name *ʾIȝt.*

2. Presumably of the sun.

Spell 670

VI, 298 A Great Lady and[1] a Great Lady appear, a Great Lady is exalted[2] above her son, (even) Ḥatḥōr, Lady of the sky, Mistress of all the gods. She finds her son and his brother; his cattle[3] are strong, and Rēʿ has seen what he wished.

Hail to you, Eye of Horus! The whole of(?)[4] the sky is given to you, the earth is given to you to its thickness and the snakes which are in it; see, Rēᶜ has given to you those two knots of yours which are in front of the Cow, Thoth has given to you those two knots of yours which are in front of [. . .], Neith has given to you those two knots of yours which are in front of the Ibis, Atum has given to you those two (rays of) light of yours which are in front of the Vulture, and every god in your retinue is completed, spiritualized and equipped. Turn your face, that your face may be strong, that your horns may be strong, that your . . .[5] may be complete; it means that N will be among them.[6]

1. The preposition *ḥr* here and in 298*d* appears to have the role of co-ordination, cf. *Eg. Gramm.*[3] §165,10, in which case the two great ladies will be Ḥatḥōr and Neith, named respectively in 298*c* and *l*, and associated already in Spell 669.

2. 𓇋𓀁 appears to stand for the prothetic *ỉ*; cf. *ỉmrt.n.f* in 298*f*.

3. For *ỉwꜣt* cf. Mar. *Mast.* D52; Leps. *Denkm.* II, 45; 84. It appears to be a fem. collective.

4. Reading *pt n ḏrw.s*, cf. de Buck, n. 1*.

5. *Kꜣkꜣ*.

6. *Sn* 'them' could refer either to the suite of Ḥatḥōr or to the gods named above. The former is the more probable.

Spell 671

N has gone forth and has passed by pure, he has come about the Companionship,[1] VI, 299
N has come and a path is made for him and music for him.

O Sufferer, few and small are the threshing-floors for bread because of(?) the hacking up of land which is deficient. Go away as a heron, for it is the phoenix which passes by.[2]

1. A concrete term expressing the corresponding abstraction; compare *ṯꜣty*, meaning both 'vizier' and 'vizierate'.

2. The text from 299*e* onward is most obscure, and there is an abrupt change of topic.

Spell 672

O Kite[1] of the sky in breathlessness, go, show N to those mansions so that he may see today those things which he does not want and those things which do not please him.[2] N is a black jackal, a kite of the jackal-post; he has come today[3] that he may wield the knife[4] when he makes use of(?) . . .[5] He will open you up,

VI, 300 O western horizon; N's fields are in Dep[1] and his mansion is in the firmament. (As for) N, if the god should move about, if the sky should move about, if the earth[6] should quake, the sky will move about for him, the earth will quake for him, and he will give(?) [. . .] every time and completely(?)[7] at twilight for the document which is in(?) the twilight at the place where the lightning-flashes(?)[8] dart about. N has appeared in the presence of them of the West, the two *mnḥwt*.[9] It is N who cuts short the raging of any god, any spirit or any dead, and he ferries himself over as N in his (own) shape. TO OPEN UP THE DESERT OF THE KNIVES.

1. Masculine. The female 'kites' are much more commonly named.

2. For this translation cf. the nominal phrase *šsp ỉb*, var. *šsp n ỉb*, *Pyr.* §510; *CT* II, 29*b*; III, 199*h*; 363*e*; VI, 176*c*.

3. Or 'here', cf. James, *Ḥeḳanakhte*, pp. 111–2.

4. *ʿḏ* 'hack up', 'destroy', *Concise Dict.* 51, used here with object of the instrument of destruction.

5. For *ẖꜣ* 'make use of(?)' cf. *CT* II, 49*b*. *Rt* is incomprehensible.

6. Read as *gb*, see also VI, 293*e*.

7. I find 300*e-f* incomprehensible, and translate the words as they occur without understanding.

8. Cf. *ḥnbw* 'lightning', *Pyr.* §§324; 1212. The det. here suggests that the meaning of an archaic word has been forgotten.

9. Hardly 'slayers'; for this meaning of the stem *mnḥ* cf. *CT* III, 285*a*.

Spell 673

Hail to you,[1] Attendant who allots what is just, who guides every god and every
VI, 301 goddess,[2] I look on the face of the Great One . . .[3] darkness. It is the face of Rēʿ-Atum, and Rēʿ rejoices at it on the day of his festival; it is the third face.[4]

O You whose head is raised,[5] there has been given to him[6] the nobility of Ḥatḥōr; it is the fourth face.

O You who see backward, whose lamp is behind you, may you guide the gods.

O you two female guides of the gods, daughter(s) of the West and of the Lord of the West, who were born in the night and were conceived in the day, possessors of great *ꜣtf*-crowns[7] ⟨ . . . ⟩

O You who are greater than they, who are to the fore; O *Dwꜣ* who are to the fore, whose right leg adorns the Castle of the Sun, come to Her who makes examination among the gods and nobles.

O You whose name was made in the body of your mother before you went forth upon earth, who guided Osiris in his paths, who controlled the gods through dread of seeing you, to whom the mighty one is brought; O you who know the secret path of the portals in the Netherworld; O . . . ,[8] whose name is not known in the mansion of the Great One, whose name is not known by the gods, N knows you, he knows the names of the gods who are before, behind and beneath you; see, what he has said in his heart will not issue from his lips.

1. Note masc. suffix in *ỉnḏ ḥr.k* followed by a fem. vocative *ḫnmt*.
2. Reading the last group in 300*n* as *nṯrwt nbwt*.
3. *Wr* is followed by an obscure animal sign which de Buck cannot transcribe, see his n.1*. This sign and the following *kkw* are the last remnant of an omitted text, see n.4.
4. The meaning of this is obscure. The allusions to a third face here and a fourth face in 301*c* indicate that the first and second faces had been mentioned previously in a passage that has been omitted.
5. A mythological serpent in attitude 𓆙; cf. e.g. *Pyr.* §§401; 438; 679.
6. Presumably the deceased, who will have been first mentioned in the passage omitted from 301*a*.
7. The topic of this invocation has been omitted.
8. *Bsn* with det. 𓂻.

Spell 674

TO LIVE IN THE WEST AND TO WALK UPRIGHT. Spell for N with his knife and with the Cerastes-Mountain-knife in the hands of the living. . . .[1] it is the priest who eats the bread, being what the god gives; it is the kindly one who permits N to come with the potter whose arm is extended, and they have given him to Rēʿ-Atum, they have assigned N to the . . . ,[2] the two great and mighty gods who are brought down to the meal of their lord in the festival of the seventh day in Ōn, when they descend as snakes and N descends on their coils; they rise up as falcons, and he descends (*sic*)[3] on their wings. | The sixth-day festival is given for N's breakfast, the seventh-day festival for his supper, by the command of Rēʿ-Atum in Ōn; bread is given to N when he ascends on the ladder, having ferried across on the two routes[4] of Rēʿ-Atum. Take N's hand[5] and navigate him ⟨to⟩ the Wall so that he may join with his double as God of the Field. VI, 302 303

N is the . . .[6] and the *wrrt*-crown which are on the head of Rēʿ and the oar-butt of Nūt which belongs to the Great One; N has come so that he may repeat the matter, and exalted is he who hears it. O Cat of Ōn,[7] their[8] tribunal favours[9] N, and his right-hand fingernail(s) support Shu. He will not suffer, he will not be upside down, for N is Babi.

NOT TO WALK UPSIDE DOWN.

1. 302*e-f* is quite unintelligible to me, but it seems to concern two unidentified insects, *ḫspr* and *ht* or *mht*.

2. *ꜣdmw*.

3. *Hꜣꜣ* in 302*p* is certainly an error, having been copied from 302*n*; *ṯss* 'rises up' is what should stand here. Note the intransitive use of the verb *ṯsy*.

4. Cf. *pẖrty* 'traveller', *Urk.* IV, 1112,6.

5. The common corruption with papyrus-roll determinative for ꜥ 'hand', 'arm'.

6. Both *rrt* and *drt* (de Buck, n.1*) are *voces nihili,* and it is possible that the original reading may have been *dšrt* 'Red Crown', a natural counterpart of *wrrt*, though the peculiar det. is not accounted for.

7. An epithet of Rēꜥ, cf. *CT* IV, 283–9.

8. Suffix 3rd plur. without antecedent, which appears to point to a preceding textual omission.

9. Lit. 'is toward'.

Spell 675

O Anubis, Anubis; O *'Inw, 'Inw*; O Releaser, may you release N; O you who loose, may you loose N.

Spell 676

VI, 304 N's eye is in his face, his complete eye is in potency(?);[1] he was judged yesterday, and his power is in the tribunal; N is complete, having ferried over because of the guidance of Nūt. He speaks, but is unseen. TO HAVE POWER IN THE SKY AND IN THE REALM OF THE DEAD.

1. For the obscure word *kꜣꜣ* cf. *Pyr.* §2087; *CT* IV, 8*e*; VI, 66*g*.

Spell 677

N has spent the night as yonder Great One who fell on his side, he passes the day as the vulture[1] which is feared, being mighty by means of what is on him.[2] Those who weep for[3] him are the two Female Companions,[4] but N has not died the death;[5] he laments the two Female Companions, he has not died the death. TO SAVE THE HEAD AND NOT TO DIE THE DEATH.

1. Written with the vulture-ideogram ꜣ.
2. I.e. his protective amulets, which could include a vulture.
3. One *n* is superfluous.
4. Isis and Nephthys.
5. *Mny* here and *mn* in 304*m.o* are taken to be miswritings of *mny* 'moor' in its figurative sense of 'die'.

Spell 678

N is a swallow with divided tail which sleeps throughout the land, but N will not sleep throughout the land; O Boaster(?) who issues from the Abyss, the riparian lands do not lack the *hdn*-plant which follows after him who cooks, the strangers will not have power over N, whom the people see. N is a king, a possessor of striking-power, sharp-horned, and he whom he shoots will not live; he whom he decapitates, his head will not be knit on. N has gone out of the House of Thoth, he has broken up the fight and has quelled the uproar; the southerners are in fetters and the northerners are in bonds at N's enclosure, his house and his cavern of life. TO BECOME A SWALLOW IN THE REALM OF THE DEAD. VI, 305

Spell 679

I am the Double Lion whom the god's father sees; I sit on the great throne, my face is in the west of the horizon. O you who are censed for me, I will not kill you.

Spell 680

O you who are before N, the Sole One comes into being and grows; N has fashioned . . .[1] N brought the gods into being at his birth, for N is the Sole One, Osiris in this land. The waters have overflowed for him, the herbage has grown for him, the life of men has come into being, and (as for) rebellion, it came into being after Horus; the efflux of Osiris flooded out when he was buried, and N is one who turned aside toward it[2] for life, welfare and health. VI, 306

1. *N swꜣt nṯ ḫt* defeats me, and the reading with *s* is not certain, see de Buck, n. 2*.
2. *R.f* could stand also for the enclitic particle.

Spell 681

Hail to you, Thoth! It means that you are exalted ⟨ in ⟩[1] the mouth of Gēb.

Your *wrt*-crown is given to Horus and Osiris – may you live, have permanence and dominion.

O my son, they will save you from the stroke of Seth in the great storm.

See, N has come.

May you display your noble rank, may he establish your permanence, ⟨may you⟩ be saved ⟨from⟩[2] the stroke of Seth at the shrine(?).[3]

VI, 307 It is N who has brought the Sacred Eye from the mansion of Him of the *ḏd*-pillar.

She who is in the mouth of Gēb is she who makes the serpent of Thoth to appear in the storm. O[4] Gēb and *Hnhnw,* go down to Neith . . . for those who spit(?).[5]

N is . . . ,[6] the warm-hearted one who unites and equips those who nurse their children.

O Thoth, son of the Harpooner, brother of Horus and Seth, who are on your throne, silence Seth.

The dignity of Him who is on his throne.

'O *Dty*' says Thoth, who examines Him who is on the throne of the two Distant Ones(?).

The Great Ones are advanced (in rank).

Nu.

N.

Dty.

The name of Nūt is revealed.

Those who dispel bleariness.

Nūt[7] has set him in front of the horizon, and he controls gifts.

308 He hits with the strength of the Great Ones.

He divides those who tremble according to their gifts.

He who is at the head of the two Conclaves, Bull of Star-town.

It is N who performs the service due to[8] the two crowns when he passes by; he will not drown[9] the great warrior of Khem as on the first occasion of attaching the thigh.

N has attacked him.[10]

The cord of Maʿet is strong.

(As for) ʿApep, N has attacked him.

1. At least a preposition has been omitted here; possibly more, because the sentence does not seem to make much sense. The whole spell consists of a collection of apparently entirely unrelated sentences, and in places the text is clearly defective.

2. Emend into *nḥm⟨.k m⟩*, cf. 306*l*.

3. *'Ibsw* is not recorded, but the det. points to a shrine or coffin.

4. The interjection *ỉ* is repeated in a dittograph on passing from line to line.

5. *Bnw šbt* is unintelligible to me, and the translation of *fꜣḫw* rests solely on the determinative.

6. *Hnhnw* with det. .

7. Or 'the Ennead', see de Buck, n.2*.

8. Cf. *mḏdw* 'service due', *Urk.* I, 12,7; 210,4; 211,17.

9. Lit. 'immerse'.

10. There is no mention of whoever is attacked, and this sentence looks like an anticipation of 308*j*.

Spell 682

The foretellers of the great storm go forth from within the inner horizon of the sky; they foretell the festival of the braziers at the birth of the god before you, whose breast is great and who is in front of his offerings(?).[1] You will find N here on the front of the record(?)[2] among those who make their names, | because VI, 309
N is a god who judges the Contestants and separates the two parties;[3] his mother Nūt bore him in the Field of Tamarisk which protected the god in the nest.[4]

O Thoth, part the waters which are in the Abyss at the sound of the cry of [his] mother Nūt when she bears him and arrays him as the great heron which went forth from the gods when N's mother Isis and his (*sic*) sister Nephthys came for him, and she says: 'Who pray is born to you ⟨ in ⟩ this thicket(?)[5] as the great heron[6] which went forth from the gods?'

'There shall be brought the egg which belongs to him who was knit together within my arms;[7] there shall be brought the wonderful one who is in the bow of the *ḥnw*-bark, and it is he who will do the knitting together[8] within his arms'.

'[To] what [purpose], pray?'[9]

'So that N's arms and legs may be strong'.

'By what means will he fly up?'

'The two plumes will hurry to him from the *ḥnw*-bark'.

'Who pray will act for him?' 310

'My great guardian who is among the gods has made sharp points(?),[10] and long is the session in front of the Conclave of the House of the Great Lady'.

The form of their waterways is that of the head of a *ḥn*-bird(?).[11] N has placed the south-wind toward his *ꜣṯwt*-nurse and the north-wind is toward his *mnᶜt*-nurse, he has gone within his soul, and it is his power which takes him to and fro.[12] If he be weary, he will come to rest on the plumes of Gēb, the hands of his mother being (extended) toward him, (even) she the greatly protective, disordered of breasts. He has flown and soared as that great falcon which is on the battlements of the mansion of Him whose name is hidden, who takes what belongs to those who are yonder to Him who separated the sky from the earth and the Abyss.

N's eyes are the Bull of the crocodile-spirits;[13] his lips are the Bull of the two
311 Enneads; his horn is the Lady of Fire north of his shrine; ˡhis seed is the Bull of the Sunshine; his hoofs (*sic*) are the Lord of the Evening; his plumage is She who was in charge of his germination(?).[14] He has gone forth, turning back to the boundary of those who are in the presence of those who are in the Abyss. He has placed Ḥu among the offerings, his aspect is great in the presence of the great ones, the lords of the sky; it is Nu who gives him vision on the field of the Sunshine-god, and he alights . . .[15] as one stronger than their companions.

It is the holy ones who embalm her(?),[16] and (it is) the Oldest One who makes summons to the companions of those who are with the Red Crown. She ⟨ . . . ⟩[17] him whom he fashioned at the decree of the Eternal in front of the Pillar of Nu.

N is on high and has power [18] over and above Him who is on high at his upper shrine among the lotus-flowers of Him who is wakeful. N has opened his arms over the circumference of the firmament in the north of Those who send out; he has flown up to the sky as Shu the great, when they testify concerning
312 him(?),[19] the Great One. ˡN has inherited the sky by means of his uraeus and his children who are upon ⟨ . . . ⟩.[20] He has sown the earth, he has reached the horizon, he flies up [21] as a divine falcon. They have named N as a divine falcon, for they know that he is one of them, one older that the wakeful ones when circumambulating the Mansion. N's seat is what is in Malachite-land, north of . . . ;[22] the food of the two Fields of Offerings is the meal of Her of turquoise, and it is her female children who please(?) ⟨ . . . ⟩.[23] N eats of . . .[24] which are in the Red Crown; N is the Watcher who goes forth from food-offerings, Babi who goes forth from the Castle; N is firm in the sky and established in the sky as him who despatches the Great One and as Him who causes Rēᶜ to go up to his two Truth-goddesses,[25] who sends the Eternal to Him who brings the year to an end.

1. *'Iᶜbt,* lit. perhaps 'what is heaped up'.
2. Hardly a miswriting of ᶜ 'arm' here.
3. Lit. 'crowds'.

4. *R.s* is probably the enclitic particle.

5. This question apparently is addressed to Isis by Nephthys. A preposition, probably *m*, has been omitted before *ỉꜣr* 'rush', which here seems to stand for the thicket of rushes in the Field of Tamarisk where the young god (= the deceased) was hidden.

6. *Nwrw,* determined as usual with a crested bird in 309*g*, is determined here with an insect of some kind.

7. Read *ṯs m-ḥnw ꜥwy.s,* cf. 309*n.* For the suffix *.s* read *.ỉ.* Apparently Isis is replying to the question by Nephthys.

8. Lit. 'he will knit a knitting', i.e. of the young god born to Isis = N.

9. Read [*r*] *m tr,* cf. de Buck, n. 4*.

10. *Nꜣš(w) spdw*; the translation is a guess. Possibly the reference may be to a thorn zareba about the child.

11. Translation uncertain. There is a complete break with what has preceded, and it looks as if the spell has passed to a fresh text of which the beginning has been lost or omitted. This spell gives the impression of having been compiled from several such unrelated excerpts.

12. On the significance of the association of *ỉṯ* and *ỉn* cf. *JEA* 24, 124 f.

13. Another abrupt change of topic.

14. Reading *ḫnt(t) nḫbt.f*; For the reading *nḫbt* cf. Gardiner, *Eg. Gramm.*[3] Sign-list, M22. The signs appear commonly in the name of the goddess Nekhbet.

15. *'Iṯ,* which recurs in VII, 200*l*, is untranslatable; there appears to have been some loss of text here, for the reference to 'their companions' at the end of 311*g* shows no connection with anything that has gone before.

16. Apparently so, but who is embalmed? B1Bo is a man's coffin. The change to 3rd fem. here and in 311*j* is inexplicable, except on the assumption that we have here an extract from a woman's coffin taken over unaltered. The following *smsw nys r.f,* et., seems to be dependent on the same particle *ỉn* as *ḏsrw* above.

17. Something has been lost between *ỉw.s* and *msy.f*; the masc. gender of *msy* precludes any connection between them.

18. De Buck has made a slip here in his marginal lettering and has *i. j. k. l,* repeating *i. j. k*; these letters should read *l. m. n. o.*

19. Very doubtful, but no other translation offers itself.

20. Again something seems to be missing; *r* at the beginning of 312*b* is quite isolated.

21. Emending *ỉṯṯwt.f* to read *iṯt.f.*

22. *Wpt* as written is surely corrupt, for it makes no sense; perhaps we should read *wp tꜣ* 'Horn of Earth', i.e. the southern limit of the known world.

23. The sentence of 312*j* is left unfinished.

24. *Sbšw*; cf. *Pyr.* §411, where the king dislikes them; here the knife-det. suggests something sharp, with an acid taste. In both Pyr. and CT the *sbšw* are associated with the Red Crown.

25. An inversion of the normal procedure, in which images of Maꜥet are raised up to Rēꜥ.

Spell 683

Hail to you, Bright One! Hail to you, Fair One!

Spell 684

VI, 313 O you two vultures of Rēʿ, you two who conceived Rēʿ in the night, you two who bore him in the morning, may you conceive me in the night, may you bear me in the morning like Rēʿ every day. May I ascend up above, may I seek out[1] the riparian lands, may I hear the word of the god, may I become one of them. When you[2] find me, I will request a position on the path when conveying[3] Rēʿ. O![4] You[5] are I and I am bound for Atum(?)[6] at Ōn, at the place where Rēʿ is, at the horizon. The two who beg have beseeched(?) Horus[7] and his tongue is on his clothes(?).[8] He has come so that he may repress the transgressors, knit the Great One together and ennoble those who are yonder. The bark of Rēʿ travels in the Abyss, and it is I who take her bow-warp. My mother fashioned
314 me, and a falcon is in me, my flame is behind her, | my shout is in her brow.[9] The Red Crown has appeared on my head, and it makes me live, it makes me hale, it ties up life for me,[10] it presents it to my nose in the morning every day.

'O you who requisition, bring me this'.[11]

'Who pray are you?'

'I am *Nt*'.[12]

'O *Nt*, who pray is he who has come to you for you?'[13]

TO RECEIVE GIFTS IN THE REALM OF THE DEAD.

1. An inverted writing of *sḫn*.
2. Masc. sing.
3. Read *m ẖnyt Rʿ*; for the det. of three boats cf. *sḳddw* in 287*u*, also in BiBo. The reference to a position on the path suggests that the bark of Rēʿ is being towed from the bank.
4. The isolated interjection suggests the omission of a noun in the vocative.
5. Masc. sing.
6. See de Buck, n.4*.
7. *Sꜣš* is not known, but the dets. suggest that it may be a metathesis of *sšꜣ* 'beseech', 'pray', and that meaning would accord with the subject *dbḥwty,* though *sšꜣ* more commonly takes the dative of the person addressed rather than the objective as here, cf. *Concise Dict.* 247.
8. Is this obscure sentence a popular metaphor? For *wʿb* cf. op. cit. 53.
9. Compare the English saying about a noise being in one's head.
10. A dittograph of the preposition *n*.
11. *Swr* does not appear to be recorded, and its translation is a guess.
11. 'Bring me this' is the regular formula for demanding the celestial ferry-boat. This dialogue shows that the 1st person must have been original, for the deceased speaks directly to the being addressed.

12. An unknown being. With this writing and context the reference can hardly be to Neith.

13. The spell leaves this last question unanswered, and thus is incomplete.

Spell 685[1]

N says: Hail to you, Cavern! I have come to see the gods within you. [They have] opened their arms, ⟨ they ⟩ have uncovered their faces, when meeting me; I have come that I may offer [cakes to you, but] you [will not have power] over me,[2] for I live on the offerings which are with you; [the slayers will not pursue me, the adversaries will not pursue me].[3]

1. Cf. *BD* Spell 149, VI = p. 371,16 ff.
2. Cf. *BD* 372, 3–5.
3. Cf. *BD* 372, 5–6.

Spell 686

To drive away snakes [. . .] which are in the garden in the realm of the dead VI, 315
⟨by⟩[1] him who worships in it[2] and drinks in it. Down on your faces, you who are in the West . . .[3] I[4] have taken possession of my throne, I have received my robes of dignity, I have gone up from the lands, I am a marvel as one who is within the egg. The firmament has not split, and She who is in Ōn has not seen that I belong to him, (even) He who is in all Ōn. Rēʿ has done it for me, and his power is in me; I will not do it ⟨for⟩[5] him who rebels against him. (As for) me, my magic comes[6] into this land; (as for) me, *snwt*-cakes are made for me, my seventh-day festival is repeated for me. It is commanded that there be done[7] for me what Rēʿ knows. Gēb has opened his arm(s) to me, a path is made for me and for my entourage, he has raised[8] my gates for my robes of dignity, he has extended my movements, he has opened the land to its full extent, and movements have
been granted to me by Him whose sandals are great – |so says the Long-horn; a 316
path has been cleared(?)[9] for me by Seth, and the Nile-god has doffed his kilts for me – so says Anubis; throw-sticks have been presented to me by the great West, and the hearts of the gods are glad when they see me on that day of smashing the heads of the mottled snakes with these throw-sticks which belong to me.

This is the pool [10] which was dug ⟨in⟩ [11] the riparian lands; the brim is strong; the waters in it are the tears of the Eye of Horus in a rage; its lotus-leaves are a hail-storm (*sic*); its lands are the slices [12] from a knife; its threshing-floors are the Cerastes-Mountain-knife; Isis herself wiped over her thighs in it when she bore her son Horus. 'Go down', say the gods to me.

'Do you say that I shall go down to bathe in the presence of that *ỉšnw*,
317 the Lord of destruction, who speaks and seed is cut off? I will drive him off, like that tom-cat which conjures up a smell. Do you say that I shall bathe in the presence of that *mnš* who is loud-voiced and foul of seed? I will drive him off from himself, I will bathe in the pool in safety, the gods will serve me, I will enter and breathe the air of the cool place at his mansion, I will bathe at dusk'.

. . .[13] Maʿet. O . . . , O . . . ,[14] do not go down on my account, for I am . . . [15]

1. *'In* 'by' has been omitted after *ḫrt-nṯr*; 315*b* is part of the title of the spell.
2. The masc. suffix in *ỉm.f* must refer to *š* 'garden'; *ḫrt-nṯr* is fem.
3. *R-gs.ṯn šnwt* makes no sense; we have here yet another example of the omissions or corruptions characteristic of BiBo.
4. For the 1st person cf. 317*k.l.*
5. The preposition *n* is elided after *N pn.* The ancient editor has failed to remove the original suffix 1st sing. in *ỉr. ỉ.*
6. *'Ir* in 315*l* can hardly be the conditional particle, because an apodosis is lacking. It may stand for the enclitic *ỉr.(ỉ)* which has been overlooked in conversion into the 3rd person.
7. Reading *wḏ.tw ỉrt* (infin.), etc., but this interpretation is not certain.
8. *Sbwꜣ* is not recorded, but it is clearly the causative of *bwꜣ* 'be high', *Wb.* I, 454,10.
9. The garment-det. of *sʿḥ* is borrowed from the word for 'robe of dignity' occurring above in 315*e.q*; we may have here the causative of *ʿḥ* 'wipe over', *Wb* I, 214, 2.3.
10. Read *š pw nn.* Here the spell enters on a new topic.
11. Preposition *m* omitted.
12. Lit. 'cuttings'.
13. *Gb kt sp 2 gb* [*n*] *t sp 2*; untranslatable.
14. *'Ik . . . w,* cf. de Buck, n. 3*.
15. *Ḏʿʿmw*; cf. *Pyr.* §§439; 670; 671; 692; 693.

Spell 687

Hail to you, you god who are in the mount of the *Nt*-crown! I have come to you so that you may cause me to have power by means of your water, that I may drink of your flood, just as you did for that great god to whom the Nile comes, for whom herbage comes into being, for whom green stuff grows,[1] for I am your bodily ⟨son⟩[2] for ever.

1. Cf. de Buck, n. 4*.
2. Omitted, but supplied from *BD* 379,10; note that the *BD* text is in the 1st person.

Spell 688

To drive off a vulture and to avoid(?)[1] a scribe of the House of the Thirty who is in charge of standards and sceptres. N sits in the presence of Rēʿ; he wanders towards you[2] in the presence of the Two Enneads. N tells this name of yours, which he knows, in the Island of Fire to the two bull-vultures who will break your pen, smash your ink-wells[3] and tear up your papers because of what you have said you will do against N. VI, 318

Get back, you black bird who incurs being embroiled (in quarrels) (?);[4] hear the magic which his heart sends out. Tell him who sent[5] you that he whom you cannot find is N, she whom you cannot find is N; your dues[6] are faeces.

Get back, you black bird which issued from Ursa Major, who speak on account of your[7] father, who demand what he needs; an obstacle to him is set in the Night-bark, and your dues are faeces.

1. *Sḳd* is shown by the following text to have as object 'a scribe of the House of the Thirty' who is unfriendly to the deceased, so that, despite the determinative, I have taken it to be a causative of *ḳd* 'go round', with a sense of avoidance.
2. *Sbnbn* 'wander' elsewhere only in *Pyr.* §936.
3. In *Pyr.* §2030 the det. suggests a mussel-shell as a primitive ink-well, cf. *Pyr. Transl.* Utt. 678, n. 5. Here the det. is a fish-scale.
4. For *ʿpr* 'incur' cf. *P. Ed. Smith,* 1,4; for *skn* 'embroil(?)' cf. *Concise Dict.* 251.
5. The unfriendly scribe of 318*a*.
6. For a similar writing of *gȝwt>gyt* 'dues' cf. *Urk.* I, 289,8. The sense is that faeces are the only reward the bird will get.
7. Lit. 'his'.

Spell 689

Orion speaks: 'He is my son,[1] older than I (*sic*)' – so says Orion. ' . . .[2] N, who is pure and young, and Sothis bore him, (even) she the young, she of the year,[3] a goddess from her birth who is at the start of the year, and N is ennobled by those who are over the righteous. She is Maʿet, a possessor of offerings which are before her;[4] N is censed by those who see and those who are over the righteous. She is Maʿet, a possessor of god's offerings which are before her(?)[5] for N; he has VI, 319 become heir to[6] the lords of [. . .][7] and the lord(s) of the *wtnw* who are in the dusk. N has eaten the Chaos-gods and Ḥu, he has swallowed Sia, he has eaten magic from the magician; N has cut up [the foes(?)][8] of the Great Lady, the companion of the Lord of the shrine'.

The deceased: 'What is it?' I shall say to those in charge of cutting:[9] 'Come,
320 you lords of [. . .], for I will not be ignored[10] in the Island of Fire |when the cutting is [set aside(?)][11] for me'.

Orion: 'See, I have indeed come'[12] – so says Orion. I bring to you the two shares of [the cutting][13] which you have asked for from me and those in charge of them. Let me know what those two have done ⟨about⟩[14] what you asked for' – so says Orion.

The deceased: Ḥu is in my body, dread[15] is in my heart, Sia is in my heart, Edjō is on my head, the uraeus is on my forehead, the guiding-serpent is in front of me, the awe of me is on my lips, might is on my throat, fear is on my flesh, strength is in my arm and power is in my legs. I am a god ruling with my arm, might is in my heart, and I have taken possession of the intelligence of every god, it having been placed within my body for me. The Chaos-gods display the great secret, I have driven off ⌜Apep in his striking power; there is no god who can do what I have done, and all power has been given to me by those who are about
321 the flame. |It means that the Companions have been given to me,[16] the eater of magic in the presence of both the Barks; I have eaten them,[17] I have taken away their souls, I have taken possession of their powers, I have provided every spirit with ⟨ . . . ⟩[18] who are behind my power over them, I have brought everything, and I have not permitted myself[19] to stray from the company of all the spirits.

1. This spell consists of speeches by Orion and by the deceased; the first speech, down to 319*o*, is by Orion, setting forth the qualifications of the deceased. Spell 469, in the latter part, has likewise a dialogue between Orion and the deceased. At the beginning of the present spell, for *sꜣt* 'daughter' read *sꜣ* 'son'; the deceased was a man.
2. *Tw n* is corrupt, but it is not obvious what ought to stand here.
3. For *rnpt* as a name of Sothis, the personified year, cf. *Pyr.* §965.
4. Reading *ḫntw.s* ⟨*s*⟩*nṯr N pn* with elision of one *s*.
5. See de Buck, n. 3*, but it is difficult to see what could be the function of *n* here.
6. For this translation of *ỉwꜥ* cf. 233*k*.
7. Cf. de Buck, n. 5*.
8. There is perhaps room for *ḫftyw*, but the traces shown by de Buck hardly suit.
9. From here on the deceased originally spoke in the 1st person, of which a trace survives in 320*u*, and this is confirmed by the fact that Orion addresses him in the 2nd person
10. Emending into *nn smḫ.f*; it is possible that *n* before the suffix may have been repeated from the negation *nn* at the beginning of the clause.

11. *Ns[n]rw* or possibly *ns[s]rw*; the suggested meaning is entirely conjectural.

12. Reading *ỉy.ky*, cf. de Buck, n. 6*.

13. Cf. de Buck, nn. 3*. 4*.

14. Apparent omission of the preposition *ḥr*.

15. I.e. of N; it is not the deceased who is afraid. See also 320*p*.

16. A superfluous *m* follows *rḥwy*.

17. The Companions, not the Barks.

18. After *m* comes a certain omission, where de Buck notes a small blank space, possibly to mark a lacuna in the scribe's copy.

19. The original text probably read *n rdy.ỉ nwḏ.ỉ*.

Spell 690

Words spoken by N so that he may pass by the mound of Keset: Hail to you, O god who are in your egg! I[1] have come to you in order to be in your retinue so that you may let me come and go in Keset; the gates [of Keset] will be opened for [me, I will snuff][2] the air in it, I will have power by means of all kinds of offerings [. . .] for that august god who is in his [egg(?)[3] . . .] Keset. Its heights are opened to me, its [. . .] are thrown open to me, [its] fields are presented [to me . . .] me [for] my mouth which(?) I receive [. . .], I raise you[4] [. . .]. I will enter into the place[5] where is that august [god] who is in [. . .]; he will open my eyes for me [that I may see with them],[6] he will split open my mouth [that I may speak][7] with it; he will open up my nostrils that I may breathe [with them].[8]

1. This spell is said to have been spoken by the deceased himself, which shows that it must have stood originally in the 1st person; so too *BD* 374, 14–16.

2. For the restorations cf. loc. cit.

3. Cf. 321*j*; *BD* 374, 5.10, though the traces shown by de Buck hardly suit.

4. Cf. de Buck, n. 6*.

5. Emending into *ỉw.ỉ r ʿḳ r bw*.

6. Cf. de Buck, n. 7*.

7. Cf. de Buck, n. 8*.

8. The *m* between *nf* and *N* is superfluous. For the restoration *ỉm.sn* in the final lacuna cf. de Buck, n. 10*.

Spell 691[1]

VI, 322 Speech by N; he says: 'O Pure One, O [Falcon] rising [from the Abyss], Lord of the celestial kine,[2] make [me] hale even as you make yourself hale; may you [release] me, may you [loose] me'.

'Release him, loose him, [put] him on the earth, grant[3] his desire' – so says the [One]-faced Lord concerning me.

'I am a falcon within the shrine,[4] [I divide(?)][5] the earth for him on whom is the fringed garment' – so says Horus, son of Isis.

'O Horus son of Isis, make me hale even as you make yourself hale; may you release me, may you loose me'.

'Release [him, loose him], put him on the earth, grant his desire' – so says the [One-faced] Lord concerning me.

'I am a falcon [in the southern sky] and Thoth [in the] northern [sky], I pacify the raging fiery serpent, I raise up Maʿet to him whom [she] loves' – so says Thoth.

'O Thoth, [make] me hale even as [you] make [yourself] hale; may you release me, may you loose me'.

'Release [him], loose him, [put] him on the earth, grant [his] desire' – [so says] the One-faced Lord concerning me.

'I am the *wnb*-flower of Naref, the *nbḥḥ*-flower of the western horizon' – so says Osiris.

['O Osiris], make me hale even as you make yourself hale; may you release me, may you loose me'.

'Release him, loose him, put [him] on the earth, grant his desire' – so says the One-faced Lord concerning me.

323 'O You with terror(?)[6] in your feet, who are in action, possessor of your twin souls,[7] who live on your twin fledgelings, make me hale even as you make yourself hale; may you release me, may you loose me'.

'Release him, loose him, put him on the earth, grant his desire' – so says the One-faced Lord concerning me.

'O You who travel around[8] who are in your egg, may you make me hale even as you make yourself hale; may you release me, may you loose me'.

'Release him, loose him, put him on the earth, grant his desire' – so says the One-faced Lord concerning me.

'Rise up, O Sobk, in the midst of your high land;[9] rise up, O Neith, in the midst of your riparian land; may you[10] release me, may you loose me'.

'Release him; loose him, put him on the earth, grant his desire' – so says the

One-faced Lord concerning me.

O you seven [knots], the arms of the balance on the night of setting the Sacred Eye in order, who cut off heads, who [sever] necks, who take away hearts, who snatch [hearts], who [make] a slaughter ⟨in⟩ the Islands of Fire,[11] I know you and I know your names. May you know me[12] even as I know you, may you know my name even as I know your names; if I reach you, may you reach me; if you live through me, I will live through you. May you assign me to the life which is in your hands and the dominion which is in your grasp, may you destine [me] to annual life, |may he[13] cause many years to be added to[14] my 324
years of life, may he cause many [months] to be added to my months of life, may [he] cause many days to be added to my days of life, may he cause many nights to be added to my nights of life, until I depart. May I arise to be a likeness of myself, with breath in my nose, and may my eyes see in company with those who are in the horizon[15] on that day of dooming the robber.

1. Older version of *BD* Ch. 71 (p. 156 ff.); the restorations of lacunae have been made either from the later text or from frequent repetitions in this spell.
2. *Mḥt-wrt* with god-det. and plural strokes.
3. A series of plural imperatives; for the last two commands cf. e.g. 322*m.n*. Note the rare imperative *rdyw* 'put' beside *ỉmy* 'grant' in 322*m.dd*; 323*e.j.o*; here only the initial *r* is preserved.
4. Cf. de Buck, n. 4*.
5. A verb beginning with *p*, possibly *pss̆*. *BD* 156,9 has *wbꜣ.ỉ n ntt ḥr* [*s*]*db*.
6. *Nrw*.
7. Reading *bꜣ.fy*. *BD* 157,10 has *ṯꜣ.fy* 'his twin fledgelings'.
8. *BD* 157,14 has 'O you of Nekhen'.
9. Cf. de Buck, n. 9*.
10. Masc. sing.
11. *'Iwy n sḏt*; *BD* 158,9 has *š* (read *ỉw*) *n nsrsr*.
12. A 'liaison' *n* before *wỉ*; so too 323*cc*.
13. Suffix 3rd. sing. This refers to an unspecified deity, perhaps the One-faced Lord.
14. Lit. 'go down upon'.
15. Read *mm nw n ỉmyw ꜣḫt*;  is due to confusion with *m* 'take'.

Spell 692

I [go][1] and return between them both,[2] my hair stands up, because I am[3] he on whom are his testicles in Ōn; it is they who are potent(?) who [. . .] Thoth. I go and [return] between them, the two *ḏd*-pillars, my hair is on me at my . . .[4] in [. . .].

1. Cf. de Buck, n. 3*; for the 1st person cf. *šnw.ỉ* in 324*i*.

2. For the suffix *ny* cf. *Eg. Gramm.*^{3} §34, Obs. 3. The two *ḏd*-pillars of 324*m* are probably to be understood here.

3. The defective word following *n ntt* in 324*f* could well be a partly deleted *ỉnk* overlooked by the ancient editor, *N tn* having been substituted for it.

4. *Ṯꜣtꜣ*.

Spell 693

VI, 325 'Hail to you four times, N!' [says] Rēʿ when he rises in the sky and shines in the eastern horizon.[1]

'Hail to you four times, N!' says Rēʿ-Atum, Bull of the two great Enneads who show forth[2] the awe of you. He has decapitated . . .[3] for you.

'Hail to you, N!' says Horus, having inherited the thrones of his brothers the gods and the Enneads.

'Hail to [you] four times, N!' says Thoth, chiefest of the gods, whom the Great Ones do not know. 'May you bind fast(?)[4] those who rebel against you'.

'Hail to you, N!' [. . .]. 'May you make fast for yourself the bonds of Seth and his sisters, may the Double Crown have power over him'.

'Hail to you four times, N!' say your two great and mighty sisters who clear [Osiris(?)] of weakness by means of your sceptre. 'May you open up your holy things and your insignia . . . ;[5] may your sisters be glad at you [. . .], may you pass ⟨on⟩ the path in the sky'.[6]

'Hail to you four times, N, being in the heart of *Ḥnw*'.

326 'Hail to you, N, who set fire [to] those who creep about(?).[7] He is still(?) and he will protect you,[8] N, and fair is the Great One with many names. O N, I am your son whom he put together for the gods'.

'Hail to you, N!' 'O you Great One who are over the fair-faced one who is among the jackals, may you commend N to the two peaceful(?) Companions'.

'Hail to you four times, N!' says Rēʿ. 'The gods will love you, the patricians will adore you, the plebs will serve you, the sun-folk will extol you daily, and all the gods will cause you to appear(?). They will fell your foes for you in this happy day, and you shall appear in it with the gods, the lords of those who are in sky and earth [. . .] you shall traverse(?)[9] the sky, Rēʿ having attained to the two Truth-goddesses.

Ho N! I give his sceptre to you, and you shall have praise by means of it [. . .] in the midst of his firmament, your bones are those of divine falcons, you shall exist indeed(?),[10] and your soul shall never perish.

1. Written *ꜣḫy,* without the fem. ending, but the adjective *ỉꜣbtt* is fem.

2. *Dty,* dual fem. participle; lit. 'who place'; the figurative sense 'show forth' has not hitherto been noted for this verb.

3. *Ḥsḳ.n.f n.k* is followed by a group of signs which make no sense, and which may be a misreading in the hand-copy which was all de Buck had to use, see his n. 1*.

4. No verb *sꜣm* in this spelling appears to be known; it would seem to be connected with *sꜣmt* 'lock of hair'. The preceding negation *n* is an error derived from *ỉḫmw.*

5. I cannot translate *ỉḫmmtyw.f* at the end of 325*p.*

6. Read *swꜣ.k* ⟨*m* or *ḥr*⟩ *wꜣt m pt*; a preposition has been omitted after *swꜣ.k.*

7. Doubtful. The restoration of the lacuna is uncertain and the sense of *ỉw gr.f*(?) at the beginning of 326*b* is uncertain.

8. Note *kw* in 326*b.i.j.l* for the dep. pron. 2nd masc. sing., suggesting a very considerable age for this spell. 326*k* has *ṯw.*

9. Restore as [*nm*]*y.k*?

10. An obscure play on the stem *wn*; *wnṯ wnṯ* looks like a repeated emphasizing particle.

Spell 694

Hail to you, you gods and you spirits[1] whose speech is potent, you lords of great VI, 327
sceptres who keep(?)[2] doors because of N! ⟨Ho N!⟩[3] I have put the fear of you into those who are on earth like Horus among the gods; I have put the awe of you into the spirits like Seth among the gods.

Ho N! I have put the fear of you into those who are on earth and your strength over those who are in the Netherworld.

Ho N! I have set your striking-power into the disaffected and those who are on earth come to you bowing as to [. . .] and the sun-folk [who give][4] you worship as to one vindicated; they see you when you go down among the spirits, for you are equipped as the god himself.

1. Note the fem. plur. demonstrative *ỉptw* qualifying the masc. plur. noun *ꜣḫw*; the interpretation of this latter word as 'spirits' is enforced by the fact that this is a vocative parallel to *nṯrw ỉpw* preceding.

2. Regarding  as a miswriting of ; the 'making' of doors is inappropriate here.

3. The switch of person to 2nd masc. sing. for the person addressed in 327*d* suggests that *hꜣ Wsyr N pn* has been omitted before this sentence, cf. 327f.h.

4. Restoring  in the lacuna; this restoration seems enforced, despite de Buck's uncertain traces, cf. his n. 2.

Spell 695

VI, 328 Burial in the West as a blessed one, quelling strife in order that he may go down to his possessions which belong to the West. O Wilful One(?)[1] who are in charge of litters,[2] send to Osiris pre-eminent in Abydos and say to him: 'Open the chest of writings so that you may hear the word of this god whose face is hidden, pre-eminent in the eastern desert, who says that he is knitting me together in order to complete those parts of me which should be knit together.[3] See, a . . .[4] is made for me among the blessed ones who watch over your name. See, there are brought to me those who would approach who came out of Gold(?),[5] who did this in the festival in Khemennu'.

It was I who made my offering from out of what the god brought forth(?),[6] and there is brought to me what is prepared for the dawn among those who proceed to the festival. I reached out ⟨my⟩ mouth to the brightness,[7] it having been set in the pure place;[8] I nullified the striking-power of the . . .[9] of the walls of the pure place, I made firm the wounds of the Inert One on the day of putting the Great Hall in order and of quelling the strife of the gods attached thereto.

329 My herbage [10] is what the king desires, and your herbage is not with me, O Wilful One(?) who are in charge of litters; the place of herbage is in the [. . .] of the West. I am the child of Ḥa [11] in his desert, and there have been created those who stand in the presence of Osiris among those who exist. My seat is his desert, the western desert is my horizon, and I am among those who are in it, the kings of Egypt; none shall make an order against me, and there shall be no strife of the god(s) against me.

THE MAN SHALL RECITE THIS SPELL WHEN HE SEES WORK IN HIS TREASURE(?)[12] WHICH BELONGS TO THE REALM OF THE DEAD, BEING PROPERTY WHICH GOES DOWN TO THE REALM OF THE DEAD. THE MAN SHALL BE CLAD AND CAUSED TO FARE UPSTREAM, HIS HANDS BEING FULL OF THE MILK OF BULLS,[13] SO THAT HE MAY DRIP(?) IT ON TO HIS . . .[14] WHICH BELONG TO THE REALM OF THE DEAD. TO BE DONE [15] IN THE PRESENCE OF THE MAN, WHO SHALL STAND FOR SEVEN DAYS WHILE THIS IS BEING DONE DAILY, WHILE YOU ARE WEEPING, SO THAT ⟨TEARS⟩ FALL FROM YOUR EYES. YOU SHALL DO WHAT IS TO BE DONE AGAIN WHILE RECITING THIS MATTER IN THE MONTHLY FESTIVAL AND THE HALF-MONTHLY FESTIVAL.

1. *Mr.f*; this god is doubtless identical with *'Imr.f* of *CT* I, 45*a*; 170*g*; cf. *CT Transl.* Spell 14, n. 5. The initial *'I* here is the interjection.

2. For *ḫwdt* 'litter' cf. *Urk.* I, 43, 15; *D. el Geb.* II,8.

3. Note the demonstrative *ptf* qualifying what is apparently a passive participle + possessive suffix.

4. *Ppt*; possibly a preparation of the *ppt*-plant, for which see *Wb.* I, 507, 2–3.

5. Possibly a miswriting of *Nbt* 'Ombos', but cf. *Horus and Seth,* 12, 11.

6. This apparent transitive use of *pr* recalls the construction of *Pyr.* §23*b*, cf. *Pyr. Transl.* Utt. 32, n. 1. An alternative would be to emend into *m prt m nṯr* 'from what came forth from the god'.

7. Or 'whiteness', perhaps as a term for milk.

8. *Dy* is probably perfective passive participle qualifying *rꜣ*, lit. 'which was set'; *wꜥbt* could mean 'tomb' or 'place of embalming'.

9. *Ḥwnw* with skin-det.; compare *ḥwnt* in *CT* V, 210*k*; VII, 163*j*; after it read *ỉnbw,* see de Buck, n. 7*.

10. So rather than *sm* 'help, 'succour', cf. 329*c*. It is not clear what all this means.

11. The desert god. Perhaps should be restored in the lacuna.

12. Cf. de Buck, n. 2*. Possibly valuable tomb goods, cf. *Sin.* B287.

13. Probably refers to bulls' semen.

14. Quite obscure; the word is feminine, see the genitive adjective *nt* which follows. It is tempting to read it as *kꜣt* 'work', but de Buck's n. 3* hardly supports this.

15. Read *ỉrt* (infinitive) rather than *ỉrrt.*

Spell 696

I have gone in to you[1] with my Eye behind me . . .[2] tears; I have nourished my[3] VI, 330
members and I make myself flourishing; my 'mat'[4] is on me, my staff is in my
hand [by means of] my twin powers, and I have gone in and out so that I may
surpass persons(?). I am a worshipper(?)[5] of the god who is in my heart. I have
gone in and out, I have travelled the air and have traversed the storm of the polar
region of the sky;[6] the *ỉꜣd*-star[7] is in my hand by means of my twin powers. I
have gone in and out and have surpassed persons(?), I have travelled the air and
have traversed the orbit(?)[8] of the *ỉꜣd*-star. The doors of . . .[9] are opened, the
three doors of Rēʿ which are fair of being. There has been given to me ⟨ . . . ⟩;[10]
it is Ḥatḥōr who raises me, the impediment is removed for me, and I am set in
the presence of Rēʿ; her hand is under the branches of the *iṯnws*-tree.[11] I ascend
to the sky as the gods, the flood is fostered for me and is brought to me;|abund- 331
ance is confirmed to me[12] and vegetation is planted in this garden by this Horus(?),
Neith is sated in Sais and the flood brings its speech(?). You shall prepare a path
for me to it in the plot of the Field of Offerings, you shall plant trees in this
garden of mine among the waterways of Them of turquoise; it is the Two Companions who shall plant[13] it with their mighty arms. O you Keepers of the Man-

sion, make pleasant the courts(?)[14] which were constructed(?)[15] when Ḥatḥōr travelled and which she adorned;[16] which the . . .[17] placed, which my foot brought, and which the . . .[18] gave, and I depart to those who are yonder.

1. Plural.
2. *R sꜣty*, meaning unknown.
3. The 1st person is original; the suffix *.f* lacks an antecedent.
4. For *p* 'mat' cf. Breasted, *P. Ed. Smith*, 481; here a kind of garment.
5. The reading of what follows *ink* is uncertain, cf. de Buck, nn. 2*. 3*, and the translation 'worshipper' is a guess based on the determinative.
6. Cf. de Buck, n. 7*. A variant of this passage occurs in 330*m*; on *wꜥrt* 'polar region' cf. *Komm. Pyr.* III, 393.
7. This star is named in *Pyr.* §280; *CT* VI, 141*a*; 341*l*.
8. Hardly 'entourage', despite the det.; the verb *nmt* requires a spatial object.
9. *Wdnwdn,* det. lost.
10. The sentence is unfinished.
11. Cf. spell 1029, n. 8.
12. Read probably *smn n.i,* cf. 330*u*.
13. Note *srd.ty* as a writing of the prospective active participle, cf. *GES* Ch. III.
14. *Nmꜥ*; for this det. cf. the homophones of *CT* IV, 99*c*; *Siut,* Pl. V, 249, with meanings which do not suit here.
15. It is not clear how the first word of 331*h* is to be read; *ḫwsy* seems a possibility.
16. Read *sḫws.s*? Cf. de Buck, n. 1*.
17. Obscure; *ꜥšꜣ* so spelt is not known.
18. *Šsmy*; the translation of 331*g-i* is quite uncertain.

Spell 697

A boon which the king grants. Osiris commands[1] that N shall enter into his house, inspect his nest[2] and do what is pleasant in his plantation[3] in company with those who are on earth for ever and ever. May he achieve all the transformations which he desires to make, for the august god who is in his egg has commanded that N shall breathe the air on the day of the great deed.

1. Cf. de Buck, n. 3*. *Iꜣ* here and in 331*p* appears to be an error for *iw*.
2. Read *syp.f šš.f* with *CT* III, 330*b*; cf. de Buck, n. 5*.
3. Read *ir.f nḏmt m šsp.f*; there is a play on *nḏmmt* 'sexual passion'.

Spell 698

TO MAKE OPPOSITION IN THE REALM OF THE DEAD[1] AGAINST HIM WHO COMES TO CLOSE A MAN'S MOUTH. O you of the expanses of Shu who close the mouth for him who points[2] his finger against him who shall see, your eye shall be broken and your finger fractured, for the Sistrum-player has turned you back, and Rēʿ has set his sun-folk as a protection against you, your tongue being in your crutch(?)[3] and your phallus in your mouth. VI, 332

Get you back, you club-wielder,[4] who live on your urine! I am saved from you by the Faceless One who was born in front of his father; such is your nature, but it is not my nature; such is your image, but it is not my image; your mouth has overcome me, but your foot will not have power over me, because I have come here from . . . ,[5] I have risen up, I have joined myself together; my members are your members, while Rēʿ lives in his mother.[6]

1. The det. of *ẖrt-nṯr* is displaced; read *ẖrt-nṯr r ỉw r,* etc.
2. Lit. 'sends', probably with a nuance of accusation.
3. *Ṯt*; not recorded, but 'crutch' or 'pubes' seems probable, cf. 332*h*. This appears to be a curse to the effect that the tongue and the phallus shall change places.
4. Cf. *Pyr.* §264, where the det. is a club-head.
5. A place-name, cf. de Buck, n. 3*.
6. This sentence is so at variance with what has preceded as to suggest that something has been left out.

Spell 699

I will go forth on the earth, I will climb up[1] on the air, and my foot will not be opposed[2] even to the limit of the horizon. Remove yourself, for it is he who will remove.[3]

1. Read *ḥfd,* cf. *Pyr.* §751; *CT* II, 25*f*; 145*c*; 146*c*.
2. I read the beginning of 332*v* as *n* (negation) *ḫsf rd.ỉ r.ỉ*, it being assumed that the position of the tall *ḫsf* sign is due to the desire for a neat square; *r.ỉ* has been taken to be the enclitic.
3. It is not clear to whom the pronoun *ṯw* refers; the change of person in *swt šd.f* suggests that a new speaker has come on the scene.

Spell 700

VI, 333 A MAN SHALL BE AMONG THE LIVING. O you who are between the two cows[1] of Gēb, I escape(?)[2] thence, and Gēb is cleansed.[3] He will grant to me his appearings in glory and will put down for me the plant[4] which is between his lips;[5] his phallus is between the buttocks of his son and heir. If there be not a son for a man, he will act behind the back of the daughter of the phoenix.

1. Cf. *Eg. Gramm.*^{3} Sign-list F 45.
2. B2L: *nhp*; Sq5Sq: [*n*]*h*.
3. So B2L; Sq5Sq had something more which is lost and then ended. Note the writing of the name of Gēb in the latter text; compare *CT* III, 112*c* (T1C).
4. *Šsm,* not identified.
5. Lit. 'on his mouth'.

Spell 701

TO EAT WITH HIS MOUTH AND ⟨TO DEFECATE⟩ WITH HIS HINDER PARTS.[1] My head is that of Rēʿ on the day of putting Atum together; a quartette of my spirits are there. My mouth speaks to me with a knife[2] on the day of the union of the Two Lands.

1. Some such word as *fgn* 'defecate' must have been omitted before *m pḥwy*.
2. *S3ḫ*, cf. *CT* II, 61*e*; 107*b*.

Spell 702

VI, 334 When indeed you have come, I will see you at the dawn of the day of this call(?)[1] of yours. Who is he who provides(?)[2] what is pleasing, the beer of the nobles? Your bread and your meal are laid on the ground; come to the front of your (offering-)slab. Your spirit is seated;[3] ⟨ . . . ⟩[4] your wishes and your equipment. I know everything.

1. An obscure spell. *H3* is difficult; it could conceivably be the interjection 'Ho!' used as a noun.
2. Cf. *JEA* 16, 196.
3. For *ḥfd* 'sit' cf. *BD* 212, 8; 'climb' makes no sense. The det. is borrowed from *fd* 'pull up' plants.
4. There must be an omission after *ḥfd*; 334*g* makes no sense as it stands.

Spell 703

SPELL FOR BECOMING A LOTUS-TANK BIRD.[1] I am indeed a lotus-tank bird which fishes in the plains. [I] go up ⟨ . . . ⟩,[2] I eat according as I wish in the plains of Osiris, I eat natron,[3] I am a possessor of shapes, I go up as I wish from the western horizon, I fish in the waters of the Abyss, I eat of pure things in the plains,[4] | and VI, 335
they enter into this body of mine as Rēʿ's food-offerings and as the . . .[5] of Ḥatḥōr. I am one who is transformed into the spirits who have gone to their doubles, I have assumed the forms of Atum, and it means that I eat of those living doubles of mine, (namely) the spirits.

I am a spirit who ascended from the Netherworld, I am indeed a god who lives in all his shapes, which are brought together in the plains, for ⟨whom⟩[6] are performed all presentations; my spirits are in my body, I cleanse my bones, I rest on my corpse at will.

BECOMING A LOTUS-TANK BIRD IN THE REALM OF THE DEAD, SO THAT A MAN MAY BE EQUIPPED WITH HIS SPIRITS.

1. Cf. *CT* V, 45*g*.
2. A blank space.
3. Read *ḥsmn.*
4. *Nb* after *wꜥrwt* is a subsequent addition and has been ignored in the translation.
5. *Nšfwt.*
6. Read *ỉr n⟨.f⟩ fꜣt nbt.*

Spell 704

DRIVING OUT TERROR FROM THE REALM OF THE DEAD. Rēʿ cries out within his holy place. Those who are below tremble at them(?).[1] Her strong arms are praised(?). The eastern hills cry out at the sound of the storm. Their faces have brought[2] the flaming one.

I travel around in the northern sky, and praise is given to me, a stairway to VI, 336
the sky is set up for me; all the gods go about in my retinue, Ḥu takes away their utterance for me. Take my thrones from ʿApep for me, for all the gods who are in my retinue have given me their staffs. May he[3] not drive me off from the northern sky, because I am indeed a god mighty of deeds, greatly majestic, who sits in front of the great ones in the tribunal of Horus, Lord of appearings in glory.

1. Apparently the suffix 3rd plur., cf. de Buck, n. 1. The word-order is unusual, and there is no antecedent for the suffix. 335*o-s* is obscure and somewhat incoherent; it appears to consist of a series of unrelated sentences. The continuation in 336*a* ff. is more coherent.

2. Read *sḫp.n ḥrw.sn.*

3. ʿApep.

Spell 705

THE MAN SHALL HAVE POWER THROUGH HIS MAGIC SO THAT THE MAN MAY PUT HIS MAGIC WITH HIM. Be far from me, O *Mspr* yonder, for I am the Eyeless One, the son of Osiris, my face is the wig(?)[1] of the god in Ōn, my lips are Her of the
VI, 337 Cerastes Mountain who is before . . .[2] and *Ḫrs.* I have gone up on the ladder, I have crossed over in the travelling boats of the Songstress, and it is granted to me to make you go grey, O Burnt One(?)[3] ⟨ . . . ⟩[4] at the wall of eating, my bread is in the riparian land of the god. O Sistrum-player, Anointer(?),[5] Traveller(?), . . .[6] my heart for me, for I have power by means of my magic.

1. For *ḫnswt* 'wig(?)' cf. *Pyr.* §456; *Komm. Pyr.* II, 249f.
2. An indecipherable name.
3. Perhaps a *m*-formative from *hwt* 'burn', *Siut,* pl. 13, 14; *CT* II, 73*a*; V, 244*d*; 247*a*.
4. A blank space.
5. Reading doubtful, perhaps *mrḥw*; cf. de Buck, n. 4*.
6. *Bḥ* or *bḥḳ,* meaning unknown.

Spell 706

TO BECOME A SEAL-BEARER(?) IN THE SKY. O Red Goddess! O You of the Mansions! O Precise One! I have received a seal with you alone[1] at the birth of the Planner, and the snake(?)[2] is struck down for me by the nobles of the horizon.

1. We would have expected *wʿ.tywn* here.
2. *Sꜣ-tꜣ,* but the writing is abnormal.

Spell 707

VI, 338 [. . .] my name(?); he is the sore heat of(?)[1] the Sole One when he ascends to the sky, and I myself ascend with him to the sky. I have climbed up on the sunbeams, one who crept jackal-wise on your arms which belong to the sky.[2]

O *Hꜣnyt,* bring me this,[3] for I am that jackal which went out from the leaf[4] and that lion which presides over Upper Egypt. Open the doors of the sky for me, turn back[5] from the towers of vision[6] which are yours,[7] for indeed I am not ⟨ . . . ⟩.[8] I am a lotus-tank bird(?),[9] I indeed am one who is ⟨ . . . ⟩[10]

'Where have you come from?'

'I have come from behind *Nḫb* of the Island of Fire'.

'What do you want?'[11]

'I will worship [. . .]'.

'[On] what will you live?'[12]

'I will eat of the flood, I will live on its produce;[13] . . . me as those who dwell in the Netherworld and who greet(?)[14] my father Rēꜥ, and I will live thereby.

1. Reading *tꜣw mr nt, pace* de Buck, n. 2*. The lost sign is indecipherable, but *n* would have no function between noun and adjective. Possibly the traces may belong to a second det. of *tꜣw. Nt* must surely be the genitive adjective, but it is out of concord, *tꜣw* being masc. This suggests the possibility of an omission after *mr.*

2. *Sꜣbw* has been taken to be a participle of *sꜣb* 'creep like a jackal', cf. Wb. III, 420,15; in 338*h* the deceased avers that he *is* a jackal. *ꜥwy.ṯn nw pt* may be an allusion to the sunbeams to be seen stretching from sky to earth when the sun itself is behind the edge of a cloud. The suffix *ṯn* lacks an antecedent unless it is used of the sunbeams.

3. *'In n.ỉ nw* is the regular formula for demanding a ferry-boat.

4. Cf. *Eg. Gramm.*[3] Sign-list F21. The jackal seems to be envisaged as emerging from a clump of leaves.

5. Cf. *Pyr.* §246.

6. Apparently 'watch-towers' of the desert borders were in mind, to judge by the det. of *swnw.*

7. *Ṯwwt* is probably the same as *ṯwyt* 'what belongs to you', var. *ṯwt, Pyr.* §648, cf. also §613. Although this is addressed to the female being *Hꜣnyt,* the masc. form has been used; there seem to be no recorded instances of the possessive use of the corresponding fem. form *ṯmt,* and it may be questioned whether there ever was such use.

8. On the assumption that the negation before *ỉnk* is correct, there must be an omission of the rest of the clause.

9. *Šsnty* for *sšnty*?

10. Another omission after *nty.*

11. Lit. 'you are for what?'; for *sbw* as a var. of *sy* 'who?', 'what?' cf. *CT* V, 46*a*; VI, 57*f* (BIBo).

12. Restoring as *ꜥnḫ.k ỉr.f m ỉšst,* cf. 284*m.p.*

13. *Mꜣg* has been taken to be an *m*-formation from *ꜣg* 'make to sprout', *Pyr.* §513. The *f* is surely a misplaced suffix. I cannot translate *bsn* in 338*u.*

14. *Snnw,* meaning doubtful.

Spell 708

VI, 339 My house is built by Atum, my mansion is founded by the Double Lion on the east side of the House of *Swswt* [. . .] above and below. I will go and ascend high in order to climb ⟨to⟩ the mansions and to crawl ⟨into⟩ the houses, for I am that wall which separates the sky from the body of the god, and I have gone up. There are invocation-offerings for me by[1] the lords of offerings when they enlist Him of eternity[2] for me just as he provided the perfume of Horus ⟨ . . . ⟩ in giving his . . .

1. Or perhaps 'so say'.
2. Read *nḥḥw*.

Spell 709

TO BUILD A MANSION IN THE WEST. The sky trembles, the earth quakes[1] at the voices of Ḥu and Him who awakes hale; they mould the bricks for this mansion which is in the Field of Offerings, and the gods who preside over the Mansions of the Red Crown come to them. I know them and I know those names of theirs,
VI, 340 (namely) the great ones who strike (the bricks) and Atum invisible of shape;| they carry the bricks for this mansion of mine which is in the Field of Offerings.

Come, O Greatly Mysterious, with your[2] sole brother *Bnḏ*, bring the Hale One and Seshat, that they may build this mansion which is in the Field of Offerings. 'I will help him' says Atum; [. . .] which has been done for him by Shu and *'Idn,* its site is given by Gēb, it is confirmed in my possession, I will go in and out of it joyfully(?). O Skull, go and tell the Lord of Eternity that I go up as a falcon because I am wiped down(?)[3] in the House of the Souls; I have seen Him whose face is hidden, who presides over the Mansion of [. . .], my eyes are raised on high to the singing goddess(?); I am a possessor of food[4] in Ōn, and the Great One is content in front of the horizon. I have appeared in front of the Mansion of the Trappers, I [have] made my father who is on his belly, my mansion is within the limit of the horizon on a (legal) deed of the West . . .[5] I have appeared as Lord of eternity, I have been wiped down(?)[6] at the great stairway, I am
341 greater ⟨than⟩[7] the *wrdnw*-bird. |My mansion is within the limit of the horizon, for I am Atum, Lord to the limit of the sky, and the entire limit is given to me by Atum.

1. *'Iḳy* is not recorded, but its meaning is hardly in doubt.

2. Emend into *sn.k.*
3. Read ⟨*n*⟩-*ntt ỉw.ỉ sk.ky* (old perfective 1st sing. with elision of a *k*).
4. Cf. *dwnw* 'Spiesen', *Wb.* V, 433,11.
5. *Nhy nyš,* incomprehensible.
6. Read *sk.ky,* cf. n. 3 above.
7. *R* of comparison omitted.

Spell 710

TO BE IN THE RETINUE OF ḤATḤŌR.[1] O Ḥatḥōr who are under the trees, your . . . ,[2] I eat of food,[3] live poultry and fish in the hidden places which are on the earth; I travel and traverse the circuit,[4] I tread the *ỉꜣd*-star, I climb the sunbeams in the retinue of Ḥatḥōr.

1. The rubric is out of place, cf. de Buck, n. 2*.
2. *Snṯntyw,* incomprehensible.
3. *Šn* is not recorded, but compare *šnt* 'food', *BD* 305,13.
4. Presumably of the sun.

Spell 711

TO GO OUT INTO THE DAY . . .[1] O Wounds! O [. . .]. My striking-power is VI, 342
Sakhmet the divine; my eyes are Ḥatḥōr; my arms are Rēꜥ; my strength is Gēb. My brazier spurts fire and my water is on my mouth, for I am Ḥu, my power chooses as the Sole One(?), I give heat(?)[2] to . . .[3] [. . .].

I place maggots in the Eye of Atum, I am Rēꜥ [. . .], I have come that I may repeat his tears for him,[4] for I am Rēꜥ who weeps for himself with his sole Eye. The fire is quenched with my Eye, the ways are cooled with my tears. I am the [. . .] of Rēꜥ who lifts up Rēꜥ daily; I have washed myself,[5] I am possessed with tears, I go forth from it, (namely) this fire, and I am hale, I am not cut down.[6]

1. See de Buck, n. 1*.
2. Restoring as *tꜣw.*
3. *Swt* with fire-det., cf. de Buck, n. 2*.
4. The repeated references here and below to the tears of Rēꜥ and of the deceased, identified with Rēꜥ, seems to have no connection with what has preceded, and it is possible that 342*i* ff. may originally have been part of a different text.
5. Read *ỉꜥn.ỉ wỉ.*
6. Read *m*⟨*d*⟩*s.ỉ.*

Spell 712

VI, 343 To be made whole as a god in the sky. The *pꜣt*-loaf is that which flies up to the two mansions, they are the places of destruction(?) which belong to the Red Crown. As for him who knows this spell[1] in the Field of Offerings, he will do everything that he desires just as when he was on earth, having gone to his double.

1. Read *ỉr rḫ rꜣ pn,* disregarding *ỉw rꜣ,* which has been inserted in error.

Spell 713

I ferment(?)[1] with dates.

1. Unrecorded; the meaning given is a guess, but the det. of *ḫnt* suggests a culinary operation, perhaps the preparation of date-wine.

Spell 714

I am Nu, the Sole One who has no equal, and I came into being yonder on the great occasion of my flood,[1] when I came into being. I am he who flew up, whose shape is (that of) *Ḏbnn* who is in his egg; I am he who originated in the
VI, 344 Abyss, and see, the Chaos-god came out to me; | see, I am hale. I brought my body into being through my power; I am one who made myself, and I formed myself at my will according to my desire. What went forth from me was under my supervision; it means that tears are what I created in him who was angry[2] with me, and men of the blind ones[3] are my cattle[4] . . . [5]

1. Reading *n mḥt,* cf. de Buck, 343, n. 2*.
2. See de Buck, 344, n. 1*.
3. See de Buck, n. 2*.
4. For this interpretation of *ḥrw-sꜣ* cf. *P. Kah.* 16,14; *Urk.* IV, 1134,8. In *Pyr.* §1544 *ḥry-sꜣ* stands for 'subjected bull', i.e. Seth subjected to Osiris, cf. *Pyr. Transl.* Utt. 580, n. 1.
5. *Sk* followed by a short lacuna.

Spell 715

[NOT TO PERMIT THAT A MAN'S HEART BE TAKEN FROM] [1] HIM IN THE REALM OF
THE DEAD. O you [who take away] hearts (*ỉbw*) and who accuse [hearts
(*ḥꜣtyw*) . . .], who re-create a man's heart ⟨in respect of(?)⟩ what he has done,
see, he is unconscious through what you have done. Hail to you, Lords [of
Eternity, Founders of] Everlasting! Do not reject my heart (*ỉb*), do not accuse
my heart (*ḥꜣty*). O you who re-create [this heart of mine], I [am accused] wrong-
fully, because [as for] this heart of mine, it is the heart of Him whose names are
great, | [who speaks about] his own [members], who sends out his heart which is VI, 345
in [his] body, and he is proclaimed to the god. I possess my heart, [I have]
power [in it], and it will forbid what has been done to me. I am one having
strength in my own members, and my heart will obey me, [for I am] its [lord],
and it is in [this] body of mine; it will not turn against me, for I am he [to whom]
it was commanded that [it should] obey.

1. Restored from *BD* 90,8–9 (Spell 27). There is perhaps insufficient room in the lacuna for the introductory *rꜣ n* 'Spell for . . . '. For the other restorations see de Buck's notes.

Spell 716

I am this child who slept and was helpless in his mother's entrails; what I remember and what I forget, I will say in Ōn.

Spell 717

A woman is not to be eaten by a snake. Atum has bitten and has filled his[1] VI, 346
mouth, and he coils up.

Cool is she who is in the town and warm is she who is in the country.
Do not take hold of N, do not grasp or grip her.

1. Cf. *Pyr.* §425*a-b,* which I translated rather differently there. In Pyr. the owner of the mouth is the deceased; in that case *rꜣ.f* should have read *rꜣ.s,* for this is a woman's coffin.

Spell 718

To go about in the sky. N has descended with you[1] in cloud, she has ascended with you as one in the midst of the doubles. The gods(?) and Khnum are with her(?),[2] she herself shoots in the place of decapitation(?),[3] and N has issued thence ⟨as⟩ one who is worshipped.

1. Feminine singular.
2. *'Imty.s.*
3. Emend into *st tn n ḥsḳ*?

Spell 719

VI, 347 To dispel anger in the heart of a god against me.[1] Woe to you, O you who send out power and who preside over all mysteries. See, a word is spoken against me by a god who is angry with me, but wrongdoing is washed away, and it falls into the hands of the Lord of Justice, since you evilly do harm to me.[2] He who is respected(?)[3] has joined with Maᶜet, this god is gracious to me, and my impediment is imposed on someone else.[4] O Lord of offerings in *Gn-wr*(?),[5] see, I am brought to you, and life is provided by means of it; may you partake of it. Be gracious to me and dispel all anger which is in your heart against me.

1. For the 1st person cf. *BD* Spell 14.
2. *BD* 34,15 omits *wd.*
3. *Tr.*
4. Read *wd sḏb⟨i⟩ r ky*; de Buck's *d,* which makes no sense, could well be an ancient misreading of hieratic *r. BD* 35, 1–2 has *dr sdb.ỉ n.k.*
5. *Gn-wr* is probably a place-name, see the preposition *m*; the god-det. is assumed to cover the whole phrase.

Spell 720

To become a dawn-god and to live by means of magicians. Those who are in (a state of) trembling are thrown down, I[1] [have] opened the double door of Him
VI, 348 who shines.[2] The rulers[3] of . . .[4] who watch over the two fields of locusts tremble; ¹one thunders and the plume(?)[5] trembles. What the Great One possesses is given, but the Lesser One will never be content; he who stands up gave to me, to me(?)[6] in the Island of Fire when his going to rest was not yet known, and furthermore when the Lesser One had not yet seen what he possessed. I know that your water is complete,[7] and see, they[8] know that I am a ruler of farm-lands, because Rēᶜ is against them.[9] I am not satisfied with my entourage, for I cannot see [10] what

they have done for me. I give away what the Great One possesses, I pacify the
Lesser One, for see, they know that I am a dawn-god, and it is permitted that I
see my retinue and look at my entourage. Farm-lands are given and pools planned,
for Rēʿ has commanded that I give to them. See, I am content, for they know
me;[11] I am a dawn-god. The plumes tremble when Nūt ascends, those who are in
the storm tremble. Groaning is in the sky since the night, for I starve the Great
Ones and kill the Lesser Ones by the command of Rēʿ.[l] I will act as one [who is 349
sent(?)][12] to them, (namely) the gods, and my voice is (that of) *Wnwt*; Rēʿ has
commanded that my father(?) be [. . .]. He is a dawn-god; see, his robes are
granted to him, he has received his *ꜣtf*-crown, his entourage move about for him.
I regard myself[13] (as) a dawn-god,[14] as a god in his own shape, one equipped and
flourishing in the bow of the bark of Rēʿ. I have brought my documents which
confirm my offerings for me, my possessions are put into the shambles of the
Wine-press god and I am content in my hour, because[15] I am one who gives orders
to Rēʿ and despatches to Ḥatḥōr; I have made the bearer of my offerings[16] content within my body,[17] for Rēʿ knows that I am indeed a dawn-god.

1. For the 1st person cf. 348*h.w.x*; 349*a.h.l.* This spell is obscure and even self-contradictory, compare e.g. 348*k* with 348*x*.

2. For *wbg* 'shine' cf. *Wb.* I, 296,14. The dual strokes after *wbg* may imply that both leaves of the door belong to him: it is less likely that there should be two beings with that designation.

3. Feminine.

4. The loss of the end of *ḏny* leaves us in the dark as to which of the various words from this stem was intended.

5. Read *šw*[*t*]? Cf. 348*t*.

6. Cf. de Buck, n. 2*.

7. The meaning of 348*e* escapes me; there is no antecedent for the suffix in *mw.k,* and it looks as if corruption had crept in.

8. The suffix *.sn* likewise has no antecedent.

9. Translation doubtful.

10. Reading *n mꜣ*[*.n*].

11. On my interpretation *N tn* should be allotted to 348*r,* as being apparently the object of *rḫ.n.sn.* Possibly we should read *N tn* twice, in both 348*r* and *s.*

12. Cf. de Buck, 349, n. 1*.

13. Lit. 'N sees N'.

14. A dittograph of *ḥḏ-tꜣ* in 349*g.* For *mm* following read simply *m.*

15. Read as *n-ntt*; in *tn n-ntt* one *n* has been elided.

16. *Ḳny ḥtpt.ỉ*; can this be a metaphor for 'stomach'?

17. Restoring the demonstrative *tn* in the lacuna in 349*m,* cf. de Buck, n. 5*.

Spell 721

VI, 350 Hail to you, you double of N, of her body; you [. . .] in peace, in peace.
[. . .] make content [. . .] for the Great One, [. . .] make content [. . .]
the Great One.

Spell 722

To become the Morning Star. The paths of the Netherworld are opened for N,
the gates of those who are in the horizon are opened for her, the beautiful star[1]
[. . .] which(?) his earth-gods who are in his darkness eat. He(?) makes bright
[. . .], he has revealed those who were forgotten, for N is the Morning Star, N
is the beautiful *wꜥꜣ*-star of gold which went up alone from the horizon; one
multiple[2] of uraei whom his mother bore, who consumed yon Destroyers.
N is the Lone Star[3] on the horizon, and her father Rēꜥ has given her the whole
VI, 351 of the sky when he brightens. | He has given N his living beings for their protec-
tion; he has made spirits for N in order to[4] have power over them; he has made
gods for N in order to be in N's retinue; Anubis, Lord of burial, has brought
⟨ . . . ⟩,[5] having fallen on his face before N.

1. Perhaps nothing lost in the small lacuna before *sḥd.*
2. Masculine; probably therefore an epithet of the star.
3. Cf. *JNES* 25, 160 ff.
4. *R* repeated in passing from line to line.
5. Name of the being brought has been omitted; possibly Seth should have been named.

Spell 723

[It is a cake-offering] to Rēꜥ, to the great god, to Anubis who presides over the god's booth, and to Osiris, which his son N has given to him on the days of the monthly festival, the festival of the New Moon, and the half-monthly festival, for N is the butler[1] of Rēꜥ; who will never die, Maꜥet is raised up to him, *šꜥt*- and *pꜣt*-cakes are raised up to him, a leg (of beef) is extended to him.

These are the four cake-offerings[2] which the great god gave to his eldest
VI, 353 son on the day of death, | which N gave to him on this day; O Primeval One,
your *nḥrw*-loaf is in the *ṯnnt*-shrine. Ho N! The sixth-day festival[3] is for your
(main) meal and the seventh-day festival is for your supper. May you ascend to
the sky on the air, may you climb up on the sunbeams, for a *nḥrw*-loaf and white
bread are in the Broad Hall.

Your *nḥrw*-loaf is in the *ṯnnt*-shrine, and bread will be given to you at the sycamore in which Rēʿ is sheltered. Every good meal goes up to you in the presence of the *smn*-goose in the *ṯnnt*-shrine, but N is not the one who asks that she may see you[4] in this shape of yours in which you are; it is Horus who asks that he may see you in this shape of yours in which you are when ascending [to] the celestial kine. May the doors of the sky be opened for you[5] as for Horus of the gods; may the doors of the firmament be thrown open for you as
for Horus of the East when he goes down to bathe in the Field of Rushes. |May 354
the doors of the sky be opened for you, may the gates of the horizon be thrown open for you as for Horus of the gods and for N herself,[6] and you shall go up to the altars of Rēʿ.

Ho N! May you cross the lake, may [you] traverse [. . .], may you obstruct the foot of *ʾImtt* at the following of the god, may N turn aside from it.

1. The *n* under *wdpw* in B3Bo is superfluous. This text is followed, because T2C, which has minor variants, is fragmentary.

2. The text continues in 352*o*.

3. Written as *snwt* 'shrine', but this makes no sense.

4. There is confusion of pronouns from here on, see de Buck, n. 1*; it is by no means clear at times who is being addressed, and there is no antecedent for the masculine suffixes. The correction of *ṯn* to *ṯw* in 353*m* shows that the scribe also was confused. Some of the muddle may have arisen from adapting the text from a man's coffin to a woman's.

5. The masculine pronouns continue until 354*c*.

6. 354*b* is largely a dittograph of 354*a*; only *n N tn ḏs.s* is new, and this is probably to be appended to 354*a*. It has been translated thus.

Spell 724

A boon which Anubis who presides over the Sacred Land gives, that you may go all over the sky with your little finger like *Swn*. The *ỉmꜣ*-tree attends you, the zizyphus-tree turns its top to you, you go up as the Morning Star, and the plebs worship you daily. You escort [. . .] behind him who does this for you. Such am I![1]

1. A final boast by the deceased in person. The rest of the spell will have been recited by the lector at the funeral.

Spell 725

VI, 355 Ho N! He who presides over the Two Conclaves finds you in Ōn, the *ḫntyw-š* kneel to you, the Imperishable Stars fall on their faces to you.

Ho N! Receive [your] thousand [of] bread and beer, oxen and fowl, alabaster and clothing, your thousand of wine, your thousand of grapes, and your thousand of everything good and pure of which men eat. Receive [your] joints (of meat) [from upon] the slaughtering-block of the god; the foreleg and the hindleg are the joints upon the slaughtering-block of the god. May your heart be glad[1] and may your feet dance, may [your tomb(?)][2] be as well-founded as the tomb of Horus and the burial-place of Seth[3] who is in *Ḥnt*, may you bathe[4] in the celestial expanses, may you bathe in the pool of the firmament, may you be purified in the pool of [. . .] you [. . .] you [in] life, and you will not die. Receive these four cake-offerings which your father [Osiris(?)] of the Great Mansion has given to you.

O N, raise yourself on your left side, put yourself on your right side.

O N-Atum,[5] the flowing of water has made the cultivation of emmer, and you have joy(?)[6] [through] it wherever you may be.

356 O N-Shu, receive this bread of yours which is brought to you. I have placed sky and earth for you under ⟨your⟩ son Horus, your heir;[7] may you be glad by means of it.

O N-Gēb, receive this pure bread of yours which was issued from upon the great offering-slab. I have given you the rulership of the Two Banks, O my son Horus, who shall appear on your throne.

O N-Thoth, receive these two cake-offerings; may the rib of the Bright One[8] be lengthy for you upon the altar of Atum; bread, torch, water, take and drink![9] May your two great ones make greeting to the Eye of Horus so that it may rejoice over you; provide yourself with the ferment(?) which issued from you, and which I myself have given to you as a boon which the king gives. You yourself shall watch over yourself; take bread, and you will not hunger. I[10] have given to you from the offering which was given by the Mysterious Ones, and your warrant is in respect of this bread of yours which I have given to you because of Him who goes and returns,[11] (even) Horus in the Night-bark, and he gives bread to [. . .] bread [. . .].

1. The sudden reversion to the 3rd person is out of place, and the original 2nd person has been restored in the translation.

2. Restore a word for 'tomb' in the lacuna?

3. Restore as *S*[*t*]*š*; note the parallel with Horus and the epithet *ỉmy Ḫnt*.
4. One water-sign too many.
5. Compare 'N-Shu', 'N-Gēb', 'N-Thoth' in 356*a-i*.
6. Note the masc. suffix in *ḥnkt n.k*; the scribe has forgotten to change it to *.ṯ*.
7. Supply *.ṯ* after *sȝ* 'son' and emend *.k* into *.ṯ* after *ỉwʿ*.
8. Compare *ḳȝḥyt* in *BD* 355,3.
9. An admonition addressed to the deceased.
10. Read the 1st person here. The officiant is speaking.
11. For *prt* read *prr*? An alternative would be to take *prt* as a *sḏmt.f* form with *ỉww* as nominal subject: 'since he who comes goes forth'.

Spell 726

Gēb is aroused by the Languid One so that he may convey the daughters of the VI, 357
Two who fish up; he has found me in [. . .], and my horn is that of a wild bull; I go to yonder portal as a king, and the great offering is what the god confirms.

Spell 727

O you two crews of Shu; O Osiris the father of N, arise, arise in the Great Booth; the movements of the sunshine are freed for you[1] by those who are in the sky until those who are in . . .[2] come to you and those who are in . . . travel to you. you.

1. Masc. sing.
2. *Nnwtyw.*

Spell 728

O Cloth, the Great One stands up, for he has received his staff, he has sub- VI, 358
dued those who conspired against him in this his name of 'Loin-cloth', so that he may set his protection about N's bed.

O Cloth, the Great One awakes and the serpents rouse, for they look on the mothers of those who preceded the Great Lady, ⟨ . . . ⟩ [she] ferries across in it[1] in this her name of 'Two-weave cloth'. You[2] are the protection of N's bed.

O Cloth, arouse Osiris on his throne, for he has recovered his senses, and presented ⟨N⟩[3] to himself. Arouse N on his throne, for he has recovered his senses, and has presented Osiris to himself. He has found the great ones who are in the

secret places [because of(?)] their power, he has bound(?) his own body and is
unconscious through it in this his name of 'Three-weave cloth' which those who
are over the healing[4] of backbones bring. He has collected [his] members to-
gether, and he sets his protection[5] about N's bed. May he have power over
[his foes(?)].
O Cloth, the Great One travels . . .[6] multitudes; those who are among
359 those who fly up(?) in front of Isis go to him [. . .] in wrath. She causes that
her brother Osiris[7] be made to travel about, she fights on behalf of her son Horus
[. . .] Imsety, Ḥapy, Duamūtef, Ḳebḥsenuf, in this his name of 'Three-weave
cloth' [. . .] which is on the back of Osiris; there is none who [. . .], there is
none who will rob you, O N, for ever.
O Cloth, a seat is allotted by the Bull [. . .] the secret shambles [. . .]
their great ones(?) at the voice of the Five(?)[8] who were allotted to the body of
Nūt in this your name of 'Four-weave cloth'. The need of Osiris[9] is the allotting
of a place so that they may spread their protection about N's bed for ever.
O Cloth, go [. . .] the great ones who are in the sky that he may see [. . .]
great, dread [. . .] in his place. He whose face is hidden who is in the horizon,
360 for whom the sky is hidden, to whom the earth is allotted, whose place is pre-
pared [. . .] gods, the god[s] know that he will give his testimony(?). Clothe
[. . .] clothe [. . .] he will put himself in the mansion of the seven-weave cloth
which encloses Osiris [. . .] which is collected [. . .] his powers as a protection
about N's bed for ever.
O Cloth, you Great One, a protection for N, clothe [. . .] who are hidden
[. . .] Great One [. . .] five days. They mourned(?)[10] Osiris in it in his robe of
the *sndw*-garment[11] which they have given to their(?) sister [. . .] in this its
name of 'Five-weave cloth'. You are the protection of [N's] bed [. . .] N in
361 [. . .] Lord of Assembly at his voice. The Enneads greet him, the Great One
is [glad], his foe is overturned in their presence [. . .], he drags in his . . . ,[12] N
[. . .] 'Seven-weave cloth'. Your cloth is the protection of N's ⟨bed⟩[13] for ever.
O Cloth [. . .] Great One, herdsman(?) of Sia, look at him [. . .] in the
Conclaves of the Ennead [. . .] in his presence, (even) Rēʿ-Atum; his face shines
in [this] his name [of] 'Six-weave cloth';[14] you are the protection of N's [bed]
for ever.
O Cloth, the great ones stand up in their places, the Enneads are joyful, so
362 that they are not afraid ⟨in⟩ their majesty when they see [. . .] offerings. His
bones are reckoned, [. . .], his back is pressed [. . .] 'Nine-weave cloth', for
you are the protection of N's bed for ever.

1. 'It' presumably refers to a celestial boat of which the previous mention has been omitted.
2. Masc. sing., presumably addressed to *'Idmy* invoked in 358*c*.
3. The name of the deceased has been omitted; for the converse of this passage cf. 358*i.j*.
4. Read *s(w)ḏꜣ*.
5. Reading *dy.f sꜣ.f* as in 358*c*. It is doubtful if the lacuna shown after *dy.f* actually exists, for it comes at the bottom of line 364, so that it may well be that nothing has been lost. At this point de Buck had to depend on an earlier copy.
6. *N bẖš*.
7. The name of the deceased is superfluous here, and it is omitted.
8. or 'Seven'. Only 'Five' or 'Seven' are possible; note the grouping of the extant strokes.
9. The name of the deceased omitted?
10. Cf. de Buck, n. 13*; *ḥꜣ* 'mourn' seems more probable than *ḥw* 'smite'.
11. For the reading *sndw* of the name of this garment cf. *CT.* I, 109*a*; III, 82*a*.
12. *Ḫmwt.*
13. *Ḥnkyt nt* omitted between *sꜣ* and *Wsyr.*
14. One would expect 'Eight-weave'.

Spell 729

O N, you are a double which satisfies its[1] lord; seven portions are in Ōn, four portions are in the sky and three are on earth,[2] the . . .[3] shouts, the altar has on it the water[4] of oblation. RECEIVING GIFTS WHICH ARE GIVEN TO A MAN IN THE REALM OF THE DEAD.

1. A fem. suffix because this is a woman's coffin.
2. Slightly corrupt; after *pt* read simply *ḫmt r tꜣ*.
3. *'Ign.*
4. So rather than 'is on the water', which makes no sense. Compare *ḥr rn* 'having on it the name', *ḥr ḫtm* 'having on it the seal', *Eg. Gramm.*[3] §165,9.

Spell 730

[. . .] I support the White Crown, I receive the *wrrt*-crown of Thoth, for I am VI, 363
his paternal brother. I have come against you, you foe yonder who are black beneath me in the tribunal; O Thoth, equip, equip, so that I may go to and fro in the face of [. . .]. I support a single bowl(?),[1] for the West belongs to me.

1. Tentatively connecting *ḏny* here with *ḏnyw* 'bowl', *CT* II, 203*a*.

Spell 731

[. . .] sky [. . .] for me [at(?)] the horizon which is yonder in my mansion. Mine is protection, mine is magic, mine is his club, mine is [his staff . . .] god, I know you . . .[1] every day, the . . .[2] of the good god is clad as the Two Ladies. [I] myself(?),[3] I have spent time as the Sacred Eye, and the blast of fire(?)[4] has arisen.

1. *Nḫꜣ ꜣty nṯrty wtt,* unintelligible.
2. *Byt syꜣ.*
3. Reading *ỉ[nk] ḏs.⟨ỉ⟩*.
4. Reading *ns* 'fire' rather than *ns* 'knife'.

Spells 732–4 are almost entirely lost. A god Hndd *is named in 365k.*

Spell 735

VI, 366 NOT TO LET A MAN'S HEART BE TAKEN [FROM HIM]. *The rest is lost except for a few words.*

Spell 736

[. . . s knife(?)] against you, and . . . has seen you.[1]

1. Apparently a spell against a dangerous animal, which is not identified.

Spell 737

VI, 367 'What will you live on?' say the vatmen of Rēʿ. 'I will live on what they live on'.[1]

1. For *ṯnmw* 'vatmen' cf. *CT* IV, 303*a*. What follows must have been originally in the 1st person, as the question is addressed directly to the deceased. This spell is clearly but a fragment of a longer text.

Spell 738

THE NORTHERN EXPANSE.[1] O Ptah-Sokar who appears in the *Ḥnw*-bark . . .[2]

1. Cf. *pḏw* 'open space(?)', *CT* VI, 4*h*.
2. Cf. de Buck, n. 3*.

Spell 739

TO CAUSE A MAN TO RECEIVE PROVISIONS IN THE REALM OF THE DEAD. As for ⟨N⟩, give to N, guard N.

Spell 740

O you Radiant Ones, you of the Armpit who belong to the god . . . VI, 368

Spell 741

The sky thunders, the earth quakes [. . .] my[1] local(?)[2] god for me, the Hand-filler who is in the tribunal [. . .] he remembers my name. He has taken thought for me, he has called out to me as to a potentate [. . .] die [. . .] the silent ones through fear lest the plebs should go forth, while darkness is in [. . .].

Get back, you Disturber, and tell what you[3] have seen. An impediment is set up against you on my account [. . .] my father who is in the tribunal is
in front of you, | and he who is vindicated is my champion against you [. . .] VI, 369
my father against you, and you shall be unaware[4] of me [. . . I am] without my father who is among the gods. See, Rēʿ has imposed an obstacle [. . .] he speaks to the gods who are about his shrine, and they have smitten [. . .] mysterious [words(?)] which are in the mouth of Anubis. The terror of you is in front of my[5] shape, [and I see(?)][6] what has been done to you because of your evil affair. You are enwrapped,[7] and the Great One is in [. . .] the Great One stands up with his sceptre directing an arm against you because (someone) comes against you. You have no bread [. . .] you have no *ḥbnnt*-cakes in the realm of the dead; see, you belong to him, the king who acts [. . .] Osiris against you, and your affair shall not escape from him for ever.

1. For the 1st person cf. 369*a*.

2. Cf. de Buck, n. 2*.

3. Lit. 'he'.

4. An odd construction; assuming *ỉḫ* to be the non-enclitic particle, one would have expected *ỉḫ ḫm.k*, cf. *Eg. Gramm.*[3] §450, 5(*a*). Probably the scribe has misplaced the suffix.

5. For *ỉrw.f* read *ỉrw.i*, see n. 1 above; strictly this should have read *ỉrw.s*, but the scribe has forgotten that this is a woman's coffin. The owner of it is still speaking to the Disturber of 369*o*.

6. Restore as *mꜣꜣ.f* (for *mꜣꜣ.ỉ*)?

7. Lit. 'mummy-wrappings are yours'.

Spell 742

VI, 370 O father of N [. . .] for you her foes, etc., who come against her wrongfully [. . .] N in the realm of the dead. See, he is yours; let him be taken to the House of the Smiter [. . .] whom he conducts to the House of the Year(?), whom he judges in it before the knees [of . . .] who ferried the boatless across when the day had not yet come [. . .] bread, who has no runnel(?)[1] or marsh; he makes [. . .] what she chews is his ear of corn. He who speaks to you is he who fills her hand, who is in the tribunal [. . .] the fledgelings were nursed before she was nursed, before [. . .] were pressed out(?) [. . .] Thoth; he it is who will protect her. Your glance is on her, and hers is the sweat of the flesh of [. . .] yonder foe, etc., who shall pursue her; you have put him under [. . .].

371 Speak a word behind his shrine to ʿApep, you being rejuvenated [. . .] N, he has spoken evil against her to [. . .] cutting off(?) hair after her head was cut off and after [her(?)] inertia was removed [. . .] outside; do what has not been done [. . .] loud of voice; who was commanded to do his slaughter on her account by night, bright [. . .] who do your slaughter by night. You are destined(?) to [. . .] your speech which has come into being in their presence. Get back, be on guard! Swallow[2] all [that you devised(?)] which was in your heart against N [. . .] this place to which you were destined. It is he who commands that N shall be [. . .] she serves her god, and she does all that
372 the lords of [. . .] desire [. . .] she will plaster their stairway, she will maintain their gates in front of [. . .] they have acted behind you, having been cut off with her; [. . .] do not know [. . .] you have no bread, you have no *pꜣḳ*-cakes, you have no *ḥbnnt*-cakes, you have no *pꜣd*-cakes, you have no invocation-offerings [from(?)] N in this land. You are in the land [. . .] N. A MAN SHALL SAY THIS SPELL AT TIME OF NIGHT.

1. *T3ḥt*; cf. also 206*h*. This is said of the deceased.

2. Imperative with reinforcing dative and enclitic particle; what follows could be restored as *sḫ3.n.k*.

Spell 743

SPELL FOR BEING IN [. . .] water. N has come to you,[1] for N is this Great One,
[she] is not weak [. . .] N is Maʿet for Rēʿ [. . .]. | The staff is in good condi- VI, 373
tion, the sceptre of Anubis is the backbone(?)[2] of N's double [. . .] you, who
splits up(?) the power of your heat, who knots up [. . .] of electrum(?) in his
riparian land; she fashions the offerings of Maʿet,[3] [she is] joyful [. . .] N sees
[. . .] N against(?) you.[4] May you[5] be high as that which is on your[6] head, may
the year be joyful[7] in life in [. . .] N; she gives respect [. . .] the god is conjured
in her shape. Pursue yesterday; the young one(?) will not vacillate [. . .] wrong-
doing. The god bows to N[8] [. . .] yesterday; see, she rises up pregnant.

1. Plural.
2. Read *psḏ*?
3. Read *ms.s ḥtpw M3ʿt* with honorific transposition.
4. Plural.
5. Fem. sing.
6. Plural. Emend to sing. *ṯ*?
7. For *ḥk* read *ḥkn*.
8. Read *ks nṯr n N*; *f3* is an erroneous interpolation, or possibly the first signs of a passage which has been omitted.

Spell 744

O N, Bull of the dappled [cattle . . .] her [three portions] are in the sky with VI, 374
Rēʿ, her four portions are on earth with Gēb. N will not eat faeces, she will not
drink urine [. . .].

Spell 745

N [. . .] the Ennead with your foe under you.[1] He has said: 'I will act in this
your[2] name of Osiris'; Horus(?) has placed [. . .] your magic in your name of
'Great of magic'. You are the great god [. . .] as Sokar, he is a son who wears
his father's Red Crown, | which has power as a god [. . .] you will have power VI, 375
thereby; you will have power to protect yourself through [. . .] the Great One
who travels about as he who travels about the Isles. May the living one live.

1. Fem. sing.; the female deceased is addressed.

2. Masc. sing.; the genders of pronouns in this coffin are apt to be confused, partly because the editorial change from masc. to fem. has often been ineffectively carried out, and partly because the identification of the dead woman with a male god, e.g. Osiris, faces the editor with an insoluble problem.

Spell 746

I am Atum who came into being [. . .] me on the Supports of Shu, and the flames of my eye are about me, [I am(?)] not unaware of those who are about my shrine; [. . .] has no power [over me(?) . . .] over me, because I walk within the firmament, and his thickness is my thickness; he will make division for those who are before me, and he will make completion for those who are behind [me[1]
VI, 376 . . .] my paths to them; they will watch over my ways, and their magic will watch over my paths, because I [. . .] this your[1] name of Lord of All. I walk to and fro at the head of my bodies in Ōn, because I am Rēʿ at the head of the plebs, who live [. . .] men [. . .][2] who go up on account of their tongues. I wash myself(?),[3] I worship Rēʿ, I exalt Ḥatḥōr, [I(?)] go up [. . .], I have wands(?), and they support(?) my arms in the basket(?) of . . .[4] My hands are those of Seshat who is in my mouth as the Sistrum-player, and I am pure for Ḥatḥōr . . . upon earth.

1. Fem. sing.
2. See de Buck, n. 6*.
3. Lit. 'she washes(?) N'.
4. Cf. de Buck, n. 9*.

Spell 747

VI, 377 GUIDE TO[1] THE PATHS OF THE NETHERWORLD. O Cropped One(?)![2] O Terrible One![3] The boatless one has gone astray [. . .] on the paths of the dead(?).[4]

1. Direct genitive, lit. 'of'.
2. Cf. *BD* 401,16.
3. Cf. *CT* IV, 159*b*.
4. *Ppw* is not recorded; it could be a corruption of *ḫpw*.

Spell 748

Do not take her on an unknown path, do not take her on a meandering path of . . .[1] which goes round about . . .[2]

She who receives from the satchels is she who possesses the ends[3] of its cloth strip because of what is in it. Depth below, height above are(?) what the owner cares for(?) concerning his property.[4]

She who is in pain is under terror, the terror of the years; she whose knives are sharp is she who cuts hair for her shrine(?).

She who goes about, who is behind Him who is respected, who exhales and . . .[5] behind . . .[6]

You shall guide her on the path of offerings(?); guide[7] her on the path to 378
[. . .] who fashioned the falcons who are vigilant when they see N [. . .] she will turn aside, for you know this(?)[8] which they know, and N knows [. . . within(?)][9] the egg with the father-of-children-bird[10] which is in the thickets of rushes, who lives [. . .] N as Rēᶜ, she shines as Rēᶜ, she has copulated(?) in the Mansion of [. . .] in the sky as Rēᶜ, the dread of N is that of the great god; [she(?)] goes [. . .] born [again(?)][11] on this day, N is delivered of the two embryos of Shu.[12] As for any god who shall oppose himself to these [. . .] the two daughters of the Lord of the Thunderbolt(?), (namely) the two women in bright red linen, and the Sunshine-god.

1. *Tp dmḏt.* The tabular part of this spell is mostly unintelligible to me, and the renderings are wholly tentative.
2. *Ḫr ỉm.s.*
3. Lit. 'the two heads'.
4. The relationship to the context is quite obscure.
5. *Nmᶜ.*
6. *ꜣsytyw.*
7. Imperative with reinforcing dative.
8. Regarding *nnṯn* as a miswriting of *nn.*
9. Restoring *m-ẖnw* before *swḥt.*
10. For this bird, a heron or bittern, cf. *Pyr.* §1225.
11. Restore as [*wḥ*] *mt mst*?
12. *Bkꜣty* appears to mean not 'pregnant women', which would make no sense, but rather the results of pregnancy, the embryos. Here the deceased woman appears in the role of Tefēnet, who gave birth to Gēb and Nūt, presumably the *bkꜣty* of this text.

Spell 749

VI, 379 HASTEN, COME . . . him who rises for her. She is made bright and shining by the glitter on the brow of the Sunshine-god; N has gone up in the red hour[1] [. . .] between them every day. N has gone up as one who is stared at on that bright day when N passed away because of those who are in [. . .] you have passed away.

1. Probably sunset.

Spell 750

TO DRIVE OFF THE SLAYERS. O you slayers yonder of the Lord of Life [. . .] who make presentation of the legs of children to the Lord of Life, be far from N, do not make presentation of her [. . .] be far from her; see, she will let him
VI,380 know, | she will slay his foes for him, she will shoot(?) for him those who rebel against him. O N [. . .] N, depart alive, you shall not depart dead.

Spell 751

O Imsety, Ḥapy, Duamūtef, Ḳebḥsenuf, seek me out for this bread of mine, my heirs(?)[1] reap for ⟨me⟩, (namely) my surviving children.

I, even I,[2] will make a spirit of you, I give water to Thoth that he may make you[3] content with it and you shall eat of bread of white emmer and beer of red emmer, for I give you your bread which will not go stale and your beer which will not go sour; be content with the king's boon and go [. . .].[4]

1. A corruption of *ỉwʿw*?

2. The officiant speaks; the invocation of the four children of Horus was deemed to have been uttered by the deceased.

3. In 380*k* the name of the deceased should be replaced by the dependent pronoun *ṯw*.

4. The end of the spell is unintelligible.

Spell 752

O you gods [who keep] the doors of [. . .] of the *rꜣ*-goose and who watch over the portal of Her who ascends to the sky, open to me so that I may breathe the breezes which are in the midst of the waters and that the bark may convey me[1] in her bow, for I am he who has charge of the rigging[2] in the god's bark, and I row, for I know how to pull, and my seat is in the bark. I am skilled in the craft of Her who permits throats to breathe; therefore I will drive off ⸢Apep, ferrying across the firmament; I will not be replaced in the streams which are above, for I know the food(?)[3] of the god of offerings, and I have shown it to the gods. VI, 381

O you Souls of the Westerners who are on yonder mountain of *Bꜣẖw,* it is 300 rods long and 120 rods wide.[4]

SPELL FOR ENTERING INTO THE WEST DAILY IN THE RETINUE OF RĒʿ.

1. Abnormal word order; one would expect *ḏꜣ wỉ wyꜣ.*
2. Cf. de Buck, n. 5; the correct det. of *smyw* is the rope, cf. *CT II, 366b.*
3. *Nmy*; the crosshatched signs in 381*l* look like further dets. of this word.
4. Compare *CT* II, 375*c*–376*c*.

Spell 753

TO GO ABOARD THE BARK OF RĒʿ WHEN HE[1] HAS GONE TO HIS DOUBLE. VI, 382
O So-and-so(?),[2] where are you?

I have come into the Island of Fire, I allot well-being, for I know that I will give a son to his father and I will give a daughter to her mother. I do wish that (someone) would come to me so that I might tie up(?)[3] a bundle and lift up the mooring-ropes, for I have tied the knot for Ḥatḥōr, for Him who strews the sky with your (*sic*) beauty. The year is at peace because of your goodness, and I will wash my hands, for I have taken my oars so that I may convey Ḥatḥōr to the horizon, to the pure places. Command was made to Atum, and I have come that I may appear in glory and go aboard the bark on the starboard side and on the larboard side. I have come that I may guide the waters and control the voyages in the bark of Ḥatḥōr; I will fare southward in order to be far ⟨from⟩ the back part,[4] I will sit with those who are between the steering-oars. I will fare southward at the bow, I will sit ⟨ . . . ⟩[5] among your[6] powerful ones, for I am one of these powerful ones of yours. | I am the one who guides the waters, I control the 383
voyages in the bark of Ḥatḥōr. I have come, having appeared in glory; I will go aboard the bark, I will sit on the throne, I will receive *sẖt,*[7] and I will eat . . . of these gifts to me.[8]

1. The deceased.
2. *Pwy* and *Wy* are terms for the deceased, perhaps meaning 'So-and-so'.
3. A guess based on the context.
4. I.e. the northern regions.
5. An omission between *r* and *m-m* on passing from line to line.
6. Fem. sing., presumably referring to Ḥatḥōr, so also 382*j*, end.
7. *Sẖt* is doubtless a var. of *sšt* in *Pyr.* §§96; 108; Mr. Spaull has pointed out to me that the item in question seems to be grain rather than fruit.
8. Lit. 'the *mnw* of these my gifts'; the meaning of *mnw* is not clear.

Spell 754

SPELL FOR THE BEING OF A MAN AND WHAT IS IN HIS HOUSE. Osiris speaks to his son Horus,[1] for he has nullified what was done to him on his eighth day, he has removed the sweat which was on his flesh on his fourth day. Those who should come[2] will come to you[3] in the garden, for you are alive and cleansed in the pool of cold water, and your son Horus will guide you. How happy are those who see, how content are those who hear, when Horus is seen extending
VI, 384 the *wꜣs*-staff to his father Osiris! | Your libation is poured[4] by Isis, Nephthys cleanses you, (even) your two sisters great of magic. Your bones are knit together for you, your members are collected for you, your eyes are set in your face for you ⟨by⟩ the Night-bark and the Day-bark.[5]

1. This spell is a version of *Pyr.* §§1978–82.
2. Fem. plural.
3. The deceased in the role of Osiris, cf. 383*n*.
4. Read *zꜣṯ zꜣṯ.k ỉn ꜣst* with *Pyr.* §1981*a*. 384*a* reads nonsensically: 'See, your servitor is your daughter by Isis'.
5. With 384*b-g* compare *Pyr.* §§1981*b*–1982*a*.

Spell 755

A MAN IS NOT TO PUTREFY IN THE REALM OF THE DEAD. The members in Osiris are inert, but ⟨they⟩ shall not be inert, they shall not putrefy or shake, [they shall] not [swell up or] make[1] foul fluid. O you who come from the [acacia-tree] of the Double Lion [to Horus in the midst of] his corruption,[2] may [you(?)][3] come and see me at the house of Him who approaches his father(?).[4] Say:[5] Do not choke in this your name of Him of Oxyrhynchus; do not putrefy in this your name of Ḥa; do not decay in this your name of Anubis; do not drip on the ground in this your name of 'Jackal'.[6]

O Great One, weep; I do wish that this Great One who weeps were one who weeps for the two Sisterly Companions, West and East, when they weep [for(?)] themselves at the coffin. The tears of the god are the putrefaction of the member in me, and it shall not putrefy, it shall not rot, [it] shall not become maggoty, it shall not become corrupt(?). The great ones shall not have power thereby, the mighty ones shall not have power thereby, the great bulls are approached, having gone forth from the nose of the Eldest One (and from) the acacia-tree of the Double Lion to Horus in the midst of his corruption [. . .] which is in Ōn. VI, 385

There is put together for me the worm of Him who approaches his father(?).[7] Weep! I do wish that the Great One who weeps were one [who weeps for] them, the two Sisterly Companions, West and East – and *vice versa* – when they go out weeping and lamenting – and *vice versa* – for the Great One and for their father and their son; they weep [for him who is(?)][8] behind them on the mountain when they say: [May the putrefaction] of Osiris [be stopped(?)].[9]

1. Restore 384*l* as *n* [*bn.sn n*] *ỉr*⟨*.sn*⟩ *mw ḏw*; for *bn.sn* cf. *BD* 120,8.
2. Cf. 385*j*.
3. De Buck's n. 4* questions the reading *ỉw.f*; *ỉw*[*.k*] seems to me more probable, as following up the vocative *ỉww* of 384*m*.
4. *H̱n ỉt.f*, translation doubtful, for *ẖn* 'approach' is normally constructed with *m*.
5. An imperative addressed to 'you who come'?
6. Compare *Pyr.* §1257.
7. See n. 4 above.
8. Restore *ỉmy* in the lacuna?
9. Restore as *ỉh*[*m ḥw*] *ꜣ*?

Spell 756

Do not putrefy in this your name of Ḥa; do not be maggoty in this your name of 'Maggot'; do not choke in this your name of Him of Oxyrhynchus; [do not] rot in this your name of Anubis; do not drip your corruption which is in them (*sic*) in this your name of 'Jackal'. VI, 386

I do wish that he[1] were slain with knives quivering(?) in the members in the presence of Anubis who presides over his god's booth in his . . .[2]

1. Presumably an anonymous being hostile to the deceased.
2. *Gg* with lost det. Neither *ggt* 'kidney' nor *ggw* 'stare' make sense.

Spell 757

My White Crown is Sakhmet, my Red Crown is Edjō, and I will not be disturbed.

Spell 758[1]

VI, 387 A. *On the throne of the god*: Myriads of years.[2]

B. *On the right edge of the ovals*: The paths of fire. These paths guard the larboard side of the bark of the Coiled One, who makes a circle in a myriad after a myriad (of years). The gates are confused, the bow of the bark[3] of the Coiled One has swung round.[4] This is the seat of the Shining[5] Sun which these gates guard;[6] it is a myriad of a myriad after a myriad (of years).

C. *On the left edge of the ovals*: The gates are confused, the starboard side of the bark belongs to the right side of the Coiled One. The paths of fire go round about the seat of the Shining Sun, who guards the paths for the great bark of the Coiled One, who makes a circle for myriad after myriad.[7]

1. This spell and the first lines of Spell 759 belong to the vignette on p. 386. The enthroned god enclosed in a series of ovals is Rēʿ within his coils; cf. 'Rēʿ who is in his coils' in *Th.T.S.* I, pl 37, middle horizontal band.

2. We have here a variant of the hieroglyph  in which the year-sign is separated from the head of the human figure.

3. Read *ỉm(w)*; for the word cf. *Concise Dict.* 20, bottom.

4. The bark has changed course owing to the confusion of the gates.

5. *Psḏ*, written as the numeral 9.

6. *Nw* at the end of 387*g* governs the entire clause.

7. *Ḥḥ m-sꜣ ḥḥ* used adverbially, cf. *Eg. Gramm.*[3] §205,6 (p. 156, bottom).

Spell 759[1]

As for this Coiled One,[2] he is ⟨the Coiled One(?)⟩[3] of Rēʿ, ⟨and Rēʿ is(?)⟩ this myriad (of years).[4] He is this myriad (of years) . . .[5] after a myriad.[6]

A million (cubits) are a half of the length of the bark;[7] starboard, bow, stern and larboard[8] are four million (cubits); the crawler(?), who is he?[9] All the
VI, 388 Ennead are in this, on every side of it, and there is a division into these four parts;[10] every fiery path is between each million (of cubits) in this and its counterpart;[11] it means that the four paths are of fire and that they turn about in fire behind it.[12] I know these firmaments(?) over which the winds blow(?)[13] daily,

and my father Rēʿ sees. Such am I,[14] (even) I whom the winds blow(?). I will not make opposition on account of[15] Rēʿ within his coils, for I am one who is in his body. Moreover I know the dark paths by which Ḥu and Sia come in with the four dark snakes which are made bright for those who follow them and those who precede them, and I come in between them, being in possession of the secret path in which is the vertex of Rēʿ, and these four knots which belong to the celestial kine are hidden(?) because of them. I also know those secret paths by means of which the she-cat comes in daily; what is removed(?)[16] for it is upon the head, what is loosed for it is the backbone, when Rēʿ speaks about it. See(?), you[17] are lifted up alive; . . .[18] and she lives.

Prepare paths for me, open for me the gates which are among the Coiled 389
Ones, for I know the circuit of Rēʿ and of those who are with him, I know his foes who are in the gates, I know the paths [. . .]. Prepare a path for me, for I am indeed alive, the heir of eternity, who passes everlasting, whom Rēʿ has placed over you. It is I who see [your] births, but you do not see [my] birth.[19] I am one whose name is secret who is in the boundary of the gods, and your hands make acclamation to me.[20] I am the Inert One who issued from the Eye, I am he who fashioned fire about the Coiled One who makes a circle; I am the corded ferry-boat[21] which the Coiled One encircles every day. I come to land because of the celestial kine;[22] the lords of the Coiled One are within the abode of the flood. I make Maʿet to flourish, and I am content that you should live in my time; when I am angry, I will not give to you, (but) I will not oppose(?) the living Lord of All.

1. This spell begins with the short vertical lines above and below the ovals in the figure on p. 386, but they are hardly intelligible; in fact, de Buck was even uncertain of the sequence of the lines, see his n. 6* on p. 387. We can now be confident that the sequence is 1, 1*a*; 2, 2*a* and so on, but understanding them is another matter. Allen tackled this problem in dealing with Ch. 131 in his 1960 translation of the BD, but I do not find myself entirely in accord with him; individual points will be dealt with below. See also Zandee, *De reis van de dode*; Assmann, *Liturgische Lieder an den Sonnengott,* 51; Hornung, *Am Duat,* 130; *JEOL* 15,65.

2. Cf. 390*a*; *wnnt* is the enclitic particle.

3. *Ỉr wnnt mhn pwy* is straightforward, but it is followed by *pw n Rʿ*, where the predicate has been omitted. The missing word may well have been *mḥn,* the scribe avoiding repetition of this word owing to shortage of space, so that probably we should read ⟨*mḥn*⟩ *pw n Rʿ*.

4. At the beginning of 387*p, w* is in the air, and something has clearly been omitted before it; perhaps here we have another case of the avoidance of repetition and should read ⟨*Rʿ p*⟩*w*. Allen's suggestion of ⟨*ỉ*⟩*w ḥḥ pw* contravenes the rules of grammar; in Middle Egyptian *ỉw* does not introduce *pw* clauses. For *ḥḥ* he suggests 'a million (cubits)' of thickness of the sun-snake's body, basing his view on a dubious interpretation of 387*r*, see n. 5 below. I

believe *ḥḥ* here to refer to years, as in Spell 758, the *w* before it to be the remnant of another *Rꜥ pw*, and *p pw* after *ḥḥ* to be in this case a miswriting of simple *pw*. The transliteration of 387*p* would then be ⟨*Rꜥ p*⟩ *w ḥḥ pw.*

5. Reading *ḥḥ pw* ⟨*p*⟩ *w m* . . . in 387*q-r*; Allen's view that *w m* stands for *wmt* 'thick' cannot be maintained. *Wmt* is written always with  , and the final *t* is radical. In any case, if a linear dimension of the snake were needed, it would surely be its length rather than its thickness. I suggest that the second *w* (387*r*) stands for ⟨*p*⟩*w* and that *m* following it is the preposition, but I cannot guess what  may represent.

6. *Sꜣ* in 387*t* is taken to be a dittograph on passing from line to line.

7. *Ḥḥ* in 387*u* stands here not for years but for units of length of the solar bark, i.e. 'a million (cubits) are a half of its length, the bark', the last word being added in order to account for the suffix in *ꜣw.f.*

8. Read *ỉmy-wrt ꜥꜣt wꜣḏt ꜥꜣt ỉmy-nḏs(t) tꜣ-wr ꜥꜣ.*

9. Allen's translation of *ḥnmw* as 'crawler' is probably not far wrong, for it appears to be formed from the simplex of *ḥnmnm* 'creep'; his translation of *nm sw* as 'who is he?' is justified by *m tr tw* 'who are you?', *Eg. Gramm.*[3] §495; for the use of *nm* instead of simple *m* in this class of sentence cf. op. cit. §256, end.

10. Lit. 'sides', i.e. starboard, larboard, bow and stern. So already Allen.

11. Emending into *snnw.f* with Allen.

12. I.e. the bark.

13. *'Iptw byꜣ ỉtp* appears to be corrupt; read as *byꜣw ỉptw*? *Tt* (again 388*g*) is not recorded elsewhere; the translation as 'blow(?)' is a guess, but what else could the winds do?

14. Lit. 'N is N'; emended into the 1st person.

15. *Ḫsf ḥr,* lit. 'oppose because of'; hardly 'defend' as in *Pr.* 7,9; *Leb.* 24.

16. Causative of *nḥm* 'take away'? These sentences are incomprehensible.

17. The suffix *ṯn* here and recurrently hereafter lacks an antecedent, which points to an omission from the preceding text. The *m* before *ṯs.ṯn* may belong to the missing text or may stand for *m* 'see' used without suffix.

18. I can make nothing of most of 388*u*.

19. Cf. de Buck, nn. 5*. 6*.

20. I.e. by clapping.

21. *Sic,* not 'ferryman'; note the fem. relative form *dbnt.*

22. Restored as in 388*n*.

Spell 760

VI, 390 As for this Coiled One whom Isis brought to her son Horus, who is in the bow of the bark which her word brought into being on his account in the presence of the Sole Lord, because of her bringing him[1] to Horus, she spoke of[2] the Coiled One to Rēꜥ, and it goes well with Horus son of Isis since he went in; he has become lord of the bark and he has inherited the sky. He has become the double[3] of the Lord of All since he entered into it, and it is this Horus son of Isis who rules[4] all the skies and their gods who are in them.[5] As for any spirit who knows the name of the Shining Sun, he knows his (own) name; the gate [. . .] in the twilight. Come ⟨ . . . ⟩.[6] As for him who knows[7] the names of those paths of his, it is he who will go in to the Coiled One. As for him who knows this spell, he will never perish. He will live on what Rēʿ lives ⟨on⟩[8] in the seat of the Shining Sun which guards these gates in myriad after myriad (of years).[9]

1. The Coiled One.
2. Cf. *Wb.* IV, 335,12.
3. *Wḥmw,* lit. 'repetition', physical, not spiritual, double.
4. For *srỉ* 'rule' a region cf. *CT* VI, 182*e*; 268*i.*
5. For the suffix *.s* read *.sn.*
6. There has been an omission after the imperative *m.*
7. Reading *ỉr ⟨r⟩ḫ*, cf. 390*m.*
8. Supply *ỉm* after 'Rēʿ'.
9. Compare 387*g.h.*

Spell 761

TO ASSEMBLE A SPIRIT'S MEMBERS FOR HIM IN THE REALM OF THE DEAD. Wake! VI, 391
Wake! O N, wake! See what your son Horus has done for you, hear what your father Gēb has done for you; he has set your foes beneath you for you. Go up and bathe in the Lake of Life; what is evil on you will be purged in the Lake of the Firmament. You have come into being complete as any god; your head is Rēʿ, your face is Wepwawet, your nose is the Jackal, your lips are the Twins, your ears are Isis and Nephthys, your eyes are the twin children of Rēʿ-Atum, your tongue is Thoth, your throat is Nūt, your neck is Gēb, your shoulders are Horus, your chest is He who pleases the spirit of Rēʿ, the great god who is in you, your flanks are Ḥu and Khopri, your navel is the Jackal of the Double Lion, your back is Anubis,[1] your belly is the Double Lion, your arms are the two sons of Horus,
Ḥapy and Imsety, your fingers and your finger-nails are the Children of Horus,[1] 392
your back is the Extender of the Sunshine, your legs are Anubis, your buttocks are Isis and Nephthys, your feet are Duamūtef and Ḳebḥsenuf, and there is no member in you which lacks a god; raise yourself, N!

1. Cf. 392*a*: 'your back is the Extender of the Sunshine' and 392*b*: 'your legs are Anubis'; this reference to the back is out of place, coming as it does between 'navel' and 'belly'.

Spell 762

Ho N! You are Neḥebkau, son of Gēb, born of your mother Ernūtet; you are indeed the double of every god, having power in your heart. Stand up; Horus has greeted you, for he recognizes(?)[1] you as the double of all the gods; there is no god who has not his double in you. You have come into being and have become on high in company with your father Horus who is in the sky, the Great One who is among the gods.

1. Emending *ỉt.n.f*, which has no meaning, into *ỉp.f*; de Buck's n. 2* shows how the corruption could have come about.

Spell 763

VI, 393 Ho N! Go to the front of the horizon, join the circuit(?)[1] with Rēʿ; you shall sit in it[2] with Khopri, you shall tread it[3] and travel all over it with Rēʿ-Atum, for Rēʿ has given you your fair paths which are therein. The gates of the sky are thrown open for you, for Rēʿ has commanded that you shall be there as ruler of his thrones, for he[4] is the chiefest of his nobles.

1. Reading uncertain; possibly *šnwt*, referring to the path of the sun.
2. *Ḥms* used as a transitive verb, 'sit in' or 'on'. So also 407e.
3. For a similar transitive use of *šm* cf. *CT* IV, 353*c* (S1C, S2C).
4. *Swt* 'he' may be an error for *ṯwt* 'you'.

Spell 764

Ho N! The watchers of the gods shall attend on you,[1] those who are in their primeval state shall fear you, those who are in their towns shall dread you,[2] the gods shall come to you at the stairway of your throne, the multitudinous sun-folk who are in the god's castle shall rejoice at you. Lift yourself up! Be
VI, 394 greater than he who spends the day, | be mightier than he who spends the night, for you are the great god, and Horus has gathered your members together for you.

You are a jackal (lying) on your side, whose shape is revealed against your foes; yours is the sky, and there is given to you the earth to the width of your domain(?). You are bound ⟨for⟩[3] the Fields of Offerings in company with

Nephthys and Osiris, you shall mount up to Rēʿ in the sky, and the gods who are in it will obey you, for the power of the Foremost of the Westerners has been given to you[4], and your bread is good in the presence of the gods, your food-offerings are in the presence of the two great Enneads and in the presence of Anubis who is over the gods. May you remove all your bonds, may guardians be assigned to you, may the efflux which is on your flesh be cast to the ground for you, for Ḥarakhti has commanded that there be given to you this right-dealing which you desire wherever you may go.

1. Cf. *Pyr.* §656; for the bier as det. of *wrš* cf. §875. The future tense is indicated by the prospective forms *ỉwt* in 393*n* and *ḥʿw* in 393*o*.
2. Read *nr* ⟨*n.*⟩*k*; the preposition has been omitted.
3. The preposition *r* has been omitted.
4. In 394*j* there is a superfluous *n* after *rdy*; read *rdy n.k,* passive *sḏm.f* + dative.

Spell 765

Ho N! You are the eldest son ⟨of⟩ the Great One in the company of those who are VI, 395
greater than he in the assembly which is in the Night-bark. You have come into being and have become on high in company with Atum in your fair places which are in the flood. You are with Rēʿ in the Field of Rushes, and you will find the gods joyful at meeting you like Rēʿ, Lord of people.[1] Nūt the great will raise you in your beauty, she will enclose you in her arms which nurse, (i.e.) the two ladies of Dep, like Horus son of Osiris; they will extend their hands to you, and they will set your heart in your body for you.

1. Lit. 'heads'.

Spell 766

[. . .][1] at your side(?) [. . .] in the sky. One goes [. . .] goes out [. . .] lack, VI, 396
foulness, smoke [. . .]. (Someone) comes for N, N has searched out[2] what has been brought to him from the Eye of Rēʿ, and the Milk-goddess [. . .] N at the Jackal Lakes and at the marshes of the floor of the sky, the two [. . .] the efflux of the two who nourish this disemboweller(?)[3] who went forth and travelled with his White Crown on his head. He has given [. . .] to the eyes of N, and N has brought Osiris to life, N has made Osiris grow, he has seen his seats which are in the upper sky, he has purged his efflux, he has knocked(?)[4] his blow-fly(?)[5] to

the ground. He has surpassed the great ones so that he may be at the head of the Ennead, he has no hindrance.[6]

N has come today into the horizon of the sky [. . .] on account of what is in it, N has found [. . .] which opens hearts in their places, N has turned aside today in order to make their names secret, being unknown to them, in the Field of *Smw*.

397 N has come [today . . .] he has seen the deeds of their hearts, N has found the head, the long neck is knit on, the owners of offering-slabs are at their offerings, N has turned aside today in order to close the mouth of[7] the baboon because of what he knows.

N has come girded(?)[8] and alive by means of those who make N's name to flourish,[9] N has found those who appear on their thrones, ⟨whose⟩ members are hale(?),[10] N has turned aside today in order to protect the grey-haired ones.[11]

N has come today from Ombos, N has fashioned [. . .], N has consumed the day (*sic*), N has found [. . .], N [has] counted and has put a period to eternity,[12] N has turned aside today in order to put joy into wombs.

N [has] come today into rulership and its god, he has found him who put seed [. . .], he has found the winds which are given ⟨to⟩ the noses which were
398 open, N has turned aside today in order to [. . .] [1]storm on the day of judging [. . .] of her who ate(?).

[N has] found that the great ones are raised up and the lesser ones stand up.

N has found fish-scales in the living waters which came into being at the river banks.

N [has] found a feather which grew [. . .] dead.

N has found praise which was given ⟨in⟩ the empty boat.

1. Cf. de Buck, n. 1*.

2. Reading *dꜥr.n N.*

3. Reading *bsk,* assuming confusion between the knife-det. and *k*; for the verb cf. ***Pyr.*** §1286.

4. Reading and meaning both doubtful; cf. de Buck, n. 10*.

5. No such word with insect-det. is recorded, but *Wb.* III, 150,3 has *ḥrrt* with snake-det used for crawling creatures; here it may perhaps stand for the kind of insect which infests rotting flesh.

6. For *ỉmy-rd* 'hindrance' cf. *Pyr.* §§322; 417; 2247; in §§211; 2202 the possessive suffix follows the whole expression; the form *ỉmy.f-rd* found here does not seem to recur.

7. Dittograph of genitive *n.*

8. If the reading be *šsmtt* or *šsmty,* as suggested in de Buck's n. 1*, the word could be related to *šsmt* 'sacred girdle', *Concise Dict.* 272.

9. See de Buck, n. 3*.

10. Read *ʿwt.s⟨n⟩ w3ḏyt*?
11. The repeated *skm* is a dittograph.
12. Read *ḥts.n.f nḥḥ*.

Spell 767

Those who are content are in the sky, those who are joyful are on earth, because the god has inherited the horizon, and a voice is sent out; content [. . .] Osiris daily because of N. He gives him his double for his body, for N is he who looses, lord of the affairs(?) of the place of the four pillars,[1] who pleases Osiris every day. One who makes Osiris content, to whom Osiris gives bread daily, | and who gives VI, 399
bread to Osiris daily. Speak on N's behalf in the sky, for he speaks on your[2] behalf on the sand.

May N live! When he speaks of the morrow, speak to N, for he has taken possession of eternity and has put a period to everlasting,[3] N will not die again among the dead.

1. Cf. *Pyr.* §152.
2. Plural.
3. Cf. 397*l*; Spell 766, n. 12.

Spell 768

O You who see all,
O You who work the destruction of all,
If you see N, he will see you;
If N be aware, do not be unaware of him.[1]
If you know N, N will know you.

O You whose heart aches for the Sacred Eye,
If N be aware, do not be unaware of him.
If you know N, N will know you.

Let N know of the tens, hundreds,
Thousands, tens of thousands,
Hundreds of thousands, millions,
All the universe[2] about you.
If N be aware, do not be unaware of him.
If you know N, N will know you.

O You with a perceiving heart which is in the body,
If N be aware, do not be unaware of him.
VI, 400 If you know N, N ⟨will know you⟩.

O You who measure everything,
O You who number those who sleep,
He will number those who sleep.
O You who know what is in hearts,
If N be aware, etc.

O You who have come into being,
Khopri who is in the flood,
Whom Nu made as Onuris(?),
If N be aware, etc.

O You whose name is one
And whose faces are four,[3]
If N be aware, etc.

[. . .] Elephantine.
If N be aware, etc.

Speak, O You who go and return safely,
If N be aware, etc.

Do not be ignorant of your names,
For Maʿet is over the uplifting of Rēʿ daily.
O Provider, Lord of all,
If N be aware, etc.

401 Do not be unaware of N, O Thoth;
If you know N, N will know you.

Do not be unaware of N, O Thoth;
Speak, O Unpleasant One.
Do not be unaware of N, O Ḥar-Sopd;
If you know N, N will know you.

Do not be unaware of N, O Ḥar-Sopd;
Speak, O You who satisfy the One.
Do not be unaware of N, O You who are in the Netherworld;
[If you know N], N will know you.

Do not be unaware of N, O You who are in the Netherworld;
Speak, O You who awake hale.
Do not be unaware of N, O You who are in the Netherworld.

Speak, O Old One, when you come;[4] see, N comes and goes. If he himself does
not come, it is a message[5] which will come for him. N has passed by yon House
of Danger(?),[6] | and those who have gone for them have missed him. They bring 402
him these four spirits, the Elders who are before them of the braided locks, [who
stand] in the eastern side of the sky, who are upraised on their *ḏʿm*-staffs. They
will tell N's fair name to Rēʿ, they will announce him to Neḥebkau, they will be
on guard when N enters into the east side of the sky; N will be ferried across to
the east side of the horizon [. . .] to be ferried across to the east side of the sky;
it is his sister Sothis who bore[7] and worshipped him.

1. Cf. *Pyr.* Utt. 262.
2. *Šn.*
3. Lit. 'his four faces'.
4. The crosshatched *w* in 401*l* seems superfluous.
5. *Sic,* not 'messenger'; the participle is feminine.
6. Cf. *Pyr.* §334; on the rare sign cf. above, Spell 576, n. 4. In 403*f* (Spell 769) it is distinct from *bꜣ* in 403*k*.
7. For *mstwt* read *mswṯ*. Sothis appears as both sister and mother.

Spell 769

Stand up, O Ladder of Horus! Stand up, O Ladder of Seth![1] Stand up, O great
and mighty ladder which was made for Osiris, so that he might ascend on it to the
sky. I am your son,[2] I am Horus; give me the ladder which you gave to my father,[3]
so that I may ascend on it to the sky and escort [Rēʿ],[4] the great god, and those
gods, the great and mighty ones who have gone to their doubles | and who have VI, 403
departed to yonder side of the Field of the Ladder. The serpent is in the sky,
[the centipede of Horus][5] is on earth, the Eye of Horus raises ⟨itself⟩,[6] having
awakened in peace, the ladder [stands up(?)] in peace, the Dangerous One(?)[7]
awakes, having passed by(?) in peace. May you[8] give me the ladder which you

gave to Osiris, so that he might ascend on it to the sky. As for any god who shall oppose [himself] to me, he shall have no bread, he shall have no white bread, he shall have no supplies,[9] he shall have no soul, he shall not go up to Ḥatḥōr[10] who is in the sky; but as for any god who shall not oppose himself to me, he shall indeed [have] his [bread], he shall indeed have his white bread, he shall indeed have his supplies, he shall have his soul, and he shall indeed go up to Ḥatḥōr who is in the sky, and he who pleases [his] mother's double shall protect him [by
404 means of it | . . . for] the god's ladder which is set up. I am he who shall ascend on it to the sky.

Your head shall be knit to your bones,[11] your members[12] shall be brought together as for Horus who stands in front of the Field of the Ladder; he will give you your double exactly[13] for your body, and great will be your [. . .] for(?) the great titulary(?). You [. . .] for the cable(?)[14] of the net of [. . .] dead for the living, and they help(?)[15] the breaking of the execution block(?).

You[16] shall provide the . . . of the net(?)[17] and the [. . .] are raised up [. . .] The Lords of ʿAnpet are those who blind your heads for you, your staffs shall be raised(?)[18] for you. Since Osiris will pass by you and since I will pass by you, go, that I may pass; go, that Osiris may pass.

You[19] shall divide them as Shu, you shall penetrate(?)[20] them as Tefēnet, those two great and mighty gods who are at the head of the Souls of Ōn.

1. Cf. *Pyr.* Utt. 478.
2. Read *sꜣ.k,* cf. de Buck, n. 6*.
3. The fem. *dyt.n.ṯ* 'which you gave' probably refers to Isis, while *ỉt.k* should be emended into *ỉt.ỉ* 'my father', i.e. Osiris.
4. Restore *stp* [*sꜣ r Rꜥ*], cf. *Pyr.* §974*c*.
5. Restored from *Pyr.* §244*a*.
6. Read *ḏsr.s* ⟨*sy*⟩.
7. Cf. Spell 768, n. 6.
8. Plural.
9. Determined with a bread-sign in 403*o*; for *spd* 'supply' food cf. *Siut,* pl. 19,27.
10. Cf. *Pyr.* §§1026–7; but the woman-det. to *Ḥwt-ḥr* makes it clear that the original *Ḥwt Ḥr* 'Mansion of Horus' has to be taken here as the name of the goddess.
11. The officiant is now addressing the deceased.
12. Compound expression *rꜣ-ꜥwt.*
13. For *r mtr.k* cf. *Wb.* II, 174,1.
14. *Nynt* looks like a variant of *nynṯ* 'cable(?)', *CT* V, 74*aa*.
15. Reading *sm.sn swꜣ n ḫbt* and assuming that *sm* is the verb for 'help' deprived of its determinatives.
16. Plural, but it is not clear who is addressed.

17. 404*j* is obscure. I have read it as *dbꜣ.ṯn ḏsṯ i̓nt,* where *ḏsṯ* may perhaps stand for part of a net, and *i̓nt* (or *i̓ntt*) may be identical with *i̓nyt* 'purse-net(?)', *CT* IV, 348*a*.

18. For this writing of *ssšw* 'lift up' cf. *Pyr.* §275*f* (T).

19. The deceased is addressed.

20. Cf. *ḏfy* 'penetrate', *P. Ed. Smith,* 337.

Spell 770

To cause a child to breathe.[1] I am the Ram of the West, the helper(?) of a corpse,[2] VI, 405
and Horus has spat – and *vice versa.* If Horus can go upright, then I can go upright, and I *will* go upright; even if he goes upside down, I will go upright, I will breathe the air of him who is in . . .[3] for I have gone forth from the upper sky to the lower sky.

1. This title suggests that we have here a spell originally intended for childbirth used on behalf of the dead.

2. See de Buck, n. 1*; nevertheless the word must surely be *ẖꜣt* 'corpse'. The preceding *smty* or *smtt* has been connected with *sm* 'help'.

3. *Htt-š*; apparently a compound term for a part of the body, possibly the lungs, though the etymology is quite obscure.

Spell 771

Not to go upside down and not ⟨to eat⟩[1] faeces in the realm of the dead. I fly up as a swallow,[2] I have cackled as a goose, I have trodden on the Mound of the Dancer,[3] I will play music because of him, and he will not shake, nor will it[4] be upset. I will appear as a god, for the banks of the sky have sought for me on account of the Eye of Horus; I will go down pure, I will inspire fear of(?)[5] myself because of the reeds of the Lake of the God.[6]

1. *Wnm* omitted in error.

2. As often, confused with *wr* 'great one'.

3. Sing., despite the plur. strokes, cf. the sing. suffix in *ḥr.f,* 405*o*.

4. Fem., presumably in reference to the mound.

5. *Snšnš⟨.i⟩wi̓*; for this verb cf. *CT* IV, 59*c*; Spell 305, n. 5.

6. Reading simply as *š nṯr*; the final *nṯrw* is a kind of dittograph.

Spell 772

VI, 406 What I doubly detest I will not eat;[1] faeces is what I detest, and I will not eat it, filth shall not fall[2] from my belly, I will not go up to it with my fingers,[3] I will not touch on ⟨it⟩ with my toes.

'What will you live on',[4] say the gods,[5] spirits and dead, 'in this place where you have been brought?'

'I will live on seven portions which are being brought; their seven loaves are with Horus[6] and with Seth'.[7]

'Where has it been granted to you to eat?' say the gods to me.

⟨'I will eat under the sycamore of Ḥatḥōr my mistress, for I have placed my deeds there for her pleasure'⟩.[8]

I have divided[9] my lands in Djedu and my green-stuffs in Ōn; I will live on red barley, I will swallow white barley, which one gave to my family, my father and my mother. O you janitors of Him who speaks in the Two Lands, open to me, prepare a path for me, extend and prepare a path for me, so that my double may sit[10] where it wishes to be, for my soul lives and is not driven away.

1. *Bwt.ỉ* in 406*b* is superfluous. The text of this spell is far from accurate.
2. Read *ḥtp- kꜣ nn ḫr.f*; cf. de Buck, n. 2* and *BD* 123,16.
3. Read *nn ꜥr.i n.f m ḏbꜥw.ỉ*; cf. *CT* III, 98*f*; compare also *BD* 124,1.
4. Read *ꜥnh.k ỉr.f m m* (interrogative); cf. *BD* 124, 2–3, which, however, has *ỉšst* instead of *m*.
5. Read *ḫr.sn nṯrw* with *BD* 124,3; cf. also 406*l* below.
6. The suffix after 'Horus' is superfluous.
7. Woman(!)-det. with Seth-head superimposed. *BD* 124,5 substitutes 'Thoth'.
8. The passage in pointed brackets is supplied from *BD* 124,7–8. It has been omitted from the *CT* text, leaving the preceding question unanswered. The last word in the passage, here translated as 'pleasure', is *ḫnyt,* lit. 'music'.
9. Read *ỉw wḏꜥ.n.ỉ* with BD 124, 8–9.
10. Read *ḥmsw* with *BD* 124,14.

Spell 773

VI, 407 O you who are . . . ,[1] they of Elephantine groan; may you[2] guard the wearers of the head-cloth[3] for(?) those who bow[4] the knee, who see the body and what is in it, who see the bark of the Inert One on the night of sitting on the thrones in order to lament those who make report and those who groan loudly(?),[5] they of Abydos doing reverence, and brightness having gone all over the Great Hall.

O you who view the corpse and deal with[6] corruption and who go all over the Great Hall, set me among you; O you who hear the Companions, O Edjō who makes my neck firm, I am a loving son.

1. I can make nothing of the opening words of this spell except that *wnw* appears to be a participle; it may be that the true beginning has been lost. The mention of the Great Hall below and the general trend of the text show that it has to do with the embalming of the corpse, the speaker being not the deceased but the *s3-mr.f* priest.

2. Plural.

3. Read *ʿfnwtyw*.

4. For *ḳfn* cf. *Pyr.* §§460; 1008; 1213. *M3st* of 407*c* is the object of *ḳfnw*.

5. *M hnw* can hardly mean 'jubilation' here. The basic meaning of *hnw* may have been simply 'loud cry', indifferently for joy or sorrow, though it came to be used almost exclusively of the former.

6. Lit. 'go round'.

Spell 774

O you who make firm the necks of those who are in the sky and of those who are on earth because of what is in them,[1] I know you[2] and I know the four falcon gods who are in charge of the chest of Atum. VI, 408

1. Apparently *s* for *sn*.

2. A superfluous *n* before *ṯn*.

Spell 775

The ferry-boat is ferried across . . .[1] run, O you who are in the suite of Horus, run, O you who are in the suite of Seth.[2] He cannot reach him,[3] (though) he has run before Rēʿ to the great city, he has found a ferry-boat[4] in yonder ⟨side⟩, having been boatless.

Horus: He is angry with me[5] and he attacks me – so says Horus the boatless. I wish that that mother of mine would speak to me,[6] because[7] I am very much afraid; I am stranded on yonder side because the Outcast is angry with me.

Isis: See [I am(?) a protection] from fear, for I am your mother, I am Isis; I summon the Day-bark(?)[8] which is in the midst of the waters of . . .[9] VI, 409

Horus: See, I knew your name[10] before I was boatless; come and row me, come and ferry me over, come and bring me to land at the great city before Rēʿ. The tears of the cackler are in my eyes, my hunger is in my belly, my tears are in my eyes, my tears are in my throat(?).

Isis: See, I bring you the best of the *ḥn*-bird,[11] and the choice joints which are with the very great lady are standing on the standard.

1. Cf. de Buck, 408, n. 3*; 409, n. 2*.
2. The Seth-animal has been marked out and *Wdꜥ* 'the Outcast' substituted.
3. The deceased?
4. Note the writing of *mḫnt.*
5. Note the transitive use of *ꜣd.*
6. Reading *ḥw ꜣ ḏd n⟨.ỉ⟩ mwt⟨.ỉ⟩ tw.*
7. Read *⟨n⟩ ntt* here and in 408*q*.
8. Cf. de Buck, 409, n. 1*.
9. Cf. n. 1 above.
10. Addressed to Isis.
11. Cf. *Pyr.* §1970.

Spell 776

O you who are among the . . . ,[1] He of the two staffs[2] appears in the sky, my feet are on earth, my staff [. . .].[3]

1. *ꜥpꜥw,* unidentified.
2. Probably masculine; S10C uses the woman-det. for both genders.
3. The spell was left unfinished.

Spell 777

VI, 410 O N, Isis has come so that she may cause air to go forth, for she wants it to enter into the holes which are in your head, so that you may live and speak to her, O N. There are brought to her these two *krm*-birds of yours on the day when you have joined them together for meat(?).[1]

1. T6C stops short at *krmwy.k pn.* At end, read *r ỉf*?

Spell 778

O N, Horus has protected you;[1] he has caused Nephthys to put you together, and she will put you together; she will mould you in her name of Seshat, Mistress of potters, for such is this great lady, a possessor of life in the Night-bark, who raises up Horus, and she will bring to you.[2]

1. T10C omits *nḏ.n tw.*
2. T6C stops at *nn nbt*; in 410*l* it looks as if *sw* 'him' has been omitted.

Spell 779

O N, Horus has protected you, he makes you joyful by means of his woven Eye which he has allotted in every place. O N, take your linen, being what was given to Ernūtet[1] who is on the brow of Horus, so that you may be cheerful and content.[2] VI, 411

1. The name is bungled in T6C.
2. T10C adds 'in your name of *Ḥḏ-ḥtp*', which seems superfluous.

Spell 780

Words spoken by the Souls of the Westerners: N has come on the hidden paths, he has opened[1] the gates of the Abyss, he has reached the gate of Her who ascends to the celestial expanse, who knows the rope(s) and who teaches to row.[2] His wand is given to him and he strikes with it when he announces[3] the day in the bow of the sacred bark.[4]

1. Written as *sn* 'smell', which makes no sense.
2. *'Iḥ* 'rope', *BD* 393,7; 505,11, is a var. of *ꜥḥ* 'rope', *Pyr.* §§1376; 1742. To take this passage at the foot of the letter yields poor sense, and a more rational result is obtained by emending the masc. *sbꜣ* into the fem. *sbꜣt.*
3. Read *sr.f.*
4. Following T10C.

Spell 781

O N, Anubis stands up, having stocked[1] himself with milk which he will give, and he allots its jars[2] to you; he cuts off what those who are over the watchers may do against you. How happy are you! You are supported on the *wꜣs*-staff, and Horus has smitten those who would smite you,[3] he has slain those who would slay you.[4] VI, 412

1. Lit. 'filled'.
2. Reading *mhrw.sn* 'their milk-jars'; *ỉrtt,* being a fluid, is construed as plural. *'Ibw.sn* is a reading which makes no sense; nor does *ỉbw n.sn* of T10C.
3. Read *ḥyw* with T10C; T6C inserts a superfluous *n.*
4. T6C is corrupt after *smꜣ.n.f.*

Spell 782

Words spoken by those whose doubles are happy, the owners of possessions, who exist for ever: O N, O you for whom the Netherworld has been opened,[1] and on whose account those who would keep the gates have been driven away, enter into the secret place[2] of the Milky Way(?) and behold for yourself[3] the god therein.[4]

1. The unusual signs in 412*h* may well be writings of *wbꜣ*, cf. 414*f*, and compare Möller, *Pal.* I, no. 487. The ending *.tyw* is unexpected, but it could well have originated in confusion of the *ꜣ*-bird (Gardiner, Sign-list G1) and the *tyw*-bird (Gardiner, G4), as from the earliest times they were not always clearly distinguished. If such be the case, the true reading would be *wbꜣw*, plural passive participle, which yields good sense. Cf. 414*f*.
2. T6C omits *ḥr* after *ʿḳ* and T10C stops short at *štꜣ*.
3. *N.f* is an error for *n.k*.
4. At the end, for *m* read *ỉm*, unless a noun has been omitted after it.

Spell 783

VI, 413 O N, Horus has protected you and he has caused the gods to go forth, and you shall desire that . . .[1] be opened. O N, how happy are you who see![2] Your vision is cleared[3] by the right Eye of Rēʿ which is on the left of Her who is in the sun(?).

How happy are they who see, how pleased are they who behold,[4] when Horus takes his thrones! N forms himself so that his double may exist thereby; N is your son, O Horus, and he has formed you.[5] O you twins Shu and Tefēnet, form yourselves'.[6]

O N, Horus has protected you and he has shut fast the jaws of your foes; he has seized him who would take ⟨you⟩[7] to his place of slaughter. Your protection[8] comes to you and your son Sopd the sharp-toothed acts as protector from[9] whoever would harm you in the eastern desert.

1. *Ḫw n ḥg.f* T6C; *ḫw ḥg.f* T10C. This is quite obscure; for the form of *g* in *ḥg* cf. *dg* 'behold' in 412*k*.
2. T6C (woman's coffin) has *nfrt* for the predicative adjective here and in 413*e*; here the intensive particle *wy* is followed by the enclitic *ꜣ*, which is lacking elsewhere. The fem. participle *mꜣt* in T6C shows that it refers to the deceased and not to onlookers; in 413*e* the masc. imperfective form *mꜣꜣ* and the masc. *ḥtp* in both texts shows that here onlookers are envisaged.
3. T6C has the passive form *wn.t(w)* whereas T10C has the passive *sḏm.f*.
4. Cf. n. 2 above.
5. *Sic*; what one would expect is 'you have formed him'. The pronouns may have become confused.

6. Reading *ḳd tw* with T6C; note the use of the singular pronoun in reference to the dual *s3ty*.

7. T6C has 'N' here, but the 2nd person is needed; T10C omits it.

8. For the compound word *gs-dpt* cf. *CT* IV, 88*k*; 94*b*; VI, 75*e*, *BD* 18,9–10; T6C omits the suffix. The fact that in T10C the suffix follows *gs*, as also in 75*e* above, shows that the meaning 'protection' derives from the notion of a ship's side as a bulwark against danger.

9. The Egyptian uses the direct genitive.

Spell 784

Words spoken by the Souls of Ōn: O N, our son, our beloved, we have commanded that you go into us and rest[1] ⟨in⟩ our peace. Mnevis grants[2] ascent to the sky and the Netherworld is opened up for the term of eternity. To go out into the day. O N, Horus has protected you.[3] VI, 414

1. Emend into *ꜥk.k*, *ḥtp.k; ꜥḳ* has been miswritten in both texts as *nk*.
2. For *dd.n* of T6C read *dd.f* with T10C.
3. T6C only; note the miswriting of the pronoun *tw*, as already in 413*j*.

Spell 785

O N, indeed you have not changed in your name of Father of the gods.[1] You have gone and will return whether you have slept or whether you have waked.[2] Remove the efflux which exuded(?)[3] from your flesh, you being filled and provided with the Eye of Horus.

Stand up, N, for Horus has protected you; he gives the gods to you, so take possession of them in your name of Prince-mansion. They have loved you and they draw near to you;[4] your face is illumined in the Castle of the Mace. O mighty of magic, greatly strong, the gods, the lords of all things, circulate about you[5] in your name of Him who goes round about the Isles.

O N, Anubis indeed forms you, so that you may be on earth through him, you being alive so that you may travel about daily; your vision is restored so that you may see the sun; be a spirit, O Baboon(?) ⟨ . . . ⟩[6] of what is given in your name of Horizon. He lifts bread to him who has no bread in the second hour of the night, O N.[7]

1. Cf. Gilula, *JEA* 60,249. He translates the passage rather differently.

2. Reading *šm.n.t ỉwt.t sḏr.n.t rs.n.t* as T6C, but ignoring the apparently superfluous *r* before *sḏr*, which is absent in T10C. The meaning of the passage seems to be that come life, come death, N will remain unchanged.

3. Apparently an extended use of *ḏbꜣ* 'replace', etc., *Concise Dict.* 321.

4. Both texts are slightly at fault; read *ꜥr.sn ⟨n⟩.t(k) m ꜥrw,* lit. 'they approach you in nearness'.

5. Read *šnn n.k(t) nṯrw nbw ḫt nbt is* with T10C except for *isṯ,* which is an error for the enclitic *is* of T6C; this latter omits *nbw ḫt.*

6. Something appears to be missing from both texts after *ꜥn(n),* for there is no antecedent for the plural genitive.

7. So T10C; T6C stops short at *fꜣ t m(?).*

Spell 786

VI, 415 TO MOUNT UP TO THE GOD IN THE REALM OF THE DEAD. [My cavern][1] is opened, my [spirit falls into the darkness, the Eye of Horus] raises [me], Wepwawet [caresses] me, and I have established myself [among you,] you six Imperishable Stars. Everything that is good [. . .].[2]

1. The restorations are from *BD* 119, 9 ff. (*BD* Ch. 44, 1st part).
2. *CT* and *BD* differ in 415*g*.

Spell 787

NOT TO DIE A SECOND TIME.[1] ⟨My vision⟩ is cleared, my heart is in its place[2] which is on the White Crown which is with me; I am Rēꜥ, who himself protects himself, and I am not harmed.[3] Live, [O my father],[4] the son of Nūt, for I am [your eldest son][5] who sees the secret things; I appear as king of the gods, and I will not die a second time.

1. This rubric corresponds to that in *BD* 119, 8.
2. This corresponds to *BD* 119, 13.
3. Read *ḥm.t(w.i).* *BD* 119, 14–15 has corruptly *n ḥm.i tw* 'I am not ignorant of you'.
4. Restored from *BD* 119,15, except that for *it.k* we must read *it.i.*
5. Restored from *BD* 119, 16.

THE ANCIENT EGYPTIAN COFFIN TEXTS

Volume III Spells 788–1185 & Indexes

PREFACE

The present volume completes the translation into English of the Ancient Egyptian Coffin Texts. It corresponds to Vol. VII of de Buck's edition of the Egyptian text, comprising Spells 788 – 1185. For the student of religion and mythology the most important part consists of Spells 1029 – 1185, which record a composition which has interested scholars ever since Schack-Schackenborg in 1903 published *Das Buch von den Zwei Wegen des seligen Toten.* But the interest of the Coffin Texts as a whole does not rest solely on their religious and mythological content, although that, of course, gives them their major importance to the reader. They also shed light, albeit a dim and flickering glimmer, on other aspects of ancient Egyptian life. There are spells clearly adapted or borrowed for the benefit of the dead from the rituals of the death or accession of the king; for those who are interested in ancient boat-building there are references to the construction of canoes made from reeds, together with long lists of the component parts of a sailing boat and its gear, the terms for which will be found collected in Index VI at the end of this book. There are also spells which are concerned with fishing-nets and their gear, or with the preparation of the catch for table; one spell even has to do with various grades of woven cloth. In attempting to interpret such texts the translator's greatest obstacle is our ignorance of the meanings of so many Egyptian technical terms; sometimes the context or an inherent probability may provide a clue to the meaning, but too often the would-be interpreter has to abandon the attempt.

The philology of the Coffin Texts offers a wide field of study. Falling as they do between Old Egyptian on the one hand and the classical literary idiom on the other, constructions and usages referable to both phases of the language are found, but there is a tendency for the older element to predominate. Thus the older independent pronouns *ṯwt, swt* (very rarely also *stt*) are preferred to the *ntf* paradigm, though that also is present; the writing out of the weak final radical in the prospective tense of *infirmae* verbs is common; the earlier combination *hꜣy m* 'go down into' competes on equal terms with the later *hꜣy r*; and perhaps most significant of all, the negative construction *n sḏm.f* used with reference to future time is much more common than the classical *nn sḏm.f.* In orthography the distinction between *z* and *s* is largely preserved, even though it is evident that they have been fairly completely merged in speech; also the distinction between *t* and *ṯ* is fairly consistently observed, and the same is true of *d* and *ḏ*, though in both cases there are exceptions. Instances of cryptic writing also occur, while there are not a few new words to be inserted in our dictionaries, and the grammatical usages provide a fruitful field for research.

No task like that just completed could come to fruition in isolation, without the sympathy and support of colleagues, so once again I express my deep appreciation of the help and encouragement I have received on all hands, notably those of Professor Harry Smith, Mr. C. H. S. Spaull, Dr. David Dixon and Mr. Adrian Phillips of Aris and Phillips Ltd., to whom has fallen the heavy task of printing these three volumes. Also I gratefully acknowledge again the generosity of the Sir Alan Gardiner Settlement for Egyptological Purposes and of the Committee of the British Academy in the very considerable financial support which has rendered it possible to publish these volumes at what for these days is a modest cost.

R. O. Faulkner
Woodbridge, Suffolk.
September 1977.

Spell 788

N's vision is cleared so that he may see the Lord of the horizon and cross over the VII,1
sky, he[1] causes him to appear as the great god, the Lord of eternity, who will
never[2] perish, and he will be worshipped in the starry sky. O you who are over
those who have gone before ⟨ . . . ⟩.[3]

1. The Lord of the horizon. For the following *ḫꜥ.f* two texts have *ḫpr.f.*
2. *'Iḫm* in three texts, *ỉtm* in Da1C. The sense is not affected.
3. 1*u* only in L2Li; 1*v* only in Da3C, which is incomplete.

Spell 789

Hail to you, you gods who are in the beautiful West! N has come that he may VII, 2
greet you, for N knows you and N knows your shapes; may you grant that N
may go to rest in his fair place among the possessors of doubles; see, N's sitting
and resting[1] are with provisions. N has done what is right, for he detests wrong-
doing and never sees it; N rows the bark of Rēꜥ, N has acquired his throne, N is
one of those who are in the retinue of Horus, who go to the *ṯnnt*-shrine.

O you who are in charge of the Milky Way(?). who guard the gates of the Netherworld, prepare a fair path for N, so that N may enter and that N may worship Osiris, and (himself) be a god for ever.

1. *Ḥmswt* and *ḥtp* appear to be infinitives.

Spell 790

Words spoken by N: See, I have come that I may open up the Netherworld and that I may see my father Osiris who has flown up. I am a son beloved of my father; I have come so that I may protect Osiris from Seth. I open all the paths which are in the sky, I open all the paths which are on earth, I open all the paths which are in the Netherworld, and I have entered into the horizon, for I know my way and I am one who equips his spirits.

Spell 791

A boon which the king grants, a boon which Osiris grants, a boon which Rēꜥ- VII, 3

Ḥarakhti grants, that he (*sic*) may permit N to be in company with the nobles who once existed, that he may see Rēʿ every day, that N may ferry across to the Field of Rushes, that he may receive offerings there daily among the possessors of offerings through the command of the great god, the Lord of Offerings.

Spell 792

Words spoken by Nūt: O N, I am your mother, I am Nūt, and I have come so that I may enfold and protect you from all things evil.

Words spoken by Isis: O N, I am your sister Isis; I have come so that I may lay hold of you, I have come so that I may protect you.[1]

1. Read *3n* as *ỉw.n.ỉ ḫw.ỉ tw*.

Spell 793

⌈A boon which the king⌉ grants, a boon which Osiris grants, (and also) ⌈the god⌉ who is in the Mound of the *Nt*-crown, that he may permit N to have power over cold water at his desire, being what was commanded for ever [. . .] what is good. N has invocation-offerings by favour of [. . .].

A boon which the king grants (and also) Gēb, Lord of the lands, of what is under the ribs.

A boon which Osiris grants, that he may permit N to be a spirit and to be at the head of the spirits for ever.

Spell 794

VII, 4 TO BE SPLENDID OF SHAPE IN THE REALM OF THE DEAD. [. . .] I have taken possession of the *wrrt*-crown of every god, I am [. . .]. *The rest of the spell is lost except for a few fragments.*

***Spell** 795 is almost entirely lost.*

Spell 796

VII, 5 NOT TO GO UPSIDE DOWN ON THE PART OF A MAN IN THE REALM OF THE DEAD. *The rest of the spell is lost.*

Spell 797

TO BE GIVEN BREAD IN DJEDU. *The rest of the spell is nearly all lost, but there are mentions of the Bull of the Ennead, of the town of Djedu and of the Mansion of Thoth.*

Spell 798

TO RISE UP FROM UPON THE LEFT SIDE ON TO THE RIGHT SIDE. *Of the rest of the* VII, 6
spell only fragments remain.

Spell 799

TO ESCAPE FROM THE FIRE AND TO SAVE A MAN FROM HIS FOE. *The rest of the* VII, 7
spell is nearly all lost, but there is a mention of Gēb in 7a. i.

Spell 800

NOT TO PERISH(?), BUT TO BE GUIDED(?) IN SKY AND EARTH. *What follows is* VII, 8
fragmentary; the Ennead and Thoth are named.

Spell 801

[A boon which the king grants(?)], which the god of linen(?) grants, which Osiris the god of the marshland[1] grants; going out into the day by[2] N. N is this lone spirit, this [. . .] on [. . .],[3] N has come into this land, being spiritualized through magic and being worthy through magic; there is nothing unknown to N in the sky,[4] there is nothing unknown[5] to N on earth, there is nothing unknown to N in the waters, there is nothing unknown to him at [. . .], there is nothing unknown to [him as(?)] a god,[6] there is ⟨nothing⟩[7] unknown to N
[. . .], because N ⟨knows the names of⟩[8] the two Sisterly Companions [. . .].[9] | VII, 9
N [will] not fall[10] into the *ḫns*- and *ḥtmt*-waters, for N knows the name of [. . .] who sits at the gate; 'He who fashioned[11] the god' is his name in it; ⟨N[12]⟩ knows the name of another [. . .];[13] 'Dancer of the god' is his name. ⟨N knows⟩[14] the name of the [Valley(?)[15] . . .] the name of the West in which he is [. . .].[16]

1. Reading *mḥw* and emending  into .
2. For *n* read *ỉn.*
3. 8*l* is broken and unintelligible, but compare *CT* V, 303*c*–304*a.*
4. Compare V, 305*b* ff.; Spell 443, n. 5.
5. The fem. ending of *ḫmt* has been omitted.
6. Restoring tentatively as *nn ḫmt n* [*.f m*] *nṯr.*
7. The negative word has been omitted.
8. An omission supplied from V, 306*c*–307*a.* The text here makes no sense as it stands.
9. Broken and unintelligible; originally perhaps a version of V, 306 *a* or *c.*
10. Read *n ḫr* [*.n*] *N*; compare V, 308*b.*
11. The det. of *ms* is lost.
12. The subject of *rḫ*, i.e. the name of the deceased, has been omitted.
13. A tall sign lost after *ỉ.*
14. *Ỉw N rḫ* omitted, cf. 9*b.*
15. Restore as *ỉnt*?
16. The rest of the spell is too much broken to yield a coherent sense.

Spell 802

Do not come down on N, do not [. . .] the brother of the two gods who have come in. N has come to this land as owner [of] his magic.[1]

1. The final *n ḥkꜣw* looks like a dittograph.

Spell 803

Words spoken by Nūt who enfolds [him(?)] and who puts ⟨her⟩ arm(s) about N [in] life: N will not die.

O Nūt, you have carried off Horus[1] and his greatly magical; you have carried off Seth and his greatly magical; enfold N with life [in] your [name] of Great Protectress.[2]

1. Cf. *Pyr.* §823; de Buck, n. 5*.
2. Cf. *Pyr.* §638; de Buck, n. 6*.

Spell 804

VII, 10 N's protection is with Osiris, N[. . .]. The name of the cord is 'The god who pervades [. . .]'. *The rest of the spell is too fragmentary to translate, but it appears to have enumerated the parts of a boat; ḥmw 'steering-oar' occurs in 10d, with probably mḏꜣbt 'bailer' in 10f.*

Spell 805

Rise up(?) to the god who is pre-eminent in the [*ṯnnt*-shrine(?)[1] . . .] Lord of eternity, who celebrates the Festival of the New Moon for [Osiris(?)] after . . . ,[2] having travelled around for it(?).[3] One honoured by Osiris, the great god, Lord of eternity; the vindicated N, Lord of [. . .].

1. Cf. de Buck, n. 3*.
2. The group following *m-ḫt* defeats me.
3. For what? There is no fem. antecedent for the suffix.

Spell 806

[. . .] you[1] bathe in the Lake of *nw*-birds,[2] your springs of water [are in] the VII, 11
Field [of Rushes(?) . . .] this tree of yours which is south of the house, and the
Lingerer is he who goes up to it. You will not die, (namely) you who expel [. . .
you have been] made to appear [as the great god[3] . . .] you [grow] as a growing-
bird.[4] You travel to and fro as Khons[5] and glitter as a glitter-bird[6] [. . .] you
see, you eat bread in the isles of the sky [. . .].

1. The 2nd person is original, cf. 11*e.i.*
2. Cf. *Wb.* II, 217,15. In *CT* IV, 26*a* the corresponding word is *nw* 'Abyss'.
3. Compare IV, 26*k* – 27*a*.
4. Compare IV, 26*c*.
5. Compare IV, 26*j*.
6. Compare IV, 26*d*.

Spell 807

[. . .] Osiris knows [his name(?)];[1] may he not fall into [it,] because he knows his name. N knows him and N knows [his name . . .].[2]

1. Cf. de Buck, n. 9*.
2. Of the rest of the spell only a few odd words survive.

Spell 808

VII, 12 [. . .] seeking [. . .] N's lips; the offering-stone of the tomb [. . .].

Spell 809 is entirely lost.

Spell 810

[. . .] N [will not] putrefy,[1] [. . .] N's efflux[2] is like that of Anubis, N is Osiris, Lord of burial, N will not putrefy [. . .].

1. Cf. 12*q*.
2. Read [*r*]*ḏw*.

Spell 811

VII, 13 [. . .] N [has] sat [. . .].

Spell 812

[. . .] N has spent the night [. . .] fast asleep(?)[1] [. . .].

1. Cf. de Buck, n. 2*.

Spell 813

[. . .][1] N is the god of the twilight[2] [. . .], N grasps the sky as the Sunshine god, N has travelled and traversed [. . .].

1. The first word in the lost rubric could have been *ỉꜥr* 'ascend'; *ỉꜥ* 'wash' is less likely.
2. Reading *ỉḫḫ*[*w*], cf. 13*o*.

Spell 814

VII, 14 [. . .] N; grant(?) that you rest in eternity.

Spell 815

⟨ . . . ⟩ IN THE TOMB.[1] O you who are in the Abyss beside the sky,[2] equip the vessel beneath me as the Night-bark(?),[3] and I will steer straight for(?)[4] the land, I will land at the horizon, I will drink deep and sit in front, I will open up my place on the banks of the sky, because[5] I am . . .[6] the great, the son of Nūt. I take the bow-warp in the Day-bark as Horus the great at the evening meals[7] of Rēʿ-Atum; because I am a limb of[8] this Great One of yours, whose soul does not know his name; (I am) one who cuts off[9] the heads of the gods, knowing my name and guarding my name from the bands which are on the *wrt*-crowns(?).[10]

1. Apparently the greater part of the rubric has been omitted. *ʾIs* 'tomb' is followed by an illegible sign in red.
2. *Pt* miswritten as *tp*.
3. Cf. de Buck, n. 4*.
4. Regarding *mtr* as a writing of *mty* 'straight', 'exact' used as a verb; cf. *mty* 'straight on', *CT* I, 251*c*, used of the movement of a boat.
5. Read *n ntt,* cf. de Buck, n. 5*.
6. An unintelligible compound name.
7. Reading *mšrwt*; the *t* is misplaced.
8. For a similar 'genitival' use of *m* after *ʿt* 'limb' cf. *Pyr.* §966*d; CT* V, 8*e*; 24*b*; VII, 39e.
9. A participial predicate of *ỉnk* in 14*p*.
10. Cf. de Buck, nn. 9*. 10*.

Spell 816

The iron is broken by Anubis in the sky. Ho, iron which opened up the West! VII, 15
This is the iron which is on my mouth,[1] which Sokar spiritualized in Ōn, which makes the water of my mouth to rise;[2] the iron is washed, and it is sharp and strong.

This is the iron which Sokar raised on high in the name of the Great One in it in Ōn, the iron which raises me up, which lifts me up[3] so that I may open the land of the West ⟨in⟩ which I dwelt.[4] If Maʿet alights, I will alight[5] on . . .[6] of the gods; I have seen Sia, and he opens my mouth and tells a true matter to the Lord of All, who goes round about the land of the thrones of the West in the retinue of those who shine and of the Permanent One who goes forth anew every day: so say(?)[7] the young folk and those who are dead who come for me, (even) the messengers of the king of the dead.

O Rēʿ, hasten and move along; O Rēʿ roam your land, not 〈 . . . 〉.[8]

1. A reference to the ritual of 'Opening the Mouth' with an adze of iron, cf. *Pyr.* §§13; 14.
2. Read *swb〈n〉 mw rꜣ.ỉ.* There is a dittograph of the suffix on passing from line to line.
3. Reading *sšw wỉ,* cf. de Buck, n. 5*.
4. *'Im* or *ỉm.f* omitted after *ḥmswt.n.ỉ.*
5. For *ḫn.ny.ỉ* read *ḫn.ỉ.*
6. *Kmkꜣt,* meaning unknown.
7. Emend into  .
8. The spell breaks off short.

Spell 817

VII, 16 NOT TO GO UPSIDE DOWN, (BUT) TO BE A FOLLOWER(?).[1] I am the living uraeus which is pre-eminent in the Bark of Flesh on the vertex of its lord; I have come today into the horizon of the sky, and there are given to me the seats of those who are in the Presence, I control the gifts to the gods among those who account for the land of the Great One.

I am unique among those with whom Ptaḥ is pleased at the ferrying of the Souls of Ōn, for I put a stop to the contending of the Rivals on the day of judgement, I have put a stop to mourning and have brought joy.

I am one who performed governance because there was no-one who satisfied(?) the gods about what I had said.

I am mistress of the flame of the great ewe(?),[2] and the sun-folk come bowing to me; the fear of me is in [their] hearts (*ỉbw*), and the awe of me is in their hearts (*ḥꜣtyw*), and I will be in the bow of the Bark as mistress of the flame.

I am one who is before my lord, and I will be the guide [. . .] there. I eat of food-offerings and I am rich in your (*sic*)[3] provisions like Him who dwells in his Eye, who fashions those who see every day.

1. The construction of 16*b* is abnormal,since the *m* of predication is absent; *wnn* is almost certainly the infinitive, while the following word was probably the noun *šmsw.* If so, we can conclude only that *m* was inadvertently omitted after *wnn.*
2. Woman's coffin. With *ʿꜣt* 'ewe(?) compare 18*v*; 26*s*.
3. Fem. sing., but who is meant?

Spell 818

TO CAUSE A WOMAN TO BE A SPIRIT [. . .] IN THE SKY, WITH GREAT PROTECTION. VII, 17
I am Rēʿ, Lord of the sunshine; authority is in my hand, and I will cross the sky by means of it. See, I enter into the secret places, the Field of Offerings serves me, and I myself make provision. I am pure for my double, I make firm the heads, vertebrae and necks of the gods, I spit on their shoulders.[1] I provide a harpoon in the evening, for I know that I shall be opposed[2] in the bark; I observe for it[3] the ways of eternity and the paths of everlasting.

I will do work for Him who is in his circle, and his primeval ones will be made to grow; the bark will rejoice at meeting me, those who row him will take me, and I will grasp the *dbḥw* and support the yards(?) through the great strength of Shu.[4] I will see the shapes of those who follow after Rēʿ, I will eat and I will speak in [. . .], and it means that he will tell his name which is in his hand.[5] My protection is the protection of Shu and Tefēnet on that night of dragging the boats from(?) that on account of which heads are cut off with the knife which is in his[6] hand. This protection of mine is the protection of Rēʿ and
Tefēnet on that night of dragging the boats; | I will speak of the requirements of 18
this Great One of yours[7] who is in his shrine,[8] and he will speak and induct himself into the tribunal in company with the Ennead which is about the shrine; they will be saved from the crocodile-spirits on the day in which I spiritualize him. Such is my magic and my magic lives – so says Rēʿ on the day of showing respect to him.[9] You are Authority – so says the magic – my soul is stronger than he who guards it. I am a possessor of a braided lock, I clear the sky for its lord; he is happy among the gods in the western horizon, and he goes to rest in the horizon with Nu. See, he has saved me from all things evil.

1. After *psg* 'spit on' *rmn.s⟨n⟩* is to be read, restoring  in the lacuna. The spitting is prophylactic in purpose.
2. Read *rḫ.ỉ ḫsf(w).ỉ.*
3. Presumably the bark.
4. The deceased will hold the yards aloft just as Shu holds up the sky.
5. Reading *ỉmy-ʿ.f*; cf. de Buck, n. 10*.
6. Shu's.
7. Plural!
8. Read *kȝr.f.*
9. Reading as *hrw twr n.f,* with  for later , cf. *Concise Dict.* 295.

Spell 819

NOT TO GO UPSIDE DOWN, NOT TO [. . .]. O you who are in(?)[1] the granite bowl
in Ōn, I travel around(?)[2] with Khopri; I am one who will sail because of(?) what
I have done, and there is no company of any kind which is about [me(?)].[3] He
who turns himself about to face me[4] shall not stand, and I will open the firma-
ment against his bull. I am he who made himself, I am he who raised the fore-
heads of the great ewes(?).[5] I am not dead nor one whose speech is forgotten, I
am one who was known on his earth, whom the West remembers. I have restrained
VII, 19 the foes of Osiris, | and I worship him in the pure firmament which Rēʿ gave to
him. It has been granted to me to go forth, and I have adored Rēʿ at his rising; I
have conducted him[6] in the ceremony of reverence[7] at the western horizon, and
my head has not been taken away in the entourage(?) of the Foremost of the
Westerners. [. . .] I draw the winds with my arms just as I used to do on earth.
Beware of me, O you who cut off limbs, for my limbs are Rēʿ when he goes
down to Ōn in order to weep for his corpse.[8] Rēʿ stands in the midst of the sky,
and I will lift up my brow,[9] my feet are swift, I will not be killed, and the god
will not be eaten.

1. Perhaps a variant of *ỉmyt* 'you (fem.) who are in'.
2. *Pḫry* is obscure, but it may be a miswriting of *pḫr.ỉ*.
3. *Nn ḫt nb ḥꜣt*[.*ỉ*]. For the restored suffix cf. de Buck, n. 7*.
4. For *ḥs m* 'turn to face' cf. *AEO* I, 159.
5. *ꜥꜣꜣt.f*, var. *ꜥꜣt* in 16*n* above. Cf. Spell 825, n. 9.
6. *N* before *sw* seems superfluous; it may be a 'liaison' *n*.
7. Either *r* or *m* before *sꜣ-tꜣ* is superfluous; the tick on *r* suggests that it is the sign to be discarded, but cf. de Buck, n. 3*. For *sꜣ-tꜣ* cf. *D. el B.* 114; *CT* VI, 158*j*; 407*g*; but with the festival-det. only here.
8. *Sic*, but 'my corpse' should perhaps be read.
9. Read probably *ỉnk ṯs.ỉ ḥꜣt.ỉ*.

Spell 820

TO BE FAVOURED AMONG [THE GODS] IN [ŌN] (?).[1] I have sent forth worship by
means of the mouths of the two Conclaves of Nu, I have healed(?)[2] after wound-
ings, I have broken up the fight for him, I have driven off the disorderly for him,
VII, 20 for I am his son who issued from Isis, whom Nūt bore | within the secret places of
the House of Gēb. I am one who is blind, one who is bleary-eyed;[3] ⟨ . . . ⟩[4] bore
me blind. I have protected my father Rēʿ from those who conspired against him;

I have never deprived . . . of it(?)[5] through desire to greet him, I have decapitated every evil thing which was in existence with the knife which is in my hand.[6] He has given me his awesomeness(?),[7] and no-one has been found who can face me, because so great is my power and so mighty(?)[8] is my strength.

I am Horus who went out from Khem; I removed(?) myself to Upper Egypt[9] because of the creation of[10] the *wnr*-priest of Upper Egypt; I removed(?) myself to Lower Egypt because of the creation of the *wnr*-priest of Lower Egypt,[11] and my father Rēʿ gave me the strength of sky and earth in my members, for I am his son who issued from him.

I am unique among those who serve you, O Rēʿ; I have come in your train, O Rēʿ.

I am a spirit who went up from the Nile and who went up from the Abyss, my seat is beneath me, my throne is in my possession. I am uniquely joyous in my spirit, and mine are the two knots which were in(?)[12] the mouth of Rēʿ-Atum.

You have your soul, you have your power, you have your movements; O Rēʿ, you have your strength; O Rēʿ, the Nine Bows are felled for you, | your two 21
fair barks have acclaimed you today even more than yesterday.

Hail to you,[13] O you who are in the Abyss, you snakes and crocodiles of Neith,[14] the possessors of souls in the waters, who sit on the sides of the canoe of Neith of Sais.

Hail to you, O you tribunals which are in the sky, on earth and upon the waters. I have come to you that I may greet you, O you who reckon up those who act on behalf of Nu; (I am) one honoured with his Ennead, I am a lord of streams, having power over the waters; I am one who is firm-footed on the verge of the horizon; I am in good order and the two knots which are on the mouth of [Nu(?)][15] are in good order;[16] I am in balance(?) and my mouth is in balance(?).[17] I pass by hale like the Sacred Eye, I direct the winds for the Lord of the Sun-disk, the protection of Nu is about me [just as][18] the protection of Nu was about the egg from which I issued . . .[19] I am in good order. I come to life;[20] I am rejuvenated[21] and am hale, for I am one who went forth from the belly.

[HAVING POWER][22] OVER WATER, BEING WITH NEITH, GOING DOWN TO THE ISLAND [. . .][23] IN ORDER TO DO WHAT HE WISHES IN IT IN EVERY STREAM AND EVERY ISLAND.

1. Conjectural restoration of the damaged rubric as *ḥst mm nṯrw m ʾIwnw.*
2. *ʿb.n.ỉ* may be a var. of *ỉʿb.n.ỉ,* with a nuance of closing, 'reuniting' wounds.
3. Cf. *ḥ3ty* 'bleariness', *Concise Dict.* 163; *CT* VII, 441*a*.

4. The subject of *ms.n* has been omitted in passing from line to line.

5. The absence of a subject to *kf.n* presumably implies the 1st person singular; the object of the verb is indecipherable, see de Buck, n. 4*; and the reference of *ỉm* is obscure.

6. *Wn* after *wnt* may be a partial dittograph; at bottom read *ꜥ.ỉ* 'my hand', not 'his hand'; as in 20*g*, the scribe has confused his pronouns.

7. *Srwdt* is not recorded, and the translation is a guess; the etymology may be 'what has been made to grow (of fear)', this last being implied by the determinative.

8. I do not understand *nkꜣs n,* but a synonym of *wrr n* above seems needed.

9. *Wnrw.n s(y)* is to be understood as *wnrw.n.ỉ wỉ* as in 20*j*, the pronoun of the 3rd person having been substituted for the original 1st person. The meaning of *wnrw* is uncertain, but there is an obvious pun on the priestly title *wnr* below, on which cf. *Wb.* I, 323, 5–7. *Šms* is an error for *šmꜥ*, cf. 20*i*, end, and compare *mḥw* in 20*j*.

10. Disregarding *n m* after *sḫpr,* cf. 20*j*.

11. *Ḥr.s* at the end of 20*j* seems to be but an echo of *ḥr sḫpr* above, and has been disregarded.

12.  probably stands for *ỉmyw*; compare 18*p*.

13. Plural. We may have here the beginning of what once was a separate spell.

14. For Neith and crocodiles cf. *Pyr.* §§489; 510; Lanzone, *Mitologia,* pl. 175,3; *PSBA* 35, 50.

15. Cf. de Buck, n. 2*.

16. Read as *wḏꜣ*.

17. Cf. the noun *ḏꜣt* 'balance' in accounts, *Concise Dict.* 318.

18. Restore *my* 'like' as de Buck, n. 3*.

19. Cf. de Buck, n. 5*.

20. Lit. 'I cause life to live'.

21. A dittograph of *snḫḫ.ỉ*.

22. Restoring *sḫm* in the lacuna.

23. There is not room for *nsrsr* in the lacuna.

Spell 821

VII, 22 Provide for my father N [. . .] my father N [. . .]. Betake yourselves to him, grasp him by his legs [. . .] you shall live [. . .]. Someone has gone to his double,[1] Horus has gone to his double, Seth has gone to [his double, Thoth has gone] to his double, *Dwn-ꜥnwy* has gone [to his double, Osiris has gone] to his double, the Eyeless One has gone to his double. Ho [N]! You have departed living, and you shall not depart [dead]; your mother has come to you, Nūt has come to you so that [she may] cleanse [you][2] and provide for you as a god, for you are the greatest of her children. ⟨Gēb⟩ is gracious to you,[3] he loves you and ⟨he⟩ will protect ⟨you⟩.[4]

1. 22*f-h* corresponds to Pyr. §§16–17.
2. Restore as *swᶜb.s ṯw.*
3. Read *ṯwt wr imy msw⟨s⟩ ḥtp n.k ⟨Gb⟩*, cf. de Buck, n. 5*.
4. Cf. *Pyr.* §639.

Spell 822

[SPELL FOR NOT LETTING] CORPSES PERISH IN THE EARTH. I am he who assesses the allotment which was given by Gēb when the ruler(?) was born [. . .] great bull. I am the tooth of Sopd, I am the throat of Neḥebkau, I am the hair of the Great One, Lord of [. . . , I am] the phallus of Babi, I am the knee of the Bull in Khem. | [My] corpse will not putrefy in the earth, [I] will be hale [. . .] my VII, 23
neck is devoid of all baseness, I am the breast of Her who is weary under [. . .] who is mighty of magic. I will not go [. . .] the . . .[1] of my flesh [goes up(?)]. I am a Great One; a spirit goes up [. . .], a meal is given to him in the *ṯnnt*-shrine [. . .] command [. . .] is given to you on earth [. . .] you have made an occasion of . . .[2] [. . .] for him who is limp. I am the remnant(?) from out of(?) the hale ones . . .[3] N.

1. *ʾIdw.*
2. *Sppy.*
3. *Tnwy.*

Spell 823

SPELL FOR GIVING A HEADREST TO N. Horus stands up(?)[1] [at the head of(?)[2]] the trappers(?);[3] he saves N, who says: O you gods[4] who sail within the Lake of the Knife[5] and whose faces meet on the day of removing the hearts and cutting off the heads of the living, | you cannot do this[6] to me because of what the gods VII, 24
say. I am his (*sic*) *ᶜmᶜ*-plant(?),[7] a god(?)[8] who created himself, one mysterious of shapes. May you live, O my father, may you raise my head, for your knives will not [be effective][9] against me.

1. Cf. de Buck, n. 13*.  following *Ḥr* stands for , as also after *ʾInpw* in 24*p* (Spell 824); similarly as det. of the expression *ir ḏs.f* in 24*b*; and it stands for  in *ink* in in 24*b*, top. In 23*o* it is the interjection 'O!' and in 24*a.d.e.f* it is the suffix 1st sing. After *ᶜmᶜ.f* in 24*b* it seems to stand for *nṯr* 'god'.  stands for  or  in *ibtyw* in 23*m* and *wrw* in 24*k* (Spell 824). These eccentric usages seem peculiar to T1Be.

2. Restoring *ḥr tp* in the lacuna, cf. de Buck, n. 14*.

3. *'Ibtyw*; the translation is doubtful, but the word could be a derivative of *ỉbṯ* 'trap', cf. *Wb.* I, 65, 3.

4. Note *nw n* used to express a plural vocative instead of the more usual *ỉpw.*

5. The sign after the knife is obscure, but may be a miswriting of a determinative. Cf. de Buck, n. 15*.

6. An unusual construction, lit. 'there is not that you do this'.

7. Cf. de Buck, n. 2* and *Pyr.* §524.

8. See n. 1 above. Read *nṯr* here?

9. Cf. de Buck, nn. 4*. 5*. For this sense of *ḫpr* cf. *Pr.* 6, 10.

Spell 824

SPELL FOR EMPOWERING N'S SOUL as a gift for him in the realm of the dead. Rēʿ rises, the mysterious one goes forth, my soul is a possessor of power in its primeval form. O Moon,[1] the great ones and those who are in the Night-bark are content, Gēb and Anubis are in attendance[2] at the great shrine,[3] offerings are given to the great [ones], and my soul is in the seal-ring.[4] If Gēb be content, this soul of mine will be content; if Anubis be content, this double of mine will be content, for I have directed foodstuffs into the shrine(?).[5]

VII, 25 I am one who makes report, and I lack nothing;[6] my shares are in the Night-bark, and my (priestly) service is in the Sun-bark, and the throne of the land belongs to me.[7] O you who come in peace to this house of mine, this soul of mine exists and what is in it exists; there comes Atum who is in his disk(?) [. . .] his horizon. The moon rises on the nostril of the mysterious one, Thoth is the great Bull who sees[8] the sun-folk and who attacks[9] those who belong to the Netherworld with his arms outstretched; who gives commands ⟨to⟩ the lips and who overthrows the long-nailed dead;[10] who sends out the soul who reckons up the deeds[11] of those who belong to the totality of the hale; who knows [. . .] the Great One who has nothing; the Great Lady has propitiated her lord on the paths of Him who prohibits utterance.

You[12] shall establish my double, you shall obstruct[13] my foes [. . .], you shall give a command and my possessions will be in the horizon; I will be vindicated there today [. . .].

1. *24j* is shown by the det. to be a corruption of *psd* 'moon', *Wb.* I, 557, 4.

2. Lit. 'in a state of standing', old perfective, without indication of the dual ending. Note that *ỉw* is repeated before each of the two subjects.

3. More probably so than 'the shrine of the great one', since *wr* lacks a determinative. De Buck's marginal *m* would have been better placed by *rdy.t(w).*

4. *Ỉ* before *ḏbꜥyt* is obscure and seems superfluous.
5. Equating *snt* with *snwt* 'shrine', discussed in *SDT* 234.
6. Lit. 'there is not my need'.
7. Regarding *nw.ỉ* as an abnormal writing of *n wỉ* 'belongs to me'.
8. Read *mꜣ,* not *mꜣ*[*.f*], cf. the parallel participle *shdd* in 25*j*.
9. Cf. *shd* '(den Frevler) strafen o.ä.', *Wb.* IV, 209, 6.
10. Lit. 'those who are long of nails of the dead', with two direct genitives.
11. Read *ỉrwt*; note the fem. adjective *ẖrt* next below.
12. Thoth(?); cf. 25*h.*
13. For this use of *ḏr* cf. *Pyr.* §§625; 1715.

Spell 825

SPELL FOR ENTERING THE GATE OF THE NETHERWORLD [. . .] OF HIM WHO IS IN HIS . . .[1]. Your condition is that of one who lives[2] fully, and those who are in the Netherworld will act on your behalf, so that you will be content, be a spirit[3] and be glad for ever; you shall have your tall standard,[4] which does not part from its ground. The Abyss gives you water, He who is over the Nile worships you when you sustain eternity for its lord. You shall report the governance of the masses in accordance with what belongs to the issues of every day.[5] VII, 26

I have come as an equipped [and worthy(?)][6] spirit, I heal my members, and my (priestly) service is in this house. I have come in order to do my duty and in order to enter into the gate which is under the care of Anubis. I have not eaten what remains over of the stretched bull[7] after the share-out, and I have not repeated what I heard in the Presence. I am the embalmer[8] of Anubis, I have come that I may cover up what I found missing, for I am a warden who spent his day so that [. . .] was reckoned up before Rēꜥ daily, and I have not eaten the black ewes(?),[9] I have not bathed in the waters of Nedit.

1. *Whm.f*; note the det., characteristic of T1Be, cf. Spell 823, n. 1; so also *nb.f*, 26*g*; *Rꜥ*, 26*r*.

2. The formula *ỉw ḫrt.k m ꜥnḫ* is familiar from letters to the dead, cf. *L. to D.* p. 14.

3. The suffix *.k* has been omitted after *ꜣḫ*.

4. Read *wnn* ⟨*n*⟩*.k wnn*; the second *wnn* appears to be an enclitic particle like *wnnt*; in this context *ḳꜣt* can hardly be a var. of *ḳꜣꜣt* <*ḳꜣrt* 'door-bolt'. *Ṯn* is an error for *.k*.

5. Translation not certain. *Nt* before *rꜥ nb* should read *n*, in concord with *prw*; the fem. ending is perhaps under the influence of *ẖrt*.

6. Restoring *ỉḳr* within the lacuna, cf. *BD* 443,16; 461,4; 470,11.

7. For the *pḏty*-bull cf. *Pyr.* §1545. The significance of the term is not clear, but it could

perhaps refer to the legs of the bull being stretched taut prior to lashing them together before butchery. In *Pyr.* §§1544–5 we seem to have allusions to the operations of slaughtering; the subduing of the animal (*ḥry-s3*). Its stretching (*pḏty*), its lashing(?) (*šsr*, translated by me as 'shot(?)', probably wrongly), and its stunning (*ỉd*, lit 'deaf'), cf. my *Pyr. Transl.* 234–5, where I had not realized the meaning of this sequence of terms.

8. The *ỉ* after *wt* represents the man (or god) determinative. The speaker is an embalmer serving Anubis, not one who embalms him.

9. *ꜥ3ty* is a var. of *ꜥ3t* determined with a ram's head, cf. 16*n* above; var. *ꜥ33t* 18*v*. The adj. *km* lacks the fem. ending.

Spell 826

VII, 27 Complete is he who eats[1] the bread of Gēb and swallows the beer of the Milk-goddess; my face is that of a bull, my teeth are those of Sopd,[2] I am the great god in the horizon, and I will not live on what the gods detest; mine are the waters(?)[3] of Osiris, and my name is true. O you whom your shrine protects, Lord of offerings in the places of the horizon in which I am(?),[4] present offerings [on][5] the altars and partake(?) [of . . .] for me, for I[6] know the name of [. . .] the *bhh*-plant[7] for me. I am pure for [Gēb(?)],[8] a god whose utterance has power, I am a soul [. . .].[9]

1. Reading as *t(w)t 3 wnm t*; for the writing of *twt* cf. *Pyr.* §81; *Urk.* I, 105,1. *3* is the enclitic.

2. Emended to read *ỉbḥw.ỉ ⟨m⟩ Spdw*, cf. 22*t* above.

3. Reading *n(y) wỉ nwyt nt Wsyr*, with the words before *nt* merged by haplography; the signs before *nt* suggest a word for water, and it is difficult otherwise to account for the fem. genitive adjective *nt*.

4. *Nty.ỉ m* [. . .] is obscure; what one would expect would be *ntt wỉ ỉm*[.*sn*], and I have translated accordingly.

5. Restore *ḥr* in the lacuna.

6. Restoring *ỉw*[.*ỉ*] at the beginning of 27*j*.

7. Cf. *Wb.* I, 469, 3.

8. Cf. de Buck, n. 8*. The *ỉ* following the lacuna could well have stood for the det. of *Gb*.

9. The spell ends with two stock *ỉm3ḫy ḫr* formulae which have not been translated, one referring to the original owner of the coffin and the other to a woman, possibly his wife.

Spell 827

SPELL FOR ENTERING [THE FIELD] OF RUSHES. N says: I am a god and I will continue to exist; [I] came into being yesterday with the great ones, I came into

being so that I might exist, I was on high among [the servitors(?)] of the Lord of
the land of the living, and you[1] were with me, (but) I am not with [. . .]. I VII, 28
am he who made offering of the funeral meal in Khem on that night of the
lamps(?),[2] I know what Gēb knows, I am the unique one among you, I have sought[3] the horizon, I have seen the opening up,[4] I am Osiris [. . . me(?)] at *Rꜣ-ꜣyf*[5] in peace [. . .] what is good as a spirit in the Field of Rushes. The gods who act on [my(?)] behalf [. . .] as Lord of eternity. I wish that you would give me a god-like body[6] [. . .]. I am Horus the beloved whose name is Lord of All [. . .]. I am known to [him(?)] in the presence of the tribunal of the Seven(?).[7] What was said: Be hale [. . .].

1. Plural; presumably the 'great ones' of 27*t*.
2. *Nḫbw* determined with the night-sign; for *nḫb* 'lamp' cf. *Wb.* II, 308, 12.
3. Restoring *w* in the lacuna.
4. Of the horizon?
5. An unidentified locality.
6. *Ḏt nṯrty*.
7. Reading *ỉw rḫ(w.i) n*[*.f*] *m-bꜣḥ ḏꜣḏꜣt 7*; the writing of *ḏꜣḏꜣt* is abnormal and the whole passage is obscure.

Spell 828

[. . .] OF THE BACK OF THE HEAD [. . .]. I come that I may greet you,[1] you Mourner of Osiris, who conceal [the Great One][2] from the flood of ill;[3] Mistress of thrones who makes a spirit of the Bull of the West, at seeing whom the Wester-
ners rejoice; Mistress of All[4] in the secret places; watch over [me],[5] for I am
Osiris whom I (*sic*) have spiritualized. | O you who split open my mouth for me[6] VII, 29
and gathered together for me what issued from my flesh,[7] grant to me offerings
among the great ones,[8] for I see the god in charge of the oblations to his father which the Sacred Eye sanctified after . . . .[9] Many mouths are content which I have satisfied, for I am one who knows his utterance, I have come so that my face may have power [. . .] and there is no sort of suffering which is on me.[10]

I come that I may greet you, O Great Lady who are behind your [lord];[11] raise him up at his time of inertness(?).[12] [O you who gathered][13] my body together for me and who pulled [my] flesh together,[14] spiritualize yourself,[15] split open my mouth for me, grant my name and gifts for my mouth [. . .][16] on every day of giving[17] food-supplies; I satisfy [many][18] mouths. I am Osiris, I am bound for Abydos,[19] [. . .] the shrine and those who are in it, for I am he who protects the air[20] [. . .].

1. Reading as *ỉy⟨.ỉ n⟩ḏ⟨.ỉ⟩ ḥr.t,* cf. 29*j*, which also omits the *n* of *nḏ*; so too 31*a*. This spell is a variant of parts of Spells 237 and 238, cf. *CT Transl.* I, 185 ff.

2. Restore the *wr*-sign in the lacuna, cf. de Buck, 28, n.14*.

3. *ꜣgbw* determined with the 'bad' bird.

4. Read *nbt* [*r*] *ḏr,* cf. de Buck, n. 15* and *CT* III, 307*e*.

5. Read *rs ḥr*[*.ỉ*], cf. III, 309*a*.

6. Read *wpt n⟨.ỉ⟩ rꜣ.ỉ*, cf. III, 312*g*; 316*a*.

7. Read *ỉnḳt n.ỉ prt m ỉf.ỉ.*

8. Cf. III, 313*b*. The partitive *m* before *ḥtpw* seems superfluous.

9. *ꜥsg.s.* Compare III, 316*g*.

10. Restore *n šnnt* at the beginning of 29*i*, cf. de Buck, 29, n. 3*. The x recorded by de Buck after the lacuna could perhaps represent the lower part of 𓎛.

11. On 29*j* see n. 1 above. At the end of the sentence restore *nb* in the lacuna, the *ỉ* before the suffix standing for the falcon-on-perch determinative.

12. Read *bꜣg*? Cf. de Buck, n. 6*.

13. *CT* III, 316*m* has *ỉnḳt*.

14. *Sꜣḳ.n* should be emended into *sꜣḳt*. Restore the suffix *ỉ* in the lacuna.

15. For the masc. *ṯw* read the fem. *ṯn*; the 'Great Lady' (*wrt*) of 29*j* is being addressed.

16. 29*n* is a corrupt version of III, 316*o*, but an attempt has been made to render the passage as it stands.

17. For *dy r* read *dyt.* Cf. III, 316*p*.

18. Restore the lizard *ꜥšꜣ* in the lacuna, cf. loc. cit; de Buck, n. 7*.

19. Cf. III, 313*c*; 317*a*.

20. Compare III. 311*g*; a corrupt version in 317*c*.

Spell 829

VII, 30 SPELL FOR ENTERING INTO THE EARTH AND BEING TRANSFORMED INTO [. . .] (spoken) by N. He says:-

I am the Lion.

I am the Double Lion.[1]

I am the greatest of his priesthood.

I am Horus, the uniter of [. . .].[2]

I am the second of four, two of three of his four, who offer a god's ewer to him who served these god's ewers(?).[3]

I am he who makes calm after storm.[4]

I am Isis [when she was] in Chemmis,[5] and I will listen[6] like him who was deaf(?) and who stared.[7]

I am Gēb, who entered into the earth.

I am he who assesses whoever serves him.

I am transformed ⟨into⟩ one whose spirits are mighty.

I am Rēʿ, Lord of his Two Lands.

I am he who is put behind him, I will not place you[8] behind me, I will not place you behind him. The waters and the earth are joined together, presentation is made[9] of the waters and the earth, and your [10]hands shall be laid bare[11] because of what is in you; I will see(?)[12] the house thereof.

I am the waters and the earth; The Bitter Lakes and the Great Bull are [my] name[s]. I will travel and enter into that place which I know.

I am yonder bearer of a staff(?).[13]

I am he who unites the earth to himself.[14]

1. Cf. Spell 1.

2. Cf. *Ḥr zmꜣw* in *Pyr.* §1831.

3. *30h* is most obscure. The meaning of the progression of numerals is not clear, though it is possible that this may be an allusion to the four children of Horus, and what follows is even more difficult. The sign rendered by 'god's ewer' consists of the *nṯr*-sign mounted on an ewer or spouted vessel; and *nw* in *ỉr n nw* before the repetition of this sign has been taken to be the demonstrative *nw* before a plural noun, though if so, we would have to restore the plural strokes in the lacuna at the end of *30h*. But the rendering of the whole passage must be regarded as highly doubtful.

4. The reading of the sign following *ỉr* is uncertain; de Buck, n. 1*, suggests *smꜣ*, but *nfr* seems possible also. The translation of the word as 'calm' depends on the interpretation of *ẖnnw* as 'storm', i.e. 'uproar' determined with the sky pouring rain. Note the slightly abnormal spelling of *ẖnnw*.

5. The reading *ꜣs*[*t*] 'Isis' is indicated by the following allusion to Chemmis, where she took refuge from Seth, but the following *sy* is a problem. It cannot be a normal dependent pronoun, for to serve as subject such a pronoun must be preceded by a non-enclitic particle such as *mk* or *ỉsṯ*, for which there is no room in the preceding lacuna, assuming that *ꜣs*[*t*] had a normal determinative. It would seem, therefore, that we have here a hitherto unknown use of the archaic paradigm *sw, sy, sn* noted in *Eg. Gramm.*[3] p. 424, but with adverbial predicate and in a virtual clause of circumstance; Gardiner records it only before *sḏm.f.*

6. Read *sḏm.ḫr*⟨*.ỉ*⟩.

7. Regarding *ỉdn* as an error for *ỉd* 'be deaf'. Gilula, *JEA* 61, 251, translates differently.

8. See de Buck, n. 4*.; neither here nor just below is it clear who is being addressed in the 2nd person sing.

9. Reading *ʿbꜣ.t(w)*.

10. Plural, but whose hands?

11. Read *ḥꜣ.t(w)*, transitive (passive) use of *ḥꜣ* 'naked'.

12. Read *ptr.ỉ*(?).

13. In the absence of a det., *ʿbw* is hard to interpret; provisionally I have regarded it as a derivative of *ʿbw* 'staff', on which see *Concise Dict.* 41. See also *Wb.* I, 176, 15.

14. Again there is no det., but I have taken *ʿb* to be a var. of *ỉʿb* 'unite', and a participial predicate of *ỉnk*; the dative has been postponed. The sentence probably refers to burial and would thus be in accord with the introductory rubric.

Spell 830

VII, 31 I COME THAT I MAY GREET [YOU];[1] I AM RAISED UP[2] BY MEANS OF WHAT IS PROFITABLE TO THOSE WHO LEAD; WAKE [ME] SO THAT MY[3] MEMBERS MAY BE AT EASE FOR ME THEREBY AND THAT I MAY HAVE POWER THEREAFTER, YOU BEING ALIVE, FOR I KNOW THAT I AM THE SON OF HIM IN WHOM IS AN EYE. My heart is assessed, my members are gathered together; I am raised up[4] thereby, you being alive for ever(?).[5] I am one profitable of speech who went forth from Gēb to [. . .] in the great bark; I have come so that I may be in your[6] protection. Join my members together when yonder [potent(?)][7] god looks at you,[8] when he has protected this land for him who lives for ever. N is vindicated.

1. Cf. Spell 828, n. 1.
2. Read *wṯs.t(w).i.*
3. Read as 1st person.
4. See n. 2 above.
5. Cf. de Buck, n. 2*.
6. Masc. sing.
7. Restoring as *mn*[*ḫ*].
8. Plural without antecedent. Either there has been an omission or else the copyist has blundered.

Spell 831

Choice joints which are brought before the offering-table.[1] The king's gift:[2] pure[3] is everything which is done for me.[4] The king's gift: pure[5] is everything which is done for my double,[6] and I am pure and vindicated.[7]

1. So T3Be; T2Be (31*n*) reads: 'I am pure, I cleanse the offering-table with cold water and incense'; the single *w* at the beginning is a slip for *ỉw*. T1Be omits all this and begins in 31*o* with *n N* 'for N' etc., i.e. 'for me'.
2. *'Iḫt nyswt.* T3Be alone writes the initial *ỉ* of *ỉḫt,* but omits the *t*.
3. T3B and T1Be needlessly insert *ỉw* before *wꜥb*.
4. Read *ỉrrt n.ỉ,* see the stroke after *n*; the following name of the deceased is doubtless an ancient editorial addition. T2Be has the name alone, while the text of T1Be properly belongs to 31*p*; it omits one of the two virtually identical clauses.
5. T3Be has inserted *ỉw* after *wꜥb,* probably with the idea of correcting its omission before *wꜥb*, but it is meaningless here.
6. T2Be has *kꜣ.k* 'your double' in error.
7. So T3Be; the parallels omit *mꜣꜥ ḫrw*.

Spell 832

'How lovely to see! How pleasant to hear!'[1] – so says Isis the divine.[2] This god VII, 32
ascends[3] to the sky with his soul at his head, the dread of him at his mouth and
his magic on his hands. He has been helped by Atum in accordance with the
manner in which he should have helped him.[4] He[5] has brought to him the gods
the Souls of Pe, he has brought to him the gods the Souls of Nekhen, he has
brought to him the gods the Souls of Ōn,[6] he has gathered together for him the
gods who are in the sky and who are on earth; they make supports for him with[7]
their arms, | ⟨May he ascend to the sky⟩[8] and mount up on it in this its[9] name of 33
'Ladder'.

What you have said, you gods: 'Towns are given to you and you have travel-
led about the nomes' – so says Atum; it means that Gēb speaks about it.[10] Sky
and earth and the Mounds of Horus have been given to you, you have travelled
about the Mounds of Seth.[11] They worship you in this your name of *Dwꜣw*[12] and
as *ꜣḥs* and Dedwen pre-eminent in Zety-land[13] and Sopd who is beneath his
ksbt-trees.[14] | Has he[15] slain you or does he desire your death?[16] You shall not 34
die:[17] see, you have become the enduring one of the wild bull(s).[18] Endure, O
enduring Bull, at the head of the gods in yonder[19] land for ever.

1. A version of *Pyr.* Utt. 306. Note that in T1C the enclitic *ꜣ* is written as *n*.
2. T1C omits *ỉt ỉn ꜣst*; *nṯrt* 'divine' is in T9C only.
3. The best reading is *pr r.f* of B10C; *Pyr.* §476*b* has the *sḏmt.f* form *prt r.f nṯr pn*. 'This god' is the deceased.
4. Read *ỉrw n.f ỉn ʾItm*, lit. 'there has been done for him by Atum', see T9C and originally B10C. After *my ḳd, ỉr.n.f* is perfective relative form. T2C begins at 32*g*, cf. de Buck, n. 6*, and has bungled the passage. Cf. *Pyr.* §477*c*.
5. Atum.
6. T1C omits the reference to the Souls of Ōn. Cf. *Pyr.* §478*a*.
7. 'With' seems a better translation for *ḥr* than 'upon'; the arms themselves are the supports in question.
8. Omitted here but supplied from *Pyr.* §479*a*;
9. Read *rn.s* for *rn.ṯ* in accord with loc. cit. T2C has *rn.f* and at the end of the sentence has repeated *mꜣḳt*.
10. With 33*c-f* compare *Pyr.* §480*a-b*.
11. Var. B10C: 'the Mounds of the Outcast have been given to you'.
12. Cf. *Pyr.* §480*d*.
13. Not in Pyr.
14. Cf. *Pyr.* loc.cit.
15. Seth.
16. Lit. 'Has his heart said that you shall die?' Compare *Pyr.* §481*a*.

17. So 34*d.* in 34*c* T1C precedes this with *n rdy mt.k n mt,* lit. 'your dying for death will not be permitted'; B10C has *n mt.k* 'you shall not die' and repeats it in 34*d.*

18. With 34*e.f* compare *Pyr.* §481*b-d.* *Ḫpr.t(y) r.f* of T9C is correct.

19. *T3 pf* 'yonder land' of T1C is to be preferred to *t3 pn* 'this land' of T9C; the end of B10C is lost.

Spell 833

Water for Horus! Water for Horus! Give him the water of his father Osiris! Ho N! You have your water, you have your cold water, the efflux[1] which issued from the god, the putrescence which issued from Osiris.

VII, 35 O N! You depart living, you do not[2] depart dead. | O N, may you ferry over the Great Bull to the Green Pillar, to the fields of the Great Bull, and do what he wishes. Raise yourself, N; live, for you are not dead.

1. *Pdw* is a corruption of *rḏw* 'efflux', cf. *Pyr.* §788*b.*
2. Read as the negation *n.*

Spell 834

Ho N! Are you in the sky?[1] Are you on earth? Your mother Nūt will[2] throw open for you the doors of the firmament, your father Gēb will open[3] his doors for you. Are you in your southern mounds? Are you in your northern mounds? Are you in ⟨your⟩ eastern mounds? Are you in your western mounds? You shall come in safety, you shall have power in your body, the doors shall be turned back,[4] and the gates of the tomb shall be opened. Ho N! You shall go out thence spirit-like, mighty and honoured.

1. T1C writes *ỉn* of *ỉn ỉw* with the negation *n*; so also five times below.
2. For the future tense cf. the prospective *sḏm.f* form *ỉwt.k* in 35*m.*
3. Read *wn n.k,* passing over the superfluous *n.* The *sḏm.n.f* form is out of consideration here.
4. *Ngbgb* is not recorded, but cf. *ngb* 'turn aside', *Concise Dict.* 141, bottom.

Spell 835

VII, 36 O N, Horus will not let you perish;[1] Horus has set your foes under you, Horus has given you the gods that they may serve you,[2] and that [you] may have power over them; none of them will dance. O Thoth, reassemble him,[3] so that what is on him may cease to be.

1. This spell is made up of extracts, somewhat garbled, from the Pyramid Texts, see de Buck's notes.

2. Note the archaic pronoun *kw*; *Pyr.* §620*a* has *ṯw*.

3. *Sn* in 36*h* is obviously corrupt, and it has been emended to the 3rd sing. as *Pyr.* §830; it is not the deceased who is speaking. *Mk* before 'Thoth' is surely corrupt; it is not in Pyr.

Spell 836

The staff(?) of *Smy* is broken(?),[1] and it means(?)[2] that the Elder is brought to him; the mouth is hale, it recites a water-spell(?)[3] for us; your mouth is hale . . .[4] Your bull is in the place of your . . . ,[5] the fear of you has perished, respect for you has gone, the storm of Her who is mighty of dread, Mistress of the land, is quelled(?).[6] At dawn, very early, he crossed over, and a thousand joined together in unison(?).[7]

1. 36*i* is unintelligible to me; the version given above is but a precarious guess. It is possible that this spell may have lost its beginning and that it starts here with only the latter part of a passage, since there are apparently no antecedents for the suffixes *.f* in 36*j* or *.n* in 36*l*; *smy* in 36*i* could be a place-name, see de Buck, n. 8*. The whole spell gives the impression of being but a fragment of a longer text.

2. The reading *pw* is not certain, cf. de Buck, n. 9*.

3. *Ḥsw-m-mw,* lit. perhaps 'spell consisting of water'; cf. *ḥsw* 'water-spell', *Concise Dict.* 177. 36*n-p* reads like a spell against some being.

4. What follows *wḏꜣ rꜣ.k* in 36*m* defeats me.

5. Cf. de Buck, n. 12*.

6. A guess; the opening of 36*q* is obscure in both reading and meaning; cf. de Buck, 13* – 14*.

7. *Smꜣ ḫꜣ m smꜣ*; there must surely have been originally a continuation of the text.

Spell 837

Opening the doors of the sky, throwing open the doors of the firmament. Horus VII, 37
appears, Thoth comes, they come to Osiris[1] and they cause him to go forth at the head of the Enneads. Remember, Seth, and put in your heart[2] this word which Gēb spoke against you, this threat[3] which the gods made against you in the Mansion of the Prince[4] which is in Ōn when you felled Osiris to the earth in Nedit,[5]

when you said, Seth, 'I did not do this',[6] so that you might have power over him, that you might be saved and that you might have power over Horus;[7] when you said, Seth,[8] 'It was he who attacked me', when there came into being his name of 'Earth-attacker(?)';[9] when you said, Seth, 'It was he who kicked me', when there came into being his name of 'Osiris as Orion,[10] long of leg and lengthy of stride, who presides over Upper Egypt'.

Rise up, Osiris, on your side in Geḥesty;[11] Isis has your arm and Nephthys
38 has your hand, so go between them.[12] | Sky and earth are given to you,[13] the Field of Rushes is given to you; go all over the Mounds of Horus, travel about the Mounds of Seth[14] in the presence of the two gods,[15] the two lords who give judgement.

Live, Osiris! I am holy, being pure;[16] I have come that I may make for you the surplus[17] which your son Horus made for you, I have come that I may make for you the great meal which Gēb commanded to be made for you. Lift up your hand which bears (the sign of) life, make firm your hand which bears the *wꜣs*-staff,[18] so that you may be the *ḏd*-pillar of the gods. You shall go hence, for you have gone as Lord of the horn.[19]

I have come to you,[20] my lord, I have come to you, my god, I have come to you, Osiris, that I may clothe you with your clothing; may you be pure in Djedet.
39 It is your daughter Sothis who sits for you and who prepares for ⟨you⟩[21] your yearly sustenance in her name of 'Year', | and who guides me.[22]

I have come to you, my lord, I have come[23] to you, Osiris, that I may wipe your face and clothe you with the clothing of a god. I will eat a limb of[24] him who would harm you, I will carve it ⟨for⟩ you, O Osiris,[25] I have been put (*sic*) at the head of its carvers.[26]

I have come to you, my lord, I have come to you, my god, I have come to you, Osiris, that I may wipe your face and clothe you with the clothing of a god. Priestly service will be done for you by Horus your son whom you fashioned.[27] I will remove you from the dead and put you at the head of your runners, who are spirits yonder, and who make spirits of those who are yonder.[28] My bread is the bread of the gods, ⟨my beer is⟩ the beer of the gods[29] on which they live, and I will live thereon.[30] What Horus did for his father Osiris, I will do likewise for you.[31]

1. Read *ỉw.sn n Wsyr,* cf. de Buck, n. 1*. With this spell compare *Pyr.* Utt. 477.
2. Read *d r ỉb.k* with T9C and *Pyr.* §957*a*.
3. Cf. loc. cit.
4. B10C: 'the great Mansion of the Prince'.
5. *Ndy n.k* is a corruption of the place-name Nedit, where Osiris was killed.

6. Read *n ỉr.n.ỉ ỉs nw* with *Pyr.* §958*a*.

7. Read *nḥm.k sḫm.k n Ḥr*, combining both texts; the *m* before *nḥm.k* in T9C is superfluous. Compare Pyr. §958*b*.

8. T9C represents the name of the god with an oblique stroke.

9. *'Ikw-tꜣ* is determined with a beetle in T9C. With 37*k-p* compare *Pyr.* §959; for *rn.k* read *rn.f*, as also in 37*o*, cf. n. 10 below.

10. T9C has *rn.k*, B10C simply *rn*; read *rn.f*.

11. With 37*q-s* compare *Pyr.* §960.

12. So B10C correctly; T9C has *šm.k ỉmy mkt.sn*, 'go, you who are in their protection'.

13. With 38*a-c* compare *Pyr.* §961. The *r* before *pt* in 38*a* (T9C) is to be disregarded; it appears to be the *r* of *rdy* which has strayed from its proper place.

14. *Dbn* and *pḫr* appear to be imperatives with reinforcing dative, except that T9C has *rk* after *dbn* instead of *n.k*; this text represents the names of both gods by a single oblique stroke.

15. Here the spell temporarily diverges from *Pyr.* Utt. 477.

16. Following B10C and reading *wꜥb.k(y)*, old perfective, after *ḏsr*; T9C has miswritten this verb.

17. For *prw* 'surplus' see *Concise Dict.* 91; the reference will be to food-offerings.

18. Cf. *Pyr.* §967*d*.

19. So T9C; B10C may have read *nb sꜣ*. Cf. de Buck, nn. 1*. 4*.

20. With 38*k* to 39*n* compare *Pyr.* §§964 ff.

21. Omission of suffix *.k*.

22. Emend *sšmt sw* into *sšmt wỉ*. Before this read *snt* 'sister'(?); cf. de Buck, 39, n 1*.

23. For *ỉw.n.f* read *ỉw.n.ỉ*; so also 39*h*.

24. Another instance of 'genitival' *m* after *ꜥt*, cf. Spell 815, n. 8. *.K* is an error.

25. Read *ḥnṯ.⟨.ỉ⟩ ⟨n⟩.k sy Wsyr*, cf. *Pyr.* §966*e*; for the verb cf. also *Adm.* 8, 11 (var. *ḥntꜣ*).

26. Cf. loc. cit. (N), which has *d.f ỉw m ḫnt n ḥnṯtyw* 'he (read 'I') will put myself at the head of the carvers'; read accordingly in my *Pyr. Transl.*

27. Supply *wꜥb* 'do priestly service' at the beginning of 39*k* in T9C, though the suffix *.k* which actually stands there is superfluous, since the deceased can hardly perform his own service, while B10C seems to have had two datives *n.k*; the correct reading is probably *wꜥb n.k ỉn Ḥr ms.n.k*; with 39*k-n* cf. *Pyr.* §§969-70.

28. So T9C; B10C runs: 'your runners, who are your spirits, and the gods who are spirits yonder, who make spirits of those who are yonder'. Note the play on the stem *ꜣḫ*. *'Imy* has been taken to be a *nisba* of the *m* of predication.

29. T9C simply 'bread and beer of the gods' and stops. B10C should have read *ḥnkt.ỉ ḥnkt nt nṯrw*; the scribe has omitted one *ḥnkt* and has written the masc. gemitive *n* for the fem. *nt*.

30. Restore as *ꜥnḫ.ỉ ỉm*.

31. The text has the name of the dead man, but from the end of p. 37 the deceased, in his identification with Osiris, is addressed in the 2nd person.

Spell 838

VII, 40 The Great One falls on his side, He who is in Nedit[1] quakes. 'Raise your head', says Rēʿ; 'you shall detest sleep and hate[2] inertness' [. . .] Nūt; the nurse[3] has suckled him, [. . .] will not wean him with you, you gods. This is Osiris who comes to you, you gods; Osiris indeed(?)[4] is devoid of his flesh, and Isis has stopped for herself his flesh and his efflux (from falling) to the ground.[5] You shall complete what is on them[6] in this your name of 'Northerner';[7] the gods are astonished at you, the gods are astonished at you[8] in this your name of *wꜣs*-staff'.[9] May you stand up at the head of the Conclave of Upper Egypt as Horus, for the Nine Gods come to you bowing as (to) Min[10] who is in his house and Seth of *Ḥnt*. Smite him[11] in his (*sic*) name of 'Bull of the sky', kick him in your name of Orion, for Horus will capture[12] Seth in order to raise up your [corpse(?)][13] bearing this staff(?).[14]

1. *Ndyt* here and in 41*a* has an additional determinative, of water.
2. Restore as *msḏ*, cf. Pyr. §721*d*.
3. *Ḫsmy* is masc. and thus can hardly be subject of the verb *snḳ* 'suckle'. It is surely a corruption of *ḫnmyt* 'nurse'.
4. The initial sign of T9C in 39*i* is the slanting stroke, which could stand here for the name of Osiris; it stands for various gods' names, cf. 37*k.n*; 40*l.r.* while *ms* might well be the enclitic particle. B10C lacks a subject for *šwy*, which looks like a participle, and reads perhaps 'he who is devoid of his flesh'. in T9C *šw* is old perfective.
5. *Snḥm* (T9C) and *sḥm* (B10C) are synonyms; *snḥm* means 'stop' or 'prevent' movements, cf. *CT* I, 52*a*, and *sḥm* is likewise used of stopping movements in *BD* 211,1 and of putting a stop to ill deeds in *RB* 111,11; *Urk.* IV, 1683,13. *Ḫr* 'fall' is not written in either text, but is surely implied by *r tꜣ* 'to the ground' at the end of the sentence; it is difficult to see what else Isis could 'stop'.
6. T9C has *mḥ n.k*, imperative with reflexive dative, B10C has the optative *sḏm.f* form *mḥ.k*, and there is little to choose between them; the suffix in *ḥr.sn* apparently refers to the 'flesh' and the 'efflux' of 40*j*.
7. Read *mḥty*, a fem. word such as *mḥt* would be out of place in referring to a god. Note the obscure scribble which follows the word in T9C.
8. Cf. *gꜣw* with eye-det. in *Wb.* V, 151, 2–4. This makes better sense than equating *gꜣyw* with *gꜣw* 'be narrow', etc., *Concise Dict.* 287–8.
9. T9C represents the *wꜣs*-staff with the characteristic slanting stroke. We would have expected a pun on *gꜣyw* here, and the reference to the *wꜣs* is a little obscure, unless indeed we should read *wꜣsy* 'he of the *wꜣs*-staff'.
10. Represented in T9C by the slanting stroke.
11. Imperative with reflexive dative.
12. Read *nḥm* with B10C.
13. Restore as [*ẖꜣt*].*k*? There is room in the lacuna in T9C.

14. Read *ẖr w3ʿ.k pw*? *W3ʿ* could mean 'staff' or 'baton' of authority, cf. *w3ʿw* 'captain' of ship, *Urk.* IV, 996,1. The reading *ẖr,* however, is not certain, cf. de Buck, n. 10*. The last words of the spell have been omitted in T9C.

Spell 839

The Great One falls on his side, He who is in Nedit quakes; '[Lift up(?)] [1] your VII, 41
hand', says Rēʿ, and your hand is taken by his Enneads. O my father, see, this is
Osiris. The gods come [to you[2] . . .] in putrescence [. . .] who removes what
the god who is in [. . .] detests [. . .]. O N, beware of the Great Lake,[3] beware
of [. . .] beware of [. . .] spirits, beware of those men who are over [. . .]
you exclude(?) [. . .] as Rēʿ [. . .].[4] Go down on to the deck of [this] bark in
which Rēʿ rows to the horizon. O my father Osiris,[5] [go down on to the
bow(?)] [6] of this bark of Rēʿ; you and Rēʿ shall go aboard her, you and Rēʿ shall
sit in her, you and Rēʿ shall take your [seat(?)] in [her], you shall sit on this 42
throne of Rēʿ [. . .] on your south side, [. . . on] your north side, Shu on your
east side and Tefēnet on your west side [. . .] Rēʿ. They [will cause] [7] you to
take possession of the *wrt*-crown at the head of the Enneads just as they caused
Rēʿ to take possession of the *wrrt*-crown at the head of [the Enneads(?)].[8]
They will lead you to the seats of Rēʿ [. . .]; they will receive [. . .] as a spirit
[just as] they receive [. . .] who(?) have power over [. . .].

I have come, O my father Osiris, for I am your son, I am Horus, [I] have
come [that I may bring(?)[9] to you] this [foe(?)] of yours, and the Enneads
[have] put him beneath you [for] you[10] [. . .] a long-horn [. . .][11] in this his 43
name of [. . .]; Atum has [. . .] him for you as one who is evil. He will be
bound, the sun-folk being with him, in this his name of 'Sacrificial Bull''.[12] I bring
him to you as a bull with a duct(?) in its neck.[13] Eat it, taste[14] its head at all your
meals belonging to you, for your heritage belongs to me; I am your heir upon
your throne,[15] while you are perpetuated in front of your shrine(?) yonder which
is on earth. May you speak with the great and mighty gods who are in the session
in front of Ōn, may your power be greater than that of the gods of the Wester-
ners, [16] may the dread of you be mightier than that of your (*sic*) gods of the West-
erners. May the silent ones go to you, Osiris(?), [17] may the dread of you be on
them and the awe of you be on their hearts; may your bonds be cut as Horus who 44
is in his house [18] and your cords hewn asunder [19] as Seth who is in *Ḥnt.* O my
father Osiris, be a spirit, be awake, be wise(?),[20] be effective,[21] and walk the earth
by day in your stride. May you travel by day, may you open up a path(?),[22] may
you go to rest on the pillow(?)[23] of Rēʿ which separates the Day-bark[24] from the

Night-bark in which Rēʿ rows; the darkness of the two gods in which they go to rest is what the two gods seek when ⟨they(?)⟩ go to rest(?).[25] Go aboard the Day-bark on the day when the Lord of the horizon is spiritualized(?) so that he may
45 row you [26] | in the Night-bark and the Day-bark like Rēʿ every day. Stand up, Osiris, living for ever and ever![27]

1. Restored according to de Buck, n. 1*.
2. Compare 40*h.r.*
3. Cf. *Pyr.* §§872*d*; 885; 1752*c*.
4. A long lacuna extending over *ỉ-m,* with a few signs surviving.
5. 'N' is superfluous here, cf. 42*l.*
6. Cf. de Buck, n. 12*.
7. Cf. de Buck, 42, n. 1*.
8. If the proposed restoration be correct, *psḏt* must have been written as 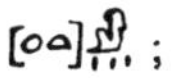 ; in its favour is the fem. determinative and the space available. Cf. 41*b*; 42*p* for a similar writing of *psḏt*.
9. Cf. de Buck, n. 7*.
10. Cf. de Buck, n. 8*.
11. T9C comes in at 43*b*; 43*a* and *b* are damaged in B10C.
12. Compare *Pyr.* §1545 and cf. above, spell 825, n. 7. Following *šsrw.f* we have an allusion to the sun-folk in *ḥnmmt ỉm.f*; this seems to have no relation to the context, despite the fact that it occurs in both texts; one suspects an early interpolation from elsewhere.
13. For *mt* 'vessel', 'duct', 'muscle' cf. *Concise Dict.* 120, but what *mt n ḫḫ.f* means in this context is not clear; is the *mt* a blood-vessel to be cut after the stunning, or does it refer to the windpipe which is to be strangled? 43*e* suggests that the killing of the bull is being referred to obliquely, so that one operation or the other seem to be implied.
14. For *ỉdp.f* read *ỉdp.k*; the scribe himself has corrected *ỉšt.f* into *ỉšt.k,* cf. de Buck, 43, n.4*.
15. The latter part of 43*e* is certainly corrupt; read probably *ỉšt.k nbt n.k ỉmy.* The B10C version of 43*f* shows that in 43*e ỉʿrw.f n.ỉ* should read as *ỉwʿ.k n.ỉ,* and 43*f* should read *ỉnk ỉwʿ.k ḥr nst.k.*
16. Hardly 'the western gods', cf. *nṯrw.k n* (sic) *ỉmntyw* below. B10C has bungled *ỉmntyw* in both places.
17. 53*j* seems corrupt in T9C; B10C is damaged. *'Igrtt* of T9C appears to stand for a plural, since it is referred to by *sn* in 43*k*; I conjecturally suggest the emendation *sb ỉgrw n.k Wsyr* 'may the silent ones go to you, Osiris'.
18. Followed in T9C by the figure of a pig.
19. In T9C *ỉntwt* is followed by a superfluous *r.*
20. *ʿw,* written with the sign employed for *ʿw* 'interpreter', 'dragoman'.
21. Emend into *spd n.k,* imperative with reflexive dative in accord with what precedes and follows.
22. *Ṯn* after *wbꜣ.k* is obscure; it may be a remnant of *mṯn* 'path', which would make sense.
23. For *ḏdyt* read *ḏnyt,* and for the meaning 'pillow(?)' cf. *CT* III. 297*i.*

24. Reading *mꜥnḏt,* cf. de Buck, n. 3*.

25. Emend as *sḏrt⟨.sn⟩*? 44*g* is obscure and seems irrelevant. *R.s⟨n⟩* at the end could be the enclitic.

26. 44*j*–45*c* is a repetition of 43*c* ff. The present text resumes in 45*d*, cf. de Buck, nn. 44,4*; 45,1*. *Ḫn.f ṯw* is repeated in 45*d.*

27. The spell ends with *r rnpt* and an unintelligible group; after *nḥḥ ḥnꜥ ḏt* a reference to 'years' is surely superfluous. *N* between *ꜥnḫt* and *r nḥḥ* is likewise to be disregarded.

Spell 840

O N, may it go well with you, your double being your protection, your soul being within you and your feet being in your place, you being renewed[1] and young in this your name of 'Fresh Water',[2] you being raised up on this happy day in which you appeared in glory. Your mother Nūt comes to you in it[3] with your sister Nephthys, and they bring (something) like the Eye of Horus; fair is their perfume on you, and the perfume of the Eye of Horus is on you.

1. Reading *mꜣw.ty* 'renewed', not *mꜣ.ty* 'seen'; cf. *rnp.ty* 'young' in the next clause.
2. Corrupt; emend as *m rn.k pw n mw rnpw,* cf. *Pyr.* §25*c.*
3. I.e. 'this happy day'.

Spell 841

Am I guarded? Am I released?[1] [Does one bind][2] his hand [to me] and thrust his VII, 46
hand into me on earth? The knot is tied [. . .] who has no bark. Seth is released from bonds [. . .] Seth is released from the Eye of Horus, who is firmly established [. . .] this head of mine for me. There is no god who stands at the rope [. . .] which was spoken in my defence(?).[3] I am [. . .] Rēꜥ, and you do not break (*sic*) against me; not [. . .]. I am the great one who issued from the horizon(?) [. . .] I am Horus who absorbed the Chaos-god, [I have(?)] come into being[4] [. . .] since a hand was extended to me. I am [. . .] I am content. You have your double, and your soul is within [you . . .].

1. Cf. *CT* III, 216*a*; de Buck, n. 1*. Read *ỉn sꜣꜣ.tw.i, ỉn sfḫ.⟨t⟩w.ỉ.*

2. Cf. de Buck, n. 3*; 46*b* must have been corrupt, for there is not enough space in the first lacuna for *ỉn my* (=*mr*) or for *ỉm.ỉ* in the second lacuna; there can be little doubt that this clause originally was virtually identical with the corresponding part of III, 216*b.*

3. *Mꜥnḏt* with papyrus-roll determinative appears to be unrecorded; the translation 'defence(?)' rests on the idea of 'safety' apparently embodied in the word *mꜥnḏt* as a deriva-

tive of *ʿ(n)ḏ* 'safe'.

4. Restoring as the old perfective *ḫpr.k[y]*.

Spell 842

VII, 47 Recitation of many incantations for[1] him who is vindicated in the realm of the dead, for N's double. Ho N! Are you in the sky? [Are you on earth?[2] . . .] Are you in the wind?[3] [. . .].

1. Lit. 'of', direct genitive.
2. Restoring *în î.k m t3*.
3. From here on, only disjointed fragments of the spell remain.

Spell 843

VII, 48 [. . .][1] incantations[2] which are given for N. This *ḥwg*-cake(?)[3] is upon Anubis. The confederacy of Horus and Seth has no power over him, they being far removed[4] from this which is given to you (*sic*) for this bread and this beer.

1. A long lacuna, extending over 18 lines. All that survives is *ḥnḳt* 'beer' at the top of l. 228 and *m* at the top of l. 229.
2. Read *s3ḫw-r3* as in 47*a*.
3. Read *ḥwg pw pw*?
4. Old perfective 3rd plural.

Spell 844 *is almost entirely destroyed. See de Buck's nn. 5*. 6*.*

Spell 845

VII, 49 O Osiris, Horus has filled his Eye with ointment.[1] O N,[2] take the Eye of Horus, the ointment, in its name of 'Ointment'. O Horus who is N, take the Eye of Horus on account of which he suffered(?) in this its name of '*sfṯ*-oil'. I put[3] it on your brow for you, (even) the Eye of Horus which cooks your foes. Gēb has given you his heritage and your[4] vindication, Wepwawet separates your paths from your foes.

Take the Eye of Horus and be pleased with it,[5] put the Eye of Horus on your brow.[6] O Horus who is N, take the Eye of Horus, for it belongs to you, it belongs to your body,[7] put it on yourself, provide yourself with it, for it will provide you as a god; lift up what is on you, which is on the brow of Horus.[8]

1. With 49*a-d* compare Pyr. §§50 and 51.
2. Sq3C has 'O Horus who is N'.
3. Sq3C has the imperative *m*, but *dy(.ỉ)* in T1C is the better reading.
4. T1C omits the suffix.
5. T1C omits 49*j*.
6. So Sq3C; T1C: 'put it on you, the Eye of Horus, on your brow'.
7. T1C omits 49*l*, has slightly garbled 49*m* and omits 49*n*.
8. So T1C in 49*q*; Sq3C substitutes in 49*r*: 'you shall take the *wrrt*-crown by means of it before the Great Ennead'.

Spell 846

Get back, Black-front, skilled in perfume [. . .] the Mansion of the Lion, VII, 50
Disturber who is sent in storm, messenger[1] of Seth living on what you[2] steal: oppose your face to the earth-god [. . .].

O you who oppose N ⟨in⟩ . . .[3] I am in front of you, so turn yourself about; you shall not allow anyone to come to you about it who comes from . . .[4] If you go, Shu(?) will go [. . .]; tell this name of yours [to(?)] the copulator multitudinous[5] of begettings; that is your need(?).

The fire goes forth against the temple of the desert-goddess who goes forth [. . .] before him, and he shall not put danger[6] about N. N's . . .[7] is under him among [. . .] in Sais. The Great Lady [whose(?)] horns [. . .] adorned with two stars;[8] N's lips [. . .] N has brought [. . .] N his powers; N has not given [. . .] TAKE AWAY MAGIC.

1. Read *wpty*, masc.; cf. the masc. suffix in *ꜥwꜣ.f* below.
2. English demands the 2nd person, as this is a vocative phrase.
3. Obscure; *mtš* (or *mt* with lake det.) at the end of 50*f* suggests that we have a superfluous *n* here and that we should read ⟨*m*⟩ *mtš n ḏbꜣw*, which I cannot translate.
4. *Mtš*.
5. For *ꜥšꜣt* read the participle *ꜥšꜣ*.
6. For *swt* 'danger' cf. *Pyr.* §652.
7. *Nḏd*, an unidentified part of the body.
8. Compare the Ḥatḥōr head in *JEA* 43, pl. 9, 3, which, however, shows five stars; one on each horn, one between the horns, and one at each ear.

Spell 847

VII, 51 O you who are satisfied with(?) [. . .] seasons of birds(?),[1] raise yourself[2] [in] your shape, for that is your body. O N, [you are] the Saviour-god [. . .] your shape. The Skilled One[3] has smitten you,[4] and you[5] are in your . . .[6] The Sole One asks for what belongs to(?) [the mother(?)] of the Bald One [. . .] his mansion, who passes the night and returns, and he apportions for N what is given. O N, you are he who gives [. . .] to N. O N, you are one who is in the protection of Him who comes crawling everywhere.[7] Speak your speech(?), N,[8] you shall not hide(?)[9] him; you shall hear it;[10] speak [. . .] who sees your pubes(?)[11] on the day of dividing the boundary [12] in the presence of the Lord of [. . .] [13] O Great One, O N [. . . cavern] [14] who goes forth in order to see between them. N has come into the Island of Fire, and great is N when [he] sees Osiris;[15] N is ennobled as a lord, and it is your [16] Great One who cries 'Woe!'. O man, O men(?)[17] who live on [. . .], N draws near to you [18] but your hand is not for N . . .[19] your face; so do not pass by, N.

[. . .] WHO ARE IN THEIR CAVERN[S], WHO ARE NOT IGNORANT OF THEIR SPELL.

1. Read *ỉtrw pꜣw*? Cf. *pꜣyw* 'birds', *Wb* I, 494, 15.
2. For *sw* read *ṯw*; cf. *ỉm.k* and *ḥꜥ.k* below.
3. *Ḥmt* with woman-det.
4. Again for *sw* read *ṯw*.
5. For *tṯw* read *ṯwt* + adverbial predicate?
6. *'Irṯw.*
7. *Ḫtḫt sp 2,* lit. 'throughout, throughout'.
8. Regarding *ry* as a miswriting of *rꜣ; r.k* is taken to be the enclitic reinforcing the imperative.
9. A guess; the det. has not been confirmed by de Buck. Note the rare enclitic negation *w* after *ỉmn.k.*
10. Not 'him', which would require *n.f.*
11. With *b(ꜣ)gt* 'pubes(?)' compare *bꜣgw* 'privy parts(?)', *CT* I, 141*g*, var. *bꜣgg* II, 162*ỉ*.
12. *'Ist*; probably identical with *ỉst* 'boundary-stone', 'landmark', *Concise Dict.* 29, but one cannot divide a boundary stone.
13. *Ḥnts.*
14. At the end of the lacuna restore *ṯpḥt,* cf. 51*x*.
15. For 'Osiris N' read simply 'Osiris'.
16. Plural.
17. *S* with god-det. could be a writing for 'man' deceased; *sy* as a plural of *s* is much more questionable, as the normal 'plural' of *s* is *rmṯt* 'men'. However, the singular is written 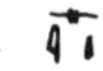 in *CT* V, 115*c* (T1Be).
18. Singular.

19. *Pḥꜣ ṯn* is incomprehensible.

Spell 848

O Horn, ferry across Him who is in his shrine; O you with eyes in the back of VII, 52
your head, beware [. . .] N when going forth with these peaceful ones of his, for your mouth is stopped up. O N, you are fully conscious,[1] there is no-one who will turn you back, for your horns are hidden(?), the . . . for Him who cuts off faces,[2] and *Npt* approves(?)[3] what was done in his presence.

Turn yourself about, that you may see the Great Provider who spends the night . . . with asses.[4] They are sorry for you, and they see ⟨ . . . ⟩[5] who sees by means of it. Do you speak to him, or have they heard? The Greyhaired Ones have taken away ⟨ . . . ⟩[6] in the early morning. Be happy, for he equips you; look out for(?) the dangerous one who copulates[7] with his mother. If you become unconscious, you will not be able to [settle(?)] yourself among the owners of names in the presence of Sia-Rēʿ on the day of dividing the shrine. N is benefitted(?)[8] by means of the horns of the giraffe(?).[9]

O N, you are the Bull of the *iḫmwt*-women, but not Anubis, nor the face of N.[10] You have come into being in the presence of the [. . .]-bird, and the [. . .] is the plain. N is indeed in the presence of Him who constructs his mansion in the presence of the Tribunal.[11] | It is Khopri who sees you and informs the guinea- 53
fowl[12] about you; also N knows the name of that on which you live among them.[13] He who lives on the dead is the [. . .] of the fly which spends the night and is born daily. O you who make offering to the Vigilant One, your horn is in your side, your horn is in you behind your face, for[14] your horn is what ferries over Him who is in your (*sic*) shrine.

TO APPROACH THE HORN WHICH IS FERRIED OVER IN THE BARK OF RĒʿ AND TO SEE THE SAME.[15]

1. *Ṯwt rḫ ṯw*, lit. 'you are one who knows yourself'.
2. The translation of 52*e* is doubtful, and *sḫꜣwtt* is quite obscure.
3. *Ṯmꜣ*; the translation 'approve' is a guess.
4. There is corruption here; *wy* after *sḏr* is meaningless, and the suffixes 3rd plural in 52*i* lack an antecedent, unless it be 'asses', which I find hard to believe.
5. An omission before *nwꜣ*, which is left in the air.
6. *Nḥm.n* lacks its object; yet another omission.
7. For as det. of *nhp* 'copulate' cf. *CT* VI, 191*a*.
8. For *iḫm* 'benefit(?)' cf. *Pyr.* §§1264; 1265.

9. Or is this a miswriting of *sr* 'ram'?

10. 52*t* is incomprehensible; not only does it seem meaningless in itself, but also it lacks any connection with the context. I have therefore rendered it just as it stands, as an apparently senseless interpolation.

11. Reading the last group as *ḏꜣḏꜣt*.

12. *N* is taken to be the initial of *nḥw* 'guinea-fowl'.

13. The frequent changes of person from 52*u* onward make it impossible to extract a coherent sense from the text, which appears to be much garbled. *Mm sp 2* at the end of 53*b* probably represents an adverbial use of the preposition.

14. Reading the negation-sign as the preposition *n*.

15. *My*.

Spell 849

N has come to you, O You who erase destruction, warden in charge of the ferry-boat 'She who turns back(?)', Lord of the gate of Him who . . .[1] him. It is he who opens in the presence of Sopd of the East.

N has come to you equipped as the great Hidden One who is in the corner of the Mansion of the Divine Images.

VII, 54 N has come to you pure as the black bird;[1] he is sadly devoid of offerings.

N has come to you so that you may open the gate for him and that you may throw open for him the great double door;[2] let N see Rēʿ in his shape and hear what is said to him, (namely) N. You shall bring Thoth to him in his shape and Seshat in her shape, and they shall bring to him this writing. it is his recognition, it is his being made a spirit in the Island of Fire, the Mighty One helps N by means of it, so that N may see those who are yonder among the blessed.

TO OPEN THE TOMB AND TO BRING WRITINGS TO A MAN IN THE REALM OF THE DEAD.

1. *Bsnw*.
2. Cf. *Pyr.* §416; *CT* VII, 243*h*.

Spell 850

O N, your mother comes to you; see, Nūt has come so that she may join your bones together, knit up your sinews, make your members firm, take away your corruption and take hold of your hand, so that you may live in your name of 'Living One'. May you live for ever!

NOT TO PERMIT A SPIRIT TO BE ALLOTTED TO WORK IN THE REALM OF THE DEAD.

Spell 851

[. . .] which issued from the Eye of Atum. N has issued thence [. . .] Horus. VII, 55
O N, you are the living uraeus which went forth [. . .] N at the bow of his bark which is in the Abyss.

Spell 852

[. . .] Horus who sowed[1] the land of his father, who divided linen(?) in the land [. . .] his phallus which the gods grasped, [whom][2] the dead fear when [they] see [N(?)[3] . . .] male. The . . .[4] who are all over the land see him; [. . .] VII, 56
with blood. May N live on the entrails [. . .] all the dead, male and female, when they see N. Down on your faces! [. . .] your souls.

1. For this writing of *sty* 'sow' cf. *CT* V, 366*a*.
2. Read *snḏ* [*n.*]*f mtw.*
3. Cf. de Buck, 55, n. 5*.
4. *ꜥḳnw-ḥr.*

Spell 853

'The god comes in peace',[1] say those who are in the full moon; they grant to him appearings in glory[2] with the red ones who are over the horizon-dwellers(?)[3] [. . .] they grant dignities [to] N, and N has assumed his *wrrt*-crown in com- VII, 57
pany with the Sole Lord at the birth of Orion; the doers of reverence(?)[4] are presented to N by those who dedicate white loaves.

TO BECOME A DIGNITARY.

1. Following *CT* III, 62*f*, cf. de Buck, 56, n. 4*.
2. Emending into *rdyn.sn n.f ḫꜥw* as III, 62*h.*
3. Conjecturally restoring as *dšrw ḥr(yw) ꜣḫtyw.*
4. Reading *sḳr.t(w) sꜣ*[w]*-tꜣ*; cf. *sꜣ-tꜣ* 'reverence(?)' *Concise Dict.* 211; *CT* VI, 158*j*.

Spell 854

N is Khopri, the lord(?) who [created] himself in [. . .] those modes of being of his [. . .] Sha in the Field of God. N will not be taken to the shambles [. . .], he has become [. . .] in front of [his(?)] seats more than(?) the gods. O N, may you [go forth(?)], may the sun appear over N [. . .].

TO BECOME KHOPRI.

Spell 855

VII, 58 Ho N! Take the water which is in the Eye of Horus, do not let go of it. O Horus who is N, I bring to you the bodily Eyes of Horus; seize them and join them to yourself.

O N, I bring to you those things which expand the heart of Seth; seize them.

Spell 856

O N, take the Eye of Horus; prevent him[1] from consuming it.

O N, take the Eye of Horus, the garment[2] of which the gods are afraid.

O N, Horus has attached his Eye to your forehead for you in its name of 'Great of Magic'.

O N, take that of which the gods are afraid just as they are afraid of Horus.

O N, take the Eye of Horus, against which Seth acted.

O N, take the Eye of Horus, the half of which he saw in the hand of Seth when he snatched it.

O N, take the white Eye of Horus which he rescued from Seth when he snatched it.

VII, 59 O N, take the Eye of Horus, some of which he[3] stole.

O N, let him be far from you.

O N, take the Eye of Horus which hung from the hands of his children.

O N, take the water which is in the Eye of Horus, do not let go[4] of it.

1. Seth.

2. *Tꜣtt* is identical with *tꜣytt,* translated as 'woven fabric' in *Pyr.* §2094; cf. also 64*a* below.

3. Seth.

4. Read *sfḫḫ.k* as 58*b*.

Spell 857

There is double satisfaction for the *ꜣms*-club of tamarisk which smites the disaffected, and he who controls[1] the land is powerful. You have the soul of Horus, you have the strength of Seth,[2] | may you control this land, O N, as Horus, may VII, 60
there be given to you the water which issued from the Eye of Horus, the name of which was made out as '*ꜣms*-club' when it was turned about[3] throughout the deserts under the fingers of Seth.

Raise yourself![4] May you protect N from those who would do anything evil against her. There is double satisfaction for the white Eye of Horus which smites the plebs, and N is protected from those who would do anything evil against her.[5] He will not live, (namely) him whom you[6] strike, his head will not be knit on.

1. Read *ỉtḥ*, cf. 60*a*; for the translation 'control' cf. *CT* V, 160*a*.
2. Sq10C adds *Ḥr ỉs* 'as Horus' at the end of 59*i*. Sq1Sq reads: 'you have the soul and you have the acuity of Horus, you have the strength of Seth, O N' and the two damaged texts follow it.
3. For *ỉnn* 'turn about' cf. *Pyr.* §214; *CT* I, 306*a*.
4. Addressed to the deceased; what follows is said to a god, probably Horus, who is prayed to protect N from harm.
5. Sq10C reads *m-ꜥ ḫt nb ỉḏwt* 'from anything evil'.
6. Feminine.

Spell 858[1]

O N, take the Eye of Horus, the water in which Thoth has seen.

Go behind me, N, for I am Isis. Osiris, take your son, put him within yourself. You are secluded(?) because of him. See, you have brought him to naught.[2] You shall love him,[3] | for he is Horus. Make the Eye of Horus come back to you. VII, 61

O N, do not let your face be blind(?), for I place it in your hand . . .[4] for you.

Ho N! Take the water which is in the Eye of Horus, fill your hand with the sceptre, provide yourself with it, and it will equip you as a god.

O N, take the finger of Seth which causes the white Eye of Horus to see.

O N, take the white Eye of Horus, which illumines the tip of the finger of Seth.

O N, take hold of his hand.

O N, take the hand of Nephthys, prevent her from putting[5] it on them.

O N, I give it to you; put it in your possession, for you are a Great One.[6]

Bring the two Eyes of Horus into the place of which they spoke.[7] Take them, (namely) what I give you, and put them on the ground for him.

I bring what expands the heart of Seth, I give what expands the heart of Seth, I give them to you, so seize them and join them to yourself.[8]

Ho N! I bring to you the two Eyes of Horus from the place ⟨where⟩ his body is.[9] I bring them to you; join them to yourself and bring them together. Horus has put them on N's feet that they may guide her, N, to the firmament, to Horus who is in the sky and to the great god, and they will protect N against all her foes.

62 O N, I bring to you the two Eyes of Horus which expand his heart; lay hold of them and join them to yourself, for they are complete for Horus who is N.[10]

1. This spell consists of sentences from part of the Ritual of Offering, cf. *Pyr. Suppl.* 1 ff. For cross-references to the Pyr. cf. de Buck's textual notes.

2. Emend *pš* into *šp* as *Pyr.* §45*b*. 'Him' refers to Seth both here and in the previous sentence.

3. Read *mr.k* ⟨*s*⟩*w*; the reference is now to Horus.

4. *Ndsḏsw.*

5. For *rdy.sn* read *rdy.s*; 62*s* (Spell 859) has the correct suffix. 61*o-p* is a dittograph of *m-n*.

6. For *wr.f* read *wr* without the suffix.

7. Cf. *Pyr.* §40+2 = *Suppl.* 1. *Ḫr* is taken to be a writing of *ḫr(w)* 'speak'. In my translation of the *Pyr.* I failed to understand §40+2, not recognizing that *b* stood for *bw* 'place', cf. 61*s*; my original version should be corrected accordingly.

8. The lacunae in *Pyr.* §§40+6 – 40+8 (*Suppl.* 1 – 2) can be restored from 61*w-x*, but 61*y* clearly differs somewhat from *Pyr.* §40+9.

9. A garbled version of *Pyr.* §69*b*. As the *CT* text stands the adverb *ỉm* is needed after *ḏt.f*.

10. 62*e-g* are a dittograph of *a-c*, except that the masc. suffix 2nd sing. is used in error. This is a woman's coffin.

Spell 859[1]

O N, take the water which is in the Eye of Horus; do not let go of it.[2]

O N, take the Eye of Horus, the water in which Thoth has seen.

O N, take the ⟨white⟩ Eye of Horus which illumines the tip of the finger of Seth; O N, grasp his hand; O N, do not let it be far from you. Be holy(?)[3] upon his fingers, and live, live![4]

O N, take the Eye of Horus which hung from the hands of his children.

O N, take the hand of Nephthys, prevent her from putting it on them.

A *pḏ-ꜥḥꜥ* mantlet: O Thoth, bring it thence, lay hold of it there. I give it to you; put it in your possession, for it is yours.[5]

I bring to ⟨you⟩ the two Eyes of Horus at the place of which they spoke.[6] Take them, (namely) what I give you, and put ⟨them⟩ on the ground for him.

O N, I bring to you the two Eyes of Horus, I bring what expands the heart of Seth, I give what expands the heart of Seth, I give them to you.

1. Again a series of extracts from the Ritual of Offering.
2. The plur. suffix *.sn* is used because *mw* 'water' is construed as a plural, as also in 58*b*.
3. Cf. *Pyr. Transl.* Utt. 71B, n. 1. The verb-form is hortative old perfective.
4. Hortative old perfectives.
5. Cf. op. cit. Utt. 71G, n. 3.
6. Cf. Spell 858, n. 7.

Spell 860

O ⟨N⟩, take the white Eye of Horus, [provide yourself with it[1]. .] them for you for VII, 63
ever and ever [. . .] who work evil against the Eye of Horus [. . .].

1. Restore *ḫtm ṯw ỉm.s.*

Spell 861

Horus has put gold on his Eye. O Horus who is N, take the Eye of Horus on which he has put gold, for it[1] is yours for ever.

O Horus who is N, I cause the two Eyes of Horus to go up for you to your face, I place for you the pupils which are in the Eyes of Horus in your head, I place for you their [. . .] on you in their name of the Two Great of Magic.

O Horus who is N, Horus gives you his Eye, and it will guide you on the path, your throat will be opened by means of it, and the water in it is yours for ever.[2]

1. A dittograph of *s(y)* after *n.k ỉm(y).*
2. Emend 63*r* to read *mw ỉm.s n.k ỉmy ḏt ḏt.* Cf. 63*j*, which is also slightly garbled.

Spell 862

O N, I have clad you in the Eye of Horus, which is the garment in which he clad VII, 64 his father, in which he clad Osiris; provide yourself with it, and it will equip you as a god. O N, may it belong to you, to you(?)[1] [. . .] as your protection.

O N, take the Eye of Horus, on account of which [he suffered(?)].[2]

Rejoice(?)[3] as a god when he sees ⟨himself⟩ made [more] hale [than(?)][4] the august gods with him, which[5] Horus granted to his father [. . . among] the spirits. Take [him], N, may he [make][6] your members hale [. . .] spirits.

If you awake [in peace(?)],[7] Ernūtet will awake; receive the Sole Town (*sic*) in peace [. . .] gods [. . .] Osiris; Horus will act at(?)[8] the Chapel [of Lower Egypt].[9] Take it, N, that it may ennoble you [among] the gods.

O N, I give [you the Eye of] Horus that it may adorn [you as] the primeval goddess who is in Pe and the Bright One who is in [Nekhen(?) . . .] you in the eyes of all the spirits when they look at you.

O N, receive this brightness of yours which is on you; may you live on the great Eye of Horus [which is in] the *pr-wr,* of the terror of which the gods are afraid.

O N, take the milk when he provides your flesh with milk[10] so that he may make you greater and your members mightier than the gods in this his name of 'Provider of Milk'.

65 O N, take the Eye of Horus over which he rejoiced(?),[11] which is in the chapel of Lower Egypt, for I give to you[12] your place in which your father Osiris was drowned. O N, be vindicated!

What is given to the god is his protection, and also (to) Isis with him; what Horus has granted to his father is a strengthening of his members. O N, take it as your protection so that your members may be strong.

O N, take all the clothing which is in the chapel of Lower Egypt, for the gods have given to you what is in it. It will cause you to appear from its egg,[13] it will place you as King of Upper and Lower Egypt, for you are Lord of its god. O N, be vindicated!

O N, take the Eye of Horus, prevent him from consuming it.[14]

O N, take the Eye of Horus which he has made hale.

O N, take the Eye of Horus which he gave to his father.

O N, take the Eye of Horus, that its perfume may be sweet on you![15]

O N, take these pieces of linen which are in the Mansion of Ptaḥ, which are great and mighty ⟨for⟩ this Ernūtet,[16] Mistress of dread, greatly majestic, so that she may cause your foes to fear and dread,[17] and so that you may be potent through her in her name of 'Linen', fine garments which he who is in the temple brings to the Eyeless One for everything which Horus has given to his father. Take it, N!

O N, take the Eye of Horus which combines your flesh and pulls together your members which are in the outer chamber of the *ṯnnt*-shrine; it will distinguish you above the gods in its name of 'She who presides over the *ṯnnt*-shrine'.

O N, take what is in the Mansion of Ptaḥ, for it will join you together; may 66
your limbs not be weak, may the langour of faintness not be in you. O N, take him, that he may make you divine and ward off your foes, for he will not forsake you[18] for ever. O N, be vindicated!

O N, take the Eye of Horus which is in the two chapels; it will ennoble you and it will adorn you in its name of 'Garment which is in the two chapels'.

1. De Buck, n. 3* quotes *Pyr.* §1068*c.*
2. Cf. de Buck, n. 5*.
3. Read *ḥꜥ n*[*.k*], imperative + reflexive dative?
4. The dependent pronoun *sw* has been elided between *mꜣ.f* and *swḏꜣ.f.* Restore the *r* of comparison after *swḏꜣ.f*?
5. *Rdy.n* appears to be a relative form with *swḏꜣ.f* as antecedent.
6. Read [*s*] *wḏꜣ.f.*
7. Restore as *m* [*ḥtp*] ?
8. For *rt* after *Ḥr* read *r* alone? The *t* is cross hatched and suspect. De Buck had to take the whole of this spell at second hand.
9. *Sic,* not 'conclave' here; in 65*h* it is a sacred building containing clothing. For the restoration 'of Lower Egypt' cf. 65*a.h.*
10. For the meaning of *bsꜣ* cf. *mw.k ỉpn bzꜣw* 'this milky fluid of yours', *Pyr.* §1873; the literal translation here is 'take the milk when he milk-provides your flesh'.
11. Cf. *Pyr.* §40 + 17 = *Suppl.* 3.
12. Read *rdy.n*⟨*.i*⟩ *n.k* as elsewhere. Note the eccentric use of the negation *n.*
13. 'It' refers to the 'chapel'; note also the writing of the dep. pron. 2nd masc. sing. as *tw* instead of *ṯw* as mostly elsewhere in this spell. The suffix in *m swḥt.s* 'from *its* egg' may be a slip, for 'from *the* egg' is more usual; furthermore, a chapel can hardly produce an egg.
14. Cf. *Pyr.* §40+11 = Suppl. 2; 'him' refers to Seth.
15. Read *nḏm sṯy.s r.k,* cf. de Buck, n. 6*.
16. Read *r Rnnwtt*; one *r* has been elided.
17. Corrupt; read *dy.s snḏ nr ḫftyw.k.*
18. Lit. 'run from under you'; the *t* in *bṯ(t)* is superfluous.

Spell 863

The dead are swallowed for you,[1] the cakes of your eating are freshly made(?);[2] N will live because of your offerings with me.[3] If N be hungry, Nekhbet will be hungry; if N be thirsty, Nekhbet will be thirsty. Food which the king gives (and also) Nūt, mother of the gods, for your provision . . .[4] perform rites for the vulture of whom the gods are afraid and whom the souls fear in N's abode(?), just as they are afraid of the Eye of Horus.

1. Cf. *ʿm mt* 'Swallower of the dead' who in BD waits in the Hall of Judgement to devour the rejected dead.

2. Cf. *snḫ̮* 'sich verjüngen', *Wb.* IV, 169, 7.

3. Read *ḥr.ỉ*; the second *r* is superfluous.

4. There is an omission after *ḥw.k*, of which plural strokes and suffix alone are preserved. I can make nothing of what immediately follows.

Spell 864 is fragmentary and yields no connected sense.

Spell 865

VII, 69 SPELL FOR A COFFIN. O *Rnn*(?), I make my coffin firm [. . .]. I am detained, I am the . . .[1]

1. *Ḏʿʿmw*; cf. *Pyr.* §§439; 670; 671; 692; 693.

Spell 866

70 TO GIVE A MAN POWER OVER [. . .]. The doors of the sky are opened for Rēʿ, the doors [of the firmament][1] are thrown open for Thoth, so that they may bring to me [. . .] he gives me power over [. . .] my fathers [. . .] for women
71 [. . .].| The Great One will say [. . .] West, having bathed in the waters of the horizon. See, [it is well with me(?)][2] in the Island of Fire. Let him know my names;[3] he does not know the place where we are. Go down into [. . .] you will govern with your rod, you will rule over the Unwearying Stars; the abode of the god [. . .].

72 I am the helmsman of Rēʿ | when he rows therein [. . .] scorched [. . .]. I am [. . .] within the house of his dignity. I am the Great One at the head of the Souls of Ōn, and no god has power to do what I do. I am [. . .] Great One [. . .] god. The doors of Osiris are opened for me, the doors of the firmament are thrown open for me.

O Thoth, O Nile-god [. . .] in this your name of 'He who wounds the land'. Water is given to me, and I have power over it like the robber-god, namely he who

rebelled on the day of the storm of the Two Lands | [. . . Thoth(?)] has power 73
over him who would [harm(?)] him.[4]

1. Restore *ḳbḥw,* cf. 72*i.*
2. Restore *ꜣḫ n.ỉ*?
3. Read *rdy* (rare imperative) *rḫ.f* with S2 Chass.
4. Cf. de Buck, 73, nn. 1*. 2*.

Spells 867 – 870 are fragmentary.

Spell 871

[. . .]. TO BECOME AN IBIS. I am an ibis [. . .], I have come [. | .] red. I am VII, 76
the . . .[1] [. . .] hidden paths[2] [on which(?)] a god lives [. . .] strewing its fire.

1. *Ḥr* [*r*] *wt.*
2. Restore as *wꜣwt.*

Spells 872 and 873 are fragmentary. 873 is undoubtedly concerned with the identification of the deceased with the snake-god Neḥebkau, and thus closely related to Spells 85 – 87. A conjectural restoration of 873 suggests that it was very similar to Spell 86.

Spell 874

[. . .] the great Inert One who dwells in [. . .] in peace – so says [Ḥatḥōr(?)
who dwells in the] beautiful [desert].[1] | She has come favouring me[2] [. . .] in VII, 79
the West [. . .]. She has loosed Osiris who dwells in the beautiful desert from her dress,[3] she has heaped up the oblations of those who are attached to her, consisting of natron and incense, in accordance with the word of the Great One who presides over the West and who dwells in the beautiful desert. Indeed, my
living soul will be announced | when it goes forth on earth and while it is there[4] 80
it will copulate and stride forth among men – [so says][5] Osiris and also so say the gods. It is permitted that I return to[6] my living soul when it goes forth on earth and while it is among men, and it will copulate and stride forth – so say [the gods].[7]

1. S2C*b* shows that the name of a goddess followed *ỉt ỉn,* and the space suits *Ḥwt-ḥr*; cf. the reference to the *ṯstn*-dress in 79*c,* which in Spells 483, 484 and 486 is associated with Ḥatḥōr; it belongs to Nūt in *Pyr.* §1426, and to Shesmetet in *CT* Spell 485. Nūt is ruled out here on the grounds of occupying too little space, and Shesmētet seems unlikely. For the restoration of what follows cf. 79*c.f.*

2. Read *ỉy.n.s* [*ḥr*] *ḥst.ỉ*?

3. *S* at the beginning of 79*d* should surely be attached to the preceding *ṯstn,* as de Buck has suspected in his n. 4*.

4. *Prt.f* and *wnnt.f* are *sḏmt.f* forms.

5. Restoring *ỉ* [*.ỉn*] *Wsyr.*

6. S2C*b* omits *r.*

7. Reading *ỉn.sn* [*nṯrw*] in S1C.

Spell 875

VII, 81 I am a noble [. . . I(?)] live [. . .], I am the Double Bull(?) [. . .] | I live on
[. . .] god [. . .] in the Netherworld according to your(?)[1] word, and I have
life in accordance with what was commanded. The gate in the sky(?) is set open
for me, I open the caverns [. . .], the primeval ones are united for me(?),[2]
[. . .] are joined together for me [. . .], the ferry-boat is made ready for me,
the ropes are cast off(?)[3] for me, I have traversed the lands, I have ferried across,
82 I have knotted [. . .] the celestial kine(?) [. . .] my majesty is upon me,| be-
cause I am the great soul[4] of Osiris [. . .] he has power over [. . .] in accord-
ance with the word of the gods. I am [announced(?)],[5] and I go out into the
day in my living shape among [the patricians, the sun-folk(?)][6] and the plebs.
I nourish [. . .] I have gone out [. . .] as the Double Lion [. . .] the god who
83 rebelled [. . . with(?)] me. | I [go out(?)] seeing [Osiris], I [recite(?) his] word
[to] the judges. [. . . has caused] the word [to enter(?)] for me Him whose
throat is constricted, [because][7] I am [. . .] who is sent(?) [to] me – [so
says(?)][8] Khopri. I live, I [live on(?)[9] . . .], I am(?) [. . .], I live as Rēʿ lives
84 every day, and it is Nu [. . .]. | I set my raging among [. . . the dread] of me
[and the terror][10] of me(?) are in those who dwell in the [Netherworld(?)] in
this my dignity of Lord. I am [. . . the soul of Osiris . . .] by day – so says
Thoth who presides over my mansion [. . .] for me. My water-courses [. . .]
Great One [. . .] striking power [. . .] shall not take away [. . .] acts as my
85 protection [. . .] those who dwell in [the Netherworld(?) . . .]. | I ferry across
[. . .] the ferry-boat is made ready for me [. . .].

1. Plural; cf. de Buck, 81, n. 1*.

2. Reading *smꜣw n.ỉ pꜣwtyw*; cf. de Buck, nn. 3* – 5*.
3. *Sb,* lit. 'sent out'.
4. S2C^{b} has an unexplained [hieroglyph] before *bꜣ*.
5. Reading [*ḥ*] *ww.ỉ*.
6. Restoring *ḥnmmt* alone in the left-hand column; there is not enough space for *pꜥt*; this latter, however, may well have stood in S2C^{b}.
7. Read [*n n*] *tt*.
8. The space is right for the restoration *ỉ.ỉn*.
9. Cf. de Buck, 83, n. 1*; *m* seems likely.
10. Cf. de Buck, 84, n. 1*. I suggest restoring *nrw.ỉ* after [*šꜥt*].

Spell 876

TO MAKE OSIRIS'S NECK FIRM FOR HIM. Hail to you, my father Osiris Onnophris! I have come so that I may protect you, that I may make [your] members comfortable for you, that I may knit on [your face for you(?)],[1] | that I may make VII, 86
your [neck firm for] you, that I may make your flesh strong, that [I may cause] your skin [to be permanent(?)[2] . . . your neck] will be made firm [. . .] for Rēꜥ-Atum.

Take [. . .] Nūt, they are Isis and Nephthys [. . .] they will be pleased. [They] have received[3] their garments, they have heaped up [the oblations of those who are attached to them(?),[4] . . .], they have removed(?) their [. . .].|
The god [. . .] good, [your flesh(?)][5] is hale, [. . .] good, [your flesh(?)] is 87
hale [. . .] Rēꜥ-Atum in the place in which [your] brother [Seth] set you [. . .] at(?) the riparian land, [whom Horus smote(?)][6] at the back-land of [ꜥAndjet[7] . . .] him.

[Osiris] Onnophris stands up[8] [. . .] who is in charge of [. . .], whom I detain among(?) your successors(?).[9] [This] shape of mine(?)[10] which is in
[. . .] who are in [. | . .] your [brother] Seth [. . .] your mother Nūt [. . .] 88
the land in [. . . you(?) are born . . .[11] and fashioned [. . .] like Rēꜥ every day.

Your mother Nūt puts [her hands on you(?)[12] . . .] like Rēꜥ every day.

Your mother Nūt puts her hands on you [. . .] path [. . .] like Rēꜥ every day.

Row[13] in [. . | .] like Rēꜥ every day. 89

[May you] cross the [sky . . .] your [mother] Nūt, may you [grasp(?) . . .] like Rēꜥ every day.

[. . . like] Rēꜥ every day.

[. . .] as the second of Rēꜥ, the companion [of Thoth(?). You(?)] have purity [. . .] the Great City, may you moor at the plain of [the pure place of(?)] [14] the sky [. . .] like Rēʿ every day.

VII, 90 [. . .] as your [mother] Nūt [. . .] the Great Lady who dwells in [. . .] Sothis [sharp][15] of horns, high of disk, . . . [16] [. . . who dwells in Ōn][17] [. . .] like Rēʿ every day. May she guide you on the path [of the living] like Rēʿ every day.

1. Cf. de Buck, 85, nn. 4*. 5*. There is space for *n.k* in 52c^a but not in S2C^b.
2. Reading *sw3*[*ḥ.i*] *inm.k.*
3. Cf. de Buck, 86, n. 4*.
4. Restored from 79*d*, cf. de Buck, n. 5*.
5. Restoring *ḥ*[*ʿw.k*] after *w3ḏ.*
6. Restoring at conjecture *ḥ*[*w.n Ḥr*]; the space seems about right, and this restoration puts two birds at the places noted by de Buck, 87, n. 2*.
7. Cf. de Buck, n. 3*.
8. The space in the lacuna after *ʿḥʿ* is adequate for 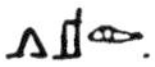.
9. Reading *ḥnḥn.i m-*[*m*] *styw.k.*
10. The sign at the beginning of 87*g* could read either *im* 'shape' or *gs* 'side'. The trace of a bird-sign seen by de Buck, n. 2*, could perhaps be the *w* of *pw.*
11. Cf. de Buck, 88, n. 2*. The *ḥḥ*-sign after *ms*[*.k(?)*] is obscure.
12. Cf. 88*f.* 88*e* only in S2C^b; it reads '[. . .] like Rēʿ every day'
13. Probably imperative with reflexive dative.
14. Cf. de Buck, 89, nn. 7*. 8*.
15. Restoring *spdwt.*
16. *Ḫ3sf,* here hardly 'krankhaften Zustand', *Wb.* III, 236, 3.
17. Cf. de Buck, 90, n. 4*.

Spells 877 and 878 are fragmentary; the former refers to 'the movements of Shu'.

Spell 879

VII, 91 O you who set Rēʿ in Ōn, the Beauteous One of Rēʿ has made contentment for me,[1] and he[2] will not turn aside from what he says. The fire scorches [Babi(?)] with what issued from his Eye.[3] Have power over water.

1. Cf. de Buck, n. 6*.
2. Cf. de Buck, n. 7* He favours *n* rather than *f* after *nwḏ,* but the verb needs a subject, which as the text stands can hardly be other than *.f.* What function *n* could have here is not clear to me.
3. Presumably of Rēʿ.

Spell 880 is fragmentary.

Spell 881

NOT TO TAKE A MAN'S [. . .] FROM HIM IN THE REALM OF THE DEAD. My bones VII, 92
are broken [. . .].

Spell 882

I am the twilight on the shoulders of the Great One, and I have come so that I VII, 93
may travel the sky, for I have traversed the twilight of the flashing Rēʿ; I am he who is behind those two fingers of his [. . .].[1] There is issued the announcement(?)[2] which made me angry(?)[3] with Shu. I have climbed on to . . . ,[4] I have [extended(?)][5] my foot to the fire which shines[6] in the East. The potters' wheels are broken, I reveal the disk on his [. . .] which are on my hands, and I will create him who should go forth at this time to the rays(?) of my sun(?), my sole knot being on me.[7] Horus secures the rope of Seth when he ferries him across, and see, my bark is placed on ⟨those who⟩ are yonder(?).[8]

1. 93*e* looks like a dittograph of *pyw* in 93*d*.
2. *Ḥwt; wdt* 'command' is also a possibility.
3. Lit. perhaps 'which made anger for me'.
4. *Ḳnḳn . . . ;* cf. *ḳnḳnt, CT* V, 352, I; 358, XXI.
5. Restore [*ḏ3*]*.n.ỉ*?
6. For *wpš* 'shine' cf. *Pyr.* §1328.
7. The translation of 93*l* is highly speculative.
8. The latter part of 93*o* seems corrupt. Perhaps we should read *dy tp ntyw ỉm.*

Spells 883 and 884 are fragmentary.

Spell 885[1]

TO DRIVE OFF A SNAKE. Rēʿ arises with his uraeus upon him, Mafdet[2] leaps at the neck of the *'In-dy.f*-snake.

[One face] falls on another,[3] the bull-snake falls to the *sḏḥ*-snake – and *vice versa.*[4]

[. . .] his father Atum; the bull-snake falls to the *sḏḥ*-snake – and *vice versa.*

O fat one of the earth, my heart is yonder, my heart is yonder.

VII, 95 O you who are all-pervading, this hand of mine[5] is what has come upon you. Fall, you snake which issued from ⟨ . . . ⟩[6] which Atum has bitten.[7]

. . . the viper is in the sky.[8]

The head of the bull is broken[9] again because of you . . .[10]

O *ttw*-snake, rise up(?); [11] you shall not move, your actions(?) [12] shall be annulled.

O soul of my *moringa*-tree [. . .] inert.

. . . Get back, you attacker-snake; I am an attacker[-snake. The viper] is in the sky and Horus is on earth. [13]

O monster, lie down;[14] O bull-snake, crawl away, for I am he who will survive. The knife[15] goes out [against it], it has [swallowed] you.

O poison, O monster, die! [16] O . . .[17] I have woven(?) the White Crown in Khem; fall down, crawl away on both sides of the path.

Beware, O blind one, for your mother Nūt sees you; fall down, crawl away! Someone coils himself up[18] because of reconciliation[19] . . .[20]

O lion, be off! [21] [Beware] of the Great Door! You shall [not] [22] draw near, . . . ,[23] you monster which are in . . . ;[24] crawl away over the Abyss!

96 O Horus [who is on] earth [25] ⟨ . . . ⟩. O monster, crawl away, slide into the earth, for I have said this against you.

O monster, lie down! [26] Your face is pierced,[27] and [my] odour is [against] you,[28] for I prophesy what he will want in Ōn.

. . . red ochre;[29] O monster, lie down! I am sated, and I say: ‘I am the [. . .]-snake which came forth from the *fnṯ*-snake in your mother’s house’.

O *Wnty*, O sailor(?), [30] the garments are put in the Day-bark. How honoured is he who has done this! As for the attacker, I have devoured him piecemeal(?). [31] The knife falls and his power is assaulted(?).[32] Where indeed is he who created a storm and started a fire?[33] See, it is extinguished.

O you who are fair of face,[34] what I shave is my cheeks.[35] O you who sit on the horns of the earth-god,[36] fell for me every snake which is in this house, and in this [room] in which I am. As for you who today will not fell every snake, etc., for me, I will indeed tell this name of yours to her who will act, who bears her throwstick.[37] . . . [38]

97 The fields are demolished, the caverns are burst open(?)[39] [on(?)] the arms of the spirits.

Down on your [40] faces, the two of you! Be off! [41] Beware! Be off! Your fate(?)[42] is against you, you *nt*(?)-animal.

O . . . ,[43] for what purpose have you come here? O goddess, you shall bring(?) your eye-trouble(?)[44] – and *vice versa* – until you have passed by this house of . . .[45]

Rēʿ is bitten by the *nʿw*-snake – and *vice versa* – . . .[46]

Get back! The mounds are flattened(?),[47] the caverns are burst open(?).

O son of Rēʿ-Atum, come, for I am seen; even if you have not come(?),[48] I am seen in the House of Gold, my pillar-amulets are of turquoise, my cavern is (that of) Selḳet, the snake is in my hand and cannot bite me,[49] and so forth – two *sf*-cakes.

O . . . ,[50] get far away from me, for I am one who attacks[51] with his Eye, who is in his mansion.

O you who are distinguished, dwelling in the Mansion of Fire, the *nʿw*-snake is within the sacred things.

O Shu, the earth is against you; the son-of-earth-snake is against you.

O Who-is-on-his-bush-snake, he has filled your mouth with earth.

Get back, you necklace-snake, the bush is green; O creeping-snake, the *sḫm*-field is green, | and your teeth are broken. 98

The poison of him who would harm you is weak.

Plough into the earth,[52] for [I] am far away.

One face falls on another; the Great One has seen the meal which issued from him who is on earth, which he has swallowed.[53] The bull-snake falls to the *sḏḥ*-snake – and *vice versa*. The fire goes forth against the earth-god;[54] be consumed, O Neḥebkau.

Fall, O son-of-earth-snake, on [your] back(?).[55] O monster, fall, lie down,[56] crawl away!

Rēʿ is bitten by the *nʿw*-snake – and *vice versa*. The bull-snake falls to the *sḏḥ*-snake[57] – and *vice versa*. Fall down, crawl away! . . .[58]

O great bull-snake, curl yourself into your coil, for your winding is brought to you for you.

1. This spell consists of disconnected sentences taken from a collection of spells against snakes, many from the Pyr., and mostly garbled, so that there is no connected sense to be obtained. For the majority of references to the Pyr. see de Buck's notes, though a few have been added below. In the translations the most corrupt and unintelligible passages have been given footnote references only.

2. Written *m3dt* with skin-det. It is the animal, perhaps a mongoose, which is envisaged here rather than the divinity.

3. I.e. glance crosses glance, cf. *Pyr. Transl.* Utt. 228, n. 1.

4. This bull-snake spell recurs below in 94*v*; 98*f.l.*

5. At the beginning of 95*a* read *ḥtḥt,* lit. 'throughout', as a vocative. *N* between *ḥtḥt* and *ḏryt* 'hand' is due to a recollection of *nḏr* 'seize' and is to be disregarded.

6. After *pr m* the source whence the snake came is omitted; the horizontal sign of de Buck, n. 2* is the sole survivor of what should have stood there.

7. Cf. *Pyr.* §425*a.*

8. 95*c.d* are untranslatable except for *ḏt r pt* at the end. For 95*c* cf. *Pyr.* §§428*a*; 2256 (*Suppl.* 77), and with 95*d* compare *Pyr.* §2261 (*Suppl.* 78).

9. Read *sḏ*; cf. *sḏt* 'fire' in 98*g.*

10. From here to the end of 95*i* the text is altogether corrupt. With 95*f* compare *Pyr.* §684*b,* and with 95*g* compare *Pyr.* §2259 (Suppl. 78). 95*h* has an echo of *Pyr.* §2260 (loc. cit.)

11. 95*j*. For *ṯs* 'rise up' cf. *CT* VI, 302*o*; 332*r.*

12. Cf. *Wb.* III, 179, 4–5.

13. 95*l* is a misinterpretation of the opening words of *Pyr.* Utt. 376; the rest of the spell is omitted. The untranslatable *iḫ3stnr* of 95*m* represents the opening of *Pyr.* Utt. 282. For the restorations cf. de Buck, n. 18* (on p. 92). *Ḥr* in *ḥr t3* (95*n*) is oddly written.

14. Read *hyw sḏr,* cf. Pyr. §443*c*; for this writing of *sḏr* see also 96*c.e*; 98*j.*

15. Read *nm* 'knife', corrupted here into *ỉnm* 'skin', cf. *Pyr.* §431*a.*

16. Hortative old perfective.

17. *Nʿwty ỉty.*

18. Read *ʿnn sw ʿnnt,* cf. *Pyr.* §425*b.*

19. Cf. *Pyr.* §§26*e*; 488*a.*

20. 95*w.*

21. Cf. Pyr. §428*b.*

22. Restoring the negation *n* in the lacuna.

23. *'Ikn.*

24. *N3 nnt.*

25. Cf. 95*n.* The context of this invocation of Horus has been omitted.

26. Read *sḏr*; cf. n. 14 above.

27. Reading *ḥr.k tḫn*; the det. of *tḫn* derives from *tḫn* 'ibis'.

28. Read *ỉw sṯ*[.*ỉ r.*]*k*; there is an unnecessary *ỉ* before *st.*

29. For *dd* 'red ochre' cf. Harris, *Minerals,* 155. The words preceding it are unintelligible.

30. Cf. *Pyr.* §661*b.c.*

31. In Pyr. 1772*c tkkt* has a bee- or wasp-det., and is translated by me as 'hornet'. Here, however, *tkkt* seems rather to belong to *wnm.ỉ sw,* despite the lack of concord of gender, and one can hardly devour a stinging insect. The last group reads *mwmw* 'piecemeal(?)'.

32. For *mds* 'knife cf. *Pyr.* §1999*c*; for *ỉd* 'assault(?)' cf. *CT* III, 365*b*; 387*d. 3t* 'power is determined with a burning lamp.

33. Read *wd sḏt* or *wd ḫt.*

34. Feminine.

35. Determined with three door-signs! The relevance of this remark is not obvious.

36. *3kr.*

37. Not 'who is on her throwstick', which makes no sense, but 'on whom is a throwstick', i.e. bearing it.

38. 96*t-u* consists of disjointed phrases which yield no coherent sense.
39. *Ḥmr*; the verb is not recorded and the translation is a guess.
40. For *.f* read *.k*; this is a direct order.
41. Cf. 95*x*.
42. *'Iskt*; the translation is a guess.
43. *Swḥ*.
44. *Rpwt* is fem., but is referred to by a masc. suffix in *in.k* unless, as is quite possible in this text, the connection is apparent only. For *bꜣẖt* cf. *bꜣẖ* 'a disorder of the eye', *Wb*. I, 422, 7.
45. *Dygg*.
46. I can make nothing of 97*h*.
47. Lit. 'wide', as a mound would be if squashed flat.
48. Something has been omitted after *tm.ỉn.k*, which itself looks strange; possibly we should emend into *tm.n.k i*[*w*].
49. Emend as *n psḥ*⟨*.n.f*⟩ *wỉ*.
50. A fantastic name *ỉbhꜣhty*.
51. For *ỉk* 'attack' cf. *Pyr*. §§806*b*; 959*a.b*.
52. In *Pyr*. §670*c nny* 'the wandering snake' is addressed.
53. *ʿmʿ.n.f* presumably refers to the meal; in strict concord of gender it should have read *ʿmʿt.n.f*.
54. Read *pr sḏt r ꜣk*⟨*r*⟩.
55. Lit. 'on [your] lower spine'.
56. Read *sḏr*; cf. n. 14 above.
57. Written *sḥ* in error.
58. *Rnpw* of 98*m* and all of 98*n* yield no coherent sense.

Spell 886

The doors of the sky are opened for the Double Lion, the doors of the [firmament are thrown open . . .] having power over water in the realm of the dead through the word of those gods whose coming into being [was primeval].[1] [. . .].

1. in 98*t*, after *ỉpw* restore .

Spell 887

I have come from Pe, I have gone down into Dep, [I] am a knife, my members VII,99
are of iron, I will be exalted like [Nūt(?)], I will be enduring like Ḥatḥōr, my [arms] will be strong like [. . .], I will look at the Great Lady, a path to the Field of [. . .] is prepared for me, I will fortify him whose horn is pulled off, I

will clothe [. . .], I will see the fields, I(?) will regard him who pulled Osiris apart[1] [. . .]. O great Wakeful One, beware of the two mansions of Sokar, for I am this one whom he sought; life is allotted [to me[2] . . .].

1. The suffix *.f* in *mꜣ.f* seems out of place; emend into *mꜣ.ỉ n fd Wsyr*(?).
2. Restoring as *ỉp*[*n.ỉ*] *ʿnḫ*. The restoration of the rest of 99*p* is uncertain.

Spell 888

To be buried in the necropolis. O *Rrw*, you who mount up into the West on [the
throne(?)] of the doors of him who is smaller than(?) them of darkness, at whom
the Westerners are limp with dread(?)[1] because of the sound of thunder when he
VII, 100 goes forth from [. . .] you. | You are happy when he is bound, Rēʿ rejoices at it
when he is stretched out; there is no foe of yours in the sky, and indeed the sky
will not contend against you. Your will is done . . .[2] the king is on the water. Do
not come or oppose the movements of Rēʿ in his broad hall.[3] While Rēʿ is in [his]
broad hall [. . .] paths, the steering-oars are broken.[4] O Lord of lords, I am
Ndd[5] who establishes(?) Rēʿ within the Mansion of the Sacred Images, and I
will not be given over to ʿApep; there is no-one whom I will give over to ʿApep.

1. For *nhd* 'dread(?)' cf. *CT* IV, 21*d*.
2. I do not understand *nw ỉrr.k r ỉb.k*, and the nexus of *nswt ḥr mw* in 100*f* with what precedes and follows is quite obscure.
3. Reading the last word of 100g as *wsḫt.f*.
4. We have here a kind of dittograph; *swꜣ* 'break' is followed by *swꜣ* 'pass'. The former is clearly what is meant.
5. According to *Wb*. II, 369, 1 the *ndd* are foes of the sun-god, but that meaning can hardly apply here.

Spell 889[1]

Woe to you, you who are on your belly in front of the Two Companions; see, I take the fire(?) of Thoth(?)[2] in the darkness of the evildoers, which is done against the . . .[3] There are driven off your . . .[4] from upon the Eye of Horus, (and also) those who come from the confederacy of the Outcast on those nights when hearts are judged.

1. Another snake-spell.

2. The words following *ỉṯ.ỉ* in 100*p* are obscure, but there is certainly a reference to fire. The last word could read *tḫ* = 'Thoth', cf. *Wb.* 325, 17.

3. *ʾIḫmw.*

4. *Trwt.*

Spell 890

I am he who sought her who is far away on the day of the festival of red linen[1] in VII,101
the early morning. O Bull [. . .].[2]

1. 101*c* is obscure, and the reading of the last group is doubtful; *p* preceding Ol suggests that the writer was thinking of the town of Pe, which makes no sense here. I would emend 101*c-d* into *nw* ⟨*n*⟩ *rꜥ n ḥb ỉns.*

2. The rest of the spell is lost.

Spell 891

TO DRIVE AWAY THOSE WHO WOULD CUT OFF [. . .]. Raise yourselves, O you who are in your caverns; beware of me, you gods. I have come and I am great, I seek(?) and I am seen. I have seen the holy things of Anubis, and I have come so that I may hear the voice of the monster, I [have] broken the bonds of [. . .], I am cleansed in the Lake of the Netherworld in the place where you were a spirit;[1] your perfume was made by him who was honoured in [. . .] the praised one. It is
he of the braided lock who will guide you[2] into the place where I am – so says(?) VII,102
he who hearkens to me.[3] | You shall break [. . .] your protection against him shall be made for you. Shout against(?)[4] this one whom he hates; he will see the primeval one who is in [. . .].[5] It means that he will break him,[6] and you shall see the secret things.

What is it against me? What can I do?[7]

1. There seems to be some confusion in the pronouns of this spell which I cannot unravel; who for example is 'you' (sing.)?

2. Reading *ỉn ḥnskt(y) sšm.f ṯn.* Who are the beings addressed as 'you' (plur.)?

3. Reading 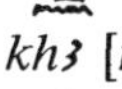 *smt r.ỉ*, cf. de Buck, n. 11*.

4. Reading *khȝ* [*r*] *nw msḏ.f* with [*r*] displaced, cf. de Buck, n. 2*.

5. The trace after *ỉmy* does not suit *kȝr* 'shrine'.

6. Restore as *swȝ*; there is a dittograph of the pronoun *sw*.

7. *Sšst* is a var. of *ỉšst*; Gilula, *JEA* 62, 175, reads *sšst pwỉ* (= *pw wỉ*) and translates as 'What am I?', but to my mind this question does not suit the context. I suggest that is

intrusive, through confusion with *wỉ*, and that we should read 102*g* as 'What is it against me?', *ỉr.ỉ m* 'What can I do?' which follows makes a natural continuation of this question.

Spell 892

You[1] will find [. . .] who puts out fire, whose hinder parts [are made hale(?)].[2]
What was said by the Potent One: O you[3] who see my langour, the robed ones
lament(?) you; I [will][4] take away this hair which is on her (*sic*) neck and the
hair which is on her lips, and she will tear out her hair(?) for me,[5] which will be
tied on your [neck] for you.[6] You [shall cause(?)][7] a covering of your face, lest
VII, 103 those who are on their faces should hear and cover you with the hair [of(?) . . .]
your hand on me. Cover your face, for I will cover you with my skin, and you
shall see the great hidden lady, for my name is on the clothing which the gods
have given. It means that I have seen your[8] Great One, for I am Gēb, uniquely
alone; I am [spiritualized] in my dignity. I open the gates of Gēb, I kiss her who
rebelled(?) against the Great Ones, I [. . .] my two *tḫbt*-birds which are alive in
the West. I live on air, I govern those who are in the full moon(?)[9] on the bark of
Khopri, and I have given orders to the crew of Rēꜥ-Atum in the evening.

1. Masc. sing.
2. Conjecturally restoring *s*[*wꜣḏ*]*w*.
3. Fem. sing.
4. Cf. de Buck, n. 8*.
5. 102*p* is certainly corrupt; read *fdd.s šn.s n.ỉ*?
6. Masc. sing.
7. Restoring [*dy.kꜣ*].*k*. The space is about right; perhaps a little short.
8. Plural.
9. Corrupt for *ỉꜥḥ wr*?

Spell 893 consists only of a broken rubric.

Spell 894

VII, 104 SPELL FOR NOT EATING FAECES IN THE REALM OF THE DEAD. Ho N! You have
your power among the gods, O N, in life in front of one like him(?) yonder.

A boon which the king grants, and also Thoth and the great gods who are in Ōn; a meal is prepared for you[1] in accordance with the writing which Thoth made for Osiris in the scriptorium of the god.[2]

Hands are what they give ⟨to⟩ Gēb,[3] and Plenty is he who makes the king's offering pure, and pure is N's utterance for N (*sic*).

1. So S5C; S14C reads: 'A boon which the king grants, and also Thoth, the Conclaves of Upper and Lower Egypt and the Great Ennead which is in Ōn; they prepare a meal for you'.
2. Var. S14C: 'in accordance with the writing which Thoth placed in the scriptorium of the god when she (the deceased) went to the sky among the gods – an invocation-offering for N's double'. This text confines itself to the developed *ḥtp-dy-nswt* formula.
3. Read *dy.sn ⟨n⟩ Gb.*

Spell 895

SPELL FOR NOT GOING UPSIDE DOWN. How cold is this water of yours here,[1] O N, which went up to your father, which went up to Gēb, which went up to Horus, and which went up to Osiris; you are refreshed possessing it.

I have come and I bring to you the Eye [of Horus], and you are refreshed possessing it . . .[2] | Take the efflux which issued from you, for your heart will not be inert, possessing it. See, see! Be young, be young![3] in this your name of VII, 105
Him who is in cold water. Horus has felled your foes in your presence; take what comes forth at the voice to you[4] – an invocation-offering of bread and beer, oxen and fowl, for N.

1. For the combination *pw nn,* cf. *Pyr.* §§167 ff.
2. Cf. de Buck, nn. 5*; 7*; 8*.
3. Hortative old perfectives.
4. Cf. *Pyr. Transl.* Utt. 32, n. 1.

Spell 896

SPELL FOR NOT DYING A SECOND TIME IN THE REALM OF THE DEAD. Ho N! If every good thing belongs to Osiris, every good thing will belong to N before all the gods.

Spell 897

Unguent with N. Ointment, where are you?[1] O you who should be on the brow, where are you?

If I be on the brow of Horus, I will be on N's brow, vindicating him and felling his foes in(?)[2] the realm of the dead.

Ho N! You have your heart in your body, N.

1. Cf. *Pyr. Transl.* Utt. 77, of which this is a garbled version.
2. *'Iw* before *ẖrt-nṯr* is either corrupt for the preposition *m* or the start of a new clause which has not been completed.

Spells 898 and 899 are lost except for odd fragments.

Spell 900

VII, 107 I am the maiden [. . .] and enduring, who fought Seth and ⟨his⟩ confederacy.

Spell 901

SPELL FOR PROCEEDING TO THE GATES (AND TO) [THOSE WHO ARE IN CHARGE OF THE GATES][1] OF THE TOMB. [. . .] the knife is sharp. There shall be no repelling on my part with a knife . . . who will not repel them by means of it. Do
VII, 108 not come down upon me, for [I am] vigilant [. . .].[2] | ⌜Apep is taken and darkness(?) is [. . .] by means of it. [. . .] the chest of him who is protected(?) and my father annuls(?) the reckoning of the place.[3]

The first room. The secret room of her who possesses beer-jars(?)[4] before the god.[5]

The second [room]. The room of . . . ,[6] Mistress of the blessed.

The [third] room. The room of the Great Lady, mistress of the shrine, whom Rēꜥ knows in his bark.

The fourth room. The room of the fiery one, Lady of punishment(?), the protectress who gives bread to those who are on [their bellies(?)].

The fifth room. The room of the Lady of life, mistress of provisions, who succoured the gods.

The sixth room. The room of Maꜥet(?), Lady of the House of the horizon, whom Rēꜥ knows in his name [of . . .].

The seventh room. The room of Her who is hidden(?), mistress of paths, who guides Horus and Seth when the bark passes by.

1. Restoring 901*l* as *ỉr[yw ꜥrr]wt ḥꜣt*.
2. I do not understand 107*r*.

3. 108*a-b* are difficult and the translation is provisional. *Ḫwy* in 108*b* looks like a passive participle, and after *ḥḏ* we should read *ỉt.ỉ*, in accord with 107*n.p.*

4. Or 'knives'? The papyrus-roll determinative suits neither interpretation.

5. The house-sign after *nṯr* is employed here regularly as a determinative of the entire clause.

6. I cannot read the first sign in . . . *sbt.*

Spell 902

The hand is washed, the hand is waved.[1] O *Hꜣrwty* [. . .]. Are you in the sky or VII, 109
on earth when those who went out approach? [. . .]. I bring you ⟨to⟩ your feet[2] that you may see this house of yours [. . .]. Khnum has arisen over his court. [The doors of the sky are] opened,[3] the doors of the firmament are thrown open by Horus [. . .] his father's son. He is spiritualized by his son [. . .]. You are examined before Thoth, who examines [. . .] West, your bread of the Broad Hall [. . .] in front of you [. . .] walk to and fro [. . . the sun-folk extend] arms to you and stamp [feet for you . . . the sun-folk][4] burn(?) for you, [. . .] and Nephthys. O N,[5] [. . .].

1. For *ḏꜣm* 'wave' hands, cf. *Pyr.* §§743; 1366.
2. *Sic.* One *r* in *r rdwy.k* has been elided.
3. Cf. de Buck, n. 3*.
4. Cf. de Buck, n. 8* in respect of 109*n.o.*
5. Cf. de Buck, n. 9.

Spell 903 is almost entirely lost.

Spell 904

TO SAVE THE NECK FROM HIM WHO WOULD CUT IT. [. . .] N today[1] [. . .] the VII, 110
god of offerings whom N has met(?). N lifts up [. . .] with gold and electrum(?) [. . .] whom N has bound(?).[2] N is on his way to the Garden of [. . .],[3] N will drive in the mooring-post in the Waterway of Horus, N will dispel the storm. N has formerly waged war against his horn,[4] and he cannot lift up his face, he will be rightly broken. The . . .[5] worship N, and it is Shu who has prepared a path for ⟨him⟩ and for his great double(?);[6] the associates(?)[7] are they who take N from the Ennead(?) in front of Her who fares upstream, and who gives air to the Ennead for N.

1. Cf. de Buck, n. 2*. Read *N pn myn.*

2. *Sf.n N; sf* is not recorded.

3. Apparently not *š* [*Ḥr*], cf. de Buck, n. 5*.

4. *Šd.n N pn ḫrw r ᶜb.f*; cf. *šd.n.f ḫrwyt r* 'he has waged war against', *CT* II, 130*d.* There must have been an omission before this sentence, because there is no antecedent for the suffixes *.f* here and in 110*j.k.*

5. *Ṯstyw.*

6. 110*m* seems corrupt; we might expect *in Šw ir n.f w3t,* and the passage has been translated in that sense, but the sign drawn in de Buck's n. 9* is obscure.

7. *Snsnw.*

Spell 905

[. . .][1] the water of N's mouth;[2] O you who are little,[3] it means that the Eyes of Horus speak to you. N shall go forth upon the battlements of the northern sky, N has put this water in N's intestines.

VII, 111 O you Souls of Dep, you Lords of Pe, quench (thirst) with the water of N's mouth; it is the Winding Waterway. O Rēᶜ! O Horus of the desert(?), a son who protects his father! O you of the sharp knives! O you who rule the slayers, who say that they will rob N! Their faces are like . . .[4] The long-horn which is on the mounds of the food of those who are accused[5] will gore; the . . .-bird[6] has sucked, they swallow the fiery Eye of Horus.[7] See, they know,[8] but they forget it.[9] See, N is the hale Eye of Horus. O Coiled One ⟨ . . . ⟩.[10]

1. 110*p-r* yields no connected sense, owing to damage.
2. Cf. 111*b.*
3. Feminine plural.
4. *Mt iw* defeats me. Can it be a cryptogram for *myw* 'cat'?
5. *Wnmt smywt* is obscure.
6. *Snb-i3y.*
7. Read *irt tw nt Ḥr,* ignoring the first *Ḥr,* which is superfluous; cf. 111*k.*
8. Old perfective 3rd plural.
9. Read *sḫm.sn s(y),* but the relevance of 111*j* is not clear.
10. The spell breaks off short.

Spell 906

N has gone up into the horizon as the front of a lion(?),[1] N's gifts go forth in front of N, who issued from the god's egg. N is the Bull of Kenzet, which is known in Ōn. There is bread on earth with Horus, great loaves are with the god, and ⟨it(?)⟩

is for N. You are the double of every god, the first-born, the eldest son of Atum, the image of him(?).[2] Stand up and sit down (at) a thousand of bread, a thousand of beer, [a thousand of] oxen, poultry, alabaster and clothing which the god provides in these offerings.

1. Taking *ḥꜣ* to be an ideogram; *sp 2* is regarded, here and elsewhere, as a mark of emphasis.

2. *Wt.f* is assumed to be an error for *twt.f* 'his image'; it can hardly be intended for *wtw* 'eldest son' as in *Pyr.* §593, since that term is a synonym of *wt(w)ty* just above, and would be superfluous here.

Spell 907 is fragmentary.

Spell 908

A boon which the king grants (and also) Anubis who presides over the god's VII, 112
booth, Lord of the Netherworld, to whom the Westerners give worship; Lord of Sepa, pre-eminent in the Sacred Land; [. . .][1] who dwells in the middle sky, the fourth of the Children of Rēʿ, who was caused to descend from the sky to put Osiris in order, because he was so highly regarded by Rēʿ and the gods. May he grant that N's tomb will benefit. The land will come to him, his [. . .] bearing bread;[2] he will drink of the waters of his well,[3] he will go down to his garden for what is given at his desire; he will speak about his house in the necropolis; he will be vindicated on account of his children in the presence of the Company of the Mat(?).[4] Ḥatḥōr will hear all that he says in the Tribunal of the Two Gods, (even) N whom Ḥatḥōr loves, the companion of *Ḥḏ-ḥtp.*[5]

1. *Sw* after *tꜣ-ḏsr* is corrupt; *ḥr-ỉb pt* which follows shows that a name of Anubis must have stood here.

2. A feminine noun must have stood in the lacuna to account for the fem. *ẖrt.*

3. Note *ḫnmt* 'well' spelt with *ḫ.*

4. *Šnyt tmꜣ*(?) appears to be the designation of a body of judges in the Beyond.

5. 112*x.y* are concerned only with N's wife and are no more parts of the actual spell than are the *ỉmꜣḫ* formulae of 112*n.u.*

Spell 909

This day of N is renewing(?) the heart in the early morning[1] for N by means of VII, 113 your writings. [It will go well with(?)] N, N is pure;[2] the mighty ones of Horus speak to N, who is afraid of him[3] and of [them(?) . . .] Sepa. Those who are in [. . .] speak to N [. . .] the Great Ones. He who is in authority over speech greets N . . . behind N,[4] and there will be no trouble ⟨among⟩ those who are in the Presence on her account. EACH ONE OF THEM [IS YOUNG(?) . . .] THOSE WHO ARE IN SILENCE ARE SILENT FOR YOU AT THE TIME [OF] THE SPIRIT.[5] THERE COMES [. . .], THE GOD COMES IN PEACE.

The Great One hears [. . .][6] N a path in company with you,[7] and the god is loud-voiced. Stand at the portal [. . .] your two faces(?). N is in front of the gods, and N is raised on high. Your[8] face is that of Sia who ⟨ . . . ⟩ his cloak.[9] He
114 has caused N to receive [. . .] who is before you, the Elder of the tribunal; he gives a mat(?) to N in company with you in order to go into N's presence[10] in your company, N will not sit in your . . . ,[11] your mighty ones shall not stand on the heads of(?) [. . .].[12]

1. For *n nhpw* read *nhpw* only.
2. Restoring [*ꜣḫ n*] *N tn wꜥb*[*n*] *N tn.*
3. The suffix in *snḏ n.f* presumably refers to Horus; N is a woman.
4. I do not understand 113*g*.
5. 113*j* may well be corrupt. The initial *ỉ* seems without function; it appears to be neither the interjection, nor the verb 'says', nor the prothetic *ỉ*. The dative after *ỉ gr* has a plural suffix. *Imyw gr* looks strange, but 'those who are in silence' is perhaps not impossible. *Sp* [*n*(?)] *ꜣḫ* also looks strange, and its relevance is not clear.
6. Cf. de Buck, nn. 15*; 16*. The traces of 113*m* do not suit *ỉr n* 'there is made for'.
7. Plural, so that the suffix cannot refer to *nṯr* following.
8. Plural!
9. Something has been omitted between *Syꜣ* and *syꜣt*, A possible restoration is *Syꜣ* ⟨*syꜣ*⟩ *syꜣt.f*; this would stress the pun.
10. Emending into *r ꜥḳ* ⟨*m-*⟩*bꜣḥ N.*
11. *Nwt.*
12. The rest of the spell is too much broken to translate.

Spell 910

N [is clad(?)] as [Horus], N [is robed(?)] as Osiris,[1] N [has come(?)] in the morning, N has gone forth in [the night(?), N] is brighter than a rod, N's rank is (that of) [her][2] father Atum, N has uncovered [. . .] the place of embalming, N has broken up[3] the mansions of the Old One for [. . .], N has travelled [the land(?)] of the sleepers who belong to Thoth [. . .].

Hail to you, tooth(?)[4] of the Great One [. . .] the striking-power of the

Great One [. . .] which was said: 'You shall come for her'. A Great One comes VII, 115
to N; may Sobk not be aggressive [. . .] I wish that he were dead! O you who take away knees, go upside down, do not take away my knees [. . .] in these two great chapels ⟨in⟩[5] which are the Souls of Ōn. N will not[6] eat faeces, N will not drink urine for them, N will not go upside down for them.[7] May you[8] be pure and clean, O N, among the pure ones who are in their [places(?)].

1. See de Buck, nn. 10* ff. The restoration 'is robed(?)' in 114*i* is a guess.
2. De Buck suggests restoring *ỉt*[*.f*] in n. 16*, no doubt rightly, cf. the masc. suffix in 115*l*, but the deceased was a woman.
3. *Gmgm* is doubtless to be understood as a *sḏm.n.f* form, since it comes between two such forms. The omission of the *n*-formative may well be a slip.
4. Reading ⟨*ỉ*⟩*bḥ* 'tooth'.
5. Supply *ỉm.sn* after *bꜣw 'Iwnw*. *'Itrty* seems here to mean 'chapel'.
6. On the use of the archaic enclitic negative *w* reinforced by *ỉs* see my Brief Communication in *JEA* 62, 176.
7. The name of the deceased is inserted superfluously at the end of 115*k*.
8. Masc. suffix, though this is a woman's coffin.

Spell 911 is fragmentary. Shu is named in 116f.

Spell 912

N is young [. . .] by[1] this god who is in the heart of *'Iꜣdw*, more secret than VII,117
the gods, (although) his name is known. N has come so that she may order the paths; N allots [. . .] their [. . .], N has power over *'Iꜣdw*, and he has no power over her [. . .] for N,[2] [. . .] will not obstruct(?)[3] N's movements, they will [not] oppose N's staff, N has eaten [of] the uraeus yesterday, N [has] swallowed [. . .] today [. . .] N's breath [. . .] the Lord of *'Iꜣdw*.

1. Or perhaps 'so says'.
2. Note the writing of *N tn* as N *ṯn*; so also in Spell 913.
3. Reading *ḥn* 'obstruct'; for this verb cf. *Concise Dict.* 171.

Spell 913

The mighty one speaks to N, and N will replace air, N will smite[1] [. . .]. N will not ignore(?)[2] you, O *Wꜣmmw*, when he passes the [. . .] of Rēꜥ on his throne; [N] will live [on bread(?)], N [will breathe(?)] air, N [will have] a soul(?),[3] N will be clad in what she grasps [. . .].

1. Prospective *sḏm.f.*
2. Restoring conjecturally as *n sẖ*[*m.n*].
3. Restoring 117*r-t* as *ꜥnḫ*[*N m t, sn*] *N ṯꜣw, bꜣ*[*n*] *N.*

Spell 914

VII,118 To be with the Great Ones. Hail to you, you souls of the lords of terror in the waters! I have come to you, for I am the [pupil(?)] which is in the midst of his Eye,[1] who will not be driven away(?).[2] I have come and brought Truth to the contented wife of[3] Thoth, ⟨to⟩ the Eye of Horus the Red, to the magician, the staff of Him of the flood, the [. . .] of Anubis [. . .]. The fillet of Thoth is tied, and he and she who taste are not exalted(?),[4] the *sꜣꜣ*-plant is on its river-bank [. . .] you by means of it. See me, you gods[5] who are on [. . .] I am high[6] in [. . .] I am(?) [. . .] for my name. O you who are clean [. . .] for my command(?) in everything which [you(?)] have done [. . .] I go after . . . ,[7] [I] will not go astray [. . .] because of youthfulness(?) [. . .] while I am . . . within(?) *Hnhnw.*[8] [. . .] make content . . . within(?) *Hnhnw.*

1. Conjecturally restoring *ḥwnt* in the lacuna in 118*d*; the space and the det. suit. The suffix in *ỉrt.f* doubtless refers to Horus, though an antecedent is lacking.

2. As it stands, I cannot translate 118*e*, which except for the first group is not confirmed by de Buck. A possible emendation may be *ỉwty ẖsf.f,* referring to the deceased.

3. Reading *n ḥmt ḥtpt*; this last is determined with a sign which may well be a distorted papyrus-roll. The obscure sign which follows perhaps stands for the genitive adjective.

4. In B1C the latter part of 118*i* seems corrupt; in D1C what follows *ṯs mḏḥ* is certainly corrupt.

5. In B1C read *ỉ*[*r.ṯ*]*n* after *mꜣw wỉ.*

6. The first group in 118*l* appears to be prothetic *ỉ.*

7. *Sf nn,* var. *sfꜣ nn* in 119*e,* defeats me; see also 119*f.*

8. For this god see also *CT* VI, 307*e.*

Spell 915

[. . .] I have acted on behalf of your heart, I enter into [. . .] I am a Power [. . .].

Spell 916 is largely illegible and yields no coherent sense, but Thoth, Isis, Nephthys and Nūt are named.

Spell 917

His arms are about you,[1] N [. . .] N who acts in his [. . .] in every place where VII, 120
you are. Ho[N! . . .] the realm of the dead. O N, turn yourself to Nūt when she unites the Two Lands of Gēb and the land of your West. Your mother has given you her hands for life [. . .]. O N, [raise][2] yourself on your left side, having been placed on your right side, worship(?) the Great Lady [. . .] and live for ever.

An invocation-offering of bread and beer, oxen and fowl for N! [. . .]. O N, I place your heart in your body for you, for you are Osiris [. . .] for Nūt. Nephthys brings to you [your daily ration(?)[3] . . .] ⟨N⟩.[4] May you ferry across [. . .] N in the western desert of [N . . .].

A boon which the king grants, (and also) Anubis [. . .], of a fair burial. Your son is with N.[5] Gēb, chiefest[6] of the gods, will accompany you, for he is your son, O N, [. . .] you shall nourish ⟨your son⟩ [with it];[7] he has made you hale, and you are powerful and able(?).[8] Atum himself is with them.[9] Gēb [. . .] life, permanence and dominion for ever [. . .] N. May you protect him(?)[10] . . . life, permanence and dominion for ever.

O N [. . .] N, you standing on the earth that you may govern at the head of the gods [11] who are before Anubis wherever he may be. An invocation offering of
bread and beer, oxen and fowl [. . . ⌈A boon which the king grants⌉ (and also) 122
Duamūtef and Ḳebḥsenuf. A boon which the king grants (and also) Isis and Nephthys. A boon which the king grants (and also) Imsety and [Ḥapy]. A boon which the king grants (and also) the god [. . .]. A boon which the king grants [. . .] at the head of the gods. O N, you [12]are [. . .] Gēb [. . .].

1. Whose arms? The beginning of this spell has been omitted.

2. Restore [*t*]*s ṯw*.

3. Read *ẖrt hrw*? De Buck, n. 3*, is uncertain about the reading *tp*.

4. The name of the deceased has been omitted.

5. *Sw* at the beginning of 121*h* is probably the rare particle of *Eg. Gramm.*[3] §240 used with a non-verbal sentence, but it is not clear to whom the suffix in *sꜣ.k* applies, unless it be to Anubis, which seems unlikely.

6. Read *rp*[*ꜥt*], cf. *Pyr.* §1620*a*.

7. 121*j* has been restored as *Pyr.* §1620*b*, but there must have been garbling. The lacuna after 'N' has no counterpart in Pyr., while that after *sꜥnḫ.k* is too small to take *sꜣ.k ỉm.f* of Pyr., and may have read *ỉm* only, cf. de Buck, n. 8*.

8. A corrupt version of *Pyr.* §1618.

9. Cf. *Pyr.* §1617*b*; 'them' in *Pyr.* refers to the Ennead.

10. For *nḫ* see *Concise Dict.* 137.  is incomprehensible as it stands, but could have arisen from a miswriting of *sw*. What follows is surely corrupt.

11. Cf. *Pyr.* § 1619*a*.

12. Read *ṯw*[*t*].

Spells 918 and 919 are fragmentary. Spell 918 mentions the town of Djedu (123b) and from 123p onward it is a broken variant of CT II, 230a ff. cf. de Buck, n. 19.*

Spell 920

VII, 125 NOT TO DIE AGAIN. O you living one who are in the horizon, O Osiris![1] Reach[2] the Great Provider with whom is a staff, reach the two Songstresses, the two female [Companions],[3] your two [Sisters(?)], appear in your great crown. May your mother Nūt bear you, may Pe be yours,[4] may (something) be given to you ⟨by⟩[5] Dep. May you see [. . .] in Ōn, may life be established in you through the Souls of Pe and through the Souls of Nekhen. Your foes, O Rēʿ, are turned about; the spirits in the West serve you, [. . .] serve [. . .] their heads and their skins [. . .] bearing life. Ho [N!] ⟨ . . . ⟩.[6]

1. *H3 Wsyr pn* refers to the deceased, despite the absence of the name.
2. Probably imperative with reflexive dative, cf. the certain imperative *ḫʿ ỉr.k* in 125*f*.
3. Cf. de Buck, n. 3*.
4. Read *n.k ỉmy P*?
5. Supplying *m-ʿ* before *Dpw*.
6. The spell is unfinished.

Spell 921 is much damaged and yields no connected sense.

Spell 922[1]

VII, 126 O you Great Lady[2] with whom they are angered,[3] may you fare upstream to the great throne so that you may bring to me all my magic,[4] and it will be well with you.[5] O you who are in throats, you children of men,[6] Powers, [. . .], Khopri and his companions whose thrones are hidden,[7] I have passed by you [. . .], I am exalted [. . .] fillet about her who is [. . .]. The Red One[8] who is in [. . .]

opens to me [. . .] Osiris. ⟨I have(?)⟩ passed ⟨ . . . ⟩.[9]

1. This spell falls into two distinct parts, the first from M44C and the other from M13C, the two overlapping only at 126*j*, which is in lacuna in M13C, to 126*l*. There is also some corruption; 126*g-i* ⟨M44C⟩ contains two virtually identical passages concerning the 'building up' of Isis after being 'cut up' which have every appearance of being an interpolation from an entirely unconnected source; see n. 7 below.

2. It seems certain that nothing has been lost in the small lacunae at the beginnings of lines 1–3 of M44C. Note that de Buck was entirely dependent for this spell on Lacau's copy, cf. his n. 1*.

3. Lit. 'who is in the anger of their hearts'. There is nothing to show who 'they' may be, which suggests that the beginning of this spell has been lost.

4. The *n* after *ḥkꜣ* is in error and should be ignored.

5. Lit. 'benefit on your heart'. On the interpretation of what follows see nn. 6 and 7 below.

6. *Smrw.f štꜣ swt* is isolated as it stands and is better placed after *Ḫpry* in 126*m*. On the omission from the translation of 126*g-j* see n. 7 below.

7. As noted in n. 1, 126*g-i* appear to be irrelevant interpolations and therefore have been omitted from the translation. The passages in question run: 'O Satis, Isis is built up after her cutting up; Isis is built up after he cut her up'. After this M44C has 'Bring me honour', which looks like a variant of 126*c*. M13C has a lacuna at this point, of which the initial *i͗n* is preserved, but follows with a duplicate of 126*d* and of the first part of 126*e*, which constitutes the only overlap between the two texts.

8. Feminine.

9. The spell is unfinished.

Spell 923

O so-and-so, take the Eye of Horus, that I may put it in your mouth for you – a portion of white *sẖt*-grain, a portion of[1] green *sẖt*-grain, a scorching[2] of wheat, a scorching of barley, a portion of *bꜣbꜣt*, a portion of zizyphus fruit, a portion of zizyphus bread, | all kinds of sweet fruits, all kinds of [fresh vegetables], all kinds VII, 127
of *ḥnkt*, all kinds of sweet things, split earth-almonds,[3] choice joints of the forepart from[4] the offering-tables, all pure and abundant[5] for So-and-so. Take the Eye of Horus which the gods have collected for it according to what they have created.

1. For this sense of *ʿ* cf. *Concise Dict.* 36.

2. *ʿg*, var. *ʿwg* 'scorch' occurs in *CT* V, 10*g*; 12*a*; *BD* 133, 5.

3. Cf. Edel, *Qubbet el Kawa*, Abt. II, Bd. I, Teil 2, p. 22. I owe this reference to Mr. Spaull. *Pdyw*, which I translate as 'split', is lit. 'extended, stretched out', which in this context probably means 'split open and extended' like an open book. In 127*r* is a reference to halves of an earth-almond.

4. Lit. 'of'.

5. *Ḥwy,* lit 'overflowing', but here only solid foods are mentioned.

Spell 924

O N, take the sweet Eye of Horus; I put it in your mouth for you – a portion of [white *sḫt*]-grain, a portion of green [*sḫt*]-grain,[1] a scorching of wheat, a scorching of barley, [a portion of] *bꜣꜣwt*, a portion of [zizyphus fruit], a portion of [zizyphus] bread,[2] all kinds of sweet [fruits] and of fresh vegetables, all kinds of *ḥnkt,* halves of earth-almonds. I cause choice joints to come, I bring[3] forepart-meat from the offering-tables, for N has purity.

They give a duck, he purifies an ibis,[4] he makes offering of everything on which a god lives, [and he(?)] proclaims(?) blessedness for N.

1. This spell is a variant of 923. The name of the grain is incomplete in both instances, but is surely *sḫt,* a var. of *sẖt,* cf. 126*v.w* above.

2. Restored from 126*aa*.

3. Restore as *ṣḫp,* cf. 128*b*.

4. Not 'Thoth', despite the determinative. 'They' may be the mourners at the funeral and 'he' the officiant.

Spell 925

VII, 128 O Companion, open the chest and bring ointment before N's face for N in all his dignities and in all his places which he desires; may he have happiness yonder with the god, with Anubis and with his double, (even) N.

Spell 926

Wash yourself, sit down at the meal, put your hands on it; divert the god's-offerings, break the red pots, give cold water, purify the offering-tables with [. . .],[1]
VII, 129 make libation; fire and incense are for N in all his dignities and in all his places which he desires [. . .] at [the temple(?)]. May you appear in the retinue of the king [. . .].

Spells 927–931 are fragmentary.

Spell 932

Hail to you, Successor[1] of the Great One, Lady of All, who lift up everyone, VII, 132
who open your arms to Him who is inert, on whom it is granted to Him to rest, who collects efflux, who gathers putrescence together, Successor in [. . .] life, what she commanded ⟨for⟩ her lord[2] when he embraces in this her name of Lady
of All [. . .]. I am Osiris, I am languid . . . [. . .]. | I have come equipped with 133
magic, and my utterance has protected me. I am indeed a twin-plumed falcon,[3] [I(?)] foretell [. . .] my heart is in my possession.

O you slayers[4] who belong to Osiris, who fish the earth[5] and who traverse [. . .] in the tombs(?) [. . .] this head of mine. I am one great of soul in front of the mountain,[6] I shall not be taken for your poison(?),[7] for I have seen the cavern [. . .] I am a god [. . .] in it. Open the paths for me, for I am a possessor of Right.

1. Read *stt,* cf. de Buck, n. 5*.
2. The det.  of *wḏt* is a very easy error for  in hieratic; read *wḏt.s ⟨n⟩ nb.s.*
3. *Nt* after *byk* is curious; if it represents the genitive it is in error, for the masc. *n* is needed; if it stands for *nty,* the predicate of the relative clause it should introduce has been omitted.
4. *Tmw,* see also *CT* VI, 379*k.l.*
5. For victims?
6. A small obscure sign after *ḏw,* see de Buck, 133, n. 7*.
7. Read *n ỉṯ.t(w).ỉ r mtwt*(?)*.ṯn*, see de Buck, n. 8*.

Spell 933

As for [. . .] a seal has been given to me [. . .] consisting of clothing, of [eye-paint(?)],[1] of ointment, and everything which she brings,[2] saying . . .[3]

1. Restore .
2. Read *ỉnt.s nbt.*
3. *Fnw.* The spell is unfinished.

Spell 934[1]

Festival perfume. O N, I give you the Eye of Horus, and its perfume is on you. VII, 134
Sfṯ-oil. O N, I give you the Eye of Horus on account of which he suffered(?).[2]
Ḥknw-oil. O N, I give you the Eye of Horus; be joyful by means of it.

Nḫnm-oil. O N, I give you the Eye of Horus, with which he brought and protected the gods.

First quality pine-oil. O N, I give you the Eye of Horus, with which he brought and supported the gods.[3]

First quality oil of Libya.[4] Ointment! Ointment! What is in the Eye[5] of Horus is what is in N's eye; may you give pleasure [to][6] him.

Myrrh. What he receives is your[7] perfume.

A bag of green eyepaint and a bag of black eyepaint. O N, I give you the Eye(s) of Horus, (both) black and white, that they may paint your face and illumine your face.

Twꜣwt-oil. O N, I give you the Eye of Horus, which the winds bring to you for your nose.[8]

135 A *ꜥbt*-vase (of water).[9] O N, I give you the Eye of Horus; there is collected for you the water which is in it.

A *smꜣ*.[10] O N, I give you the Eye of Horus; Horus has united his Two Lands for you.

A *ꜥprt*-jar. Horus has equipped his Two Lands for you.

Two bags of linen. O N, I give you the Eye(s) of Horus, (both) white and green, that they may paint your face[11] and that they may illumine your face.

. . .[12] Awake in peace, awake in peace, O Eye of Horus which is in Dep!

Two crossed clubs.[13] O N, grasp your foes!

O N, the Imperishable Stars fear you.

May you be content with the king's boons, which are sent on account of you yourself.

O N, I give you the Eye of Horus, which is pointed(?)[14] against your foes.

O N, I give you the Eye of Horus, for Horus has seen his father Osiris.[15]

O N, I give you the white Eye of Horus that you may live by means of it.[16]

O N, I give you the Eye of Horus, I provide for you the water which is in it.

O N, I give you the white Eye of Horus, and it will be behind you.

136 O N, I raise your head for you;[17] you shall live, your soul shall live, and you shall be a god.

O Osiris, I make these nails of yours firm for you.

An ornament for his arms.[18] O N, I give you the Eye of Horus, an ornament for your arms.

Giving a collar of turquoise.[19] O N, I give you the Eye of Horus, so that you may be rich[20] by means of it.

O N, I give you the beautiful right eye of Horus, so that your soul may live on it.

1. This spell is part of the Ritual of Offering, with reference to perfumes, cosmetics and dress, each utterance being associated with a title and picture of the relevant item, with the exception of 135*g-n*; it is not clear to which items these utterances refer.

2. Cf. *Pyr. Transl.* Utt.74, n. 1.

3. This text belongs properly to *twꜣwt*-oil, cf. *Pyr.* §51*c*. Here this oil is in 134*j* with the text *ỉnt n.k ṯꜣw r fnḏ.k* 'which the winds bring to you for your nose'.

4. A1C has misunderstood the *ṯhn*-sign and reads *msnw*. The text which follows is a garbled version of *Pyr.* §52; G1T is followed.

5. The 'Eye' is represented by its inner corner, drawn as , see also below in line 9*b* of G1T and in 137*q*; 138*a.g*; 140*l*; note that the text of *Pyr.* §52*b* makes no mention of the Eye of Horus.

6. There hardly seems space in the lacuna for de Buck's *w*, see his n. 2*; the restoration of *n* is according to *Pyr.* §52*c*. A1C is damaged but is even more corrupt than G1T; *snḏm.ṯ* of loc. cit. has been changed in A1C into *sṯ* 'perfume'. The suffix in *snḏm.ṯ* refers to the Eye.

7. Again the Eye of Horus.

8. See n. 3 Above.

9. The contents of the vase are indicated by the following text; the vase itself cannot be connected with the *ꜥbt* used in 'Opening the Mouth', for which see *Th. T.S.* I, p. 59; *Meir* III, p. 28, n. 8.

10. This object probably represents the 'union of the Two Lands' group.

11. For 'face' G1T has both *ḥr* and *mḫnt*; one of them is superfluous.

12. An item of clothing resembling the *ms*-sign. Cf. Jequier, *Frises,* fig. 28?

13. Mr. Spaull suggests the crossed bands on the chest, but de Buck's drawing and the reference to 'foes' seems to favour clubs.

14. *Gnt* here is an attribute hostile to N's foes, and the translation 'pointed(?)' rests on the harpoon-like det. The word certainly has nothing to do with *gnwt* 'annals'.

15. So G1T; A1C reads *mꜣṯ ỉt.f* 'who proclaims his father'.

16. So G1T; A1C is corrupt.

17. After N's name, A1C automatically inserts 'I give you the Eye of Horus', although nothing is given at this point. This spell may belong to the pictures of two headrests or two heads, which occur with the legend 'Giving him his head that he may live', see de Buck, 136, n. 1*.

18. See de Buck, n. 2*.

19. The object in de Buck, n. 3* apparently reads *wsḫw,* cf. 136*h,* and it has therefore been taken to be the *wsḫ*-collar, though here it looks more like a pectoral with necklace.

20. Lit. 'wide'; of girth or of property?

Spell 935

O N, I give you the Eye of Horus, because of which the gods were merciful.

O N, I give you the Eye of Horus; betake yourself to it.

O N, I give you the Eye of Horus which they guarded(?).[1]
O N, I give you the lesser Eye of Horus, of which Seth ate.
O N, I give you the Eye of Horus, with which your mouth is opened. The pupil[2] which is in the Eye of Horus, eat it.
O N, I give you the Eye of Horus, and you will not be ill(?)

1. Read  for  .
2. Read *ḥwnw,* cf. 141*g.* It is a masc. var. of the commoner *ḥwnt* 'pupil' of the eye, for which see e.g. *Pyr.* §§93*a*; 2278*a* (*Suppl.* p. 84).

Spell 936

VII, 137 A boon which the king grants (and also) Anubis, Lord of the coffin, Lord of interment, Lord of invocation-offerings in the *wȝg*-festival, in the Thoth-festival, in the Sokar-festival, in the festival of the First of the Year, in the festival of the Opening of the Year, and in all the goodly festivals of Osiris, for N.

A boon of the king for[1] the sky, that the mouth and eyes may be opened by means of the foreleg by the lector: a thousand of bread and beer, oxen, fowl, alabaster and clothing for N, consisting of everything which Osiris desires and which comes forth to him (at) the voice, he being rich thereby.[2]

The opening of the mouth with the iron chisel. As for all that you do for yourselves,[3] you shall do (it) for N.

From here on the texts 137g ff. are referred to the table of offerings on de Buck's p. 143, and they are translated under the respective headings. The marginal page-numbers refer to the main text.

Water of libation.[4] Incense. Ho Osiris,[5] [hasten, carry off] him who speaks evilly against his name. [O Thoth, hasten], bring away him who is harmful to Osiris,[6] bring away him who speaks against the king's name; do not let go of him, do not let go of him. O N, go also with your double;[7] O N, the hands of your double are before you, the feet of your double are behind you. I come and I bring you the Eye of Horus, that your face may be provided with it, doubly diffused; I bring the perfume of the Eye of Horus, and it will not be far from you.

Cold water. O Osiris, this cold water of yours, Osiris, is the cold water which went forth to the Great One, which went forth to Horus.

Incense of Upper Egypt. O N, I give you the Upper Egyptian Eye of Horus that it may cense your face and cense your eyes, and it may give you Upper

Egypt in worship.

Incense of Lower Egypt. O N, I give you the Eye of Horus which censes what is in his Eye;[8] it will unite Lower Egypt for you and it, (namely) the perfume, will sweeten your face and your eyes.

Incense of [. . .]. O N, take the Eye of Horus, that your face may be censed 138
and your eyes censed by means of it; it will be in your eye.

Ḥknw-oil. O N, take the Eye of Horus; be joyful by means of it.

Festival perfume. O N, take(?) the Eye of Horus as the hale Eye.[9]

Nḫnm-oil. O N, I give you the Eye of Horus with which he protected the gods.

Twꜣw[t]-oil. O N, I give you the Eye of Horus with which he supported the gods.

Sfṯ-oil. O N, I give you the Eye of Horus, (even) its oil which is on it.

First quality pine-oil. Ointment, ointment which is in the Eye of Horus! You shall be on N's brow, you shall put his soul, his strength and the dread of him in the eyes of all spirits who shall see him and who shall hear his name.

First quality oil of Libya. Forward, forward to Osiris![10] I give you the Eye of Horus which he has taken to ⟨your⟩ brow.

A bag of green eyepaint. O N, I paint an uninjured Eye of Horus on your face for you.

A bag of black eyepaint. O N, I paint the Eye of Horus on your face for you, that you may be vindicated.

Clothing, fire and incense. O N, awake in peace! Awake, O Tayt, in peace! Awake, O Eye of Horus, in peace! ⟨Awake⟩, O you who are in Dep and in the Mansions of the Red Crown, in peace! O you who receive a shape and who adorn the Great One, may you cause the Two Lands to bow to N just as they bow[11] to Horus; may you cause the Two Lands to fear N just as they fear[12] the Outcast; may you cause him to sit in [. . .][13] and to open up his place to the spirits and Anubis, Foremost of the Westerners, who presides over the nomes, may you place his soul ⟨at the head of⟩[14] those spirits.

Give cold water of the Northland.[15] O N, I will come and bring you your 139
feet and your testicles; I give you the efflux which issued from you, and by means of it you will not be inert.

Iron, a *ḥnw*-bowl; do not(?) lift up. O N, I give you the *ḥnw*-bowl which issued from the Eye of Horus; provide yourself with it.

A chest of goods(?).[16] *There is no corresponding utterance.*

Srw of Upper and Lower Egypt. *There is no corresponding utterance.*

A fresh *pꜣt*-cake. O N, I give you the Eye of Horus; Rēʿ who is in the sky [17] is gracious to you, he propitiates for you the beneficial Eye of Horus which you glorify(?) and choose.[18]

A *pꜣt*-cake spread into two halves. O N, I give you the Eye of Horus, because of which he once flew up that he might eat.

Five bundles of onions. O N, I bring you your white teeth, which come intact, that your face may be brightened thereby.

Two *hꜣṯs*-jars of *mnw*-stone containing wine. O N, I give you the Eye of Horus which was wrested [19] from Seth, and your mouth is opened with it.

A bowl of *mnw*-stone containing wine. O N, I give you the Eye of Horus which is firm on Horus's brow, and your mouth is opened with it.

A bowl of *mnw*-stone containing beer. O N, I give you the Eye of Horus, and your heart is provided with it.

Give loaves and lift up before ⟨him⟩. O N, I give you the Eye of Horus, which is potent and sacred and which is on Atum; it will be in your eye(?) before you.

Two king's boons which consist of a sack(?) of bread. Bring him with it, for he has gone forth with the Eye of Horus, which was given to him. (As for) the Eye of Horus, he is pleased with it, and I give you the Eye [of Horus] which[20] he pulled out.

Presentation of an invocation offering. O N, I give you the Eye of Horus; quench thirst with it.

Sit down and eat the invocation offering. O N, I give you the Eye of Horus; sit down at your [bread(?)].

Bread, two loaves. O N, I give you the Eye of Horus, with which . . . [. . .]. [21]

'Itḥ-bread. O N, I give you the Eye of Horus, which he pulled out, [namely (?)] Seth.

Four *ỉdtt*-loaves.[22] O N, I give you the Eye of Horus, take it.

Three *prsn*-loaves.[23] O N, I give you the Eye of Horus on which [he] flew up.[24]

[Three] *šns*-loaves. O N, I give you the Eye of Horus which received heads from(?) Seth.[25]

140 An *ỉmy-tꜣ* loaf. O N, I give you the Eye of Horus which is on Horus's brow.

Four *ḥnfw*-loaves. O N, I give you the Eye of Horus [which he has] baked(?) [. . .].

Four *ỉḥbnnt*-loaves. O N, I give you the Eye of Horus which is in [. . .].

Four *pꜣwt*-loaves. O N, I give you the Eye of Horus [. . .].

Four toasted loaves. O N, I give you the Eye of Horus, which he has pulled out [. . .].

Four *ḳmḥw*-loaves. O N, I give you the Eye of Horus, which hammered its foes.

A fore-leg (of beef). O N, I give you the Eye of Horus, of which the gods shared out for you.

A hind-leg. O N, [, . .] Gēb with the hind-leg.[26]

A *sḫn*-joint. O N, I give you the Eye of Horus which he sought out, being pleased with it.

A *swt*-joint. O N, I give you the Eye of Horus, the full equivalent of(?)[27] the Eye of Horus.

Four ribs.[28] O N, I give you the Eye of Horus . . .[29]

A liver. O N, I give you the Eye of Horus for which ⟨the gods⟩[30] went and over which the gods rejoiced, (namely) what is in the Eye of Horus.

A *ḥꜥ*-joint. O N, I give you the Eye of Horus which he(?) ate and at which he was joyful.

Meat of the forepart. O N, I give you the Eye of Horus [which is on][31] the brow of Seth.

A goose. O N, I give you the Eye of Horus, for which [he] came when they prophesied.

A *sr*-bird. O N, I come and I foretell [the Eye(?)] which is on the brow of Horus; take it to your brow.

A *ṯrp*-bird.[32] O N, I give you the Eye of Horus; take the end(?) of your [heart].[33]

A duck. O N, I give you the Eye of Horus; [betake][34] yourself to it.

A pigeon. O N, I give you the Eye of Horus, [. . .] those who would harm 141
it.

A *syf*-loaf. O N, I give you the Eye of Horus, because of which the gods were merciful.[35]

Four *msyt*-cakes. O N, I give you the Eye of Horus, [the water in which he] has squeezed out. Betake yourself to it.[36]

Two *msḏrt*.[37] *There is no corresponding utterance.*

Three bowls of milky ale(?). O N, I give you the Eye of Horus which they have guarded(?).

Three bowls of strong ale. O N, I give [you] the Eye of Horus; [little] is that which Seth has eaten of it.[38]

Two bowls of beer. O N, [I give you the Eye of Horus], and you are [provided] with the . . . which issued from it.

Two portions of wine. O N, I give you the Eye of Horus, that your [mouth] may be opened by means of it, (namely) the pupil which is in the Eye of Horus;

eat it.

Two portions of *ḥꜣmy*-wine. O N, I give you [the Eye of] Horus which he has snatched away from Seth.

Two portions of *swny*-wine. O N, [I give] you the Eye of Horus; having it you [will not be ill(?)] [39] and you will not be passed over, but your mouth will be opened by means of it.

Two portions of *ỉšd*-fruit. O N, I give you the Eye of Horus [which he rescued] from Seth. [40]

Two portions of zizyphus-fruit. [O N, I give you the Eye of] Horus [which] they [have licked] [41] . . .

Green *sẖt*-grain. O N, I give you the Eye of Horus that you may be made fresh by means of it.

White *sẖt*-grain. O N, I give you the Eye of Horus that your [face(?)] may be made bright and your mouth freshened by means of it.

Two portions of *npꜣt*. O N, I give you the Eye of Horus, I allot it [to] you, I fly up in order to devour him who would harm it. [42]

Two portions of *sḫpt*-drink. O N, [I give] you the Eye of Horus that it may [protect(?)] your face.

Two portions of figs. O N, I give you the Eye of Horus [. . .] your mother's breast for you.

142 Two portions of scorched wheat. O N, I give you the Eye of Horus, that its foes may be scorched with its fire.

Scorched barley. O N, I give you the Eye of Horus which smote Seth.

Bꜣbꜣwt. O N, I give you the Eye of Horus which . . . [43] Seth.

H̱nms-beer. O N, I give you the Eye of Horus which it has reft(?) from him; [44] befriend it.

Grapes. O N, I give [you] the Eye of Horus which was torn(?) [45] from Seth, which he ejected to the ground through it. [46]

Two portions of earth-almonds. O N, I give you the Eye of Horus [. . .].

. . . [47] of wine. O N, I give you the Eye of Horus [. . .] which he has guarded and [saved(?)] from Seth.

A jar of *šns*-loaves. O N, I give you the Eye of Horus; join it to your mouth.

Two *ḥrṯ*-loaves. [48] O N, I give you the Eye of Horus; take it before you.

Two *nḥrw*-loaves. O N, I give you the Eye of Horus, by means of which he has . . . [49]

Four *dptt*-loaves. O N, I give you the Eye of Horus which is in Dep.

All kinds of sweet fruit and all kinds of fresh vegetables. O N, he [50] is pure and also N. I give you the sweet Eye of Horus, by means of which the gods have made strength for you and sweetness for you,[51] (namely) all kinds of sweet things which Osiris and N have found, a thousand of bread and beer, ⟨a thousand of oxen and fowl⟩, a thousand of alabaster and clothing for Osiris and N; may he have power over his foes.

The reversion of the offering(?).[52]

The front of the offering-table.

The back of the offering-table.

The list on de Buck, p. 143 ends here; there are no utterances corresponding to the last three entries.

Someone goes with his double;
Osiris goes with his double.
Someone goes with his double;
Thoth goes with his double.
Someone goes with his double;
Seth goes with his double.
Someone goes with his double;
Dwn-ꜥnwy goes with his double.
Someone goes with his double;
The Eyeless One goes with his double.
Someone goes with his double;
N goes with his double.

1. *Nw,* lit. 'of', plural.
2. Read *wsẖ ỉm.*
3. Read *ir(t).ṯn ⟨n⟩.ṯn nbt.*
4. In the first entry on p. 143, read *mw sꜣ*[*ṯ*].
5. Cf de Buck, n. 4*; but it is probable that the name of the deceased was omitted, as in 137*o*, and that *ỉ* is the initial sign of *ỉs* 'hasten', see n. 6 below.
6. 137*g-i* is a version of *Pyr.* §16*b-d* and I suggest restoring 137*g-h* as *hꜣ Wsyr ỉ*[*s ỉṯ*] *mdw m rn.f ḏw,* [*Ḏḥwty ỉs*] *ỉn sw n Wsyr.*
7. For *ḏdk* 'also' cf. *Pyr.* §17*c*.
8. On this writing of *ỉrt* 'eye' cf. Spell 934, n. 5.
9. *M snw(?) n.k* is obscure, cf. de Buck, 138, n. 2*. The group might conceivably be a cryptogram for *mnk* in the formula *m n.k* 'take'.
10. This occurs in *Pyr.* §57*e* in a different context.
11. Read *my ks.sn* with *Pyr.* 57*a*.
12. Note the *ꜥḥꜣ*-sign as a det. of *nr* 'fear'.
13. Obscure and damaged, cf. de Buck, n. 4*.

14. Omission of *m-ḥꜣt*.

15. Corrupt version of *Pyr.* §23*b* (N 260), itself apparently a corruption of W 32*a*.

16. A corruption of *ꜥfdt ḫt*? The fact that this entry and the next lack their respective utterances suggests that the scribe was at a loss to identify these items.

17. Emend into *Rꜥ ỉmy pt*, cf. *Pyr.* §34*a*.

18. At the end of 139*c*, for *ꜣḫt.k* read *sꜣḫt.k*; this is a relative form referring back to *ỉrt Ḥr*, which speaks against the simplex *ꜣḫt*, which is intransitive. Following it, *stpt.k* could have the alternative meaning 'which you cut up'.

19. For *nhpt* read *hpt* with *Pyr.* §§36; 39.

20. Seth.

21. Possibly a corruption of *Pyr.* Utt. 88.

22. Cf. *Pyr.* §77*d*. *Ḥꜣ.k* is obscure; in N 424*a* there occurs  , which looks like a kind of determinative.

23. The enigmatic *ḥꜣ.k* does not appear in *Pyr.* §74*f*, which uses the older spelling *pzn* for the name of the loaf.

24. A corruption of *Pyr.* §74*e*, which reads *ḫw pꜣz.f ḥr.s* 'prevent him from suffering because of it'.

25. Corrupted from *šzp n.k tpy.k* 'receive what should be on you', *Pyr.* §75*a*. At the end of 139*q* we should perhaps restore *m*[-ꜥ]*Stẖ*.

26. A corruption of *n ỉzf Gb m ỉwꜥ.f ỉwꜥ* 'Gēb will not do wrong to his rightful heir', *Pyr.* §80*a*.

27.  in 140*j* is obscure, but it occupies the place of *(ỉ)sw* 'equivalent' in Pyr. §81*a*.

28. *Spḥt n spr*, lit. perhaps 'rib-meat of rib'; for *spḥt* cf. *CT* V, 203*d*; VI, 38*e*; *Meir*, III, 2; *D. el B.* 110.

29. Untranslatable.

30. The subject of *šmt.n* is omitted; it is assumed that *nṯrw* is the joint subject of *šmt.n* and *ḥꜥt.n*.

31. Cf. de Buck, 140, n. 6* and *Pyr.* §84*a*.

32. According to *Bibl. Or.* 21,32 the birds listed in the last three entries are all different species of goose.

33. A version of *Pyr.* §85*a*.

34. *M*[s]; cf. de Buck, 140, n. 7*.

35. Cf. 136*j*.

36. *Pyr.* §88*a* reads *szwnt.n.f mw ỉm.s* 'the water in which he has squeezed out'. The damaged CT version has not room in the lacuna for all this *plus* the *m* of *ms k⟨w⟩* at the end, and may have read *swn*[*t.f mw m*]*s k⟨w⟩ r.s*, omitting *ỉm.s* through confusion with *ms* 'betake'.

37. *Msḏrt* in the table on p. 143 is not recorded. It appears to be a *vox nihili* made up of the *m* of *msyt* immediately preceding and of *ḏsrt* 'strong ale' in *Pyr.* §88*d*, which there follows on *mzt*. That it is not a real word is confirmed by the facts that it has no det., no corresponding utterance, and that the genuine *ḏsrt* appears in the table two compartments further on.

38. Restore as *dy⟨.ỉ⟩ n*[*.k*] *ỉrt Ḥr* [*nḏs*] *wnmt.n Stẖ ỉm.s* as *Pyr.* §88*c*.

39. Restore [*n mr(?)*]*.k*; see de Buck, n. 7*.

40. Restored from *Pyr.* §95*c*.

41. Restored from *Pyr.* §98*c*. I cannot translate the following *nbsbs ḏs.s*.

42. At the end of 141*n*, emend *ỉrtw* into *ỉrrw* or *ỉrw*.

43. *Snbꜣbꜣ,* meaning unknown, cf. *Pyr.* §98*a*.

44. Cf. Pyr. §89*c*.

45. A sense of *ỉꜣrr* hitherto unrecorded, but there is little doubt as to the meaning.

46. For *m-ꜥ.f* at the end of 142*e* read *m-ꜥ.s* or *ỉm.s*; presumably the reference is to the Eye of Horus.

47. *ꜥršw* is not known; the corresponding utterance, although damaged and corrupt, suggests that this intended to be a version of *Pyr.* 92*d,* where the T-text has *ỉrp ꜥbš,* N has *ꜥbš* and W has *ꜥš.* The meaning of *ꜥbš* is not clear, and *Wb* I, 179,1 adds after a variant a note: 'und ähnliche verderbte Schreibungen'.

48. *Pyr.* §73*f* reads *ḥt.*

49. The meaning of *nẖrt.n.f* is obscure; *Pyr.* §74*a* has *in⟨.i⟩ n.k nẖrw ḥr.k* 'I bring you that which resembles (?) your face', but *nẖrt.n.f ỉm.s* can hardly bear any such meaning.

50. 'He' stands for Osiris, see 142*n.o*.

51. Compare *Pyr.* Utt. 169–70.

52. Read *wḏb pḏyt.* This corresponds to *wḏb ḥtpw-nṯr* 'the reversion of the god's offering' in *Pyr.* 115*c*; the CT version may perhaps mean 'the reversion of what is extended', i.e. what has been offered. On the meaning of *wḏb* in this context cf. *JEA* 24,83 ff.

Spell 937

[. . .] my head, I am strong in my brow [. . .] which is on Rēꜥ-Atum. I am a VII, 144
soul, I have appeared [. . .] I am strong [. . .] Horus the Elder. Nūt comes to
me [. . .] He whose scalp is comfortable opens to me his arms which open the
years, Satis opens to me, [. . .] opens to me the cleared paths, and my glance
falls on all of them(?),[1] the evil ones who are in their caverns. I have taken, for I
was strong(?)[2] while I was in my father's nest, and no-one saw him on her
mouth.[3]

I spiritualized myself as Her who is a spirit, | I have strength by means of my 145
utterance. These harmful(?)[4] gods come to me trembling(?), they have taken me
into the firmament(?) [. . .] water, they have put me [. . .] which are in the
Netherworld. I have gone all over the sky [. . .] me as the opener(?) who is at
the heart of the dawn [. . .] whose shapes are mysterious. Make a path for me
that there may come to me those who would meet ⟨me⟩, who did not obey Gēb
aforetime(?). I have gathered together the fiery breath(?)[5] for the blast of this
spirit of fire; I will leave them[6] on the threshing-floors, I will uncover the points
of Shu, | all those whom I have seen will come to me [. . .] who are upon the 146
powerful ones who make my soul. I have [. . .] Rēꜥ [. . .], I have taken possession of the *wrrt*-crown of my father, I have [satisfied(?)] my mother with
plenty, I have put my raging among them. Horus laments him – so says the

Chaos-god; he has carried off the primeval one [. . .]. The Chaos-god serves me, his father is [yonder(?)]. I raise high(?)[7] the praise of me(?),[8] a multitude serves me in my suite, and I will make a path there for my father; he shall have his soul, and the sky shall be protected. I have acclaim, and men will bring to me from the reaping, for I have taken possession of strength.

1. According to de Buck, nn. 8* – 10*, the reading *r ꜣw nbw* is not certain.
2. Restoring tentatively as *ỉṯ.n.ỉ wsr.ỉ*.
3. Apparently so, but what can it mean?
4. Reading *snk⟨n⟩tyw*?
5. Reading *nsfy* with dets. of both fire and air.
6. Who? The *ỉmyw-ḫsfw* of 145*j*?
7. Read *ỉꜣd* 'mount', 'climb up'(?), used figuratively and transitively.
8. Reading uncertain, cf. de Buck, n. 5*.

Spell 938

VII, 147 The god is knit together within the egg, the god is formed and comes into being within the [nest(?)[1] . . .], the god is raised up, *Knnḥ* has formed me, the Watcher has moulded me, [. . .] has conceived me [. . .], her womb [fashioned(?)] me, my two mothers bore me, [. . .], they saw her who bore the god in me, who knew [me(?)]. I am the Primeval One, greatly powerful and loud-voiced, weighty
148 [of majesty[2] . . .] who make [. . .] of this my great majesty | [. . .] open [. . .] greatly powerful, loud-voiced, weighty of majesty, [. . .] great of power, loud of voice, [whom(?) . . .] fear [. . .] the *mnsꜣ*-jar which is in [. . .]. I am he who has power through it, I am the great Power of the horizon [. . .].

[Come],[3] you gods, and see me, for I have come on your account as Lord of
149 the great *wrrt*-crown, | I have circumambulated the Great Throne [. . .] Great One of the horizon, and none second to me came into being in it.

[Come, you gods, and see] me,[4] for I have come on your account, manifested and besouled, and He who was in the beginning has ennobled me; He who is on his block(?) has enfolded me. She who bore Horus bore me, the god's nest created me; I am . . .[5] in my shape, I am [. . .] in the horizon, a path is made for me into the gate of Him who smote the Great One, no celebration of the rebellious has been made against me [. . .] the god's nest, I am one who is great.

1. *Šs* restored conjecturally from 149*h*.
2. *Šfšft* restored from 148*c*.
3. Restored as plural imperative *myw*.

4. Restored after 148*h-i*.
5. I cannot translate *n ꜣ.ky*.

Spell 939

[. . .] I have established my fledgeling on my thrones. VII, 150

O Thoth who made order for the Great One and who made nourishment for the multitude; O Lord of Strength who acquired strength for me; O Ptah the Coiled One; O Horus of Nekhen, taken to your blinded ones(?), hearts are mine.

O you great gods [. . .], you who are in [. . .], I am he whom the god pacified.

O Maʿet in front of the place of complaint in the tribunal, I am he who was pleasing to the god.

O sick scalp [. . .] the horizon, who raised up the sky, whose flame is Lord of the sunshine(?).

O you jackal(?),[1] doubly long, who cannot see the brow of Rēʿ-Atum[2] when he guides[3] the inert one of the gods who are among those who are made to fly.

[. . .] you shall sit [. . .][4] who are on thrones before all the gods, and I 151
am . . .[5] by night among them in company with the son of the Sistrum-player. I have departed wakeful, I have returned wakeful, I have attained the sky, I have taken possession of the earth, I have set up the jackal-headed posts of the Imperishable Stars. I am one who is in front of Tjenēnet, one greater than my father; my bread is the Eye, my beer is the Eye, I have seen the heart of *Tywtyw*, and I am content every day; it is the nameless one who speaks, and I will never speak the boon-which-the-king-grants formula, for see, the Baboon is with me – four times.

1. ʿḏ; the det. suggests a jackal, and so does its description below as nocturnal or semi-nocturnal, not seeing the sun.
2. Note the honorific transposition: 'Rēʿ-Atum, his brow'.
3. *'Ir.f* is perhaps an early use of *ỉry* as an auxiliary verb.
4. Reading doubtful, see de Buck, nn. 2*. 3*.
5. *Ssšn.* [*k*]*y(?)*

Spell 940

. . . beautiful, the beautiful golden rod. May acclamation be given, may prophecy VII, 152
be created; may you arise as a vulture, may you be terrible [. . .] Sakhmet, may you have power over them, may the Anointer come to you bowing [. . .] the

Great Lady [. . .] the Joyful One – four times.

I am Ḥatḥōr, I am swift[1] as the Great Wild Bull who runs on his body. O men, gods, spirits, [see], I am [mighty(?)], manifest, besouled, spiritualized, [favoured],[2] assigned (a place),[3] beloved [. . .]; my magic is pure with men and
153 gods; those above and those below. | See [. . .] this day.

1. Lit. perhaps: 'I hasten myself'.
2. Read [*m.*]*ṯn wỉ* [*sḫm(?)*] *.ky ḫꜥ.ky bꜣ.ky ꜣḫ*[*.ky . . . ḥ*] *s.ky.*
3. For the sense of *mṯn* cf. *Pyr.* §2040; here the object is left unexpressed.

Spell 941

[. . .] wake [. . .] on this throne of mine. I am new, young, swift, spiritualized, besouled, [strong], powerful, favoured, beloved, assigned (a place), protected, fathered(?), and manifest as a young god [. . .]. I have waked as He who wakes
VII, 154 hale, the son of Sokar, I am swift as *Wnty,* | who is set in the mouth of [. . .] the Lion who presides over the Mansion of Natron [. . .] the Great One [. . .] the great Conclave; my seat(?) [. . .] in my hand, and my goods of my estate are brought to me. There is given to me what was taken from me, and what I said about it has been circulated for me [. . .] the Powers are pleased at it, the tribunal is in acclamation, those who bear witness [are in joy].[1] I have arisen as Ptaḥ, greatly strong; [I] appoint [. . .] me as Thoth who is in the peace of the gods, I propitiate the god for(?) the god in his power and [his] might [. . .]. I propitiate *Sd*[2] with right as Maꜥet, he opens [. . .] for me, he(?) [. . .] the Two Conclaves for me, he breaks rebellion for me, he drives off the turbulent ones for
155 me, he repels the raging ones for me, | [. . .] peace. The terror of me is behind me, my majesty is upon me, the Chaos-gods are controlled for me, so that they of the celestial expanses quake for me,[3] the company of Seth is [. . .] for me, [. . .] their shrines [. . .] his head, the greyhaired one uncovers his arms for me [. . .] one brotherly [. . .] peace [. . .] the Angry Ones(?).

1. Restore as *m* [*ḥꜥꜥ*]*wt.*
2. Reading [*s*]*ḥtp.ỉ Sd,* cf. de Buck, n. 10*.
3. Read *r ꜣwr n.ỉ pḏtyw.*

Spell 942

My going forth is the going forth of Him who smote the Great One, the mans-

ion(?) . . .[1] Seth who turned the land upside down [. . .] dances(?) [. . .] the horns of Him who smote the Great One are bent in the eastern gate of the sky [. .[1] .] her tress of fire is quenched [. . . ; he(?)] praises them of Khemennu VII, 156
[. . .] they spit out(?)[2] the two powers when I go forth and when this goddess goes forth, having appeared as Rēʿ [. . .] the Sole Lord, she has taken away the flame of the sunshine, she has shaved the side-whiskers[3] of ʿAnti, who is adorned on [. . .] she has nothing which has been done against her[4] in [this her name][5] of *Wnwt*; Seth has been placed beneath her coils for her [. . .] this name of hers is in his hand. Offering-slabs have been made [. . .] them in these names of theirs; if I live, they will live; if I am hale, they will be hale.

1. The beginning of 155*l* is obscure; *ḥwt* 'mansion', if that indeed be the reading, has no apparent relevance to what precedes, and the following *sꜣ* is untranslatable.

2. Cf. *Pyr.* §1628.

3. *'Iꜣrty* is dual, so that the translation as 'side-whiskers' seems enforced, especially in view of the reference to shaving. *Wb.* I, 32,3 records this word in the singular as 'Stirnschlange des Re', but it is possible that 'forelock' may be a better translation, on account of the hair-determinative.

4. Reading *n⟨n⟩ n.s ỉryt r.s.*

5. Cf. de Buck, n. 11*.

Spell 943

O you who eat,[1] speak ⟨to⟩ her who casts[2] the Two Baboons (in gold); I have VII, 157
appeared as the Eye of [Horus], and the Eye of Horus [has appeared] as I;[3] I am it and it is I.[4]

I eat, I speak, I cast the Two Baboons; the Eye of Horus appears as I, and I appear as the Eye of Horus; I [am it and it is] I.[5]

O you who celebrate the [. . .] of Rēʿ, I have appeared, etc.[6]

I celebrate my [. . .], for I am [. . .]; the Eye of Horus appears, etc.[7]

O Mistress of past time(?)[8] who swallowed the Vulture, I have appeared, etc.

[. . .] it is I who bore Sakhmet; the Eye of Horus appears, etc.

[. . .] the Sole Lord. I have appeared, etc.

O you who ran from me, I guide the Sole Lord; the Eye of Horus appears, etc.

[. . .] my two doubles(?). O you who make the land bright, I have appeared, etc.

Mine is the double(?) [. . .]; the Eye of Horus appears, etc.

[. . .] in front of Her who swallowed her sister; I have appeared, etc.
I have swallowed [. . .]; the Eye of Horus appears, etc.
158 O you who eat, whose speech is not opposed, I have appeared, etc.
I live as Khons, I am Neḥebkau; the Eye of Horus appears, etc.

1. Feminine. For the restoration *wnm* see de Buck, n. 1*.
2. For this writing of *nby* 'cast' gold, cf. *BH* II, 4.
3. Restoring the lacuna in 157*b* as *Ḥ*[*r ḫʿ.n*].
4. Note the rare use of the pronoun *stt*, otherwise recorded only in *Pyr.* §131*e*; *Urk.* I, 163,17. Also abnormal is the attaching a suffix to *pw* in *pw.s*, *pw.ỉ*, but construction and meaning alike seem certain. *Ṯs pẖr* here is no more than a visual note of the inversion already expressed in the text, and it has not been translated.
5. Restoring 157*f* as 157*c*.
6. Repetition of 157*b-c*, and so regularly below.
7. Repetition of 157*e-f*, and so regularly below, in alternation with 157*b-c*.
8. *Tpy-ʿ* with temporal meaning? Read perhaps *tpy-ʿ* ⟨*ʿ*⟩*mt*.

Spell 944

I am Khopri[1] who is over the Lord of [. . .], I have opened up the darkness, I have fashioned my father, I have conceived(?)[2] my mother, [I] have taken possession of [. . .] whose scalp is shaven[3] in front of the upper sky, I grant powers, [I take away(?)] powers, my face is Horus the Elder, my heart is the Wine-press god who is in . . .[4] My arm is not opposed,[5] and I appear as the Eye of Horus; I am fire [. . .] my arm is not opposed at all [. . . one who knows] that from this[6] among them, I know [. . .].

1. Reading not certain, cf. de Buck, n. 2*.
2. Restoring as *ỉ*[*wr.*]*n.ỉ*.
3. *Fk*.
4. *Tyṯnt*; unknown.
5. Read *ḫsf ʿ.ỉ* without the papyrus-roll.
6. Cf. de Buck, n. 8*.

Spell 945

VII, 159 My face is Rēʿ.
My hair is Horus.
My eyes are the God of Magic.

My ears are the Great Hearer.
My eyebrows are the Two Powers.
My [. . .] is Wepwawet.
My [. . . is *G*] *spn*(?).[1]
My [. . .] are the Two Enneads.
My [. . .] is Sakhmet.
My [. . .] is He who is wise and acute.
My teeth are Sopd.
My tusks are Shesmētet.
My throat is Rēʿ.
My [. . .] is Ḥatḥōr.
My lungs are [Isis].
My liver is the *nšmt*-bark.
My spleen is Maʿet and(?) the god.
My [. . .] is the Great Pathfinder.
My [. . .] is He who awakes hale.
My heart is Neḥebkau.
My spine is the Twin Souls.
My shoulders are [. . .].
My arms are [. . .].
My armpits are [. . .].
My hands are the Bull of Governance.
My fingers are the *nʿw*-snake.
My nails are Gēb.
My [. . .] are Khopri.
My [. . .] is the Destroyer.[2]
My [. . .] are the Two Conclaves.
My sides are the wands.
My ribs are Neith.
My chest is [. . .].
My mammae are [. . .].
My belly is the motion of Rēʿ(?).
My shorn parts are The-god-is-content.
My [. . .] is [. . .].
My vessels[3] are Rēʿ who is gracious to Iunmūtef.
My testicles are the Centipede(?).[4]
My . . .[5] is Maʿet who supports Horus.
My anus is the Frog-goddess.

161 My lower-legs are the Two Baboons,
My buttocks are Isis and Nephthys.
My thighs are Shu and Tefēnet.
[. . .].
The soles of my feet are the birth of the god.
My toes are the ordinance of Osiris.
My [. . .] is Ḥa of the West.
My striking-power is Khons.
My strength is Seth.
My protection is Babi.
My [. . .] is Neith.
[. . .].
My path is Nūt.

1. Cf. de Buck, n. 2*.
2. *Tšts̆*, determined by a feline(?) of obscure species. Compare perhaps *CT* IV, 94*t*.
3. *Mt*; perhaps collective for the whole vascular system.
4. The sign for the name of the god could be a corruption of the sign of the centipede.
5. *Gꜣs*.

Spell 946

VII, 162 My love is my . . . , my kindness is my . . . , Horus will favour me, Nūt . . . is for my reward(?);[1] all that ⟨I(?)⟩ desire is the overflowing of what I request[2] by means of my seekers and my bringers.[3] They will bring me[4] [what I] desire and what my heart requests; the god's reward is in the storehouses of the nobles [. . . the provisions] of those who provide. My heart is determined,[5] my foes are under my left sandal, for I am the Eye of Horus [. . . the Eye of] Horus, the Lady of All. The Eye of Horus has gone out after(?)[6] [. . .] the lord. I am a fire in sky and earth, and all my foes are under my flame. I did not know that from this [. . .] the great rod[7] which controls the patricians and spits out the plebs
163 [. . .]. O you who rage, the retinue of the god, O you gods, spirits and the dead who serve me and worship me,[8] I will give you air, for I am [. . .], I am Edjō, I have possessions(?),[9] I am a monkey.

1. The beginning of this spell is incomprehensible to me, and also I do not understand the placing of de Buck's marginal *b*. To me it looks as if his 162*a-b* should be divided into four clauses: *mrwt.ỉ kyt.ỉ, ỉmꜣt.ỉ kyt.ỉ, Ḥr r ḥswt.ỉ, Nwt ḏrt r mṯnwt.ỉ*. I cannot interpret *kyt* or *ḏrt*; *mṯnwt* is taken to be a writing of *mṯnwt* 'reward'.

2. Lit. perhaps 'all that I desire is that what-I-request-overflows (*ḥw*)'.
3. I.e. those who collect and bring what the deceased requires.
4. Read *ỉnn.sn* ⟨*n*⟩.*ỉ*.
5. Cf. the similar expression *mds byt* 'forceful of character', *Les.* 79,7.
6. Interpreting the trace after *ḫt* as  rather than  as de Buck, n. 9*.
7. Cf. de Buck's fragment of P. Gard. IV on p. 163.
8. The P. Gard. IV fragment reads: 'O you gods, spirits and the dead who fear me, who tremble at me, and who burn incense (*ỉd*) to me, [. . .], you gods, [spirits and the dead] who serve me [. . .]'.
9. Reading *g(ꜣ)w* 'a bundle'.

Spell 947

O you who lack(?), [. . .], you who are pure, you who are primeval(?), you who are enduring [. . .] . . .[1] I am Edjō, I am [. . .][2] pre-eminent in the *pr-wr,* the fiery serpent pre-eminent in the *pr-nsr,* I have appeared that I may control those who make offering, and my foundation is made for me among the kings. I will not protect a misdeed(?); is there any protection by me for his misdeed?[3]

1. Again the opening words of the spell are obscure; the various fem. verb-forms have been assumed to be participles, epithets of the beings addressed; the word *sšsš* with head-rest(?) det. appears to be unknown.
2. For the *ḥwnt*-animal, species unknown, cf. also *CT* V, 210*k*.
3. 163*m.n* are difficult; if the translation be even approximately correct, these two clauses seem devoid of connection with what precedes. *'In rf ỉw wn* is a strange combination, apparently interrogative, and there is no clue to the meaning of *sp* as object of *mk* except that it is something not to be protected.

Spell 948

[. . .] the Four,[1] living and equipped, who went out from Dep, the supports of VII, 164
the sky, the company of the gods, and Bubastis [. . .] he who is worshipped and her greedy ones,[2] who fetched her possessions.

1. Feminine.
2. These last two words are on the fragment of P. Gard. IV. For *ḥty* 'worship' cf. *ḥtt* 'adoration', *RB* 114,11; for *ḫntw.s* 'her greedy ones' cf. *ḫnt* 'greed', *Concise Dict.* 173.

Spell 949

I know you,[1] I know your names, I live as you, I come into being as you, I will leap up[2] and I will run to you. (As for) you older gods who would oppose(?) me,[3] I will be conducted on the path of my warrant.

1. This spell is but a fragment of a longer text of which the beginning is lost; the pronouns *ṯn* lack an antecedent.
2. With fish-det., perhaps derived from fish leaping out of the water or rising to the surface.
3. Restore as *ḫs*[*f.ty.sn*]?

Spell 950

VII, 165 [. . .] spirits who went forth adorned in the two sun-barks of Rēʿ, my pillar-amulet of life is in my hand and I make the plebs flourish;[1] I am [on high(?)],[2] I am Edjō. O you gods, spirits and dead, come to me [. . .] in my presence, for I am Edjō; [O you gods, goddesses(?)],[3] Powers, men, spirits, the dead [. . .] burn incense and [. . .] for me [. . .] or(?) I will kill you. O you whom I wish to serve me, come [. . .]. O you servitors who are well-disposed to me and whom
166 I love, my life will be made pleasant and I will be made glad,[4] I will be lovable [1]and the sweet breath of life will be given to me. He knows and she knows that I am Edjō, living and equipped, I have possessions(?),[5] I am a monkey.

1. For the transitive use of *w3ḏ* cf. *Urk.* IV 132,12; 2157,15.
2. Restore as [*k3*]*y n.ỉ*?
3. Restoration conjectural.
4. Restore as *snḏm* [*ỉb*].*ỉ*.
5. Cf. Spell 946, n. 9.

Spell 951

[. . .]. I am she who has come into being, (even) Edjō; I am the great flame which shines over Nūt, I am the great rod which governs [. . .], which controls the patricians [and spits out the plebs[1] . . .], I am lovable, [my] portion is made [. . .].

1. Restored from 162*q* above.

Spell 952

O Pe, [O Dep . . .], O you who are afraid of me, who tremble at me, who burn VII,167
incense to me and who are under my great power, see, I have appeared to you as Edjō of Pe and Dep, the slayer pre-eminent in the Mansions of the Red Crown, who herself strews well-being(?), who protects the gods from those who would harm them, I [. . .] there, I have seen the pillar [. . .] the kite, by means of which [the patricians(?)] and the plebs flourish, [by means of which . . .] flourish [. . . I am] Edjō who dwells in the starry sky [. . .].

Spell 953

O you tribunal which sits in front of the Great One – and *vice versa* – if you send VII,168
your messengers for me, I will not come to you. If I move about, I will move about as Min, I will travel as Horus who is in Ut, I have opened up my path as Wepwawet. My face is Sakhmet, my [. . .] is Nekhbet, my nails are the pigeon[1] of the gods; I will not come to you, I will not return to you until I act the fighter(?)[2] [. . .] me – and *vice versa*; I go all over the Two Lands, I possess my river-banks, I will point a finger to Edjō.

1. For this bird cf. *CT* VI, 278*k*; Edel, *Weltkammer*, I, 229.
2. *ʾIꜣꜣw*, written twice with two different spellings, may possibly be connected with *i͗ꜣꜣwy* 'pair of combatants', *Pyr.* §264.

Spell 954

[. . .] Nekhbet, evil [. . .] [1]there is made for me . . .[1] [. . .]. I am in the dark, VII,169
I am allotted into the hand of the Great Lady, I am [Horus(?) . . . , alive[2]] and young on the night when I departed and returned in the bark of Rēʿ that I might give thrones to Neḥebkau. My utterance is made, earth is upon me, Gēb is on my vertex, and I will be Edjō; I WILL SPEAK ABOUT wood for the fire, incense, myrrh, ladanum(?), *ḥknw*-oil, *šsꜣt*-oil,[3] 'vulture-dirt', 'feather-of-the-field',[4] all heaped together, so that ⟨my⟩ flesh may be anointed with it, and that the Great Lady may be pure.[5]

1. *Ppw.*
2. Cf. de Buck, n. 3*.
3. Cf. *Wb.* IV, 543, 4.

4. Two names for ritual materials which are unidentified.
5. Regarding *r.s* as the enclitic.

Spell 955

[. . .] Edjō who lives on . . .[1] [. . .] with the Mistress of Pe there; [I am
VII,170 Sakhmet],[2] | Bastet the beloved(?)[3] [. . .]. I am Edjō when she is sick(?), she who guards the seasons(?) on the day of [. . . , living and] equipped on the vertex of the silent ones from whom I have flown up. The gods have served me, they have seen my soul at my throat as the Mistress of All Years. [BECOMING] A VULTURE.

1. *ꜣrwtyw*.
2. Cf. de Buck, n. 8*.
3. Restore *mrwtt*?

Spell 956

[Shout!][1] I have taken acclamation, I have ascended to the upper sky of Rēᶜ, I have fashioned Nekhbet, I [have descended][2] to the lower sky, I have fashioned
VII,171 [Sakhmet[3] . . .], I have nourished Rēᶜ. | The guardian of the [complete(?)][4] Vulture [. . .] Rēᶜ lives in me every day; if life be at his nose, life will be at my nose; if he be a noble, I will be a noble; the love of him will be the love of me. My mother [has installed me][5] in the midst of herself, because what is disliked is that Seth should see me when I reappear.

O you who are in the Suite, [who see][6] the young Horus every day as a protection for his Eye, I [will be a child][7] every day – so says Rēᶜ of me. If I do not place [him, he will not place me(?)],[8] and *Ḥng* will be astray(?) [. . . you fear] Rēᶜ and Horus, and Horus is content [. . .] the powers of Seth are sealed off(?), and I will be a child[9] – so says Rēᶜ of me. He does not place me because I see(?) what Rēᶜ desires every day [. . .] on which Rēᶜ lives every day [. . .] the Mistress[10] of Eternity, [the Mistress of] the limits of the sky, who will not die, perish, be destroyed or come to nothing because of it; (therefore) I will not die, perish, be destroyed or come to nothing.

172 Rēᶜ [has installed me][11] within Nekhbet [. . . I have guided my father(?)][12] Rēᶜ, and he has given me the year's bread [. . .] this my [. . .] which is in Nekhbet. May I ascend to the sky as the young Horus, may I descend to the earth

as *Šstt*,[13] for my wand is mightier than his wand. I am the heir of eternity, I have passed everlasting.

1. Restored as 172*l*.
2. Restored as 173*a*.
3. Restored as 173*b*.
4. Cf. de Buck, 171, n. 1*.
5. Restored as 173*m* + 175*e*.
6. Restored as 174*a*.
7. Restored from 174*b*.
8. Restoring as 174*c.d*.
9. With *ny* compare the passage regarding a new-born child in *Eb.* 97,13: 'if he says *ny* means he will live'. 174*o* has *nny*.
10. Cf. 175*b*.
11. Restored as 175*e*.
12. Conjecturally restored as 175*l*.
13. We should surely emend to the 1st person here.

Spell 957

TO BECOME MAʿET. Shout! I have taken the bark of acclamation. Shout! I have fashioned the bark of acclamation. I have ascended to the upper sky,[1] and I have fashioned Nekhbet; I have descended to the lower sky of Rēʿ, and I have fash- VII,173
ioned Sakhmet. I have power in the shrine, for I have nourished Rēʿ; I have traversed the middle sky [. . .] Rēʿ-Atum for him, because I am Maʿet in these manifestations of hers which are upon and in the middle of Nekhbet, the entire Vulture. [Her(?) wings] are opened [to(?)] me, and Rēʿ lives thereby every day; if life be at his nose, life will be at my nose; if he be a noble, I will be a noble, the love of him will be the love of me. Nekhbet has [installed] me in the midst of herself, because what is disliked is that [Seth] should see me when I reappear.[2]

O you who are in the Suite who see the young Horus on the lap of Rēʿ as 174
a protection for his Eye, if I be a child, he will be a child to Rēʿ every day – so says Rēʿ of me. If I do not place [him], *Ḥng* who is astray(?) will not place me. May my[3] eyes be open and may he clear my vision, so that I may not fear ʿApep the Wanderer(?), and he[4] will never see Maʿet or Rēʿ, so that you may not be afraid, O Rēʿ; if Horus be content, Maʿet will be content. O you who are on high within the doors [. . . of] Nekhbet, the double doors will be opened, Rēʿ will shine, the powers of Seth will be sealed off(?). O you who are in the Suite who see the young Horus, if he be a child, I will be a child [. . .] so that I may not be

175 afraid.[1] I will not perish, die, come to nothing or be destroyed, I am that Maʿet who is in the midst of Nekhbet, who loves Rēʿ, Mistress of eternity, Mistress of the limits of [sky] and earth, who will not perish, die, come to nothing or [be destroyed,] because she sees.[5] I am within my mother the Mistress of Pe and mine is her Pe.[6] Rēʿ has installed me within Nekhbet, in the midst of Nekhbet, because what is disliked is that the great ones should have power over me. If I see Rēʿ, Rēʿ will see me; may Rēʿ flourish and be glad, for I myself am alive and glad. I will reappear, for I have guided my father Rēʿ, I have received his year's bread and his thrice daily beer.

176 O every god and every spirit [who shall speak][7] my fair and true name when I appear ⟨as⟩ him who is in Nekhbet; may I[8] ascend to the sky as Horus of the Netherworld, may I descend to the lower sky as *Šstt*, [may my power be greater(?)][9] than his power, for I am one who passes eternity [. . .] within [. . .] . . .[10] sky and earth, your (masc.!) deserts of the nomads come to you (fem.).[11] [. . .]

1. Cf. 170*k* and the reference to the lower sky in 173*a*.
2. Cf. 171*g-h*.
3. For *ỉrty.k* read *ỉrty.ỉ*; there is no-one addressed in the 2nd person.
4. For *sp.k* read *sp.f,* in reference to ʿApep.
5. Following P. Gard. IV.
6. Lit. 'your Pe'; confusion of suffix again.
7. Restore *ḏd.ty.fy,* cf. de Buck, 176, n. 5*.
8. Emend into 1st person.
9. Conjectural restoration as *wr sḫm.ỉ.*
10. *Ppy* is not recorded, but cf. *ppw*, 169*b*.
11. Note the confusion of suffixes within a single sentence.

Spell 958

To become Sia who belongs to Rēʿ. Dread has fallen on the gods of the horizon,
177 so stand up, O you who dwell in your shrines! They see their joy in me, for [1]I appear as Sia [. . .] they have [. . .] those who are in mourning, because he goes to and fro[1] for them; those who are in the limits of the horizon rejoice because he judges business [. . .] my lips speak ⟨to⟩[2] the Great Lady, seeing that Thoth writes therein. It is I who despatch Maʿet to the horizon, and my name is injured(?) [. . .] Sia who belongs to Rēʿ.

1. The *n* at the beginning of 177*c* is probably the preposition, as in *n wpp.f* in 177*e*;

no verb *nmnmn* appears to be known. It is not clear who 'he' may be; possibly it is an editorial change from the 1st person.

2. Elision of *n* after *sn.*

Spell 959

To become the scribe of the great god, the greatest of [the tribunal of the god].[1] I am Rēʿ, the great one in the midst of his Eye, who went forth separated(?);[2] I cause [. . .] to be separated(?) [. . .] from the horizon [. . . I(?)] have come on your account. | O you who are on the willow(?), I am he who excludes(?)[3] VII,178
(men) from Maʿet. See, I know and I have spoken; I have come and surpassed the great ones. I sit on the bench(?)[4] and deliver my judgements, my retainers are the sun-folk, for I will be the scribe of the great god, the greatest of the tribunal of the god.

1. For the restoration cf. 178*g*.
2. Cf. *ỉw* 'abtrennen', Wb. I, 48,1.
3. Perhaps in the sense of 'condemns'.
4. In the literal sense, note the long narrow determinative.

Spell 960

[. . .] Rēʿ who excludes the sun-folk, [who] all belong to me[1][. . .] who (fem.) displays beauty and who kicks Seth. O You (fem.) who go round about, I have come that I may see, in company with my double, and I am content with my meal [. . .] great and [small], I have brought up(?) the two Ḥu-gods with the aid of my meat(?),[2] and there is no god or goddess who can oppose himself (or herself) to me | [. . .] being what she did for me. Good [. . .] I am not [. . .] who VII,179
can oppose himself to me.

1. Reading *ḏr.sn.*
2. Lit. perhaps: 'by means of my two shins (of beef)'.

Spell 961 is lost.

Spell 962

[. . .] the sunshine falls within my course, I caress the Eye of Horus [. . .] every day [. . .].

Spell 963 is lost.

Spell 964

VII,180 [I will go aboard the bark which is tied up][1] at the stairway, I [have] removed the trouble [of the larboard watch, and the starboard watch] is under my command[2] [. . . it means that speech(?)] will come into being behind the mansion of Khopri [. . .] his shape is like that of *Swnṯ*.

1. Restored from *CT* VI, 282*l-n*, cf. de Buck, n. 5*.
2. Restored from VI, 280*f-g*.

Spell 965

VII,181 I [. . .] as Thoth, I have taken the strength of Rēʿ-Atum, I am Shu, Lord of All, I have come on foot so that I may be strong, [. . .] I have come against that foe of mine, and he is put an end to beneath me, even he whom I have placed in the tribunal.

Spell 966 is fragmentary.

Spell 967

VII,182 [I am][1] the Ram, I am primeval(?), my phallus is primeval(?),[2] my seed is that of the Bull of the sun-folk [. . .] to his double. I have travelled to Osiris and to his double, and he has given me his house and his seed that I may copulate with it [. . .] what I desire [. . .]. I traverse Upper Egypt [. . .] by my horn(?) and my lasso. It means that(?) [. . .] is strong and that what is damaged is the thigh of Osiris. My phallus is that of Min on the day of [. . .]-birds, I am the Ram, and I have come that I may be a crocodile-spirit.

1. Restored from 182*n.*

2. *P3wt* is feminine. We have here the anomaly of a spell essentially masculine being spoken by a woman.

Spell 968 is fragmentary, but it names Rēʿ-Atum and Neḥebkau.

Spell 969

[I am a crocodile][1] immersed in his blood [. . . I am][2] he who brings this which was stolen, [I am] the Great Fish, my face is toward the region of the Two Bulls,[3] I am the Lord of strength in Khem.[4] VII,183

1. Restored as de Buck, n. 6*.
2. Restore *ink* in both 183*i* and *j*, Compare *BD* 188, 12–13.
3. *BD* 188,14 has *Km-wr*; here it is just possible that Xois was meant, cf. Gauthier, *Dict. géogr.* V, 185, top. The damaged version of 203*h* in Spell 991 seems to be slightly corrupt, and shows but one bull-on-standard.
4. On *ks* cf. *JEA* 57,18 (31). *BD* 188, 14–15 has: 'I am the Lord of those who bow down in Khem'.

Spell 970

[. . .] I . . .[1] and I strike [. . .], | I [eat] with my mouth and defecate [with] my anus, I follow what Osiris tore off(?)[2] among what is burnt [. . .] who acted at their desire. VII,184

1. *Nsḳ*; cf. *Wb.* II, 336,15.
2. Not 'the four'; there are only three strokes.

Spell 971

[. . .] long of temple (of head) (?) [. . .] painful of tress(?).[1] I have come to you that I may nourish your great ones [. . .] the keeper of linen for the uraei on the night of the great flood which issued from the Great Lady. I have come [. . .] who washed(?) me that I might drive out crookedness, and I will do what is right. I am the guardian of the nose of the Great Power, for he has placed me [. . .].

1. For *swt* 'tress(?)' cf. *CT* VI, 124*d*; 250*d*.

Spell 978 is almost entirely lost.

Spell 979

[. . .] the great Wild Bull. I will appear as the great Wild Bull, Lord of the Man-
sions of the West; my horns are the two tails[1] [. . .] the gods; | my eyes are VII,189
[. . .]; my hoofs are the hoofs of Isis;[2] [. . .] at the Mansions of the Red Crown.[3] I eat and drink[4] in the Mansions of [. . .]; I traverse the fish-ponds[5] [. . .], I [travel(?)] the waterways of the Field of Offerings, [. . .], I traverse the river-banks [. . .]; my [eyes][6] are the . . .[7] of the Eye of Horus; my wings are those of the Bull of the crocodile-spirits [. . .] eat; he goes to rest, having done what he wished,[8] and my wings are those of ⟨the Bull of⟩ the crocodile-spirits.[9]

1. Apparently so, though the det. is that of *sd* 'clothe'.
2. As cow-goddess.
3. The water-sign is borrowed from *nt* 'water'.
4. Read *wnm swr.*
5. *Swnw,* cf. *Concise Dict.* 217, though the fish-det. is unusual.
6. Cf. de Buck, n. 8*.
7. *Ṯpṯt.*
8. Perhaps we should emend into the 1st person.
9. Supply *kꜣ* 'bull' before *ʿšmw,* cf. 189*j*.

Spell 980

[. . .] . . .[1] I will not be repelled from sky or earth. My mother bore me [. . .], VII,190
and him whom I find in my way, I will devour him.

1. *R mst.ỉ ỉn* 190*e* is obscure to me.

Spell 981 is fragmentary.

Spell 982

[I am][1] the son of Isis who inflames(?)[2] sky and earth, my wings are [. . .] I fly VII,191
up(?) [. . .], I land as Rēʿ in the West. O you men, spirits, gods or powers who

would oppose yourselves to me [. . .] ascend as Shu. 'O my son, use your feet' says my mother Isis to me [. . .] when he reaches [. . .] says my mother [Isis to me . . .] use your feet, hurry, hurry, run, for you will not be named if he has not yet reached you – so says my mother Isis to me.

1. Cf. de Buck, n. 1*.
2. Cf. *JEA* 35,96, n. 7.

Spell 983

VII,192 [. . .] for providing for living. The whole of the two skies comes to him,[1] (and also) [the Lord(?)] of the Fields of Offerings and of Rushes [. . .] who is in the Netherworld.

1. Possibly to be understood in the 1st person.

Spell 984

[. . .] horizon [. . .] Horus son of Isis. His gods and spirits will come behind and before him, and there are no souls or gods who will oppose him, (so also) there are
VII,193 no souls or gods who will oppose me; my eye [. . .] any foe who may come to oppose me. O Bald-pate, ferryman of the Winding Waterway [. . .] I am manifest, exalted and existent as a possessor of powers. I have gone in that I may count [. . .].

Spell 985

Thoth goes forth in his brightness with his ritual-book in his hands, and praise is given to him, offerings are presented to him by those who are in the great castle [. . .].

Spell 986 is fragmentary.

Spell 987

To become [. . .] a path is made for me [. . .] the gods will come[1] [. . .]. O Bald-pate, [ferryman of the Winding Waterway[2] . . .] of the Winding Waterway[1] [. . .] they rejoice[3] because of me [. . .]. Here am I; I have come [. . .], I am VII,195 manifest, exalted and existent as a possessor of [powers[4] . . . Thoth has gone forth in his brightness][5] with his ritual-book[6] in [his] hands [. . . offerings are presented][7] to me by those who are in the great castle [. . .] the two Enneads, and I am uplifted on the throne [. . .], I am he who swallowed [. . .].

1. Cf. de Buck, n. 7*.
2. Cf. de Buck, n. 8*.
3. Read perhaps *ḥꜥ.sn* rather than *sḥꜥ.sn*; the *s* may have belonged to the preceding clause.
4. Cf. de Buck, 195, n. 5*.
5. Cf. de Buck, n. 6*.
6. Read *ḥbt* with 193*m*.
7. Cf. de Buck, n. 10*.

Spell 988

To become air. I have come from the limits of the lands [. . .], I have passed by VII,196 [. . .] whom the Chastiser smites.[1] [I have upraised(?)[2] the corners] of the zenith(?)[3] in the house of those who suffer beatings, I have glimpsed[4] the booths which they sanctified, I have whitened my wall for the disembowelling of the Baboon [. . .] I found him in company with the Double Lion, and the river was placed for them on the top of Gēb [. . .] of Shu [. . .] whom I found there. [I have(?)] come [. . .] the living ones who are in [. . .].

1. For *rmrm* 'chastise' cf. Urk. IV, 1076,5.
2. Restore as *ỉw skꜣ.n.ỉ*?
3. Cf. *Komm. Pyr.* II, 338.
4. Cf. *Wb.* I, 426, 1.

Spell 989

TO BECOME A FALCON. The announcers of the great storm-cloud go forth from VII,197 the horizon, the inner apartment of Her who bore the gods on the five epagomenal days, (even) they who are before you [. . .] before your hand(?)[1] among those who make [. . .] at the sound of the cry[2] of my mother [. . .] who bore [me(?) . . .] as this her great and mighty *nwr*-fish(?) which is in the sky. [My] mother bore me [. . .] within the god's tamarisk[-clump(?)] which enfolds Thoth when Isis comes, and she says: 'Semen shall be destroyed for you and . . . before your days have come.[3]

What is to be done about this?[4]

198 The god shall ejaculate semen and . . . | and I will have brought to you this iron which is in the bow of the bark of *Ḥnw*. They shall knit together [. . .] within the arms of [. . . within] the arms of Khopri as a god.

Who will break the god's egg?

I will cause [. . .] his bones shall be moulded[5] for him [. . .] he will break the egg and split the iron [. . .] my guardian who is among the gods. O [. . .], you shall guide him who has served you, and I will fly up as [. . .]. The plumes of[6] *Ḥnw* shall be given to you, and their . . .[7] shall be on top of *Ḥnw*.

The south-wind shall be given to you for your henchman and the north-wind for your nurse; the plume of the Beauteous One shall be tied on her sister, |
199 [. . .] which is between them both. I will make ascents to the horizon, for I reached the horizon as a uraeus when I was born.

1. So rather than ʿ 'warrant'; this is a common corruption.
2. *'Iṯn*, unrecorded.
3. I do not understand 197*h*, but there is clearly a reference to the sexual act, see 197*i*. The meaning of the fem. word *ʿȝʿt* is obscure, and the dative before it either is a dittograph of *n.ṯ* following *ḥḏ*, or else a verb has been omitted.
4. Lit. 'What is the thing of doing about this?'
5. *Nb*, lit. 'cast' in metal.
6. Apparently an instance of genitival *m*; cf. Spell 356, n. 5.
7. *Ḳdmw*.

Spell 990

I am the great falcon which is on the battlements of the Mansion [of Him whose name is hidden, taking what belongs to Atum][1] to Him who separates the [sky(?)][2] from the earth and the Abyss. My eyes are the Bull of the Sunshine
VII,200 [. . .] my wing[3] is He who is foremost [. . .]; | they make out my name as Divine Falcon, they raise me up to Reʿ-Atum, my father who fashioned me. I have come to my seat which is in Malachite-land north of [. . .],[4] my food is in the Fields of Offerings, in the waterways of turquoise, and it is the *ḏsytt*[5] who

will feed me [. . .]. I possess my spirit, I possess my soul as the bull of his stall(?)[6] on the boat [. . .]. I have flown up to the sky as Shu the great[7] [. . .] on the northern shore(?)[8] of the Island of Dancers(?),[9] and I will alight on
. . .[10] [. . .] the storm will be high(?) among the innumerable(?).[11] | See, I will 201
endure[12] [. . .] my year is complete and my guide [is] Maꜥet(?).[13]

1. Restored as *Pyr.* §1778, cf. de Buck, n. 3*.
2. Presumably *pt* 'sky' should be restored before *r tꜣ*, despite the extant determinative, cf. *Pyr.* §1778*b*; *CT* VI, 310*l*.
3. For the hair-det. of *dmꜣt,* cf. *šwt* 'feather', *M.u.K.* 1, 2; *ḏnḥ* 'wing', *CT* VII, 191*b*.
4. Cf. de Buck, 200, n. 4*. On *Šsmt* cf. *Stud. Griff.* 321.
5. Hardly to be connected with *ḏsw* 'call', 'shout'.
6. *Ḳrrt*; hardly 'cavern' in this context.
7. Cf. de Buck, 200, n. 1*.
8. *Mdb.*
9. *Hꜣbw*; compare *ỉhbw,* var. *ỉhꜣbw,* 'dancers', *Concise Dict.* 28.
10. Cf. Spell 682, n. 15.
11. The translation of 200*m* is doubtful.
12. Read *sk wỉ mn. ỉ.*
13. Restore as *sšmw. ỉ m Mꜣꜥt*?

Spell 991

TO BECOME SOBK. I am the seed which issued from the encircling wrapping.[1]

I am he who broke the teeth of him who cut away the iron.[2]

I am the Lord of strength and might who took crocodile-shape.[3]

I am the Lord of wrong who lives on woe.

I am that crocodile[4] whose tongue was cut out because of the mutilation of Osiris.

I am he who puts fear [into . . .] whom the Ennead fear. VII,202

I am Lord of the Nile [. . .].

I am that god who rises in the East and sets in the West, to whom the Niles are given.

I am he who rises, who has no weakness because of the gods of the nomes.

I am that god whom the eight row.

I am Sobk, the rebel who is among you, [you gods];[5] you cannot do anything against me, you spirits or you dead, for I have taken possession of the sky and have taken possession of the earth.

I am a possessor of worship [. . .] to whom are given his *smwt*-women[6] and their hair.

203 I am [. . .] a multitude.
I am Sobk, Lord of strife, who lingers [. . .].
I am Sobk, Lord of the river-banks [. . .] his blood.
I am he who impregnates[7] *smwt*-women.
I am he who has recourse to robbery.
I am [the Great Fish] giving to the region of the Bull.[8]
I am a possessor of strength in Khem.[9]

1. The seed of the dead and enwrapped Osiris. For *sḥw dbn* cf. *sḥ* 'enwrap' a mummy, *CT* I, 205*d*.
2. Or 'the firmament'.
3. Lit. 'who received crocodile'.
4. The sense of the passage and the use of *pw* point to *sbk* here being the common noun 'crocodile' rather than the name of the god; cf. the clear instances *CT* IV, 2*e*; 3*b*; 4*g* (where the word is in parallel with *msḥ*), all in the crocodile-spell no. 268.
5. Cf. de Buck, n. 7*.
6. The *smwt*-women are mentioned again in 203*f*, and there is a more elaborate writing in *CT* IV, 2*a* (Spell 268). The determinatives in all three instances suggest persons doomed to an unpleasant fate.
7. For *sṯw* 'impregnate' with *ḥr* + object cf. *Urk.* IV, 238,8.
8. Compare 183*j*.
9. See also 183*k*.

Spell 992

TO BECOME THE SECRETARY OF THOTH AND TO OPEN WHAT HIS BOX[1] CONTAINS.
VII,204 My *nt*-crown is my reward, my reward.[2] | I am [. . .] Rēʿ-Atum, I have come so that I may reckon up the signs [. . .] I will open what it contains. The seal is broken, [the cord(?)] is cut[3] [. . .] words. I am he who is over exhaling, Lord of the breath of the Great One [. . . I] sit [. . .] I open the chest of the Great One, I break the seal [. . .] the Lord of Right. I open what the boxes of the god contain,[4] I lift out the documents, for I am a lord who exhales.

1. The determinative of *ʿ* seems to represent a shallow box or tray on legs with a lift-out lid.
2. This seems quite irrelevant to the rest of the spell.
3. For *sš* 'cut' cf. *JEA* 37, 51(*o*). The reference may have been to the cord tied round the roll.
4. Var. P. Gard. III: 'I open what the documents contain'.

Spell 993

TO BECOME HIM OF THE TWO WANDS. The skies are uncovered, the clouds disperse,[1] [. . .] he who counts(?), who see what he has desired. Rēʿ appears with this Ennead[2] of his, Lord of [the Sunshine(?)[3] . . .] which she put on herself. What Horus brought to him was what the Two Lands gave to him[4] [. . .]. VII,205

She whose head was cut off with a knife.[5]
She of the papyrus-plant[6] whose milk is sweet.
She of vegetation(?) which her lord divided.[7]
She whom Horus examined(?) . . .[8]
Mistress of herbage who makes the Two Lands green.
Mistress of the night who takes possession of the Two Lands.
She who bent Seth on account of her utterance.
She who cleared Horus's vision for him.
She who placed her lord in her embrace for herself.

Hail to you,[9] Horus [. . .] Horus in [Pe] on the day of pain(?) [. . . and of] 206
the night of [cutting off(?)] heads and of having power over the lesser ones and the great ones.

'WHO IS[10] THIS SPIRIT' SAYS RĒʿ-ATUM OF ME.
'HE IS(?)[11] MY SON' SAYS OSIRIS.
I am [. . .].
'PE BELONGS TO YOU' SAY THE GREAT ONES.
'YOU SHALL BRING ME THIS MY ENNEAD' SAYS RĒʿ TO ME.

I am Thoth [. . .] Rēʿ has power when he is bright [. . .]. I am [. . .].
'Who is [boatless[12] . . . ?' . . .]. He shall ferry over [. . .]|in the way [. . .] I 207
taste [you(?)].[13] O Image(?),[14] you have no knife, you have no fire. O hunter(?),[15] I will not fall because of you.[16] O shambles of the god, I will not enter into you. My seat is in the sun-disk; how firm is my seat in the sun-disk! I am [. . .] I am he who is in charge of the seats of the gods, a star which is joyful in [. . .], because if I live, Rēʿ will live – and *vice versa*; the Ennead [. . .].

1. *ʿḏwt* appears not to be recorded, but the sense is hardly in doubt; *nwr* normally means 'quake', 'tremble', *Pyr.* §§143; 581; 2109, or 'cease', 789, and a cessation, i.e. dispersal of cloud is certainly meant here.

2. *N* is prefixed to *psḏt* also in 206*g*; 207*l*, but the reason is not clear.

3. Restoring the second word in 205*e* as *i͗ꜣḫw*.

4. Reading as *dyt.n ⟨n.⟩f tꜣwy*.

5. Here begins a series of epithets of a female deity, probably Isis, cf. 205*p.q*. A refer-

ence to the decapitation of Isis occurs in Chester Beatty Papyrus No. I, 9,9. For *wḏꜥt* 'knife' cf. *Wb.* I, 406,14.

6. Written as a derivative of *mnḥ* 'papyrus', *Concise Dict.* 109. This may be the origin of the term *mnḥyt* recorded in *Wb.* II, 84,3–8 as applicable to a number of goddesses, who are not infrequently depicted as bearing a papyrus-stem staff.

7. Quite obscure. Is it the vegetation which is divided?

8. I can make nothing of this.

9. Here the text begins a new topic.

10. The apparent negation of 206*d* makes no sense as such; it is taken to be an abnormal writing of *ỉn m tr* 'who is . . . ?'. For other eccentric writings of this interrogative phrase cf. de Buck, *Archiv Orientální,* 20, 397 ff.

11. I cannot suggest a plausible reading for the group marked 6* by de Buck; the context demands 'he is', but I can read neither *swt, ntf* nor *ỉw.f m* into the group in question. Why cryptic writings should be adopted for 'who is' and 'he is' is not known.

12. Conjecturally restoring *ỉw* 'be boatless', in view of the reference to ferrying below.

13. Cf. de Buck, 207, n. 4*.

14. Cf. de Buck, 207, n. 1*. The word could be *ỉrw* or *twt.*

15. Cf. *ḫdd,* var. *ḫdḏ,* Wb. III, 355,15.

16. For *ỉm.ṯ* read *ỉm.k.*

Spell 994

VII,208 SPELL FOR THE GOVERNANCE OF THE RIVER-BANKS OF THE IBIS. Hail to you, Thoth, in your power in the midst of the river-banks [. . .]. Find[1] Edjō in it, and she will make you flourish; find the Eye of Horus in it, and you will be strong by means of it. I have come that I may see you, that I may recognise your beauty, that I may send your foreleg-offering [. . .] and that I may send your word. O White Crown, Mistress of Pe for Edjō, make light [for me], so that I may have light and be high(?) [. . .] my mother who bore her thousand for the Devouring Flame, Lady of [. . .] in her name [. . .].

209 I copulate with you[2] for Horus who protects his father, so that he may do for me what you have done for him. I will live on heads, for I am Khons; my lake is dug, my pond is excavated, I [have given birth to(?)][3] my heir, namely he who issued[4] from me. It is Horus who is on his coils(?)[5] who permits me to speak.[6] Might is created for me [. . .] in the river-bank of the ibis; I have power over them, and they [will] not ⸢have power⸣ over[7] me; I have equipped(?)[8] [. . .].

1. Imperative with reflexive dative.

2. Masc., but who is meant? Possibly Osiris, with the deceased woman in the role of

Isis, for apparently Horus is to be the offspring of this act.

3. Restoring conjecturally *ms.n.ỉ* in the lacuna.

4. Fem. participle!

5. *Nnt* with rope- or curl-det. seems not to be known. There is probably no connection with *nn* of *BD* 340,2, which may be a garment or material.

6. So P. Gard. II; in P. Gard. III there is a lacuna after *nn*[*t*] which ends with the name of Thoth.

7. Cf. de Buck, n. 7*.

8. Or 'equipment is mine'? P. Gard. II has a reference to an obscure word *ssw,* which occurs again in 212*b*, see de Buck, n. 2*, and continues: 'I will not perish, I will not [. . .]'.

Spell 995

THE TWO KNOTS OF THE IBIS. O Rēʿ-Atum, I have seen these Twins of yours VII,210
[. . .] he speaks and guides them both to the middle of the East.

'REJOICE!'[1] SAYS RĒʿ-ATUM TO[2] THESE ENDURING THINGS. I am an enduring thing; let the two knots of the ibis be given to me. I will bring to you [. . .] in due course(?).[3]

'ARE YOU AN EQUIPPED SPIRIT?' SAYS RĒʿ-ATUM.

'BE PLEASED'[4] – REPEAT FOUR TIMES – SAYS SIA [TO ME]. ALL MAGIC IS BROUGHT TO ME FROM THE UTTERMOST PARTS(?)[5] [. . .] DAUGHTER. HE HAS OCCUPIED HIS THRONE, HE HAS COME ON ACCOUNT OF ONE WHO GIVES PRAISES TO OSIRIS, FOR HE KNOWS THE NAME [. . .] WHO IS IN THE TWO BARKS OF RIGHT.
THERE ARE GIVEN TO HIM THE TWO KNOTS OF THE IBIS SO THAT HE MAY BRING 211
TO ME THE DAUGHTER(?) [. . .].

The Great One comes with his knife in his hand and he severs the spine of Rēʿ whom he sees. The Shining One comes with his horn in his hand so that he may remove the heart of Rēʿ whom he sees. Great is *'Iw* who falls for me, mighty is *'Iw* who looks on me. I am an equipped spirit, there are brought to me the Twins of Rēʿ; Rēʿ-Atum [. . .]; if Rēʿ be content with them, then will Rēʿ-Atum be content with them, and I will have power (over them) and be content with them [. . .] Rēʿ-Atum. See, I know the two knots of the ibis – REPEAT FOUR TIMES.

1. *Hrhr* is presumably an intensive reduplication of *hr* 'be pleased'.

2. *Ḫr* has been taken to be the preposition.

3. *M ꜣwt,* lit. 'in length'.

4. *'Ihr* has been taken to be the imperative of *hr* with prothetic *ỉ*.

5. *Ḏrwt* with the same determinative as *pḥww* 'far north'.

Spell 996

VII,212 [. . .] I have come here with a skin-bottle(?);[1] the beer[2] in it is stale, the cup in it is broken, the vessel in it is the . . .[3] of Khnum in his mouth. He has moulded me [. . .] he has treated me ill for a year.

'WHAT IS IT INTO WHICH YOU HAVE LOOKED?' SAYS THOTH [. . .] drinking water for that pregnant woman and beer for this pregnant woman – and *vice* [*versa*(?)[4] . . .] who(?) permits Seth to breathe because he is dishevelled through them; Seth will come [. . .]. As for my restraint(?) of *Nrt,*[5] that hoof (*sic*) which is in the coil of Rēʿ will be given to him who comes for it, and he will have power
213 over [. . .], | the great ones shall become lesser ones, and it shall not come to pass that I speak but am not heard. Shall I who say this be opposed when *Ḥnnsw* speaks? [. . .].

1. *Ssw* has the skin-det., and 212*c* shows that it contained drink.
2. *Tꜣḥḳt* of the text is a conflation of *tꜣḥt* 'dregs' and of *ḥnḳt* 'beer'.
3. I do not understand the kiln-sign before the name of Khnum.
4. Cf. de Buck, n. 3*.
5. A place-name. This passage is quite obscure.

Spell 997

[. . .] GOD [. . . IN(?)] THE BARK OF RĒʿ. O you gods who are in the bow of the bark of Rēʿ, I know you [and I know your names which] the god [made][1] for Him who is in darkness; the name of Him who is among the gods is secret, for
VII,214 he is a spirit. I am he who made you, | and I am he who is; I am Rēʿ-Atum dwelling in my flood, I am the seventh of the [seven] names which are in the chest of the Lord of the sunshine. I came into being in the Mansion of Him whose face is removed(?) in company with the earth-god [. . .] fallen on his face in the presence of Him who created his father.

'Whence have you come?' says the Great Flood who dwells in his enclosure.

'I have come from the circle(?) of the Pillar of Horus[2] which is north of the opening of darkness, and praise has gone forth to me from the mouths of the sceptred ones who are in the presence of Him who is in [. . .]. I have overturned the sky, and the sky has ceased[3] for me before his two faces'.

The *ʿnn*-snake [. . .] the Red Crown which is in the forefront. My shape is
215 sculpted(?)[4] for the two great Enneads of Rēʿ-Atum, | and I am your leader; I receive the dread(?)[5] which is in the hand[6] of Horus, and the impure ones are

repelled by means of it, (even) they who are in her (*sic*) great water. I am the vigilant one, the son of *ꜣsb* the great; my mother [. . .].

1. Restored according to de Buck, n. 7*.
2. Or 'the upper pillar'?
3. Or 'has stayed'.
4. *Ṯn* with knife-det. Not recorded.
5. *Nhd*; cf. *CT* IV, 21*d*.
6. The common corruption of ʿ 'document' for ʿ 'hand', 'arm'.

Spell 998

TO KNOW THE NAME OF THE MANSIONS OF REʿ(?).[1] This *pꜣt*-cake is a *pꜣt*-cake for the upper gate and for the lower gate of the ⟨upper(?)⟩[2] mansions and the lower mansions. The name is 'The Lower Mansions'.

This *pꜣt*-cake[3] is a *pꜣt*-cake for the upper gate and for the lower gate of the mansions of the Bulls. The name is 'The Mansions of the Bulls'.

1. Cf. de Buck, n. 5*. This spell is obscure and the translation doubtful.
2. Either *ḥrt* 'upper' has been omitted, or else there is a dittograph of *ḥwwt*. 215*j* seems to point rather to a dittograph.
3. Read *pꜣt tn* as in 215*h*.

Spell 999

TO KNOW THE NAME OF [. . .] LIFE. Hail to you, Reʿ, in this city of yours which VII,216
is in the middle of [. . .] when you put female images(?)[1] in a jar in it; I know its name, and I will not die. Its new-moon festival is stopped(?),[2] and weary is he who . . . ,[3] so that I may not be afraid and my wounds will be cooled. You make fast (your boat) at the banks(?)[4] and he who lives will enter into it.[5]

1. *Dyt.k* is taken to be the *sḏmt.f* form. For *ḥmwt*, cf. the masc. *ḥmw*, *Urk.* IV, 576,10.
2. Reading as *ỉw psḏntyw.s ỉs ḫnt*, but the translation is quite uncertain.
3. I do not understand *nhy n.f.*
4. On *hy* 'make fast', elsewhere of a rope, cf. *JEA* 57, 202; with the unrecorded word *bnḏwt* compare *bnd* 'Acker o.a.', *Wb.* I, 464,13.
5. The suffix *.s* may refer to the postulated boat or to the city of 216*b*.

Spell 1000

SPELL FOR ENTERING INTO THE SUN-DISK. O you who are strong in your striking-power, who do not turn aside because of what he[1] would do, here am I; I
VII,217 have come and have recognized the Great Lady, | I have established Right for Rēʿ-Khopri, I have opened that mysterious Eye of yours which is behind the Double Lion, I am saved from the wrath of Him who is joined to his body, and he is strong by means of it. I go forth in company with the creator of the god who goes about in the train of Rēʿ-Atum; I(?)[2] [. . .] Horus the Elder within his shrine, and the uraeus which is on my vertex is joyful just as Rēʿ-Atum was joyful at the raging of his White Crown(?)[3] by means of which Shu was strong.

O You who are strong in striking-power, who sit on your coils and who hear [the speech(?)[4]] of the great ones in the place where Rēʿ-Atum speaks: I wish that my eye [. . .] the Great One speaks. It is the Westerners who display
218 and see your power, and I display your power | and lay hold of your brow, I send you the words of Him whose face is hidden, I lament the Great One with grief(?),[5] the . . .[6] [who hide(?)][7] their seats from the gods of the horizon. I am one who enters into his great Eye.

1. Seth?
2. The 1st person seems required here.
3. Emend *tpt* to *ḥḏt*?
4. Restore *mdt*(?)
5. *Nyfyf,* not recorded.
6. Reading doubtful, see de Buck, 281, n. 1*.
7. Restore *ỉmnw*?

Spell 1001

TO OPEN THE INNER[1] GATES OF [. . .]. I have come into this Island of Fire, and I am content with the manifestations of the ithyphallic ones(?).[2] O Grain-god,
VII,219 open the gates for me, | open out the ritual book [for] me,[3] for I have come so that those whose mouths are hidden may have abundance.

1. Lit. 'which are behind'.
2. Cf. *Wb.* I, 167, 1.
3. Restore as *sn n.ỉ ḥbt.*

Spell 1002

NOT TO GO INTO [THE SHAMBLES] [1] OF THE HOUSE OF HIM WHO IS FOREMOST. The brick grows[2] in the Eye of Horus, and Osiris cleanses it;[3] he comes into being[4] in the presence of Rēᶜ-Khopri.

1. Cf. de Buck, n. 4*.
2. The bird seems to be an additional determinative of *rd. Ḏbt* 'brick' could perhaps be used by hyperbole of a speck of grit in Horus's eye, where it might well feel like a brick, the 'brick' being removed by Osiris (219*f*).
3. On *sw* before a *sḏm.f* form cf. *Eg. Gramm.* [3] p. 424.
4. A false gemination *ḫprr.f* in P. Gard II (219*g*) is perhaps due to a memory of *ḫprr* 'scarab-beetle'.

Spell 1003

Prepare a path for me, for I am a bull on whom are testicles; open the door of the VII,220
blue sky,[1] for I have come so that I may open the door of the Great One and make content[2] him who takes possession of his house. The Lord of those with braided locks has gone out to meet me, and he causes me to enter on the secret paths of the Double Lion on which the gods fear to enter. I will make acclamation with the few within the god's shrine before Him who goes forth who shall burn on the battlements of the sky, and the sky will set me beside the . . .[3] in the north. Praise will be given to me within my power,[4] for I am exalted over my Two Lands and pre-eminent in the Two Conclaves of the sky.

1. Cf. *ṯfrr* 'lapis lazuli'. *Minerals,* 134; *ṯfrr* 'blue', *CT* II, 214*c*; *Ṯfrrt* 'Blue Land' of lapis lazuli, VI, 213*c*; *'Iṯfrrt* 'Blue Goddess' of the sky, II, 208*c*.
2. Cf. de Buck, n. 2*; but *snḏm* is surely what was meant.
3. *Spw,* meaning unknown.
4. Meaning perhaps 'within the limit of what is due to me'.

Spell 1004

TO GO TO ŌN. The Bull is dead, (even) he who presided over those who are in the Abyss, lying on his two faces. He has taken possession for himself of the throne which is in front of the portal, (even) he who guards the living, and the Great One has stood up for what is to be said to him ⌈when arranging(?)⌉[1] the VII,221 years. A spirit who is in his hidden shape is in the secret of the Great One, who . . .[2] himself on behalf of Rēʿ in the presence of the Bull of the horizon in the Mansion of Khnum: He of the New Moon is he who serves him in Ōn, (even) he who crosses the sky with the Great Wanderer in the year of giving Sothis to Ḥarakhti. O you of Ōn, move on after them in the year of ascending to the sky; greet Rēʿ in [. . .]. Come,[3] join [. . .] who makes offering of his hinder parts in the middle of the vertex of Nūt, who . . .[4] the Living One in the morning in the presence of Him who is in . . .[5] Go to Ōn, that he may come to Kherʿaḥa, and the Sixth-day Festival shall be celebrated for him by the secluded ones(?).

1. *Stwt,* lit. 'making smooth', cf. *JEA* 9, 17, n. 2.
2. *Sn* with det. of a man making an offering.
3. Plural imperative.
4. *Sn* with fish-det.
5. *Nhd.f.*

Spell 1005

Hail to you, Nome of Silence! Hail to you, . . . ![1] Hail to you, Thorn-bush,[2] servitor of the gods who guides the spirits! May you guide me to the Field of Offerings, may I be passed again,[3] may I speak with the Westerner in the Field of [Rushes].[4]

1. Cf. de Buck, n. 10*.
2. *B3gs,* named also in *Pyr.* §1083.
3. I do not grasp the meaning of this.
4. At the end, restore *i3rw.*

Spell 1006

VII,222 SIA [IN THE MIDST] OF THE EYE OF RĒʿ. I go up that I may give you your plume; I have gone down that I may create Ḥu and that a god may be diverted by a god. I run[1] and I fetch Ḥu; I have propitiated Rēʿ-Atum in Ōn.

Hail to you, Rēʿ-Atum in Ōn,[2] for I am Sia who is in the midst of your Eye, and you shall not give me to *B . . . rt, Ḫ3mt* shall not have power over me, for I am your image(?)[3] in the midst of your shrine, I have placed . . .[4] on the throne(?) of the sky, I have duplicated your soul for your power. I am he who makes content, and it is your wand which does it again.[5] Guard this power of mine,[6] give me air, and I will give you what is in the offering(?); my sacrificial cattle are in it, duly equipped. I am he who is over the Mansion of the Six; (as for) him who helps me, I will help him. I am he who gives orders, and I am he who acts as one who gives orders. I will take myself off into the midst of the Eye of Rēʿ-Atum.

1. Regarding *btꜣ* as the known var. of *bṯ* 'run', cf. *Concise Dict.* 86.
2. *M 'Iwnw* is repeated by dittograph.
3. Taking *tty* as standing for *tyt,* op. cit. 294.
4. *Srf* with animal det., cf. de Buck, nn. 6*; 7*.
5. Lit. 'which repeats'.
6. Emending into the 1st person; the 3rd is out of place, for the deceased is asking a boon of the god.

Spell 1007

TO OPEN THE GATE OF THE HORIZON. Open, O Atum, the outer door; throw VII,223 open, O Khons, the great door. I will swim by means of you, I will pass therein as Thoth, I will fill my mouth with the braided lock of the god. Ho![1] Lift me up! Ho! Raise me aloft!.

1. The *whm* sign after *hy* appears to be an emphatic particle, and to be a synonym of *sp 2.*

Spell 1008

See, he[1] comes that he may wade in blood; he will scratch in his gore,[2] he will seek to extinguish the Eye of Horus, he will grind it in its extinguished state, and it is he who will strew(?)[3] it.

1. The identity of the being is not disclosed.
2. The future tense of what follows is suggested by the undoubted future of 223*m*. *Ṯr* is another word for 'blood' and for a red substance, cf. *Pyr.* §§451; 1263; Harris, *Minerals,* 154.
3. The determinative of *sty* suggests the translation 'kindle', but it appears that the Eye of Horus is ground to powder to strew abroad.

Spell 1009

TO EXTINGUISH THE FIRE. The fire shall not go forth against the temple of VII,224 Ḥatḥōr which is in *Smnw.*[1] A bowl(?)[2] is what I will make for the two attendants of the god who dwell in the temple.

1. Probably Gebelēn; cf. Gardiner, *On. Am.* II, 20*; on the cult of Ḥatḥōr in the locality cf. op. cit. 17*, s.v. *Pr-Ḥtḥr*.

2. Cf. *ḫꜣw* 'bowl', *Concise Dict.* 184.

Spell 1010

TO GO DOWN STRONG INTO THE TRIBUNAL OF THE GOD. What those who are in *Rmyꜣ* do shall be stopped, (even) the . . .[1] who stand before Anubis. O enduring(?) youth, have you come that you may embrace[2] the Sole One, and do you bring me to do harm(?)[3] to you? If you cross me,[4] the Little One will be against you as a hornet(?);[5] if you oppose me, the Images(?)[6] will be against you in the Night-bark. *Ḫnty-mnt,f* will cross him who would cross me.

1. *ꜣḫbw,* unidentified.

2. Or 'seek'.

3. *Nknkw r.k* looks corrupt. It is just possible that we may have here a bungled writing of *nkn⟨.ỉ⟩ nknw r.k,* lit. 'that I may inflict injury on you'; the leg-dets. support the notion that the stem *nkn* is involved.

4. I.e. get in my way, hinder me; lit. 'cross yourself in me'.

5. Masc. *byw,* therefore not 'bee', but probably an aggressive insect of the same general type.

6. Cf. de Buck, n. 7*.

Spell 1011

VII,225 SPELL FOR NOT EATING FAECES IN THE REALM OF THE DEAD. What I doubly detest, I will not eat. What I detest is faeces, and I will not eat; filth, I will not eat; the vulture, the servitor of the dead, shall not bring to me, he shall not wipe his lips on me, he shall not coil his neck on me, because[1] I sit between the two great gods, I live on bread of white emmer, my altars [. . .], I sit in the Field of Rushes, and my abundance is in the Field of Offerings. I will not go up with my fingers, I will not tread on it with my sandals, because I am the Bull of the Pregnant Woman in Ōn, (I am) he who is at seven portions in the god's booth; three portions of mine are in the sky with Rēʿ, four portions of mine are on earth with Gēb [. . .], and it is the Day-bark which will convey them to me in Ōn. I have acclaim and my double has acclaim, for I have honour; I live on the sweet-stuffs which are issued from the four shrines of . . .[2]

The statue(?)[3] of the shrine of the Sistrum-player is firm in front of the Sistrum-
player, the arms(?) are firm in front of the Sistrum-player, | and the Sistrum- 226
player goes round about. The arms of the horizon are opened to me, the Great
Lady throws open the darkness(?)[4] to me.

O you two pillars of Rēʿ, I go up and enter between you. My hair stands up, my braided tress is disordered,[5] because I am one whose mouth is pure and whose teeth are strong, and what I detest is wrongdoing against[6] Atum, because I have honour and I am a *tknw,* a possessor of seven portions in Ōn; three portions of mine are in the House of Horus, two portions of mine are in the House of Seth, two portions of mine are on earth with Gēb, and it is the Day-bark which will bring (them) to me upon the altars of the gods.

O you great gods who are on your standards, I will not eat faeces for you nor drink urine, I will not go to you upside down, because I am Rēʿ, a possessor of eyes, I will not eat what Gēb lifts up,[7] I will not be harmed by that on which those who are in the Abyss live.

O you doorkeeper plundering the Two Lands, prepare a path for me in it
that I may pass, for I am one of those who wash (their) mouths and who chew
myrrh, who live on Right. Prepare a path for me, for I live on what they live
on, | and I am alive and flourishing for ever and ever. I come and go between the 227
two pillars of Rēʿ and the two djed-pillars of Gēb; my hair stands up and my
braided tress is disordered.

What I detest is efflux, and I will not eat [. . .], I will live on the sweet-stuffs which are issued from the shrine. Awake, O you who rise early! Be high, O Thoth! Awake, O you who rise early, O you who are in Kenzet, who are before the Egret which went up from the cultivation, and Wepwawet who issued from Asyut.[8] I ward off faeces, I reject urine just as Thoth protects the dead.[9]

O you great and mighty gods who traverse the sky, take me with you, that I may eat of what you eat, that I may drink of what you drink, that I may gorge on that on which you gorge, that I may eat goose and slaughter the *ḥḏw*-bird. My booth is in the Field of Rushes, my abundance is in the Field of Offerings, I go all over the sky like Rēʿ, and I will be like Rēʿ, I will have acclaim like Thoth.[10]

1. Read *n ntt* 'because', as in 225*p*; 226*r*.
2. Indecipherable, cf. de Buck, 225, n. 6*.
3. Read *ẖnty* 'statue'? But cf. de Buck, n. 7*.
4. Regarding *kk* as an unfinished *kkw*.
5. See also 227*c*.
6. Lit. 'of'.
7. Wind-raised dust?

8. A bungled version of *Pyr.* §126. The fallen-man sign, which probably originated in *sḏrw* 'sleepers' in Pyr., is used here as a determinative of *rs* 'wake'. *Nhpw,* which here appears to derive from *nhz,* in this context doubtless refers to early rising.

9. With 227*j* compare *Pyr.* §§127*c* – 128*b.*

10. With 227*k-t* compare *Pyr.* §§128*b* – 130*d.*

Spell 1012

VII,228 NOT TO EAT FAECES IN THE REALM OF THE DEAD. What I doubly detest, I will not eat. What I detest is faeces, and I will not eat; filth, ⟨I will not eat⟩.[1] I will not go up [to it] with my fingers, I will not tread on it with my sandals, I will not be satisfied with filth. O Greatest of those who are content, see, my equipped spirit will come.[2]

'Open the gate and issue from it', says *Ḫrḫr*; 'join the twilight of[3] Him who is pure'.

'I have opened the gate so that I may issue from it'.

'Let me see you go out, let me see you come in'.

'I have gone out with Him whose vision is cleared'.

'You were born of his seed, you were conceived of his seed'.

'I was born in sleep, I was conceived in darkness before sky and earth were in being, before the jaws of *Mꜣṯ⟨r⟩t* the daughter of Rēꜥ[4] were bound up'.

'Tell me your name, the name which was given to you'.[5]

'I have begged from Him who is great in power, and it is he who gives to me'.

'What will you live on in this place into which you have come?'

'I will live on bread of white emmer washed down with zizyphus-beer. If I be warm, warm will be ⟨the food of⟩ the Enneads[6] on the altars of the Souls
229 of Ōn, (namely) the foreleg, the hindleg(?)[7] and the haunch. I will eat what is on the rushes[8] under the branches of the *ỉṯns*-tree, and I will be conveyed in the 'How-happy-is-he' bark on the day of [. . .]. I will call for a boat, for so Rēꜥ has commanded'.

1. *N wnm.ỉ* omitted.

2. Prospective *sḏm.f,* more commonly written *ỉwt.*

3. *N* before *wꜥb* is written as the negation, but in fact is the genitive.

4. Cf. de Buck, n. 1*; for *nnt* read *ꜥnnt* and for *Mꜣtt* read *Mꜣṯrt,* as in *CT* II, 401*a.*

5. The *n* between *rn* and *rdy* is superfluous.

6. An omission of a word for food between *srf r.f.* and *psḏty* seems certain; the Enneads could hardly themselves be warm on the altars. The missing word will have formed an apposition with the joints of meat named in 226*y.*

7. Cf. *Wb.* IV, 379, 16.
8. 229*b* is a dittograph.

Spell 1013

SPELL FOR NOT EATING FAECES IN THE REALM OF THE DEAD. What I doubly detest, I will not eat. What I detest is faeces, and I will not eat; filth, and I will not eat. I cross the sky like Rēʿ, I worship her[1] like *Dwꜣ-wr.* I come to land in the southern sky; beware of me, you who are in the enclosure(?) of their arms;[2] I live on the food-portion which is in the shrine, [I live on bread of][3] white emmer washed down with zizyphus-beer.

I have come and I have . . .[4] in the Island of Fire; make for me this which VII,230
you made for the judging of the land when you judged between it and ⟨its⟩ foe.[5]

O you who lean on it ⟨ . . . ⟩[6] by means of(?) it, for I am bound for those who are in the Presence. Prepare a path for me that I may pass, O strong one, for I am Thoth, and I testify concerning the Eye of Horus to him. What is brought to you from out of it? I have filled it with the monthly festival [. . .].

O you who are at the head of the Chaos-gods, who guide them of the celestial expanses, do not let me pass into the tomb against(?) Rēʿ [. . .] among the confederacy of Seth.

O you who are over Shusety,[7] let me take possession of my body ⟨ . . . ⟩ Gēb ⟨ . . . ⟩[8] for I have made Horus triumphant over Seth.

O you who are over your adornments(?), who guide souls, give me acclaim through the proclamation of the Vulture-festival which came forth ⟨at⟩ my voice.[9]

O Lord of majesty, lector of Rēʿ-Atum, if you do not write, truth will not be found in you with me.

Do not take possession of the *nt*-crown of Rēʿ or his uraeus which is on his 231
vertex.[10]

O *Ḥmmf,* greater than the Ennead, sit in front of the great ones in Ōn.

I AM the *wrrt*-crown which is upon Rēʿ; the Bull, Lord of the *snwt*-shrine; Lord of those with braided tresses; and a possessor of five portions. My five portions are in the house of Horus-Atum.

I will not eat faeces for you;[11] I will not drink urine for you, I will not go upside down for you [. . .], I will lift up the air-gods ⟨to(?)⟩ Rēʿ; my wailing-women are silent.[12]

See me, I have come here with Ptaḥ, I am seated[13] between the Enneads; the great ones of the horizon have been brought to them, and a writing of what I have said has been brought which has been placed for them in their remembrance. They

Spell 972 is almost entirely lost.

Spell 973

VII,185 [. . . the representatives(?)][1] of Rēʿ who go all over the sky in [. . .] for ever
[. . .]. Sky and earth [come(?)] to you, the deserts of them of Kenzet come to you [. . .] Maʿet [. . .] before the wind[2] [. . .] her whose arms are outstretched(?). I have lain on [my] right side [. . .].

1. Read *stywy,* dual?
2. Cf. de Buck, n. 10*.

Spells 974 and 975 are largely lost.

Spell 976

VII,186 [. . .] whom I burned(?),[1] you (pl.) shall not oppose him, (even) this one whom I
187 burned(?). I appear as a snake-goddess [. . .] in redness.|My protection is the leaping fish, I will tread on grief(?),[2] I will set my course, I will take my panoply [. . .] his spirits. What was fashioned in the firmament was the utterance of Rēʿ-Atum [. . .] the Rivals.

1. Assuming that *wht* is a var of *hwt* 'burn', 'burning', *Siut* pl. 13,14; *CT* II, 73*a*; V, 244*d*; 247*a*.
2. *Sꜣmt* with weeping-eye det.

Spell 977

[. . .] within Khem, the loud-voiced, greatly majestic; I am one who travels alone [. . .] who is lifted up to the sky that he may eat at the shambles of his
VII,188 father Horus [. | . .]yon crocodile[1] who dwells in the castle. The representatives of Horus love me [. . .] you [shall slay(?)] all my foes and him who would destroy[2] me.

1. Restore as *msḥ*.
2. Interpreting *ḥmwt.f* as a *sḏm.ty.fy* form.

have made me into a baton which smote their nobles; they have made a seat on
232 which I sit on the block [which is in(?)] the horizon, ꜥand I sit on the block. My
face is that of a god, my flesh is that of a man; I have appeared and have been
on high as a male . . .[14] and I hold my bow and arrows in my grasp. I will not eat
faeces for you, I will not drink urine for you; O hearts, follow after me . . .[15] I
have gone about as a follower of Shu, there has been given to me all that there is[16]
He is the one who greatly surpasses(?) for the Double Lion.[17] Come to me bowing
down, you being greatly afraid; I have done what I found you had done for the
male . . .[18] I have gone down to him, because[19] I am that one who creeps in the
middle of his . . . [20]

1. Apparently referring to *pt,* which is not usually an object of worship; perhaps there has been confusion between *pt* and *nwt.* The whole spell is somewhat incoherent, and from 231*a* onward it is a miscellany of unconnected extracts.

2. *Ḏrt* is obscure, but may be related to *ḏryt* 'wall(?)', *Concise Dict.* 323. There is no antecedent for the suffix *.sn.*

3. Restored from 228*v.*

4. *Sw* with hair-det., which is not known otherwise. The usual formula is *ỉy.n.ỉ myn m ꜥIw Nsrsr* 'I have come here into the Island of Fire'.

5. The division lines recorded here and below in de Buck, 230, n. 2*; 231, n. 1*, mark separate sections of text.

6. There has certainly been an omission here, for ꜥ between *ḥr.f* and *ỉm.f* conveys nothing.

7. *Šwsty* recalls the goddess *Šwst* in *Pyr.* §123.

8. The name of Gēb is quite isolated, and again there must have been omissions of text.

9. The translation of this section is uncertain.

10. 231*a* is difficult. *M* at the beginning looks like a negative imperative, and *ỉṯ* may be a writing of *ỉṯy* 'take' without the legs usually attached to the *ṯ*-sign, but there is no clue as to whom such a prohibition could be addressed.

11. Plural, but there is no antecedent.

12. *Mꜣṯrw* is a corruption of *mꜣṯrwt* 'female mourners', *CT* IV, 122*h*; cf. Spell 317, n. 45; the word appears to be the subject of an old perfective.

13. A confused writing of the old perfective 1st sing.

14. On *bꜣty ṯꜣy* cf. Spell 584, n. 1.

15. *Snfw* 'blood-cakes(?)' is isolated and devoid of context; there has certainly been an omission here.

16. Lit. 'There has been given to me to the limit of all'.

17. For 'he is' understand 'I am'? This passage seems out of context.

18. *Bꜣt(y) ṯꜣy.*

19. Read *n ntt* in the affirmative, 'because'.

20. On the obscure word *kꜣꜣ* cf. Spell 487, n. 3. Its meaning here is quite uncertain; it lacks a determinative and is not in an 'eye' context.

Spell 1014

What I doubly detest, I will not eat. I detest faeces, and I will not eat; filth, ⟨and
I will not eat⟩. I will not go up to it with [my hands],[1] I will not tread ⟨on it⟩ with
my sandals. I cross ⟨the sky⟩ like Rēꜥ, I worship her like *Dwȝ-wr.* If I have acclaim
you will have acclaim.[2] | O you who are in your efflux, be very far from me, for I VII,233
live on the food-portion which is in his shrine.[3] I will walk upright, I will not walk
upside-down.[4]

1. The trace after *m* looks like ꜥ 'hand' rather than *ḏbꜥ* 'finger', the more usual word in this context. 232*p-u* are a version of 229*i-m,* but with omissions.
2. *'I* after *hny n.k* is superfluous, and arises from confusion with the ending of the old perfective 1st sing.
3. De Buck notes a division-line here, cf. 233, n. 4*.
4. The rest of the spell is a dittograph of 232*t*-233*b*.

Spell 1015

TO BECOME A FOWLER OF THE GREAT GOD WHO GIVES WATER AND WATCHES
OVER WATER. Greeting to you whose face is cut(?),[1] fowler of fresh water; turn
your face and look at me with both your faces, for I am a heron which went up
in distress(?)[2] when the shambles of the gods were uncovered. The ducks[3] who
are in their marshy pools(?)[4] come to me in order to . . . for the fourth of the
faces.[5] | The bag(?) for it is of skin;[6] the Fen-goddess binds Shu in darkness(?);[7] VII,234
its fastenings(?) are two stakes in the ground;[8] the Fen-goddess has put (something) for me at the tops of the nets. The doors of the bird-trap(?)[9] are opened, the cord is set aright, the great ones rejoice. My servitor belongs to the fourth of the faces,[10] and [he] brings [what is good(?)].[11] I expel the evil which is on the face of *Sḫȝs*; their arms are behind her;[12] those who see her are turned upside down because of the young [fowler(?)]; it is his fowler who calls out(?).[13] I have set aright the two stakes(?)[14] which are on the . . .[15] which are brought to me from the marshes of the north for the tops of my nets. I give (something) in my hands to the great god for his nose within yonder bark of his; I have sat down in it with my back to the great Broad Hall. The Nile-god[s] go forth, and I prepare a gift for the god.[16]

1. *Sš* with cord-det. Cf. Spell 992, n. 3.
2. Cf. *ḳmw* 'distress(?)', 'confusion(?)', *CT* I, 26*c*; V, 176*j,* with bird-det.
3. Reading *ȝpdw,* cf. de Buck, n. 5*.

4. *H̱ꜣẖꜣwt,* perhaps a reduplicated plural derived from *ẖꜣt* 'marsh'.

5. Quite obscure. For the allusion to *fdnw ḥrw* cf. also 234*h* and n. 10 below.

6. Reading 234*a* as *šṯw r.s. m ỉnm,* but the relation with the preceding context appears to be non-existent, suggesting a considerable textual omission. *Šṯw* may be identical with *šṯ* 'scrip', 'satchel', *CT* I, 71*h*; IV, 115*g*; since this spell is concerned with fowling, a skin bag could well be part of a fowler's equipment. 'It' could well refer to an unmentioned snare or trap.

7. Cf. *tnmw* 'darkness', *Concise Dict.* 299. Not much weight can be attached to the det. of *tnm* here; P. Gard. II is far from precise in its use of the seated-god sign.

8. Reading perhaps [*s*]*mn.s ꜣ,* the latter apparently being the enclitic particle. In this sentence the suffix *.s* could refer to a net, cf. 234*d*, where the det. of *ỉꜣdwt* shows a net secured between two stakes.

9. *Wptt* is not recorded, but the determinative and the context suggest that it may be a kind of bird-trap with its entrances covered by movable flaps.

10. For *fdnw ḥrw* see also 233*p* above. While the numeral is written clearly as the ordinal *fdnw* 'fourth' in both cases, it would make better sense if the text were emended into *fdw ḥrw* '(him of) the four faces'.

11. Cf. de Buck, 234, n. 5*.

12. The pronouns *.s* and *.sn* lack antecedents.

13. *ꜥgꜥg*; not recorded and meaning quite uncertain.

14. Wooden articles of unknown nature; possibly the stakes of a net.

15. *Sṯꜣw,* plural with bird and seated-god determinatives.

16. For *ꜣwtwt* read *ꜣwt*; the direct genitive following may imply a gift intended for the god.

Spell 1016

VII,235 TO BECOME HORUS OF NEKHEN. O you who are hateful, you who are hateful of character, you who are hateful of character, prepare a path for me, for I have laid your rank on the ground.[1] If ⟨you⟩ do not prepare a path for me or lay your rank on the ground for me, I will come against you as the Great One, Lord of strength, mighty in my (capacity for) harm; I give your face to my mighty Eye, and it has wound about you, because its [. . .][2] is against the Primeval One and its flood is against the doer of (ill) deeds. I put my hands on the jar in the bounds of which you[3] sit; it descends to your faces, and the Great One runs[4] within the horizon; he has laid his rank on the ground. I have taken possession of Ḥu, I have power over Sia, I possess acclaim, I have taken possession of the horizon. He of the *swnt*-plant is not in the horizon; I consult(?) with Rēꜥ against the hateful ones, for I am Horus.

1. I.e. degraded or cancelled it.

2. Probably a noun is lost in the lacuna, cf. *ḫfḫft.s* below.
3. Plural in reference to *ỉrw* of 235*h*.
4. Regarding *r.f* as the enclitic.

Spell 1017

SPELL FOR LIVING BY MEANS OF MAGIC AND BY MEANS OF PROTECTION[1] IN THE TWO HOUSES. O Orion, here am I; I have come as ruler of the *moringa*-tree, I have eaten the doubles, I have fed on those who sit, I live on the spirits and the elder gods, those whose names are secret have been brought to me, I have joined in the protection in the Two Houses. O you who unite, I have had recourse to the sky, I have had recourse to him who sits ⟨on⟩ my neck(?),[2] and what was taken for me from the throat of the mighty one is lifted up. I have joined with my body [. . .] in my throat, I have joined the Ptaḥ-gods; O you who unite, who have put (something) together for me, I have joined the spirits, I have joined the Powers[3] and the Elders. I am one stronger than my forefathers, I am one mightier that those who are older than I, I am equipped with all that they know, (namely) the gods who are in the Presence. I have taken their might, I have swallowed their spirits, I have eaten their magic, I have made a holocaust of gleaming blood, and I come as an equipped spirit. VII,236

Thus says Orion to me:[4] You have acquired all their powers,[5] you have forgotten nothing. See, you have come spiritualized and equipped; establish yourself on this throne of yours which is superior to (all) thrones, for there is no god who can surpass you.[6] Let me know what you have done on earth and in the Island of Fire;[7] because[8] there is one who makes offerings(?)[9] for you and speaks to you when going to the earth; because someone comes indeed with you to this throne of yours [on which] one has sat(?); [10] because there is one who will do for you what Horus did for [his father] Osiris; because someone made him firm thereby;[11] because someone comes indeed with him to the coffin of ferrying;[12] because you[13] come indeed with him into the Island of Fire on his day of coming. He who turns back spirits will come behind him; he has made staffs, sceptres, [. . .] images. 237

I have glorified my soul,[14] I have made my staffs strong, I have freshened the earth-hair into something which [my] father did not know,[15] because Osiris is established thereby, my soul is a spirit, my staff is strong, and because there is benefit thereby for my father Osiris.

Thus says Orion to me: Come and tell what the god does who comes equipped and who opens the earth for himself through what he knows on the day when he desires to come thence. Pure and noble are you; sit on your throne [which is in the *Ḥꜣw*]-*nbwt*(?)[16] that the gods may turn the meal to you. Speak, that I may hear what you have done over and above what you have not done – so says Orion [to] me.

238 I have come and I have done what brings everything[17] into being; I have
given milk, I have impregnated the egg, I have eaten Right, I have swallowed
magic, I have made the soul of the images in the standing-place of my father, I
have life before him; because I have done it for my dead father (although) he was
vexed with me. He [has set] me [upright] on account of it with the god, because
I have glorified his soul into something which he did not know, [my] staff [is
strong],[18] because I have freshened his earth-hair, I have clothed myself, I have
scattered water for my dead father, and he has invocation-offerings, being what
goes down before me to my dead father. My wrapping(?)[19] is the Great Comm-
ander, I give incense and water to my dead father, because I have offered an
imꜣ-tree, because I have uprooted an acacia, because it is I who see my pool, for
I have dug it in company with Seth; because [. . .] who dug his canal, who
guided his measuring-cord. I have put in my mouth what I found, I have filled
[my] mouth with the powers[20] of the fathers of the great one[s];[21] I have taken
possession of the place of their great ones, I have acquired all spirits,[22] I have
fettered(?)[23] the Chaos-gods,[24] I have subdued the sun-folk. O you southern,
239 northern, western and eastern gods, | silence is mine and my retainers worship.

Thus says Orion concerning me; This god is equipped, he has come equipped [. . .] the elder gods; he has eaten their magic, he has swallowed their powers, [he has] opened [the earth] by means of what he knows on the day when he desired [to come] thence,[25] he has cleansed all that he has done in the Island of Fire for his dead [father] because he sees the pool; because he digs it and has dug his canal; he has done his just deeds which ennoble him and which establish him on his throne.

O you who are high on your block! ⟨ . . . ⟩.[26]

Thus says Orion to me: O you who have appeared, may you be strong and [live(?)] on your food. Come, come,[27] O you spirit whom the god equipped[28] as one who is attached to the great god who has no equal [. . .]. Receive your offerings, for the Two Ladies will establish you; O you who have appeared,[29] the elder gods will ennoble you. Appear[30] as the great god whose father ate and fed on his companions. Appear, be content, be exalted, for you have come manifested, spiritualized, crowned.[31] Go all over the celestial expanses[32] of the gods, for you will rest because you appear in his place which belongs to you both.[33] You have taken possession of the limits of the horizon, for there comes [. . .] Osiris.

So says Orion to me. [34]

1. The dual *gswy-dpt* is a variant of the singular *gs-dpt* 'protection'; the literal 'two sides of a boat' makes no sense.

2. The deceased may be referring to an amuletic image worn on the neck.

3. A dittograph of *sḫmw*.

4. The context shows that *ỉn S3ḥ r.ỉ* refers to the speech which follows, not to what precedes, which is more usual; cf. however *JEA* 21, 181, top. In two cases below, 237*s-z* and 238*k-x*, this expression appears at both the beginning and the end of the speech.

5. So, rather then 'spirits', despite the determinative; cf. 236*q* above.

6. The fem. pronoun in the 3rd person shows some confusion; the gender is correct, for the owner of this papyrus was a woman, but the person should be the 2nd. References to the sex of the deceased in this spell are few; for the most part the scribe has faithfully copied the original masculine pronouns of his text.

7. At the bottom of 237*e* read *ỉw* ⟨*n*⟩*sysy*; it is doubtful if anything has been lost in the small lacuna between it and *n wnn*.

8. The apparent negation which appears frequently from 237*f* onward represents the preposition *n* used as a conjunction at the head of a clause; to interpret it as a negative makes no sense.

9. *Snwt* with bowl-det.

10. Read *ḥmst.n.tw*[*ỉm*]?

11. Cf. 237*q*; in 237*i* ff. the pronouns refer to Osiris.

12. Lit. perhaps 'for the purpose of ferrying'; the allusion may be to the coffin on board the funeral barge.

13. The fem. suffix in *ỉw.s* refers to the deceased, and should be emended into the 2nd person, for Orion is still addressing her.

14. The change to the 1st person indicates that the deceased is now speaking; hence the suffixes of the 3rd person must be read as the 1st person.

15. Cf. 238*j-k*.

16. The restoration is conjectural, but fits the space in the lacuna. The *Ḥ3w-nbwt* are named in the related Spell 469 (*CT* V, 392*d*) and in Spell 594 (VI, 213*a*).

17. Restore as [*ntt*] *ỉwtt*, lit. 'what is and what is not'.

18. Restored from 237*q* end.

19. *Swḏ* 'wrapping(?)' is not recorded, but cf. *swdwd* 'bandage' (vb.), *ZAS* 57,7*. The following name *wḏ-wr*, with its partial pun, precludes the emendation into *swḥ* 'loincloth', *Concise Dict.* 217.

20. 'Powers' makes better sense than 'spirits'. This papyrus is not at all critical in its use of seated-god dets.

21. Following *wr* in 238*w*, bottom, there may well have been plural strokes now lost, cf. 238*x*.

22. Or 'all powers'.

23. *Ḳ3ḥ* may be the original form of the stem *ḳḥ* 'fetter' (n.), cf. *JEA* 21, 31, n. 7.

24. Or 'myriads'.

25. Restored as *wp*[*.n.f t3*] *m rḫt.n.f hrw mrr*[*w.f ỉwt*] *ỉm*, following 237*u*.

26. This may well have been addressed to Orion, and to have been the start of a speech by the deceased which otherwise has been entirely omitted, for a new speech by Orion to the deceased in the 2nd person follows directly, and nowhere else in this spell do we find two consecutive speeches by the same speaker.

27. Imperative *ỉy* with reflexive dative.

28. Note the fem. gender of *ꜣḫt ꜥprt.n*; cf. n. 6 above.

29. *Ḫꜥw* of 239*o* seems to belong rather to the start of 239*p,* cf. 239*l.*

30. Regarding *ḫꜥ.ty* as hortative old perfective.

31. For *sbn* 'crown' (vb.) cf. *Pyr.* §§409; 1854; 2036.

32. Written as if it meant 'bowmen', which would not make sense in view of the verb *pḫr* 'go all over' a place.

33. Presumably the dead father already mentioned and the deceased.

34. *Sp 4* at the end of the spell may reflect the fact that there are four speeches by Orion.

Spell 1018

VII,240 SPELL FOR PASSING [OVER][1] THE BOUNDARY SOUTH ⟨OF THE SKY⟩.[2] O you who are south of the storm,[3] let me pass to Abydos, to the place where Osiris is; I will speak to him before [the gods(?)] who mourn, I will recite to him the words of those whose places are secret, who are in Rostau.

THE BOUNDARY EAST OF THE SKY. O you two powers of the air, you two easterners of the Mansion of Uproar, let me pass over the boundary, for I have circled round the Vulture [. . .] the Great One who has bound on the fillet.

THE BOUNDARY WEST OF THE SKY. O western sky, O you who mourn, let me [. . .] *Ḥsddt* who is in the secret place; its supporter(?)[4] is in company with him who opens up the shallows(?) of the boundary.[5] The boundary [. . .] Rēꜥ-Atum passed over them in the evening.

THE BOUNDARY NORTH OF THE SKY. Hail to you, my father Osiris, in this field of yours which belongs to the Mistress of [eternity(?) . . .][6] Shu the young. The two cords(?)[7] of the earth-god are my protection [. . .] my foot – FOUR TIMES – the wind is with me.

1. Restore *ḥr* after *šwꜣ* as in 240*f.*
2. 'Of the sky' is supplied from 240*e.i.m.*
3. For *ḫꜣpt* cf. *Pyr.* §500 (*šꜣpt*); P. Bremner Rhind, 23, 9.
4. The meaning of *rmn* and the relevance of the suffix *.f* are alike not clear.
5. For *šꜣwt* cf. *Wb.* IV, 401, 9; this word occurs also in *CT* IV, 349*c.*
6. Reading *sḫt.k tn* ⟨*nt*⟩ *nbt nḥḥ*(?).
7. *Fnḫwy,* meaning doubtful.

Spell 1019

TO PASS [OVER] THE PLAIN. O Anubis on your mountain, lay your hand[1] on the two bowls [. . .] you are saved from the cutting-table(?),[2] you are taken from the coil [1] together with [. . .] of the Mound. I have come to you spiritualized, VII,241 besouled, pure, clean [. . .] the Powers speak to me, and there is no god who will cross me, for I am . . .[3] [. . .].

1. Written as ꜥ 'warrant'.
2. *Snt* may be a derivative of *sn* 'cut off', *Concise Dict.* 230.
3. *ꜣdmw,* cf. de Buck, n. 2*.

Spell 1020

SPELL FOR GOING FORTH [. . .]. *Rrty* receives me, *Rrty* puts her hands on [me . . .] because(?)[1] it is Rēꜥ who went forth from the yoke and because(?) I am [. . .] I have led[2] her whom he saw into the limits of the sky.

1. Read as the preposition *n* in 241*k.* In 241*l* the loss of the following words makes it impossible to decide whether the *n* before *ink* is or is not a true negative, 241*k* suggests that the latter is the case.
2. Cf. de Buck, n. 14*.

Spell 1021

[SPELL] FOR [BEING SAVED] FROM SLAUGHTER,[1] The son of Nūt lives indeed;[2] VII,242 see[3] Rēꜥ [. . .] their [mourners].[4] I have seen these great ones who extend the Eye of the Mysterious One [. . .] the limits of the horizon, I have seen those who are in the horizon, I have looked on those who are in [. . .] who are in [. . .] in joy; they see for themselves that the limb belonging to me[5] is a god [. . .], and there are none who see the slaughtering of the great Broad Hall. As for those who would inflict great injury on me in [. . . I will guard][6] the female falcon who dwells in Ōnet on that day of [lassoing the long-horn,[7] while Rēꜥ][8] stands on the bonds[9] of Seth. My knife is broken, my shield is split [. . .] Horus, Lord of the great one[s].

1. Restoring the rubric as [*rꜣ*] *n* [*n*]*ḥm m-ꜥ ꜥḏt.*
2. Regarding *rk* as the enclitic, in view of the loose use by P. Gard. II of the seated-god

determinative. No god *Rk* is recorded.

3. Imperative with reflexive dative?
4. Restoring as *ỉꜣḳbw.sn*; cf. 240*c.f.*
5. Cf. Spell 356, n. 5.
6. Restored from *CT* V, 21*d*, cf. de Buck, n. 4*.
7. Restored from V, 23*j*, cf. de Buck, n. 5*.
8. Restoring *ỉsṯ Rꜥ* as V, 21*e.f.*
9. Cf. de Buck, n. 6*.

Spell 1022

VII,243 [SPELL] FOR [. . .] UPON OSIRIS. I have come to you, O you who oppose destruction,[1] ⟨you who are in charge of⟩ the ferry-boat 'She-who-turns-back(?)'[2] [. . .][3] who watches over the . . .[4] of my right side. I have come to you [equipped][5] as the executioner(?)[6] who is with the great Hidden One who is in the corner of the Mansion [of the Divine Images[7] . . .]. Throw open the great double doors for me, let [me] see [Rēꜥ in his shape],[8] let him [hear] what I shall say to him. He shall bring Thoth to me in his shape, he shall bring [Seshat] to me [in] her [shape],[9] he shall bring [this writing to me],[10] for it is my recognition which is made for me in the Island of Fire. Remembrance[11] is made for me so that I may see you [among] the blessed.[12]

1. *Ḏꜣw sk*; compare *wḫꜣ sk* in 53*j*.
2. A corrupt version of 53*k*, emended into *ỉry mẖnt ỉnnwt.*
3. The lacuna may have contained a version of part of 53*l-m.*
4. In 243*d* read as *ḥwnw,* meaning unknown.
5. Restored as 53*p.*
6. Cf. *wd nkn* 'execute', *JEA* 22,42.
7. For *ꜥẖmw* cf. 53*q*; the initial *ꜥ* is preserved here.
8. Cf. 54*e.*
9. Cf. 54*h.*
10. cf. 54*i.*
11. Read *sḫꜣ*[*t*].
12. Compare 54*l.*

Spell 1023

VII,244 [SPELL] FOR [BRINGING][1] WHAT I HAVE WRITTEN TO HIM IN THE REALM OF THE DEAD. O *Skt,*[2] *Ṯwtyw,* Locust, *Btꜣy*-snake, *ꜥfꜥft*, Robber, You of Dep: go with your feet that you may bring [. . .] you find [. . .] beneath the earth-god; it is he who will give [. . .] beneath Tayt; it is she who will open it for you [. . .] oars in [your] hands [. . .] the son of him who is in the rope(?). You shall say: 'I am summoned(?)[3] [. . .] in his true name'. The writing shall not be opposed [. . .] I put it(?)[4] within [. . .].

1. See de Buck, p. 243, n. 1*.
2. 244*b-h* consists of a series of proper names.
3. Restoring tentatively as [*wn*].*ky ỉs nys*[.*ky*], but the traces recorded by de Buck, n. 12*, hardly suit.
4. Cf. de Buck, n. 13*.

Spell 1024

[SPELL] FOR [. . .]. I have stood up in the tribunal, I have trembled [. . .] your vertebrae and heads, O god[s]. I have taken Pe from Ōn. | Come,[1] you nobles, VII,245
enter [. . .].

The land is cleared for Gēb, the way to Sais is opened [. . .]. Prepare a path for me, for I am the earth-god and *ꜣks*. I have gone all over [. . .], I have seen the great Entrapper(?) in his shape of the *hnhnw*-bark [. . .] at the place where Gēb is. His fiery breath is what guides me(?) ⟨to⟩ the court(?)[2] [. . .] who releases Him of the knife(?), and it is he whom I have put on the way [. . .] in the plenty of the *hnhnw*-bark within its abundance. [I(?)] sit [. . .] I betake myself[3] within the secret place, I judge [. . .] their names, who are in the walls.[4] I have come into being with the Great One [. . .] within the seed of the great god. | . . .[5] 246
[. . .] the *pꜣt*-cake is put together [. . .] who are at the head of eternity, who eat . . . of those who weep [. . .] you open [. . .] your *pꜣt*-cakes.

1. Read *m r.k r.k*, imperative.
2. For *nmʿ*, cf. *CT* VI, 331*g*.
3. Read *šm*⟨.*ỉ*⟩ *wỉ*.
4. Read *ỉmyw ỉnbw*; the writing as *wnmw ỉnbw* makes no sense.
5. I can make nothing of *ỉsmw* in 246*a*.

Spell 1025

[SPELL] FOR GIVING AIR TO A MAN IN THE REALM OF THE DEAD.[1] The breath(?) of the gullet is hot;[2] the throat [. . .] the breath(?) of Rēʿ is hot[3] on the day of [. . .] who opens up the air.[4] Rēʿ has put the north-wind in order in the gullet;[5]

VII,247 his lungs [. . .] he has given air to the lungs,[6] | he has given his hand to the lungs [. . .].[7] The lungs are on high, for he has united the Two Lands.[8] May you mould(?) [your] child, [may] you [hold(?)] your power in your grasp[9] [like] Edjō [. . .].[10]

1. So P. Gard. II; var. Sq4C: 'To breathe the air in the West'. P. Gard. II is followed in the translation; de Buck was unable to collate Sq4C, see his p. 246, n. 10*.

2. Var. Sq4C 'the breath(?) is hot, the gullet is dry'. For *šꜣm* 'be hot', 'burn', cf. Breasted, *P. Ed. Smith,* 366; 376. To translate *ḫrw* as 'voice' makes no sense, and it would seem that the word is used figuratively of breath exhaled from the throat.

3. Var. Sq4C: 'the smoke of its heat is the breath(?) of Rēᶜ'.

4. Sq4C: 'he protects contentment, he has released breath, and the air is opened up'.

5. Var. Sq4C: 'Rēᶜ has put life in order [. . .] in the gullet'.

6. *Smꜣ* here is certainly the word for 'lungs'; this is a spell for breathing. Sq4C has: '[. . .] Rēᶜ is content with [. . .]'.

7. In P. Gard. II *ᶜ* 'hand' has the common erroneous papyrus-roll det.; Sq4C has the correct form, but after the following *n* this text is lost in a lacuna which has preserved only three signs before *hrw n* 'the day of' in 247*b.* See also de Buck, 247, n. 1*.

8. Sq4C seems to convey the same sense, but the writing is eccentric. The play on *smꜣ* seems inevitable.

9. With *nḫn.k* 'your child' as object it is tempting to translate *wḏḥ.k* in P. Gard. II as 'may you wean', but since the subject of *wḏḥ* is masculine, this translation seems ruled out. We may perhaps have here a figurative use of *wḏḥ* 'cast' metal, in the sense of 'moulding' the child. The Sq4C text runs: *swḏnḏ nḫn.k n m twꜣ N pn n.k ꜣt.f m ḫfᶜ.k,* which at first glance looks unintelligible, but if *swḏnḏ* be accepted as a possible corruption of *wḏḥ,* with *s* for *ḥ* and *nḏ* as a blunder for the fire-sign, and if the negation *n* + *m* be accepted as a cryptic writing of *în m* 'who?', we arrive at the translation 'O you who mould(?) your child, who is he who supports N for you, his power being in your grasp?'

10. Reading P. Gard. II as [*m*]*y Wꜣḏt* [. . .]. Sq4C has 'like the green-stone (or 'column'), like Rēᶜ'.

Spell 1026

THE SAME. Your breathing has come to an end(?), the garment of darkness is [your(?)] garment [. . .]. You shall have air for what is in my body; fly up, O Shu! [. . .].

Spell 1027

SPELL FOR DEMANDING A COFFIN IN THE BEAUTIFUL WEST. O Incense, put VII,248
yourself on your mother; [her(?)] eye[s[1] . . .] she watches over those who are in the sky, namely those who fly up [. . .]. O you seven gods, the western eastern, southern and northern hunters who hunt [. . .] in the wall [. . .]. Atum stands upon [. . .]. May you command that I come and see [. . .] in these seven days of yours [. . .] in the beautiful West; go [. . .].

1. The trace shown in de Buck, n. 3* could have been the top of a second eye-sign.

Spell 1028

To show the path to acclaim. [A path] is opened [. . .] the living White Crown is established for him on his bull's vertex [. . .] in his hands, and he is distinguished above the gods.

O Bull of myrrh [. . .] who is in . . .[1] at(?) the filling of his mansion with those who have come into being [. . .]. O you of myrrh who issued from the Netherworld because of [. . .] in his thousands. Mine are the necklaces which VII,249
you (fem.) have made [. . .].

I am he who is pre-eminent on his throne, the gatekeeper of [. . .] the day when I ascend thence to the sky. I fall to [. . .] the day when I descend thence to the earth, for I have appeared [. . .] the bull-god who issued from the womb of his mother [Nūt(?)[2] . . .] my sandal was set for me in the bark of Rēʿ [. . .] within the shrine.

Prepare a path for me [. . .] my place and she brings me the myrrh which is from Punt [. . .] Rēʿ himself; he sees me as a god, [my] body[3] [. . .] the entire land at my gates which are in the Island of Fire [. . .] my [father(?)] of the West and my mother of the West who fare southward to the throne [. . .] the sky at my birth, and those who are in the Island of Fire [. . .] at the middle of the day.

I am the Sole Horn which stopped the gods, I am [. . .] god [. . .]. 250

I am one multitudinous of uraei of living flesh [. . .] what men and gods eat; they are driven off from me by means of [. . .].

[I am][4] one who is uplifted on his foreland, the Great One of the sky, and a path has been prepared for ⟨me⟩ [. . .] who chew;[5] the standards of the possessor of mansions are in front of [. . .]; the possessor of great striking-power which I have caused to be high[6] upon him; see [. . .] which are placed beneath

[. . .] vindication. He has removed the plumes, which are set in [my(?)] grasp [. . .]. The Wine-press God[7] has seen me on the eastern side of the sky, and [I(?)] have come [. . .] in order to slaughter for me the elders of the sky upon the [altar(?)[8] . . .] as the Lord of all.

I am indeed one whom they have served; acclamation [. . .] uplifted on your throne; the voice of their lesser ones [. . .] at the place where [he(?)] is. I have found Seth in the House of the Watchers [. . .] she will not tell it to him,
251 while I am the Bull [. . .] |powers [of my mother(?)].[9]

I am he who protects the Sole One who is in [. . .] as uraei; I send my mother of the West [. . .] who eat everything, and I will not be opposed.

I am one truly wakeful [. . .], I am one [rich] in food offerings; the great ones of the sky have said to me [. . .] eat [. . .] the Two Fields of Offerings.

I am a god, Thoth of Ōn,[10] [. . .] who (fem.) reduces to order men and gods who oppose [. . .] who presents Maꜥet.

I am on the face of Him who supports [. . .] within the Two Conclaves.

I am the Lord of terror, and [I] am not driven off [. . .].

I am exalted by those who exist [. . .]. See,[11] the throat of Seth is brought to me, and it is I who present [. . .].

I am exalted beneath the horns of the Lord of the *ꜣtf*-crown [. . .] on the day when he was born(?)[12] [. . .] eternity [. . .] Sokar the side-locks of the gods.[13] O Horus-Rēꜥ in [. . .] she who dwells in Ōnet the great, companion of his mother who is pre-eminent in [. . .] I speak concerning the true pillar of the abode which is placed [. . .].

1. An indecipherable place-name.
2. Cf. de Buck, 249, n. 6*.
3. Cf. de Buck, n. 11*.
4. Cf. de Buck, p. 250, n. 1*.
5. The sense seems to demand that *wšꜥ* 'chew' should stand at the end of 250*d*.
6. The suffix *.s* omitted after *ḳꜣꜣ*.
7. Reading the name as *Šsmw*.
8. Cf. de Buck, n. 9*.
9. Cf. de Buck, 251, n. 1*.
10. For this writing of the name of Thoth cf. Boylan, *Thoth,* 3, n. 1.
11. Read *mk* [*wī*].
12. Cf. de Buck, n. 9*. The sign may read *ms.*
13. Sokar appears to be the subject and *smꜣw* the object of a verb which is lost. For *smꜣw* 'side-locks' cf. *Pyr.* §§1005; 1974.

Spell 1029[1]

Trembling falls on the eastern horizon of the sky at the voice of Nūt, and she VII,252
clears the paths of Rēʿ before the Great One when he goes around.
Raise yourself, Rēʿ; raise yourself, you who are in your shrine; may you 253
snuff the air,[2] | swallow the backbones, spit out the day,[3] and kiss Maʿet; may 254
the Suite go about,[4] may your[5] bark travel to Nūt, | may the great ones quake 255
at your voice, may you count your bones and gather your members together,
may you turn your face to the beautiful West and return anew every day,
because you are indeed that fair[6] image of gold[7] under the branches of the 256
ỉṯnws-tree(?);[8] sky and earth[9] fall to you, being possessed with trembling at
your travelling around anew every day. | The horizon is joyful[10] and acclama- 257
tion is at your tow-rope.

SPELL FOR NAVIGATING IN THE GREAT BARK OF RĒʿ.[11]

1. This spell begins the long series of 'The Book of the Two Ways', of which the most recent translations both appeared in 1972; one by Piankoff in his book *The Wandering of the Soul,* and another by Lesko, *The Ancient Egyptian Book of Two Ways*; the latter is the more intensive study, so that it is to it that references are made in the notes below. For practical convenience and for the sake of uniformity with my other work on the Coffin Texts, I have translated the relevant spells strictly in de Buck's numerical order, and not in the revised order adopted by Lesko.

2. The B1L group adds 'swallow the north-wind'.

3. The B1L group has 'entrap the day'.

4. *Pẖr*; B4Bo and the B1L group have *pšn* 'split up'.

5. B3C, B4Bo and the B1L group omit the suffix in *wyꜣ.k*.

6. *Nfr* 'fair' in seven texts only.

7. For *nbw* 'gold' B1C has *šsmtt* 'malachite'. The rest of the B1L group seem doubtful about the reading and compromise with a *vox nihili* which looks like *nbtwt.*

8. *'Iṯnwt,* varr. *ỉṯnw, ỉtnw,* is obscure, but the original reading of the text may well have been *ẖr smꜣw ỉṯnws* 'under the branches of the *ỉṯnws*-tree', cf. *CT* VI, 138*b*; 140*d*; VII 229*c.* In III, 87*c*; VI, 330*s, ỉṯnws* in this expression has the town-det., as if there were a locality named after the tree, cf. III, 241*a*; and it appears as the name of a god in III, 51*g*; VI, 297*n.* In III, 203*b* the name is that of a tree, but in a different context; in *CT* III, 1*e* we should read 'Ḥatḥōr who is in front of the *ỉṯnws*-tree.' The corruption into *ỉṯnwt* may have come about through the final *s* being mistaken for the fem. suffix; note the writing of VII, 229*c,* where the *s* is written after the determinative.

9. The B1L group omit *tꜣ ḥr.sn n.k.*

10. Before this sentence B9C inserts 'Maʿet is joyful at meeting you'.

11. The rubric is in the B1L group only.

Spell 1030

VII,258 See, its[1] starry sky is in Ōn, the sun-folk are in Kherʿaha, because its thousand gods are born, because their[2] fillets are bound on, because their oars are grasped.[3]

259 | I will go[4] with them aboard the lotus-bark[5] at the dockyard of the gods, I will take possession of the bark with lotus-leaves on her ends, I will ascend in her to

260 the sky,[6] | I will navigate in her in company with Rēʿ,[7] I will navigate in her with

261 *Mgf-ỉb*,| I will act as pilot in her to the polar region of the sky,[8] to the stairway of the bark of Mercury.[9]

SPELL FOR NAVIGATING IN THE GREAT BARK OF RĒʿ.[10]

1. *Ḫꜣ.s-bꜣs* 'its starry sky' has the fem. sing. suffix after *ḫꜣ*, lit. 'its "thousand-are-her-souls" ', the suffix referring in anticipation to *'Iwnw*, which as a town-name has fem. gender; some texts, however, lack this suffix.

2. The masc. sing. suffix in *sšd.f* and *dpw.f* refers to *ḫꜣ* 'thousand', but English demands the plural.

3. *Nḏr* with adze-det. in B9C, B1L, and B3L is due to mistaking *nḏr* 'grasp' for its homophone meaning 'hew', which makes no sense here.

4. In 259*a* ff. we have a series of verbs in the prospective *sḏm.f*, many texts showing the ending *y* or in 259*a* the ending *w* in *hꜣw* (B2Bo and B4Bo). For *hꜣy.ỉ r.f ḥnʿ.sn* of the B3C group, B9C ff. have *wḏʿ.ỉ ḥnʿ.sn* 'I will have judgement with them', which is surely an inferior reading.

5. For *sšnt* 'lotus-bark' B12C has *nšmt*, the name of the bark of Osiris.

6. So B2Bo ff.

7. B2L ff. insert before 260*b*: 'I will navigate in her to the sky'; B1L: 'I will navigate with Rēʿ', omitting the next clause; similarly B9C: 'I will navigate in her to the sky with Rēʿ'.

8. So the B3C group; B1L ff. have shortly: 'on the *wʿrt* of Nūt'. *Wʿrt* here appears to stand for 'polar region', cf. Sethe, *Komm. Pyr.* III, 393.

9. *Sbg* with simple bark-det. in B6C, B4L, B4Bo; with falcon-in-bark det. in B3C and B2Bo, with seated-god det. elsewhere. B12C has *sbꜣ n wyꜣ* 'gate of the bark', so too probably B13C.

10. The B1L group only; B1C appends *rʿ nb* 'every day'.

Spell 1031 is in fact the end of the B3C text of Spell 1130, inserted here because a blank space on the coffin was available, cf. de Buck, 470, n. 1. The translation will be found in its proper place below.*

Spell 1032

Circle of fire.[1] VII,262

1. Repeated four times, see de Buck, n. 2*. Lesko translates *šnwt* as 'entourage', but the real meaning is made clear by 276*c*, where it is something to be traversed. Similarly 278*a*.

Spell 1033

The fire which is about Rēʿ is bright against you,[1] being bound about him; the VII,263
Lord[2] of Storm fears the bark of Rēʿ, and you shall join the fire.[3] | I have come 264
here with him whose face is wiped,[4] I have seen him who has gone to Maʿet, |
having fallen by the hand of those whose shapes are sacred who are in the midst 265
of the sacred lake,[5] the companions of the reed-dwellers[6] of the Lake of Rushes. |
I have seen them there, and we shall give ⟨to(?)⟩ them;[7] their great ones are in joy 266
and their lesser ones in happiness.

Prepare a path for me into the bow of his bark;[8] brightness is in his disk and 267
power is in his shape.[9] I will rise up in front of his uraei, | and he will partake of 268
the meal as the Lord of Right![10] I have ejected[11] what was amiss in him, | I have 270
brought Maʿet to him,[12] so that he may live by means of her.

Go and return, and tell the state of his father in the Abyss.[13] You shall send 271
out his voice in the evening,[14] for see, I have come,[15] | I have brought ʿApep to 273
him,[16] I have spat on his wounds for him;[17] prepare a path for me that I may
pass,[18] | for I am the greatest of the gods. 274

Come, pass by, that your bark may be rowed, O Lord of Wisdom, for you are the heir of the Great One.

Swamp[19] the fire, quench the fire, prepare a path for me, for it is he who 275
mixes them[20] who presents the horizon to me.[21] | I have passed by the great ones, 276
I have instructed Him of the West who is in his bark, I have traversed the circle
of fire | which is about the Lord of them of the braided locks. 277

'Pass!' says Harakhti, 'that you may command the boat which your father built'.[22]

SPELL FOR PASSING OVER THE CIRCLE OF FIRE OF THE CABIN(?) OF THE 278
BARK OF RĒʿ.[23]

1. Read *sḏt tw* ⟨*w*⟩*bḫt*; *tw* after *sḏt* has been regarded as the definite article. On grounds of sense there is little to choose between *wbḫ.t(y)* 'is bright' and *wbd.t(y)* 'is burning'; the former is supported by the varr. of B2Bo, B4Bo and B9C, with merging of the successive

w's, while B12C is supported by B4L and B1Bo, and thus is slightly in the minority, for what that is worth; *tw nn* of B4L may stand for 'this (fire) here'. *ꜣbḫ* of the B1L group may well derive from a miswriting of *wbḫ* in a MS ancestral to this group, and to some extent supports *wbḫ* as against *wbd*; *wbḫ>ꜣbḫ* would be an easy corruption, and the genuine transitive *ꜣbḫ* of 263*c* may have had some influence. I have the impression that the B1L group of texts descends from a secondary and inferior source.

2. The B1L group omit *nb* 'lord'.

3. I.e. be burnt in it. For *sḏt* 'fire' B9C ff. have *ḏsrt,* translated by Lesko as 'what is sacred', but which appears to me to be but a corruption of *sḏt,* perhaps influenced by *š ḏsr* in 264*a.* Lesko's rendering seems out of accord with the context.

4. B9C ff. add *m-ḳꜣb n š (n) ḏsr* 'in the midst of the sacred lake', which properly belongs to 265*a.*

5. The reading of the end of B3C is uncertain; in B4Bo *ḏsr* is reduced to the determinative. The B1L group have *ỉrw ỉmyw ḏbꜣwt*; the meaning of the last word is obscure, but Lesko tentatively suggests 'sarcophagi'.

6. *Swtyw,* a plural *nisba* form of *swt* 'reed'. B12C–B4Bo have confused this word with *swt* 'tress(?)', *CT* VI, 124*d*; 250*s.* For *smꜣw* the B1L group has predicative *ꜥšꜣ* 'many are . . . '.

7. Cf. Lesko, 18, n.*j*, but his translation has its difficulties. The suffixes *.sn* presumably refer to 'those whose shapes are sacred . . . the companions of the reed-dwellers', who appear as friendly to the deceased, so why are they to be handed over, and to whom? I would suggest that the preposition *n* has been displaced in B3C and dropped elsewhere, and that we should read *ỉw.n r rdyt n.sn.* Another question is: to whom does 'we' refer? There are errors in B12C, B4L and B4Bo, and the B1L group is corrupt.

8. 'His' presumably refers to Rēꜥ; B4Bo has 'your bark', and B9C ff. omit the suffix at the end of 267*a.*

9. For *bꜣ* = 'shape' cf. vol. I, Spell 312, n. 2.

10. The B1L group reads: 'he will partake of the meal, being sheltered as the Lord of Right', var. B1C: 'as Lord of the uraei of the two Rights'; this final dual is also in B3L. At this point B9C + B1L ff. insert 268*b*–269*b*: 'What is it?' 'A shrine'.'I am he who goes around (var. B9C: 'the Destroyer'), the Bull of the great ones, the son of the Kite of Osiris; see, he has testified concerning his father, the Lord of what is yonder (*ỉmywt*)'. For *nb ỉmywt* B9C appears to have *nb nnw* 'Lord of the inert ones'. Cf. Lesko, 19, *ap* – *aq.*

11. Lit. 'pitchforked'; note the det. in B1Bo and B9C (269*c*), The B1L group has *wḏꜥ.n.ỉ* 'I have cut out'.

12. The B1L group introduces this clause with a rubric *idnt* 'Alternative', and for 'Maꜥet' have 'Tefēnet'. There are also some minor errors.

13. This is an instruction to the deceased, whose reply comes in 271*b. Sp 2* has been regarded, as often, as a visual indication of emphasis rather than as a mark of repetition. The suffix in *ỉt.k* 'your father' in B12C is a slip. The B1L group makes a rubric of 270*c* and writes: 'Go and return and tell his state'. 271*a* is an insertion confined to B9C ff.: 'Maꜥet bears witness to the Lord of All'.

14. The B1L group reads: 'Go and make invocation in the evening'.

15. A long insertion (272*a* – *c*) by B9C ff.: 'I have brought to him his jaws which were in Rostau, I have brought to him the spine which was in Ōn, and I have joined his multitudes to him'.

16. Var. B9C ff.: 'I have repelled ꜥApep for him'.

17. I.e. the wounds inflicted by ꜥApep. Several texts omit the suffix of *nspw*.

18. The B1L group add 'among you'. B6C adds obscurely *ỉm.s*.

19. Cf. *ỉdt* 'downpour' of rain, *Urk.* IV, 615, 15.

20. The meaning of *ꜣbḫ* is not entirely clear, nor is the reference of *.sn* 'them'. Lesko, 18, n.*y*, plausibly suggests that possibly *wbḫ* 'brighten' should be read here. B9C ff. substitute *wbnw* for *ꜣbḫ*, which tends to support Lesko's suggestion.

21. The B1L group has *sꜥḳ ꜣḫt* 'who cause the horizon to come in', which seems an inferior reading.

22. The B3C group has *ḫrp* for 'command', the B1L group has the near synonym *sꜥbꜣ*. It also appends in B3L the suffix *.k* to *dpt* (for the reading see the fem. participle *ỉrt* in B3C ff.) and corrupts *ỉrt ỉt.k* 'which your father built' into the meaningless *ỉrt.k ỉt.f* 'your eye of his father'.

23. This rubric in B1L ff. only. Lesko's translation of *rꜣ-ỉwꜣ* as 'cabin(?)' clearly rests on the determinative in B2L, see his note 20*bf*.

Spell 1034

Down on your faces, you snakes of . . . ;[1] let me pass, | for I am a mighty one, VII,279
a Lord of might,[2] I am a noble of Rēꜥ[3], a lord of righteousness whom Edjō creat-
ed, and my protection is | the protection of Rēꜥ.[4] See, he has gone all over the 280
Field of Offerings, which belongs to me, for I am Rēꜥ, a greater god than you;[5] | 281
he assesses his Enneads in giving offerings.

GUIDANCE TO THE PATHS OF ROSTAU.

1. The meaning of *ꜥftt* is not known. It occurs in *sḏtyw ỉmyw ꜥftt* 'the *sḏtyw* who are in . . . ', *CT* I, 182*d-e*; *wꜣwt ꜥftt* 'the paths of . . . ', 208*c*; *ꜥpr ꜥftt* 'acquire . . . ', III, 329*b*; IV, 401*e*; V, 271*g*; 278*a*; VII, 470*b*; *wn.ỉ ꜥftt* 'I open . . . ', III, 376*a*; *nṯrw ꜥftt* 'the gods of . . . ', V, 245*c*; *nṯr ḏs.f m-ḫn ꜥftt* 'the god himself within . . . ', VI, 157*d*; *ḥfꜣw* (var. *ḥfꜣwt*) *ꜥftt* 'the snakes of . . . ', VII, 278*c*; 468*e*; 518*a*; *ꜥftt nw mꜣꜥt* 'this is the true . . . ', VII, 447*e*. The word appears to be a feminine substantive, but I can offer no suggestion as to its meaning. Lesko's 'mysterious(?)' must be discarded.

2. Var. B1Bo ff.: 'a lord of mighty men'.

3. B1Bo omits *ỉnk sꜥḥ*, reading *Rꜥ pw* 'he is Rēꜥ'; B9C ff. read: 'I am the son of a noble of Rēꜥ'.

4. B3C and B4C omit *mkt.ỉ pw*; B1Bo reads tautologically (279*d* – 280*a*): 'her protection is the protection of Rēꜥ and the protection of N'.

5. For *ꜥꜣ r.k* B12C has corruptly *sꜥr.k*.

Spell 1035

VII,282 I have passed over[1] the paths of Rostau, whether on water or on land, and these are the paths of Osiris; they are in the limit of the sky. As for him who knows
283 this spell for going down into them, he himself is a god, in the suite of Thoth;[2] he will go down to any sky | to which he wishes to go down. But as for him who does not know this spell for passing over these paths, he shall be taken into the infliction(?) of the dead[3] which is ordained, as one who is non-existent, who shall never have rightness.

1. *Swꜣ* in transitive sense; var. B9C: *sšm* 'are shown'. For this sense of *sšm* cf. *Concise Dict.* 247; 283*b*, however, indicates that *swꜣ.n.ỉ* of the other texts is to be preferred.

2. B9C seems here to have the better reading, except that it has one *m* too many; B1L ff. have *nṯr ḏsr m šmsw Ḏḥwty* 'a holy god in the suite of Thoth'. To me the combination *nṯr ḏsr* 'holy god' seems tautological and suspect.

3. 'Of the dead' is preferable to 'of death'; *mt* has the plural strokes in all intact instances. Before *m ꜥꜣbt* B1C has *ỉṯ.f*; so too B9C.

Spell 1036

VII,284 Here am I, I have come in the dignity of Shu,[1] I have restored Osiris to health;[2]
285 prepare a path for me, that I may pass.[3] |Clap your hands, for the best of the maces of Rēꜥ is what is in my hand.[4] Go away![5]

IT IS A SPELL FOR PASSING BY HIM.[6]

1. Var. 'My dignity is that of Shu'. B9C ff. have a garbled version of 498*a* (Spell 1147) which appears to read:'⟨I⟩ will be in the sky of Osiris, my heritage being the rank of the head', i.e. of the headman.

2. For this sense of *srwḫ* cf. *CT* III, 322*b.e*; V, 320*d*.

3. *Swꜣ.ỉ* 'that I may pass' in three texts only.

4. A difficult sentence; B1L ff. omit *ꜥ* and read 'It means that the best of the maces which are in my hand strike for you'; *ḥḏw* 'maces' has the seated-god det. after it as the last remnant of the genitive *Rꜥ* which is still present in B9C ff. Lesko, 40–41, translates rather differently.

5. B9C ff. have confused *rw* 'go away' with *rww* 'lions', a nonsense.

6. It is not clear to whom or to what the suffix in *ḥr.f* refers; it has been taken to be to a warden of the path.

Spell 1037

Fire.[1] I have seen what I have restored to health in Osiris, so do not mourn(?)[2] over his flesh. His name is[3] 'He who drives off those who would demolish'. VII,286
The gate of fire and THE GATE OF DARKNESS.[4] 287

1. Only in B6C and the B1L group.
2. Cf. Lesko, 42, n.*c*.
3. *Rn.f pw* only in the B1L group.
4. B13C and B4L omit 'gate of fire' and add 'Spell for the Lake of . . . , the name of which is . . . '; the final *ỉpty* may be a variant of the demonstrative *ỉptw*. But cf. Lesko, 42, n.*e*. 287*a-b* appear to serve as the heading for Spell 1038, and perhaps should be transferred there.

Spell 1038

Its keeper is the sad-voiced one.[1]

1. B4Bo adds: 'This is a spell for passing by him,(even) this which is beneath him,' perhaps with reference to the following spell.

Spell 1039

Those who are in it are: Leaper;[1] Fiery;[2] She of the knife(?); Robber (?);[3]He who curses;[4] . . .[5] VII,288

1. Cf. Lesko, 44, n. *b*.
2. Cf. *Pyr.* §324; *CT* II, 135*b*; VI, 24*h*; 39*u*; *Urk.* V, 43, 11.
3. B4L[b] writes *ṯ3* as if it were the word for 'pellet'; B4L[a] has *hyw* 'monster', *Pyr.* §§ 245; 435; *CT* III, 396*e*; IV, 325*c*.
4. Cf. *Concise Dict.* 57. B4L[a] has *3sty* 'trembler(?)', cf. *Wb.* I, 20, 17.
5. *ʿ3ty*, var. *ʿ3tym*, meaning unknown; B4L[a] has *š3m* 'He who is hot'.

Spell 1040

I am one who was born in Rostau,[1] and power is given to me by my lord Rēʿ- VII,289
Harakhti;[2] my dignity is in Pe | when I cleanse Osiris.[3] I have received acclamation[4] 290
in Rostau in the guidance of the gods on their mounds,[5] | for I am one of their 291
guides.

1. Varr. B3C; B4C; B1Bo: 'Rostau of Pe'; hardly 'Rostau *and* Pe', since one could hardly be born in two places at once; *rꜣ-stꜣw* is the term for a ramp or slide for moving the sarcophagus into a tomb, transferred to a region of the Beyond, cf. *JEA* 4,137, so that there could be a Rostau at any important cult-centre.

2. Var. B1L ff.: 'Lord of the horizon'.

3. Var. B1L ff.: 'just as Osiris is pure'; B9C has: 'Osiris the noble is pure'.

4. *Kyw,* cf. *ky* 'cry out'; *kyt* 'shout of acclaim', *Concise Dict.* 285.

5. B9C ff. have: 'on the horizon in the entourage which is about Osiris'.

Spell 1041

VII,292 Its keeper is Scowler.[1] Those who are in it are: He whose face is hot(?);[2] | He of the loud voice; Oppressor;[3] Monster;[4] Trembler(?);[5] He who is hot.[6]

1. Lit. 'accursed of face'. B9Bo follows 291*b* with 'This is a spell for passing by him which is beneath him', and ends.

2. The B1L group have *'In-ḥr.*

3. For *ꜣy<ꜣr* the B1L group has *my.*

4. The B1L group has *shyw.*

5. Cf. Spell 1039, n. 4.

6. 292*f* is absent from the B12C group and lost in B1L ff.

Spell 1042

VII,293 I am a spirit and a lord of spirits; the spirit whom I will create will indeed exist;[1]
294 the spirit whom I hate will not exist.[2] | I am one who goes all over his lake in fire, a lord of light;[3] I circle around with the Eye of Horus at hand;[4] | Thoth crosses the
295 sky[5] in my presence,[6] and I pass safely.

1. *Wn* in *ỉw.f wn* is the old perfective, as a participle, being a nominal form, would require the *m* of predication; on the other hand, in 293*c ntf* requires a nominal predicate, so that *wn* here is participial. Lesko is surely right in taking *ꜣḫ* at the end of 293*b* as the first word of 293*c*.

2. For *n ntf wn* the B1L group (except B1C) have *n wnt.f.*

3. The B1L group substitutes: 'I am he who celebrates the monthly festival and announces the half-monthly festival'.

4. Var. B4L: 'at the hand of Thoth'; so also the B1L group. B1L and B2L append to this: 'at night'.

5. Var. 'the lake'.

6. B1L and B2L after 295*a* have 'his throne is my throne'.

Spell 1043

The keeper is He whose face is covered(?),[1] and this is its path; you should not pass on it.[2] VII,296

1. For *šṯ* 'cover(?)' cf. *CT* IV, 66*a*; 67*a*, where *šṯ.i m šṯw* would be better translated as 'I am covered as a tortoise'.

2. B1C ff. substitute in 296*c*: 'A spell for passing by him'.

Spell 1044

He who swallows(?);[1] He who is alert; He who is vigilant; He who is sharp-sighted; He who is acute;[2] He who listens.

1. For *3šbw* cf. *CT* VI, 39*u*, where it is a variant of *3ḫbw*, VI, 18*l*; 24*h*; for the rare verb *3ḫb* 'swallow' cf. *BD* 397, 9. No weight can be attached to the fire-dets., as they are used indiscriminately.

2. For *spdw* of the other texts, B2Bo has *ḫrw*.

Spell 1045

Flesh of the foe who lives in the Fledgeling-lake;[1] He whose face is dreadful(?) for her;[2] He who . . .[3] in beauty. This is the path which I know on the river bank.[4] VII,297

1. Varr. 'who lives beside the Fledgeling-lake'; 'who lives in silence'.

2. So B3C and B4C; for *nhd* 'dread'(?)' cf. *CT* IV, 21*d*. B9C and varr. read: 'dreadful(?) of fire'.

3. *3dmw*, with varr. Lesko suggests 'glowing'.

4. 297*e* is in B9C ff only. At the end, *ḥr wḏbw* 'on the river bank' seems the simplest interpretation of the rather muddled texts; I find it hard to accept Lesko's and Piankoff's idea of a reference to reversion-offerings, which seems to me quite out of context in a sentence concerned with a path; note that the true expression for 'reversion' is *wḏb-rd* and not *rd-wḏb*. This seems to me a typical example of scribal muddle; note that in 298*a*, where there definitely is a reference to reversion-offerings, the spelling is a recognized variant of *wdb-rd*, though in most cases the leg-sign *rd* has been omitted, and in the other instances it has been corrupted into something else.

Spell 1046

VII,298 He who grants benefits, the Lord of reversion-offerings, is in it[1] among the reti-
nue of Osiris; the retainers who are in it are the spirits who dwell in it | after they
299 have done escort duty there for their lords.

1. In what? Apparently a locality, but the lack of an antecedent leaves us in the dark. Perhaps *dwꜣt* 'Netherworld' was what the scribe had in mind.

Spell 1047

What Anubis bewails is the offerings in the day of straw[1] among those who make
VII,300 *ḫnmt*-cakes[2] for Osiris. I am he who is at the hand of Thoth, | I am he who cooks[3]
a *ḫnmt*-cake for Osiris among those who make offerings; what Anubis bewails is
the offerings on the day of straw.[4]

1. Cf. Lesko, 53, nn. *b.c.*
2. The meaning of *ḫnmt* is doubtful, cf. op. cit. n.*e.*
3. Var. *swꜣ* 'who passes'.
4. B3C omits *m htpw,* probably a purely scribal error.

Spell 1048

I am the pure one who cooks for Osiris daily. My lands are in the Field of Offer-
VII,301 ings among the Wise Ones, | among those who prepare *ḫnmt*-cakes for Osiris. I am
the scribe of lands at the hand of Thoth, I am the attendant of Osiris among those
who prepare offerings. What Anubis bewails is the offerings, but there is nothing
which can be taken from me.

Spell 1049

A basket of offerings.[1] A *ḫnmt*-cake is in it for its owner;[2] he who is in the Field
VII,302 of Offerings is its owner, who eats bread in it with Osiris every day.[3] | Its owner
has gone forth, and a *ḫnmt*-cake is issued from it for Osiris every day.[4] Offerings.[5]

1. So B2Bo; varr. B1C: 'a field of offerings'; B1L to B2P: 'a field of the Eye'.
2. So B2Bo, which omits 301*h*-302*a*; varr. B1C: 'an attendant (*ḫnmt*) will be in it for Osiris'; B2L and B2P: 'an owner of an attendant is in it for Osiris'.

3. This clause in B1C only.
4. So B2Bo; varr. B1L and B2L: 'a *ḫnmt*-cake is made from it for Osiris every day'.
5. A title for the spell, not in B2Bo.

Spell 1050

Spell for being a god for Osiris.[1] He who sees the dead Osiris will never die. The gatekeeper is one who will gain through robbery.[2]

1. *Sp 2* has been regarded as merely a mark of emphasis.
2. Presumably the gatekeeper is set to plunder the traveller. For *ms* in the sense of 'bring away' booty, cf. *Urk.* IV, 1308, 10. Compare 303*c*.

Spell 1051

The inert ones(?) are with the offerings[1] which are with the retinue of Osiris VII,303
every day, and they shall eat bread among the living for ever.[2] His[3] lands will
be yonder, | he is with Thoth, and he will not be driven off by any destroyer.[4] 304

1. *Nn* at the beginning of B3C – B4L can hardly be the demonstrative, on the grounds both of writing and of construction; the suffix in *wnm.sn* in 303*b* shows that *nn* must refer to beings who can eat. I have guessed *nn* to be a miswriting of *nnyw* 'the dead'. The group B1C – B2P, which writes this spell entirely in red ink, opens it with 'Spell for being with the offerings among the gods', continuing 303*a* with *ntyw m šmsw,* etc., as in B3C ff.
2. B1C – B2L insert (303*d*): 'and they shall never die'.
3. The suffix in *ꜣḥt.f* is a puzzle; the only apparent antecedent for it is 'Osiris' in 303*a*, but the probability is that it refers to the deceased, who has not been named. Lesko's 'the one whose plots of land will be there' (p. 55) would require *nty* after *wnn.*
4. B1C – B2L add (304*c*): 'the lords of the gates are those who gain through robbery'; cf. 302*f.* B1C and B2L insert the *m* of predication before *ms.*

Spell 1052

The snakes of . . . are the keepers of the gates.[1] The place of herbage. The place of fields. The place of sand. The place of stones(?).[2] The house of herbage(?)[3] of *'Iḫt-wtt*(?).[4] This is the spell which is above the waterways.

1. On *ꜥftt* cf. Spell 1034, n. 1.
2. Cf. Lesko, 57, n.*c*, who suggests a corruption of *ỉnrw.*

3. Reading the sign after *pr* 'house' as an abbreviation of *smw* 'herbage'.
4. Cf. Lesko, 57, n.*d.*

Spell 1053

VII,305 This is the path to the abodes of[1] those who live on sweet things(?).[2] This is a spell for passing on it which is before ⟨me⟩,[3] a spell for passing by the abodes of the knife-wielders and of those who shout.

This is its lower path, and you should not pass on it.[4]

Spell for passing on the path of the fiery ones. I am the Eye of Horus, bene-
306 ficial in the night, which makes fire with its beauty;[5] | I am the Lord of the horizon, and the daily flame licks me.[6] As for him who passes on the path, his foes will be felled and ⌜Apep will be driven off.[7]

Spell for reaching those who squat,[8] the keepers of the gates.

1. *Wꜣt nw r nywt nt* only in B2Bo.
2. *Bnt* may be a writing of *bnrt*; so already Lesko, 58, n.*d.*
3. Reading *tp-ꜥwy.ỉ*, cf. Spell 1064, 323*a.*
4. Not in B2Bo.
5. Following B2Bo, which has the most intelligible text.
6. *Nsbw* of B2Bo should be emended into *nsb.s* (so too Lesko) with *sḏt rꜥ nb* in anticipatory emphasis. The other texts have 'Khopri shines and licks me'. We have here an allusion to the sun rising past the horizon.
7. No two texts are in accord, and all are damaged in some degree. The most intelligible is B1C, if *ḫsf* be restored before *ꜥꜣpp*; the sign in de Buck, n. 1*, is indecipherable as it stands, but the broad top with a vertical tail suggests a distorted *ḫsf*-sign. Perhaps also the enclitic *wnnt* should be supplied after *sḫr.t(w),* though it is not essential to the sense.
8. So B2Bo; the attitude implied is that of the seated-god sign. The other texts substitute *smswty* 'the elders'.

Spell 1054

Its name is 'The lake of fire[1] of the knife-wielders'. There is no-one who knows how to enter the fire, for he is turned back from it; it means that he inherits the path. Spell[2] for the true lake.

1. B13C and B4L show only *š* 'lake.
2. Reading *rꜣ n* 'spell for' as B1C and B2L rather than *rn n* 'name of' in B3L.

Spell 1055

This is a spell for passing by; what is beneath it is the lake.[1] Let me pass safely, VII,307
prepare a way for me, so that I may navigate the bark, | for its protection is my 308
protection, and what will happen to me will also happen to it as a result of(?)
what you can do.[2]

1. *Ḫry.f š*, corrupted into *ḫry n* in B3C.

2. Lesko, p. 75, has 'if you act' at the end of the spell, but this translation takes no account of the ending *-w* in *ḏr ỉrw.k,* which looks like a relative form. The literal sense seems to be 'at the end of (= as the result of?) what you can do'. In the extended text of B1C–B2L *ỉrw.k* stands for a *sḏm.f* form with direct object, the ending *-w* being erroneously retained from the apparently older version; B3L drops the ending. These last four texts read: 'since you act against me, I am he who drives off the aggressors'; B2L inserts the adverb *ḏw* 'evilly' after *irw.k ḥt nbt ỉr.ỉ.*

Spell 1056

Great-face who repels the aggressors is the keeper of this bend. VII,309

Spell 1057

He of the sharp knife is the keeper of the waterway[1] and the keeper of this bend.

1. The reference to a bend suggests that *š* (or *mr*?) stands here for a meandering strip of water rather than a lake.

Spell 1058

I am one who drives off the opposition[1] of the aggressors who travel in order to VII,310
capture.[2] I am he who possesses the egg, and his dignity[3] is here when he appears
in the early morning. | Beware of his dignity,[4] because I have attained it;[5] when he 311
shall appear,[6] I will see him.[7] What I detest is delay,[8] since I know him, | and he 312
who would exclude me and the young god shall not live in the horizon.[9]

1. Four texts duplicate *ḫsf.*

2. *'Ir* of purpose + *ỉtt.* B9C ff. have *ỉṯṯwt,* by confusion with *ỉṯt* 'fly up'; and B9C and B1L of this group show the *r* of purpose.

3. After *swḥt* Lesko translates *sꜥḥ.f* as 'whose dignity', presumably with reference to the speaker, but what follows strongly suggests that the suffix refers to Rēꜥ, and this is confirmed by 510*f* in Spell 1168.

4. B3C and B4Bo have *sꜣ ṯw sꜥḥ.f*; B12C–B2Bo have *sꜣ sꜥḥ.f*, which with Lesko I interpret as a passive, 'his dignity is guarded'; while B4L ff. read *sꜣ.tw sꜥḥ.f* with the same meaning. B3C and B4Bo may well preserve the archetypal reading.

5. The apparent negations before *pḥ* in B12C and B4L are the known fanciful writing of the preposition *n*, which appears as *ỉn* in B1C ff. Lesko's rendering 'by him who attacked him' is ruled out by the 3rd person texts of B3C and B1Bo, where *pḥ* is a *sḏm.f* form with nominal subject; the other texts have the *sḏm.f* of the 1st person.

6. B12C and B4Bo show the prospective *sḏm.f* form *ḫꜥy.f*.

7. So B3C and four other texts; the negation *n* before *mꜣ* on three texts here and in 311*e* makes no sense.

8. B9C here inserts 311*e*.

9. *Ḫmwt.f*, apparently *sḏmty.fy* form, is in apposition to the suffix in *ꜥnḫ.f*, lit. 'he shall not live, (namely) he who would exclude me', etc. B9C ff. have the participle *ḫsf* instead of *ḫmwt(y).f(y)*. For *nṯr nḫn* three texts have *nṯr.ỉ nywtyw nḫn* 'my local young god'.

Spell 1059

VII,313 His name is Protector-of-the-two-gods. He is the keeper of this bend, and it is he who guards those who go down to it.

Spell 1060

VII,314 I have come here from the lifting up[1] of the horizon | that I may show[2] Rēꜥ at the gates of the sky and that the gods may be joyful at meeting me. The perfume
315 of a god is on me, | and the destroyers will not attack me,[3] nor will the gatekeepers
316 exclude me, for I am he who is hidden[4] within the shrine, | who is in charge of the
317 chapel[5] of Him who is bound, for this is the shrine which I have reached[6] in the land of tombs.

1. Lesko's (p. 71) 'numbering' of the horizon gives poor sense, for what could such 'numbering' mean? The real meaning of *ṯnw* is shown by *dsrw>ḏsrw* of B1C ff., both stems having 'raise', 'lift up' as the basic meaning; 314*a* indicates that a reference to the 'lifting up' or 'clearing' of the horizon at dawn is what is meant.

2. For *sr* 'show' cf. *CT* I, 191*e*; 211*a*; 229*d*; 404*c*.

3. Read *n pḥ wỉ nbḏw* with B12C, B9C, B1C, B1L and B3L.

4. Var. 'He whose face is hidden within the shrine'.

5. Varr. 'of his chapel'; 'of the chapel of the gods'; 'of the chapel of the god at the

proper time to which I have attained'; for *r nw* 'at the proper time' cf. *CT* IV, 115*a*; *Urk.* IV, 1105, 2.3; 1106, 9.10; B1C–B2L add (316*b*): 'after Ḥatḥōr is pure'.

6. *N ḳꜣss* in B1C ff. looks like a genitive referring to *ḫm* in 316*a*. B9C and B1C read: 'she binds the shrine in the time when I reached'. For *ḳꜣs.s* 'she binds' B1L and B2L have *ḳꜣb.s* 'she doubles', etc.

Spell 1061

I am Great-name; you have aided me on the right path; executioners are what I
detest. | The protection of Harwerrēꜥ is my protection, for I am one who acted VII,318
according to his desire,[1] and I will not be hindered,[2] I will not be opposed at the
gates of the sky; | it was I who equipped the Double Lion,[3] the Frog-goddess and 319
the gods of the living, so do not exclude me.[4]

1. So B3C. The other texts of this group inexplicably omit *ỉr* 'one who acted'; B1C ff. omit *ỉnk*.

2. Lit. 'my foot will not be grasped'. B1C ff. omit *rd* 'foot' and read: 'I will not be grasped'.

3. Var. B12C: 'the gods'.

4. B3C–B4L are to be read: *ỉm.k ḫmw wỉ*; B9C ff. have corrupted this into *ꜥnḫ.ỉ m ḫm sw* 'I live by excluding him', which makes no sense.

Spell 1062

His name is Hippotamus-face, bellowing of power; it is his lustral basin(?).[1] Spell VII,320
for going about[2] by day, since a man knows this spell.[3]

1. *Šꜣsw*, varr. *ḫꜣs*, *ẖꜣsw*, occurs here, in 323*b*, 513*b*, 514*b* and II, 257*b*; this last reads *hꜣ.n.ỉ m ẖꜣsw* 'I have descended into the lustral basins(?)'. On what grounds Lesko conjectures 'corpse(?)' is not clear. B4L is corrupt.

2. B9C ff. insert *sn* after *pẖr*.

3. So B2L and B3L; see also B12C. *Rḫ s* demands an object.

Spell 1063

I have inherited the horizon of Rēꜥ. See, I am indeed the Lord of All;[1] I am one VII,321
who reveals[2] what has been said to him, for I am heir of the horizon. | A path is 322
prepared for Rēꜥ when he comes to a halt. O . . . ,[3] I know your name.

1. Varr. 'Lord of wounds', 'Lord of Kenzet'.

2. *Sn*; cf. *Urk.* IV, 1381, 16.

3. B3C ff.: *ʿwnt*; B9C ff.: *ỉwʿt*; Lesko (p. 67) translates the former as 'plunderer', the latter as 'heir', though 'heiress' would be more exact. Neither of these readings makes sense, nor does *ʿw* with cord-det. in B1Bo; *ʿwnt* is without det. One has the impression of an ancient corruption.

Spell 1064

VII,323 His name is Dog-face,[1] whose shape is big. | This is a spell for passing by him which is before me;[2] it is a spell for the . . .[3] of her who divides the lustral basins(?).[4]

This is a spell for passing by him.

1. Var. B9C ff.: 'Great-face'.

2. *Tp-ʿwy.ỉ* is taken as referring to the spell which is in front of the deceased for him to read.

3. *ʿwʿw* with papyrus-roll det.

4. Cf. Spell 1062, n. 1.

Spell 1065

VII,324 Open, O sky and earth; open, O western and eastern horizons; open, you chapels
325 of Upper and Lower Egypt; open, you doors; | open, you eastern gates of Rēʿ, that he may issue from the horizon. Open to him, you double doors of the Night-
326 bark; open to him, you gates of the Day-bark, that he may kiss Shu, | that he may create Tefēnet. Those who are in the Suite will serve him, and they will serve me like Rēʿ daily.

Spell 1066

VII,327 His name is 'He who is driven off with two faces in dung(?)',[1] and he is the keeper of this bend. It is a spell for passing by him.

1. So Lesko, 64, n.*c.* B4L is corrupt; B9C ff. have: 'he who is driven off, a face which lives on dung(?)'.

Spell 1067

It is I who send the word of a god to a god; O Rēᶜ,[1] I have come that I may VII,328
report(?)[2] a message to its recipient.[3]

1. Var. BɪBo: 'Atum'.
2. a guess based on the context.
3. Lit. 'lord' or 'owner'.

Spell 1068

Hail to you, Rēᶜ! May you make Osiris content because of me,[1] so that those VII,329
who are in the tomb may worship you| and that those who who are in the 330
Netherworld may glorify you. They shall give you praise, and you shall come in peace so that you may give offerings to the great ones and satisfaction to the
lesser ones, | and give content to me; I shall attain to blessedness like Rēᶜ every 331
day.

1. Var. 'may you make contentment for me because of Osiris'.

Spell 1069

Great-face who opposes the aggressors and who guards them in his house; he it is
who enters beneath this bend. O Selḳet, I shall exist for ever!| HE IS THE KEEPER VII,332
OF THIS BEND, overbearing(?) of form whose mother speaks like a . . .| HE IS THE KEEPER OF THIS BEND, HE IS THIS GUARDIAN WITHIN HIS SHRINE. THIS IS A SPELL FOR PASSING ON IT[2] WHICH IS BEFORE ME.[3]

I am the lizard[4] which created thunder, who lifts up Maᶜet to Rēᶜ and repels the strength of ᶜApep, who splits up the sky and drives away the storm, and who nourishes the crews of Rēᶜ.

My two *šspt*-garments and my rod have been given to me,[5] I have raised up 333
Ḥetep as warden,[6] and I have caused the Bark to make a good voyage; prepare a path for me, that I may pass.

1. At the beginning of 332*b* read *ḫnfꜣ* in all texts; for the profile-face sign as phon. *ḫn* cf. *Eg. Gramm.*[3], Sign-list, D19-20. Lesko, p. 63, has misread the word in BɪÇ and BɪL as *nfꜣ*. The precise meaning of *ḫnfꜣ* is not certain, but the stem may mean 'overbearing', 'arrogant', cf. *Bersh.* II, 21, lower, 12. The sign of the mace in BɪC and BɪL looks like a det. of

ḫnfꜣ; B2L has *ḫnfꜣ ỉrw,* which may be the better reading. Following this, B2L reads *ḏdw mwt.f my šft*; for the last word B1C has *šwt* with lion-det. and woman-det., and B1L has *wšft*; the meanings of these are not known. Lesko has entirely misunderstood this passage.

2. Fem., in reference to the path (*wꜣt*), in B1L; masc. *ḥr.f* 'by him', referring to the keeper, in B2L.

3. At the end of 332*e,* for *.f* read *.ỉ,* cf. 323*a* (B2Bo).

4. For *ꜥšꜣ* 'lizard' cf. P. Ram. V, 21.

5. B1C omitted *šspty.ỉ*; there is no room for it in the lacuna.

6. So B1L; B3L has *m ỉrt.f* 'in his duty', cf. also B1C, B2L.

Spell 1070

It is fire which opposes the one (written three times)[1]

1. In 333*f* B9C omits *wꜥ* 'the one'. Lesko, p. 77, notes that this repeated passage refers to walls of fire that divide Spell 1071 in the coffins.

Spell 1071

VII,334 His name is High-of-winds.[1] This a spell for passing on it which is beneath it.[2]
335 His name is Lord-of-striking-power. O you who watch,| I am loud-voiced in the horizon, as your Great One.[3] Down on your faces, you watchers; prepare a path for your lord, for such am I. His[4] name is Flame.

336 This is a spell for passing on it which is beneath it. His name is Fiery-of-faces. O you possessors of power, my face is that of a Great One,| my hinder-parts are
337 those of the *wrrt*-crown, I am a lord of mighty ones.[5] His name is Diseased(?)-of-shape.[6]

This is a spell for passing on it[7] which is beneath it. His name is |Snake(?)-
338 face,[8] Lord of aggressors.[9] I am he who sits on the Eye of Horus, first of the three(?),[10] who judges the gods as the companion of Thoth.[11] |The protection of
339 Thoth is my protection from you.[12]

1. For the participle *ḳꜣ* of B3C ff., three texts have an unusual writing of the *sḏm.f* form *ḳꜣy.f*; this is confirmed by the fem. *ḳꜣ.s* of B1C, though why the feminine here is obscure; Lesko, 78, has 'high of flesh and(?) of winds', but does not suggest what this might mean.

2. Fem., therefore *wꜣt* 'way' presumably is implied; three texts have *.sn* after *ẖr* instead of *.s.* B4Bo has: 'This is a spell for passing by him (i.e. the keeper of the way) which is beneath him'.

3. Lesko's 'a great one like you' implies an unparalled and probably impossible use of *ỉs* 'like', 'as' after a dependent pronoun; *ỉs* surely refers to *wr.ṯn* 'your great one' as a whole; so too Piankoff, p. 41.

4. I.e. of the keeper of the way.

5. Var. 'power belongs to me'.

6. Cf. *ḫꜣsf* 'als krankhafter Zustand', *Wb.* III, 236, 3.

7. B12C has *ḥr.f* instead of *ḥr.s* of the other texts.

8. Reading *ḥꜣf* as *ḥfꜣ,* following Lesko, 79, n.*n.* B4Bo has *nḥꜣ.f* he is dangerous'.

9. So B12C, which alone is intelligible. B13C–B4L + B1C have *nbw nꜣw*; B9C + B1L – B3L have *nḫꜣw.* After 338*b* B9C inserts 'what(?) they see is . . . in the distance'.

10. B1L ff. have the ordinal *ḫmtnw* 'third'. B12C and B4L append *rꜥ nb* 'every day'.

11. B9C ff. omit *nṯrw.*

12. B9C adds in 339*b*: 'N's protection is from you'; an addition in B3L (339*c*) is lost.

Spell 1072

Spell for the paths of Rostau.[1] These paths here are in confusion;[2] every one of VII,340
them is opposed to its fellow.[3] It is those who know them[4] who will find their
paths.[5] | They[6] are high on the flint walls which are ⟨in⟩ Rostau, which is both on 341
water and on land.[7]

1. B3C has only: 'Spell for the paths'. B1C ff. precede the title with 'Fire'.

2. B1C has: 'these paths are the paths which reach here in confusion'; B1L, B2L: 'these paths which reach here are these paths in confusion'; for the idiom *pḥ nn* 'reach here', cf. *Sin.* B34. In 340*a*, for *m stnm* 'in confusion' B9C has corruptly *m sš*(?) 'in writing(?)', cf. de Buck, n. 1*, and B1C has *m stn.*

3. B3C–B4Bo add superfluously *m stnm* at the end; it is absent from the other texts and has been omitted from the translation. The reading of B9C is doubtful, cf. de Buck, n. 3*, but it appears to omit *ḫsft m* 'is opposed to'.

4. The paths. B3C and B4C have *.s* for *.sn.*

5. So B3C–B9C; B1C–B3L have: 'as for those who know them, who will find their paths'; the reading with *ỉr* seems to be secondary and an error.

6. The paths.

7. In B3C–B4Bo read *nt⟨y⟩ ⟨r⟩ Rꜣ-sṯꜣw*; B9C has *nt⟨y⟩ n R.*, B2L *m R.*, and in B3L *nt⟨y⟩ m R.* B9C omits *ḥrt mw tꜣ* at the end; the fact that *ḥrt* is feminine shows that it refers to Rostau and not to the walls.

Spell 1073

Be weary, you squatting gods, whose faces are hidden, who live by means of your VII,342
throw-sticks;[1] I am a mighty one,[2] | weighty of striking-power, preparing my path 343

in the fire. I have restored Osiris to health, so prepare a path for me that I may
344 pass,[3] | for I will save Osiris;[4] then shall I see the Sole One who circles around, (namely) Rēꜥ, among those who have made offerings, who will prepare a path
345 for me and who will let me | pass quite safely.

1. B9C ff. have not understood *ꜥmꜥꜣwt* 'throwsticks' and have corrupted it into *mꜣꜥt* followed by 'their fingers', not recognizing the throwsticks-det.
2. B3C–B4Bo have *wsr*; B9C ff. have *wsr-ỉb* 'stouthearted'.
3. Var. B9C ff.: 'so that I may be allowed to pass'.
4. Only in B9C ff.

Spell 1074

The paths by water and by land which belong to Rostau.

Spell 1075

VII,346 I am he who limited the flood, who judged between the Rivals; I have come that I may remove the humiliation from upon Osiris.

Spell 1076

VII,347 His name is 'One who spits out the Nile', who gives himself. Neḥebkau. He who eats his fathers. He who eats his mothers. He who drives off Seth when he is angry. He who begot the Bull of Ōn. He who swallowed the flood.[1] Falcon-face who issued from Edjō. Four-faces who issued from the horizon.

1. For *ḥḥw* 'flood' cf. *CT* V, 166*h*. The god-det. in B2Bo is borrowed from *ḥḥ* 'chaos-god'.

Spell 1077

Multiple-of-faces who hears the *ḏꜣdwt*-snake,[1] for much is the speech of the
VII,348 *ḏꜣdwt*-snake. He who meets him of the cow(?).[2] | He who sets down Khopri. He who stretches out the leg. The *ḏꜣdwt*-snake which fishes up multitudes.

1. *Sḏm* is corrupted in B9C. For *ḏꜣdwt* we have the varr. *ḏꜣdwtt, ḏꜣdt* and *ḏꜣd.*

2. Quite uncertain. For *ḫpy* as transitive verb cf. *Concise Dict.* 188; the reading of the second word is doubtful, as is its meaning, but it has been guessed to be a *nisba*-form of *ḥmt* 'cow'. The single determinative speaks against it being a dual 'two cows'.

Spell 1078

The paths by water which belong to Rostau.

Spell 1079

I am he who wrapped his standard, | who issued from the *wrrt*-crown; I have VII,349
come that I may establish offerings in Abydos; I have opened up Rostau that I
may ease the suffering of Osiris. | It was I who created water, who assigned my 350
standards, and who prepared my path in the Valley. O Great One, prepare a
bright path for me, that I may be allowed to pass, | and I will remove pain from 351
the Self-created. AS FOR THOSE WHO SQUAT, IT IS GĒB WHO WILL ESTABLISH THEM IN ROSTAU IN THE REALM OF HIS SON OSIRIS FOR FEAR OF HIS BROTHER SETH; MAY HE NOT HARM HIM. AS FOR ANYONE WHO KNOWS THE NAMES OF THOSE WHO SQUAT, HE WILL BE WITH OSIRIS FOR EVER AND HE WILL NEVER PERISH.

Spell 1080

This is the sealed thing[1] which is in darkness, with fire about it, which contains VII,352
the efflux of Osiris, and it is put[2] in Rostau; | it has been hidden since it fell from 353
him,[3] and it is what came down from him on to the desert of sand; it means that what belonged to him was put in Rostau.

1. Following B3C; *ḫtmt* is the true reading, note the fem. *ntt* in all texts of this group. B9C ff. are slightly garbled.

2. In B12C *rdy* is corrupted into *dr*; cf. *Stud. Griff.* 72.

3. For *ỉm.f* at the end of 353*a* B3C and B9C have *ỉm.s* in error; Osiris is meant.

Spell 1081

As for any man who is seen yonder alive, he will never perish, since he knows the VII,354 spell for passing by those who squat, the keepers of the gates.[1]

1. Following the B3C group.

Spell 1082

SPELL FOR BEING IN ROSTAU. I am Great-name who created his brightness, I have
VII,355 come to you, Osiris, | that I may worship you and that I may cause your efflux to raise itself.

Spell 1083

Fire.

Spell 1084

I am a possessor of blood on the days of those who come into being,[1] I am he of the sharp knives, and I will not be robbed.[2] A path is prepared for me in front of
VII,356 the temple, and the embalmer belongs to those who are in[3] the date-palm(?). | There will be brought to me what appertains to the Red Crown. To pass safely into the protection of Osiris and to pass the gates.

1. With 355*d*–356*a* compare VI, 193*d-i*.
2. B2L omits the negation, perhaps by confusion with *n* of *pn* preceding.
3. Reading *ỉmyw* with B2L; *sw* of the other two texts is a miswriting of *ỉmyw*.

Spell 1085

Spell for existing in Rostau, for living on plenty in the presence of Osiris, and for
VII,357 seeing ⟨ . . . ⟩.[1] | I am[2] Great-name who created his brightness, I have come to you,
358 Osiris, that I may worship you, and you have not driven me off.[3] | I will cause your efflux which flowed from you to raise itself, and I will recite the name of Rostau, since I fell in it.[4]

359 Hail to you, Osiris! | Raise yourself, have power and might,[5] have power by
360 means of this wand of yours which belongs to Rostau,[6] | in this power of yours which belongs to Abydos. Travel around, O Sole One,[7] as Rēʿ goes about. May

you speak, Osiris,[8] for I am a dignitary of the god.[9] | What I say comes to pass,[10] 362
and I will not be driven off because of you, Rēʿ. [11]

1. B1L^{a} adds *mꜣꜣ* at the end of 356*e*, apparently the first word of an incomplete sentence. B3L–B2P omit 256*d-e*. B5C ff. have the titles of the preceding spell 1084, which does not occur in these coffins.

2. B5C and B1P^{b} use a cryptic sign for *ỉnk* which resembles the ideogram of *sḫꜣk* 'squeeze out', *Concise Dict.* 244; so also in 361*e* (B1L^{b}); 520*i* (B5C)

3. 357*c* makes poor sense as it stands, but if *rdy* be emended to *dr* the passage becomes intelligible. This is the reverse of the corruption noted in 352*c* (B12C), and the error in both directions is known elsewhere, cf. *Stud. Griff.* 72. In B1L^{a} – B9C, 357*c* and 358*a* follow one another; 357*c* does not occur in B1L^{b} – B1P^{b}, which have (357*d*): 'I am pure because of your efflux'. In 358*a* B5C – B1P^{b} omit the passage and in 358*b* instead of *sṯꜣ ỉm.k* have *sṯs.ỉ* 'I am raised up'.

4. For *ỉm.f* B9C has *ỉm.s*. This is technically correct; a town-name is *ipso facto* feminine in Egyptian, though the rule is not always observed.

5. Var. 'in your power and might, and in life, prosperity and health'.

6. Var. 'have power in Rostau'.

7. A considerable omission from B1L^{a} – B3L, comprising 360*c* – 361*b*. B9C ff. omit 360*b*, but from 360*c* on they read: 'May your forehead go all over the sky in front of Rēʿ, may you see all the plebs. O Sole One, may you invoke Rēʿ when sweeping over the sky, that he may go all over the horizon'. There are minor variants in this group of texts, which omits 361*c*. All versions come together in 361*d*.

8. Varr. 'do not speak, Osiris'; 'I speak like Osiris'.

9. Varr. 'I am his dignitary and his mighty one';'I am his soul and his mighty one' (B5C).

10. Var. 'what I say comes to pass, just as he has said'.

11. Var. 'Osiris'.

Spell 1086

The walls are of charcoal. I open the way in Rostau, | I ease the suffering of VII,363
Osiris, I am he who created what exists, who assigned his standard, who made his
path in the Valley, a great one who made a bright path[1] for myself, | and I will 364
be allowed to pass.

1. B5C ff. omit *ššpt* 'bright' and add in 363*f*: 'I remove its brightness'. Instead of this the B1L group has 364*a*, which makes better sense.

Spell 1087

THIS IS THE WORD WHICH WAS IN DARKNESS. AS FOR ANY SPIRIT WHO KNOWS IT, HE WILL LIVE AMONG THE LIVING. FIRE IS ABOUT IT,[1] WHICH CONTAINS
VII,365 THE EFFLUX OF OSIRIS. | AS FOR ANY MAN WHO SHALL KNOW IT, HE WILL NEVER PERISH THERE, SINCE HE KNOWS WHAT SHALL BE IN ROSTAU.[2] ROSTAU IS HIDDEN SINCE HE FELL THERE, FOR HE IS ONE WHO HAS COME DOWN FROM UPON THE DESERT, AND HE POSSESSES WRITING MATERIALS IN DJEDU. ROSTAU
366 IS THE CORRUPTION OF OSIRIS. AS FOR ANY MAN WHO IS THERE, | HE WILL SEE OSIRIS EVERY DAY, HIS BREATH WILL BE IN HIS NOSE, AND HE WILL NEVER DIE, since he knows the spell for passing on it.[3]

1. The 'word'.
2. Read *wnty.sy m Rꜣ-sṯꜣw* with B5C ff.
3. An addition in black ink in three texts only.

Spell 1088

Head-bringer. Fiery One. Head-bringer bearing the *bnwt* of Rostau.[1] Baboon. He who bears the *bnw*.[2] Fire.

1. The first element of the name is omitted, but Rostau is surely meant.
2. At the beginning and end of 366*i* are jottings which I cannot read.

Spell 1089

VII,367 Permit that I be brought to you, O Thoth,[1] for I am he who opened the Netherworld.[2] O Rēʿ, I will lift up your head and I will navigate in your bark. | I will
368 prepare your path in the sky,[3] and its waters will come down[4] so that you may
369 navigate your bark in it by night. | I am one who makes silent the waters of the pool(?) of the plain.[5] A path is prepared for the rod-bearer of *Nḥbty,* and a path
370 is prepared for me, so that I may dispel the bleariness of the Lord of All | and spit on the wounds of Rēʿ, who will live[6] content, for I am one who knows how to repel ʿApep, who will turn back, having come.[7]

1. For the name of Thoth B9C ff. substitute 'Bull of the stars';
2. B12C has a superfluous *n* after *dꜣt.* B9C ff. omit 367*b*.
3. Var. 'I will prepare your path in this sky, the mistress of your plain'. It is possible,

however, that *wˁrt* here and below may refer to the polar region.

4. B1L ff. omit the *h* of *h3*.

5. The absence of a determinative renders the meaning of *šdw* uncertain, but 'pool' or 'lake' seems more likely in this context than Lesko's 'plot' of land. B12C reads: 'I am one who makes silence within the plain of waters'. At this point 369*e* is inserted in B9C–B1L, the texts of which differ from each other, but which all refer to preparing a path in the fire.

6. For *ˁnḫ* B1Bo has *rḫ*, perhaps influenced in advance by 370*b*.

7. B2Bo adds meaninglessly *m ḥtp m ḥtp*. B12C omits *ḫsf* after *rḫ*.

Spell 1090

Nḥbty. Fierce-face. Possessor of joy. Possessor of rain. Possessor of worship. *Nḥbty*. Fire. Fire. His name is Fierce-face. Possessor of wrong(?). Possessor of worship.

Spell 1091

O fire, go back, O you who burn(?)[1] there! I will not be burnt(?), for I am wear- VII,371
ing the wig-cover and wearing the White Crown. The *ṯnnw* have come into being, having come into being as Khopri.

1. *3t* or *3ṯ* (371*b*) is unknown, and the translation as 'burn' is a guess. So already Lesko, p. 98.

Spell 1092

HAIL TO YOU, THOTH, WHO WAS CHOSEN AS LORD OF THE MORNING. I POSSESS RIGHTEOUSNESS, AND WHAT I DETEST [IS WRONG(?)]. MY(?) LIGHT IS MY OPENING UP OF THE DARKNESS.

Spell 1093

This is the path of Thoth to the House of Maˁet,[1] and I will be in the suite of VII,372
Thoth at night, assembling[1] them. I possess Maˁet, I detest darkness, I open up(?) the night.[2] Fire.

1. Reading *nw* with B12C; the last signs in B1L–B2P appear to be corrupt, and the reading *nwḥ* 'bind' does not make good sense.

2. 372*b* is in B9C alone.

Spell 1094

VII,373 Hail to you, Thoth, in the suite of Rēʿ! | It is I who bring the bright Sacred Eye,
it is I who dispel[1] the bleariness which is on the injured Eye so that it may be
374 bright. | See, I have come to you in this nightly suite of yours among those who
375 make offerings. I have gone aboard your bark, O Rēʿ.[2] |I have swamped[3] the
fire, I have lightened the darkness among those who come with offerings when
376 Maʿet is brought to Him who crosses the waterway[4] | when he has heard the
noise[5] of the monster on the great plain north of Stretching-the-bows. It is I
377 who save Rēʿ from the storm of ʿApep, | and he[6] will not fall into his[7] bonds. It
is I who make disturbance, I cleanse the injured Eye, I go round about the door,
378 I adorn[8] the god with what was made for him. | Let me bring Thoth to you, for
he cannot defend you by night.[9] It is I who bring the Sacred Eye, having saved it
379 from him who would conquer it. | The Mansion of the Moon is a witness.[10]

1. For *dr* B1Bo has *wḏʿ*. B9C is corrupt.
2. Var. 'the bark of Rēʿ'.
3. Reading *mwy.n.ỉ sḏt*, lit. 'I have watered the fire'.
4. Var. B2Bo and B4Bo: 'the sky'.
5. B3C–B4Bo have *mdw* 'speech', but *ḫrw* 'noise' of B9C ff. makes better sense.
6. Rēʿ.
7. ʿApep's.
8. B9C ff. have *ʿpr* 'equip'.
9. For *ḥsf ḥr* 'defend' cf. *Leb.* 24; *Pr.* 7, 9. After *ḥr.k* B9C ff. insert the name of Thoth. For the 3rd person of B1Bo–B6C the remaining four texts have the 1st.
10. Compare 380*b* (Spell 1096).

Spell 1095

This is Isis who is before him[1] as Maʿet, she shows him the paths when crossing the sky, that he may imitate what Rēʿ does.[2]

1. The deceased.
2. So B2Bo; B1L and B2L have *stwt Rʿ* 'resembling Rēʿ'.

Spell 1096

VII,380 This is Thoth[1] who is in the sky; the Eye of Horus is on his hands in the Mansion
of the Moon.

1. Var. B1L: 'Moon-Thoth'.

Spell 1097

He who possesses joy. Fire. Fire.

Spell 1098

As for the Coiled One[1] which is on his head,[2] it was Isis who brought it to him. VII,381
Thus says Horus the Elder:[3] Proclaim his name for him on the day when they
do escort duty yonder for him | in the horizon when dividing the Entourage in 382
the horizon, when they bring their great ones, when his father who is with the
gods speaks. | The Entourage will act for you among your plebs;[4] I will cause 383
them to watch over you.[5] It is Rēʿ who shines in the night.[6] | As for anyone who 384
is in his suite, he will live for ever among the suite of Thoth. | It will be permitted 385
that he appear by night, and Osiris will be made glad,[7] since he is the Sole One
who suffered more than he,[8] (even) he who was placed among his servitors in the
Entourage.[9]

1. Var. B3L: 'the living one'.

2. Var. 'on him'. Lesko, 100, thinks that 'him' refers to Thoth.

3. Normally *ḫr Ḥr* 'thus says Horus' would follow the quoted speech, but here it clearly precedes it; so already Lesko.

4. There is much confusion of gender and number here; two texts show *ỉr n.ṯ*, one *ỉr n.k*, two *ỉr n.ṯn*, one *ỉr r.ṯ* and two *ỉr r.ṯn*. In five texts *šnwt* has no suffix, one has *šnwt.k*, one has *šnwt.ṯ*, with *šnwt.f* in three certain and two damaged instances. At the end of 383*a* we have *rḫyt.ṯ* in four certain cases, while in B9C ff. we have five instances of *.f* attached to a garbled version of *rḫyt*. It is impossible to disentangle this confusion, but it is possible that B3C may preserve the archetypal reading, in which case the fem. suffixes must refer to Isis, named in 381*b*.

5. Fem. except B4Bo, which is masc. B9C ff. have a different text: 'when they make splendid on his account', referring perhaps to *rḫyt* (in its garbled form in 383*a*).

6. B9C ff. insert (384*a*): 'this is the Great One for whom the sky came into being'.

7. Var. 'in the gladness of Osiris'.

8. Var. B1L: 'you are he who suffered alone'; B2L ff.: 'you are the son of him who suffered alone'. *Ṯtt* in two texts is a corruption of *ṯwt*. The first 'he' seems to refer to Osiris, and that at the end of 385*c* to the deceased.

9. Var. B9C ff. 'his father Rēʿ was placed for him among the members of the Entourage', with minor varr.

Spell 1099

VII, 386 I am a servitor of Rēʿ who receives his iron[1] and adorns the god in his chapel;
387 (I am) Horus who approaches his lord,[2] whose throne is hidden | in the purifica-
tion of the shrine;[3] a messenger[4] of the god to Her whom he loved. It was I who
388 nurtured Maʿet, and I caused her to ascend into his presence.[5] | It was I who
knotted the rope and who bound up his shrine. What I detest is storm, and there
389 shall be no heaping up of water[6] in my presence, | I will not be opposed because
of Rēʿ, I will not be turned back by him who acts with his hands, I will not walk
390 in the Valley of Darkness, | I will not enter into the Lake of Criminals,[7] I will not
391 be in the heat of (a god's) striking-power, I will not fall as Her who is plundered[8] |
when she enters among those who are taken[9] to Him whose face is behind the
chopping-block of the shambles of Her who is sharp.[10]

392 Hail to you, you of the mat(?);[11] the private matters of the god | are in the
secret places, and the hands of Gēb support [12] the dawn. Who is he who will lead
393 the great ones and will count[13] the children at his due time? | See, Thoth is within
the secret places, and he will do priestly service for him who counts the myriads
who are to be counted; who [14] splits open the firmament and dispels cloudiness in
394 his realm. | I have reached him in his place, so that I may grasp the staff and receive
the wig-cover of Rēʿ,[15] whose fair movements will be extensive.[16]

395 Horus swells up around his Eye,[17] but his Enneads are about his throne, and
they will get rid of the severe pain which he suffers. I (too) will get rid of the
396 pain, | and I will comfort him who has it. I have opened up the horizon for Rēʿ,
397 I have built his boat,[18] which travels smoothly. | Thoth's face is bright for me
when I worship Rēʿ by serving him, and he listens to me; he has removed my
398 impediment, and I will not be boatless, | I will not be turned away from the hori-
zon, for I am Rēʿ, I will not be boatless in the great crossing. It is he whose face
399 is on his knees [19] who extends his arm, | because the name of Rēʿ is in my body
and his dignity is in my mouth. I say it to him and I hear his words.

400 Praise to you, Rēʿ, Lord of the horizon; hail to you for whom the sun-folk
are pure, for whom the sky controls those who are in charge of the great striking-
401 power, | and the oars of those who are hostile are broken.[20] See, I have come
402 among those who show forth truth, since He who is far distant is in the West. | I
break up the storm of ʿApep; O Double Lion, I am he who prophesies to you.
403 See, I have come; O You who are before the great throne, hearken to me, | for I
will go down into your tribunal. I save [21] Rēʿ from ʿApep daily, but I will not
404 attack him when he awakens me.[22] | I will hold[23] the writing so that I may receive
offerings and equip Thoth with what was made for him,[24] I will cause Maʿet to

travel around at the head of the great bark,[25] | I will go down vindicated into the 405
tribunal, I will establish the Chaos-gods, I will lead the Entourage, I will grant to
them | to voyage in high delight, and the crew of Rēʿ will travel around in charge 406
of his beauty. Maʿet will be exalted and she will reach her lord, | praise will be
given to the Lord of All, and I will receive the staff; I will sweep over the sky with 407
it, and the sun-folk will give me praise as to Him who stands and will never tire. | I 408
will exalt Rēʿ with what I have done for him, I will dispel cloudiness so that I may
see his beauty and display the terror of him, I will fix his course, | so that his bark 409
may traverse the sky at dawn, for I am the Great One in the midst of his Eye;[26] I
will sit or kneel at the head of the great bark of Khopri the self-created; | I will 410
come into being and what I say will come to pass. I am this one who travels
around the sky to the West, and those who heap up the air(?)[27] will stand up in
joy; | they have taken the bow-warp of Rēʿ into the hands of his crew, and at my 411
command Rēʿ will travel all over the sky safely and happily(?). I will not be
opposed, | and the blast of your (*sic*)[28] power shall not carry me off, and nothing 412
repellent shall issue from your mouth against me, I will not walk on the paths of
downpour,[29] | for what my double detests is to fall into it; what I detest is a flood, 413
and it shall not reach me. I will go aboard your bark,[30] I will occupy your 414
throne,[31] | I will receive my dignity, I will show the paths of Rēʿ and the stars.
I am he who opposed the destroyer who came setting fire to your bark[32] | on the 415
great polar quarter. I am he who knows them[33] by their names, and they shall not
attack your bark while I am in it, for it is I who make offerings.

1. The ritual adze? Cf. *Pyr.* §13.

2. 386*d* is taken to be an epithet of the deceased; for 'Horus' B12C has *wr* 'great one', and B9C, B2L and B3L have *ḏr* 'kite'. At the end of the clause, for *nb.f* B3L has a group which looks like a bungle for *nḫny* 'he of Nekhen'.

3. Varr. 'your purification' and 'his shrine'.

4. *Wpty* 'messenger', like Horus in 386*d*, is taken to refer to the deceased.

5. *S(y) m-bꜣḥ.f* has been corrupted in five texts into *sšm.f.*

6. The negation *n* at the beginning of this and subsequent clauses has been regarded as the equivalent of Middle Egyptian *nn*; the translation in the future tense yields better sense than Lesko's present perfect, for the deceased will be more concerned with what shall not happen to him than what has not happened. *N wnn.ỉ* of 390*b* supports this view. For *wbs* 'heap up' cf. n. 17 below; B3C has *bsw* 'influx'.

7. Where the bodies of executed criminals were dumped? Cf. 'there is no tomb for him who rebels against His Majesty, his corpse is thrown into the water', Cairo 20538, II, 19 = *Les.* 69, 1.

8. B2Bo inserts *m-m ỉṯ n ḥr.f* between 390*b* and *c,* anticipating the same phrase in 391*a.*

9. *Ṯn* after *m-m* in B3C is a corruption of *ỉṯ n* of the other texts. After this read *ḥr.f*

ḥ3 nmt; B1Bo has *Ḥr.f-ḥ3.f,* the name of the celestial ferryman.

10. Hardly 'Sothis' as Lesko, 101; out of ten instances not one shows either star- or goddess-dets. 'Her who is sharp' may well be an epithet of the knife used on the chopping-block.

11. Lesko: 'judges'.

12. Lit. 'are on'.

13. B4C has *m ip.f* 'when he was counting'.

14. Thoth?

15. Although all texts except B3C and B12C (corrupt at end) read *nms r Rꜥ*, the preposition is hard to interpret convincingly, and I suspect it to be a corruption of long standing. I therefore have accepted the direct genitive of B3C, which makes good sense, despite its being in a minority of one.

16. The B1C text mentions Rēꜥ in this clause.

17. The root-meaning of *wbs* is 'heap up' corn, Dav. *Ptaḥ.* II,8, hence of water in storm, *CT* VII, 388*c*; of air(?), 410*c*; here the verb may refer to a painful swelling about the eye; 395*d* refers clearly to the alleviation of severe pain. *Wbn* of B3L looks like a scribal substitute for a verb which the copyist did not understand.

18. *Dpt* here, not *wy3*; note the fem. endings in *sḏ3t nfrt.*

19. *M3st* 'knee' of most texts is to be preferred to *rd* 'leg' of B3C–B1Bo.

20. Lesko, 105, has: 'which the courses of the rebellious pass', but *sw3* is written in all texts but one as the verb for 'break', and in that case *ḥpwt,* which lacks the det. of motion, must mean 'oars'; for *snṯ* 'hostile' cf. Spell 1100, n. 5.

21. B12C is slightly corrupt, having *nḥm.kw* instead of *nḥm. i.*

22. So B9L–B3L; B3C–B12C are obscure and probably corrupt. Could the archetypal reading have been *n is rs.f wi* 'if he does not awaken me'? It would yield better sense.

23. For the translation in the future tense see the prospective *sḏm.f* form *h3y.⟨i⟩* in 405*a*; so too *ḳ3y* in 406*c*; *sḳ3y* in 408*a*; *rdy* in 408*d.* For *nḏr* B4C has *ḏr*; B9C has *šsp. i* 'I will receive'.

24. Not 'what he has made', Lesko, 103; if he had made something, he would not need equipping with it; it would already be in his possession.

25. B1L ff. in 405*a* have *ḫr m3ꜥ-ḫrw* 'having vindication', with reference to *m3ꜥt* in 404*d.*

26. Var. B1Bo: 'in the midst of his bark, in the midst of his eye'.

27. Cf. n. 17 above.

28. ꜥApep presumably is addressed in this sudden switch to the 2nd person. Read *n iṯ wi hh n 3t.k* as B1L ff.

29. So rather than 'pestilence' as Lesko, 104. What we would expect in this solar context is a reference to bad weather, cf. the related word *idt* in *Urk.* IV, 615,15. This is borne out by the mention of flood in 413*b.* B1Bo has 'on the mound of downpour'.

30. The second person here can refer only to Rēꜥ, and the negation in four texts is certainly an error, probably under the influence of 413*c*, where the negation is correct; the other four texts are in the affirmative prospective *sḏm.f* form, which is what the sense demands. Cf. also *BD* 284, 2.

31. Cf. *Pyr.* §§906; 1171; 1325.

32. *'Iḳ3y* of B9C is a misreading of *iy*; B6C has 'the destroyer on the throne of your bark'. *Ns* appears to be a verb derived from *ns(r)* 'fire'.

33. The beings hostile to the sun.

Spell 1100

HE WHO STRETCHES OUT THE BOW-WARP[1] IS THE KEEPER OF THE OUTER GATE. VII,416
I have come here into the great valley, I have taken the knives[2] of the knife-wielder from him, | (even) the butcher, acute of striking-power, who has not 417
been repelled, for I am he who repels the destroyers who have not been repelled. Do not come down on me; | O you who stretch out the bow-warp, be vigilant, and 418
do not let cloudiness come into being among the sun-folk on the day of clearing the god.[3] If you should come against me[4] | as any kind of snake, Rēʿ will die and 419
ʿApep will be hostile.[5] Ritual is to be performed in the matter[6] within the shambles of the Protector(?)[7] by him who destroyed his father.[8]

1. For *ḥꜣt* read *ḥꜣtt* as Lesko, 109.

2. Cf. loc. cit. n.*f.* The *ꜣ*-vulture in B2Bo, B9C and B12C may be due to confusion with the *tyw*-bird.

3. I take 'the god' as referring to the sun, and the whole clause as a demand that the sky be kept clear of cloud. For *ḏsr* 'clear' the sky, cf. *CT* I, 223*a*.

4. *R.ỉ* 'against me' in B9C—B3L only.

5. For *snṯ* 'hostile', cf. *Pyr.* §1837; *CT* IV, 115*f*; V, 308*a*; VII, 401*a*. Lesko has 'slaughtered'.

6. Lit. 'in it'.

7. So Lesko, but the determinatives in some texts, especially B1Bo, speak against this. The copyists seem quite confused as to what was meant.

8. The significance of the last words of this spell is obscure.

Spell 1101

'IKNTY[1] IS THE KEEPER OF THE SECOND GATE. May you guard him who turns VII,420
aside to you; what is on me spreads protection over me. | The monster stands up 421
when meeting you, and the bark has fallen into the waters of weakness.[2] You are . . .[3] in the mouth of Rēʿ, | you shall not die(?) at the hands of his Suite;[4] 422
striking-power is on you(?) . . . ,[5] and you shall not come[6] in his time(?).[7] You are seen, | O you aggressor who are below, because the Great Lady comes. 423

1. Var. *mds sn* 'he who cuts them down'.

2. *Sic,* but the meaning is obscure. B9C ff. have 'the waters on the flood', the last word being *ꜣgb.* The final *nw* suggests a corruption of *gnnw* of B3C – B12C.

3. *'Iw.k sṯntf,* which I cannot translate. Lesko, 111, n.*f,* emends this into *ỉw.k* (*ḥr*) *s(ꜣ)ṯ ntf,* which he translates as 'you pour out that which is(?)' followed by 'in the mouth of Reʿ', but this does not account for the arm-sign in various forms which follows his *ntf* in

several texts, nor can *ntf m* stand for 'which is in'; *nty m* is what would be required. Further, in B12C and B1L, the walking legs displace the arm-sign. As it stands the text is unintelligible.

4. B3C and B1Bo have *wḏꜣ* without det., assumed to mean 'go' in the figurative sense of 'die'; this yields a better sense than *ḏꜣ* with boat-det. of the other texts of this group, and allows a literal translation of *m-ꜥ* as 'at the hand of' rather than Lesko's 'you have not travelled with his suite'. B1L ff. determine *ḏꜣ* with the papyrus-roll, which could yield 'you shall not be opposed by the hand of his suite'.

5. I can make little of 422*b*. B3C and B12C read *ꜣt ḥr.k,* but six texts omit the suffix, and it is by no means clear to whom it refers. If the reading *ḥr.k* be accepted, it could mean that *ꜣt* is 'on to you', in the sense of 'against you', 'you' being possibly the gatekeeper, threatened if he does not let the deceased pass. The following *nṯ* is equated by Lesko with *nṯ* 'tongue' of *Pyr.* §1088, but the word has not the tongue-det. here. He translates the section as 'the striking force (of God) is before you, his tongue against you', but the doubt as to the meaning of *nṯ.f r.k* and the fact that B12C follows *ḥr.k* with *ỉw nṯrr r.k, nṯrr* having both god- and snake-dets., speak against Lesko's rendering. My own impression is that 422*b-c* is quite corrupt.

6. B1L shows the prospective *sḏm.f* form *ỉwt.k.*

7. *Sp.f* is used adverbially, cf. *Eg. Gramm.*³ §88.

Spell 1102

HE WHO EATS THE DROPPINGS[1] OF HIS HINDER PARTS IS THE KEEPER OF THE
VII,424 THIRD GATE. Get back, | you aggressor, for your arm is as a *ꜣbḥw*-plant, your backbone is as a red *b̆bt*-plant, you shall eat of what the *mmt*-plant eats.[2] | I know
425 you, and I know the name of this throwstick of yours which is thrown behind
426 you. Down on your face! Lay out your arms! | Light shall go forth that it may open up the firmament, and bleariness of vision will be dispelled.[3]

1. *Ḥꜣmt* is not recorded, but there is no doubt as to its meaning.

2. Lesko compares *mmt* with *Pyr.* §1362, but there the reading is *m mt* 'with a throw-stick', cf. *Pyr. Transl.* Spell 553, n. 9.

3. Following B1L and B3L in reading *ḫsr ḥꜣty* 'bleariness will be dispelled'. If *sw* in *ḫsr sw ḥꜣty* of the other texts be regarded as the dependent pronoun, object of *ḫsr,* we must translate as 'bleariness of vision will dispel it', i.e. the light, which in this context seems to be nonsense, yet the presence of *sw* calls for explanation. Is it possible that *sw* here may be the particle of *Eg. Gramm.*³ §240, but used enclitically?

Spell 1103

VII,427 HE WHO GLOWERS,[1] THE VOLUBLE ONE, IS THE KEEPER OF THE FOURTH GATE. O Shu and Double Lion, Shu in the sky and the Double Lion on earth, it is you[2]

who tell me that sky and earth are cleared. Down on your face![3] The White Crown
and the Wig-cover have retreated. | I am made to enter,[4] and I make him who 428
glowers tremble behind the sacred matters of the god; I am made known in the
Above.[5] Who is he who goes around the Coiled One?[6] | One whose rank is high, 429
whom Thoth will judge in the morning. The bark has been broken up since you
came in opposition to me.[7]

1. *Ḥsf ḥr* does not mean 'defend' here, but is in itself an epithet of the gatekeeper, cf. 428*a*. Lesko renders it as 'Opposed-face'.

2. *Ṯwt,* lacking a form for the dual, refers to the two gods Shu and the Double Lion.

3. Presumably addressed to the gatekeeper.

4. Var. 'he enters'. The suffixes here refer to the deceased, cf. *ỉm.ỉ* in 429*d* in B9C, and should be transposed to the 1st person; see also the absence of suffixes to *sˁḳ* and *ssḏꜣ* in B3C and to *ssḏꜣ.n* in all other texts except B9C.

5. *ꜣsrt* with sky-det. may be an invented word intended to make a pun on *sr* 'make known'. The var. *ꜣrt* is due to a miscopying and can be ignored.

6. The signs at the end of 428*c* in B3C and B1Bo are probably distortions of the det. of *mḥn* in B1L ff., and so to be read.

7. Or 'meeting me'. 'You' apparently refers to the gatekeeper.

Spell 1104

I have come joyfully that I may announce the number of the appearings[1] of Rēˁ VII,430
as Khopri when Horus the first-born of Rēˁ goes around the sky, | and he will 431
see me among those who are at the steering-oars (of the solar bark).

1. So B1Bo; the other texts have *mḥw* 'cubits', which yields poor sense.

Spell 1105

I have come into[1] the sky of the Double Lion, | I have nurtured Maˁet; prepare a VII,432
path for me, that I may receive the *wrrt*-crown which is on Horus the first-born of 433
Rēˁ from her into my hand,[2] so bring it to me. | Prepare a path for me that I may
pass on it, that I may set Maˁet aright,[3] and that I may split open the darkness.

1. Or perhaps 'from'. B3C omits *m pt* and B3L has corruptly *m ḥtp*.

2. After Rēˁ' read *m-ˁ.s m-ˁ.ỉ* 'from her into my hand' as B9C and B3L; Lesko's '(from) myself' for the second instance is not possible, for one cannot receive from oneself.

3. Var. 'put right what is on Maˁet'.

Spell 1106

VII,434 I have come to you, O Horus[1] | the first-born among those who split open the firmament, so that you may save me from the claws of him who takes for him-
435 self what he sees, | and the blast of his mouth shall not carry me off, his striking-power shall not drive me away; I am admitted because of him who is over *nṯ*.[2] Let me pass, so that I may split open the darkness.

1. B3C has *wr,* a not uncommon corruption of the falcon-sign.
2. On *nṯ* see Spell 1101, n. 5. Here it has the var. *nṯnṯ*.

Spell 1107

VII,436 Darkness, darkness, darkness. THE GATE OF DARKNESS.[1] Fire, fire, fire.

1. In B1L only.

Spell 1108

HE WHOSE FACE IS INVERTED, THE MANY-SHAPED, IS THE KEEPER OF THE FIRST
VII,437 GATE. He lives on the excluded ones | who do not know how to pass over it. This is a spell for passing by him which is before me, my protection from him,[1] for I know that he who acts on his own behalf is ferried over.

1. *Mkt* is in apposition to *r3* 'spell'. 'Him' is the gatekeeper.

Spell 1109

HE WHO LIVES ON MAGGOTS[1] IS THE KEEPER OF THE MIDDLE GATE. He lives on
VII,438 him who does not know how to go[2] to | the sky of Horus the first-born, the third one who approaches his lord that he may live.[3] As for him who comes into being among maggots,[4] he shall eat them, since he does not know that this is the spell for passing by him[5] which is before him,[6] my protection from him.[7] I am in the midst of his firmament,[8] and he is my brother,[9] (namely) the Coiled One, when sailing, and I am ⟨in⟩ his suite.[10]

1. For this translation of *fnṯw* cf. *CT* VI, 386*b*, where it is enforced by the connection

with *ḥwꜣ* 'putrefy' in 386*a*.

2. Var. 'the spell for going'.

3. In B3C only. Probably borrowed from Spell 1110, 439*b*.

4. 438*c* seems to refer to the ignorant traveller, who has failed to learn his spell (438*d*) and is therefore condemned to the same unpleasant diet as the gatekeeper, Lesko has 'As for what becomes worms', but perhaps a better sense is obtained by translating *ḫpr m* as 'him who comes into being among'.

5. The gatekeeper.

6. The deceased.

7. 'Him' is the gatekeeper.

8. Var. B3L: 'his bark'. Here the suffix can refer only to the sun-god. 438*d-g* show the vague way in which these texts sometimes use their pronouns.

9. B9C–B3L have corrupted *swt sn.ỉ* into *swt ꜥnḫ n.ỉ* (B9C) and variants.

10. Not in the B3C group. B9C and B1L omit the preposition *m* and B3L is corrupt.

Spell 1110

'IKNTY WHO BELLOWS IN THE FIRE IS THE KEEPER OF THE THIRD GATE, the VII,439
third one who approaches his lord that he may live in the fire. This is the fire which is on his mouth, this is a spell for passing by him which is before him, my protection from him.[1] I am in the midst of his[2] firmament as Horus the first-
born; | I cannot be attacked by those who live or those who have passed away.[3] 440
It is his entourage which has given me prosperity(?).[4]

1. Cf. Spell 1108, n. 1.

2. The sun-god's.

3. Reading *ꜥnḫ(w) sbw* with Lesko. B9C and B1L are corrupt.

4. The rope-det. of *wḏꜣw,* which is common to all texts where it is preserved, raises a doubt as to the meaning of the word. That the determinative is not a misreading of the cursive *w* is shown by B4C and B1L, which write both the ending -*w* and the rope, as also in the damaged B3C.

Spell 1111

Fire. THE GATE OF DARKNESS.

Spell 1112

Open yourself, O storm, | you who are cloudy! Rēꜥ is covered, but Horus proceeds VII,441
happily every day, (even he) the great of shape and weighty of striking-power,

442 who dispels cloudiness with his fiery breath.[1] | See, O Rēʿ, I have come voyaging, for I am one of those four gods who are at the side of the sky,[2] and I show you Him who is present by day.

443 Make your cable fast,[3] for there is no opposition to you.

1. Varr. B9C: 'with what is in the midst'; B1L, B3L: 'with his two faces.'
2. The gods of the four cardinal points.
3. Apparently Rēʿ is speaking. On the translation of 443a cf. *Pyr.* Utt. 256, n. 6; *JEA* 57, 202; cf. also *CT* IV, 15*e*; V, 66*d*; VI, 280*l*.

Spell 1113

VII,444 Be high,[1] that I may approach you; be high,[2] O you who are high.[3] | I am one whom ʿApep detests, since I know how to spit on your wounds; I see, for I am
445 one who spits on wounds which will heal, | and I will not oppose you, O Rēʿ.

1. Imperative with reflexive dative.
2. B3C and B2P have *ḳꜣ n.k*; the other four texts have *ḳꜣ.k*. B1Bo precedes this with *pr.k* 'may you go up'; B9C has *ḳꜣt* only.
3. *Ḳꜣt*, var. *ḳꜣyt* with doubled det., probably stands for an original old perfective 2nd sing. *ḳꜣ.ty* 'being high'.

Spell 1114

This is Horus the first-born who is in all parts of the sky.[1] As for anyone who knows this spell which is before Him whose shape is great, he will be yonder as one whose shape is great.

VII,446 Hail to you, Rēʿ! May I see your beauty, may you not reach the destroyer who is against you.

1. Lit. 'all this sky of every sky'. Varr. B9C: 'this sky': B1L 'all the sky'.

Spell 1115

This is the drinking-bowl of the sky which belongs to the god's booth, and it endures in the sky; its front is fire, its back is darkness.

Spell 1116

He who bears her unguent jar(?), the best of the Sistrum-player(?).[1] This is the VII,447
seat of a spirit who knows how to enter into the fire and split open the darkness, but who does not know how to go up to the sky of Rēꜥ and of Horus the first-born among the suite of Rēꜥ and of Horus the first-born by means of offerings in
the horizon of Rēꜥ and of Horus the first-born. This is the true . . .[2] of Rēꜥ, | the 448
seat of a truly equipped spirit who will never die, and there is no god whom he will recognize as superior to himself; the seat of an equipped spirit who will himself be a god.

1. 447*a* is most obscure. The first group may read *ẖr(y) mrḥt.s*; Lesko, p. 120, plausibly suggests that the fem. suffix may refer to Ḥatḥōr. *Mrḥt*(?) is written with the ideogram of a man pouring fluid, which in B1L–B3L is determined with an ointment-jar. My version of the rest of the passage is close to that of Lesko, but neither is entirely convincing. For the reading *'Iḥy* 'Sistrum-player' cf. B9C ff. B3C and B9C end with strange groups which I am unable to interpret.

2. *ꜥftt*; cf. Spell 1034, n.1.

Spell 1117

As for anyone who knows what is sealed, he will become more glorious thereby
than Osiris. | He has passed every tribunal in which Thoth is, but Thoth will be VII,449
in the tribunal of Osiris. If there be a man, a Great One, who is on his waterway of death to the beautiful West, the man shall read it at the quadruple purifica-
tion, and he shall depart in four days, | being correct in everything; but if he 450
wishes to know how to survive on his feet, he shall read it daily, having rubbed his flesh with . . .[1] of a girl who is . . .[2] and with the flakes of skin(?)[3] of a bald man who is . . .[4]

1. *Bꜣd,* a substance of unknown nature.

2. *ꜥmꜥt*; cf. *Wb* I, 185, 15. The word may be connected with *ꜥmꜥ* 'smear', *AEO* I, 11*. Piankoff, p. 32, translates it as 'uncircumcised'. Cf. Spell 1145, n.2.

3. Cf. *šnft* 'scales' of fish, *Amarna,* III, 29, 8 (restd).

4. *ꜥmꜥ*; cf. n. 2 above.

Spell 1118

The Mansion of Osiris. The land of spirits. Seth of the land of spirits. VII,451

Spell 1119

This is he who proclaims Osiris; water[1] is about him and life is on his mouth.[2] As for Osiris who was made(?)[3] in the field, his arms drive off(?) Seth for him,[4]
VII,452 and every limb of his[5] | is in the place which they[6] reached. The limbs of his which he allots to his semblance(?) are necessary.[7]

Hail to you, Osiris, possessing your mansions,[8] you who endure; the ill-disposed is inert, but your heart is stout, O you who do not fight, but drive off uproar. I speak of the content of the chest of red stuff(?) of him who is spiteful.[9] Assess me,[10] Osiris, for I have assessed you; may my bones be hale and my limbs strong.

1. B1L and B3L have *ṯn* 'you', an easy corruption in hieratic from *mw* 'water'.
2. So B3C; minor varr. in B9C and B3L.
3. *'Iry* has the appearance of a perfective passive participle.
4. On *sꜣš*, var. *sꜣẖ*, see Lesko, 123, *n.f.* However, Piankoff's 'repulse(?)' makes better sense. He refers the suffix in *sꜣš ꜥwy.f* to 'him who proclaims' in 451*c*. In that case the dative *n.f* will refer to Osiris. Note its unusual position following a noun-subject.
5. On *ỉm.f* after *ꜥt* cf. Spell 356, n. 5.
6. The suffix *.s* is singular because *ꜥt* in *ꜥt nbt* is singular, but in English 'they' is enforced. B3L in fact has 'they'.
7. Lit. 'beneficial'.
8. B3C has a superfluous *n* between *ẖr* and *ḥwt.f.*
9. B3C has *sꜣrt* without det.; B9C and B1L have *sꜣyt* with box- and wood-dets.; B3L has *sꜣt* with wood-det. alone. For *ṯr* 'red stuff(?)' of B3C, cf. Harris, *Minerals,* 154; B9C has *ṯꜣw,* B3L and probably B1L have *ṯrꜣw,* both unidentified and probably corruptions of *ṯr.* For *mds ỉb* 'spiteful' cf. *Urk.* IV, 969, 1; the other texts have simply *mds,* meaning in this context perhaps 'he who is forceful'.
10. B9C has *sḳd n.k* ⟨w⟩*ỉ*; the verb may be a derivative of *ḳd* '(good) character' with the meaning 'give me a good character' *'Ip* 'assess' appears to be used in the sense of 'summing one up'.

Spell 1120

VII,453 I stand up with Osiris when he stands up; O Osiris, your soul comes to you and your throat is opened. Come, Osiris[1] – four times – that the sweet breezes may come to you, for his[2] power is laid low, and they have forsaken the wrath which is on him for ever.[3]

1. So B9C and B3L. B3C and B4C have 'Come, Osiris, for Osiris', which is meaningless.

2. Seth's.
3. B1L and B3L have corrupted *bṯ* into *ỉṯ*. B1L has 'they have forsaken the wrath of Seth'.

Spell 1121

The Centipede-god. Osiris. The earth-god. | 'Enduring and living' is the name of VII,454
this bark.

Spell 1122

He does not know Seth because of Osiris. Stand, that I may raise you; open your ears, for I give you the Sacred Eye.[1]

1. Var. *ḥtpw* 'offerings'.

Spell 1123

I am he who went forth from you. Give the Eye of Horus to Osiris. Your eye is clean; rise up that you may live. I am satisfied, for (something) has been given to me.

Spell 1124

I am pure in my own sarcophagus; I am Thoth, a possessor of offerings to Osiris VII,455
and a possessor of offerings to myself. These[1] belong to my father Osiris who is on the high ground (and to) the Coiled One.[2]

1. B3C omits *nn* 'these'.
2. B9C and B1L add 'the Earth-god (*ꜣkr*)' before 'the Coiled One'; cf. de Buck, n. 5*.

Spell 1125

Hail to you, you gates whose names are secret, whose sites are sacred! | May VII,456
you save me from him who would impose any evil obstacle of the mighty ones who are before you until I come into the presence of the Lord of All. I have pacified the Two Warriors, I have raised up the orphan so that he may make

complaint about the injury which was inflicted on his father by *Ṯbhꜣ* when his body was slain.

Spell 1126

VII,457 ⌜Apep and his backbone. Imsety, Ḥapy, Duamūtef, Ḳebḥsenuf. He who sees his father. He who made his own name. The sun-folk. The crew of Rēʿ, whose number is unknown.

Spell 1127

Words spoken by the elder magician: 'You shall go,[1] for he who sees his father is fallen[2] because of you; the bowmen shot him[3] and the spearmen felled him'.

1. *Sbw* apparently is infinitive after the *r* of futurity, but one would have expected the fem. *sbt.* Lesko, 127, translates this as a question, 'Will you travel?', but the particle *tr* is not necessarily interrogative in meaning.

2. Reading *ỉw mꜣꜣw ỉt.f* with B3C; B9C has confused the suffixes. B3C, however, has the fem. *ḫr.t(y)* in error, perhaps because this is a woman's coffin.

3. *Ỉ* at the beginning of 457*m* may be the prothetic *ỉ* or conceivably may mean 'it is said that . . . '. The sense demands that the *sḏm.f* forms here and in 457*n* should be taken as referring to past time. At the end of 457*m*, *wꜣwt* of B9C is an error for *pḏwt.*

Spell 1128

VII,458 Circle of fire. [Circle] of fire. Fires.[1] The fire of the Night-bark.[2] The company which is in the bow is Isis, Seth and Horus. The company which is in the stern is Ḥu, Sia and Rēʿ.

1. So B3C; B1L has again 'circle of fire'.

2. Read *sḏt (m)sktt.*

Spell 1129

The north bank of the Winding Waterway,[1] the towns of which are unnumbered.
VII,459 A million cubits are about it in the flame of a torch.

Hail to you, Protectress of its blast, which its fire extended[2] far beyond it;

save me from him who would impose any kind of evil obstacle because of Him whose name is 'Secret-of-wisdom', for I have come into being from his flesh. He has created me from his members, but it was not my father who caused her to fly
up(?),[3] | and there was nothing which came forth to me from her body. She raises 460
my name above the stare(?)[4] of her face, the number of my limbs is at her will[5] according to[6] what is good in my sight. This portal has closed on me as on the body of the egg from which I have emerged. It is the darkness of my father Nu
which does it, being far from this portal.[7] | I have made a million cubits into my 461
own cubit[8] when flying up to this place of mine.

1. So B3C. The other texts have 'arriving at the north of'.

2. Lit. 'made'.

3. Reading *nn ỉt.ỉ rdy sḥr.s* with B3C, but putting it in the 1st person. B9C, the only other intact version, reads *n it.i rdy.ỉ hr.s* 'it is not my father whom I put on her'. B1L must have read something like *n ỉt*[*.ỉ rdy*] *wỉ ḥr.s.* It is clear that the passage became corrupted early, and it is doubtful if either version really reproduces the archetype.

4. *Stw* in B3C and B4C; cf. the verb *sty* 'stare' in *Concise Dict.* 252. B9C is corrupt; B1L has 'she raises my name in order to please my face'. There is nothing to show which of the two versions is to be preferred.

5. So B3C. B9C is again corrupt; B1L and B3L read 'you make my limbs distinguished at my desire'.

6. *R* only in B3C and B4C.

7. So B3C; B4C is similar. The varr. add *ḥr.ỉ* 'on my account' at the end of 461*f.* This passage is unintelligible to me.

8. So B3C, B1L and B3L. B9C is corrupt.

Spell 1130

WORDS SPOKEN BY HIM WHOSE NAMES ARE SECRET, the Lord of All, who said to
the Silent Ones who raged when the Entourage sailed: | Go in peace! I will relate VII,462
to you the two good deeds[1] which my own heart did for me within the Coiled One in order that falsehood might be silenced.[2] I have done four good deeds
within the portal of the horizon. I made the four winds | that everyone might 463
breathe[3] in his time. Such was my deed in the matter. I made a great flood so that the poor as well as the great might be strong.[4] Such was my deed in the
matter. I made every man equal to his fellow, | and I forbade them to do wrong,[5] 464
but their hearts disobeyed what I had said. Such was my deed in the matter. I made their hearts not to forget the West, in order to make god's-offerings to the gods of the nomes. Such was my deed in the matter.

I created the gods from my sweat, | and mankind from the tears of my eye; 465

I will shine[6] anew daily in [their] booth for the Lord of All,[7] I made night for Him who was languid. I will navigate aright in my bark, for I am the Lord of
466 waters when crossing the sky,[8] | I am not rejected(?) because of any member of mine.[9] Ḥu is in company with Magic, felling yonder Ill-disposed One for me,[10] I see the horizon, [11] I sit before it, I judge between the wretched and the wealthy; |
467 so also as regards the evildoers. I possess life, because I am its lord, and my staff will not be taken away. [12] I have passed myriads of years between myself and
468 yonder Inert One, [13] the son of Gēb; I will sit with him in the one place, | and mounds will be towns and towns will be mounds; mansion will desolate mansion.

I AM THE LORD OF FIRE WHO LIVES BY TRUTH, LORD OF ETERNITY,[14] WHO CREATES JOY, AND THE SNAKES OF . . .[15] WILL NOT REBEL AGAINST ME: MY SHRINE
469 BELONGS TO ME,[16] THE LORD OF WOUNDS WHO PUTS A STOP TO THE RAGING, | WHO DRIVES OUT SNAKES FOR HIM WHOSE NAMES ARE MANY, WHO GOES FORTH FROM HIS SHRINE; LORD OF THE WINDS WHO FORETELLS THE NORTH-WIND, WHOSE NAMES ARE MANY IN THE MOUTHS OF THE ENNEAD; LORD OF THE HORIZON WHO CREATES LIGHT AND ILLUMINES THE SKY WITH HIS OWN BEAUTY. SUCH AM I;
470 PREPARE A PATH FOR ME THAT I MAY SEE *NYW* AND AMŪN. I AM A SPIRIT WHO HAS ACQUIRED . . . [17] I PASS BY THE . . . [18]⟨AND THEY WILL⟩ NOT ⟨SPEAK⟩ THE WORD(?) [19]WHICH IS ON THE BACK OF THE ROLL, THEY WILL NOT SPEAK THROUGH
471 FEAR OF HIM WHOSE NAME IS SECRET WHO IS WITHIN MY BELLY. | KNOW HIM AND AM NOT IGNORANT OF HIM, I AM ONE WHO IS EQUIPPED, SKILLED IN OPENING PORTALS.[20]

As for anyone who knows this spell, he will be like Rēꜥ in the east of the sky [21] like Osiris within the Netherworld, and he will go down to the circle of fire; there will never be a flame against him for ever.

It has come happily to an end.

1. Var. B6C: 'four good deeds'; *sp* in B9C has the normal plural determinative.

2. Var. B1L: 'because I desire that falsehood be silenced'.

3. B6C has *ssnsn* and B9C has *snsn* for *ssn*; B1L has *sn.* B6C has *s* 'man' without the following *nb* and substitutes *ỉm my snw.f* 'there like his fellows'.

4. B6C and B1L insert *ỉm.f* after *ḥwr.*

5. Var. B1L: 'I forbade the doing of wrong'.

6. *'Iw. ỉ psḏ. ỉ* has been corrupted into *spd.i* in B1L. *Pace* Lesko, 131, n.*l*, it seems to me better if the translation in the 1st person be maintained, since the deceased is identified with the Lord of All, and one cannot satisfactorily distinguish between them.

7. So B3C. B1Bo reads: 'I shine and am seen daily in the dignity of the Lord of All'; so also probably B4C. For *sꜥḥ* 'dignity' the much damaged B1C has obscurely *sḥr,* while B6C–B1L have *sḥḏ* 'one who makes brightness'; B1L omits *m* after *rꜥ nb.*

8. For *ḥḥw* 'waters' cf. *CT* V, 166*h* and the late word *ḥḥ* 'inundation-water', *Wb.* III, 153, 13. For *nb ḥḥw* B9C has corruptly *nb nḥḥ* 'lord of eternity; so also B6C, which omits *ỉnk* or *N pn* at the beginning of the clause. B1L has *ỉnk nb dd mw* 'I am the lord who gives water'.

9. The meaning of *tr* is not clear; I have tentatively connected it with *tr* 'reject', *Wb.* V, 318, 12. On *ʿt ỉm.ỉ* cf. Spell 356, n. 5.

10. For *ỉw Ḥw* B4C has *ỉw.ỉ.* B6C expands 'felling yonder Ill-disposed One for me' into 'felling N's foes and felling yonder Ill-disposed One for him'.

11. B3C omits *ȝḫt* 'horizon'.

12. Var. 'the staff will not be taken from my hand'.

13. I.e. between the coming into existence of the two beings.

14. B1L has only *mȝʿt nb nḥḥ.*

15. *ʿftt*; cf. Spell 1034, n. 1.

16. Var. B1L: 'I am he who is in his [shrine]'.

17. *ʿftt*; cf. Spell 1034, n. 1.

18. *Nhȝw*, varr. *hnw, msw.*

19. From here on the text of B3C will be found under Spell 1031 (p. 262), cf. de Buck, 470, n. 1*. From the shortness of the lacuna in B3C after the negation *n* in 470*d* it is obvious that something has been omitted between this and *ḥrt pḥwy n mḏȝt* in 262*a* which is not in the parallel versions. *Ḥrt* may well be an adjective qualifying a lost preceding noun, and I have conjecturally restored the sentence as *n ⟨mdw.n.sn mdt⟩ ḥrt pḥwy n mḏȝt*; it is difficult to think what else could be on the back of the roll but a word or sentence (*mdt*).

20. B9C here inserts the damaged 471*b*, of which there remains the sentence 'he will pass safely'.

21. Cf. 262*g*. B1L in 471*c* has corrupted *m ỉȝbt pt* into *m pt ỉpt.*

Spell 1131

Hail to you, my father, and to the Companions in your beautiful field, Lord of VII,472
those who give to him who disregards(?)[1] your putrefaction in it. Its light is in the sky as your soul, and Rēʿ stands up in the midst of the sky in order to give guidance to his attendants. His back, (even) Rēʿ-Atum's, is turned to the smells; a lock of hair is cut off, and the eye is closed because of (?) . . .[2] May the fledgeling which issued from you live, may the tip of a fingernail be covered, may a fly fly up, may Osiris live, may the great ones, the Celestial Kine, be gathered together.[3]

I am a builder and I have knowledge; | I am a builder and I raise up my father; 473
I have built up the Great One and the Great Lady, I have built up the sea and the flood, I am this defiant one(?)[4] of Khnum who takes away enmity(?). This is the builder who cuts off . . .[5] I have come that I may see Osiris, and I will live beside him and putrefy beside him, I am your[6] semblance, I am the image of you.

GUIDE TO THE DOUBLE DOORS OF THE HORIZON WHEN THEY CLOSED ON ACCOUNT OF THE GODS. THIS IS THE NAME[7] OF THEIR KEEPERS WHICH IS IN

WRITING AND THIS IS THEIR ENTIRE NATURE. AS FOR ANYONE WHO DOES NOT
KNOW WHAT THEY SPEAK, HE SHALL FALL INTO THE NETS[8] OF THOSE WHO NET
474 THERE(?) . . .[9] | AS FOR ANYONE WHO SHALL KNOW WHAT THEY SPEAK, HE SHALL
PASS BY, AND HE SHALL SIT BESIDE THE GREAT GOD WHEREVER HE MAY BE, AND
HE SHALL GIVE RESPECT TO HIM, FOR HE IS ONE WHOLLY EQUIPPED AND SPIRITUALIZED. AS FOR A MAN WHO SHALL KNOW, HE WILL NEVER PERISH, AND THEIR SEAL SHALL BE ON HIM LIKE ANY GOD FOR WHOM THEY DO IT AMONG ALL THE GODS.

1. *Btn* without determinative, lit. perhaps 'defies'.

2. *Ṯꜣ n bꜣbꜣ.f* (or *nbꜣbꜣ.f*). I cannot make anything of this. To me Lesko's version (p. 23) 'the eye which this pellet in its socket sealed' does not carry conviction. *Ṯꜣ* lacks the pellet-det., and *bꜣbꜣ* or *nbꜣbꜣ* has no det. at all. In 472*g* *ṯꜣ* may well be the word for 'fledgeling', since it can live. *Nbꜣbꜣ* occurs as a verb of unknown meaning in *Pyr.* §104; see also 480*g* below.

3. The significance of 472 *f-k* escapes me.

4. *Btnn.*

5. *Ynysf pr.*

6. *Sic.* The 2nd person presumably refers to Osiris.

7. Apparently 473*j* is a joint name of the keepers.

8. *'Innwt* may be a variant of *ỉnyt* 'purse-net(?)', *CT* IV, 348*a*; for the vine-prop as determinative of a word for 'net', cf. *ỉꜣdt,* loc. cit.; 354*a*; VI, 3*a*; cf. also *ỉssyt* 'fish-trap', loc. cit.

9. 473*n* is too badly damaged to yield a clear sense. Lesko's version seems to me questionable, especially his translation of *hbw* as 'have been written'. It seems better to wait on the chance of a more complete version coming to light.

Spell 1132

A gate with fire in front and hidden at the back, with a man in it who is bound,
VII,475 and it is a marvel for the length of a day(?).[1] I am Nu, Lord of darkness; | I have
come that I may have power over the path, and he who has two faces[2] is afraid of me. I am one who is heavy on your shoulders for you,[3] and who . . . shoulders for you . . .[4] I have come here from Ōn that I may be . . .[5] as the Mighty Lady; that I may see the Bull of Ōn in their (*sic!*) shape, that I may see my water in darkness. I speak to them, for I know them by their images, I saw their mother's delivery, and I guide them to you in(?) my name of Bull of Ōn,[6] that they may illumine me . . .[7]

1. Lit. 'in a day on length'.

2. Reading *ḥry ḥrwy.f,* lit. 'he on whom are two faces'.

3. It is not clear to whom 'you', 'your' refer.

4. 475*d* is corrupt. *Nsḥwḥ* is a *vox nihili* which Lesko, 26, n. *f*, suggests may possibly be a corruption of *snḥ* 'bind'; *rmnwy,* following the dative *n.k,* lacks the suffix *.k* as in 475*c,* which seems to have been displaced to follow *pḥ*, while *ḏd n pḥ ỉt.f* is nonsense, as is *pḥ.k ỉt.f.*

5. *Tfꜣ* is not known. Lesko, loc. cit., hesitatingly follows Kees in suggesting that the word may be a corruption of *ꜣtf* 'be crowned'. The objection to this interpretation is the feminine noun *wsrt* 'Mighty Lady', with the implication that she too wore the *ꜣtf*-crown, but this crown was not normally worn by goddesses.

6. 475*l* appears to be corrupt. Perhaps one should emend as *šsm.ỉ n.k sn m rn.ỉ n*; it does not seem possible otherwise to make good sense of the passage. Lesko proposes an alternative: 'May I draw for you among(?) them the name of', but I question his translation of *sšm*; by 'draw' he appears to mean 'depict'. For *N kꜣ 'Iwnw* of 475*m,* in my view we should emend by omitting *N.*

7. The three water-signs which end the spell are obscure; Lesko, 26, n.*l*, would read them as *m-ẖnw* 'inside(?)'.

Spell 1133

I will show the way and pass on it. I am *Wsrnn,* Lord of the secret things; one VII,476
mightier ⟨than⟩[1] all the *ṯnnwt*-gods. I am the . . .[2] of the lungs of Shu when he
passes the liver on the . . .[3] My father belongs to me.

1. Read perhaps *wsr* ⟨*r*⟩.

2. *Btkw* with flesh-det. Lesko, p. 26 has 'squalor of the lungs', but not only does this fail to make much sense, but the determinative here is wrong for *btk* 'squalor', cf. *Concise Dict.* 86.

3. The end of 476*e* is quite obscure. Lesko suggests either 'on the sledge' or 'first of all', but neither conveys much meaning; furthermore 'sledge' is *tmt,* not *tm,* cf. op. cit. 298.

Spell 1134

Open to me, and I will sleep; open to me, and I will be protected[1] from them. It
is an equipped spirit who guards the gate of the mansion of Many-faced. I have
come and I have traversed the swamp, I have moved about[2] since you . . . ,[3] and VII,477
I pass by the shoulders of Osiris, for he knows that the . . . who are in[4] the gates
who shall guard them, belong to me. See, I am a Lord of motion, and my back is
not opposed(?).[5] I have gone straight ahead(?),[6] everything(?) being about you[7]
like *ꜣṯn* and the Companions. Movements here are mine, and he grants my dignity
like one who raises himself; I am more of a spirit than the Lord of thrones, and I
see him making them into their shapes.[8]

I have come here from Dep that I may see the growing plant and see it in my 478 day; the mansions belong to his face.[9] My head is on me, my arms are on me, my legs are on me, I am the wearer of the royal headcloth[10] who is in Dep; Dep is on him, having become him. I am he, I am the wearer of the royal headcloth who is in darkness.

1. Cf. Lesko, 27, n.*b*.
2. So Lesko.
3. Lesko proposes either *dr ꜥšt.k* 'until you called', with metathesis of *ꜥšt* into *ꜥtš*, or *ḏr dyt š.k* 'since your lake was given'. Neither proposal is impossible, but nevertheless I am sceptical; of the two the second seems the more probable, but in that case the absence of a dative *n.k* and of any determinative to the supposed *š* 'lake' is curious, and I suspect corruption.
4. Cf. de Buck, 477, n. 2*. The doubtful sign looks like a dittograph of *ỉmy*.
5. Reading *ḫsff sꜣ.ỉ*. Lesko has 'who was not opposed afterward'.
6. Lit. 'after my face', i.e. looking ahead.
7. Reading *tm m-ḥꜣ.k*. All this is most obscure; one can only attempt to render the words. Lesko's version of 477*e* -*f* is quite different.
8. There is no antecedent for 'them', their', which suggests that there has been an omission between 477*i* and *j*.
9. The meaning of this escapes me.
10. Read *ꜥfnwt(y)*; the word has the seated-god det. in all texts and is qualified by a masc. adjective *ỉmy*, miswritten in two texts as *sw m*; cf. also 478*j*. Lesko reads *ꜥfnwt* and translates it as 'wrapped up'.

Spell 1135

VII,479 The Souls of Nekhen. Those who lay hold, the guardians of my[1] limbs in rage; see, they are dangerous. Fire. Fire.

Hail to you (plur.) who lay hold of my Two Lands for me, you guardians of my limbs in storm. I am the Nekhenite who fashioned your snakes, I am the torch which is with you. I will pass with Shu into the Abyss, I am one who makes himself content after the Mistress,[2] I am he who will restore the sky to order, I am he who will have power over darkness, one mightier of striking-power than
480 the Mighty One; | mine are those who exist,[3] the possessors of what is required, I am his protection in darkness, the Terrible One who issued from his[4] Eye.

I have come here from Abydos, and I have found his waters descending; the worms . . .[5] in a canoe, and he goes down paying honour to Her who guides the head of the Protector ⟨ . . . ⟩ their shoulders.[6] I am he who is pre-eminent in Abydos; I have bound my horn in the fight,[7] and the pure path belongs to me.

1. A better sense is obtained by reading the suffixes of the 3rd person as the 1st; 480*h* is a clear example.

2. So BiP; the parallels determine *ḥnwt* with the papyrus-roll.

3. Lesko's 'those who are possessors' would require the *m* of predication; *ntyw m nbw.*

4. Here we must accept the 3rd person; the reference must be to Horus or to Rēʿ.

5. For *nbꜣbꜣ* cf. *Pyr.* §104; its meaning is not known.

6. *Rmnw.sn* 'their shoulders' is entirely devoid of context, so that there must have been an omission before it. The passages 480*f-i* are hard to understand.

7. Here English clearly demands the 1st person, since the reference is to the speaker.

Spell 1136

VII,481 Fire. Fire. He who mounts up(?). The sealed document of Stern-face. I have come here on the wind,[1] for I am the leg(?)[2] of Shu with which the Abyss was filled within Soul-of-Powers House.[3] Ḥu who speaks in darkness belongs to me, (even) he who is rich in hours, who opens a path that I may pass to you on it; do not tell my name.

I have come here from Sepa,[4] I have seen what is in it, it was I who saw and beheld,[5] I encountered the *dom*-palm(?),[6] I made Sepa inaccessible, I attended(?) to you in (my own) name(?).[7] | What I said to you there is an enduring act.[8] I am 482
. . .[9] the north-wind of Sepa, I am the horizon which they . . .[10] My path is pure.

1. Var. 'I have come on the north-wind'.

2. Cf. Lesko, 29, n.*e*. The doubt as to Lesko's 'mine is(?) the place' is that these texts prefer *nnk* to *ink* as a possessive, cf. 481*g*.

3. B5C omits *bꜣ*.

4. The 'squiggle' before the det. in the place-name in B1C is probably a contraction of the centipede-sign; it is further corrupted into *n* in B5C.

5. B1P adds *irw* 'shape' in error, making the single eye-sign do duty for both *ptr* and *irw*.

6. *Mꜣ sp 2* = *mꜣmꜣ*(?) without det.

7. *Sm.n.i n.k m rn* is difficult. Lesko's 'I have aided you as a youth' is questionable, for *rn* is used only of the young of animals as a prefix to the name of the animal, cf. *Wb.* II, 429, 1. In his p. 30, n.*k* he suggests the alternative of 'in name', but this would make better sense if read as *rn* ⟨*.i*⟩'⟨my (own)⟩ name', perhaps with the meaning 'in person'. At the beginning of the sentence the verb *sm* is not recorded with hair-det.; we could have here either *sm* 'help' (so Lesko) or *sm* 'achten', *Wb.* IV, 120, 7.

8. Read *ḏdt.i n.k im* ⟨*m*⟩ *irw mn*; the *m* of predication is required.

9. The word after *ink* may be *ḫbt* 'place of execution'; note the butcher's-block ideogram. Lesko reads *ḥt* 'carve', but neither interpretation makes sense, and corruption is certain.

10. *Ndpt.sn,* meaning unknown. Lesko has 'which they experienced(?)', reading presumably *n dpt.sn,* but the function of *n* in his interpretation is not clear.

Spell 1137

They who attack. I am the Power who robbed Him who was strong,[1] a Power who is in darkness who will never permit that you (pl.) have power over him among those who make every kind of accusation and those who are on the necks of . . .[2] who are with the honoured one(?)[3] who is in darkness.

VII,483 I have come here from Kherᶜaḥa, having found the sealed box which extended(?) under . . .[4] It is he who goes down who testifies to me concerning the path on which I pass by by reason of my power in company with those who are in the Abyss,[5] and it is I who guard the trap with two mouths in the middle(?).[6] CROSS THE PLACE(?).[7] Light belongs to me.

1. For *ks* with crocodile-det. cf. *JEA* 57, 18 (31).
2. *Ṯpw*; unintelligible and apparently corrupt.
3. Cf. *mḫ* 'jem. ehren o. a.', *Wb.* II, 129, 12.
4. *Ḥts.*
5. Var. B1P: 'the sky'.
6. *'Ibṯ rꜣwy ḥr-ỉb*; var. B1Be: *ỉbṯ sp 2 rꜣ ḥr-ỉb.*
7. Translation doubtful. In B5C the *ḏꜣ*-sign is followed by one resembling the forepart of a lion.

Spell 1138

Rēᶜ-Atum is dead![1] Fire. Fire. I have come that I may be strong in your company.
VII,484 It is the Aggressor who joined the Scowler[1] when Seth who made the Eye of Darkness passed by. I am a destroyer with the Lord of robbery following me, I am he who passes by and splits open the darkness, and fire has no power over me[2] as over anyone else who belongs to the night. The *t*-bird belongs to me,[3] and I have split open the darkness.

1. Lesko, p. 31, has 'the sledge of Re'.
2. Lit. 'fire is that which has no power over him', but the sense demands the 1st person.
3. B1Be precedes this clause with an unexplained *ḥ*, and B1P and B5C with an obscure sign, cf. de Buck, nn. 2*; 3*.

Spell 1139

The ramparts are high,[1] and I die in their limit.[2] Fire. Fire. The mouths of their snakes guard it.[3] Reveal their names, you Companions ⟨who are in⟩ his high ram-

part.[4] | Prepare a pure path for me, O Lord of eternity who is in righteousness. VII,485
The breadth of the path is the trail(?) of the snakes. May darkness come to an end and light come into being, for movement is mine. I have come here into this pure land, O Apis, and I have found a herb there which is green; it is small, but it grows, I smell[5] it and I breathe. I am he to whom his wall(?) was given, I am the knife which is in the hand of Him whose mouth is open in darkness. My finger-nail. The motherless one[6] is He whose mouth is open; may I be mighty by means of my horn and your (*sic*) nail.

1. Cf. *ỉmḏr* 'rampart', *P. Kah.* 2, 14.
2. *S* for *sn*; cf. *JEA* 16,64 (5). So also 484*k* (B5C).
3. B1P has *fnḏ* 'nose'. What is protected is presumably the fire. The plural suffix to *ḥfꜣw* may refer to the ramparts.
4. Read ⟨*ỉmy*⟩ *ỉmḏr.f*? But to whom does the suffix refer?
5. So B5C. The other texts have less well: 'I created it', which contradicts *gm.n.ỉ* 'I found it' of 485*h*. In B1P read *ỉw sn.ỉ sw ỉw sn.ỉ*.
6. Var. B1P: *ỉwty bꜣ.f* 'the soulless one'.

Spell 1140

He is in darkness. It is his horn which gives darkness, pain and death. These are VII,486
those things(?) which are on the heat of its great fiery doors,[1] and this name of his is He whose mouth is open in darkness.[2]

O Rēʿ, Atum, Nu, Old One, Isis the divine, I have come here in fear of the Fiery Ones; I am the Power which issued from the Vultures on the day when I was superior to *Ḥḏn*; it means that his horns were cut off in darkness. It was your arm | which slew when it cut off the head of him who came that he might oppose the god, I am he whom the goddess[3] bore, and it was Imsety who cleansed me when the hand of him who would destroy my power raged.[4]

1. An obscure passage. To what *ỉmywt* (or *swt*) refers is not clear, *nt tp* has been assumed to stand for *nty tp,* while the position of the suffix *.s* suggests that the fire-sign determines the whole phrase *srf r-ʿꜣw ʿꜣ*.
2. Lesko, pl. 32, suggests that the masc. suffix in 486*a* refers to a bull, which may be *Ḥbḏ-rꜣ* named here; but in 485*m* (B5C) this being has a ram-det.
3. *Nṯrt-ḥmt,* cf. *JEA* 58, 300. B5C has corrupted *ḥmt* into *nbt*.
4. *M nšn ḏrt* has been bungled in B5C.

Spell 1141

I am the torch and the flame, I am the spear which is in the hand which is stabbed at those who are below.[1] O you of fire(?),[2] beware of me, for I am the knife
VII,488 which pierces the middle of his head.[3] | It is I who repel her[4] and give her to the earth-gods who are in the lake.

Gēb is your protector;[5] down on your face! Do not frustrate(?) his action.

1. This sentence is perhaps an image drawn from the spearing of fish by torchlight. *Šnpw* is not recorded, but the harpoon-sign would suit a fish-spear, 'those who are below' being likened to the fish in the water. ʿ with papyrus-roll is a common miswriting of ʿ 'arm', 'hand'.

2. Lesko translates *nfw* as 'sailors', which is quite out of context. The strange determinative in B1P and B5P corresponds to the sign for fire not only here, but also in 486*f* and 487*h*. No word *nf* with fire-det., however, appears to be known.

3. Translation doubtful, but the text may be maintaining the figure of a fish stabbed in the head. For *s3ḫ* 'knife' cf. *CT* II, 61*e*; 107*b*; VII, 485*l*. What a sign of fire is doing in *sttw* is not clear.

4. Whom?

5. The change of person to the 2nd suggests that the deceased is now being addressed.

Spell 1142

Do not send her name into the midst of the fire(?)[1] They guard his house and her fire, (namely) the . . .[2] Be far away, O earth-gods in the *ḏtn*-bark.[3] Arise and succour, O Rēʿ, Atum, Nu, the Old One, Shu, *'Ikw, Nmw, Ḥtp.* | The woman has
VII,489 driven off . . .[4] I am he whom Rēʿ built up, whom Shu built up, and Right belongs to that god who is in the midst of the fire, who will never place the just with him; . . . a command[5] which issued from his mouth on the day of protection. His soul has protected me . . .[6] I am Maʿet who is in . . .[7] If you advance to meet me, the Terrible One will be driven away from the earth-god together with Him of
490 the sharp knife as an aggressor, | since I stop(?)[8] movements.

1. Quite obscure. It is not clear whether we should read *m sb rn.s* as a negative imperative or *ms rn.s* 'her name is brought'. Lesko, p. 34, has 'she whose name was presented'. So also B1Be, but with *ḫt.s* 'her fire'. B5C is damaged, but was not entirely identical with the other two texts. This is a very difficult spell, apart from its manifold corruptions; it gives the impression of being a medley of unconnected extracts.

2. *Sẖwt* with rope-det. in two texts and flesh-det. in one. Meaning unknown. For various attempts at translating this word see Lesko, 32, n.*b*.

3. Var. B1P: *ḏdtn*-bark.

4. *Wmrw*(?), var. B1Be: *mhḏw*; I find the rest of 489*a* untranslatable.

5. *M ky n ḥnwt* cannot mean 'with another command' (Lesko), which would require *m kt ḥnwt*. I cannot translate *m ky* (or *mky*) *n*.

6. 489*g* is unintelligible. It is in the 2nd person, but the number changes from singular to plural, and there is no clue as to who is being addressed, while, despite Lesko's valiant effort, one cannot even guess at the meaning of the passage; it seems to be utterly corrupt.

7. *ʿnṯ*. Lesko's 'the nail' would require *ʿnt* with appropriate determinative.

8. Assuming a transitive meaning for *ḫt*.

Spell 1143

Drive off the terrible ones from the earth-gods,[1] protect the Great Lady, separate the two Combatants in 603 storms (*sic*). There are 600 in the breadth of what is over this lake.[2] O Shu, Nu, Atum, Rēʿ, Old One, I have passed by Shu, Nu, Atum, Rēʿ, the Old One, the four Seths, |Ptaḥ, Sia who is in his Eye,[3] the torch and the VII,491
fire; his[4] power is the terror of Nu who fashioned[5] the body of Horus, more potent than his fellows; the Falcon, the Duck and the Plume on the Day of Scratching; they are safe after the destruction,[6] and what they pray for is eternity.[7] Scatter(?)[8] toward them, O you whose face is hidden; make a plan for ⟨your⟩ arms[9] according to your movements,[10] Horus the Elder is in the middle of the upper stars and opposite the lower ones.

1. Reading *dr nrw m ꜣkrw* with B1P; B1Be has *ḏrw ꜣkrw*, B5C has *d nrw m ꜣkrw*.

2. This passage reads strangely; are the 600 storms viewed as still raging over the lake? And what has happened to the odd three? It looks rather as if a clause has been omitted after 490*e*. We should read *sḫw n ḥry š* with B1Be.

3. In Ptaḥ's eye.

4. Sia's?

5. Not 'she who has borne' as Lesko, p. 35; *msw* is a masculine participle. B1Be has a superfluous *ḥr* between *msw* and *ẖt*. 491*b* looks like a kind of parenthesis inserted into the series of entities invoked, unless the clause itself is to be regarded as an entity in its own right.

6. *Ḫrḫr* in B5C; *ḫrḫrt* in B1Be. B1P omits *pꜣḫw ʿḏ.sn*.

7. As Lesko points out, *r* after *nḥt* in B1P and B5C may well be a miswriting of the papyrus-roll determinative.

8. Lesko takes *bnš* to read *bn* as a metathesis of *nby* 'swim', but this seems improbable. The determinative of the word is not that of swimming, but is identical with that of *sṯy* 'strew', 'scatter', cf. *Pyr.* §567; *Urk.* IV, 615,14. *Bnš* 'scatter(?)' is not recorded, and what is scattered is not stated; it could be corn-seed, precious substances as in *Pyr.* §567, or even the stars, cf. 491*h*.

9. The suffix *.k* is required after *ʿwy*.

10. B1P has *sšmwt.kk* (*sic*) in error for *šmwt.k*.

Spell 1144

VII,492 He whose anger is sharp. He who reveals(?) the warden.

Spell 1145

O you protectors of his[1] . . .[2] who fight and guard him within his shrine, he being . . .[3] within his shrine; O *Nkmy* hearing the Sistrum-player;[4] O YOU PHYSICIANS, PROTECT ME EVERY DAY FROM THOSE WHOSE NAMES ARE UNKNOWN, THE LORDS OF LIFE EVERY DAY; THOSE WHO OPPOSE THEM ARE THOSE WHO ARE INSIGNIFICANT.[5]

O you four gods whom the goddess bore, see, he who comes to meet me is
He of the shrine,[6] and I will inform him that it is I whom you have fashioned. O
VII,493 Sole One, I pass by | that I may satisfy the maker of traps, so that you may en-
trap the shining sun. He is one who is blind as to the fingers in front of him and
(as to) his hand.[7] Stand up, O Red Ōn;[8] I repeat your course when he[9] has shot
at you, in accordance with your desire.

Your heart has been taken[10] by Shu, and I am in the spirit-state when I pass safely. Peace be to you![11] Your spirits have been divided up, and it is they of angry speech who extinguish your striking-power; it is those who are in front of Shu who strike and raise an uproar in the Abyss.

494 I am one mighty and aggressive, and this is your primeval(?) shrine. I am
one more powerful than you, so prepare a path for me. I am a vindicated one who
serves Him of blood; I am a man of a million who cannot be seen by those about
him who shoot arrows. Your mouth was silenced[12] by those (in the service) of
Osiris. Swallow and chew this slice[13] of your meat from the middle of *Btḳtḳw*.[14] If
you should come against me or if an arrow should come, miss, and continue its
495 course behind me, | then ʿApep will thrust[15] at you,[16] having coiled round the
hole which is his. I will speak: Isis the great whose house is hers will thrust at you,
for it is you who speak against me; it is the great baboon who eats[17] the gods who
thrusts at me beneath him with a crane and a danger-bird(?).[18] May you fall[19] on
your face; take yourself off! The god will come in peace, (even he) the Lord of the
Red Mansion which is in the horizon. I am . . . ,[20] I pass the *nwr*-fish(?)[21] when
Rēʿ shines in peace.

1. Whose? This too is a somewhat incoherent spell, which gives the impression of being a miscellany of perhaps four excerpts.

2. For *ʿmʿ* cf. Piankhi Stela, 151, as well as *CT* V, 24*d*. The instance Lesko, 37, n *c*,

quotes from *Pyr.* §2206 is but a restoration by Sethe based on B1C of the *CT* example; in the Nt parallel (l. 7 = Faulkner, *Pyr. Suppl.* 61), the word is lost except for an indeterminate sign at the end. Lesko's suggestion that *ꜥmꜥ* may be a miswriting of *ꜥm* 'know' seems to me highly improbable.

3. The meaning of *nkm* is not known. This clause is only in B1P.

4. Cf. *Nkmy* 'Wesen im Jenseits', *Wb.* II, 356, 6, which supports the readings of B1P and B1Be. *Skmy* of B5C would be an easy corruption of *nkmy. Sḏm* with direct object of the person heard is rare; the dative is usual.

5. This rubric, which is absent from B1Be, is retrograde except for the last clause, which is probably to be read as *ḫsf r.sn m nḏs; nfs* of B5C is an easy corruption of *nḏs.*

6. *Ḫmy,* derived by Lesko from *ḫm* 'destroy', 'demolish', but more probably here from *ḫm* 'shrine'.

7. Read *ḏryt.f* in all texts, though only B1Be spells the word correctly; *ḏryt* appears to be in apposition to *ḏbꜥw.* Is this passage intended to say that the trapper is blinded by the shining sun he has caught?

8. Apparently an epithet of the sun; cf. 493*e.f.*

9. Presumably ⸢Apep.

10. *H̱n* of B5C is a corruption of *ꞽṯ*; there is some resemblance between the two signs.

11. Lit. 'in your peace' ', perhaps a euphemism for a curse, in view of what follows.

12. Lit. 'extinguished'.

13. Cf. *nkt* 'cut' of meat, *CT* V, 394*a.* Note the masculine gender.

14. Not 'the Escaper' as Lesko; *btktk* 'escape' is written with the basket *k.*

15. Read *wdꞽ* 'thrust' rather than *wdn* 'offer' (Lesko), cf. B1Be; in all texts the *n* is lacking.

16. This is translated in the 2nd person because it refers to the hostile being addressed in 494*j.k*; 495*d*; a clear case of the confusion of suffixes to which de Buck refers in *JEA* 35, 89.

17. So B5C; the papyrus-roll determinative in the other texts points to *wnm* rather than *ꞽmy,* which does not normally take a determinative.

18. *Swtt*; cf. *swty* 'dangerous', *CT* IV, 346*b*; *swt* 'danger', *Pyr.* §652; *CT* VII, 50*l.*

19. So B1Be. B1P has an obscure word *ḫdw* instead of *ḫr.* B5C has *ḫw.k,* but the following *ḥr ḥr.k* 'on your face' speaks for the reading *ḫr.*

20. *'Ink wꞽ* of B5C looks like 'I am myself' and is so translated by Lesko; but the fact that *wꞽ* also follows *N* in B1P rather speaks against this interpretation, which in any case would be a strange remark; in B1Be the reading is *N w.* If the speaker wished to assert his identity, *ꞽnk pw* 'Such am I' would be a more normal expression, cf. e.g. *CT* V, 24*c*, and I suspect that what follows *ꞽnk* or *N* may be the ending and determinative of a noun that has been lost, e.g. *sḫmw* 'mighty one' or some such appellation.

21. *Nwr* is determined with a fish in B1P, with an arrow in B1Be, and with the 'bad' bird and an indeterminate sign in B5C, cf. de Buck, 495, n. 7*. For *nwr,* probably with fish-det., cf. *CT* VII, 197*e.*

Spell 1146

The image of a mansion. He[1] will sleep, and he will wake at the First of the Year, VII,496
when his entourage will see him. It is a voice which is heard; it is the place of the

destroyer who puts himself[2] in the limit of his vision of an equipped spirit.[3]

The way for passing by him on which he sails.[4] I have opened up the sky, the earth and the horizon.

The place of a spirit, the place of potent magic. He is a man a million (cubits) tall, he is within the darkness, and he is invisible. It means that the river is far removed from him; as for his entourage, he is invisible.

497 What is in them, (namely) their mansions, is the path of the goddess, the Sacred Eye. Baboon. Chaos-god. Ḥu. Destroyer. Hound. Protector. She is joyful. He is prosperous. He is firm. The sky, the earth and the horizon, and what is in them are the path of the goddess, the Sacred Eye.

1. The deceased identified with the sun-god.
2. Var. B1Be: 'who is put'.
3. After *dd sw* B5C is corrupt.
4. The suffix in *ḥr.f* may refer to the 'destroyer' in 496*e*; in *sḳdd.f* it presumably refers to the sun-god = the deceased.

Spell 1147

VII,498 The sky is opened for Osiris before me as a noble; strike your hand, O Rēʿ, into my hand;[1] rise up so that I MAY PASS THE TWO WATERWAYS OF SHU. It was I who restored Osiris to health.

1. *M-ʿ.ỉ* belongs to the end of 498*b*.

Spell 1148

O Fire, prepare a path for me so that I may pass. I restore Osiris to health, so do

VII,499 not mourn over his flesh.[1] Shu ploughs with a knife ⌈and the destroyers are driven off. ITS NAME IS GATE-OF-DARKNESS. THIS IS A SPELL FOR RECOGNIZING(?)[2] HIS NAME.

1. B1P is bungled, cf. de Buck, n. 6*.
2. For *s3y* = *sy3* cf. *Sin.* B25; *Urk.* IV, 248, 15. The sign resembling *š* may well be a misunderstanding of the fringed-cloth sign. B4L is incomprehensible.

Spell 1149

THE NAMES OF THE SPIRITS WHO GUARD THESE PATHS. Those who are in them. *ꜥtyꜣḥwt.* He who grasps. Knife-wielder. *ꜥbs.*[1] *Pgpy.*[2] HIS NAME IS Large-Face AND HE IS ITS GATEKEEPER.

1. Var. B4L: *ꜣsb* 'fiery one'.
2. On the var. of B4L cf. de Buck, n. 5*.

Spell 1150

I am one who was born in Rostau of the horizon, and the horizon was given to VII,500
me by the Lord of the horizon. My dignity is in Pe like the purity of Osiris. The worship ⟨of me⟩ in Rostau is the guidance of the gods of the paths in the entourage which is about Osiris, and I am one of those who guide them.

Spell 1151

I am a spirit, a lord of spirits;[1] may I have spirit-power[2] and may I act therewith VII,501
so that they exist, but the spirit whom I hate[3] shall not exist. I am he who celebrates the monthly festival, who perpetuates the half-monthly festival, and who examines the 'eighth'-garment(?). I am circling round because[4] the Eye of Horus is with the retinue of Thoth. I have caused it to cross the sky when I pass, and I will not be afraid.

1. So all texts except B1Be, which is corrupt.
2. B4L omits *ꜣḫ.ỉ* in 501*b*.
3. B4L omits *ꜣḫ sfꜣ.ỉ* and substitutes *ṯn.ỉ* 'he whom I mark'.
4. I take the negation *n* here to be a writing of the preposition *n*.

Spell 1152

⟨Those who are in it⟩.[1] Hot of face. Loud of voice. Oppressor. Monster. His name is 'he who is hot'.

1. Emending into *ỉw ntyw ỉm.s* as Lesko, cf. 499*b*.

Spell 1153

VII,502 This is the path to [the abodes][1] of those who live on their sweet things. THIS IS A SPELL FOR PASSING ON IT WHICH IS BEFORE ME; IT IS A SPELL FOR PASSING BY THOSE OF THE SHARP KNIVES. I AM . . . THESE ARE . . .[2] WHO ARE OVER THE CHAPEL(?).

1. Restored after 305*a*.
2. 502*d* is mostly untranslatable.

Spell 1154

Šb. He who is vigilant. He who is sharp-sighted. The noisy one . . .

Spell 1155

VII,503 The two whose faces were covered in order to pass by him.

Spell 1156

This is its path which is in the Mansion of Incense;[1] you should not walk on it. MY FLESH IS AFIRE. He should not go back on it. THIS NAME OF HIS IS Aggressor. HE AND HIS POWER HAVE GONE DOWN.[2] This name of his is 'Dreadful(?) of fire'.

1. Read *ḥwt bd*.
2. Lesko's 'he will charge down upon' is grammatically impossible; assuming that a construction with *ỉw.f* is to be used, to obtain his rendering it would have to be *ỉw.f r h3t; ỉw.f h3* is a construction with the old perfective and cannot take a direct object. Unless we assume an omission after *h3*, *3t* can only be in parallel with *ỉw.f*.

Spell 1157

VII,504 A spell for passing toward the path[1] of fire. I am that Eye of Horus[2] which is effective at night, namely the Eye of Fire in its beauty.

1. Var. B4L: *nywt* 'abode'.
2. 'Horus' is omitted from B1P.

Spell 1158

HE WHO GIVES REAL[1] BENEFITS AND REVERSION OFFERINGS IN IT AMONG THE GODS. SUCH IS OSIRIS WHO IS IN IT, WHO IS BENEFITTED AND DWELLS IN IT AFTER THEY HAVE REACHED THEIR OWNERS.

1. Var. BıBe: 'benefits and vindication'.

Spell 1159

My two plots are in the Field of Offerings among those who know, and I care for VII,505
Osiris there; I am the land-scribe of Ḥetep at the hand of Thoth; I am a pure one who cooks for Osiris daily among those who know offerings.

Spell 1160

The field which makes offerings; I make Osiris glad in it, from which the Field of Offerings goes up daily to Osiris.

Spell 1161

My two plots are safe,[1] and no-one can take ⟨them⟩ from me. VII,506

1. Lit. 'in peace'. *Ḥtp* is corrupt in BıP and in BıBe is written like the word for offerings.

Spell 1162

SPELL FOR BEING IN THE FIELD OF OFFERINGS AMONG THE RETINUE OF OSIRIS AND AMONG THE RETINUE OF THOTH EVERY DAY. THEY WILL EAT BREAD AMONG THE LIVING, AND THEY WILL NEVER DIE, BREATH BEING IN THEIR NOSES.

Spell 1163

Her name is *'Iḫyt*. As for this which is on her head, it is the Two Waterways[1] of VII,507
Shu(?).

1. Following B1Be. At end, read *šwy Šw pw*; cf. 498*d*.

Spell 1164

IT IS THE SEAT OF A SPIRIT WHO WILL NEVER DIE. As for anyone whose plots are in the Field of Offerings, he shall see Osiris and Thoth every day, and he shall not be opposed by the destroyers who keep the gates among those who send out robbers.

Spell 1165

VII,508 As for [anyone] who shall pass the bend of this waterway, he shall learn[1] that there are none who will oppose that man. THE MAN SHALL SAY: 'Depart(?)[2] [. . .], you keepers of the gates'.

1. For *ḫr* of B1P read *rḫ*, cf. B4L.
2. Restore as [*r*] *w*?

Spell 1166

This is the lake of fire of the knife-wielders;[1] there is no-one who shall fall into the fire, for he will be turned away from it. O you four *nm*-fish, the true name[2] is Inheritance.

1. Cf. 306*d* (Spell 1054).
2. So B4L; it seems a reading to be preferred to *š* 'lake' of B1P and B5C.

Spell 1167

VII,509 His name is Large-face who drives off aggressors. It is a spell for this bend of his; this is a spell for passing by him which is below the waterway, and I permit myself to pass in peace when Rēʿ proceeds. Prepare a path for me, that I may sail and proceed,[1] for the protection of Rēʿ is my protection; (as for) anything that may happen to me, the same will happen to Rēʿ; if anything be done to me, I will drive off the aggressors.

1. For the 3rd person in 509*g* read the 1st; B4L has both suffixes to *sḳd*.

Spell 1168

Your god has come into being, and HIS NAME IS Khopri. HE IS THE KEEPER OF VII,510
THE BEND OF THIS WATERWAY, AND HIS NAME IS SHARP OF VISION. FIRE IS
THIS WHICH IS ON HIM. I am he who gets rid of him who opposes the opponent
of the aggressor who moves in order to run.[1] I possess the egg of Rēꜥ and my
dignity[2] is like that of Rēꜥ when he appears in the early morning; my dignity[3]
is guarded for me when I reach it. What I detest is flesh which goes forth to those
who are in the horizon[4] who are in a hurry, | since I know that he is in the hori-
zon. I and my god, the youth *Ḫḫt(y)*, are ⟨not(?)⟩ opposed.[5] 511

1. Lesko, p. 73, translates as 'who walks rather than runs', but to me it is more likely that *bṯ* is infinitive after *r*, giving a purpose to *ḫp*. I take *ḫp r bṯ* to be a description of the aggressor.

2. In 501*g* B1P is the best text, but *sꜥh.f* should be read as *sꜥḥ.ỉ*. B5C omits the name of Rēꜥ after *mr* = *my*, and B4L has instead *myn* 'today', which makes poor sense.

3. Here again the emendation into *sꜥḥ.ỉ* gives better sense; why should Rēꜥ's dignity be guarded for the deceased? One would expect the latter to be more vulnerable than the sun-god.

4. Something has happened to the text here; *pr ḫr sw ꜣḫt* is meaningless as it stands. Lesko, 73, n.*x* suggests emending into *pr.ḫr ỉmyw ꜣḫt* 'those who are in the horizon go forth'; for confusion of *sw* and *ỉmy* cf. 486*e*. But the appearance of a *sḏm.ḫr.f* form here is unexpected; I think that we have the preposition *ḫr*.

5. The clause 511*b* as it stands is so opposed to the context that I suspect the omission of the negation *n*; otherwise the clause does not make sense.

Spell 1169

I have come here as a primeval one[1] that I may announce Rēꜥ at the gates of the sky, and the gods will be joyful at meeting me. The odour of a god is on me, the Destroyer cannot attack me, and the wardens of the rooms[2] cannot exclude me.
I am he whose face was hidden within the shrine | at the time when I attained to it, VII,512
after the purification of the mansion on account of[3] the chapel of the god which
was lashed together.

THIS IS A SPELL FOR PASSING BY HIM WHICH IS BEFORE ME. WHAT IS UNDER THE WATERWAY IS THE NAME OF THIS BEND. IT WAS HE[4] WHO GUARDED THIS WATERWAY at the time when I attained to it in the land of food,[5] the Mansions of [the Red Crown(?)].[6]

1. Reading *m pꜣwt(y)*; Lesko has 'from primeval time'.

2. So BıBe; B4L has ꜥwt 'limbs' (of Osiris?).
3. Lesko, p. 71: 'after Ḥatḥōr had purified herself'.
4. Presumably the anonymous keeper.
5. *Bꜥt* with loaf-det.
6. Cf. de Buck, n. 6*.

Spell 1170

O Hippotamus-face, wakeful of power, recognize him, for this is his face; 'Lustral basin(?)' is his name.[1]

1. On *šꜣs* see Spell 1062, n. 1.

Spell 1171

VII,513 This is a spell for passing on it; it is his lustral basin(?). His name is Dog-face, whose shape is big.

Spell 1172

I am Great-name whom you (plur.) made, I am bound for the Way of Right. The place of execution is what I detest, the protection of Horus the Elder is my protection.

Spell 1173

Spell for travelling around [in] one day, [. . .].[1]

1. Reading the title as *rꜣ n pẖr* [*m*] *hrw wꜥ*, combining the damaged B5C with BıP, which makes merely a token appearance. 513*i* following is too badly damaged to be sure what stood there. Lesko, p. 68, has 'if [one knows] ·this spell', reading perhaps *ḏr* [*rḫ.tw*] *rꜣ pn*, but *r.f* of B4L does not fit into this scheme. BıP has simply *ḏr rꜣ pn*.

Spell 1174

VII,514 He will reach this waterway, and he will never die. Spell for the heritage of the fugitive because of the lustral basins(?). O heir of the horizon of Rēꜥ, I am

Atum, Lord of Kenz(et), and I have spoken, for I am the heir of the horizon. I prepare a path for Rēʿ when he comes to a halt; O heritage, I know your name.

Spell 1175

O Horus the first-born of Rēʿ, I am one who acts on behalf of his desire; I will not be seized and I will not be turned back at the approaches(?) of the gates. | I
am he who equipped the Double Lion,[1] who lives on those who would destroy VII,515
him.

SPELL FOR PASSING BY HIM; HE IS THE KEEPER OF THIS BEND OF THE WATERWAY.

1. BɪP inserts *wʿrwt* between *ʿpr* and *Rwty*; it is displaced from 514*k*.

Spell 1176

This is one who enters beneath this bend of the waterway. O Selḳet, I shall exist for ever; I am he who despatches the word of the gods to Rēʿ, I have come that I may report(?) a message to its recipient.

Spell 1177

He who is driven off, with two faces in dung(?). HE IS THE KEEPER OF THIS BEND VII,516
OF THE WATERWAY. THIS IS A SPELL FOR PASSING BY HIM ON ACCOUNT OF IT.

Spell 1178

HE IS THE KEEPER OF THIS BEND OF THE WATERWAY. Great-face who opposes the aggressor. HE IS THE KEEPER OF THIS BEND OF THE WATERWAY. An overbearing one(?) whose mother speaks like a . . . ,[1] who guards her in his house, against whom I am placed.

1. Cf. Spell 1069, n. 1.

Spell 1179

VII,517 I am Many-faced who created thunder, who mounts up to Rēʿ and repels the strength of ʿApep, who splits open the sky and drives away storm, and who nourishes the crews[1] of Rēʿ. My two *šspt*-garments and my rod have been given to me, I have made Ḥetep great as its keeper, and it has been granted to me that the Bark shall make a good voyage. Prepare a path for me, O you who guard him within his shrine.

THIS IS A SPELL FOR PASSING ON IT WHICH IS BEFORE ME.[2]

1. *Yt* is a corruption of *ỉswt* 'crews', cf. 332*i* (Spell 1069).
2. Lit. 'him'.

Spell 1180

VII,518 The snakes of . . .[1] are the keepers of the gates, who keep my way.

1. *ʿftt,* cf. Spell 1034, n. 1.

Spell 1181

Spell for passing on it. O you who are exalted and equipped, possessors of striking-power, I am loud-voiced in the horizon, its Great One. Down on your faces, you watchers!

Spell for passing on it. My face is that of Horus, my hinder-parts are those of the *wrrt*-crown, mine are the mighty ones.[1]

Spell for passing on it. I am he who sits on the Eye of Horus as the third,[1]
VII,519 who judges with the gods on the second day. My protection from you is the protection of Thoth.

1. Or 'mine is power'.

Spell 1182

IT IS A SPELL FOR THE PATH. THESE PATHS ARE THUS:[1] ONE OF THEM IS OPPOSED TO ITS FELLOW IN CONFUSION. AS FOR THOSE WHO KNOW THEM, THEY SHALL FIND THEIR PATHS. THEIR WALLS OF FLINT ARE HIGH IN ROSTAU.

1. Reading 519*a-b* as *r3 n w3t pw w3wt pw iptw my-nw.*

Spell 1183

Be weary, you squatting gods, whose faces are hidden, who live by means of VII,520
your throwsticks, who strike your sticks; O you who are stout-hearted,[1] weighty of striking-power, preparing my path in the fire,[2] I will restore Osiris to health. Prepare a path for me and let me pass, for I am he who saved Osiris and who saw the Sole One alone when Rēʿ travelled around among those who act alone.

1. *Wsrt-ib* is out of concord, read as masculine; B1P has *wsrt* and stops.
2. Read *wdn 3t ir w3t⟨.i⟩ m sdt,* cf. 343*a*; B1Be omits *3t* and B5C omits *ir.*

Spell 1184

I am he who limited the flood,[1] who judged the Rivals; I have come that I may
remove the humiliation from upon Osiris. THE PATH TO ROSTAU WHICH IS ON VII,521
LAND.

1. 520*i* is a corruption of 346*a* and is translated accordingly. Note the cryptic writing of *ink* in B5C.

Spell 1185

I[1] am he who wrapped the standard, who issued from the *wrrt*-crown; I have come that I may drive out pain, ease the suffering of Osiris, and establish offerings in Abydos. THE WAYS BY WATER WHICH BELONG TO ROSTAU.

1. B5C has again the cryptic writing of *ink.*

INDEXES

I. MAJOR DIVINITIES

References are to volume and page of the translations.

II. VARIOUS MINOR DIVINITIES

III. LOCALITIES

IV. CELESTIAL BODIES

V. SELECTED WORDS DISCUSSED IN NOTES

References are to Spell-number and note.

VI. CATALOGUE OF COMPONENT PARTS OF BOATS AND GEAR

References are to de Buck's text.

wdwt steering-posts(?), **V**, 189*d*; cf. Sp. 404, n. 32.
wdyt helm, **VI**, 264*m*; cf. loc. cit.
byw meaning unknown, **V**, 94*b*.
bdꜣ masthead, **V**, 132*a.b*; 205*f*; **VI**, 12*d*; 38*x*; cf. Sp. 398, n. 25.
pḥwy stern, **V**, 89*f*; 230*i*.
pḥwtt stern-warp, **III**, 301*b*; **V**, 148*b*; 168*e*.
psd 'spine' of boat = hogging-beam(?), **V**, 96*c*; cf. Sp. 397, n. 43.
pgꜣw bowls, **V**, 98*e*.
pd decking(?), **V**, 74*u.cc*; cf. Spell 396, n.23.
mꜣ-pḥwty sternpiece, **V**, 125*b*.
mꜣ-ḥꜣty bowpiece, **V**, 125*a*.
mꜣꜥw meaning unknown, **V**, 136*a.b*.
mꜥwḥ oar, **V**, 12*e*. 19*e*; **VI**, 382*m* (var. *mywḥ*).
mnyt mooring-post, **III**, 77*m*; 301*b*; **V**, 111*b* and often; with rope-det. for mooring-rope, **VI**, 382*i*.
mnty 'haunches', unidentified part of boat, **V**, 92*g*.
mhy meaning unknown, **V**, 205*h*.
mhnnw meaning unknown, **V**, 190*a*.
mḫsf var. of *ḫsf* below.
msrt meaning unknown, **V**, 135*a*.
mkrt meaning unknown, **V**, 74*t*.
mdꜣm lacings(?). **V**, 74*s*; 129*a*; **VI**, 39*o*; cf. Sp. 396, n. 20.
mdw 'staff', unidentified part of boat, **V**, 231*k*.
mdꜣt meaning unknown, **V**, 134*a*; cf. Sp. 398, n. 29.
mdꜣbt bailer, **V**, 109*j*; 138*b*; 139*a*; 170*a*; 191*e*; 204*m*; **VI**, 12*a*; 39*m*; **VII**, 10*f*.
nyn a rope, **VI**, 38*x*; cf. Sp. 479, n.16.
nynṯ a rope, **V**, 74*aa*.
nwḥ ỉtḥ tow-rope, **VI**, 39*k*.
nprt deck(?), **VII**, 41*n*.
nfw meaning unknown, **V**, 141*a.b*.
nsꜣ loom(?) of oar, **V**, 137*a.b*; 193*f*; cf. Sp. 404, n. 48.
rꜣ 'opening', nature unknown, **V**, 126*b*.
rꜣ-ỉwꜣ cabin(?), **VII**, 278*b*.
ḥꜣt bow, forepart, **I**, 224*g*; 249*g*; 260*f* and often.
ḥꜣtt bow-warp, **III**, 301*b*; 371*c*; 378*b*; 394*c* and often.
ḥꜣ-ṯꜣw backstay, **V**, 142*a*; 143*a*; cf. Sp. 398, n. 44.
ḥꜥt hull(?), **V**, 189*f*.
ḥw-ỉnw 'cordage-smiter', nature doubtful, **V**, 132*b*; 133*a*; cf. Sp. 398, n. 26.
ḥpt oar, **I**, 94*b*; 244*o*; **VII**, 401*a*.
ḥpt-ḫt mast-step(?), **V**, 189*f*, cf. Sp. 404, n.34.
ḥmw steering-oar, **III**, 77*e*; **IV**, 345*a*; **V**, 139*d* and often; used exceptionally of rowing-oars, **V**, 14*d.h*.
ḥrwt ropes of some kind, **V**, 169*g*.
ḥsw meaning unknown, **VI**, 39*c*.
ḫft-ḥr forestay, **V**, 141*b*; 142*a*; cf. Sp. 398, n. 43.
ḫmt spars(?), **V**, 131*b*; 132*a*; cf. Sp. 398, n. 24.
ḫndw bent timbers, **V**, 137*b*; 138*a*, cf. Sp. 398, n. 36.
ḫndwy 'shanks', unidentified part of boat, **V**, 92*g*.
ḫrpw mallet, **V**, 149*c*; 189*b*; 204*g*.
ḫsf meaning unknown, **V**, 74*t*; 85e; 88*a*; 129*b*; 130*a*; var. *mḫsf* 74*bb*.
ḫsfwt meaning unknown, **V**, 127*b*; 128*a*.
ḫt mast, **V**, 92*b*; 233*e*.
ḫt-ṯꜣw mast, **V**, 140*b*; 169*a*; 205*d*; 232*m*; **VI**, 11*d*.
ḫry-ꜥ tiller, **III**, 77*f*; **V**, 145*a;b*. 169*e*; cf. Sp, 398, n. 48.
sꜣꜣw beams, *CT* **V**, 110*i*.
sꜥꜣ bulwark(?), **V**, 128*a*; 232*g*; cf. Sp. 398, n. 15.
swt 'reeds', unidentified part of a boat, perhaps the planking of the hull, **V**, 74*r.w;* 85*c*; 87*a*; **VI**, 12*d*; 38*x*; cf. Sp. 396, n.18.
sbꜣ door, of cabin(?), **VI**, 38*v*.
spty gunwales(?), **V**, 94*b*; 129*a*; 130*a.b*; cf. Sp. 397, n. 35.
sprwt meaning unknown, **V**, 127*b*.

smꜣyt hogging-beam(?), **V**, 192*g*; cf. Sp. 404, n. 44.
smꜣḏyt meaning unknown, **V**, 134*a.b*.
smyw rigging, **II**, 366*b*; **VI**, 381*e*.
smꜥ sounding-pole, **I**, 267*f*; **II**, 92*f*; **V**, 44*a*; 146*b*; 147*a*; 170*d*; **VI**, 11*h*; 39*g*.
smꜥ fibre lashings of reed canoe, **III**, 97*g*; 113*n.p*.
snbw meaning unknown, **V**, 139*a.b*.
sẖt meaning unknown, **V**, 138*a.b*.
ssšt tow-rope(?), **VI**, 38*x*.
sšn cordage, **V**, 98*c*.
sgrgw yards(?), **V**, 190*c*; 205*l*; **VII**, 17*q*.
šꜣ finials of hull(?), **V**, 74*r.x*; 85*d*; 86*c*; 130*b*; 131*a*; **VI**, 12*d*; 38*x*; cf. Sp. 396, n. 19.
šnnw nw ẖt rigging of the mast, **V**, 233*e*.
šspt lashing, **V**, 129*a.b*; **VI**, 39*a*; cf. Sp. 398, n. 18.
šdw lacings(?), **V**, 191*a*; 205*j*; cf. Sp. 404, n. 40.
ḳꜣsw bonding, lashing, of hull, **V**, 129*a*.
kꜣw meaning unknown, **V**, 169*c*.
kꜣ-šspt meaning unknown, **V**, 142*b*; 143*b*.
tꜣ sail, **V**, 190i; 232*m*.
tꜣ-wr larboard, **IV**, 14*b.d.*; **V**, 85*a*; 97*d*; 144*a.b*; 227*d* ff.; **VI**, 282*m*; 285*h*; 387*y*.
ṯꜣwt, varr. *tꜣywt*, sail, **IV**, 28*b*; **V**, 93*a.e*; 145*b*; 146*a*; 169*d*; 206*a*.
ṯꜣrt cabin, **V**, 145*b*.
ṯbwt 'sandal', unidentified part of boat, **V**, 147*b*; 168*g*; **VI**, 38*v*.
dbḥw meaning unknown, **V**, 190*g*; **VII**, 17*q*.
dpw oar, **VI**, 239*j*; **VII**, 258*b*.
ḏnḥ blade of oar, **V**, 193*e*; 206*j*; 229*g*.
ḏḥꜥw oar-loops(?) **V**, 74*s.y*; 86*a*; 88*b* (var. *ḏḥr*); cf. Sp. 396, n. 20.